W9-BXP-560

INTRODUCTION TO JAVA™ PROGRAMMING

COMPREHENSIVE VERSION

Ninth Edition

Y. Daniel Liang

Armstrong Atlantic State University

PEARSON

Boston Columbus Indianapolis New York San Francisco Upper Saddle River
Amsterdam Cape Town Dubai London Madrid Milan Munich Paris Montreal Toronto
Delhi Mexico City Sao Paulo Sydney Hong Kong Seoul Singapore Taipei Tokyo

Editorial Director: Marcia Horton
Editor in Chief: Michael Hirsch
Executive Editor: Tracy Dunkelberger
Associate Editor: Carole Snyder
Director of Marketing: Patrice Jones
Marketing Manager: Yez Alayan
Marketing Coordinator: Kathryn Ferranti
Marketing Assistant: Emma Snider
Director of Production: Vince O'Brien
Managing Editor: Jeff Holcomb
Production Project Manager: Kayla Smith-Tarbox
Operations Supervisor: Alan Fischer
Manufacturing Buyer: Lisa McDowell
Art Director: Anthony Gemmellaro
Cover Designer: Anthony Gemmellaro
Manager, Visual Research: Karen Sanatar
Manager, Rights and Permissions: Mike Joyce
Text Permission Coordinator: Danielle Simon and Jenn Kennett
Cover Illustration: Jason Consalvo
Lead Media Project Manager: Daniel Sandin
Project Management: Gillian Hall
Composition and Art: Laserwords
Printer/Binder: Edwards Brothers Malloy
Cover Printer: Lehigh-Phoenix Color/Hagerstown
Text Font: Times 10/12

Credits and acknowledgments borrowed from other sources and reproduced, with permission, in this textbook appear on the appropriate page within text and as follows: Table 3.2 and 10.1: Data from IRS. Figures 8.1, 8.12, 12.3, 12.5, 12.7, 12.9, 12.10, 12.12–12.21, 12.26–12.30, 13.1, 13.4, 13.9, 13.11, 13.15, 13.17, 13.19, 13.21, 13.23, 13.25–13.35, 14.10, 14.14,15.9–15.11, 16.1, 16.2, 16.8, 16.11, 16.14, 16.17, 16.19–16.35, 17.1, 17.3, 17.6, 17.9, 17.12, 17.13, 17.15, 17.17–17.32, 18.6–18.8, 18.10, 18.15–18.35, 19.19, 19.20, 19.22, 20.1, 20.9, 20.12–20.14, 20.16–20.20, 22.8, 22.17–22.21, 24.4, 24.6, 24.8, 24.11–24.17, 25.18–25.20, 27.17, 27.23-–27.25, 30.10, 30.14, 30.22, 30.23, 30.25, 31.24–31.26, 32.6, 32.7, 32.31–32.34, 33.5, 33.9–33.11, 33.16–33.22, 34.23, 34.27–34.30: Screenshots © 2011 by Oracle Corporation. Reprinted with permission.

Library of Congress Cataloging-in-Publication Data available upon request.

Prentice Hall
is an imprint of

www.pearsonhighered.com

10 9 8 7 6 5 4 3

ISBN 13: 978-0-13-293652-1
ISBN 10: 0-13-293652-6

This book is dedicated to Professor Myers Foreman. Myers used this book in CS1, CS2, and CS3 at Lamar University and provided invaluable suggestions for improving the book. Sadly, Myers passed away after he completed the review of this edition.

To Samantha, Michael, and Michelle

PREFACE

Dear Reader,

what is new?

Many of you have provided feedback on earlier editions of this book, and your comments and suggestions have greatly improved the book. This edition has been substantially enhanced in presentation, organization, examples, exercises, and supplements. We have:

- Reorganized sections and chapters to present the subjects in a more logical order
- Included many new interesting examples and exercises to stimulate interests
- Updated to Java 7
- Created animations for algorithms and data structures to visually demonstrate the concepts
- Redesigned the support Website to make it easier to navigate

problem-driven

This book teaches programming in a problem-driven way that focuses on problem solving rather than syntax. We make introductory programming interesting by using thought-provoking problems in a broad context. The central thread of early chapters is on problem solving. Appropriate syntax and library are introduced to enable readers to write programs for solving the problems. To support the teaching of programming in a problem-driven way, the book provides a wide variety of problems at various levels of difficulty to motivate students. To appeal to students in all majors, the problems cover many application areas, including math, science, business, financial, gaming, animation, and multimedia.

fundamentals-first

The book focuses on fundamentals first by introducing basic programming concepts and techniques before designing custom classes. The fundamental concepts and techniques of loops, methods, and arrays are the foundation for programming. Building this strong foundation prepares students to learn object-oriented programming and advanced Java programming.

comprehensive version

brief version

This *comprehensive version* covers fundamentals of programming, object-oriented programming, GUI programming, algorithms and data structures, concurrency, networking, internationalization, advanced GUI, database, and Web programming. It is designed to prepare students to become proficient Java programmers. A *brief version* (*Introduction to Java Programming*, Brief Version, Ninth Edition) is available for a first course on programming, commonly known as CS1. The brief version contains the first 20 chapters of the comprehensive version.

examples and exercises

The best way to teach programming is *by example*, and the only way to learn programming is *by doing*. Basic concepts are explained by example, and a large number of exercises with various levels of difficulty are provided for students to practice. For our programming courses, we assign programming exercises after each lecture.

Our goal is to produce a text that teaches problem solving and programming in a broad context using a wide variety of interesting examples. If you have any comments on and suggestions for improving the book, please email me.

Sincerely,

Y. Daniel Liang
y.daniel.liang@gmail.com
www.cs.armstrong.edu/liang
www.pearsonhighered.com/liang

What's New in This Edition?

This edition substantially improves *Introduction to Java Programming*, Eighth Edition. The major improvements are as follows:

- This edition is completely revised in every detail to enhance clarity, presentation, content, examples, and exercises. complete revision
- New examples and exercises are provided to motivate and stimulate student interest in programming. new problems
- Each section starts with a Key Point that highlights the important concepts covered in the section. key point
- Check Points provide review questions to help students track their progress and evaluate their learning after a major concept or example is covered. check point
- Each chapter provides test questions online. They are grouped by sections for students to do self-test. The questions are graded online. test questions
- New VideoNotes provide short video tutorials designed to reinforce code. VideoNotes
- The Java GUI API is an excellent example of how the object-oriented principle is applied. Students learn better with concrete and visual examples. So basic GUI/Graphics is moved before introducing abstract classes and interfaces. You can however still choose to cover abstract classes and interfaces before GUI or skip GUI. basic GUI and graphics early
- The numeric wrapper classes, `BigInteger`, and `BigDecimal` are now introduced in Chapter 10 to enable students to write code using these classes early. numeric classes covered early
- Exception handling is covered before abstract classes and interfaces so that students can build robust programs early. The instructor can still choose to cover exception handling later. Text I/O is now combined with exception handling to form a new chapter. exception handling earlier
- Simple use of generics is introduced along with `ArrayList` in Chapter 11 and with `Comparable` in Chapter 15 while the complex detail on generics is still kept in Chapter 21. simple generics early
- Chapter 22 is split into two chapters (Chapter 22 and Chapter 23) to make room for incorporating three new case studies to demonstrate effective use of data structures. splitting Chapter 22
- Chapter 24 is expanded to introduce algorithmic techniques: dynamic programming, divide-and-conquer, backtracking, and greedy algorithm with new examples to design efficient algorithms. developing efficient algorithms
- Visual animations are created to show how data structures and algorithms work. data structures and algorithm animation
- A common problem with a data structures course is lack of good examples and exercises. This edition added many new interesting examples and exercises. new data structures materials
- Parallel programming techniques are introduced in Chapter 32, Multithreading and Parallel Programming. parallel programming
- Chapter 44 is completely new to introduce the latest standard on JSF. new JSF chapter
- Chapter 50 is completely new to introduce testing using JUnit. new JUnit chapter

Please visit www.cs.armstrong.edu/liang/intro9e/newfeatures.html for a complete list of new features as well as correlations to the previous edition.

Pedagogical Features

The book uses the following elements to help students get the most from the material:

- The **Objectives** at the beginning of each chapter list what students should learn from the chapter. This will help them determine whether they have met the objectives after completing the chapter.
- The **Introduction** opens the discussion with representative problems to give the reader an overview of what to expect from the chapter.
- **Key Points** highlight the important concepts covered in each section.
- **Check Points** provide review questions to help students track their progress as they read through the chapter and evaluate their learning.
- **Problems and Case Studies**, carefully chosen and presented in an easy-to-follow style, teach problem solving and programming concepts. The book uses many small, simple, and stimulating examples to demonstrate important ideas.
- The **Chapter Summary** reviews the important subjects that students should understand and remember. It helps them reinforce the key concepts they have learned in the chapter.
- **Test Questions** are accessible online, grouped by sections, for students to do self-test on programming concepts and techniques.
- **Programming Exercises** are grouped by sections to provide students with opportunities to apply the new skills they have learned on their own. The level of difficulty is rated as easy (no asterisk), moderate (*), hard (**), or challenging (***). The trick of learning programming is practice, practice, and practice. To that end, the book provides a great many exercises.
- **Notes**, **Tips**, **Cautions**, and **Design Guides** are inserted throughout the text to offer valuable advice and insight on important aspects of program development.

Note
Provides additional information on the subject and reinforces important concepts.

Tip
Teaches good programming style and practice.

Caution
Helps students steer away from the pitfalls of programming errors.

Design Guide
Provides guidelines for designing programs.

Flexible Chapter Orderings

The book is designed to provide flexible chapter orderings to enable GUI, exception handling, recursion, generics, and the Java Collections Framework to be covered earlier or later. The diagram on the next page shows the chapter dependencies.

Organization of the Book

The chapters can be grouped into five parts that, taken together, form a comprehensive introduction to Java programming, data structures and algorithms, and database and Web programming. Because knowledge is cumulative, the early chapters provide the conceptual basis

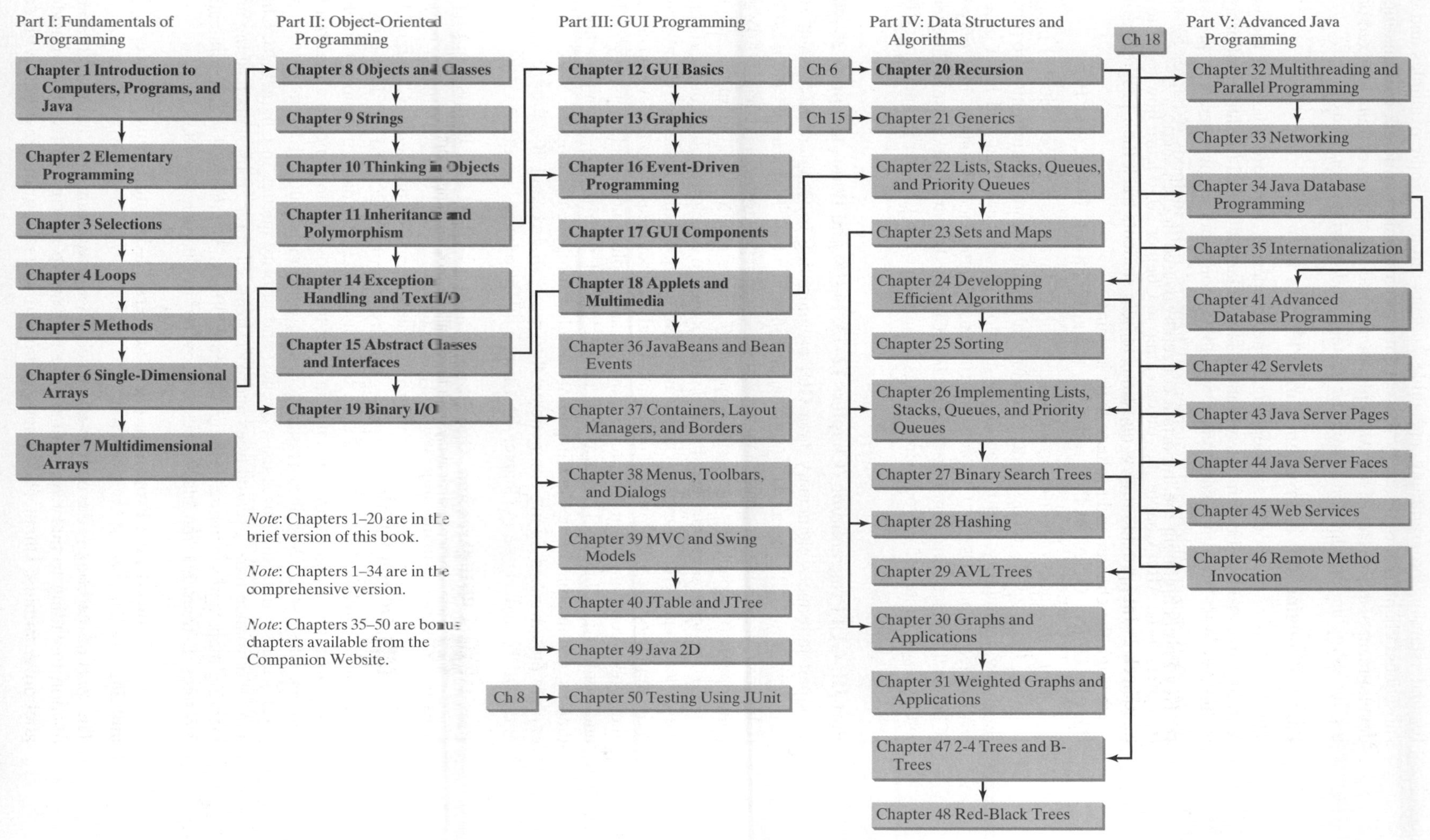
Part I: Fundamentals of Programming
Chapter 1 Introduction to Computers, Programs, and Java
Chapter 2 Elementary Programming
Chapter 3 Selections
Chapter 4 Loops
Chapter 5 Methods
Chapter 6 Single-Dimensional Arrays
Chapter 7 Multidimensional Arrays
Part II: Object-Oriented Programming
Chapter 8 Objects and Classes
Chapter 9 Strings
Chapter 10 Thinking in Objects
Chapter 11 Inheritance and Polymorphism
Chapter 14 Exception Handling and Text I/O
Chapter 15 Abstract Classes and Interfaces
Chapter 19 Binary I/O
Part III: GUI Programming
Chapter 12 GUI Basics
Chapter 13 Graphics
Chapter 16 Event-Driven Programming
Chapter 17 GUI Components
Chapter 18 Applets and Multimedia
Chapter 36 JavaBeans and Bean Events
Chapter 37 Containers, Layout Managers, and Borders
Chapter 38 Menus, Toolbars, and Dialogs
Chapter 39 MVC and Swing Models
Chapter 40 JTable and JTree
Chapter 49 Java 2D
Ch 8
Chapter 50 Testing Using JUnit
Ch 6
Ch 15
Part IV: Data Structures and Algorithms
Chapter 20 Recursion
Chapter 21 Generics
Chapter 22 Lists, Stacks, Queues, and Priority Queues
Chapter 23 Sets and Maps
Chapter 24 Developping Efficient Algorithms
Chapter 25 Sorting
Chapter 26 Implementing Lists, Stacks, Queues, and Priority Queues
Chapter 27 Binary Search Trees
Chapter 28 Hashing
Chapter 29 AVL Trees
Chapter 30 Graphs and Applications
Chapter 31 Weighted Graphs and Applications
Chapter 47 2-4 Trees and B-Trees
Chapter 48 Red-Black Trees
Ch 18
Part V: Advanced Java Programming
Chapter 32 Multithreading and Parallel Programming
Chapter 33 Networking
Chapter 34 Java Database Programming
Chapter 35 Internationalization
Chapter 41 Advanced Database Programming
Chapter 42 Servlets
Chapter 43 Java Server Pages
Chapter 44 Java Server Faces
Chapter 45 Web Services
Chapter 46 Remote Method Invocation
Note: Chapters 1–20 are in the brief version of this book.
Note: Chapters 1–34 are in the comprehensive version.
Note: Chapters 35–50 are bonus chapters available from the Companion Website.

for understanding programming and guide students through simple examples and exercises; subsequent chapters progressively present Java programming in detail, culminating with the development of comprehensive Java applications. The appendixes contain a mixed bag of topics, including an introduction to number systems and bitwise operations.

Part I: Fundamentals of Programming (Chapters 1–7)

The first part of the book is a stepping stone, preparing you to embark on the journey of learning Java. You will begin to learn about Java (Chapter 1) and fundamental programming techniques with primitive data types, variables, constants, assignments, expressions, and operators (Chapter 2), control statements (Chapters 3–4), methods (Chapter 5), and arrays (Chapters 6–7). After Chapter 6, you can jump to Chapter 20 to learn how to write recursive methods for solving inherently recursive problems.

Part II: Object-Oriented Programming (Chapters 8–11, 14–15, and 19)

This part introduces object-oriented programming. Java is an object-oriented programming language that uses abstraction, encapsulation, inheritance, and polymorphism to provide great flexibility, modularity, and reusability in developing software. You will learn programming with objects and classes (Chapters 8–10), class inheritance (Chapter 11), polymorphism (Chapter 11), exception handling and text I/O (Chapter 14), abstract classes (Chapter 15), and interfaces (Chapter 15). Processing strings is introduced in Chapter 9, and binary I/O is discussed in Chapter 19.

Part III: GUI Programming (Chapters 12–13, 16–18, and Bonus Chapters 36–40 and 49)

This part introduces elementary Java GUI programming in Chapters 12–13 and 16–18 and advanced Java GUI programming in Chapters 36–40 and 49. Major topics include GUI basics (Chapter 12), drawing shapes (Chapter 13), event-driven programming (Chapter 16), using GUI components (Chapter 17), and writing applets (Chapter 18). You will learn the architecture of Java GUI programming and use the GUI components to develop applications and applets from these elementary GUI chapters. The advanced GUI chapters discuss Java GUI programming in more depth and breadth. You will delve into JavaBeans and learn how to develop custom events and source components in Chapter 36, review and explore new containers, layout managers, and borders in Chapter 37, learn how to create GUI with menus, popup menus, toolbars, dialogs, and internal frames in Chapter 38, develop components using the MVC approach and explore the advanced Swing components `JSpinner`, `JList`, and `JComboBox` in Chapter 39, and `JTable` and `JTree` in Chapter 40. Chapter 49 introduces Java 2D.

Part IV: Data Structures and Algorithms (Chapters 20–31 and Bonus Chapters 47–48)

This part covers the main subjects in a typical data structures course. Chapter 20 introduces recursion to write methods for solving inherently recursive problems. Chapter 21 presents how generics can improve software reliability. Chapters 22 and 23 introduce the Java Collection Framework, which defines a set of useful API for data structures. Chapter 24 discusses measuring algorithm efficiency in order to choose an appropriate algorithm for applications. Chapter 25 describes classic sorting algorithms. You will learn how to implement several classic data structures lists, queues, and priority queues in Chapter 26. Chapters 27 and 29 introduce binary search trees and AVL trees. Chapter 28 presents hashing and implementing maps and sets using hashing. Chapters 30 and 31 introduce graph applications. The 2-4 trees, B-trees, and red-black trees are covered in Chapters 47–48.

Part V: Advanced Java Programming (Chapters 32–33 and Bonus Chapters 35, 41–46, and 50)

This part of the book is devoted to advanced Java programming. Chapter 32 treats the use of multithreading to make programs more responsive and interactive and introduces parallel programming. Chapter 33 discusses how to write programs that talk with each other over the Internet. Chapter 34 introduces the use of Java to develop database projects, and Chapter 35 covers the use of internationalization support to develop projects for international audiences. Chapter 41 delves into advanced Java database programming. Bonus Chapters 42, 43 and 44 introduce how to use Java servlets, JavaServer Pages, and JavaServer Faces to generate dynamic content from Web servers. Chapter 45 discusses Web services, and Chapter 46 introduces remote method invocation. Chapter 50 introduces testing Java programs using JUnit.

Appendixes

This part of the book covers a mixed bag of topics. Appendix A lists Java keywords. Appendix B gives tables of ASCII characters and their associated codes in decimal and in hex. Appendix C shows the operator precedence. Appendix D summarizes Java modifiers and their usage. Appendix E discusses special floating-point values. Appendix F introduces number systems and conversions among binary, decimal, and hex numbers. Finally, Appendix G introduces bitwise operations.

Java Development Tools

You can use a text editor, such as the Windows Notepad or WordPad, to create Java programs and to compile and run the programs from the command window. You can also use a Java development tool, such as TextPad, NetBeans, or Eclipse. These tools support an integrated development environment (IDE) for developing Java programs quickly. Editing, compiling, building, executing, and debugging programs are integrated in one graphical user interface. Using these tools effectively can greatly increase your programming productivity. TextPad is a primitive IDE tool. NetBeans and Eclipse are more sophisticated, but they are easy to use if you follow the tutorials. Tutorials on TextPad, NetBeans, and Eclipse can be found in the supplements on the Companion Website www.cs.armstrong.edu/liang/intro9e.

IDE tutorials

Online Practice and Assessment with MyProgrammingLab

MyProgrammingLab™

MyProgrammingLab helps students fully grasp the logic, semantics, and syntax of programming. Through practice exercises and immediate, personalized feedback, MyProgrammingLab improves the programming competence of beginning students who often struggle with the basic concepts and paradigms of popular high-level programming languages.

A self-study and homework tool, a MyProgrammingLab course consists of hundreds of small practice problems organized around the structure of this textbook. For students, the system automatically detects errors in the logic and syntax of their code submissions and offers targeted hints that enable students to figure out what went wrong—and why. For instructors, a comprehensive gradebook tracks correct and incorrect answers and stores the code inputted by students for review.

MyProgrammingLab is offered to users of this book in partnership with Turing's Craft, the makers of the CodeLab interactive programming exercise system. For a full demonstration, to see feedback from instructors and students, or to get started using MyProgrammingLab in your course, visit www.myprogramminglab.com.

VideoNotes

VideoNote

We are excited about the new VideoNotes feature that is found in this new edition. These videos provide additional help by presenting examples of key topics and showing how to solve problems completely, from design through coding. VideoNotes are free to first time users and can be accessed by redeeming the access code in the front of this book at www.pearsonhighered.com/liang.

LiveLab

This book is accompanied by a complementary Web-based course assessment and management system for instructors. The system has four main components:

- The **Automatic Grading System** can automatically grade programs.
- The **Quiz Creation/Submission/Grading System** enables instructors to create and modify quizzes that students can take and be graded upon automatically.
- The **Peer Evaluation System** enables peer evaluations.
- **Tracking grades, attendance, etc.,** lets students track their grades, and enables instructors to view the grades of all students and to track students' attendance.

The main features of the Automatic Grading System include:

- Students can run and submit exercises. (The system checks whether their program runs correctly—students can continue to run and resubmit the program before the due date.)
- Instructors can review submissions, run programs with instructor test cases, correct them, provide feedback to students, and check plagiarism.
- Instructors can create/modify their own exercises, create public and secret test cases, assign exercises, and set due dates for the whole class or for individuals.
- Instructors can assign all the exercises in the text to students. Additionally, LiveLab provides extra exercises that are not printed in the text.
- Instructors can sort and filter all exercises and check grades (by time frame, student, and/or exercise).
- Instructors can delete students from the system.
- Students and instructors can track grades on exercises.

The main features of the Quiz System are:

- Instructors can create/modify quizzes from the test bank or a text file or create completely new tests online.
- Instructors can assign the quizzes to students and set a due date and test time limit for the whole class or for individuals.
- Students and instructors can review submitted quizzes.
- Instructors can analyze quizzes and identify students' weaknesses.
- Students and instructors can track grades on quizzes.

The main features of the Peer Evaluation System include:

- Instructors can assign peer evaluation for programming exercises.
- Instructors can view peer evaluation reports.

Student Resource Website

The Student Resource Website (www.cs.armstrong.edu/liang/intro9e) contains the following resources:

- Access to VideoNotes (www.pearsonhighered.com/liang).
- Answers to check point questions

- Solutions to even-numbered programming exercises
- Source code for the examples in the book
- Interactive self-testing (organized by sections for each chapter)
- Data structures and algorithm animations
- Errata

Instructor Resource Website

The Instructor Resource Website, accessible from www.cs.armstrong.edu/liang/intro9e, contains the following resources:

- Microsoft PowerPoint slides with interactive buttons to view full-color, syntax-highlighted source code and to run programs without leaving the slides.
- Solutions to all programming exercises. Students will have access to the solutions of even-numbered programming exercises.
- Web-based quiz generator. (Instructors can choose chapters to generate quizzes from a large database of more than two thousand questions.)
- Sample exams. Most exams have four parts:
    - Multiple-choice questions or short-answer questions
    - Correct programming errors
    - Trace programs
    - Write programs
- Projects. In general, each project gives a description and asks students to analyze, design, and implement the project.

Some readers have requested the materials from the Instructor Resource Website. Please understand that these are for instructors only. Such requests will not be answered.

Algorithm Animations

We have provided numerous animations for algorithms. These are valuable pedagogical tools to demonstrate how algorithms work. Algorithm animations can be accessed from the Companion Website.

Acknowledgments

I would like to thank Armstrong Atlantic State University for enabling me to teach what I write and for supporting me in writing what I teach. Teaching is the source of inspiration for continuing to improve the book. I am grateful to the instructors and students who have offered comments, suggestions, bug reports, and praise.

This book has been greatly enhanced thanks to outstanding reviews for this and previous editions. The reviewers are: Elizabeth Adams (James Madison University), Syed Ahmed (North Georgia College and State University), Omar Aldawud (Illinois Institute of Technology), Yang Ang (University of Wollongong, Australia), Kevin Bierre (Rochester Institute of Technology), David Champion (DeVry Institute), James Chegwidden (Tarrant County College), Anup Dargar (University of North Dakota), Charles Dierbach (Towson University), Frank Ducrest (University of Louisiana at Lafayette), Erica Eddy (University of Wisconsin at Parkside), Deena

Engel (New York University), Henry A. Etlinger (Rochester Institute of Technology), James Ten Eyck (Marist College), Myers Foreman (Lamar University), Olac Fuentes (University of Texas at El Paso), Edward F. Gehringer (North Carolina State University), Harold Grossman (Clemson University), Barbara Guillot (Louisiana State University), Stuart Hansen (University of Wisconsin, Parkside), Dan Harvey (Southern Oregon University), Ron Hofman (Red River College, Canada), Stephen Hughes (Roanoke College), Vladan Jovanovic (Georgia Southern University), Edwin Kay (Lehigh University), Larry King (University of Texas at Dallas), Nana Kofi (Langara College, Canada), George Koutsogiannakis (Illinois Institute of Technology), Roger Kraft (Purdue University at Calumet), Norman Krumpe (Miami University), Hong Lin (DeVry Institute), Dan Lipsa (Armstrong Atlantic State University), James Madison (Rensselaer Polytechnic Institute), Frank Malinowski (Darton College), Tim Margush (University of Akron), Debbie Masada (Sun Microsystems), Blayne Mayfield (Oklahoma State University), John McGrath (J.P. McGrath Consulting), Hugh McGuire (Grand Valley State), Shyamal Mitra (University of Texas at Austin), Michel Mitri (James Madison University), Kenrick Mock (University of Alaska Anchorage), Frank Murgolo (California State University, Long Beach), Jun Ni (University of Iowa), Benjamin Nystuen (University of Colorado at Colorado Springs), Maureen Opkins (CA State University, Long Beach), Gavin Osborne (University of Saskatchewan), Kevin Parker (Idaho State University), Dale Parson (Kutztown University), Mark Pendergast (Florida Gulf Coast University), Richard Povinelli (Marquette University), Roger Priebe (University of Texas at Austin), Mary Ann Pumphrey (De Anza Junior College), Pat Roth (Southern Polytechnic State University), Amr Sabry (Indiana University), Carolyn Schauble (Colorado State University), David Scuse (University of Manitoba), Ashraf Shirani (San Jose State University), Daniel Spiegel (Kutztown University), Joslyn A. Smith (Florida Atlantic University) , Lixin Tao (Pace University), Ronald F. Taylor (Wright State University), Russ Tront (Simon Fraser University), Deborah Trytten (University of Oklahoma), Kent Vidrine (George Washington University), and Bahram Zartoshty (California State University at Northridge).

It is a great pleasure, honor, and privilege to work with Pearson. I would like to thank Tracy Dunkelberger and her colleagues Marcia Horton, Michael Hirsch, Matt Goldstein, Carole Snyder, Tim Huddleston, Yez Alayan, Jeff Holcomb, Kayla Smith-Tarbox, Gillian Hall, Rebecca Greenberg, and their colleagues for organizing, producing, and promoting this project.

As always, I am indebted to my wife, Samantha, for her love, support, and encouragement.

BRIEF CONTENTS

Chapters 35–50 are bonus Web chapters

CONTENTS

Bonus Chapters 35–50 are available from the companion Website at www.pearsonhighered.com/liang:

VideoNotes

Locations of **VideoNotes**
http://www.pearsonhighered.com/liang

CHAPTER 1

INTRODUCTION TO COMPUTERS, PROGRAMS, AND JAVA

Objectives

- To understand computer basics, programs, and operating systems (§§1.2–1.4).
- To describe the relationship between Java and the World Wide Web (§1.5).
- To understand the meaning of Java language specification, API, JDK, and IDE (§1.6).
- To write a simple Java program (§1.7).
- To display output on the console (§1.7).
- To explain the basic syntax of a Java program (§1.7).
- To create, compile, and run Java programs (§1.8).
- To display output using the `JOptionPane` message dialog boxes (§1.9).
- To become familiar with Java programming style and documentation (§1.10).
- To explain the differences between syntax errors, runtime errors, and logic errors (§1.11).

1.1 Introduction

The central theme of this book is to learn how to solve problems by writing a program.

what is programming?
programming
program

This book is about programming. So, what is programming? The term *programming* means to create (or develop) software, which is also called a *program.* In basic terms, software contains the instructions that tell a computer—or a computerized device—what to do.

Software is all around you, even in devices that you might not think would need it. Of course, you expect to find and use software on a personal computer, but software also plays a role in running airplanes, cars, cell phones, and even toasters. On a personal computer, you use word processors to write documents, Web browsers to explore the Internet, and e-mail programs to send messages. These programs are all examples of software. Software developers create software with the help of powerful tools called *programming languages.*

This book teaches you how to create programs by using the Java programming language. There are many programming languages, some of which are decades old. Each language was invented for a specific purpose—to build on the strengths of a previous language, for example, or to give the programmer a new and unique set of tools. Knowing that there are so many programming languages available, it would be natural for you to wonder which one is best. But, in truth, there is no "best" language. Each one has its own strengths and weaknesses. Experienced programmers know that one language might work well in some situations, whereas a different language may be more appropriate in other situations. For this reason, seasoned programmers try to master as many different programming languages as they can, giving them access to a vast arsenal of software-development tools.

If you learn to program using one language, you should find it easy to pick up other languages. The key is to learn how to solve problems using a programming approach. That is the main theme of this book.

You are about to begin an exciting journey: learning how to program. At the outset, it is helpful to review computer basics, programs, and operating systems. If you are already familiar with such terms as CPU, memory, disks, operating systems, and programming languages, you may skip the review in Sections 1.2–1.4.

1.2 What Is a Computer?

A computer is an electronic device that stores and processes data.

hardware
software

A computer includes both *hardware* and *software.* In general, hardware comprises the visible, physical elements of the computer, and software provides the invisible instructions that control the hardware and make it perform specific tasks. Knowing computer hardware isn't essential to learning a programming language, but it can help you better understand the effects that a program's instructions have on the computer and its components. This section introduces computer hardware components and their functions.

A computer consists of the following major hardware components (Figure 1.1):

- A central processing unit (CPU)
- Memory (main memory)
- Storage devices (such as disks and CDs)
- Input devices (such as the mouse and keyboard)
- Output devices (such as monitors and printers)
- Communication devices (such as modems and network interface cards)

bus

A computer's components are interconnected by a subsystem called a *bus.* You can think of a bus as a sort of system of roads running among the computer's components; data and

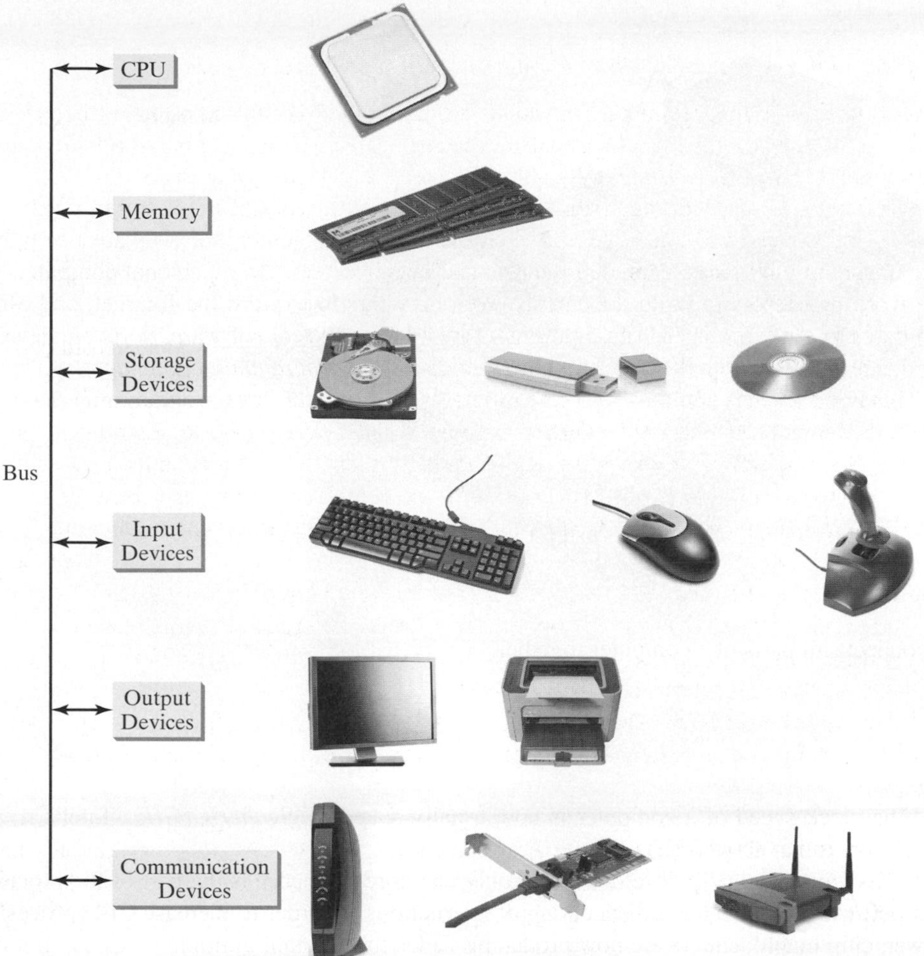

FIGURE 1.1 A computer consists of a CPU, memory, storage devices, input devices, output devices, and communication devices.

power travel along the bus from one part of the computer to another. In personal computers, the bus is built into the computer's *motherboard,* which is a circuit case that connects all of the parts of a computer together, as shown in Figure 1.2.

motherboard

1.2.1 Central Processing Unit

CPU

The *central processing unit (CPU)* is the computer's brain. It retrieves instructions from memory and executes them. The CPU usually has two components: a *control unit* and an *arithmetic/logic unit.* The control unit controls and coordinates the actions of the other components. The arithmetic/logic unit performs numeric operations (addition, subtraction, multiplication, division) and logical operations (comparisons).

Today's CPUs are built on small silicon semiconductor chips that contain millions of tiny electric switches, called *transistors,* for processing information.

speed

hertz

megahertz

Every computer has an internal clock, which emits electronic pulses at a constant rate. These pulses are used to control and synchronize the pace of operations. A higher clock *speed* enables more instructions to be executed in a given period of time. The unit of measurement of clock speed is the *hertz (Hz)*, with 1 hertz equaling 1 pulse per second. In the 1990s computers measured clocked speed in *megahertz (MHz)*, but CPU speed has been improving continuously,

FIGURE 1.2 The motherboard connects all parts of a computer together.

gigahertz

and the clock speed of a computer is now usually stated in *gigahertz (GHz).* Intel's newest processors run at about 3 GHz.

core

CPUs were originally developed with only one core. The *core* is the part of the processor that performs the reading and executing of instructions. In order to increase CPU processing power, chip manufacturers are now producing CPUs that contain multiple cores. A multicore CPU is a single component with two or more independent processors. Today's consumer computers typically have two, three, and even four separate cores. Soon, CPUs with dozens or even hundreds of cores will be affordable.

1.2.2 Bits and Bytes

Before we discuss memory, let's look at how information (data and programs) are stored in a computer.

A computer is really nothing more than a series of switches. Each switch exists in two states: on or off. Storing information in a computer is simply a matter of setting a sequence of switches on or off. If the switch is on, its value is 1. If the switch is off, its value is 0.

bits

These 0s and 1s are interpreted as digits in the binary number system and are called *bits* (binary digits).

byte

The minimum storage unit in a computer is a *byte.* A byte is composed of eight bits. A small number such as `3` can be stored as a single byte. To store a number that cannot fit into a single byte, the computer uses several bytes.

Data of various kinds, such as numbers and characters, are encoded as a series of bytes. As a programmer, you don't need to worry about the encoding and decoding of data, which the

encoding scheme

computer system performs automatically, based on the encoding scheme. An *encoding scheme* is a set of rules that govern how a computer translates characters, numbers, and symbols into data the computer can actually work with. Most schemes translate each character into a predetermined string of numbers. In the popular ASCII encoding scheme, for example, the character `C` is represented as `01000011` in one byte.

A computer's storage capacity is measured in bytes and multiples of the byte, as follows:

- A *kilobyte (KB)* is about 1,000 bytes. kilobyte (KB)
- A *megabyte (MB)* is about 1 million bytes. megabyte (MB)
- A *gigabyte (GB)* is about 1 billion bytes. gigabyte (GB)
- A *terabyte (TB)* is about 1 trillion bytes. terabyte (TB)

A typical one-page word document might take 20 KB. Therefore, 1 MB can store 50 pages of documents and 1 GB can store 50,000 pages of documents. A typical two-hour high-resolution movie might take 8 GB, so it would require 160 GB to store 20 movies.

1.2.3 Memory

memory

A computer's *memory* consists of an ordered sequence of bytes for storing programs as well as data that the program is working with. You can think of memory as the computer's work area for executing a program. A program and its data must be moved into the computer's memory before they can be executed by the CPU.

unique address

Every byte in the memory has a *unique address*, as shown in Figure 1.3. The address is used to locate the byte for storing and retrieving the data. Since the bytes in the memory can be accessed in any order, the memory is also referred to as *random-access memory (RAM)*. RAM

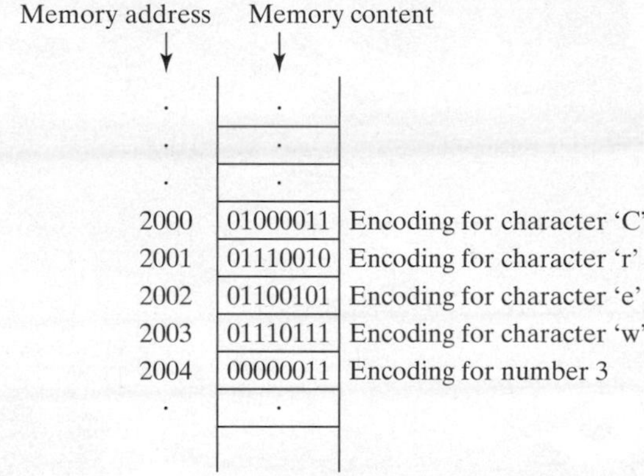

FIGURE 1.3 Memory stores data and program instructions in uniquely addressed memory locations. Each memory location can store one byte of data.

Today's personal computers usually have at least 1 gigabyte of RAM, but they more commonly have 2 to 4 GB installed. Generally speaking, the more RAM a computer has, the faster it can operate, but there are limits to this simple rule of thumb.

A memory byte is never empty, but its initial content may be meaningless to your program. The current content of a memory byte is lost whenever new information is placed in it.

Like the CPU, memory is built on silicon semiconductor chips that have millions of transistors embedded on their surface. Compared to CPU chips, memory chips are less complicated, slower, and less expensive.

1.2.4 Storage Devices

A computer's memory (RAM) is a volatile form of data storage: any information that has been stored in memory (that is, saved) is lost when the system's power is turned off. Programs and data are permanently stored on *storage devices* and are moved, when the computer actually uses them, to memory, which operates at much faster speeds than permanent storage devices can. storage devices

There are three main types of storage devices:

- Magnetic disk drives
- Optical disc drives (CD and DVD)
- USB flash drives

drive

Drives are devices for operating a medium, such as disks and CDs. A storage medium physically stores data and program instructions. The drive reads data from the medium and writes data onto the medium.

Disks

hard disk

A computer usually has at least one hard disk drive (Figure 1.4). *Hard disks* are used for permanently storing data and programs. Newer computers have hard disks that can store from 200 to 800 gigabytes of data. Hard disk drives are usually encased inside the computer, but removable hard disks are also available.

FIGURE 1.4 A hard disk is a device for permanently storing programs and data.

CDs and DVDs

CD-R

CD-RW

CD stands for compact disc. There are two types of CD drives: CD-R and CD-RW. A *CD-R* is for read-only permanent storage; the user cannot modify its contents once they are recorded. A *CD-RW* can be used like a hard disk; that is, you can write data onto the disc, and then overwrite that data with new data. A single CD can hold up to 700 MB. Most new PCs are equipped with a CD-RW drive that can work with both CD-R and CD-RW discs.

DVD

DVD stands for digital versatile disc or digital video disc. DVDs and CDs look alike, and you can use either to store data. A DVD can hold more information than a CD; a standard DVD's storage capacity is 4.7 GB. Like CDs, there are two types of DVDs: DVD-R (read-only) and DVD-RW (rewritable).

USB Flash Drives

Universal serial bus (USB) connectors allow the user to attach many kinds of peripheral devices to the computer. You can use a USB to connect a printer, digital camera, mouse, external hard disk drive, and other devices to the computer.

A USB *flash drive* is a device for storing and transporting data. A flash drive is small—about the size of a pack of gum, as shown in Figure 1.5. It acts like a portable hard drive that can be plugged into your computer's USB port. USB flash drives are currently available with up to 256 GB storage capacity.

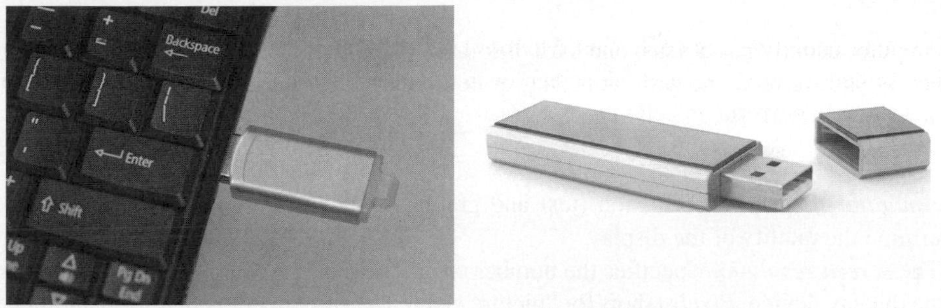

FIGURE 1.5 USB flash drives are very portable and can store a lot of data.

1.2.5 Input and Output Devices

Input and output devices let the user communicate with the computer. The most common input devices are *keyboards* and *mice.* The most common output devices are *monitors* and *printers.*

The Keyboard

A keyboard is a device for entering input. Figure 1.6 shows a typical keyboard. Compact keyboards are available without a numeric keypad.

FIGURE 1.6 A computer keyboard consists of the keys for sending input to a computer.

Function keys are located across the top of the keyboard and are prefaced with the letter *F.* Their functions depend on the software currently being used. function key

modifier key

A *modifier key* is a special key (such as the *Shift*, *Alt*, and *Ctrl* keys) that modifies the normal action of another key when the two are pressed simultaneously.

numeric keypad

The *numeric keypad*, located on the right side of most keyboards, is a separate set of keys styled like a calculator to use for entering numbers quickly.

arrow keys

Arrow keys, located between the main keypad and the numeric keypad, are used to move the mouse pointer up, down, left, and right on the screen in many kinds of programs.

Insert key
Delete key
Page Up key
Page Down key

The *Insert*, *Delete*, *Page Up*, and *Page Down keys* are used in word processing and other programs for inserting text and objects, deleting text and objects, and moving up or down through a document one screen at a time.

The Mouse

A *mouse* is a pointing device. It is used to move a graphical pointer (usually in the shape of an arrow) called a *cursor* around the screen or to click on-screen objects (such as a button) to trigger them to perform an action.

The Monitor

The *monitor* displays information (text and graphics). The screen resolution and dot pitch determine the quality of the display.

screen resolution
pixels

The *screen resolution* specifies the number of pixels in horizontal and vertical dimensions of the display device. *Pixels* (short for "picture elements") are tiny dots that form an image on the screen. A common resolution for a 17-inch screen, for example, is 1,024 pixels wide and 768 pixels high. The resolution can be set manually. The higher the resolution, the sharper and clearer the image is.

dot pitch

The *dot pitch* is the amount of space between pixels, measured in millimeters. The smaller the dot pitch, the sharper the display.

1.2.6 Communication Devices

modem

Computers can be networked through communication devices, such as a dial-up *modem* (*mo*dulator/*dem*odulator), a DSL or cable modem, a wired network interface card, or a wireless adapter.

- A dial-up modem uses a phone line and can transfer data at a speed up to 56,000 bps (bits per second).

digital subscriber line (DSL)

- A *digital subscriber line (DSL)* connection also uses a standard phone line, but it can transfer data 20 times faster than a standard dial-up modem.

cable modem

- A *cable modem* uses the cable TV line maintained by the cable company and is generally faster than DSL.

network interface card (NIC)
local area network (LAN)
million bits per second (mbps)

- A *network interface card (NIC)* is a device that connects a computer to a *local area network (LAN)*, as shown in Figure 1.7. LANs are commonly used in universities, businesses, and government agencies. A high-speed NIC called *1000BaseT* can transfer data at 1,000 million bits per second (mbps).
- Wireless networking is now extremely popular in homes, businesses, and schools. Every laptop computer sold today is equipped with a wireless adapter that enables the computer to connect to a local area network and the Internet.

Note

Answers to checkpoint questions are on the Companion Website.

Check Point
MyProgrammingLab™

1.1 What are hardware and software?

1.2 List five major hardware components of a computer.

1.3 What does the acronym "CPU" stand for?

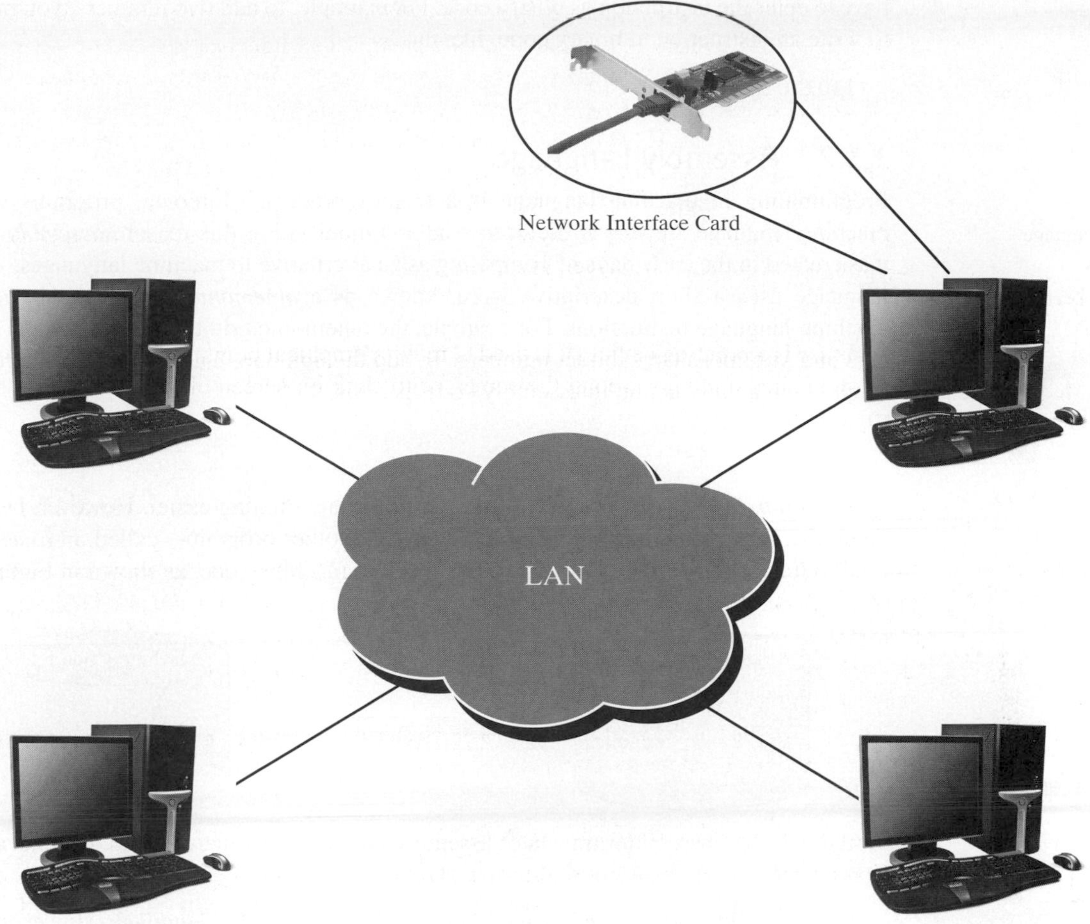

Figure 1.7 A local area network connects computers in close proximity to each other.

1.4 What unit is used to measure CPU speed?

1.5 What is a bit? What is a byte?

1.6 What is memory for? What does RAM stand for? Why is memory called RAM?

1.7 What unit is used to measure memory size?

1.8 What unit is used to measure disk size?

1.9 What is the primary difference between memory and a storage device?

1.3 Programming Languages

Computer programs, *known as* software, *are instructions that tell a computer what to do.*

Computers do not understand human languages, so programs must be written in a language a computer can use. There are hundreds of programming languages, and they were developed to make the programming process easier for people. However, all programs must be converted into a language the computer can understand.

1.3.1 Machine Language

A computer's native language, which differs among different types of computers, is its *machine language*—a set of built-in primitive instructions. These instructions are in the form of binary code, so if you want to give a computer an instruction in its native language, you

machine language

have to enter the instruction as binary code. For example, to add two numbers, you might have to write an instruction in binary code, like this:

```
1101101010011010
```

1.3.2 Assembly Language

assembly language

Programming in machine language is a tedious process. Moreover, programs written in machine language are very difficult to read and modify. For this reason, *assembly language* was created in the early days of computing as an alternative to machine languages. Assembly language uses a short descriptive word, known as a *mnemonic*, to represent each of the machine-language instructions. For example, the mnemonic **add** typically means to add numbers and **sub** means to subtract numbers. To add the numbers **2** and **3** and get the result, you might write an instruction in assembly code like this:

```
add 2, 3, result
```

assembler

Assembly languages were developed to make programming easier. However, because the computer cannot understand assembly language, another program—called an *assembler*—is used to translate assembly-language programs into machine code, as shown in Figure 1.8.

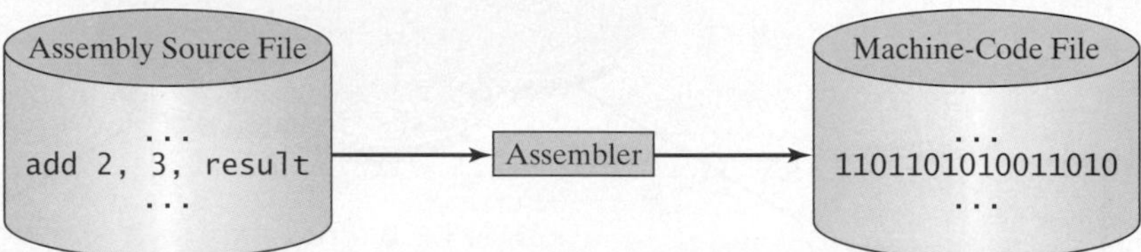

FIGURE 1.8 An assembler translates assembly-language instructions into machine code.

low-level language

Writing code in assembly language is easier than in machine language. However, it is still tedious to write code in assembly language. An instruction in assembly language essentially corresponds to an instruction in machine code. Writing in assembly requires that you know how the CPU works. Assembly language is referred to as a *low-level language*, because assembly language is close in nature to machine language and is machine dependent.

1.3.3 High-Level Language

high-level language

statement

In the 1950s, a new generation of programming languages known as *high-level languages* emerged. They are platform-independent, which means that you can write a program in a high-level language and run it in different types of machines. High-level languages are English-like and easy to learn and use. The instructions in a high-level programming language are called *statements*. Here, for example, is a high-level language statement that computes the area of a circle with a radius of **5**:

```
area = 5 * 5 * 3.1415
```

There are many high-level programming languages, and each was designed for a specific purpose. Table 1.1 lists some popular ones.

source program

source code

interpreter

compiler

A program written in a high-level language is called a *source program* or *source code*. Because a computer cannot understand a source program, a source program must be translated into machine code for execution. The translation can be done using another programming tool called an *interpreter* or a *compiler*.

- An interpreter reads one statement from the source code, translates it to the machine code or virtual machine code, and then executes it right away, as shown in Figure 1.9a.

TABLE 1.1 Popular High-Level Programming Languages

Language	*Description*
Ada	Named for Ada Lovelace, who worked on mechanical general-purpose computers. The Ada language was developed for the Department of Defense and is used mainly in defense projects.
BASIC	Beginner's All-purpose Symbolic Instruction Code. It was designed to be learned and used easily by beginners.
C	Developed at Bell Laboratories. C combines the power of an assembly language with the ease of use and portability of a high-level language.
C++	C++ is an object-oriented language, based on C.
C#	Pronounced "C Sharp." It is a hybrid of Java and C++ and was developed by Microsoft.
COBOL	COmmon Business Oriented Language. Used for business applications.
FORTRAN	FORmula TRANslation. Popular for scientific and mathematical applications.
Java	Developed by Sun Microsystems, now part of Oracle. It is widely used for developing platform-independent Internet applications.
Pascal	Named for Blaise Pascal, who pioneered calculating machines in the seventeenth century. It is a simple, structured, general-purpose language primarily for teaching programming.
Python	A simple general-purpose scripting language good for writing short programs.
Visual Basic	Visual Basic was developed by Microsoft and it enables the programmers to rapidly develop graphical user interfaces.

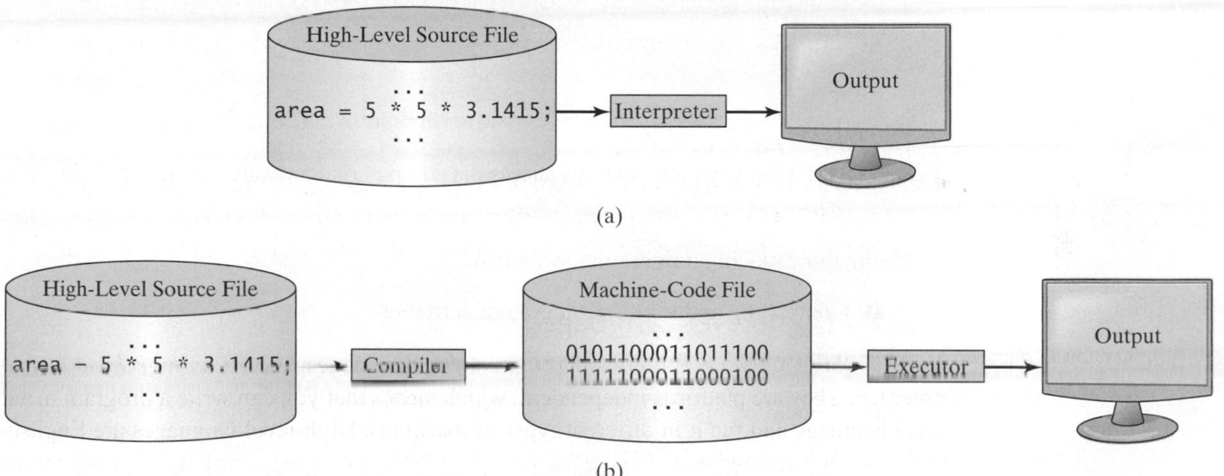

FIGURE 1.9 (a) An interpreter translates and executes a program one statement at a time. (b) A compiler translates the entire source program into a machine-language file for execution.

Note that a statement from the source code may be translated into several machine instructions.

- A compiler translates the entire source code into a machine-code file, and the machine-code file is then executed, as shown in Figure 1.9b.

1.10 What language does the CPU understand?

1.11 What is an assembly language?

MyProgrammingLab™

1.12 What is an assembler?

1.13 What is a high-level programming language?

1.14 What is a source program?

1.15 What is an interpreter?

1.16 What is a compiler?

1.17 What is the difference between an interpreted language and a compiled language?

1.4 Operating Systems

The operating system (OS) *is the most important program that runs on a computer. The OS manages and controls a computer's activities.*

operating system (OS)

The popular *operating systems* for general-purpose computers are Microsoft Windows, Mac OS, and Linux. Application programs, such as a Web browser or a word processor, cannot run unless an operating system is installed and running on the computer. Figure 1.10 shows the interrelationship of hardware, operating system, application software, and the user.

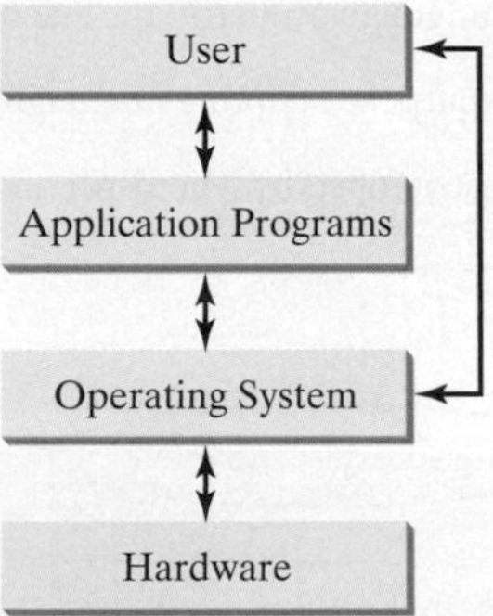

FIGURE 1.10 Users and applications access the computer's hardware via the operating system.

The major tasks of an operating system are:

- Controlling and monitoring system activities
- Allocating and assigning system resources
- Scheduling operations

1.4.1 Controlling and Monitoring System Activities

Operating systems perform basic tasks, such as recognizing input from the keyboard, sending output to the monitor, keeping track of files and folders on storage devices, and controlling peripheral devices, such as disk drives and printers. An operating system must also ensure that different programs and users working at the same time do not interfere with each other. In addition, the OS is responsible for security, ensuring that unauthorized users and programs do not access the system.

1.4.2 Allocating and Assigning System Resources

The operating system is responsible for determining what computer resources a program needs (such as CPU time, memory space, disks, input and output devices) and for allocating and assigning them to run the program.

1.4.3 Scheduling Operations

The OS is responsible for scheduling programs' activities to make efficient use of system resources. Many of today's operating systems support such techniques as *multiprogramming*, *multithreading*, and *multiprocessing* to increase system performance.

multiprogramming

Multiprogramming allows multiple programs to run simultaneously by sharing the same CPU. The CPU is much faster than the computer's other components. As a result, it is idle most of the time—for example, while waiting for data to be transferred from a disk or waiting for other system resources to respond. A multiprogramming OS takes advantage of this situation by allowing multiple programs to use the CPU when it would otherwise be idle. For example, multiprogramming enables you to use a word processor to edit a file at the same time as your Web browser is downloading a file.

multithreading

Multithreading allows a single program to execute multiple tasks at the same time. For instance, a word-processing program allows users to simultaneously edit text and save it to a disk. In this example, editing and saving are two tasks within the same application. These two tasks may run concurrently.

multiprocessing

Multiprocessing, or *parallel processing*, uses two or more processors together to perform subtasks concurrently and then combine solutions of the subtasks to obtain a solution for the entire task. It is like a surgical operation where several doctors work together on one patient.

1.18 What is an operating system? List some popular operating systems.

1.19 What are the major responsibilities of an operating system?

1.20 What are multiprogramming, multithreading, and multiprocessing?

1.5 Java, the World Wide Web, and Beyond

Java is a powerful and versatile programming language for developing software running on mobile devices, desktop computers, and servers.

This book introduces Java programming. Java was developed by a team led by James Gosling at Sun Microsystems. Sun Microsystems was purchased by Oracle in 2010. Originally called *Oak*, Java was designed in 1991 for use in embedded chips in consumer electronic appliances. In 1995, renamed *Java*, it was redesigned for developing Web applications. For the history of Java, see www.java.com/en/javahistory/index.jsp.

Java has become enormously popular. Its rapid rise and wide acceptance can be traced to its design characteristics, particularly its promise that you can write a program once and run it anywhere. As stated by its designer, Java is *simple*, *object oriented*, *distributed*, *interpreted*, *robust*, *secure*, *architecture neutral*, *portable*, *high performance*, *multithreaded*, and *dynamic*. For the anatomy of Java characteristics, see www.cs.armstrong.edu/liang/JavaCharacteristics.pdf.

Java is a full-featured, general-purpose programming language that can be used to develop robust mission-critical applications. Today, it is employed not only for Web programming, but also for developing standalone applications across platforms on servers, desktop computers, and mobile devices. It was used to develop the code to communicate with and control the robotic rover on Mars. Many companies that once considered Java to be more hype than substance are now using it to create distributed applications accessed by customers and partners across the Internet. For every new project being developed today, companies are asking how they can use Java to make their work easier.

The World Wide Web is an electronic information repository that can be accessed on the Internet from anywhere in the world. The Internet, the Web's infrastructure, has been around for more than forty years. The colorful World Wide Web and sophisticated Web browsers are the major reason for the Internet's popularity.

Java initially became attractive because Java programs can be run from a Web browser. Such programs are called *applets*. Applets employ a modern graphical interface with buttons, text fields, text areas, radio buttons, and so on, to interact with users on the Web and process their requests. Applets make the Web responsive, interactive, and fun to use. Applets are embedded in an HTML file. *HTML (Hypertext Markup Language)* is a simple scripting language for laying out documents, linking documents on the Internet, and bringing images, sound, and video alive on the Web. Figure 1.11 shows an applet running from a Web browser for playing a tic-tac-toe game.

applet

HTML

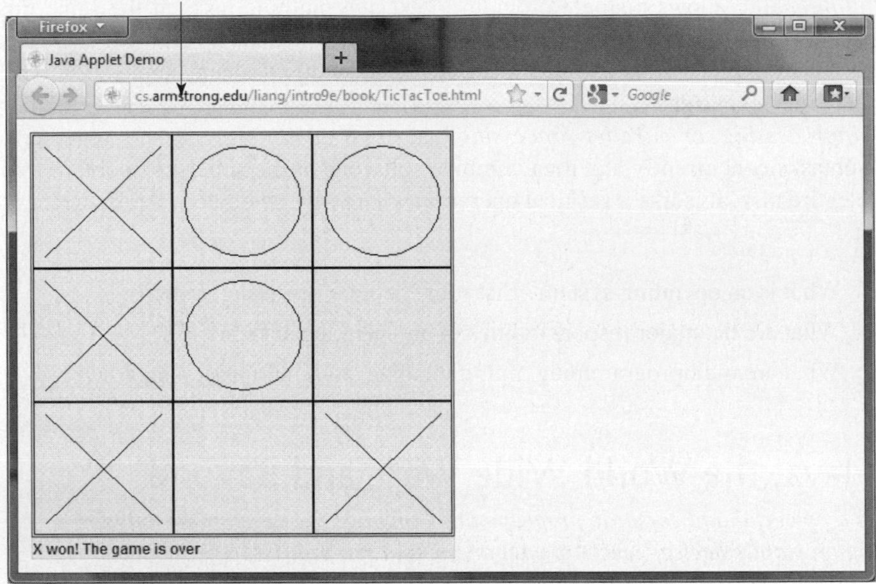

FIGURE 1.11 A Java applet for playing tic-tac-toe runs from a Web browser.

Tip

For a demonstration of Java applets, visit java.sun.com/applets. This site provides a rich Java resource as well as links to other cool applet demo sites.

Java is now very popular for developing applications on Web servers. These applications process data, perform computations, and generate dynamic Web pages. The LiveLab automatic grading system, shown in Figure 1.12 and which you can use with this book, was developed using Java.

Java is a versatile programming language: You can use it to develop applications for desktop computers, servers, and small hand-held devices. The software for Android cell phones is developed using Java. Figure 1.13 shows an emulator for developing Android phone applications.

Check Point

MyProgrammingLab™

1.21 Who invented Java? Which company owns Java now?

1.22 What is a Java applet?

1.23 What programming language does Android use?

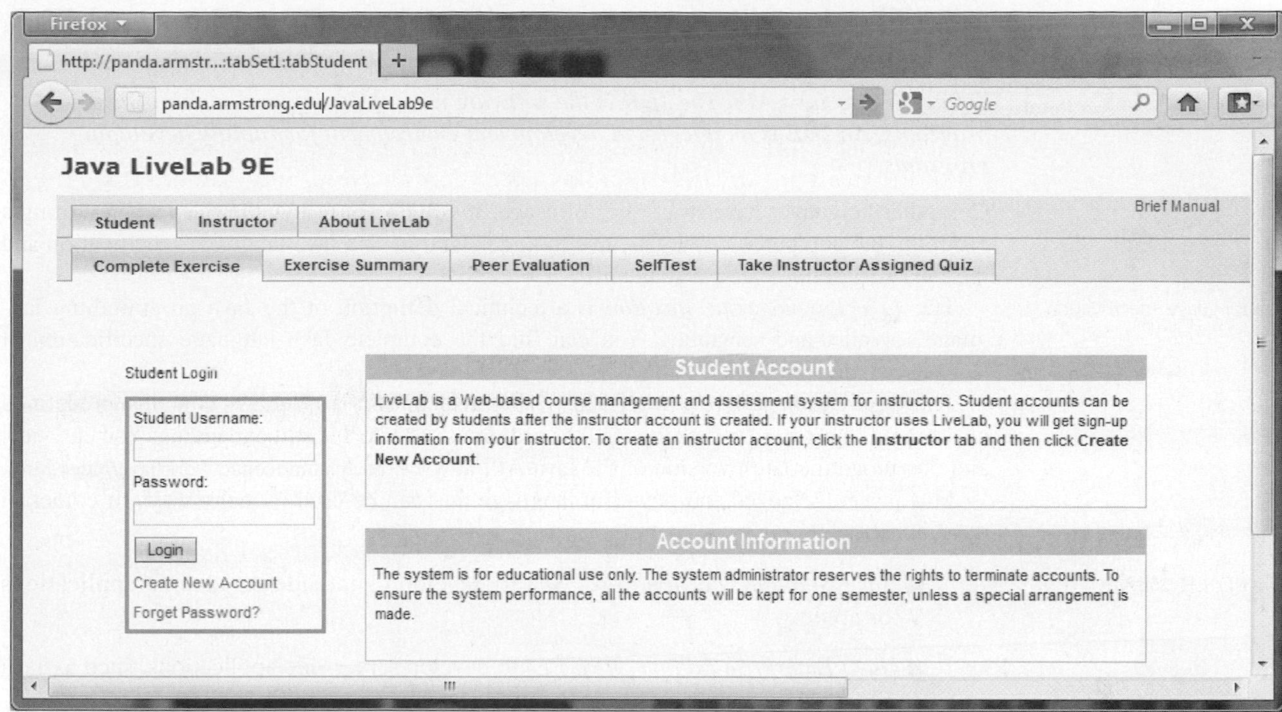

FIGURE 1.12 Java was used to develop LiveLab, the automatic grading system that accompanies this book.

FIGURE 1.13 Java is used in Android phones.

1.6 The Java Language Specification, API, JDK, and IDE

Java syntax is defined in the Java language specification, and the Java library is defined in the Java API. The JDK is the software for developing and running Java programs. An IDE is an integrated development environment for rapidly developing programs.

Computer languages have strict rules of usage. If you do not follow the rules when writing a program, the computer will not be able to understand it. The Java language specification and the Java API define the Java standards.

Java language specification

The *Java language specification* is a technical definition of the Java programming language's syntax and semantics. You can find the complete Java language specification at java.sun.com/docs/books/jls.

API
library

The *application program interface (API)*, also known as *library*, contains predefined classes and interfaces for developing Java programs. The API is still expanding. You can view and download the latest version of the Java API at www.oracle.com/technetwork/java/index.html.

Java is a full-fledged and powerful language that can be used in many ways. It comes in three editions:

Java SE, EE, and ME

- Java *Standard Edition (Java SE)* to develop client-side standalone applications or applets.
- *Java Enterprise Edition (Java EE)* to develop server-side applications, such as Java servlets, JavaServer Pages (JSP), and JavaServer Faces (JSF).
- *Java Micro Edition (Java ME)* to develop applications for mobile devices, such as cell phones.

Java Development Toolkit (JDK)
JDK 1.7 = JDK 7

This book uses Java SE to introduce Java programming. Java SE is the foundation upon which all other Java technology is based. There are many versions of Java SE. The latest, Java SE 7, is used in this book. Oracle releases each version with a *Java Development Toolkit (JDK)*. For Java SE 7, the Java Development Toolkit is called *JDK 1.7* (also known as *Java 7* or *JDK 7*).

Integrated development environment

The JDK consists of a set of separate programs, each invoked from a command line, for developing and testing Java programs. Instead of using the JDK, you can use a Java development tool (e.g., NetBeans, Eclipse, and TextPad)—software that provides an *integrated development environment (IDE)* for developing Java programs quickly. Editing, compiling, building, debugging, and online help are integrated in one graphical user interface. You simply enter source code in one window or open an existing file in a window, and then click a button or menu item or press a function key to compile and run the program.

Check Point
MyProgrammingLab™

1.24 What is the Java language specification?

1.25 What does JDK stand for?

1.26 What does IDE stand for?

1.27 Are tools like NetBeans and Eclipse different languages from Java, or are they dialects or extensions of Java?

1.7 A Simple Java Program

Key Point

A Java program is executed from the `main` method in the class.

what is a console?
console input
console output

Let's begin with a simple Java program that displays the message `Welcome to Java!` on the console. (The word *console* is an old computer term that refers to the text entry and display device of a computer. *Console input* means to receive input from the keyboard, and *console output* means to display output on the monitor.) The program is shown in Listing 1.1.

LISTING 1.1 Welcome.java

```
1 public class Welcome {
2   public static void main(String[] args) {
3     // Display message Welcome to Java! on the console
4     System.out.println("Welcome to Java!");
5   }
6 }
```

class
main method
display message

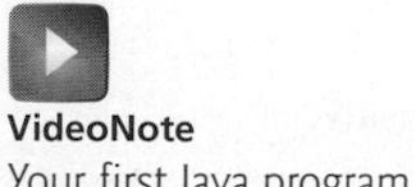

```
Welcome to Java!
```

line numbers

Note that the line numbers are for reference purposes only; they are not part of the program. So, don't type line numbers in your program.

class name

Line 1 defines a class. Every Java program must have at least one class. Each class has a name. By convention, class names start with an uppercase letter. In this example, the class name is `Welcome`.

main method

Line 2 defines the `main` method. The program is executed from the `main` method. A class may contain several methods. The `main` method is the entry point where the program begins execution.

string

A method is a construct that contains statements. The `main` method in this program contains the `System.out.println` statement. This statement displays the string `Welcome to Java!` on the console (line 4). *String* is a programming term meaning a sequence of characters. A string must be enclosed in double quotation marks. Every statement in Java ends with a semicolon (`;`), known as the *statement terminator.*

statement terminator
reserved word
keyword

Reserved words, or *keywords*, have a specific meaning to the compiler and cannot be used for other purposes in the program. For example, when the compiler sees the word `class`, it understands that the word after `class` is the name for the class. Other reserved words in this program are `public`, `static`, and `void`.

comment
line comment
block comment

Line 3 is a *comment* that documents what the program is and how it is constructed. Comments help programmers to communicate and understand the program. They are not programming statements and thus are ignored by the compiler. In Java, comments are preceded by two slashes (`//`) on a line, called a *line comment,* or enclosed between `/*` and `*/` on one or several lines, called a *block comment* or *paragraph comment.* When the compiler sees `//`, it ignores all text after `//` on the same line. When it sees `/*`, it scans for the next `*/` and ignores any text between `/*` and `*/`. Here are examples of comments:

```
// This application program displays Welcome to Java!
/* This application program displays Welcome to Java! */
/* This application program
   displays Welcome to Java! */
```

block

A pair of curly braces in a program forms a *block* that groups the program's components. In Java, each block begins with an opening brace (`{`) and ends with a closing brace (`}`). Every class has a *class block* that groups the data and methods of the class. Similarly, every method has a *method block* that groups the statements in the method. Blocks can be *nested*, meaning that one block can be placed within another, as shown in the following code.

Tip

match braces

An opening brace must be matched by a closing brace. Whenever you type an opening brace, immediately type a closing brace to prevent the missing-brace error. Most Java IDEs automatically insert the closing brace for each opening brace.

```
public class Welcome {
  public static void main(String[] args) {
    System.out.println("Welcome to Java!");
  }
}
```

Class block
Method block

Caution

case sensitive

Java source programs are case sensitive. It would be wrong, for example, to replace `main` in the program with `Main`.

special characters

You have seen several special characters (e.g., `{ }`, `//`, `;`) in the program. They are used in almost every program. Table 1.2 summarizes their uses.

TABLE 1.2 Special Characters

Character	*Name*	*Description*
{}	Opening and closing braces	Denote a block to enclose statements.
()	Opening and closing parentheses	Used with methods.
[]	Opening and closing brackets	Denote an array.
//	Double slashes	Precede a comment line.
" "	Opening and closing quotation marks	Enclose a string (i.e., sequence of characters).
;	Semicolon	Mark the end of a statement.

common errors

syntax rules

The most common errors you will make as you learn to program will be syntax errors. Like any programming language, Java has its own syntax, and you need to write code that conforms to the *syntax rules*. If your program violates a rule—for example, if the semicolon is missing, a brace is missing, a quotation mark is missing, or a word is misspelled—the Java compiler will report syntax errors. Try to compile the program with these errors and see what the compiler reports.

Note

You are probably wondering why the `main` method is defined this way and why `System.out.println(...)` is used to display a message on the console. For the time being, simply accept that this is how things are done. Your questions will be fully answered in subsequent chapters.

The program in Listing 1.1 displays one message. Once you understand the program, it is easy to extend it to display more messages. For example, you can rewrite the program to display three messages, as shown in Listing 1.2.

LISTING 1.2 WelcomeWithThreeMessages.java

class
main method
display message

```
public class WelcomeWithThreeMessages {
  public static void main(String[] args) {
    System.out.println("Programming is fun!");
    System.out.println("Fundamentals First");
    System.out.println("Problem Driven");
  }
}
```

```
Programming is fun!
Fundamentals First
Problem Driven
```

Further, you can perform mathematical computations and display the result on the console. Listing 1.3 gives an example of evaluating $\frac{10.5 + 2 \times 3}{45 - 3.5}$.

LISTING 1.3 ComputeExpression.java

```
public class ComputeExpression {
  public static void main(String[] args) {
    System.out.println((10.5 + 2 * 3) / (45 - 3.5));
  }
}
```

class
main method
compute expression

```
0.39759036144578314
```

The multiplication operator in Java is *. As you can see, it is a straightforward process to translate an arithmetic expression to a Java expression. We will discuss Java expressions further in Chapter 2.

Check Point
MyProgrammingLab™

1.28 What is a keyword? List some Java keywords.

1.29 Is Java case sensitive? What is the case for Java keywords?

1.30 What is a comment? Is the comment ignored by the compiler? How do you denote a comment line and a comment paragraph?

1.31 What is the statement to display a string on the console?

1.32 Show the output of the following code:

```
public class Test {
  public static void main(String[] args) {
    System.out.println("3.5 * 4 / 2 - 2.5 is ");
    System.out.println(3.5 * 4 / 2 - 2.5);
  }
}
```

1.8 Creating, Compiling, and Executing a Java Program

You save a Java program in a .java file and compile it into a .class file. The .class file is executed by the Java Virtual Machine.

You have to create your program and compile it before it can be executed. This process is repetitive, as shown in Figure 1.14. If your program has compile errors, you have to modify the program to fix them, then recompile it. If your program has runtime errors or does not produce the correct result, you have to modify the program, recompile it, and execute it again.

VideoNote
Eclipse brief tutorial

You can use any text editor or IDE to create and edit a Java source-code file. This section demonstrates how to create, compile, and run Java programs from a command window. If you wish to use an *IDE* such as Eclipse, NetBeans, or TextPad, refer to Supplement II for tutorials. From the command window, you can use a text editor such as Notepad to create the Java source-code file, as shown in Figure 1.15.

command window
IDE Supplements

VideoNote
NetBeans brief tutorial

Note

The source file must end with the extension **.java** and must have the same exact name as the public class name. For example, the file for the source code in Listing 1.1 should be named **Welcome.java**, since the public class name is **Welcome**.

file name

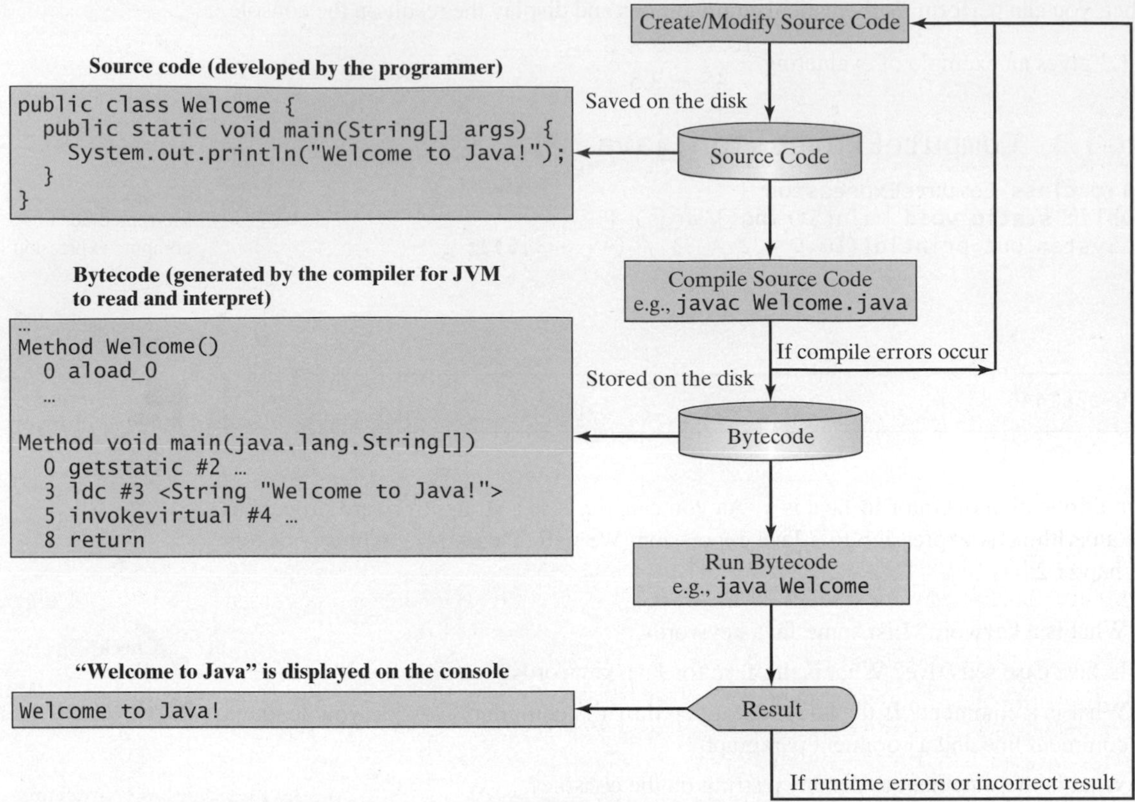

FIGURE 1.14 The Java program-development process consists of repeatedly creating/modifying source code, compiling, and executing programs.

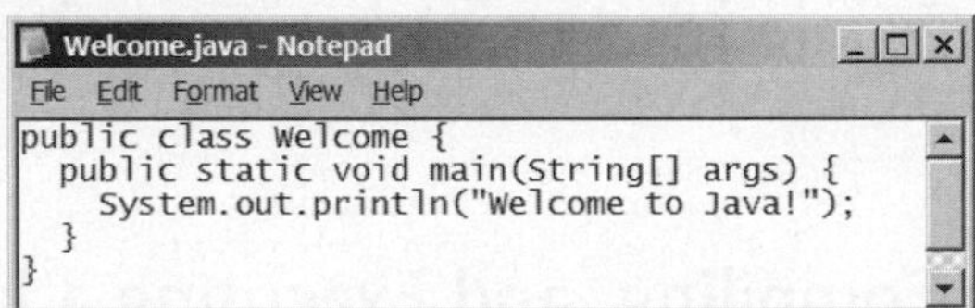

FIGURE 1.15 You can create a Java source file using Windows Notepad.

compile

A Java compiler translates a Java source file into a Java bytecode file. The following command compiles **Welcome.java**:

```
javac Welcome.java
```

Note

Supplement I.B

Supplement I.C

You must first install and configure the JDK before you can compile and run programs. See Supplement I.B, Installing and Configuring JDK 7, for how to install the JDK and set up the environment to compile and run Java programs. If you have trouble compiling and running programs, see Supplement I.C, Compiling and Running Java from the Command Window. This supplement also explains how to use basic DOS commands and how to use Windows Notepad and WordPad to create and edit files. All the supplements are accessible from the Companion Website.

`.class` bytecode file

If there aren't any syntax errors, the *compiler* generates a bytecode file with a `.class` extension. Thus, the preceding command generates a file named **Welcome.class**, as shown in

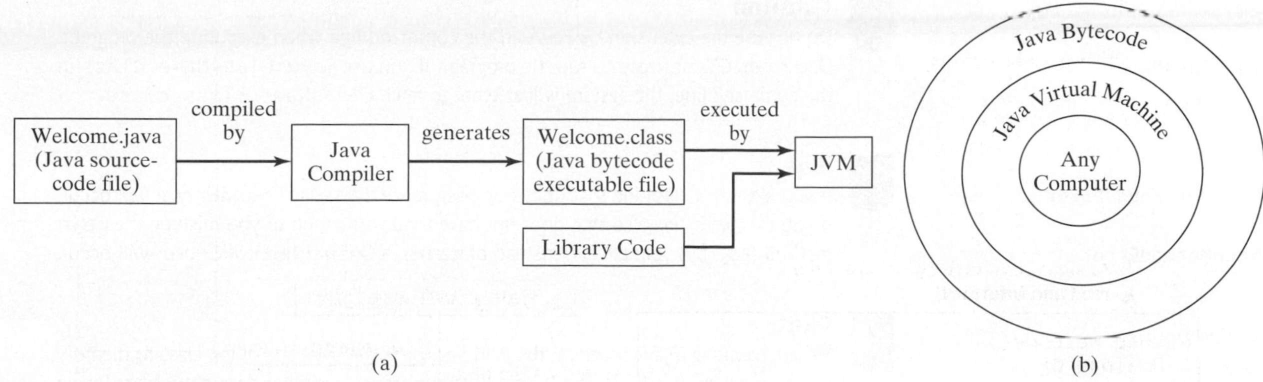

FIGURE 1.16 (a) Java source code is translated into bytecode. (b) Java bytecode can be executed on any computer with a Java Virtual Machine.

Figure 1.16a. The Java language is a high-level language, but Java bytecode is a low-level language. The *bytecode* is similar to machine instructions but is architecture neutral and can run on any platform that has a *Java Virtual Machine (JVM)*, as shown in Figure 1.16b. Rather than a physical machine, the virtual machine is a program that interprets Java bytecode. This is one of Java's primary advantages: *Java bytecode can run on a variety of hardware platforms and operating systems.* Java source code is compiled into Java bytecode and Java bytecode is interpreted by the JVM. Your Java code may use the code in the Java library. The JVM executes your code along with the code in the library.

bytecode

Java Virtual Machine (JVM)

To execute a Java program is to run the program's bytecode. You can execute the bytecode on any platform with a JVM, which is an interpreter. It translates the individual instructions in the bytecode into the target machine language code one at a time rather than the whole program as a single unit. Each step is executed immediately after it is translated.

interpret bytecode

The following command runs the bytecode for Listing 1.1:

run

```
java Welcome
```

Figure 1.17 shows the `javac` command for compiling **Welcome.java**. The compiler generates the **Welcome.class** file, and this file is executed using the `java` command.

`javac` command

`java` command

Note

For simplicity and consistency, all source-code and class files used in this book are placed under `c:\book` unless specified otherwise.

`c:\book`

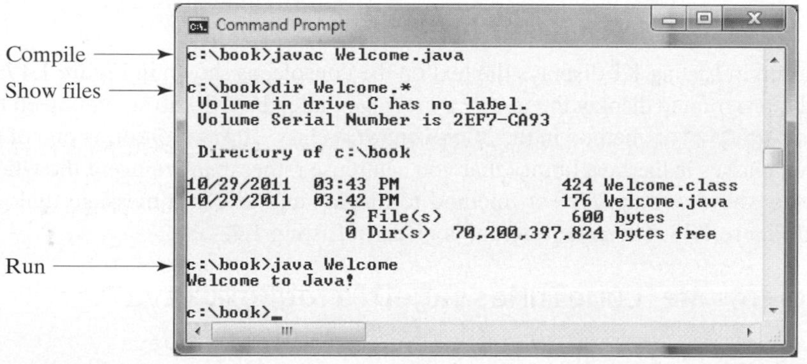

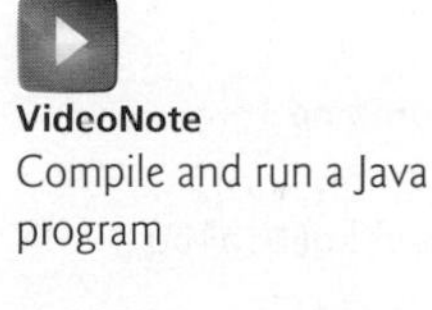

Compile and run a Java program

FIGURE 1.17 The output of Listing 1.1 displays the message "Welcome to Java!"

Caution

java ClassName

Do not use the extension `.class` in the command line when executing the program. Use `java ClassName` to run the program. If you use `java ClassName.class` in the command line, the system will attempt to fetch `ClassName.class.class`.

Tip

NoClassDefFoundError

NoSuchMethodError

If you execute a class file that does not exist, a `NoClassDefFoundError` will occur. If you execute a class file that does not have a `main` method or you mistype the `main` method (e.g., by typing `Main` instead of `main`), a `NoSuchMethodError` will occur.

Note

class loader

bytecode verifier

When executing a Java program, the JVM first loads the bytecode of the class to memory using a program called the *class loader*. If your program uses other classes, the class loader dynamically loads them just before they are needed. After a class is loaded, the JVM uses a program called the *bytecode verifier* to check the validity of the bytecode and to ensure that the bytecode does not violate Java's security restrictions. Java enforces strict security to make sure that Java class files are not tampered and do not harm your computer.

Pedagogical Note

use package

Your instructor may require you to use packages for organizing programs. For example, you may place all programs in this chapter in a package named *chapter1*. For instructions on how to use packages, see Supplement I.F, Using Packages to Organize the Classes in the Text.

Check Point

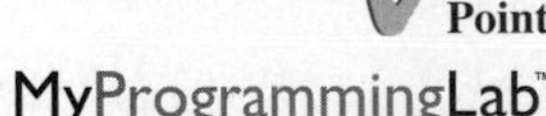

1.33 What is the Java source filename extension, and what is the Java bytecode filename extension?

1.34 What are the input and output of a Java compiler?

1.35 What is the command to compile a Java program?

1.36 What is the command to run a Java program?

1.37 What is the JVM?

1.38 Can Java run on any machine? What is needed to run Java on a computer?

1.39 If a `NoClassDefFoundError` occurs when you run a program, what is the cause of the error?

1.40 If a `NoSuchMethodError` occurs when you run a program, what is the cause of the error?

1.9 Displaying Text in a Message Dialog Box

You can display text in a graphical dialog box.

JOptionPane

showMessageDialog

The program in Listing 1.1 displays the text on the console, as shown in Figure 1.17. You can rewrite the program to display the text in a message dialog box. To do so, you need to use the `showMessageDialog` method in the `JOptionPane` class. `JOptionPane` is one of the many predefined classes in the Java library that you can reuse rather than "reinvent the wheel." You can use the `showMessageDialog` method to display any text in a message dialog box, as shown in Figure 1.18. The new program is given in Listing 1.4.

LISTING 1.4 `WelcomeInMessageDialogBox.java`

block comment

```
/*  This application program displays Welcome to Java!
 *  in a message dialog box.
 */
```

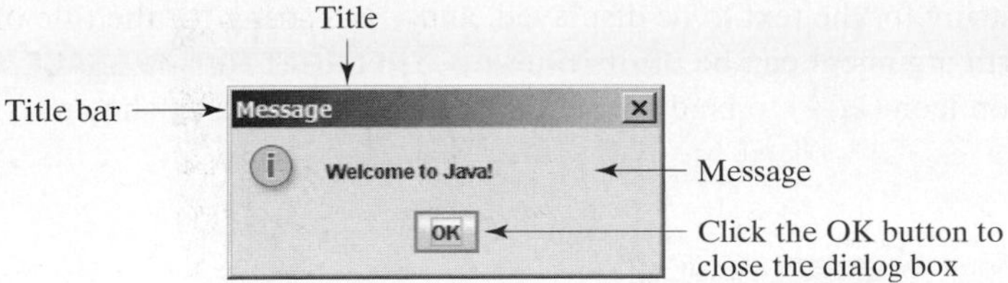

FIGURE 1.18 "Welcome to Java!" is displayed in a message box.

```
 4  import javax.swing.JOptionPane;
 5
 6  public class WelcomeInMessageDialogBox {
 7    public static void main(String[] args) {
 8      // Display Welcome to Java! in a message dialog box
 9      JOptionPane.showMessageDialog(null,"Welcome to Java!");
10    }
11  }
```

import

main method

display message

The first three lines are block comments. The first line begins with `/*` and the last line ends with `*/`. By convention, all other lines begin with an asterisk (`*`).

This program uses the Java class `JOptionPane` (line 9). Java's predefined classes are grouped into packages. `JOptionPane` is in the `javax.swing` package. `JOptionPane` is imported into the program using the `import` statement in line 4 so that the compiler can locate the class without the full name `javax.swing.JOptionPane`.

package

Note

If you replace `JOptionPane` in line 9 with `javax.swing.JOptionPane`, you don't need to import it in line 4. `javax.swing.JOptionPane` is the full name for the `JOptionPane` class.

The `showMessageDialog` method is a *static* method. Such a method should be invoked by using the class name followed by a dot operator (`.`) and the method name with arguments. Details of methods will be discussed in Chapter 5. The `showMessageDialog` method can be invoked with two arguments, as shown below.

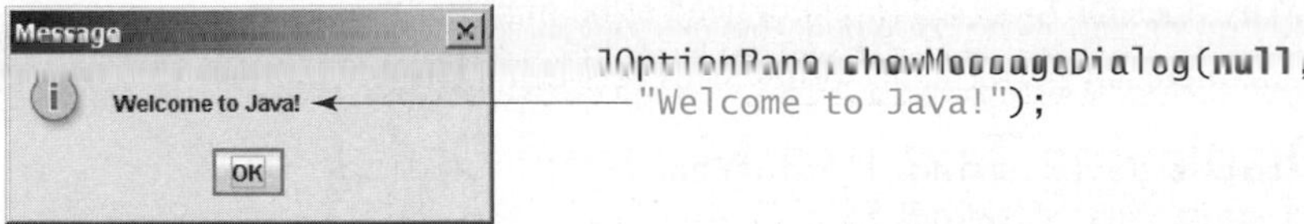

The first argument can always be `null`. `null` is a Java keyword that will be fully discussed in Chapter 8. The second argument is a string for text to be displayed.

There are several ways to use the `showMessageDialog` method. For the time being, you need to know only two ways. One is to use a statement, as shown in the example:

two versions of `showMessageDialog`

```
JOptionPane.showMessageDialog(null, x);
```

where `x` is a string for the text to be displayed.

The other is to use a statement like this one:

```
JOptionPane.showMessageDialog(null, x,
  y, JOptionPane.INFORMATION_MESSAGE);
```

where x is a string for the text to be displayed, and y is a string for the title of the message box. The fourth argument can be JOptionPane.INFORMATION_MESSAGE, which causes the information icon () to be displayed in the message box, as shown in the following example.

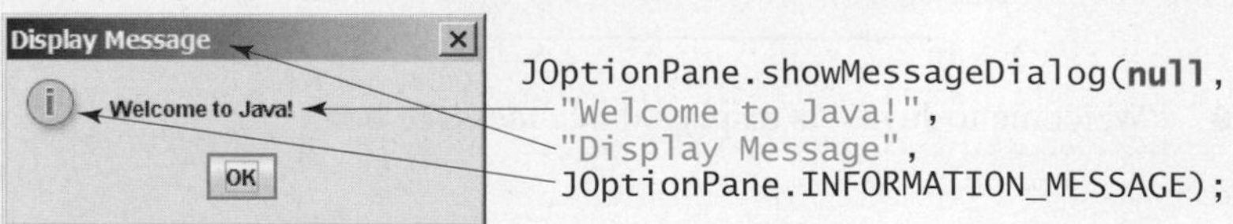

Note

specific import

There are two types of import statements: *specific import* and *wildcard import*. The *specific import* specifies a single class in the import statement. For example, the following statement imports JOptionPane from the package javax.swing.

```
import javax.swing.JOptionPane;
```

wildcard import

The *wildcard import* imports all the classes in a package by using the asterisk as the wildcard. For example, the following statement imports all the classes from the package javax.swing.

```
import javax.swing.*;
```

no performance difference

The information for the classes in an imported package is not read in at compile time or runtime unless the class is used in the program. The import statement simply tells the compiler where to locate the classes. There is no performance difference between a specific import and a wildcard import declaration.

Note

java.lang package implicitly imported

Recall that you have used the System class in the statement System.out.println("Welcome to Java"); in Listing 1.1. The System class is not imported because it is in the java.lang package. All the classes in the java.lang package are *implicitly* imported in every Java program.

MyProgrammingLab™

1.41 What is the statement to display the message "Hello world" in a message dialog box?

1.42 Why does the System class not need to be imported?

1.43 Are there any performance differences between the following two import statements?

```
import javax.swing.JOptionPane;
import javax.swing.*;
```

1.10 Programming Style and Documentation

Good programming style and proper documentation make a program easy to read and help programmers prevent errors.

programming style

documentation

Programming style deals with what programs look like. A program can compile and run properly even if written on only one line, but writing it all on one line would be bad programming style because it would be hard to read. *Documentation* is the body of explanatory remarks and comments pertaining to a program. Programming style and documentation are as important as coding. Good programming style and appropriate documentation reduce the chance of errors and make programs easy to read. This section gives several guidelines. For more detailed guidelines, see Supplement I.D, Java Coding Style Guidelines, on the Companion Website.

1.10.1 Appropriate Comments and Comment Styles

Include a summary at the beginning of the program that explains what the program does, its key features, and any unique techniques it uses. In a long program, you should also include comments that introduce each major step and explain anything that is difficult to read. It is important to make comments concise so that they do not crowd the program or make it difficult to read.

In addition to line comments (beginning with //) and block comments (beginning with /*), Java supports comments of a special type, referred to as *javadoc comments*. javadoc comments begin with /** and end with */. They can be extracted into an HTML file using the JDK's javadoc command. For more information, see java.sun.com/j2se/javadoc.

javadoc comment

Use javadoc comments (/** ... */) for commenting on an entire class or an entire method. These comments must precede the class or the method header in order to be extracted into a javadoc HTML file. For commenting on steps inside a method, use line comments (//). To see an example of a javadoc HTML file, check out www.cs.armstrong.edu/liang/javadoc/Exercise1.html. Its corresponding Java code is shown in www.cs.armstrong.edu/liang/javadoc/Exercise1.java.

1.10.2 Proper Indentation and Spacing

A consistent indentation style makes programs clear and easy to read, debug, and maintain. *Indentation* is used to illustrate the structural relationships between a program's components or statements. Java can read the program even if all of the statements are on the same long line, but humans find it easier to read and maintain code that is aligned properly. Indent each subcomponent or statement at least *two* spaces more than the construct within which it is nested.

indent code

A single space should be added on both sides of a binary operator, as shown in the following statement:

```
System.out.println(3+4*4);          <-- Bad style

System.out.println(3 + 4 * 4);      <-- Good style
```

1.10.3 Block Styles

A *block* is a group of statements surrounded by braces. There are two popular styles, *next-line* style and *end-of-line* style, as shown below.

```
public class Test
{
  public static void main(String[] args)
  {
    System.out.println("Block Styles");
  }
}
```

Next-line style

```
public class Test {
  public static void main(String[] args) {
    System.out.println("Block Styles");
  }
}
```

End-of-line style

The next-line style aligns braces vertically and makes programs easy to read, whereas the end-of-line style saves space and may help avoid some subtle programming errors. Both are acceptable block styles. The choice depends on personal or organizational preference. You should use a block style consistently—mixing styles is not recommended. This book uses the *end-of-line* style to be consistent with the Java API source code.

MyProgrammingLab™

1.44 Reformat the following program according to the programming style and documentation guidelines. Use the end-of-line brace style.

```
public class Test
{
  // Main method
  public static void main(String[] args) {
  /** Display output */
  System.out.println("Welcome to Java");
  }
}
```

1.11 Programming Errors

Programming errors can be categorized into three types: syntax errors, runtime errors, *and* logic errors.

1.11.1 Syntax Errors

syntax errors
compile errors

Errors that are detected by the compiler are called *syntax errors* or *compile errors*. Syntax errors result from errors in code construction, such as mistyping a keyword, omitting some necessary punctuation, or using an opening brace without a corresponding closing brace. These errors are usually easy to detect, because the compiler tells you where they are and what caused them. For example, the program in Listing 1.5 has a syntax error, as shown in Figure 1.19.

Listing 1.5 ShowSyntaxErrors.java

```
1 public class ShowSyntaxErrors {
2   public static main(String[] args) {
3     System.out.println("Welcome to Java);
4   }
5 }
```

Four errors are reported, but the program actually has two errors:

- The keyword `void` is missing before `main` in line 2.
- The string `Welcome to Java` should be closed with a closing quotation mark in line 3.

Since a single error will often display many lines of compile errors, it is a good practice to fix errors from the top line and work downward. Fixing errors that occur earlier in the program may also fix additional errors that occur later.

Compile

```
Administrator: Command Prompt
c:\book>javac ShowSyntaxErrors.java
ShowSyntaxErrors.java:2: error: invalid method declaration; return type required
  public static main(String[] args) {
                ^
ShowSyntaxErrors.java:3: error: unclosed string literal
    System.out.println("Welcome to Java);
                       ^
ShowSyntaxErrors.java:3: error: ';' expected
    System.out.println("Welcome to Java);
                                         ^
ShowSyntaxErrors.java:5: error: reached end of file while parsing
}
 ^
4 errors

c:\book>_
```

Figure 1.19 The compiler reports syntax errors.

Tip

If you don't know how to correct it, compare your program closely, character by character, with similar examples in the text. In the first few weeks of this course, you will probably spend a lot of time fixing syntax errors. Soon you will be familiar with Java syntax and can quickly fix syntax errors.

fix syntax errors

1.11.2 Runtime Errors

runtime errors

Runtime errors are errors that cause a program to terminate abnormally. They occur while a program is running if the environment detects an operation that is impossible to carry out. Input mistakes typically cause runtime errors. An *input error* occurs when the program is waiting for the user to enter a value, but the user enters a value that the program cannot handle. For instance, if the program expects to read in a number, but instead the user enters a string, this causes data-type errors to occur in the program.

Another example of runtime errors is division by zero. This happens when the divisor is zero for integer divisions. For instance, the program in Listing 1.6 would cause a runtime error, as shown in Figure 1.20.

LISTING 1.6 ShowRuntimeErrors.java

```
public class ShowRuntimeErrors {
  public static void main(String[] args) {
    System.out.println(1 / 0);
  }
}
```

runtime error

Administrator: Command Prompt

Run →

```
c:\book>java ShowRuntimeErrors
Exception in thread "main" java.lang.ArithmeticException: / by zero
        at ShowRuntimeErrors.main(ShowRuntimeErrors.java:4)

c:\book>_
```

FIGURE 1.20 The runtime error causes the program to terminate abnormally.

1.11.3 Logic Errors

logic errors

Logic errors occur when a program does not perform the way it was intended to. Errors of this kind occur for many different reasons. For example, suppose you wrote the program in Listing 1.7 to convert Celsius 35 degrees to a Fahrenheit degree:

LISTING 1.7 ShowLogicErrors.java

```
public class ShowLogicErrors {
  public static void main(String[] args) {
    System.out.println("Celsius 35 is Fahrenheit degree ");
    System.out.println((9 / 5) * 35 + 32);
  }
}
```

```
Celsius 35 is Fahrenheit degree
67
```

You will get Fahrenheit `67` degrees, which is wrong. It should be `95.0`. In Java, the division for integers is an integer—the fractional part is truncated—so in Java `9 / 5` is `1`. To get the correct result, you need to use `9.0 / 5`, which results in `1.8`.

In general, syntax errors are easy to find and easy to correct, because the compiler gives indications as to where the errors came from and why they are wrong. Runtime errors are not difficult to find, either, since the reasons and locations for the errors are displayed on the console when the program aborts. Finding logic errors, on the other hand, can be very challenging. In the upcoming chapters, you will learn the techniques of tracing programs and finding logic errors.

MyProgrammingLab™

1.45 What are syntax errors (compile errors), runtime errors, and logic errors?

1.46 Give examples of syntax errors, runtime errors, and logic errors.

1.47 If you forget to put a closing quotation mark on a string, what kind error will be raised?

1.48 If your program needs to read integers, but the user entered strings, an error would occur when running this program. What kind of error is this?

1.49 Suppose you write a program for computing the perimeter of a rectangle and you mistakenly write your program so that it computes the area of a rectangle. What kind of error is this?

1.50 Identify and fix the errors in the following code:

```
public class Welcome {
  public void Main(String[] args) {
    System.out.println('Welcome to Java!);
  }
}
```

1.51 The following program is wrong. Reorder the lines so that the program displays `morning` followed by `afternoon`.

```
  public static void main(String[] args) {
  }
public class Welcome {
    System.out.println("afternoon");
    System.out.println("morning");
}
```

Key Terms

Application Program Interface (API) 16
assembler 10
assembly language 10
bit 4
block 17
block comment 17
bus 2
byte 4
bytecode 21
bytecode verifier 22
cable modem 8
central processing unit (CPU) 3
class loader 22
comment 17
compiler 10
console 16
dot pitch 8
DSL (digital subscriber line) 8
encoding scheme 4
hardware 2
high-level language 10
integrated development environment (IDE) 16
interpreter 10
`java` command 21
Java Development Toolkit (JDK) 16
Java language specification 16
Java Virtual Machine (JVM) 21
`javac` command 21
keyword (or reserved word) 17
library 16
line comment 17

logic error 27	programming 2
low-level language 10	runtime error 27
machine language 9	screen resolution 8
`main` method 17	software 2
memory 5	source code 10
modem 8	source program 10
motherboard 3	specific import 24
network interface card (NIC) 8	statement 10
operating system (OS) 12	storage devices 5
pixel 8	syntax error 26
program 2	wildcard import 24

Note

The above terms are defined in this chapter. Supplement I.A, Glossary, lists all the key terms and descriptions in the book, organized by chapters.

Supplement I.A

Chapter Summary

1. A computer is an electronic device that stores and processes data.

2. A computer includes both *hardware* and *software*.

3. Hardware is the physical aspect of the computer that can be touched.

4. Computer *programs*, known as *software*, are the invisible instructions that control the hardware and make it perform tasks.

5. Computer *programming* is the writing of instructions (i.e., code) for computers to perform.

6. The *central processing unit (CPU)* is a computer's brain. It retrieves instructions from *memory* and executes them.

7. Computers use zeros and ones because digital devices have two stable states, referred to by convention as zero and one.

8. A *bit* is a binary digit 0 or 1.

9. A *byte* is a sequence of 8 bits.

10. A kilobyte is about 1,000 bytes, a megabyte about 1 million bytes, a gigabyte about 1 billion bytes, and a terabyte about 1,000 gigabytes.

11. Memory stores data and program instructions for the CPU to execute.

12. A memory unit is an ordered sequence of bytes.

13. Memory is volatile, because information is lost when the power is turned off.

14. Programs and data are permanently stored on *storage devices* and are moved to memory when the computer actually uses them.

15. The *machine language* is a set of primitive instructions built into every computer.

16. *Assembly language* is a *low-level programming language* in which a mnemonic is used to represent each machine-language instruction.

17. *High-level languages* are English-like and easy to learn and program.

18. A program written in a high-level language is called a *source program.*

19. A *compiler* is a software program that translates the source program into a *machine-language program.*

20. The *operating system (OS)* is a program that manages and controls a computer's activities.

21. Java is platform independent, meaning that you can write a program once and run it on any computer.

22. Java programs can be embedded in HTML pages and downloaded by Web browsers to bring live animation and interaction to Web clients.

23. The Java source file name must match the public class name in the program. Java source code files must end with the `.java` extension.

24. Every class is compiled into a separate bytecode file that has the same name as the class and ends with the `.class` extension.

25. To compile a Java source-code file from the command line, use the ***javac** command.*

26. To run a Java class from the command line, use the ***java** command.*

27. Every Java program is a set of class definitions. The keyword `class` introduces a class definition. The contents of the class are included in a *block.*

28. A block begins with an opening brace (`{`) and ends with a closing brace (`}`).

29. Methods are contained in a class. To run a Java program, the program must have a `main` method. The `main` method is the entry point where the program starts when it is executed.

30. Every *statement* in Java ends with a semicolon (`;`), known as the *statement terminator.*

31. *Reserved words,* or *keywords,* have a specific meaning to the compiler and cannot be used for other purposes in the program.

32. In Java, comments are preceded by two slashes (`//`) on a line, called a *line comment,* or enclosed between `/*` and `*/` on one or several lines, called a *block comment* or *paragraph comment*. Comments are ignored by the compiler.

33. Java source programs are case sensitive.

34. There are two types of `import` statements: *specific import* and *wildcard import*. The specific import specifies a single class in the import statement; the wildcard import imports all the classes in a package.

35. Programming errors can be categorized into three types: *syntax errors*, *runtime errors*, and *logic errors*. Errors that occur during compilation are called syntax errors or *compile errors*. Runtime errors are errors that cause a program to terminate abnormally. Logic errors occur when a program does not perform the way it was intended to.

Test Questions

Do the test questions for this chapter online at www.cs.armstrong.edu/liang/intro9e/test.html.

Programming Exercises

MyProgrammingLab™

Note

Solutions to even-numbered exercises are on the Companion Website. Solutions to all exercises are on the Instructor Resource Website. The level of difficulty is rated easy (no star), moderate (*), hard (**), or challenging (***).

level of difficulty

1.1 (*Display three messages*) Write a program that displays `Welcome to Java`, `Welcome to Computer Science`, and `Programming is fun`.

1.2 (*Display five messages*) Write a program that displays `Welcome to Java` five times.

*1.3 (*Display a pattern*) Write a program that displays the following pattern:

```
    J     A     V     V     A
    J    A A     V   V     A A
J   J   AAAAA     V V     AAAAA
 J J   A     A     V     A     A
```

1.4 (*Print a table*) Write a program that displays the following table:

```
a      a^2     a^3
1      1       1
2      4       8
3      9       27
4      16      64
```

1.5 (*Compute expressions*) Write a program that displays the result of

$$\frac{9.5 \times 4.5 - 2.5 \times 3}{45.5 - 3.5}.$$

1.6 (*Summation of a series*) Write a program that displays the result of

$$1 + 2 + 3 + 4 + 5 + 6 + 7 + 8 + 9.$$

1.7 (*Approximate* π) π can be computed using the following formula:

$$\pi = 4 \times \left(1 - \frac{1}{3} + \frac{1}{5} - \frac{1}{7} + \frac{1}{9} - \frac{1}{11} + \ldots\right)$$

Write a program that displays the result of $4 \times \left(1 - \frac{1}{3} + \frac{1}{5} - \frac{1}{7} + \frac{1}{9} - \frac{1}{11}\right)$ and $4 \times \left(1 - \frac{1}{3} + \frac{1}{5} - \frac{1}{7} + \frac{1}{9} - \frac{1}{11} + \frac{1}{13}\right)$. Use `1.0` instead of `1` in your program.

1.8 (*Area and perimeter of a circle*) Write a program that displays the area and perimeter of a circle that has a radius of `5.5` using the following formula:

$$perimeter = 2 \times radius \times \pi$$

$$area = radius \times radius \times \pi$$

1.9 (*Area and perimeter of a rectangle*) Write a program that displays the area and perimeter of a rectangle with the width of `4.5` and height of `7.9` using the following formula:

$$area = width \times height$$

1.10 (*Average speed in miles*) Assume a runner runs `14` kilometers in `45` minutes and `30` seconds. Write a program that displays the average speed in miles per hour. (Note that `1` mile is `1.6` kilometers.)

***1.11** (*Population projection*) The U.S. Census Bureau projects population based on the following assumptions:

- One birth every 7 seconds
- One death every 13 seconds
- One new immigrant every 45 seconds

Write a program to display the population for each of the next five years. Assume the current population is 312,032,486 and one year has 365 days. *Hint*: In Java, if two integers perform division, the result is an integer. The fraction part is truncated. For example, `5 / 4` is `1` (not `1.25`) and `10 / 4` is `2` (not `2.5`).

1.12 (*Average speed in kilometers*) Assume a runner runs `24` miles in `1` hour, `40` minutes, and `35` seconds. Write a program that displays the average speed in kilometers per hour. (Note that `1` mile is `1.6` kilometers.)

CHAPTER

2

Elementary Programming

Objectives

- To write Java programs to perform simple computations (§2.2).
- To obtain input from the console using the `Scanner` class (§2.3).
- To use identifiers to name variables, constants, methods, and classes (§2.4).
- To use variables to store data (§§2.5–2.6).
- To program with assignment statements and assignment expressions (§2.6).
- To use constants to store permanent data (§2.7).
- To name classes, methods, variables, and constants by following their naming conventions (§2.8).
- To explore Java numeric primitive data types: `byte`, `short`, `int`, `long`, `float`, and `double` (§2.9.1).
- To perform operations using operators `+`, `-`, `*`, `/`, and `%` (§2.9.2).
- To perform exponent operations using `Math.pow(a, b)` (§2.9.3).
- To write integer literals, floating-point literals, and literals in scientific notation (§2.10).
- To write and evaluate numeric expressions (§2.11).
- To obtain the current system time using `System.currentTimeMillis()` (§2.12).
- To use augmented assignment operators (§2.13).
- To distinguish between postincrement and preincrement and between postdecrement and predecrement (§2.14).
- To cast the value of one type to another type (§2.15).
- To describe the software development process and apply it to develop the loan payment program (§2.16).
- To represent characters using the `char` type (§2.17).
- To represent a string using the `String` type (§2.18).
- To obtain input using the `JOptionPane` input dialog boxes (§2.19).

2.1 Introduction

The focus of this chapter is on learning elementary programming techniques to solve problems.

In Chapter 1 you learned how to create, compile, and run very basic Java programs. Now you will learn how to solve problems by writing programs. Through these problems, you will learn elementary programming using primitive data types, variables, constants, operators, expressions, and input and output.

Suppose, for example, that you need to take out a student loan. Given the loan amount, loan term, and annual interest rate, can you write a program to compute the monthly payment and total payment? This chapter shows you how to write programs like this. Along the way, you learn the basic steps that go into analyzing a problem, designing a solution, and implementing the solution by creating a program.

2.2 Writing a Simple Program

Writing a program involves designing a strategy for solving the problem and then using a programming language to implement that strategy.

problem

Let's first consider the simple problem of computing the area of a circle. How do we write a program for solving this problem?

algorithm

pseudocode

Writing a program involves designing algorithms and translating algorithms into programming instructions, or code. An *algorithm* describes how a problem is solved by listing the actions that need to be taken and the order of their execution. Algorithms can help the programmer plan a program before writing it in a programming language. Algorithms can be described in natural languages or in *pseudocode* (natural language mixed with some programming code). The algorithm for calculating the area of a circle can be described as follows:

1. Read in the circle's radius.
2. Compute the area using the following formula:

$$area = radius \times radius \times \pi$$

3. Display the result.

Tip

It's always good practice to outline your program (or its underlying problem) in the form of an algorithm before you begin coding.

When you *code*—that is, when you write a program—you translate an algorithm into a program. You already know that every Java program begins with a class definition in which the keyword `class` is followed by the class name. Assume that you have chosen `ComputeArea` as the class name. The outline of the program would look like this:

```
public class ComputeArea {
  // Details to be given later
}
```

As you know, every Java program must have a `main` method where program execution begins. The program is then expanded as follows:

```
public class ComputeArea {
  public static void main(String[] args) {
    // Step 1: Read in radius

    // Step 2: Compute area
```

```
    // Step 3: Display the area
  }
}
```

The program needs to read the radius entered by the user from the keyboard. This raises two important issues:

- Reading the radius.
- Storing the radius in the program.

Let's address the second issue first. In order to store the radius, the program needs to declare a symbol called a *variable*. A variable represents a value stored in the computer's memory.

variable

Rather than using `x` and `y` as variable names, choose descriptive names: in this case, `radius` for radius, and `area` for area. To let the compiler know what `radius` and `area` are, specify their data types. That is the kind of the data stored in a variable, whether integer, *floating-point number*, or something else. This is known as *declaring variables.* Java provides simple data types for representing integers, floating-point numbers (i.e., numbers with a decimal point), characters, and Boolean types. These types are known as *primitive data types* or *fundamental types.*

descriptive names
data type
declare variables
floating-point number
primitive data types

Declare `radius` and `area` as double-precision floating-point numbers. The program can be expanded as follows:

```
public class ComputeArea {
  public static void main(String[] args) {
    double radius;
    double area;

    // Step 1: Read in radius

    // Step 2: Compute area

    // Step 3: Display the area
  }
}
```

The program declares `radius` and `area` as variables. The reserved word `double` indicates that `radius` and `area` are double-precision floating-point values stored in the computer.

The first step is to prompt the user to designate the circle's `radius`. You will learn how to prompt the user for information shortly. For now, to learn how variables work, you can assign a fixed value to `radius` in the program as you write the code; later, you'll modify the program to prompt the user for this value.

The second step is to compute `area` by assigning the result of the expression `radius * radius * 3.14159` to `area`.

In the final step, the program will display the value of `area` on the console by using the `System.out.println` method.

Listing 2.1 shows the complete program, and a sample run of the program is shown in Figure 2.1.

Listing 2.1 ComputeArea.java

```
public class ComputeArea {
  public static void main(String[] args) {
    double radius; // Declare radius
    double area; // Declare area

    // Assign a radius
    radius = 20; // radius is now 20
```

```
 8
 9      // Compute area
10      area = radius * radius * 3.14159;
11
12      // Display results
13      System.out.println("The area for the circle of radius " +
14        radius + " is " + area);
15    }
16  }
```

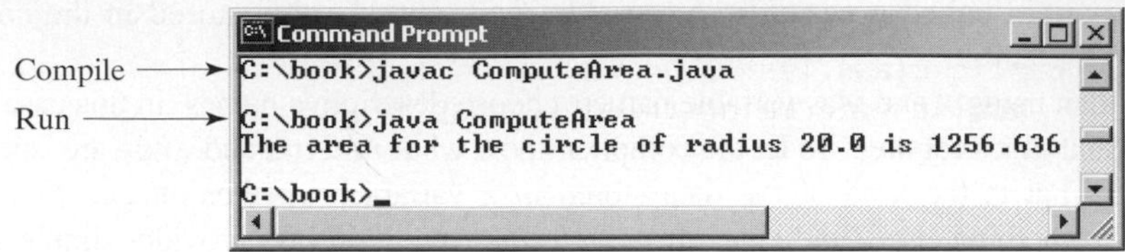

FIGURE 2.1 The program displays the area of a circle.

declare variable

assign value

tracing program

Variables such as **radius** and **area** correspond to memory locations. Every variable has a name, a type, a size, and a value. Line 3 declares that **radius** can store a **double** value. The value is not defined until you assign a value. Line 7 assigns **20** into variable **radius**. Similarly, line 4 declares variable **area**, and line 10 assigns a value into **area**. The following table shows the value in the memory for **area** and **radius** as the program is executed. Each row in the table shows the values of variables after the statement in the corresponding line in the program is executed. This method of reviewing how a program works is called *tracing a program.* Tracing programs are helpful for understanding how programs work, and they are useful tools for finding errors in programs.

line#	radius	area
3	no value	
4		no value
7	20	
10		1256.636

concatenate strings

concatenate strings with numbers

The plus sign (+) has two meanings: one for addition and the other for concatenating (combining) strings. The plus sign (+) in lines 13–14 is called a *string concatenation operator.* It combines two strings into one. If a string is combined with a number, the number is converted into a string and concatenated with the other string. Therefore, the plus signs (+) in lines 13–14 concatenate strings into a longer string, which is then displayed in the output. Strings and string concatenation will be discussed further in Section 2.18.

Caution

A string cannot cross lines in the source code. Thus, the following statement would result in a compile error:

```
System.out.println("Introduction to Java Programming,
  by Y. Daniel Liang");
```

To fix the error, break the string into separate substrings, and use the concatenation operator (+) to combine them:

break a long string

```
System.out.println("Introduction to Java Programming, " +
  "by Y. Daniel Liang");
```

Tip

This example consists of three steps. It is a good approach to develop and test these steps incrementally by adding them one at a time.

incremental development and testing

2.1 Identify and fix the errors in the following code:

MyProgrammingLab™

```
public class Test {
  public void main(string[] args) {
    int i;
    int k = 100.0;
    int j = i + 1;

    System.out.println("j is " + j + " and
      k is " + k);
  }
}
```

2.3 Reading Input from the Console

Reading input from the console enables the program to accept input from the user.

VideoNote
Obtain input

In Listing 2.1, the radius is fixed in the source code. To use a different radius, you have to modify the source code and recompile it. Obviously, this is not convenient, so instead you can use the `Scanner` class for console input.

Java uses `System.out` to refer to the standard output device and `System.in` to the standard input device. By default, the output device is the display monitor and the input device is the keyboard. To perform console output, you simply use the `println` method to display a primitive value or a string to the console. Console input is not directly supported in Java, but you can use the `Scanner` class to create an object to read input from `System.in`, as follows:

```
Scanner input = new Scanner(System.in);
```

The syntax `new Scanner(System.in)` creates an object of the `Scanner` type. The syntax `Scanner input` declares that `input` is a variable whose type is `Scanner`. The whole line `Scanner input = new Scanner(System.in)` creates a `Scanner` object and assigns its reference to the variable `input`. An object may invoke its methods. To invoke a method on an object is to ask the object to perform a task. You can invoke the methods listed in Table 2.1 to read various types of input.

For now, we will see how to read a number that includes a decimal point by invoking the `nextDouble()` method. Other methods will be covered when they are used. Listing 2.2 rewrites Listing 2.1 to prompt the user to enter a radius.

LISTING 2.2 ComputeAreaWithConsoleInput.java

```
import java.util.Scanner; // Scanner is in the java.util package

public class ComputeAreaWithConsoleInput {
  public static void main(String[] args) {
    // Create a Scanner object
    Scanner input = new Scanner(System.in);

```

import class

create a Scanner

TABLE 2.1 Methods for Scanner Objects

Method	*Description*
`nextByte()`	reads an integer of the `byte` type.
`nextShort()`	reads an integer of the `short` type.
`nextInt()`	reads an integer of the `int` type.
`nextLong()`	reads an integer of the `long` type.
`nextFloat()`	reads a number of the `float` type.
`nextDouble()`	reads a number of the `double` type.
`next()`	reads a string that ends before a whitespace character.
`nextLine()`	reads a line of text (i.e., a string ending with the *Enter* key pressed).

read a double

```
 8     // Prompt the user to enter a radius
 9     System.out.print("Enter a number for radius: ");
10     double radius = input.nextDouble();
11 
12     // Compute area
13     double area = radius * radius * 3.14159;
14 
15     // Display results
16     System.out.println("The area for the circle of radius " +
17       radius + " is " + area);
18   }
19 }
```

```
Enter a number for radius: 2.5 ↵Enter
The area for the circle of radius 2.5 is 19.6349375
```

```
Enter a number for radius: 23 ↵Enter
The area for the circle of radius 23.0 is 1661.90111
```

The `Scanner` class is in the `java.util` package. It is imported in line 1. Line 6 creates a `Scanner` object.

The statement in line 9 displays a message to prompt the user for input.

```
System.out.print ("Enter a number for radius: ");
```

print vs. println

The `print` method is identical to the `println` method except that `println` moves to the beginning of the next line after displaying the string, but `print` does not advance to the next line when completed.

The statement in line 10 reads input from the keyboard.

```
double radius = input.nextDouble();
```

After the user enters a number and presses the *Enter* key, the program reads the number and assigns it to `radius`.

More details on objects will be introduced in Chapter 8. For the time being, simply accept that this is how to obtain input from the console.

Listing 2.3 gives an example of reading multiple input from the keyboard. The program reads three numbers and displays their average.

LISTING 2.3 ComputeAverage.java

```
1  import java.util.Scanner; // Scanner is in the java.util package
2
3  public class ComputeAverage {
4    public static void main(String[] args) {
5      // Create a Scanner object
6      Scanner input = new Scanner(System.in);
7
8      // Prompt the user to enter three numbers
9      System.out.print("Enter three numbers: ");
10     double number1 = input.nextDouble();
11     double number2 = input.nextDouble();
12     double number3 = input.nextDouble();
13
14     // Compute average
15     double average = (number1 + number2 + number3) / 3;
16
17     // Display results
18     System.out.println("The average of " + number1 + " " + number2
19       + " " + number3 + " is " + average);
20   }
21 }
```

import class

create a Scanner

read a double

```
Enter three numbers: 1 2 3 ↵Enter
The average of 1.0 2.0 3.0 is 2.0
```

enter input in one line

```
Enter three numbers: 10.5 ↵Enter
11 ↵Enter
11.5 ↵Enter
The average of 10.5 11.0 11.5 is 11.0
```

enter input in multiple lines

The code for importing the Scanner class (line 1) and creating a Scanner object (line 6) are the same as in the preceding example as well as in all new programs you will write for reading input from the keyboard.

Line 9 prompts the user to enter three numbers. The numbers are read in lines 10–12. You may enter three numbers separated by spaces, then press the *Enter* key, or enter each number followed by a press of the *Enter* key, as shown in the sample runs of this program.

If you entered an input other than a numeric value, a runtime error would occur. In Chapter 14, you will learn how to handle the exception so that the program can continue to run.

runtime error

Note

Most of the programs in the early chapters of this book perform three steps: input, process, and output, called *IPO*. Input is receiving input from the user; process is producing results using the input; and output is displaying the results.

IPO

MyProgrammingLab™

2.2 How do you write a statement to let the user enter an integer or a double value from the keyboard?

2.3 What happens if you entered `5a` when executing the following code?

```
double radius = input.nextDouble();
```

2.4 Identifiers

Identifiers are the names that identify the elements such as classes, methods, and variables in a program.

identifiers
identifier naming rules

As you see in Listing 2.3, `ComputeAverage`, `main`, `input`, `number1`, `number2`, `number3`, and so on are the names of things that appear in the program. In programming terminology, such names are called *identifiers*. All identifiers must obey the following rules:

- An identifier is a sequence of characters that consists of letters, digits, underscores (_), and dollar signs ($).
- An identifier must start with a letter, an underscore (_), or a dollar sign ($). It cannot start with a digit.
- An identifier cannot be a reserved word. (See Appendix A for a list of reserved words.)
- An identifier cannot be `true`, `false`, or `null`.
- An identifier can be of any length.

For example, `$2`, `ComputeArea`, `area`, `radius`, and `showMessageDialog` are legal identifiers, whereas `2A` and `d+4` are not because they do not follow the rules. The Java compiler detects illegal identifiers and reports syntax errors.

case sensitive

Note

Since Java is case sensitive, `area`, `Area`, and `AREA` are all different identifiers.

descriptive names

Tip

Identifiers are for naming variables, constants, methods, classes, and packages. Descriptive identifiers make programs easy to read. Avoid using abbreviations for identifiers. Using complete words is more descriptive. For example, `numberOfStudents` is better than `numStuds`, `numOfStuds`, or `numOfStudents`. We use descriptive names for complete programs in the text. However, we will occasionally use variables names such as `i`, `j`, `k`, `x`, and `y` in the code snippets for brevity. These names also provide a generic tone to the code snippets.

the $ character

Tip

Do not name identifiers with the `$` character. By convention, the `$` character should be used only in mechanically generated source code.

2.4 Which of the following identifiers are valid? Which are Java keywords?

```
miles, Test, a++, --a, 4#R, $4, #44, apps
class, public, int, x, y, radius
```

2.5 Variables

Variables are used to represent values that may be changed in the program.

why called variables?

As you see from the programs in the preceding sections, variables are used to store values to be used later in a program. They are called variables because their values can be changed. In the program in Listing 2.2, `radius` and `area` are variables of the double-precision, floating-point type. You can assign any numerical value to `radius` and `area`, and the values of `radius` and `area` can be reassigned. For example, in the following code, `radius` is initially `1.0` (line 2) and then changed to `2.0` (line 7), and area is set to `3.14159` (line 3) and then reset to `12.56636` (line 8).

```
1 // Compute the first area
2 radius = 1.0;                                    radius: 1.0
3 area = radius * radius * 3.14159;                  area: 3.14159
4 System.out.println("The area is "+ area +" for radius "+ radius);
5
6 // Compute the second area
7 radius = 2.0;                                    radius: 2.0
8 area = radius * radius * 3.14159;                  area: 12.56636
9 System.out.println("The area is "+ area +" for radius "+ radius);
```

Variables are for representing data of a certain type. To use a variable, you declare it by telling the compiler its name as well as what type of data it can store. The *variable declaration* tells the compiler to allocate appropriate memory space for the variable based on its data type. The syntax for declaring a variable is

```
datatype variableName;
```

declare variable

Here are some examples of variable declarations:

```
int count;            // Declare count to be an integer variable
double radius;        // Declare radius to be a double variable
double interestRate; // Declare interestRate to be a double variable
```

These examples use the data types `int` and `double`. Later you will be introduced to additional data types, such as `byte`, `short`, `long`, `float`, `char`, and `boolean`.

If variables are of the same type, they can be declared together, as follows:

```
datatype variable1, variable2, ..., variablen;
```

The variables are separated by commas. For example,

```
int i, j, k; // Declare i, j, and k as int variables
```

initialize variables

Variables often have initial values. You can declare a variable and initialize it in one step. Consider, for instance, the following code:

```
int count = 1;
```

This is equivalent to the next two statements:

```
int count;
count = 1;
```

You can also use a shorthand form to declare and initialize variables of the same type together. For example,

```
int i = 1, j = 2;
```

Tip

A variable must be declared before it can be assigned a value. A variable declared in a method must be assigned a value before it can be used.

Whenever possible, declare a variable and assign its initial value in one step. This will make the program easy to read and avoid programming errors.

scope of a variable

Every variable has a scope. The *scope of a variable* is the part of the program where the variable can be referenced. The rules that define the scope of a variable will be introduced gradually later in the book. For now, all you need to know is that a variable must be declared and initialized before it can be used. Consider the following code:

```
double interestRate = 0.05
double interest = interestrate * 45
```

This code is wrong, because `interestRate` is assigned a value `0.05`, but `interestrate` has not been declared and initialized. Java is case sensitive, so it considers `interestRate` and `interestrate` to be two different variables.

2.6 Assignment Statements and Assignment Expressions

An assignment statement designates a value for a variable. An assignment statement can be used as an expression in Java.

assignment statement
assignment operator

After a variable is declared, you can assign a value to it by using an *assignment statement*. In Java, the equal sign (=) is used as the *assignment operator*. The syntax for assignment statements is as follows:

```
variable = expression;
```

expression

An *expression* represents a computation involving values, variables, and operators that, taking them together, evaluates to a value. For example, consider the following code:

```
int y = 1;              // Assign 1 to variable y
double radius = 1.0;    // Assign 1.0 to variable radius
int x = 5 * (3 / 2);    // Assign the value of the expression to x
x = y + 1;              // Assign the addition of y and 1 to x
area = radius * radius * 3.14159; // Compute area
```

You can use a variable in an expression. A variable can also be used in both sides of the = operator. For example,

```
x = x + 1;
```

In this assignment statement, the result of `x + 1` is assigned to `x`. If `x` is `1` before the statement is executed, then it becomes `2` after the statement is executed.

To assign a value to a variable, you must place the variable name to the left of the assignment operator. Thus, the following statement is wrong:

```
1 = x; // Wrong
```

Note

In mathematics, `x = 2 * x + 1` denotes an equation. However, in Java, `x = 2 * x + 1` is an assignment statement that evaluates the expression `2 * x + 1` and assigns the result to `x`.

assignment expression

In Java, an assignment statement is essentially an expression that evaluates to the value to be assigned to the variable on the left side of the assignment operator. For this reason, an assignment statement is also known as an *assignment expression*. For example, the following statement is correct:

```
System.out.println(x = 1);
```

which is equivalent to

```
x = 1;
System.out.println(x);
```

If a value is assigned to multiple variables, you can use this syntax:

```
i = j = k = 1;
```

which is equivalent to

```
k = 1;
j = k;
i = j;
```

Note

In an assignment statement, the data type of the variable on the left must be compatible with the data type of the value on the right. For example, `int x = 1.0` would be illegal, because the data type of `x` is `int`. You cannot assign a `double` value (`1.0`) to an `int` variable without using type casting. Type casting is introduced in Section 2.15.

2.7 Named Constants

A named constant is an identifier that represents a permanent value.

Key Point

The value of a variable may change during the execution of a program, but a *named constant*, or simply *constant*, represents permanent data that never changes. In our `ComputeArea` program, π is a constant. If you use it frequently, you don't want to keep typing `3.14159`; instead, you can declare a constant for π. Here is the syntax for declaring a constant:

constant

```
final datatype CONSTANTNAME = value;
```

A constant must be declared and initialized in the same statement. The word `final` is a Java keyword for declaring a constant. For example, you can declare π as a constant and rewrite Listing 2.1 as follows:

final keyword

```
// ComputeArea.java: Compute the area of a circle
public class ComputeArea {
  public static void main(String[] args) {
    final double PI = 3.14159; // Declare a constant

    // Assign a radius
    double radius = 20;

    // Compute area
    double area = radius * radius * PI;

    // Display results
    System.out.println("The area for the circle of radius " +
      radius + " is " + area);
  }
}
```

There are three benefits of using constants: (1) You don't have to repeatedly type the same value if it is used multiple times; (2) if you have to change the constant value (e.g., from `3.14` to `3.14159` for `PI`), you need to change it only in a single location in the source code; and (3) a descriptive name for a constant makes the program easy to read.

benefits of constants

2.8 Naming Conventions

Sticking with the Java naming conventions makes your programs easy to read and avoids errors.

Make sure that you choose descriptive names with straightforward meanings for the variables, constants, classes, and methods in your program. As mentioned earlier, names are case sensitive. Listed below are the conventions for naming variables, methods, and classes.

name variables and methods

- Use lowercase for variables and methods. If a name consists of several words, concatenate them into one, making the first word lowercase and capitalizing the first letter of each subsequent word—for example, the variables `radius` and `area` and the method `showMessageDialog`.

name classes

- Capitalize the first letter of each word in a class name—for example, the class names `ComputeArea`, `System`, and `JOptionPane`.

name constants

- Capitalize every letter in a constant, and use underscores between words—for example, the constants `PI` and `MAX_VALUE`.

It is important to follow the naming conventions to make your programs easy to read.

name classes

Caution

Do not choose class names that are already used in the Java library. For example, since the `System` class is defined in Java, you should not name your class `System`.

MyProgrammingLab™

2.5 What are the benefits of using constants? Declare an `int` constant `SIZE` with value `20`.

2.6 What are the naming conventions for class names, method names, constants, and variables? Which of the following items can be a constant, a method, a variable, or a class according to the Java naming conventions?

```
MAX_VALUE, Test, read, readInt
```

2.7 Translate the following algorithm into Java code:

Step 1: Declare a `double` variable named `miles` with initial value `100`.

Step 2: Declare a `double` constant named `KILOMETERS_PER_MILE` with value `1.609`.

Step 3: Declare a `double` variable named `kilometers`, multiply `miles` and `KILOMETERS_PER_MILE`, and assign the result to `kilometers`.

Step 4: Display `kilometers` to the console.

What is kilometers after Step 4?

2.9 Numeric Data Types and Operations

*Java has six numeric types for integers and floating-point numbers with operators +, -, *, /, and %.*

2.9.1 Numeric Types

Every data type has a range of values. The compiler allocates memory space for each variable or constant according to its data type. Java provides eight primitive data types for numeric values, characters, and Boolean values. This section introduces numeric data types and operators.

Table 2.2 lists the six numeric data types, their ranges, and their storage sizes.

TABLE 2.2 Numeric Data Types

Name	*Range*	*Storage Size*
`byte`	-2^7 to 2^7-1 (-128 to 127)	8-bit signed
`short`	-2^{15} to $2^{15}-1$ (-32768 to 32767)	16-bit signed
`int`	-2^{31} to $2^{31}-1$ (-2147483648 to 2147483647)	32-bit signed
`long`	-2^{63} to $2^{63}-1$ (i.e., -9223372036854775808 to 9223372036854775807)	64-bit signed
`float`	Negative range: $-3.4028235E+38$ to $-1.4E-45$ Positive range: $1.4E-45$ to $3.4028235E+38$	32-bit IEEE 754
`double`	Negative range: $-1.7976931348623157E+308$ to $-4.9E-324$ Positive range: $4.9E-324$ to $1.7976931348623157E+308$	64-bit IEEE 754

`byte` type

`short` type

`int` type

`long` type

`float` type

`double` type

Note

IEEE 754 is a standard approved by the Institute of Electrical and Electronics Engineers for representing floating-point numbers on computers. The standard has been widely adopted. Java uses the 32-bit **IEEE 754** for the **`float`** type and the 64-bit **IEEE 754** for the **`double`** type. The **IEEE 754** standard also defines special floating-point values, which are listed in Appendix E.

integer types

Java uses four types for integers: **`byte`**, **`short`**, **`int`**, and **`long`**. Choose the type that is most appropriate for your variable. For example, if you know an integer stored in a variable is within a range of a byte, declare the variable as a **`byte`**. For simplicity and consistency, we will use **`int`** for integers most of the time in this book.

floating-point types

Java uses two types for floating-point numbers: **`float`** and **`double`**. The **`double`** type is twice as big as **`float`**, so the **`double`** is known as *double precision* and **`float`** as *single precision*. Normally you should use the **`double`** type, because it is more accurate than the **`float`** type.

Caution

what is overflow?

When a variable is assigned a value that is too large (*in size*) to be stored, it causes *overflow*. For example, executing the following statement causes overflow, because the largest value that can be stored in a variable of the **`int`** type is **`2147483647`**. **`2147483648`** will be too large for an **`int`** value.

```
int value = 2147483647 + 1;
// value will actually be -2147483648
```

Likewise, executing the following statement causes overflow, because the smallest value that can be stored in a variable of the **`int`** type is **`-2147483648`**. **`-2147483649`** will be too large in size to be stored in an **`int`** variable.

```
int value = -2147483648 - 1;
// value will actually be 2147483647
```

Java does not report warnings or errors on overflow, so be careful when working with numbers close to the maximum or minimum range of a given type.

what is underflow?

When a floating-point number is too small (i.e., too close to zero) to be stored, it causes *underflow*. Java approximates it to zero, so normally you don't need to be concerned about underflow.

2.9.2 Numeric Operators

operators +, -, *, /, %

operands

The operators for numeric data types include the standard arithmetic operators: addition (+), subtraction (–), multiplication (*), division (/), and remainder (%), as shown in Table 2.3. The *operands* are the values operated by an operator.

TABLE 2.3 Numeric Operators

Name	*Meaning*	*Example*	*Result*
+	Addition	34 + 1	35
-	Subtraction	34.0 – 0.1	33.9
*	Multiplication	300 * 30	9000
/	Division	1.0 / 2.0	0.5
%	Remainder	20 % 3	2

integer division

When both operands of a division are integers, the result of the division is an integer and the fractional part is truncated. For example, `5 / 2` yields `2`, not `2.5`, and `–5 / 2` yields `-2`, not `–2.5`. To perform regular mathematical division, one of the operands must be a floating-point number. For example, `5.0 / 2` yields `2.5`.

The `%` operator, known as *remainder* or *modulo* operator, yields the remainder after division. The operand on the left is the dividend and the operand on the right is the divisor. Therefore, `7 % 3` yields `1`, `3 % 7` yields `3`, `12 % 4` yields `0`, `26 % 8` yields `2`, and `20 % 13` yields `7`.

```
  2          0          3          3                       1  <--- Quotient
3)7        7)3        4)12       8)26     Divisor ---> 13)20  <--- Dividend
  6          0          12         24                      13
 --         --          --         --                      --
  1          3          0          2                       7  <--- Remainder
```

The % operator is often used for positive integers, but it can also be used with negative integers and floating-point values. The remainder is negative only if the dividend is negative. For example, `-7 % 3` yields `-1`, `-12 % 4` yields `0`, `-26 % -8` yields `-2`, and `20 % -13` yields `7`.

Remainder is very useful in programming. For example, an even number `% 2` is always `0` and an odd number `% 2` is always `1`. Thus, you can use this property to determine whether a number is even or odd. If today is Saturday, it will be Saturday again in 7 days. Suppose you and your friends are going to meet in 10 days. What day is in 10 days? You can find that the day is Tuesday using the following expression:

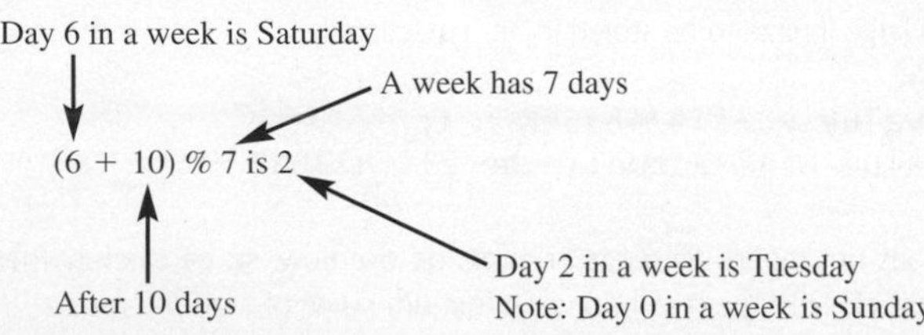

The program in Listing 2.4 obtains minutes and remaining seconds from an amount of time in seconds. For example, 500 seconds contains 8 minutes and 20 seconds.

LISTING 2.4 DisplayTime.java

```
 1 import java.util.Scanner;
 2
 3 public class DisplayTime {
 4   public static void main(String[] args) {
 5     Scanner input = new Scanner(System.in);
 6     // Prompt the user for input
 7     System.out.print("Enter an integer for seconds: ");
 8     int seconds = input.nextInt();
 9
10     int minutes = seconds / 60; // Find minutes in seconds
11     int remainingSeconds = seconds % 60; // Seconds remaining
12     System.out.println(seconds + " seconds is " + minutes +
13       " minutes and " + remainingSeconds + " seconds");
14   }
15 }
```

import Scanner

create a Scanner

read an integer

divide

remainder

```
Enter an integer for seconds: 500 ↵Enter
500 seconds is 8 minutes and 20 seconds
```

line#	seconds	minutes	remainingSeconds
8	500		
10		8	
11			20

The `nextInt()` method (line 8) reads an integer for `seconds`. Line 10 obtains the minutes using `seconds / 60`. Line 11 (`seconds % 60`) obtains the remaining seconds after taking away the minutes.

unary operator

binary operator

The `+` and `-` operators can be both unary and binary. A *unary* operator has only one operand; a *binary* operator has two. For example, the `-` operator in `-5` is a unary operator to negate number `5`, whereas the `-` operator in `4 - 5` is a binary operator for subtracting `5` from `4`.

Note

floating-point approximation

Calculations involving floating-point numbers are approximated because these numbers are not stored with complete accuracy. For example,

```
System.out.println(1.0 - 0.1 - 0.1 - 0.1 - 0.1 - 0.1);
```

displays `0.5000000000000001`, not `0.5`, and

```
System.out.println(1.0 - 0.9);
```

displays `0.09999999999999998`, not `0.1`. Integers are stored precisely. Therefore, calculations with integers yield a precise integer result.

2.9.3 Exponent Operations

Math.pow(a, b) method

The Math.pow(a, b) method can be used to compute a^b. The pow method is defined in the Math class in the Java API. You invoke the method using the syntax Math.pow(a, b) (i.e., Math.pow(2, 3)), which returns the result of a^b (2^3). Here a and b are parameters for the pow method and the numbers 2 and 3 are actual values used to invoke the method. For example,

```
System.out.println(Math.pow(2, 3)); // Displays 8.0
System.out.println(Math.pow(4, 0.5)); // Displays 2.0
System.out.println(Math.pow(2.5, 2)); // Displays 6.25
System.out.println(Math.pow(2.5, -2)); // Displays 0.16
```

Chapter 5 introduces more details on methods. For now, all you need to know is how to invoke the pow method to perform the exponent operation.

MyProgrammingLab™

2.8 Find the largest and smallest byte, short, int, long, float, and double. Which of these data types requires the least amount of memory?

2.9 Show the result of the following remainders.

```
56 % 6
78 % -4
-34 % 5
-34 % -5
5 % 1
1 % 5
```

2.10 If today is Tuesday, what will be the day in 100 days?

2.11 What is the result of 25 / 4? How would you rewrite the expression if you wished the result to be a floating-point number?

2.12 Are the following statements correct? If so, show the output.

```
System.out.println("25 / 4 is " + 25 / 4);
System.out.println("25 / 4.0 is " + 25 / 4.0);
System.out.println("3 * 2 / 4 is " + 3 * 2 / 4);
System.out.println("3.0 * 2 / 4 is " + 3.0 * 2 / 4);
```

2.13 Write a statement to display the result of $2^{3.5}$.

2.14 Suppose m and r are integers. Write a Java expression for mr^2 to obtain a floating-point result.

2.10 Numeric Literals

A literal is a constant value that appears directly in a program.

literal

For example, 34 and 0.305 are literals in the following statements:

```
int numberOfYears = 34;
double weight = 0.305;
```

2.10.1 Integer Literals

An integer literal can be assigned to an integer variable as long as it can fit into the variable. A compile error will occur if the literal is too large for the variable to hold. The statement byte b = 128, for example, will cause a compile error, because 128 cannot be stored in a variable of the byte type. (Note that the range for a byte value is from -128 to 127.)

An integer literal is assumed to be of the `int` type, whose value is between -2^{31} (−2147483648) and $2^{31} - 1$ (2147483647). To denote an integer literal of the `long` type, append the letter `L` or `l` to it. For example, to write integer `2147483648` in a Java program, you have to write it as `2147483648L` or `2147483648l`, because `2147483648` exceeds the range for the `int` value. `L` is preferred because `l` (lowercase `L`) can easily be confused with 1 (the digit one).

`long` type

Note

By default, an integer literal is a decimal integer number. To denote an octal integer literal, use a leading *0* (zero), and to denote a hexadecimal integer literal, use a leading *0x* or *0X* (zero x). For example, the following code displays the decimal value `65535` for hexadecimal number `FFFF`.

octal and hex literals

```
System.out.println(0xFFFF);
```

Hexadecimal numbers, binary numbers, and octal numbers are introduced in Appendix F.

2.10.2 Floating-Point Literals

Floating-point literals are written with a decimal point. By default, a floating-point literal is treated as a `double` type value. For example, `5.0` is considered a `double` value, not a `float` value. You can make a number a `float` by appending the letter `f` or `F`, and you can make a number a `double` by appending the letter `d` or `D`. For example, you can use `100.2f` or `100.2F` for a `float` number, and `100.2d` or `100.2D` for a `double` number.

suffix f or F

suffix d or D

Note

The `double` type values are more accurate than the `float` type values. For example,

`double` vs. `float`

```
System.out.println("1.0 / 3.0 is " + 1.0 / 3.0);
```

displays `1.0 / 3.0 is 0.3333333333333333`.

```
System.out.println("1.0F / 3.0F is " + 1.0F / 3.0F);
```

displays `1.0F / 3.0F is 0.33333334`.

2.10.3 Scientific Notation

Floating-point literals can be written in scientific notation in the form of $a \times 10^b$. For example, the scientific notation for 123.456 is 1.23456×10^2 and for 0.0123456 is 1.23456×10^{-2}. A special syntax is used to write scientific notation numbers. For example, 1.23456×10^2 is written as `1.23456E2` or `1.23456E+2` and 1.23456×10^{-2} as `1.23456E-2`. `E` (or `e`) represents an exponent and can be in either lowercase or uppercase.

Note

The `float` and `double` types are used to represent numbers with a decimal point. Why are they called *floating-point numbers*? These numbers are stored in scientific notation internally. When a number such as `50.534` is converted into scientific notation, such as `5.0534E+1`, its decimal point is moved (i.e., floated) to a new position.

why called floating-point?

2.15 Which of the following are correct literals for floating-point numbers?

`12.3, 12.3e+2, 23.4e-2, -334.4, 20.5, 39F, 40D`

2.16 Which of the following are the same as `52.534`?

`5.2534e+1, 0.52534e+2, 525.34e-1, 5.2534e+0`

2.11 Evaluating Expressions and Operator Precedence

Java expressions are evaluated in the same way as arithmetic expressions.

Writing a numeric expression in Java involves a straightforward translation of an arithmetic expression using Java operators. For example, the arithmetic expression

$$\frac{3 + 4x}{5} - \frac{10(y - 5)(a + b + c)}{x} + 9\left(\frac{4}{x} + \frac{9 + x}{y}\right)$$

can be translated into a Java expression as:

```
(3 + 4 * x) / 5 - 10 * (y - 5) * (a + b + c) / x +
9 * (4 / x + (9 + x) / y)
```

evaluating an expression

operator precedence rule

Though Java has its own way to evaluate an expression behind the scene, the result of a Java expression and its corresponding arithmetic expression are the same. Therefore, you can safely apply the arithmetic rule for evaluating a Java expression. Operators contained within pairs of parentheses are evaluated first. Parentheses can be nested, in which case the expression in the inner parentheses is evaluated first. When more than one operator is used in an expression, the following operator precedence rule is used to determine the order of evaluation.

- Multiplication, division, and remainder operators are applied first. If an expression contains several multiplication, division, and remainder operators, they are applied from left to right.
- Addition and subtraction operators are applied last. If an expression contains several addition and subtraction operators, they are applied from left to right.

Here is an example of how an expression is evaluated:

```
3 + 4 * 4 + 5 * (4 + 3) - 1
                   (1) inside parentheses first
3 + 4 * 4 + 5 * 7 - 1
                   (2) multiplication
3 + 16 + 5 * 7 - 1
                   (3) multiplication
3 + 16 + 35 - 1
                   (4) addition
19 + 35 - 1
                   (5) addition
   54 - 1
                   (6) subtraction
   53
```

Listing 2.5 gives a program that converts a Fahrenheit degree to Celsius using the formula $celsius = (\frac{5}{9})(fahrenheit - 32)$.

LISTING 2.5 FahrenheitToCelsius.java

```
import java.util.Scanner;

public class FahrenheitToCelsius {
  public static void main(String[] args) {
    Scanner input = new Scanner(System.in);

    System.out.print("Enter a degree in Fahrenheit: ");
```

```
8       double fahrenheit = input.nextDouble();
9
10      // Convert Fahrenheit to Celsius
11      double celsius = (5.0 / 9) * (fahrenheit - 32);
12      System.out.println("Fahrenheit " + fahrenheit + " is " +
13        celsius + " in Celsius");
14    }
15  }
```

divide

```
Enter a degree in Fahrenheit: 100 [Enter]
Fahrenheit 100.0 is 37.77777777777778 in Celsius
```

line#	fahrenheit	celsius
8	100	
11		37.77777777777778

Be careful when applying division. Division of two integers yields an integer in Java. $\frac{5}{9}$ is translated to `5.0 / 9` instead of `5 / 9` in line 11, because `5 / 9` yields `0` in Java.

integer vs. decimal division

2.17 How would you write the following arithmetic expression in Java?

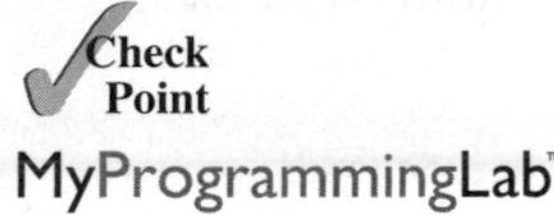

$$\frac{4}{3(r + 34)} - 9(a + bc) + \frac{3 + d(2 + a)}{a + bd}$$

2.12 Case Study: Displaying the Current Time

You can invoke `System.currentTimeMillis()` to return the current time.

The problem is to develop a program that displays the current time in GMT (Greenwich Mean Time) in the format hour:minute:second, such as 13:19:8.

VideoNote
Use operators / and %

The `currentTimeMillis` method in the `System` class returns the current time in milliseconds elapsed since the time `00:00:00` on January 1, 1970 GMT, as shown in Figure 2.2. This time is known as the *UNIX epoch*. The epoch is the point when time starts, and `1970` was the year when the UNIX operating system was formally introduced.

`currentTimeMillis`
UNIX epoch

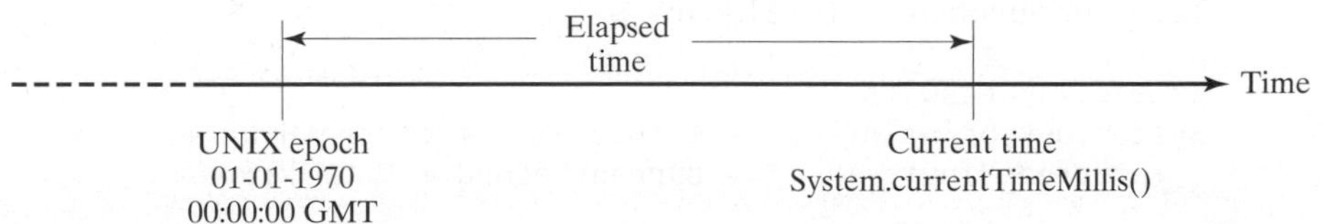

FIGURE 2.2 The `System.currentTimeMillis()` returns the number of milliseconds since the UNIX epoch.

You can use this method to obtain the current time, and then compute the current second, minute, and hour as follows.

1. Obtain the total milliseconds since midnight, January 1, 1970, in `totalMilliseconds` by invoking `System.currentTimeMillis()` (e.g., `1203183068328` milliseconds).

2. Obtain the total seconds `totalSeconds` by dividing `totalMilliseconds` by `1000` (e.g., `1203183068328` milliseconds / `1000` = `1203183068` seconds).

3. Compute the current second from `totalSeconds % 60` (e.g., `1203183068` seconds % `60` = `8`, which is the current second).

4. Obtain the total minutes `totalMinutes` by dividing `totalSeconds` by `60` (e.g., `1203183068` seconds / `60` = `20053051` minutes).

5. Compute the current minute from `totalMinutes % 60` (e.g., `20053051` minutes % `60` = `31`, which is the current minute).

6. Obtain the total hours `totalHours` by dividing `totalMinutes` by `60` (e.g., `20053051` minutes / `60` = `334217` hours).

7. Compute the current hour from `totalHours % 24` (e.g., `334217` hours % `24` = `17`, which is the current hour).

Listing 2.6 gives the complete program.

LISTING 2.6 ShowCurrentTime.java

totalMilliseconds (line 4); totalSeconds (line 7); currentSecond (line 10); totalMinutes (line 13); currentMinute (line 16); totalHours (line 19); currentHour (line 22); preparing output (line 25)

```
1  public class ShowCurrentTime {
2    public static void main(String[] args) {
3      // Obtain the total milliseconds since midnight, Jan 1, 1970
4      long totalMilliseconds = System.currentTimeMillis();
5
6      // Obtain the total seconds since midnight, Jan 1, 1970
7      long totalSeconds = totalMilliseconds / 1000;
8
9      // Compute the current second in the minute in the hour
10     long currentSecond = totalSeconds % 60;
11
12     // Obtain the total minutes
13     long totalMinutes = totalSeconds / 60;
14
15     // Compute the current minute in the hour
16     long currentMinute = totalMinutes % 60;
17
18     // Obtain the total hours
19     long totalHours = totalMinutes / 60;
20
21     // Compute the current hour
22     long currentHour = totalHours % 24;
23
24     // Display results
25     System.out.println("Current time is " + currentHour + ":"
26       + currentMinute + ":" + currentSecond + " GMT");
27   }
28 }
```

```
Current time is 17:31:8 GMT
```

Line 4 invokes `System.currentTimeMillis()` to obtain the current time in milliseconds as a long value. Thus, all the variables are declared as the long type in this program. The seconds, minutes, and hours are extracted from the current time using the `/` and `%` operators (lines 6–22).

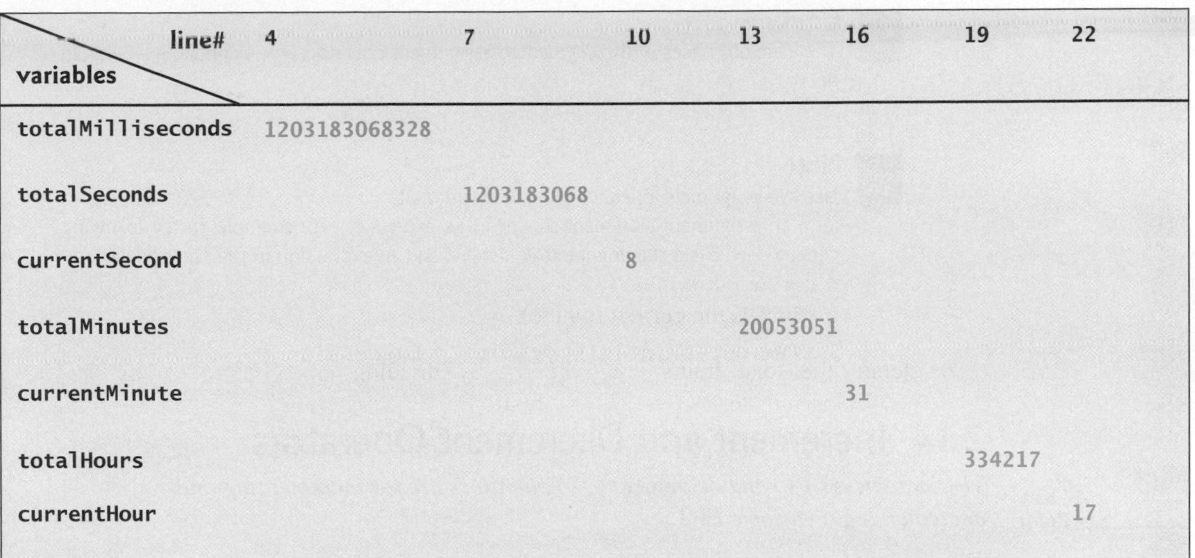

variables \ line#	4	7	10	13	16	19	22
totalMilliseconds	1203183068328						
totalSeconds		1203183068					
currentSecond			8				
totalMinutes				20053051			
currentMinute					31		
totalHours						334217	
currentHour							17

In the sample run, a single digit `8` is displayed for the second. The desirable output would be `08`. This can be fixed by using a function that formats a single digit with a prefix `0` (see Exercise 5.37).

2.13 Augmented Assignment Operators

*The operators +, -, *, /, and % can be combined with the assignment operator to form augmented operators.*

Very often the current value of a variable is used, modified, and then reassigned back to the same variable. For example, the following statement increases the variable `count` by `1`:

```
count = count + 1;
```

Java allows you to combine assignment and addition operators using an augmented (or compound) assignment operator. For example, the preceding statement can be written as:

```
count += 1;
```

The `+=` is called the *addition assignment operator.* Table 2.4 shows other augmented assignment operators. addition assignment operator

TABLE 2.4 Augmented Assignment Operators

Operator	*Name*	*Example*	*Equivalent*
+=	Addition assignment	i += 8	i = i + 8
-=	Subtraction assignment	i -= 8	i = i - 8
*=	Multiplication assignment	i *= 8	i = i * 8
/=	Division assignment	i /= 8	i = i / 8
%=	Remainder assignment	i %= 8	i = i % 8

Caution

There are no spaces in the augmented assignment operators. For example, + = should be +=.

Note

Like the assignment operator (=), the operators (+=, -=, *=, /=, %=) can be used to form an assignment statement as well as an expression. For example, in the following code, x += 2 is a statement in the first line and an expression in the second line.

```
x += 2; // Statement
System.out.println(x += 2); // Expression
```

2.14 Increment and Decrement Operators

The increment (++) and decrement (−−) operators are for incrementing and decrementing a variable by 1.

increment operator (++)
decrement operator (−−)

The ++ and −− are two shorthand operators for incrementing and decrementing a variable by 1. These are handy, because that's often how much the value needs to be changed in many programming tasks. For example, the following code increments i by 1 and decrements j by 1.

```
int i = 3, j = 3;
i++; // i becomes 4
j--; // j becomes 2
```

postincrement
postdecrement

i++ is pronounced as i plus plus and i−− as i minus minus. These operators are known as *postfix increment* (or postincrement) and *postfix decrement* (or postdecrement), because the operators ++ and −− are placed after the variable. These operators can also be placed before the variable. For example,

```
int i = 3, j = 3;
++i; // i becomes 4
--j; // j becomes 2
```

preincrement
predecrement

++i increments i by 1 and −−j decrements j by 1. These operators are known as *prefix increment* (or preincrement) and *prefix decrement* (or predecrement).

As you see, the effect of i++ and ++i or i−− and −−i are the same in the preceding examples. However, their effects are different when they are used in statements that do more than just increment and decrement. Table 2.5 describes their differences and gives examples.

TABLE 2.5 Increment and Decrement Operators

Operator	*Name*	*Description*	*Example (assume i = 1)*
++var	preincrement	Increment var by 1, and use the new var value in the statement	int j = ++i; // j is 2, i is 2
var++	postincrement	Increment var by 1, but use the original var value in the statement	int j = i++; // j is 1, i is 2
--var	predecrement	Decrement var by 1, and use the new var value in the statement	int j = --i; // j is 0, i is 0
var--	postdecrement	Decrement var by 1, and use the original var value in the statement	int j = i--; // j is 1, i is 0

Here are additional examples to illustrate the differences between the prefix form of ++ (or −−) and the postfix form of ++ (or −−). Consider the following code:

```
int i = 10;
int newNum = 10 * i++;          Same effect as   int newNum = 10 * i;
                                                 i = i + 1;
System.out.print("i is " + i
  + ", newNum is " + newNum);
```

```
i is 11, newNum is 100
```

In this case, i is incremented by 1, then the *old* value of i is used in the multiplication. So newNum becomes 100. If i++ is replaced by ++i as follows,

```
int i = 10;
int newNum = 10 * (++i);        Same effect as   i = i + 1;
                                                 int newNum = 10 * i;
System.out.print("i is " + i
  + ", newNum is " + newNum);
```

```
i is 11, newNum is 110
```

i is incremented by 1, and the new value of i is used in the multiplication. Thus newNum becomes 110.

Here is another example:

```
double x = 1.0;
double y = 5.0;
double z = x-- + (++y);
```

After all three lines are executed, y becomes 6.0, z becomes 7.0, and x becomes 0.0.

Tip

Using increment and decrement operators makes expressions short, but it also makes them complex and difficult to read. Avoid using these operators in expressions that modify multiple variables or the same variable multiple times, such as this one: int k = ++i + i.

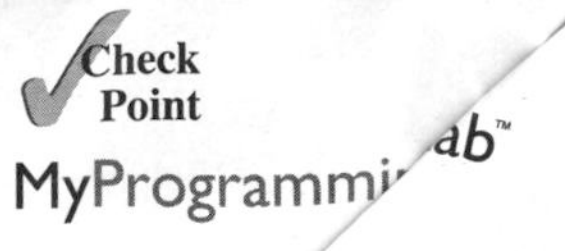

2.18 Which of these statements are true?

a. Any expression can be used as a statement.

b. The expression x++ can be used as a statement.

c. The statement x = x + 5 is also an expression.

d. The statement x = y = x = 0 is illegal.

2.19 Assume that int a = 1 and double d = 1.0, and that each expression is independent. What are the results of the following expressions?

```
a = 46 / 9;
a = 46 % 9 + 4 * 4 - 2;
a = 45 + 43 % 5 * (23 * 3 % 2);
a %= 3 / a + 3;
d = 4 + d * d + 4;
d += 1.5 * 3 + (++a);
d -= 1.5 * 3 + a++;
```

2.20 How do you obtain the current minute using the `System.currentTimeMillis()` method?

2.15 Numeric Type Conversions

Floating-point numbers can be converted into integers using explicit casting.

Can you perform binary operations with two operands of different types? Yes. If an integer and a floating-point number are involved in a binary operation, Java automatically converts the integer to a floating-point value. So, `3 * 4.5` is same as `3.0 * 4.5`.

You can always assign a value to a numeric variable whose type supports a larger range of values; thus, for instance, you can assign a `long` value to a `float` variable. You cannot, however, assign a value to a variable of a type with a smaller range unless you use *type casting*. *Casting* is an operation that converts a value of one data type into a value of another data type. Casting a type with a small range to a type with a larger range is known as *widening a type*. Casting a type with a large range to a type with a smaller range is known as *narrowing a type*. Java will automatically widen a type, but you must narrow a type explicitly.

casting

widening a type

narrowing a type

The syntax for casting a type is to specify the target type in parentheses, followed by the variable's name or the value to be cast. For example, the following statement

```
System.out.println((int)1.7);
```

displays `1`. When a `double` value is cast into an `int` value, the fractional part is truncated.

The following statement

```
System.out.println((double)1 / 2);
```

displays `0.5`, because `1` is cast to `1.0` first, then `1.0` is divided by `2`. However, the statement

```
System.out.println(1 / 2);
```

displays `0`, because `1` and `2` are both integers and the resulting value should also be an integer.

possible loss of precision

Caution

Casting is necessary if you are assigning a value to a variable of a smaller type range, such as assigning a `double` value to an `int` variable. A compile error will occur if casting is not used in situations of this kind. However, be careful when using casting, as loss of information might lead to inaccurate results.

Note

Casting does not change the variable being cast. For example, `d` is not changed after casting in the following code:

```
double d = 4.5;
int i = (int)d;  // i becomes 4, but d is still 4.5
```

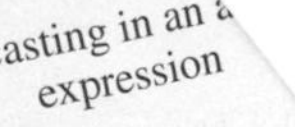

casting in an expression

Note

In Java, an augmented expression of the form `x1 op= x2` is implemented as `x1 = (T)(x1 op x2)`, where `T` is the type for `x1`. Therefore, the following code is correct.

```
int sum = 0;
sum += 4.5; // sum becomes 4 after this statement
```

`sum += 4.5` is equivalent to `sum = (int)(sum + 4.5)`.

Note

To assign a variable of the `int` type to a variable of the `short` or `byte` type, explicit casting must be used. For example, the following statements have a compile error:

```
int i = 1;
byte b = i; // Error because explicit casting is required
```

However, so long as the integer literal is within the permissible range of the target variable, explicit casting is not needed to assign an integer literal to a variable of the `short` or `byte` type (see Section 2.10, Numeric Literals).

The program in Listing 2.7 displays the sales tax with two digits after the decimal point.

LISTING 2.7 `SalesTax.java`

```
1  import java.util.Scanner;
2
3  public class SalesTax {
4    public static void main(String[] args) {
5      Scanner input = new Scanner(System.in);
6
7      System.out.print("Enter purchase amount: ");
8      double purchaseAmount = input.nextDouble();
9
10     double tax = purchaseAmount * 0.06;
11     System.out.println("Sales tax is $" + (int)(tax * 100) / 100.0);
12   }
13 }
```

casting

```
Enter purchase amount: 197.55 ↵Enter
Sales tax is $11.85
```

line#	purchaseAmount	tax	output
8	197.55		
10		11.853	
11			11.85

formatting numbers

The variable `purchaseAmount` is `197.55` (line 8). The sales tax is `6%` of the purchase, so the `tax` is evaluated as `11.853` (line 10). Note that

`tax * 100` is `1185.3`
`(int)(tax * 100)` is `1185`
`(int)(tax * 100) / 100.0` is `11.85`

So, the statement in line 11 displays the tax `11.85` with two digits after the decimal point.

2.21 Can different types of numeric values be used together in a computation?

2.22 What does an explicit casting from a `double` to an `int` do with the fractional part of the `double` value? Does casting change the variable being cast?

2.23 Show the following output:

```
float f = 12.5F;
int i = (int)f;
```

```
System.out.println("f is " + f);
System.out.println("i is " + i);
```

2.24 If you change `(int)(tax * 100) / 100.0` to `(int)(tax * 100) / 100` in line 11 in Listing 2.7, what will be the output for the input purchase amount of `197.556`?

2.16 Software Development Process

The software development life cycle is a multi-stage process that includes requirements specification, analysis, design, implementation, testing, deployment, and maintenance.

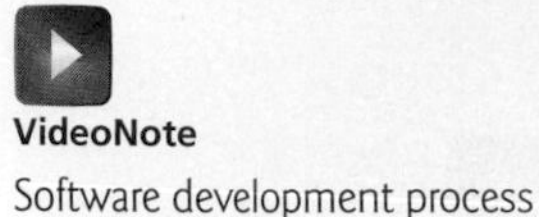

Developing a software product is an engineering process. Software products, no matter how large or how small, have the same life cycle: requirements specification, analysis, design, implementation, testing, deployment, and maintenance, as shown in Figure 2.3.

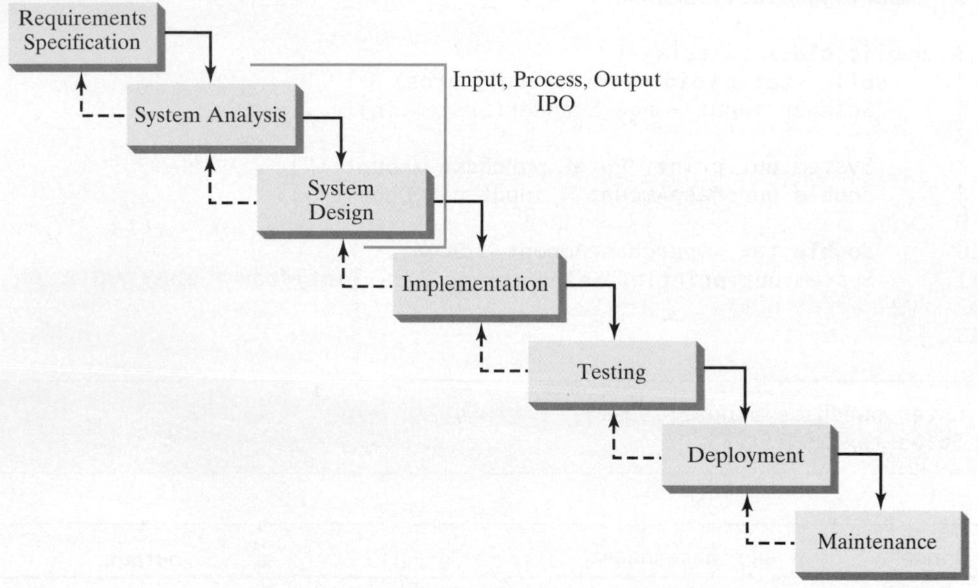

FIGURE 2.3 At any stage of the software development life cycle, it may be necessary to go back to a previous stage to correct errors or deal with other issues that might prevent the software from functioning as expected.

requirements specification

Requirements specification is a formal process that seeks to understand the problem that the software will address and to document in detail what the software system needs to do. This phase involves close interaction between users and developers. Most of the examples in this book are simple, and their requirements are clearly stated. In the real world, however, problems are not always well defined. Developers need to work closely with their customers (the individuals or organizations that will use the software) and study the problem carefully to identify what the software needs to do.

system analysis

System analysis seeks to analyze the data flow and to identify the system's input and output. When you do analysis, it helps to identify what the output is first, and then figure out what input data you need in order to produce the output.

system design

System design is to design a process for obtaining the output from the input. This phase involves the use of many levels of abstraction to break down the problem into manageable components and design strategies for implementing each component. You can view each component as a subsystem that performs a specific function of the system. The essence of system analysis and design is input, process, and output (IPO).

IPO

Implementation involves translating the system design into programs. Separate programs are written for each component and then integrated to work together. This phase requires the use of a programming language such as Java. The implementation involves coding, self-testing, and debugging (that is, finding errors, called *bugs*, in the code).

implementation

Testing ensures that the code meets the requirements specification and weeds out bugs. An independent team of software engineers not involved in the design and implementation of the product usually conducts such testing.

testing

Deployment makes the software available for use. Depending on the type of the software, it may be installed on each user's machine or installed on a server accessible on the Internet.

deployment

Maintenance is concerned with updating and improving the product. A software product must continue to perform and improve in an ever-evolving environment. This requires periodic upgrades of the product to fix newly discovered bugs and incorporate changes.

maintenance

To see the software development process in action, we will now create a program that computes loan payments. The loan can be a car loan, a student loan, or a home mortgage loan. For an introductory programming course, we focus on requirements specification, analysis, design, implementation, and testing.

VideoNote

Compute loan payments

Stage 1: Requirements Specification

The program must satisfy the following requirements:

- It must let the user enter the interest rate, the loan amount, and the number of years for which payments will be made.
- It must compute and display the monthly payment and total payment amounts.

Stage 2: System Analysis

The output is the monthly payment and total payment, which can be obtained using the following formulas:

$$monthlyPayment = \frac{loanAmount \times monthlyInterestRate}{1 - \frac{1}{(1 + monthlyInterestRate)^{numberOfYears \times 12}}}$$

$$totalPayment = monthlyPayment \times numberOfYears \times 12$$

So, the input needed for the program is the monthly interest rate, the length of the loan in years, and the loan amount.

Note

The requirements specification says that the user must enter the annual interest rate, the loan amount, and the number of years for which payments will be made. During analysis, however, it is possible that you may discover that input is not sufficient or that some values are unnecessary for the output. If this happens, you can go back and modify the requirements specification.

Note

In the real world, you will work with customers from all walks of life. You may develop software for chemists, physicists, engineers, economists, and psychologists, and of course you will not have (or need) complete knowledge of all these fields. Therefore, you don't have to know how formulas are derived, but given the monthly interest rate, the number of years, and the loan amount, you can compute the monthly payment in this program. You will, however, need to communicate with customers and understand how a mathematical model works for the system.

Stage 3: System Design

During system design, you identify the steps in the program.

Step 1. Prompt the user to enter the annual interest rate, the number of years, and the loan amount.

Step 2. The input for the annual interest rate is a number in percent format, such as 4.5%. The program needs to convert it into a decimal by dividing it by `100`. To obtain the monthly interest rate from the annual interest rate, divide it by `12`, since a year has 12 months. So, to obtain the monthly interest rate in decimal format, you need to divide the annual interest rate in percentage by `1200`. For example, if the annual interest rate is 4.5%, then the monthly interest rate is $4.5/1200 = 0.00375$.

Step 3. Compute the monthly payment using the preceding formula.

Step 4. Compute the total payment, which is the monthly payment multiplied by `12` and multiplied by the number of years.

Step 5. Display the monthly payment and total payment.

Stage 4: Implementation

`Math.pow(a, b)` method

Implementation is also known as *coding* (writing the code). In the formula, you have to compute $(1 + monthlyInterestRate)^{numberOfYears \times 12}$, which can be obtained using `Math.pow(1 + monthlyInterestRate, numberOfYears * 12)`.

Listing 2.8 gives the complete program.

LISTING 2.8 ComputeLoan.java

import class; create a `Scanner`; enter interest rate; enter years; enter loan amount; `monthlyPayment`; `totalPayment`

```
import java.util.Scanner;

public class ComputeLoan {
  public static void main(String[] args) {
    // Create a Scanner
    Scanner input = new Scanner(System.in);

    // Enter annual interest rate in percentage, e.g., 7.25%
    System.out.print("Enter annual interest rate, e.g., 7.25%: ");
    double annualInterestRate = input.nextDouble();

    // Obtain monthly interest rate
    double monthlyInterestRate = annualInterestRate / 1200;

    // Enter number of years
    System.out.print(
      "Enter number of years as an integer, e.g., 5: ");
    int numberOfYears = input.nextInt();

    // Enter loan amount
    System.out.print("Enter loan amount, e.g., 120000.95: ");
    double loanAmount = input.nextDouble();

    // Calculate payment
    double monthlyPayment = loanAmount * monthlyInterestRate / (1
      - 1 / Math.pow(1 + monthlyInterestRate, numberOfYears * 12));
    double totalPayment = monthlyPayment * numberOfYears * 12;

    // Display results
```

```
30         System.out.println("The monthly payment is $" +
31           (int)(monthlyPayment * 100) / 100.0);
32         System.out.println("The total payment is $" +
33           (int)(totalPayment * 100) / 100.0);
34     }
35   }
```

casting

casting

```
Enter annual interest rate, e.g., 5.75%: 5.75 ↵Enter
Enter number of years as an integer, e.g., 5: 15 ↵Enter
Enter loan amount, e.g., 120000.95: 250000 ↵Enter
The monthly payment is $2076.02
The total payment is $373684.53
```

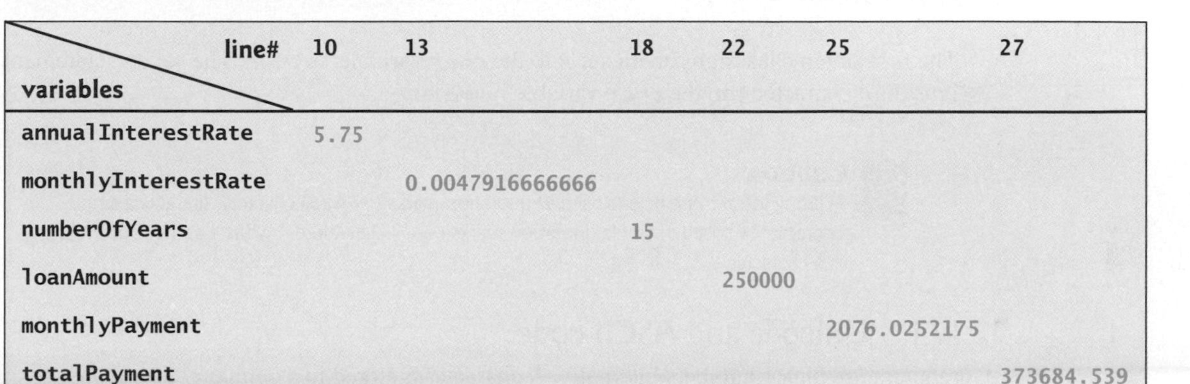

variables \ line#	10	13	18	22	25	27
annualInterestRate	5.75					
monthlyInterestRate		0.0047916666666				
numberOfYears			15			
loanAmount				250000		
monthlyPayment					2076.0252175	
totalPayment						373684.539

Line 10 reads the annual interest rate, which is converted into the monthly interest rate in line 13.

Choose the most appropriate data type for the variable. For example, `numberOfYears` is best declared as an `int` (line 18), although it could be declared as a `long`, `float`, or `double`. Note that `byte` might be the most appropriate for `numberOfYears`. For simplicity, however, the examples in this book will use `int` for integer and `double` for floating-point values.

The formula for computing the monthly payment is translated into Java code in lines 25–27.

Casting is used in lines 31 and 33 to obtain a new `monthlyPayment` and `totalPayment` with two digits after the decimal points.

The program uses the `Scanner` class, imported in line 1. The program also uses the `Math` class, and you might be wondering why that class isn't imported into the program. The `Math` class is in the `java.lang` package, and all classes in the `java.lang` package are implicitly imported. Therefore, you don't need to explicitly import the `Math` class.

`java.lang` package

Stage 5: Testing

After the program is implemented, test it with some sample input data and verify whether the output is correct. Some of the problems may involve many cases, as you will see in later chapters. For these types of problems, you need to design test data that cover all cases.

Tip

The system design phase in this example identified several steps. It is a good approach to developing and testing these steps incrementally by adding them one at a time. This approach makes it much easier to pinpoint problems and debug the program.

incremental development and testing

MyProgrammingLab™

2.25 How would you write the following arithmetic expression?

$$\frac{-b + \sqrt{b^2 - 4ac}}{2a}$$

2.17 Character Data Type and Operations

A character data type represents a single character.

char type

In addition to processing numeric values, you can process characters in Java. The character data type, `char`, is used to represent a single character. A character literal is enclosed in single quotation marks. Consider the following code:

```
char letter = 'A';
char numChar = '4';
```

The first statement assigns character `A` to the `char` variable `letter`. The second statement assigns digit character `4` to the `char` variable `numChar`.

char literal

Caution

A string literal must be enclosed in quotation marks (" "). A character literal is a single character enclosed in single quotation marks (' '). Therefore, `"A"` is a string, but `'A'` is a character.

2.17.1 Unicode and ASCII code

encoding

Computers use binary numbers internally. A character is stored in a computer as a sequence of 0s and 1s. Mapping a character to its binary representation is called *encoding*. There are different ways to encode a character. How characters are encoded is defined by an *encoding scheme.*

Unicode

original Unicode

Java supports *Unicode,* an encoding scheme established by the Unicode Consortium to support the interchange, processing, and display of written texts in the world's diverse languages. Unicode was originally designed as a 16-bit character encoding. The primitive data type `char` was intended to take advantage of this design by providing a simple data type that could hold any character. However, it turned out that the 65,536 characters possible in a 16-bit encoding are not sufficient to represent all the characters in the world. The Unicode standard therefore has been extended to allow up to 1,112,064 characters. Those characters that go beyond the original 16-bit limit are called *supplementary characters.* Java supports the supplementary characters. The processing and representing of supplementary characters are beyond the scope of this book. For simplicity, this book considers only the original 16-bit Unicode characters. These characters can be stored in a `char` type variable.

supplementary Unicode

A 16-bit Unicode takes two bytes, preceded by `\u`, expressed in four hexadecimal digits that run from `\u0000` to `\uFFFF`. Hexadecimal numbers are introduced in Appendix F, Number Systems. For example, the English word `welcome` is translated into Chinese using two characters, 欢迎. The Unicodes of these two characters are `\u6B22\u8FCE`.

Listing 2.9 gives a program that displays two Chinese characters and three Greek letters.

LISTING 2.9 `DisplayUnicode.java`

```
import javax.swing.JOptionPane;

public class DisplayUnicode {
  public static void main(String[] args) {
    JOptionPane.showMessageDialog(null,
      "\u6B22\u8FCE \u03b1 \u03b2 \u03b3",
      "\u6B22\u8FCE Welcome",
```

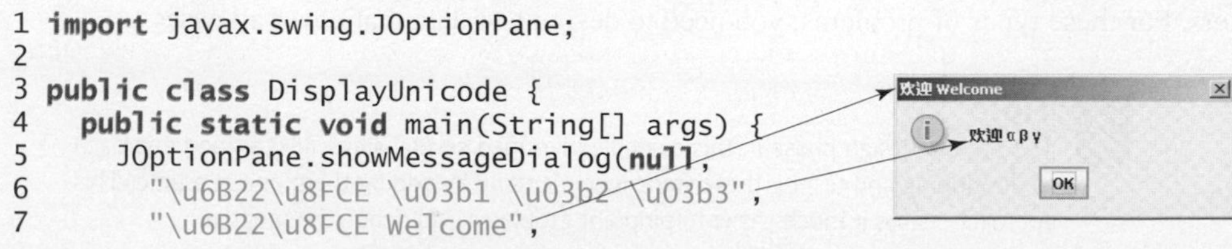

```
        JOptionPane.INFORMATION_MESSAGE);
  }
}
```

If no Chinese font is installed on your system, you will not be able to see the Chinese characters. The Unicodes for the Greek letters α β γ are `\u03b1 \u03b2 \u03b3`.

ASCII

Most computers use *ASCII (American Standard Code for Information Interchange)*, a 7-bit encoding scheme for representing all uppercase and lowercase letters, digits, punctuation marks, and control characters. Unicode includes ASCII code, with `\u0000` to `\u007F` corresponding to the 128 ASCII characters. (See Appendix B for a list of ASCII characters and their decimal and hexadecimal codes.) You can use ASCII characters such as `'X'`, `'1'`, and `'$'` in a Java program as well as Unicodes. Thus, for example, the following statements are equivalent:

```
char letter = 'A';
char letter = '\u0041'; // Character A's Unicode is 0041
```

Both statements assign character `A` to the `char` variable `letter`.

Note

`char` increment and decrement

The increment and decrement operators can also be used on `char` variables to get the next or preceding Unicode character. For example, the following statements display character `b`.

```
char ch = 'a';
System.out.println(++ch);
```

2.17.2 Escape Characters

Suppose you want to print a message with quotation marks in the output. Can you write a statement like this?

```
System.out.println("He said "Java is fun"");
```

No, this statement has a compile error. The compiler thinks the second quotation character is the end of the string and does not know what to do with the rest of the characters.

escape character

To overcome this problem, Java uses a special notation to represent special characters, as shown in Table 2.6. This special notation, called an *escape character*, consists of a backslash (\) followed by a character or a character sequence. For example, `\t` is an escape character for the Tab character and an escape character such as `\u03b1` is used to represent a Unicode. The symbols in an escape character are interpreted as a whole rather than individually.

So, now you can print the quoted message using the following statement:

```
System.out.println("He said \"Java is fun\"");
```

The output is

```
He said "Java is fun"
```

Note that the symbols \ and " together represent one character.

2.17.3 Casting between `char` and Numeric Types

A `char` can be cast into any numeric type, and vice versa. When an integer is cast into a `char`, only its lower 16 bits of data are used; the other part is ignored. For example:

```
char ch = (char)0XAB0041; // The lower 16 bits hex code 0041 is
                          // assigned to ch
System.out.println(ch);   // ch is character A
```

TABLE 2.6 Escape Characters

Escape Character	*Name*	*Unicode Code*	*Decimal Value*
`\b`	Backspace	`\u0008`	8
`\t`	Tab	`\u0009`	9
`\n`	Linefeed	`\u000A`	10
`\f`	Formfeed	`\u000C`	12
`\r`	Carriage Return	`\u000D`	13
`\\`	Backslash	`\u005C`	92
`\"`	Double Quote	`\u0022`	34

When a floating-point value is cast into a `char`, the floating-point value is first cast into an `int`, which is then cast into a `char`.

```
char ch = (char)65.25;     // Decimal 65 is assigned to ch
System.out.println(ch);    // ch is character A
```

When a `char` is cast into a numeric type, the character's Unicode is cast into the specified numeric type.

```
int i = (int)'A'; // The Unicode of character A is assigned to i
System.out.println(i);  // i is 65
```

Implicit casting can be used if the result of a casting fits into the target variable. Otherwise, explicit casting must be used. For example, since the Unicode of `'a'` is `97`, which is within the range of a byte, these implicit castings are fine:

```
byte b = 'a';
int i = 'a';
```

But the following casting is incorrect, because the Unicode `\uFFF4` cannot fit into a byte:

```
byte b = '\uFFF4';
```

To force this assignment, use explicit casting, as follows:

```
byte b = (byte)'\uFFF4';
```

Any positive integer between `0` and `FFFF` in hexadecimal can be cast into a character implicitly. Any number not in this range must be cast into a `char` explicitly.

numeric operators on characters

Note

All numeric operators can be applied to `char` operands. A `char` operand is automatically cast into a number if the other operand is a number or a character. If the other operand is a string, the character is concatenated with the string. For example, the following statements

```
int i = '2' + '3'; // (int)'2' is 50 and (int)'3' is 51
System.out.println("i is " + i); // i is 101
```

```
int j = 2 + 'a'; // (int)'a' is 97
System.out.println("j is " + j); // j is 99
System.out.println(j + " is the Unicode for character "
  + (char)j); // j is the Unicode for character c
System.out.println("Chapter " + '2');
```

display

```
i is 101
j is 99
99 is the Unicode for character c
Chapter 2
```

Note

The Unicodes for lowercase letters are consecutive integers starting from the Unicode for `'a'`, then for `'b'`, `'c'`, . . . , and `'z'`. The same is true for the uppercase letters. Furthermore, the Unicode for `'a'` is greater than the Unicode for `'A'`, so `'a' - 'A'` is the same as `'b' - 'B'`. For a lowercase letter *ch*, its corresponding uppercase letter is `(char)('A' + (ch - 'a'))`.

2.17.4 Case Study: Counting Monetary Units

Suppose you want to develop a program that changes a given amount of money into smaller monetary units. The program lets the user enter an amount as a **`double`** value representing a total in dollars and cents, and outputs a report listing the monetary equivalent in the maximum number of dollars, quarters, dimes, nickels, and pennies, in this order, to result in the minimum number of coins, as shown in the sample run.

Here are the steps in developing the program:

1. Prompt the user to enter the amount as a decimal number, such as `11.56`.
2. Convert the amount (e.g., `11.56`) into cents (`1156`).
3. Divide the cents by `100` to find the number of dollars. Obtain the remaining cents using the cents remainder `100`.
4. Divide the remaining cents by `25` to find the number of quarters. Obtain the remaining cents using the remaining cents remainder `25`.
5. Divide the remaining cents by `10` to find the number of dimes. Obtain the remaining cents using the remaining cents remainder `10`.
6. Divide the remaining cents by `5` to find the number of nickels. Obtain the remaining cents using the remaining cents remainder `5`.
7. The remaining cents are the pennies.
8. Display the result.

The complete program is given in Listing 2.10.

LISTING 2.10 ComputeChange.java

import class

```
import java.util.Scanner;

public class ComputeChange {
  public static void main(String[] args) {
    // Create a Scanner
    Scanner input = new Scanner(System.in);

    // Receive the amount
    System.out.print(
```

enter input · dollars · quarters · dimes · nickels · pennies · output

```
10          "Enter an amount, for example, 11.56: ");
11        double amount = input.nextDouble();
12
13        int remainingAmount = (int)(amount * 100);
14
15        // Find the number of one dollars
16        int numberOfOneDollars = remainingAmount / 100;
17        remainingAmount = remainingAmount % 100;
18
19        // Find the number of quarters in the remaining amount
20        int numberOfQuarters = remainingAmount / 25;
21        remainingAmount = remainingAmount % 25;
22
23        // Find the number of dimes in the remaining amount
24        int numberOfDimes = remainingAmount / 10;
25        remainingAmount = remainingAmount % 10;
26
27        // Find the number of nickels in the remaining amount
28        int numberOfNickels = remainingAmount / 5;
29        remainingAmount = remainingAmount % 5;
30
31        // Find the number of pennies in the remaining amount
32        int numberOfPennies = remainingAmount;
33
34        // Display results
35        System.out.println("Your amount " + amount + " consists of \n" +
36          "\t" + numberOfOneDollars + " dollars\n" +
37          "\t" + numberOfQuarters + " quarters\n" +
38          "\t" + numberOfDimes + " dimes\n" +
39          "\t" + numberOfNickels + " nickels\n" +
40          "\t" + numberOfPennies + " pennies");
41      }
42    }
```

```
Enter an amount, for example, 11.56: 11.56 ↵Enter
Your amount 11.56 consists of
        11 dollars
        2 quarters
        0 dimes
        1 nickels
        1 pennies
```

variables \ line#	11	13	16	17	20	21	24	25	28	29	32
amount	11.56										
remainingAmount		1156		56		6		6		1	
numberOfOneDollars			11								
numberOfQuarters					2						
numberOfDimes							0				
numberOfNickels									1		
numberOfPennies											1

The variable amount stores the amount entered from the console (line 11). This variable is not changed, because the amount has to be used at the end of the program to display the results. The program introduces the variable remainingAmount (line 13) to store the changing remaining amount.

The variable amount is a double decimal representing dollars and cents. It is converted to an int variable remainingAmount, which represents all the cents. For instance, if amount is 11.56, then the initial remainingAmount is 1156. The division operator yields the integer part of the division, so 1156 / 100 is 11. The remainder operator obtains the remainder of the division, so 1156 % 100 is 56.

The program extracts the maximum number of singles from the remaining amount and obtains a new remaining amount in the variable remainingAmount (lines 16–17). It then extracts the maximum number of quarters from remainingAmount and obtains a new remainingAmount (lines 20–21). Continuing the same process, the program finds the maximum number of dimes, nickels, and pennies in the remaining amount.

loss of precision

One serious problem with this example is the possible loss of precision when casting a double amount to an int remainingAmount. This could lead to an inaccurate result. If you try to enter the amount 10.03, 10.03 * 100 becomes 1002.9999999999999. You will find that the program displays 10 dollars and 2 pennies. To fix the problem, enter the amount as an integer value representing cents (see Exercise 2.24).

As shown in the sample run, 0 dimes, 1 nickels, and 1 pennies are displayed in the result. It would be better not to display 0 dimes, and to display 1 nickel and 1 penny using the singular forms of the words. You will learn how to use selection statements to modify this program in the next chapter (see Exercise 3.7).

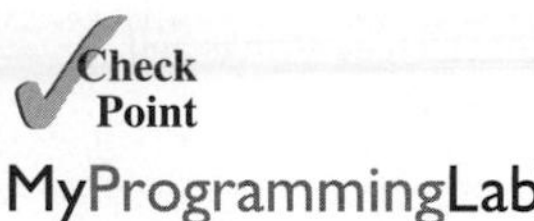

2.26 Use print statements to find out the ASCII code for '1', 'A', 'B', 'a', and 'b'. Use print statements to find out the character for the decimal codes 40, 59, 79, 85, and 90. Use print statements to find out the character for the hexadecimal code 40, 5A, 71, 72, and 7A.

2.27 Which of the following are correct literals for characters?
'1', '\u345dE', '\u3fFa', '\b', '\t'

2.28 How do you display the characters \ and "?

2.29 Evaluate the following:

```
int i = '1';
int j = '1' + '2' * ('4' - '3') + 'b' / 'a';
int k = 'a';
char c = 90;
```

2.30 Can the following conversions involving casting be allowed? If so, find the converted result.

```
char c = 'A';
int i = (int)c;

float f = 1000.34f;
int i = (int)f;

double d = 1000.34;
int i = (int)d;

int i = 97;
char c = (char)i;
```

2.31 Show the output of the following program:

```
public class Test {
  public static void main(String[] args) {
    char x = 'a';
    char y = 'c';

    System.out.println(++x);
    System.out.println(y++);
    System.out.println(x - y);
  }
}
```

2.18 The String Type

A string is a sequence of characters.

The char type represents only one character. To represent a string of characters, use the data type called String. For example, the following code declares the message to be a string with the value "Welcome to Java".

```
String message = "Welcome to Java";
```

String is a predefined class in the Java library, just like the classes System, JOptionPane, and Scanner. The String type is not a primitive type. It is known as a *reference type.* Any Java class can be used as a reference type for a variable. Reference data types will be thoroughly discussed in Chapter 8, Objects and Classes. For the time being, you need to know only how to declare a String variable, how to assign a string to the variable, and how to concatenate strings.

concatenate strings and numbers

As first shown in Listing 2.1, two strings can be concatenated. The plus sign (+) is the concatenation operator if one of the operands is a string. If one of the operands is a nonstring (e.g., a number), the nonstring value is converted into a string and concatenated with the other string. Here are some examples:

```
// Three strings are concatenated
String message = "Welcome " + "to " + "Java";

// String Chapter is concatenated with number 2
String s = "Chapter" + 2; // s becomes Chapter2

// String Supplement is concatenated with character B
String s1 = "Supplement" + 'B'; // s1 becomes SupplementB
```

If neither of the operands is a string, the plus sign (+) is the addition operator that adds two numbers.

The augmented += operator can also be used for string concatenation. For example, the following code appends the string "and Java is fun" with the string "Welcome to Java" in message.

```
message += " and Java is fun";
```

So the new message is "Welcome to Java and Java is fun".

If i = 1 and j = 2, what is the output of the following statement?

```
System.out.println("i + j is " + i + j);
```

The output is "i + j is 12" because "i + j is " is concatenated with the value of i first. To force i + j to be executed first, enclose i + j in the parentheses, as follows:

```
System.out.println("i + j is " + (i + j));
```

To read a string from the console, invoke the `next()` method on a `Scanner` object. For example, the following code reads three strings from the keyboard: read strings

```
Scanner input = new Scanner(System.in);
System.out.println("Enter three words separated by spaces: ");
String s1 = input.next();
String s2 = input.next();
String s3 = input.next();
System.out.println("s1 is " + s1);
System.out.println("s2 is " + s2);
System.out.println("s3 is " + s3);
```

```
Enter three words separated by spaces: Welcome to Java ↵Enter
s1 is Welcome
s2 is to
s3 is Java
```

The `next()` method reads a string that ends with a whitespace character. The characters `' '`, `\t`, `\f`, `\r`, or `\n` are known as *whitespace characters*. whitespace character

You can use the `nextLine()` method to read an entire line of text. The `nextLine()` method reads a string that ends with the *Enter* key pressed. For example, the following statements read a line of text.

```
Scanner input = new Scanner(System.in);
System.out.println("Enter a line: ");
String s = input.nextLine();
System.out.println("The line entered is " + s);
```

```
Enter a line: Welcome to Java ↵Enter
The line entered is Welcome to Java
```

Important Caution

To avoid input errors, do not use `nextLine()` after `nextByte()`, `nextShort()`, `nextInt()`, `nextLong()`, `nextFloat()`, `nextDouble()`, or `next()`. The reasons will be explained in Section 14.11.3, "How Does `Scanner` Work?" avoid input errors

2.32 Show the output of the following statements (write a program to verify your results):

```
System.out.println("1" + 1);
System.out.println('1' + 1);
System.out.println("1" + 1 + 1);
System.out.println("1" + (1 + 1));
System.out.println('1' + 1 + 1);
```

2.33 Evaluate the following expressions (write a program to verify your results):

```
1 + "Welcome " + 1 + 1
1 + "Welcome " + (1 + 1)
1 + "Welcome " + ('\u0001' + 1)
1 + "Welcome " + 'a' + 1
```

2.19 Getting Input from Input Dialogs

An input dialog box prompts the user to enter an input graphically.

JOptionPane class

You can obtain input from the console. Alternatively, you can obtain input from an input dialog box by invoking the `JOptionPane.showInputDialog` method, as shown in Figure 2.4.

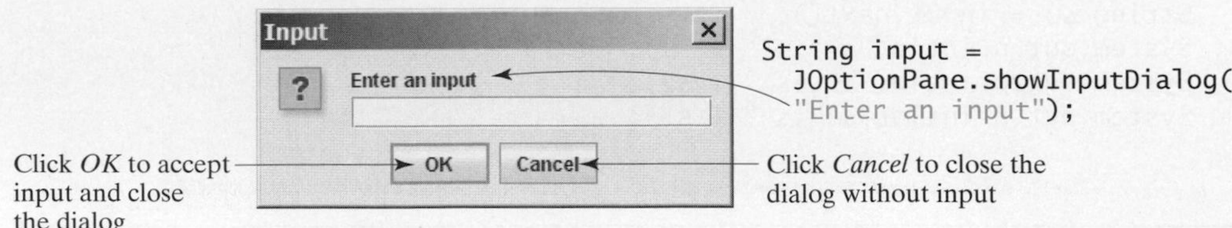

FIGURE 2.4 The input dialog box enables the user to enter a string.

When this method is executed, a dialog is displayed to enable you to enter an input value. After entering a string, click *OK* to accept the input and close the dialog box. The input is returned from the method as a string.

showInputDialog method

There are several ways to use the `showInputDialog` method. For the time being, you need to know only two ways to invoke it.

One is to use a statement like this one:

```
JOptionPane.showInputDialog(x);
```

where `x` is a string for the prompting message.

The other is to use a statement such as the following:

```
String string = JOptionPane.showInputDialog(null, x,
  y, JOptionPane.QUESTION_MESSAGE);
```

where `x` is a string for the prompting message and `y` is a string for the title of the input dialog box, as shown in the example below.

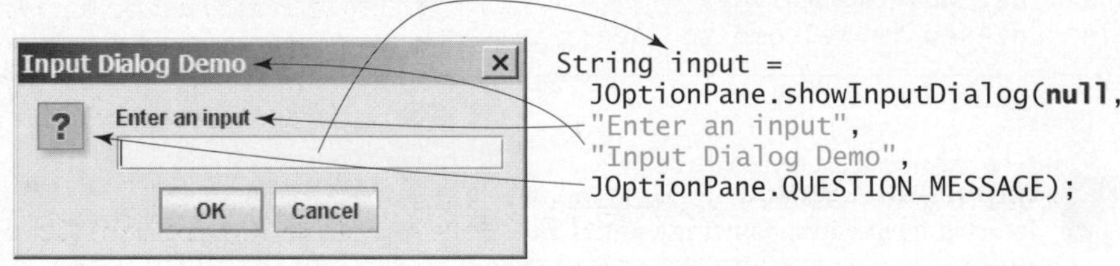

2.19.1 Converting Strings to Numbers

The input returned from the input dialog box is a string. If you enter a numeric value such as `123`, it returns `"123"`. You have to convert a string into a number to obtain the input as a number.

Integer.parseInt method

To convert a string into an `int` value, use the `Integer.parseInt` method, as follows:

```
int intValue = Integer.parseInt(intString);
```

where `intString` is a numeric string such as `123`.

Double.parseDouble method

To convert a string into a `double` value, use the `Double.parseDouble` method, as follows:

```
double doubleValue = Double.parseDouble(doubleString);
```

where `doubleString` is a numeric string such as `123.45`.

The `Integer` and `Double` classes are both included in the `java.lang` package, and thus they are automatically imported.

2.19.2 Using Input Dialog Boxes

Having learned how to read input from an input dialog box, you can rewrite the program in Listing 2.8, ComputeLoan.java, to read from input dialog boxes rather than from the console. Listing 2.11 gives the complete program. Figure 2.5 shows a sample run of the program.

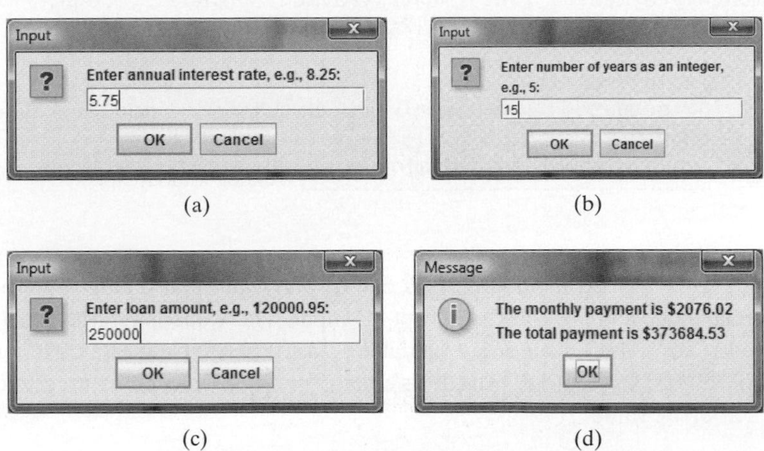

FIGURE 2.5 The program accepts the annual interest rate (a), number of years (b), and loan amount (c), then displays the monthly payment and total payment (d).

LISTING 2.11 ComputeLoanUsingInputDialog.java

```
import javax.swing.JOptionPane;

public class ComputeLoanUsingInputDialog {
  public static void main(String[] args) {
    // Enter annual interest rate
    String annualInterestRateString = JOptionPane.showInputDialog(
      "Enter annual interest rate, for example, 8.25:");

    // Convert string to double
    double annualInterestRate =
      Double.parseDouble(annualInterestRateString);

    // Obtain monthly interest rate
    double monthlyInterestRate = annualInterestRate / 1200;

    // Enter number of years
    String numberOfYearsString = JOptionPane.showInputDialog(
      "Enter number of years as an integer, for example, 5:");

    // Convert string to int
    int numberOfYears = Integer.parseInt(numberOfYearsString);

    // Enter loan amount
    String loanString = JOptionPane.showInputDialog(
      "Enter loan amount, for example, 120000.95:");

    // Convert string to double
    double loanAmount = Double.parseDouble(loanString);

```

enter interest rate

convert string to double

monthlyPayment

totalPayment

preparing output

```
30        // Calculate payment
31        double monthlyPayment = loanAmount * monthlyInterestRate / (1
32          - 1 / Math.pow(1 + monthlyInterestRate, numberOfYears * 12));
33        double totalPayment = monthlyPayment * numberOfYears * 12;
34
35        // Format to keep two digits after the decimal point
36        monthlyPayment = (int)(monthlyPayment * 100) / 100.0;
37        totalPayment = (int)(totalPayment * 100) / 100.0;
38
39        // Display results
40        String output = "The monthly payment is $" + monthlyPayment +
41          "\nThe total payment is $" + totalPayment;
42        JOptionPane.showMessageDialog(null, output);
43      }
44    }
```

The `showInputDialog` method in lines 6–7 displays an input dialog. Enter the interest rate as a double value and click *OK* to accept the input. The value is returned as a string that is assigned to the `String` variable `annualInterestRateString`. The `Double.parseDouble (annualInterestRateString)` (line 11) is used to convert the string into a `double` value.

JOptionPane or Scanner?

Pedagogical Note

For obtaining input you can use either `JOptionPane` or `Scanner`—whichever is more convenient. For consistency and simplicity, the examples in this book use `Scanner` for getting input. You can easily revise the examples using `JOptionPane` for getting input.

MyProgrammingLab™

2.34 Why do you have to import `JOptionPane` but not the `Math` class?

2.35 How do you prompt the user to enter an input using a dialog box?

2.36 How do you convert a string to an integer? How do you convert a string to a double?

Key Terms

algorithm 34
assignment operator (=) 42
assignment statement 42
`byte` type 45
casting 56
`char` type 62
constant 43
data type 35
declare variables 35
decrement operator (−−) 54
`double` type 45
encoding 62
escape character 63
expression 42
`final` keyword 43
`float` type 45
floating-point number 35
identifier 40
increment operator (++) 54
incremental development and testing 37
`int` type 45
IPO 39
literal 48
`long` type 45
narrowing (of types) 56
operands 46
operator 46
overflow 45
postdecrement 54
postincrement 54
predecrement 54
preincrement 54
primitive data type 35
pseudocode 34
requirements specification 58

Chapter Summary

1. *Identifiers* are names for naming elements such as variables, constants, methods, classes, packages in a program.
2. An identifier is a sequence of characters that consists of letters, digits, underscores (_), and dollar signs ($). An identifier must start with a letter or an underscore. It cannot start with a digit. An identifier cannot be a reserved word. An identifier can be of any length.
3. *Variables* are used to store data in a program.
4. To declare a variable is to tell the compiler what type of data a variable can hold.
5. In Java, the equal sign (=) is used as the *assignment operator.*
6. A variable declared in a method must be assigned a value before it can be used.
7. A *named constant* (or simply a *constant*) represents permanent data that never changes.
8. A named constant is declared by using the keyword `final`.
9. Java provides four integer types (`byte`, `short`, `int`, and `long`) that represent integers of four different sizes.
10. Java provides two *floating-point types* (`float` and `double`) that represent floating-point numbers of two different precisions.
11. Java provides *operators* that perform numeric operations: + (addition), – (subtraction), * (multiplication), / (division), and % (remainder).
12. Integer arithmetic (/) yields an integer result.
13. The numeric operators in a Java expression are applied the same way as in an arithmetic expression.
14. Java provides the augmented assignment operators += (addition assignment), –= (subtraction assignment), *= (multiplication assignment), /= (division assignment), and %= (remainder assignment).
15. The *increment operator* (++) and the *decrement operator* (––) increment or decrement a variable by `1`.
16. When evaluating an expression with values of mixed types, Java automatically converts the operands to appropriate types.
17. You can explicitly convert a value from one type to another using the `(type)value` notation.

18. *Casting* a variable of a type with a small range to a variable of a type with a larger range is known as *widening a type.*

19. Casting a variable of a type with a large range to a variable of a type with a smaller range is known as *narrowing a type.*

20. Widening a type can be performed automatically without explicit casting. Narrowing a type must be performed explicitly.

21. The character type `char` represents a single character.

22. An *escape character* is a notation for representing a special character. An escape character consists of a backslash (\) followed by a character or a character sequence.

23. The characters `' '`, `\t`, `\f`, `\r`, and `\n` are known as the whitespace characters.

24. In computer science, midnight of January 1, 1970, is known as the *UNIX epoch.*

Test Questions

Do the test questions for this chapter online at www.cs.armstrong.edu/liang/intro9e/test.html.

MyProgrammingLab™

Programming Exercises

sample runs

Note

You can run all exercises by downloading **exercise9e.zip** from www.cs.armstrong.edu/liang/intro9e/exercise9e.zip and use the command `java -cp exercise9e.zip Exercisei_j` to run Exercise*i_j*. For example, to run Exercise 2.1, use

```
java -cp exercise9e.zip Exercise02_01
```

This will give you an idea how the program runs.

learn from examples

Debugging TIP

The compiler usually gives a reason for a syntax error. If you don't know how to correct it, compare your program closely, character by character, with similar examples in the text.

document analysis and design

Pedagogical Note

Instructors may ask you to document your analysis and design for selected exercises. Use your own words to analyze the problem, including the input, output, and what needs to be computed, and describe how to solve the problem in pseudocode.

Sections 2.2–2.12

2.1 (*Convert Celsius to Fahrenheit*) Write a program that reads a Celsius degree in a `double` value from the console, then converts it to Fahrenheit and displays the result. The formula for the conversion is as follows:

```
fahrenheit = (9 / 5) * celsius + 32
```

Hint: In Java, `9 / 5` is `1`, but `9.0 / 5` is `1.8`.

Here is a sample run:

```
Enter a degree in Celsius: 43 ↵Enter
43 Celsius is 109.4 Fahrenheit
```

2.2 (*Compute the volume of a cylinder*) Write a program that reads in the radius and length of a cylinder and computes the area and volume using the following formulas:

```
area = radius * radius * π
volume = area * length
```

Here is a sample run:

```
Enter the radius and length of a cylinder: 5.5 12 ↵Enter
The area is 95.0331
The volume is 1140.4
```

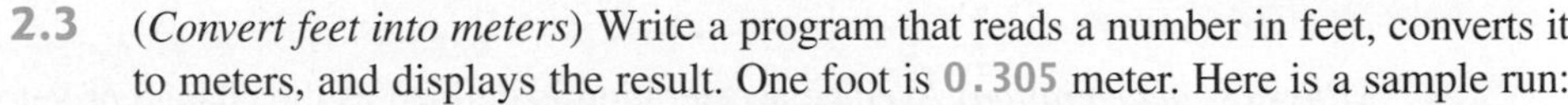

2.3 (*Convert feet into meters*) Write a program that reads a number in feet, converts it to meters, and displays the result. One foot is `0.305` meter. Here is a sample run:

```
Enter a value for feet: 16.5 ↵Enter
16.5 feet is 5.0325 meters
```

2.4 (*Convert pounds into kilograms*) Write a program that converts pounds into kilograms. The program prompts the user to enter a number in pounds, converts it to kilograms, and displays the result. One pound is `0.454` kilograms. Here is a sample run:

```
Enter a number in pounds: 55.5 ↵Enter
55.5 pounds is 25.197 kilograms
```

***2.5** (*Financial application: calculate tips*) Write a program that reads the subtotal and the gratuity rate, then computes the gratuity and total. For example, if the user enters `10` for subtotal and `15%` for gratuity rate, the program displays `$1.5` as gratuity and `$11.5` as total. Here is a sample run:

```
Enter the subtotal and a gratuity rate: 10 15 ↵Enter
The gratuity is $1.5 and total is $11.5
```

****2.6** (*Sum the digits in an integer*) Write a program that reads an integer between `0` and `1000` and adds all the digits in the integer. For example, if an integer is `932`, the sum of all its digits is `14`.

Hint: Use the `%` operator to extract digits, and use the `/` operator to remove the extracted digit. For instance, `932 % 10 = 2` and `932 / 10 = 93`.

Here is a sample run:

```
Enter a number between 0 and 1000: 999 ↵Enter
The sum of the digits is 27
```

*2.7 (*Find the number of years*) Write a program that prompts the user to enter the minutes (e.g., 1 billion), and displays the number of years and days for the minutes. For simplicity, assume a year has 365 days. Here is a sample run:

```
Enter the number of minutes: 1000000000 ↵Enter
1000000000 minutes is approximately 1902 years and 214 days
```

*2.8 (*Current time*) Listing 2.6, ShowCurrentTime.java, gives a program that displays the current time in GMT. Revise the program so that it prompts the user to enter the time zone offset to GMT and displays the time in the specified time zone. Here is a sample run:

```
Enter the time zone offset to GMT: -5 ↵Enter
The current time is 4:50:34
```

2.9 (*Physics: acceleration*) Average acceleration is defined as the change of velocity divided by the time taken to make the change, as shown in the following formula:

$$a = \frac{v_1 - v_0}{t}$$

Write a program that prompts the user to enter the starting velocity v_0 in meters/second, the ending velocity v_1 in meters/second, and the time span t in seconds, and displays the average acceleration. Here is a sample run:

```
Enter v0, v1, and t: 5.5 50.9 4.5 ↵Enter
The average acceleration is 10.0889
```

2.10 (*Science: calculating energy*) Write a program that calculates the energy needed to heat water from an initial temperature to a final temperature. Your program should prompt the user to enter the amount of water in kilograms and the initial and final temperatures of the water. The formula to compute the energy is

```
Q = M * (finalTemperature - initialTemperature) * 4184
```

where M is the weight of water in kilograms, temperatures are in degrees Celsius, and energy Q is measured in joules. Here is a sample run:

```
Enter the amount of water in kilograms: 55.5 ↵Enter
Enter the initial temperature: 3.5 ↵Enter
Enter the final temperature: 10.5 ↵Enter
The energy needed is 1625484.0
```

2.11 (*Population projection*) Rewrite Exercise 1.11 to prompt the user to enter the number of years and displays the population after the number of years. Here is a sample run of the program:

```
Enter the number of years: 5 ↵Enter
The population in 5 years is 325932970
```

2.12 (*Physics: finding runway length*) Given an airplane's acceleration *a* and take-off speed *v*, you can compute the minimum runway length needed for an airplane to take off using the following formula:

$$length = \frac{v^2}{2a}$$

Write a program that prompts the user to enter *v* in meters/second (m/s) and the acceleration *a* in meters/second squared (m/s^2), and displays the minimum runway length. Here is a sample run:

```
Enter speed and acceleration: 60 3.5 ↵Enter
The minimum runway length for this airplane is 514.286
```

****2.13** (*Financial application: compound value*) Suppose you save $100 *each* month into a savings account with the annual interest rate 5%. Thus, the monthly interest rate is 0.05/12 = 0.00417. After the first month, the value in the account becomes

```
100 * (1 + 0.00417) = 100.417
```

After the second month, the value in the account becomes

```
(100 + 100.417) * (1 + 0.00417) = 201.252
```

After the third month, the value in the account becomes

```
(100 + 201.252) * (1 + 0.00417) = 302.507
```

and so on.

Write a program that prompts the user to enter a monthly saving amount and displays the account value after the sixth month. (In Exercise 4.30, you will use a loop to simplify the code and display the account value for any month.)

```
Enter the monthly saving amount: 100 ↵Enter
After the sixth month, the account value is $608.81
```

***2.14** (*Health application: computing BMI*) Body Mass Index (BMI) is a measure of health on weight. It can be calculated by taking your weight in kilograms and dividing by the square of your height in meters. Write a program that prompts the user to enter a weight in pounds and height in inches and displays the BMI. Note that one pound is 0.45359237 kilograms and one inch is 0.0254 meters. Here is a sample run:

VideoNote
Compute BMI

```
Enter weight in pounds: 95.5 ↵Enter
Enter height in inches: 50 ↵Enter
BMI is 26.8573
```

***2.15** (*Geometry: area of a triangle*) Write a program that prompts the user to enter three points `(x1, y1)`, `(x2, y2)`, `(x3, y3)` of a triangle and displays its area. The formula for computing the area of a triangle is

$$s = (side1 + side2 + side3)/2;$$

$$area = \sqrt{s(s - side1)(s - side2)(s - side3)}$$

Here is a sample run:

```
Enter three points for a triangle: 1.5 -3.4 4.6 5 9.5 -3.4 ↵Enter
The area of the triangle is 33.6
```

2.16 (*Geometry: area of a hexagon*) Write a program that prompts the user to enter the side of a hexagon and displays its area. The formula for computing the area of a hexagon is

$$Area = \frac{3\sqrt{3}}{2}s^2,$$

where s is the length of a side. Here is a sample run:

```
Enter the side: 5.5 ↵Enter
The area of the hexagon is 78.5895
```

***2.17** (*Science: wind-chill temperature*) How cold is it outside? The temperature alone is not enough to provide the answer. Other factors including wind speed, relative humidity, and sunshine play important roles in determining coldness outside. In 2001, the National Weather Service (NWS) implemented the new wind-chill temperature to measure the coldness using temperature and wind speed. The formula is:

$$t_{wc} = 35.74 + 0.6215t_a - 35.75v^{0.16} + 0.4275t_a v^{0.16}$$

where t_a is the outside temperature measured in degrees Fahrenheit and v is the speed measured in miles per hour. t_{wc} is the wind-chill temperature. The formula cannot be used for wind speeds below 2 mph or temperatures below −58°F or above 41°F.

Write a program that prompts the user to enter a temperature between −58°F and 41°F and a wind speed greater than or equal to `2` and displays the wind-chill temperature. Use `Math.pow(a, b)` to compute $v^{0.16}$. Here is a sample run:

```
Enter the temperature in Fahrenheit: 5.3 ↵Enter
Enter the wind speed in miles per hour: 6 ↵Enter
The wind chill index is -5.56707
```

2.18 (*Print a table*) Write a program that displays the following table:

```
a     b     pow(a, b)
1     2     1
2     3     8
3     4     81
4     5     1024
5     6     15625
```

2.19 (*Geometry: distance of two points*) Write a program that prompts the user to enter two points `(x1, y1)` and `(x2, y2)` and displays their distance between them. The formula for computing the distance is $\sqrt{(x_2 - x_1)^2 + (y_2 - y_1)^2}$. Note that you can use `Math.pow(a, 0.5)` to compute $\sqrt{a}$. Here is a sample run:

```
Enter x1 and y1: 1.5 -3.4 [Enter]
Enter x2 and y2: 4 5 [Enter]
The distance between the two points is 8.764131445842194
```

Sections 2.13–2.16

***2.20** (*Financial application: calculate interest*) If you know the balance and the annual percentage interest rate, you can compute the interest on the next monthly payment using the following formula:

$$\text{interest} = \text{balance} \times (\text{annualInterestRate} / 1200)$$

Write a program that reads the balance and the annual percentage interest rate and displays the interest for the next month. Here is a sample run:

```
Enter balance and interest rate (e.g., 3 for 3%): 1000 3.5 [Enter]
The interest is 2.91667
```

***2.21** (*Financial application: calculate future investment value*) Write a program that reads in investment amount, annual interest rate, and number of years, and displays the future investment value using the following formula:

```
futureInvestmentValue =
  investmentAmount x (1 + monthlyInterestRate)^(numberOfYears*12)
```

For example, if you enter amount `1000`, annual interest rate `3.25%`, and number of years `1`, the future investment value is `1032.98`.

Here is a sample run:

```
Enter investment amount: 1000 [Enter]
Enter annual interest rate in percentage: 4.25 [Enter]
Enter number of years: 1 [Enter]
Accumulated value is $1043.34
```

Sections 2.17–2.18

2.22 (*Random character*) Write a program that displays a random uppercase letter using the `System.CurrentTimeMillis()` method.

2.23 (*Find the character of an ASCII code*) Write a program that receives an ASCII code (an integer between 0 and 127) and displays its character. For example, if the user enters `97`, the program displays character `a`. Here is a sample run:

```
Enter an ASCII code: 69 ↵Enter
The character is E
```

***2.24** (*Financial application: monetary units*) Rewrite Listing 2.10, ComputeChange.java, to fix the possible loss of accuracy when converting a `double` value to an `int` value. Enter the input as an integer whose last two digits represent the cents. For example, the input `1156` represents `11` dollars and `56` cents.

***2.25** (*Financial application: payroll*) Write a program that reads the following information and prints a payroll statement:

Employee's name (e.g., Smith)
Number of hours worked in a week (e.g., 10)
Hourly pay rate (e.g., 6.75)
Federal tax withholding rate (e.g., 20%)
State tax withholding rate (e.g., 9%)

```
Enter employee's name: Smith ↵Enter
Enter number of hours worked in a week: 10 ↵Enter
Enter hourly pay rate: 6.75 ↵Enter
Enter federal tax withholding rate: 0.20 ↵Enter
Enter state tax withholding rate: 0.09 ↵Enter

Employee Name: Smith
Hours Worked:  10.0
Pay Rate:  $6.75
Gross Pay:  $67.5
Deductions:
  Federal Withholding (20.0%):  $13.5
  State Withholding (9.0%):  $6.07
  Total Deduction:  $19.57
Net Pay:  $47.92
```

Section 2.19

***2.26** (*Use input dialog*) Rewrite Listing 2.10, ComputeChange.java, using input and output dialog boxes.

***2.27** (*Financial application: payroll*) Rewrite Exercise 2.25 using GUI input and output dialog boxes.

CHAPTER 3

SELECTIONS

Objectives

- To declare `boolean` variables and write Boolean expressions using comparison operators (§3.2).
- To implement selection control using one-way `if` statements (§3.3).
- To program using one-way `if` statements (`GuessBirthday`) (§3.4).
- To implement selection control using two-way `if-else` statements (§3.5).
- To implement selection control using nested `if` and multi-way `if` statements (§3.6).
- To avoid common errors in `if` statements (§3.7).
- To generate random numbers using the `Math.random()` method (§3.8).
- To program using selection statements for a variety of examples (`SubtractionQuiz`, `BMI`, `ComputeTax`) (§§3.8–3.10).
- To combine conditions using logical operators (`&&`, `||`, and `!`) (§3.11).
- To program using selection statements with combined conditions (`LeapYear`, `Lottery`) (§§3.12–3.13).
- To implement selection control using `switch` statements (§3.14).
- To write expressions using the conditional operator (§3.15).
- To format output using the `System.out.printf` method (§3.16).
- To examine the rules governing operator precedence and associativity (§3.17).
- To get user confirmation using confirmation dialogs (§3.18).
- To apply common techniques to debug errors (§3.19).

3.1 Introduction

The program can decide which statements to execute based on a condition.

problem

If you enter a negative value for `radius` in Listing 2.2, ComputeAreaWithConsoleInput.java, the program displays an invalid result. If the radius is negative, you don't want the program to compute the area. How can you deal with this situation?

selection statements

Like all high-level programming languages, Java provides *selection statements*: statements that let you choose actions with two or more alternative courses. You can use the following selection statement to replace lines 12–17 in Listing 2.2:

```
if (radius < 0) {
  System.out.println("Incorrect input");
}
else {
  area = radius * radius * 3.14159;
  System.out.println("Area is " + area);
}
```

Boolean expression
Boolean value

Selection statements use conditions that are Boolean expressions. A *Boolean expression* is an expression that evaluates to a *Boolean value*: `true` or `false`. We now introduce Boolean types and comparison operators.

3.2 `boolean` Data Type

A `boolean` data type declares a variable with the value either `true` or `false`.

`boolean` data type
comparison operators

How do you compare two values, such as whether a radius is greater than `0`, equal to `0`, or less than `0`? Java provides six *comparison operators* (also known as *relational operators*), shown in Table 3.1, which can be used to compare two values (assume radius is `5` in the table).

TABLE 3.1 Comparison Operators

Java Operator	*Mathematics Symbol*	*Name*	*Example (radius is 5)*	*Result*
<	<	less than	`radius < 0`	`false`
<=	≤	less than or equal to	`radius <= 0`	`false`
>	>	greater than	`radius > 0`	`true`
>=	≥	greater than or equal to	`radius >= 0`	`true`
==	=	equal to	`radius == 0`	`false`
!=	≠	not equal to	`radius != 0`	`true`

compare characters

Note

You can also compare characters. Comparing characters is the same as comparing their Unicodes. For example, `a` is larger than `A` because the Unicode of `a` is larger than the Unicode of `A`. See Appendix B, The ASCII Character Set, to find the order of characters.

== vs. =

Caution

The equality comparison operator is two equal signs (==), not a single equal sign (=). The latter symbol is for assignment.

The result of the comparison is a Boolean value: `true` or `false`. For example, the following statement displays `true`:

```
double radius = 1;
System.out.println(radius > 0);
```

A variable that holds a Boolean value is known as a *Boolean variable*. The `boolean` data type is used to declare Boolean variables. A `boolean` variable can hold one of the two values: `true` or `false`. For example, the following statement assigns `true` to the variable `lightsOn`:

Boolean variable

```
boolean lightsOn = true;
```

`true` and `false` are literals, just like a number such as `10`. They are reserved words and cannot be used as identifiers in your program.

Boolean literals

Suppose you want to develop a program to let a first-grader practice addition. The program randomly generates two single-digit integers, `number1` and `number2`, and displays to the student a question such as "What is 1 + 7?", as shown in the sample run in Listing 3.1. After the student types the answer, the program displays a message to indicate whether it is true or false.

VideoNote
Program addition quiz

There are several ways to generate random numbers. For now, generate the first integer using `System.currentTimeMillis() % 10` and the second using `System.currentTimeMillis() / 7 % 10`. Listing 3.1 gives the program. Lines 5–6 generate two numbers, `number1` and `number2`. Line 14 obtains an answer from the user. The answer is graded in line 18 using a Boolean expression `number1 + number2 == answer`.

LISTING 3.1 AdditionQuiz.java

```
 1 import java.util.Scanner;
 2
 3 public class AdditionQuiz {
 4   public static void main(String[] args) {
 5     int number1 = (int)(System.currentTimeMillis() % 10);
 6     int number2 = (int)(System.currentTimeMillis() / 7 % 10);
 7
 8     // Create a Scanner
 9     Scanner input = new Scanner(System.in);
10
11     System.out.print(
12       "What is " + number1 + " + " + number2 + "? ");
13
14     int answer = input.nextInt();
15
16     System.out.println(
17       number1 + " + " + number2 + " = " + answer + " is " +
18       (number1 + number2 == answer));
19   }
20 }
```

generate number1
generate number2

show question

display result

```
What is 1 + 7? 8 ↵Enter
1 + 7 = 8 is true
```

```
What is 4 + 8? 9 ↵Enter
4 + 8 = 9 is false
```

line#	number1	number2	answer	output
5	4			
6		8		
14			9	
16				4 + 8 = 9 is false

MyProgrammingLab™

3.1 List six comparison operators.

3.2 Show the printout of the following statements:

```
System.out.println('a' < 'b');
System.out.println('a' <= 'A');
System.out.println('a' > 'b');
System.out.println('a' >= 'A');
System.out.println('a' == 'a');
System.out.println('a' != 'b');
```

3.3 Can the following conversions involving casting be allowed? If so, find the converted result.

```
boolean b = true;
i = (int)b;

int i = 1;
boolean b = (boolean)i;
```

3.3 `if` Statements

An `if` statement executes the statements if the condition is true.

why `if` statement?

The preceding program displays a message such as "6 + 2 = 7 is false." If you wish the message to be "6 + 2 = 7 is incorrect," you have to use a selection statement to make this minor change.

Java has several types of selection statements: one-way `if` statements, two-way `if-else` statements, nested `if` statements, `switch` statements, and conditional expressions.

A one-way `if` statement executes an action if and only if the condition is `true`. The syntax for a one-way `if` statement is:

`if` statement

```
if (boolean-expression) {
  statement(s);
}
```

flowchart

The flowchart in Figure 3.1 illustrates how Java executes the syntax of an `if` statement. A *flowchart* is a diagram that describes an algorithm or process, showing the steps as boxes of various kinds, and their order by connecting these with arrows. Process operations are represented in these boxes, and arrows connecting them represent the flow of control. A diamond box is used to denote a Boolean condition and a rectangle box is for representing statements.

If the `boolean-expression` evaluates to `true`, the statements in the block are executed. As an example, see the following code:

```
if (radius >= 0) {
  area = radius * radius * PI;
  System.out.println("The area for the circle of radius " +
    radius + " is " + area);
}
```

The flowchart of the preceding statement is shown in Figure 3.1b. If the value of `radius` is greater than or equal to `0`, then the `area` is computed and the result is displayed; otherwise, the two statements in the block will not be executed.

The `boolean-expression` is enclosed in parentheses. For example, the code in (a) below is wrong. It should be corrected, as shown in (b).

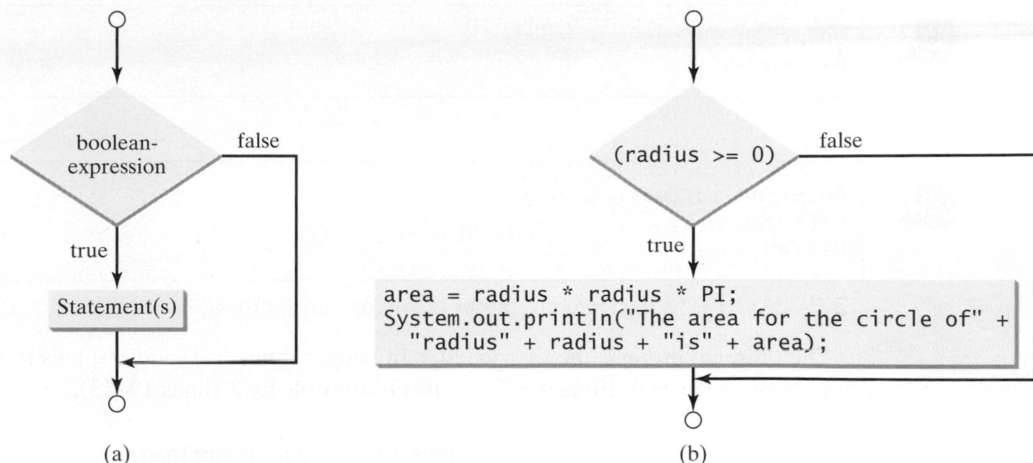

FIGURE 3.1 An `if` statement executes statements if the `boolean-expression` evaluates to `true`.

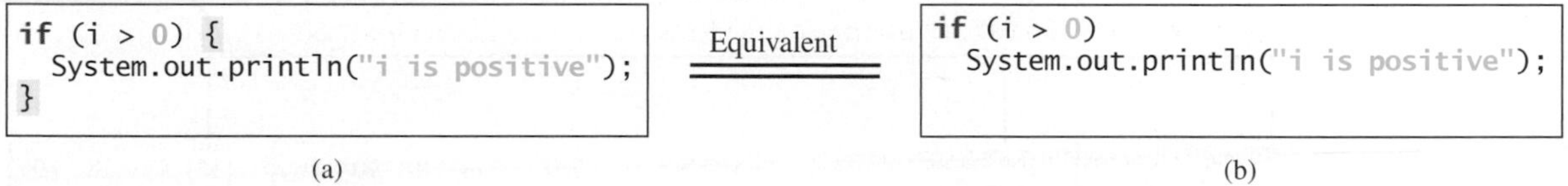

The block braces can be omitted if they enclose a single statement. For example, the following statements are equivalent.

```
if (i > 0) {
  System.out.println("i is positive");
}
```

(a)

Equivalent

```
if (i > 0)
  System.out.println("i is positive");
```

(b)

Note

Omitting braces makes the code shorter, but it is prone to errors. It is a common mistake to forget the braces when you go back to modify the code that omits the braces.

Omitting braces or not

Listing 3.2 gives a program that prompts the user to enter an integer. If the number is a multiple of `5`, the program displays `HiFive`. If the number is divisible by `2`, it displays `HiEven`.

LISTING 3.2 SimpleIfDemo.java

```
import java.util.Scanner;

public class SimpleIfDemo {
  public static void main(String[] args) {
    Scanner input = new Scanner(System.in);
    System.out.println("Enter an integer: ");
    int number = input.nextInt();

    if (number % 5 == 0)
      System.out.println("HiFive");

    if (number % 2 == 0)
      System.out.println("HiEven");
  }
}
```

enter input

check 5

check even

```
Enter an integer: 4 ↵Enter
HiEven
```

```
Enter an integer: 30 ↵Enter
HiFive
HiEven
```

The program prompts the user to enter an integer (lines 6–7) and displays `HiFive` if it is divisible by `5` (lines 9–10) and `HiEven` if it is divisible by `2` (lines 12–13).

MyProgrammingLab™

3.4 Write an `if` statement that assigns `1` to `x` if `y` is greater than `0`.

3.5 Write an `if` statement that increases pay by 3% if `score` is greater than `90`.

3.4 Case Study: Guessing Birthdays

Guessing birthdays is an interesting problem with a simple programming solution.

You can find out the date of the month when your friend was born by asking five questions. Each question asks whether the day is in one of the five sets of numbers.

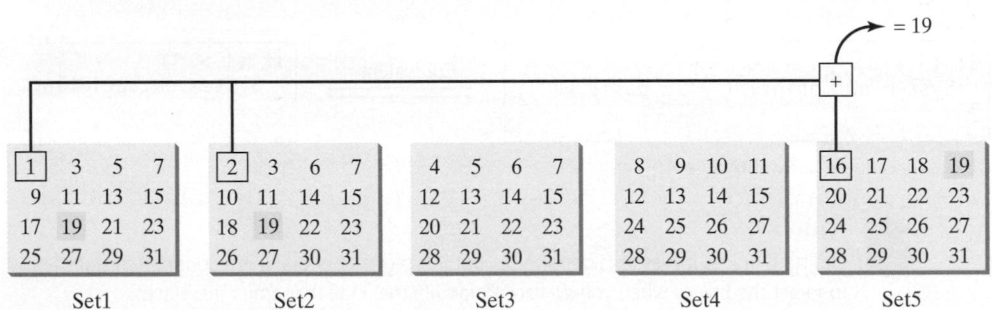

The birthday is the sum of the first numbers in the sets where the day appears. For example, if the birthday is `19`, it appears in Set1, Set2, and Set5. The first numbers in these three sets are `1`, `2`, and `16`. Their sum is `19`.

Listing 3.3 gives a program that prompts the user to answer whether the day is in Set1 (lines 41–44), in Set2 (lines 50–53), in Set3 (lines 59–62), in Set4 (lines 68–71), and in Set5 (lines 77–80). If the number is in the set, the program adds the first number in the set to `day` (lines 47, 56, 65, 74, 83).

LISTING 3.3 GuessBirthday.java

```
1  import java.util.Scanner;
2
3  public class GuessBirthday {
4    public static void main(String[] args) {
5      String set1 =
6        " 1  3  5  7\n" +
```

```
      " 9 11 13 15\n" +
      "17 19 21 23\n" +
      "25 27 29 31";

    String set2 =
      " 2  3  6  7\n" +
      "10 11 14 15\n" +
      "18 19 22 23\n" +
      "26 27 30 31";

    String set3 =
      " 4  5  6  7\n" +
      "12 13 14 15\n" +
      "20 21 22 23\n" +
      "28 29 30 31";

    String set4 =
      " 8  9 10 11\n" +
      "12 13 14 15\n" +
      "24 25 26 27\n" +
      "28 29 30 31";

    String set5 =
      "16 17 18 19\n" +
      "20 21 22 23\n" +
      "24 25 26 27\n" +
      "28 29 30 31";

    int day = 0;
```

day to be determined

```
    // Create a Scanner
    Scanner input = new Scanner(System.in);

    // Prompt the user to answer questions
    System.out.print("Is your birthday in Set1?\n");
    System.out.print(set1);
    System.out.print("\nEnter 0 for No and 1 for Yes: ");
    int answer = input.nextInt();

    if (answer == 1)
      day += 1;
```

in Set1?

```
    // Prompt the user to answer questions
    System.out.print("\nIs your birthday in Set2?\n");
    System.out.print(set2);
    System.out.print("\nEnter 0 for No and 1 for Yes: ");
    answer = input.nextInt();

    if (answer == 1)
      day += 2;
```

in Set2?

```
    // Prompt the user to answer questions
    System.out.print("Is your birthday in Set3?\n");
    System.out.print(set3);
    System.out.print("\nEnter 0 for No and 1 for Yes: ");
    answer = input.nextInt();

    if (answer == 1)
      day += 4;
```

in Set3?

```
    // Prompt the user to answer questions
    System.out.print("\nIs your birthday in Set4?\n");
    System.out.print(set4);
    System.out.print("\nEnter 0 for No and 1 for Yes: ");
    answer = input.nextInt();

    if (answer == 1)
      day += 8;

    // Prompt the user to answer questions
    System.out.print("\nIs your birthday in Set5?\n");
    System.out.print(set5);
    System.out.print("\nEnter 0 for No and 1 for Yes: ");
    answer = input.nextInt();

    if (answer == 1)
      day += 16;

    System.out.println("\nYour birthday is " + day + "!");
  }
}
```

in Set4?

in Set5?

```
Is your birthday in Set1?
 1  3  5  7
 9 11 13 15
17 19 21 23
25 27 29 31
Enter 0 for No and 1 for Yes: 1 ↵Enter

Is your birthday in Set2?
 2  3  6  7
10 11 14 15
18 19 22 23
26 27 30 31
Enter 0 for No and 1 for Yes: 1 ↵Enter

Is your birthday in Set3?
 4  5  6  7
12 13 14 15
20 21 22 23
28 29 30 31
Enter 0 for No and 1 for Yes: 0 ↵Enter

Is your birthday in Set4?
 8  9 10 11
12 13 14 15
24 25 26 27
28 29 30 31
Enter 0 for No and 1 for Yes: 0 ↵Enter

Is your birthday in Set5?
16 17 18 19
20 21 22 23
24 25 26 27
28 29 30 31
Enter 0 for No and 1 for Yes: 1 ↵Enter
Your birthday is 19!
```

line#	day	answer	output
35	0		
44		1	
47	1		
53		1	
56	3		
62		0	
71		0	
80		1	
83	19		
85			Your birthday is 19!

mathematics behind the game

This game is easy to program. You may wonder how the game was created. The mathematics behind the game is actually quite simple. The numbers are not grouped together by accident—the way they are placed in the five sets is deliberate. The starting numbers in the five sets are 1, 2, 4, 8, and 16, which correspond to 1, 10, 100, 1000, and 10000 in binary (binary numbers are introduced in Appendix F, Number Systems). A binary number for decimal integers between 1 and 31 has at most five digits, as shown in Figure 3.2a. Let it be $b_5b_4b_3b_2b_1$. Thus, $b_5b_4b_3b_2b_1 = b_50000 + b_4000 + b_300 + b_20 + b_1$, as shown in Figure 3.2b. If a day's binary number has a digit 1 in b_k, the number should appear in Set*k*. For example, number 19 is binary 10011, so it appears in Set1, Set2, and Set5. It is binary 1 + 10 + 10000 = 10011 or decimal 1 + 2 + 16 = 19. Number 31 is binary 11111, so it appears in Set1, Set2, Set3, Set4, and Set5. It is binary 1 + 10 + 100 + 1000 + 10000 = 11111 or decimal 1 + 2 + 4 + 8 + 16 = 31.

Decimal	Binary
1	00001
2	00010
3	00011
...	
19	10011
...	
31	11111

(a)

$$\begin{array}{r} b_5\,0\,0\,0\,0 \\ b_4\,0\,0\,0 \\ b_3\,0\,0 \\ b_2\,0 \\ +\quad b_1 \\ \hline b_5b_4b_3b_2b_1 \end{array} \qquad \begin{array}{r} 10000 \\ 10 \\ +\quad 1 \\ \hline 10011 \\ 19 \end{array} \qquad \begin{array}{r} 10000 \\ 1000 \\ 100 \\ 10 \\ +\quad 1 \\ \hline 11111 \\ 31 \end{array}$$

(b)

Figure 3.2 (a) A number between 1 and 31 can be represented using a 5-digit binary number. (b) A 5-digit binary number can be obtained by adding binary numbers 1, 10, 100, 1000, or 10000.

3.5 Two-Way `if-else` Statements

An `if-else` statement decides which statements to execute based on whether the condition is true or false.

A one-way `if` statement takes an action if the specified condition is `true`. If the condition is `false`, nothing is done. But what if you want to take alternative actions when the condition is `false`? You can use a two-way `if-else` statement. The actions that a two-way `if-else` statement specifies differ based on whether the condition is `true` or `false`.

Here is the syntax for a two-way `if-else` statement:

```
if (boolean-expression) {
  statement(s)-for-the-true-case;
}
else {
  statement(s)-for-the-false-case;
}
```

The flowchart of the statement is shown in Figure 3.3.

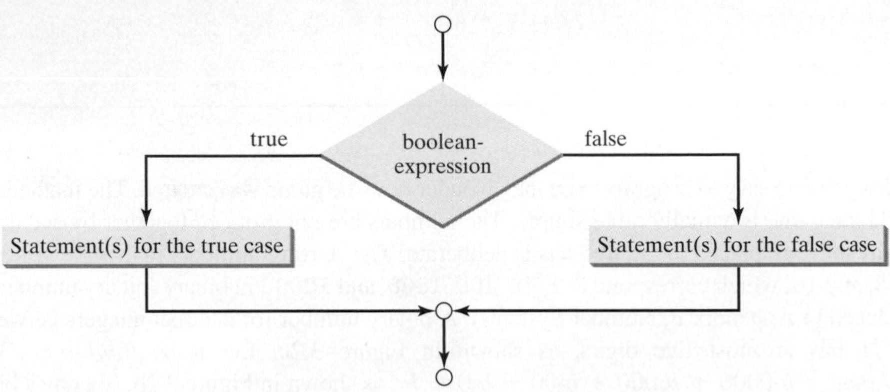

FIGURE 3.3 An `if-else` statement executes statements for the true case if the `Boolean-expression` evaluates to `true`; otherwise, statements for the false case are executed.

If the `boolean-expression` evaluates to `true`, the statement(s) for the true case are executed; otherwise, the statement(s) for the false case are executed. For example, consider the following code:

two-way `if-else` statement

```
if (radius >= 0) {
  area = radius * radius * PI;
  System.out.println("The area for the circle of radius " +
    radius + " is " + area);
}
else {
  System.out.println("Negative input");
}
```

If `radius >= 0` is `true`, `area` is computed and displayed; if it is `false`, the message `"Negative input"` is displayed.

As usual, the braces can be omitted if there is only one statement within them. The braces enclosing the `System.out.println("Negative input")` statement can therefore be omitted in the preceding example.

Here is another example of using the `if-else` statement. The example checks whether a number is even or odd, as follows:

```
if (number % 2 == 0)
  System.out.println(number + " is even.");
else
  System.out.println(number + " is odd.");
```

MyProgrammingLab™

3.6 Write an if statement that increases pay by 3% if score is greater than 90, otherwise increases pay by 1%.

3.7 What is the printout of the code in (a) and (b) if number is 30? What if number is 35?

```
if (number % 2 == 0)
  System.out.println(number + " is even.");

System.out.println(number + " is odd.");
```

(a)

```
if (number % 2 == 0)
  System.out.println(number + " is even.");
else
  System.out.println(number + " is odd.");
```

(b)

3.6 Nested **if** and Multi-Way **if-else** Statements

An if *statement can be inside another* if *statement to form a nested* if *statement.*

nested if statement

The statement in an if or if-else statement can be any legal Java statement, including another if or if-else statement. The inner if statement is said to be *nested* inside the outer if statement. The inner if statement can contain another if statement; in fact, there is no limit to the depth of the nesting. For example, the following is a nested if statement:

```
if (i > k) {
  if (j > k)
    System.out.println("i and j are greater than k");
}
else
  System.out.println("i is less than or equal to k");
```

The if (j > k) statement is nested inside the if (i > k) statement.

The nested if statement can be used to implement multiple alternatives. The statement given in Figure 3.4a, for instance, assigns a letter grade to the variable grade according to the score, with multiple alternatives.

```
if (score >= 90.0)
  grade = 'A';
else
  if (score >= 80.0)
    grade = 'B';
  else
    if (score >= 70.0)
      grade = 'C';
    else
      if (score >= 60.0)
        grade = 'D';
      else
        grade = 'F';
```

Equivalent

This is better

```
if (score >= 90.0)
  grade = 'A';
else if (score >= 80.0)
  grade = 'B';
else if (score >= 70.0)
  grade = 'C';
else if (score >= 60.0)
  grade = 'D';
else
  grade = 'F';
```

(a) (b)

FIGURE 3.4 A preferred format for multiple alternatives is shown in (b) using a multi-way if-else statement.

The execution of this if statement proceeds as shown in Figure 3.5. The first condition (score >= 90.0) is tested. If it is true, the grade becomes A. If it is false, the second condition (score >= 80.0) is tested. If the second condition is true, the grade becomes B. If that condition is false, the third condition and the rest of the conditions (if necessary) are tested until a condition is met or all of the conditions prove to be false. If all of the conditions are false, the grade becomes F. Note that a condition is tested only when all of the conditions that come before it are false.

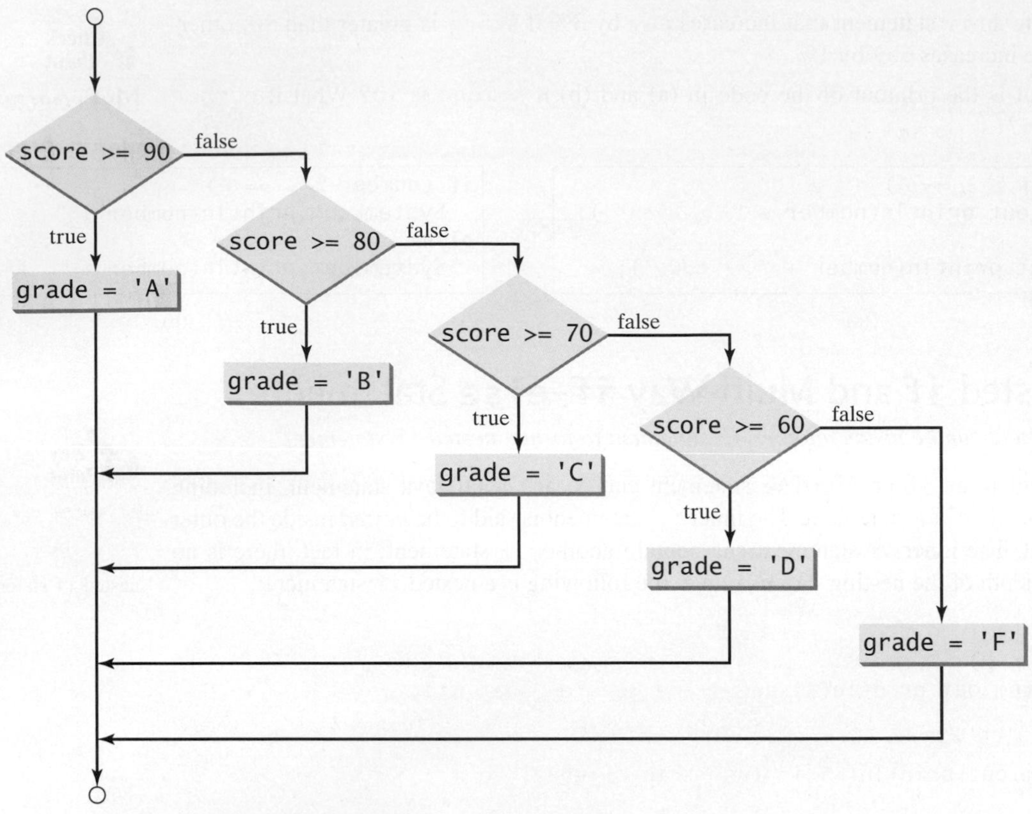

FIGURE 3.5 You can use a multi-way `if-else` statement to assign a grade.

The `if` statement in Figure 3.4a is equivalent to the `if` statement in Figure 3.4b. In fact, Figure 3.4b is the preferred coding style for multiple alternative `if` statements. This style, called *multi-way* ***`if-else`*** *statements*, avoids deep indentation and makes the program easy to read.

multi-way `if` statement

MyProgrammingLab™

3.8 Suppose `x = 3` and `y = 2`; show the output, if any, of the following code. What is the output if `x = 3` and `y = 4`? What is the output if `x = 2` and `y = 2`? Draw a flowchart of the code.

```
if (x > 2) {
  if (y > 2) {
    z = x + y;
    System.out.println("z is " + z);
  }
}
else
  System.out.println("x is " + x);
```

3.9 Suppose `x = 2` and `y = 3`. Show the output, if any, of the following code. What is the output if `x = 3` and `y = 2`? What is the output if `x = 3` and `y = 3`? (*Hint*: Indent the statement correctly first.)

```
if (x > 2)
  if (y > 2) {
    int z = x + y;
    System.out.println("z is " + z);
  }
else
  System.out.println("x is " + x);
```

3.10 What is wrong in the following code?

```
if (score >= 60.0)
  grade = 'D';
else if (score >= 70.0)
  grade = 'C';
else if (score >= 80.0)
  grade = 'B';
else if (score >= 90.0)
  grade = 'A';
else
  grade = 'F';
```

3.7 Common Errors in Selection Statements

Forgetting necessary braces, ending an `if` *statement in the wrong place, mistaking == for =, and dangling* `else` *clauses are common errors in selection statements.*

The following errors are common among new programmers.

Common Error 1: Forgetting Necessary Braces

The braces can be omitted if the block contains a single statement. However, forgetting the braces when they are needed for grouping multiple statements is a common programming error. If you modify the code by adding new statements in an `if` statement without braces, you will have to insert the braces. For example, the following code in (a) is wrong. It should be written with braces to group multiple statements, as shown in (b).

```
if (radius >= 0)
  area = radius * radius * PI;
  System.out.println("The area "
    + " is " + area);
```

(a) Wrong

```
if (radius >= 0) {
  area = radius * radius * PI;
  System.out.println("The area "
    + " is " + area);
}
```

(b) Correct

Common Error 2: Wrong Semicolon at the `if` Line

Adding a semicolon at the end of an `if` line, as shown in (a) below, is a common mistake.

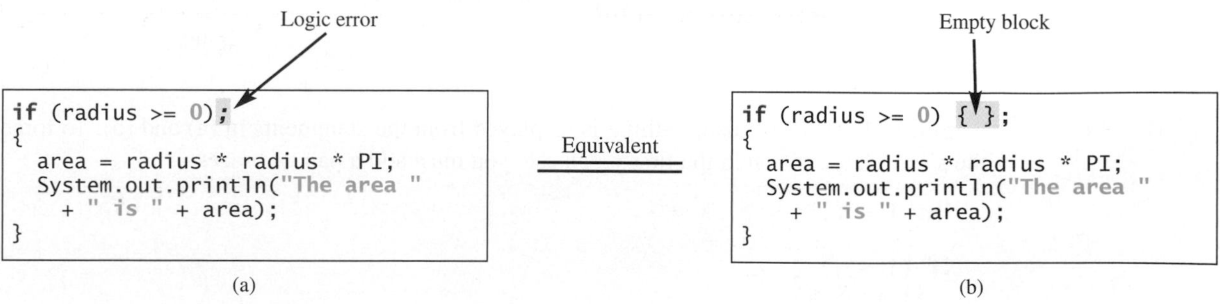

This mistake is hard to find, because it is neither a compile error nor a runtime error; it is a logic error. The code in (a) is equivalent to that in (b) with an empty block.

This error often occurs when you use the next-line block style. Using the end-of-line block style can help prevent this error.

Common Error 3: Redundant Testing of Boolean Values

To test whether a `boolean` variable is `true` or `false` in a test condition, it is redundant to use the equality comparison operator like the code in (a):

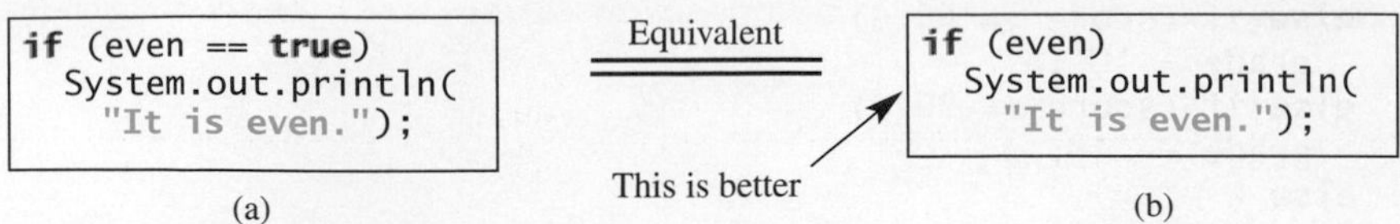

(a) (b)

Instead, it is better to test the `boolean` variable directly, as shown in (b). Another good reason for doing this is to avoid errors that are difficult to detect. Using the = operator instead of the == operator to compare the equality of two items in a test condition is a common error. It could lead to the following erroneous statement:

```
if (even = true)
  System.out.println("It is even.");
```

This statement does not have compile errors. It assigns `true` to `even`, so that `even` is always `true`.

Common Error 4: Dangling `else` Ambiguity

dangling else ambiguity

The code in (a) below has two `if` clauses and one `else` clause. Which `if` clause is matched by the `else` clause? The indentation indicates that the `else` clause matches the first `if` clause. However, the `else` clause actually matches the second `if` clause. This situation is known as the *dangling else ambiguity*. The `else` clause always matches the most recent unmatched `if` clause in the same block. So, the statement in (a) is equivalent to the code in (b).

```
int i = 1, j = 2, k = 3;

if (i > j)
  if (i > k)
    System.out.println("A");
else
    System.out.println("B");
```

(a)

Equivalent

This is better with correct indentation

```
int i = 1, j = 2, k = 3;

if (i > j)
  if (i > k)
    System.out.println("A");
  else
    System.out.println("B");
```

(b)

Since `(i > j)` is false, nothing is displayed from the statements in (a) and (b). To force the `else` clause to match the first `if` clause, you must add a pair of braces:

```
int i = 1, j = 2, k = 3;

if (i > j) {
  if (i > k)
    System.out.println("A");
}
else
  System.out.println("B");
```

This statement displays `B`.

Tip

Often new programmers write the code that assigns a test condition to a `boolean` variable like the code in (a):

assign `boolean` variable

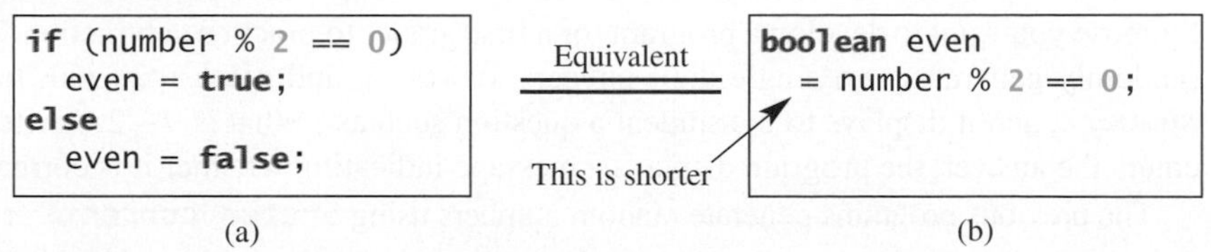

```
if (number % 2 == 0)
  even = true;
else
  even = false;
```

(a)

Equivalent

This is shorter

```
boolean even
  = number % 2 == 0;
```

(b)

The code can be simplified by assigning the test value directly to the variable, as shown in (b).

Check Point

MyProgrammingLab™

3.11 Which of the following statements are equivalent? Which ones are correctly indented?

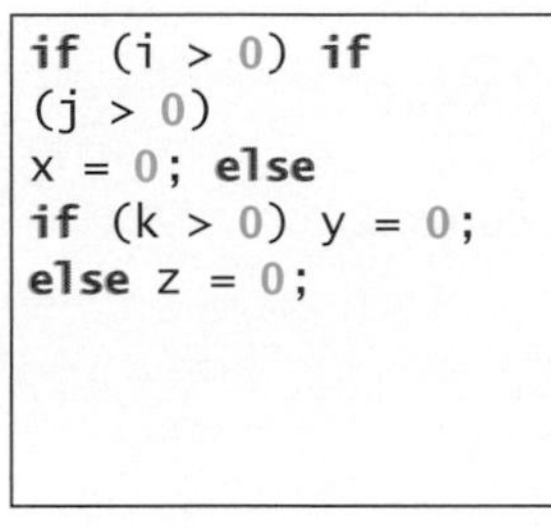

```
if (i > 0) if
(j > 0)
x = 0; else
if (k > 0) y = 0;
else z = 0;
```

(a)

```
if (i > 0) {
  if (j > 0)
    x = 0;
  else if (k > 0)
    y = 0;
}
else
  z = 0;
```

(b)

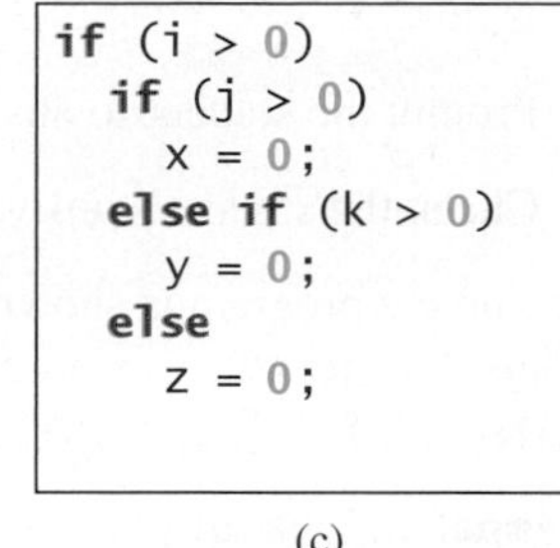

```
if (i > 0)
  if (j > 0)
    x = 0;
  else if (k > 0)
    y = 0;
  else
    z = 0;
```

(c)

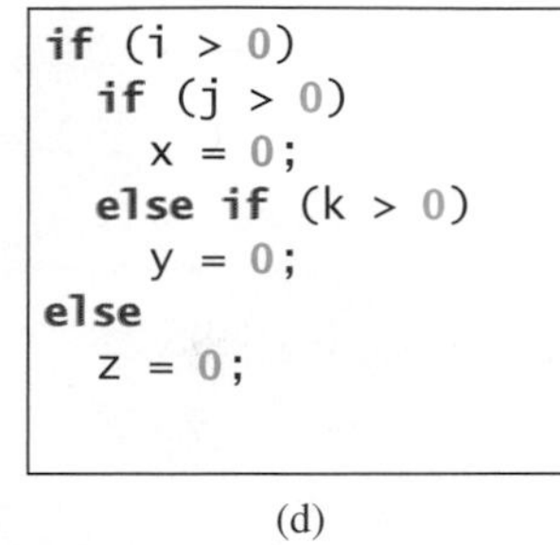

```
if (i > 0)
  if (j > 0)
    x = 0;
  else if (k > 0)
    y = 0;
else
  z = 0;
```

(d)

3.12 Rewrite the following statement using a Boolean expression:

```
if (count % 10 == 0)
  newLine = true;
else
  newLine = false;
```

3.13 Are the following statements correct? Which one is better?

```
if (age < 16)
  System.out.println
    ("Cannot get a driver's license");
if (age >= 16)
  System.out.println
    ("Can get a driver's license");
```

(a)

```
if (age < 16)
  System.out.println
    ("Cannot get a driver's license");
else
  System.out.println
    ("Can get a driver's license");
```

(b)

3.14 What is the output of the following code if `number` is `14`, `15`, and `30`?

```
if (number % 2 == 0)
  System.out.println
    (number + " is even");
if (number % 5 == 0)
  System.out.println
    (number + " is multiple of 5");
```

(a)

```
if (number % 2 == 0)
  System.out.println
    (number + " is even");
else if (number % 5 == 0)
  System.out.println
    (number + " is multiple of 5");
```

(b)

3.8 Generating Random Numbers

You can use `Math.random()` to obtain a random double value between `0.0` and `1.0`, excluding `1.0`.

VideoNote
Program subtraction quiz

Suppose you want to develop a program for a first-grader to practice subtraction. The program randomly generates two single-digit integers, `number1` and `number2`, with `number1 >= number2`, and it displays to the student a question such as "What is 9 – 2?" After the student enters the answer, the program displays a message indicating whether it is correct.

The previous programs generate random numbers using `System.currentTimeMillis()`. A better approach is to use the `random()` method in the `Math` class. Invoking this method returns a random double value `d` such that $0.0 \leq d < 1.0$. Thus, `(int)(Math.random() * 10)` returns a random single-digit integer (i.e., a number between `0` and `9`).

random() method

The program can work as follows:

1. Generate two single-digit integers into `number1` and `number2`.
2. If `number1 < number2`, swap `number1` with `number2`.
3. Prompt the student to answer, `"What is number1 – number2?"`
4. Check the student's answer and display whether the answer is correct.

The complete program is shown in Listing 3.4.

LISTING 3.4 SubtractionQuiz.java

random number

get answer

check the answer

```
import java.util.Scanner;

public class SubtractionQuiz {
  public static void main(String[] args) {
    // 1. Generate two random single-digit integers
    int number1 = (int)(Math.random() * 10);
    int number2 = (int)(Math.random() * 10);

    // 2. If number1 < number2, swap number1 with number2
    if (number1 < number2) {
      int temp = number1;
      number1 = number2;
      number2 = temp;
    }

    // 3. Prompt the student to answer "What is number1 - number2?"
    System.out.print
      ("What is " + number1 + " - " + number2 + "? ");
    Scanner input = new Scanner(System.in);
    int answer = input.nextInt();

    // 4. Grade the answer and display the result
    if (number1 - number2 == answer)
      System.out.println("You are correct!");
    else
      System.out.println("Your answer is wrong\n" + number1 + " - "
        + number2 + " is " + (number1 - number2));
  }
}
```

```
What is 6 - 6? 0 ↵Enter
You are correct!
```

```
What is 9 - 2? 5 ↵Enter
Your answer is wrong
9 - 2 is 7
```

line#	number1	number2	temp	answer	output
6	2				
7		9			
11			2		
12	9				
13		2			
20				5	
26					Your answer is wrong 9 - 2 should be 7

To swap two variables `number1` and `number2`, a temporary variable `temp` (line 11) is used to first hold the value in `number1`. The value in `number2` is assigned to `number1` (line 12), and the value in `temp` is assigned to `number2` (line 13).

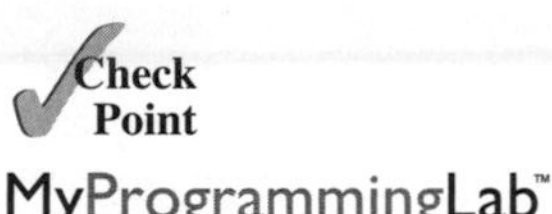

3.15 Which of the following is a possible output from invoking `Math.random()`?

`323.4, 0.5, 34, 1.0, 0.0, 0.234`

3.16 a. How do you generate a random integer `i` such that $0 \leq i < 20$?

b. How do you generate a random integer `i` such that $10 \leq i < 20$?

c. How do you generate a random integer `i` such that $10 \leq i \leq 50$?

3.9 Case Study: Computing Body Mass Index

You can use nested `if` statements to write a program that interprets body mass index.

Body Mass Index (BMI) is a measure of health based on height and weight. It can be calculated by taking your weight in kilograms and dividing it by the square of your height in meters. The interpretation of BMI for people 20 years or older is as follows:

BMI	Interpretation
BMI < 18.5	Underweight
18.5 ≤ BMI < 25.0	Normal
25.0 ≤ BMI < 30.0	Overweight
30.0 ≤ BMI	Obese

Write a program that prompts the user to enter a weight in pounds and height in inches and displays the BMI. Note that one pound is `0.45359237` kilograms and one inch is `0.0254` meters. Listing 3.5 gives the program.

LISTING 3.5 ComputeAndInterpretBMI.java

input weight
input height
compute bmi
display output

```
 1 import java.util.Scanner;
 2
 3 public class ComputeAndInterpretBMI {
 4   public static void main(String[] args) {
 5     Scanner input = new Scanner(System.in);
 6
 7     // Prompt the user to enter weight in pounds
 8     System.out.print("Enter weight in pounds: ");
 9     double weight = input.nextDouble();
10
11     // Prompt the user to enter height in inches
12     System.out.print("Enter height in inches: ");
13     double height = input.nextDouble();
14
15     final double KILOGRAMS_PER_POUND = 0.45359237; // Constant
16     final double METERS_PER_INCH = 0.0254; // Constant
17
18     // Compute BMI
19     double weightInKilograms = weight * KILOGRAMS_PER_POUND;
20     double heightInMeters = height * METERS_PER_INCH;
21     double bmi = weightInKilograms /
22       (heightInMeters * heightInMeters);
23
24     // Display result
25     System.out.println("BMI is " + bmi);
26     if (bmi < 18.5)
27       System.out.println("Underweight");
28     else if (bmi < 25)
29       System.out.println("Normal");
30     else if (bmi < 30)
31       System.out.println("Overweight");
32     else
33       System.out.println("Obese");
34   }
35 }
```

```
Enter weight in pounds: 146 ↵Enter
Enter height in inches: 70 ↵Enter
BMI is 20.948603801493316
Normal
```

line#	weight	height	weightInKilograms	heightInMeters	bmi	output
9	146					
13		70				
19			66.22448602			
20				1.778		
21					20.9486	
25						BMI is 20.95
31						Normal

The constants KILOGRAMS_PER_POUND and METERS PER INCH are defined in lines 15–16. Using constants here makes programs easy to read.

3.10 Case Study: Computing Taxes

You can use nested `if` statements to write a program for computing taxes.

VideoNote

Use multi-way `if-else` statements

The United States federal personal income tax is calculated based on filing status and taxable income. There are four filing statuses: single filers, married filing jointly or qualified widow(er), married filing separately, and head of household. The tax rates vary every year. Table 3.2 shows the rates for 2009. If you are, say, single with a taxable income of $10,000, the first $8,350 is taxed at 10% and the other $1,650 is taxed at 15%, so, your total tax is $1,082.50.

TABLE 3.2 2009 U.S. Federal Personal Tax Rates

Marginal Tax Rate	*Single*	*Married Filing Jointly or Qualifying Widow(er)*	*Married Filing Separately*	*Head of Household*
10%	$0 – $8,350	$0 – $16,700	$0 – $8,350	$0 – $11,950
15%	$8,351– $33,950	$16,701 – $67,900	$8,351 – $33,950	$11,951 – $45,500
25%	$33,951 – $82,250	$67,901 – $137,050	$33,951 – $68,525	$45,501 – $117,450
28%	$82,251 – $171,550	$137,051 – $208,850	$68,526 – $104,425	$117,451 – $190,200
33%	$171,551 – $372,950	$208,851 – $372,950	$104,426 – $186,475	$190,201 – $372,950
35%	$372,951+	$372,951+	$186,476+	$372,951+

You are to write a program to compute personal income tax. Your program should prompt the user to enter the filing status and taxable income and compute the tax. Enter 0 for single filers, 1 for married filing jointly or qualified widow(er), 2 for married filing separately, and 3 for head of household.

Your program computes the tax for the taxable income based on the filing status. The filing status can be determined using `if` statements outlined as follows:

```
if (status == 0) {
  // Compute tax for single filers
}
else if (status == 1) {
  // Compute tax for married filing jointly or qualifying widow(er)
}
else if (status == 2) {
  // Compute tax for married filing separately
}
else if (status == 3) {
  // Compute tax for head of household
}
else {
  // Display wrong status
}
```

For each filing status there are six tax rates. Each rate is applied to a certain amount of taxable income. For example, of a taxable income of $400,000 for single filers, $8,350 is taxed at 10%, (33,950 – 8,350) at 15%, (82,250 – 33,950) at 25%, (171,550 – 82,250) at 28%, (372,950 – 171,550) at 33%, and (400,000 – 372,950) at 35%.

Listing 3.6 gives the solution for computing taxes for single filers. The complete solution is left as an exercise.

LISTING 3.6 ComputeTax.java

input status
input income
compute tax
exit program
display output

```
import java.util.Scanner;

public class ComputeTax {
  public static void main(String[] args) {
    // Create a Scanner
    Scanner input = new Scanner(System.in);

    // Prompt the user to enter filing status
    System.out.print(
      "(0-single filer, 1-married jointly or qualifying widow(er),
      + "\n2-married separately, 3-head of household)\n" +
      "Enter the filing status: ");
    int status = input.nextInt();

    // Prompt the user to enter taxable income
    System.out.print("Enter the taxable income: ");
    double income = input.nextDouble();

    // Compute tax
    double tax = 0;

    if (status == 0) { // Compute tax for single filers
      if (income <= 8350)
        tax = income * 0.10;
      else if (income <= 33950)
        tax = 8350 * 0.10 + (income - 8350) * 0.15;
      else if (income <= 82250)
        tax = 8350 * 0.10 + (33950 - 8350) * 0.15 +
          (income - 33950) * 0.25;
      else if (income <= 171550)
        tax = 8350 * 0.10 + (33950 - 8350) * 0.15 +
          (82250 - 33950) * 0.25 + (income - 82250) * 0.28;
      else if (income <= 372950)
        tax = 8350 * 0.10 + (33950 - 8350) * 0.15 +
          (82250 - 33950) * 0.25 + (171550 - 82250) * 0.28 +
          (income - 171550) * 0.33;
      else
        tax = 8350 * 0.10 + (33950 - 8350) * 0.15 +
          (82250 - 33950) * 0.25 + (171550 - 82250) * 0.28 +
          (372950 - 171550) * 0.33 + (income - 372950) * 0.35;
    }
    else if (status == 1) { // Left as exercise
      // Compute tax for married file jointly or qualifying widow(er)
    }
    else if (status == 2) { // Compute tax for married separately
      // Left as exercise
    }
    else if (status == 3) { // Compute tax for head of household
      // Left as exercise
    }
    else {
      System.out.println("Error: invalid status");
      System.exit(1);
    }

    // Display the result
    System.out.println("Tax is " + (int)(tax * 100) / 100.0);
  }
}
```

```
(0-single filer, 1-married jointly or qualifying widow(er),
2-married separately, 3-head of household)
Enter the filing status: 0 ↵Enter
Enter the taxable income: 400000 ↵Enter
Tax is 117683.5
```

line#	status	income	tax	output
13	0			
17		400000		
20			0	
38			117683.5	
57				Tax is 117683.5

The program receives the filing status and taxable income. The multi-way `if-else` statements (lines 22, 42, 45, 48, 51) check the filing status and compute the tax based on the filing status.

`System.exit(status)` (line 53) is defined in the `System` class. Invoking this method terminates the program. The status `0` indicates that the program is terminated normally. A nonzero status code indicates abnormal termination.

System.exit(status)

An initial value of `0` is assigned to `tax` (line 20). A compile error would occur if it had no initial value, because all of the other statements that assign values to `tax` are within the `if` statement. The compiler thinks that these statements may not be executed and therefore reports a compile error.

To test a program, you should provide the input that covers all cases. For this program, your input should cover all statuses (`0`, `1`, `2`, `3`). For each status, test the tax for each of the six brackets. So, there are a total of 24 cases.

test all cases

Tip

For all programs, you should write a small amount of code and test it before moving on to add more code. This is called *incremental development and testing*. This approach makes testing easier, because the errors are likely in the new code you just added.

incremental development and testing

3.17 Are the following two statements equivalent?

Check Point

MyProgrammingLab™

```
if (income <= 10000)
  tax = income * 0.1;
else if (income <= 20000)
  tax = 1000 +
    (income - 10000) * 0.15;
```

```
if (income <= 10000)
  tax = income * 0.1;
else if (income > 10000 &&
         income <= 20000)
  tax = 1000 +
    (income - 10000) * 0.15;
```

3.11 Logical Operators

The logical operators !, &&, ||, and ^ can be used to create a compound Boolean expression.

Key Point

Sometimes, whether a statement is executed is determined by a combination of several conditions. You can use logical operators to combine these conditions to form a compound Boolean expression. *Logical operators*, also known as *Boolean operators*, operate on Boolean values to create a new Boolean value. Table 3.3 lists the Boolean operators. Table 3.4 defines the not (`!`) operator, which negates `true` to `false` and `false` to `true`. Table 3.5 defines the and (`&&`) operator. The and (`&&`) of two Boolean operands is `true` if and only if both operands are `true`. Table 3.6 defines the or (`||`) operator. The or (`||`) of two Boolean operands is `true` if at least one of the operands is `true`. Table 3.7 defines the exclusive or (`^`) operator. The exclusive or (`^`) of two Boolean operands is `true` if and only if the two operands have different Boolean values. Note that `p1 ^ p2` is the same as `p1 != p2`.

TABLE 3.3 Boolean Operators

Operator	*Name*	*Description*
`!`	not	logical negation
`&&`	and	logical conjunction
`||`	or	logical disjunction
`^`	exclusive or	logical exclusion

TABLE 3.4 Truth Table for Operator `!`

p	!p	*Example (assume* `age = 24, gender = 'F'`*)*
`true`	`false`	`!(age > 18)` is `false`, because `(age > 18)` is `true`.
`false`	`true`	`!(gender == 'M')` is `true`, because `(gender == 'M')` is `false`.

TABLE 3.5 Truth Table for Operator `&&`

p_1	p_2	p_1 && p_2	*Example (assume* `age = 24, gender = 'F'`*)*
`false`	`false`	`false`	`(age > 18) && (gender == 'F')` is `true`, because `(age > 18)` and `(gender == 'F')` are both `true`.
`false`	`true`	`false`	
`true`	`false`	`false`	`(age > 18) && (gender != 'F')` is `false`, because `(gender != 'F')` is `false`.
`true`	`true`	`true`	

TABLE 3.6 Truth Table for Operator `||`

p_1	p_2	p_1 || p_2	*Example (assume* `age = 24, gender = 'F'`*)*
`false`	`false`	`false`	`(age > 34) || (gender == 'F')` is `true`, because `(gender == 'F')` is `true`.
`false`	`true`	`true`	
`true`	`false`	`true`	`(age > 34) || (gender == 'M')` is `false`, because `(age > 34)` and `(gender == 'M')` are both `false`.
`true`	`true`	`true`	

TABLE 3.7 Truth Table for Operator ^

p_1	p_2	p_1 ^ p_2	*Example (assume* `age = 24, gender = 'F'`*)*
`false`	`false`	`false`	`(age > 34) ^ (gender == 'F')` is `true`, because `(age > 34)` is `false` but `(gender == 'F')` is `true`.
`false`	`true`	`true`	
`true`	`false`	`true`	`(age > 34) ^ (gender == 'M')` is `false`, because `(age > 34)` and `(gender == 'M')` are both `false`.
`true`	`true`	`false`	

Listing 3.7 gives a program that checks whether a number is divisible by 2 and 3, by 2 or 3, and by 2 or 3 but not both:

LISTING 3.7 `TestBooleanOperators.java`

```
 1 import java.util.Scanner;
 2
 3 public class TestBooleanOperators {
 4   public static void main(String[] args) {
 5     // Create a Scanner
 6     Scanner input = new Scanner(System.in);
 7
 8     // Receive an input
 9     System.out.print("Enter an integer: ");
10     int number = input.nextInt();
11
12     if (number % 2 == 0 && number % 3 == 0)
13       System.out.println(number + " is divisible by 2 and 3.");
14
15     if (number % 2 == 0 || number % 3 == 0)
16       System.out.println(number + " is divisible by 2 or 3.");
17
18     if (number % 2 == 0 ^ number % 3 == 0)
19       System.out.println(number +
20         " is divisible by 2 or 3, but not both.");
21   }
22 }
```

import class (line 1) · input (line 10) · and (line 12) · or (line 15) · exclusive or (line 18)

```
Enter an integer: 4 ↵Enter
4 is divisible by 2 or 3.
4 is divisible by 2 or 3, but not both.
```

```
Enter an integer: 18 ↵Enter
18 is divisible by 2 and 3.
18 is divisible by 2 or 3.
```

`(number % 2 == 0 && number % 3 == 0)` (line 12) checks whether the number is divisible by both 2 and 3. `(number % 2 == 0 || number % 3 == 0)` (line 15) checks whether the number is divisible by 2 and/or by 3. `(number % 2 == 0 ^ number % 3 == 0)` (line 18) checks whether the number is divisible by 2 or 3, but not both.

Caution

In mathematics, the expression

```
1 <= numberOfDaysInAMonth <= 31
```

is correct. However, it is incorrect in Java, because `1 <= numberOfDaysInAMonth` is evaluated to a `boolean` value, which cannot be compared with `31`. Here, two operands (a `boolean` value and a numeric value) are *incompatible*. The correct expression in Java is

incompatible operands

```
(1 <= numberOfDaysInAMonth) && (numberOfDaysInAMonth <= 31)
```

Note

cannot cast boolean

As shown in the preceding chapter, a `char` value can be cast into an `int` value, and vice versa. A `boolean` value, however, cannot be cast into a value of another type, nor can a value of another type be cast into a `boolean` value.

Note

De Morgan's law

De Morgan's law, named after Indian-born British mathematician and logician Augustus De Morgan (1806–1871), can be used to simplify Boolean expressions. The law states:

`!(condition1 && condition2)` is the same as
  `!condition1 || !condition2`
`!(condition1 || condition2)` is the same as
  `!condition1 && !condition2`

For example,

```
! (number % 2 == 0 && number % 3 == 0)
```

can be simplified using an equivalent expression:

```
(number % 2 != 0 || number % 3 != 0)
```

As another example,

```
!(number == 2 || number == 3)
```

is better written as

```
number != 2 && number != 3
```

If one of the operands of an `&&` operator is `false`, the expression is `false`; if one of the operands of an `||` operator is `true`, the expression is `true`. Java uses these properties to improve the performance of these operators. When evaluating `p1 && p2`, Java first evaluates `p1` and then, if `p1` is `true`, evaluates `p2`; if `p1` is `false`, it does not evaluate `p2`. When evaluating `p1 || p2`, Java first evaluates `p1` and then, if `p1` is `false`, evaluates `p2`; if `p1` is `true`, it does not evaluate `p2`. Therefore, `&&` is referred to as the *conditional* or *short-circuit AND* operator, and `||` is referred to as the *conditional* or *short-circuit OR* operator. Java also provides the conditional AND (`&`) and OR (`|`) operators, which are covered in Supplement III.C and III.D for advanced readers.

conditional operator
short-circuit operator

MyProgrammingLab™

3.18 Assuming that `x` is `1`, show the result of the following Boolean expressions.

```
(true) && (3 > 4)
!(x > 0) && (x > 0)
(x > 0) || (x < 0)

(x != 0) || (x == 0)
(x >= 0) || (x < 0)
(x != 1) == !(x == 1)
```

3.19 Write a Boolean expression that evaluates to `true` if a number stored in variable `num` is between `1` and `100`.

3.20 Write a Boolean expression that evaluates to `true` if a number stored in variable `num` is between `1` and `100` or the number is negative.

3.21 Assume that x and y are int type. Which of the following are legal Java expressions?

```
x > y > 0
x = y && y
x /= y
x or y
x and y
(x != 0) || (x = 0)
```

3.22 Suppose that x is 1. What is x after the evaluation of the following expression?

```
a. (x >= 1) && (x++ > 1)
b. (x > 1) && (x++ > 1)
```

3.23 What is the value of the expression ch >= 'A' && ch <= 'Z' if ch is 'A', 'p', 'E', or '5'?

3.24 Suppose, when you run the program, you enter input 2 3 6 from the console. What is the output?

```
public class Test {
  public static void main(String[] args) {
    java.util.Scanner input = new java.util.Scanner(System.in);
    double x = input.nextDouble();
    double y = input.nextDouble();
    double z = input.nextDouble();

    System.out.println("(x < y && y < z) is " + (x < y && y < z));
    System.out.println("(x < y || y < z) is " + (x < y || y < z));
    System.out.println("!(x < y) is " + !(x < y));
    System.out.println("(x + y < z) is " + (x + y < z));
    System.out.println("(x + y < z) is " + (x + y < z));
  }
}
```

3.25 Write a Boolean expression that evaluates true if age is greater than 13 and less than 18.

3.26 Write a Boolean expression that evaluates true if weight is greater than 50 pounds or height is greater than 60 inches.

3.27 Write a Boolean expression that evaluates true if weight is greater than 50 pounds and height is greater than 60 inches.

3.28 Write a Boolean expression that evaluates true if either weight is greater than 50 pounds or height is greater than 60 inches, but not both.

3.12 Case Study: Determining Leap Year

A year is a leap year *if it is divisible by* 4 *but not by* 100, *or if it is divisible by* 400.

You can use the following Boolean expressions to check whether a year is a leap year:

```
// A leap year is divisible by 4
boolean isLeapYear = (year % 4 == 0);

// A leap year is divisible by 4 but not by 100
isLeapYear = isLeapYear && (year % 100 != 0);

// A leap year is divisible by 4 but not by 100 or divisible by 400
isLeapYear = isLeapYear || (year % 400 == 0);
```

Or you can combine all these expressions into one like this:

```
isLeapYear = (year % 4 == 0 && year % 100 != 0) || (year % 400 == 0);
```

Listing 3.8 gives the program that lets the user enter a year and checks whether it is a leap year.

LISTING 3.8 LeapYear.java

input

leap year?

display result

```
import java.util.Scanner;

public class LeapYear {
  public static void main(String[] args) {
    // Create a Scanner
    Scanner input = new Scanner(System.in);
    System.out.print("Enter a year: ");
    int year = input.nextInt();

    // Check if the year is a leap year
    boolean isLeapYear =
      (year % 4 == 0 && year % 100 != 0) || (year % 400 == 0);

    // Display the result
    System.out.println(year + " is a leap year? " + isLeapYear);
  }
}
```

```
Enter a year: 2008 ↵Enter
2008 is a leap year? true
```

```
Enter a year: 1900 ↵Enter
1900 is a leap year? false
```

```
Enter a year: 2002 ↵Enter
2002 is a leap year? false
```

3.13 Case Study: Lottery

The lottery program involves generating random numbers, comparing digits, and using Boolean operators.

Suppose you want to develop a program to play lottery. The program randomly generates a lottery of a two-digit number, prompts the user to enter a two-digit number, and determines whether the user wins according to the following rules:

1. If the user input matches the lottery number in the exact order, the award is $10,000.
2. If all the digits in the user input match all the digits in the lottery number, the award is $3,000.
3. If one digit in the user input matches a digit in the lottery number, the award is $1,000.

The complete program is shown in Listing 3.9.

LISTING 3.9 Lottery.java

```
import java.util.Scanner;

public class Lottery {
  public static void main(String[] args) {
    // Generate a lottery number
```

```
6       int lottery = (int)(Math.random() * 100);
7
8       // Prompt the user to enter a guess
9       Scanner input = new Scanner(System.in);
10      System.out.print("Enter your lottery pick (two digits): ");
11      int guess = input.nextInt();
12
13      // Get digits from lottery
14      int lotteryDigit1 = lottery / 10;
15      int lotteryDigit2 = lottery % 10;
16
17      // Get digits from guess
18      int guessDigit1 = guess / 10;
19      int guessDigit2 = guess % 10;
20
21      System.out.println("The lottery number is " + lottery);
22
23      // Check the guess
24      if (guess == lottery)
25        System.out.println("Exact match: you win $10,000");
26      else if (guessDigit2 == lotteryDigit1
27              && guessDigit1 == lotteryDigit2)
28        System.out.println("Match all digits: you win $3,000");
29      else if (guessDigit1 == lotteryDigit1
30              || guessDigit1 == lotteryDigit2
31              || guessDigit2 == lotteryDigit1
32              || guessDigit2 == lotteryDigit2)
33        System.out.println("Match one digit: you win $1,000");
34      else
35        System.out.println("Sorry, no match");
36    }
37  }
```

generate a lottery number

enter a guess

exact match?

match all digits?

match one digit?

```
Enter your lottery pick (two digits): 45 ↵Enter
The lottery number is 12
Sorry, no match
```

```
Enter your lottery pick: 23 ↵Enter
The lottery number is 34
Match one digit: you win $1,000
```

line# / variable	6	11	14	15	18	19	33
lottery	34						
guess		23					
lotteryDigit1			3				
lotteryDigit2				4			
guessDigit1					2		
guessDigit2						3	
Output							Match one digit: you win $1,000

The program generates a lottery using the `random()` method (line 6) and prompts the user to enter a guess (line 11). Note that `guess % 10` obtains the last digit from `guess` and `guess / 10` obtains the first digit from `guess`, since `guess` is a two-digit number (lines 18–19).

The program checks the guess against the lottery number in this order:

1. First, check whether the guess matches the lottery exactly (line 24).
2. If not, check whether the reversal of the guess matches the lottery (lines 26–27).
3. If not, check whether one digit is in the lottery (lines 29–32).
4. If not, nothing matches and display `"Sorry, no match"` (lines 34–35).

3.14 switch Statements

A `switch` statement executes statements based on the value of a variable or an expression.

The `if` statement in Listing 3.6, ComputeTax.java, makes selections based on a single `true` or `false` condition. There are four cases for computing taxes, which depend on the value of `status`. To fully account for all the cases, nested `if` statements were used. Overuse of nested `if` statements makes a program difficult to read. Java provides a `switch` statement to simplify coding for multiple conditions. You can write the following `switch` statement to replace the nested `if` statement in Listing 3.6:

```
switch (status) {
  case 0:  compute tax for single filers;
           break;
  case 1:  compute tax for married jointly or qualifying widow(er);
           break;
  case 2:  compute tax for married filing separately;
           break;
  case 3:  compute tax for head of household;
           break;
  default: System.out.println("Error: invalid status");
           System.exit(1);
}
```

The flowchart of the preceding `switch` statement is shown in Figure 3.6.

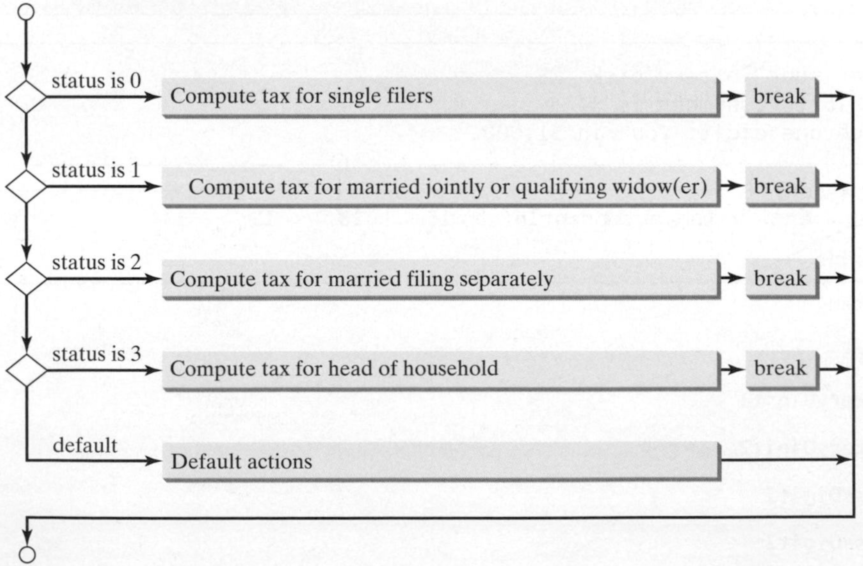

FIGURE 3.6 The `switch` statement checks all cases and executes the statements in the matched case.

This statement checks to see whether the status matches the value 0, 1, 2, or 3, in that order. If matched, the corresponding tax is computed; if not matched, a message is displayed. Here is the full syntax for the switch statement:

switch statement

```
switch (switch-expression) {
  case value1: statement(s)1;
               break;
  case value2: statement(s)2;
               break;
  ...
  case valueN: statement(s)N;
               break;
  default:     statement(s)-for-default;
}
```

The switch statement observes the following rules:

- The switch-expression must yield a value of char, byte, short, int, or String type and must always be enclosed in parentheses. (Using String type in the switch expression is new in JDK 7.)
- The value1, . . ., and valueN must have the same data type as the value of the switch-expression. Note that value1, . . ., and valueN are constant expressions, meaning that they cannot contain variables, such as 1 + x.
- When the value in a case statement matches the value of the switch-expression, the statements *starting from this case* are executed until either a break statement or the end of the switch statement is reached.
- The default case, which is optional, can be used to perform actions when none of the specified cases matches the switch-expression.
- The keyword break is optional. The break statement immediately ends the switch statement.

Caution

without break

fall-through behavior

Do not forget to use a break statement when one is needed. Once a case is matched, the statements starting from the matched case are executed until a break statement or the end of the switch statement is reached. This is referred to as *fall-through* behavior. For example, the following code displays the character a three times if ch is a:

```
switch (ch) {
  case 'a': System.out.println(ch);
  case 'b': System.out.println(ch);
  case 'c': System.out.println(ch);
}
```

Tip

To avoid programming errors and improve code maintainability, it is a good idea to put a comment in a case clause if break is purposely omitted.

Now let us write a program to find out the Chinese Zodiac sign for a given year. The Chinese Zodiac is based on a twelve-year cycle, with each year represented by an animal—monkey, rooster, dog, pig, rat, ox, tiger, rabbit, dragon, snake, horse, or sheep—in this cycle, as shown in Figure 3.7.

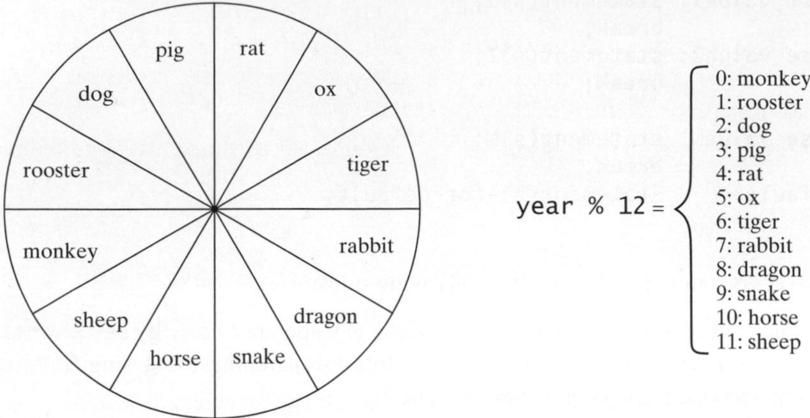

FIGURE 3.7 The Chinese Zodiac is based on a twelve-year cycle.

Note that `year % 12` determines the Zodiac sign. 1900 is the year of the rat because `1900 % 12` is `4`. Listing 3.10 gives a program that prompts the user to enter a year and displays the animal for the year.

LISTING 3.10 ChineseZodiac.java

enter year

determine Zodiac sign

```
import java.util.Scanner;

public class ChineseZodiac {
  public static void main(String[] args) {
    Scanner input = new Scanner(System.in);

    System.out.print("Enter a year: ");
    int year = input.nextInt();

    switch (year % 12) {
      case 0: System.out.println("monkey"); break;
      case 1: System.out.println("rooster"); break;
      case 2: System.out.println("dog"); break;
      case 3: System.out.println("pig"); break;
      case 4: System.out.println("rat"); break;
      case 5: System.out.println("ox"); break;
      case 6: System.out.println("tiger"); break;
      case 7: System.out.println("rabbit"); break;
      case 8: System.out.println("dragon"); break;
      case 9: System.out.println("snake"); break;
      case 10: System.out.println("horse"); break;
      case 11: System.out.println("sheep");
    }
  }
}
```

```
Enter a year: 1963 ↵Enter
rabbit
```

```
Enter a year: 1877 ↵Enter
ox
```

3.29 What data types are required for a `switch` variable? If the keyword `break` is not used after a case is processed, what is the next statement to be executed? Can you convert a `switch` statement to an equivalent `if` statement, or vice versa? What are the advantages of using a `switch` statement?

3.30 What is `y` after the following `switch` statement is executed? Rewrite the code using the `if-else` statement.

```
x = 3; y = 3;
switch (x + 3) {
  case 6:  y = 1;
  default: y += 1;
}
```

3.31 What is `x` after the following `if-else` statement is executed? Use a `switch` statement to rewrite it and draw the flowchart for the new `switch` statement.

```
int x = 1, a = 3;
if (a == 1)
  x += 5;
else if (a == 2)
  x += 10;
else if (a == 3)
  x += 16;
else if (a == 4)
  x += 34;
```

3.32 Write a `switch` statement that assigns a `String` variable `dayName` with Sunday, Monday, Tuesday, Wednesday, Thursday, Friday, Saturday, if `day` is `0`, `1`, `2`, `3`, `4`, `5`, `6`, accordingly.

3.15 Conditional Expressions

A conditional expression evaluates an expression based on a condition.

You might want to assign a value to a variable that is restricted by certain conditions. For example, the following statement assigns `1` to `y` if `x` is greater than `0`, and `-1` to `y` if `x` is less than or equal to `0`.

```
if (x > 0)
  y = 1;
else
  y = -1;
```

Alternatively, as in the following example, you can use a conditional expression to achieve the same result.

```
y = (x > 0) ? 1 : -1;
```

conditional expression

Conditional expressions are in a completely different style, with no explicit `if` in the statement. The syntax is:

```
boolean-expression ? expression1 : expression2;
```

The result of this conditional expression is `expression1` if `boolean-expression` is true; otherwise the result is `expression2`.

Suppose you want to assign the larger number of variable `num1` and `num2` to `max`. You can simply write a statement using the conditional expression:

```
max = (num1 > num2) ? num1 : num2;
```

For another example, the following statement displays the message "num is even" if `num` is even, and otherwise displays "num is odd."

```
System.out.println((num % 2 == 0) ? "num is even" : "num is odd");
```

As you can see from these examples, conditional expressions enable you to write short and concise code.

Note

The symbols `?` and `:` appear together in a conditional expression. They form a conditional operator called a *ternary operator* because it uses three operands. It is the only ternary operator in Java.

MyProgrammingLab™

3.33 Suppose that, when you run the following program, you enter input `2 3 6` from the console. What is the output?

```
public class Test {
  public static void main(String[] args) {
    java.util.Scanner input = new java.util.Scanner(System.in);
    double x = input.nextDouble();
    double y = input.nextDouble();
    double z = input.nextDouble();

    System.out.println((x < y && y < z) ? "sorted" : "not sorted");
  }
}
```

3.34 Rewrite the following `if` statements using the conditional operator.

```
if (ages >= 16)
  ticketPrice = 20;
else
  ticketPrice = 10;
```

```
if (count % 10 == 0)
  System.out.print(count + "\n");
else
  System.out.print(count);
```

3.35 Rewrite the following conditional expressions using `if-else` statements.

a. `score = (x > 10) ? 3 * scale : 4 * scale;`
b. `tax = (income > 10000) ? income * 0.2 : income * 0.17 + 1000;`
c. `System.out.println((number % 3 == 0) ? i : j);`

3.16 Formatting Console Output

You can use the `System.out.printf` method to display formatted output on the console.

Often it is desirable to display numbers in a certain format. For example, the following code computes interest, given the amount and the annual interest rate.

```
double amount = 12618.98;
double interestRate = 0.0013;
```

```
double interest = amount * interestRate;
System.out.println("Interest is " + interest);
```

```
Interest is 16.404674
```

Because the interest amount is currency, it is desirable to display only two digits after the decimal point. To do this, you can write the code as follows:

```
double amount = 12618.98;
double interestRate = 0.0013;
double interest = amount * interestRate;
System.out.println("Interest is "
  + (int)(interest * 100) / 100.0);
```

```
Interest is 16.4
```

However, the format is still not correct. There should be two digits after the decimal point: `16.40` rather than `16.4`. You can fix it by using the `printf` method, like this:

printf

```
double amount = 12618.98;
double interestRate = 0.0013;
double interest = amount * interestRate;
System.out.printf("Interest is %4.2f", interest);
```

% 4 . 2 f ← format specifier
field width
conversion code
precision

```
Interest is 16.40
```

The syntax to invoke this method is

```
System.out.printf(format, item1, item2, ..., itemk)
```

where `format` is a string that may consist of substrings and format specifiers.

A *format specifier* specifies how an item should be displayed. An item may be a numeric value, a character, a Boolean value, or a string. A simple format specifier consists of a percent sign (%) followed by a conversion code. Table 3.8 lists some frequently used simple format specifiers.

format specifier

TABLE 3.8 Frequently Used Format Specifiers

Format Specifier	*Output*	*Example*
%b	a Boolean value	true or false
%c	a character	'a'
%d	a decimal integer	200
%f	a floating-point number	45.460000
%e	a number in standard scientific notation	4.556000e+01
%s	a string	"Java is cool"

Here is an example:

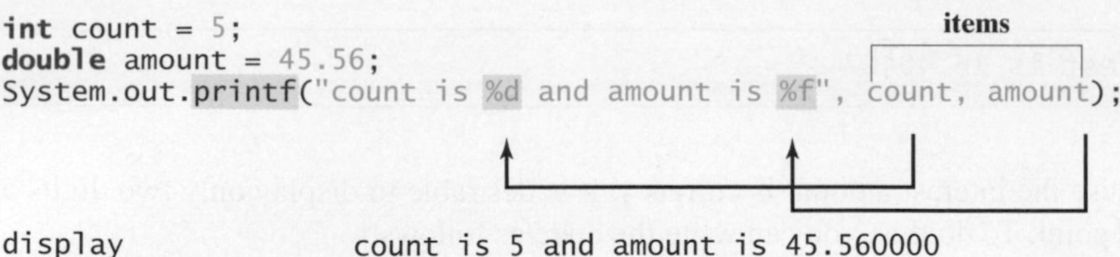

Items must match the format specifiers in order, in number, and in exact type. For example, the format specifier for `count` is `%d` and for `amount` is `%f`. By default, a floating-point value is displayed with six digits after the decimal point. You can specify the width and precision in a format specifier, as shown in the examples in Table 3.9.

TABLE 3.9 Examples of Specifying Width and Precision

Example	*Output*
`%5c`	Output the character and add four spaces before the character item, because the width is 5.
`%6b`	Output the Boolean value and add one space before the false value and two spaces before the true value.
`%5d`	Output the integer item with width at least 5. If the number of digits in the item is <5, add spaces before the number. If the number of digits in the item is >5, the width is automatically increased.
`%10.2f`	Output the floating-point item with width at least 10 including a decimal point and two digits after the point. Thus there are 7 digits allocated before the decimal point. If the number of digits before the decimal point in the item is <7, add spaces before the number. If the number of digits before the decimal point in the item is >7, the width is automatically increased.
`%10.2e`	Output the floating-point item with width at least 10 including a decimal point, two digits after the point and the exponent part. If the displayed number in scientific notation has width less than 10, add spaces before the number.
`%12s`	Output the string with width at least 12 characters. If the string item has fewer than 12 characters, add spaces before the string. If the string item has more than 12 characters, the width is automatically increased.

If an item requires more spaces than the specified width, the width is automatically increased. For example, the following code

```
System.out.printf("%3d#%2s#%3.2f\n", 1234, "Java", 51.6653);
```

displays

```
1234#Java#51.67
```

The specified width for `int` item `1234` is `3`, which is smaller than its actual size `4`. The width is automatically increased to `4`. The specified width for string item `Java` is `2`, which is smaller than its actual size `4`. The width is automatically increased to `4`. The specified width for `double` item `51.6653` is `3`, but it needs width 5 to display 51.67, so the width is automatically increased to `5`.

By default, the output is right justified. You can put the minus sign (-) in the format specifier to specify that the item is left justified in the output within the specified field. For example, the following statements

right justify
left justify

```
System.out.printf("%8d%8s%8.1f\n", 1234, "Java", 5.63);
System.out.printf("%-8d%-8s%-8.1f \n", 1234, "Java", 5.63);
```

display

```
|<-- 8 -->|<-- 8 -->|<-- 8 -->|
□□□□1234□□□□Java□□□□□5.6
1234□□□□Java□□□□5.6□□□□□
```

where the square box (□) denotes a blank space.

Caution

The items must match the format specifiers in exact type. The item for the format specifier `%f` or `%e` must be a floating-point type value such as `40.0`, not `40`. Thus, an `int` variable cannot match `%f` or `%e`.

Tip

The `%` sign denotes a format specifier. To output a literal `%` in the format string, use `%%`.

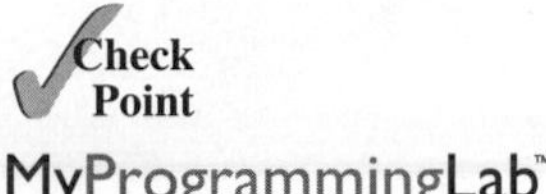

3.36 What are the format specifiers for outputting a Boolean value, a character, a decimal integer, a floating-point number, and a string?

3.37 What is wrong in the following statements?

a. `System.out.printf("%5d %d", 1, 2, 3);`

b. `System.out.printf("%5d %f", 1);`

c. `System.out.printf("%5d %f", 1, 2);`

3.38 Show the output of the following statements.

a. `System.out.printf("amount is %f %e\n", 32.32, 32.32);`

b. `System.out.printf("amount is %5.4f %5.4e\n", 32.32, 32.32);`

c. `System.out.printf("%6b\n", (1 > 2));`

d. `System.out.printf("%6s\n", "Java");`

e. `System.out.printf("%-6b%s\n", (1 > 2), "Java");`

f. `System.out.printf("%6b%-8s\n", (1 > 2), "Java");`

3.17 Operator Precedence and Associativity

Operator precedence and associativity determine the order in which operators are evaluated.

Section 2.11 introduced operator precedence involving arithmetic operators. This section discusses operator precedence in more details. Suppose that you have this expression:

```
3 + 4 * 4 > 5 * (4 + 3) - 1 && (4 - 3 > 5)
```

What is its value? What is the execution order of the operators?

The expression in the parentheses is evaluated first. (Parentheses can be nested, in which case the expression in the inner parentheses is executed first.) When evaluating an expression without parentheses, the operators are applied according to the precedence rule and the associativity rule.

The precedence rule defines precedence for operators, as shown in Table 3.10, which contains the operators you have learned so far. Operators are listed in decreasing order of precedence from top to bottom. The logical operators have lower precedence than the relational operators and the relational operators have lower precedence than the arithmetic operators. Operators with the same precedence appear in the same group. (See Appendix C, *Operator Precedence Chart*, for a complete list of Java operators and their precedence.)

operator precedence

TABLE 3.10 Operator Precedence Chart

Precedence	*Operator*
↓	var++ and var-- (Postfix)
	+, - (Unary plus and minus), ++var and --var (Prefix)
	(type) (Casting)
	! (Not)
	*, /, % (Multiplication, division, and remainder)
	+, - (Binary addition and subtraction)
	<, <=, >, >= (Comparison)
	==, != (Equality)
	^ (Exclusive OR)
	&& (AND)
	|| (OR)
	=, +=, -=, *=, /=, %= (Assignment operator)

operator associativity

If operators with the same precedence are next to each other, their *associativity* determines the order of evaluation. All binary operators except assignment operators are *left associative*. For example, since + and - are of the same precedence and are left associative, the expression

```
a - b + c - d   is equivalent to   ((a - b) + c) - d
```

Assignment operators are *right associative*. Therefore, the expression

```
a = b += c = 5   is equivalent to   a = (b += (c = 5))
```

Suppose a, b, and c are 1 before the assignment; after the whole expression is evaluated, a becomes 6, b becomes 6, and c becomes 5. Note that left associativity for the assignment operator would not make sense.

Note

Java has its own way to evaluate an expression internally. The result of a Java evaluation is the same as that of its corresponding arithmetic evaluation. Advanced readers may refer to Supplement III.B for more discussions on how an expression is evaluated in Java *behind the scenes*.

behind the scenes

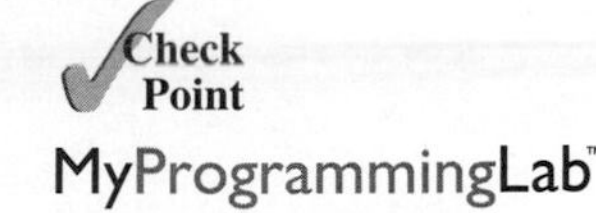

3.39 List the precedence order of the Boolean operators. Evaluate the following expressions:

```
true || true && false
true && true || false
```

3.40 True or false? All the binary operators except = are left associative.

3.41 Evaluate the following expressions:

```
2 * 2 - 3 > 2 && 4 - 2 > 5
2 * 2 - 3 > 2 || 4 - 2 > 5
```

3.42 Is `(x > 0 && x < 10)` the same as `((x > 0) && (x < 10))`? Is `(x > 0 || x < 10)` the same as `((x > 0) || (x < 10))`? Is `(x > 0 || x < 10 && y < 0)` the same as `(x > 0 || (x < 10 && y < 0))`?

3.18 Confirmation Dialogs

You can use a confirmation dialog to obtain a confirmation from the user.

You have used `showMessageDialog` to display a message dialog box and `showInputDialog` to display an input dialog box. Occasionally it is useful to answer a question with a confirmation dialog box. A confirmation dialog can be created using the following statement:

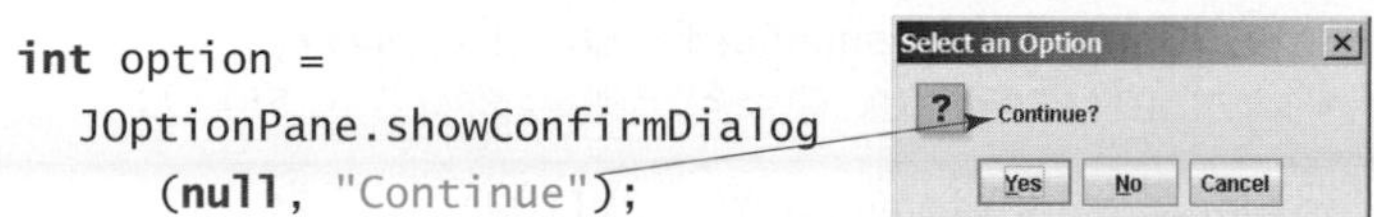

```
int option =
  JOptionPane.showConfirmDialog
    (null, "Continue");
```


When a button is clicked, the method returns an option value. The value is `JOptionPane.YES_OPTION` (0) for the *Yes* button, `JOptionPane.NO_OPTION` (1) for the *No* button, and `JOptionPane.CANCEL_OPTION` (2) for the *Cancel* button.

You may rewrite the guess-birthday program in Listing 3.3 using confirmation dialog boxes, as shown in Listing 3.11. Figure 3.8 shows a sample run of the program for the day 19.

LISTING 3.11 GuessBirthdayUsingConfirmationDialog.java

```
import javax.swing.JOptionPane;                                  // import class

public class GuessBirthdayUsingConfirmationDialog {
  public static void main(String[] args) {
    String set1 =                                                // set1
      " 1  3  5  7\n" +
      " 9 11 13 15\n" +
      "17 19 21 23\n" +
      "25 27 29 31";

    String set2 =                                                // set2
      " 2  3  6  7\n" +
      "10 11 14 15\n" +
      "18 19 22 23\n" +
      "26 27 30 31";

```

set3

```
17    String set3 =
18      " 4  5  6  7\n" +
19      "12 13 14 15\n" +
20      "20 21 22 23\n" +
21      "28 29 30 31";
22
```

set4

```
23    String set4 =
24      " 8  9 10 11\n" +
25      "12 13 14 15\n" +
26      "24 25 26 27\n" +
27      "28 29 30 31";
28
```

set5

```
29    String set5 =
30      "16 17 18 19\n" +
31      "20 21 22 23\n" +
32      "24 25 26 27\n" +
33      "28 29 30 31";
34
35    int day = 0;
36
37    // Prompt the user to answer questions
```

confirmation dialog

```
38    int answer = JOptionPane.showConfirmDialog(null,
39      "Is your birthday in these numbers?\n" + set1);
40
```

in set1?

```
41    if (answer == JOptionPane.YES_OPTION)
42      day += 1;
43
44    answer = JOptionPane.showConfirmDialog(null,
45      "Is your birthday in these numbers?\n" + set2);
46
```

in set2?

```
47    if (answer == JOptionPane.YES_OPTION)
48      day += 2;
49
50    answer = JOptionPane.showConfirmDialog(null,
51      "Is your birthday in these numbers?\n" + set3);
52
```

in set3?

```
53    if (answer == JOptionPane.YES_OPTION)
54      day += 4;
55
56    answer = JOptionPane.showConfirmDialog(null,
57      "Is your birthday in these numbers?\n" + set4);
58
```

in set4?

```
59    if (answer == JOptionPane.YES_OPTION)
60      day += 8;
61
62    answer = JOptionPane.showConfirmDialog(null,
63      "Is your birthday in these numbers?\n" + set5);
64
```

in set5?

```
65    if (answer == JOptionPane.YES_OPTION)
66      day += 16;
67
68    JOptionPane.showMessageDialog(null, "Your birthday is " +
69      day + "!");
70  }
71 }
```

The program displays confirmation dialog boxes to prompt the user to answer whether a number is in Set1 (line 38), Set2 (line 44), Set3 (line 50), Set4 (line 56), and Set5 (line 62). If the answer is Yes, the first number in the set is added to **day** (lines 42, 48, 54, 60, and 66).

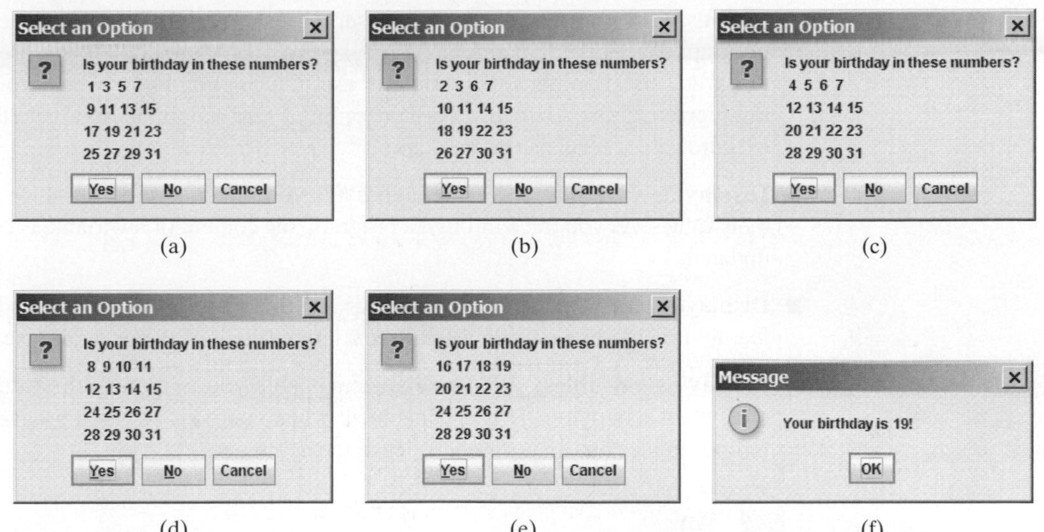

FIGURE 3.8 Click Yes in (a), Yes in (b), No in (c), No in (d), and Yes in (e).

3.43 How do you display a confirmation dialog? What value is returned when invoking `JOptionPane.showConfirmDialog`?

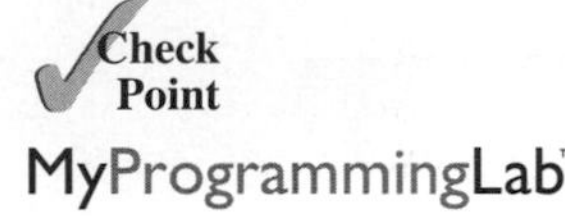

3.19 Debugging

Debugging is the process of finding and fixing errors in a program.

As mentioned in Section 1.11,1, syntax errors are easy to find and easy to correct because the compiler gives indications as to where the errors came from and why they are there. Runtime errors are not difficult to find either, because the Java interpreter displays them on the console when the program aborts. Finding logic errors, on the other hand, can be very challenging.

Logic errors are called *bugs*. The process of finding and correcting errors is called *debugging*. A common approach to debugging is to use a combination of methods to help pinpoint the part of the program where the bug is located. You can *hand-trace* the program (i.e., catch errors by reading the program), or you can insert print statements in order to show the values of the variables or the execution flow of the program. These approaches might work for debugging a short, simple program, but for a large, complex program, the most effective approach is to use a debugger utility.

bugs
debugging
hand-traces

JDK includes a command-line debugger, jdb, which is invoked with a class name. jdb is itself a Java program, running its own copy of Java interpreter. All the Java IDE tools, such as Eclipse and NetBeans, include integrated debuggers. The debugger utilities let you follow the execution of a program. They vary from one system to another, but they all support most of the following helpful features.

- **Executing a single statement at a time:** The debugger allows you to execute one statement at a time so that you can see the effect of each statement.

- **Tracing into or stepping over a method:** If a method is being executed, you can ask the debugger to enter the method and execute one statement at a time in the method, or you can ask it to step over the entire method. You should step over the entire method if you know that the method works. For example, always step over system-supplied methods, such as `System.out.println`.

- **Setting breakpoints:** You can also set a breakpoint at a specific statement. Your program pauses when it reaches a breakpoint. You can set as many breakpoints as you want. Breakpoints are particularly useful when you know where your programming error starts. You can set a breakpoint at that statement and have the program execute until it reaches the breakpoint.
- **Displaying variables:** The debugger lets you select several variables and display their values. As you trace through a program, the content of a variable is continuously updated.
- **Displaying call stacks:** The debugger lets you trace all of the method calls. This feature is helpful when you need to see a large picture of the program-execution flow.
- **Modifying variables:** Some debuggers enable you to modify the value of a variable when debugging. This is convenient when you want to test a program with different samples but do not want to leave the debugger.

Tip

debugging in IDE

If you use an IDE such as Eclipse or NetBeans, please refer to *Learning Java Effectively with Eclipse/NetBeans* in Supplements II.C and II.E on the Companion Website. The supplement shows you how to use a debugger to trace programs and how debugging can help in learning Java effectively.

Key Terms

Boolean expression 82
`boolean` data type 82
Boolean value 82
conditional operator 104
dangling else ambiguity 94
debugging 119
fall-through behavior 109
flowchart 84
format specifier 113
operator associativity 116
operator precedence 116
selection statement 82
short-circuit operator 104

Chapter Summary

1. A `boolean` type variable can store a `true` or `false` value.
2. The relational operators (<, <=, ==, !=, >, >=) work with numbers and characters, and yield a Boolean value.
3. The Boolean operators &&, ||, !, and ^ operate with Boolean values and variables.
4. When evaluating `p1 && p2`, Java first evaluates `p1` and then evaluates `p2` if `p1` is `true`; if `p1` is `false`, it does not evaluate `p2`. When evaluating `p1 || p2`, Java first evaluates `p1` and then evaluates `p2` if `p1` is `false`; if `p1` is `true`, it does not evaluate `p2`. Therefore, && is referred to as the *conditional* or *short-circuit AND operator*, and || is referred to as the *conditional* or *short-circuit OR operator*.
5. *Selection statements* are used for programming with alternative courses of actions. There are several types of selection statements: `if` statements, two-way `if-else` statements, nested `if` statements, multi-way `if-else` statements, `switch` statements, and conditional expressions.

6. The various `if` statements all make control decisions based on a *Boolean expression*. Based on the `true` or `false` evaluation of the expression, these statements take one of two possible courses.

7. The `switch` statement makes control decisions based on a switch expression of type `char`, `byte`, `short`, `int`, or `String`.

8. The keyword `break` is optional in a `switch` statement, but it is normally used at the end of each case in order to skip the remainder of the `switch` statement. If the `break` statement is not present, the next `case` statement will be executed.

9. The operators in expressions are evaluated in the order determined by the rules of parentheses, *operator precedence*, and *operator associativity*.

10. Parentheses can be used to force the order of evaluation to occur in any sequence.

11. Operators with higher precedence are evaluated earlier. For operators of the same precedence, their associativity determines the order of evaluation.

12. All binary operators except assignment operators are left-associative; assignment operators are right-associative.

Test Questions

Do the test questions for this chapter online at www.cs.armstrong.edu/liang/intro9e/test.html.

Programming Exercises

MyProgrammingLab™

Pedagogical Note

For each exercise, carefully analyze the problem requirements and design strategies for solving the problem before coding.

think before coding

Debugging Tip

Before you ask for help, read and explain the program to yourself, and trace it using several representative inputs by hand or using an IDE debugger. You learn how to program by debugging your own mistakes.

learn from mistakes

Section 3.2

*3.1 (*Algebra: solve quadratic equations*) The two roots of a quadratic equation $ax^2 + bx + c = 0$ can be obtained using the following formula:

$$r_1 = \frac{-b + \sqrt{b^2 - 4ac}}{2a} \quad \text{and} \quad r_2 = \frac{-b - \sqrt{b^2 - 4ac}}{2a}$$

$b^2 - 4ac$ is called the discriminant of the quadratic equation. If it is positive, the equation has two real roots. If it is zero, the equation has one root. If it is negative, the equation has no real roots.

Write a program that prompts the user to enter values for a, b, and c and displays the result based on the discriminant. If the discriminant is positive, display two roots. If the discriminant is `0`, display one root. Otherwise, display "The equation has no real roots".

Note that you can use `Math.pow(x, 0.5)` to compute $\sqrt{x}$. Here are some sample runs.

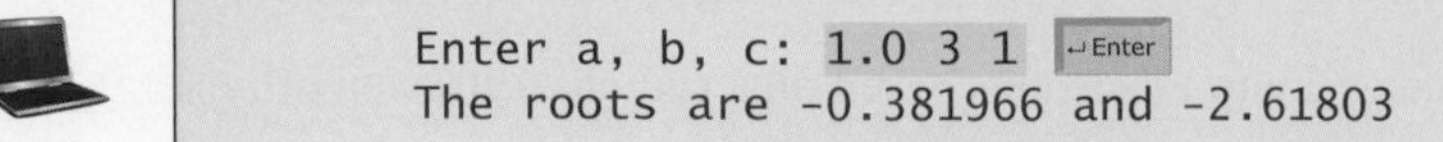

```
Enter a, b, c: 1.0 3 1
The roots are -0.381966 and -2.61803
```

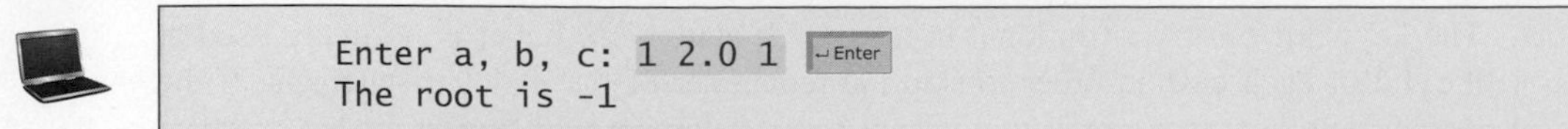

```
Enter a, b, c: 1 2.0 1
The root is -1
```

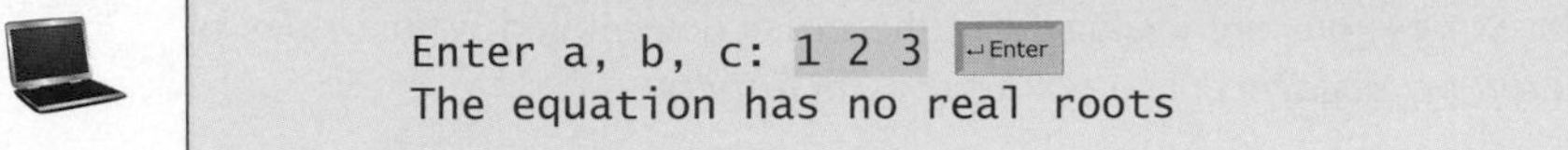

```
Enter a, b, c: 1 2 3
The equation has no real roots
```

3.2 (*Game: add three numbers*) The program in Listing 3.1 generates two integers and prompts the user to enter the sum of these two integers. Revise the program to generate three single-digit integers and prompt the user to enter the sum of these three integers.

Sections 3.3–3.8

***3.3** (*Algebra: solve* 2×2 *linear equations*) You can use Cramer's rule to solve the following 2×2 system of linear equation:

$$\begin{matrix} ax + by = e \\ cx + dy = f \end{matrix} \qquad x = \frac{ed - bf}{ad - bc} \qquad y = \frac{af - ec}{ad - bc}$$

Write a program that prompts the user to enter a, b, c, d, e, and f and displays the result. If $ad - bc$ is `0`, report that "The equation has no solution".

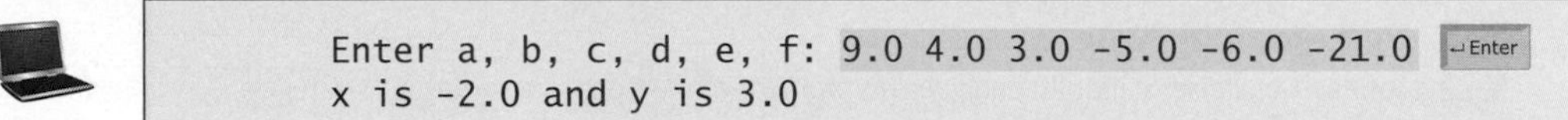

```
Enter a, b, c, d, e, f: 9.0 4.0 3.0 -5.0 -6.0 -21.0
x is -2.0 and y is 3.0
```

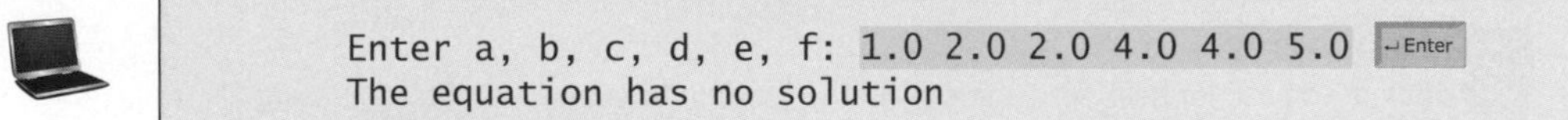

```
Enter a, b, c, d, e, f: 1.0 2.0 2.0 4.0 4.0 5.0
The equation has no solution
```

****3.4** (*Game: learn addition*) Write a program that generates two integers under 100 and prompts the user to enter the sum of these two integers. The program then reports true if the answer is correct, false otherwise. The program is similar to Listing 3.1.

***3.5** (*Find future dates*) Write a program that prompts the user to enter an integer for today's day of the week (Sunday is 0, Monday is 1, . . ., and Saturday is 6). Also prompt the user to enter the number of days after today for a future day and display the future day of the week. Here is a sample run:

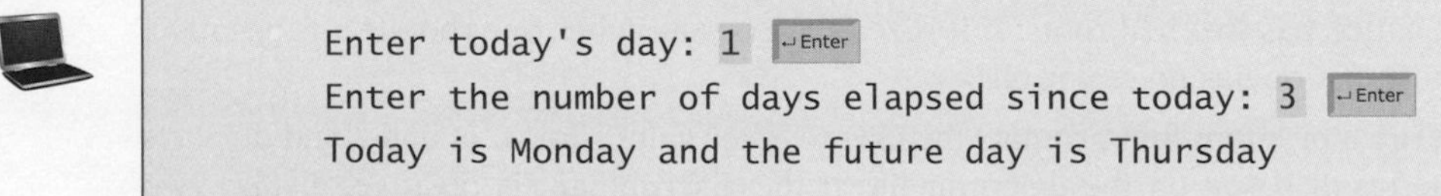

```
Enter today's day: 1
Enter the number of days elapsed since today: 3
Today is Monday and the future day is Thursday
```

```
Enter today's day: 0 ↵Enter
Enter the number of days elapsed since today: 31 ↵Enter
Today is Sunday and the future day is Wednesday
```

***3.6** (*Health application: BMI*) Revise Listing 3.5, ComputeAndInterpretBMI.java, to let the user enter weight, feet, and inches. For example, if a person is 5 feet and 10 inches, you will enter 5 for feet and 10 for inches. Here is a sample run:

```
Enter weight in pounds: 140 ↵Enter
Enter feet: 5 ↵Enter
Enter inches: 10 ↵Enter
BMI is 20.087702275404553
Normal
```

3.7 (*Financial application: monetary units*) Modify Listing 2.10, ComputeChange.java, to display the nonzero denominations only, using singular words for single units such as 1 dollar and 1 penny, and plural words for more than one unit such as 2 dollars and 3 pennies.

VideoNote
Sort three integers

***3.8** (*Sort three integers*) Write a program that sorts three integers. The integers are entered from the input dialogs and stored in variables `num1`, `num2`, and `num3`, respectively. The program sorts the numbers so that $num1 \leq num2 \leq num3$.

****3.9** (*Business: check ISBN-10*) An **ISBN-10** (International Standard Book Number) consists of 10 digits: $d_1d_2d_3d_4d_5d_6d_7d_8d_9d_{10}$. The last digit, d_{10}, is a checksum, which is calculated from the other nine digits using the following formula:

$$(d_1 \times 1 + d_2 \times 2 + d_3 \times 3 + d_4 \times 4 + d_5 \times 5 + \\ d_6 \times 6 + d_7 \times 7 + d_8 \times 8 + d_9 \times 9) \% 11$$

If the checksum is 10, the last digit is denoted as X according to the ISBN-10 convention. Write a program that prompts the user to enter the first 9 digits and displays the 10-digit ISBN (including leading zeros). Your program should read the input as an integer. Here are sample runs:

```
Enter the first 9 digits of an ISBN as integer: 013601267 ↵Enter
The ISBN-10 number is 0136012671
```

```
Enter the first 9 digits of an ISBN as integer: 013031997 ↵Enter
The ISBN-10 number is 013031997X
```

3.10 (*Game: addition quiz*) Listing 3.4, SubtractionQuiz.java, randomly generates a subtraction question. Revise the program to randomly generate an addition question with two integers less than 100.

Sections 3.9–3.19

***3.11** (*Find the number of days in a month*) Write a program that prompts the user to enter the month and year and displays the number of days in the month. For example, if the user entered month 2 and year 2012, the program should display that February 2012 had 29 days. If the user entered month 3 and year 2015, the program should display that March 2015 had 31 days.

3.12 (*Check a number*) Write a program that prompts the user to enter an integer and checks whether the number is divisible by both 5 and 6, or neither of them, or just one of them. Here are some sample runs for inputs 10, 30, and 23.

```
10 is divisible by 5 or 6, but not both
30 is divisible by both 5 and 6
23 is not divisible by either 5 or 6
```

***3.13** (*Financial application: compute taxes*) Listing 3.6, ComputeTax.java, gives the source code to compute taxes for single filers. Complete Listing 3.6 to give the complete source code.

3.14 (*Game: heads or tails*) Write a program that lets the user guess whether the flip of a coin results in heads or tails. The program randomly generates an integer 0 or 1, which represents head or tail. The program prompts the user to enter a guess and reports whether the guess is correct or incorrect.

****3.15** (*Game: lottery*) Revise Listing 3.9, Lottery.java, to generate a lottery of a three-digit number. The program prompts the user to enter a three-digit number and determines whether the user wins according to the following rules:

1. If the user input matches the lottery number in the exact order, the award is $10,000.
2. If all the digits in the user input match all the digits in the lottery number, the award is $3,000.
3. If one digit in the user input matches a digit in the lottery number, the award is $1,000.

3.16 (*Random character*) Write a program that displays a random uppercase letter using the `Math.random()` method.

***3.17** (*Game: scissor, rock, paper*) Write a program that plays the popular scissor-rock-paper game. (A scissor can cut a paper, a rock can knock a scissor, and a paper can wrap a rock.) The program randomly generates a number 0, 1, or 2 representing scissor, rock, and paper. The program prompts the user to enter a number 0, 1, or 2 and displays a message indicating whether the user or the computer wins, loses, or draws. Here are sample runs:

```
scissor (0), rock (1), paper (2): 1 ↵Enter
The computer is scissor. You are rock. You won
```

```
scissor (0), rock (1), paper (2): 2 ↵Enter
The computer is paper. You are paper too. It is a draw
```

***3.18** (*Use the input dialog box*) Rewrite Listing 3.8, LeapYear.java, using the input dialog box.

****3.19** (*Compute the perimeter of a triangle*) Write a program that reads three edges for a triangle and computes the perimeter if the input is valid. Otherwise, display that the input is invalid. The input is valid if the sum of every pair of two edges is greater than the remaining edge.

*3.20 (*Science: wind-chill temperature*) Programming Exercise 2.17 gives a formula to compute the wind-chill temperature. The formula is valid for temperatures in the range between −58ºF and 41ºF and wind speed greater than or equal to 2. Write a program that prompts the user to enter a temperature and a wind speed. The program displays the wind-chill temperature if the input is valid; otherwise, it displays a message indicating whether the temperature and/or wind speed is invalid.

Comprehensive

**3.21 (*Science: day of the week*) Zeller's congruence is an algorithm developed by Christian Zeller to calculate the day of the week. The formula is

$$h = \left(q + \frac{26(m + 1)}{10} + k + \frac{k}{4} + \frac{j}{4} + 5j\right) \% 7$$

where

- h is the day of the week (0: Saturday, 1: Sunday, 2: Monday, 3: Tuesday, 4: Wednesday, 5: Thursday, 6: Friday).
- q is the day of the month.
- m is the month (3: March, 4: April, . . ., 12: December). January and February are counted as months 13 and 14 of the previous year.
- j is the century (i.e., $\frac{year}{100}$).
- k is the year of the century (i.e., *year* % 100).

Note that the division in the formula performs an integer division. Write a program that prompts the user to enter a year, month, and day of the month, and displays the name of the day of the week. Here are some sample runs:

```
Enter year: (e.g., 2012): 2015 ↵Enter
Enter month: 1-12: 1 ↵Enter
Enter the day of the month: 1-31: 25 ↵Enter
Day of the week is Sunday
```

```
Enter year: (e.g., 2012): 2012 ↵Enter
Enter month: 1-12: 5 ↵Enter
Enter the day of the month: 1-31: 12 ↵Enter
Day of the week is Saturday
```

(*Hint*: January and February are counted as 13 and 14 in the formula, so you need to convert the user input 1 to 13 and 2 to 14 for the month and change the year to the previous year.)

VideoNote
Check point location

**3.22 (*Geometry: point in a circle?*) Write a program that prompts the user to enter a point (x, y) and checks whether the point is within the circle centered at (0, 0) with radius 10. For example, (4, 5) is inside the circle and (9, 9) is outside the circle, as shown in Figure 3.9a.

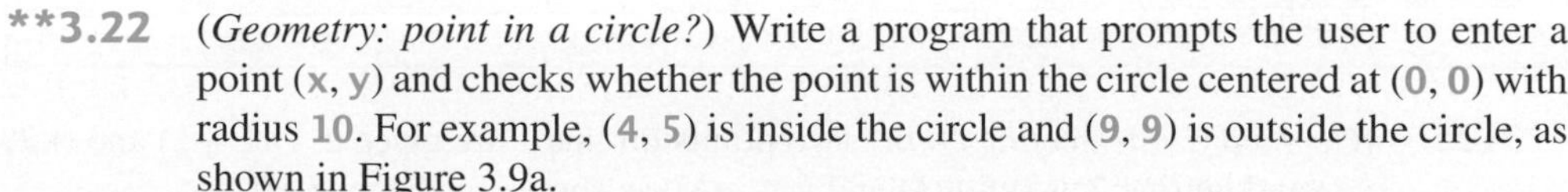

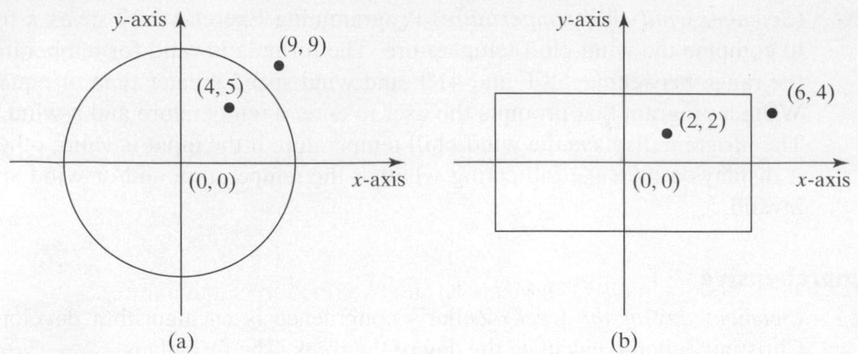

FIGURE 3.9 (a) Points inside and outside of the circle. (b) Points inside and outside of the rectangle.

(*Hint*: A point is in the circle if its distance to (**0**, **0**) is less than or equal to **10**. The formula for computing the distance is $\sqrt{(x_2 - x_1)^2 + (y_2 - y_1)^2}$. Test your program to cover all cases.) Two sample runs are shown below.

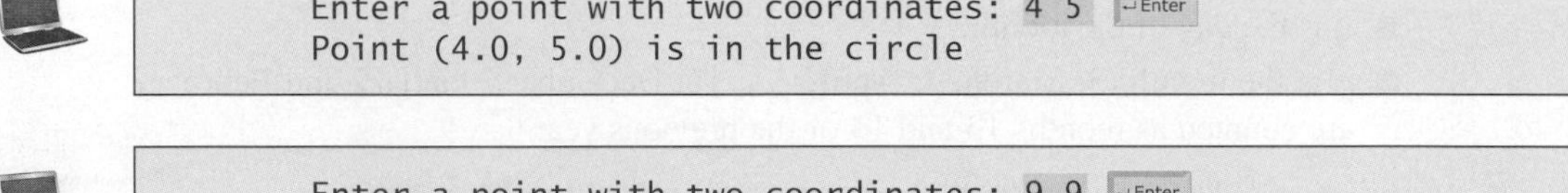

```
Enter a point with two coordinates: 4 5 [Enter]
Point (4.0, 5.0) is in the circle
```

```
Enter a point with two coordinates: 9 9 [Enter]
Point (9.0, 9.0) is not in the circle
```

****3.23** (*Geometry: point in a rectangle?*) Write a program that prompts the user to enter a point **(x, y)** and checks whether the point is within the rectangle centered at (**0**, **0**) with width **10** and height **5**. For example, (**2**, **2**) is inside the rectangle and (**6**, **4**) is outside the rectangle, as shown in Figure 3.9b. (*Hint*: A point is in the rectangle if its horizontal distance to (**0**, **0**) is less than or equal to **10 / 2** and its vertical distance to (**0**, **0**) is less than or equal to **5.0 / 2**. Test your program to cover all cases.) Here are two sample runs.

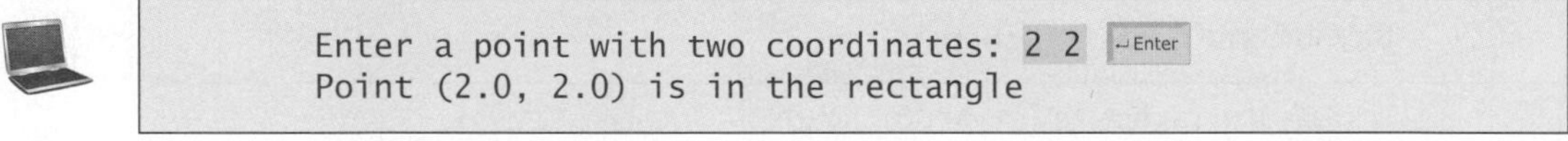

```
Enter a point with two coordinates: 2 2 [Enter]
Point (2.0, 2.0) is in the rectangle
```

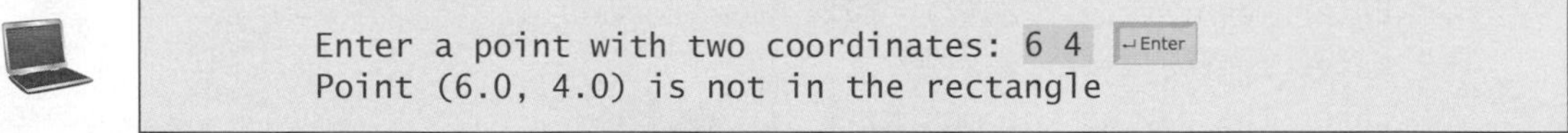

```
Enter a point with two coordinates: 6 4 [Enter]
Point (6.0, 4.0) is not in the rectangle
```

****3.24** (*Game: pick a card*) Write a program that simulates picking a card from a deck of **52** cards. Your program should display the rank (**Ace**, **2**, **3**, **4**, **5**, **6**, **7**, **8**, **9**, **10**, **Jack**, **Queen**, **King**) and suit (**Clubs**, **Diamonds**, **Hearts**, **Spades**) of the card Here is a sample run of the program:

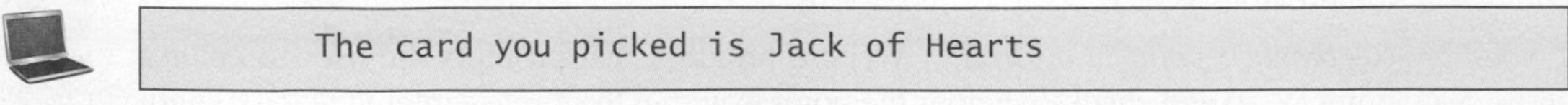

```
The card you picked is Jack of Hearts
```

***3.25** (*Geometry: intersecting point*) Two points on line 1 are given as (**x1**, **y1**) and (**x2**, **y2**) and on line 2 as (**x3**, **y3**) and (**x4**, **y4**), as shown in Figure 3.10a–b.

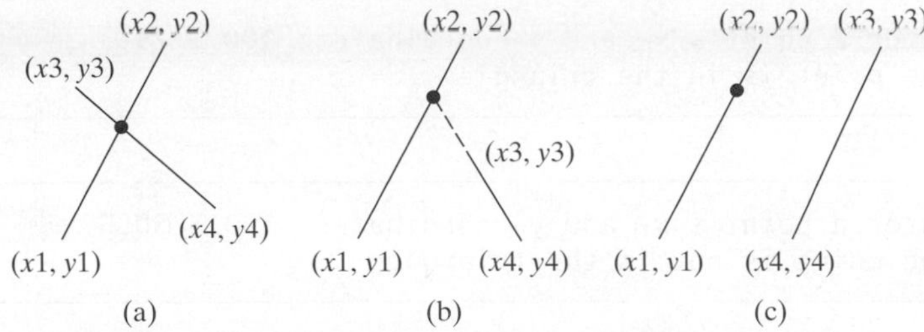

FIGURE 3.10 Two lines intersect in (a and b) and two lines are parallel in (c).

The intersecting point of the two lines can be found by solving the following linear equation:

$$(y_1 - y_2)x - (x_1 - x_2)y = (y_1 - y_2)x_1 - (x_1 - x_2)y_1$$

$$(y_3 - y_4)x - (x_3 - x_4)y = (y_3 - y_4)x_3 - (x_3 - x_4)y_3$$

This linear equation can be solved using Cramer's rule (see Exercise 3.3). If the equation has no solutions, the two lines are parallel (Figure 3.10c). Write a program that prompts the user to enter four points and displays the intersecting point. Here are sample runs:

```
Enter x1, y1, x2, y2, x3, y3, x4, y4: 2 2 5 -1.0 4.0 2.0 -1.0 -2.0 ↵Enter
The intersecting point is at (2.88889, 1.1111)
```

```
Enter x1, y1, x2, y2, x3, y3, x4, y4: 2 2 7 6.0 4.0 2.0 -1.0 -2.0 ↵Enter
The two lines are parallel
```

3.26 (*Use the &&, || and ^ operators*) Write a program that prompts the user to enter an integer and determines whether it is divisible by 5 and 6, whether it is divisible by 5 or 6, and whether it is divisible by 5 or 6, but not both. Here is a sample run of this program:

```
Enter an integer: 10 ↵Enter
Is 10 divisible by 5 and 6? false
Is 10 divisible by 5 or 6? true
Is 10 divisible by 5 or 6, but not both? true
```

****3.27** (*Geometry: points in triangle?*) Suppose a right triangle is placed in a plane as shown below. The right-angle point is placed at (0, 0), and the other two points are placed at (200, 0), and (0, 100). Write a program that prompts the user to enter a point with x- and y-coordinates and determines whether the point is inside the triangle. Here are the sample runs:

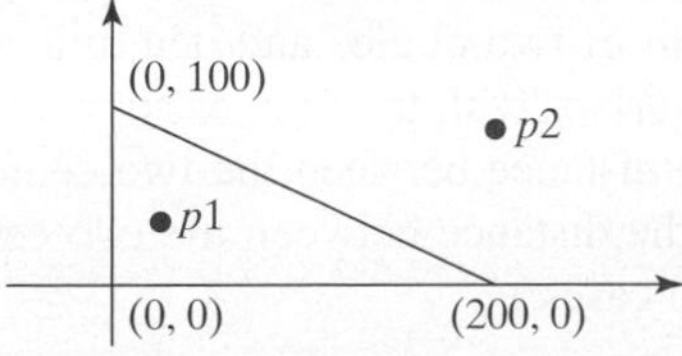

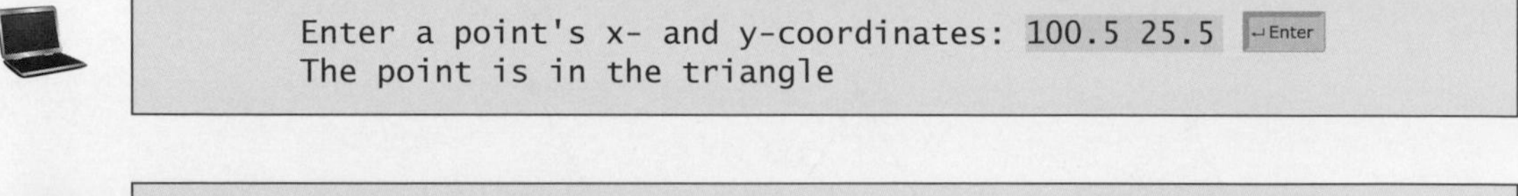

```
Enter a point's x- and y-coordinates: 100.5 25.5 ↵Enter
The point is in the triangle
```

```
Enter a point's x- and y-coordinates: 100.5 50.5 ↵Enter
The point is not in the triangle
```

****3.28** (*Geometry: two rectangles*) Write a program that prompts the user to enter the center x-, y-coordinates, width, and height of two rectangles and determines whether the second rectangle is inside the first or overlaps with the first, as shown in Figure 3.11. Test your program to cover all cases.

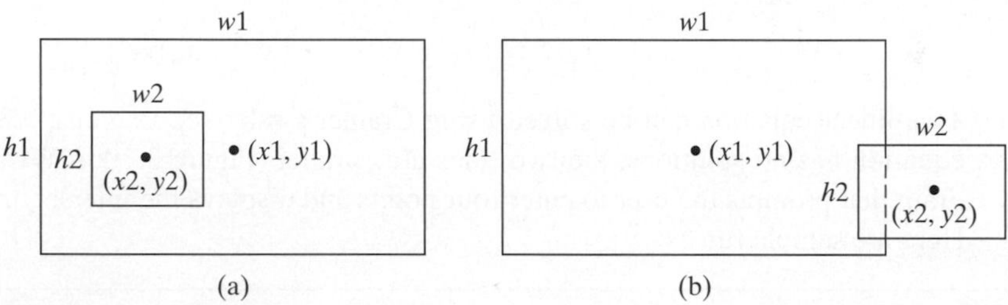

FIGURE 3.11 (a) A rectangle is inside another one. (b) A rectangle overlaps another one.

Here are the sample runs:

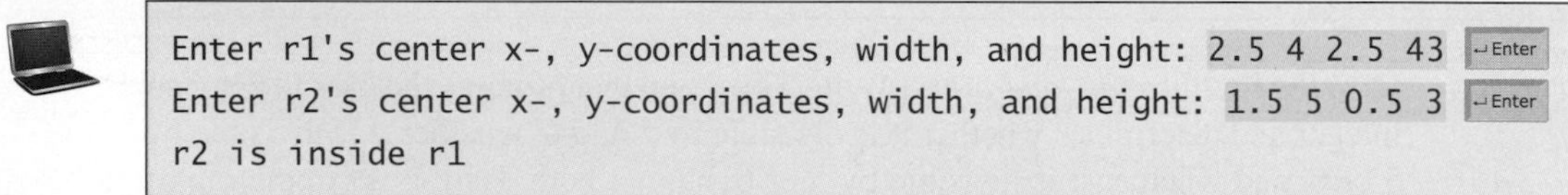

```
Enter r1's center x-, y-coordinates, width, and height: 2.5 4 2.5 43 ↵Enter
Enter r2's center x-, y-coordinates, width, and height: 1.5 5 0.5 3 ↵Enter
r2 is inside r1
```

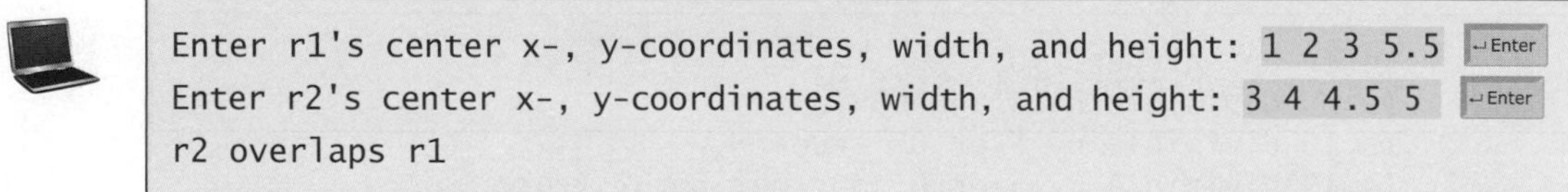

```
Enter r1's center x-, y-coordinates, width, and height: 1 2 3 5.5 ↵Enter
Enter r2's center x-, y-coordinates, width, and height: 3 4 4.5 5 ↵Enter
r2 overlaps r1
```

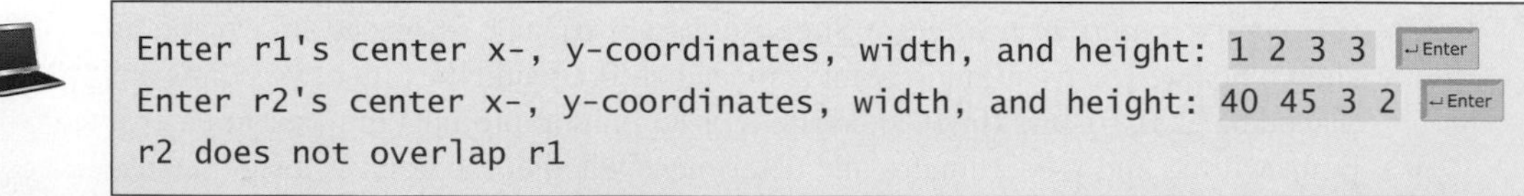

```
Enter r1's center x-, y-coordinates, width, and height: 1 2 3 3 ↵Enter
Enter r2's center x-, y-coordinates, width, and height: 40 45 3 2 ↵Enter
r2 does not overlap r1
```

****3.29** (*Geometry: two circles*) Write a program that prompts the user to enter the center coordinates and radii of two circles and determines whether the second circle is inside the first or overlaps with the first, as shown in Figure 3.12. (*Hint*: circle2 is inside circle1 if the distance between the two centers <= |`r1 - r2`| and circle2 overlaps circle1 if the distance between the two centers <= `r1 + r2`. Test your program to cover all cases.)

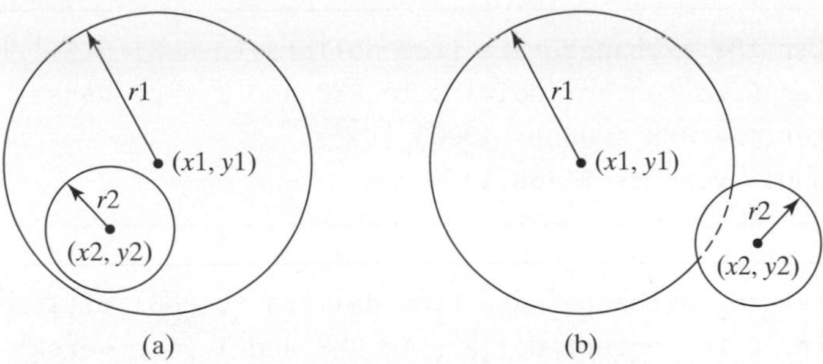

FIGURE 3.12 (a) A circle is inside another circle. (b) A circle overlaps another circle.

Here are the sample runs:

```
Enter circle1's center x-, y-coordinates, and radius: 0.5 5.1 13 [Enter]
Enter circle2's center x-, y-coordinates, and radius: 1 1.7 4.5 [Enter]
circle2 is inside circle1
```

```
Enter circle1's center x-, y-coordinates, and radius: 3.4 5.7 5.5 [Enter]
Enter circle2's center x-, y-coordinates, and radius: 6.7 3.5 3 [Enter]
circle2 overlaps circle1
```

```
Enter circle1's center x-, y-coordinates, and radius: 3.4 5.5 1 [Enter]
Enter circle2's center x-, y-coordinates, and radius: 5.5 7.2 1 [Enter]
circle2 does not overlap circle1
```

***3.30** (*Current time*) Revise Programming Exercise 2.8 to display the hour using a 12-hour clock. Here is a sample run:

```
Enter the time zone offset to GMT: -5 [Enter]
The current time is 4:50:34 AM
```

***3.31** (*Financials: currency exchange*) Write a program that prompts the user to enter the exchange rate from currency in U.S. dollars to Chinese RMB. Prompt the user to enter 0 to convert from U.S. dollars to Chinese RMB and 1 to convert from Chinese RMB and U.S. dollars. Prompt the user to enter the amount in U.S. dollars or Chinese RMB to convert it to Chinese RMB or U.S. dollars, respectively. Here are the sample runs:

```
Enter the exchange rate from dollars to RMB: 6.81 [Enter]
Enter 0 to convert dollars to RMB and 1 vice versa: 0 [Enter]
Enter the dollar amount: 100 [Enter]
$100.0 is 681.0 yuan
```

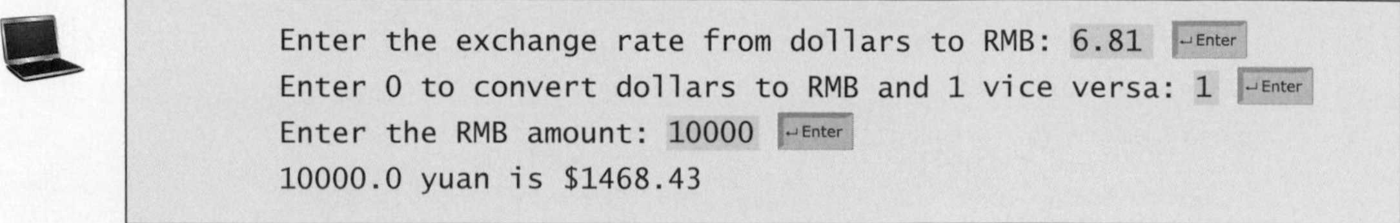

```
Enter the exchange rate from dollars to RMB: 6.81 ↵Enter
Enter 0 to convert dollars to RMB and 1 vice versa: 1 ↵Enter
Enter the RMB amount: 10000 ↵Enter
10000.0 yuan is $1468.43
```

```
Enter the exchange rate from dollars to RMB: 6.81 ↵Enter
Enter 0 to convert dollars to RMB and 1 vice versa: 5 ↵Enter
Incorrect input
```

***3.32** (*Geometry: point position*) Given a directed line from point p0(x0, y0) to p1(x1, y1), you can use the following condition to decide whether a point p2(x2, y2) is on the left of the line, on the right, or on the same line (see Figure 3.13):

$$(x1 - x0)*(y2 - y0) - (x2 - x0)*(y1 - y0) \begin{cases} >0 \text{ p2 is on the left side of the line} \\ =0 \text{ p2 is on the same line} \\ <0 \text{ p2 is on the right side of the line} \end{cases}$$

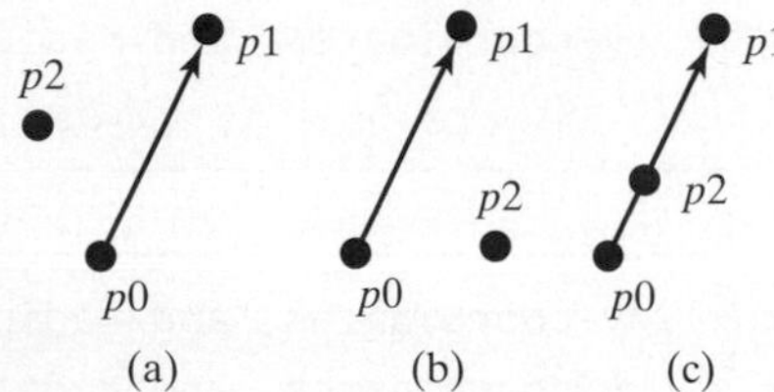

FIGURE 3.13 (a) p2 is on the left of the line. (b) p2 is on the right of the line. (c) p2 is on the same line.

Write a program that prompts the user to enter the three points for p0, p1, and p2 and displays whether p2 is on the left of the line from p0 to p1, to the right, or on the same line. Here are some sample runs:

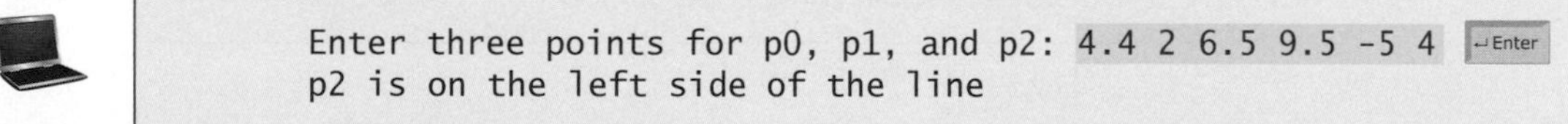

```
Enter three points for p0, p1, and p2: 4.4 2 6.5 9.5 -5 4 ↵Enter
p2 is on the left side of the line
```

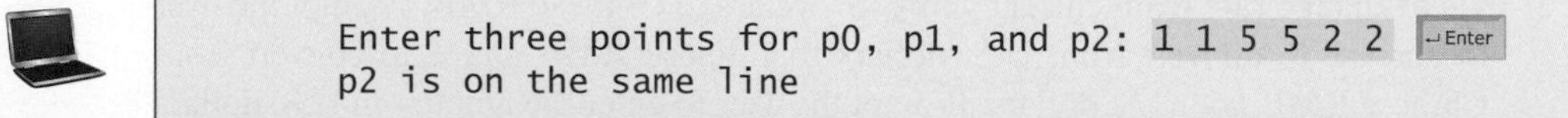

```
Enter three points for p0, p1, and p2: 1 1 5 5 2 2 ↵Enter
p2 is on the same line
```

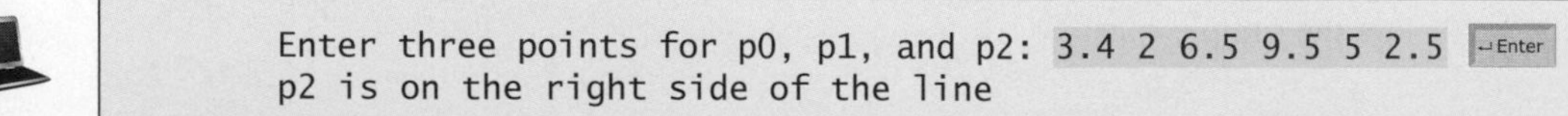

```
Enter three points for p0, p1, and p2: 3.4 2 6.5 9.5 5 2.5 ↵Enter
p2 is on the right side of the line
```

***3.33** (*Financial: compare costs*) Suppose you shop for rice in two different packages. You would like to write a program to compare the cost. The program prompts the user to enter the weight and price of the each package and displays the one with the better price. Here is a sample run:

```
Enter weight and price for package 1: 50 24.59 ↵Enter
Enter weight and price for package 2: 25 11.99 ↵Enter
Package 2 has a better price.
```

***3.34** (*Geometry: point on line segment*) Exercise 3.32 shows how to test whether a point is on an unbounded line. Revise Exercise 3.32 to test whether a point is on a line segment. Write a program that prompts the user to enter the three points for p0, p1, and p2 and displays whether p2 is on the line segment from p0 to p1. Here are some sample runs:

```
Enter three points for p0, p1, and p2: 1 1 2.5 2.5 1.5 1.5 ↵Enter
(1.5, 1.5) is on the line segment from (1.0, 1.0) to (2.5, 2.5)
```

```
Enter three points for p0, p1, and p2: 1 1 2 2 3.5 3.5 ↵Enter
(3.5, 3.5) is not on the line segment from (1.0, 1.0) to (2.0, 2.0)
```

***3.35** (*Decimal to hex*) Write a program that prompts the user to enter an integer between 0 and 15 and displays its corresponding hex number. Here are some sample runs:

```
Enter a decimal value (0 to 15): 11 ↵Enter
The hex value is B
```

```
Enter a decimal value (0 to 15): 5 ↵Enter
The hex value is 5
```

```
Enter a decimal value (0 to 15): 31 ↵Enter
Invalid input
```

CHAPTER

4

Loops

Objectives

- To write programs for executing statements repeatedly using a `while` loop (§4.2).
- To follow the loop design strategy to develop loops (§§4.2.1–4.2.3).
- To control a loop with a sentinel value (§4.2.4).
- To obtain large input from a file using input redirection rather than typing from the keyboard (§4.2.5).
- To write loops using `do-while` statements (§4.3).
- To write loops using `for` statements (§4.4).
- To discover the similarities and differences of three types of loop statements (§4.5).
- To write nested loops (§4.6).
- To learn the techniques for minimizing numerical errors (§4.7).
- To learn loops from a variety of examples (`GCD`, `FutureTuition`, `MonteCarloSimulation`) (§4.8).
- To implement program control with `break` and `continue` (§4.9).
- To write a program that displays prime numbers (§4.10).
- To control a loop with a confirmation dialog (§4.11).

4.1 Introduction

A loop can be used to tell a program to execute statements repeatedly.

problem

Suppose that you need to display a string (e.g., `Welcome to Java!`) a hundred times. It would be tedious to have to write the following statement a hundred times:

```
            System.out.println("Welcome to Java!");
            System.out.println("Welcome to Java!");
100 times   ...
            System.out.println("Welcome to Java!");
```

So, how do you solve this problem?

loop

Java provides a powerful construct called a *loop* that controls how many times an operation or a sequence of operations is performed in succession. Using a loop statement, you simply tell the computer to display a string a hundred times without having to code the print statement a hundred times, as follows:

```
int count = 0;
while (count < 100) {
  System.out.println("Welcome to Java!");
  count++;
}
```

The variable `count` is initially `0`. The loop checks whether `count < 100` is `true`. If so, it executes the loop body to display the message `Welcome to Java!` and increments `count` by `1`. It repeatedly executes the loop body until `count < 100` becomes `false`. When `count < 100` is `false` (i.e., when `count` reaches `100`), the loop terminates and the next statement after the loop statement is executed.

Loops are constructs that control repeated executions of a block of statements. The concept of looping is fundamental to programming. Java provides three types of loop statements: `while` loops, `do-while` loops, and `for` loops.

4.2 The `while` Loop

A `while` loop executes statements repeatedly while the condition is true.

The syntax for the `while` loop is:

`while` loop

```
while (loop-continuation-condition) {
  // Loop body
  Statement(s);
}
```

loop body
iteration
`loop-continuation-condition`

Figure 4.1a shows the `while`-loop flowchart. The part of the loop that contains the statements to be repeated is called the *loop body.* A one-time execution of a loop body is referred to as an *iteration* (or *repetition) of the loop.* Each loop contains a *loop-continuation-condition,* a Boolean expression that controls the execution of the body. It is evaluated each time to determine if the loop body is executed. If its evaluation is `true`, the loop body is executed; if its evaluation is `false`, the entire loop terminates and the program control turns to the statement that follows the `while` loop.

The loop for displaying `Welcome to Java!` a hundred times introduced in the preceding section is an example of a `while` loop. Its flowchart is shown in Figure 4.1b. The

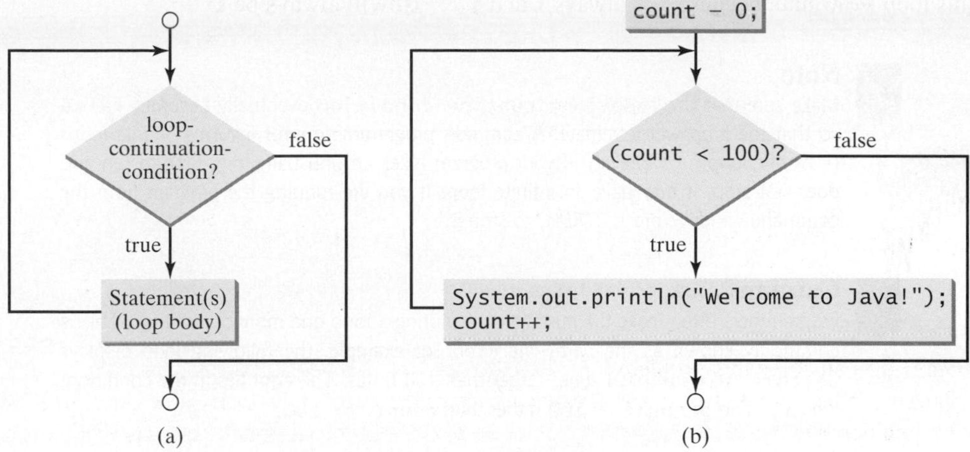

FIGURE 4.1 The `while` loop repeatedly executes the statements in the loop body when the `loop-continuation-condition` evaluates to `true`.

`loop-continuation-condition` is `count < 100` and the loop body contains the following two statements:

loop-continuation-condition

```
int count = 0;
while (count < 100) {
  System.out.println("Welcome to Java!");
  count++;
}
```

loop body

In this example, you know exactly how many times the loop body needs to be executed because the control variable `count` is used to count the number of executions. This type of loop is known as a *counter-controlled loop.*

counter-controlled loop

Note

The `loop-continuation-condition` must always appear inside the parentheses. The braces enclosing the loop body can be omitted only if the loop body contains one or no statement.

Here is another example to help understand how a loop works.

```
int sum = 0, i = 1;
while (i < 10) {
  sum = sum + i;
  i++;
}
System.out.println("sum is " + sum); // sum is 45
```

If `i < 10` is `true`, the program adds `i` to `sum`. Variable `i` is initially set to `1`, then is incremented to `2`, `3`, and up to `10`. When `i` is `10`, `i < 10` is `false`, so the loop exits. Therefore, the sum is `1 + 2 + 3 + ... + 9 = 45`.

What happens if the loop is mistakenly written as follows?

```
int sum = 0, i = 1;
while (i < 10) {
  sum = sum + i;
}
```

This loop is infinite, because `i` is always `1` and `i < 10` will always be `true`.

Note

infinite loop

Make sure that the `loop-continuation-condition` eventually becomes `false` so that the loop will terminate. A common programming error involves *infinite loops* (i. e., the loop runs forever). If your program takes an unusually long time to run and does not stop, it may have an infinite loop. If you are running the program from the command window, press *CTRL+C* to stop it.

Caution

off-by-one error

Programmers often make the mistake of executing a loop one more or less time. This is commonly known as the *off-by-one error.* For example, the following loop displays `Welcome to Java` 101 times rather than 100 times. The error lies in the condition, which should be `count < 100` rather than `count <= 100`.

```
int count = 0;
while (count <= 100) {
  System.out.println("Welcome to Java!");
  count++;
}
```

Recall that Listing 3.1, AdditionQuiz.java, gives a program that prompts the user to enter an answer for a question on addition of two single digits. Using a loop, you can now rewrite the program to let the user repeatedly enter a new answer until it is correct, as shown in Listing 4.1.

LISTING 4.1 RepeatAdditionQuiz.java

generate number1
generate number2
show question
get first answer
check answer
read an answer

```
import java.util.Scanner;

public class RepeatAdditionQuiz {
  public static void main(String[] args) {
    int number1 = (int)(Math.random() * 10);
    int number2 = (int)(Math.random() * 10);

    // Create a Scanner
    Scanner input = new Scanner(System.in);

    System.out.print(
      "What is " + number1 + " + " + number2 + "? ");
    int answer = input.nextInt();

    while (number1 + number2 != answer) {
      System.out.print("Wrong answer. Try again. What is "
        + number1 + " + " + number2 + "? ");
      answer = input.nextInt();
    }

    System.out.println("You got it!");
  }
}
```

```
What is 5 + 9? 12 ↵Enter
Wrong answer. Try again. What is 5 + 9? 34 ↵Enter
Wrong answer. Try again. What is 5 + 9? 14 ↵Enter
You got it!
```

The loop in lines 15–19 repeatedly prompts the user to enter an `answer` when `number1 + number2 != answer` is `true`. Once `number1 + number2 != answer` is `false`, the loop exits.

4.2.1 Case Study: Guessing Numbers

VideoNote
Guess a number

The problem is to guess what number a computer has in mind. You will write a program that randomly generates an integer between `0` and `100`, inclusive. The program prompts the user to enter a number continuously until the number matches the randomly generated number. For each user input, the program tells the user whether the input is too low or too high, so the user can make the next guess intelligently. Here is a sample run:

```
Guess a magic number between 0 and 100
Enter your guess: 50 ↵Enter
Your guess is too high
Enter your guess: 25 ↵Enter
Your guess is too low
Enter your guess: 42 ↵Enter
Your guess is too high
Enter your guess: 39 ↵Enter
Yes, the number is 39
```

intelligent guess

The magic number is between `0` and `100`. To minimize the number of guesses, enter `50` first. If your guess is too high, the magic number is between `0` and `49`. If your guess is too low, the magic number is between `51` and `100`. So, you can eliminate half of the numbers from further consideration after one guess.

think before coding

How do you write this program? Do you immediately begin coding? No. It is important to *think before coding*. Think how you would solve the problem without writing a program. You need first to generate a random number between `0` and `100`, inclusive, then to prompt the user to enter a guess, and then to compare the guess with the random number.

code incrementally

It is a good practice to *code incrementally* one step at a time. For programs involving loops, if you don't know how to write a loop right away, you may first write the code for executing the loop one time, and then figure out how to repeatedly execute the code in a loop. For this program, you may create an initial draft, as shown in Listing 4.2.

LISTING 4.2 GuessNumberOneTime.java

```
import java.util.Scanner;

public class GuessNumberOneTime {
  public static void main(String[] args) {
    // Generate a random number to be guessed
    int number = (int)(Math.random() * 101);              generate a number

    Scanner input = new Scanner(System.in);
    System.out.println("Guess a magic number between 0 and 100");

    // Prompt the user to guess the number
    System.out.print("\nEnter your guess: ");
    int guess = input.nextInt();                          enter a guess

    if (guess == number)
      System.out.println("Yes, the number is " + number);  correct guess?
    else if (guess > number)
      System.out.println("Your guess is too high");        too high?
    else
```

too low?

```
20        System.out.println("Your guess is too low");
21    }
22  }
```

When you run this program, it prompts the user to enter a guess only once. To let the user enter a guess repeatedly, you may put the code in lines 11–20 in a loop as follows:

```
while (true) {
  // Prompt the user to guess the number
  System.out.print("\nEnter your guess: ");
  guess = input.nextInt();

  if (guess == number)
    System.out.println("Yes, the number is " + number);
  else if (guess > number)
    System.out.println("Your guess is too high");
  else
    System.out.println("Your guess is too low");
} // End of loop
```

This loop repeatedly prompts the user to enter a guess. However, this loop is not correct, because it never terminates. When **guess** matches **number**, the loop should end. So, the loop can be revised as follows:

```
while (guess != number) {
  // Prompt the user to guess the number
  System.out.print("\nEnter your guess: ");
  guess = input.nextInt();

  if (guess == number)
    System.out.println("Yes, the number is " + number);
  else if (guess > number)
    System.out.println("Your guess is too high");
  else
    System.out.println("Your guess is too low");
} // End of loop
```

The complete code is given in Listing 4.3.

Listing 4.3 GuessNumber.java

generate a number

enter a guess

```
import java.util.Scanner;

public class GuessNumber {
  public static void main(String[] args) {
    // Generate a random number to be guessed
    int number = (int)(Math.random() * 101);

    Scanner input = new Scanner(System.in);
    System.out.println("Guess a magic number between 0 and 100");

    int guess = -1;
    while (guess != number) {
      // Prompt the user to guess the number
      System.out.print("\nEnter your guess: ");
      guess = input.nextInt();

      if (guess == number)
        System.out.println("Yes, the number is " + number);
      else if (guess > number)
```

```
20         System.out.println("Your guess is too high");
21       else
22         System.out.println("Your guess is too low");
23     } // End of loop
24   }
25 }
```

too high?

too low?

	line#	number	guess	output
	6	39		
	11		-1	
iteration 1	15		50	
	20			Your guess is too high
iteration 2	15		25	
	22			Your guess is too low
iteration 3	15		42	
	20			Your guess is too high
iteration 4	15		39	
	18			Yes, the number is 39

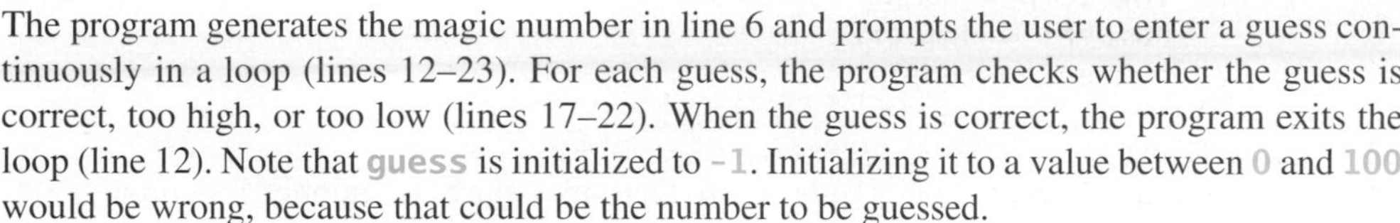

The program generates the magic number in line 6 and prompts the user to enter a guess continuously in a loop (lines 12–23). For each guess, the program checks whether the guess is correct, too high, or too low (lines 17–22). When the guess is correct, the program exits the loop (line 12). Note that `guess` is initialized to `-1`. Initializing it to a value between `0` and `100` would be wrong, because that could be the number to be guessed.

4.2.2 Loop Design Strategies

Writing a correct loop is not an easy task for novice programmers. Consider three steps when writing a loop.

Step 1: Identify the statements that need to be repeated.

Step 2: Wrap these statements in a loop like this:

```
while (true) {
  Statements;
}
```

Step 3: Code the `loop-continuation-condition` and add appropriate statements for controlling the loop.

```
while (loop-continuation-condition) {
  Statements;
  Additional statements for controlling the loop;
}
```

4.2.3 Case Study: Multiple Subtraction Quiz

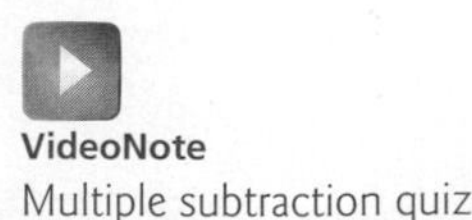

The Math subtraction learning tool program in Listing 3.4, SubtractionQuiz.java, generates just one question for each run. You can use a loop to generate questions repeatedly. How do you write the code to generate five questions? Follow the loop design strategy. First identify the statements that need to be repeated. These are the statements for obtaining two random numbers, prompting the user with a subtraction question, and grading the question. Second, wrap the statements in a loop. Third, add a loop control variable and the `loop-continuation-condition` to execute the loop five times.

Listing 4.4 gives a program that generates five questions and, after a student answers all five, reports the number of correct answers. The program also displays the time spent on the test and lists all the questions.

LISTING 4.4 SubtractionQuizLoop.java

```java
import java.util.Scanner;

public class SubtractionQuizLoop {
  public static void main(String[] args) {
    final int NUMBER_OF_QUESTIONS = 5; // Number of questions
    int correctCount = 0; // Count the number of correct answers
    int count = 0; // Count the number of questions
    long startTime = System.currentTimeMillis();
    String output = " "; // output string is initially empty
    Scanner input = new Scanner(System.in);

    while (count < NUMBER_OF_QUESTIONS) {
      // 1. Generate two random single-digit integers
      int number1 = (int)(Math.random() * 10);
      int number2 = (int)(Math.random() * 10);

      // 2. If number1 < number2, swap number1 with number2
      if (number1 < number2) {
        int temp = number1;
        number1 = number2;
        number2 = temp;
      }

      // 3. Prompt the student to answer "What is number1 - number2?"
      System.out.print(
        "What is " + number1 + " - " + number2 + "? ");
      int answer = input.nextInt();

      // 4. Grade the answer and display the result
      if (number1 - number2 == answer) {
        System.out.println("You are correct!");
        correctCount++; // Increase the correct answer count
      }
      else
        System.out.println("Your answer is wrong.\n" + number1
          + " - " + number2 + " should be " + (number1 - number2));

      // Increase the question count
      count++;

      output += "\n" + number1 + "-" + number2 + "=" + answer +
        ((number1 - number2 == answer) ? " correct" : " wrong");
    }

    long endTime = System.currentTimeMillis();
    long testTime = endTime - startTime;

    System.out.println("Correct count is " + correctCount +
      "\nTest time is " + testTime / 1000 + " seconds\n" + output);
  }
}
```

get start time

loop

display a question

grade an answer

increase correct count

increase control variable

prepare output

end loop

get end time

test time

display result

```
What is 9 - 2? 7 ↵Enter
You are correct!

What is 3 - 0? 3 ↵Enter
You are correct!

What is 3 - 2? 1 ↵Enter
You are correct!

What is 7 - 4? 4 ↵Enter
Your answer is wrong.

7 - 4 should be 3
What is 7 - 5? 4 ↵Enter

Your answer is wrong.
7 - 5 should be 2

Correct count is 3
Test time is 1021 seconds

9-2=7 correct
3-0=3 correct
3-2=1 correct
7-4=4 wrong
7-5=4 wrong
```

The program uses the control variable `count` to control the execution of the loop. `count` is initially `0` (line 7) and is increased by `1` in each iteration (line 39). A subtraction question is displayed and processed in each iteration. The program obtains the time before the test starts in line 8 and the time after the test ends in line 45, and computes the test time in line 46. The test time is in milliseconds and is converted to seconds in line 49.

4.2.4 Controlling a Loop with a Sentinel Value

Another common technique for controlling a loop is to designate a special value when reading and processing a set of values. This special input value, known as a *sentinel value*, signifies the end of the input. A loop that uses a sentinel value to control its execution is called a *sentinel-controlled loop*.

sentinel value

sentinel-controlled loop

Listing 4.5 writes a program that reads and calculates the sum of an unspecified number of integers. The input `0` signifies the end of the input. Do you need to declare a new variable for each input value? No. Just use one variable named `data` (line 12) to store the input value and use a variable named `sum` (line 15) to store the total. Whenever a value is read, assign it to `data` and, if it is not zero, add it to `sum` (line 17).

LISTING 4.5 SentinelValue.java

```
 1 import java.util.Scanner;
 2
 3 public class SentinelValue {
 4   /** Main method */
 5   public static void main(String[] args) {
 6     // Create a Scanner
 7     Scanner input = new Scanner(System.in);
 8
 9     // Read an initial data
10     System.out.print(
11       "Enter an integer (the input ends if it is 0): ");
12     int data = input.nextInt();
```

input

loop

end of loop

display result

```
13
14       // Keep reading data until the input is 0
15       int sum = 0;
16       while (data != 0) {
17         sum += data;
18
19         // Read the next data
20         System.out.print(
21           "Enter an integer (the input ends if it is 0): ");
22         data = input.nextInt();
23       }
24
25       System.out.println("The sum is " + sum);
26     }
27   }
```

```
Enter an integer (the input ends if it is 0): 2 ↵Enter
Enter an integer (the input ends if it is 0): 3 ↵Enter
Enter an integer (the input ends if it is 0): 4 ↵Enter
Enter an integer (the input ends if it is 0): 0 ↵Enter
The sum is 9
```

	line#	data	sum	output
	12	2		
	15		0	
iteration 1	17		2	
	22	3		
iteration 2	17		5	
	22	4		
iteration 3	17		9	
	22	0		
	25			The sum is 9

If `data` is not `0`, it is added to `sum` (line 17) and the next item of input data is read (lines 20–22). If `data` is `0`, the loop body is no longer executed and the `while` loop terminates. The input value `0` is the sentinel value for this loop. Note that if the first input read is `0`, the loop body never executes, and the resulting sum is `0`.

Caution

Don't use floating-point values for equality checking in a loop control. Because floating-point values are approximations for some values, using them could result in imprecise counter values and inaccurate results.

Consider the following code for computing `1 + 0.9 + 0.8 + ... + 0.1`:

```
double item = 1; double sum = 0;
while (item != 0) { // No guarantee item will be 0
  sum += item;
  item -= 0.1;
}
System.out.println(sum);
```

Variable `item` starts with `1` and is reduced by `0.1` every time the loop body is executed. The loop should terminate when `item` becomes `0`. However, there is no guarantee that item will be exactly `0`, because the floating-point arithmetic is approximated. This loop seems okay on the surface, but it is actually an infinite loop.

numeric error

4.2.5 Input and Output Redirections

In the preceding example, if you have a large number of data to enter, it would be cumbersome to type from the keyboard. You can store the data separated by whitespaces in a text file, say **input.txt**, and run the program using the following command:

```
java SentinelValue < input.txt
```

input redirection

This command is called *input redirection.* The program takes the input from the file **input.txt** rather than having the user type the data from the keyboard at runtime. Suppose the contents of the file are

```
2 3 4 5 6 7 8 9 12 23 32
23 45 67 89 92 12 34 35 3 1 2 4 0
```

The program should get `sum` to be `518`.

output redirection

Similarly, there is *output redirection,* which sends the output to a file rather than displaying it on the console. The command for output redirection is:

```
java ClassName > output.txt
```

Input and output redirection can be used in the same command. For example, the following command gets input from **input.txt** and sends output to **output.txt**:

```
java SentinelValue < input.txt > output.txt
```

Try running the program to see what contents are in **output.txt**.

Check Point

MyProgrammingLab™

4.1 Analyze the following code. Is `count < 100` always `true`, always `false`, or sometimes `true` or sometimes `false` at Point A, Point B, and Point C?

```
int count = 0;
while (count < 100) {
  // Point A
  System.out.println("Welcome to Java!\n");
  count++;
  // Point B
}
// Point C
```

4.2 What is wrong if `guess` is initialized to `0` in line 11 in Listing 4.3?

4.3 How many times are the following loop bodies repeated? What is the printout of each loop?

```
int i = 1;
while (i < 10)
  if (i % 2 == 0)
    System.out.println(i);
```

(a)

```
int i = 1;
while (i < 10)
  if (i % 2 == 0)
    System.out.println(i++);
```

(b)

```
int i = 1;
while (i < 10)
  if ((i++) % 2 == 0)
    System.out.println(i);
```

(c)

4.4 Suppose the input is 2 3 4 5 0. What is the output of the following code?

```
import java.util.Scanner;

public class Test {
  public static void main(String[] args) {

    Scanner input = new Scanner(System.in);

    int number, max;
    number = input.nextInt();
    max = number;

    while (number != 0) {
      number = input.nextInt();
      if (number > max)
        max = number;
    }

    System.out.println("max is " + max);
    System.out.println("number " + number);
  }
}
```

4.5 What is the output of the following code? Explain the reason.

```
int x = 80000000;

while (x > 0)
  x++;

System.out.println("x is " + x);
```

4.3 The do-while Loop

A do-while loop is the same as a while loop except that it executes the loop body first and then checks the loop continuation condition.

The do-while loop is a variation of the while loop. Its syntax is:

do-while loop

```
do {
  // Loop body;
  Statement(s);
} while (loop-continuation-condition);
```

Its execution flowchart is shown in Figure 4.2.

The loop body is executed first, and then the loop-continuation-condition is evaluated. If the evaluation is true, the loop body is executed again; if it is false, the do-while loop terminates. The difference between a while loop and a do-while loop is the order in which the loop-continuation-condition is evaluated and the loop body executed. You can write a loop using either the while loop or the do-while loop. Sometimes one is a more convenient choice than the other. For example, you can rewrite the while loop in Listing 4.5 using a do-while loop, as shown in Listing 4.6.

LISTING 4.6 TestDoWhile.java

```
import java.util.Scanner;

public class TestDoWhile {
```

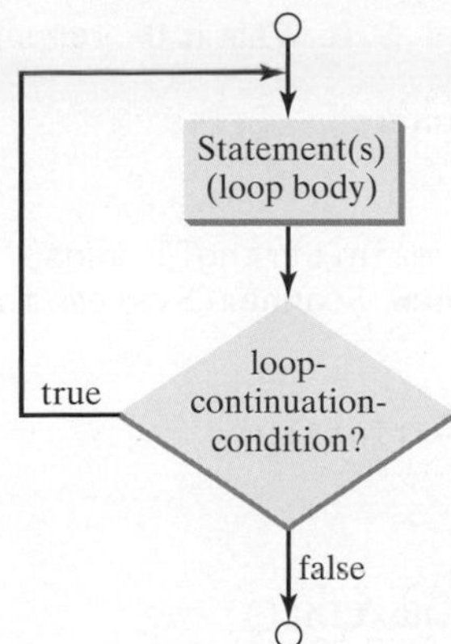

FIGURE 4.2 The `do-while` loop executes the loop body first, then checks the `loop-continuation-condition` to determine whether to continue or terminate the loop.

```
  /** Main method */
  public static void main(String[] args) {
    int data;
    int sum = 0;

    // Create a Scanner
    Scanner input = new Scanner(System.in);

    // Keep reading data until the input is 0
    do {                                                         loop
      // Read the next data
      System.out.print(
        "Enter an integer (the input ends if it is 0): ");
      data = input.nextInt();

      sum += data;
    } while (data != 0);                                         end loop

    System.out.println("The sum is " + sum);
  }
}
```

```
Enter an integer (the input ends if it is 0): 3 ↵Enter
Enter an integer (the input ends if it is 0): 5 ↵Enter
Enter an integer (the input ends if it is 0): 6 ↵Enter
Enter an integer (the input ends if it is 0): 0 ↵Enter
The sum is 14
```

Tip

Use the `do-while` loop if you have statements inside the loop that must be executed *at least once*, as in the case of the `do-while` loop in the preceding `TestDoWhile` program. These statements must appear before the loop as well as inside it if you use a `while` loop.

MyProgrammingLab™

4.6 Suppose the input is `2 3 4 5 0`. What is the output of the following code?

```
import java.util.Scanner;

public class Test {
  public static void main(String[] args) {
    Scanner input = new Scanner(System.in);

    int number, max;
    number = input.nextInt();
    max = number;

    do {
      number = input.nextInt();
      if (number > max)
        max = number;
    } while (number != 0);

    System.out.println("max is " + max);
    System.out.println("number " + number);
  }
}
```

4.7 What are the differences between a `while` loop and a `do-while` loop? Convert the following `while` loop into a `do-while` loop.

```
Scanner input = new Scanner(System.in);
int sum = 0;
System.out.println("Enter an integer " +
  "(the input ends if it is 0)");
int number = input.nextInt();
while (number != 0) {
  sum += number;
  System.out.println("Enter an integer " +
    "(the input ends if it is 0)");
  number = input.nextInt();
}
```

4.4 The for Loop

A `for` loop has a concise syntax for writing loops.

Often you write a loop in the following common form:

```
i = initialValue;  // Initialize loop control variable
while (i < endValue) {
  // Loop body
  ...
  i++; // Adjust loop control variable
}
```

A `for` loop can be used to simplify the preceding loop as:

```
for (i = initialValue; i < endValue; i++) {
  // Loop body
  ...
}
```

In general, the syntax of a `for` loop is:

for loop

```
for (initial-action; loop-continuation-condition;
     action-after-each-iteration) {
  // Loop body;
  Statement(s);
}
```

The flowchart of the `for` loop is shown in Figure 4.3a.

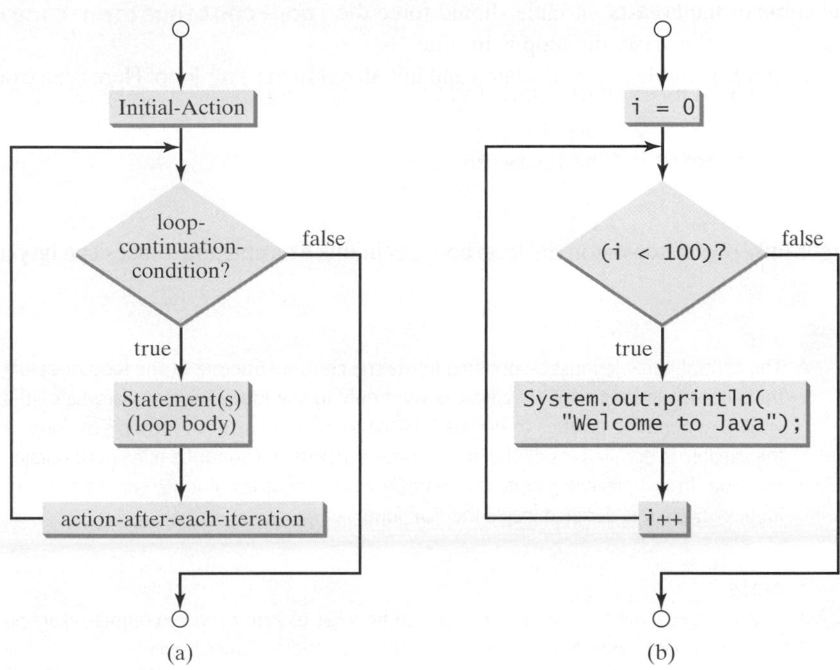

FIGURE 4.3 A `for` loop performs an initial action once, then repeatedly executes the statements in the loop body, and performs an action after an iteration when the `loop-continuation-condition` evaluates to `true`.

The `for` loop statement starts with the keyword `for`, followed by a pair of parentheses enclosing the control structure of the loop. This structure consists of `initial-action`, `loop-continuation-condition`, and `action-after-each-iteration`. The control structure is followed by the loop body enclosed inside braces. The `initial-action`, `loop-continuation-condition`, and `action-after-each-iteration` are separated by semicolons.

A `for` loop generally uses a variable to control how many times the loop body is executed and when the loop terminates. This variable is referred to as a *control variable*. The `initial-action` often initializes a control variable, the `action-after-each-iteration` usually increments or decrements the control variable, and the `loop-continuation-condition` tests whether the control variable has reached a termination value. For example, the following `for` loop prints `Welcome to Java!` a hundred times:

control variable

```
int i;
for (i = 0; i < 100; i++) {
  System.out.println("Welcome to Java!");
}
```

The flowchart of the statement is shown in Figure 4.3b. The `for` loop initializes `i` to `0`, then repeatedly executes the `println` statement and evaluates `i++` while `i` is less than `100`.

initial-action

The `initial-action`, `i = 0`, initializes the control variable, `i`. The `loop-continuation-condition`, `i < 100`, is a Boolean expression. The expression is evaluated right after the initialization and at the beginning of each iteration. If this condition is `true`, the loop body is executed. If it is `false`, the loop terminates and the program control turns to the line following the loop.

action-after-each-iteration

The `action-after-each-iteration`, `i++`, is a statement that adjusts the control variable. This statement is executed after each iteration and increments the control variable. Eventually, the value of the control variable should force the `loop-continuation-condition` to become `false`; otherwise, the loop is infinite.

The loop control variable can be declared and initialized in the `for` loop. Here is an example:

```
for (int i = 0; i < 100; i++) {
  System.out.println("Welcome to Java!");
}
```

omitting braces

If there is only one statement in the loop body, as in this example, the braces can be omitted.

declare control variable

Tip

The control variable must be declared inside the control structure of the loop or before the loop. If the loop control variable is used only in the loop, and not elsewhere, it is good programming practice to declare it in the `initial-action` of the `for` loop. If the variable is declared inside the loop control structure, it cannot be referenced outside the loop. In the preceding code, for example, you cannot reference `i` outside the `for` loop, because it is declared inside the `for` loop.

`for` loop variations

Note

The `initial-action` in a `for` loop can be a list of zero or more comma-separated variable declaration statements or assignment expressions. For example:

```
for (int i = 0, j = 0; (i + j < 10); i++, j++) {
  // Do something
}
```

The `action-after-each-iteration` in a `for` loop can be a list of zero or more comma-separated statements. For example:

```
for (int i = 1; i < 100; System.out.println(i), i++);
```

This example is correct, but it is a bad example, because it makes the code difficult to read. Normally, you declare and initialize a control variable as an initial action and increment or decrement the control variable as an action after each iteration.

Note

If the `loop-continuation-condition` in a `for` loop is omitted, it is implicitly `true`. Thus the statement given below in (a), which is an infinite loop, is the same as in (b). To avoid confusion, though, it is better to use the equivalent loop in (c).

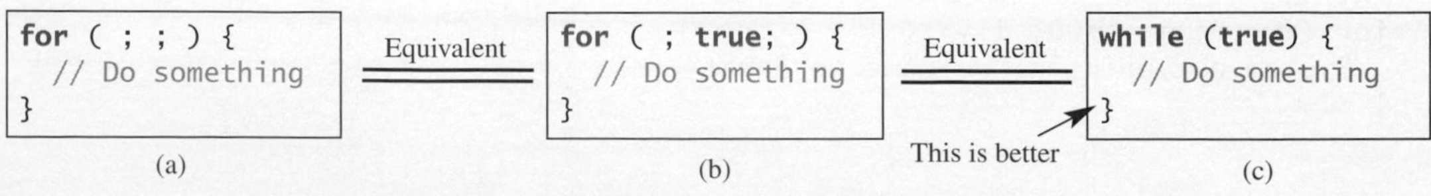

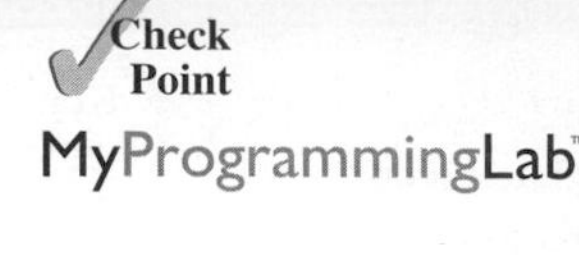

4.8 Do the following two loops result in the same value in sum?

```
for (int i = 0; i < 10; ++i) {
  sum += i;
}
```

(a)

```
for (int i = 0; i < 10; i++) {
  sum += i;
}
```

(b)

4.9 What are the three parts of a for loop control? Write a for loop that prints the numbers from 1 to 100.

4.10 Suppose the input is 2 3 4 5 0. What is the output of the following code?

```
import java.util.Scanner;

public class Test {
  public static void main(String[] args) {
    Scanner input = new Scanner(System.in);

    int number, sum = 0, count;

    for (count = 0; count < 5; count++) {
      number = input.nextInt();
      sum += number;
    }

    System.out.println("sum is " + sum);
    System.out.println("count is " + count);
  }
}
```

4.11 What does the following statement do?

```
for ( ; ; ) {
  // Do something
}
```

4.12 If a variable is declared in the for loop control, can it be used after the loop exits?

4.13 Convert the following for loop statement to a while loop and to a do-while loop:

```
long sum = 0;
for (int i = 0; i <= 1000; i++)
  sum = sum + i;
```

4.14 Count the number of iterations in the following loops.

```
int count = 0;
while (count < n) {
  count++;
}
```

(a)

```
for (int count = 0;
    count <= n; count++) {
}
```

(b)

```
int count = 5;
while (count < n) {
  count++;
}
```

(c)

```
int count = 5;
while (count < n) {
  count = count + 3;
}
```

(d)

4.5 Which Loop to Use?

You can use a `for` *loop, a* `while` *loop, or a* `do-while` *loop, whichever is convenient.*

pretest loop
posttest loop

The `while` loop and `for` loop are called *pretest loops* because the continuation condition is checked before the loop body is executed. The `do-while` loop is called a *posttest loop* because the condition is checked after the loop body is executed. The three forms of loop statements—`while`, `do-while`, and `for`—are expressively equivalent; that is, you can write a loop in any of these three forms. For example, a `while` loop in (a) in the following figure can always be converted into the `for` loop in (b).

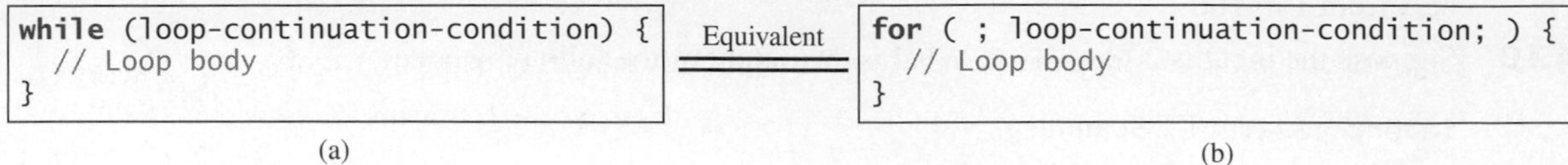

(a) (b)

A `for` loop in (a) in the next figure can generally be converted into the `while` loop in (b) except in certain special cases (see Checkpoint Question 4.23 for such a case).

```
for (initial-action;
     loop-continuation-condition;
     action-after-each-iteration) {
  // Loop body;
}
```

Equivalent

```
initial-action;
while (loop-continuation-condition) {
  // Loop body;
  action-after-each-iteration;
}
```

(a) (b)

Use the loop statement that is most intuitive and comfortable for you. In general, a `for` loop may be used if the number of repetitions is known in advance, as, for example, when you need to display a message a hundred times. A `while` loop may be used if the number of repetitions is not fixed, as in the case of reading the numbers until the input is `0`. A `do-while` loop can be used to replace a `while` loop if the loop body has to be executed before the continuation condition is tested.

Caution

Adding a semicolon at the end of the `for` clause before the loop body is a common mistake, as shown below in (a). In (a), the semicolon signifies the end of the loop prematurely. The loop body is actually empty, as shown in (b). (a) and (b) are equivalent. Both are incorrect.

Error

```
for (int i = 0; i < 10; i++);
{
  System.out.println("i is " + i);
}
```

(a)

Empty body

```
for (int i = 0; i < 10; i++) { };
{
  System.out.println("i is " + i);
}
```

(b)

Similarly, the loop in (c) is also wrong. (c) is equivalent to (d). Both are incorrect.

Error

```
int i = 0;
while (i < 10);
{
  System.out.println("i is " + i);
  i++;
}
```

(c)

Empty body

```
int i = 0;
while (i < 10) { };
{
  System.out.println("i is " + i);
  i++;
}
```

(d)

These errors often occur when you use the next-line block style. Using the end-of-line block style can avoid errors of this type.

In the case of the do-while loop, the semicolon is needed to end the loop.

```
int i = 0;
do {
  System.out.println("i is " + i);
  i++;
} while (i < 10);
```

Correct

MyProgrammingLab™

4.15 Can you convert a for loop to a while loop? List the advantages of using for loops.

4.16 Can you always convert a while loop into a for loop? Convert the following while loop into a for loop.

```
int i = 1;
int sum = 0;
while (sum < 10000) {
  sum = sum + i;
  i++;
}
```

4.17 Identify and fix the errors in the following code:

```
public class Test {
  public void main(String[] args) {
    for (int i = 0; i < 10; i++);
      sum += i;

    if (i < j);
      System.out.println(i)
    else
      System.out.println(j);

    while (j < 10);
    {
      j++;
    }

    do {
      j++;
    } while (j < 10)
  }
}
```

4.18 What is wrong with the following programs?

```
public class ShowErrors {
  public static void main(String[] args) {
    int i;
    int j = 5;

    if (j > 3)
      System.out.println(i + 4);
  }
}
```

(a)

```
public class ShowErrors {
  public static void main(String[] args) {
    for (int i = 0; i < 10; i++);
      System.out.println(i + 4);
  }
}
```

(b)

4.6 Nested Loops

A loop can be nested inside another loop.

nested loop

Nested loops consist of an outer loop and one or more inner loops. Each time the outer loop is repeated, the inner loops are reentered, and started anew.

Listing 4.7 presents a program that uses nested `for` loops to display a multiplication table.

LISTING 4.7 `MultiplicationTable.java`

table title · outer loop · inner loop

```
 1 public class MultiplicationTable {
 2   /** Main method */
 3   public static void main(String[] args) {
 4     // Display the table heading
 5     System.out.println("           Multiplication Table");
 6
 7     // Display the number title
 8     System.out.print("    ");
 9     for (int j = 1; j <= 9; j++)
10       System.out.print("   " + j);
11
12     System.out.println("\n-----------------------------------------");
13
14     // Display table body
15     for (int i = 1; i <= 9; i++) {
16       System.out.print(i + " | ");
17       for (int j = 1; j <= 9; j++) {
18         // Display the product and align properly
19         System.out.printf("%4d", i * j);
20       }
21       System.out.println();
22     }
23   }
24 }
```

```
           Multiplication Table
       1   2   3   4   5   6   7   8   9
-----------------------------------------
1 |    1   2   3   4   5   6   7   8   9
2 |    2   4   6   8  10  12  14  16  18
3 |    3   6   9  12  15  18  21  24  27
4 |    4   8  12  16  20  24  28  32  36
5 |    5  10  15  20  25  30  35  40  45
6 |    6  12  18  24  30  36  42  48  54
7 |    7  14  21  28  35  42  49  56  63
8 |    8  16  24  32  40  48  56  64  72
9 |    9  18  27  36  45  54  63  72  81
```

The program displays a title (line 5) on the first line in the output. The first `for` loop (lines 9–10) displays the numbers `1` through `9` on the second line. A dashed (`-`) line is displayed on the third line (line 12).

The next loop (lines 15–22) is a nested `for` loop with the control variable `i` in the outer loop and `j` in the inner loop. For each `i`, the product `i * j` is displayed on a line in the inner loop, with `j` being `1`, `2`, `3`, ..., `9`.

Note

Be aware that a nested loop may take a long time to run. Consider the following loop nested in three levels:

```
for (int i = 0; i < 10000; i++)
  for (int j = 0; j < 10000; j++)
    for (int k = 0; k < 10000; k++)
      Perform an action
```

The action is performed one trillion times. If it takes 1 microsecond to perform the action, the total time to run the loop would be more than 277 hours. Note that 1 microsecond is one millionth (10^{-6}) of a second.

4.19 How many times is the **println** statement executed?

```
for (int i = 0; i < 10; i++)
  for (int j = 0; j < i; j++)
    System.out.println(i * j)
```

4.20 Show the output of the following programs. (*Hint*: Draw a table and list the variables in the columns to trace these programs.)

```
public class Test {
  /** Main method */
  public static void main(String[] args) {
    for (int i = 1; i < 5; i++) {
      int j = 0;
      while (j < i) {
        System.out.print(j + " ");
        j++;
      }
    }
  }
}
```

(a)

```
public class Test {
  /** Main method */
  public static void main(String[] args) {
    int i = 0;
    while (i < 5) {
      for (int j = i; j > 1; j--)
        System.out.print(j + " ");
      System.out.println("****");
      i++;
    }
  }
}
```

(b)

```
public class Test {
  public static void main(String[] args) {
    int i = 5;
    while (i >= 1) {
      int num = 1;
      for (int j = 1; j <= i; j++) {
        System.out.print(num + "xxx");
        num *= 2;
      }

      System.out.println();
      i--;
    }
  }
}
```

(c)

```
public class Test {
  public static void main(String[] args) {
    int i = 1;
    do {
      int num = 1;
      for (int j = 1; j <= i; j++) {
        System.out.print(num + "G");
        num += 2;
      }

      System.out.println();
      i++;
    } while (i <= 5);
  }
}
```

(d)

4.7 Minimizing Numeric Errors

Key Point

Using floating-point numbers in the loop continuation condition may cause numeric errors.

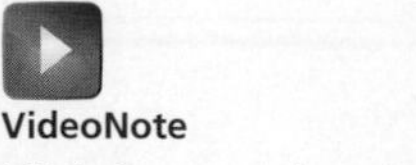

VideoNote
Minimize numeric errors

Numeric errors involving floating-point numbers are inevitable. This section discusses how to minimize such errors through an example.

Listing 4.8 presents an example summing a series that starts with 0.01 and ends with 1.0. The numbers in the series will increment by 0.01, as follows: 0.01 + 0.02 + 0.03, and so on.

LISTING 4.8 TestSum.java

loop

```
 1 public class TestSum {
 2   public static void main(String[] args) {
 3     // Initialize sum
 4     float sum = 0;
 5
 6     // Add 0.01, 0.02, ..., 0.99, 1 to sum
 7     for (float i = 0.01f; i <= 1.0f; i = i + 0.01f)
 8       sum += i;
 9
10     // Display result
11     System.out.println("The sum is " + sum);
12   }
13 }
```

```
The sum is 50.499985
```

The for loop (lines 7–8) repeatedly adds the control variable i to sum. This variable, which begins with 0.01, is incremented by 0.01 after each iteration. The loop terminates when i exceeds 1.0.

The for loop initial action can be any statement, but it is often used to initialize a control variable. From this example, you can see that a control variable can be a float type. In fact, it can be any data type.

double precision

The exact sum should be 50.50, but the answer is 50.499985. The result is imprecise because computers use a fixed number of bits to represent floating-point numbers, and thus they cannot represent some floating-point numbers exactly. If you change float in the program to double, as follows, you should see a slight improvement in precision, because a double variable holds 64 bits, whereas a float variable holds 32 bits.

```
// Initialize sum
double sum = 0;

// Add 0.01, 0.02, ..., 0.99, 1 to sum
for (double i = 0.01; i <= 1.0; i = i + 0.01)
  sum += i;
```

numeric error

However, you will be stunned to see that the result is actually 49.50000000000003. What went wrong? If you display i for each iteration in the loop, you will see that the last i is slightly larger than 1 (not exactly 1). This causes the last i not to be added into sum. The fundamental problem is that the floating-point numbers are represented by approximation. To fix the problem, use an integer count to ensure that all the numbers are added to sum. Here is the new loop:

```
double currentValue = 0.01;

for (int count = 0; count < 100; count++) {
```

```
    sum += currentValue;
    currentValue += 0.01;
  }
```

After this loop, sum is 50.50000000000003. This loop adds the numbers from smallest to biggest. What happens if you add numbers from biggest to smallest (i.e., 1.0, 0.99, 0.98, . . . , 0.02, 0.01 in this order) as follows:

```
  double currentValue = 1.0;

  for (int count = 0; count < 100; count++) {
    sum += currentValue;
    currentValue -= 0.01;
  }
```

avoiding numeric error

After this loop, sum is 50.49999999999995. Adding from biggest to smallest is less accurate than adding from smallest to biggest. This phenomenon is an artifact of the finite-precision arithmetic. Adding a very small number to a very big number can have no effect if the result requires more precision than the variable can store. For example, the inaccurate result of 100000000.0 + 0.000000001 is 100000000.0. To obtain more accurate results, carefully select the order of computation. Adding smaller numbers before bigger numbers is one way to minimize errors.

4.8 Case Studies

Loops are fundamental in programming. The ability to write loops is essential in learning Java programming.

If you can write programs using loops, you know how to program! For this reason, this section presents three additional examples of solving problems using loops.

4.8.1 Case Study: Finding the Greatest Common Divisor

gcd

The greatest common divisor (gcd) of the two integers 4 and 2 is 2. The greatest common divisor of the two integers 16 and 24 is 8. How do you find the greatest common divisor? Let the two input integers be n1 and n2. You know that number 1 is a common divisor, but it may not be the greatest common divisor. So, you can check whether k (for k = 2, 3, 4, and so on) is a common divisor for n1 and n2, until k is greater than n1 or n2. Store the common divisor in a variable named gcd. Initially, gcd is 1. Whenever a new common divisor is found, it becomes the new gcd. When you have checked all the possible common divisors from 2 up to n1 or n2, the value in variable gcd is the greatest common divisor. The idea can be translated into the following loop:

```
  int gcd = 1; // Initial gcd is 1
  int k = 2; // Possible gcd

  while (k <= n1 && k <= n2) {
    if (n1 % k == 0 && n2 % k == 0)
      gcd = k; // Update gcd
    k++; // Next possible gcd
  }

  // After the loop, gcd is the greatest common divisor for n1 and n2
```

Listing 4.9 presents the program that prompts the user to enter two positive integers and finds their greatest common divisor.

LISTING 4.9 GreatestCommonDivisor.java

input
input
gcd
check divisor
output

```
import java.util.Scanner;

public class GreatestCommonDivisor {
  /** Main method */
  public static void main(String[] args) {
    // Create a Scanner
    Scanner input = new Scanner(System.in);

    // Prompt the user to enter two integers
    System.out.print("Enter first integer: ");
    int n1 = input.nextInt();
    System.out.print("Enter second integer: ");
    int n2 = input.nextInt();

    int gcd = 1; // Initial gcd is 1
    int k = 2; // Possible gcd
    while (k <= n1 && k <= n2) {
      if (n1 % k == 0 && n2 % k == 0)
        gcd = k; // Update gcd
      k++;
    }

    System.out.println("The greatest common divisor for " + n1 +
      " and " + n2 + " is " + gcd);
  }
}
```

```
Enter first integer: 125 Enter
Enter second integer: 2525 Enter
The greatest common divisor for 125 and 2525 is 25
```

think before you type

How would you write this program? Would you immediately begin to write the code? No. It is important to *think before you type*. Thinking enables you to generate a logical solution for the problem without concern about how to write the code. Once you have a logical solution, type the code to translate the solution into a Java program. The translation is not unique. For example, you could use a `for` loop to rewrite the code as follows:

```
for (int k = 2; k <= n1 && k <= n2; k++) {
  if (n1 % k == 0 && n2 % k == 0)
    gcd = k;
}
```

multiple solutions

A problem often has multiple solutions, and the gcd problem can be solved in many ways. Programming Exercise 4.14 suggests another solution. A more efficient solution is to use the classic Euclidean algorithm (see www.cut-the-knot.org/blue/Euclid.shtml for more information).

erroneous solutions

You might think that a divisor for a number `n1` cannot be greater than `n1 / 2` and would attempt to improve the program using the following loop:

```
for (int k = 2; k <= n1 / 2 && k <= n2 / 2; k++) {
  if (n1 % k == 0 && n2 % k == 0)
    gcd = k;
}
```

This revision is wrong. Can you find the reason? See Checkpoint Question 4.21 for the answer.

4.8.2 Case Study: Predicting the Future Tuition

Suppose that the tuition for a university is $10,000 this year and tuition increases 7% every year. In how many years will the tuition be doubled?

Before you can write a program to solve this problem, first consider how to solve it by hand. The tuition for the second year is the tuition for the first year * 1.07. The tuition for a future year is the tuition of its preceding year * 1.07. Thus, the tuition for each year can be computed as follows:

```
double tuition = 10000;   int year = 0;  // Year 0
tuition = tuition * 1.07; year++;        // Year 1
tuition = tuition * 1.07; year++;        // Year 2
tuition = tuition * 1.07; year++;        // Year 3
...
```

Keep computing the tuition for a new year until it is at least 20000. By then you will know how many years it will take for the tuition to be doubled. You can now translate the logic into the following loop:

```
double tuition = 10000;   // Year 0
int year = 0;
while (tuition < 20000) {
  tuition = tuition * 1.07;
  year++;
}
```

The complete program is shown in Listing 4.10.

LISTING 4.10 FutureTuition.java

```
1  public class FutureTuition {
2    public static void main(String[] args) {
3      double tuition = 10000;   // Year 0
4      int year = 0;
5      while (tuition < 20000) {
6        tuition = tuition * 1.07;
7        year++;
8      }
9
10     System.out.println("Tuition will be doubled in "
11       + year + " years");
12     System.out.printf("Tuition will be $%.2f in %1d years",
13       tuition, year);
14   }
15 }
```

loop
next year's tuition

```
Tuition will be doubled in 11 years
Tuition will be $21048.52 in 11 years
```

The while loop (lines 5–8) is used to repeatedly compute the tuition for a new year. The loop terminates when the tuition is greater than or equal to 20000.

4.8.3 Case Study: Monte Carlo Simulation

Monte Carlo simulation uses random numbers and probability to solve problems. This method has a wide range of applications in computational mathematics, physics, chemistry, and finance. This section gives an example of using Monte Carlo simulation for estimating π.

To estimate π using the Monte Carlo method, draw a circle with its bounding square as shown below.

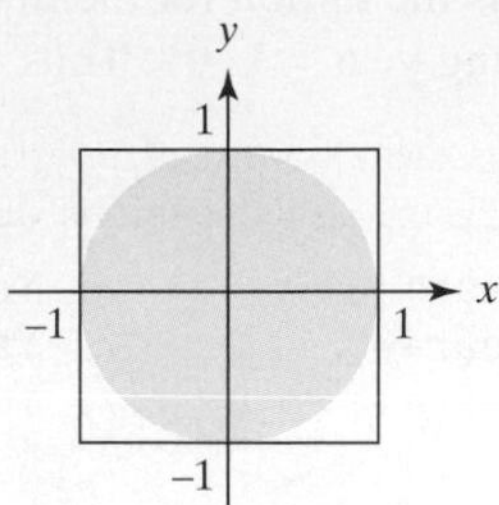

Assume the radius of the circle is `1`. Therefore, the circle area is π and the square area is `4`. Randomly generate a point in the square. The probability for the point to fall in the circle is `circleArea / squareArea = π / 4`.

Write a program that randomly generates 1,000,000 points in the square and let `numberOfHits` denote the number of points that fall in the circle. Thus, `numberOfHits` is approximately `1000000 * (π / 4)`. π can be approximated as `4 * numberOfHits / 1000000`. The complete program is shown in Listing 4.11.

LISTING 4.11 MonteCarloSimulation.java

generate random points

check inside circle

estimate pi

```
1  public class MonteCarloSimulation {
2    public static void main(String[] args) {
3      final int NUMBER_OF_TRIALS = 10000000;
4      int numberOfHits = 0;
5
6      for (int i = 0; i < NUMBER_OF_TRIALS; i++) {
7        double x = Math.random() * 2.0 - 1;
8        double y = Math.random() * 2.0 - 1;
9        if (x * x + y * y <= 1)
10         numberOfHits++;
11     }
12
13     double pi = 4.0 * numberOfHits / NUMBER_OF_TRIALS;
14     System.out.println("PI is " + pi);
15   }
16 }
```

```
PI is 3.14124
```

The program repeatedly generates a random point (`x`, `y`) in the square in lines 7–8:

```
double x = Math.random() * 2.0 - 1;
double y = Math.random() * 2.0 - 1;
```

If $x^2 + y^2 \leq 1$, the point is inside the circle and `numberOfHits` is incremented by `1`. π is approximately `4 * numberOfHits / NUMBER_OF_TRIALS` (line 13).

4.21 Will the program work if `n1` and `n2` are replaced by `n1 / 2` and `n2 / 2` in line 17 in Listing 4.9?

MyProgrammingLab™

4.9 Keywords *break* and *continue*

The **break** *and* **continue** *keywords provide additional controls in a loop.*

Pedagogical Note

Two keywords, **break** and **continue**, can be used in loop statements to provide additional controls. Using **break** and **continue** can simplify programming in some cases. Overusing or improperly using them, however, can make programs difficult to read and debug. (*Note to instructors*: You may skip this section without affecting students' understanding of the rest of the book.)

You have used the keyword **break** in a **switch** statement. You can also use **break** in a loop to immediately terminate the loop. Listing 4.12 presents a program to demonstrate the effect of using **break** in a loop.

break statement

LISTING 4.12 TestBreak.java

```
1  public class TestBreak {
2    public static void main(String[] args) {
3      int sum = 0;
4      int number = 0;
5
6      while (number < 20) {
7        number++;
8        sum += number;
9        if (sum >= 100)
10         break;
11     }
12
13     System.out.println("The number is " + number);
14     System.out.println("The sum is " + sum);
15   }
16 }
```

break

```
The number is 14
The sum is 105
```

The program in Listing 4.12 adds integers from **1** to **20** in this order to **sum** until **sum** is greater than or equal to **100**. Without the **if** statement (line 9), the program calculates the sum of the numbers from **1** to **20**. But with the **if** statement, the loop terminates when **sum** becomes greater than or equal to **100**. Without the **if** statement, the output would be:

```
The number is 20
The sum is 210
```

You can also use the **continue** keyword in a loop. When it is encountered, it ends the current iteration and program control goes to the end of the loop body. In other words, **continue** breaks out of an iteration while the **break** keyword breaks out of a loop. Listing 4.13 presents a program to demonstrate the effect of using **continue** in a loop.

continue statement

Listing 4.13 TestContinue.java

```
1  public class TestContinue {
2    public static void main(String[] args) {
3      int sum = 0;
4      int number = 0;
5
6      while (number < 20) {
7        number++;
8        if (number == 10 || number == 11)
9          continue;
10       sum += number;
11     }
12
13     System.out.println("The sum is " + sum);
14   }
15 }
```

continue

```
The sum is 189
```

The program in Listing 4.13 adds integers from `1` to `20` except `10` and `11` to `sum`. With the `if` statement in the program (line 8), the `continue` statement is executed when `number` becomes `10` or `11`. The `continue` statement ends the current iteration so that the rest of the statement in the loop body is not executed; therefore, `number` is not added to `sum` when it is `10` or `11`. Without the `if` statement in the program, the output would be as follows:

```
The sum is 210
```

In this case, all of the numbers are added to `sum`, even when `number` is `10` or `11`. Therefore, the result is `210`, which is `21` more than it was with the `if` statement.

Note

The `continue` statement is always inside a loop. In the `while` and `do-while` loops, the `loop-continuation-condition` is evaluated immediately after the `continue` statement. In the `for` loop, the `action-after-each-iteration` is performed, then the `loop-continuation-condition` is evaluated, immediately after the `continue` statement.

You can always write a program without using `break` or `continue` in a loop (see Checkpoint Question 4.24). In general, though, using `break` and `continue` is appropriate if it simplifies coding and makes programs easier to read.

Suppose you need to write a program to find the smallest factor other than `1` for an integer `n` (assume `n >= 2`). You can write a simple and intuitive code using the `break` statement as follows:

```
int factor = 2;
while (factor <= n) {
  if (n % factor == 0)
    break;
  factor++;
}
```

```
System.out.println("The smallest factor other than 1 for "
  + n + " is " + factor);
```

You may rewrite the code without using break as follows:

```
boolean found = false;
int factor = 2;
while (factor <= n && !found) {
  if (n % factor == 0)
    found = true;
  else
    factor++;
}
System.out.println("The smallest factor other than 1 for "
  + n + " is " + factor);
```

Obviously, the break statement makes this program simpler and easier to read in this case. However, you should use break and continue with caution. Too many break and continue statements will produce a loop with many exit points and make the program difficult to read.

Note

Some programming languages have a goto statement. The goto statement indiscriminately transfers control to any statement in the program and executes it. This makes your program vulnerable to errors. The break and continue statements in Java are different from goto statements. They operate only in a loop or a switch statement. The break statement breaks out of the loop, and the continue statement breaks out of the current iteration in the loop.

goto

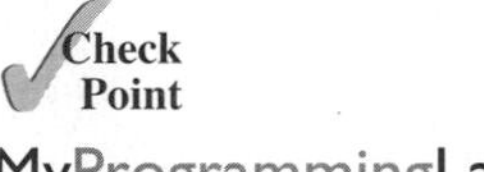

4.22 What is the keyword break for? What is the keyword continue for? Will the following programs terminate? If so, give the output.

```
int balance = 10;
while (true) {
  if (balance < 9)
    break;
  balance = balance - 9;
}

System.out.println("Balance is "
  + balance);
```

(a)

```
int balance = 10;
while (true) {
  if (balance < 9)
    continue;
  balance = balance - 9;
}

System.out.println("Balance is "
  + balance);
```

(b)

4.23 The for loop on the left is converted into the while loop on the right. What is wrong? Correct it.

```
for (int i = 0; i < 4; i++) {
  if (i % 3 == 0) continue;
  sum += i;
}
```

Converted

Wrong conversion

```
int i = 0;
while (i < 4) {
  if (i % 3 == 0) continue;
  sum += i;
  i++;
}
```

4.24 Rewrite the programs TestBreak and TestContinue in Listings 4.12 and 4.13 without using break and continue.

4.25 After the break statement in (a) is executed in the following loop, which statement is executed? Show the output. After the continue statement in (b) is executed in the following loop, which statement is executed? Show the output.

```
for (int i = 1; i < 4; i++) {
  for (int j = 1; j < 4; j++) {
    if (i * j > 2)
      break;

    System.out.println(i * j);
  }

  System.out.println(i);
}
```

(a)

```
for (int i = 1; i < 4; i++) {
  for (int j = 1; j < 4; j++) {
    if (i * j > 2)
      continue;

    System.out.println(i * j);
  }

  System.out.println(i);
}
```

(b)

4.10 Case Study: Displaying Prime Numbers

This section presents a program that displays the first fifty prime numbers in five lines, each containing ten numbers.

An integer greater than 1 is *prime* if its only positive divisor is 1 or itself. For example, 2, 3, 5, and 7 are prime numbers, but 4, 6, 8, and 9 are not.

The problem is to display the first 50 prime numbers in five lines, each of which contains ten numbers. The problem can be broken into the following tasks:

- Determine whether a given number is prime.
- For number = 2, 3, 4, 5, 6, ..., test whether it is prime.
- Count the prime numbers.
- Display each prime number, and display ten numbers per line.

Obviously, you need to write a loop and repeatedly test whether a new number is prime. If the number is prime, increase the count by 1. The count is 0 initially. When it reaches 50, the loop terminates.

Here is the algorithm for the problem:

```
Set the number of prime numbers to be printed as
  a constant NUMBER_OF_PRIMES;
Use count to track the number of prime numbers and
  set an initial count to 0;
Set an initial number to 2;

while (count < NUMBER_OF_PRIMES) {
  Test whether number is prime;

  if number is prime {
    Display the prime number and increase the count;
  }

  Increment number by 1;
}
```

To test whether a number is prime, check whether it is divisible by 2, 3, 4, and so on up to number/2. If a divisor is found, the number is not a prime. The algorithm can be described as follows:

```
Use a boolean variable isPrime to denote whether
  the number is prime; Set isPrime to true initially;

for (int divisor = 2; divisor <= number / 2; divisor++) {
  if (number % divisor == 0) {
    Set isPrime to false
    Exit the loop;
  }
}
```

The complete program is given in Listing 4.14.

LISTING 4.14 PrimeNumber.java

```java
public class PrimeNumber {
  public static void main(String[] args) {
    final int NUMBER_OF_PRIMES = 50; // Number of primes to display
    final int NUMBER_OF_PRIMES_PER_LINE = 10; // Display 10 per line
    int count = 0; // Count the number of prime numbers
    int number = 2; // A number to be tested for primeness

    System.out.println("The first 50 prime numbers are \n");

    // Repeatedly find prime numbers
    while (count < NUMBER_OF_PRIMES) {
      // Assume the number is prime
      boolean isPrime = true; // Is the current number prime?

      // Test whether number is prime
      for (int divisor = 2; divisor <= number / 2; divisor++) {
        if (number % divisor == 0) { // If true, number is not prime
          isPrime = false; // Set isPrime to false
          break; // Exit the for loop
        }
      }

      // Display the prime number and increase the count
      if (isPrime) {
        count++; // Increase the count

        if (count % NUMBER_OF_PRIMES_PER_LINE == 0) {
          // Display the number and advance to the new line
          System.out.println(number);
        }
        else
          System.out.print(number + " ");
      }

      // Check if the next number is prime
      number++;
    }
  }
}
```

count prime numbers

check primeness

exit loop

display if prime

```
The first 50 prime numbers are
2 3 5 7 11 13 17 19 23 29
31 37 41 43 47 53 59 61 67 71
73 79 83 89 97 101 103 107 109 113
127 131 137 139 149 151 157 163 167 173
179 181 191 193 197 199 211 223 227 229
```

subproblem

This is a complex program for novice programmers. The key to developing a programmatic solution for this problem, and for many other problems, is to break it into subproblems and develop solutions for each of them in turn. Do not attempt to develop a complete solution in the first trial. Instead, begin by writing the code to determine whether a given number is prime, then expand the program to test whether other numbers are prime in a loop.

To determine whether a number is prime, check whether it is divisible by a number between `2` and `number/2` inclusive (lines 16–21). If so, it is not a prime number (line 18); otherwise, it is a prime number. For a prime number, display it. If the count is divisible by `10` (lines 27–30), advance to a new line. The program ends when the count reaches `50`.

The program uses the **`break`** statement in line 19 to exit the **`for`** loop as soon as the number is found to be a nonprime. You can rewrite the loop (lines 16–21) without using the **`break`** statement, as follows:

```
for (int divisor = 2; divisor <= number / 2 && isPrime;
    divisor++) {
  // If true, the number is not prime
  if (number % divisor == 0) {
    // Set isPrime to false, if the number is not prime
    isPrime = false;
  }
}
```

However, using the **`break`** statement makes the program simpler and easier to read in this case.

4.11 Controlling a Loop with a Confirmation Dialog

You can use a confirmation dialog to prompt the user to confirm whether to continue or exit a loop.

confirmation dialog

A sentinel-controlled loop can be implemented using a confirmation dialog. The answers *Yes* or *No* continue or terminate the loop. The template of the loop may look as follows:

```
int option = JOptionPane.YES_OPTION;
while (option == JOptionPane.YES_OPTION) {
  System.out.println("continue loop");
  option = JOptionPane.showConfirmDialog(null, "Continue?");
}
```

Listing 4.15 rewrites Listing 4.5, SentinelValue.java, using a confirmation dialog box. A sample run is shown in Figure 4.4.

LISTING 4.15 SentinelValueUsingConfirmationDialog.java

```
import javax.swing.JOptionPane;

public class SentinelValueUsingConfirmationDialog {
  public static void main(String[] args) {
    int sum = 0;
```

```
6
7       // Keep reading data until the user answers No
8       int option = JOptionPane.YES_OPTION;
9       while (option == JOptionPane.YES_OPTION) {
10        // Read the next data
11        String dataString = JOptionPane.showInputDialog(
12          "Enter an integer: ");
13        int data = Integer.parseInt(dataString);
14
15        sum += data;
16
17        option = JOptionPane.showConfirmDialog(null, "Continue?");
18      }
19
20      JOptionPane.showMessageDialog(null, "The sum is " + sum);
21    }
22  }
```

confirmation option
check option
input dialog
confirmation dialog
message dialog

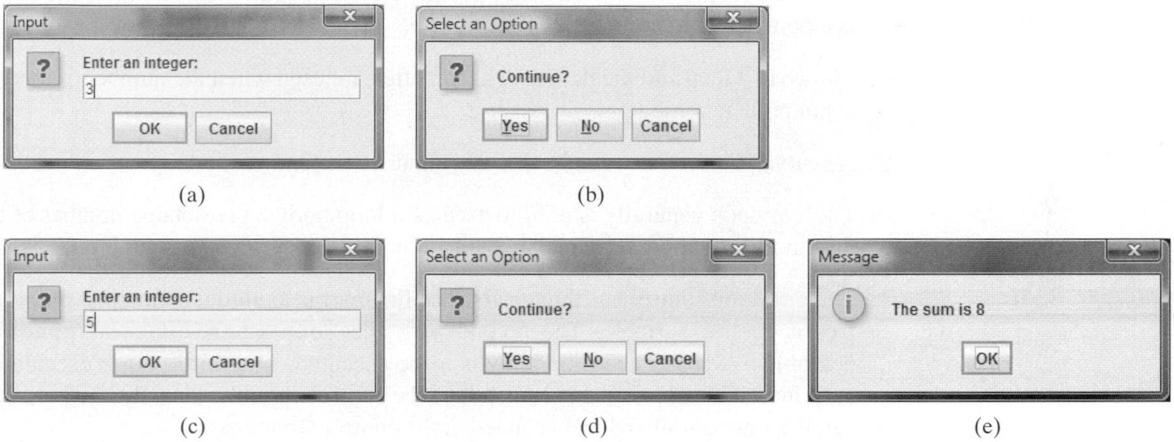

(a) (b) (c) (d) (e)

FIGURE 4.4 The user enters 3 in (a), clicks Yes in (b), enters 5 in (c), clicks No in (d), and the result is shown in (e).

The program displays an input dialog to prompt the user to enter an integer (line 11) and adds it to `sum` (line 15). Line 17 displays a confirmation dialog to let the user decide whether to continue the input. If the user clicks *Yes,* the loop continues; otherwise, the loop exits. Finally, the program displays the result in a message dialog box (line 20).

The `showConfirmDialog` method (line 17) returns an integer `JOptionPane.YES_OPTION`, `JOptionPane.NO_OPTION`, or `JOptionPane.CANCEL_OPTION`, if the user clicks *Yes*, *No*, or *Cancel*. The return value is assigned to the variable `option` (line 17). If this value is `JOptionPane.YES_OPTION`, the loop continues (line 9).

Key Terms

- `break` statement 159
- `continue` statement 159
- `do-while` loop 144
- `for` loop 147
- infinite loop 136
- input redirection 143
- iteration 134
- loop 134
- loop body 134
- nested loop 152
- off-by-one error 136
- output redirection 143
- posttest loop 150
- pretest loop 150
- sentinel value 141
- `while` loop 134

Chapter Summary

1. There are three types of repetition statements: the `while` loop, the `do-while` loop, and the `for` loop.
2. The part of the loop that contains the statements to be repeated is called the *loop body.*
3. A one-time execution of a loop body is referred to as an *iteration of the loop.*
4. An *infinite loop* is a loop statement that executes infinitely.
5. In designing loops, you need to consider both the *loop control structure* and the loop body.
6. The `while` loop checks the `loop-continuation-condition` first. If the condition is `true`, the loop body is executed; if it is `false`, the loop terminates.
7. The `do-while` loop is similar to the `while` loop, except that the `do-while` loop executes the loop body first and then checks the `loop-continuation-condition` to decide whether to continue or to terminate.
8. The `while` loop and the `do-while` loop often are used when the number of repetitions is not predetermined.
9. A *sentinel value* is a special value that signifies the end of the loop.
10. The `for` loop generally is used to execute a loop body a predictable number of times; this number is not determined by the loop body.
11. The `for` loop control has three parts. The first part is an initial action that often initializes a control variable. The second part, the `loop-continuation-condition`, determines whether the loop body is to be executed. The third part is executed after each iteration and is often used to adjust the control variable. Usually, the loop control variables are initialized and changed in the control structure.
12. The `while` loop and `for` loop are called *pretest loops* because the continuation condition is checked before the loop body is executed.
13. The `do-while` loop is called a *posttest loop* because the condition is checked after the loop body is executed.
14. Two keywords, `break` and `continue`, can be used in a loop.
15. The `break` keyword immediately ends the innermost loop, which contains the break.
16. The `continue` keyword only ends the current iteration.

Test Questions

Do the test questions for this chapter online at www.cs.armstrong.edu/liang/intro9e/test.html.

MyProgrammingLab™

Programming Exercises

Pedagogical Note

read and think before coding

Read each problem several times until you understand it. Think how to solve the problem before starting to write code. Translate your logic into a program.

explore solutions

A problem often can be solved in many different ways. Students are encouraged to explore various solutions.

Sections 4.2–4.7

***4.1** (*Count positive and negative numbers and compute the average of numbers*) Write a program that reads an unspecified number of integers, determines how many positive and negative values have been read, and computes the total and average of the input values (not counting zeros). Your program ends with the input 0. Display the average as a floating-point number. Here is a sample run:

```
Enter an integer, the input ends if it is 0: 1 2 -1 3 0 ↵Enter
The number of positives is 3
The number of negatives is 1
The total is 5
The average is 1.25
```

```
Enter an integer, the input ends if it is 0: 0 ↵Enter
No numbers are entered except 0
```

4.2 (*Repeat additions*) Listing 4.4, SubtractionQuizLoop.java, generates five random subtraction questions. Revise the program to generate ten random addition questions for two integers between 1 and 15. Display the correct count and test time.

4.3 (*Conversion from kilograms to pounds*) Write a program that displays the following table (note that 1 kilogram is 2.2 pounds):

```
Kilograms     Pounds
1               2.2
3               6.6
...
197           433.4
199           437.8
```

4.4 (*Conversion from miles to kilometers*) Write a program that displays the following table (note that 1 mile is 1.609 kilometers):

```
Miles       Kilometers
1           1.609
2           3.218
...
9           14.481
10          16.090
```

4.5 (*Conversion from kilograms to pounds and pounds to kilograms*) Write a program that displays the following two tables side by side (note that 1 kilogram is 2.2 pounds):

```
Kilograms   Pounds    |   Pounds        Kilograms
1             2.2     |   20               9.09
3             6.6     |   25              11.36
...
197         433.4     |   510            231.82
199         437.8     |   515            234.09
```

4.6 (*Conversion from miles to kilometers*) Write a program that displays the following two tables side by side (note that 1 mile is 1.609 kilometers):

```
Miles      Kilometers  |  Kilometers     Miles
1          1.609       |  20             12.430
2          3.218       |  25             15.538
...
9          14.481      |  60             37.290
10         16.090      |  65             40.398
```

****4.7** (*Financial application: compute future tuition*) Suppose that the tuition for a university is $10,000 this year and increases 5% every year. Write a program that computes the tuition in ten years and the total cost of four years' worth of tuition starting ten years from now.

4.8 (*Find the highest score*) Write a program that prompts the user to enter the number of students and each student's name and score, and finally displays the name of the student with the highest score.

***4.9** (*Find the two highest scores*) Write a program that prompts the user to enter the number of students and each student's name and score, and finally displays the student with the highest score and the student with the second-highest score.

4.10 (*Find numbers divisible by 5 and 6*) Write a program that displays all the numbers from 100 to 1,000, ten per line, that are divisible by 5 and 6. Numbers are separated by exactly one space.

4.11 (*Find numbers divisible by 5 or 6, but not both*) Write a program that displays all the numbers from 100 to 200, ten per line, that are divisible by 5 or 6, but not both. Numbers are separated by exactly one space.

4.12 (*Find the smallest* `n` *such that* $n^2 > 12{,}000$) Use a `while` loop to find the smallest integer `n` such that n^2 is greater than 12,000.

4.13 (*Find the largest* `n` *such that* $n^3 < 12{,}000$) Use a `while` loop to find the largest integer `n` such that n^3 is less than 12,000.

Sections 4.8–4.10

***4.14** (*Compute the greatest common divisor*) Another solution for Listing 4.9 to find the greatest common divisor of two integers `n1` and `n2` is as follows: First find `d` to be the minimum of `n1` and `n2`, then check whether `d`, `d-1`, `d-2`, ..., `2`, or `1` is a divisor for both `n1` and `n2` in this order. The first such common divisor is the greatest common divisor for `n1` and `n2`. Write a program that prompts the user to enter two positive integers and displays the gcd.

***4.15** (*Display the ASCII character table*) Write a program that prints the characters in the ASCII character table from `!` to `~`. Display ten characters per line. The ASCII table is shown in Appendix B. Characters are separated by exactly one space.

***4.16** (*Find the factors of an integer*) Write a program that reads an integer and displays all its smallest factors in increasing order. For example, if the input integer is `120`, the output should be as follows: `2, 2, 2, 3, 5`.

****4.17** (*Display pyramid*) Write a program that prompts the user to enter an integer from `1` to `15` and displays a pyramid, as shown in the following sample run:

```
Enter the number of lines: 7
                        1
                     2  1  2
                  3  2  1  2  3
               4  3  2  1  2  3  4
            5  4  3  2  1  2  3  4  5
         6  5  4  3  2  1  2  3  4  5  6
      7  6  5  4  3  2  1  2  3  4  5  6  7
```

***4.18** (*Display four patterns using loops*) Use nested loops that display the following patterns in four separate programs:

```
Pattern A      Pattern B      Pattern C      Pattern D
1              1 2 3 4 5 6              1    1 2 3 4 5 6
1 2            1 2 3 4 5              2 1      1 2 3 4 5
1 2 3          1 2 3 4              3 2 1        1 2 3 4
1 2 3 4        1 2 3              4 3 2 1          1 2 3
1 2 3 4 5      1 2              5 4 3 2 1            1 2
1 2 3 4 5 6    1              6 5 4 3 2 1              1
```

****4.19** (*Display numbers in a pyramid pattern*) Write a nested `for` loop that prints the following output:

```
                              1
                          1   2   1
                      1   2   4   2   1
                  1   2   4   8   4   2   1
              1   2   4   8  16   8   4   2   1
          1   2   4   8  16  32  16   8   4   2   1
      1   2   4   8  16  32  64  32  16   8   4   2   1
  1   2   4   8  16  32  64 128  64  32  16   8   4   2   1
```

***4.20** (*Display prime numbers between 2 and 1,000*) Modify Listing 4.14 to display all the prime numbers between 2 and 1,000, inclusive. Display eight prime numbers per line. Numbers are separated by exactly one space.

Comprehensive

****4.21** (*Financial application: compare loans with various interest rates*) Write a program that lets the user enter the loan amount and loan period in number of years and displays the monthly and total payments for each interest rate starting from 5% to 8%, with an increment of 1/8. Here is a sample run:

```
Loan Amount: 10000
Number of Years: 5
Interest Rate    Monthly Payment    Total Payment
5.000%           188.71             11322.74
5.125%           189.28             11357.13
5.250%           189.85             11391.59
...
7.875%           202.17             12129.97
8.000%           202.76             12165.83
```

For the formula to compute monthly payment, see Listing 2.8, ComputeLoan.java.

VideoNote
Display loan schedule

****4.22** (*Financial application: loan amortization schedule*) The monthly payment for a given loan pays the principal and the interest. The monthly interest is computed by multiplying the monthly interest rate and the balance (the remaining principal). The principal paid for the month is therefore the monthly payment minus the monthly interest. Write a program that lets the user enter the loan amount, number of years, and interest rate and displays the amortization schedule for the loan. Here is a sample run:

```
Loan Amount: 10000 ↵Enter
Number of Years: 1 ↵Enter
Annual Interest Rate: 7 ↵Enter

Monthly Payment: 865.26
Total Payment: 10383.21

Payment#      Interest      Principal      Balance
1             58.33         806.93         9193.07
2             53.62         811.64         8381.43
...
11            10.0          855.26          860.27
12             5.01         860.25            0.01
```

Note

The balance after the last payment may not be zero. If so, the last payment should be the normal monthly payment plus the final balance.

Hint: Write a loop to display the table. Since the monthly payment is the same for each month, it should be computed before the loop. The balance is initially the loan amount. For each iteration in the loop, compute the interest and principal, and update the balance. The loop may look like this:

```
for (i = 1; i <= numberOfYears * 12; i++) {
  interest = monthlyInterestRate * balance;
  principal = monthlyPayment - interest;
  balance = balance - principal;
  System.out.println(i + "\t\t" + interest
    + "\t\t" + principal + "\t\t" + balance);
}
```

***4.23** (*Obtain more accurate results*) In computing the following series, you will obtain more accurate results by computing from right to left rather than from left to right:

$$1 + \frac{1}{2} + \frac{1}{3} + \ldots + \frac{1}{n}$$

Write a program that computes the results of the summation of the preceding series from left to right and from right to left with `n = 50000`.

VideoNote
Sum a series

***4.24** (*Sum a series*) Write a program to sum the following series:

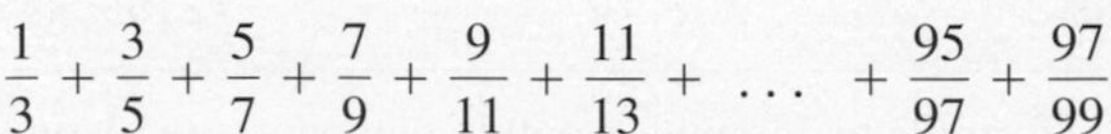

$$\frac{1}{3} + \frac{3}{5} + \frac{5}{7} + \frac{7}{9} + \frac{9}{11} + \frac{11}{13} + \ldots + \frac{95}{97} + \frac{97}{99}$$

**4.25 (*Compute* π) You can approximate π by using the following series:

$$\pi = 4\left(1 - \frac{1}{3} + \frac{1}{5} - \frac{1}{7} + \frac{1}{9} - \frac{1}{11} + \ldots + \frac{(-1)^{i+1}}{2i-1}\right)$$

Write a program that displays the π value for `i = 10000, 20000, ...,` and `100000`.

**4.26 (*Compute e*) You can approximate `e` using the following series:

$$e = 1 + \frac{1}{1!} + \frac{1}{2!} + \frac{1}{3!} + \frac{1}{4!} + \ldots + \frac{1}{i!}$$

Write a program that displays the `e` value for `i = 10000, 20000, ...,` and `100000`. (*Hint*: Because $i! = i \times (i-1) \times \ldots \times 2 \times 1$, then

$$\frac{1}{i!} \text{ is } \frac{1}{i(i-1)!}$$

Initialize `e` and `item` to be `1` and keep adding a new `item` to `e`. The new item is the previous item divided by `i` for `i = 2, 3, 4, ...`.)

**4.27 (*Display leap years*) Write a program that displays all the leap years, ten per line, in the twenty-first century (from 2001 to 2100), separated by exactly one space.

**4.28 (*Display the first days of each month*) Write a program that prompts the user to enter the year and first day of the year, and displays the first day of each month in the year on the console. For example, if the user entered the year `2013`, and `2` for Tuesday, January 1, 2013, your program should display the following output:

```
January 1, 2013 is Tuesday
...
December 1, 2013 is Sunday
```

**4.29 (*Display calendars*) Write a program that prompts the user to enter the year and first day of the year and displays the calendar table for the year on the console. For example, if the user entered the year `2013`, and `2` for Tuesday, January 1, 2013, your program should display the calendar for each month in the year, as follows:

January 2013

Sun	Mon	Tue	Wed	Thu	Fri	Sat
		1	2	3	4	5
6	7	8	9	10	11	12
13	14	15	16	17	18	19
20	21	22	23	24	25	26
27	28	29	30	31		

⋮

December 2013

Sun	Mon	Tue	Wed	Thu	Fri	Sat
1	2	3	4	5	6	7
8	9	10	11	12	13	14
15	16	17	18	19	20	21
22	23	24	25	26	27	28
29	30	31				

***4.30** (*Financial application: compound value*) Suppose you save $100 *each* month into a savings account with the annual interest rate 5%. So, the monthly interest rate is `0.05 / 12 = 0.00417`. After the first month, the value in the account becomes

```
100 * (1 + 0.00417) = 100.417
```

After the second month, the value in the account becomes

```
(100 + 100.417) * (1 + 0.00417) = 201.252
```

After the third month, the value in the account becomes

```
(100 + 201.252) * (1 + 0.00417) = 302.507
```

and so on.

Write a program that prompts the user to enter an amount (e.g., `100`), the annual interest rate (e.g., `5`), and the number of months (e.g., `6`) and displays the amount in the savings account after the given month.

***4.31** (*Financial application: compute CD value*) Suppose you put $10,000 into a CD with an annual percentage yield of 5.75%. After one month, the CD is worth

```
10000 + 10000 * 5.75 / 1200 = 10047.91
```

After two months, the CD is worth

```
10047.91 + 10047.91 * 5.75 / 1200 = 10096.06
```

After three months, the CD is worth

```
10096.06 + 10096.06 * 5.75 / 1200 = 10144.43
```

and so on.

Write a program that prompts the user to enter an amount (e.g., `10000`), the annual percentage yield (e.g., `5.75`), and the number of months (e.g., `18`) and displays a table as shown in the sample run.

```
Enter the initial deposit amount: 10000 ↵Enter
Enter annual percentage yield: 5.75 ↵Enter
Enter maturity period (number of months): 18 ↵Enter

Month  CD Value
1      10047.91
2      10096.06
...
17     10846.56
18     10898.54
```

****4.32** (*Game: lottery*) Revise Listing 3.9, Lottery.java, to generate a lottery of a two-digit number. The two digits in the number are distinct. (*Hint*: Generate the first digit. Use a loop to continuously generate the second digit until it is different from the first digit.)

**4.33 (*Perfect number*) A positive integer is called a *perfect number* if it is equal to the sum of all of its positive divisors, excluding itself. For example, 6 is the first perfect number because `6 = 3 + 2 + 1`. The next is `28 = 14 + 7 + 4 + 2 + 1`. There are four perfect numbers less than 10,000. Write a program to find all these four numbers.

***4.34 (*Game: scissor, rock, paper*) Exercise 3.17 gives a program that plays the scissor-rock-paper game. Revise the program to let the user continuously play until either the user or the computer wins more than two times.

*4.35 (*Summation*) Write a program to compute the following summation.

$$\frac{1}{1 + \sqrt{2}} + \frac{1}{\sqrt{2} + \sqrt{3}} + \frac{1}{\sqrt{3} + \sqrt{4}} + \ldots + \frac{1}{\sqrt{624} + \sqrt{625}}$$

**4.36 (*Business application: checking ISBN*) Use loops to simplify Exercise 3.9.

**4.37 (*Decimal to binary*) Write a program that prompts the user to enter a decimal integer and displays its corresponding binary value. Don't use Java's `Integer.toBinaryString(int)` in this program.

**4.38 (*Decimal to hex*) Write a program that prompts the user to enter a decimal integer and displays its corresponding hexadecimal value. Don't use Java's `Integer.toHexString(int)` in this program.

*4.39 (*Financial application: find the sales amount*) You have just started a sales job in a department store. Your pay consists of a base salary and a commission. The base salary is $5,000. The scheme shown below is used to determine the commission rate.

Sales Amount	Commission Rate
$0.01–$5,000	8 percent
$5,000.01–$10,000	10 percent
$10,000.01 and above	12 percent

Your goal is to earn $30,000 a year. Write a program that finds out the minimum number of sales you have to generate in order to make $30,000.

4.40 (*Simulation: heads or tails*) Write a program that simulates flipping a coin one million times and displays the number of heads and tails.

**4.41 (*Occurrence of max numbers*) Write a program that reads integers, finds the largest of them, and counts its occurrences. Assume that the input ends with number `0`. Suppose that you entered `3 5 2 5 5 5 0`; the program finds that the largest is `5` and the occurrence count for `5` is `4`.

(*Hint*: Maintain two variables, `max` and `count`. `max` stores the current max number, and `count` stores its occurrences. Initially, assign the first number to `max` and `1` to `count`. Compare each subsequent number with `max`. If the number is greater than `max`, assign it to `max` and reset `count` to `1`. If the number is equal to `max`, increment `count` by `1`.)

```
Enter numbers: 3 5 2 5 5 5 0 ↵Enter
The largest number is 5
The occurrence count of the largest number is 4
```

***4.42** (*Financial application: find the sales amount*) Rewrite Exercise 4.39 as follows:

- Use a `for` loop instead of a `do-while` loop.
- Let the user enter `COMMISSION_SOUGHT` instead of fixing it as a constant.

***4.43** (*Simulation: clock countdown*) Write a program that prompts the user to enter the number of seconds, displays a message at every second, and terminates when the time expires. Here is a sample run:

```
Enter the number of seconds: 3 ↵Enter
2 seconds remaining
1 second remaining
Stopped
```

****4.44** (*Monte Carlo simulation*) A square is divided into four smaller regions as shown below in (a). If you throw a dart into the square 1,000,000 times, what is the probability for a dart to fall into an odd-numbered region? Write a program to simulate the process and display the result.

(*Hint*: Place the center of the square in the center of a coordinate system, as shown in (b). Randomly generate a point in the square and count the number of times for a point to fall into an odd-numbered region.)

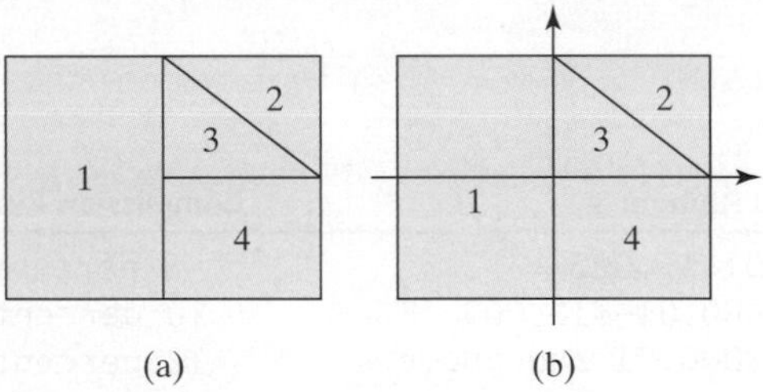

(a) (b)

***4.45** (*Math: combinations*) Write a program that displays all possible combinations for picking two numbers from integers `1` to `7`. Also display the total number of all combinations.

```
1 2
1 3
...
...

The total number of all combinations is 21
```

***4.46** (*Computer architecture: bit-level operations*) A `short` value is stored in `16` bits. Write a program that prompts the user to enter a short integer and displays the `16` bits for the integer. Here are sample runs:

```
Enter an integer: 5 ↵Enter
The bits are 0000000000000101
```

```
Enter an integer: -5 ↵Enter
The bits are 1111111111111011
```

(*Hint*: You need to use the bitwise right shift operator (>>) and the bitwise **AND** operator (&), which are covered in Appendix G, Bitwise Operations.)

****4.47** (*Statistics: compute mean and standard deviation*) In business applications, you are often asked to compute the mean and standard deviation of data. The mean is simply the average of the numbers. The standard deviation is a statistic that tells you how tightly all the various data are clustered around the mean in a set of data. For example, what is the average age of the students in a class? How close are the ages? If all the students are the same age, the deviation is 0.

Write a program that prompts the user to enter ten numbers, and displays the mean and standard deviations of these numbers using the following formula:

$$mean = \frac{\sum_{i=1}^{n} x_i}{n} = \frac{x_1 + x_2 + \ldots + x_n}{n} \qquad deviation = \sqrt{\frac{\sum_{i=1}^{n} x_i^2 - \frac{\left(\sum_{i=1}^{n} x_i\right)^2}{n}}{n-1}}$$

Here is a sample run:

```
Enter ten numbers: 1 2 3 4.5 5.6 6 7 8 9 10 ↵Enter
The mean is 5.61
The standard deviation is 2.99794
```

CHAPTER 5

METHODS

Objectives

- To define methods with formal parameters (§5.2).
- To invoke methods with actual parameters (i.e., arguments) (§5.2).
- To define methods with a return value (§5.3).
- To define methods without a return value (§5.4).
- To pass arguments by value (§5.5).
- To develop reusable code that is modular, easy to read, easy to debug, and easy to maintain (§5.6).
- To write a method that converts decimals to hexadecimals (§5.7).
- To use method overloading and understand ambiguous overloading (§5.8).
- To determine the scope of variables (§5.9).
- To solve mathematics problems using the methods in the `Math` class (§§5.10–5.11).
- To apply the concept of method abstraction in software development (§5.12).
- To design and implement methods using stepwise refinement (§5.12).

5.1 Introduction

Methods can be used to define reusable code and organize and simplify code.

problem

Suppose that you need to find the sum of integers from 1 to 10, from 20 to 37, and from 35 to 49, respectively. You may write the code as follows:

```
int sum = 0;
for (int i = 1; i <= 10; i++)
  sum += i;
System.out.println("Sum from 1 to 10 is " + sum);

sum = 0;
for (int i = 20; i <= 37; i++)
  sum += i;
System.out.println("Sum from 20 to 37 is " + sum);

sum = 0;
for (int i = 35; i <= 49; i++)
  sum += i;
System.out.println("Sum from 35 to 49 is " + sum);
```

why methods?

You may have observed that computing these sums from 1 to 10, from 20 to 37, and from 35 to 49 are very similar except that the starting and ending integers are different. Wouldn't it be nice if we could write the common code once and reuse it? We can do so by defining a method and invoking it.

The preceding code can be simplified as follows:

define sum method

main method

invoke sum

```
1  public static int sum(int i1, int i2) {
2    int result = 0;
3    for (int i = i1; i <= i2; i++)
4      result += i;
5
6    return result;
7  }
8
9  public static void main(String[] args) {
10   System.out.println("Sum from 1 to 10 is " + sum(1, 10));
11   System.out.println("Sum from 20 to 37 is " + sum(20, 37));
12   System.out.println("Sum from 35 to 49 is " + sum(35, 49));
13 }
```

Lines 1–7 define the method named sum with two parameters i1 and i2. The statements in the main method invoke sum(1, 10) to compute the sum from 1 to 10, sum(20, 37) to compute the sum from 20 to 37, and sum(35, 49) to compute the sum from 35 to 49.

method

A *method* is a collection of statements grouped together to perform an operation. In earlier chapters you have used predefined methods such as System.out.println, JOptionPane.showMessageDialog, System.exit, Math.pow, and Math.random. These methods are defined in the Java library. In this chapter, you will learn how to define your own methods and apply method abstraction to solve complex problems.

5.2 Defining a Method

A method definition consists of its method name, parameters, return value type, and body.

The syntax for defining a method is:

```
modifier returnValueType methodName(list of parameters) {
  // Method body;
}
```

Let's look at a method defined to find the larger between two integers. This method, named `max`, has two `int` parameters, `num1` and `num2`, the larger of which is returned by the method. Figure 5.1 illustrates the components of this method.

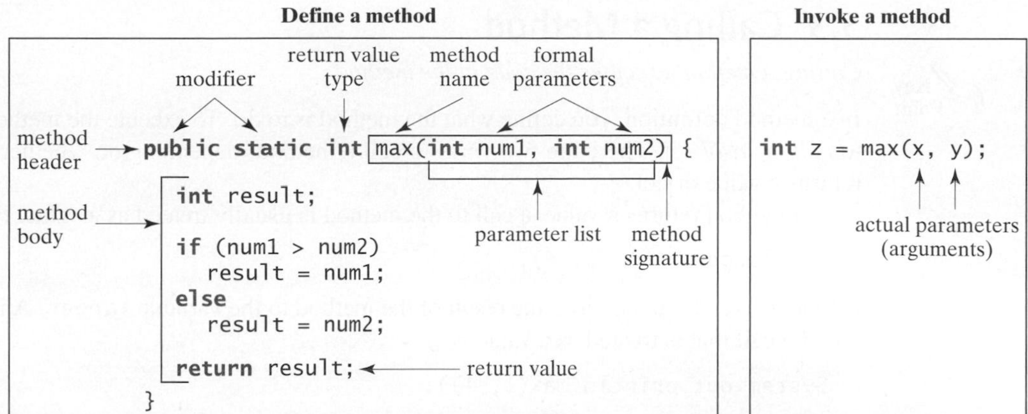

FIGURE 5.1 A method definition consists of a method header and a method body.

The *method header* specifies the *modifiers*, *return value type*, *method name*, and *parameters* of the method. The `static` modifier is used for all the methods in this chapter. The reason for using it will be discussed in Chapter 8, Objects and Classes.

method header
modifier

A method may return a value. The `returnValueType` is the data type of the value the method returns. Some methods perform desired operations without returning a value. In this case, the `returnValueType` is the keyword `void`. For example, the `returnValueType` is `void` in the `main` method, as well as in `System.exit`, `System.out.println`, and `JOptionPane.showMessageDialog`. If a method returns a value, it is called a *value-returning method*, otherwise it is called a *void method.*

value-returning method
void method

The variables defined in the method header are known as *formal parameters* or simply *parameters.* A parameter is like a placeholder: When a method is invoked, you pass a value to the parameter. This value is referred to as an *actual parameter or argument.* The *parameter list* refers to the method's type, order, and number of the parameters. The method name and the parameter list together constitute the *method signature.* Parameters are optional; that is, a method doesn't have to contain any parameters. For example, the `Math.random()` method has no parameters.

formal parameter
parameter
actual parameter
argument
parameter list
method signature

The method body contains a collection of statements that implement the method. The method body of the `max` method uses an `if` statement to determine which number is larger and return the value of that number. In order for a value-returning method to return a result, a return statement using the keyword `return` is *required.* The method terminates when a return statement is executed.

Note

Some programming languages refer to methods as *procedures* and *functions.* In those languages, a value-returning method is called a *function* and a void method is called a *procedure.*

Caution

In the method header, you need to declare each parameter separately. For instance, `max(int num1, int num2)` is correct, but `max(int num1, num2)` is wrong.

define vs. declare

Note

We say "*define* a method" and "*declare* a variable." We are making a subtle distinction here. A definition defines what the defined item is, but a declaration usually involves allocating memory to store data for the declared item.

5.3 Calling a Method

Key Point

Calling a method executes the code in the method.

In a method definition, you define what the method is to do. To execute the method, you have to *call* or *invoke* it. There are two ways to call a method, depending on whether the method returns a value or not.

If a method returns a value, a call to the method is usually treated as a value. For example,

```
int larger = max(3, 4);
```

calls `max(3, 4)` and assigns the result of the method to the variable `larger`. Another example of a call that is treated as a value is

```
System.out.println(max(3, 4));
```

which prints the return value of the method call `max(3, 4)`.

If a method returns `void`, a call to the method must be a statement. For example, the method `println` returns `void`. The following call is a statement:

```
System.out.println("Welcome to Java!");
```

Note

A value-returning method can also be invoked as a statement in Java. In this case, the caller simply ignores the return value. This is not often done, but it is permissible if the caller is not interested in the return value.

When a program calls a method, program control is transferred to the called method. A called method returns control to the caller when its return statement is executed or when its method-ending closing brace is reached.

Listing 5.1 shows a complete program that is used to test the `max` method.

VideoNote
Define/invoke `max` method

LISTING 5.1 TestMax.java

main method · invoke max · define method

```
public class TestMax {
  /** Main method */
  public static void main(String[] args) {
    int i = 5;
    int j = 2;
    int k = max(i, j);
    System.out.println("The maximum of " + i +
      " and " + j + " is " + k);
  }

  /** Return the max of two numbers */
  public static int max(int num1, int num2) {
    int result;

    if (num1 > num2)
      result = num1;
    else
      result = num2;

    return result;
  }
}
```

```
The maximum of 5 and 2 is 5
```

	line#	i	j	k	num1	num2	result
	4	5					
	5		2				
Invoking max	12				5	2	
	13						undefined
	16						5
	6			5			

This program contains the `main` method and the `max` method. The `main` method is just like any other method except that it is invoked by the JVM to start the program.

`main` method

The `main` method's header is always the same. Like the one in this example, it includes the modifiers `public` and `static`, return value type `void`, method name `main`, and a parameter of the `String[]` type. `String[]` indicates that the parameter is an array of `String`, a subject addressed in Chapter 6.

The statements in `main` may invoke other methods that are defined in the class that contains the `main` method or in other classes. In this example, the `main` method invokes `max(i, j)`, which is defined in the same class with the `main` method.

When the `max` method is invoked (line 6), variable `i`'s value `5` is passed to `num1`, and variable `j`'s value `2` is passed to `num2` in the `max` method. The flow of control transfers to the `max` method, and the `max` method is executed. When the `return` statement in the `max` method is executed, the `max` method returns the control to its caller (in this case the caller is the `main` method). This process is illustrated in Figure 5.2.

`max` method

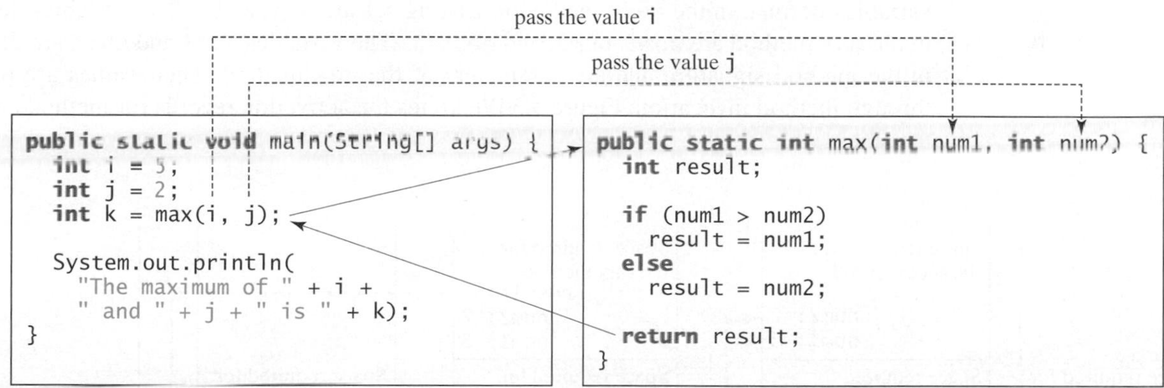

FIGURE 5.2 When the `max` method is invoked, the flow of control transfers to it. Once the `max` method is finished, it returns control back to the caller.

Caution

A `return` statement is required for a value-returning method. The method shown below in (a) is logically correct, but it has a compile error because the Java compiler thinks that this method might not return a value.

```
public static int sign(int n) {
  if (n > 0)
    return 1;
  else if (n == 0)
    return 0;
  else if (n < 0)
    return -1;
}
```

(a)

Should be

```
public static int sign(int n) {
  if (n > 0)
    return 1;
  else if (n == 0)
    return 0;
  else
    return -1;
}
```

(b)

To fix this problem, delete `if (n < 0)` in (a), so the compiler will see a `return` statement to be reached regardless of how the `if` statement is evaluated.

Note

reusing method

Methods enable code sharing and reuse. The `max` method can be invoked from any class, not just `TestMax`. If you create a new class, you can invoke the `max` method using `ClassName.methodName` (i.e., `TestMax.max`).

activation record

call stack

Each time a method is invoked, the system creates an *activation record* (also called an *activation frame*) that stores parameters and variables for the method and places the activation record in an area of memory known as a *call stack*. A call stack is also known as an *execution stack*, *runtime stack*, or *machine stack*, and it is often shortened to just "the stack." When a method calls another method, the caller's activation record is kept intact, and a new activation record is created for the new method called. When a method finishes its work and returns to its caller, its activation record is removed from the call stack.

A call stack stores the activation records in a last-in, first-out fashion: The activation record for the method that is invoked last is removed first from the stack. For example, suppose method `m1` calls method `m2`, and then `m3`. The runtime system pushes `m1`'s activation record into the stack, then `m2`'s, and then `m3`'s. After `m3` is finished, its activation record is removed from the stack. After `m2` is finished, its activation record is removed from the stack. After `m1` is finished, its activation record is removed from the stack.

Understanding call stacks helps you to comprehend how methods are invoked. The variables defined in the `main` method in Listing 5.1 are `i`, `j`, and `k`. The variables defined in the `max` method are `num1`, `num2`, and `result`. The variables `num1` and `num2` are defined in the method signature and are parameters of the `max` method. Their values are passed through method invocation. Figure 5.3 illustrates the activation records for method calls in the stack.

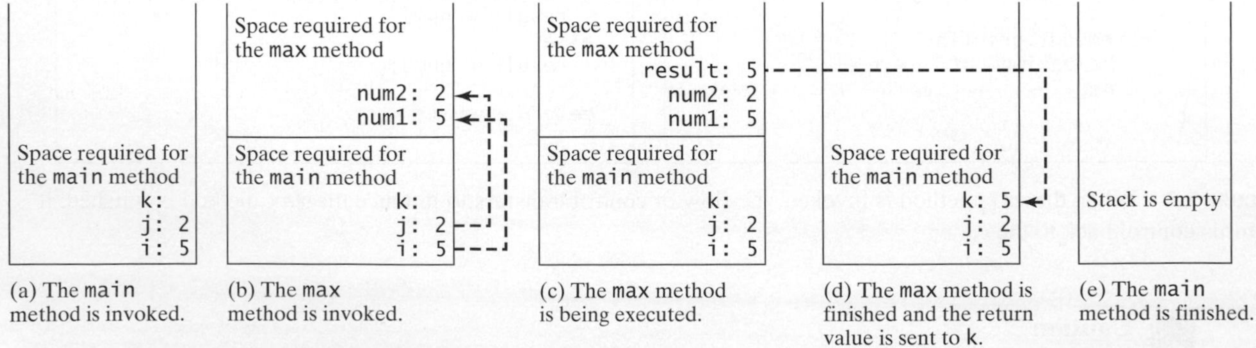

FIGURE 5.3 When the `max` method is invoked, the flow of control transfers to the `max` method. Once the `max` method is finished, it returns control back to the caller.

5.4 void Method Example

A `void` *method does not return a value.*

Key Point

The preceding section gives an example of a value-returning method. This section shows how to define and invoke a `void` method. Listing 5.2 gives a program that defines a method named `printGrade` and invokes it to print the grade for a given score.

VideoNote
Use `void` method

LISTING 5.2 TestVoidMethod.java

```
1  public class TestVoidMethod {
2    public static void main(String[] args) {
3      System.out.print("The grade is ");
4      printGrade(78.5);
5
6      System.out.print("The grade is ");
7      printGrade(59.5);
8    }
9
10   public static void printGrade(double score) {
11     if (score >= 90.0) {
12       System.out.println('A');
13     }
14     else if (score >= 80.0) {
15       System.out.println('B');
16     }
17     else if (score >= 70.0) {
18       System.out.println('C');
19     }
20     else if (score >= 60.0) {
21       System.out.println('D');
22     }
23     else {
24       System.out.println('F');
25     }
26   }
27 }
```

`main` method
invoke `printGrade`
`printGrade` method

```
The grade is C
The grade is F
```

invoke `void` method

The `printGrade` method is a `void` method because it does not return any value. A call to a `void` method must be a statement. Therefore, it is invoked as a statement in line 4 in the `main` method. Like any Java statement, it is terminated with a semicolon.

void vs. value-returned

To see the differences between a void and value-returning method, let's redesign the `printGrade` method to return a value. The new method, which we call `getGrade`, returns the grade as shown in Listing 5.3.

LISTING 5.3 TestReturnGradeMethod.java

```
public class TestReturnGradeMethod {
  public static void main(String[] args) {
    System.out.print("The grade is " + getGrade(78.5));
    System.out.print("\nThe grade is " + getGrade(59.5));
  }

```

`main` method
invoke `getGrade`

getGrade method

```
 7   public static char getGrade(double score) {
 8     if (score >= 90.0)
 9       return 'A';
10     else if (score >= 80.0)
11       return 'B';
12     else if (score >= 70.0)
13       return 'C';
14     else if (score >= 60.0)
15       return 'D';
16     else
17       return 'F';
18   }
19 }
```

```
The grade is C
The grade is F
```

The `getGrade` method defined in lines 7–18 returns a character grade based on the numeric score value. The caller invokes this method in lines 3–4.

The `getGrade` method can be invoked by a caller wherever a character may appear. The `printGrade` method does not return any value, so it must be invoked as a statement.

return in void method

Note

A `return` statement is not needed for a `void` method, but it can be used for terminating the method and returning to the method's caller. The syntax is simply

```
return;
```

This is not often done, but sometimes it is useful for circumventing the normal flow of control in a `void` method. For example, the following code has a return statement to terminate the method when the score is invalid.

```
public static void printGrade(double score) {
  if (score < 0 || score > 100) {
    System.out.println("Invalid score");
    return;
  }

  if (score >= 90.0) {
    System.out.println('A');
  }
  else if (score >= 80.0) {
    System.out.println('B');
  }
  else if (score >= 70.0) {
    System.out.println('C');
  }
  else if (score >= 60.0) {
    System.out.println('D');
  }
  else {
    System.out.println('F');
  }
}
```

Check Point

MyProgrammingLab™

5.1 What are the benefits of using a method?

5.2 How do you define a method? How do you invoke a method?

5.3 How do you simplify the `max` method in Listing 5.1 using the conditional operator?

5.4 True or false? A call to a method with a `void` return type is always a statement itself, but a call to a value-returning method cannot be a statement by itself.

5.5 What is the `return` type of a `main` method?

5.6 What would be wrong with not writing a `return` statement in a value-returning method? Can you have a `return` statement in a `void` method? Does the `return` statement in the following method cause syntax errors?

```
public static void xMethod(double x, double y) {
  System.out.println(x + y);
  return x + y;
}
```

5.7 Define the terms parameter, argument, and method signature.

5.8 Write method headers (not the bodies) for the following methods:

a. Compute a sales commission, given the sales amount and the commission rate.

b. Display the calendar for a month, given the month and year.

c. Compute a square root of a number.

d. Test whether a number is even, and returning `true` if it is.

e. Display a message a specified number of times.

f. Compute the monthly payment, given the loan amount, number of years, and annual interest rate.

g. Find the corresponding uppercase letter, given a lowercase letter.

5.9 Identify and correct the errors in the following program:

```
public class Test {
  public static method1(int n, m) {
    n += m;
    method2(3.4);
  }

  public static int method2(int n) {
    if (n > 0) return 1;
    else if (n == 0) return 0;
    else if (n < 0) return -1;
  }
}
```

5.10 Reformat the following program according to the programming style and documentation guidelines proposed in Section 1.10, Programming Style and Documentation. Use the next-line brace style.

```
public class Test {
  public static double method1(double i, double j)
  {
  while (i < j) {
    j--;
  }

  return j;
  }
}
```

5.5 Passing Parameters by Values

The arguments are passed by value to parameters when invoking a method.

parameter order association

The power of a method is its ability to work with parameters. You can use `println` to print any string and `max` to find the maximum of any two `int` values. When calling a method, you need to provide arguments, which must be given in the same order as their respective parameters in the method signature. This is known as *parameter order association.* For example, the following method prints a message `n` times:

```
public static void nPrintln(String message, int n) {
  for (int i = 0; i < n; i++)
    System.out.println(message);
}
```

You can use `nPrintln("Hello", 3)` to print `Hello` three times. The `nPrintln("Hello", 3)` statement passes the actual string parameter `Hello` to the parameter `message`, passes `3` to `n`, and prints `Hello` three times. However, the statement `nPrintln(3, "Hello")` would be wrong. The data type of `3` does not match the data type for the first parameter, `message`, nor does the second argument, `Hello`, match the second parameter, `n`.

Caution

The arguments must match the parameters in *order, number,* and *compatible type,* as defined in the method signature. Compatible type means that you can pass an argument to a parameter without explicit casting, such as passing an `int` value argument to a `double` value parameter.

pass-by-value

When you invoke a method with an argument, the value of the argument is passed to the parameter. This is referred to as *pass-by-value.* If the argument is a variable rather than a literal value, the value of the variable is passed to the parameter. The variable is not affected, regardless of the changes made to the parameter inside the method. As shown in Listing 5.4, the value of `x` (`1`) is passed to the parameter `n` to invoke the `increment` method (line 5). The parameter `n` is incremented by `1` in the method (line 10), but `x` is not changed no matter what the method does.

LISTING 5.4 `Increment.java`

invoke increment

increment n

```
1  public class Increment {
2    public static void main(String[] args) {
3      int x = 1;
4      System.out.println("Before the call, x is " + x);
5      increment(x);
6      System.out.println("After the call, x is " + x);
7    }
8
9    public static void increment(int n) {
10     n++;
11     System.out.println("n inside the method is " + n);
12   }
13 }
```

```
Before the call, x is 1
n inside the method is 2?
After the call, x is 1
```

Listing 5.5 gives another program that demonstrates the effect of passing by value. The program creates a method for swapping two variables. The swap method is invoked by passing two arguments. Interestingly, the values of the arguments are not changed after the method is invoked.

LISTING 5.5 TestPassByValue.java

```
1  public class TestPassByValue {
2    /** Main method */
3    public static void main(String[] args) {
4      // Declare and initialize variables
5      int num1 = 1;
6      int num2 = 2;
7
8      System.out.println("Before invoking the swap method, num1 is " +
9        num1 + " and num2 is " + num2);
10
11     // Invoke the swap method to attempt to swap two variables
12     swap(num1, num2);
13
14     System.out.println("After invoking the swap method, num1 is " +
15       num1 + " and num2 is " + num2);
16   }
17
18   /** Swap two variables */
19   public static void swap(int n1, int n2) {
20     System.out.println("\tInside the swap method");
21     System.out.println("\t\tBefore swapping, n1 is " + n1
22       + " and n2 is " + n2);
23
24     // Swap n1 with n2
25     int temp = n1;
26     n1 = n2;
27     n2 = temp;
28
29     System.out.println("\t\tAfter swapping, n1 is " + n1
30       + " and n2 is " + n2);
31   }
32 }
```

false swap

```
Before invoking the swap method, num1 is 1 and num2 is 2
  Inside the swap method
    Before swapping, n1 is 1 and n2 is 2
    After swapping, n1 is 2 and n2 is 1
After invoking the swap method, num1 is 1 and num2 is 2
```

Before the swap method is invoked (line 12), num1 is 1 and num2 is 2. After the swap method is invoked, num1 is still 1 and num2 is still 2. Their values have not been swapped. As shown in Figure 5.4, the values of the arguments num1 and num2 are passed to n1 and n2, but n1 and n2 have their own memory locations independent of num1 and num2. Therefore, changes in n1 and n2 do not affect the contents of num1 and num2.

Another twist is to change the parameter name n1 in swap to num1. What effect does this have? No change occurs, because it makes no difference whether the parameter and the argument have the same name. The parameter is a variable in the method with its own memory space. The variable is allocated when the method is invoked, and it disappears when the method is returned to its caller.

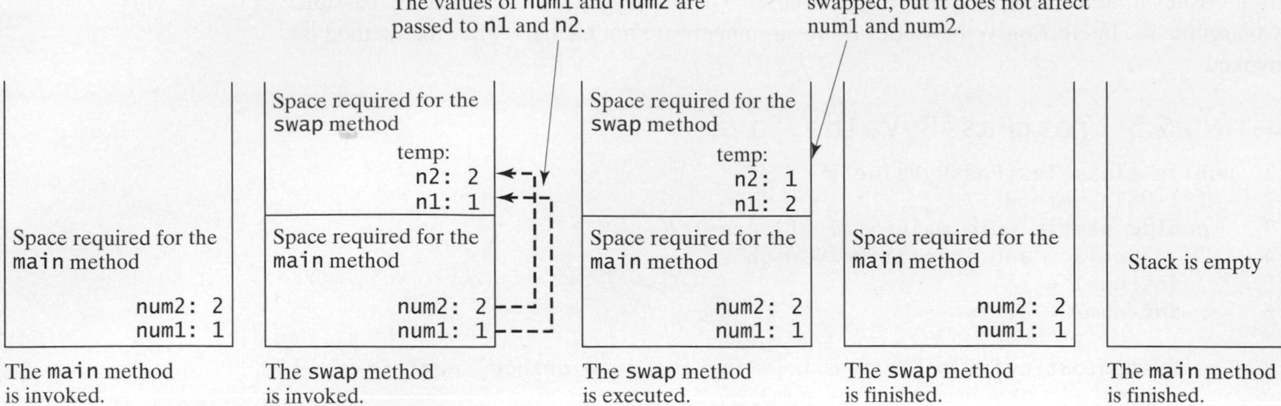

FIGURE 5.4 The values of the variables are passed to the method's parameters.

Note

For simplicity, Java programmers often say *passing* **x** to **y**, which actually means *passing the value of argument* **x** *to parameter* **y**.

Check Point

MyProgrammingLab™

5.11 How is an argument passed to a method? Can the argument have the same name as its parameter?

5.12 Identify and correct the errors in the following program:

```
public class Test {
  public static void main(String[] args) {
    nPrintln(5, "Welcome to Java!");
  }

  public static void nPrintln(String message, int n) {
    int n = 1;
    for (int i = 0; i < n; i++)
      System.out.println(message);
  }
}
```

5.13 What is pass-by-value? Show the result of the following programs.

```
public class Test {
  public static void main(String[] args) {
    int max = 0;
    max(1, 2, max);
    System.out.println(max);
  }

  public static void max(
      int value1, int value2, int max) {
    if (value1 > value2)
      max = value1;
    else
      max = value2;
  }
}
```

(a)

```
public class Test {
  public static void main(String[] args) {
    int i = 1;
    while (i <= 6) {
      method1(i, 2);
      i++;
    }
  }

  public static void method1(
      int i, int num) {
    for (int j = 1; j <= i; j++) {
      System.out.print(num + " ");
      num *= 2;
    }

    System.out.println();
  }
}
```

(b)

```
public class Test {
  public static void main(String[] args) {
    // Initialize times
    int times = 3;
    System.out.println("Before the call,"
      + " variable times is " + times);

    // Invoke nPrintln and display times
    nPrintln("Welcome to Java!", times);
    System.out.println("After the call,"
      + " variable times is " + times);
  }

  // Print the message n times
  public static void nPrintln(
      String message, int n) {
    while (n > 0) {
      System.out.println("n = " + n);
      System.out.println(message);
      n--;
    }
  }
}
```

(c)

```
public class Test {
  public static void main(String[] args) {
    int i = 0;
    while (i <= 4) {
      method1(i);
      i++;
    }

    System.out.println("i is " + i);
  }

  public static void method1(int i) {
    do {
      if (i % 3 != 0)
        System.out.print(i + " ");
      i--;
    }
    while (i >= 1);

    System.out.println();
  }
}
```

(d)

5.14 For (a) in the preceding question, show the contents of the activation records in the call stack just before the method max is invoked, just as max is entered, just before max is returned, and right after max is returned.

5.6 Modularizing Code

Modularizing makes the code easy to maintain and debug and enables the code to be reused.

Methods can be used to reduce redundant code and enable code reuse. Methods can also be used to modularize code and improve the quality of the program.

Modularize code

Listing 4.9 gives a program that prompts the user to enter two integers and displays their greatest common divisor. You can rewrite the program using a method, as shown in Listing 5.6.

LISTING 5.6 GreatestCommonDivisorMethod.java

```
import java.util.Scanner;

public class GreatestCommonDivisorMethod {
  /** Main method */
  public static void main(String[] args) {
    // Create a Scanner
    Scanner input = new Scanner(System.in);

    // Prompt the user to enter two integers
    System.out.print("Enter first integer: ");
    int n1 = input.nextInt();
    System.out.print("Enter second integer: ");
    int n2 = input.nextInt();

```

invoke gcd

compute gcd

return gcd

```
    System.out.println("The greatest common divisor for " + n1 +
      " and " + n2 + " is " + gcd(n1, n2));
  }

  /** Return the gcd of two integers */
  public static int gcd(int n1, int n2) {
    int gcd = 1; // Initial gcd is 1
    int k = 2;  // Possible gcd

    while (k <= n1 && k <= n2) {
      if (n1 % k == 0 && n2 % k == 0)
        gcd = k; // Update gcd
      k++;
    }

    return gcd; // Return gcd
  }
}
```

```
Enter first integer: 45 ↵Enter
Enter second integer: 75 ↵Enter
The greatest common divisor for 45 and 75 is 15
```

By encapsulating the code for obtaining the gcd in a method, this program has several advantages:

1. It isolates the problem for computing the gcd from the rest of the code in the main method. Thus, the logic becomes clear and the program is easier to read.
2. The errors on computing the gcd are confined in the gcd method, which narrows the scope of debugging.
3. The gcd method now can be reused by other programs.

Listing 5.7 applies the concept of code modularization to improve Listing 4.14, PrimeNumber.java.

LISTING 5.7 PrimeNumberMethod.java

invoke printPrimeNumbers

printPrimeNumbers method

invoke isPrime

```
public class PrimeNumberMethod {
  public static void main(String[] args) {
    System.out.println("The first 50 prime numbers are \n");
    printPrimeNumbers(50);
  }

  public static void printPrimeNumbers(int numberOfPrimes) {
    final int NUMBER_OF_PRIMES_PER_LINE = 10; // Display 10 per line
    int count = 0; // Count the number of prime numbers
    int number = 2; // A number to be tested for primeness

    // Repeatedly find prime numbers
    while (count < numberOfPrimes) {
      // Print the prime number and increase the count
      if (isPrime(number)) {
        count++; // Increase the count

```

```
        if (count % NUMBER_OF_PRIMES_PER_LINE == 0) {
          // Print the number and advance to the new line
          System.out.printf("%-5s\n", number);
        }
        else
          System.out.printf("%-5s", number);
      }

      // Check whether the next number is prime
      number++;
    }
  }

  /** Check whether number is prime */
  public static boolean isPrime(int number) {
    for (int divisor = 2; divisor <= number / 2; divisor++) {
      if (number % divisor == 0) { // If true, number is not prime
        return false; // Number is not a prime
      }
    }

    return true; // Number is prime
  }
}
```

isPrime method

```
The first 50 prime numbers are

2    3    5    7    11   13   17   19   23   29
31   37   41   43   47   53   59   61   67   71
73   79   83   89   97   101  103  107  109  113
127  131  137  139  149  151  157  163  167  173
179  181  191  193  197  199  211  223  227  229
```

We divided a large problem into two subproblems: determining whether a number is a prime and printing the prime numbers. As a result, the new program is easier to read and easier to debug. Moreover, the methods printPrimeNumbers and isPrime can be reused by other programs.

5.7 Case Study: Converting Decimals to Hexadecimals

This section presents a program that converts a decimal number to a hexadecimal number.

Hexadecimals are often used in computer systems programming (see Appendix F for an introduction to number systems). To convert a decimal number d to a hexadecimal number is to find the hexadecimal digits $h_n, h_{n-1}, h_{n-2}, \ldots, h_2, h_1$, and h_0 such that

$$d = h_n \times 16^n + h_{n-1} \times 16^{n-1} + h_{n-2} \times 16^{n-2} + \ldots \\ + h_2 \times 16^2 + h_1 \times 16^1 + h_0 \times 16^0$$

These hexadecimal digits can be found by successively dividing d by 16 until the quotient is 0. The remainders are $h_0, h_1, h_2, \ldots, h_{n-2}, h_{n-1}$, and h_n. The hexadecimal digits include the decimal digits 0, 1, 2, 3, 4, 5, 6, 7, 8, and 9, plus A, which is the decimal value 10; B, which is the decimal value 11; C, which is 12; D, which is 13; E, which is 14; and F, which is 15.

For example, the decimal number 123 is 7B in hexadecimal. The conversion is done as follows. Divide 123 by 16. The remainder is 11 (B in hexadecimal) and the quotient is 7. Continue to divide 7 by 16. The remainder is 7 and the quotient is 0. Therefore 7B is the hexadecimal number for 123.

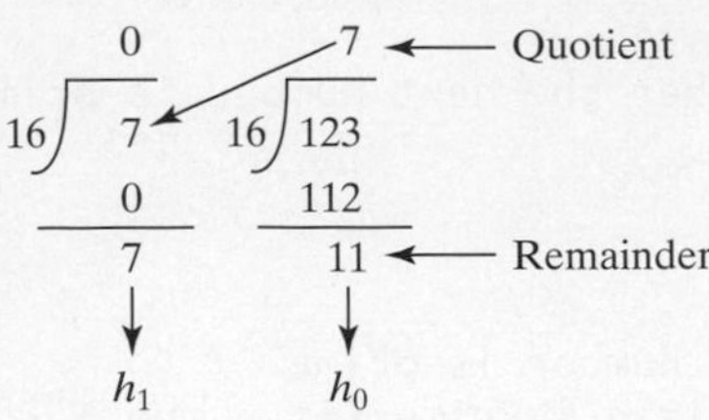

Listing 5.8 gives a program that prompts the user to enter a decimal number and converts it into a hex number as a string.

LISTING 5.8 Decimal2HexConversion.java

input decimal

decimal to hex

get a hex char

get a letter

```
import java.util.Scanner;

public class Decimal2HexConversion {
  /** Main method */
  public static void main(String[] args) {
    // Create a Scanner
    Scanner input = new Scanner(System.in);

    // Prompt the user to enter a decimal integer
    System.out.print("Enter a decimal number: ");
    int decimal = input.nextInt();

    System.out.println("The hex number for decimal " +
      decimal + " is " + decimalToHex(decimal));
  }

  /** Convert a decimal to a hex as a string */
  public static String decimalToHex(int decimal) {
    String hex = "";

    while (decimal != 0) {
      int hexValue = decimal % 16;
      hex = toHexChar(hexValue) + hex;
      decimal = decimal / 16;
    }

    return hex;
  }

  /** Convert an integer to a single hex digit in a character */
  public static char toHexChar(int hexValue) {
    if (hexValue <= 9 && hexValue >= 0)
      return (char)(hexValue + '0');
    else  // hexValue <= 15 && hexValue >= 10
      return (char)(hexValue - 10 + 'A');
  }
}
```

```
Enter a decimal number: 1234 ↵Enter
The hex number for decimal 1234 is 4D2
```

	line#	decimal	hex	hexValue	toHexChar(hexValue)
	19	1234	""		
iteration 1	22			2	
	23		"2"		2
	24	77			
iteration 2	22			13	
	23		"D2"		D
	24	4			
iteration 3	22			4	
	23		"4D2"		4
	24	0			

The program uses the `decimalToHex` method (lines 18–28) to convert a decimal integer to a hex number as a string. The method gets the remainder of the division of the decimal integer by `16` (line 22). The remainder is converted into a character by invoking the `toHexChar` method (line 23). The character is then appended to the hex string (line 23). The hex string is initially empty (line 19). Divide the decimal number by `16` to remove a hex digit from the number (line 24). The `decimalToHex` method repeatedly performs these operations in a loop until quotient becomes `0` (lines 21–25).

The `toHexChar` method (lines 31–36) converts a `hexValue` between `0` and `15` into a hex character. If `hexValue` is between `0` and `9`, it is converted to `(char)(hexValue + '0')` (line 33). Recall that when adding a character with an integer, the character's Unicode is used in the evaluation. For example, if `hexValue` is `5`, `(char)(hexValue + '0')` returns `5`. Similarly, if `hexValue` is between `10` and `15`, it is converted to `(char)(hexValue - 10 + 'A')` (line 35). For instance, if `hexValue` is `11`, `(char)(hexValue - 10 + 'A')` returns `B`.

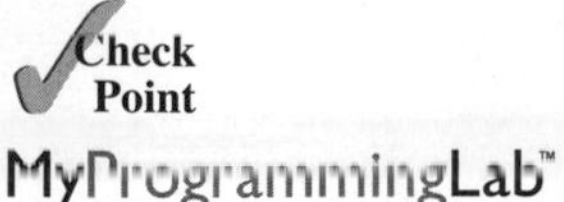

5.15 What is the return value from invoking `toHexChar(5)`? What is the return value from invoking `toHexChar(15)`?

5.16 What is the return value from invoking `decimalToHex(245)`? What is the return value from invoking `decimalToHex(3245)`?

5.8 Overloading Methods

Overloading methods enables you to define the methods with the same name as long as their signatures are different.

The `max` method that was used earlier works only with the `int` data type. But what if you need to determine which of two floating-point numbers has the maximum value? The solution is to create another method with the same name but different parameters, as shown in the following code:

```
public static double max(double num1, double num2) {
  if (num1 > num2)
    return num1;
  else
    return num2;
}
```

method overloading

If you call `max` with `int` parameters, the `max` method that expects `int` parameters will be invoked; if you call `max` with `double` parameters, the `max` method that expects `double` parameters will be invoked. This is referred to as *method overloading*; that is, two methods have the same name but different parameter lists within one class. The Java compiler determines which method to use based on the method signature.

Listing 5.9 is a program that creates three methods. The first finds the maximum integer, the second finds the maximum double, and the third finds the maximum among three double values. All three methods are named `max`.

Listing 5.9 TestMethodOverloading.java

```
1  public class TestMethodOverloading {
2    /** Main method */
3    public static void main(String[] args) {
4      // Invoke the max method with int parameters
5      System.out.println("The maximum of 3 and 4 is "
6        + max(3, 4));
7
8      // Invoke the max method with the double parameters
9      System.out.println("The maximum of 3.0 and 5.4 is "
10       + max(3.0, 5.4));
11
12     // Invoke the max method with three double parameters
13     System.out.println("The maximum of 3.0, 5.4, and 10.14 is "
14       + max(3.0, 5.4, 10.14));
15   }
16
17   /** Return the max of two int values */
18   public static int max(int num1, int num2) {
19     if (num1 > num2)
20       return num1;
21     else
22       return num2;
23   }
24
25   /** Find the max of two double values */
26   public static double max(double num1, double num2) {
27     if (num1 > num2)
28       return num1;
29     else
30       return num2;
31   }
32
33   /** Return the max of three double values */
34   public static double max(double num1, double num2, double num3) {
35     return max(max(num1, num2), num3);
36   }
37 }
```

overloaded max (line 18)

overloaded max (line 26)

overloaded max (line 34)

```
The maximum of 3 and 4 is 4
The maximum of 3.0 and 5.4 is 5.4
The maximum of 3.0, 5.4, and 10.14 is 10.14
```

When calling `max(3, 4)` (line 6), the `max` method for finding the maximum of two integers is invoked. When calling `max(3.0, 5.4)` (line 10), the `max` method for finding the maximum of two doubles is invoked. When calling `max(3.0, 5.4, 10.14)` (line 14), the `max` method for finding the maximum of three double values is invoked.

Can you invoke the `max` method with an `int` value and a `double` value, such as `max(2, 2.5)`? If so, which of the `max` methods is invoked? The answer to the first question is yes. The answer to the second question is that the `max` method for finding the maximum of two `double` values is invoked. The argument value `2` is automatically converted into a `double` value and passed to this method.

You may be wondering why the method `max(double, double)` is not invoked for the call `max(3, 4)`. Both `max(double, double)` and `max(int, int)` are possible matches for `max(3, 4)`. The Java compiler finds the most specific method for a method invocation. Since the method `max(int, int)` is more specific than `max(double, double)`, `max(int, int)` is used to invoke `max(3, 4)`.

Tip

Overloading methods can make programs clearer and more readable. Methods that perform the same function with different types of parameters should be given the same name.

Note

Overloaded methods must have different parameter lists. You cannot overload methods based on different modifiers or return types.

Note

ambiguous invocation

Sometimes there are two or more possible matches for an invocation of a method, but the compiler cannot determine the most specific match. This is referred to as *ambiguous invocation*. Ambiguous invocation causes a compile error. Consider the following code:

```
public class AmbiguousOverloading {
  public static void main(String[] args) {
    System.out.println(max(1, 2));
  }

  public static double max(int num1, double num2) {
    if (num1 > num2)
      return num1;
    else
      return num2;
  }

  public static double max(double num1, int num2) {
    if (num1 > num2)
      return num1;
    else
      return num2;
  }
}
```

Both `max(int, double)` and `max(double, int)` are possible candidates to match `max(1, 2)`. Because neither is more specific than the other, the invocation is ambiguous, resulting in a compile error.

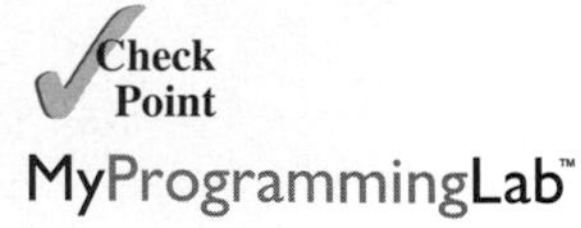

5.17 What is method overloading? Is it permissible to define two methods that have the same name but different parameter types? Is it permissible to define two methods in a class that have identical method names and parameter lists but different return value types or different modifiers?

5.18 What is wrong in the following program?

```
public class Test {
  public static void method(int x) {
  }
```

```
    public static int method(int y) {
      return y;
    }
  }
```

5.19 Given two method definitions,

```
public static double m(double x, double y)

public static double m(int x, double y)
```

tell which of the two methods is invoked for:

a. `double z = m(4, 5);`

b. `double z = m(4, 5.4);`

c. `double z = m(4.5, 5.4);`

5.9 The Scope of Variables

The scope of a variable *is the part of the program where the variable can be referenced.*

scope of a variable
local variable

Section 2.5 introduced the scope of a variable. This section discusses the scope of variables in more details. A variable defined inside a method is referred to as a *local variable*. The scope of a local variable starts from its declaration and continues to the end of the block that contains the variable. A local variable must be declared and assigned a value before it can be used.

A parameter is actually a local variable. The scope of a method parameter covers the entire method. A variable declared in the initial-action part of a `for`-loop header has its scope in the entire loop. However, a variable declared inside a `for`-loop body has its scope limited in the loop body from its declaration to the end of the block that contains the variable, as shown in Figure 5.5.

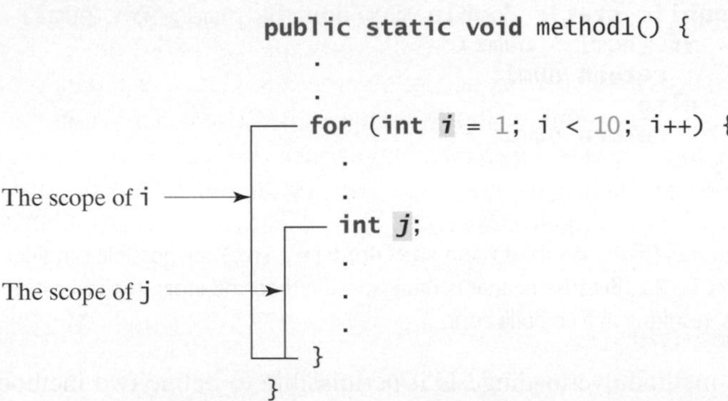

FIGURE 5.5 A variable declared in the initial action part of a `for`-loop header has its scope in the entire loop.

You can declare a local variable with the same name in different blocks in a method, but you cannot declare a local variable twice in the same block or in nested blocks, as shown in Figure 5.6.

It is fine to declare `i` in two nonnested blocks.

```
public static void method1() {
  int x = 1;
  int y = 1;

  for (int i = 1; i < 10; i++) {
    x += i;
  }

  for (int i = 1; i < 10; i++) {
    y += i;
  }
}
```

It is wrong to declare `i` in two nested blocks.

```
public static void method2() {

  int i = 1;
  int sum = 0;

  for (int i = 1; i < 10; i++)
    sum += i;
  }

}
```

FIGURE 5.6 A variable can be declared multiple times in nonnested blocks, but only once in nested blocks.

Caution

Do not declare a variable inside a block and then attempt to use it outside the block. Here is an example of a common mistake:

```
for (int i = 0; i < 10; i++) {
}

System.out.println(i);
```

The last statement would cause a syntax error, because variable `i` is not defined outside of the `for` loop.

Check Point

MyProgrammingLab™

5.20 What is a local variable?

5.21 What is the scope of a local variable?

5.10 The Math Class

Key Point

The `Math` class contains the methods needed to perform basic mathematical functions.

You have already used the `pow(a, b)` method to compute a^b in Section 2.9.3, Exponent Operations, and the `Math.random()` method in Section 3.8, Generating Random Numbers. This section introduces other useful methods in the `Math` class. They can be categorized as *trigonometric methods*, *exponent methods*, and *service methods*. Service methods include the rounding, min, max, absolute, and random methods. In addition to methods, the `Math` class provides two useful `double` constants, `PI` and `E` (the base of natural logarithms). You can use these constants as `Math.PI` and `Math.E` in any program.

5.10.1 Trigonometric Methods

The `Math` class contains the following trigonometric methods:

```
/** Return the trigonometric sine of an angle in radians */
public static double sin(double radians)

/** Return the trigonometric cosine of an angle in radians */
public static double cos(double radians)

/** Return the trigonometric tangent of an angle in radians */
public static double tan(double radians)
```

```
/** Convert the angle in degrees to an angle in radians */
public static double toRadians(double degree)

/** Convert the angle in radians to an angle in degrees */
public static double toDegrees(double radians)

/** Return the angle in radians for the inverse of sin */
public static double asin(double a)

/** Return the angle in radians for the inverse of cos */
public static double acos(double a)

/** Return the angle in radians for the inverse of tan */
public static double atan(double a)
```

The parameter for `sin`, `cos`, and `tan` is an angle in radians. The return value for `asin`, `acos`, and `atan` is a degree in radians in the range between $-\pi/2$ and $\pi/2$. One degree is equal to $\pi/180$ in radians, 90 degrees is equal to $\pi/2$ in radians, and 30 degrees is equal to $\pi/6$ in radians.

For example,

```
Math.toDegrees(Math.PI / 2) returns 90.0
Math.toRadians(30) returns 0.5236 (same as π/6)
Math.sin(0) returns 0.0
Math.sin(Math.toRadians(270)) returns -1.0
Math.sin(Math.PI / 6) returns 0.5
Math.sin(Math.PI / 2) returns 1.0
Math.cos(0) returns 1.0
Math.cos(Math.PI / 6) returns 0.866
Math.cos(Math.PI / 2) returns 0
Math.asin(0.5) returns 0.523598333 (same as π/6)
```

5.10.2 Exponent Methods

There are five methods related to exponents in the `Math` class:

```
/** Return e raised to the power of x (e^x) */
public static double exp(double x)

/** Return the natural logarithm of x (ln(x) = log_e(x)) */
public static double log(double x)

/** Return the base 10 logarithm of x (log_10(x)) */
public static double log10(double x)

/** Return a raised to the power of b (a^b) */
public static double pow(double a, double b)

/** Return the square root of x √x for x >= 0 */
public static double sqrt(double x)
```

For example,

```
Math.exp(1) returns 2.71828
Math.log(Math.E) returns 1.0
Math.log10(10) returns 1.0
Math.pow(2, 3) returns 8.0
Math.pow(3, 2) returns 9.0
Math.pow(3.5, 2.5) returns 22.91765
```

```
Math.sqrt(4) returns 2.0
Math.sqrt(10.5) returns 3.24
```

5.10.3 The Rounding Methods

The `Math` class contains five rounding methods:

```
/** x is rounded up to its nearest integer. This integer is
  * returned as a double value. */
public static double ceil(double x)

/** x is rounded down to its nearest integer. This integer is
  * returned as a double value. */
public static double floor(double x)

/** x is rounded to its nearest integer. If x is equally close
  * to two integers, the even one is returned as a double. */
public static double rint(double x)

/** Return (int)Math.floor(x + 0.5). */
public static int round(float x)

/** Return (long)Math.floor(x + 0.5). */
public static long round(double x)
```

For example,

```
Math.ceil(2.1) returns 3.0
Math.ceil(2.0) returns 2.0
Math.ceil(-2.0) returns -2.0
Math.ceil(-2.1) returns -2.0
Math.floor(2.1) returns 2.0
Math.floor(2.0) returns 2.0
Math.floor(-2.0) returns -2.0
Math.floor(-2.1) returns -3.0
Math.rint(2.1) returns 2.0
Math.rint(-2.0) returns -2.0
Math.rint(-2.1) returns -2.0
Math.rint(2.5) returns 2.0
Math.rint(3.5) returns 4.0
Math.rint(-2.5) returns -2.0
Math.round(2.6f) returns 3 // Returns int
Math.round(2.0) returns 2  // Returns long
Math.round(-2.0f) returns -2  // Returns int
Math.round(-2.6) returns -3  // Returns long
Math.round(-2.4) returns -2  // Returns long
```

5.10.4 The `min`, `max`, and `abs` Methods

The `min` and `max` methods are overloaded to return the minimum and maximum numbers of two numbers (`int`, `long`, `float`, or `double`). For example, `max(3.4, 5.0)` returns `5.0`, and `min(3, 2)` returns `2`.

The `abs` method is overloaded to return the absolute value of the number (`int`, `long`, `float`, or `double`). For example,

```
Math.max(2, 3) returns 3
Math.max(2.5, 3) returns 3.0
Math.min(2.5, 3.6) returns 2.5
```

```
Math.abs(-2) returns 2
Math.abs(-2.1) returns 2.1
```

5.10.5 The random Method

You have used the `random()` method to generate a random `double` value greater than or equal to `0.0` and less than `1.0` (`0 <= Math.random() < 1.0`). This method is very useful. You can use it to write a simple expression to generate random numbers in any range. For example,

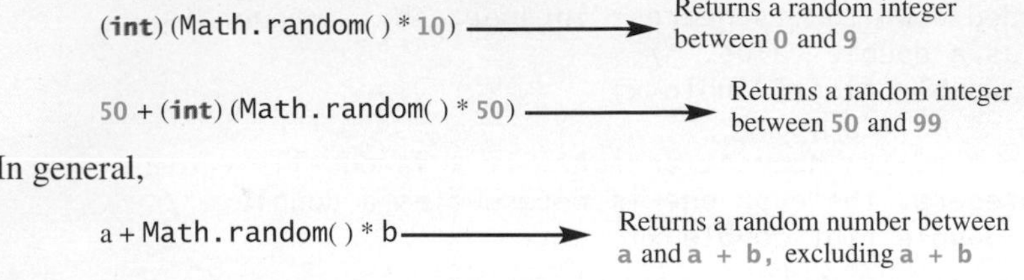

In general,

a + Math.random() * b → Returns a random number between a and a + b, excluding a + b

Tip

You can view the complete documentation for the `Math` class online at **download.oracle.com/javase/7/docs/api**, as shown in Figure 5.7.

Note

Not all classes need a `main` method. The `Math` class and the `JOptionPane` class do not have `main` methods. These classes contain methods for other classes to use.

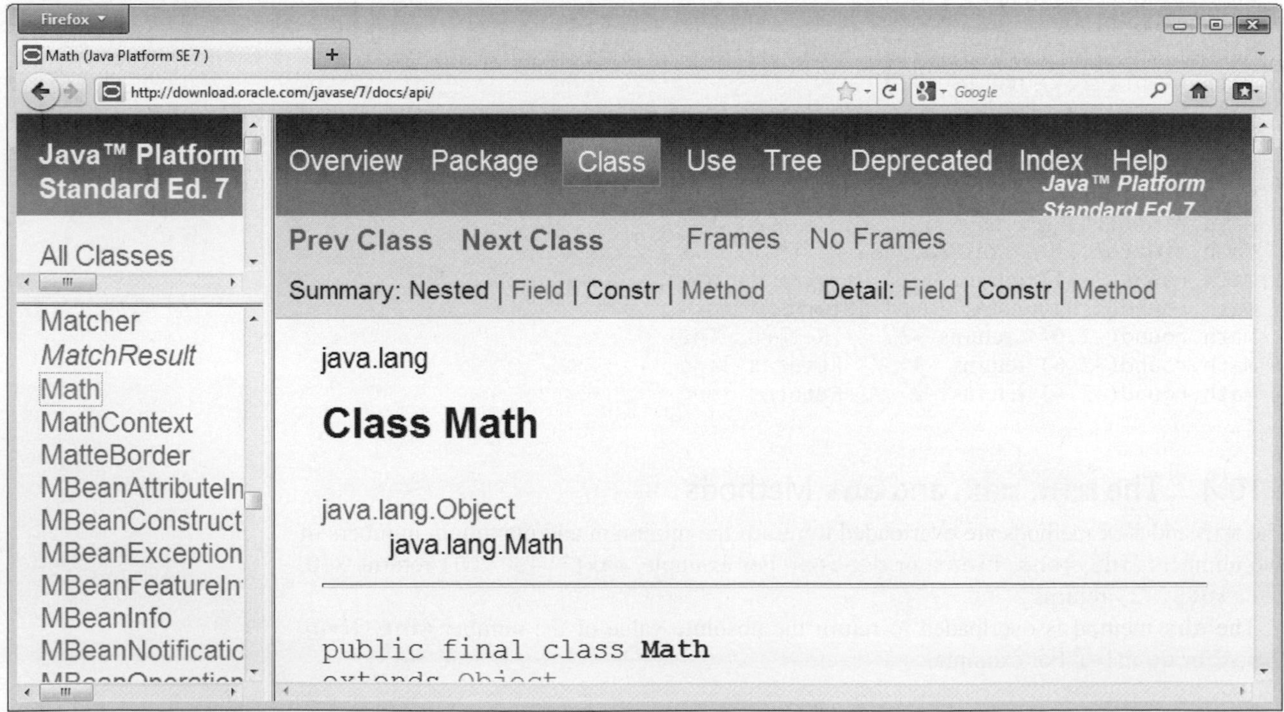

FIGURE 5.7 You can view the documentation for the Java API online.

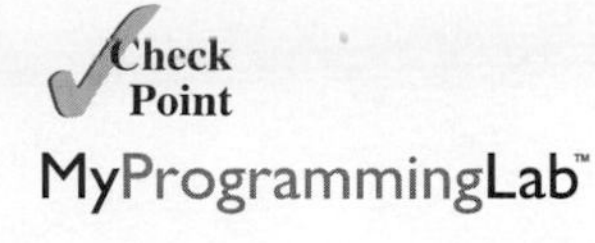

5.22 True or false? The argument for trigonometric methods is an angle in radians.

5.23 Write an expression that obtains a random integer between 34 and 55. Write an expression that obtains a random integer between 0 and 999. Write an expression that obtains a random number between 5.5 and 55.5. Write an expression that obtains a random lowercase letter.

5.24 Evaluate the following method calls:

a. `Math.sqrt(4)`
b. `Math.sin(2 * Math.PI)`
c. `Math.cos(2 * Math.PI)`
d. `Math.pow(2, 2)`
e. `Math.log(Math.E)`
f. `Math.exp(1)`
g. `Math.max(2, Math.min(3, 4))`
h. `Math.rint(-2.5)`
i. `Math.ceil(-2.5)`
j. `Math.floor(-2.5)`
k. `Math.round(-2.5f)`
l. `Math.round(-2.5)`
m. `Math.rint(2.5)`
n. `Math.ceil(2.5)`
o. `Math.floor(2.5)`
p. `Math.round(2.5f)`
q. `Math.round(2.5)`
r. `Math.round(Math.abs(-2.5))`

5.11 Case Study: Generating Random Characters

A character is coded using an integer. Generating a random character is to generate an integer.

Computer programs process numerical data and characters. You have seen many examples that involve numerical data. It is also important to understand characters and how to process them. This section presents an example of generating random characters.

As introduced in Section 2.17, every character has a unique Unicode between 0 and FFFF in hexadecimal (65535 in decimal). To generate a random character is to generate a random integer between 0 and 65535 using the following expression (note that since `0 <= Math.random() < 1.0`, you have to add 1 to 65535):

```
(int)(Math.random() * (65535 + 1))
```

Now let's consider how to generate a random lowercase letter. The Unicodes for lowercase letters are consecutive integers starting from the Unicode for a, then that for b, c, . . . , and z. The Unicode for a is

```
(int)'a'
```

Thus, a random integer between `(int)'a'` and `(int)'z'` is

```
(int)((int)'a' + Math.random() * ((int)'z' - (int)'a' + 1))
```

As discussed in Section 2.17.3, all numeric operators can be applied to the char operands. The char operand is cast into a number if the other operand is a number or a character. Therefore, the preceding expression can be simplified as follows:

```
'a' + Math.random() * ('z' - 'a' + 1)
```

and a random lowercase letter is

```
(char)('a' + Math.random() * ('z' - 'a' + 1))
```

Hence, a random character between any two characters **ch1** and **ch2** with **ch1 < ch2** can be generated as follows:

```
(char)(ch1 + Math.random() * (ch2 - ch1 + 1))
```

This is a simple but useful discovery. Listing 5.10 creates a class named **RandomCharacter** with five overloaded methods to get a certain type of character randomly. You can use these methods in your future projects.

LISTING 5.10 RandomCharacter.java

getRandomCharacter
getRandomLowerCaseLetter()
getRandomUpperCaseLetter()
getRandomDigitCharacter()
getRandomCharacter()

```
public class RandomCharacter {
  /** Generate a random character between ch1 and ch2 */
  public static char getRandomCharacter(char ch1, char ch2) {
    return (char)(ch1 + Math.random() * (ch2 - ch1 + 1));
  }

  /** Generate a random lowercase letter */
  public static char getRandomLowerCaseLetter() {
    return getRandomCharacter('a', 'z');
  }

  /** Generate a random uppercase letter */
  public static char getRandomUpperCaseLetter() {
    return getRandomCharacter('A', 'Z');
  }

  /** Generate a random digit character */
  public static char getRandomDigitCharacter() {
    return getRandomCharacter('0', '9');
  }

  /** Generate a random character */
  public static char getRandomCharacter() {
    return getRandomCharacter('\u0000', '\uFFFF');
  }
}
```

Listing 5.11 gives a test program that displays 175 random lowercase letters.

LISTING 5.11 TestRandomCharacter.java

constants
lower-case letter

```
public class TestRandomCharacter {
  /** Main method */
  public static void main(String[] args) {
    final int NUMBER_OF_CHARS = 175;
    final int CHARS_PER_LINE = 25;

    // Print random characters between 'a' and 'z', 25 chars per line
    for (int i = 0; i < NUMBER_OF_CHARS; i++) {
      char ch = RandomCharacter.getRandomLowerCaseLetter();
      if ((i + 1) % CHARS_PER_LINE == 0)
        System.out.println(ch);
      else
        System.out.print(ch);
    }
  }
}
```

```
gmjsohezfkgtazqgmswfclrao
pnrunulnwmaztlfjedmpchcif
lalqdgivxkxpbzulrmqmbhikr
lbnrjlsopfxahssqhwuuljvbe
xbhdotzhpehbqmuwsfktwsoli
cbuwkzgxpmtzihgatdslvbwbz
bfesoklwbhnooygiigzdxuqni
```

Line 9 invokes `getRandomLowerCaseLetter()` defined in the `RandomCharacter` class. Note that `getRandomLowerCaseLetter()` does not have any parameters, but you still have to use the parentheses when defining and invoking the method.

parentheses required

5.12 Method Abstraction and Stepwise Refinement

The key to developing software is to apply the concept of abstraction.

Key Point

VideoNote

Stepwise refinement

You will learn many levels of abstraction from this book. *Method abstraction* is achieved by separating the use of a method from its implementation. The client can use a method without knowing how it is implemented. The details of the implementation are encapsulated in the method and hidden from the client who invokes the method. This is also known as *information hiding* or *encapsulation.* If you decide to change the implementation, the client program will not be affected, provided that you do not change the method signature. The implementation of the method is hidden from the client in a "black box," as shown in Figure 5.8.

method abstraction

information hiding

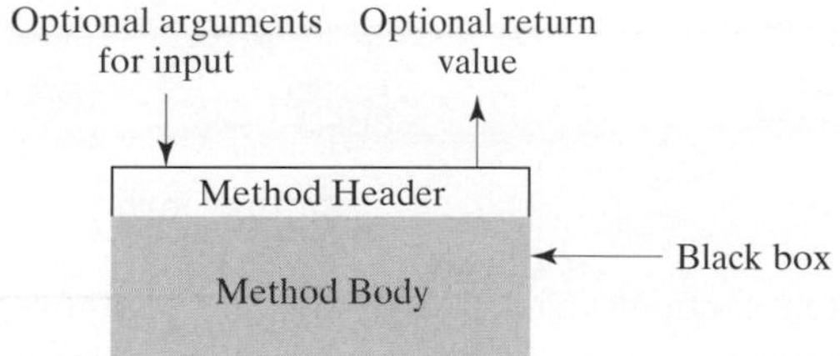

FIGURE 5.8 The method body can be thought of as a black box that contains the detailed implementation for the method.

You have already used the `System.out.print` method to display a string and the `max` method to find the maximum number. You know how to write the code to invoke these methods in your program, but as a user of these methods, you are not required to know how they are implemented.

The concept of method abstraction can be applied to the process of developing programs. When writing a large program, you can use the *divide-and-conquer* strategy, also known as *stepwise refinement*, to decompose it into subproblems. The subproblems can be further decomposed into smaller, more manageable problems.

divide and conquer

stepwise refinement

Suppose you write a program that displays the calendar for a given month of the year. The program prompts the user to enter the year and the month, then displays the entire calendar for the month, as shown in the following sample run.

```
Enter full year (e.g., 2012): 2012 ↵Enter
Enter month as a number between 1 and 12: 3 ↵Enter
         March 2012
-----------------------------
 Sun Mon Tue Wed Thu Fri Sat
                   1   2   3
   4   5   6   7   8   9  10
  11  12  13  14  15  16  17
  18  19  20  21  22  23  24
  25  26  27  28  29  30  31
```

Let us use this example to demonstrate the divide-and-conquer approach.

5.12.1 Top-Down Design

How would you get started on such a program? Would you immediately start coding? Beginning programmers often start by trying to work out the solution to every detail. Although details are important in the final program, concern for detail in the early stages may block the problem-solving process. To make problem solving flow as smoothly as possible, this example begins by using method abstraction to isolate details from design and only later implements the details.

For this example, the problem is first broken into two subproblems: get input from the user, and print the calendar for the month. At this stage, you should be concerned with what the subproblems will achieve, not with how to get input and print the calendar for the month. You can draw a structure chart to help visualize the decomposition of the problem (see Figure 5.9a).

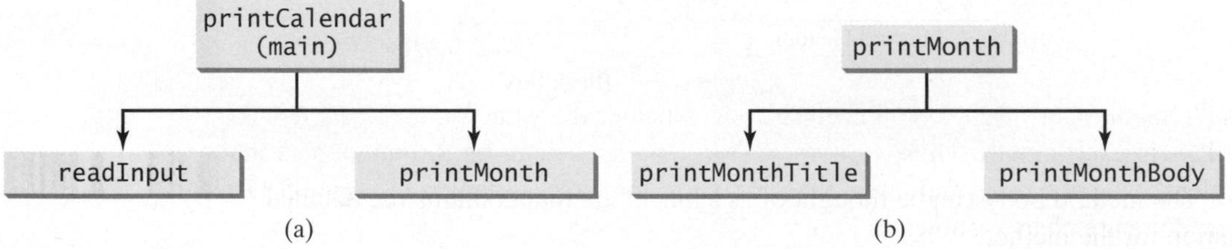

FIGURE 5.9 The structure chart shows that the `printCalendar` problem is divided into two subproblems, `readInput` and `printMonth` in (a), and that `printMonth` is divided into two smaller subproblems, `printMonthTitle` and `printMonthBody` in (b).

You can use `Scanner` to read input for the year and the month. The problem of printing the calendar for a given month can be broken into two subproblems: print the month title, and print the month body, as shown in Figure 5.9b. The month title consists of three lines: month and year, a dashed line, and the names of the seven days of the week. You need to get the month name (e.g., January) from the numeric month (e.g., 1). This is accomplished in `getMonthName` (see Figure 5.10a).

In order to print the month body, you need to know which day of the week is the first day of the month (`getStartDay`) and how many days the month has (`getNumberOfDaysInMonth`),

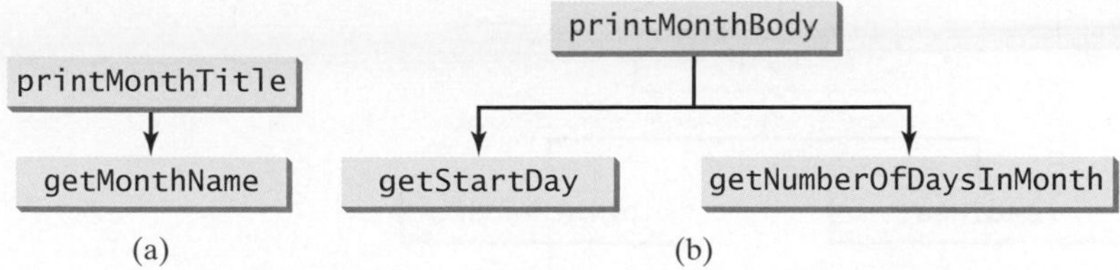

FIGURE 5.10 (a) To `printMonthTitle`, you need `getMonthName`. (b) The `printMonthBody` problem is refined into several smaller problems.

as shown in Figure 5.10b. For example, December 2013 has 31 days, and December 1, 2013, is a Sunday.

How would you get the start day for the first date in a month? There are several ways to do so. For now, we'll use an alternative approach. Assume you know that the start day for January 1, 1800, was a Wednesday (`START_DAY_FOR_JAN_1_1800 = 3`). You could compute the total number of days (`totalNumberOfDays`) between January 1, 1800, and the first date of the calendar month. The start day for the calendar month is `(totalNumberOfDays + startDay1800) % 7`, since every week has seven days. Thus, the `getStartDay` problem can be further refined as `getTotalNumberOfDays`, as shown in Figure 5.11a.

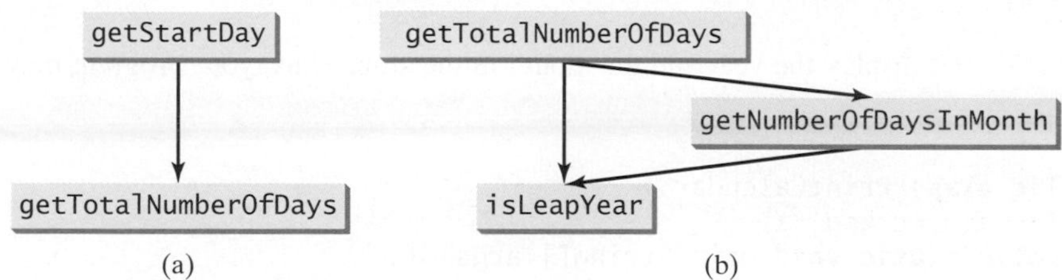

FIGURE 5.11 (a) To `getStartDay`, you need `getTotalNumberOfDays`. (b) The `getTotalNumberOfDays` problem is refined into two smaller problems.

To get the total number of days, you need to know whether the year is a leap year and the number of days in each month. Thus, `getTotalNumberOfDays` can be further refined into two subproblems: `isLeapYear` and `getNumberOfDaysInMonth`, as shown in Figure 5.11b. The complete structure chart is shown in Figure 5.12.

5.12.2 Top-Down and/or Bottom-Up Implementation

Now we turn our attention to implementation. In general, a subproblem corresponds to a method in the implementation, although some are so simple that this is unnecessary. You would need to decide which modules to implement as methods and which to combine in other methods. Decisions of this kind should be based on whether the overall program will be easier to read as a result of your choice. In this example, the subproblem `readInput` can be simply implemented in the `main` method.

You can use either a "top-down" or a "bottom-up" approach. The top-down approach implements one method in the structure chart at a time from the top to the bottom. *Stubs*—a simple but incomplete version of a method—can be used for the methods waiting to be implemented. The use of stubs enables you to quickly build the framework of the program. Implement the `main` method first, then use a stub for the `printMonth` method. For example,

top-down approach

stub

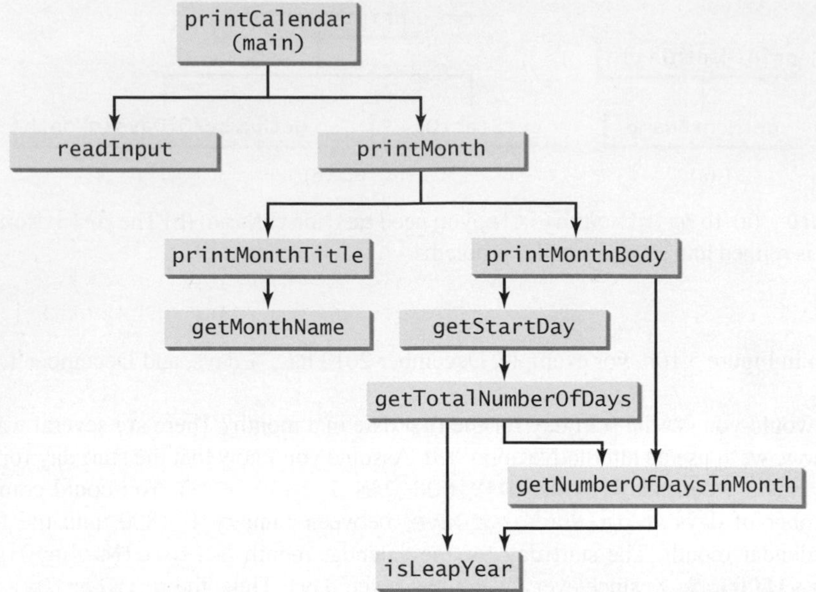

FIGURE 5.12 The structure chart shows the hierarchical relationship of the subproblems in the program.

let `printMonth` display the year and the month in the stub. Thus, your program may begin like this:

```
public class PrintCalendar {
  /** Main method */
  public static void main(String[] args) {
    Scanner input = new Scanner(System.in);

    // Prompt the user to enter year
    System.out.print("Enter full year (e.g., 2012): ");
    int year = input.nextInt();

    // Prompt the user to enter month
    System.out.print("Enter month as a number between 1 and 12: ");
    int month = input.nextInt();

    // Print calendar for the month of the year
    printMonth(year, month);
  }

  /** A stub for printMonth may look like this */
  public static void printMonth(int year, int month) {
    System.out.print(month + " " + year);
  }

  /** A stub for printMonthTitle may look like this */
  public static void printMonthTitle(int year, int month) {
  }

  /** A stub for getMonthBody may look like this */
  public static void printMonthBody(int year, int month) {
  }
```

```
  /** A stub for getMonthName may look like this */
  public static String getMonthName(int month) {
    return "January"; // A dummy value
  }

  /** A stub for getStartDay may look like this */
  public static int getStartDay(int year, int month) {
    return 1; // A dummy value
  }

  /** A stub for getTotalNumberOfDays may look like this */
  public static int getTotalNumberOfDays(int year, int month) {
    return 10000; // A dummy value
  }

  /** A stub for getNumberOfDaysInMonth may look like this */
  public static int getNumberOfDaysInMonth(int year, int month) {
    return 31; // A dummy value
  }

  /** A stub for isLeapYear may look like this */
  public static Boolean isLeapYear(int year) {
    return true; // A dummy value
  }
}
```

Compile and test the program, and fix any errors. You can now implement the `printMonth` method. For methods invoked from the `printMonth` method, you can again use stubs.

bottom-up approach

driver

The bottom-up approach implements one method in the structure chart at a time from the bottom to the top. For each method implemented, write a test program, known as the *driver*, to test it. The top-down and bottom-up approaches are equally good: Both approaches implement methods incrementally, help to isolate programming errors, and make debugging easy. They can be used together.

5.12.3 Implementation Details

The `isLeapYear(int year)` method can be implemented using the following code from Section 3.12:

```
return (year % 400 == 0 || (year % 4 == 0 && year % 100 != 0));
```

Use the following facts to implement `getTotalNumberOfDaysInMonth(int year, int month)`:

- January, March, May, July, August, October, and December have 31 days.
- April, June, September, and November have 30 days.
- February has 28 days during a regular year and 29 days during a leap year. A regular year, therefore, has 365 days, a leap year 366 days.

To implement `getTotalNumberOfDays(int year, int month)`, you need to compute the total number of days (`totalNumberOfDays`) between January 1, 1800, and the first day of the calendar month. You could find the total number of days between the year 1800 and the calendar year and then figure out the total number of days prior to the calendar month in the calendar year. The sum of these two totals is `totalNumberOfDays`.

To print a body, first pad some space before the start day and then print the lines for every week.

The complete program is given in Listing 5.12.

LISTING 5.12 PrintCalendar.java

```
import java.util.Scanner;

public class PrintCalendar {
  /** Main method */
  public static void main(String[] args) {
    Scanner input = new Scanner(System.in);

    // Prompt the user to enter year
    System.out.print("Enter full year (e.g., 2012): ");
    int year = input.nextInt();

    // Prompt the user to enter month
    System.out.print("Enter month as a number between 1 and 12: ");
    int month = input.nextInt();

    // Print calendar for the month of the year
    printMonth(year, month);
  }

  /** Print the calendar for a month in a year */
```

printMonth

```
  public static void printMonth(int year, int month) {
    // Print the headings of the calendar
    printMonthTitle(year, month);

    // Print the body of the calendar
    printMonthBody(year, month);
  }

  /** Print the month title, e.g., March 2012 */
```

printMonthTitle

```
  public static void printMonthTitle(int year, int month) {
    System.out.println("         " + getMonthName(month)
      + " " + year);
    System.out.println("-----------------------------");
    System.out.println(" Sun Mon Tue Wed Thu Fri Sat");
  }

  /** Get the English name for the month */
```

getMonthName

```
  public static String getMonthName(int month) {
    String monthName = "";
    switch (month) {
      case 1: monthName = "January"; break;
      case 2: monthName = "February"; break;
      case 3: monthName = "March"; break;
      case 4: monthName = "April"; break;
      case 5: monthName = "May"; break;
      case 6: monthName = "June"; break;
      case 7: monthName = "July"; break;
      case 8: monthName = "August"; break;
      case 9: monthName = "September"; break;
      case 10: monthName = "October"; break;
      case 11: monthName = "November"; break;
      case 12: monthName = "December";
    }

    return monthName;
  }

  /** Print month body */
```

printMonthBody

```
  public static void printMonthBody(int year, int month) {
    // Get start day of the week for the first date in the month
    int startDay = getStartDay(year, month);

    // Get number of days in the month
    int numberOfDaysInMonth = getNumberOfDaysInMonth(year, month);

    // Pad space before the first day of the month
    int i = 0;
    for (i = 0; i < startDay; i++)
      System.out.print("    ");

    for (i = 1; i <= numberOfDaysInMonth; i++) {
      System.out.printf("%4d", i);

      if ((i + startDay) % 7 == 0)
        System.out.println();
    }

    System.out.println();
  }

  /** Get the start day of month/1/year */
```

getStartDay

```
  public static int getStartDay(int year, int month) {
    final int START_DAY_FOR_JAN_1_1800 = 3;
    // Get total number of days from 1/1/1800 to month/1/year
    int totalNumberOfDays = getTotalNumberOfDays(year, month);

    // Return the start day for month/1/year
    return (totalNumberOfDays + START_DAY_FOR_JAN_1_1800) % 7;
  }

  /** Get the total number of days since January 1, 1800 */
```

getTotalNumberOfDays

```
  public static int getTotalNumberOfDays(int year, int month) {
    int total = 0;

    // Get the total days from 1800 to 1/1/year
    for (int i = 1800; i < year; i++)
      if (isLeapYear(i))
        total = total + 366;
      else
        total = total + 365;

    // Add days from Jan to the month prior to the calendar month
    for (int i = 1; i < month; i++)
      total = total + getNumberOfDaysInMonth(year, i);

    return total;
  }

  /** Get the number of days in a month */
```

getNumberOfDaysInMonth

```
  public static int getNumberOfDaysInMonth(int year, int month) {
    if (month == 1 || month == 3 || month == 5 || month == 7 ||
      month == 8 || month == 10 || month == 12)
      return 31;

    if (month == 4 || month == 6 || month == 9 || month == 11)
      return 30;

    if (month == 2) return isLeapYear(year) ? 29 : 28;
```

```java

        return 0; // If month is incorrect
    }

    /** Determine if it is a leap year */
    public static boolean isLeapYear(int year) {
        return year % 400 == 0 || (year % 4 == 0 && year % 100 != 0);
    }
}
```

isLeapYear

The program does not validate user input. For instance, if the user enters either a month not in the range between 1 and 12 or a year before 1800, the program displays an erroneous calendar. To avoid this error, add an `if` statement to check the input before printing the calendar.

This program prints calendars for a month but could easily be modified to print calendars for a whole year. Although it can print months only after January 1800, it could be modified to print months before 1800.

5.12.4 Benefits of Stepwise Refinement

Stepwise refinement breaks a large problem into smaller manageable subproblems. Each subproblem can be implemented using a method. This approach makes the program easier to write, reuse, debug, test, modify, and maintain.

Simpler Program

The print calendar program is long. Rather than writing a long sequence of statements in one method, stepwise refinement breaks it into smaller methods. This simplifies the program and makes the whole program easier to read and understand.

Reusing Methods

Stepwise refinement promotes code reuse within a program. The **isLeapYear** method is defined once and invoked from the **getTotalNumberOfDays** and **getNumberOfDayInMonth** methods. This reduces redundant code.

Easier Developing, Debugging, and Testing

Since each subproblem is solved in a method, a method can be developed, debugged, and tested individually. This isolates the errors and makes developing, debugging, and testing easier.

incremental development and testing

When implementing a large program, use the top-down and/or bottom-up approach. Do not write the entire program at once. Using these approaches seems to take more development time (because you repeatedly compile and run the program), but it actually saves time and makes debugging easier.

Better Facilitating Teamwork

When a large problem is divided into subprograms, subproblems can be assigned to different programmers. This makes it easier for programmers to work in teams.

Key Terms

actual parameter 179
ambiguous invocation 195
argument 179
divide and conquer 203
formal parameter (i.e., parameter) 179
information hiding 203
method 178
method abstraction 203
method overloading 194
method signature 179
modifier 179
parameter 179
pass-by-value 186
scope of a variable 196
stepwise refinement 203
stub 205

Chapter Summary

1. Making programs modular and reusable is one of the central goals in software engineering. Java provides many powerful constructs that help to achieve this goal. *Methods* are one such construct.

2. The method header specifies the *modifiers*, *return value type*, *method name*, and *parameters* of the method. The `static` modifier is used for all the methods in this chapter.

3. A method may return a value. The `returnValueType` is the data type of the value the method returns. If the method does not return a value, the `returnValueType` is the keyword `void`.

4. The *parameter list* refers to the type, order, and number of a method's parameters. The method name and the parameter list together constitute the *method signature.* Parameters are optional; that is, a method doesn't need to contain any parameters.

5. A return statement can also be used in a `void` method for terminating the method and returning to the method's caller. This is useful occasionally for circumventing the normal flow of control in a method.

6. The arguments that are passed to a method should have the same number, type, and order as the parameters in the method signature.

7. When a program calls a method, program control is transferred to the called method. A called method returns control to the caller when its return statement is executed or when its method-ending closing brace is reached.

8. A value-returning method can also be invoked as a statement in Java. In this case, the caller simply ignores the return value.

9. A method can be overloaded. This means that two methods can have the same name, as long as their method parameter lists differ.

10. A variable declared in a method is called a local variable. The *scope of a local variable* starts from its declaration and continues to the end of the block that contains the variable. A local variable must be declared and initialized before it is used.

11. *Method abstraction* is achieved by separating the use of a method from its implementation. The client can use a method without knowing how it is implemented. The details of the implementation are encapsulated in the method and hidden from the client who invokes the method. This is known as *information hiding* or *encapsulation.*

12. Method abstraction modularizes programs in a neat, hierarchical manner. Programs written as collections of concise methods are easier to write, debug, maintain, and modify than would otherwise be the case. This writing style also promotes method reusability.

13. When implementing a large program, use the top-down and/or bottom-up coding approach. Do not write the entire program at once. This approach may seem to take more time for coding (because you are repeatedly compiling and running the program), but it actually saves time and makes debugging easier.

Test Questions

Do the test questions for this chapter online at www.cs.armstrong.edu/liang/intro9e/test.html.

MyProgrammingLab™

Programming Exercises

Sections 5.2–5.9

5.1 (*Math: pentagonal numbers*) A pentagonal number is defined as $n(3n–1)/2$ for $n = 1, 2, \ldots$, and so on. Therefore, the first few numbers are 1, 5, 12, 22, ... Write a method with the following header that returns a pentagonal number:

```
public static int getPentagonalNumber(int n)
```

Write a test program that uses this method to display the first 100 pentagonal numbers with 10 numbers on each line.

***5.2** (*Sum the digits in an integer*) Write a method that computes the sum of the digits in an integer. Use the following method header:

```
public static int sumDigits(long n)
```

For example, `sumDigits(234)` returns `9` (2 + 3 + 4). (*Hint*: Use the `%` operator to extract digits, and the `/` operator to remove the extracted digit. For instance, to extract 4 from 234, use `234 % 10` (= 4). To remove 4 from 234, use `234 / 10` (= 23). Use a loop to repeatedly extract and remove the digit until all the digits are extracted. Write a test program that prompts the user to enter an integer and displays the sum of all its digits.

****5.3** (*Palindrome integer*) Write the methods with the following headers

```
// Return the reversal of an integer, i.e., reverse(456) returns 654
public static int reverse(int number)

// Return true if number is a palindrome
public static boolean isPalindrome(int number)
```

Use the `reverse` method to implement `isPalindrome`. A number is a palindrome if its reversal is the same as itself. Write a test program that prompts the user to enter an integer and reports whether the integer is a palindrome.

VideoNote
Reverse an integer

***5.4** (*Display an integer reversed*) Write a method with the following header to display an integer in reverse order:

```
public static void reverse(int number)
```

For example, `reverse(3456)` displays `6543`. Write a test program that prompts the user to enter an integer and displays its reversal.

***5.5** (*Sort three numbers*) Write a method with the following header to display three numbers in increasing order:

```
public static void displaySortedNumbers(
  double num1, double num2, double num3)
```

Write a test program that prompts the user to enter three numbers and invokes the method to display them in increasing order.

***5.6** (*Display patterns*) Write a method to display a pattern as follows:

```
              1
            2 1
          3 2 1
...
n n-1 ... 3 2 1
```

The method header is

```
public static void displayPattern(int n)
```

***5.7** (*Financial application: compute the future investment value*) Write a method that computes future investment value at a given interest rate for a specified number of years. The future investment is determined using the formula in Programming Exercise 2.21.

Use the following method header:

```
public static double futureInvestmentValue(
  double investmentAmount, double monthlyInterestRate, int years)
```

For example, `futureInvestmentValue(10000, 0.05/12, 5)` returns `12833.59`.

Write a test program that prompts the user to enter the investment amount (e.g., 1000) and the interest rate (e.g., 9%) and prints a table that displays future value for the years from 1 to 30, as shown below:

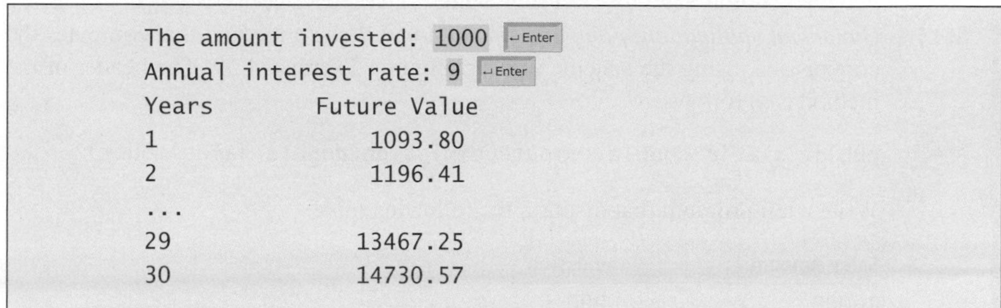

```
The amount invested: 1000 ↵Enter
Annual interest rate: 9 ↵Enter
Years         Future Value
1                1093.80
2                1196.41
...
29              13467.25
30              14730.57
```

5.8 (*Conversions between Celsius and Fahrenheit*) Write a class that contains the following two methods:

```
/** Convert from Celsius to Fahrenheit */
public static double celsiusToFahrenheit(double celsius)

/** Convert from Fahrenheit to Celsius */
public static double fahrenheitToCelsius(double fahrenheit)
```

The formula for the conversion is:

```
fahrenheit = (9.0 / 5) * celsius + 32
celsius = (5.0 / 9) * (fahrenheit – 32)
```

Write a test program that invokes these methods to display the following tables:

Celsius	Fahrenheit	|	Fahrenheit	Celsius
40.0	104.0	|	120.0	48.89
39.0	102.2	|	110.0	43.33
...				
32.0	89.6	|	40.0	4.44
31.0	87.8	|	30.0	-1.11

5.9 (*Conversions between feet and meters*) Write a class that contains the following two methods:

```
/** Convert from feet to meters */
public static double footToMeter(double foot)
```

```
/** Convert from meters to feet */
public static double meterToFoot(double meter)
```

The formula for the conversion is:

```
meter = 0.305 * foot
foot = 3.279 * meter
```

Write a test program that invokes these methods to display the following tables:

Feet	Meters	Meters	Feet
1.0	0.305	20.0	65.574
2.0	0.610	25.0	81.967
...			
9.0	2.745	60.0	196.721
10.0	3.050	65.0	213.115

5.10 (*Use the* `isPrime` *Method*) Listing 5.7, PrimeNumberMethod.java, provides the `isPrime(int number)` method for testing whether a number is prime. Use this method to find the number of prime numbers less than `10000`.

5.11 (*Financial application: compute commissions*) Write a method that computes the commission, using the scheme in Programming Exercise 4.39. The header of the method is as follows:

```
public static double computeCommission(double salesAmount)
```

Write a test program that displays the following table:

Sales Amount	Commission
10000	900.0
15000	1500.0
...	
95000	11100.0
100000	11700.0

5.12 (*Display characters*) Write a method that prints characters using the following header:

```
public static void printChars(char ch1, char ch2, int
  numberPerLine)
```

This method prints the characters between `ch1` and `ch2` with the specified numbers per line. Write a test program that prints ten characters per line from `1` to `Z`. Characters are separated by exactly one space.

***5.13** (*Sum series*) Write a method to compute the following series:

$$m(i) = \frac{1}{2} + \frac{2}{3} + \ldots + \frac{i}{i+1}$$

Write a test program that displays the following table:

i	m(i)
1	0.5000
2	1.1667
...	
19	16.4023
20	17.3546

***5.14** (*Estimate π*) π can be computed using the following series:

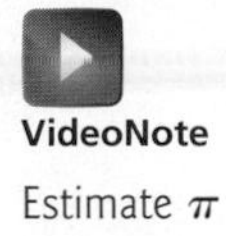

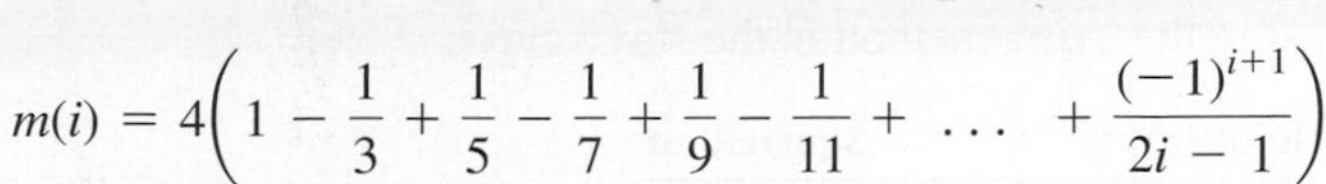

$$m(i) = 4\left(1 - \frac{1}{3} + \frac{1}{5} - \frac{1}{7} + \frac{1}{9} - \frac{1}{11} + \ \ldots \ + \frac{(-1)^{i+1}}{2i - 1}\right)$$

Write a method that returns `m(i)` for a given `i` and write a test program that displays the following table:

i	m(i)
1	4.0000
101	3.1515
201	3.1466
301	3.1449
401	3.1441
501	3.1436
601	3.1433
701	3.1430
801	3.1428
901	3.1427

***5.15** (*Financial application: print a tax table*) Listing 3.6 gives a program to compute tax. Write a method for computing tax using the following header:

```
public static double computetax(int status, double taxableIncome)
```

Use this method to write a program that prints a tax table for taxable income from $50,000 to $60,000 with intervals of $50 for all the following statuses:

Taxable Income	Single	Married Joint or Qualifying Widow(er)	Married Separate	Head of a House
50000	8688	6665	8688	7352
50050	8700	6673	8700	7365
...				
59950	11175	8158	11175	9840
60000	11188	8165	11188	9852

***5.16** (*Number of days in a year*) Write a method that returns the number of days in a year using the following header:

```
public static int numberOfDaysInAYear(int year)
```

Write a test program that displays the number of days in year from 2000 to 2020.

Sections 5.10–5.11

***5.17** (*Display matrix of 0s and 1s*) Write a method that displays an *n*-by-*n* matrix using the following header:

```
public static void printMatrix(int n)
```

Each element is 0 or 1, which is generated randomly. Write a test program that prompts the user to enter `n` and displays an *n*-by-*n* matrix. Here is a sample run:

```
Enter n: 3 ↵Enter
0 1 0
0 0 0
1 1 1
```

5.18 (*Use the* `Math.sqrt` *method*) Write a program that prints the following table using the `sqrt` method in the `Math` class.

Number	SquareRoot
0	0.0000
2	1.4142
...	
18	4.2426
20	4.4721

***5.19** (*The* `MyTriangle` *class*) Create a class named `MyTriangle` that contains the following two methods:

```
/** Return true if the sum of any two sides is
 *  greater than the third side. */
public static boolean isValid(
  double side1, double side2, double side3)

/** Return the area of the triangle. */
public static double area(
  double side1, double side2, double side3)
```

Write a test program that reads three sides for a triangle and computes the area if the input is valid. Otherwise, it displays that the input is invalid. The formula for computing the area of a triangle is given in Programming Exercise 2.15.

5.20 (*Use trigonometric methods*) Print the following table to display the `sin` value and `cos` value of degrees from 0 to 360 with increments of 10 degrees. Round the value to keep four digits after the decimal point.

Degree	Sin	Cos
0	0.0000	1.0000
10	0.1736	0.9848
...		
350	-0.1736	0.9848
360	0.0000	1.0000

***5.21** (*Geometry: great circle distance*) The great circle distance is the distance between two points on the surface of a sphere. Let (x1, y1) and (x2, y2) be the geographical latitude and longitude of two points. The great circle distance between the two points can be computed using the following formula:

$$d = radius \times \arccos(\sin(x_1) \times \sin(x_2) + \cos(x_1) \times \cos(x_2) \times \cos(y_1 - y_2))$$

Write a program that prompts the user to enter the latitude and longitude of two points on the earth in degrees and displays its great circle distance. The average earth radius is 6,371.01 km. Note that you need to convert the degrees into radians using the `Math.toRadians` method since the Java trigonometric methods use radians. The latitude and longitude degrees in the formula are for North and West. Use negative to indicate South and East degrees. Here is a sample run:

```
Enter point 1 (latitude and longitude) in degrees:
  39.55 -116.25 [Enter]
Enter point 2 (latitude and longitude) in degrees:
  41.5 87.37 [Enter]
The distance between the two points is 10691.79183231593 km
```

**5.22 (*Math: approximate the square root*) There are several techniques for implementing the `sqrt` method in the `Math` class. One such technique is known as the *Babylonian method.* It approximates the square root of a number, `n`, by repeatedly performing a calculation using the following formula:

```
nextGuess = (lastGuess + n / lastGuess) / 2
```

When `nextGuess` and `lastGuess` are almost identical, `nextGuess` is the approximated square root. The initial guess can be any positive value (e.g., `1`). This value will be the starting value for `lastGuess`. If the difference between `nextGuess` and `lastGuess` is less than a very small number, such as `0.0001`, you can claim that `nextGuess` is the approximated square root of `n`. If not, `nextGuess` becomes `lastGuess` and the approximation process continues. Implement the following method that returns the square root of `n`.

```
public static double sqrt(long n)
```

*5.23 (*Geometry: display angles*) Write a program that prompts the user to enter three points of a triangle and displays the angles in degrees. Round the value to keep two digits after the decimal point. The formula to compute angles A, B, and C are as follows:

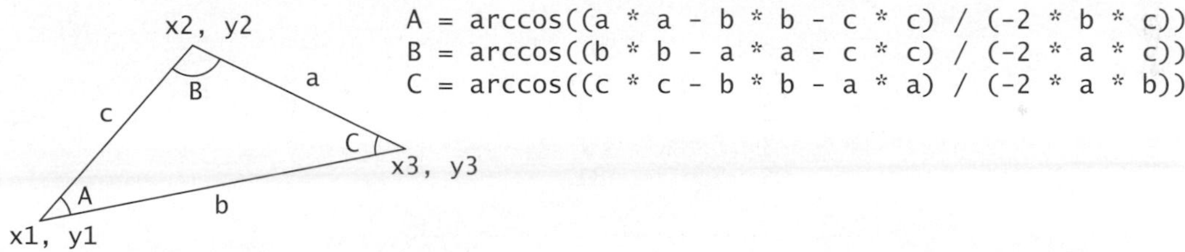

Here is a sample run of the program:

```
Enter three points: 1 1 6.5 1 6.5 2.5 ↵Enter
The three angles are 15.26 90.0 74.74
```

Sections 5.10–5.12

**5.24 (*Display current date and time*) Listing 2.6, ShowCurrentTime.java, displays the current time. Improve this example to display the current date and time. The calendar example in Listing 5.12, PrintCalendar.java, should give you some ideas on how to find the year, month, and day.

**5.25 (*Convert milliseconds to hours, minutes, and seconds*) Write a method that converts milliseconds to hours, minutes, and seconds using the following header:

```
public static String convertMillis(long millis)
```

The method returns a string as *hours:minutes:seconds*. For example, `convertMillis(5500)` returns a string 0:0:5, `convertMillis(100000)` returns a string `0:1:40`, and `convertMillis(555550000)` returns a string `154:19:10`.

Comprehensive

****5.26** (*Palindromic prime*) A *palindromic prime* is a prime number and also palindromic. For example, 131 is a prime and also a palindromic prime, as are 313 and 757. Write a program that displays the first 100 palindromic prime numbers. Display 10 numbers per line, separated by exactly one space, as follows:

```
2 3 5 7 11 101 131 151 181 191
313 353 373 383 727 757 787 797 919 929
...
```

****5.27** (*Emirp*) An *emirp* (prime spelled backward) is a nonpalindromic prime number whose reversal is also a prime. For example, 17 is a prime and 71 is a prime, so 17 and 71 are emirps. Write a program that displays the first 100 emirps. Display 10 numbers per line, separated by exactly one space, as follows:

```
13 17 31 37 71 73 79 97 107 113
149 157 167 179 199 311 337 347 359 389
...
```

****5.28** (*Mersenne prime*) A prime number is called a *Mersenne prime* if it can be written in the form $2^p - 1$ for some positive integer p. Write a program that finds all Mersenne primes with $p \leq 31$ and displays the output as follows:

```
    p        2^p - 1

    2           3
    3           7
    5          31
...
```

****5.29** (*Twin primes*) Twin primes are a pair of prime numbers that differ by 2. For example, 3 and 5 are twin primes, 5 and 7 are twin primes, and 11 and 13 are twin primes. Write a program to find all twin primes less than 1,000. Display the output as follows:

```
(3, 5)
(5, 7)
...
```

****5.30** (*Game: craps*) Craps is a popular dice game played in casinos. Write a program to play a variation of the game, as follows:

Roll two dice. Each die has six faces representing values 1, 2, . . ., and 6, respectively. Check the sum of the two dice. If the sum is 2, 3, or 12 (called *craps*), you lose; if the sum is 7 or 11 (called *natural*), you win; if the sum is another value (i.e., 4, 5, 6, 8, 9, or 10), a point is established. Continue to roll the dice until either a 7 or the same point value is rolled. If 7 is rolled, you lose. Otherwise, you win.

Your program acts as a single player. Here are some sample runs.

```
You rolled 5 + 6 = 11
You win
```

```
You rolled 1 + 2 = 3
You lose
```

```
You rolled 4 + 4 = 8
point is 8
You rolled 6 + 2 = 8
You win
```

```
You rolled 3 + 2 = 5
point is 5
You rolled 2 + 5 = 7
You lose
```

****5.31** (*Financial: credit card number validation*) Credit card numbers follow certain patterns. A credit card number must have between 13 and 16 digits. It must start with:

- 4 for Visa cards
- 5 for Master cards
- 37 for American Express cards
- 6 for Discover cards

In 1954, Hans Luhn of IBM proposed an algorithm for validating credit card numbers. The algorithm is useful to determine whether a card number is entered correctly or whether a credit card is scanned correctly by a scanner. Credit card numbers are generated following this validity check, commonly known as the *Luhn check* or the *Mod 10 check,* which can be described as follows (for illustration, consider the card number 4388576018402626):

1. Double every second digit from right to left. If doubling of a digit results in a two-digit number, add up the two digits to get a single-digit number.

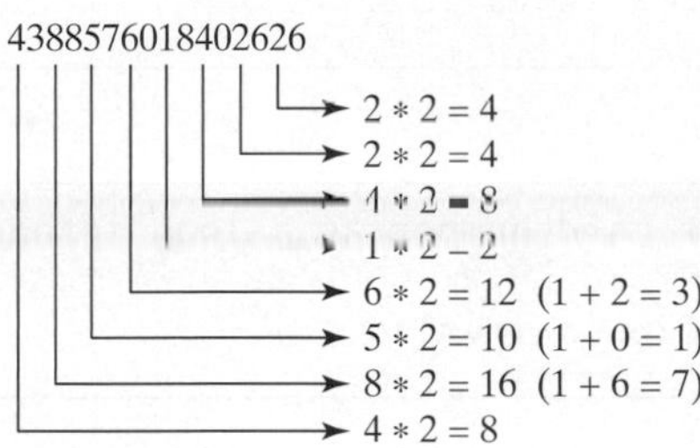

2. Now add all single-digit numbers from Step 1.

$$4 + 4 + 8 + 2 + 3 + 1 + 7 + 8 = 37$$

3. Add all digits in the odd places from right to left in the card number.

$$6 + 6 + 0 + 8 + 0 + 7 + 8 + 3 = 38$$

4. Sum the results from Step 2 and Step 3.

$$37 + 38 = 75$$

5. If the result from Step 4 is divisible by 10, the card number is valid; otherwise, it is invalid. For example, the number 4388576018402626 is invalid, but the number 4388576018410707 is valid.

Write a program that prompts the user to enter a credit card number as a `long` integer. Display whether the number is valid or invalid. Design your program to use the following methods:

```
/** Return true if the card number is valid */
public static boolean isValid(long number)

/** Get the result from Step 2 */
public static int sumOfDoubleEvenPlace(long number)

/** Return this number if it is a single digit, otherwise,
 * return the sum of the two digits */
public static int getDigit(int number)

/** Return sum of odd-place digits in number */
public static int sumOfOddPlace(long number)

/** Return true if the digit d is a prefix for number */
public static boolean prefixMatched(long number, int d)

/** Return the number of digits in d */
public static int getSize(long d)

/** Return the first k number of digits from number. If the
 * number of digits in number is less than k, return number. */
public static long getPrefix(long number, int k)
```

Here are sample runs of the program:

```
Enter a credit card number as a long integer:
  4388576018410707 ↵Enter
4388576018410707 is valid
```

```
Enter a credit card number as a long integer:
  4388576018402626 ↵Enter
4388576018402626 is invalid
```

****5.32** (*Game: chance of winning at craps*) Revise Exercise 5.30 to run it 10,000 times and display the number of winning games.

****5.33** (*Current date and time*) Invoking `System.currentTimeMillis()` returns the elapsed time in milliseconds since midnight of January 1, 1970. Write a program that displays the date and time. Here is a sample run:

```
Current date and time is May 16, 2012 10:34:23
```

**5.34 (*Print calendar*) Programming Exercise 3.21 uses Zeller's congruence to calculate the day of the week. Simplify Listing 5.12, PrintCalendar.java, using Zeller's algorithm to get the start day of the month.

5.35 (*Geometry: area of a pentagon*) The area of a pentagon can be computed using the following formula:

$$Area = \frac{5 \times s^2}{4 \times \tan\left(\frac{\pi}{5}\right)}$$

Write a program that prompts the user to enter the side of a pentagon and displays the area. Here is a sample run:

```
Enter the side: 5.5 ↵Enter
The area of the pentagon is 52.04444136781625
```

*5.36 (*Geometry: area of a regular polygon*) A regular polygon is an n-sided polygon in which all sides are of the same length and all angles have the same degree (i.e., the polygon is both equilateral and equiangular). The formula for computing the area of a regular polygon is

$$Area = \frac{n \times s^2}{4 \times \tan\left(\frac{\pi}{n}\right)}$$

Write a method that returns the area of a regular polygon using the following header:

```
public static double area(int n, double side)
```

Write a main method that prompts the user to enter the number of sides and the side of a regular polygon and displays its area. Here is a sample run:

```
Enter the number of sides: 5 ↵Enter
Enter the side: 6.5 ↵Enter
The area of the polygon is 72.69017017488385
```

5.37 (*Format an integer*) Write a method with the following header to format the integer with the specified width.

```
public static String format(int number, int width)
```

The method returns a string for the number with one or more prefix `0`s. The size of the string is the width. For example, `format(34, 4)` returns `0034` and `format(34, 5)` returns `00034`. If the number is longer than the width, the method returns the string representation for the number. For example, `format(34, 1)` returns `34`.

Write a test program that prompts the user to enter a number and its width and displays a string returned by invoking `format(number, width)`.

***5.38** (*Generate random characters*) Use the methods in `RandomCharacter` in Listing 5.10 to print 100 uppercase letters and then 100 single digits, printing ten per line.

5.39 (*Geometry: point position*) Programming Exercise 3.32 shows how to test whether a point is on the left side of a directed line, on the right, or on the same line. Write the methods with the following headers:

```
/** Return true if point (x2, y2) is on the left side of the
 *  directed line from (x0, y0) to (x1, y1) */
public static boolean leftOfTheLine(double x0, double y0,
  double x1, double y1, double x2, double y2)

/** Return true if point (x2, y2) is on the same
 *  line from (x0, y0) to (x1, y1) */
public static boolean onTheSameLine(double x0, double y0,
  double x1, double y1, double x2, double y2)

/** Return true if point (x2, y2) is on the
 *  line segment from (x0, y0) to (x1, y1) */
public static boolean onTheLineSegment(double x0, double y0,
  double x1, double y1, double x2, double y2)
```

Write a program that prompts the user to enter the three points for `p0`, `p1`, and `p2` and displays whether `p2` is on the left of the line from `p0` to `p1`, right, the same line, or on the line segment. Here are some sample runs:

```
Enter three points for p0, p1, and p2: 1 1 2 2 1.5 1.5 [Enter]
(1.5, 1.5) is on the line segment from (1.0, 1.0) to (2.0, 2.0)
```

```
Enter three points for p0, p1, and p2: 1 1 2 2 3 3 [Enter]
(3.0, 3.0) is on the same line from (1.0, 1.0) to (2.0, 2.0)
```

```
Enter three points for p0, p1, and p2: 1 1 2 2 1 1.5 [Enter]
(1.0, 1.5) is on the left side of the line
  from (1.0, 1.0) to (2.0, 2.0)
```

```
Enter three points for p0, p1, and p2: 1 1 2 2 1 -1 [Enter]
(1.0, -1.0) is on the right side of the line
  from (1.0, 1.0) to (2.0, 2.0)
```

CHAPTER 6

SINGLE-DIMENSIONAL ARRAYS

Objectives

- To describe why arrays are necessary in programming (§6.1).
- To declare array reference variables and create arrays (§§6.2.1–6.2.2).
- To obtain array size using `arrayRefVar.length` and know default values in an array (§6.2.3).
- To access array elements using indexed variables (§6.2.4).
- To declare, create, and initialize an array using an array initializer (§6.2.5).
- To program common array operations (displaying arrays, summing all elements, finding the minimum and maximum elements, random shuffling, and shifting elements) (§6.2.6).
- To simplify programming using the for-each loops (§6.2.7).
- To apply arrays in application development (`LottoNumbers`, `DeckOfCards`) (§§6.3–6.4).
- To copy contents from one array to another (§6.5).
- To develop and invoke methods with array arguments and return values (§§6.6–6.8).
- To define a method with a variable-length argument list (§6.9).
- To search elements using the linear (§6.10.1) or binary (§6.10.2) search algorithm.
- To sort an array using the selection sort approach (§6.11.1).
- To sort an array using the insertion sort approach (§6.11.2).
- To use the methods in the `java.util.Arrays` class (§6.12).

6.1 Introduction

A single array variable can reference a large collection of data.

problem

why array?

Often you will have to store a large number of values during the execution of a program. Suppose, for instance, that you need to read 100 numbers, compute their average, and find out how many numbers are above the average. Your program first reads the numbers and computes their average, then compares each number with the average to determine whether it is above the average. In order to accomplish this task, the numbers must all be stored in variables. You have to declare 100 variables and repeatedly write almost identical code 100 times. Writing a program this way would be impractical. So, how do you solve this problem?

what is array?

An efficient, organized approach is needed. Java and most other high-level languages provide a data structure, the *array*, which stores a fixed-size sequential collection of elements of the same type. In the present case, you can store all 100 numbers into an array and access them through a single array variable. The solution may look like this:

create array

store number in array

get average

above average?

```
1  public class AnalyzeNumbers {
2    public static void main(String[] args) {
3      final int NUMBER_OF_ELEMENTS = 100;
4      double[] numbers = new double[NUMBER_OF_ELEMENTS];
5      double sum = 0;
6
7      java.util.Scanner input = new java.util.Scanner(System.in);
8      for (int i = 0; i < NUMBER_OF_ELEMENTS; i++) {
9        System.out.print("Enter a new number: ");
10       numbers[i] = input.nextDouble();
11       sum += numbers[i];
12     }
13
14     double average = sum / NUMBER_OF_ELEMENTS;
15
16     int count = 0; // The number of elements above average
17     for (int i = 0; i < NUMBER_OF_ELEMENTS; i++)
18       if (numbers[i] > average)
19         count++;
20
21     System.out.println("Average is " + average);
22     System.out.println("Number of elements above the average "
23       + count);
24   }
25 }
```

numbers array

numbers[0]:
numbers[1]:
numbers[2]:
.
numbers[i] .
.
numbers[97]:
numbers[98]:
numbers[99]:

The program creates an array of **100** elements in line 4, stores numbers into the array in line 10, adds each number to **sum** in line 11, and obtains the average in line 14. It then compares each number in the array with the average to count the number of values above the average (lines 16–19).

This chapter introduces single-dimensional arrays. The next chapter will introduce two-dimensional and multidimensional arrays.

6.2 Array Basics

Once an array is created, its size is fixed. An array reference variable is used to access the elements in an array using an index.

index

An array is used to store a collection of data, but often we find it more useful to think of an array as a collection of variables of the same type. Instead of declaring individual variables, such as **number0**, **number1**, . . . , and **number99**, you declare one array variable such as **numbers** and use **numbers[0]**, **numbers[1]**, . . . , and **numbers[99]** to represent individual variables.

This section introduces how to declare array variables, create arrays, and process arrays using indexed variables.

6.2.1 Declaring Array Variables

To use an array in a program, you must declare a variable to reference the array and specify the array's *element type*. Here is the syntax for declaring an array variable:

element type

```
elementType[] arrayRefVar;
```

The `elementType` can be any data type, and all elements in the array will have the same data type. For example, the following code declares a variable `myList` that references an array of double elements.

```
double[] myList;
```

Note

You can also use `elementType arrayRefVar[]` to declare an array variable. This style comes from the C language and was adopted in Java to accommodate C programmers. The style `elementType[] arrayRefVar` is preferred.

preferred syntax

6.2.2 Creating Arrays

Unlike declarations for primitive data type variables, the declaration of an array variable does not allocate any space in memory for the array. It creates only a storage location for the reference to an array. If a variable does not contain a reference to an array, the value of the variable is `null`. You cannot assign elements to an array unless it has already been created. After an array variable is declared, you can create an array by using the `new` operator with the following syntax:

null

```
arrayRefVar = new elementType[arraySize];
```

new operator

This statement does two things: (1) it creates an array using `new elementType[arraySize]`; (2) it assigns the reference of the newly created array to the variable `arrayRefVar`.

Declaring an array variable, creating an array, and assigning the reference of the array to the variable can be combined in one statement as:

```
elementType[] arrayRefVar = new elementType[arraySize];
```

or

```
elementType arrayRefVar[] = new elementType[arraySize];
```

Here is an example of such a statement:

```
double[] myList = new double[10];
```

This statement declares an array variable, `myList`, creates an array of ten elements of `double` type, and assigns its reference to `myList`. To assign values to the elements, use the syntax:

```
arrayRefVar[index] = value;
```

For example, the following code initializes the array.

```
myList[0] = 5.6;
myList[1] = 4.5;
myList[2] = 3.3;
myList[3] = 13.2;
```

```
myList[4] = 4.0;
myList[5] = 34.33;
myList[6] = 34.0;
myList[7] = 45.45;
myList[8] = 99.993;
myList[9] = 11123;
```

This array is illustrated in Figure 6.1.

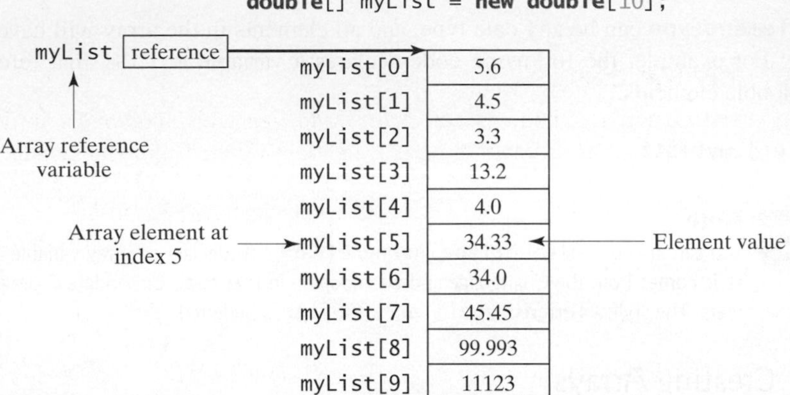

FIGURE 6.1 The array `myList` has ten elements of `double` type and `int` indices from `0` to `9`.

array vs. array variable

> **Note**
> An array variable that appears to hold an array actually contains a reference to that array. Strictly speaking, an array variable and an array are different, but most of the time the distinction can be ignored. Thus it is all right to say, for simplicity, that `myList` is an array, instead of stating, at greater length, that `myList` is a variable that contains a reference to an array of ten double elements.

6.2.3 Array Size and Default Values

array length

When space for an array is allocated, the array size must be given, specifying the number of elements that can be stored in it. The size of an array cannot be changed after the array is created. Size can be obtained using `arrayRefVar.length`. For example, `myList.length` is `10`.

default values

When an array is created, its elements are assigned the default value of `0` for the numeric primitive data types, `\u0000` for `char` types, and `false` for `boolean` types.

6.2.4 Array Indexed Variables

0 based

The array elements are accessed through the index. Array indices are `0` based; that is, they range from `0` to `arrayRefVar.length-1`. In the example in Figure 6.1, `myList` holds ten `double` values, and the indices are from `0` to `9`.

indexed variable

Each element in the array is represented using the following syntax, known as an *indexed variable*:

```
arrayRefVar[index];
```

For example, `myList[9]` represents the last element in the array `myList`.

> **Caution**
> Some programming languages use parentheses to reference an array element, as in `myList(9)`, but Java uses brackets, as in `myList[9]`.

After an array is created, an indexed variable can be used in the same way as a regular variable. For example, the following code adds the values in myList[0] and myList[1] to myList[2].

```
myList[2] = myList[0] + myList[1];
```

The following loop assigns 0 to myList[0], 1 to myList[1], . . . , and 9 to myList[9]:

```
for (int i = 0; i < myList.length; i++) {
  myList[i] = i;
}
```

6.2.5 Array Initializers

Java has a shorthand notation, known as the *array initializer*, which combines the declaration, creation, and initialization of an array in one statement using the following syntax:

array initializer

```
elementType[] arrayRefVar = {value0, value1, ..., valuek};
```

For example, the statement

```
double[] myList = {1.9, 2.9, 3.4, 3.5};
```

declares, creates, and initializes the array myList with four elements, which is equivalent to the following statements:

```
double[] myList = new double[4];
myList[0] = 1.9;
myList[1] = 2.9;
myList[2] = 3.4;
myList[3] = 3.5;
```

Caution

The new operator is not used in the array-initializer syntax. Using an array initializer, you have to declare, create, and initialize the array all in one statement. Splitting it would cause a syntax error. Thus, the next statement is wrong:

```
double[] myList;
myList = {1.9, 2.9, 3.4, 3.5};
```

6.2.6 Processing Arrays

When processing array elements, you will often use a for loop—for two reasons:

- All of the elements in an array are of the same type. They are evenly processed in the same fashion repeatedly using a loop.
- Since the size of the array is known, it is natural to use a for loop.

Assume the array is created as follows:

```
double[] myList = new double[10];
```

The following are some examples of processing arrays.

1. *Initializing arrays with input values:* The following loop initializes the array myList with user input values.

```
java.util.Scanner input = new java.util.Scanner(System.in);
System.out.print("Enter " + myList.length + " values: ");
for (int i = 0; i < myList.length; i++)
  myList[i] = input.nextDouble();
```

2. *Initializing arrays with random values:* The following loop initializes the array `myList` with random values between `0.0` and `100.0`, but less than `100.0`.

```
for (int i = 0; i < myList.length; i++) {
  myList[i] = Math.random() * 100;
}
```

3. *Displaying arrays:* To print an array, you have to print each element in the array using a loop like the following:

```
for (int i = 0; i < myList.length; i++) {
  System.out.print(myList[i] + " ");
}
```

print character array

Tip

For an array of the `char[]` type, it can be printed using one print statement. For example, the following code displays `Dallas`:

```
char[] city = {'D', 'a', 'l', 'l', 'a', 's'};
System.out.println(city);
```

4. *Summing all elements:* Use a variable named `total` to store the sum. Initially `total` is `0`. Add each element in the array to `total` using a loop like this:

```
double total = 0;
for (int i = 0; i < myList.length; i++) {
  total += myList[i];
}
```

5. *Finding the largest element:* Use a variable named `max` to store the largest element. Initially `max` is `myList[0]`. To find the largest element in the array `myList`, compare each element with `max`, and update `max` if the element is greater than `max`.

```
double max = myList[0];
for (int i = 1; i < myList.length; i++) {
  if (myList[i] > max) max = myList[i];
}
```

6. *Finding the smallest index of the largest element:* Often you need to locate the largest element in an array. If an array has more than one largest element, find the smallest index of such an element. Suppose the array `myList` is {`1, 5, 3, 4, 5, 5`}. The largest element is `5` and the smallest index for `5` is `1`. Use a variable named `max` to store the largest element and a variable named `indexOfMax` to denote the index of the largest element. Initially `max` is `myList[0]`, and `indexOfMax` is `0`. Compare each element in `myList` with `max`, and update `max` and `indexOfMax` if the element is greater than `max`.

```
double max = myList[0];
int indexOfMax = 0;
for (int i = 1; i < myList.length; i++) {
  if (myList[i] > max) {
    max = myList[i];
    indexOfMax = i;
  }
}
```

VideoNote
Random shuffling

7. *Random shuffling:* In many applications, you need to randomly reorder the elements in an array. This is called *shuffling*. To accomplish this, for each element

myList[i], randomly generate an index j and swap myList[i] with myList[j], as follows:

```
for (int i = 0; i < myList.length; i++) {
  // Generate an index j randomly
  int j = (int) (Math.random()
    * mylist.length);

  // Swap myList[i] with myList[j]
  double temp = myList[i];
  myList[i] = myList[j];
  myList[j] = temp;
}
```

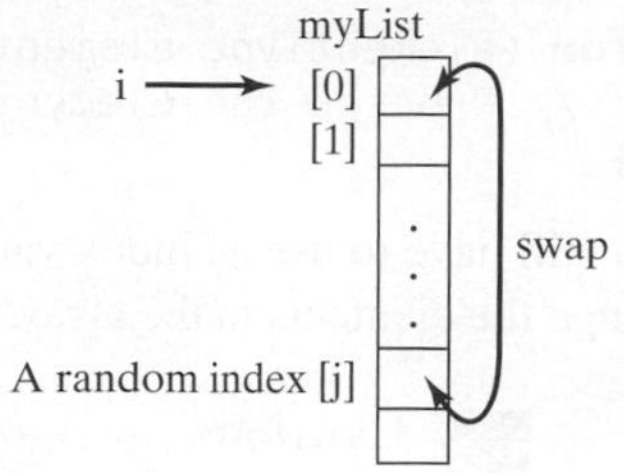

8. *Shifting elements:* Sometimes you need to shift the elements left or right. Here is an example of shifting the elements one position to the left and filling the last element with the first element:

```
double temp = myList[0]; // Retain the first element

// Shift elements left
for (int i = 1; i < myList.length; i++) {
  myList[i - 1] = myList[i];
}

// Move the first element to fill in the last position
myList[myList.length - 1] = temp;
```

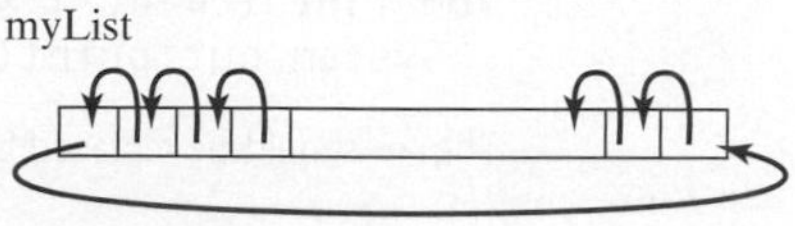

9. *Simplifying coding:* Arrays can be used to greatly simplify coding for certain tasks. For example, suppose you wish to obtain the English name of a given month by its number. If the month names are stored in an array, the month name for a given month can be accessed simply via the index. The following code prompts the user to enter a month number and displays its month name:

```
String[] months = {"January", "February", ..., "December"};
System.out.print("Enter a month number (1 to 12): ");
int monthNumber = input.nextInt();
System.out.println("The month is " + months[monthNumber - 1]);
```

If you didn't use the months array, you would have to determine the month name using a lengthy multi-way if-else statement as follows:

```
if (monthNumber == 1)
  System.out.println("The month is January");
else if (monthNumber == 2)
  System.out.println("The month is February");
...
else
  System.out.println("The month is December");
```

6.2.7 for-each Loops

Java supports a convenient for loop, known as a *for-each loop* or *enhanced for loop*, which enables you to traverse the array sequentially without using an index variable. For example, the following code displays all the elements in the array myList:

```
for (double u: myList) {
  System.out.println(u);
}
```

You can read the code as "for each element u in myList, do the following." Note that the variable, u, must be declared as the same type as the elements in myList.

In general, the syntax for a for-each loop is

```
for (elementType element: arrayRefVar) {
  // Process the element
}
```

You still have to use an index variable if you wish to traverse the array in a different order or change the elements in the array.

ArrayIndexOutOfBounds-Exception

Caution

Accessing an array out of bounds is a common programming error that throws a runtime ArrayIndexOutOfBoundsException. To avoid it, make sure that you do not use an index beyond arrayRefVar.length - 1.

off-by-one error

Programmers often mistakenly reference the first element in an array with index 1, but it should be 0. This is called the *off-by-one error*. Another common error in a loop is using <= where < should be used. For example, the following loop is wrong.

```
for (int i = 0; i <= list.length; i++)
  System.out.print(list[i] + " ");
```

The <= should be replaced by <.

MyProgrammingLab™

6.1 How do you declare an array reference variable and how do you create an array?

6.2 When is the memory allocated for an array?

6.3 What is the printout of the following code?

```
int x = 30;
int[] numbers = new int[x];
x = 60;
System.out.println("x is " + x);
System.out.println("The size of numbers is " + numbers.length);
```

6.4 Indicate true or false for the following statements:

- Every element in an array has the same type.
- The array size is fixed after an array reference variable is declared.
- The array size is fixed after it is created.
- The elements in an array must be a primitive data type.

6.5 Which of the following statements are valid?

```
int i = new int(30);
double d[] = new double[30];
char[] r = new char(1..30);
int i[] = (3, 4, 3, 2);
float f[] = {2.3, 4.5, 6.6};
char[] c = new char();
```

6.6 How do you access elements in an array? What is an array indexed variable?

6.7 What is the array index type? What is the lowest index? What is the representation of the third element in an array named a?

6.8 Write statements to do the following:

a. Create an array to hold 10 double values.

b. Assign the value 5.5 to the last element in the array.

c. Display the sum of the first two elements.

d. Write a loop that computes the sum of all elements in the array.

e. Write a loop that finds the minimum element in the array.

f. Randomly generate an index and display the element of this index in the array.

g. Use an array initializer to create another array with the initial values `3.5`, `5.5`, `4.52`, and `5.6`.

6.9 What happens when your program attempts to access an array element with an invalid index?

6.10 Identify and fix the errors in the following code:

```
public class Test {
  public static void main(String[] args) {
    double[100] r;

    for (int i = 0; i < r.length(); i++);
      r(i) = Math.random * 100;
  }
}
```

6.11 What is the output of the following code?

```
public class Test {
  public static void main(String[] args) {
    int list[] = {1, 2, 3, 4, 5, 6};
    for (int i = 1; i < list.length; i++)
      list[i] = list[i - 1];

    for (int i = 0; i < list.length; i++)
      System.out.print(list[i] + " ");
  }
}
```

6.3 Case Study: Lotto Numbers

The problem is to write a program that checks if all the input numbers cover 1 to 99.

Lotto numbers

Each ticket for the Pick-10 lotto has 10 unique numbers ranging from 1 to 99. Suppose you buy a lot of tickets and like to have them cover all numbers from 1 to 99. Write a program that reads the ticket numbers from a file and checks whether all numbers are covered. Assume the last number in the file is 0. Suppose the file contains the numbers

```
80 3 87 62 30 90 10 21 46 27
12 40 83 9 39 88 95 59 20 37
80 40 87 67 31 90 11 24 56 77
11 48 51 42 8 74 1 41 36 53
52 82 16 72 19 70 44 56 29 33
54 64 99 14 23 22 94 79 55 2
60 86 34 4 31 63 84 89 7 78
43 93 97 45 25 38 28 26 85 49
47 65 57 67 73 69 32 71 24 66
92 98 96 77 6 75 17 61 58 13
35 81 18 15 5 68 91 50 76
0
```

Your program should display

```
The tickets cover all numbers
```

Suppose the file contains the numbers

```
11 48 51 42 8 74 1 41 36 53
52 82 16 72 19 70 44 56 29 33
0
```

Your program should display

```
The tickets don't cover all numbers
```

How do you mark a number as covered? You can create an array with `99` `boolean` elements. Each element in the array can be used to mark whether a number is covered. Let the array be `isCovered`. Initially, each element is `false`, as shown in Figure 6.2a. Whenever a number is read, its corresponding element is set to `true`. Suppose the numbers entered are `1`, `2`, `3`, `99`, `0`. When number `1` is read, `isCovered[0]` is set to `true` (see Figure 6.2b). When number `2` is read, `isCovered[2 - 1]` is set to `true` (see Figure 6.2c). When number `3` is read, `isCovered[3 - 1]` is set to `true` (see Figure 6.2d). When number `99` is read, `isCovered[98]` is set to `true` (see Figure 6.2e).

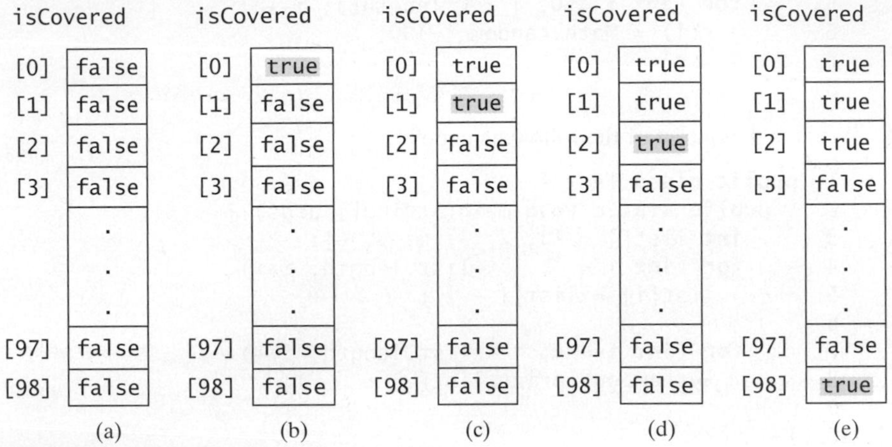

isCovered	(a)	(b)	(c)	(d)	(e)
[0]	false	true	true	true	true
[1]	false	false	true	true	true
[2]	false	false	false	true	true
[3]	false	false	false	false	false
	. . .	. . .	. . .	. . .	. . .
[97]	false	false	false	false	false
[98]	false	false	false	false	true

FIGURE 6.2 If number `i` appears in a Lotto ticket, `isCovered[i-1]` is set to `true`.

The algorithm for the program can be described as follows:

```
for each number k read from the file,
  mark number k as covered by setting isCovered[k - 1] true;
if every isCovered[i] is true
  The tickets cover all numbers
else
  The tickets don't cover all numbers
```

The complete program is given in Listing 6.1.

LISTING 6.1 LottoNumbers.java

create and initialize array

read number

mark number covered

read number

```
import java.util.Scanner;

public class LottoNumbers {
  public static void main(String[] args) {
    Scanner input = new Scanner(System.in);
    boolean[] isCovered = new boolean[99]; // Default is false

    // Read each number and mark its corresponding element covered
    int number = input.nextInt();
    while (number != 0) {
      isCovered[number - 1] = true;
      number = input.nextInt();
    }

```

```
15      // Check whether all covered
16      boolean allCovered = true; // Assume all covered initially
17      for (int i = 0; i < isCovered.length; i++)
18        if (!isCovered[i]) {
19          allCovered = false; // Find one number not covered
20          break;
21        }
22
23      // Display result
24      if (allCovered)
25        System.out.println("The tickets cover all numbers");
26      else
27        System.out.println("The tickets don't cover all numbers");
28    }
29  }
```

check `allCovered`?

Suppose you have created a text file named LottoNumbers.txt that contains the input data `2 5 6 5 4 3 23 43 2 0`. You can run the program using the following command:

```
java LottoNumbers < LottoNumbers.txt
```

The program can be traced as follows:

Line#	Representative elements in array isCovered							number	allCovered
	[1]	[2]	[3]	[4]	[5]	[22]	[42]		
6	false	false	false	false	false	false	false		
9								2	
11	true								
12								5	
11				true					
12								6	
11					true				
12								5	
11				true					
12								4	
11			true						
12								3	
11		true							
12								23	
11						true			
12								43	
11							true		
12								2	
11	true								
12								0	
16									true
18(i=0)									false

The program creates an array of `99` `boolean` elements and initializes each element to `false` (line 6). It reads the first number from the file (line 9). The program then repeats the following operations in a loop:

- If the number is not zero, set its corresponding value in array `isCovered` to `true` (line 11);
- Read the next number (line 12).

When the input is `0`, the input ends. The program checks whether all numbers are covered in lines 16–21 and displays the result in lines 24–27.

6.4 Case Study: Deck of Cards

The problem is to create a program that will randomly select four cards from a deck of cards.

Say you want to write a program that will pick four cards at random from a deck of `52` cards. All the cards can be represented using an array named `deck`, filled with initial values `0` to `51`, as follows:

```
int[] deck = new int[52];
// Initialize cards
for (int i = 0; i < deck.length; i++)
  deck[i] = i;
```

Card numbers `0` to `12`, `13` to `25`, `26` to `38`, and `39` to `51` represent 13 Spades, 13 Hearts, 13 Diamonds, and 13 Clubs, respectively, as shown in Figure 6.3. `cardNumber / 13` determines the suit of the card and `cardNumber % 13` determines the rank of the card, as shown in Figure 6.4. After shuffling the array `deck`, pick the first four cards from `deck`. The program displays the cards from these four card numbers.

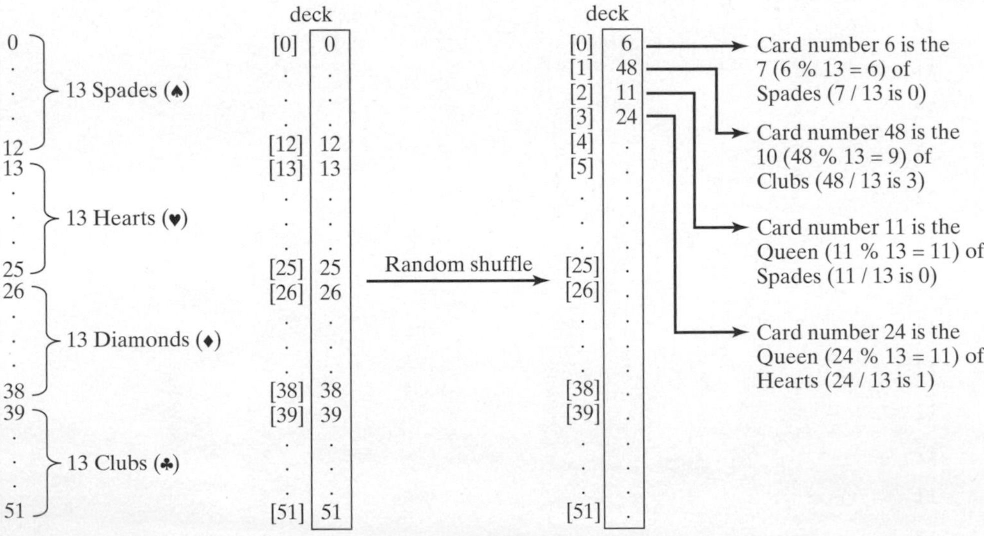

FIGURE 6.3 52 cards are stored in an array named `deck`.

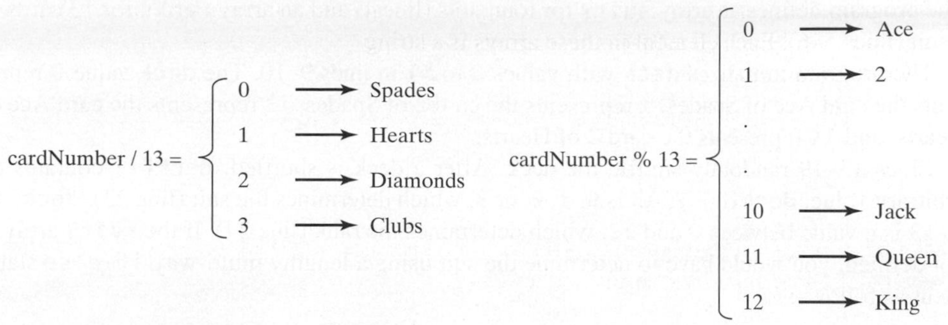

cardNumber / 13 =
- 0 → Spades
- 1 → Hearts
- 2 → Diamonds
- 3 → Clubs

cardNumber % 13 =
- 0 → Ace
- 1 → 2
- .
- .
- 10 → Jack
- 11 → Queen
- 12 → King

FIGURE 6.4 How `cardNumber` identifies a card's suit and rank number.

Listing 6.2 gives the solution to the problem.

LISTING 6.2 DeckOfCards.java

```
public class DeckOfCards {
  public static void main(String[] args) {
    int[] deck = new int[52];
    String[] suits = {"Spades", "Hearts", "Diamonds", "Clubs"};
    String[] ranks = {"Ace", "2", "3", "4", "5", "6", "7", "8", "9",
      "10", "Jack", "Queen", "King"};

    // Initialize the cards
    for (int i = 0; i < deck.length; i++)
      deck[i] = i;

    // Shuffle the cards
    for (int i = 0; i < deck.length; i++) {
      // Generate an index randomly
      int index = (int)(Math.random() * deck.length);
      int temp = deck[i];
      deck[i] = deck[index];
      deck[index] = temp;
    }

    // Display the first four cards
    for (int i = 0; i < 4; i++) {
      String suit = suits[deck[i] / 13];
      String rank = ranks[deck[i] % 13];
      System.out.println("Card number " + deck[i] + ": "
        + rank + " of " + suit);
    }
  }
}
```

create array deck
array of strings
array of strings
initialize deck
shuffle deck
suit of a card
rank of a card

```
Card number 6: 7 of Spades
Card number 48: 10 of Clubs
Card number 11: Queen of Spades
Card number 24: Queen of Hearts
```

The program defines an array **suits** for four suits (line 4) and an array **ranks** for 13 cards in a suit (lines 5–6). Each element in these arrays is a string.

The program initializes **deck** with values **0** to **51** in lines 9–10. The **deck** value **0** represents the card Ace of Spades, **1** represents the card 2 of Spades, **13** represents the card Ace of Hearts, and **14** represents the card 2 of Hearts.

Lines 13–19 randomly shuffle the deck. After a deck is shuffled, **deck[i]** contains an arbitrary value. **deck[i] / 13** is **0**, **1**, **2**, or **3**, which determines the suit (line 23). **deck[i] % 13** is a value between **0** and **12**, which determines the rank (line 24). If the **suits** array is not defined, you would have to determine the suit using a lengthy multi-way **if-else** statement as follows:

```
if (deck[i] / 13 == 0)
  System.out.print("suit is Spades");
else if (deck[i] / 13 == 1)
  System.out.print("suit is Hearts");
else if(deck[i] / 13 == 2)
  System.out.print("suit is Diamonds");
else
  System.out.print("suit is Clubs");
```

With **suits = {"Spades", "Hearts", "Diamonds", "Clubs"}** created in an array, **suits[deck / 13]** gives the suit for the **deck**. Using arrays greatly simplifies the solution for this program.

6.5 Copying Arrays

To copy the contents of one array into another, you have to copy the array's individual elements into the other array.

Often, in a program, you need to duplicate an array or a part of an array. In such cases you could attempt to use the assignment statement (=), as follows:

```
list2 = list1;
```

copy reference

garbage collection

However, this statement does not copy the contents of the array referenced by **list1** to **list2**, but instead merely copies the reference value from **list1** to **list2**. After this statement, **list1** and **list2** reference the same array, as shown in Figure 6.5. The array previously referenced by **list2** is no longer referenced; it becomes garbage, which will be automatically collected by the Java Virtual Machine (this process is called *garbage collection*).

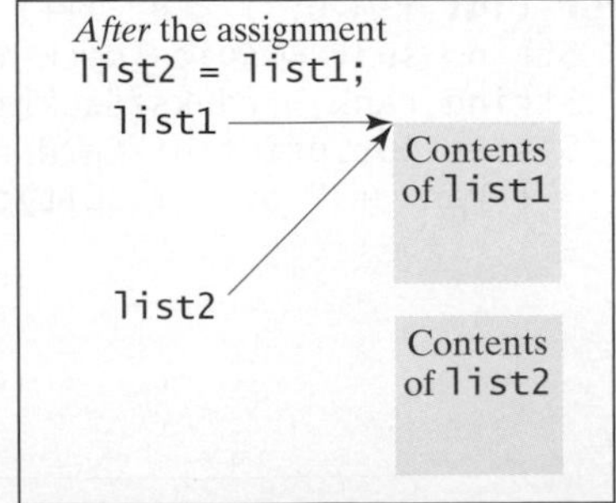

FIGURE 6.5 Before the assignment statement, **list1** and **list2** point to separate memory locations. After the assignment, the reference of the **list1** array is passed to **list2**.

In Java, you can use assignment statements to copy primitive data type variables, but not arrays. Assigning one array variable to another array variable actually copies one reference to another and makes both variables point to the same memory location.

There are three ways to copy arrays:

- Use a loop to copy individual elements one by one.
- Use the static arraycopy method in the System class.
- Use the clone method to copy arrays; this will be introduced in Chapter 15, Abstract Classes and Interfaces.

You can write a loop to copy every element from the source array to the corresponding element in the target array. The following code, for instance, copies sourceArray to targetArray using a for loop.

```
int[] sourceArray = {2, 3, 1, 5, 10};
int[] targetArray = new int[sourceArray.length];
for (int i = 0; i < sourceArray.length; i++) {
  targetArray[i] = sourceArray[i];
}
```

Another approach is to use the arraycopy method in the java.lang.System class to copy arrays instead of using a loop. The syntax for arraycopy is:

arraycopy method

```
arraycopy(sourceArray, src_pos, targetArray, tar_pos, length);
```

The parameters src_pos and tar_pos indicate the starting positions in sourceArray and targetArray, respectively. The number of elements copied from sourceArray to targetArray is indicated by length. For example, you can rewrite the loop using the following statement:

```
System.arraycopy(sourceArray, 0, targetArray, 0, sourceArray.length);
```

The arraycopy method does not allocate memory space for the target array. The target array must have already been created with its memory space allocated. After the copying takes place, targetArray and sourceArray have the same content but independent memory locations.

Note

The arraycopy method violates the Java naming convention. By convention, this method should be named arrayCopy (i.e., with an uppercase C).

6.12 Use the arraycopy() method to copy the following array to a target array t:

```
int[] source = {3, 4, 5};
```

6.13 Once an array is created, its size cannot be changed. Does the following code resize the array?

```
int[] myList;
myList = new int[10];
// Sometime later you want to assign a new array to myList
myList = new int[20];
```

6.6 Passing Arrays to Methods

When passing an array to a method, the reference of the array is passed to the method.

Just as you can pass primitive type values to methods, you can also pass arrays to methods. For example, the following method displays the elements in an int array:

```
public static void printArray(int[] array) {
  for (int i = 0; i < array.length; i++) {
```

```
        System.out.print(array[i] + " ");
    }
  }
```

You can invoke it by passing an array. For example, the following statement invokes the `printArray` method to display 3, 1, 2, 6, 4, and 2.

```
printArray(new int[]{3, 1, 2, 6, 4, 2});
```

Note

The preceding statement creates an array using the following syntax:

```
new elementType[]{value0, value1, ..., valuek};
```

anonymous array

There is no explicit reference variable for the array. Such array is called an *anonymous array*.

pass-by-value

Java uses *pass-by-value* to pass arguments to a method. There are important differences between passing the values of variables of primitive data types and passing arrays.

- For an argument of a primitive type, the argument's value is passed.
- For an argument of an array type, the value of the argument is a reference to an array; this reference value is passed to the method. Semantically, it can be best described as *pass-by-sharing*, that is, the array in the method is the same as the array being passed. Thus, if you change the array in the method, you will see the change outside the method.

pass-by-sharing

Take the following code, for example:

```
public class Test {
  public static void main(String[] args) {
    int x = 1; // x represents an int value
    int[] y = new int[10]; // y represents an array of int values

    m(x, y); // Invoke m with arguments x and y

    System.out.println("x is " + x);
    System.out.println("y[0] is " + y[0]);
  }

  public static void m(int number, int[] numbers) {
    number = 1001; // Assign a new value to number
    numbers[0] = 5555; // Assign a new value to numbers[0]
  }
}
```

```
x is 1
y[0] is 5555
```

You may wonder why after `m` is invoked, `x` remains `1`, but `y[0]` become `5555`. This is because `y` and `numbers`, although they are independent variables, reference the same array, as illustrated in Figure 6.6. When `m(x, y)` is invoked, the values of `x` and `y` are passed to `number` and `numbers`. Since `y` contains the reference value to the array, `numbers` now contains the same reference value to the same array.

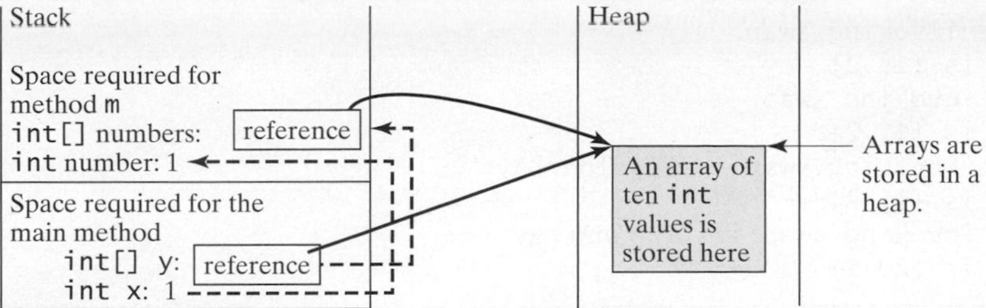

FIGURE 6.6 The primitive type value in **x** is passed to **number**, and the reference value in **y** is passed to **numbers**.

Note

Arrays are objects in Java (objects are introduced in Chapter 8). The JVM stores the objects in an area of memory called the *heap*, which is used for dynamic memory allocation.

heap

Listing 6.3 gives another program that shows the difference between passing a primitive data type value and an array reference variable to a method.

The program contains two methods for swapping elements in an array. The first method, named **swap**, fails to swap two **int** arguments. The second method, named **swapFirstTwoInArray**, successfully swaps the first two elements in the array argument.

LISTING 6.3 TestPassArray.java

```
public class TestPassArray {
  /** Main method */
  public static void main(String[] args) {
    int[] a = {1, 2};

    // Swap elements using the swap method
    System.out.println("Before invoking swap");
    System.out.println("array is {" + a[0] + ", " + a[1] + "}");
    swap(a[0], a[1]);
    System.out.println("After invoking swap");
    System.out.println("array is {" + a[0] + ", " + a[1] + "}");

    // Swap elements using the swapFirstTwoInArray method
    System.out.println("Before invoking swapFirstTwoInArray");
    System.out.println("array is {" + a[0] + ", " + a[1] + "}");
    swapFirstTwoInArray(a);
    System.out.println("After invoking swapFirstTwoInArray");
    System.out.println("array is {" + a[0] + ", " + a[1] + "}");
  }

  /** Swap two variables */
  public static void swap(int n1, int n2) {
    int temp = n1;
    n1 = n2;
    n2 = temp;
  }

  /** Swap the first two elements in the array */
  public static void swapFirstTwoInArray(int[] array) {
    int temp = array[0];
    array[0] = array[1];
    array[1] = temp;
  }
}
```

false swap

swap array elements

```
Before invoking swap
array is {1, 2}
After invoking swap
array is {1, 2}
Before invoking swapFirstTwoInArray
array is {1, 2}
After invoking swapFirstTwoInArray
array is {2, 1}
```

As shown in Figure 6.7, the two elements are not swapped using the `swap` method. However, they are swapped using the `swapFirstTwoInArray` method. Since the parameters in the `swap` method are primitive type, the values of `a[0]` and `a[1]` are passed to `n1` and `n2` inside the method when invoking `swap(a[0], a[1])`. The memory locations for `n1` and `n2` are independent of the ones for `a[0]` and `a[1]`. The contents of the array are not affected by this call.

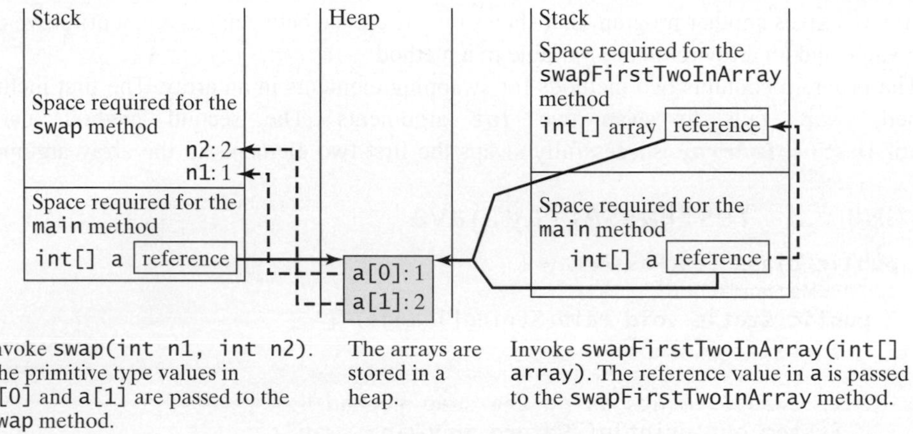

Figure 6.7 When passing an array to a method, the reference of the array is passed to the method.

The parameter in the `swapFirstTwoInArray` method is an array. As shown in Figure 6.7, the reference of the array is passed to the method. Thus the variables `a` (outside the method) and `array` (inside the method) both refer to the same array in the same memory location. Therefore, swapping `array[0]` with `array[1]` inside the method `swapFirstTwoInArray` is the same as swapping `a[0]` with `a[1]` outside of the method.

6.7 Returning an Array from a Method

Key Point

When a method returns an array, the reference of the array is returned.

You can pass arrays when invoking a method. A method may also return an array. For example, the following method returns an array that is the reversal of another array.

create array

return array

```
public static int[] reverse(int[] list) {
  int[] result = new int[list.length];

  for (int i = 0, j = result.length - 1;
       i < list.length; i++, j--) {
    result[j] = list[i];
  }

  return result;
}
```

list

result

Line 2 creates a new array `result`. Lines 4–7 copy elements from array `list` to array `result`. Line 9 returns the array. For example, the following statement returns a new array `list2` with elements 6, 5, 4, 3, 2, 1.

```
int[] list1 = {1, 2, 3, 4, 5, 6};
int[] list2 = reverse(list1);
```

6.8 Case Study: Counting the Occurrences of Each Letter

This section presents a program to count the occurrences of each letter in an array of characters.

The program given in Listing 6.4 does the following:

1. Generates 100 lowercase letters randomly and assigns them to an array of characters, as shown in Figure 6.8a. You can obtain a random letter by using the `getRandomLowerCaseLetter()` method in the `RandomCharacter` class in Listing 5.10.
2. Count the occurrences of each letter in the array. To do so, create an array, say `counts`, of 26 `int` values, each of which counts the occurrences of a letter, as shown in Figure 6.8b. That is, `counts[0]` counts the number of a's, `counts[1]` counts the number of b's, and so on.

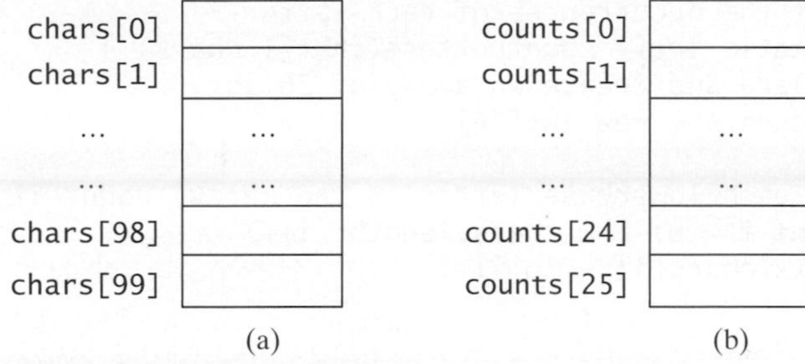

FIGURE 6.8 The `chars` array stores 100 characters, and the `counts` array stores 26 counts, each of which counts the occurrences of a letter.

LISTING 6.4 CountLettersInArray.java

```
public class CountLettersInArray {
  /** Main method */
  public static void main(String[] args) {
    // Declare and create an array
    char[] chars = createArray();

    // Display the array
    System.out.println("The lowercase letters are:");
    displayArray(chars);

    // Count the occurrences of each letter
    int[] counts = countLetters(chars);

    // Display counts
    System.out.println();
    System.out.println("The occurrences of each letter are:");
    displayCounts(counts);
  }

  /** Create an array of characters */
```

create array

pass array

return array

pass array

increase count

```
  public static char[] createArray() {
    // Declare an array of characters and create it
    char[] chars = new char[100];

    // Create lowercase letters randomly and assign
    // them to the array
    for (int i = 0; i < chars.length; i++)
      chars[i] = RandomCharacter.getRandomLowerCaseLetter();

    // Return the array
    return chars;
  }

  /** Display the array of characters */
  public static void displayArray(char[] chars) {
    // Display the characters in the array 20 on each line
    for (int i = 0; i < chars.length; i++) {
      if ((i + 1) % 20 == 0)
        System.out.println(chars[i]);
      else
        System.out.print(chars[i] + " ");
    }
  }

  /** Count the occurrences of each letter */
  public static int[] countLetters(char[] chars) {
    // Declare and create an array of 26 int
    int[] counts = new int[26];

    // For each lowercase letter in the array, count it
    for (int i = 0; i < chars.length; i++)
      counts[chars[i] - 'a']++;

    return counts;
  }

  /** Display counts */
  public static void displayCounts(int[] counts) {
    for (int i = 0; i < counts.length; i++) {
      if ((i + 1) % 10 == 0)
        System.out.println(counts[i] + " " + (char)(i + 'a'));
      else
        System.out.print(counts[i] + " " + (char)(i + 'a') + " ");
    }
  }
}
```

```
The lowercase letters are:
e y l s r i b k j v j h a b z n w b t v
s c c k r d w a m p w v u n q a m p l o
a z g d e g f i n d x m z o u l o z j v
h w i w n t g x w c d o t x h y v z y z
q e a m f w p g u q t r e n n w f c r f

The occurrences of each letter are:
5 a 3 b 4 c 4 d 4 e 4 f 4 g 3 h 3 i 3 j
2 k 3 l 4 m 6 n 4 o 3 p 3 q 4 r 2 s 4 t
3 u 5 v 8 w 3 x 3 y 6 z
```

The **createArray** method (lines 21–32) generates an array of **100** random lowercase letters. Line 5 invokes the method and assigns the array to **chars**. What would be wrong if you rewrote the code as follows?

```
char[] chars = new char[100];
chars = createArray();
```

You would be creating two arrays. The first line would create an array by using **new char[100]**. The second line would create an array by invoking **createArray()** and assign the reference of the array to **chars**. The array created in the first line would be garbage because it is no longer referenced, and as mentioned earlier Java automatically collects garbage behind the scenes. Your program would compile and run correctly, but it would create an array unnecessarily.

Invoking **getRandomLowerCaseLetter()** (line 28) returns a random lowercase letter. This method is defined in the **RandomCharacter** class in Listing 5.10.

The **countLetters** method (lines 46–55) returns an array of **26 int** values, each of which stores the number of occurrences of a letter. The method processes each letter in the array and increases its count by one. A brute-force approach to count the occurrences of each letter might be as follows:

```
for (int i = 0; i < chars.length; i++)
  if (chars[i] == 'a')
    counts[0]++;
  else if (chars[i] == 'b')
    counts[1]++;
  ...
```

But a better solution is given in lines 51–52.

```
for (int i = 0; i < chars.length; i++)
  counts[chars[i] - 'a']++;
```

If the letter (**chars[i]**) is **a**, the corresponding count is **counts['a' - 'a']** (i.e., **counts[0]**). If the letter is **b**, the corresponding count is **counts['b' - 'a']** (i.e., **counts[1]**), since the Unicode of **b** is one more than that of **a**. If the letter is **z**, the corresponding count is **counts['z' - 'a']** (i.e., **counts[25]**), since the Unicode of **z** is **25** more than that of **a**.

Figure 6.9 shows the call stack and heap *during* and *after* executing **createArray**. See Checkpoint Question 6.16 to show the call stack and heap for other methods in the program.

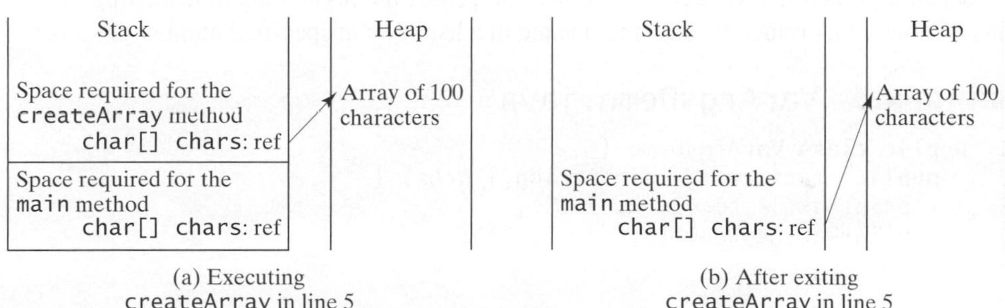

FIGURE 6.9 (a) An array of 100 characters is created when executing **createArray**. (b) This array is returned and assigned to the variable **chars** in the **main** method.

MyProgrammingLab™

6.14 True or false? When an array is passed to a method, a new array is created and passed to the method.

6.15 Show the output of the following two programs:

```
public class Test {
  public static void main(String[] args) {
    int number = 0;
    int[] numbers = new int[1];

    m(number, numbers);

    System.out.println("number is " + number
      + " and numbers[0] is " + numbers[0]);
  }

  public static void m(int x, int[] y) {
    x = 3;
    y[0] = 3;
  }
}
```

(a)

```
public class Test {
  public static void main(String[] args) {
    int[] list = {1, 2, 3, 4, 5};
    reverse(list);
    for (int i = 0; i < list.length; i++)
      System.out.print(list[i] + " ");
  }

  public static void reverse(int[] list) {
    int[] newList = new int[list.length];

    for (int i = 0; i < list.length; i++)
      newList[i] = list[list.length - 1 - i];

    list = newList;
  }
}
```

(b)

6.16 Where are the arrays stored during execution? Show the contents of the stack and heap during and after executing `displayArray`, `countLetters`, `displayCounts` in Listing 6.4.

6.9 Variable-Length Argument Lists

A variable number of arguments of the same type can be passed to a method and treated as an array.

You can pass a variable number of arguments of the same type to a method. The parameter in the method is declared as follows:

```
typeName... parameterName
```

In the method declaration, you specify the type followed by an ellipsis (`...`). Only one variable-length parameter may be specified in a method, and this parameter must be the last parameter. Any regular parameters must precede it.

Java treats a variable-length parameter as an array. You can pass an array or a variable number of arguments to a variable-length parameter. When invoking a method with a variable number of arguments, Java creates an array and passes the arguments to it. Listing 6.5 contains a method that prints the maximum value in a list of an unspecified number of values.

LISTING 6.5 VarArgsDemo.java

pass variable-length arg list

pass an array arg

a variable-length arg parameter

```
public class VarArgsDemo {
  public static void main(String[] args) {
    printMax(34, 3, 3, 2, 56.5);
    printMax(new double[]{1, 2, 3});
  }

  public static void printMax(double... numbers) {
    if (numbers.length == 0) {
      System.out.println("No argument passed");
```

```
10          return;
11        }
12
13        double result = numbers[0];
14
15        for (int i = 1; i < numbers.length; i++)
16          if (numbers[i] > result)
17            result = numbers[i];
18
19        System.out.println("The max value is " + result);
20      }
21    }
```

Line 3 invokes the **printMax** method with a variable-length argument list passed to the array **numbers**. If no arguments are passed, the length of the array is **0** (line 8).

Line 4 invokes the **printMax** method with an array.

6.17 What is wrong in the following method header?

```
public static void print(String... strings, double... numbers)
public static void print(double... numbers, String name)
public static double... print(double d1, double d2)
```

6.18 Can you invoke the **printMax** method in Listing 6.5 using the following statements?

```
printMax(1, 2, 2, 1, 4);
printMax(new double[]{1, 2, 3});
printMax(new int[]{1, 2, 3});
```

6.10 Searching Arrays

If an array is sorted, binary search is more efficient than linear search for finding an element in the array.

Searching is the process of looking for a specific element in an array—for example, discovering whether a certain score is included in a list of scores. Searching is a common task in computer programming. Many algorithms and data structures are devoted to searching. This section discusses two commonly used approaches, *linear search* and *binary search*.

linear search

binary search

6.10.1 The Linear Search Approach

The linear search approach compares the key element **key** sequentially with each element in the array. It continues to do so until the key matches an element in the array or the array is exhausted without a match being found. If a match is made, the linear search returns the index of the element in the array that matches the key. If no match is found, the search returns **-1**. The **linearSearch** method in Listing 6.6 gives the solution.

linear search animation on Companion Website

LISTING 6.6 LinearSearch.java

```
public class LinearSearch {
  /** The method for finding a key in the list */
  public static int linearSearch(int[] list, int key) {
    for (int i = 0; i < list.length; i++) {
      if (key == list[i])
        return i;
    }
    return -1;
  }
}
```

[0] [1] [2] ...

list

key Compare key with list[i] for i = 0, 1, ...

To better understand this method, trace it with the following statements:

```
int[] list = {1, 4, 4, 2, 5, -3, 6, 2};
int i = linearSearch(list, 4);  // Returns 1
int j = linearSearch(list, -4); // Returns -1
int k = linearSearch(list, -3); // Returns 5
```

The linear search method compares the key with each element in the array. The elements can be in any order. On average, the algorithm will have to examine half of the elements in an array before finding the key, if it exists. Since the execution time of a linear search increases linearly as the number of array elements increases, linear search is inefficient for a large array.

6.10.2 The Binary Search Approach

Binary search is the other common search approach for a list of values. For binary search to work, the elements in the array must already be ordered. Assume that the array is in ascending order. The binary search first compares the key with the element in the middle of the array. Consider the following three cases:

- If the key is less than the middle element, you need to continue to search for the key only in the first half of the array.
- If the key is equal to the middle element, the search ends with a match.
- If the key is greater than the middle element, you need to continue to search for the key only in the second half of the array.

Clearly, the binary search method eliminates at least half of the array after each comparison. Sometimes you eliminate half of the elements, and sometimes you eliminate half plus one. Suppose that the array has *n* elements. For convenience, let `n` be a power of `2`. After the first comparison, `n/2` elements are left for further search; after the second comparison, `(n/2)/2` elements are left. After the `k`th comparison, $n/2^k$ elements are left for further search. When $k = \log_2 n$, only one element is left in the array, and you need only one more comparison. Therefore, in the worst case when using the binary search approach, you need $\log_2 n+1$ comparisons to find an element in the sorted array. In the worst case for a list of `1024` (2^{10}) elements, binary search requires only `11` comparisons, whereas a linear search requires `1023` comparisons in the worst case.

binary search animation on Companion Website

The portion of the array being searched shrinks by half after each comparison. Let `low` and `high` denote, respectively, the first index and last index of the array that is currently being searched. Initially, `low` is `0` and `high` is `list.length-1`. Let `mid` denote the index of the middle element, so `mid` is `(low + high)/2`. Figure 6.10 shows how to find key `11` in the list {`2`, `4`, `7`, `10`, `11`, `45`, `50`, `59`, `60`, `66`, `69`, `70`, `79`} using binary search.

You now know how the binary search works. The next task is to implement it in Java. Don't rush to give a complete implementation. Implement it incrementally, one step at a time. You may start with the first iteration of the search, as shown in Figure 6.11a. It compares the key with the middle element in the list whose `low` index is `0` and `high` index is `list.length - 1`. If `key < list[mid]`, set the `high` index to `mid - 1`; if `key == list[mid]`, a match is found and return `mid`; if `key > list[mid]`, set the `low` index to `mid + 1`.

Next consider implementing the method to perform the search repeatedly by adding a loop, as shown in Figure 6.11b. The search ends if the key is found, or if the key is not found when `low > high`.

why not –1?

When the key is not found, `low` is the insertion point where a key would be inserted to maintain the order of the list. It is more useful to return the insertion point than `-1`. The method must return a negative value to indicate that the key is not in the list. Can it simply return `-low`? No. If the key is less than `list[0]`, `low` would be `0`. `-0` is `0`. This would

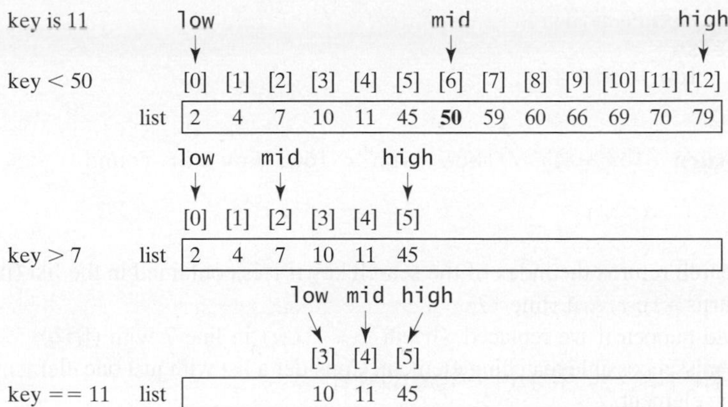

FIGURE 6.10 Binary search eliminates half of the list from further consideration after each comparison.

```
public static int binarySearch(
    int[] list, int key) {
  int low = 0;
  int high = list.length - 1;


    int mid = (low + high) / 2;
    if (key < list[mid])
      high = mid - 1;
    else if (key == list[mid])
      return mid;
    else
      low = mid + 1;



}
```

(a) Version 1

```
public static int binarySearch(
    int[] list, int key) {
  int low = 0;
  int high = list.length - 1;

  while (high >= low) {
    int mid = (low + high) / 2;
    if (key < list[mid])
      high = mid - 1;
    else if (key == list[mid])
      return mid;
    else
      low = mid + 1;
  }

  return -1; // Not found
}
```

(b) Version 2

FIGURE 6.11 Binary search is implemented incrementally.

indicate that the key matches `list[0]`. A good choice is to let the method return `–low – 1` if the key is not in the list. Returning `–low – 1` indicates not only that the key is not in the list, but also where the key would be inserted.

The complete program is given in Listing 6.7.

LISTING 6.7 BinarySearch.java

```
public class BinarySearch {
  /** Use binary search to find the key in the list */
  public static int binarySearch(int[] list, int key) {
    int low = 0;
    int high = list.length - 1;

    while (high >= low) {
      int mid = (low + high) / 2;
      if (key < list[mid])
        high = mid - 1;
      else if (key == list[mid])
```

first half

second half

```
12         return mid;
13       else
14         low = mid + 1;
15     }
16
17     return -low - 1; // Now high < low, key not found
18   }
19 }
```

The binary search returns the index of the search key if it is contained in the list (line 12). Otherwise, it returns `-low - 1` (line 17).

What would happen if we replaced `(high >= low)` in line 7 with `(high > low)`? The search would miss a possible matching element. Consider a list with just one element. The search would miss the element.

Does the method still work if there are duplicate elements in the list? Yes, as long as the elements are sorted in increasing order. The method returns the index of one of the matching elements if the element is in the list.

To better understand this method, trace it with the following statements and identify `low` and `high` when the method returns.

```
int[] list = {2, 4, 7, 10, 11, 45, 50, 59, 60, 66, 69, 70, 79};
int i = BinarySearch.binarySearch(list, 2); // Returns 0
int j = BinarySearch.binarySearch(list, 11); // Returns 4
int k = BinarySearch.binarySearch(list, 12); // Returns -6
int l = BinarySearch.binarySearch(list, 1); // Returns -1
int m = BinarySearch.binarySearch(list, 3); // Returns -2
```

Here is the table that lists the `low` and `high` values when the method exits and the value returned from invoking the method.

Method	Low	High	Value Returned
`binarySearch(list, 2)`	0	1	0
`binarySearch(list, 11)`	3	5	4
`binarySearch(list, 12)`	5	4	-6
`binarySearch(list, 1)`	0	-1	-1
`binarySearch(list, 3)`	1	0	-2

Note

binary search benefits

Linear search is useful for finding an element in a small array or an unsorted array, but it is inefficient for large arrays. Binary search is more efficient, but it requires that the array be presorted.

6.11 Sorting Arrays

There are many strategies for sorting elements in an array. Selection sort and insertion sort are two common approaches.

selection sort

insertion sort

Sorting, like searching, is a common task in computer programming. Many different algorithms have been developed for sorting. This section introduces two simple, intuitive sorting algorithms: *selection sort* and *insertion sort*.

6.11.1 Selection Sort

VideoNote
Selection sort

selection sort animation on Companion Website

Suppose that you want to sort a list in ascending order. Selection sort finds the smallest number in the list and swaps it with the first element. It then finds the smallest number remaining and swaps it with the second element, and so on, until only a single number remains. Figure 6.12 shows how to sort the list {2, 9, 5, 4, 8, 1, 6} using selection sort.

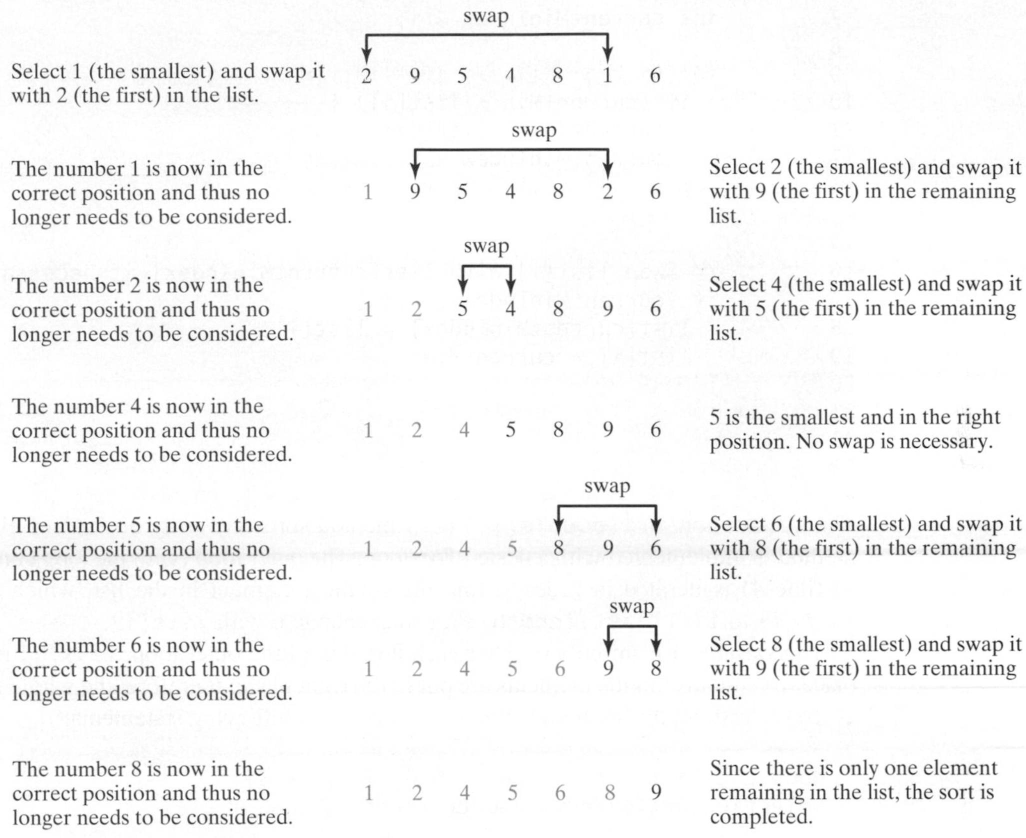

FIGURE 6.12 Selection sort repeatedly selects the smallest number and swaps it with the first number in the list.

You know how the selection-sort approach works. The task now is to implement it in Java. Beginners find it difficult to develop a complete solution on the first attempt. Start by writing the code for the first iteration to find the smallest element in the list and swap it with the first element, and then observe what would be different for the second iteration, the third, and so on. The insight this gives will enable you to write a loop that generalizes all the iterations.

The solution can be described as follows:

```
for (int i = 0; i < list.length - 1; i++) {
  select the smallest element in list[i..list.length-1];
  swap the smallest with list[i], if necessary;
  // list[i] is in its correct position.
  // The next iteration apply on list[i+1..list.length-1]
}
```

Listing 6.8 implements the solution.

LISTING 6.8 SelectionSort.java

```
1  public class SelectionSort {
2    /** The method for sorting the numbers */
3    public static void selectionSort(double[] list) {
4      for (int i = 0; i < list.length - 1; i++) {
5        // Find the minimum in the list[i..list.length-1]
6        double currentMin = list[i];
7        int currentMinIndex = i;
8
9        for (int j = i + 1; j < list.length; j++) {
10         if (currentMin > list[j]) {
11           currentMin = list[j];
12           currentMinIndex = j;
13         }
14       }
15
16       // Swap list[i] with list[currentMinIndex] if necessary
17       if (currentMinIndex != i) {
18         list[currentMinIndex] = list[i];
19         list[i] = currentMin;
20       }
21     }
22   }
23 }
```

select

swap

The `selectionSort(double[] list)` method sorts any array of `double` elements. The method is implemented with a nested `for` loop. The outer loop (with the loop control variable `i`) (line 4) is iterated in order to find the smallest element in the list, which ranges from `list[i]` to `list[list.length-1]`, and exchange it with `list[i]`.

The variable `i` is initially `0`. After each iteration of the outer loop, `list[i]` is in the right place. Eventually, all the elements are put in the right place; therefore, the whole list is sorted.

To understand this method better, trace it with the following statements:

```
double[] list = {1, 9, 4.5, 6.6, 5.7, -4.5};
SelectionSort.selectionSort(list);
```

6.11.2 Insertion Sort

insertion sort animation on Companion Website

Suppose that you want to sort a list in ascending order. The insertion-sort algorithm sorts a list of values by repeatedly inserting a new element into a sorted sublist until the whole list is sorted. Figure 6.13 shows how to sort the list {2, 9, 5, 4, 8, 1, 6} using insertion sort.

The algorithm can be described as follows:

```
for (int i = 1; i < list.length; i++) {
  insert list[i] into a sorted sublist list[0..i-1] so that
  list[0..i] is sorted.
}
```

To insert `list[i]` into `list[0..i-1]`, save `list[i]` into a temporary variable, say `currentElement`. Move `list[i-1]` to `list[i]` if `list[i-1] > currentElement`, move `list[i-2]` to `list[i-1]` if `list[i-2] > currentElement`, and so on, until `list[i-k] <= currentElement` or `k > i` (we pass the first element of the sorted list). Assign `currentElement` to `list[i-k+1]`. For example, to insert `4` into {`2, 5, 9`} in Step 4 in Figure 6.14, move `list[2]` (`9`) to `list[3]` since `9 > 4`, and move `list[1]` (`5`) to `list[2]` since `5 > 4`. Finally, move `currentElement` (`4`) to `list[1]`.

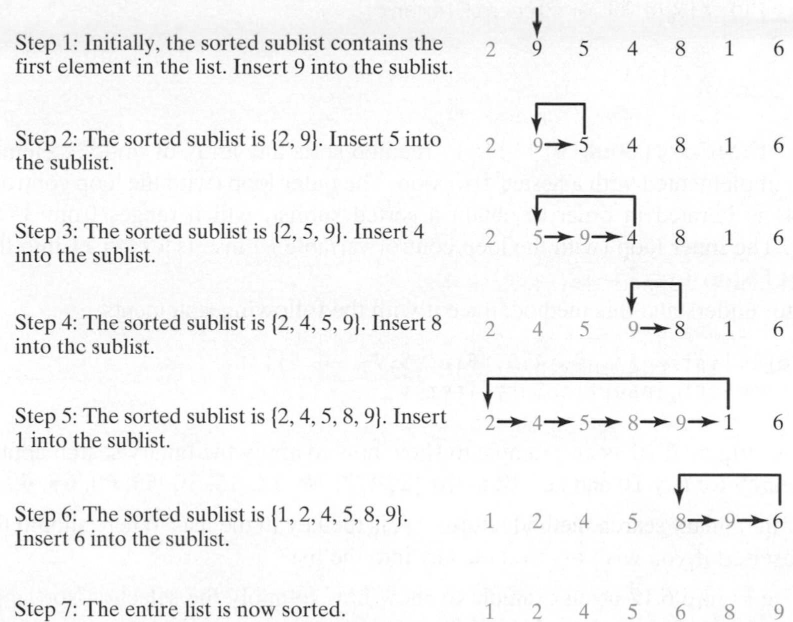

FIGURE 6.13 Insertion sort repeatedly inserts a new element into a sorted sublist.

```
      [0][1][2][3][4][5][6]
list | 2  5  9  4          |   Step 1: Save 4 to a temporary variable currentElement

      [0][1][2][3][4][5][6]
list | 2  5     9          |   Step 2: Move list[2] to list[3]

      [0][1][2][3][4][5][6]
list | 2     5  9          |   Step 3: Move list[1] to list[2]

      [0][1][2][3][4][5][6]
list | 2  4  5  9          |   Step 4: Assign currentElement to list[1]
```

FIGURE 6.14 A new element is inserted into a sorted sublist.

The algorithm can be expanded and implemented as in Listing 6.9.

LISTING 6.9 InsertionSort.java

```
public class InsertionSort {
  /** The method for sorting the numbers */
  public static void insertionSort(double[] list) {
    for (int i = 1; i < list.length; i++) {
      /** Insert list[i] into a sorted sublist list[0..i-1] so that
           list[0..i] is sorted. */
      double currentElement = list[i];
      int k;
      for (k = i - 1; k >= 0 && list[k] > currentElement; k--) {
        list[k + 1] = list[k];
      }

      // Insert the current element into list[k + 1]
```

shift

insert

```
14         list[k + 1] = currentElement;
15       }
16     }
17 }
```

The `insertionSort(double[] list)` method sorts any array of `double` elements. The method is implemented with a nested `for` loop. The outer loop (with the loop control variable `i`) (line 4) is iterated in order to obtain a sorted sublist, which ranges from `list[0]` to `list[i]`. The inner loop (with the loop control variable `k`) inserts `list[i]` into the sublist from `list[0]` to `list[i-1]`.

To better understand this method, trace it with the following statements:

```
double[] list = {1, 9, 4.5, 6.6, 5.7, -4.5};
InsertionSort.insertionSort(list);
```

MyProgrammingLab™

6.19 Use Figure 6.10 as an example to show how to apply the binary search approach to a search for key `10` and key `12` in list {`2`, `4`, `7`, `10`, `11`, `45`, `50`, `59`, `60`, `66`, `69`, `70`, `79`}.

6.20 If the binary search method returns `-4`, is the key in the list? Where should the key be inserted if you wish to insert the key into the list?

6.21 Use Figure 6.12 as an example to show how to apply the selection-sort approach to sort {`3.4`, `5`, `3`, `3.5`, `2.2`, `1.9`, `2`}.

6.22 Use Figure 6.13 as an example to show how to apply the insertion-sort approach to sort {`3.4`, `5`, `3`, `3.5`, `2.2`, `1.9`, `2`}.

6.23 How do you modify the `selectionSort` method in Listing 6.8 to sort numbers in decreasing order?

6.24 How do you modify the `insertionSort` method in Listing 6.9 to sort numbers in decreasing order?

6.12 The Arrays Class

The `java.util.Arrays` class contains useful methods for common array operations such as sorting and searching.

The `java.util.Arrays` class contains various static methods for sorting and searching arrays, comparing arrays, filling array elements, and returning a string representation of the array. These methods are overloaded for all primitive types.

sort

You can use the `sort` method to sort a whole array or a partial array. For example, the following code sorts an array of numbers and an array of characters.

```
double[] numbers = {6.0, 4.4, 1.9, 2.9, 3.4, 3.5};
java.util.Arrays.sort(numbers); // Sort the whole array

char[] chars = {'a', 'A', '4', 'F', 'D', 'P'};
java.util.Arrays.sort(chars, 1, 3); // Sort part of the array
```

Invoking `sort(numbers)` sorts the whole array `numbers`. Invoking `sort(chars, 1, 3)` sorts a partial array from `chars[1]` to `chars[3-1]`.

binarySearch

You can use the `binarySearch` method to search for a key in an array. The array must be presorted in increasing order. If the key is not in the array, the method returns `-(insertionindex + 1)`. For example, the following code searches the keys in an array of integers and an array of characters.

```
int[] list = {2, 4, 7, 10, 11, 45, 50, 59, 60, 66, 69, 70, 79};
System.out.println("(1) Index is " +
      java.util.Arrays.binarySearch(list, 11));
```

```
System.out.println("(2) Index is " +
      java.util.Arrays.binarySearch(list, 12));

char[] chars = {'a', 'c', 'g', 'x', 'y', 'z'};
System.out.println("(3) Index is " +
      java.util.Arrays.binarySearch(chars, 'a'));
System.out.println("(4) Index is " +
      java.util.Arrays.binarySearch(chars, 't'));
```

The output of the preceding code is

1. Index is 4
2. Index is –6
3. Index is 0
4. Index is –4

You can use the `equals` method to check whether two arrays are equal. Two arrays are equal if they have the same contents. In the following code, `list1` and `list2` are equal, but `list2` and `list3` are not. `equals`

```
int[] list1 = {2, 4, 7, 10};
int[] list2 = {2, 4, 7, 10};
int[] list3 = {4, 2, 7, 10};
System.out.println(java.util.Arrays.equals(list1, list2)); // true
System.out.println(java.util.Arrays.equals(list2, list3)); // false
```

You can use the `fill` method to fill in all or part of the array. For example, the following code fills `list1` with `5` and fills `8` into elements `list2[1]` and `list2[3-1]`. `fill`

```
int[] list1 = {2, 4, 7, 10};
int[] list2 = {2, 4, 7, 10};
java.util.Arrays.fill(list1, 5); // Fill 5 to the whole array
java.util.Arrays.fill(list2, 1, 3, 8); // Fill 8 to a partial array
```

You can also use the `toString` method to return a string that represents all elements in the array. This is a quick and simple way to display all elements in the array. For example, the following code `toString`

```
int[] list = {2, 4, 7, 10};
System.out.println(Arrays.toString(list));
```

displays `[2, 4, 7, 10]`.

MyProgrammingLab™

6.25 What types of array can be sorted using the `java.util.Arrays.sort` method? Does this `sort` method create a new array?

6.26 To apply `java.util.Arrays.binarySearch(array, key)`, should the array be sorted in increasing order, in decreasing order, or neither?

6.27 Show the output of the following code:

```
int[] list1 = {2, 4, 7, 10};
java.util.Arrays.fill(list1, 7);
System.out.println(java.util.Arrays.toString(list1));

int[] list2 = {2, 4, 7, 10};
System.out.println(java.util.Arrays.toString(list2));
System.out.print(java.util.Arrays.equals(list1, list2));
```

Key Terms

Chapter Summary

1. A variable is declared as an *array* type using the syntax `elementType[] arrayRefVar` or `elementType arrayRefVar[]`. The style `elementType[] arrayRefVar` is preferred, although `elementType arrayRefVar[]` is legal.

2. Unlike declarations for primitive data type variables, the declaration of an array variable does not allocate any space in memory for the array. An array variable is not a primitive data type variable. An array variable contains a reference to an array.

3. You cannot assign elements to an array unless it has already been created. You can create an array by using the `new` operator with the following syntax: `new elementType[arraySize]`.

4. Each element in the array is represented using the syntax `arrayRefVar[index]`. An *index* must be an integer or an integer expression.

5. After an array is created, its size becomes permanent and can be obtained using `arrayRefVar.length`. Since the index of an array always begins with `0`, the last index is always `arrayRefVar.length - 1`. An out-of-bounds error will occur if you attempt to reference elements beyond the bounds of an array.

6. Programmers often mistakenly reference the first element in an array with index `1`, but it should be `0`. This is called the index *off-by-one error*.

7. When an array is created, its elements are assigned the default value of `0` for the numeric primitive data types, `\u0000` for char types, and `false` for `boolean` types.

8. Java has a shorthand notation, known as the *array initializer*, which combines declaring an array, creating an array, and initializing an array in one statement, using the syntax `elementType[] arrayRefVar = {value0, value1, ..., valuek}`.

9. When you pass an array argument to a method, you are actually passing the reference of the array; that is, the called method can modify the elements in the caller's original array.

10. If an array is sorted, *binary search* is more efficient than *linear search* for finding an element in the array.

11. *Selection sort* finds the smallest number in the list and swaps it with the first element. It then finds the smallest number remaining and swaps it with the first element in the remaining list, and so on, until only a single number remains.

12. The *insertion-sort algorithm* sorts a list of values by repeatedly inserting a new element into a sorted sublist until the whole list is sorted.

Test Questions

Do the test questions for this chapter online at **www.cs.armstrong.edu/liang/intro9e/test.html**.

Programming Exercises

MyProgrammingLab™

Sections 6.2–6.5

***6.1** (*Assign grades*) Write a program that reads student scores, gets the best score, and then assigns grades based on the following scheme:

Grade is A if score is >= best − 10

Grade is B if score is >= best − 20;

Grade is C if score is >= best − 30;

Grade is D if score is >= best − 40;

Grade is F otherwise.

The program prompts the user to enter the total number of students, then prompts the user to enter all of the scores, and concludes by displaying the grades. Here is a sample run:

```
Enter the number of students: 4 [Enter]
Enter 4 scores: 40 55 70 58 [Enter]
Student 0 score is 40 and grade is C
Student 1 score is 55 and grade is B
Student 2 score is 70 and grade is A
Student 3 score is 58 and grade is B
```

6.2 (*Reverse the numbers entered*) Write a program that reads ten integers and displays them in the reverse of the order in which they were read.

****6.3** (*Count occurrence of numbers*) Write a program that reads the integers between 1 and 100 and counts the occurrences of each. Assume the input ends with 0. Here is a sample run of the program:

```
Enter the integers between 1 and 100: 2 5 6 5 4 3 23 43 2 0 [Enter]
2 occurs 2 times
3 occurs 1 time
4 occurs 1 time
5 occurs 2 times
6 occurs 1 time
23 occurs 1 time
43 occurs 1 time
```

Note that if a number occurs more than one time, the plural word "times" is used in the output.

6.4 (*Analyze scores*) Write a program that reads an unspecified number of scores and determines how many scores are above or equal to the average and how many scores are below the average. Enter a negative number to signify the end of the input. Assume that the maximum number of scores is 100.

****6.5** (*Print distinct numbers*) Write a program that reads in ten numbers and displays distinct numbers (i.e., if a number appears multiple times, it is displayed only once). (*Hint*: Read a number and store it to an array if it is new. If the number is already in the array, ignore it.) After the input, the array contains the distinct numbers. Here is the sample run of the program:

```
Enter ten numbers: 1 2 3 2 1 6 3 4 5 2 ↵Enter
The distinct numbers are: 1 2 3 6 4 5
```

***6.6** (*Revise Listing 4.14, PrimeNumber.java*) Listing 4.14 determines whether a number `n` is prime by checking whether `2`, `3`, `4`, `5`, `6`, ..., `n/2` is a divisor. If a divisor is found, `n` is not prime. A more efficient approach is to check whether any of the prime numbers less than or equal to $\sqrt{n}$ can divide `n` evenly. If not, `n` is prime. Rewrite Listing 4.14 to display the first 50 prime numbers using this approach. You need to use an array to store the prime numbers and later use them to check whether they are possible divisors for `n`.

***6.7** (*Count single digits*) Write a program that generates 100 random integers between 0 and 9 and displays the count for each number. (*Hint*: Use `(int)(Math.random() * 10)` to generate a random integer between 0 and 9. Use an array of ten integers, say `counts`, to store the counts for the number of 0s, 1s, ..., 9s.)

Sections 6.6–6.8

6.8 (*Average an array*) Write two overloaded methods that return the average of an array with the following headers:

```
public static int average(int[] array)
public static double average(double[] array)
```

Write a test program that prompts the user to enter ten double values, invokes this method, and displays the average value.

6.9 (*Find the smallest element*) Write a method that finds the smallest element in an array of double values using the following header:

```
public static double min(double[] array)
```

Write a test program that prompts the user to enter ten numbers, invokes this method to return the minimum value, and displays the minimum value. Here is a sample run of the program:

```
Enter ten numbers: 1.9 2.5 3.7 2 1.5 6 3 4 5 2 ↵Enter
The minimum number is: 1.5
```

6.10 (*Find the index of the smallest element*) Write a method that returns the index of the smallest element in an array of integers. If the number of such elements is greater than 1, return the smallest index. Use the following header:

```
public static int indexOfSmallestElement(double[] array)
```

Write a test program that prompts the user to enter ten numbers, invokes this method to return the index of the smallest element, and displays the index.

***6.11** (*Statistics: compute deviation*) Programming Exercise 5.37 computes the standard deviation of numbers. This exercise uses a different but equivalent formula to compute the standard deviation of **n** numbers.

$$mean = \frac{\sum_{i=1}^{n} x_i}{n} = \frac{x_1 + x_2 + \ldots + x_n}{n} \quad deviation = \sqrt{\frac{\sum_{i=1}^{n}(x_i - mean)^2}{n-1}}$$

To compute the standard deviation with this formula, you have to store the individual numbers using an array, so that they can be used after the mean is obtained.

Your program should contain the following methods:

```
/** Compute the deviation of double values */
public static double deviation(double[] x)

/** Compute the mean of an array of double values */
public static double mean(double[] x)
```

Write a test program that prompts the user to enter ten numbers and displays the mean and standard deviation, as shown in the following sample run:

```
Enter ten numbers: 1.9 2.5 3.7 2 1 6 3 4 5 2 ↵Enter
The mean is 3.11
The standard deviation is 1.55738
```

***6.12** (*Reverse an array*) The **reverse** method in Section 6.7 reverses an array by copying it to a new array. Rewrite the method that reverses the array passed in the argument and returns this array. Write a test program that prompts the user to enter ten numbers, invokes the method to reverse the numbers, and displays the numbers.

Section 6.9

***6.13** (*Random number chooser*) Write a method that returns a random number between 1 and 54, excluding the numbers passed in the argument. The method header is specified as follows:

```
public static int getRandom(int... numbers)
```

6.14 (*Computing gcd*) Write a method that returns the gcd of an unspecified number of integers. The method header is specified as follows:

```
public static int gcd(int... numbers)
```

Write a test program that prompts the user to enter five numbers, invokes the method to find the gcd of these numbers, and displays the gcd.

Sections 6.10–6.12

6.15 (*Eliminate duplicates*) Write a method that returns a new array by eliminating the duplicate values in the array using the following method header:

```
public static int[] eliminateDuplicates(int[] list)
```

Write a test program that reads in ten integers, invokes the method, and displays the result. Here is the sample run of the program:

```
Enter ten numbers: 1 2 3 2 1 6 3 4 5 2 [Enter]
The distinct numbers are: 1 2 3 6 4 5
```

6.16 (*Execution time*) Write a program that randomly generates an array of 100,000 integers and a key. Estimate the execution time of invoking the `linearSearch` method in Listing 6.6. Sort the array and estimate the execution time of invoking the `binarySearch` method in Listing 6.7. You can use the following code template to obtain the execution time:

```
long startTime = System.currentTimeMillis();
perform the task;
long endTime = System.currentTimeMillis();
long executionTime = endTime - startTime;
```

****6.17** (*Sort students*) Write a program that prompts the user to enter the number of students, the students' names, and their scores, and prints student names in decreasing order of their scores.

****6.18** (*Bubble sort*) Write a sort method that uses the bubble-sort algorithm. The bubble-sort algorithm makes several passes through the array. On each pass, successive neighboring pairs are compared. If a pair is not in order, its values are swapped; otherwise, the values remain unchanged. The technique is called a *bubble sort* or *sinking sort* because the smaller values gradually "bubble" their way to the top and the larger values "sink" to the bottom. Write a test program that reads in ten double numbers, invokes the method, and displays the sorted numbers.

****6.19** (*Sorted?*) Write the following method that returns true if the list is already sorted in increasing order.

```
public static boolean isSorted(int[] list)
```

Write a test program that prompts the user to enter a list and displays whether the list is sorted or not. Here is a sample run. Note that the first number in the input indicates the number of the elements in the list.

```
Enter list: 8 10 1 5 16 61 9 11 1 [Enter]
The list is not sorted
```

```
Enter list: 10 1 1 3 4 4 5 7 9 11 21 [Enter]
The list is already sorted
```

***6.20** (*Revise selection sort*) In Section 6.11.1, you used selection sort to sort an array. The selection-sort method repeatedly finds the smallest number in the current array and swaps it with the first. Rewrite this program by finding the largest number and swapping it with the last. Write a test program that reads in ten double numbers, invokes the method, and displays the sorted numbers.

*****6.21** (*Game: bean machine*) The bean machine, also known as a quincunx or the Galton box, is a device for statistics experiments named after English scientist Sir Francis Galton. It consists of an upright board with evenly spaced nails (or pegs) in a triangular form, as shown in Figure 6.15.

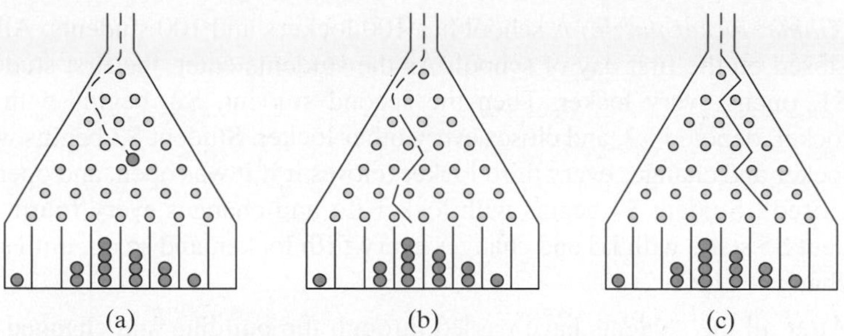

FIGURE 6.15 Each ball takes a random path and falls into a slot.

Balls are dropped from the opening of the board. Every time a ball hits a nail, it has a 50% chance of falling to the left or to the right. The piles of balls are accumulated in the slots at the bottom of the board.

Write a program that simulates the bean machine. Your program should prompt the user to enter the number of the balls and the number of the slots in the machine. Simulate the falling of each ball by printing its path. For example, the path for the ball in Figure 6.15b is LLRRLLR and the path for the ball in Figure 6.15c is RLRRLRR. Display the final buildup of the balls in the slots in a histogram. Here is a sample run of the program:

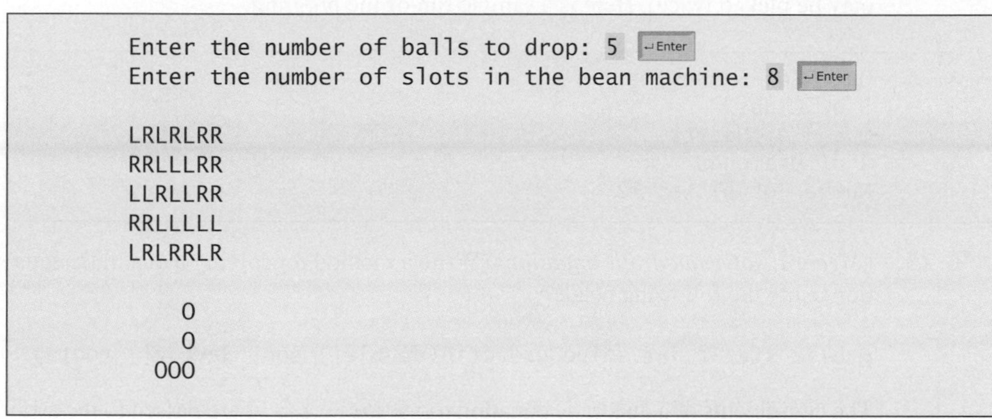

```
Enter the number of balls to drop: 5 ↵Enter
Enter the number of slots in the bean machine: 8 ↵Enter

LRLRLRR
RRLLLRR
LLRLLRR
RRLLLLL
LRLRRLR

    O
    O
   OOO
```

(*Hint*: Create an array named `slots`. Each element in `slots` stores the number of balls in a slot. Each ball falls into a slot via a path. The number of Rs in a path is the position of the slot where the ball falls. For example, for the path LRLRLRR, the ball falls into `slots[4]`, and for the path is RRLLLLL, the ball falls into `slots[2]`.)

*****6.22** (*Game: Eight Queens*) The classic Eight Queens puzzle is to place eight queens on a chessboard such that no two queens can attack each other (i.e., no two queens are on the same row, same column, or same diagonal). There are many possible solutions. Write a program that displays one such solution. A sample output is shown below:

```
|Q| | | | | | | |
| | | | |Q| | | |
| | | | | | | |Q|
| | | | | |Q| | |
| | |Q| | | | | |
| | | | | | |Q| |
| |Q| | | | | | |
| | | |Q| | | | |
```

****6.23** (*Game: locker puzzle*) A school has 100 lockers and 100 students. All lockers are closed on the first day of school. As the students enter, the first student, denoted S1, opens every locker. Then the second student, S2, begins with the second locker, denoted L2, and closes every other locker. Student S3 begins with the third locker and changes every third locker (closes it if it was open, and opens it if it was closed). Student S4 begins with locker L4 and changes every fourth locker. Student S5 starts with L5 and changes every fifth locker, and so on, until student S100 changes L100.

After all the students have passed through the building and changed the lockers, which lockers are open? Write a program to find your answer.

(*Hint*: Use an array of 100 Boolean elements, each of which indicates whether a locker is open (`true`) or closed (`false`). Initially, all lockers are closed.)

VideoNote
Coupon collector's problem

****6.24** (*Simulation: coupon collector's problem*) Coupon collector is a classic statistics problem with many practical applications. The problem is to pick objects from a set of objects repeatedly and find out how many picks are needed for all the objects to be picked at least once. A variation of the problem is to pick cards from a shuffled deck of 52 cards repeatedly and find out how many picks are needed before you see one of each suit. Assume a picked card is placed back in the deck before picking another. Write a program to simulate the number of picks needed to get four cards from each suit and display the four cards picked (it is possible a card may be picked twice). Here is a sample run of the program:

```
Queen of Spades
5 of Clubs
Queen of Hearts
4 of Diamonds
Number of picks: 12
```

6.25 (*Algebra: solve quadratic equations*) Write a method for solving a quadratic equation using the following header:

```
public static int solveQuadratic(double[] eqn, double[] roots)
```

The coefficients of a quadratic equation $ax^2 + bx + c = 0$ are passed to the array `eqn` and the noncomplex roots are stored in roots. The method returns the number of roots. See Programming Exercise 3.1 on how to solve a quadratic equation.

Write a program that prompts the user to enter values for a, b, and c and displays the number of roots and all noncomplex roots.

6.26 (*Strictly identical arrays*) The arrays `list1` and `list2` are *strictly identical* if their corresponding elements are equal. Write a method that returns `true` if `list1` and `list2` are strictly identical, using the following header:

```
public static boolean equals(int[] list1, int[] list2)
```

Write a test program that prompts the user to enter two lists of integers and displays whether the two are strictly identical. Here are the sample runs. Note that the first number in the input indicates the number of the elements in the list.

```
Enter list1: 5 2 5 6 1 6 ↵Enter
Enter list2: 5 2 5 6 1 6 ↵Enter
Two lists are strictly identical
```

```
Enter list1: 5 2 5 6 6 1 ↵Enter
Enter list2: 5 2 5 6 1 6 ↵Enter
Two lists are not strictly identical
```

6.27 (*Identical arrays*) The arrays `list1` and `list2` are *identical* if they have the same contents. Write a method that returns `true` if `list1` and `list2` are identical, using the following header:

```
public static boolean equals(int[] list1, int[] list2)
```

Write a test program that prompts the user to enter two lists of integers and displays whether the two are identical. Here are the sample runs. Note that the first number in the input indicates the number of the elements in the list.

```
Enter list1: 5 2 5 6 6 1 ↵Enter
Enter list2: 5 5 2 6 1 6 ↵Enter
Two lists are identical
```

```
Enter list1: 5 5 5 6 6 1 ↵Enter
Enter list2: 5 2 5 6 1 6 ↵Enter
Two lists are not identical
```

***6.28** (*Math: combinations*) Write a program that prompts the user to enter 10 integers and displays all combinations of picking two numbers from the 10.

***6.29** (*Game: pick four cards*) Write a program that picks four cards from a deck of 52 cards and computes their sum. An Ace, King, Queen, and Jack represent 1, 13, 12, and 11, respectively. Your program should display the number of picks that yields the sum of 24.

***6.30** (*Pattern recognition: consecutive four equal numbers*) Write the following method that tests whether the array has four consecutive numbers with the same value.

Consecutive four

```
public static boolean isConsecutiveFour(int[] values)
```

Write a test program that prompts the user to enter a series of integers and displays true if the series contains four consecutive numbers with the same value. Otherwise, display false. Your program should first prompt the user to enter the input size—i.e., the number of values in the series.

****6.31** (*Merge two sorted lists*) Write the following method that merges two sorted lists into a new sorted list.

```
public static int[] merge(int[] list1, int[] list2)
```

Implement the method in a way that takes `list1.length + list2.length` comparisons. Write a test program that prompts the user to enter two sorted lists and displays the merged list. Here is a sample run. Note that the first number in the input indicates the number of the elements in the list.

```
Enter list1: 5 1 5 16 61 111
Enter list2: 4 2 4 5 6
The merged list is 1 2 4 5 5 6 16 61 111
```

**6.32 (*Partition of a list*) Write the following method that partitions the list using the first element, called a *pivot*.

```
public static int partition(int[] list)
```

After the partition, the elements in the list are rearranged so that all the elements before the pivot are less than or equal to the pivot and the elements after the pivot are greater than the pivot. The method returns the index where the pivot is located in the new list. For example, suppose the list is {5, 2, 9, 3, 6, 8}. After the partition, the list becomes {3, 2, 5, 9, 6, 8}. Implement the method in a way that takes `list.length` comparisons. Write a test program that prompts the user to enter a list and displays the list after the partition. Here is a sample run. Note that the first number in the input indicates the number of the elements in the list.

```
Enter list: 8 10 1 5 16 61 9 11 1
After the partition, the list is 9 1 5 1 10 61 11 16
```

*6.33 (*Culture: Chinese Zodiac*) Simplify Listing 3.10 using an array of strings to store the animal names.

***6.34 (*Game: multiple Eight Queens solutions*) Exercise 6.22 finds one solution for the Eight Queens problem. Write a program to count all possible solutions for the Eight Queens problem and display all solutions.

CHAPTER

7

Multidimensional Arrays

Objectives

- To give examples of representing data using two-dimensional arrays (§7.1).
- To declare variables for two-dimensional arrays, create arrays, and access array elements in a two-dimensional array using row and column indexes (§7.2).
- To program common operations for two-dimensional arrays (displaying arrays, summing all elements, finding the minimum and maximum elements, and random shuffling) (§7.3).
- To pass two-dimensional arrays to methods (§7.4).
- To write a program for grading multiple-choice questions using two-dimensional arrays (§7.5).
- To solve the closest-pair problem using two-dimensional arrays (§7.6).
- To check a Sudoku solution using two-dimensional arrays (§7.7).
- To use multidimensional arrays (§7.8).

7.1 Introduction

Data in a table or a matrix can be represented using a two-dimensional array.

problem

The preceding chapter introduced how to use one-dimensional arrays to store linear collections of elements. You can use a two-dimensional array to store a matrix or a table. For example, the following table that lists the distances between cities can be stored using a two-dimensional array named **distances**.

Distance Table (in miles)

	Chicago	Boston	New York	Atlanta	Miami	Dallas	Houston
Chicago	0	983	787	714	1375	967	1087
Boston	983	0	214	1102	1763	1723	1842
New York	787	214	0	888	1549	1548	1627
Atlanta	714	1102	888	0	661	781	810
Miami	1375	1763	1549	661	0	1426	1187
Dallas	967	1723	1548	781	1426	0	239
Houston	1087	1842	1627	810	1187	239	0

```
double[][] distances = {
  {0, 983, 787, 714, 1375, 967, 1087},
  {983, 0, 214, 1102, 1763, 1723, 1842},
  {787, 214, 0, 888, 1549, 1548, 1627},
  {714, 1102, 888, 0, 661, 781, 810},
  {1375, 1763, 1549, 661, 0, 1426, 1187},
  {967, 1723, 1548, 781, 1426, 0, 239},
  {1087, 1842, 1627, 810, 1187, 239, 0},
};
```

7.2 Two-Dimensional Array Basics

An element in a two-dimensional array is accessed through a row and column index.

How do you declare a variable for two-dimensional arrays? How do you create a two-dimensional array? How do you access elements in a two-dimensional array? This section addresses these issues.

7.2.1 Declaring Variables of Two-Dimensional Arrays and Creating Two-Dimensional Arrays

The syntax for declaring a two-dimensional array is:

```
elementType[][] arrayRefVar;
```

or

```
elementType arrayRefVar[][]; // Allowed, but not preferred
```

As an example, here is how you would declare a two-dimensional array variable **matrix** of **int** values:

```
int[][] matrix;
```

or

```
int matrix[][]; // This style is allowed, but not preferred
```

You can create a two-dimensional array of 5-by-5 `int` values and assign it to `matrix` using this syntax:

```
matrix = new int[5][5];
```

Two subscripts are used in a two-dimensional array, one for the row and the other for the column. As in a one-dimensional array, the index for each subscript is of the `int` type and starts from `0`, as shown in Figure 7.1a.

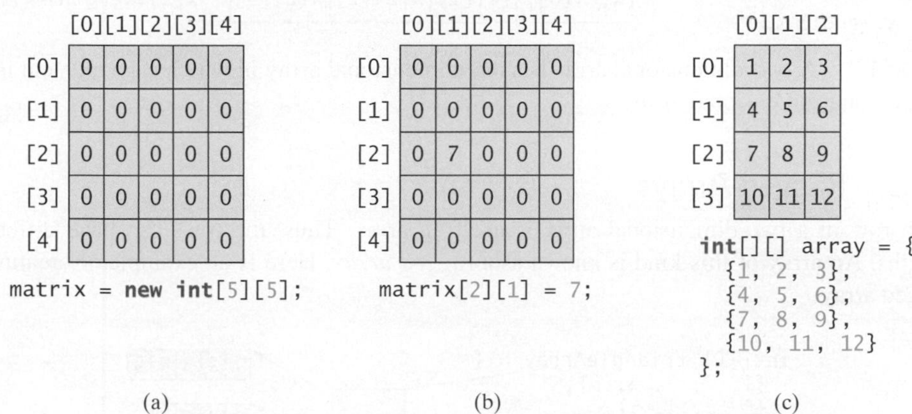

FIGURE 7.1 The index of each subscript of a two-dimensional array is an `int` value, starting from `0`.

To assign the value `7` to a specific element at row `2` and column `1`, as shown in Figure 7.1b, you can use the following syntax:

```
matrix[2][1] = 7;
```

Caution

It is a common mistake to use `matrix[2, 1]` to access the element at row `2` and column `1`. In Java, each subscript must be enclosed in a pair of square brackets.

You can also use an array initializer to declare, create, and initialize a two-dimensional array. For example, the following code in (a) creates an array with the specified initial values, as shown in Figure 7.1c. This is equivalent to the code in (b).

```
int[][] array = {
  {1, 2, 3},
  {4, 5, 6},
  {7, 8, 9},
  {10, 11, 12}
};
```

(a)

Equivalent

```
int[][] array = new int[4][3];
array[0][0] = 1; array[0][1] = 2; array[0][2] = 3;
array[1][0] = 4; array[1][1] = 5; array[1][2] = 6;
array[2][0] = 7; array[2][1] = 8; array[2][2] = 9;
array[3][0] = 10; array[3][1] = 11; array[3][2] = 12;
```

(b)

7.2.2 Obtaining the Lengths of Two-Dimensional Arrays

A two-dimensional array is actually an array in which each element is a one-dimensional array. The length of an array `x` is the number of elements in the array, which can be obtained using `x.length`. `x[0]`, `x[1]`, . . . , and `x[x.length-1]` are arrays. Their lengths can be obtained using `x[0].length`, `x[1].length`, . . . , and `x[x.length-1].length`.

For example, suppose `x = new int[3][4]`, `x[0]`, `x[1]`, and `x[2]` are one-dimensional arrays and each contains four elements, as shown in Figure 7.2. `x.length` is `3`, and `x[0].length`, `x[1].length`, and `x[2].length` are `4`.

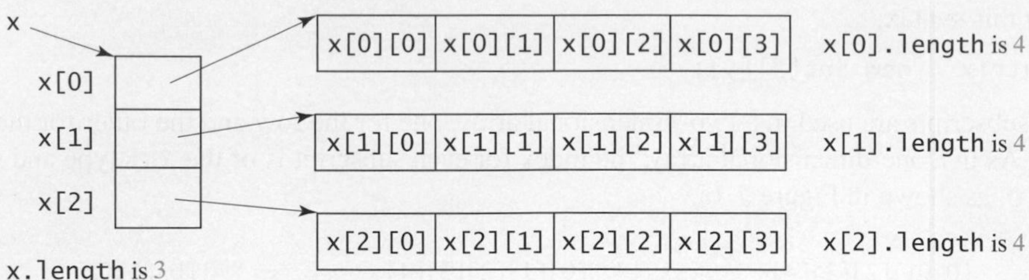

FIGURE 7.2 A two-dimensional array is a one-dimensional array in which each element is another one-dimensional array.

7.2.3 Ragged Arrays

ragged array

Each row in a two-dimensional array is itself an array. Thus, the rows can have different lengths. An array of this kind is known as a *ragged array*. Here is an example of creating a ragged array:

```
int[][] triangleArray = {
  {1, 2, 3, 4, 5},
  {2, 3, 4, 5},
  {3, 4, 5},
  {4, 5},
  {5}
};
```

1 2 3 4 5
2 3 4 5
3 4 5
4 5
5

As you can see, `triangleArray[0].length` is 5, `triangleArray[1].length` is 4, `triangleArray[2].length` is 3, `triangleArray[3].length` is 2, and `triangle-Array[4].length` is 1.

If you don't know the values in a ragged array in advance, but do know the sizes—say, the same as before—you can create a ragged array using the following syntax:

```
int[][] triangleArray = new int[5][];
triangleArray[0] = new int[5];
triangleArray[1] = new int[4];
triangleArray[2] = new int[3];
triangleArray[3] = new int[2];
triangleArray[4] = new int[1];
```

You can now assign values to the array. For example,

```
triangleArray[0][3] = 50;
triangleArray[4][0] = 45;
```

Note

The syntax `new int[5][]` for creating an array requires the first index to be specified. The syntax `new int[][]` would be wrong.

7.1 Declare an array reference variable for a two-dimensional array of `int` values, create a 4-by-5 `int` matrix, and assign it to the variable.

7.2 Can the rows in a two-dimensional array have different lengths?

7.3 What is the output of the following code?

```
int[][] array = new int[5][6];
int[] x = {1, 2};
array[0] = x;
System.out.println("array[0][1] is " + array[0][1]);
```

7.4 Which of the following statements are valid?

```
int[][] r = new int[2];
int[] x = new int[];
int[][] y = new int[3][];
int[][] z = {{1, 2}};
int[][] m = {{1, 2}, {2, 3}};
int[][] n = {{1, 2}, {2, 3}, };
```

7.3 Processing Two-Dimensional Arrays

Nested `for` *loops are often used to process a two-dimensional array.*

Key Point

Suppose an array `matrix` is created as follows:

```
int[][] matrix = new int[10][10];
```

The following are some examples of processing two-dimensional arrays.

1. *Initializing arrays with input values.* The following loop initializes the array with user input values:

```
java.util.Scanner input = new Scanner(System.in);
System.out.println("Enter " + matrix.length + " rows and " +
  matrix[0].length + " columns: ");
for (int row = 0; row < matrix.length; row++) {
  for (int column = 0; column < matrix[row].length; column++) {
    matrix[row][column] = input.nextInt();
  }
}
```

2. *Initializing arrays with random values.* The following loop initializes the array with random values between `0` and `99`:

```
for (int row = 0; row < matrix.length; row++) {
  for (int column = 0; column < matrix[row].length; column++) {
    matrix[row][column] = (int)(Math.random() * 100);
  }
}
```

3. *Printing arrays.* To print a two-dimensional array, you have to print each element in the array using a loop like the following:

```
for (int row = 0; row < matrix.length; row++) {
  for (int column = 0; column < matrix[row].length; column++) {
    System.out.print(matrix[row][column] + " ");
  }

  System.out.println();
}
```

4. *Summing all elements.* Use a variable named **total** to store the sum. Initially **total** is 0. Add each element in the array to **total** using a loop like this:

```
int total = 0;
for (int row = 0; row < matrix.length; row++) {
  for (int column = 0; column < matrix[row].length; column++) {
    total += matrix[row][column];
  }
}
```

5. *Summing elements by column.* For each column, use a variable named **total** to store its sum. Add each element in the column to **total** using a loop like this:

```
for (int column = 0; column < matrix[0].length; column++) {
  int total = 0;
  for (int row = 0; row < matrix.length; row++)
    total += matrix[row][column];
  System.out.println("Sum for column " + column + " is "
    + total);
}
```

VideoNote

Find the row with the largest sum

6. *Which row has the largest sum?* Use variables **maxRow** and **indexOfMaxRow** to track the largest sum and index of the row. For each row, compute its sum and update **maxRow** and **indexOfMaxRow** if the new sum is greater.

```
int maxRow = 0;
int indexOfMaxRow = 0;

// Get sum of the first row in maxRow
for (int column = 0; column < matrix[0].length; column++) {
  maxRow += matrix[0][column];
}

for (int row = 1; row < matrix.length; row++) {
  int totalOfThisRow = 0;
  for (int column = 0; column < matrix[row].length; column++)
    totalOfThisRow += matrix[row][column];

  if (totalOfThisRow > maxRow) {
    maxRow = totalOfThisRow;
    indexOfMaxRow = row;
  }
}

System.out.println("Row " + indexOfMaxRow
  + " has the maximum sum of " + maxRow);
```

7. *Random shuffling.* Shuffling the elements in a one-dimensional array was introduced in Section 6.2.6. How do you shuffle all the elements in a two-dimensional array? To accomplish this, for each element **matrix[i][j]**, randomly generate indices **i1** and **j1** and swap **matrix[i][j]** with **matrix[i1][j1]**, as follows:

```
for (int i = 0; i < matrix.length; i++) {
  for (int j = 0; j < matrix[i].length; j++) {
    int i1 = (int)(Math.random() * matrix.length);
    int j1 = (int)(Math.random() * matrix[i].length);

    // Swap matrix[i][j] with matrix[i1][j1]
    int temp = matrix[i][j];
    matrix[i][j] = matrix[i1][j1];
    matrix[i1][j1] = temp;
  }
}
```

7.5 Show the printout of the following code:

Check Point
MyProgrammingLab™

```
int[][] array = {{1, 2}, {3, 4}, {5, 6}};
for (int i = array.length - 1; i >= 0; i--) {
  for (int j = array[i].length - 1; j >= 0; j--)
    System.out.print(array[i][j] + " ");
  System.out.println();
}
```

7.6 Show the printout of the following code:

```
int[][] array = {{1, 2}, {3, 4}, {5, 6}};
int sum = 0;
for (int i = 0; i < array.length; i++)
  sum += array[i][0];
System.out.println(sum);
```

7.4 Passing Two-Dimensional Arrays to Methods

When passing a two-dimensional array to a method, the reference of the array is passed to the method.

Key Point

You can pass a two-dimensional array to a method just as you pass a one-dimensional array. You can also return an array from a method. Listing 7.1 gives an example with two methods. The first method, `getArray()`, returns a two-dimensional array, and the second method, `sum(int[][] m)`, returns the sum of all the elements in a matrix.

LISTING 7.1 PassTwoDimensionalArray.java

```
import java.util.Scanner;

public class PassTwoDimensionalArray {
  public static void main(String[] args) {
    int[][] m = getArray(); // Get an array

    // Display sum of elements
    System.out.println("\nSum of all elements is " + sum(m));
  }

  public static int[][] getArray() {
    // Create a Scanner
    Scanner input = new Scanner(System.in);

    // Enter array values
    int[][] m = new int[3][4];
    System.out.println("Enter " + m.length + " rows and "
      + m[0].length + " columns: ");
    for (int i = 0; i < m.length; i++)
      for (int j = 0; j < m[i].length; j++)
        m[i][j] = input.nextInt();

    return m;
  }

  public static int sum(int[][] m) {
    int total = 0;
    for (int row = 0; row < m.length; row++) {
      for (int column = 0; column < m[row].length; column++) {
        total += m[row][column];
      }
```

get array
pass array
`getArray` method
return array
`sum` method

```
32       }
33
34       return total;
35     }
36   }
```

```
Enter 3 rows and 4 columns:
1 2 3 4 [Enter]
5 6 7 8 [Enter]
9 10 11 12 [Enter]

Sum of all elements is 78
```

The method **getArray** prompts the user to enter values for the array (lines 11–24) and returns the array (line 23).

The method **sum** (lines 26–35) has a two-dimensional array argument. You can obtain the number of rows using **m.length** (line 28) and the number of columns in a specified row using **m[row].length** (line 29).

MyProgrammingLab™

7.7 Show the printout of the following code:

```
public class Test {
  public static void main(String[] args) {
    int[][] array = {{1, 2, 3, 4}, {5, 6, 7, 8}};
    System.out.println(m1(array)[0]);
    System.out.println(m1(array)[1]);
  }

  public static int[] m1(int[][] m) {
    int[] result = new int[2];
    result[0] = m.length;
    result[1] = m[0].length;
    return result;
  }
}
```

7.5 Case Study: Grading a Multiple-Choice Test

The problem is to write a program that will grade multiple-choice tests.

VideoNote

Grade multiple-choice test

Suppose you need to write a program that grades multiple-choice tests. Assume there are eight students and ten questions, and the answers are stored in a two-dimensional array. Each row records a student's answers to the questions, as shown in the following array.

Students' Answers to the Questions:

	0	1	2	3	4	5	6	7	8	9
Student 0	A	B	A	C	C	D	E	E	A	D
Student 1	D	B	A	B	C	A	E	E	A	D
Student 2	E	D	D	A	C	B	E	E	A	D
Student 3	C	B	A	E	D	C	E	E	A	D
Student 4	A	B	D	C	C	D	E	E	A	D
Student 5	B	B	E	C	C	D	E	E	A	D
Student 6	B	B	A	C	C	D	E	E	A	D
Student 7	E	B	E	C	C	D	E	E	A	D

The key is stored in a one-dimensional array:

Key to the Questions:

	0	1	2	3	4	5	6	7	8	9
Key	D	B	D	C	C	D	A	E	A	D

Your program grades the test and displays the result. It compares each student's answers with the key, counts the number of correct answers, and displays it. Listing 7.2 gives the program.

LISTING 7.2 GradeExam.java

```
 1 public class GradeExam {
 2   /** Main method */
 3   public static void main(String[] args) {
 4     // Students' answers to the questions
 5     char[][] answers = {
 6       {'A', 'B', 'A', 'C', 'C', 'D', 'E', 'E', 'A', 'D'},
 7       {'D', 'B', 'A', 'B', 'C', 'A', 'E', 'E', 'A', 'D'},
 8       {'E', 'D', 'D', 'A', 'C', 'B', 'E', 'E', 'A', 'D'},
 9       {'C', 'B', 'A', 'E', 'D', 'C', 'E', 'E', 'A', 'D'},
10       {'A', 'B', 'D', 'C', 'C', 'D', 'E', 'E', 'A', 'D'},
11       {'B', 'B', 'E', 'C', 'C', 'D', 'E', 'E', 'A', 'D'},
12       {'B', 'B', 'A', 'C', 'C', 'D', 'E', 'E', 'A', 'D'},
13       {'E', 'B', 'E', 'C', 'C', 'D', 'E', 'E', 'A', 'D'}};
14
15     // Key to the questions
16     char[] keys = {'D', 'B', 'D', 'C', 'C', 'D', 'A', 'E', 'A', 'D'};
17
18     // Grade all answers
19     for (int i = 0; i < answers.length; i++) {
20       // Grade one student
21       int correctCount = 0;
22       for (int j = 0; j < answers[i].length; j++) {
23         if (answers[i][j] == keys[j])
24           correctCount++;
25       }
26
27       System.out.println("Student " + i + "'s correct count is " +
28         correctCount);
29     }
30   }
31 }
```

2-D array

1-D array

compare with key

```
Student 0's correct count is 7
Student 1's correct count is 6
Student 2's correct count is 5
Student 3's correct count is 4
Student 4's correct count is 8
Student 5's correct count is 7
Student 6's correct count is 7
Student 7's correct count is 7
```

The statement in lines 5–13 declares, creates, and initializes a two-dimensional array of characters and assigns the reference to **answers** of the **char[][]** type.

The statement in line 16 declares, creates, and initializes an array of **char** values and assigns the reference to **keys** of the **char[]** type.

Each row in the array **answers** stores a student's answer, which is graded by comparing it with the key in the array **keys**. The result is displayed immediately after a student's answer is graded.

7.6 Case Study: Finding the Closest Pair

This section presents a geometric problem for finding the closest pair of points.

closest-pair animation on the Companion Website

Given a set of points, the closest-pair problem is to find the two points that are nearest to each other. In Figure 7.3, for example, points `(1, 1)` and `(2, 0.5)` are closest to each other. There are several ways to solve this problem. An intuitive approach is to compute the distances between all pairs of points and find the one with the minimum distance, as implemented in Listing 7.3.

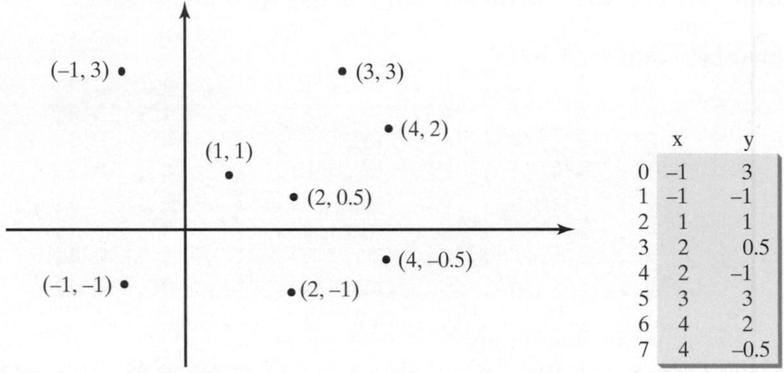

FIGURE 7.3 Points can be represented in a two-dimensional array.

LISTING 7.3 FindNearestPoints.java

```java
import java.util.Scanner;

public class FindNearestPoints {
  public static void main(String[] args) {
    Scanner input = new Scanner(System.in);
    System.out.print("Enter the number of points: ");
    int numberOfPoints = input.nextInt();

    // Create an array to store points
    double[][] points = new double[numberOfPoints][2];
    System.out.print("Enter " + numberOfPoints + " points: ");
    for (int i = 0; i < points.length; i++) {
      points[i][0] = input.nextDouble();
      points[i][1] = input.nextDouble();
    }

    // p1 and p2 are the indices in the points' array
    int p1 = 0, p2 = 1; // Initial two points
    double shortestDistance = distance(points[p1][0], points[p1][1],
      points[p2][0], points[p2][1]); // Initialize shortestDistance

    // Compute distance for every two points
    for (int i = 0; i < points.length; i++) {
```

number of points

2-D array

read points

track two points

track `shortestDistance`

for each point `i`

- Check each cell. Each cell must be a number from `1` to `9` and the cell must be unique on every row, every column, and every small box.

```
A solution grid is
  {{5, 3, 4, 6, 7, 8, 9, 1, 2},
   {6, 7, 2, 1, 9, 5, 3, 4, 8},
   {1, 9, 8, 3, 4, 2, 5, 6, 7},
   {8, 5, 9, 7, 6, 1, 4, 2, 3},
   {4, 2, 6, 8, 5, 3, 7, 9, 1},
   {7, 1, 3, 9, 2, 4, 8, 5, 6},
   {9, 6, 1, 5, 3, 7, 2, 8, 4},
   {2, 8, 7, 4, 1, 9, 6, 3, 5},
   {3, 4, 5, 2, 8, 6, 1, 7, 9}
  };
```

FIGURE 7.6 A solution is stored in `grid`.

The program in Listing 7.4 prompts the user to enter a solution and reports whether it is valid. We use the second approach in the program to check whether the solution is correct.

LISTING 7.4 CheckSudokuSolution.java

```java
import java.util.Scanner;

public class CheckSudokuSolution {
  public static void main(String[] args) {
    // Read a Sudoku solution
    int[][] grid = readASolution();

    System.out.println(isValid(grid) ? "Valid solution" :
      "Invalid solution");
  }

  /** Read a Sudoku solution from the console */
  public static int[][] readASolution() {
    // Create a Scanner
    Scanner input = new Scanner(System.in);

    System.out.println("Enter a Sudoku puzzle solution:");
    int[][] grid = new int[9][9];
    for (int i = 0; i < 9; i++)
      for (int j = 0; j < 9; j++)
        grid[i][j] = input.nextInt();

    return grid;
  }

  /** Check whether a solution is valid */
  public static boolean isValid(int[][] grid) {
    for (int i = 0; i < 9; i++)
      for (int j = 0; j < 9; j++)
        if (grid[i][j] < 1 || grid[i][j] > 9
            || !isValid(i, j, grid))
          return false;
    return true; // The solution is valid
  }

  /** Check whether grid[i][j] is valid in the grid */
  public static boolean isValid(int i, int j, int[][] grid) {
    // Check whether grid[i][j] is valid in i's row
```

read input

solution valid?

read solution

check solution

check rows

check columns

check small boxes

```
39      for (int column = 0; column < 9; column++)
40        if (column != j && grid[i][column] == grid[i][j])
41          return false;
42
43      // Check whether grid[i][j] is valid in j's column
44      for (int row = 0; row < 9; row++)
45        if (row != i && grid[row][j] == grid[i][j])
46          return false;
47
48      // Check whether grid[i][j] is valid in the 3-by-3 box
49      for (int row = (i / 3) * 3; row < (i / 3) * 3 + 3; row++)
50        for (int col = (j / 3) * 3; col < (j / 3) * 3 + 3; col++)
51          if (row != i && col != j && grid[row][col] == grid[i][j])
52            return false;
53
54      return true; // The current value at grid[i][j] is valid
55    }
56  }
```

```
Enter a Sudoku puzzle solution:
9 6 3 1 7 4 2 5 8 ↵Enter
1 7 8 3 2 5 6 4 9 ↵Enter
2 5 4 6 8 9 7 3 1 ↵Enter
8 2 1 4 3 7 5 9 6 ↵Enter
4 9 6 8 5 2 3 1 7 ↵Enter
7 3 5 9 6 1 8 2 4 ↵Enter
5 8 9 7 1 3 4 6 2 ↵Enter
3 1 7 2 4 6 9 8 5 ↵Enter
6 4 2 5 9 8 1 7 3 ↵Enter
Valid solution
```

The program invokes the **readASolution()** method (line 6) to read a Sudoku solution and return a two-dimensional array representing a Sudoku grid.

isValid method

The **isValid(grid)** method checks whether the values in the grid are valid by verifying that each value is between **1** and **9** and that each value is valid in the grid (lines 27–34).

overloaded isValid method

The **isValid(i, j, grid)** method checks whether the value at **grid[i][j]** is valid. It checks whether **grid[i][j]** appears more than once in row **i** (lines 39–41), in column **j** (lines 44–46), and in the 3 × 3 box (lines 49–52).

How do you locate all the cells in the same box? For any **grid[i][j]**, the starting cell of the 3 × 3 box that contains it is **grid[(i / 3) * 3][(j / 3) * 3]**, as illustrated in Figure 7.7.

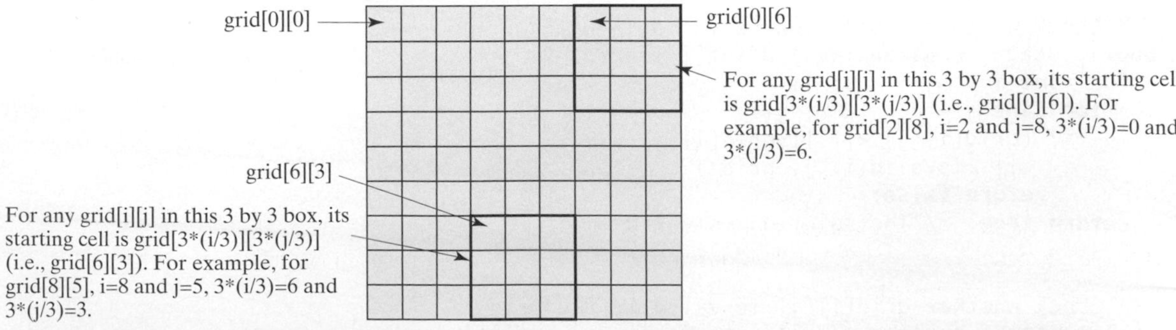

FIGURE 7.7 The location of the first cell in a 3 × 3 box determines the locations of other cells in the box.

With this observation, you can easily identify all the cells in the box. For instance, if grid[r][c] is the starting cell of a 3 × 3 box, the cells in the box can be traversed in a nested loop as follows:

```
// Get all cells in a 3-by-3 box starting at grid[r][c]
for (int row = r; row < r + 3; row++)
  for (int col = c; col < c + 3; col++)
    // grid[row][col] is in the box
```

It is cumbersome to enter 81 numbers from the console. When you test the program, you may store the input in a file, say **CheckSudokuSolution.txt** (see www.cs.armstrong.edu/liang/data/CheckSudokuSolution.txt), and run the program using the following command: input file

```
java CheckSudokuSolution < CheckSudokuSolution.txt
```

7.8 Multidimensional Arrays

A two-dimensional array consists of an array of one-dimensional arrays and a three-dimensional array consists of an array of two-dimensional arrays.

In the preceding section, you used a two-dimensional array to represent a matrix or a table. Occasionally, you will need to represent *n*-dimensional data structures. In Java, you can create *n*-dimensional arrays for any integer *n*.

The way to declare two-dimensional array variables and create two-dimensional arrays can be generalized to declare *n*-dimensional array variables and create *n*-dimensional arrays for *n* >= 3. For example, you may use a three-dimensional array to store exam scores for a class of six students with five exams, and each exam has two parts (multiple-choice and essay). The following syntax declares a three-dimensional array variable scores, creates an array, and assigns its reference to scores.

```
double[][][] scores = new double[6][5][2];
```

You can also use the short-hand notation to create and initialize the array as follows:

```
double[][][] scores = {
  {{7.5, 20.5}, {9.0, 22.5}, {15, 33.5}, {13, 21.5}, {15, 2.5}},
  {{4.5, 21.5}, {9.0, 22.5}, {15, 34.5}, {12, 20.5}, {14, 9.5}},
  {{6.5, 30.5}, {9.4, 10.5}, {11, 33.5}, {11, 23.5}, {10, 2.5}},
  {{6.5, 23.5}, {9.4, 32.5}, {13, 34.5}, {11, 20.5}, {16, 7.5}},
  {{8.5, 26.5}, {9.4, 52.5}, {13, 36.5}, {13, 24.5}, {16, 2.5}},
  {{9.5, 20.5}, {9.4, 42.5}, {13, 31.5}, {12, 20.5}, {16, 6.5}}};
```

scores[0][1][0] refers to the multiple-choice score for the first student's second exam, which is 9.0. scores[0][1][1] refers to the essay score for the first student's second exam, which is 22.5. This is depicted in the following figure:

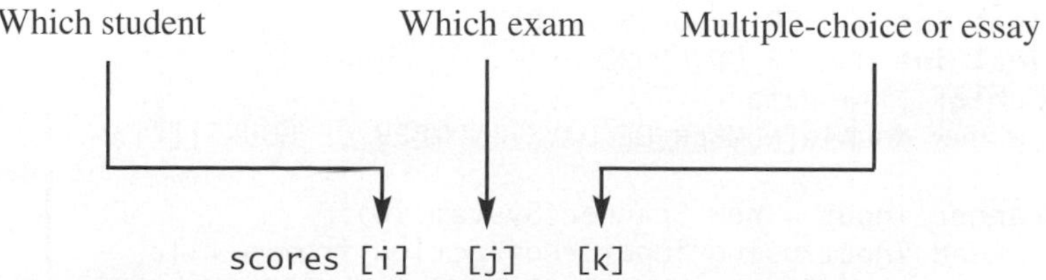

A multidimensional array is actually an array in which each element is another array. A three-dimensional array consists of an array of two-dimensional arrays. A two-dimensional array consists of an array of one-dimensional arrays. For example, suppose x = new int[2][2][5], and x[0] and x[1] are two-dimensional arrays. X[0][0], x[0][1], x[1][0], and x[1][1] are one-dimensional arrays and each contains five elements.

`x.length` is `2`, `x[0].length` and `x[1].length` are `2`, and `X[0][0].length`, `x[0][1].length`, `x[1][0].length`, and `x[1][1].length` are `5`.

7.8.1 Case Study: Daily Temperature and Humidity

Suppose a meteorology station records the temperature and humidity every hour of every day and stores the data for the past ten days in a text file named **Weather.txt** (see www.cs.armstrong.edu/liang/data/Weather.txt). Each line of the file consists of four numbers that indicate the day, hour, temperature, and humidity. The contents of the file may look like the one in (a).

Day	Hour	Temperature	Humidity
1	1	76.4	0.92
1	2	77.7	0.93
...			
10	23	97.7	0.71
10	24	98.7	0.74

(a)

Day	Hour	Temperature	Humidity
10	24	98.7	0.74
1	2	77.7	0.93
...			
10	23	97.7	0.71
1	1	76.4	0.92

(b)

Note that the lines in the file are not necessarily in increasing order of day and hour. For example, the file may appear as shown in (b).

Your task is to write a program that calculates the average daily temperature and humidity for the `10` days. You can use the input redirection to read the file and store the data in a three-dimensional array named `data`. The first index of `data` ranges from `0` to `9` and represents `10` days, the second index ranges from `0` to `23` and represents `24` hours, and the third index ranges from `0` to `1` and represents temperature and humidity, as depicted in the following figure:

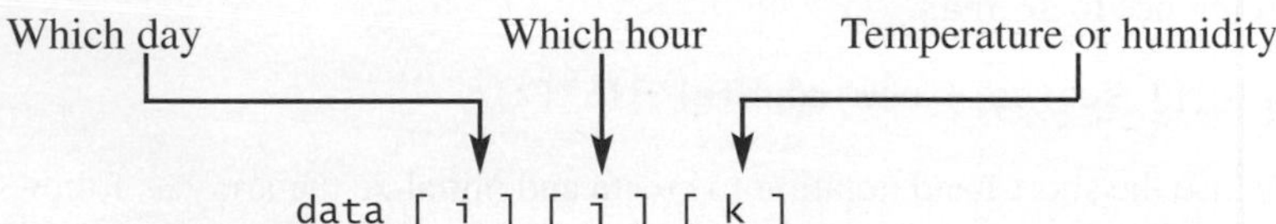

Note that the days are numbered from `1` to `10` and the hours from `1` to `24` in the file. Because the array index starts from `0`, `data[0][0][0]` stores the temperature in day `1` at hour `1` and `data[9][23][1]` stores the humidity in day `10` at hour `24`.

The program is given in Listing 7.5.

LISTING 7.5 Weather.java

three-dimensional array

```java
import java.util.Scanner;

public class Weather {
  public static void main(String[] args) {
    final int NUMBER_OF_DAYS = 10;
    final int NUMBER_OF_HOURS = 24;
    double[][][] data
      = new double[NUMBER_OF_DAYS][NUMBER_OF_HOURS][2];

    Scanner input = new Scanner(System.in);
    // Read input using input redirection from a file
    for (int k = 0; k < NUMBER_OF_DAYS * NUMBER_OF_HOURS; k++) {
      int day = input.nextInt();
      int hour = input.nextInt();
      double temperature = input.nextDouble();
      double humidity = input.nextDouble();
      data[day - 1][hour - 1][0] = temperature;
```

```
18          data[day - 1][hour - 1][1] = humidity;
19        }
20
21        // Find the average daily temperature and humidity
22        for (int i = 0; i < NUMBER_OF_DAYS; i++) {
23          double dailyTemperatureTotal = 0, dailyHumidityTotal = 0;
24          for (int j = 0; j < NUMBER_OF_HOURS; j++) {
25            dailyTemperatureTotal += data[i][j][0];
26            dailyHumidityTotal += data[i][j][1];
27          }
28
29          // Display result
30          System.out.println("Day " + i + "'s average temperature is "
31            + dailyTemperatureTotal / NUMBER_OF_HOURS);
32          System.out.println("Day " + i + "'s average humidity is "
33            + dailyHumidityTotal / NUMBER_OF_HOURS);
34        }
35      }
36    }
```

```
Day 0's average temperature is 77.7708
Day 0's average humidity is 0.929583
Day 1's average temperature is 77.3125
Day 1's average humidity is 0.929583
. . .
Day 9's average temperature is 79.3542
Day 9's average humidity is 0.9125
```

You can use the following command to run the program:

java Weather < Weather.txt

A three-dimensional array for storing temperature and humidity is created in line 8. The loop in lines 12–19 reads the input to the array. You can enter the input from the keyboard, but doing so will be awkward. For convenience, we store the data in a file and use input redirection to read the data from the file. The loop in lines 24–27 adds all temperatures for each hour in a day to `dailyTemperatureTotal` and all humidity for each hour to `dailyHumidityTotal`. The average daily temperature and humidity are displayed in lines 30–33.

7.8.2 Case Study: Guessing Birthdays

Listing 3.3, GuessBirthday.java, gives a program that guesses a birthday. The program can be simplified by storing the numbers in five sets in a three-dimensional array, and it prompts the user for the answers using a loop, as shown in Listing 7.6. The sample run of the program can be the same as shown in Listing 3.3.

LISTING 7.6 GuessBirthdayUsingArray.java

three-dimensional array

```
import java.util.Scanner;

public class GuessBirthdayUsingArray {
  public static void main(String[] args) {
    int day = 0; // Day to be determined
    int answer;

    int[][][] dates = {
      {{ 1,  3,  5,  7},
       { 9, 11, 13, 15},
```

```
11          {17, 19, 21, 23},
12          {25, 27, 29, 31}},
13        {{ 2,  3,  6,  7},
14          {10, 11, 14, 15},
15          {18, 19, 22, 23},
16          {26, 27, 30, 31}},
17        {{ 4,  5,  6,  7},
18          {12, 13, 14, 15},
19          {20, 21, 22, 23},
20          {28, 29, 30, 31}},
21        {{ 8,  9, 10, 11},
22          {12, 13, 14, 15},
23          {24, 25, 26, 27},
24          {28, 29, 30, 31}},
25        {{16, 17, 18, 19},
26          {20, 21, 22, 23},
27          {24, 25, 26, 27},
28          {28, 29, 30, 31}}};
29
30      // Create a Scanner
31      Scanner input = new Scanner(System.in);
32
33      for (int i = 0; i < 5; i++) {
34        System.out.println("Is your birthday in Set" + (i + 1) + "?");
35        for (int j = 0; j < 4; j++) {
36          for (int k = 0; k < 4; k++)
37            System.out.printf("%4d", dates[i][j][k]);
38          System.out.println();
39        }
40
41        System.out.print("\nEnter 0 for No and 1 for Yes: ");
42        answer = input.nextInt();
43
44        if (answer == 1)
45          day += dates[i][0][0];
46      }
47
48      System.out.println("Your birthday is " + day);
49    }
50  }
```

Set i

add to day

A three-dimensional array **dates** is created in Lines 8–28. This array stores five sets of numbers. Each set is a 4-by-4 two-dimensional array.

The loop starting from line 33 displays the numbers in each set and prompts the user to answer whether the birthday is in the set (lines 41–42). If the day is in the set, the first number (**dates[i][0][0]**) in the set is added to variable **day** (line 45).

MyProgrammingLab™

7.8 Declare an array variable for a three-dimensional array, create a $4 \times 6 \times 5$ **int** array, and assign its reference to the variable.

7.9 Assume **int[][][] x = new char[12][5][2]**, how many elements are in the array? What are **x.length**, **x[2].length**, and **x[0][0].length**?

7.10 Show the printout of the following code:

```
int[][][] array = {{{1, 2}, {3, 4}}, {{5, 6},{7, 8}}};
System.out.println(array[0][0][0]);
System.out.println(array[1][1][1]);
```

Chapter Summary

1. A two-dimensional array can be used to store a table.
2. A variable for two-dimensional arrays can be declared using the syntax: `elementType[][] arrayVar`.
3. A two-dimensional array can be created using the syntax: `new elementType[ROW_SIZE][COLUMN_SIZE]`.
4. Each element in a two-dimensional array is represented using the syntax: `arrayVar[rowIndex][columnIndex]`.
5. You can create and initialize a two-dimensional array using an array initializer with the syntax: `elementType[][] arrayVar = {{row values}, . . . , {row values}}`.
6. You can use arrays of arrays to form multidimensional arrays. For example, a variable for three-dimensional arrays can be declared as `elementType[][][] arrayVar`, and a three-dimensional array can be created using `new elementType[size1][size2][size3]`.

Test Questions

Do the test questions for this chapter online at www.cs.armstrong.edu/liang/intro9e/test.html.

Programming Exercises

MyProgrammingLab™

***7.1** (*Sum elements column by column*) Write a method that returns the sum of all the elements in a specified column in a matrix using the following header:

```
public static double sumColumn(double[][] m, int columnIndex)
```

Write a test program that reads a 3-by-4 matrix and displays the sum of each column. Here is a sample run:

```
Enter a 3-by-4 matrix row by row:
1.5 2 3 4 ↵Enter
5.5 6 7 8 ↵Enter
9.5 1 3 1 ↵Enter
Sum of the elements at column 0 is 16.5
Sum of the elements at column 1 is 9.0
Sum of the elements at column 2 is 13.0
Sum of the elements at column 3 is 13.0
```

***7.2** (*Sum the major diagonal in a matrix*) Write a method that sums all the numbers in the major diagonal in an $n \times n$ matrix of integers using the following header:

```
public static double sumMajorDiagonal(double[][] m)
```

Write a test program that reads a 4-by-4 matrix and displays the sum of all its elements on the major diagonal. Here is a sample run:

```
Enter a 4-by-4 matrix row by row:
1 2 3 4.0 ↵Enter
5 6.5 7 8 ↵Enter
9 10 11 12 ↵Enter
13 14 15 16 ↵Enter
Sum of the elements in the major diagonal is 34.5
```

***7.3** (*Sort students on grades*) Rewrite Listing 7.2, GradeExam.java, to display the students in increasing order of the number of correct answers.

****7.4** (*Compute the weekly hours for each employee*) Suppose the weekly hours for all employees are stored in a two-dimensional array. Each row records an employee's seven-day work hours with seven columns. For example, the following array stores the work hours for eight employees. Write a program that displays employees and their total hours in decreasing order of the total hours.

	Su	M	T	W	Th	F	Sa
Employee 0	2	4	3	4	5	8	8
Employee 1	7	3	4	3	3	4	4
Employee 2	3	3	4	3	3	2	2
Employee 3	9	3	4	7	3	4	1
Employee 4	3	5	4	3	6	3	8
Employee 5	3	4	4	6	3	4	4
Employee 6	3	7	4	8	3	8	4
Employee 7	6	3	5	9	2	7	9

7.5 (*Algebra: add two matrices*) Write a method to add two matrices. The header of the method is as follows:

```
public static double[][] addMatrix(double[][] a, double[][] b)
```

In order to be added, the two matrices must have the same dimensions and the same or compatible types of elements. Let **c** be the resulting matrix. Each element c_{ij} is $a_{ij} + b_{ij}$. For example, for two 3×3 matrices **a** and **b**, **c** is

VideoNote
Multiply two matrices

$$\begin{pmatrix} a_{11} & a_{12} & a_{13} \\ a_{21} & a_{22} & a_{23} \\ a_{31} & a_{32} & a_{33} \end{pmatrix} + \begin{pmatrix} b_{11} & b_{12} & b_{13} \\ b_{21} & b_{22} & b_{23} \\ b_{31} & b_{32} & b_{33} \end{pmatrix} = \begin{pmatrix} a_{11}+b_{11} & a_{12}+b_{12} & a_{13}+b_{13} \\ a_{21}+b_{21} & a_{22}+b_{22} & a_{23}+b_{23} \\ a_{31}+b_{31} & a_{32}+b_{32} & a_{33}+b_{33} \end{pmatrix}$$

Write a test program that prompts the user to enter two 3×3 matrices and displays their sum. Here is a sample run:

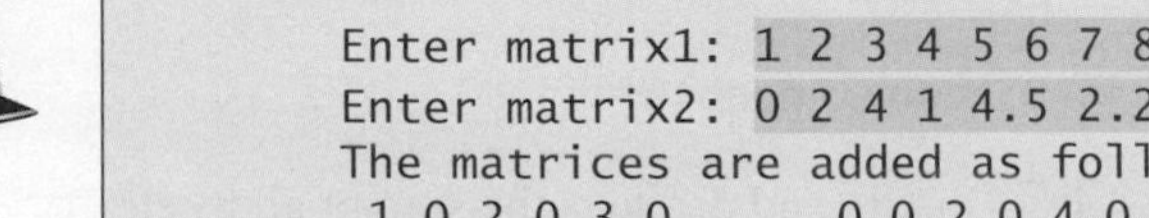

```
Enter matrix1: 1 2 3 4 5 6 7 8 9 ↵Enter
Enter matrix2: 0 2 4 1 4.5 2.2 1.1 4.3 5.2 ↵Enter
The matrices are added as follows
  1.0 2.0 3.0          0.0 2.0 4.0          1.0 4.0 7.0
  4.0 5.0 6.0    +     1.0 4.5 2.2    =     5.0 9.5 8.2
  7.0 8.0 9.0          1.1 4.3 5.2          8.1 12.3 14.2
```

****7.6** (*Algebra: multiply two matrices*) Write a method to multiply two matrices. The header of the method is:

```
public static double[][]
   multiplyMatrix(double[][] a, double[][] b)
```

To multiply matrix a by matrix b, the number of columns in a must be the same as the number of rows in b, and the two matrices must have elements of the same or compatible types. Let c be the result of the multiplication. Assume the column size of matrix a is n. Each element c_{ij} is $a_{i1} \times b_{1j} + a_{i2} \times b_{2j} + \ldots + a_{in} \times b_{nj}$. For example, for two 3 × 3 matrices a and b, c is

$$\begin{pmatrix} a_{11} & a_{12} & a_{13} \\ a_{21} & a_{22} & a_{23} \\ a_{31} & a_{32} & a_{33} \end{pmatrix} \times \begin{pmatrix} b_{11} & b_{12} & b_{13} \\ b_{21} & b_{22} & b_{23} \\ b_{31} & b_{32} & b_{33} \end{pmatrix} = \begin{pmatrix} c_{11} & c_{12} & c_{13} \\ c_{21} & c_{22} & c_{23} \\ c_{31} & c_{32} & c_{33} \end{pmatrix}$$

where $c_{ij} = a_{i1} \times b_{1j} + a_{i2} \times b_{2j} + a_{i3} \times b_{3j}$.

Write a test program that prompts the user to enter two 3 × 3 matrices and displays their product. Here is a sample run:

```
Enter matrix1: 1 2 3 4 5 6 7 8 9 [Enter]
Enter matrix2: 0 2 4 1 4.5 2.2 1.1 4.3 5.2 [Enter]
The multiplication of the matrices is
 1 2 3       0 2.0 4.0        5.3 23.9 24
 4 5 6   *   1 4.5 2.2   =    11.6 56.3 58.2
 7 8 9       1.1 4.3 5.2      17.9 88.7 92.4
```

***7.7** (*Points nearest to each other*) Listing 7.3 gives a program that finds two points in a two-dimensional space nearest to each other. Revise the program so that it finds two points in a three-dimensional space nearest to each other. Use a two-dimensional array to represent the points. Test the program using the following points:

```
double[][] points = {{-1, 0, 3}, {-1, -1, -1}, {4, 1, 1},
  {2, 0.5, 9}, {3.5, 2, -1}, {3, 1.5, 3}, {-1.5, 4, 2},
  {5.5, 4, 0.5}},
```

The formula for computing the distance between two points (x1, y1, z1) and (x2, y2, z2) is $\sqrt{(x_2 - x_1)^2 + (y_2 - y_1)^2 + (z_2 - z_1)^2}$.

****7.8** (*All closest pairs of points*) Revise Listing 7.3, FindNearestPoints.java, to find all closest pairs of points with the same minimum distance.

*****7.9** (*Game: play a tic-tac-toe game*) In a game of tic-tac-toe, two players take turns marking an available cell in a 3 × 3 grid with their respective tokens (either X or O). When one player has placed three tokens in a horizontal, vertical, or diagonal row on the grid, the game is over and that player has won. A draw (no winner) occurs when all the cells on the grid have been filled with tokens and neither player has achieved a win. Create a program for playing tic-tac-toe.

The program prompts two players to enter an X token and O token alternately. Whenever a token is entered, the program redisplays the board on the console and determines the status of the game (win, draw, or continue). Here is a sample run:

```
-------------
|   |   |   |
-------------
|   |   |   |
-------------
|   |   |   |
-------------
Enter a row (0, 1, or 2) for player X: 1 ↵Enter
Enter a column (0, 1, or 2) for player X: 1 ↵Enter

-------------
|   |   |   |
-------------
|   | X |   |
-------------
|   |   |   |
-------------
Enter a row (0, 1, or 2) for player O: 1 ↵Enter
Enter a column (0, 1, or 2) for player O: 2 ↵Enter

-------------
|   |   |   |
-------------
|   | X | O |
-------------
|   |   |   |
-------------
Enter a row (0, 1, or 2) for player X:

  . . .

-------------
| X |   |   |
-------------
| O | X | O |
-------------
|   |   | X |
-------------
X player won
```

***7.10** (*Largest row and column*) Write a program that randomly fills in 0s and 1s into a 4-by-4 matrix, prints the matrix, and finds the first row and column with the most 1s. Here is a sample run of the program:

```
0011
0011
1101
1010
The largest row index: 2
The largest column index: 2
```

****7.11** (*Game: nine heads and tails*) Nine coins are placed in a 3-by-3 matrix with some face up and some face down. You can represent the state of the coins using a 3-by-3 matrix with values 0 (heads) and 1 (tails). Here are some examples:

```
0 0 0    1 0 1    1 1 0    1 0 1    1 0 0
0 1 0    0 0 1    1 0 0    1 1 0    1 1 1
0 0 0    1 0 0    0 0 1    1 0 0    1 1 0
```

Each state can also be represented using a binary number. For example, the preceding matrices correspond to the numbers

```
000010000 101001100 110100001 101110100 100111110
```

There are a total of 512 possibilities, so you can use decimal numbers 0, 1, 2, 3, . . . , and 511 to represent all states of the matrix. Write a program that prompts the user to enter a number between 0 and 511 and displays the corresponding matrix with the characters H and T. Here is a sample run:

```
Enter a number between 0 and 511: 7 ↵Enter
H H H
H H H
T T T
```

The user entered 7, which corresponds to 000000111. Since 0 stands for H and 1 for T, the output is correct.

****7.12** (*Financial application: compute tax*) Rewrite Listing 3.6, ComputeTax.java, using arrays. For each filing status, there are six tax rates. Each rate is applied to a certain amount of taxable income. For example, from the taxable income of $400,000 for a single filer, $8,350 is taxed at 10%, (33,950 – 8,350) at 15%, (82,250 – 33,950) at 25%, (171,550 – 82,550) at 28%, (372,550 – 82,250) at 33%, and (400,000 – 372,950) at 36%. The six rates are the same for all filing statuses, which can be represented in the following array:

```
double[] rates = {0.10, 0.15, 0.25, 0.28, 0.33, 0.35};
```

The brackets for each rate for all the filing statuses can be represented in a two-dimensional array as follows:

```
int[][] brackets = {
  {8350, 33950, 82250, 171550, 372950}, // Single filer
  {16700, 67900, 137050, 20885, 372950}, // Married jointly
                                         // or qualifying widow(er)
  {8350, 33950, 68525, 104425, 186475}, // Married separately
  {11950, 45500, 117450, 190200, 372950} // Head of household
};
```

Suppose the taxable income is $400,000 for single filers. The tax can be computed as follows:

```
tax = brackets[0][0] * rates[0] +
  (brackets[0][1] - brackets[0][0]) * rates[1] +
  (brackets[0][2] - brackets[0][1]) * rates[2] +
  (brackets[0][3] - brackets[0][2]) * rates[3] +
  (brackets[0][4] - brackets[0][3]) * rates[4] +
  (400000 - brackets[0][4]) * rates[5]
```

***7.13** (*Locate the largest element*) Write the following method that returns the location of the largest element in a two-dimensional array.

```
public static int[] locateLargest(double[][] a)
```

The return value is a one-dimensional array that contains two elements. These two elements indicate the row and column indices of the largest element in the two-dimensional array. Write a test program that prompts the user to enter a two-dimensional array and displays the location of the largest element in the array. Here is a sample run:

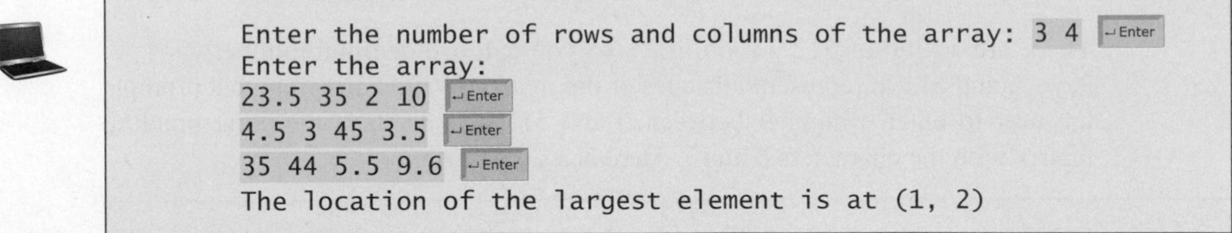

```
Enter the number of rows and columns of the array: 3 4 ↵Enter
Enter the array:
23.5 35 2 10 ↵Enter
4.5 3 45 3.5 ↵Enter
35 44 5.5 9.6 ↵Enter
The location of the largest element is at (1, 2)
```

****7.14** (*Explore matrix*) Write a program that prompts the user to enter the length of a square matrix, randomly fills in `0`s and `1`s into the matrix, prints the matrix, and finds the rows, columns, and diagonals with all `0`s or `1`s. Here is a sample run of the program:

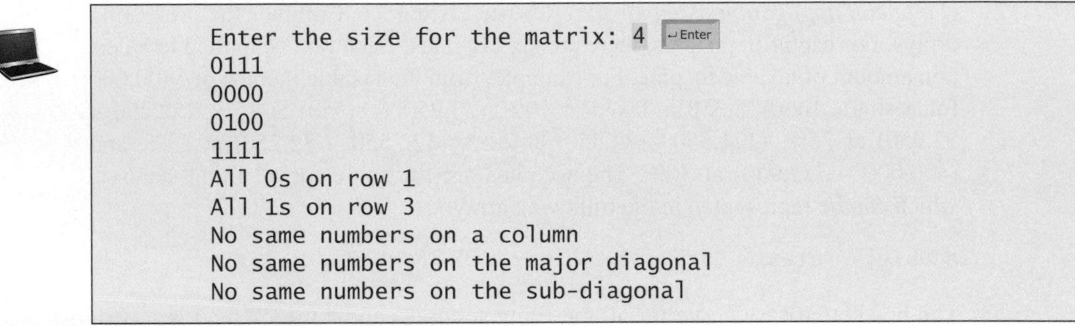

```
Enter the size for the matrix: 4 ↵Enter
0111
0000
0100
1111
All 0s on row 1
All 1s on row 3
No same numbers on a column
No same numbers on the major diagonal
No same numbers on the sub-diagonal
```

***7.15** (*Geometry: same line?*) Programming Exercise 5.39 gives a method for testing whether three points are on the same line.

Write the following method to test whether all the points in the array `points` are on the same line.

```
public static boolean sameLine(double[][] points)
```

Write a program that prompts the user to enter five points and displays whether they are on the same line. Here are sample runs:

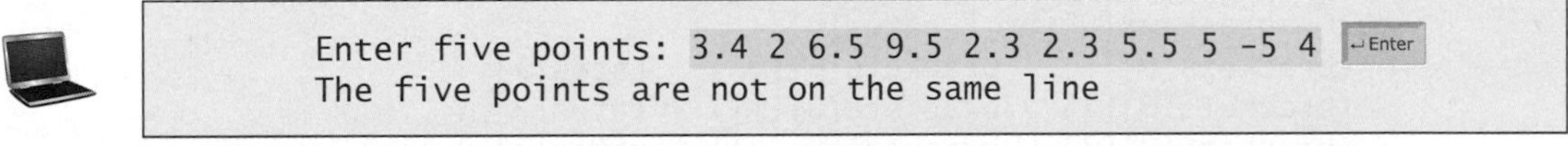

```
Enter five points: 3.4 2 6.5 9.5 2.3 2.3 5.5 5 -5 4 ↵Enter
The five points are not on the same line
```

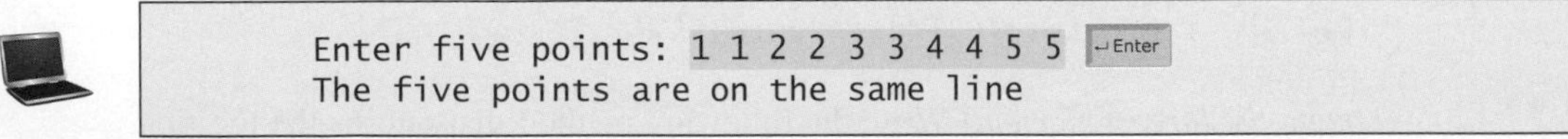

```
Enter five points: 1 1 2 2 3 3 4 4 5 5 ↵Enter
The five points are on the same line
```

***7.16** (*Sort two-dimensional array*) Write a method to sort a two-dimensional array using the following header:

```
public static void sort(int m[][])
```

The method performs a primary sort on rows and a secondary sort on columns. For example, the following array

```
{{4, 2},{1, 7},{4, 5},{1, 2},{1, 1},{4, 1}}
```

will be sorted to

```
{{1, 1},{1, 2},{1, 7},{4, 1},{4, 2},{4, 5}}.
```

***7.17 (*Financial tsunami*) Banks lend money to each other. In tough economic times, if a bank goes bankrupt, it may not be able to pay back the loan. A bank's total assets are its current balance plus its loans to other banks. The diagram in Figure 7.8 shows five banks. The banks' current balances are 25, 125, 175, 75, and 181 million dollars, respectively. The directed edge from node 1 to node 2 indicates that bank 1 lends 40 million dollars to bank 2.

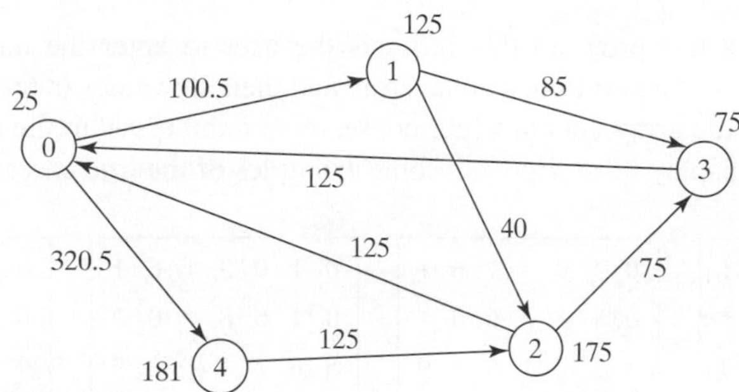

Figure 7.8 Banks lend money to each other.

If a bank's total assets are under a certain limit, the bank is unsafe. The money it borrowed cannot be returned to the lender, and the lender cannot count the loan in its total assets. Consequently, the lender may also be unsafe, if its total assets are under the limit. Write a program to find all the unsafe banks. Your program reads the input as follows. It first reads two integers `n` and `limit`, where `n` indicates the number of banks and `limit` is the minimum total assets for keeping a bank safe. It then reads `n` lines that describe the information for `n` banks with IDs from `0` to `n-1`.

The first number in the line is the bank's balance, the second number indicates the number of banks that borrowed money from the bank, and the rest are pairs of two numbers. Each pair describes a borrower. The first number in the pair is the borrower's ID and the second is the amount borrowed. For example, the input for the five banks in Figure 7.8 is as follows (note that the limit is 201):

```
5 201
25 2 1 100.5 4 320.5
125 2 2 40 3 85
175 2 0 125 3 75
75 1 0 125
181 1 2 125
```

The total assets of bank 3 are (75 + 125), which is under 201, so bank 3 is unsafe. After bank 3 becomes unsafe, the total assets of bank 1 fall below (125 + 40). Thus, bank 1 is also unsafe. The output of the program should be

```
Unsafe banks are 3 1
```

(*Hint*: Use a two-dimensional array `borrowers` to represent loans. `borrowers[i][j]` indicates the loan that bank `i` loans to bank `j`. Once bank `j` becomes unsafe, `borrowers[i][j]` should be set to `0`.)

***7.18** (*Shuffle rows*) Write a method that shuffles the rows in a two-dimensional `int` array using the following header:

```
public static void shuffle(int[][] m)
```

Write a test program that shuffles the following matrix:

```
int[][] m = {{1, 2}, {3, 4}, {5, 6}, {7, 8}, {9, 10}};
```

****7.19** (*Pattern recognition: four consecutive equal numbers*) Write the following method that tests whether a two-dimensional array has four consecutive numbers of the same value, either horizontally, vertically, or diagonally.

```
public static boolean isConsecutiveFour(int[][] values)
```

Write a test program that prompts the user to enter the number of rows and columns of a two-dimensional array and then the values in the array and displays true if the array contains four consecutive numbers with the same value. Otherwise, display false. Here are some examples of the true cases:

0	1	0	3	1	6	1
0	1	6	8	6	0	1
5	6	2	1	8	2	9
6	5	6	1	1	9	1
1	3	6	1	4	0	7
3	3	3	3	4	0	7

0	1	0	3	1	6	1
0	1	6	8	6	0	1
5	5	2	1	8	2	9
6	5	6	1	1	9	1
1	5	6	1	4	0	7
3	5	3	3	4	0	7

0	1	0	3	1	6	1
0	1	6	8	6	0	1
5	6	2	1	6	2	9
6	5	6	6	1	9	1
1	3	6	1	4	0	7
3	6	3	3	4	0	7

0	1	0	3	1	6	1
0	1	6	8	6	0	1
9	6	2	1	8	2	9
6	9	6	1	1	9	1
1	3	9	1	4	0	7
3	3	3	9	4	0	7

*****7.20** (*Game: connect four*) Connect four is a two-player board game in which the players alternately drop colored disks into a seven-column, six-row vertically suspended grid, as shown below.

The objective of the game is to connect four same-colored disks in a row, a column, or a diagonal before your opponent can do likewise. The program prompts two players to drop a red or yellow disk alternately. In the preceding figure, the red disk is shown in a dark color and the yellow in a light color. Whenever a disk is dropped, the program redisplays the board on the console and determines the status of the game (win, draw, or continue). Here is a sample run:

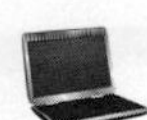

```
| | | | | | | |
| | | | | | | |
| | | | | | | |
| | | | | | | |
| | | | | | | |
| | | | | | | |
———————————————
Drop a red disk at column (0-6): 0 ↵Enter

| | | | | | | |
| | | | | | | |
| | | | | | | |
| | | | | | | |
| | | | | | | |
|R| | | | | | |
———————————————
Drop a yellow disk at column (0-6): 3 ↵Enter

| | | | | | | |
| | | | | | | |
| | | | | | | |
| | | | | | | |
| | | | | | | |
|R| | |Y| | | |

. . .
. . .
. . .

Drop a yellow disk at column (0-6): 6 ↵Enter
| | | | | | | |
| | | | | | | |
| | | |R| | | |
| | | |Y|R|Y| |
| | |R|Y|Y|Y|Y|
|R|Y|R|Y|R|R|R|
———————————————
The yellow player won
```

***7.21** (*Central city*) Given a set of cities, the central point is the city that has the shortest total distance to all other cities. Write a program that prompts the user to enter the number of the cities and the locations of the cities (coordinates), and finds the central city.

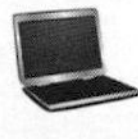

```
Enter the number of cities: 5 ↵Enter
Enter the coordinates of the cities:
  2.5 5 5.1 3 1 9 5.4 54 5.5 2.1 ↵Enter
The central city is at (2.5, 5.0)
```

***7.22** (*Even number of 1s*) Write a program that generates a 6-by-6 two-dimensional matrix filled with 0s and 1s, displays the matrix, and checks if every row and every column have an even number of 1s.

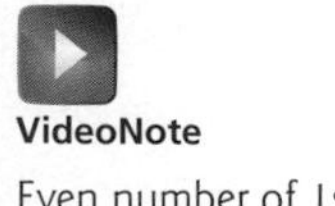

VideoNote
Even number of 1s

***7.23** (*Game: find the flipped cell*) Suppose you are given a 6-by-6 matrix filled with 0s and 1s. All rows and all columns have an even number of 1s. Let the user flip one cell (i.e., flip from 1 to 0 or from 0 to 1) and write a program to find which cell was flipped. Your program should prompt the user to enter a 6-by-6 array with 0s and 1s and find the first row *r* and first column *c* where the even number of the 1s property is violated (i.e., the number of 1s is not even). The flipped cell is at (*r*, *c*).

***7.24** (*Check Sudoku solution*) Listing 7.4 checks whether a solution is valid by checking whether every number is valid in the board. Rewrite the program by checking whether every row, every column, and every small box has the numbers 1 to 9.

***7.25** (*Markov matrix*) An $n \times n$ matrix is called a *positive Markov matrix* if each element is positive and the sum of the elements in each column is 1. Write the following method to check whether a matrix is a Markov matrix.

```
public static boolean isMarkovMatrix(double[][] m)
```

Write a test program that prompts the user to enter a 3×3 matrix of double values and tests whether it is a Markov matrix. Here are sample runs:

```
Enter a 3-by-3 matrix row by row:
0.15 0.875 0.375 ↵Enter
0.55 0.005 0.225 ↵Enter
0.30 0.12 0.4 ↵Enter
It is a Markov matrix
```

```
Enter a 3-by-3 matrix row by row:
0.95 -0.875 0.375 ↵Enter
0.65 0.005 0.225 ↵Enter
0.30 0.22 -0.4 ↵Enter
It is not a Markov matrix
```

***7.26** (*Row sorting*) Implement the following method to sort the rows in a two-dimensional array. A new array is returned and the original array is intact.

```
public static double[][] sortRows(double[][] m)
```

Write a test program that prompts the user to enter a 3×3 matrix of double values and displays a new row-sorted matrix. Here is a sample run:

```
Enter a 3-by-3 matrix row by row:
0.15 0.875 0.375 ↵Enter
0.55 0.005 0.225 ↵Enter
0.30 0.12 0.4 ↵Enter

The row-sorted array is
0.15 0.375 0.875
0.005 0.225 0.55
0.12 0.30 0.4
```

***7.27** (*Column sorting*) Implement the following method to sort the columns in a two-dimensional array. A new array is returned and the original array is intact.

```
public static double[][] sortColumns(double[][] m)
```

Write a test program that prompts the user to enter a 3 × 3 matrix of double values and displays a new column-sorted matrix. Here is a sample run:

```
Enter a 3-by-3 matrix row by row:
0.15 0.875 0.375 ↵Enter
0.55 0.005 0.225 ↵Enter
0.30 0.12 0.4 ↵Enter

The column-sorted array is
0.15 0.0050 0.225
0.3  0.12   0.375
0.55 0.875  0.4
```

7.28 (*Strictly identical arrays*) The two-dimensional arrays `m1` and `m2` are *strictly identical* if their corresponding elements are equal. Write a method that returns `true` if `m1` and `m2` are strictly identical, using the following header:

```
public static boolean equals(int[][] m1, int[][] m2)
```

Write a test program that prompts the user to enter two 3 × 3 arrays of integers and displays whether the two are strictly identical. Here are the sample runs.

```
Enter list1: 51 22 25 6 1 4 24 54 6 ↵Enter
Enter list2: 51 22 25 6 1 4 24 54 6 ↵Enter
The two arrays are strictly identical
```

```
Enter list1: 51 25 22 6 1 4 24 54 6 ↵Enter
Enter list2: 51 22 25 6 1 4 24 54 6 ↵Enter
The two arrays are not strictly identical
```

7.29 (*Identical arrays*) The two-dimensional arrays `m1` and `m2` are *identical* if they have the same contents. Write a method that returns `true` if `m1` and `m2` are identical, using the following header:

```
public static boolean equals(int[][] m1, int[][] m2)
```

Write a test program that prompts the user to enter two arrays of integers and displays whether the two are identical. Here are the sample runs.

```
Enter list1: 51 25 22 6 1 4 24 54 6 ↵Enter
Enter list2: 51 22 25 6 1 4 24 54 6 ↵Enter
The two arrays are identical
```

```
Enter list1: 51 5 22 6 1 4 24 54 6 ↵Enter
Enter list2: 51 22 25 6 1 4 24 54 6 ↵Enter
The two arrays are not identical
```

***7.30** (*Algebra: solve linear equations*) Write a method that solves the following 2 × 2 system of linear equations:

$$a_{00}x + a_{01}y = b_0 \qquad x = \frac{b_0 a_{11} - b_1 a_{01}}{a_{00}a_{11} - a_{01}a_{10}} \qquad y = \frac{b_1 a_{00} - b_0 a_{10}}{a_{00}a_{11} - a_{01}a_{10}}$$
$$a_{10}x + a_{11}y = b_1$$

The method header is

```
public static double[] linearEquation(double[][] a, double[] b)
```

The method returns `null` if $a_{00}a_{11} - a_{01}a_{10}$ is `0`. Write a test program that prompts the user to enter a_{00}, a_{01}, a_{10}, a_{11}, b_0, and b_1, and displays the result. If $a_{00}a_{11} - a_{01}a_{10}$ is `0`, report that "The equation has no solution." A sample run is similar to Programming Exercise 3.3.

***7.31** (*Geometry: intersecting point*) Write a method that returns the intersecting point of two lines. The intersecting point of the two lines can be found by using the formula shown in Programming Exercise 3.25. Assume that (`x1`, `y1`) and (`x2`, `y2`) are the two points on line 1 and (`x3`, `y3`) and (`x4`, `y4`) are on line 2. The method header is

```
public static double[] getIntersectingPoint(double[][] points)
```

The points are stored in a 4-by-2 two-dimensional array `points` with (`points[0][0]`, `points[0][1]`) for (`x1`, `y1`). The method returns the intersecting point or `null` if the two lines are parallel. Write a program that prompts the user to enter four points and displays the intersecting point. See Programming Exercise 3.25 for a sample run.

***7.32** (*Geometry: area of a triangle*) Write a method that returns the area of a triangle using the following header:

```
public static double getTriangleArea(double[][] points)
```

The points are stored in a 3-by-2 two-dimensional array `points` with `points[0][0]` and `points[0][1]` for (`x1`, `y1`). The triangle area can be computed using the formula in Programming Exercise 2.15. The method returns `0` if the three points are on the same line. Write a program that prompts the user to enter two lines and displays the intersecting point. Here is a sample run of the program:

```
Enter x1, y1, x2, y2, x3, y3: 2.5 2 5 -1.0 4.0 2.0 [Enter]
The area of the triangle is 2.25
```

```
Enter x1, y1, x2, y2, x3, y3: 2 2 4.5 4.5 6 6 [Enter]
The three points are on the same line
```

***7.33** (*Geometry: polygon subareas*) A convex 4-vertex polygon is divided into four triangles, as shown in Figure 7.9.

Write a program that prompts the user to enter the coordinates of four vertices and displays the areas of the four triangles in increasing order. Here is a sample run:

```
Enter x1, y1, x2, y2, x3, y3, x4, y4:
  -2.5 2 4 4 3 -2 -2 -3.5 [Enter]
The areas are 6.17 7.96 8.08 10.42
```

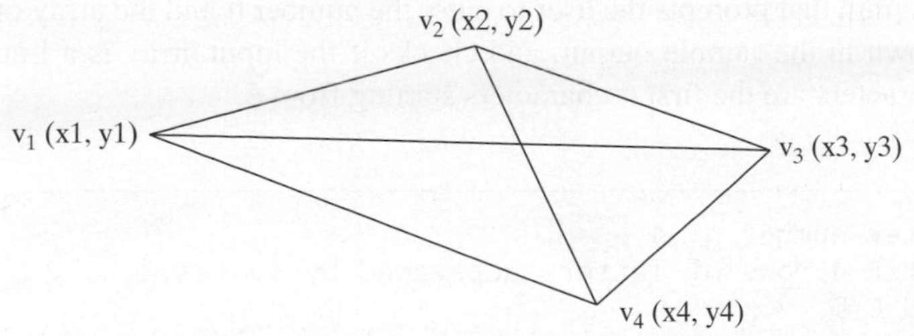

FIGURE 7.9 A 4-vertex polygon is defined by four vertices.

***7.34** (*Geometry: rightmost lowest point*) In computational geometry, often you need to find the rightmost lowest point in a set of points. Write the following method that returns the rightmost lowest point in a set of points.

```
public static double[]
      getRightmostLowestPoint(double[][] points)
```

Write a test program that prompts the user to enter the coordinates of six points and displays the rightmost lowest point. Here is a sample run:

```
Enter 6 points: 1.5 2.5 -3 4.5 5.6 -7 6.5 -7 8 1 10 2.5 ↵Enter
The rightmost lowest point is (6.5, -7.0)
```

****7.35** (*Largest block*) Given a square matrix with the elements 0 or 1, write a program to find a maximum square submatrix whose elements are all 1s. Your program should prompt the user to enter the number of rows in the matrix. The program then displays the location of the first element in the maximum square submatrix and the number of the rows in the submatrix. Here is a sample run:

```
Enter the number of rows in the matrix: 5 ↵Enter
Enter the matrix row by row:
1 0 1 0 1 ↵Enter
1 1 1 0 1 ↵Enter
1 0 1 1 1 ↵Enter
1 0 1 1 1 ↵Enter
1 0 1 1 1 ↵Enter

The maximum square submatrix is at (2, 2) with size 3
```

Your program should implement and use the following method to find the maximum square submatrix:

```
public static int[] findLargestBlock(int[][] m)
```

The return value is an array that consists of three values. The first two values are the row and column indices for the first element in the submatrix, and the third value is the number of the rows in the submatrix.

****7.36** (*Latin square*) A Latin square is an n-by-n array filled with **n** different Latin letters, each occurring exactly once in each row and once in each column. Write a program that prompts the user to enter the number n and the array of characters, as shown in the sample output, and checks if the input array is a Latin square. The characters are the first n characters starting from A.

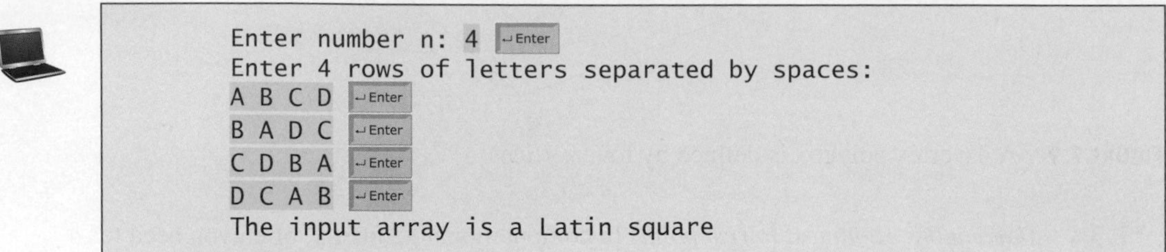

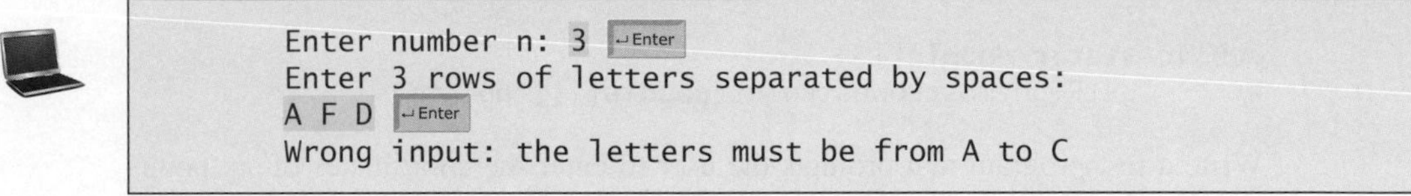

CHAPTER

8

OBJECTS AND CLASSES

Objectives

- To describe objects and classes, and use classes to model objects (§8.2).
- To use UML graphical notation to describe classes and objects (§8.2).
- To demonstrate how to define classes and create objects (§8.3).
- To create objects using constructors (§8.4).
- To access objects via object reference variables (§8.5).
- To define a reference variable using a reference type (§8.5.1).
- To access an object's data and methods using the object member access operator (`.`) (§8.5.2).
- To define data fields of reference types and assign default values for an object's data fields (§8.5.3).
- To distinguish between object reference variables and primitive data type variables (§8.5.4).
- To use the Java library classes `Date`, `Random`, and `JFrame` (§8.6).
- To distinguish between instance and static variables and methods (§8.7).
- To define private data fields with appropriate `get` and `set` methods (§8.8).
- To encapsulate data fields to make classes easy to maintain (§8.9).
- To develop methods with object arguments and differentiate between primitive-type arguments and object-type arguments (§8.10).
- To store and process objects in arrays (§8.11).

8.1 Introduction

Object-oriented programming enables you to develop large-scale software and GUIs effectively.

Having learned the material in the preceding chapters, you are able to solve many programming problems using selections, loops, methods, and arrays. However, these Java features are not sufficient for developing graphical user interfaces and large-scale software systems. Suppose you want to develop a graphical user interface (GUI, pronounced *goo-ee*) as shown in Figure 8.1. How would you program it? You will learn how in this chapter.

why OOP?

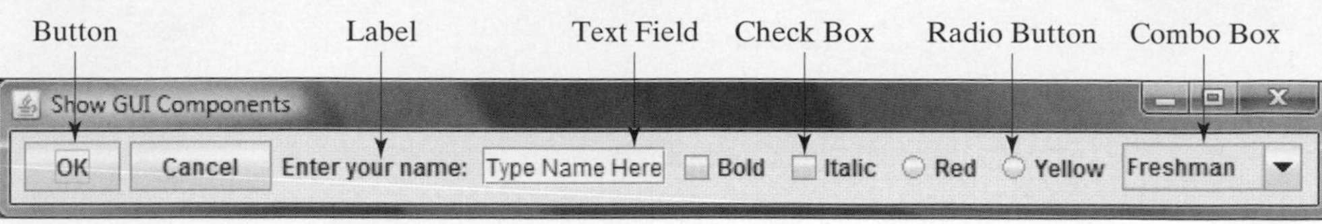

FIGURE 8.1 The GUI objects are created from classes.

This chapter introduces object-oriented programming, which you can use to develop GUI and large-scale software systems.

8.2 Defining Classes for Objects

A class defines the properties and behaviors for objects.

VideoNote
Define classes and objects

Object-oriented programming (OOP) involves programming using objects. An *object* represents an entity in the real world that can be distinctly identified. For example, a student, a desk, a circle, a button, and even a loan can all be viewed as objects. An object has a unique identity, state, and behavior.

object
state of an object
properties
attributes
data fields
behavior
actions

- The *state* of an object (also known as its *properties* or *attributes*) is represented by *data fields* with their current values. A circle object, for example, has a data field `radius`, which is the property that characterizes a circle. A rectangle object has the data fields `width` and `height`, which are the properties that characterize a rectangle.
- The *behavior* of an object (also known as its *actions*) is defined by methods. To invoke a method on an object is to ask the object to perform an action. For example, you may define methods named `getArea()` and `getPerimeter()` for circle objects. A circle object may invoke `getArea()` to return its area and `getPerimeter()` to return its perimeter. You may also define the `setRadius(radius)` method. A circle object can invoke this method to change its radius.

class
contract
instantiation
instance

Objects of the same type are defined using a common class. A *class* is a template, blueprint, or *contract* that defines what an object's data fields and methods will be. An object is an instance of a class. You can create many instances of a class. Creating an instance is referred to as *instantiation*. The terms *object* and *instance* are often interchangeable. The relationship between classes and objects is analogous to that between an apple-pie recipe and apple pies: You can make as many apple pies as you want from a single recipe. Figure 8.2 shows a class named `Circle` and its three objects.

data field
method
constructors

A Java class uses variables to define data fields and methods to define actions. Additionally, a class provides methods of a special type, known as *constructors*, which are invoked to create a new object. A constructor can perform any action, but constructors are designed to perform initializing actions, such as initializing the data fields of objects. Figure 8.3 shows an example of defining the class for circle objects.

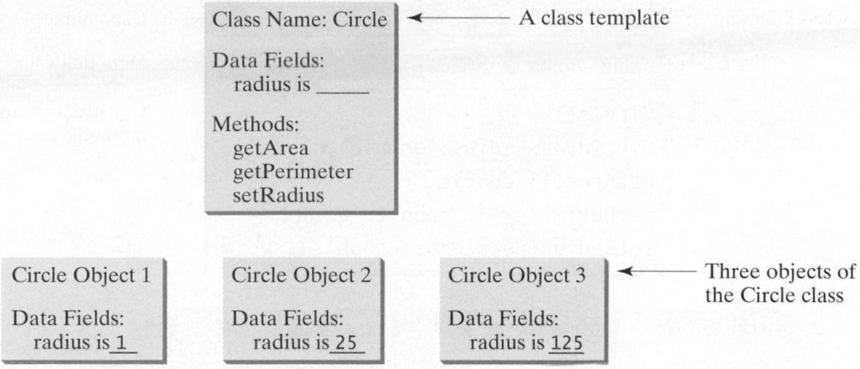

FIGURE 8.2 A class is a template for creating objects.

```
class Circle {
  /** The radius of this circle */
  double radius = 1;                                    ← Data field

  /** Construct a circle object */
  Circle() {
  }
                                                        ← Constructors
  /** Construct a circle object */
  Circle(double newRadius) {
    radius = newRadius;
  }

  /** Return the area of this circle */
  double getArea() {
    return radius * radius * Math.PI;
  }

  /** Return the perimeter of this circle */
  double getPerimeter() {                               ← Method
    return 2 * radius * Math.PI;
  }

  /** Set new radius for this circle */
  double setRadius(double newRadius) {
    radius = newRadius;
  }
}
```

FIGURE 8.3 A class is a construct that defines objects of the same type.

The `Circle` class is different from all of the other classes you have seen thus far. It does not have a `main` method and therefore cannot be run; it is merely a definition for circle objects. The class that contains the `main` method will be referred to in this book, for convenience, as the *main class*. main class

The illustration of class templates and objects in Figure 8.2 can be standardized using *Unified Modeling Language (UML)* notation. This notation, as shown in Figure 8.4, is called a *UML class diagram*, or simply a *class diagram*. In the class diagram, the data field is denoted as

Unified Modeling Language (UML)

class diagram

```
dataFieldName: dataFieldType
```

The constructor is denoted as

```
ClassName(parameterName: parameterType)
```

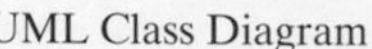

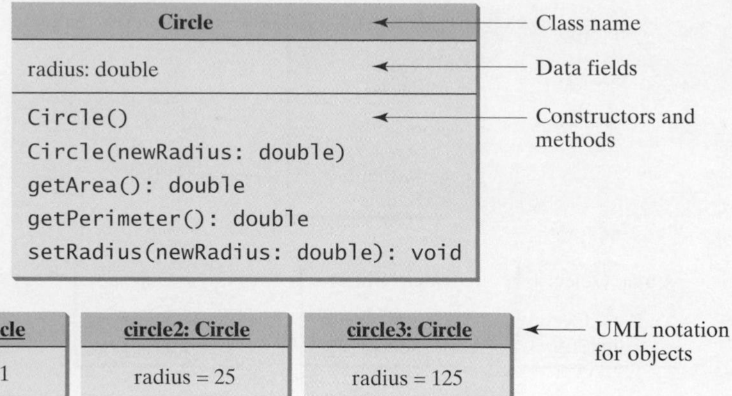

FIGURE 8.4 Classes and objects can be represented using UML notation.

The method is denoted as

```
methodName(parameterName: parameterType): returnType
```

8.3 Example: Defining Classes and Creating Objects

Key Point

Classes are definitions for objects and objects are created from classes.

This section gives two examples of defining classes and uses the classes to create objects. Listing 8.1 is a program that defines the `Circle` class and uses it to create objects. The program constructs three circle objects with radius `1`, `25`, and `125` and displays the radius and area of each of the three circles. It then changes the radius of the second object to `100` and displays its new radius and area.

avoid naming conflicts

Note

To avoid a naming conflict with several enhanced versions of the `Circle` class introduced later in the chapter, the `Circle` class in this example is named `SimpleCircle`. For simplicity, we will still refer to the class in the text as `Circle`.

LISTING 8.1 TestSimpleCircle.java

main class; main method; create object; create object; create object

```
public class TestSimpleCircle {
  /** Main method */
  public static void main(String[] args) {
    // Create a circle with radius 1
    SimpleCircle circle1 = new SimpleCircle();
    System.out.println("The area of the circle of radius "
      + circle1.radius + " is " + circle1.getArea());

    // Create a circle with radius 25
    SimpleCircle circle2 = new SimpleCircle(25);
    System.out.println("The area of the circle of radius "
      + circle2.radius + " is " + circle2.getArea());

    // Create a circle with radius 125
    SimpleCircle circle3 = new SimpleCircle(125);
    System.out.println("The area of the circle of radius "
      + circle3.radius + " is " + circle3.getArea());

    // Modify circle radius
    circle2.radius = 100; // or circle2.setRadius(100)
    System.out.println("The area of the circle of radius "
      + circle2.radius + " is " + circle2.getArea());
  }
```

```
}

// Define the circle class with two constructors
class SimpleCircle {
  double radius;

  /** Construct a circle with radius 1 */
  SimpleCircle() {
    radius = 1;
  }

  /** Construct a circle with a specified radius */
  SimpleCircle(double newRadius) {
    radius = newRadius;
  }

  /** Return the area of this circle */
  double getArea() {
    return radius * radius * Math.PI;
  }

  /** Return the perimeter of this circle */
  double getPerimeter() {
    return 2 * radius * Math.PI;
  }

  /** Set a new radius for this circle */
  void setRadius(double newRadius) {
    radius = newRadius;
  }
}
```

class `SimpleCircle`
data field
no-arg constructor
second constructor
`getArea`
`getPerimeter`
`setRadius`

```
The area of the circle of radius 1.0 is 3.141592653589793
The area of the circle of radius 25.0 is 1963.4954084936207
The area of the circle of radius 125.0 is 49087.385212340516
The area of the circle of radius 100.0 is 31415.926535897932
```

The program contains two classes. The first of these, `TestSimpleCircle`, is the main class. Its sole purpose is to test the second class, `SimpleCircle`. Such a program that uses the class is often referred to as a *client* of the class. When you run the program, the Java runtime system invokes the `main` method in the main class.

client

You can put the two classes into one file, but only one class in the file can be a *public class*. Furthermore, the public class must have the same name as the file name. Therefore, the file name is **TestSimpleCircle.java**, since `TestSimpleCircle` is public. Each class in the source code is compiled into a **.class** file. When you compile **TestSimpleCircle.java**, two class files **TestSimpleCircle.class** and **SimpleCircle.class** are generated, as shown in Figure 8.5.

public class

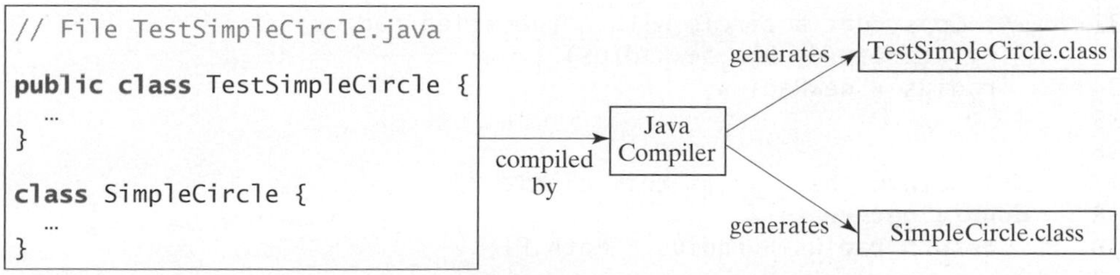

```
// File TestSimpleCircle.java
public class TestSimpleCircle {
  ...
}

class SimpleCircle {
  ...
}
```


FIGURE 8.5 Each class in the source code file is compiled into a **.class** file.

The main class contains the `main` method (line 3) that creates three objects. As in creating an array, the `new` operator is used to create an object from the constructor. `new SimpleCircle()` creates an object with radius `1` (line 5), `new SimpleCircle(25)` creates an object with radius `25` (line 10), and `new SimpleCircle(125)` creates an object with radius `125` (line 15).

These three objects (referenced by `circle1`, `circle2`, and `circle3`) have different data but the same methods. Therefore, you can compute their respective areas by using the `getArea()` method. The data fields can be accessed via the reference of the object using `circle1.radius`, `circle2.radius`, and `circle3.radius`, respectively. The object can invoke its method via the reference of the object using `circle1.getArea()`, `circle2.getArea()`, and `circle3.getArea()`, respectively.

These three objects are independent. The radius of `circle2` is changed to `100` in line 20. The object's new radius and area are displayed in lines 21–22.

There are many ways to write Java programs. For instance, you can combine the two classes in the example into one, as shown in Listing 8.2.

LISTING 8.2 SimpleCircle.java

main method (line 3); data field (line 25); no-arg constructor (line 28); second constructor (line 33); method (line 38)

```
 1 public class SimpleCircle {
 2   /** Main method */
 3   public static void main(String[] args) {
 4     // Create a circle with radius 1
 5     SimpleCircle circle1 = new SimpleCircle();
 6     System.out.println("The area of the circle of radius "
 7       + circle1.radius + " is " + circle1.getArea());
 8
 9     // Create a circle with radius 25
10     SimpleCircle circle2 = new SimpleCircle(25);
11     System.out.println("The area of the circle of radius "
12       + circle2.radius + " is " + circle2.getArea());
13
14     // Create a circle with radius 125
15     SimpleCircle circle3 = new SimpleCircle(125);
16     System.out.println("The area of the circle of radius "
17       + circle3.radius + " is " + circle3.getArea());
18
19     // Modify circle radius
20     circle2.radius = 100;
21     System.out.println("The area of the circle of radius "
22       + circle2.radius + " is " + circle2.getArea());
23   }
24
25   double radius;
26
27   /** Construct a circle with radius 1 */
28   SimpleCircle() {
29     radius = 1;
30   }
31
32   /** Construct a circle with a specified radius */
33   SimpleCircle(double newRadius) {
34     radius = newRadius;
35   }
36
37   /** Return the area of this circle */
38   double getArea() {
39     return radius * radius * Math.PI;
40   }
41
```

```
  /** Return the perimeter of this circle */
  double getPerimeter() {
    return 2 * radius * Math.PI;
  }

  /** Set a new radius for this circle */
  void setRadius(double newRadius) {
    radius = newRadius;
  }
}
```

Since the combined class has a `main` method, it can be executed by the Java interpreter. The `main` method is the same as in Listing 8.1. This demonstrates that you can test a class by simply adding a `main` method in the same class.

As another example, consider television sets. Each TV is an object with states (current channel, current volume level, power on or off) and behaviors (change channels, adjust volume, turn on/off). You can use a class to model TV sets. The UML diagram for the class is shown in Figure 8.6.

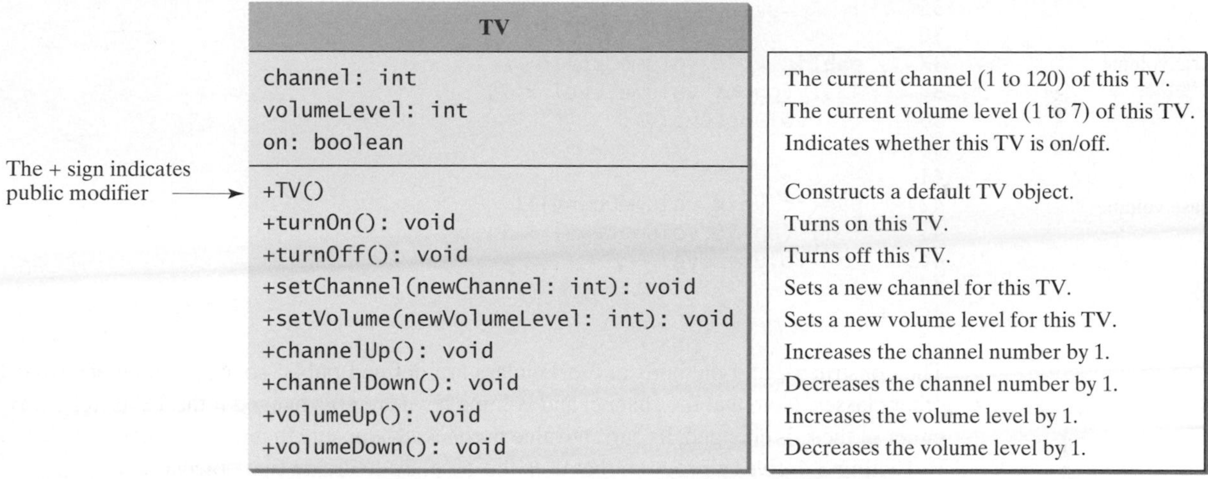

FIGURE 8.6 The TV class models TV sets.

Listing 8.3 gives a program that defines the `TV` class.

LISTING 8.3 TV.java

```
public class TV {
  int channel = 1; // Default channel is 1
  int volumeLevel = 1; // Default volume level is 1
  boolean on = false; // TV is off

  public TV() {
  }

  public void turnOn() {
    on = true;
  }

  public void turnOff() {
```

data fields

constructor

turn on TV

turn off TV

set a new channel
set a new volume
increase channel
decrease channel
increase volume
decrease volume

```
    on = false;
  }

  public void setChannel(int newChannel) {
    if (on && newChannel >= 1 && newChannel <= 120)
      channel = newChannel;
  }

  public void setVolume(int newVolumeLevel) {
    if (on && newVolumeLevel >= 1 && newVolumeLevel <= 7)
      volumeLevel = newVolumeLevel;
  }

  public void channelUp() {
    if (on && channel < 120)
      channel++;
  }

  public void channelDown() {
    if (on && channel > 1)
      channel--;
  }

  public void volumeUp() {
    if (on && volumeLevel < 7)
      volumeLevel++;
  }

  public void volumeDown() {
    if (on && volumeLevel > 1)
      volumeLevel--;
  }
}
```

The constructor and methods in the TV class are defined public so they can be accessed from other classes. Note that the channel and volume level are not changed if the TV is not on. Before either of these is changed, its current value is checked to ensure that it is within the correct range.

Listing 8.4 gives a program that uses the TV class to create two objects.

LISTING 8.4 TestTV.java

main method
create a TV
turn on
set a new channel
set a new volume
create a TV
turn on
increase channel
increase volume
display state

```
public class TestTV {
  public static void main(String[] args) {
    TV tv1 = new TV();
    tv1.turnOn();
    tv1.setChannel(30);
    tv1.setVolume(3);

    TV tv2 = new TV();
    tv2.turnOn();
    tv2.channelUp();
    tv2.channelUp();
    tv2.volumeUp();

    System.out.println("tv1's channel is " + tv1.channel
      + " and volume level is " + tv1.volumeLevel);
    System.out.println("tv2's channel is " + tv2.channel
      + " and volume level is " + tv2.volumeLevel);
  }
}
```

```
tv1's channel is 30 and volume level is 3
tv2's channel is 3 and volume level is 2
```

The program creates two objects in lines 3 and 8 and invokes the methods on the objects to perform actions for setting channels and volume levels and for increasing channels and volumes. The program displays the state of the objects in lines 14–17. The methods are invoked using syntax such as `tv1.turnOn()` (line 4). The data fields are accessed using syntax such as `tv1.channel` (line 14).

These examples have given you a glimpse of classes and objects. You may have many questions regarding constructors, objects, reference variables, accessing data fields, and invoking object's methods. The sections that follow discuss these issues in detail.

8.1 Describe the relationship between an object and its defining class.

8.2 How do you define a class?

8.3 How do you declare an object's reference variable?

8.4 How do you create an object?

8.4 Constructing Objects Using Constructors

A constructor is invoked to create an object using the `new` *operator.*

Key Point

Constructors are a special kind of method. They have three peculiarities:

- A constructor must have the same name as the class itself. (constructor's name)
- Constructors do not have a return type—not even `void`. (no return type)
- Constructors are invoked using the `new` operator when an object is created. Constructors play the role of initializing objects. (new operator)

The constructor has exactly the same name as its defining class. Like regular methods, constructors can be overloaded (i.e., multiple constructors can have the same name but different signatures), making it easy to construct objects with different initial data values. (overloaded constructors)

It is a common mistake to put the `void` keyword in front of a constructor. For example,

no `void`

```
public void Circle() {
}
```

In this case, `Circle()` is a method, not a constructor.

Constructors are used to construct objects. To construct an object from a class, invoke a constructor of the class using the `new` operator, as follows: (constructing objects)

```
new ClassName(arguments);
```

For example, `new Circle()` creates an object of the `Circle` class using the first constructor defined in the `Circle` class, and `new Circle(25)` creates an object using the second constructor defined in the `Circle` class.

A class normally provides a constructor without arguments (e.g., `Circle()`). Such a constructor is referred to as a *no-arg* or *no-argument constructor*. (no-arg constructor)

A class may be defined without constructors. In this case, a public no-arg constructor with an empty body is implicitly defined in the class. This constructor, called a *default constructor*, is provided automatically *only if no constructors are explicitly defined in the class*. (default constructor)

Check Point MyProgrammingLab™

8.5 What are the differences between constructors and methods?

8.6 When will a class have a default constructor?

8.5 Accessing Objects via Reference Variables

An object's data and methods can be accessed through the dot (`.`) operator via the object's reference variable.

Newly created objects are allocated in the memory. They can be accessed via reference variables.

8.5.1 Reference Variables and Reference Types

reference variable

Objects are accessed via the object's *reference variables*, which contain references to the objects. Such variables are declared using the following syntax:

```
ClassName objectRefVar;
```

reference type

A class is essentially a programmer-defined type. A class is a *reference type*, which means that a variable of the class type can reference an instance of the class. The following statement declares the variable `myCircle` to be of the `Circle` type:

```
Circle myCircle;
```

The variable `myCircle` can reference a `Circle` object. The next statement creates an object and assigns its reference to `myCircle`:

```
myCircle = new Circle();
```

You can write a single statement that combines the declaration of an object reference variable, the creation of an object, and the assigning of an object reference to the variable with the following syntax:

```
ClassName objectRefVar = new ClassName();
```

Here is an example:

```
Circle myCircle = new Circle();
```

The variable `myCircle` holds a reference to a `Circle` object.

object vs. object reference variable

Note

An object reference variable that appears to hold an object actually contains a reference to that object. Strictly speaking, an object reference variable and an object are different, but most of the time the distinction can be ignored. Therefore, it is fine, for simplicity, to say that `myCircle` is a `Circle` object rather than use the longer-winded description that `myCircle` is a variable that contains a reference to a `Circle` object.

array object

Note

Arrays are treated as objects in Java. Arrays are created using the `new` operator. An array variable is actually a variable that contains a reference to an array.

8.5.2 Accessing an Object's Data and Methods

dot operator (.)

In OOP terminology, an object's member refers to its data fields and methods. After an object is created, its data can be accessed and its methods invoked using the *dot operator* (`.`), also known as the *object member access operator*:

- `objectRefVar.dataField` references a data field in the object.
- `objectRefVar.method(arguments)` invokes a method on the object.

For example, `myCircle.radius` references the radius in `myCircle`, and `myCircle.getArea()` invokes the `getArea` method on `myCircle`. Methods are invoked as operations on objects.

The data field `radius` is referred to as an *instance variable*, because it is dependent on a specific instance. For the same reason, the method `getArea` is referred to as an *instance method*, because you can invoke it only on a specific instance. The object on which an instance method is invoked is called a *calling object*.

instance variable

instance method

calling object

Caution

Recall that you use `Math.methodName(arguments)` (e.g., `Math.pow(3, 2.5)`) to invoke a method in the `Math` class. Can you invoke `getArea()` using `Circle.getArea()`? The answer is no. All the methods in the `Math` class are static methods, which are defined using the `static` keyword. However, `getArea()` is an instance method, and thus nonstatic. It must be invoked from an object using `objectRefVar.methodName(arguments)` (e.g., `myCircle.getArea()`). Further explanation is given in Section 8.7, Static Variables, Constants, and Methods.

invoking methods

Note

Usually you create an object and assign it to a variable, and then later you can use the variable to reference the object. Occasionally an object does not need to be referenced later. In this case, you can create an object without explicitly assigning it to a variable using the syntax:

```
new Circle();
```

or

```
System.out.println("Area is " + new Circle(5).getArea());
```

The former statement creates a `Circle` object. The latter creates a `Circle` object and invokes its `getArea` method to return its area. An object created in this way is known as an *anonymous object*.

anonymous object

8.5.3 Reference Data Fields and the `null` Value

The data fields can be of reference types. For example, the following `Student` class contains a data field `name` of the `String` type. `String` is a predefined Java class.

reference data fields

```
class Student {
  String name; // name has the default value null
  int age; // age has the default value 0
  boolean isScienceMajor; // isScienceMajor has default value false
  char gender; // gender has default value '\u0000'
}
```

If a data field of a reference type does not reference any object, the data field holds a special Java value, `null`. `null` is a literal just like `true` and `false`. While `true` and `false` are Boolean literals, `null` is a literal for a reference type.

`null` value

The default value of a data field is `null` for a reference type, `0` for a numeric type, `false` for a `boolean` type, and `\u0000` for a `char` type. However, Java assigns no default value to a local variable inside a method. The following code displays the default values of the data fields `name`, `age`, `isScienceMajor`, and `gender` for a `Student` object:

default field values

```
class Test {
  public static void main(String[] args) {
    Student student = new Student();
    System.out.println("name? " + student.name);
```

```
    System.out.println("age? " + student.age);
    System.out.println("isScienceMajor? " + student.isScienceMajor);
    System.out.println("gender? " + student.gender);
  }
}
```

The following code has a compile error, because the local variables x and y are not initialized:

```
class Test {
  public static void main(String[] args) {
    int x; // x has no default value
    String y; // y has no default value
    System.out.println("x is " + x);
    System.out.println("y is " + y);
  }
}
```

NullPointerException

Caution

NullPointerException is a common runtime error. It occurs when you invoke a method on a reference variable with a **null** value. Make sure you assign an object reference to the variable before invoking the method through the reference variable.

8.5.4 Differences between Variables of Primitive Types and Reference Types

Every variable represents a memory location that holds a value. When you declare a variable, you are telling the compiler what type of value the variable can hold. For a variable of a primitive type, the value is of the primitive type. For a variable of a reference type, the value is a reference to where an object is located. For example, as shown in Figure 8.7, the value of int variable i is int value 1, and the value of Circle object c holds a reference to where the contents of the Circle object are stored in memory.

When you assign one variable to another, the other variable is set to the same value. For a variable of a primitive type, the real value of one variable is assigned to the other variable. For a variable of a reference type, the reference of one variable is assigned to the other variable. As shown in Figure 8.8, the assignment statement i = j copies the contents of j into i for

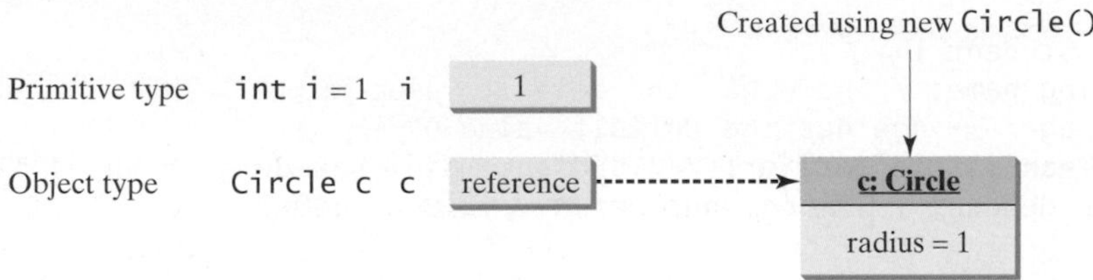

FIGURE 8.7 A variable of a primitive type holds a value of the primitive type, and a variable of a reference type holds a reference to where an object is stored in memory.

Primitive type assignment i = j

	Before:		After:
i	1	i	2
j	2	j	2

FIGURE 8.8 Primitive variable j is copied to variable i.

primitive variables. As shown in Figure 8.9, the assignment statement `c1 = c2` copies the reference of `c2` into `c1` for reference variables. After the assignment, variables `c1` and `c2` refer to the same object.

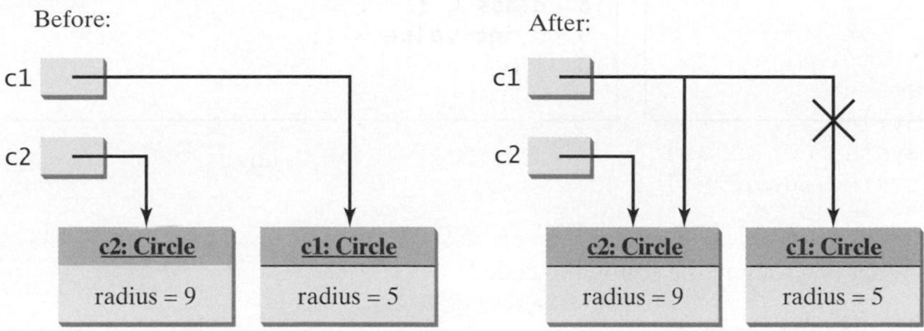

FIGURE 8.9 Reference variable `c2` is copied to variable `c1`.

Note

As illustrated in Figure 8.9, after the assignment statement `c1 = c2`, `c1` points to the same object referenced by `c2`. The object previously referenced by `c1` is no longer useful and therefore is now known as *garbage*. Garbage occupies memory space, so the Java runtime system detects garbage and automatically reclaims the space it occupies. This process is called *garbage collection*.

garbage

garbage collection

Tip

If you know that an object is no longer needed, you can explicitly assign `null` to a reference variable for the object. The JVM will automatically collect the space if the object is not referenced by any reference variable.

Check Point
MyProgrammingLab™

8.7 Which operator is used to access a data field or invoke a method from an object?

8.8 What is an anonymous object?

8.9 What is `NullPointerException`?

8.10 Is an array an object or a primitive type value? Can an array contain elements of an object type as well as a primitive type? Describe the default value for the elements of an array.

8.11 What is wrong with each of the following programs?

```
public class ShowErrors {
  public static void main(String[] args) {
    ShowErrors t = new ShowErrors(5);
  }
}
```

(a)

```
public class ShowErrors {
  public static void main(String[] args) {
    ShowErrors t = new ShowErrors();
    t.x();
  }
}
```

(b)

```
public class ShowErrors {
  public void method1() {
    Circle c;
    System.out.println("What is radius "
      + c.getRadius());
    c = new Circle();
  }
}
```

(c)

```
public class ShowErrors {
  public static void main(String[] args) {
    C c = new C(5.0);
    System.out.println(c.value);
  }
}

class C {
  int value = 2;
}
```

(d)

8.12 What is wrong in the following code?

```
class Test {
  public static void main(String[] args) {
    A a = new A();
    a.print();
  }
}

class A {
  String s;

  A(String newS) {
    s = newS;
  }

  public void print() {
    System.out.print(s);
  }
}
```

8.13 What is the printout of the following code?

```
public class A {
  private boolean x;

  public static void main(String[] args) {
    A a = new A();
    System.out.println(a.x);
  }
}
```

8.6 Using Classes from the Java Library

The Java API contains a rich set of classes for developing Java programs.

Listing 8.1 defined the `SimpleCircle` class and created objects from the class. You will frequently use the classes in the Java library to develop programs. This section gives some examples of the classes in the Java library.

8.6.1 The `Date` Class

In Listing 2.6, ShowCurrentTime.java, you learned how to obtain the current time using `System.currentTimeMillis()`. You used the division and remainder operators to extract the current second, minute, and hour. Java provides a system-independent encapsulation of date and time in the **java.util.Date** class, as shown in Figure 8.10.

java.util.Date class

java.util.Date	
+Date()	Constructs a Date object for the current time.
+Date(elapseTime: long)	Constructs a Date object for a given time in milliseconds elapsed since January 1, 1970, GMT.
+toString(): String	Returns a string representing the date and time.
+getTime(): long	Returns the number of milliseconds since January 1, 1970, GMT.
+setTime(elapseTime: long): void	Sets a new elapse time in the object.

FIGURE 8.10 A **Date** object represents a specific date and time.

You can use the no-arg constructor in the **Date** class to create an instance for the current date and time, the **getTime()** method to return the elapsed time since January 1, 1970, GMT, and the **toString()** method to return the date and time as a string. For example, the following code

```
java.util.Date date = new java.util.Date();                      // create object
System.out.println("The elapsed time since Jan 1, 1970 is " +
  date.getTime() + " milliseconds");                             // get elapsed time
System.out.println(date.toString());                             // invoke toString
```

displays the output like this:

```
The elapsed time since Jan 1, 1970 is 1324903419651 milliseconds
Mon Dec 26 07:43:39 EST 2011
```

The **Date** class has another constructor, **Date(long elapseTime)**, which can be used to construct a **Date** object for a given time in milliseconds elapsed since January 1, 1970, GMT.

8.6.2 The Random Class

You have used **Math.random()** to obtain a random **double** value between **0.0** and **1.0** (excluding **1.0**). Another way to generate random numbers is to use the **java.util.Random** class, as shown in Figure 8.11, which can generate a random **int**, **long**, **double**, **float**, and **boolean** value.

java.util.Random	
+Random()	Constructs a Random object with the current time as its seed.
+Random(seed: long)	Constructs a Random object with a specified seed.
+nextInt(): int	Returns a random int value.
+nextInt(n: int): int	Returns a random int value between 0 and n (excluding n).
+nextLong(): long	Returns a random long value.
+nextDouble(): double	Returns a random double value between 0.0 and 1.0 (excluding 1.0).
+nextFloat(): float	Returns a random float value between 0.0F and 1.0F (excluding 1.0F).
+nextBoolean(): boolean	Returns a random boolean value.

FIGURE 8.11 A **Random** object can be used to generate random values.

When you create a Random object, you have to specify a seed or use the default seed. A seed is a number used to initialize a random number generator. The no-arg constructor creates a Random object using the current elapsed time as its seed. If two Random objects have the same seed, they will generate identical sequences of numbers. For example, the following code creates two Random objects with the same seed, 3.

```
Random random1 = new Random(3);
System.out.print("From random1: ");
for (int i = 0; i < 10; i++)
  System.out.print(random1.nextInt(1000) + " ");

Random random2 = new Random(3);
System.out.print("\nFrom random2: ");
for (int i = 0; i < 10; i++)
  System.out.print(random2.nextInt(1000) + " ");
```

The code generates the same sequence of random int values:

```
From random1: 734 660 210 581 128 202 549 564 459 961
From random2: 734 660 210 581 128 202 549 564 459 961
```

same sequence

Note

The ability to generate the same sequence of random values is useful in software testing and many other applications. In software testing, often you need to reproduce the test cases from a fixed sequence of random numbers.

8.6.3 Displaying GUI Components

Pedagogical Note

Graphical user interface (GUI) components are good examples for teaching OOP. Simple GUI examples are introduced here for this purpose. The full introduction to GUI programming begins with Chapter 12, GUI Basics.

When you develop programs to create graphical user interfaces, you will use Java classes such as JFrame, JButton, JRadioButton, JComboBox, and JList to create frames, buttons, radio buttons, combo boxes, lists, and so on. Listing 8.5 is an example that creates two windows using the JFrame class. The output of the program is shown in Figure 8.12.

FIGURE 8.12 The program creates two windows using the JFrame class.

LISTING 8.5 TestFrame.java

create an object
invoke a method

```
import javax.swing.JFrame;

public class TestFrame {
  public static void main(String[] args) {
    JFrame frame1 = new JFrame();
    frame1.setTitle("Window 1");
    frame1.setSize(200, 150);
    frame1.setLocation(200, 100);
    frame1.setDefaultCloseOperation(JFrame.EXIT_ON_CLOSE);
    frame1.setVisible(true);
```

```
11
12       JFrame frame2 = new JFrame();
13       frame2.setTitle("Window 2");
14       frame2.setSize(200, 150);
15       frame2.setLocation(410, 100);
16       frame2.setDefaultCloseOperation(JFrame.EXIT_ON_CLOSE);
17       frame2.setVisible(true);
18     }
19   }
```

create an object
invoke a method

This program creates two objects of the `JFrame` class (lines 5, 12) and then uses the methods `setTitle`, `setSize`, `setLocation`, `setDefaultCloseOperation`, and `setVisible` to set the properties of the objects. The `setTitle` method sets a title for the window (lines 6, 13). The `setSize` method sets the window's width and height (lines 7, 14). The `setLocation` method specifies the location of the window's upper-left corner (lines 8, 15). The `setDefaultCloseOperation` method terminates the program when the frame is closed (lines 9, 16). The `setVisible` method displays the window.

You can add graphical user interface components, such as buttons, labels, text fields, check boxes, and combo boxes to the window. The components are defined using classes. Listing 8.6 gives an example of creating a graphical user interface, as shown in Figure 8.1.

LISTING 8.6 GUIComponents.java

VideoNote
Use classes

```java
import javax.swing.*;

public class GUIComponents {
  public static void main(String[] args) {
    // Create a button with text OK
    JButton jbtOK = new JButton("OK");

    // Create a button with text Cancel
    JButton jbtCancel = new JButton("Cancel");

    // Create a label with text "Enter your name: "
    JLabel jlblName = new JLabel("Enter your name: ");

    // Create a text field with text "Type Name Here"
    JTextField jtfName = new JTextField("Type Name Here");

    // Create a check box with text Bold
    JCheckBox jchkBold = new JCheckBox("Bold");

    // Create a check box with text Italic
    JCheckBox jchkItalic = new JCheckBox("Italic");

    // Create a radio button with text Red
    JRadioButton jrbRed = new JRadioButton("Red");

    // Create a radio button with text Yellow
    JRadioButton jrbYellow = new JRadioButton("Yellow");

    // Create a combo box with several choices
    JComboBox jcboColor = new JComboBox(new String[]{"Freshman",
      "Sophomore", "Junior", "Senior"});

    // Create a panel to group components
    JPanel panel = new JPanel();
    panel.add(jbtOK); // Add the OK button to the panel
    panel.add(jbtCancel); // Add the Cancel button to the panel
```

create a button
create a button
create a label
create a text field
create a check box
create a check box
create a radio button
create a radio button
create a combo box
create a panel
add to panel

create a frame
add panel to frame
display frame

```
37     panel.add(jlblName); // Add the label to the panel
38     panel.add(jtfName); // Add the text field to the panel
39     panel.add(jchkBold); // Add the check box to the panel
40     panel.add(jchkItalic); // Add the check box to the panel
41     panel.add(jrbRed); // Add the radio button to the panel
42     panel.add(jrbYellow); // Add the radio button to the panel
43     panel.add(jcboColor); // Add the combo box to the panel
44
45     JFrame frame = new JFrame(); // Create a frame
46     frame.add(panel); // Add the panel to the frame
47     frame.setTitle("Show GUI Components");
48     frame.setSize(450, 100);
49     frame.setLocation(200, 100);
50     frame.setDefaultCloseOperation(JFrame.EXIT_ON_CLOSE);
51     frame.setVisible(true);
52   }
53 }
```

This program creates GUI objects using the classes **JButton**, **JLabel**, **JTextField**, **JCheckBox**, **JRadioButton**, and **JComboBox** (lines 6–31). Then, using the **JPanel** class (line 34), it then creates a panel object and adds the button, label, text field, check box, radio button, and combo box to it (lines 35–43). The program then creates a frame and adds the panel to the frame (line 45). The frame is displayed in line 51.

MyProgrammingLab™

8.14 How do you create a **Date** for the current time? How do you display the current time?

8.15 How do you create a **JFrame**, set a title in a frame, and display a frame?

8.16 Which packages contain the classes **Date**, **JFrame**, **JOptionPane**, **System**, and **Math**?

8.7 Static Variables, Constants, and Methods

A static variable is shared by all objects of the class. A static method cannot access instance members of the class.

VideoNote
Static vs. instance

instance variable

The data field **radius** in the circle class is known as an *instance variable*. An instance variable is tied to a specific instance of the class; it is not shared among objects of the same class. For example, suppose that you create the following objects:

```
Circle circle1 = new Circle();
Circle circle2 = new Circle(5);
```

The **radius** in **circle1** is independent of the **radius** in **circle2** and is stored in a different memory location. Changes made to **circle1**'s **radius** do not affect **circle2**'s **radius**, and vice versa.

static variable

If you want all the instances of a class to share data, use *static variables*, also known as *class variables*. Static variables store values for the variables in a common memory location. Because of this common location, if one object changes the value of a static variable, all objects of the same class are affected. Java supports static methods as well as static variables. *Static methods* can be called without creating an instance of the class.

static method

Let's modify the **Circle** class by adding a static variable **numberOfObjects** to count the number of circle objects created. When the first object of this class is created, **numberOfObjects** is **1**. When the second object is created, **numberOfObjects** becomes **2**. The UML of the new circle class is shown in Figure 8.13. The **Circle** class defines the instance variable **radius** and the static variable **numberOfObjects**, the instance methods **getRadius**, **setRadius**, and **getArea**, and the static method **getNumberOfObjects**. (Note that static variables and methods are underlined in the UML class diagram.)

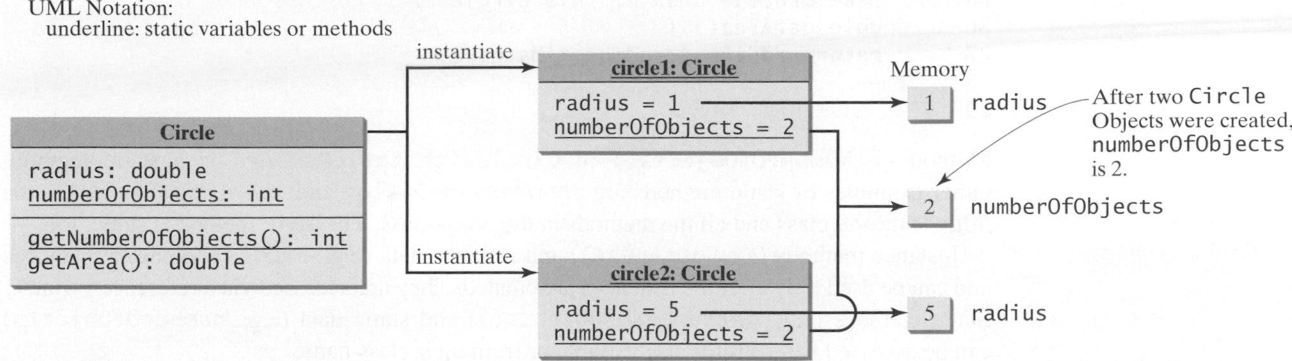

FIGURE 8.13 Instance variables belong to the instances and have memory storage independent of one another. Static variables are shared by all the instances of the same class.

To declare a static variable or define a static method, put the modifier `static` in the variable or method declaration. The static variable `numberOfObjects` and the static method `getNumberOfObjects()` can be declared as follows:

```
static int numberOfObjects;

static int getNumberObjects() {
  return numberOfObjects;
}
```

declare static variable

define static method

Constants in a class are shared by all objects of the class. Thus, constants should be declared as `final static`. For example, the constant `PI` in the `Math` class is defined as:

declare constant

```
final static double PI = 3.14159265358979323846;
```

The new circle class, named `CircleWithStaticMembers`, is defined in Listing 8.7:

LISTING 8.7 CircleWithStaticMembers.java

```
public class CircleWithStaticMembers {
  /** The radius of the circle */
  double radius;

  /** The number of objects created */
  static int numberOfObjects = 0;

  /** Construct a circle with radius 1 */
  CircleWithStaticMembers() {
    radius = 1;
    numberOfObjects++;
  }

  /** Construct a circle with a specified radius */
  CircleWithStaticMembers(double newRadius) {
    radius = newRadius;
    numberOfObjects++;
  }

  /** Return numberOfObjects */
  static int getNumberOfObjects() {
    return numberOfObjects;
  }

```

static variable

increase by 1

increase by 1

static method

```
  /** Return the area of this circle */
  double getArea() {
    return radius * radius * Math.PI;
  }
}
```

Method `getNumberOfObjects()` in `CircleWithStaticMembers` is a static method. Other examples of static methods are `showMessageDialog` and `showInputDialog` in the `JOptionPane` class and all the methods in the `Math` class. The `main` method is static, too.

Instance methods (e.g., `getArea()`) and instance data (e.g., `radius`) belong to instances and can be used only after the instances are created. They are accessed via a reference variable. Static methods (e.g., `getNumberOfObjects()`) and static data (e.g., `numberOfObjects`) can be accessed from a reference variable or from their class name.

The program in Listing 8.8 demonstrates how to use instance and static variables and methods and illustrates the effects of using them.

LISTING 8.8 TestCircleWithStaticMembers.java

static variable
instance variable
static variable
instance variable
static variable
static variable

```
public class TestCircleWithStaticMembers {
  /** Main method */
  public static void main(String[] args) {
    System.out.println("Before creating objects");
    System.out.println("The number of Circle objects is " +
      CircleWithStaticMembers.numberOfObjects);

    // Create c1
    CircleWithStaticMembers c1 = new CircleWithStaticMembers();

    // Display c1 BEFORE c2 is created
    System.out.println("\nAfter creating c1");
    System.out.println("c1: radius (" + c1.radius +
      ") and number of Circle objects (" +
      c1.numberOfObjects + ")");

    // Create c2
    CircleWithStaticMembers c2 = new CircleWithStaticMembers(5);

    // Modify c1
    c1.radius = 9;

    // Display c1 and c2 AFTER c2 was created
    System.out.println("\nAfter creating c2 and modifying c1");
    System.out.println("c1: radius (" + c1.radius +
      ") and number of Circle objects (" +
      c1.numberOfObjects + ")");
    System.out.println("c2: radius (" + c2.radius +
      ") and number of Circle objects (" +
      c2.numberOfObjects + ")");
  }
}
```

```
Before creating objects
The number of Circle objects is 0
After creating c1
c1: radius (1.0) and number of Circle objects (1)
After creating c2 and modifying c1
c1: radius (9.0) and number of Circle objects (2)
c2: radius (5.0) and number of Circle objects (2)
```

When you compile `TestCircleWithStaticMembers.java`, the Java compiler automatically compiles `CircleWithStaticMembers.java` if it has not been compiled since the last change.

Static variables and methods can be accessed without creating objects. Line 6 displays the number of objects, which is `0`, since no objects have been created.

The `main` method creates two circles, `c1` and `c2` (lines 9, 18). The instance variable `radius` in `c1` is modified to become `9` (line 21). This change does not affect the instance variable `radius` in `c2`, since these two instance variables are independent. The static variable `numberOfObjects` becomes `1` after `c1` is created (line 9), and it becomes `2` after `c2` is created (line 18).

Note that `PI` is a constant defined in `Math`, and `Math.PI` references the constant. `c1.numberOfObjects` (line 27) and `c2.numberOfObjects` (line 30) are better replaced by `CircleWithStaticMembers.numberOfObjects`. This improves readability, because other programmers can easily recognize the static variable. You can also replacc `CircleWithStaticMembers.numberOfObjects` with `CircleWithStaticMembers.getNumberOfObjects()`.

Tip

Use `ClassName.methodName(arguments)` to invoke a static method and `ClassName.staticVariable` to access a static variable. This improves readability, because other programmers can easily recognize the static method and data in the class.

use class name

An instance method can invoke an instance or static method and access an instance or static data field. A static method can invoke a static method and access a static data field. However, a static method cannot invoke an instance method or access an instance data field, since static methods and static data fields don't belong to a particular object. The relationship between static and instance members is summarized in the following diagram:

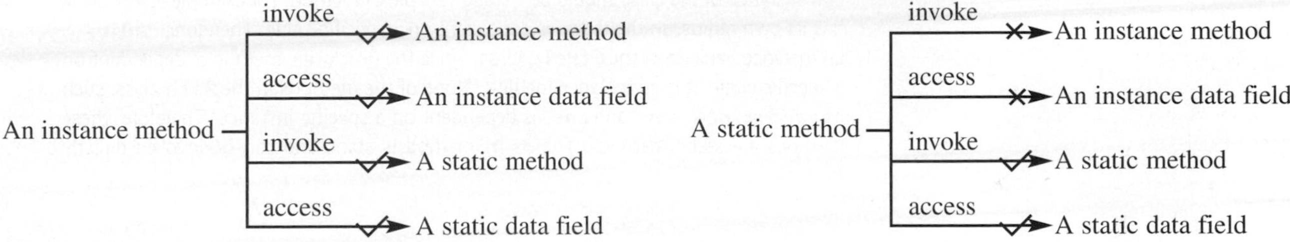

For example, the following code is wrong.

```
public class A {
  int i = 5;
  static int k = 2;

  public static void main(String[] args) {
    int j = i; // Wrong because i is an instance variable
    m1(); // Wrong because m1() is an instance method
  }

  public void m1() {
    // Correct since instance and static variables and methods
    // can be used in an instance method
    i = i + k + m2(i, k);
  }

  public static int m2(int i, int j) {
    return (int)(Math.pow(i, j));
  }
}
```

Note that if you replace the preceding code with the following new code, the program would be fine, because the instance data field `i` and method `m1` are now accessed from an object `a` (lines 7–8):

```
1  public class A {
2    int i = 5;
3    static int k = 2;
4
5    public static void main(String[] args) {
6      A a = new A();
7      int j = a.i; // OK, a.i accesses the object's instance variable
8      a.m1(); // OK. a.m1() invokes the object's instance method
9    }
10
11   public void m1() {
12     i = i + k + m2(i, k);
13   }
14
15   public static int m2(int i, int j) {
16     return (int)(Math.pow(i, j));
17   }
18 }
```

instance or static?

Design Guide

How do you decide whether a variable or method should be an instance one or a static one? A variable or method that is dependent on a specific instance of the class should be an instance variable or method. A variable or method that is not dependent on a specific instance of the class should be a static variable or method. For example, every circle has its own radius, so the radius is dependent on a specific circle. Therefore, `radius` is an instance variable of the `Circle` class. Since the `getArea` method is dependent on a specific circle, it is an instance method. None of the methods in the `Math` class, such as `random`, `pow`, `sin`, and `cos`, is dependent on a specific instance. Therefore, these methods are static methods. The `main` method is static and can be invoked directly from a class.

common design error

Caution

It is a common design error to define an instance method that should have been defined as static. For example, the method `factorial(int n)` should be defined as static, as shown next, because it is independent of any specific instance.

```
public class Test {
  public int factorial(int n) {
    int result = 1;
    for (int i = 1; i <= n; i++)
      result *= i;

    return result;
  }
}
```

(a) Wrong design

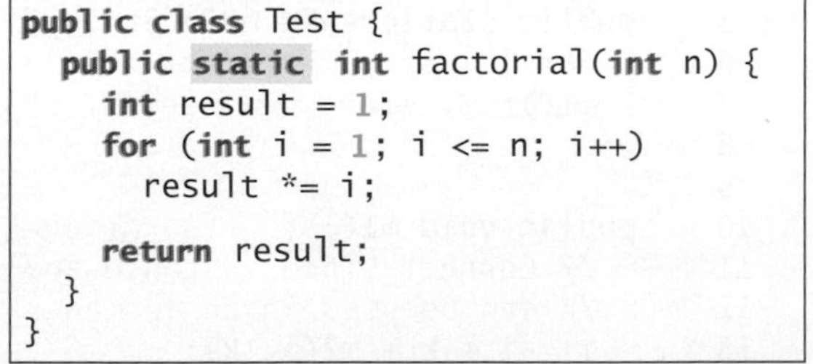

```
public class Test {
  public static int factorial(int n) {
    int result = 1;
    for (int i = 1; i <= n; i++)
      result *= i;

    return result;
  }
}
```

(b) Correct design

8.17 Suppose that the class `F` is defined in (a). Let `f` be an instance of `F`. Which of the statements in (b) are correct?

```
public class F {
  int i;
  static String s;

  void imethod() {
  }

  static void smethod() {
  }
}
```

(a)

```
System.out.println(f.i);
System.out.println(f.s);
f.imethod();
f.smethod();
System.out.println(F.i);
System.out.println(F.s);
F.imethod();
F.smethod();
```

(b)

8.18 Add the `static` keyword in the place of `?` if appropriate.

```
public class Test {
  private int count;

  public ? void main(String[] args) {
    ...
  }

  public ? int getCount() {
    return count;
  }

  public ? int factorial(int n) {
    int result = 1;
    for (int i = 1; i <= n; i++)
      result *= i;

    return result;
  }
}
```

8.19 Can you invoke an instance method or reference an instance variable from a static method? Can you invoke a static method or reference a static variable from an instance method? What is wrong in the following code?

```
public class C {
  public static void main(String[] args) {
    method1();
  }

  public void method1() {
    method2();
  }

  public static void method2() {
    System.out.println("What is radius " + c.getRadius());
  }

  Circle c = new Circle();
}
```

8.8 Visibility Modifiers

Visibility modifiers can be used to specify the visibility of a class and its members.

You can use the `public` visibility modifier for classes, methods, and data fields to denote that they can be accessed from any other classes. If no visibility modifier is used, then by default the classes, methods, and data fields are accessible by any class in the same package. This is known as *package-private* or *package-access*.

package-private (or package-access)

using packages

Note

Packages can be used to organize classes. To do so, you need to add the following line as the first noncomment and nonblank statement in the program:

```
package packageName;
```

If a class is defined without the package statement, it is said to be placed in the *default package*.

Java recommends that you place classes into packages rather using a default package. For simplicity, however, this book uses default packages. For more information on packages, see Supplement III.G, Packages.

In addition to the `public` and default visibility modifiers, Java provides the `private` and `protected` modifiers for class members. This section introduces the `private` modifier. The `protected` modifier will be introduced in Section 11.13, The `protected` Data and Methods.

The `private` modifier makes methods and data fields accessible only from within its own class. Figure 8.14 illustrates how a public, default, and private data field or method in class `C1` can be accessed from a class `C2` in the same package and from a class `C3` in a different package.

```
package p1;

public class C1 {
  public int x;
  int y;
  private int z;

  public void m1() {
  }
  void m2() {
  }
  private void m3() {
  }
}
```

```
package p1;

public class C2 {
  void aMethod() {
    C1 o = new C1();
    can access o.x;
    can access o.y;
    cannot access o.z;

    can invoke o.m1();
    can invoke o.m2();
    cannot invoke o.m3();
  }
}
```

```
package p2;

public class C3 {
  void aMethod() {
    C1 o = new C1();
    can access o.x;
    cannot access o.y;
    cannot access o.z;

    can invoke o.m1();
    cannot invoke o.m2();
    cannot invoke o.m3();
  }
}
```

FIGURE 8.14 The private modifier restricts access to its defining class, the default modifier restricts access to a package, and the public modifier enables unrestricted access.

If a class is not defined as public, it can be accessed only within the same package. As shown in Figure 8.15, `C1` can be accessed from `C2` but not from `C3`.

```
package p1;

class C1 {
  ...
}
```

```
package p1;

public class C2 {
  can access C1
}
```

```
package p2;

public class C3 {
  cannot access C1;
  can access C2;
}
```

FIGURE 8.15 A nonpublic class has package-access.

inside access

A visibility modifier specifies how data fields and methods in a class can be accessed from outside the class. There is no restriction on accessing data fields and methods from inside the class. As shown in Figure 8.16b, an object `c` of class `C` cannot access its private members, because `c` is in the `Test` class. As shown in Figure 8.16a, an object `c` of class `C` can access its private members, because `c` is defined inside its own class.

```java
public class C {
  private boolean x;

  public static void main(String[] args) {
    C c = new C();
    System.out.println(c.x);
    System.out.println(c.convert());
  }

  private int convert() {
    return x ? 1 : -1;
  }
}
```

(a) This is okay because object c is used inside the class C.

```java
public class Test {
  public static void main(String[] args) {
    C c = new C();
    System.out.println(c.x);
    System.out.println(c.convert());
  }
}
```

(b) This is wrong because x and convert are private in class C.

FIGURE 8.16 An object can access its private members if it is defined in its own class.

Caution

The `private` modifier applies only to the members of a class. The `public` modifier can apply to a class or members of a class. Using the modifiers `public` and `private` on local variables would cause a compile error.

Note

In most cases, the constructor should be public. However, if you want to prohibit the user from creating an instance of a class, use a *private constructor*. For example, there is no reason to create an instance from the `Math` class, because all of its data fields and methods are static. To prevent the user from creating objects from the `Math` class, the constructor in `java.lang.Math` is defined as follows:

private constructor

```java
private Math() {
}
```

8.9 Data Field Encapsulation

Making data fields private protects data and makes the class easy to maintain.

VideoNote

Data field encapsulation

The data fields `radius` and `numberOfObjects` in the `CircleWithStaticMembers` class in Listing 8.7 can be modified directly (e.g., `c1.radius = 5` or `CircleWithStaticMembers.numberOfObjects = 10`). This is not a good practice—for two reasons:

- First, data may be tampered with. For example, `numberOfObjects` is to count the number of objects created, but it may be mistakenly set to an arbitrary value (e.g., `CircleWithStaticMembers.numberOfObjects = 10`).
- Second, the class becomes difficult to maintain and vulnerable to bugs. Suppose you want to modify the `CircleWithStaticMembers` class to ensure that the radius is nonnegative after other programs have already used the class. You have to change not only the `CircleWithStaticMembers` class but also the programs that use it, because the clients may have modified the radius directly (e.g., `c1.radius = -5`).

To prevent direct modifications of data fields, you should declare the data fields private, using the `private` modifier. This is known as *data field encapsulation*.

data field encapsulation

A private data field cannot be accessed by an object from outside the class that defines the private field. However, a client often needs to retrieve and modify a data field. To make a private data field accessible, provide a *get* method to return its value. To enable a private data field to be updated, provide a *set* method to set a new value.

getter (or accessor)
setter (or mutator)

Note

Colloquially, a `get` method is referred to as a *getter* (or *accessor*), and a `set` method is referred to as a *setter* (or *mutator*).

A `get` method has the following signature:

```
public returnType getPropertyName()
```

boolean accessor

If the `returnType` is `boolean`, the `get` method should be defined as follows by convention:

```
public boolean isPropertyName()
```

A `set` method has the following signature:

```
public void setPropertyName(dataType propertyValue)
```

Let's create a new circle class with a private data-field radius and its associated accessor and mutator methods. The class diagram is shown in Figure 8.17. The new circle class, named `CircleWithPrivateDataFields`, is defined in Listing 8.9:

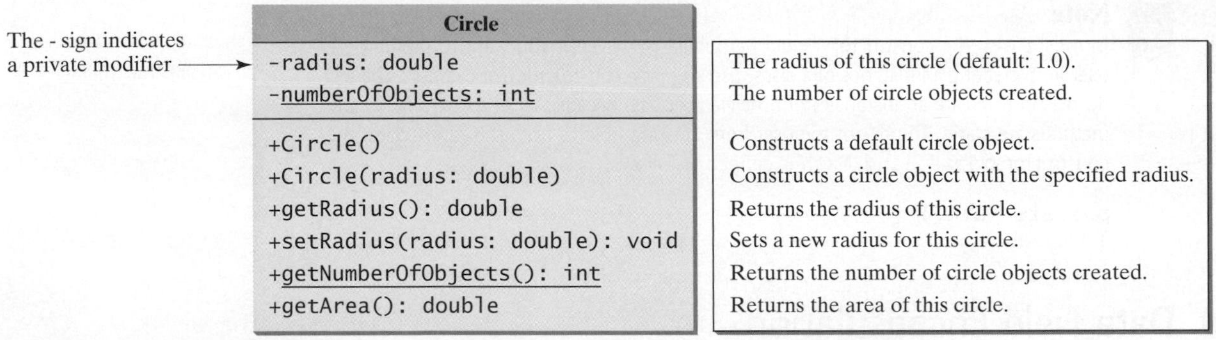

The - sign indicates a private modifier →

Circle	
-radius: double	The radius of this circle (default: 1.0).
-numberOfObjects: int	The number of circle objects created.
+Circle()	Constructs a default circle object.
+Circle(radius: double)	Constructs a circle object with the specified radius.
+getRadius(): double	Returns the radius of this circle.
+setRadius(radius: double): void	Sets a new radius for this circle.
+getNumberOfObjects(): int	Returns the number of circle objects created.
+getArea(): double	Returns the area of this circle.

FIGURE 8.17 The `Circle` class encapsulates circle properties and provides get/set and other methods.

LISTING 8.9 CircleWithPrivateDataFields.java

encapsulate `radius`

encapsulate `numberOfObjects`

```
public class CircleWithPrivateDataFields {
  /** The radius of the circle */
  private double radius = 1;

  /** The number of objects created */
  private static int numberOfObjects = 0;

  /** Construct a circle with radius 1 */
  public CircleWithPrivateDataFields() {
    numberOfObjects++;
  }

  /** Construct a circle with a specified radius */
  public CircleWithPrivateDataFields(double newRadius) {
    radius = newRadius;
```

```
16     numberOfObjects++;
17   }
18 
19   /** Return radius */
20   public double getRadius() {
21     return radius;
22   }
23 
24   /** Set a new radius */
25   public void setRadius(double newRadius) {
26     radius = (newRadius >= 0) ? newRadius : 0;
27   }
28 
29   /** Return numberOfObjects */
30   public static int getNumberOfObjects() {
31     return numberOfObjects;
32   }
33 
34   /** Return the area of this circle */
35   public double getArea() {
36     return radius * radius * Math.PI;
37   }
38 }
```

accessor method

mutator method

accessor method

The `getRadius()` method (lines 20–22) returns the radius, and the `setRadius(newRadius)` method (line 25–27) sets a new radius for the object. If the new radius is negative, `0` is set as the radius for the object. Since these methods are the only ways to read and modify the radius, you have total control over how the `radius` property is accessed. If you have to change the implementation of these methods, you don't need to change the client programs. This makes the class easy to maintain.

Listing 8.10 gives a client program that uses the `Circle` class to create a `Circle` object and modifies the radius using the `setRadius` method.

LISTING 8.10 TestCircleWithPrivateDataFields.java

```
public class TestCircleWithPrivateDataFields {
  /** Main method */
  public static void main(String[] args) {
    // Create a circle with radius 5.0
    CircleWithPrivateDataFields myCircle =
      new CircleWithPrivateDataFields(5.0);
    System.out.println("The area of the circle of radius "
      + myCircle.getRadius() + " is " + myCircle.getArea());

    // Increase myCircle's radius by 10%
    myCircle.setRadius(myCircle.getRadius() * 1.1);
    System.out.println("The area of the circle of radius "
      + myCircle.getRadius() + " is " + myCircle.getArea());

    System.out.println("The number of objects created is "
      + CircleWithPrivateDataFields.getNumberOfObjects());
  }
}
```

invoke public method

invoke public method

invoke public method

The data field `radius` is declared private. Private data can be accessed only within their defining class, so you cannot use `myCircle.radius` in the client program. A compile error would occur if you attempted to access private data from a client.

Since `numberOfObjects` is private, it cannot be modified. This prevents tampering. For example, the user cannot set `numberOfObjects` to `100`. The only way to make it `100` is to create `100` objects of the `Circle` class.

Suppose you combined `TestCircleWithPrivateDataFields` and `Circle` into one class by moving the `main` method in `TestCircleWithPrivateDataFields` into `Circle`. Could you use `myCircle.radius` in the `main` method? See Checkpoint Question 8.22 for the answer.

Design Guide

To prevent data from being tampered with and to make the class easy to maintain, declare data fields private.

MyProgrammingLab™

8.20 What is an accessor method? What is a mutator method? What are the naming conventions for accessor methods and mutator methods?

8.21 What are the benefits of data field encapsulation?

8.22 In the following code, `radius` is private in the `Circle` class, and `myCircle` is an object of the `Circle` class. Does the highlighted code cause any problems? If so, explain why.

```
public class Circle {
  private double radius = 1;

  /** Find the area of this circle */
  public double getArea() {
    return radius * radius * Math.PI;
  }

  public static void main(String[] args) {
    Circle myCircle = new Circle();
    System.out.println("Radius is " + myCircle.radius);
  }
}
```

8.10 Passing Objects to Methods

Passing an object to a method is to pass the reference of the object.

You can pass objects to methods. Like passing an array, passing an object is actually passing the reference of the object. The following code passes the `myCircle` object as an argument to the `printCircle` method:

pass an object

```
public class Test {
  public static void main(String[] args) {
    // CircleWithPrivateDataFields is defined in Listing 8.9
    CircleWithPrivateDataFields myCircle = new
      CircleWithPrivateDataFields(5.0);
    printCircle(myCircle);
  }

  public static void printCircle(CircleWithPrivateDataFields c) {
    System.out.println("The area of the circle of radius "
      + c.getRadius() + " is " + c.getArea());
  }
}
```

pass-by-value

Java uses exactly one mode of passing arguments: pass-by-value. In the preceding code, the value of `myCircle` is passed to the `printCircle` method. This value is a reference to a `Circle` object.

The program in Listing 8.11 demonstrates the difference between passing a primitive type value and passing a reference value.

LISTING 8.11 TestPassObject.java

```
1  public class TestPassObject {
2    /** Main method */
3    public static void main(String[] args) {
4      // Create a Circle object with radius 1
5      CircleWithPrivateDataFields myCircle =
6        new CircleWithPrivateDataFields(1);
7
8      // Print areas for radius 1, 2, 3, 4, and 5.
9      int n = 5;
10     printAreas(myCircle, n);
11
12     // See myCircle.radius and times
13     System.out.println("\n" + "Radius is " + myCircle.getRadius());
14     System.out.println("n is " + n);
15   }
16
17   /** Print a table of areas for radius */
18   public static void printAreas(
19     CircleWithPrivateDataFields c, int times) {
20     System.out.println("Radius \t\tArea");
21     while (times >= 1) {
22       System.out.println(c.getRadius() + "\t\t" + c.getArea());
23       c.setRadius(c.getRadius() + 1);
24       times--;
25     }
26   }
27 }
```

pass object

object parameter

```
Radius      Area
1.0         3.141592653589793
2.0         12.566370614359172
3.0         29.274333882308138
4.0         50.26548245743669
5.0         79.53981633974483
Radius is 6.0
n is 5
```

The `CircleWithPrivateDataFields` class is defined in Listing 8.9. The program passes a `CircleWithPrivateDataFields` object `myCircle` and an integer value from `n` to invoke `printAreas(myCircle, n)` (line 9), which prints a table of areas for radii `1`, `2`, `3`, `4`, `5`, as shown in the sample output.

Figure 8.18 shows the call stack for executing the methods in the program. Note that the objects are stored in a heap (see Section 6.6).

When passing an argument of a primitive data type, the value of the argument is passed. In this case, the value of `n` (`5`) is passed to `times`. Inside the `printAreas` method, the content of `times` is changed; this does not affect the content of `n`.

When passing an argument of a reference type, the reference of the object is passed. In this case, `c` contains a reference for the object that is also referenced via `myCircle`. Therefore, changing the properties of the object through `c` inside the `printAreas` method has the same effect as doing so outside the method through the variable `myCircle`. Pass-by-value on references can be best described semantically as *pass-by-sharing*; that is, the object referenced in the method is the same as the object being passed.

pass-by-sharing

FIGURE 8.18 The value of `n` is passed to `times`, and the reference to `myCircle` is passed to `c` in the `printAreas` method.

MyProgrammingLab™

8.23 Describe the difference between passing a parameter of a primitive type and passing a parameter of a reference type. Show the output of the following programs:

```
public class Test {
  public static void main(String[] args) {
    Count myCount = new Count();
    int times = 0;

    for (int i = 0; i < 100; i++)
      increment(myCount, times);

    System.out.println("count is " + myCount.count);
    System.out.println("times is " + times);
  }

  public static void increment(Count c, int times) {
    c.count++;
    times++;
  }
}
```

```
public class Count {
  public int count;

  public Count(int c) {
    count = c;
  }

  public Count() {
    count = 1;
  }
}
```

8.24 Show the output of the following program:

```
public class Test {
  public static void main(String[] args) {
    Circle circle1 = new Circle(1);
    Circle circle2 = new Circle(2);

    swap1(circle1, circle2);
    System.out.println("After swap1: circle1 = " +
      circle1.radius + " circle2 = " + circle2.radius);

    swap2(circle1, circle2);
    System.out.println("After swap2: circle1 = " +
      circle1.radius + " circle2 = " + circle2.radius);
  }

  public static void swap1(Circle x, Circle y) {
    Circle temp = x;
    x = y;
    y = temp;
```

```
  }

  public static void swap2(Circle x, Circle y) {
    double temp = x.radius;
    x.radius = y.radius;
    y.radius = temp;
  }
}

class Circle {
  double radius;

  Circle(double newRadius) {
    radius = newRadius;
  }
}
```

8.25 Show the printout of the following code:

```
public class Test {
  public static void main(String[] args) {
    int[] a = {1, 2};
    swap(a[0], a[1]);
    System.out.println("a[0] = " + a[0]
      + " a[1] = " + a[1]);
  }

  public static void swap(int n1, int n2) {
    int temp = n1;
    n1 = n2;
    n2 = temp;
  }
}
```

(a)

```
public class Test {
  public static void main(String[] args) {
    int[] a = {1, 2};
    swap(a);
    System.out.println("a[0] = " + a[0]
      + " a[1] = " + a[1]);
  }

  public static void swap(int[] a) {
    int temp = a[0];
    a[0] = a[1];
    a[1] = temp;
  }
}
```

(b)

```
public class Test {
  public static void main(String[] args) {
    T t = new T();
    swap(t);
    System.out.println("e1 = " + t.e1
      + " e2 = " + t.e2);
  }

  public static void swap(T t) {
    int temp = t.e1;
    t.e1 = t.e2;
    t.e2 = temp;
  }
}

class T {
  int e1 = 1;
  int e2 = 2;
}
```

(c)

```
public class Test {
  public static void main(String[] args) {
    T t1 = new T();
    T t2 = new T();
    System.out.println("t1's i = " +
      t1.i + " and j = " + t1.j);
    System.out.println("t2's i = " +
      t2.i + " and j = " + t2.j);
  }
}

class T {
  static int i = 0;
  int j = 0;

  T() {
    i++;
    j = 1;
  }
}
```

(d)

8.26 What is the output of the following programs?

```
import java.util.Date;

public class Test {
  public static void main(String[] args) {
    Date date = null;
    m1(date);
    System.out.println(date);
  }

  public static void m1(Date date) {
    date = new Date();
  }
}
```

(a)

```
import java.util.Date;

public class Test {
  public static void main(String[] args) {
    Date date = new Date(1234567);
    m1(date);
    System.out.println(date.getTime());
  }

  public static void m1(Date date) {
    date = new Date(7654321);
  }
}
```

(b)

```
import java.util.Date;

public class Test {
  public static void main(String[] args) {
    Date date = new Date(1234567);
    m1(date);
    System.out.println(date.getTime());
  }

  public static void m1(Date date) {
    date.setTime(7654321);
  }
}
```

(c)

```
import java.util.Date;

public class Test {
  public static void main(String[] args) {
    Date date = new Date(1234567);
    m1(date);
    System.out.println(date.getTime());
  }

  public static void m1(Date date) {
    date = null;
  }
}
```

(d)

8.11 Array of Objects

An array can hold objects as well as primitive type values.

Chapter 6, Single-Dimensional Arrays, described how to create arrays of primitive type elements. You can also create arrays of objects. For example, the following statement declares and creates an array of ten `Circle` objects:

```
Circle[] circleArray = new Circle[10];
```

To initialize `circleArray`, you can use a `for` loop like this one:

```
for (int i = 0; i < circleArray.length; i++) {
  circleArray[i] = new Circle();
}
```

An array of objects is actually an *array of reference variables*. So, invoking `circleArray[1].getArea()` involves two levels of referencing, as shown in Figure 8.19. `circleArray` references the entire array; `circleArray[1]` references a `Circle` object.

Note

When an array of objects is created using the `new` operator, each element in the array is a reference variable with a default value of `null`.

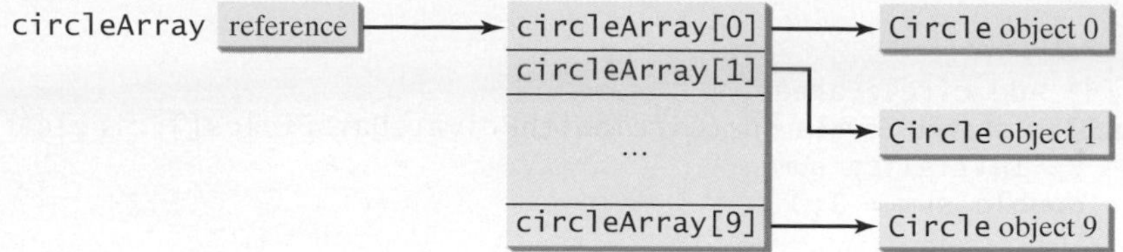

FIGURE 8.19 In an array of objects, an element of the array contains a reference to an object.

Listing 8.12 gives an example that demonstrates how to use an array of objects. The program summarizes the areas of an array of circles. The program creates `circleArray`, an array composed of five `Circle` objects; it then initializes circle radii with random values and displays the total area of the circles in the array.

LISTING 8.12 TotalArea.java

```
public class TotalArea {
  /** Main method */
  public static void main(String[] args) {
    // Declare circleArray
    CircleWithPrivateDataFields[] circleArray;

    // Create circleArray
    circleArray = createCircleArray();

    // Print circleArray and total areas of the circles
    printCircleArray(circleArray);
  }

  /** Create an array of Circle objects */
  public static CircleWithPrivateDataFields[] createCircleArray() {
    CircleWithPrivateDataFields[] circleArray =
      new CircleWithPrivateDataFields[5];

    for (int i = 0; i < circleArray.length; i++) {
      circleArray[i] =
        new CircleWithPrivateDataFields(Math.random() * 100);
    }

    // Return Circle array
    return circleArray;
  }

  /** Print an array of circles and their total area */
  public static void printCircleArray(
      CircleWithPrivateDataFields[] circleArray) {
    System.out.printf("%-30s%-15s\n", "Radius", "Area");
    for (int i = 0; i < circleArray.length; i++) {
      System.out.printf("%-30f%-15f\n", circleArray[i].getRadius(),
        circleArray[i].getArea());
    }

    System.out.println("-----------------------------------------");

    // Compute and display the result
    System.out.printf("%-30s%-15f\n", "The total area of circles is",
      sum(circleArray) );
```

array of objects

return array of objects

pass array of objects

pass array of objects

```
42   }
43
44   /** Add circle areas */
45   public static double sum(CircleWithPrivateDataFields[] circleArray) {
46     // Initialize sum
47     double sum = 0;
48
49     // Add areas to sum
50     for (int i = 0; i < circleArray.length; i++)
51       sum += circleArray[i].getArea();
52
53     return sum;
54   }
55 }
```

```
Radius                       Area
70.577708                    15648.941866
44.152266                    6124.291736
24.867853                    1942.792644
 5.680718                    101.380949
36.734246                    4239.280350
-----------------------------------------
The total area of circles is 28056.687544
```

The program invokes `createCircleArray()` (line 8) to create an array of five circle objects. Several circle classes were introduced in this chapter. This example uses the `CircleWithPrivateDataFields` class introduced in Section 8.9, Data Field Encapsulation.

The circle radii are randomly generated using the `Math.random()` method (line 21). The `createCircleArray` method returns an array of `CircleWithPrivateDataFields` objects (line 25). The array is passed to the `printCircleArray` method, which displays the radius and area of each circle and the total area of the circles.

The sum of the circle areas is computed by invoking the `sum` method (line 41), which takes the array of `CircleWithPrivateDataFields` objects as the argument and returns a `double` value for the total area.

MyProgrammingLab™

8.27 What is wrong in the following code?

```
public class Test {
  public static void main(String[] args) {
    java.util.Date[] dates = new java.util.Date[10];
    System.out.println(dates[0]);
    System.out.println(dates[0].toString());
  }
}
```

Key Terms

action 296
anonymous object 305
attribute 296
behavior 296
class 296
client 299
constructor 296
data field 296
data field encapsulation 319
default constructor 303
dot operator (`.`) 304
getter (or accessor) 320

CHAPTER SUMMARY

1. A *class* is a template for *objects*. It defines the *properties* of objects and provides *constructors* for creating objects and methods for manipulating them.

2. A class is also a data type. You can use it to declare object *reference variables*. An object reference variable that appears to hold an object actually contains a reference to that object. Strictly speaking, an object reference variable and an object are different, but most of the time the distinction can be ignored.

3. An object is an *instance* of a class. You use the `new` operator to create an object, and the *dot operator* (`.`) to access members of that object through its reference variable.

4. An *instance variable* or *method* belongs to an instance of a class. Its use is associated with individual instances. A *static variable* is a variable shared by all instances of the same class. A *static method* is a method that can be invoked without using instances.

5. Every instance of a class can access the class's static variables and methods. For clarity, however, it is better to invoke static variables and methods using `ClassName.variable` and `ClassName.method`.

6. Modifiers specify how the class, method, and data are accessed. A `public` class, method, or data is accessible to all clients. A `private` method or data is accessible only inside the class.

7. You can provide a `get` method or a `set` method to enable clients to see or modify the data. Colloquially, a `get` method is referred to as a *getter* (or *accessor*), and a `set` method as a *setter* (or *mutator*).

8. A `get` method has the signature `public returnType getPropertyName()`. If the `returnType` is `boolean`, the `get` method should be defined as `public boolean isPropertyName()`. A `set` method has the signature `public void setPropertyName(dataType propertyValue)`.

9. All parameters are passed to methods using pass-by-value. For a parameter of a primitive type, the actual value is passed; for a parameter of a *reference type*, the reference for the object is passed.

10. A Java array is an object that can contain primitive type values or object type values. When an array of objects is created, its elements are assigned the default value of `null`.

Test Questions

Do the test questions for this chapter online at www.cs.armstrong.edu/liang/intro9e/test.html.

MyProgrammingLab™

Programming Exercises

three objectives

Pedagogical Note

The exercises in Chapters 8–11, 15 help you achieve three objectives:

- Design classes and draw UML class diagrams
- Implement classes from the UML
- Use classes to develop applications

Students can download solutions for the UML diagrams for the even-numbered exercises from the Companion Website, and instructors can download all solutions from the same site.

Sections 8.2–8.5

8.1 (*The `Rectangle` class*) Following the example of the `Circle` class in Section 8.2, design a class named `Rectangle` to represent a rectangle. The class contains:

- Two `double` data fields named `width` and `height` that specify the width and height of the rectangle. The default values are `1` for both `width` and `height`.
- A no-arg constructor that creates a default rectangle.
- A constructor that creates a rectangle with the specified `width` and `height`.
- A method named `getArea()` that returns the area of this rectangle.
- A method named `getPerimeter()` that returns the perimeter.

Draw the UML diagram for the class and then implement the class. Write a test program that creates two `Rectangle` objects—one with width `4` and height `40` and the other with width `3.5` and height `35.9`. Display the width, height, area, and perimeter of each rectangle in this order.

8.2 (*The `Stock` class*) Following the example of the `Circle` class in Section 8.2, design a class named `Stock` that contains:

- A string data field named `symbol` for the stock's symbol.
- A string data field named `name` for the stock's name.
- A `double` data field named `previousClosingPrice` that stores the stock price for the previous day.
- A `double` data field named `currentPrice` that stores the stock price for the current time.
- A constructor that creates a stock with the specified symbol and name.
- A method named `getChangePercent()` that returns the percentage changed from `previousClosingPrice` to `currentPrice`.

Draw the UML diagram for the class and then implement the class. Write a test program that creates a `Stock` object with the stock symbol `ORCL`, the name `Oracle Corporation`, and the previous closing price of `34.5`. Set a new current price to `34.35` and display the price-change percentage.

Section 8.6

***8.3** (*Use the `Date` class*) Write a program that creates a `Date` object, sets its elapsed time to `10000`, `100000`, `1000000`, `10000000`, `100000000`, `1000000000`, `10000000000`, and `100000000000`, and displays the date and time using the `toString()` method, respectively.

***8.4** (*Use the* **Random** *class*) Write a program that creates a `Random` object with seed `1000` and displays the first 50 random integers between `0` and `100` using the `nextInt(100)` method.

***8.5** (*Use the* **GregorianCalendar** *class*) Java API has the `GregorianCalendar` class in the `java.util` package, which you can use to obtain the year, month, and day of a date. The no-arg constructor constructs an instance for the current date, and the methods `get(GregorianCalendar.YEAR)`, `get(GregorianCalendar.MONTH)`, and `get(GregorianCalendar.DAY_OF_MONTH)` return the year, month, and day. Write a program to perform two tasks:

- Display the current year, month, and day.
- The `GregorianCalendar` class has the `setTimeInMillis(long)`, which can be used to set a specified elapsed time since January 1, 1970. Set the value to `1234567898765L` and display the year, month, and day.

Sections 8.7–8.9

****8.6** (*Display calendars*) Rewrite the `PrintCalendar` class in Listing 5.12 to display calendars in a message dialog box. Since the output is generated from several static methods in the class, you may define a static `String` variable `output` for storing the output and display it in a message dialog box.

8.7 (*The* **Account** *class*) Design a class named `Account` that contains:

- A private `int` data field named `id` for the account (default `0`).
- A private `double` data field named `balance` for the account (default `0`).
- A private `double` data field named `annualInterestRate` that stores the current interest rate (default `0`). Assume all accounts have the same interest rate.
- A private `Date` data field named `dateCreated` that stores the date when the account was created.
- A no-arg constructor that creates a default account.
- A constructor that creates an account with the specified id and initial balance.
- The accessor and mutator methods for `id`, `balance`, and `annualInterestRate`.
- The accessor method for `dateCreated`.
- A method named `getMonthlyInterestRate()` that returns the monthly interest rate.
- A method named `getMonthlyInterest()` that returns the monthly interest.
- A method named `withdraw` that withdraws a specified amount from the account.
- A method named `deposit` that deposits a specified amount to the account.

Draw the UML diagram for the class and then implement the class. (*Hint*: The method `getMonthlyInterest()` is to return monthly interest, not the interest rate. Monthly interest is `balance * monthlyInterestRate`. `monthlyInterestRate` is `annualInterestRate / 12`. Note that `annualInterestRate` is a percentage, e.g.,like 4.5%. You need to divide it by 100.)

Write a test program that creates an `Account` object with an account ID of 1122, a balance of $20,000, and an annual interest rate of 4.5%. Use the `withdraw` method to withdraw $2,500, use the `deposit` method to deposit $3,000, and print the balance, the monthly interest, and the date when this account was created.

8.8 (*The* **Fan** *class*) Design a class named `Fan` to represent a fan. The class contains:

VideoNote
The Fan class

- Three constants named `SLOW`, `MEDIUM`, and `FAST` with the values `1`, `2`, and `3` to denote the fan speed.

- A private `int` data field named `speed` that specifies the speed of the fan (the default is `SLOW`).
- A private `boolean` data field named `on` that specifies whether the fan is on (the default is `false`).
- A private `double` data field named `radius` that specifies the radius of the fan (the default is `5`).
- A string data field named `color` that specifies the color of the fan (the default is `blue`).
- The accessor and mutator methods for all four data fields.
- A no-arg constructor that creates a default fan.
- A method named `toString()` that returns a string description for the fan. If the fan is on, the method returns the fan speed, color, and radius in one combined string. If the fan is not on, the method returns the fan color and radius along with the string "fan is off" in one combined string.

Draw the UML diagram for the class and then implement the class. Write a test program that creates two `Fan` objects. Assign maximum speed, radius `10`, color `yellow`, and turn it on to the first object. Assign medium speed, radius `5`, color `blue`, and turn it off to the second object. Display the objects by invoking their `toString` method.

****8.9** (*Geometry: n-sided regular polygon*) In an *n*-sided regular polygon, all sides have the same length and all angles have the same degree (i.e., the polygon is both equilateral and equiangular). Design a class named `RegularPolygon` that contains:

- A private `int` data field named `n` that defines the number of sides in the polygon with default value `3`.
- A private `double` data field named `side` that stores the length of the side with default value `1`.
- A private `double` data field named `x` that defines the *x*-coordinate of the polygon's center with default value `0`.
- A private `double` data field named `y` that defines the *y*-coordinate of the polygon's center with default value `0`.
- A no-arg constructor that creates a regular polygon with default values.
- A constructor that creates a regular polygon with the specified number of sides and length of side, centered at (`0`, `0`).
- A constructor that creates a regular polygon with the specified number of sides, length of side, and *x*-and *y*-coordinates.
- The accessor and mutator methods for all data fields.
- The method `getPerimeter()` that returns the perimeter of the polygon.
- The method `getArea()` that returns the area of the polygon. The formula for computing the area of a regular polygon is $Area = \dfrac{n \times s^2}{4 \times \tan\left(\dfrac{\pi}{n}\right)}$.

Draw the UML diagram for the class and then implement the class. Write a test program that creates three `RegularPolygon` objects, created using the no-arg constructor, using `RegularPolygon(6, 4)`, and using `RegularPolygon(10, 4, 5.6, 7.8)`. For each object, display its perimeter and area.

***8.10** (*Algebra: quadratic equations*) Design a class named `QuadraticEquation` for a quadratic equation $ax^2 + bx + x = 0$. The class contains:

- Private data fields `a`, `b`, and `c` that represent three coefficients.
- A constructor for the arguments for `a`, `b`, and `c`.

- Three `get` methods for a, b, and c.
- A method named `getDiscriminant()` that returns the discriminant, which is $b^2 - 4ac$.
- The methods named `getRoot1()` and `getRoot2()` for returning two roots of the equation

$$r_1 = \frac{-b + \sqrt{b^2 - 4ac}}{2a} \quad \text{and} \quad r_2 = \frac{-b - \sqrt{b^2 - 4ac}}{2a}$$

These methods are useful only if the discriminant is nonnegative. Let these methods return 0 if the discriminant is negative.

Draw the UML diagram for the class and then implement the class. Write a test program that prompts the user to enter values for *a*, *b*, and *c* and displays the result based on the discriminant. If the discriminant is positive, display the two roots. If the discriminant is 0, display the one root. Otherwise, display "The equation has no roots." See Programming Exercise 3.1 for sample runs.

***8.11** (*Algebra: 2 × 2 linear equations*) Design a class named `LinearEquation` for a 2 × 2 system of linear equations:

$$\begin{aligned} ax + by &= e \\ cx + dy &= f \end{aligned} \qquad x = \frac{ed - bf}{ad - bc} \qquad y = \frac{af - ec}{ad - bc}$$

The class contains:

- Private data fields a, b, c, d, e, and f.
- A constructor with the arguments for a, b, c, d, e, and f.
- Six `get` methods for a, b, c, d, e, and f.
- A method named `isSolvable()` that returns true if $ad - bc$ is not 0.
- Methods `getX()` and `getY()` that return the solution for the equation.

Draw the UML diagram for the class and then implement the class. Write a test program that prompts the user to enter a, b, c, d, e, and f and displays the result. If $ad - bc$ is 0, report that "The equation has no solution." See Programming Exercise 3.3 for sample runs.

****8.12** (*Geometry: intersection*) Suppose two line segments intersect. The two endpoints for the first line segment are (x1, y1) and (x2, y2) and for the second line segment are (x3, y3) and (x4, y4). Write a program that prompts the user to enter these four endpoints and displays the intersecting point. (*Hint*: Use the `LinearEquation` class in Exercise 8.11.)

```
Enter the endpoints of the first line segment: 2.0 2.0 0 0 ↵Enter
Enter the endpoints of the second line segment: 0 2.0 2.0 0 ↵Enter
The intersecting point is: (1.0, 1.0)
```

****8.13** (*The `Location` class*) Design a class named `Location` for locating a maximal value and its location in a two-dimensional array. The class contains public data fields `row`, `column`, and `maxValue` that store the maximal value and its indices in a two-dimensional array with `row` and `column` as `int` types and `maxValue` as a `double` type.

Write the following method that returns the location of the largest element in a two-dimensional array:

```
public static Location locateLargest(double[][] a)
```

The return value is an instance of `Location`. Write a test program that prompts the user to enter a two-dimensional array and displays the location of the largest element in the array. Here is a sample run:

```
Enter the number of rows and columns in the array: 3 4 ↵Enter
Enter the array:
23.5 35 2 10 ↵Enter
4.5 3 45 3.5 ↵Enter
35 44 5.5 9.6 ↵Enter
The location of the largest element is 45 at (1, 2)
```

***8.14** (*Stopwatch*) Design a class named `StopWatch`. The class contains:

- Private data fields `startTime` and `endTime` with get methods.
- A no-arg constructor that initializes `startTime` with the current time.
- A method named `start()` that resets the `startTime` to the current time.
- A method named `stop()` that sets the `endTime` to the current time.
- A method named `getElapsedTime()` that returns the elapsed time for the stopwatch in milliseconds.

Draw the UML diagram for the class and then implement the class. Write a test program that measures the execution time of sorting 100,000 numbers using selection sort.

CHAPTER

9

STRINGS

Objectives

- To use the `String` class to process fixed strings (§9.2).
- To construct strings (§9.2.1).
- To understand that strings are immutable and to create an interned string (§9.2.2).
- To compare strings (§9.2.3).
- To get string length and characters, and combine strings (§9.2.4).
- To obtain substrings (§9.2.5).
- To convert, replace, and split strings (§9.2.6).
- To match, replace, and split strings by patterns (§9.2.7).
- To search for a character or substring in a string (§9.2.8).
- To convert between a string and an array (§9.2.9).
- To convert characters and numbers into a string (§9.2.10).
- To obtain a formatted string (§9.2.11).
- To check whether a string is a palindrome (§9.3).
- To convert hexadecimal numbers to decimal numbers (§9.4).
- To use the `Character` class to process a single character (§9.5).
- To use the `StringBuilder` and `StringBuffer` classes to process flexible strings (§9.6).
- To distinguish among the `String`, `StringBuilder`, and `StringBuffer` classes (§9.2–9.6).
- To learn how to pass arguments to the `main` method from the command line (§9.7).

9.1 Introduction

The classes `String`, `StringBuilder`, and `StringBuffer` are used for processing strings.

A *string* is a sequence of characters. Strings are frequently used in programming. In many languages, strings are treated as an array of characters, but in Java a string is treated as an object. This chapter introduces the classes for processing strings.

9.2 The String Class

A `String` object is immutable: Its content cannot be changed once the string is created.

The `String` class has 13 constructors and more than 40 methods for manipulating strings. Not only is it very useful in programming, but it is also a good example for learning classes and objects.

9.2.1 Constructing a String

You can create a string object from a string literal or from an array of characters. To create a string from a string literal, use the syntax:

```
String newString = new String(stringLiteral);
```

The argument `stringLiteral` is a sequence of characters enclosed inside double quotes. The following statement creates a `String` object `message` for the string literal `"Welcome to Java"`:

```
String message = new String("Welcome to Java");
```

string literal object

Java treats a string literal as a `String` object. Thus, the following statement is valid:

```
String message = "Welcome to Java";
```

You can also create a string from an array of characters. For example, the following statements create the string `"Good Day"`:

```
char[] charArray = {'G', 'o', 'o', 'd', ' ', 'D', 'a', 'y'};
String message = new String(charArray);
```

`String` variable, `String` object, string value

Note

A `String` variable holds a reference to a `String` object that stores a string value. Strictly speaking, the terms *`String` variable*, *`String` object*, and *string value* are different, but most of the time the distinctions between them can be ignored. For simplicity, the term *string* will often be used to refer to `String` variable, `String` object, and string value.

9.2.2 Immutable Strings and Interned Strings

immutable

A `String` object is immutable; its contents cannot be changed. Does the following code change the contents of the string?

```
String s = "Java";
s = "HTML";
```

The answer is no. The first statement creates a `String` object with the content `"Java"` and assigns its reference to `s`. The second statement creates a new `String` object with the content

"HTML" and assigns its reference to s. The first String object still exists after the assignment, but it can no longer be accessed, because variable s now points to the new object, as shown in Figure 9.1.

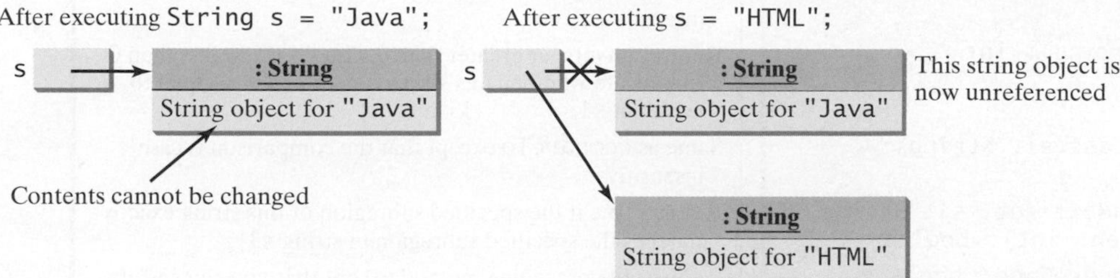

FIGURE 9.1 Strings are immutable; once created, their contents cannot be changed.

Because strings are immutable and are ubiquitous in programming, the JVM uses a unique instance for string literals with the same character sequence in order to improve efficiency and save memory. Such an instance is called an *interned string*. For example, the following statements:

interned string

```
String s1 = "Welcome to Java";

String s2 = new String("Welcome to Java");

String s3 = "Welcome to Java";

System.out.println("s1 == s2 is " + (s1 == s2));
System.out.println("s1 == s3 is " + (s1 == s3));
```

s1
s3
: String
Interned string object for "Welcome to Java"
s2
: String
A string object for "Welcome to Java"

display

```
s1 == s2 is false
s1 == s3 is true
```

In the preceding statements, s1 and s3 refer to the same interned string—"Welcome to Java"—so s1 == s3 is true. However, s1 == s2 is false, because s1 and s2 are two different string objects, even though they have the same contents.

9.2.3 String Comparisons

The String class provides the methods for comparing strings, as shown in Figure 9.2.

How do you compare the contents of two strings? You might attempt to use the == operator, as follows:

==

```
if (string1 == string2)
  System.out.println("string1 and string2 are the same object");
else
  System.out.println("string1 and string2 are different objects");
```

However, the == operator checks only whether string1 and string2 refer to the same object; it does not tell you whether they have the same contents. Therefore, you cannot use the == operator to find out whether two string variables have the same contents. Instead, you should use the equals method. The following code, for instance, can be used to compare two strings:

string1.equals(string2)

```
if (string1.equals(string2))
  System.out.println("string1 and string2 have the same contents");
else
  System.out.println("string1 and string2 are not equal");
```

java.lang.String	
`+equals(s1: Object): boolean`	Returns true if this string is equal to string `s1`.
`+equalsIgnoreCase(s1: String): boolean`	Returns true if this string is equal to string `s1` case insensitive.
`+compareTo(s1: String): int`	Returns an integer greater than 0, equal to 0, or less than 0 to indicate whether this string is greater than, equal to, or less than `s1`.
`+compareToIgnoreCase(s1: String): int`	Same as `compareTo` except that the comparison is case insensitive.
`+regionMatches(index: int, s1: String, s1Index: int, len: int): boolean`	Returns true if the specified subregion of this string exactly matches the specified subregion in string `s1`.
`+regionMatches(ignoreCase: boolean, index: int, s1: String, s1Index: int, len: int): boolean`	Same as the preceding method except that you can specify whether the match is case sensitive.
`+startsWith(prefix: String): boolean`	Returns true if this string starts with the specified prefix.
`+endsWith(suffix: String): boolean`	Returns true if this string ends with the specified suffix.

FIGURE 9.2 The `String` class contains the methods for comparing strings.

Note that parameter type for the `equals` method is `Object`. We will introduce the `Object` class in Chapter 11. For now, you can replace `Object` by `String` for using the `equals` method to compare two strings. For example, the following statements display `true` and then `false`.

```
String s1 = new String("Welcome to Java");
String s2 = "Welcome to Java";
String s3 = "Welcome to C++";
System.out.println(s1.equals(s2)); // true
System.out.println(s1.equals(s3)); // false
```

The `compareTo` method can also be used to compare two strings. For example, consider the following code:

s1.compareTo(s2)

```
s1.compareTo(s2)
```

The method returns the value `0` if `s1` is equal to `s2`, a value less than `0` if `s1` is lexicographically (i.e., in terms of Unicode ordering) less than `s2`, and a value greater than `0` if `s1` is lexicographically greater than `s2`.

The actual value returned from the `compareTo` method depends on the offset of the first two distinct characters in `s1` and `s2` from left to right. For example, suppose `s1` is `abc` and `s2` is `abg`, and `s1.compareTo(s2)` returns `-4`. The first two characters (`a` vs. `a`) from `s1` and `s2` are compared. Because they are equal, the second two characters (`b` vs. `b`) are compared. Because they are also equal, the third two characters (`c` vs. `g`) are compared. Since the character `c` is `4` less than `g`, the comparison returns `-4`.

Caution

Syntax errors will occur if you compare strings by using comparison operators `>`, `>=`, `<`, or `<=`. Instead, you have to use `s1.compareTo(s2)`.

Note

The `equals` method returns `true` if two strings are equal and `false` if they are not. The `compareTo` method returns `0`, a positive integer, or a negative integer, depending on whether one string is equal to, greater than, or less than the other string.

The `String` class also provides the `equalsIgnoreCase`, `compareToIgnoreCase`, and `regionMatches` methods for comparing strings. The `equalsIgnoreCase` and

java.lang.String	
+indexOf(ch: char): int	Returns the index of the first occurrence of ch in the string. Returns -1 if not matched.
+indexOf(ch: char, fromIndex: int): int	Returns the index of the first occurrence of ch after fromIndex in the string. Returns -1 if not matched.
+indexOf(s: String): int	Returns the index of the first occurrence of string s in this string. Returns -1 if not matched.
+indexOf(s: String, fromIndex: int): int	Returns the index of the first occurrence of string s in this string after fromIndex. Returns -1 if not matched.
+lastIndexOf(ch: int): int	Returns the index of the last occurrence of ch in the string. Returns -1 if not matched.
+lastIndexOf(ch: int, fromIndex: int): int	Returns the index of the last occurrence of ch before fromIndex in this string. Returns -1 if not matched.
+lastIndexOf(s: String): int	Returns the index of the last occurrence of string s. Returns -1 if not matched.
+lastIndexOf(s: String, fromIndex: int): int	Returns the index of the last occurrence of string s before fromIndex. Returns -1 if not matched.

FIGURE 9.8 The **String** class contains the methods for matching substrings.

For example,

indexOf

```
"Welcome to Java".indexOf('W') returns 0.
"Welcome to Java".indexOf('o') returns 4.
"Welcome to Java".indexOf('o', 5) returns 9.
"Welcome to Java".indexOf("come") returns 3.
"Welcome to Java".indexOf("Java", 5) returns 11.
"Welcome to Java".indexOf("java", 5) returns -1.
```

lastIndexOf

```
"Welcome to Java".lastIndexOf('W') returns 0.
"Welcome to Java".lastIndexOf('o') returns 9.
"Welcome to Java".lastIndexOf('o', 5) returns 4.
"Welcome to Java".lastIndexOf("come") returns 3.
"Welcome to Java".lastIndexOf("Java", 5) returns -1.
"Welcome to Java".lastIndexOf("Java") returns 11.
```

9.2.9 Conversion between Strings and Arrays

Strings are not arrays, but a string can be converted into an array, and vice versa. To convert a string into an array of characters, use the **toCharArray** method. For example, the following statement converts the string **Java** to an array.

toCharArray

```
char[] chars = "Java".toCharArray();
```

Thus, **chars[0]** is **J**, **chars[1]** is **a**, **chars[2]** is **v**, and **chars[3]** is **a**.

You can also use the **getChars(int srcBegin, int srcEnd, char[] dst, int dstBegin)** method to copy a substring of the string from index **srcBegin** to index **srcEnd-1** into a character array **dst** starting from index **dstBegin**. For example, the following code copies a substring **"3720"** in **"CS3720"** from index **2** to index **6-1** into the character array **dst** starting from index **4**.

getChars

```
char[] dst = {'J', 'A', 'V', 'A', '1', '3', '0', '1'};
"CS3720".getChars(2, 6, dst, 4);
```

Thus, **dst** becomes **{'J', 'A', 'V', 'A', '3', '7', '2', '0'}**.

To convert an array of characters into a string, use the `String(char[])` constructor or the `valueOf(char[])` method. For example, the following statement constructs a string from an array using the `String` constructor.

```
String str = new String(new char[]{'J', 'a', 'v', 'a'});
```

valueOf

The next statement constructs a string from an array using the `valueOf` method.

```
String str = String.valueOf(new char[]{'J', 'a', 'v', 'a'});
```

9.2.10 Converting Characters and Numeric Values to Strings

overloaded `valueOf`

The static `valueOf` method can be used to convert an array of characters into a string. There are several overloaded versions of the `valueOf` method that can be used to convert a character and numeric values to strings with different parameter types, `char`, `double`, `long`, `int`, and `float`, as shown in Figure 9.9.

java.lang.String	
+valueOf(c: char): String	Returns a string consisting of the character c.
+valueOf(data: char[]): String	Returns a string consisting of the characters in the array.
+valueOf(d: double): String	Returns a string representing the double value.
+valueOf(f: float): String	Returns a string representing the float value.
+valueOf(i: int): String	Returns a string representing the int value.
+valueOf(l: long): String	Returns a string representing the long value.
+valueOf(b: boolean): String	Returns a string representing the boolean value.

FIGURE 9.9 The `String` class contains the static methods for creating strings from primitive type values.

For example, to convert a `double` value `5.44` to a string, use `String.valueOf(5.44)`. The return value is a string consisting of the characters `'5'`, `'.'`, `'4'`, and `'4'`.

Note

You can use `Double.parseDouble(str)` or `Integer.parseInt(str)` to convert a string to a `double` value or an `int` value. `Double` and `Integer` are two classes in the `java.lang` package.

9.2.11 Formatting Strings

The `String` class contains the static `format` method to create a formatted string. The syntax to invoke this method is:

```
String.format(format, item1, item2, ..., itemk)
```

This method is similar to the `printf` method except that the `format` method returns a formatted string, whereas the `printf` method displays a formatted string. For example,

```
String s = String.format("%7.2f%6d%-4s", 45.556, 14, "AB");
System.out.println(s);
```

displays

```
□□45.56□□□□14AB□□
```

Note that

```
System.out.printf(format, item1, item2, ..., itemk);
```

is equivalent to

```
System.out.printf(
   String.format(format, item1, item2, ..., itemk));
```

where the square box (□) denotes a blank space.

Check Point
MyProgrammingLab™

9.1 Suppose that **s1**, **s2**, **s3**, and **s4** are four strings, given as follows:

```
String s1 = "Welcome to Java";
String s2 = s1;
String s3 = new String("Welcome to Java");
String s4 = "Welcome to Java";
```

What are the results of the following expressions?

a. `s1 == s2`
b. `s2 == s3`
c. `s1.equals(s2)`
d. `s2.equals(s3)`
e. `s1.compareTo(s2)`
f. `s2.compareTo(s3)`
g. `s1 == s4`
h. `s1.charAt(0)`
i. `s1.indexOf('j')`
j. `s1.indexOf("to")`
k. `s1.lastIndexOf('a')`
l. `s1.lastIndexOf("o", 15)`
m. `s1.length()`
n. `s1.substring(5)`
o. `s1.substring(5, 11)`
p. `s1.startsWith("Wel")`
q. `s1.endsWith("Java")`
r. `s1.toLowerCase()`
s. `s1.toUpperCase()`
t. `"Welcome ".trim()`
u. `s1.replace('o', 'T')`
v. `s1.replaceAll("o", "T")`
w. `s1.replaceFirst("o", "T")`
x. `s1.toCharArray()`

9.2 To create the string **Welcome to Java**, you may use a statement like this:

```
String s = "Welcome to Java";
```

or:

```
String s = new String("Welcome to Java");
```

Which one is better? Why?

9.3 Suppose that **s1** and **s2** are two strings. Which of the following statements or expressions are incorrect?

```
String s = new String("new string");
String s3 = s1 + s2;
String s3 = s1 - s2;
s1 == s2;
s1 >= s2;
s1.compareTo(s2);
int i = s1.length();
char c = s1(0);
char c = s1.charAt(s1.length());
```

9.4 What is the printout of the following code?

```
String s1 = "Welcome to Java";
String s2 = s1.replace("o", "abc");
System.out.println(s1);
System.out.println(s2);
```

9.5 Let `s1` be `" Welcome "` and `s2` be `" welcome "`. Write the code for the following statements:

a. Check whether `s1` is equal to `s2` and assign the result to a Boolean variable `isEqual`.

b. Check whether `s1` is equal to `s2`, ignoring case, and assign the result to a Boolean variable `isEqual`.

c. Compare `s1` with `s2` and assign the result to an `int` variable `x`.

d. Compare `s1` with `s2`, ignoring case, and assign the result to an `int` variable `x`.

e. Check whether `s1` has the prefix `AAA` and assign the result to a Boolean variable `b`.

f. Check whether `s1` has the suffix `AAA` and assign the result to a Boolean variable `b`.

g. Assign the length of `s1` to an `int` variable `x`.

h. Assign the first character of `s1` to a `char` variable `x`.

i. Create a new string `s3` that combines `s1` with `s2`.

j. Create a substring of `s1` starting from index `1`.

k. Create a substring of `s1` from index `1` to index `4`.

l. Create a new string `s3` that converts `s1` to lowercase.

m. Create a new string `s3` that converts `s1` to uppercase.

n. Create a new string `s3` that trims blank spaces on both ends of `s1`.

o. Replace all occurrences of the character `e` with `E` in `s1` and assign the new string to `s3`.

p. Split `Welcome to Java and HTML` into an array `tokens` delimited by a space.

q. Assign the index of the first occurrence of the character `e` in `s1` to an `int` variable `x`.

r. Assign the index of the last occurrence of the string `abc` in `s1` to an `int` variable `x`.

9.6 Does any method in the `String` class change the contents of the string?

9.7 Suppose string `s` is created using `new String()`; what is `s.length()`?

9.8 How do you convert a `char`, an array of characters, or a number to a string?

9.9 Why does the following code cause a `NullPointerException`?

```
public class Test {
  private String text;

  public Test(String s) {
    String text  = s;
  }

  public static void main(String[] args) {
    Test test = new Test("ABC");
    System.out.println(test.text.toLowerCase());
  }
}
```

9.10 What is wrong in the following program?

```
public class Test {
  String text;

```

```
    public void Test(String s) {
      text = s;
    }

    public static void main(String[] args) {
      Test test = new Test("ABC");
      System.out.println(test);
    }
  }
```

9.11 Show the output of the following code.

```
public class Test {
  public static void main(String[] args) {
    System.out.println("Hi, ABC, good".matches("ABC "));
    System.out.println("Hi, ABC, good".matches(".*ABC.*"));
    System.out.println("A,B;C".replaceAll(",;", "#"));
    System.out.println("A,B;C".replaceAll("[,;]", "#"));

    String[] tokens = "A,B;C".split("[,;]");
    for (int i = 0; i < tokens.length; i++)
      System.out.print(tokens[i] + " ");
  }
}
```

9.3 Case Study: Checking Palindromes

This section presents a program that checks whether a string is a palindrome.

A string is a palindrome if it reads the same forward and backward. The words "mom," "dad," and "noon," for instance, are all palindromes.

VideoNote
Check palindrome

The problem is to write a program that prompts the user to enter a string and reports whether the string is a palindrome. One solution is to check whether the first character in the string is the same as the last character. If so, check whether the second character is the same as the second-to-last character. This process continues until a mismatch is found or all the characters in the string are checked, except for the middle character if the string has an odd number of characters.

To implement this idea, use two variables, say `low` and `high`, to denote the position of the two characters at the beginning and the end in a string `s`, as shown in Listing 9.1 (lines 22, 25). Initially, `low` is `0` and `high` is `s.length() - 1`. If the two characters at these positions match, increment `low` by `1` and decrement `high` by `1` (lines 31–32). This process continues until (`low >= high`) or a mismatch is found.

LISTING 9.1 CheckPalindrome.java

```
1  import java.util.Scanner;
2
3  public class CheckPalindrome {
4    /** Main method */
5    public static void main(String[] args) {
6      // Create a Scanner
7      Scanner input = new Scanner(System.in);
8
9      // Prompt the user to enter a string
10     System.out.print("Enter a string: ");
11     String s = input.nextLine();
12
13     if (isPalindrome(s))
```

input string

low index

high index

update indices

```
14         System.out.println(s + " is a palindrome");
15       else
16         System.out.println(s + " is not a palindrome");
17     }
18
19     /** Check if a string is a palindrome */
20     public static boolean isPalindrome(String s) {
21       // The index of the first character in the string
22       int low = 0;
23
24       // The index of the last character in the string
25       int high = s.length() - 1;
26
27       while (low < high) {
28         if (s.charAt(low) != s.charAt(high))
29           return false; // Not a palindrome
30
31         low++;
32         high--;
33       }
34
35       return true; // The string is a palindrome
36     }
37   }
```

```
Enter a string: noon [Enter]
noon is a palindrome
```

```
Enter a string: moon [Enter]
moon is not a palindrome
```

The `nextLine()` method in the `Scanner` class (line 11) reads a line into `s`, and then `isPalindrome(s)` checks whether `s` is a palindrome (line 13).

9.4 Case Study: Converting Hexadecimals to Decimals

This section presents a program that converts a hexadecimal number into a decimal number.

Section 5.7 gives a program that converts a decimal to a hexadecimal. How do you convert a hex number into a decimal?

Given a hexadecimal number $h_n h_{n-1} h_{n-2} \ldots h_2 h_1 h_0$, the equivalent decimal value is

$$h_n \times 16^n + h_{n-1} \times 16^{n-1} + h_{n-2} \times 16^{n-2} + \ldots + h_2 \times 16^2 + h_1 \times 16^1 + h_0 \times 16^0$$

For example, the hex number `AB8C` is

$$10 \times 16^3 + 11 \times 16^2 + 8 \times 16^1 + 12 \times 16^0 = 43916$$

Our program will prompt the user to enter a hex number as a string and convert it into a decimal using the following method:

```
public static int hexToDecimal(String hex)
```

A brute-force approach is to convert each hex character into a decimal number, multiply it by 16^i for a hex digit at the `i`'s position, and then add all the items together to obtain the equivalent decimal value for the hex number.

Note that

$$h_n \times 16^n + h_{n-1} \times 16^{n-1} + h_{n-2} \times 16^{n-2} + \ldots + h_1 \times 16^1 + h_0 \times 16^0$$

$$= (\ldots ((h_n \times 16 + h_{n-1}) \times 16 + h_{n-2}) \times 16 + \ldots + h_1) \times 16 + h_0$$

This observation, known as the Horner's algorithm, leads to the following efficient code for converting a hex string to a decimal number:

```
int decimalValue = 0;
for (int i = 0; i < hex.length(); i++) {
  char hexChar = hex.charAt(i);
  decimalValue = decimalValue * 16 + hexCharToDecimal(hexChar);
}
```

Here is a trace of the algorithm for hex number AB8C:

	i	hexChar	hexCharToDecimal(hexChar)	decimalValue
before the loop				0
after the 1st iteration	0	A	10	10
after the 2nd iteration	1	B	11	10 * 16 + 11
after the 3rd iteration	2	8	8	(10 * 16 + 11) * 16 + 8
after the 4th iteration	3	C	12	((10 * 16 + 11) * 16 + 8) * 16 + 12

Listing 9.2 gives the complete program.

LISTING 9.2 HexToDecimalConversion.java

```
import java.util.Scanner;

public class HexToDecimalConversion {
  /** Main method */
  public static void main(String[] args) {
    // Create a Scanner
    Scanner input = new Scanner(System.in);

    // Prompt the user to enter a string
    System.out.print("Enter a hex number: ");
    String hex = input.nextLine();

    System.out.println("The decimal value for hex number "
      + hex + " is " + hexToDecimal(hex.toUpperCase()));
  }

  public static int hexToDecimal(String hex) {
    int decimalValue = 0;
    for (int i = 0; i < hex.length(); i++) {
      char hexChar = hex.charAt(i);
      decimalValue = decimalValue * 16 + hexCharToDecimal(hexChar);
    }

    return decimalValue;
  }

```

input string

hex to decimal

hex char to decimal
to uppercase

```
27   public static int hexCharToDecimal(char ch) {
28     if (ch >= 'A' && ch <= 'F')
29       return 10 + ch - 'A';
30     else // ch is '0', '1', ..., or '9'
31       return ch - '0';
32   }
33 }
```

```
Enter a hex number: AB8C ↵Enter
The decimal value for hex number AB8C is 43916
```

```
Enter a hex number: af71 ↵Enter
The decimal value for hex number af71 is 44913
```

The program reads a string from the console (line 11), and invokes the `hexToDecimal` method to convert a hex string to decimal number (line 14). The characters can be in either lowercase or uppercase. They are converted to uppercase before invoking the `hexToDecimal` method.

The `hexToDecimal` method is defined in lines 17–25 to return an integer. The length of the string is determined by invoking `hex.length()` in line 19.

The `hexCharToDecimal` method is defined in lines 27–32 to return a decimal value for a hex character. The character can be in either lowercase or uppercase. Recall that to subtract two characters is to subtract their Unicodes. For example, `'5' - '0'` is `5`.

9.5 The **Character** Class

Key Point

You can create an object for a character using the `Character` *class. A* `Character` *object contains a character value.*

Many methods in the Java API require an object argument. To enable the primitive data values to be treated as objects, Java provides a class for every primitive data type. These classes are `Character`, `Boolean`, `Byte`, `Short`, `Integer`, `Long`, `Float`, and `Double` for `char`, `boolean`, `byte`, `short`, `int`, `long`, `float`, and `double`, respectively. These classes are called *wrapper classes* because each wraps or encapsulates a primitive type value in an object. All these classes are in the `java.lang` package, and they contain useful methods for processing primitive values. This section introduces the `Character` class. The other wrapper classes will be introduced in Chapter 10, Thinking in Objects.

wrapper class

The `Character` class has a constructor and several methods for determining a character's category (uppercase, lowercase, digit, and so on) and for converting characters from uppercase to lowercase, and vice versa, as shown in Figure 9.10.

You can create a `Character` object from a `char` value. For example, the following statement creates a `Character` object for the character `a`.

```
Character character = new Character('a');
```

The `charValue` method returns the character value wrapped in the `Character` object. The `compareTo` method compares this character with another character and returns an integer that is the difference between the Unicode of this character and the Unicode of the other character. The `equals` method returns `true` if and only if the two characters are the same. For example, suppose `charObject` is `new Character('b')`:

```
charObject.compareTo(new Character('a')) returns 1
charObject.compareTo(new Character('b')) returns 0
charObject.compareTo(new Character('c')) returns -1
```

`charObject.compareTo(new Character('d'))` returns `-2`
`charObject.equals(new Character('b'))` returns `true`
`charObject.equals(new Character('d'))` returns `false`

java.lang.Character	
`+Character(value: char)`	Constructs a character object with `char` value.
`+charValue(): char`	Returns the `char` value from this object.
`+compareTo(anotherCharacter: Character): int`	Compares this character with another.
`+equals(anotherCharacter: Character): boolean`	Returns true if this character is equal to another.
`+isDigit(ch: char): boolean`	Returns true if the specified character is a digit.
`+isLetter(ch: char): boolean`	Returns true if the specified character is a letter.
`+isLetterOrDigit(ch: char): boolean`	Returns true if the character is a letter or a digit.
`+isLowerCase(ch: char): boolean`	Returns true if the character is a lowercase letter.
`+isUpperCase(ch: char): boolean`	Returns true if the character is an uppercase letter.
`+toLowerCase(ch: char): char`	Returns the lowercase of the specified character.
`+toUpperCase(ch: char): char`	Returns the uppercase of the specified character.

FIGURE 9.10 The **Character** class provides the methods for manipulating a character.

Most of the methods in the **Character** class are static methods. The **isDigit(char ch)** method returns **true** if the character is a digit, and the **isLetter(char ch)** method returns **true** if the character is a letter. The **isLetterOrDigit(char ch)** method returns **true** if the character is a letter or a digit. The **isLowerCase(char ch)** method returns **true** if the character is a lowercase letter, and the **isUpperCase(char ch)** method returns **true** if the character is an uppercase letter. The **toLowerCase(char ch)** method returns the lowercase letter for the character, and the **toUpperCase(char ch)** method returns the uppercase letter for the character.

Now let's write a program that prompts the user to enter a string and counts the number of occurrences of each letter in the string regardless of case.

Here are the steps to solve this problem:

1. Convert all the uppercase letters in the string to lowercase using the **toLowerCase** method in the **String** class.
2. Create an array, say **counts** of **26 int** values, each of which counts the occurrences of a letter. That is, **counts[0]** counts the number of **a**s, **counts[1]** counts the number of **b**s, and so on.
3. For each character in the string, check whether it is a (lowercase) letter. If so, increment the corresponding count in the array.

Listing 9.3 gives the complete program.

LISTING 9.3 CountEachLetter.java

```
import java.util.Scanner;

public class CountEachLetter {
  /** Main method */
  public static void main(String[] args) {
    // Create a Scanner
    Scanner input = new Scanner(System.in);

```

input string

count letters

count a letter

```
9       // Prompt the user to enter a string
10      System.out.print("Enter a string: ");
11      String s = input.nextLine();
12
13      // Invoke the countLetters method to count each letter
14      int[] counts = countLetters(s.toLowerCase());
15
16      // Display results
17      for (int i = 0; i < counts.length; i++) {
18        if (counts[i] != 0)
19          System.out.println((char)('a' + i) + " appears  " +
20            counts[i] + ((counts[i] == 1) ? " time" : " times"));
21      }
22    }
23
24    /** Count each letter in the string */
25    public static int[] countLetters(String s) {
26      int[] counts = new int[26];
27
28      for (int i = 0; i < s.length(); i++) {
29        if (Character.isLetter(s.charAt(i)))
30          counts[s.charAt(i) - 'a']++;
31      }
32
33      return counts;
34    }
35  }
```

```
Enter a string: abababx ↵Enter
a appears  3 times
b appears  3 times
x appears  1 time
```

The main method reads a line (line 11) and counts the number of occurrences of each letter in the string by invoking the **countLetters** method (line 14). Since the case of the letters is ignored, the program uses the **toLowerCase** method to convert the string into all lowercase and pass the new string to the **countLetters** method.

The **countLetters** method (lines 25–34) returns an array of **26** elements. Each element counts the number of occurrences of a letter in the string **s**. The method processes each character in the string. If the character is a letter, its corresponding count is increased by **1**. For example, if the character (**s.charAr(i)**) is **a**, the corresponding count is **counts['a' - 'a']** (i.e., **counts[0]**). If the character is **b**, the corresponding count is **counts['b' - 'a']** (i.e., **counts[1]**), since the Unicode of **b** is **1** more than that of **a**. If the character is **z**, the corresponding count is **counts['z' - 'a']** (i.e., **counts[25]**), since the Unicode of **z** is **25** more than that of **a**.

MyProgrammingLab™

9.12 How do you determine whether a character is in lowercase or uppercase?

9.13 How do you determine whether a character is alphanumeric?

9.14 Show the output of the following code.

```
public class Test {
  public static void main(String[] args) {
    String s = "Hi, Good Morning";
    System.out.println(m(s));
  }
```

```
    public static int m(String s) {
      int count = 0;
      for (int i = 0; i < s.length(); i++)
        if (Character.isUpperCase(s.charAt(i)))
          count++;

      return count;
    }
  }
```

9.6 The StringBuilder and StringBuffer Classes

The `StringBuilder` *and* `StringBuffer` *classes are similar to the* `String` *class except that the* `String` *class is immutable.*

In general, the `StringBuilder` and `StringBuffer` classes can be used wherever a string is used. `StringBuilder` and `StringBuffer` are more flexible than `String`. You can add, insert, or append new contents into `StringBuilder` and `StringBuffer` objects, whereas the value of a `String` object is fixed once the string is created.

`StringBuilder`

The `StringBuilder` class is similar to `StringBuffer` except that the methods for modifying the buffer in `StringBuffer` are *synchronized*, which means that only one task is allowed to execute the methods. Use `StringBuffer` if the class might be accessed by multiple tasks concurrently. Concurrent programming will be introduced in Chapter 32. Using `StringBuilder` is more efficient if it is accessed by just a single task. The constructors and methods in `StringBuffer` and `StringBuilder` are almost the same. This section covers `StringBuilder`. You can replace `StringBuilder` in all occurrences in this section by `StringBuffer`. The program can compile and run without any other changes.

`StringBuilder` constructors

The `StringBuilder` class has three constructors and more than 30 methods for managing the builder and modifying strings in the builder. You can create an empty string builder or a string builder from a string using the constructors, as shown in Figure 9.11.

java.lang.StringBuilder	
+StringBuilder()	Constructs an empty string builder with capacity 16.
+StringBuilder(capacity: int)	Constructs a string builder with the specified capacity.
+StringBuilder(s: String)	Constructs a string builder with the specified string.

FIGURE 9.11 The `StringBuilder` class contains the constructors for creating instances of `StringBuilder`.

9.6.1 Modifying Strings in the StringBuilder

You can append new contents at the end of a string builder, insert new contents at a specified position in a string builder, and delete or replace characters in a string builder, using the methods listed in Figure 9.12.

The `StringBuilder` class provides several overloaded methods to append `boolean`, `char`, `char[]`, `double`, `float`, `int`, `long`, and `String` into a string builder. For example, the following code appends strings and characters into `stringBuilder` to form a new string, `Welcome to Java`.

`append`

```
StringBuilder stringBuilder = new StringBuilder();
stringBuilder.append("Welcome");
stringBuilder.append(' ');
stringBuilder.append("to");
stringBuilder.append(' ');
stringBuilder.append("Java");
```

java.lang.StringBuilder	
+append(data: char[]): StringBuilder	Appends a char array into this string builder.
+append(data: char[], offset: int, len: int): StringBuilder	Appends a subarray in data into this string builder.
+append(v: *aPrimitiveType*): StringBuilder	Appends a primitive type value as a string to this builder.
+append(s: String): StringBuilder	Appends a string to this string builder.
+delete(startIndex: int, endIndex: int): StringBuilder	Deletes characters from startIndex to endIndex-1.
+deleteCharAt(index: int): StringBuilder	Deletes a character at the specified index.
+insert(index: int, data: char[], offset: int, len: int): StringBuilder	Inserts a subarray of the data in the array into the builder at the specified index.
+insert(offset: int, data: char[]): StringBuilder	Inserts data into this builder at the position offset.
+insert(offset: int, b: *aPrimitiveType*): StringBuilder	Inserts a value converted to a string into this builder.
+insert(offset: int, s: String): StringBuilder	Inserts a string into this builder at the position offset.
+replace(startIndex: int, endIndex: int, s: String): StringBuilder	Replaces the characters in this builder from startIndex to endIndex-1 with the specified string.
+reverse(): StringBuilder	Reverses the characters in the builder.
+setCharAt(index: int, ch: char): void	Sets a new character at the specified index in this builder.

FIGURE 9.12 The **StringBuilder** class contains the methods for modifying string builders.

The **StringBuilder** class also contains overloaded methods to insert **boolean**, **char**, **char array**, **double**, **float**, **int**, **long**, and **String** into a string builder. Consider the following code:

insert

```
stringBuilder.insert(11, "HTML and ");
```

Suppose **stringBuilder** contains **Welcome to Java** before the **insert** method is applied. This code inserts **"HTML and "** at position 11 in **stringBuilder** (just before the **J**). The new **stringBuilder** is **Welcome to HTML and Java**.

You can also delete characters from a string in the builder using the two **delete** methods, reverse the string using the **reverse** method, replace characters using the **replace** method, or set a new character in a string using the **setCharAt** method.

For example, suppose **stringBuilder** contains **Welcome to Java** before each of the following methods is applied:

delete — **stringBuilder.delete(8, 11)** changes the builder to **Welcome Java**.
deleteCharAt — **stringBuilder.deleteCharAt(8)** changes the builder to **Welcome o Java**.
reverse — **stringBuilder.reverse()** changes the builder to **avaJ ot emocleW**.
replace — **stringBuilder.replace(11, 15, "HTML")** changes the builder to **Welcome to HTML**.
setCharAt — **stringBuilder.setCharAt(0, 'w')** sets the builder to **welcome to Java**.

All these modification methods except **setCharAt** do two things:

- Change the contents of the string builder
- Return the reference of the string builder

ignore return value

For example, the following statement

```
StringBuilder stringBuilder1 = stringBuilder.reverse();
```

reverses the string in the builder and assigns the builder's reference to `stringBuilder1`. Thus, `stringBuilder` and `stringBuilder1` both point to the same `StringBuilder` object. Recall that a value-returning method can be invoked as a statement, if you are not interested in the return value of the method. In this case, the return value is simply ignored. For example, in the following statement

```
stringBuilder.reverse();
```

the return value is ignored.

Tip

If a string does not require any change, use `String` rather than `StringBuilder`. Java can perform some optimizations for `String`, such as sharing interned strings.

`String` or `StringBuilder`?

9.6.2 The `toString`, `capacity`, `length`, `setLength`, and `charAt` Methods

The `StringBuilder` class provides the additional methods for manipulating a string builder and obtaining its properties, as shown in Figure 9.13.

java.lang.StringBuilder	
+toString(): String	Returns a string object from the string builder.
+capacity(): int	Returns the capacity of this string builder.
+charAt(index: int): char	Returns the character at the specified index.
+length(): int	Returns the number of characters in this builder.
+setLength(newLength: int): void	Sets a new length in this builder.
+substring(startIndex: int): String	Returns a substring starting at `startIndex`.
+substring(startIndex: int, endIndex: int): String	Returns a substring from `startIndex` to `endIndex-1`.
+trimToSize(): void	Reduces the storage size used for the string builder.

FIGURE 9.13 The `StringBuilder` class contains the methods for modifying string builders.

The `capacity()` method returns the current capacity of the string builder. The capacity is the number of characters the string builder is able to store without having to increase its size.

`capacity()`

The `length()` method returns the number of characters actually stored in the string builder. The `setLength(newLength)` method sets the length of the string builder. If the `newLength` argument is less than the current length of the string builder, the string builder is truncated to contain exactly the number of characters given by the `newLength` argument. If the `newLength` argument is greater than or equal to the current length, sufficient null characters (`\u0000`) are appended to the string builder so that `length` becomes the `newLength` argument. The `newLength` argument must be greater than or equal to `0`.

`length()`
`setLength(int)`

The `charAt(index)` method returns the character at a specific `index` in the string builder. The index is `0` based. The first character of a string builder is at index `0`, the next at index `1`, and so on. The `index` argument must be greater than or equal to `0`, and less than the length of the string builder.

`charAt(int)`

Note

The length of the string is always less than or equal to the capacity of the builder. The length is the actual size of the string stored in the builder, and the capacity is the current size of the builder. The builder's capacity is automatically increased if more characters are added to exceed its capacity. Internally, a string builder is an array of characters, so

length and capacity

the builder's capacity is the size of the array. If the builder's capacity is exceeded, the array is replaced by a new array. The new array size is `2 * (the previous array size + 1)`.

Tip

initial capacity

You can use `new StringBuilder(initialCapacity)` to create a `StringBuilder` with a specified initial capacity. By carefully choosing the initial capacity, you can make your program more efficient. If the capacity is always larger than the actual length of the builder, the JVM will never need to reallocate memory for the builder. On the other hand, if the capacity is too large, you will waste memory space. You can use the `trimToSize()` method to reduce the capacity to the actual size.

trimToSize()

9.6.3 Case Study: Ignoring Nonalphanumeric Characters When Checking Palindromes

Listing 9.1, CheckPalindrome.java, considered all the characters in a string to check whether it was a palindrome. Write a new program that ignores nonalphanumeric characters in checking whether a string is a palindrome.

Here are the steps to solve the problem:

1. Filter the string by removing the nonalphanumeric characters. This can be done by creating an empty string builder, adding each alphanumeric character in the string to a string builder, and returning the string from the string builder. You can use the `isLetterOrDigit(ch)` method in the `Character` class to check whether character `ch` is a letter or a digit.

2. Obtain a new string that is the reversal of the filtered string. Compare the reversed string with the filtered string using the `equals` method.

The complete program is shown in Listing 9.4.

LISTING 9.4 PalindromeIgnoreNonAlphanumeric.java

check palindrome

```
import java.util.Scanner;

public class PalindromeIgnoreNonAlphanumeric {
  /** Main method */
  public static void main(String[] args) {
    // Create a Scanner
    Scanner input = new Scanner(System.in);

    // Prompt the user to enter a string
    System.out.print("Enter a string: ");
    String s = input.nextLine();

    // Display result
    System.out.println("Ignoring nonalphanumeric characters, \nis "
      + s + " a palindrome? " + isPalindrome(s));
  }

  /** Return true if a string is a palindrome */
  public static boolean isPalindrome(String s) {
    // Create a new string by eliminating nonalphanumeric chars
    String s1 = filter(s);

    // Create a new string that is the reversal of s1
    String s2 = reverse(s1);

    // Check if the reversal is the same as the original string
```

```
27        return s2.equals(s1);
28      }
29
30      /** Create a new string by eliminating nonalphanumeric chars */
31      public static String filter(String s) {
32        // Create a string builder
33        StringBuilder stringBuilder = new StringBuilder();
34
35        // Examine each char in the string to skip alphanumeric char
36        for (int i = 0; i < s.length(); i++) {
37          if (Character.isLetterOrDigit(s.charAt(i))) {
38            stringBuilder.append(s.charAt(i));
39          }
40        }
41
42        // Return a new filtered string
43        return stringBuilder.toString();
44      }
45
46      /** Create a new string by reversing a specified string */
47      public static String reverse(String s) {
48        StringBuilder stringBuilder = new StringBuilder(s);
49        stringBuilder.reverse(); // Invoke reverse in StringBuilder
50        return stringBuilder.toString();
51      }
52    }
```

add letter or digit

```
Enter a string: ab<c>cb?a [Enter]
Ignoring nonalphanumeric characters,
is ab<c>cb?a a palindrome? true
```

```
Enter a string: abcc><?cab [Enter]
Ignoring nonalphanumeric characters,
is abcc><?cab a palindrome? false
```

The `filter(String s)` method (lines 31–44) examines each character in string `s` and copies it to a string builder if the character is a letter or a numeric character. The `filter` method returns the string in the builder. The `reverse(String s)` method (lines 47–51) creates a new string that reverses the specified string `s`. The `filter` and `reverse` methods both return a new string. The original string is not changed.

The program in Listing 9.1 checks whether a string is a palindrome by comparing pairs of characters from both ends of the string. Listing 9.4 uses the `reverse` method in the `StringBuilder` class to reverse the string, then compares whether the two strings are equal to determine whether the original string is a palindrome.

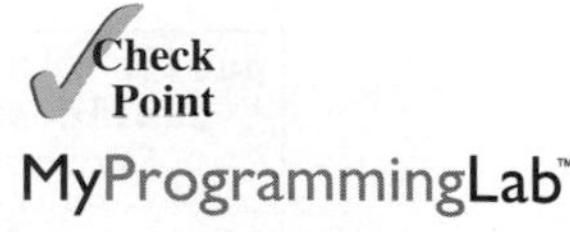

9.15 What is the difference between `StringBuilder` and `StringBuffer`?

9.16 How do you create a string builder from a string? How do you return a string from a string builder?

9.17 Write three statements to reverse a string `s` using the `reverse` method in the `StringBuilder` class.

9.18 Write three statements to delete a substring from a string `s` of `20` characters, starting at index `4` and ending with index `10`. Use the `delete` method in the `StringBuilder` class.

9.19 What is the internal storage for characters in a string and a string builder?

9.20 Suppose that `s1` and `s2` are given as follows:

```
StringBuilder s1 = new StringBuilder("Java");
StringBuilder s2 = new StringBuilder("HTML");
```

Show the value of `s1` after each of the following statements. Assume that the statements are independent.

a. `s1.append(" is fun");`
b. `s1.append(s2);`
c. `s1.insert(2, "is fun");`
d. `s1.insert(1, s2);`
e. `s1.charAt(2);`
f. `s1.length();`
g. `s1.deleteCharAt(3);`
h. `s1.delete(1, 3);`
i. `s1.reverse();`
j. `s1.replace(1, 3, "Computer");`
k. `s1.substring(1, 3);`
l. `s1.substring(2);`

9.21 Show the output of the following program:

```
public class Test {
  public static void main(String[] args) {
    String s = "Java";
    StringBuilder builder = new StringBuilder(s);
    change(s, builder);

    System.out.println(s);
    System.out.println(builder);
  }

  private static void change(String s, StringBuilder builder) {
    s = s + " and HTML";
    builder.append(" and HTML");
  }
}
```

9.7 Command-Line Arguments

The `main` method can receive string arguments from the command line.

Perhaps you have already noticed the unusual header for the `main` method, which has the parameter `args` of `String[]` type. It is clear that `args` is an array of strings. The `main` method is just like a regular method with a parameter. You can call a regular method by passing actual parameters. Can you pass arguments to `main`? Yes, of course you can. In the following examples, the `main` method in class `TestMain` is invoked by a method in `A`.

```
public class A {
  public static void main(String[] args) {
    String[] strings = {"New York",
      "Boston", "Atlanta"};
    TestMain.main(strings);
  }
}
```

```
public class TestMain {
  public static void main(String[] args) {
    for (int i = 0; i < args.length; i++)
      System.out.println(args[i]);
  }
}
```

A `main` method is just a regular method. Furthermore, you can pass arguments from the command line.

9.7.1 Passing Strings to the `main` Method

You can pass strings to a `main` method from the command line when you run the program. The following command line, for example, starts the program `TestMain` with three strings: `arg0`, `arg1`, and `arg2`:

```
java TestMain arg0 arg1 arg2
```

`arg0`, `arg1`, and `arg2` are strings, but they don't have to appear in double quotes on the command line. The strings are separated by a space. A string that contains a space must be enclosed in double quotes. Consider the following command line:

```
java TestMain "First num" alpha 53
```

It starts the program with three strings: `First num`, `alpha`, and `53`. Since `First num` is a string, it is enclosed in double quotes. Note that `53` is actually treated as a string. You can use `"53"` instead of `53` in the command line.

When the `main` method is invoked, the Java interpreter creates an array to hold the command-line arguments and pass the array reference to `args`. For example, if you invoke a program with `n` arguments, the Java interpreter creates an array like this one:

```
args = new String[n];
```

The Java interpreter then passes `args` to invoke the `main` method.

Note

If you run the program with no strings passed, the array is created with `new String[0]`. In this case, the array is empty with length `0`. `args` references to this empty array. Therefore, `args` is not `null`, but `args.length` is `0`.

9.7.2 Case Study: Calculator

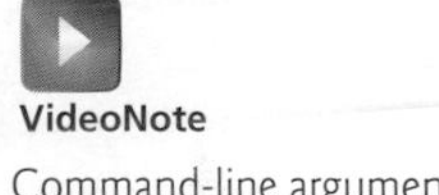

VideoNote

Command-line argument

Suppose you are to develop a program that performs arithmetic operations on integers. The program receives an expression in one string argument. The expression consists of an integer followed by an operator and another integer. For example, to add two integers, use this command:

```
java Calculator "2 + 3"
```

The program will display the following output:

```
2 + 3 = 5
```

Figure 9.14 shows sample runs of the program.

The strings passed to the main program are stored in `args`, which is an array of strings. In this case, we pass the expression as one string. Therefore, the array contains only one element in `args[0]` and `args.length` is `1`.

Here are the steps in the program:

1. Use `args.length` to determine whether the expression has been provided as one argument in the command line. If not, terminate the program using `System.exit(1)`.
2. Split the expression in the string `args[0]` into three tokens in `tokens[0]`, `tokens[1]`, and `tokens[2]`.
3. Perform a binary arithmetic operation on the operands `tokens[0]` and `tokens[2]` using the operator in `tokens[1]`.

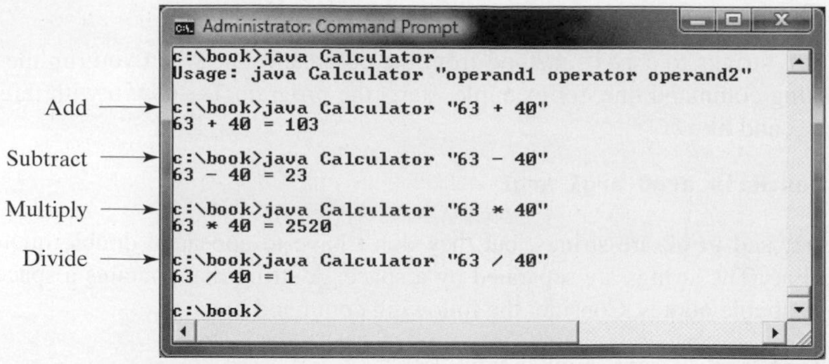

```
Administrator: Command Prompt
c:\book>java Calculator
Usage: java Calculator "operand1 operator operand2"

c:\book>java Calculator "63 + 40"
63 + 40 = 103

c:\book>java Calculator "63 - 40"
63 - 40 = 23

c:\book>java Calculator "63 * 40"
63 * 40 = 2520

c:\book>java Calculator "63 / 40"
63 / 40 = 1

c:\book>
```

Add
Subtract
Multiply
Divide

FIGURE 9.14 The program takes an expression in one argument (operand1 operator operand2) from the command line and displays the expression and the result of the arithmetic operation.

The program is shown in Listing 9.5.

LISTING 9.5 Calculator.java

check argument

split string

check operator

```
public class Calculator {
  /** Main method */
  public static void main(String[] args) {
    // Check number of strings passed
    if (args.length != 1) {
      System.out.println(
        "Usage: java Calculator \"operand1 operator operand2\"");
      System.exit(1);
    }

    // The result of the operation
    int result = 0;

    // Split items from a string
    String[] tokens = args[0].split(" ");

    // Determine the operator
    switch (tokens[1].charAt(0)) {
      case '+': result = Integer.parseInt(tokens[0]) +
                         Integer.parseInt(tokens[2]);
                break;
      case '-': result = Integer.parseInt(tokens[0]) -
                         Integer.parseInt(tokens[2]);
                break;
      case '*': result = Integer.parseInt(tokens[0]) *
                         Integer.parseInt(tokens[2]);
                break;
      case '/': result = Integer.parseInt(tokens[0]) /
                         Integer.parseInt(tokens[2]);
    }

    // Display result
    System.out.println(tokens[0] + ' ' + tokens[1] + ' '
      + tokens[2] + " = " + result);
  }
}
```

The expression is passed as a string in one argument and it is split into three parts—`tokens[0]`, `tokens[1]`, and `tokens[2]`—using the `split` method (line 15) with a space as a delimiter.

`Integer.parseInt(tokens[0])` (line 19) converts a digital string into an integer. The string must consist of digits. If it doesn't, the program will terminate abnormally.

For this program to work, the expression must be entered in the form of "operand1 operator operand2". The operands and operator are separated by exactly one space. You can modify the program to accept the expressions in different forms (see Programming Exercise 9.28).

9.22 This book declares the `main` method as

```
public static void main(String[] args)
```

Can it be replaced by one of the following lines?

```
public static void main(String args[])
public static void main(String[] x)
public static void main(String x[])
static void main(String x[])
```

9.23 Show the output of the following program when invoked using

1. **java Test I have a dream**
2. **java Test "1 2 3"**
3. **java Test**

```
public class Test {
  public static void main(String[] args) {
    System.out.println("Number of strings is " + args.length);
    for (int i = 0; i < args.length; i++)
      System.out.println(args[i]);
  }
}
```

Key Terms

interned string 337

wrapper class 350

Chapter Summary

1. Strings are objects encapsulated in the `String` class. A string can be constructed using one of the 13 constructors or simply using a string literal. Java treats a string literal as a `String` object.

2. A `String` object is immutable; its contents cannot be changed. To improve efficiency and save memory, the JVM stores two literal strings that have the same character sequence in a unique object. This unique object is called an *interned string object*.

3. You can get the length of a string by invoking its `length()` method, retrieve a character at the specified `index` in the string using the `charAt(index)` method, and use the `indexOf` and `lastIndexOf` methods to find a character or a substring in a string.

4. You can use the `concat` method to concatenate two strings, or the plus (+) operator to concatenate two or more strings.

5. You can use the `substring` method to obtain a substring from the string.

6. You can use the `equals` and `compareTo` methods to compare strings. The `equals` method returns `true` if two strings are equal, and `false` if they are not equal. The `compareTo` method returns `0`, a positive integer, or a negative integer, depending on whether one string is equal to, greater than, or less than the other string.

7. A *regular expression* (abbreviated *regex*) is a string that describes a pattern for matching a set of strings. You can match, replace, or split a string by specifying a pattern.

8. The `Character` class is a wrapper class for a single character. The `Character` class provides useful static methods to determine whether a character is a letter (`isLetter(char)`), a digit (`isDigit(char)`), uppercase (`isUpperCase(char)`), or lowercase (`isLowerCase(char)`).

9. The `StringBuilder` and `StringBuffer` classes can be used to replace the `String` class. The `String` object is immutable, but you can add, insert, or append new contents into `StringBuilder` and `StringBuffer` objects. Use `String` if the string contents do not require any change, and use `StringBuilder` or `StringBuffer` if they might change.

10. You can pass strings to the `main` method from the command line. Strings passed to the `main` program are stored in `args`, which is an array of strings. The first string is represented by `args[0]`, and `args.length` is the number of strings passed.

Test Questions

Do the test questions for this chapter online at www.cs.armstrong.edu/liang/intro9e/test.html.

MyProgrammingLab™

Programming Exercises

Sections 9.2–9.3

*9.1 (*Check SSN*) Write a program that prompts the user to enter a Social Security number in the format DDD-DD-DDDD, where D is a digit. The program displays `Valid SSN` for a correct Social Security number and `Invalid SSN` otherwise.

**9.2 (*Check substrings*) You can check whether a string is a substring of another string by using the `indexOf` method in the `String` class. Write your own method for this function. Write a program that prompts the user to enter two strings, and checks whether the first string is a substring of the second.

**9.3 (*Check password*) Some websites impose certain rules for passwords. Write a method that checks whether a string is a valid password. Suppose the password rules are as follows:

- A password must have at least eight characters.
- A password consists of only letters and digits.
- A password must contain at least two digits.

Write a program that prompts the user to enter a password and displays `Valid Password` if the rules are followed or `Invalid Password` otherwise.

9.4 (*Occurrences of a specified character*) Write a method that finds the number of occurrences of a specified character in a string using the following header:

```
public static int count(String str, char a)
```

For example, `count("Welcome", 'e')` returns `2`. Write a test program that prompts the user to enter a string followed by a character and displays the number of occurrences of the character in the string.

****9.5** (*Occurrences of each digit in a string*) Write a method that counts the occurrences of each digit in a string using the following header:

```
public static int[] count(String s)
```

The method counts how many times a digit appears in the string. The return value is an array of ten elements, each of which holds the count for a digit. For example, after executing `int[] counts = count("12203AB3")`, `counts[0]` is `1`, `counts[1]` is `1`, `counts[2]` is `2`, and `counts[3]` is `2`.

Write a test program that prompts the user to enter a string and displays the number of occurrences of each digit in the string.

***9.6** (*Count the letters in a string*) Write a method that counts the number of letters in a string using the following header:

```
public static int countLetters(String s)
```

Write a test program that prompts the user to enter a string and displays the number of letters in the string.

***9.7** (*Phone keypads*) The international standard letter/number mapping found on the telephone is:

1	2 ABC	3 DEF
4 GHI	5 JKL	6 MNO
7 PQRS	8 TUV	9 WXYZ
	0	

Write a method that returns a number, given an uppercase letter, as follows:

```
public static int getNumber(char uppercaseLetter)
```

Write a test program that prompts the user to enter a phone number as a strin input number may contain letters. The program translates a letter (upper- or case) to a digit and leaves all other characters intact. Here is a sample r program:

```
Enter a string: 1-800-Flowers [Enter]
1-800-3569377
```

```
Enter a string: 1800flowers
18003569377
```

***9.8** (*Binary to decimal*) Write a method that parses a binary number as a string into a decimal integer. The method header is:

```
public static int binaryToDecimal(String binaryString)
```

For example, binary string 10001 is 17 ($1 \times 2^4 + 0 \times 2^3 + 0 \times 2^2 + 0 \times 2 + 1 = 17$). Therefore, `binaryToDecimal("10001")` returns `17`. Note that `Integer.parseInt("10001", 2)` parses a binary string to a decimal value. Do not use this method in this exercise.

Write a test program that prompts the user to enter a binary string and displays the corresponding decimal integer value.

Section 9.4

****9.9** (*Binary to hex*) Write a method that parses a binary number into a hex number. The method header is:

```
public static String binaryToHex(String binaryValue)
```

Write a test program that prompts the user to enter a binary number and displays the corresponding hexadecimal value.

VideoNote
Number conversion

****9.10** (*Decimal to binary*) Write a method that parses a decimal number into a binary number as a string. The method header is:

```
public static String decimalToBinary(int value)
```

Write a test program that prompts the user to enter a decimal integer value and displays the corresponding binary value.

****9.11** (*Sort characters in a string*) Write a method that returns a sorted string using the following header:

```
public static String sort(String s)
```

For example, `sort("acb")` returns `abc`.

Write a test program that prompts the user to enter a string and displays the sorted string.

****9.12** (*Anagrams*) Write a method that checks whether two words are anagrams. Two words are anagrams if they contain the same letters in any order. For example, `silent` and `listen` are anagrams. The header of the method is:

```
public static boolean isAnagram(String s1, String s2)
```

Write a test program that prompts the user to enter two strings and, if they are anagrams, displays `two strings are anagrams`, and displays `two strings are not anagrams` if they are not anagrams.

tion 9.5

(*Pass a string to check palindromes*) Rewrite Listing 9.1 by passing the string as a command-line argument.

*

Sum integers) Write two programs. The first program passes an unspecified num- r of integers as separate strings to the `main` method and displays their total. The second program passes an unspecified number of integers delimited by one space in a string to the main method and displays their total. Name the two programs Exercise9_14a and Exercise9_14b, as shown in Figure 9.15.

FIGURE 9.15 The program adds all the numbers passed from the command line.

***9.15** (*Find the number of uppercase letters in a string*) Write a program that passes a string to the main method and displays the number of uppercase letters in the string.

Comprehensive

****9.16** (*Implement the String class*) The String class is provided in the Java library. Provide your own implementation for the following methods (name the new class MyString1):

```
public MyString1(char[] chars);
public char charAt(int index);
public int length();
public MyString1 substring(int begin, int end);
public MyString1 toLowerCase();
public boolean equals(MyString1 s);
public static MyString1 valueOf(int i);
```

****9.17** (*Guess the capitals*) Write a program that repeatedly prompts the user to enter a capital for a state. Upon receiving the user input, the program reports whether the answer is correct. Assume that 50 states and their capitals are stored in a two-dimensional array, as shown in Figure 9.16. The program prompts the user to answer all states' capitals and displays the total correct count. The user's answer is not case-sensitive.

```
Alabama        Montgomery
Alaska         Juneau
Arizona        Phoenix
...            ...
...            ...
```

FIGURE 9.16 A two-dimensional array stores states and their capitals.

Here is a sample run:

```
What is the capital of Alabama? Montogomery [Enter]
The correct answer should be Montgomery
What is the capital of Alaska? Juneau [Enter]
Your answer is correct
What is the capital of Arizona? ...
...
The correct count is 35
```

**9.18 (*Implement the `String` class*) The `String` class is provided in the Java library. Provide your own implementation for the following methods (name the new class `MyString2`):

```
public MyString2(String s);
public int compare(String s);
public MyString2 substring(int begin);
public MyString2 toUpperCase();
public char[] toChars();
public static MyString2 valueOf(boolean b);
```

*9.19 (*Common prefix*) Write a method that returns the longest common prefix of two strings. For example, the longest common prefix of `distance` and `disinfection` is `dis`. The header of the method is:

```
public static String prefix(String s1, String s2)
```

If the two strings don't have a common prefix, the method returns an empty string.

Write a `main` method that prompts the user to enter two strings and displays their longest common prefix.

9.20 (*Implement the `Character` class*) The `Character` class is provided in the Java library. Provide your own implementation for this class. Name the new class `MyCharacter`.

**9.21 (*New string `split` method*) The `split` method in the `String` class returns an array of strings consisting of the substrings split by the delimiters. However, the delimiters are not returned. Implement the following new method that returns an array of strings consisting of the substrings split by the matching delimiters, including the matching delimiters.

```
public static String[] split(String s, String regex)
```

For example, `split("ab#12#453", "#")` returns `ab`, `#`, `12`, `#`, `453` in an array of `String`, and `split("a?b?gf#e", "[?#]")` returns `a`, `b`, `?`, `b`, `gf`, `#`, and `e` in an array of `String`.

**9.22 (*Implement the `StringBuilder` class*) The `StringBuilder` class is provided in the Java library. Provide your own implementation for the following methods (name the new class `MyStringBuilder1`):

```
public MyStringBuilder1(String s);
public MyStringBuilder1 append(MyStringBuilder1 s);
public MyStringBuilder1 append(int i);
public int length();
public char charAt(int index);
public MyStringBuilder1 toLowerCase();
public MyStringBuilder1 substring(int begin, int end);
public String toString();
```

**9.23 (*Financial: credit card number validation*) Rewrite Programming Exercise 5.31 using a string input for the credit card number. Redesign the program using the following methods:

```
/** Return true if the card number is valid */
public static boolean isValid(String cardNumber)

/** Get the result from Step 2 */
public static int sumOfDoubleEvenPlace(String cardNumber)
```

9.4 (*Occurrences of a specified character*) Write a method that finds the number of occurrences of a specified character in a string using the following header:

```
public static int count(String str, char a)
```

For example, `count("Welcome", 'e')` returns `2`. Write a test program that prompts the user to enter a string followed by a character and displays the number of occurrences of the character in the string.

****9.5** (*Occurrences of each digit in a string*) Write a method that counts the occurrences of each digit in a string using the following header:

```
public static int[] count(String s)
```

The method counts how many times a digit appears in the string. The return value is an array of ten elements, each of which holds the count for a digit. For example, after executing `int[] counts = count("12203AB3")`, `counts[0]` is `1`, `counts[1]` is `1`, `counts[2]` is `2`, and `counts[3]` is `2`.

Write a test program that prompts the user to enter a string and displays the number of occurrences of each digit in the string.

***9.6** (*Count the letters in a string*) Write a method that counts the number of letters in a string using the following header:

```
public static int countLetters(String s)
```

Write a test program that prompts the user to enter a string and displays the number of letters in the string.

***9.7** (*Phone keypads*) The international standard letter/number mapping found on the telephone is:

1	2 ABC	3 DEF
4 GHI	5 JKL	6 MNO
7 PQRS	8 TUV	9 WXYZ
	0	

Write a method that returns a number, given an uppercase letter, as follows:

```
public static int getNumber(char uppercaseLetter)
```

Write a test program that prompts the user to enter a phone number as a string. The input number may contain letters. The program translates a letter (upper- or lowercase) to a digit and leaves all other characters intact. Here is a sample run of the program:

```
Enter a string: 1-800-Flowers ↵Enter
1-800-3569377
```

```
Enter a string: 1800flowers
18003569377
```

***9.8** (*Binary to decimal*) Write a method that parses a binary number as a string into a decimal integer. The method header is:

```
public static int binaryToDecimal(String binaryString)
```

For example, binary string 10001 is 17 ($1 \times 2^4 + 0 \times 2^3 + 0 \times 2^2 + 0 \times 2 + 1 = 17$). Therefore, `binaryToDecimal("10001")` returns `17`. Note that `Integer.parseInt("10001", 2)` parses a binary string to a decimal value. Do not use this method in this exercise.

Write a test program that prompts the user to enter a binary string and displays the corresponding decimal integer value.

Section 9.4

****9.9** (*Binary to hex*) Write a method that parses a binary number into a hex number. The method header is:

```
public static String binaryToHex(String binaryValue)
```

Write a test program that prompts the user to enter a binary number and displays the corresponding hexadecimal value.

VideoNote
Number conversion

****9.10** (*Decimal to binary*) Write a method that parses a decimal number into a binary number as a string. The method header is:

```
public static String decimalToBinary(int value)
```

Write a test program that prompts the user to enter a decimal integer value and displays the corresponding binary value.

****9.11** (*Sort characters in a string*) Write a method that returns a sorted string using the following header:

```
public static String sort(String s)
```

For example, `sort("acb")` returns `abc`.

Write a test program that prompts the user to enter a string and displays the sorted string.

****9.12** (*Anagrams*) Write a method that checks whether two words are anagrams. Two words are anagrams if they contain the same letters in any order. For example, `silent` and `listen` are anagrams. The header of the method is:

```
public static boolean isAnagram(String s1, String s2)
```

Write a test program that prompts the user to enter two strings and, if they are anagrams, displays `two strings are anagrams`, and displays `two strings are not anagrams` if they are not anagrams.

Section 9.5

***9.13** (*Pass a string to check palindromes*) Rewrite Listing 9.1 by passing the string as a command-line argument.

***9.14** (*Sum integers*) Write two programs. The first program passes an unspecified number of integers as separate strings to the `main` method and displays their total. The

```
/** Return this number if it is a single digit; otherwise,
 * return the sum of the two digits */
public static int getDigit(int number)

/** Return sum of odd-place digits in number */
public static int sumOfOddPlace(String cardNumber)
```

****9.24** (*Implement the* `StringBuilder` *class*) The `StringBuilder` class is provided in the Java library. Provide your own implementation for the following methods (name the new class `MyStringBuilder2`):

```
public MyStringBuilder2();
public MyStringBuilder2(char[] chars);
public MyStringBuilder2(String s);
public MyStringBuilder2 insert(int offset, MyStringBuilder2 s);
public MyStringBuilder2 reverse();
public MyStringBuilder2 substring(int begin);
public MyStringBuilder2 toUpperCase();
```

*****9.25** (*Game: hangman*) Write a hangman game that randomly generates a word and prompts the user to guess one letter at a time, as shown in the sample run. Each letter in the word is displayed as an asterisk. When the user makes a correct guess, the actual letter is then displayed. When the user finishes a word, display the number of misses and ask the user whether to continue to play with another word. Declare an array to store words, as follows:

```
// Add any words you wish in this array
String[] words = {"write", "that", ...};
```

```
(Guess) Enter a letter in word ******* > p [Enter]
(Guess) Enter a letter in word p****** > r [Enter]
(Guess) Enter a letter in word pr**r** > p [Enter]
      p is already in the word
(Guess) Enter a letter in word pr**r** > o [Enter]
(Guess) Enter a letter in word pro*r** > g [Enter]
(Guess) Enter a letter in word progr** > n [Enter]
      n is not in the word
(Guess) Enter a letter in word progr** > m [Enter]
(Guess) Enter a letter in word progr*m > a [Enter]
The word is program. You missed 1 time
Do you want to guess another word? Enter y or n>
```

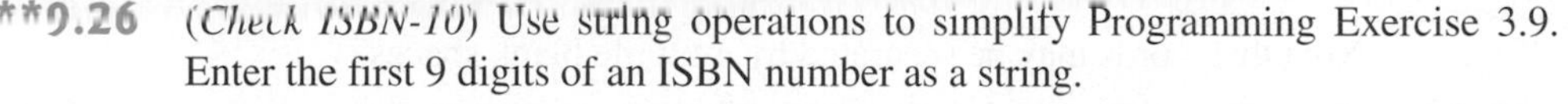

****9.26** (*Check ISBN-10*) Use string operations to simplify Programming Exercise 3.9. Enter the first 9 digits of an ISBN number as a string.

Check ISBN-10

***9.27** (*Bioinformatics: find genes*) Biologists use a sequence of the letters A, C, T, and G to model a *genome*. A *gene* is a substring of a genome that starts after a triplet ATG and ends before a triplet TAG, TAA, or TGA. Furthermore, the length of a gene string is a multiple of 3, and the gene does not contain any of the triplets ATG, TAG, TAA, or TGA. Write a program that prompts the user to enter a genome and displays all genes in the genome. If no gene is found in the input sequence, display "no gene is found". Here are the sample runs:

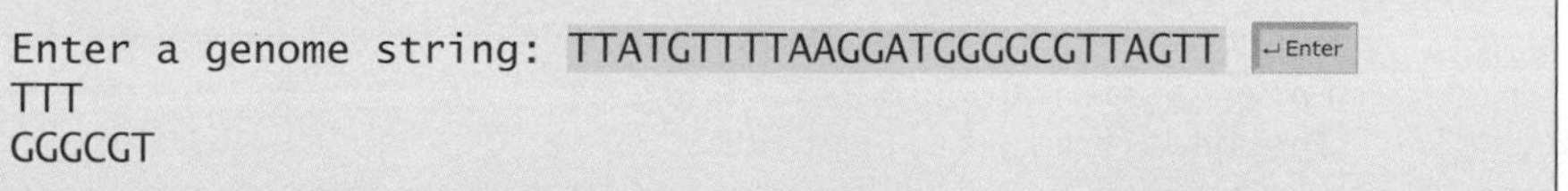

```
Enter a genome string: TTATGTTTTAAGGATGGGGCGTTAGTT [Enter]
TTT
GGGCGT
```

```
Enter a genome string: TGTGTGTATAT ↵Enter
no gene is found
```

***9.28** (*Calculator*) Revise Listing 9.5, Calculator.java, to accept an expression in which the operands and operator are separated by zero or more spaces. For example, 3+4 and 3 + 4 are acceptable expressions.

***9.29** (*Business: check ISBN-13*) **ISBN-13** is a new standard for identifying books. It uses the 13 digits $d_1d_2d_3d_4d_5d_6d_7d_8d_9d_{10}d_{11}d_{12}d_{13}$. The last digit, d_{13}, is a checksum, which is calculated from the other digits using the following formula:

$$10 - (d_1 + 3d_2 + d_3 + 3d_4 + d_5 + 3d_6 + d_7 + 3d_8 + d_9 + 3d_{10} + d_{11} + 3d_{12}) \% 10$$

If the checksum is 10, replace it with 0. Your program should read the input as a string. Here are sample runs:

```
Enter the first 12 digits of an ISBN-13 as a string:
  978013213080 ↵Enter
The ISBN-13 number is 9780132130806
```

```
Enter the first 12 digits of an ISBN-13 as a string:
  978013213079 ↵Enter
The ISBN-13 number is 9780132130790
```

***9.30** (*Capitalize first letter of each word*) Write the following method that returns a new string in which the first letter in each word is capitalized.

```
public static void title(String s)
```

Write a test program that prompts the user to enter a string and invokes this method, and displays the return value from this method. Here is a sample run:

```
Enter a string: london   england 2015 ↵Enter
The new string is: London   England 2015
```

Note that words may be separated by multiple blank spaces.

***9.31** (*Swap case*) Write the following method that returns a new string in which the uppercase letters are changed to lowercase and lowercase letters are changed to uppercase.

```
public static String swapCase(String s)
```

Write a test program that prompts the user to enter a string and invokes this method, and displays the return value from this method. Here is a sample run:

```
Enter a string: I'm here ↵Enter
The new string is: i'M HERE
```

CHAPTER

10

THINKING IN OBJECTS

Objectives

- To create immutable objects from immutable classes to protect the contents of objects (§10.2).
- To determine the scope of variables in the context of a class (§10.3).
- To use the keyword `this` to refer to the calling object itself (§10.4).
- To apply class abstraction to develop software (§10.5).
- To explore the differences between the procedural paradigm and object-oriented paradigm (§10.6).
- To develop classes for modeling composition relationships (§10.7).
- To design programs using the object-oriented paradigm (§§10.8–10.10).
- To design classes that follow the class-design guidelines (§10.11).
- To create objects for primitive values using the wrapper classes (`Byte`, `Short`, `Integer`, `Long`, `Float`, `Double`, `Character`, and `Boolean`) (§10.12).
- To simplify programming using automatic conversion between primitive types and wrapper class types (§10.13).
- To use the `BigInteger` and `BigDecimal` classes for computing very large numbers with arbitrary precisions (§10.14).

10.1 Introduction

The focus of this chapter is on class design and explores the differences between procedural programming and object-oriented programming.

The preceding two chapters introduced objects and classes. You learned how to define classes, create objects, and use objects from several classes in the Java API (e.g., `Date`, `Random`, `String`, `StringBuilder`, and `Scanner`). This book's approach is to teach problem solving and fundamental programming techniques before object-oriented programming. This chapter shows how procedural and object-oriented programming differ. You will see the benefits of object-oriented programming and learn to use it effectively.

We will use several examples to illustrate the advantages of the object-oriented approach. The examples involve designing new classes and using them in applications. We first introduce some language features supporting these examples.

10.2 Immutable Objects and Classes

You can define immutable classes to create immutable objects. The contents of immutable objects cannot be changed.

VideoNote
Immutable objects and `this` keyword

immutable object

immutable class

Normally, you create an object and allow its contents to be changed later. However, occasionally it is desirable to create an object whose contents cannot be changed once the object has been created. We call such an object an *immutable object* and its class an *immutable class*. The `String` class, for example, is immutable. If you deleted the `set` method in the `CircleWithPrivateDataFields` class in Listing 8.9, the class would be immutable, because radius is private and cannot be changed without a `set` method.

If a class is immutable, then all its data fields must be private and it cannot contain public `set` methods for any data fields. A class with all private data fields and no mutators is not necessarily immutable. For example, the following `Student` class has all private data fields and no `set` methods, but it is not an immutable class.

`Student` class

```
public class Student {
  private int id;
  private String name;
  private java.util.Date dateCreated;

  public Student(int ssn, String newName) {
    id = ssn;
    name = newName;
    dateCreated = new java.util.Date();
  }

  public int getId() {
    return id;
  }

  public String getName() {
    return name;
  }

  public java.util.Date getDateCreated() {
    return dateCreated;
  }
}
```

As shown in the following code, the data field `dateCreated` is returned using the `getDateCreated()` method. This is a reference to a `Date` object. Through this reference, the content for `dateCreated` can be changed.

```
public class Test {
  public static void main(String[] args) {
    Student student = new Student(111223333, "John");
    java.util.Date dateCreated = student.getDateCreated();
    dateCreated.setTime(200000); // Now dateCreated field is changed!
  }
}
```

For a class to be immutable, it must meet the following requirements:

- All data fields must be private.
- There can't be any mutator methods for data fields.
- No accessor methods can return a reference to a data field that is mutable.

Interested readers may refer to Supplement III.AB for an extended discussion on immutable objects.

Check Point

MyProgrammingLab™

10.1 If a class contains only private data fields and no `set` methods, is the class immutable?

10.2 If all the data fields in a class are private and primitive types, and the class doesn't contain any `set` methods, is the class immutable?

10.3 Is the following class immutable?

```
public class A {
  private int[] values;

  public int[] getValues() {
    return values;
  }
}
```

10.3 The Scope of Variables

Key Point

The scope of instance and static variables is the entire class, regardless of where the variables are declared.

Chapter 5, Methods, discussed local variables and their scope rules. Local variables are declared and used inside a method locally. This section discusses the scope rules of all the variables in the context of a class.

class's variables

Instance and static variables in a class are referred to as the *class's variables* or *data fields*. A variable defined inside a method is referred to as a *local variable*. The scope of a class's variables is the entire class, regardless of where the variables are declared. A class's variables and methods can appear in any order in the class, as shown in Figure 10.1a. The exception is when a data field is initialized based on a reference to another data field. In such cases, the

```
public class Circle {
  public double findArea() {
    return radius * radius * Math.PI;
  }

  private double radius = 1;
}
```

(a) The variable `radius` and method `findArea()` can be declared in any order.

```
public class F {
  private int i;
  private int j = i + 1;
}
```

(b) `i` has to be declared before `j` because `j`'s initial value is dependent on `i`.

FIGURE 10.1 Members of a class can be declared in any order, with one exception.

other data field must be declared first, as shown in Figure 10.1b. For consistency, this book declares data fields at the beginning of the class.

You can declare a class's variable only once, but you can declare the same variable name in a method many times in different nonnesting blocks.

hidden variables

If a local variable has the same name as a class's variable, the local variable takes precedence and the class's variable with the same name is *hidden*. For example, in the following program, x is defined both as an instance variable and as a local variable in the method.

```
public class F {
  private int x = 0; // Instance variable
  private int y = 0;

  public F() {
  }

  public void p() {
    int x = 1; // Local variable
    System.out.println("x = " + x);
    System.out.println("y = " + y);
  }
}
```

What is the printout for f.p(), where f is an instance of F? The printout for f.p() is 1 for x and 0 for y. Here is why:

- x is declared as a data field with the initial value of 0 in the class, but it is also declared in the method p() with an initial value of 1. The latter x is referenced in the System.out.println statement.
- y is declared outside the method p(), but y is accessible inside the method.

Tip

To avoid confusion and mistakes, do not use the names of instance or static variables as local variable names, except for method parameters.

Check Point

MyProgrammingLab™

10.4 What is the output of the following program?

```
public class Test {
  private static int i = 0;
  private static int j = 0;

  public static void main(String[] args) {
    int i = 2;
    int k = 3;

    {
      int j = 3;
      System.out.println("i + j is " + i + j);
    }

    k = i + j;
    System.out.println("k is " + k);
    System.out.println("j is " + j);
  }
}
```

10.4 The this Reference

The keyword `this` *refers to the object itself. It can also be used inside a constructor to invoke another constructor of the same class.*

this keyword

The `this` *keyword* is the name of a reference that an object can use to refer to itself. You can use the `this` keyword to refer to the object's instance members. For example, the following code in (a) uses `this` to reference the object's `radius` and invokes its `getArea()` method explicitly. The `this` reference is normally omitted, as shown in (b). However, the `this` reference is needed to reference hidden data fields or invoke an overloaded constructor.

```
public class Circle {
  private double radius;

  ...

  public double getArea() {
    return this.radius * this.radius
      * Math.PI;
  }

  public String toString() {
    return "radius: " + this.radius
      + "area: " + this.getArea();
  }
}
```

(a)

Equivalent

```
public class Circle {
  private double radius;

  ...

  public double getArea() {
    return radius * radius * Math.PI;
  }

  public String toString() {
    return "radius: " + radius
      + "area: " + getArea();
  }
}
```

(b)

10.4.1 Using this to Reference Hidden Data Fields

hidden data fields

The `this` keyword can be used to reference a class's *hidden data fields*. For example, a data-field name is often used as the parameter name in a `set` method for the data field. In this case, the data field is hidden in the `set` method. You need to reference the hidden data-field name in the method in order to set a new value to it. A hidden static variable can be accessed simply by using the `ClassName.staticVariable` reference. A hidden instance variable can be accessed by using the keyword `this`, as shown in Figure 10.2a.

```
public class F {
  private int i = 5;
  private static double k = 0;

  public void setI(int i) {
    this.i = i;
  }

  public static void setK(double k) {
    F.k = k;
  }

  // Other methods omitted
}
```

(a)

```
Suppose that f1 and f2 are two objects of F.

Invoking f1.setI(10) is to execute
   this.i = 10, where this refers f1

Invoking f2.setI(45) is to execute
   this.i = 45, where this refers f2

Invoking F.setK(33) is to execute
   F.k = 33. setK is a static method
```

(b)

FIGURE 10.2 The keyword `this` refers to the calling object that invokes the method.

The `this` keyword gives us a way to refer to the object that invokes an instance method. To invoke `f1.setI(10)`, `this.i = i` is executed, which assigns the value of parameter `i` to the data field `i` of this calling object `f1`. The keyword `this` refers to the object that invokes the instance method `setI`, as shown in Figure 10.2b. The line `F.k = k` means that the value in parameter `k` is assigned to the static data field `k` of the class, which is shared by all the objects of the class.

10.4.2 Using `this` to Invoke a Constructor

The `this` keyword can be used to invoke another constructor of the same class. For example, you can rewrite the `Circle` class as follows:

```
public class Circle {
  private double radius;

  public Circle(double radius) {
    this.radius = radius;
  }

  public Circle() {
    this(1.0);
  }

  ...
}
```

The `this` keyword is used to reference the hidden data field radius of the object being constructed.

The `this` keyword is used to invoke another constructor.

The line `this(1.0)` in the second constructor invokes the first constructor with a `double` value argument.

Note

Java requires that the `this(arg-list)` statement appear first in the constructor before any other executable statements.

Tip

If a class has multiple constructors, it is better to implement them using `this(arg-list)` as much as possible. In general, a constructor with no or fewer arguments can invoke a constructor with more arguments using `this(arg-list)`. This syntax often simplifies coding and makes the class easier to read and to maintain.

Check Point

MyProgrammingLab™

10.5 Describe the role of the `this` keyword.

10.6 What is wrong in the following code?

```
public class C {
  private int p;

  public C() {
    System.out.println("C's no-arg constructor invoked");
    this(0);
  }

  public C(int p) {
    p = p;
  }

  public void setP(int p) {
    p = p;
  }
}
```

10.7 What is wrong in the following code?

```
public class Test {
  private int id;

  public void m1() {
    this.id = 45;
  }

  public void m2() {
    Test.id = 45;
  }
}
```

10.5 Class Abstraction and Encapsulation

Class abstraction *is the separation of class implementation from the use of a class. The details of implementation are encapsulated and hidden from the user. This is known as* class encapsulation.

In Chapter 5, you learned about method abstraction and used it in stepwise refinement. Java provides many levels of abstraction, and *class abstraction* separates class implementation from how the class is used. The creator of a class describes the functions of the class and lets the user know how the class can be used. The collection of methods and fields that are accessible from outside the class, together with the description of how these members are expected to behave, serves as the *class's contract*. As shown in Figure 10.3, the user of the class does not need to know how the class is implemented. The details of implementation are encapsulated and hidden from the user. This is called *class encapsulation*. For example, you can create a `Circle` object and find the area of the circle without knowing how the area is computed. For this reason, a class is also known as an *abstract data type* (ADT).

class abstraction

class's contract

class encapsulation

abstract data type

FIGURE 10.3 Class abstraction separates class implementation from the use of the class.

Class abstraction and encapsulation are two sides of the same coin. Many real-life examples illustrate the concept of class abstraction. Consider, for instance, building a computer system. Your personal computer has many components—a CPU, memory, disk, motherboard, fan, and so on. Each component can be viewed as an object that has properties and methods. To get the components to work together, you need know only how each component is used and how it interacts with the others. You don't need to know how the components work internally. The internal implementation is encapsulated and hidden from you. You can build a computer without knowing how a component is implemented.

The computer-system analogy precisely mirrors the object-oriented approach. Each component can be viewed as an object of the class for the component. For example, you might have a class that models all kinds of fans for use in a computer, with properties such as fan size and speed and methods such as start and stop. A specific fan is an instance of this class with specific property values.

As another example, consider getting a loan. A specific loan can be viewed as an object of a `Loan` class. The interest rate, loan amount, and loan period are its data properties, and

VideoNote
The Loan class

computing the monthly payment and total payment are its methods. When you buy a car, a loan object is created by instantiating the class with your loan interest rate, loan amount, and loan period. You can then use the methods to find the monthly payment and total payment of your loan. As a user of the `Loan` class, you don't need to know how these methods are implemented.

Listing 2.8, ComputeLoan.java, presented a program for computing loan payments. That program cannot be reused in other programs because the code for computing the payments is in the `main` method. One way to fix this problem is to define static methods for computing the monthly payment and total payment. However, this solution has limitations. Suppose you wish to associate a date with the loan. There is no good way to tie a date with a loan without using objects. The traditional procedural programming paradigm is action-driven, and data are separated from actions. The object-oriented programming paradigm focuses on objects, and actions are defined along with the data in objects. To tie a date with a loan, you can define a loan class with a date along with other of the loan's properties as data fields. A loan object now contains data and actions for manipulating and processing data, and the loan data and actions are integrated in one object. Figure 10.4 shows the UML class diagram for the `Loan` class.

Loan	
-annualInterestRate: double	The annual interest rate of the loan (default: 2.5).
-numberOfYears: int	The number of years for the loan (default: 1).
-loanAmount: double	The loan amount (default: 1000).
-loanDate: java.util.Date	The date this loan was created.
+Loan()	Constructs a default `Loan` object.
+Loan(annualInterestRate: double, numberOfYears: int,loanAmount: double)	Constructs a loan with specified interest rate, years, and loan amount.
+getAnnualInterestRate(): double	Returns the annual interest rate of this loan.
+getNumberOfYears(): int	Returns the number of the years of this loan.
+getLoanAmount(): double	Returns the amount of this loan.
+getLoanDate(): java.util.Date	Returns the date of the creation of this loan.
+setAnnualInterestRate(annualInterestRate: double): void	Sets a new annual interest rate for this loan.
+setNumberOfYears(numberOfYears: int): void	Sets a new number of years for this loan.
+setLoanAmount(loanAmount: double): void	Sets a new amount for this loan.
+getMonthlyPayment(): double	Returns the monthly payment for this loan.
+getTotalPayment(): double	Returns the total payment for this loan.

FIGURE 10.4 The `Loan` class models the properties and behaviors of loans.

The UML diagram in Figure 10.4 serves as the contract for the `Loan` class. Throughout this book, you will play the roles of both class user and class developer. Remember that a class user can use the class without knowing how the class is implemented.

Assume that the `Loan` class is available. The program in Listing 10.1 uses that class.

LISTING 10.1 TestLoanClass.java

```
import java.util.Scanner;

public class TestLoanClass {
  /** Main method */
  public static void main(String[] args) {
```

```
6       // Create a Scanner
7       Scanner input = new Scanner(System.in);
8
9       // Enter annual interest rate
10      System.out.print(
11        "Enter annual interest rate, for example, 8.25: ");
12      double annualInterestRate = input.nextDouble();
13
14      // Enter number of years
15      System.out.print("Enter number of years as an integer: ");
16      int numberOfYears = input.nextInt();
17
18      // Enter loan amount
19      System.out.print("Enter loan amount, for example, 120000.95: ");
20      double loanAmount = input.nextDouble();
21
22      // Create a Loan object
23      Loan loan =
24        new Loan(annualInterestRate, numberOfYears, loanAmount);
25
26      // Display loan date, monthly payment, and total payment
27      System.out.printf("The loan was created on %s\n" +
28        "The monthly payment is %.2f\nThe total payment is %.2f\n",
29        loan.getLoanDate().toString(), loan.getMonthlyPayment(),
30        loan.getTotalPayment());
31    }
32  }
```

create Loan object

invoke instance method

invoke instance method

```
Enter annual interest rate, for example, 8.25: 2.5 [Enter]
Enter number of years as an integer: 5 [Enter]
Enter loan amount, for example, 120000.95: 1000 [Enter]
The loan was created on Sat Jun 16 21:12:50 EDT 2012
The monthly payment is 17.75
The total payment is 1064.84
```

The main method reads the interest rate, the payment period (in years), and the loan amount; creates a Loan object; and then obtains the monthly payment (line 29) and the total payment (line 30) using the instance methods in the Loan class.

The Loan class can be implemented as in Listing 10.2.

LISTING 10.2 Loan.java

```
public class Loan {
  private double annualInterestRate;
  private int numberOfYears;
  private double loanAmount;
  private java.util.Date loanDate;

  /** Default constructor */
  public Loan() {
    this(2.5, 1, 1000);
  }

  /** Construct a loan with specified annual interest rate,
      number of years, and loan amount
    */
```

no-arg constructor

constructor

```
  public Loan(double annualInterestRate, int numberOfYears,
      double loanAmount) {
    this.annualInterestRate = annualInterestRate;
    this.numberOfYears = numberOfYears;
    this.loanAmount = loanAmount;
    loanDate = new java.util.Date();
  }

  /** Return annualInterestRate */
  public double getAnnualInterestRate() {
    return annualInterestRate;
  }

  /** Set a new annualInterestRate */
  public void setAnnualInterestRate(double annualInterestRate) {
    this.annualInterestRate = annualInterestRate;
  }

  /** Return numberOfYears */
  public int getNumberOfYears() {
    return numberOfYears;
  }

  /** Set a new numberOfYears */
  public void setNumberOfYears(int numberOfYears) {
    this.numberOfYears = numberOfYears;
  }

  /** Return loanAmount */
  public double getLoanAmount() {
    return loanAmount;
  }

  /** Set a new loanAmount */
  public void setLoanAmount(double loanAmount) {
    this.loanAmount = loanAmount;
  }

  /** Find monthly payment */
  public double getMonthlyPayment() {
    double monthlyInterestRate = annualInterestRate / 1200;
    double monthlyPayment = loanAmount * monthlyInterestRate / (1 -
      (1 / Math.pow(1 + monthlyInterestRate, numberOfYears * 12)));
    return monthlyPayment;
  }

  /** Find total payment */
  public double getTotalPayment() {
    double totalPayment = getMonthlyPayment() * numberOfYears * 12;
    return totalPayment;
  }

  /** Return loan date */
  public java.util.Date getLoanDate() {
    return loanDate;
  }
}
```

From a class developer's perspective, a class is designed for use by many different customers. In order to be useful in a wide range of applications, a class should provide a variety of ways for customization through constructors, properties, and methods.

The `Loan` class contains two constructors, four `get` methods, three `set` methods, and the methods for finding the monthly payment and the total payment. You can construct a `Loan` object by using the no-arg constructor or the constructor with three parameters: annual interest rate, number of years, and loan amount. When a loan object is created, its date is stored in the `loanDate` field. The `getLoanDate` method returns the date. The three `get` methods—`getAnnualInterest`, `getNumberOfYears`, and `getLoanAmount`—return the annual interest rate, payment years, and loan amount, respectively. All the data properties and methods in this class are tied to a specific instance of the `Loan` class. Therefore, they are instance variables and methods.

Important Pedagogical Tip

Use the UML diagram for the `Loan` class shown in Figure 10.4 to write a test program that uses the `Loan` class even though you don't know how the `Loan` class is implemented. This has three benefits:

- It demonstrates that developing a class and using a class are two separate tasks.
- It enables you to skip the complex implementation of certain classes without interrupting the sequence of this book.
- It is easier to learn how to implement a class if you are familiar with it by using the class.

For all the class examples from now on, create an object from the class and try using its methods before turning your attention to its implementation.

10.8 If you redefine the `Loan` class in Listing 10.2 without `set` methods, is the class immutable?

10.6 Object-Oriented Thinking

The procedural paradigm focuses on designing methods. The object-oriented paradigm couples data and methods together into objects. Software design using the object-oriented paradigm focuses on objects and operations on objects.

Chapters 1–7 introduced fundamental programming techniques for problem solving using loops, methods, and arrays. Knowing these techniques lays a solid foundation for object-oriented programming. Classes provide more flexibility and modularity for building reusable software. This section improves the solution for a problem introduced in Chapter 3 using the object-oriented approach. From these improvements, you will gain insight into the differences between procedural and object-oriented programming and see the benefits of developing reusable code using objects and classes.

Listing 3.5, ComputeAndInterpretBMI.java, presented a program for computing body mass index. The code cannot be reused in other programs, because the code is in the `main` method. To make it reusable, define a static method to compute body mass index as follows:

```
public static double getBMI(double weight, double height)
```

This method is useful for computing body mass index for a specified weight and height. However, it has limitations. Suppose you need to associate the weight and height with a person's name and birth date. You could declare separate variables to store these values, but these values would not be tightly coupled. The ideal way to couple them is to create an object that contains them all. Since these values are tied to individual objects, they should be stored in instance data fields. You can define a class named `BMI` as shown in Figure 10.5.

VideoNote
The BMI class

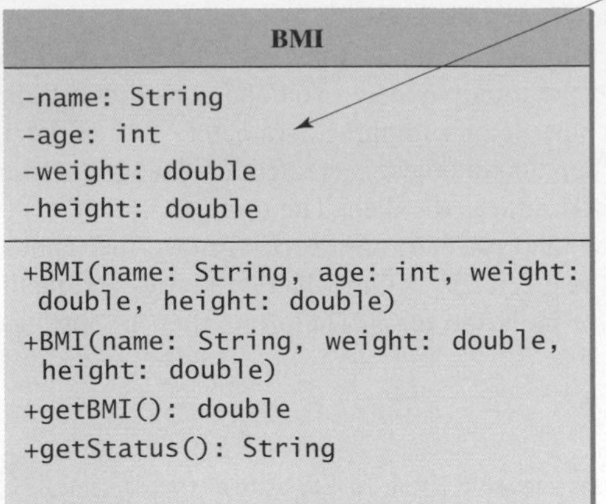

FIGURE 10.5 The `BMI` class encapsulates BMI information.

Assume that the `BMI` class is available. Listing 10.3 gives a test program that uses this class.

LISTING 10.3 UseBMIClass.java

```
 1 public class UseBMIClass {
 2   public static void main(String[] args) {
 3     BMI bmi1 = new BMI("Kim Yang", 18, 145, 70);
 4     System.out.println("The BMI for " + bmi1.getName() + " is "
 5       + bmi1.getBMI() + " " + bmi1.getStatus());
 6
 7     BMI bmi2 = new BMI("Susan King", 215, 70);
 8     System.out.println("The BMI for " + bmi2.getName() + " is "
 9       + bmi2.getBMI() + " " + bmi2.getStatus());
10   }
11 }
```

create an object
invoke instance method

create an object
invoke instance method

```
The BMI for Kim Yang is 20.81 Normal
The BMI for Susan King is 30.85 Obese
```

Line 3 creates the object `bmi1` for `Kim Yang` and line 7 creates the object `bmi2` for `Susan King`. You can use the instance methods `getName()`, `getBMI()`, and `getStatus()` to return the BMI information in a `BMI` object.

The `BMI` class can be implemented as in Listing 10.4.

LISTING 10.4 BMI.java

```
public class BMI {
  private String name;
  private int age;
  private double weight; // in pounds
  private double height; // in inches
  public static final double KILOGRAMS_PER_POUND = 0.45359237;
```

```
  public static final double METERS_PER_INCH = 0.0254;

  public BMI(String name, int age, double weight, double height) {
    this.name = name;
    this.age = age;
    this.weight = weight;
    this.height = height;
  }

  public BMI(String name, double weight, double height) {
    this(name, 20, weight, height);
  }

  public double getBMI() {
    double bmi = weight * KILOGRAMS_PER_POUND /
      ((height * METERS_PER_INCH) * (height * METERS_PER_INCH));
    return Math.round(bmi * 100) / 100.0;
  }

  public String getStatus() {
    double bmi = getBMI();
    if (bmi < 18.5)
      return "Underweight";
    else if (bmi < 25)
      return "Normal";
    else if (bmi < 30)
      return "Overweight";
    else
      return "Obese";
  }

  public String getName() {
    return name;
  }

  public int getAge() {
    return age;
  }

  public double getWeight() {
    return weight;
  }

  public double getHeight() {
    return height;
  }
}
```

The mathematical formula for computing the BMI using weight and height is given in Section 3.9. The instance method `getBMI()` returns the BMI. Since the weight and height are instance data fields in the object, the `getBMI()` method can use these properties to compute the BMI for the object.

The instance method `getStatus()` returns a string that interprets the BMI. The interpretation is also given in Section 3.9.

procedural vs. object-oriented paradigms

This example demonstrates the advantages of the object-oriented paradigm over the procedural paradigm. The procedural paradigm focuses on designing methods. The object-oriented paradigm couples data and methods together into objects. Software design using the object-oriented paradigm focuses on objects and operations on objects. The object-oriented approach combines the power of the procedural paradigm with an added dimension that integrates data with operations into objects.

In procedural programming, data and operations on the data are separate, and this methodology requires sending data to methods. Object-oriented programming places data and the operations that pertain to them in an object. This approach solves many of the problems inherent in procedural programming. The object-oriented programming approach organizes programs in a way that mirrors the real world, in which all objects are associated with both attributes and activities. Using objects improves software reusability and makes programs easier to develop and easier to maintain. Programming in Java involves thinking in terms of objects; a Java program can be viewed as a collection of cooperating objects.

MyProgrammingLab™

10.9 Is the `BMI` class defined in Listing 10.4 immutable?

10.7 Object Composition

An object can contain another object. The relationship between the two is called composition.

In Listing 10.2, you defined the `Loan` class to contain a `Date` data field. The relationship between `Loan` and `Date` is composition. In Listing 10.4, you defined the `BMI` class to contain a `String` data field. The relationship between `BMI` and `String` is composition.

aggregation
has-a relationship

Composition is actually a special case of the aggregation relationship. Aggregation models *has-a* relationships and represents an ownership relationship between two objects. The owner object is called an *aggregating object* and its class an *aggregating class*. The subject object is called an *aggregated object* and its class an *aggregated class*.

composition

An object may be owned by several other aggregating objects. If an object is exclusively owned by an aggregating object, the relationship between them is referred to as *composition*. For example, "a student has a name" is a composition relationship between the `Student` class and the `Name` class, whereas "a student has an address" is an aggregation relationship between the `Student` class and the `Address` class, because an address may be shared by several students. In UML notation, a filled diamond is attached to an aggregating class (e.g., `Student`) to denote the composition relationship with an aggregated class (e.g., `Name`), and an empty diamond is attached to an aggregating class (e.g., `Student`) to denote the aggregation relationship with an aggregated class (e.g., `Address`), as shown in Figure 10.6.

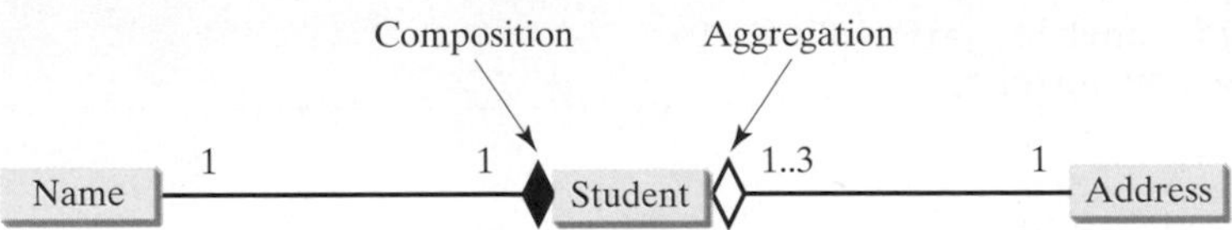

Figure 10.6 A student has a name and an address.

multiplicity

Each class involved in a relationship may specify a *multiplicity*. A multiplicity could be a number or an interval that specifies how many of the class's objects are involved in the relationship. The character * means an unlimited number of objects, and the interval `m..n` means that the number of objects should be between `m` and `n`, inclusive. In Figure 10.6, each student has only one address, and each address may be shared by up to `3` students. Each student has one name, and a name is unique for each student.

An aggregation relationship is usually represented as a data field in the aggregating class. For example, the relationship in Figure 10.6 can be represented as follows:

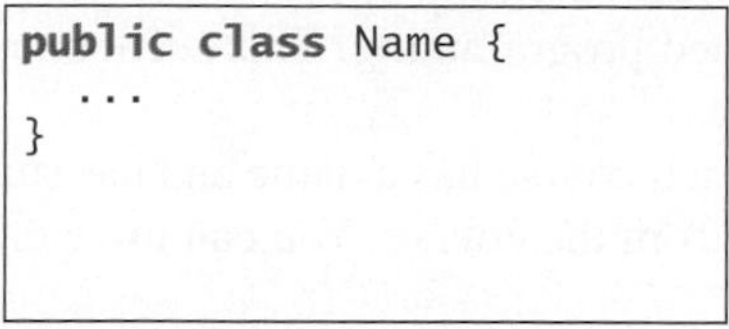

```
public class Name {
  ...
}
```

```
public class Student {
  private Name name;
  private Address address;

  ...
}
```

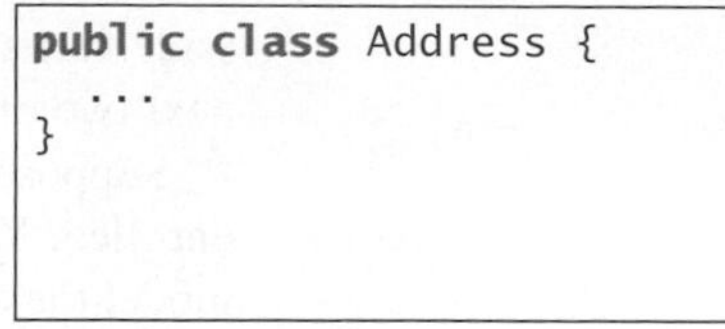

```
public class Address {
  ...
}
```

Aggregated class   Aggregating class   Aggregated class

Aggregation may exist between objects of the same class. For example, a person may have a supervisor. This is illustrated in Figure 10.7.

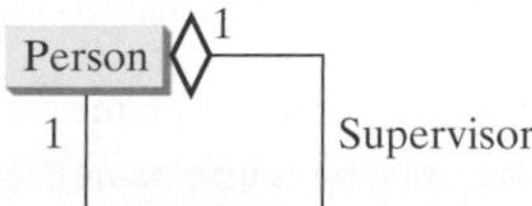

FIGURE 10.7 A person may have a supervisor.

In the relationship "a person has a supervisor," as shown in Figure 10.7, a supervisor can be represented as a data field in the `Person` class, as follows:

```
public class Person {
  // The type for the data is the class itself
  private Person supervisor;

  ...
}
```

If a person can have several supervisors, as shown in Figure 10.8a, you may use an array to store supervisors, as shown in Figure 10.8b.

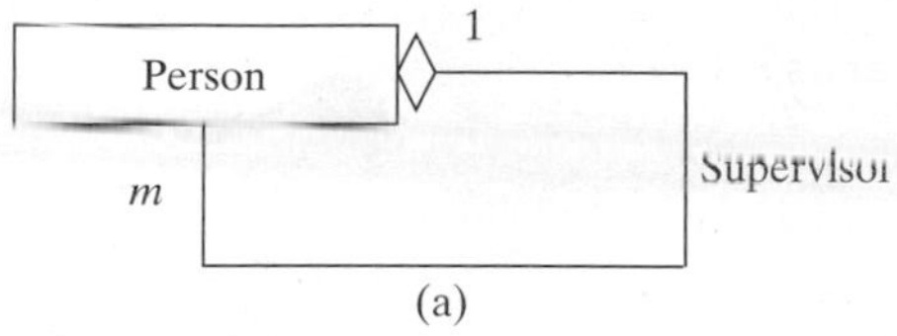

(a)

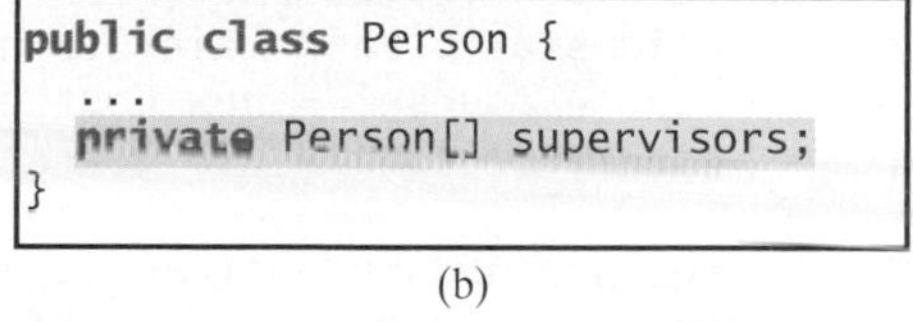

```
public class Person {
  ...
  private Person[] supervisors;
}
```

(b)

FIGURE 10.8 A person can have several supervisors.

Note

Since aggregation and composition relationships are represented using classes in the same way, many texts don't differentiate them and call both compositions. We will do the same in this book for simplicity.

aggregation or composition

Check Point

10.10 What is an aggregation relationship between two objects?

10.11 What is a composition relationship between two objects?

MyProgrammingLab™

10.8 Case Study: Designing the Course Class

This section designs a class for modeling courses.

This book's philosophy is *teaching by example and learning by doing*. The book provides a wide variety of examples to demonstrate object-oriented programming. This section and the next two offer additional examples on designing classes.

Suppose you need to process course information. Each course has a name and has students enrolled. You should be able to add/drop a student to/from the course. You can use a class to model the courses, as shown in Figure 10.9.

Course	
-courseName: String	The name of the course.
-students: String[]	An array to store the students for the course.
-numberOfStudents: int	The number of students (default: 0).
+Course(courseName: String)	Creates a course with the specified name.
+getCourseName(): String	Returns the course name.
+addStudent(student: String): void	Adds a new student to the course.
+dropStudent(student: String): void	Drops a student from the course.
+getStudents(): String[]	Returns the students for the course.
+getNumberOfStudents(): int	Returns the number of students for the course.

FIGURE 10.9 The Course class models the courses.

A Course object can be created using the constructor Course(String name) by passing a course name. You can add students to the course using the addStudent(String student) method, drop a student from the course using the dropStudent(String student) method, and return all the students in the course using the getStudents() method. Suppose the class is available; Listing 10.5 gives a test class that creates two courses and adds students to them.

LISTING 10.5 TestCourse.java

create a course

add a student

number of students

return students

```
public class TestCourse {
  public static void main(String[] args) {
    Course course1 = new Course("Data Structures");
    Course course2 = new Course("Database Systems");

    course1.addStudent("Peter Jones");
    course1.addStudent("Kim Smith");
    course1.addStudent("Anne Kennedy");

    course2.addStudent("Peter Jones");
    course2.addStudent("Steve Smith");

    System.out.println("Number of students in course1: "
      + course1.getNumberOfStudents());
    String[] students = course1.getStudents();
    for (int i = 0; i < course1.getNumberOfStudents(); i++)
      System.out.print(students[i] + ", ");

    System.out.println();
    System.out.print("Number of students in course2: "
```

```
      + course2.getNumberOfStudents());
  }
}
```

```
Number of students in course1: 3
Peter Jones, Kim Smith, Anne Kennedy,
Number of students in course2: 2
```

The **Course** class is implemented in Listing 10.6. It uses an array to store the students in the course. For simplicity, assume that the maximum course enrollment is **100**. The array is created using **new String[100]** in line 3. The **addStudent** method (line 10) adds a student to the array. Whenever a new student is added to the course, **numberOfStudents** is increased (line 12). The **getStudents** method returns the array. The **dropStudent** method (line 27) is left as an exercise.

LISTING 10.6 Course.java

```
 1 public class Course {
 2   private String courseName;
 3   private String[] students = new String[100];
 4   private int numberOfStudents;
 5
 6   public Course(String courseName) {
 7     this.courseName = courseName;
 8   }
 9
10   public void addStudent(String student) {
11     students[numberOfStudents] = student;
12     numberOfStudents++;
13   }
14
15   public String[] getStudents() {
16     return students;
17   }
18
19   public int getNumberOfStudents() {
20     return numberOfStudents;
21   }
22
23   public String getCourseName() {
24     return courseName;
25   }
26
27   public void dropStudent(String student) {
28     // Left as an exercise in Programming Exercise 10.9
29   }
30 }
```

create students

add a course

return students

number of students

The array size is fixed to be **100** (line 3), so you cannot have more than 100 students in the course. You can improve the class by automatically increasing the array size in Programming Exercise 10.9.

When you create a **Course** object, an array object is created. A **Course** object contains a reference to the array. For simplicity, you can say that the **Course** object contains the array.

The user can create a **Course** object and manipulate it through the public methods **addStudent**, **dropStudent**, **getNumberOfStudents**, and **getStudents**. However, the user doesn't need to know how these methods are implemented. The **Course** class encapsulates the internal implementation. This example uses an array to store students, but you could use a different data structure to store **students**. The program that uses **Course** does not need to change as long as the contract of the public methods remains unchanged.

10.9 Case Study: Designing a Class for Stacks

This section designs a class for modeling stacks.

stack

Recall that a *stack* is a data structure that holds data in a last-in, first-out fashion, as shown in Figure 10.10.

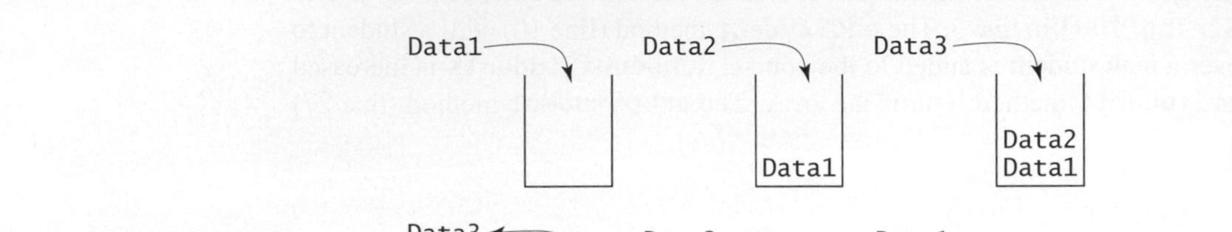

FIGURE 10.10 A stack holds data in a last-in, first-out fashion.

Stacks have many applications. For example, the compiler uses a stack to process method invocations. When a method is invoked, its parameters and local variables are pushed into a stack. When a method calls another method, the new method's parameters and local variables are pushed into the stack. When a method finishes its work and returns to its caller, its associated space is released from the stack.

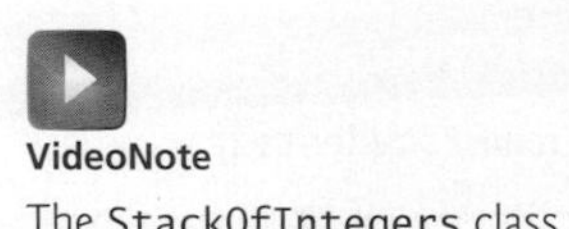

VideoNote
The StackOfIntegers class

You can define a class to model stacks. For simplicity, assume the stack holds the **int** values. So name the stack class **StackOfIntegers**. The UML diagram for the class is shown in Figure 10.11.

StackOfIntegers	
-elements: int[]	An array to store integers in the stack.
-size: int	The number of integers in the stack.
+StackOfIntegers()	Constructs an empty stack with a default capacity of 16.
+StackOfIntegers(capacity: int)	Constructs an empty stack with a specified capacity.
+empty(): boolean	Returns true if the stack is empty.
+peek(): int	Returns the integer at the top of the stack without removing it from the stack.
+push(value: int): void	Stores an integer into the top of the stack.
+pop(): int	Removes the integer at the top of the stack and returns it.
+getSize(): int	Returns the number of elements in the stack.

FIGURE 10.11 The **StackOfIntegers** class encapsulates the stack storage and provides the operations for manipulating the stack.

Suppose that the class is available. The test program in Listing 10.7 uses the class to create a stack (line 3), store ten integers **0**, **1**, **2**, . . . , and **9** (line 6), and displays them in reverse order (line 9).

LISTING 10.7 TestStackOfIntegers.java

```
public class TestStackOfIntegers {
  public static void main(String[] args) {
    StackOfIntegers stack = new StackOfIntegers();

    for (int i = 0; i < 10; i++)
      stack.push(i);

    while (!stack.empty())
      System.out.print(stack.pop() + " ");
  }
}
```

create a stack

push to stack

pop from stack

```
9 8 7 6 5 4 3 2 1 0
```

How do you implement the **StackOfIntegers** class? The elements in the stack are stored in an array named **elements**. When you create a stack, the array is also created. The no-arg constructor creates an array with the default capacity of **16**. The variable **size** counts the number of elements in the stack, and **size - 1** is the index of the element at the top of the stack, as shown in Figure 10.12. For an empty stack, **size** is **0**.

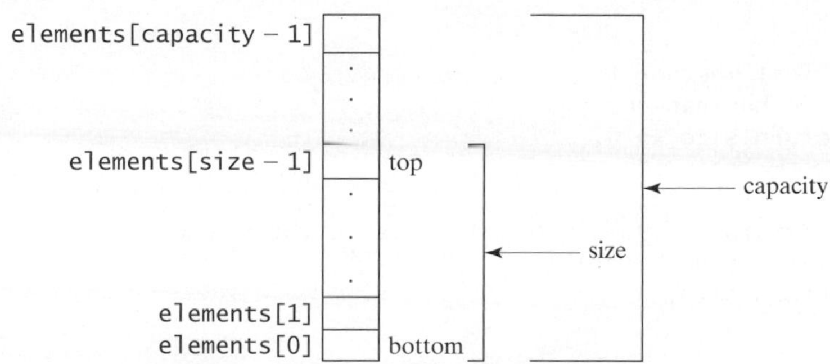

FIGURE 10.12 The **StackOfIntegers** class encapsulates the stack storage and provides the operations for manipulating the stack.

The **StackOfIntegers** class is implemented in Listing 10.8. The methods **empty()**, **peek()**, **pop()**, and **getSize()** are easy to implement. To implement **push(int value)**, assign **value** to **elements[size]** if **size < capacity** (line 24). If the stack is full (i.e., **size >= capacity**), create a new array of twice the current capacity (line 19), copy the contents of the current array to the new array (line 20), and assign the reference of the new array to the current array in the stack (line 21). Now you can add the new value to the array (line 24).

LISTING 10.8 StackOfIntegers.java

```
1 public class StackOfIntegers {
2   private int[] elements;
3   private int size;
4   public static final int DEFAULT_CAPACITY = 16;
5
6   /** Construct a stack with the default capacity 16 */
7   public StackOfIntegers() {
8     this (DEFAULT_CAPACITY);
```

max capacity 16

```
  }

  /** Construct a stack with the specified maximum capacity */
  public StackOfIntegers(int capacity) {
    elements = new int[capacity];
  }

  /** Push a new integer to the top of the stack */
  public void push(int value) {
    if (size >= elements.length) {
```

double the capacity

```
      int[] temp = new int[elements.length * 2];
      System.arraycopy(elements, 0, temp, 0, elements.length);
      elements = temp;
    }

```

add to stack

```
    elements[size++] = value;
  }

  /** Return and remove the top element from the stack */
  public int pop() {
    return elements[--size];
  }

  /** Return the top element from the stack */
  public int peek() {
    return elements[size - 1];
  }

  /** Test whether the stack is empty */
  public boolean empty() {
    return size == 0;
  }

  /** Return the number of elements in the stack */
  public int getSize() {
    return size;
  }
}
```

10.10 Case Study: Designing the **GuessDate** Class

You can define utility classes that contain static methods and static data.

Listing 3.3, GuessBirthday.java, and Listing 7.6, GuessBirthdayUsingArray.java, presented two programs for guessing birthdays. Both programs use the same data developed with the procedural paradigm. The majority of the code in these two programs is to define the five sets of data. You cannot reuse the code in these two programs, because the code is in the `main` method. To make the code reusable, design a class to encapsulate the data, as defined in Figure 10.13.

Note that `getValue` is defined as a static method because it is not dependent on a specific object of the `GuessDate` class. The `GuessDate` class encapsulates `dates` as a private member. The user of this class doesn't need to know how `dates` is implemented or even that the `dates` field exists in the class. All that the user needs to know is how to use this method to access dates. Suppose this class is available. As shown in Section 3.4, there are five sets of dates. Invoking `getValue(setNo, row, column)` returns the date at the specified row and column in the given set. For example, `getValue(1, 0, 0)` returns `2`.

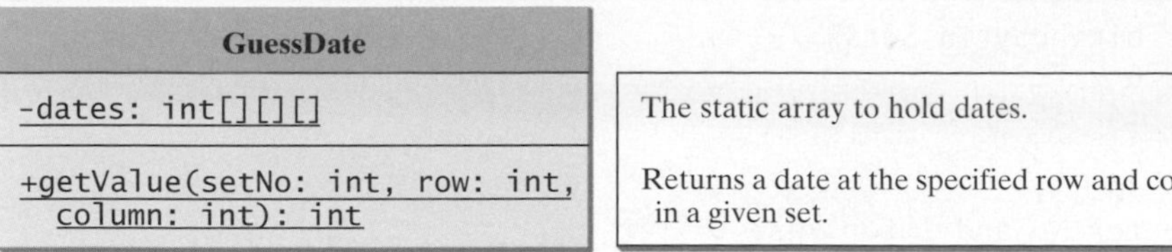

FIGURE 10.13 The GuessDate class defines data for guessing birthdays.

Assume that the GuessDate class is available. Listing 10.9 is a test program that uses this class.

LISTING 10.9 UseGuessDateClass.java

```
import java.util.Scanner;

public class UseGuessDateClass {
  public static void main(String[] args) {
    int date = 0; // Date to be determined
    int answer;

    // Create a Scanner
    Scanner input = new Scanner(System.in);

    for (int i = 0; i < 5; i++) {
      System.out.println("Is your birthday in Set" + (i + 1) + "?");
      for (int j = 0; j < 4; j++) {
        for (int k = 0; k < 4; k++)
          System.out.print(GuessDate.getValue(i, j, k) + "  ");
        System.out.println();
      }

      System.out.print("\nEnter 0 for No and 1 for Yes: ");
      answer = input.nextInt();

      if (answer == 1)
        date += GuessDate.getValue(i, 0, 0);
    }

    System.out.println("Your birthday is " + date);
  }
}
```

invoke static method

invoke static method

```
Is your birthday in Set1?
1   3   5   7
9   11  13  15
17  19  21  23
25  27  29  31
Enter 0 for No and 1 for Yes: 0 ↵Enter

Is your birthday in Set2?
2   3   6   7
10  11  14  15
18  19  22  23
26  27  30  31
Enter 0 for No and 1 for Yes: 1 ↵Enter
```

```
Is your birthday in Set3?
4   5   6   7
12  13  14  15
20  21  22  23
28  29  30  31
Enter 0 for No and 1 for Yes: 0 ↵Enter

Is your birthday in Set4?
8   9   10  11
12  13  14  15
24  25  26  27
28  29  30  31
Enter 0 for No and 1 for Yes: 1 ↵Enter

Is your birthday in Set5?
16  17  18  19
20  21  22  23
24  25  26  27
28  29  30  31
Enter 0 for No and 1 for Yes: 1 ↵Enter

Your birthday is 26
```

Since `getValue` is a static method, you don't need to create an object in order to invoke it. `GuessDate.getValue(i, j, k)` (line 15) returns the date at row `j` and column `k` in Set `i`.

The `GuessDate` class can be implemented as in Listing 10.10.

LISTING 10.10 GuessDate.java

static field

private constructor

```
public class GuessDate {
  private final static int[][][] dates = {
    {{ 1,  3,  5,  7},
     { 9, 11, 13, 15},
     {17, 19, 21, 23},
     {25, 27, 29, 31}},
    {{ 2,  3,  6,  7},
     {10, 11, 14, 15},
     {18, 19, 22, 23},
     {26, 27, 30, 31}},
    {{ 4,  5,  6,  7},
     {12, 13, 14, 15},
     {20, 21, 22, 23},
     {28, 29, 30, 31}},
    {{ 8,  9, 10, 11},
     {12, 13, 14, 15},
     {24, 25, 26, 27},
     {28, 29, 30, 31}},
    {{16, 17, 18, 19},
     {20, 21, 22, 23},
     {24, 25, 26, 27},
     {28, 29, 30, 31}}};

  /** Prevent the user from creating objects from GuessDate */
  private GuessDate() {
  }

  /** Return a date at the specified row and column in a given set */
```

```
29    public static int getValue(int setNo, int i, int j) {
30      return dates[setNo][i][j];
31    }
32  }
```

static method

This class uses a three-dimensional array to store dates (lines 2–22). You could use a different data structure (i.e., five two-dimensional arrays for representing five sets of numbers). The implementation of the **getValue** method would change, but the program that uses **GuessDate** wouldn't need to change as long as the contract of the public method **getValue** remains unchanged. This shows the benefit of data encapsulation.

benefit of data encapsulation

The class defines a private no-arg constructor (line 25) to prevent the user from creating objects for this class. Since all methods are static in this class, there is no need to create objects from this class.

private constructor

10.12 Why is the no-arg constructor in the **Math** class defined private?

MyProgrammingLab™

10.11 Class Design Guidelines

Key Point

Class design guidelines are helpful for designing sound classes.

You have learned how to design classes from the preceding two examples and from many other examples in the preceding chapters. This section summarizes some of the guidelines.

10.11.1 Cohesion

A class should describe a single entity, and all the class operations should logically fit together to support a coherent purpose. You can use a class for students, for example, but you should not combine students and staff in the same class, because students and staff are different entities.

coherent purpose

A single entity with many responsibilities can be broken into several classes to separate the responsibilities. The classes **String**, **StringBuilder**, and **StringBuffer** all deal with strings, for example, but have different responsibilities. The **String** class deals with immutable strings, the **StringBuilder** class is for creating mutable strings, and the **StringBuffer** class is similar to **StringBuilder** except that **StringBuffer** contains synchronized methods for updating strings.

separating responsibilities

10.11.2 Consistency

Follow standard Java programming style and naming conventions. Choose informative names for classes, data fields, and methods. A popular style is to place the data declaration before the constructor and place constructors before methods.

naming conventions

Make the names consistent. It is not a good practice to choose different names for similar operations. For example, the **length()** method returns the size of a **String**, a **StringBuilder**, and a **StringBuffer**. It would be inconsistent if different names were used for this method in these classes.

naming consistency

In general, you should consistently provide a public no-arg constructor for constructing a default instance. If a class does not support a no-arg constructor, document the reason. If no constructors are defined explicitly, a public default no-arg constructor with an empty body is assumed.

no-arg constructor

If you want to prevent users from creating an object for a class, you can declare a private constructor in the class, as is the case for the **Math** class and the **GuessDate** class.

10.11.3 Encapsulation

A class should use the **private** modifier to hide its data from direct access by clients. This makes the class easy to maintain.

encapsulating data fields

Provide a **get** method only if you want the field to be readable, and provide a **set** method only if you want the field to be updateable. For example, the **Course** class provides a **get** method for **courseName**, but no **set** method, because the user is not allowed to change the course name once it is created.

10.11.4 Clarity

Cohesion, consistency, and encapsulation are good guidelines for achieving design clarity. Additionally, a class should have a clear contract that is easy to explain and easy to understand.

easy to explain

Users can incorporate classes in many different combinations, orders, and environments. Therefore, you should design a class that imposes no restrictions on how or when the user can use it, design the properties in a way that lets the user set them in any order and with any combination of values, and design methods that function independently of their order of occurrence. For example, the **Loan** class contains the properties **loanAmount**, **numberOfYears**, and **annualInterestRate**. The values of these properties can be set in any order.

independent methods

Methods should be defined intuitively without causing confusion. For example, the **substring(int beginIndex, int endIndex)** method in the **String** class is somewhat confusing. The method returns a substring from **beginIndex** to **endIndex – 1**, rather than to **endIndex**. It would be more intuitive to return a substring from **beginIndex** to **endIndex**.

intuitive meaning

You should not declare a data field that can be derived from other data fields. For example, the following **Person** class has two data fields: **birthDate** and **age**. Since **age** can be derived from **birthDate**, **age** should not be declared as a data field.

independent properties

```
public class Person {
  private java.util.Date birthDate;
  private int age;

  ...
}
```

10.11.5 Completeness

Classes are designed for use by many different customers. In order to be useful in a wide range of applications, a class should provide a variety of ways for customization through properties and methods. For example, the **String** class contains more than 40 methods that are useful for a variety of applications.

10.11.6 Instance vs. Static

A variable or method that is dependent on a specific instance of the class must be an instance variable or method. A variable that is shared by all the instances of a class should be declared static. For example, the variable **numberOfObjects** in **CircleWithPrivateDataFields** in Listing 8.9 is shared by all the objects of the **CircleWithPrivateDataFields** class and therefore is declared static. A method that is not dependent on a specific instance should be defined as a static method. For instance, the **getNumberOfObjects** method in **CircleWithPrivateDataFields** is not tied to any specific instance and therefore is defined as a static method.

Always reference static variables and methods from a class name (rather than a reference variable) to improve readability and avoid errors.

Do not pass a parameter from a constructor to initialize a static data field. It is better to use a **set** method to change the static data field. Thus, the following class in (a) is better replaced by (b).

```
public class SomeThing {
  private int t1;
  private static int t2;

  public SomeThing(int t1, int t2) {
    ...
  }
}
```

(a)

```
public class SomeThing {
  private int t1;
  private static int t2;

  public SomeThing(int t1) {
    ...
  }

  public static void setT2(int t2) {
    SomeThing.t2 = t2;
  }
}
```

(b)

Instance and static are integral parts of object-oriented programming. A data field or method is either instance or static. Do not mistakenly overlook static data fields or methods. It is a common design error to define an instance method that should have been static. For example, the `factorial(int n)` method for computing the factorial of `n` should be defined static, because it is independent of any specific instance.

common design error

A constructor is always instance, because it is used to create a specific instance. A static variable or method can be invoked from an instance method, but an instance variable or method cannot be invoked from a static method.

10.13 Describe class design guidelines.

10.12 Processing Primitive Data Type Values as Objects

A primitive type value is not an object, but it can be wrapped in an object using a wrapper class in the Java API.

Owing to performance considerations, primitive data type values are not objects in Java. Because of the overhead of processing objects, the language's performance would be adversely affected if primitive data type values were treated as objects. However, many Java methods require the use of objects as arguments. Java offers a convenient way to incorporate, or wrap, a primitive data type into an object (e.g., wrapping `int` into the `Integer` class, and wrapping `double` into the `Double` class). Recall that a `char` value can be wrapped into a `Character` object in Section 9.5. By using a wrapper class, you can process primitive data type values as objects. Java provides `Boolean`, `Character`, `Double`, `Float`, `Byte`, `Short`, `Integer`, and `Long` wrapper classes in the `java.lang` package for primitive data types. The `Boolean` class wraps a Boolean value `true` or `false`. This section uses `Integer` and `Double` as examples to introduce the numeric wrapper classes.

why wrapper class?

Note

Most wrapper class names for a primitive type are the same as the primitive data type name with the first letter capitalized. The exceptions are `Integer` and `Character`.

naming convention

Numeric wrapper classes are very similar to each other. Each contains the methods `doubleValue()`, `floatValue()`, `intValue()`, `longValue()`, `shortValue()`, and `byteValue()`. These methods "convert" objects into primitive type values. The key features of `Integer` and `Double` are shown in Figure 10.14.

You can construct a wrapper object either from a primitive data type value or from a string representing the numeric value—for example, `new Double(5.0)`, `new Double("5.0")`, `new Integer(5)`, and `new Integer("5")`.

constructors

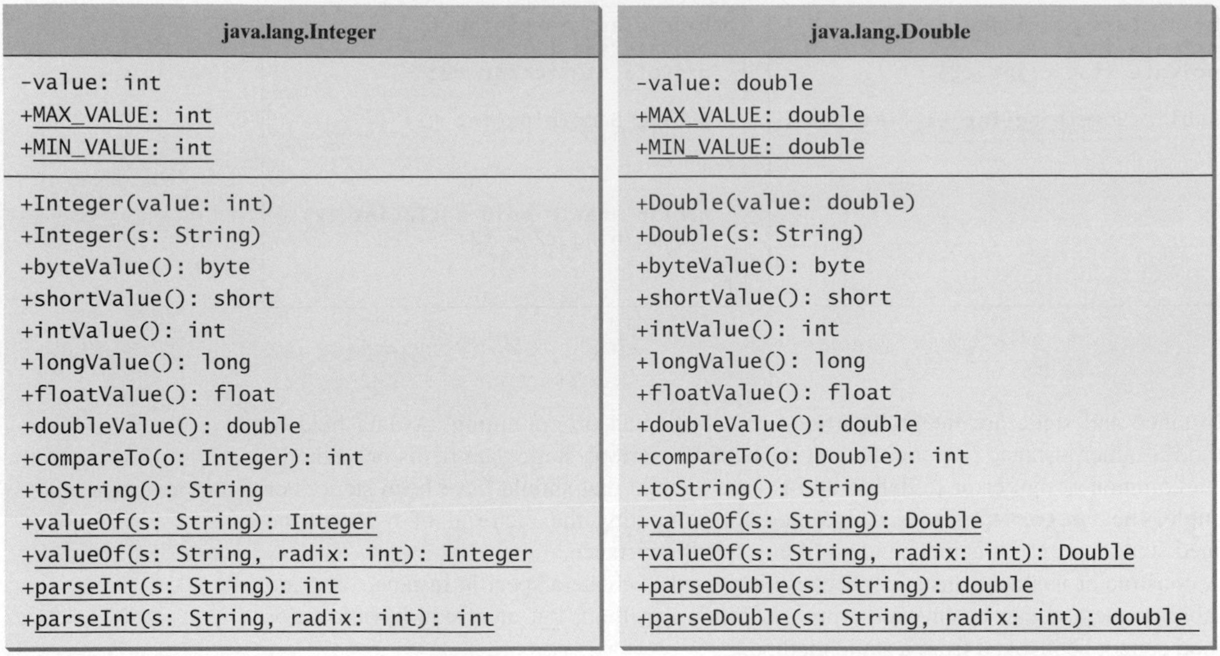

java.lang.Integer	java.lang.Double
-value: int +MAX_VALUE: int +MIN_VALUE: int	-value: double +MAX_VALUE: double +MIN_VALUE: double
+Integer(value: int) +Integer(s: String) +byteValue(): byte +shortValue(): short +intValue(): int +longValue(): long +floatValue(): float +doubleValue(): double +compareTo(o: Integer): int +toString(): String +valueOf(s: String): Integer +valueOf(s: String, radix: int): Integer +parseInt(s: String): int +parseInt(s: String, radix: int): int	+Double(value: double) +Double(s: String) +byteValue(): byte +shortValue(): short +intValue(): int +longValue(): long +floatValue(): float +doubleValue(): double +compareTo(o: Double): int +toString(): String +valueOf(s: String): Double +valueOf(s: String, radix: int): Double +parseDouble(s: String): double +parseDouble(s: String, radix: int): double

FIGURE 10.14 The wrapper classes provide constructors, constants, and conversion methods for manipulating various data types.

no no-arg constructor

immutable

The wrapper classes do not have no-arg constructors. The instances of all wrapper classes are immutable; this means that, once the objects are created, their internal values cannot be changed.

constants

Each numeric wrapper class has the constants MAX_VALUE and MIN_VALUE. MAX_VALUE represents the maximum value of the corresponding primitive data type. For Byte, Short, Integer, and Long, MIN_VALUE represents the minimum byte, short, int, and long values. For Float and Double, MIN_VALUE represents the minimum *positive* float and double values. The following statements display the maximum integer (2,147,483,647), the minimum positive float (1.4E–45), and the maximum double floating-point number (1.79769313486231570e+308d).

```
System.out.println("The maximum integer is " + Integer.MAX_VALUE);
System.out.println("The minimum positive float is " +
  Float.MIN_VALUE);
System.out.println(
  "The maximum double-precision floating-point number is " +
  Double.MAX_VALUE);
```

conversion methods

Each numeric wrapper class contains the methods doubleValue(), floatValue(), intValue(), longValue(), and shortValue() for returning a double, float, int, long, or short value for the wrapper object. For example,

```
new Double("12.4").intValue() returns 12;
new Integer("12").doubleValue() returns 12.0;
```

compareTo method

Recall that the String class contains the compareTo method for comparing two strings. The numeric wrapper classes contain the compareTo method for comparing two numbers and returns 1, 0, or -1, if this number is greater than, equal to, or less than the other number. For example,

```
new Double("12.4").compareTo(new Double("12.3")) returns 1;
new Double("12.3").compareTo(new Double("12.3")) returns 0;
new Double("12.3").compareTo(new Double("12.51")) returns -1;
```

The numeric wrapper classes have a useful static method, `valueOf (String s)`. This method creates a new object initialized to the value represented by the specified string. For example,

static `valueOf` methods

```
Double doubleObject = Double.valueOf("12.4");
Integer integerObject = Integer.valueOf("12");
```

You have used the `parseInt` method in the `Integer` class to parse a numeric string into an `int` value and the `parseDouble` method in the `Double` class to parse a numeric string into a `double` value. Each numeric wrapper class has two overloaded parsing methods to parse a numeric string into an appropriate numeric value based on `10` (decimal) or any specified radix (e.g., `2` for binary, `8` for octal, and `16` for hexadecimal). The following examples show how to use these methods.

static parsing methods

```
// These two methods are in the Byte class
public static byte parseByte(String s)
public static byte parseByte(String s, int radix)

// These two methods are in the Short class
public static short parseShort(String s)
public static short parseShort(String s, int radix)

// These two methods are in the Integer class
public static int parseInt(String s)
public static int parseInt(String s, int radix)

// These two methods are in the Long class
public static long parseLong(String s)
public static long parseLong(String s, int radix)

// These two methods are in the Float class
public static float parseFloat(String s)
public static float parseFloat(String s, int radix)

// These two methods are in the Double class
public static double parseDouble(String s)
public static double parseDouble(String s, int radix)
```

For example,

```
Integer.parseInt("11", 2) returns 3;
Integer.parseInt("12", 8) returns 10;
Integer.parseInt("13", 10) returns 13;
Integer.parseInt("1A", 16) returns 26;
```

`Integer.parseInt("12", 2)` would raise a runtime exception because `12` is not a binary number.

Note that you can convert a decimal number into a hex number using the `format` method. For example,

converting decimal to hex

```
String.format("%x", 26) returns 1A;
```

MyProgrammingLab™

10.14 Describe primitive-type wrapper classes.

10.15 Can each of the following statements be compiled?

a. `Integer i = new Integer("23");`

b. `Integer i = new Integer(23);`

c. `Integer i = Integer.valueOf("23");`

d. `Integer i = Integer.parseInt("23", 8);`

e. `Double d = new Double();`

f. `Double d = Double.valueOf("23.45");`

g. `int i = (Integer.valueOf("23")).intValue();`

h. `double d = (Double.valueOf("23.4")).doubleValue();`

i. `int i = (Double.valueOf("23.4")).intValue();`

j. `String s = (Double.valueOf("23.4")).toString();`

10.16 How do you convert an integer into a string? How do you convert a numeric string into an integer? How do you convert a double number into a string? How do you convert a numeric string into a double value?

10.17 Show the output of the following code.

```
public class Test {
  public static void main(String[] args) {
    Integer x = new Integer(3);
    System.out.println(x.intValue());
    System.out.println(x.compareTo(new Integer(4)));
  }
}
```

10.18 What is the output of the following code?

```
public class Test {
  public static void main(String[] args) {
    System.out.println(Integer.parseInt("10"));
    System.out.println(Integer.parseInt("10", 10));
    System.out.println(Integer.parseInt("10", 16));
    System.out.println(Integer.parseInt("11"));
    System.out.println(Integer.parseInt("11", 10));
    System.out.println(Integer.parseInt("11", 16));
  }
}
```

10.13 Automatic Conversion between Primitive Types and Wrapper Class Types

A primitive type value can be automatically converted to an object using a wrapper class, and vice versa, depending on the context.

boxing
unboxing

Converting a primitive value to a wrapper object is called *boxing*. The reverse conversion is called *unboxing*. Java allows primitive types and wrapper classes to be converted automatically. The compiler will automatically box a primitive value that appears in a context requiring an object, and will unbox an object that appears in a context requiring a primitive value. This is called *autoboxing* and *autounboxing*.

autoboxing
autounboxing

For instance, the following statement in (a) can be simplified as in (b) due to autoboxing.

(a)		(b)
`Integer intObject = new Integer(2);`	Equivalent	`Integer intObject = 2;`
		autoboxing

Consider the following example:

```
1 Integer[] intArray = {1, 2, 3};
2 System.out.println(intArray[0] + intArray[1] + intArray[2]);
```

In line 1, the primitive values `1`, `2`, and `3` are automatically boxed into objects `new Integer(1)`, `new Integer(2)`, and `new Integer(3)`. In line 2, the objects `intArray[0]`, `intArray[1]`, and `intArray[2]` are automatically converted into `int` values that are added together.

10.19 What are autoboxing and autounboxing? Are the following statements correct?

a. `Integer x = 3 + new Integer(5);`

b. `Integer x = 3;`

c. `Double x = 3;`

d. `Double x = 3.0;`

e. `int x = new Integer(3);`

f. `int x = new Integer(3) + new Integer(4);`

10.20 Show the output of the following code?

```
public class Test {
  public static void main(String[] args) {
    Double x = new Double(3.5);
    System.out.println(x.intValue());
    System.out.println(x.compareTo(4.5));
  }
}
```

10.14 The **BigInteger** and **BigDecimal** Classes

The `BigInteger` and `BigDecimal` classes can be used to represent integers or decimal numbers of any size and precision.

VideoNote
Process large numbers

immutable

If you need to compute with very large integers or high-precision floating-point values, you can use the `BigInteger` and `BigDecimal` classes in the `java.math` package. Both are *immutable*. The largest integer of the `long` type is `Long.MAX_VALUE` (i.e., `9223372036854775807`). An instance of `BigInteger` can represent an integer of any size. You can use `new BigInteger(String)` and `new BigDecimal(String)` to create an instance of `BigInteger` and `BigDecimal`, use the `add`, `subtract`, `multiple`, `divide`, and `remainder` methods to perform arithmetic operations, and use the `compareTo` method to compare two big numbers. For example, the following code creates two `BigInteger` objects and multiplies them.

```
BigInteger a = new BigInteger("9223372036854775807");
BigInteger b = new BigInteger("2");
BigInteger c = a.multiply(b); // 9223372036854775807 * 2
System.out.println(c);
```

The output is `18446744073709551614`.

There is no limit to the precision of a `BigDecimal` object. The `divide` method may throw an `ArithmeticException` if the result cannot be terminated. However, you can use the overloaded `divide(BigDecimal d, int scale, int roundingMode)` method to specify a scale and a rounding mode to avoid this exception, where `scale` is the maximum number of digits after the decimal point. For example, the following code creates two `BigDecimal` objects and performs division with scale `20` and rounding mode `BigDecimal.ROUND_UP`.

```
BigDecimal a = new BigDecimal(1.0);
BigDecimal b = new BigDecimal(3);
BigDecimal c = a.divide(b, 20, BigDecimal.ROUND_UP);
System.out.println(c);
```

The output is `0.33333333333333333334`.

Note that the factorial of an integer can be very large. Listing 10.11 gives a method that can return the factorial of any integer.

LISTING 10.11 LargeFactorial.java

```
1  import java.math.*;
2
3  public class LargeFactorial {
4    public static void main(String[] args) {
5      System.out.println("50! is \n" + factorial(50));
6    }
7
8    public static BigInteger factorial(long n) {
9      BigInteger result = BigInteger.ONE;              // constant
10     for (int i = 1; i <= n; i++)
11       result = result.multiply(new BigInteger(i + ""));   // multiply
12
13     return result;
14   }
15 }
```

```
50! is
30414093201713378043612608166064768844377641568960512000000000000
```

`BigInteger.ONE` (line 9) is a constant defined in the `BigInteger` class. `BigInteger.ONE` is the same as `new BigInteger("1")`.

A new result is obtained by invoking the `multiply` method (line 11).

MyProgrammingLab™

10.21 What is the output of the following code?

```
public class Test {
  public static void main(String[] args) {
    java.math.BigInteger x = new java.math.BigInteger("3");
    java.math.BigInteger y = new java.math.BigInteger("7");
    x.add(y);
    System.out.println(x);
  }
}
```

Key Terms

abstract data type (ADT) 375
aggregation 382
boxing 396
class abstraction 375
class encapsulation 375
class's contract 375
class's variable 371
composition 382
has-a relationship 382
immutable class 370
immutable object 370
multiplicity 382
stack 386
`this` keyword 373
unboxing 396

Chapter Summary

1. Once it is created, an *immutable object* cannot be modified. To prevent users from modifying an object, you can define *immutable classes*.

2. The scope of instance and static variables is the entire class, regardless of where the variables are declared. Instance and static variables can be declared anywhere in the class. For consistency, they are declared at the beginning of the class in this book.

3. The keyword `this` can be used to refer to the calling object. It can also be used inside a constructor to invoke another constructor of the same class.

4. The procedural paradigm focuses on designing methods. The object-oriented paradigm couples data and methods together into objects. Software design using the object-oriented paradigm focuses on objects and operations on objects. The object-oriented approach combines the power of the procedural paradigm with an added dimension that integrates data with operations into objects.

5. Many Java methods require the use of objects as arguments. Java offers a convenient way to incorporate, or wrap, a primitive data type into an object (e.g., wrapping `int` into the `Integer` class, and wrapping `double` into the `Double` class).

6. Java can automatically convert a primitive type value to its corresponding wrapper object in the context and vice versa.

7. The `BigInteger` class is useful for computing and processing integers of any size. The `BigDecimal` class can be used to compute and process floating-point numbers with any arbitrary precision.

Test Questions

Do the test questions for this chapter online at www.cs.armstrong.edu/liang/intro9e/test.html.

Programming Exercises

Sections 10.2–10.6

*10.1 (*The `Time` class*) Design a class named `Time`. The class contains:

- The data fields `hour`, `minute`, and `second` that represent a time.
- A no-arg constructor that creates a `Time` object for the current time. (The values of the data fields will represent the current time.)

- A constructor that constructs a `Time` object with a specified elapsed time since midnight, January 1, 1970, in milliseconds. (The values of the data fields will represent this time.)
- A constructor that constructs a `Time` object with the specified hour, minute, and second.
- Three `get` methods for the data fields `hour`, `minute`, and `second`, respectively.
- A method named `setTime(long elapseTime)` that sets a new time for the object using the elapsed time. For example, if the elapsed time is `555550000` milliseconds, the hour is `10`, the minute is `19`, and the second is `10`.

Draw the UML diagram for the class and then implement the class. Write a test program that creates two `Time` objects (using `new Time()` and `new Time(555550000)`) and displays their hour, minute, and second in the format hour:minute:second.

(*Hint*: The first two constructors will extract the hour, minute, and second from the elapsed time. For the no-arg constructor, the current time can be obtained using `System.currentTimeMillis()`, as shown in Listing 2.6, ShowCurrentTime.java.)

10.2 (*The* `BMI` *class*) Add the following new constructor in the `BMI` class:

```
/** Construct a BMI with the specified name, age, weight,
 * feet, and inches
 */
public BMI(String name, int age, double weight, double feet,
  double inches)
```

10.3 (*The* `MyInteger` *class*) Design a class named `MyInteger`. The class contains:

- An `int` data field named `value` that stores the `int` value represented by this object.
- A constructor that creates a `MyInteger` object for the specified `int` value.
- A `get` method that returns the `int` value.
- The methods `isEven()`, `isOdd()`, and `isPrime()` that return `true` if the value in this object is even, odd, or prime, respectively.
- The static methods `isEven(int)`, `isOdd(int)`, and `isPrime(int)` that return `true` if the specified value is even, odd, or prime, respectively.
- The static methods `isEven(MyInteger)`, `isOdd(MyInteger)`, and `isPrime(MyInteger)` that return `true` if the specified value is even, odd, or prime, respectively.
- The methods `equals(int)` and `equals(MyInteger)` that return `true` if the value in this object is equal to the specified value.
- A static method `parseInt(char[])` that converts an array of numeric characters to an `int` value.
- A static method `parseInt(String)` that converts a string into an `int` value.

Draw the UML diagram for the class and then implement the class. Write a client program that tests all methods in the class.

10.4 (*The* `MyPoint` *class*) Design a class named `MyPoint` to represent a point with `x`- and `y`-coordinates. The class contains:

The `MyPoint` class

- The data fields `x` and `y` that represent the coordinates with `get` methods.
- A no-arg constructor that creates a point (`0`, `0`).
- A constructor that constructs a point with specified coordinates.
- Two `get` methods for the data fields `x` and `y`, respectively.

- A method named `distance` that returns the distance from this point to another point of the `MyPoint` type.
- A method named `distance` that returns the distance from this point to another point with specified `x`- and `y`-coordinates.

Draw the UML diagram for the class and then implement the class. Write a test program that creates the two points (0, 0) and (10, 30.5) and displays the distance between them.

Sections 10.7–10.11

***10.5** (*Displaying the prime factors*) Write a program that prompts the user to enter a positive integer and displays all its smallest factors in decreasing order. For example, if the integer is 120, the smallest factors are displayed as 5, 3, 2, 2, 2. Use the `StackOfIntegers` class to store the factors (e.g., 2, 2, 2, 3, 5) and retrieve and display them in reverse order.

***10.6** (*Displaying the prime numbers*) Write a program that displays all the prime numbers less than 120 in decreasing order. Use the `StackOfIntegers` class to store the prime numbers (e.g., 2, 3, 5, . . .) and retrieve and display them in reverse order.

****10.7** (*Game: ATM machine*) Use the `Account` class created in Programming Exercise 8.7 to simulate an ATM machine. Create ten accounts in an array with id 0, 1, . . . , 9, and initial balance $100. The system prompts the user to enter an id. If the id is entered incorrectly, ask the user to enter a correct id. Once an id is accepted, the main menu is displayed as shown in the sample run. You can enter a choice 1 for viewing the current balance, 2 for withdrawing money, 3 for depositing money, and 4 for exiting the main menu. Once you exit, the system will prompt for an id again. Thus, once the system starts, it will not stop.

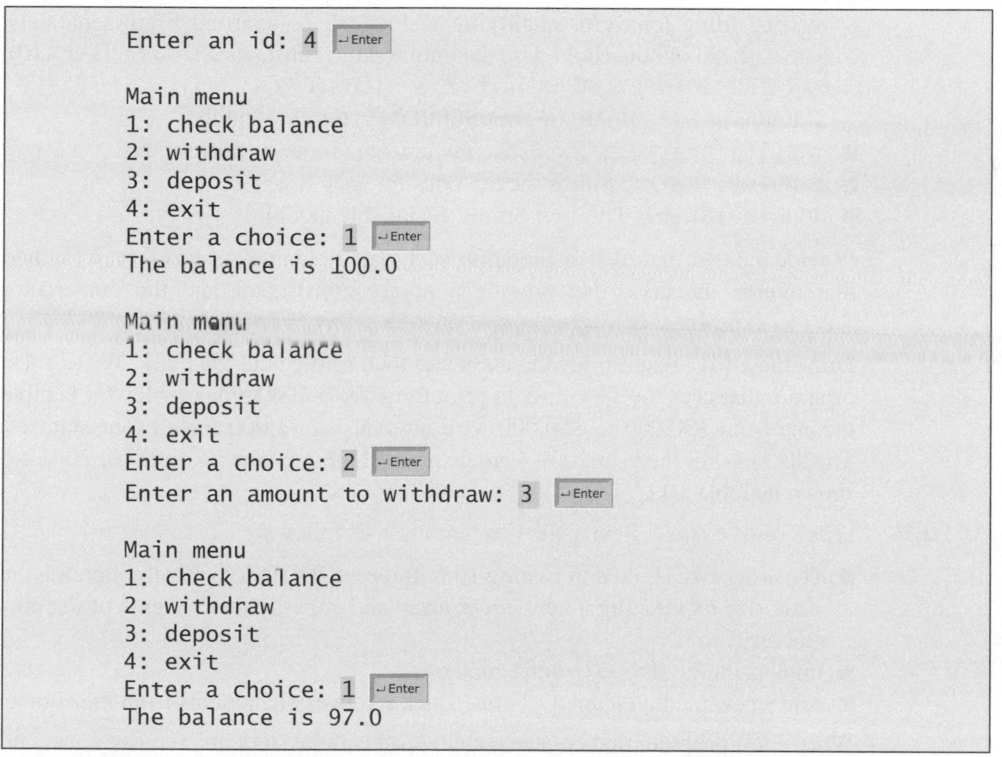

```
Enter an id: 4 ↵Enter

Main menu
1: check balance
2: withdraw
3: deposit
4: exit
Enter a choice: 1 ↵Enter
The balance is 100.0

Main menu
1: check balance
2: withdraw
3: deposit
4: exit
Enter a choice: 2 ↵Enter
Enter an amount to withdraw: 3 ↵Enter

Main menu
1: check balance
2: withdraw
3: deposit
4: exit
Enter a choice: 1 ↵Enter
The balance is 97.0
```

```
Main menu
1: check balance
2: withdraw
3: deposit
4: exit
Enter a choice: 3 ↵Enter
Enter an amount to deposit: 10 ↵Enter

Main menu
1: check balance
2: withdraw
3: deposit
4: exit
Enter a choice: 1 ↵Enter
The balance is 107.0

Main menu
1: check balance
2: withdraw
3: deposit
4: exit
Enter a choice: 4 ↵Enter

Enter an id:
```

***10.8 (*Financial: the* `Tax` *class*) Programming Exercise 7.12 writes a program for computing taxes using arrays. Design a class named `Tax` to contain the following instance data fields:

- `int filingStatus`: One of the four tax-filing statuses: `0`—single filer, `1`—married filing jointly or qualifying widow(er), `2`—married filing separately, and `3`—head of household. Use the public static constants `SINGLE_FILER` (`0`), `MARRIED_JOINTLY_OR_QUALIFYING_WIDOW(ER)` (`1`), `MARRIED_SEPARATELY` (`2`), `HEAD_OF_HOUSEHOLD` (`3`) to represent the statuses.
- `int[][] brackets`: Stores the tax brackets for each filing status.
- `double[] rates`: Stores the tax rates for each bracket.
- `double taxableIncome`: Stores the taxable income.

Provide the `get` and `set` methods for each data field and the `getTax()` method that returns the tax. Also provide a no-arg constructor and the constructor `Tax(filingStatus, brackets, rates, taxableIncome)`.

Draw the UML diagram for the class and then implement the class. Write a test program that uses the `Tax` class to print the 2001 and 2009 tax tables for taxable income from $50,000 to $60,000 with intervals of $1,000 for all four statuses. The tax rates for the year 2009 were given in Table 3.2. The tax rates for 2001 are shown in Table 10.1.

**10.9 (*The* `Course` *class*) Revise the `Course` class as follows:

- The array size is fixed in Listing 10.6. Improve it to automatically increase the array size by creating a new larger array and copying the contents of the current array to it.
- Implement the `dropStudent` method.
- Add a new method named `clear()` that removes all students from the course.

Write a test program that creates a course, adds three students, removes one, and displays the students in the course.

TABLE 10.1 2001 United States Federal Personal Tax Rates

Tax rate	*Single filers*	*Married filing jointly or qualifying widow(er)*	*Married filing separately*	*Head of household*
15%	Up to $27,050	Up to $45,200	Up to $22,600	Up to $36,250
27.5%	$27,051–$65,550	$45,201–$109,250	$22,601–$54,625	$36,251–$93,650
30.5%	$65,551–$136,750	$109,251–$166,500	$54,626–$83,250	$93,651–$151,650
35.5%	$136,751–$297,350	$166,501–$297,350	$83,251–$148,675	$151,651–$297,350
39.1%	$297,351 or more	$297,351 or more	$ 148,676 or more	$297,351 or more

***10.10** (*Game: The* **GuessDate** *class*) Modify the **GuessDate** class in Listing 10.10. Instead of representing dates in a three-dimensional array, use five two-dimensional arrays to represent the five sets of numbers. Thus, you need to declare:

```
private static int[][] set1 = {{1,  3,  5,  7}, ... };
private static int[][] set2 = {{2,  3,  6,  7}, ... };
private static int[][] set3 = {{4,  5,  6,  7}, ... };
private static int[][] set4 = {{8,  9, 10, 11}, ... };
private static int[][] set5 = {{16, 17, 18, 19}, ... };
```

***10.11** (*Geometry: The* **Circle2D** *class*) Define the **Circle2D** class that contains:

- Two **double** data fields named **x** and **y** that specify the center of the circle with **get** methods.
- A data field **radius** with a **get** method.
- A no-arg constructor that creates a default circle with (**0**, **0**) for (**x**, **y**) and **1** for **radius**.
- A constructor that creates a circle with the specified **x**, **y**, and **radius**.
- A method **getArea()** that returns the area of the circle.
- A method **getPerimeter()** that returns the perimeter of the circle.
- A method **contains(double x, double y)** that returns **true** if the specified point (**x**, **y**) is inside this circle (see Figure 10.15a).
- A method **contains(Circle2D circle)** that returns **true** if the specified circle is inside this circle (see Figure 10.15b).
- A method **overlaps(Circle2D circle)** that returns **true** if the specified circle overlaps with this circle (see Figure 10.15c).

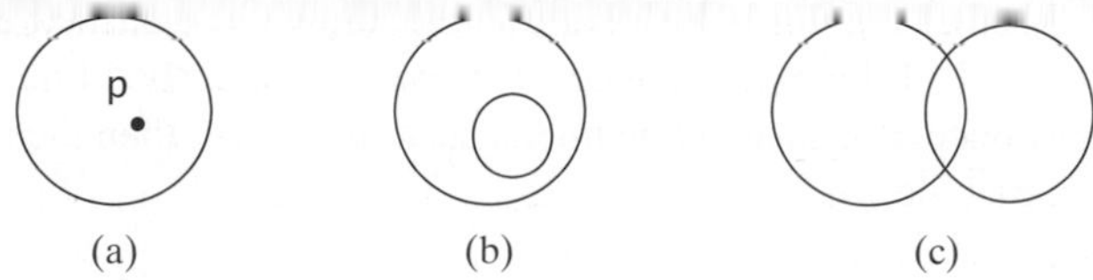

FIGURE 10.15 (a) A point is inside the circle. (b) A circle is inside another circle. (c) A circle overlaps another circle.

Draw the UML diagram for the class and then implement the class. Write a test program that creates a **Circle2D** object **c1** (**new Circle2D(2, 2, 5.5)**), displays its area and perimeter, and displays the result of **c1.contains(3, 3)**, **c1.contains(new Circle2D(4, 5, 10.5))**, and **c1.overlaps(new Circle2D(3, 5, 2.3))**.

***10.12 (*Geometry: The* `Triangle2D` *class*) Define the `Triangle2D` class that contains:

- Three points named `p1`, `p2`, and `p3` of the type `MyPoint` with `get` and `set` methods. `MyPoint` is defined in Exercise 10.4.
- A no-arg constructor that creates a default triangle with the points (`0`, `0`), (`1`, `1`), and (`2`, `5`).
- A constructor that creates a triangle with the specified points.
- A method `getArea()` that returns the area of the triangle.
- A method `getPerimeter()` that returns the perimeter of the triangle.
- A method `contains(MyPoint p)` that returns `true` if the specified point `p` is inside this triangle (see Figure 10.16a).
- A method `contains(Triangle2D t)` that returns `true` if the specified triangle is inside this triangle (see Figure 10.16b).
- A method `overlaps(Triangle2D t)` that returns `true` if the specified triangle overlaps with this triangle (see Figure 10.16c).

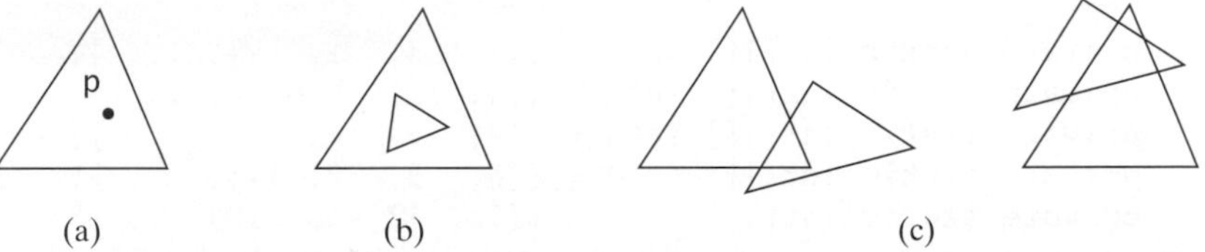

FIGURE 10.16 (a) A point is inside the triangle. (b) A triangle is inside another triangle. (c) A triangle overlaps another triangle.

Draw the UML diagram for the class and then implement the class. Write a test program that creates a `Triangle2D` objects `t1` using the constructor `new Triangle2D(new MyPoint(2.5, 2), new MyPoint(4.2, 3), new MyPoint(5, 3.5))`, displays its area and perimeter, and displays the result of `t1.contains(3, 3)`, `r1.contains(new Triangle2D(new MyPoint(2.9, 2), new MyPoint(4, 1), MyPoint(1, 3.4)))`, and `t1.overlaps(new Triangle2D(new MyPoint(2, 5.5), new MyPoint(4, -3), MyPoint(2, 6.5)))`.

(*Hint*: For the formula to compute the area of a triangle, see Programming Exercise 2.15. Use the `java.awt.geo.Line2D` class in the Java API to implement the `contains` and `overlaps` methods. The `Line2D` class contains the methods for checking whether two line segments intersect and whether a line contains a point, and so on. Please see the Java API for more information on `Line2D`. To detect whether a point is inside a triangle, draw three dashed lines, as shown in Figure 10.17. If the point is inside a triangle, each dashed line should intersect a side only once. If a dashed line intersects a side twice, then the point must be outside the triangle.)

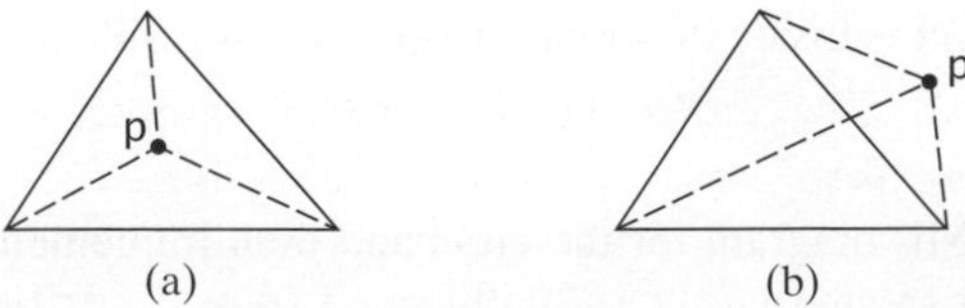

FIGURE 10.17 (a) A point is inside the triangle. (b) A point is outside the triangle.

***10.13** (*Geometry: the* `MyRectangle2D` *class*) Define the `MyRectangle2D` class that contains:

- Two `double` data fields named `x` and `y` that specify the center of the rectangle with `get` and `set` methods. (Assume that the rectangle sides are parallel to `x`- or `y`- axes.)
- The data fields `width` and `height` with `get` and `set` methods.
- A no-arg constructor that creates a default rectangle with (`0`, `0`) for (`x`, `y`) and `1` for both `width` and `height`.
- A constructor that creates a rectangle with the specified `x`, `y`, `width`, and `height`.
- A method `getArea()` that returns the area of the rectangle.
- A method `getPerimeter()` that returns the perimeter of the rectangle.
- A method `contains(double x, double y)` that returns `true` if the specified point (`x`, `y`) is inside this rectangle (see Figure 10.18a).
- A method `contains(MyRectangle2D r)` that returns `true` if the specified rectangle is inside this rectangle (see Figure 10.18b).
- A method `overlaps(MyRectangle2D r)` that returns `true` if the specified rectangle overlaps with this rectangle (see Figure 10.18c).

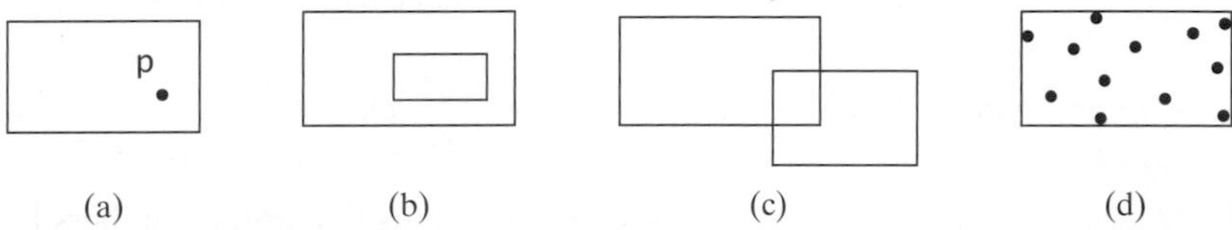

(a) (b) (c) (d)

FIGURE 10.18 A point is inside the rectangle. (b) A rectangle is inside another rectangle. (c) A rectangle overlaps another rectangle. (d) Points are enclosed inside a rectangle.

Draw the UML diagram for the class and then implement the class. Write a test program that creates a `MyRectangle2D` object `r1` (`new MyRectangle2D(2, 2, 5.5, 4.9)`), displays its area and perimeter, and displays the result of `r1.contains(3, 3)`, `r1.contains(new MyRectangle2D(4, 5, 10.5, 3.2))`, and `r1.overlaps(new MyRectangle2D(3, 5, 2.3, 5.4))`.

***10.14** (*The* `MyDate` *class*) Design a class named `MyDate`. The class contains:

- The data fields `year`, `month`, and `day` that represent a date. `month` is 0-based, i.e., `0` is for January.
- A no-arg constructor that creates a `MyDate` object for the current date.
- A constructor that constructs a `MyDate` object with a specified elapsed time since midnight, January 1, 1970, in milliseconds.
- A constructor that constructs a `MyDate` object with the specified year, month, and day.
- Three `get` methods for the data fields `year`, `month`, and `day`, respectively.
- A method named `setDate(long elapsedTime)` that sets a new date for the object using the elapsed time.

Draw the UML diagram for the class and then implement the class. Write a test program that creates two `MyDate` objects (using `new MyDate()` and `new MyDate(34355555133101L)`) and displays their year, month, and day.

(*Hint*: The first two constructors will extract the year, month, and day from the elapsed time. For example, if the elapsed time is `561555550000` milliseconds, the year is

1987, the month is 9, and the day is 18. You may use the GregorianCalendar class discussed in Programming Exercise 8.5 to simplify coding.)

***10.15** (*Geometry: finding the bounding rectangle*) A bounding rectangle is the minimum rectangle that encloses a set of points in a two-dimensional plane, as shown in Figure 10.18d. Write a method that returns a bounding rectangle for a set of points in a two-dimensional plane, as follows:

```
public static MyRectangle2D getRectangle(double[][] points)
```

The Rectangle2D class is defined in Exercise 10.13. Write a test program that prompts the user to enter five points and displays the bounding rectangle's center, width, and height. Here is a sample run:

```
Enter five points: 1.0 2.5 3 4 5 6 7 8 9 10 ↵Enter
The bounding rectangle's center (5.0, 6.25), width 8.0, height 7.5
```

Sections 10.12–10.14

***10.16** (*Divisible by 2 or 3*) Find the first ten numbers with 50 decimal digits that are divisible by 2 or 3.

***10.17** (*Square numbers*) Find the first ten square numbers that are greater than Long.MAX_VALUE. A square number is a number in the form of n^2.

***10.18** (*Large prime numbers*) Write a program that finds five prime numbers larger than Long.MAX_VALUE.

***10.19** (*Mersenne prime*) A prime number is called a *Mersenne prime* if it can be written in the form $2^p - 1$ for some positive integer p. Write a program that finds all Mersenne primes with $p \leq 100$ and displays the output as shown below. (*Hint*: You have to use BigInteger to store the number, because it is too big to be stored in long. Your program may take several hours to run.)

```
p       2^p - 1

2            3
3            7
5           31

...
```

***10.20** (*Approximate e*) Programming Exercise 4.26 approximates e using the following series:

$$e = 1 + \frac{1}{1!} + \frac{1}{2!} + \frac{1}{3!} + \frac{1}{4!} + \ \dots \ + \frac{1}{i!}$$

In order to get better precision, use BigDecimal with 25 digits of precision in the computation. Write a program that displays the e value for i = 100, 200, . . . , and 1000.

10.21 (*Divisible by 5 or 6*) Find the first ten numbers (greater than Long.MAX_VALUE) that are divisible by 5 or 6.

CHAPTER

11

INHERITANCE AND POLYMORPHISM

Objectives

- To define a subclass from a superclass through inheritance (§11.2).
- To invoke the superclass's constructors and methods using the `super` keyword (§11.3).
- To override instance methods in the subclass (§11.4).
- To distinguish differences between overriding and overloading (§11.5).
- To explore the `toString()` method in the `Object` class (§11.6).
- To discover polymorphism and dynamic binding (§§11.7–11.8).
- To describe casting and explain why explicit downcasting is necessary (§11.9).
- To explore the `equals` method in the `Object` class (§11.10).
- To store, retrieve, and manipulate objects in an `ArrayList` (§11.11).
- To implement a `Stack` class using `ArrayList` (§11.12).
- To enable data and methods in a superclass accessible from subclasses using the `protected` visibility modifier (§11.13).
- To prevent class extending and method overriding using the `final` modifier (§11.14).

11.1 Introduction

Object-oriented programming allows you to define new classes from existing classes. This is called inheritance.

inheritance

As discussed earlier in the book, the procedural paradigm focuses on designing methods and the object-oriented paradigm couples data and methods together into objects. Software design using the object-oriented paradigm focuses on objects and operations on objects. The object-oriented approach combines the power of the procedural paradigm with an added dimension that integrates data with operations into objects.

why inheritance?

Inheritance is an important and powerful feature for reusing software. Suppose you need to define classes to model circles, rectangles, and triangles. These classes have many common features. What is the best way to design these classes so as to avoid redundancy and make the system easy to comprehend and easy to maintain? The answer is to use inheritance.

11.2 Superclasses and Subclasses

Inheritance enables you to define a general class (e.g., a superclass) and later extend it to more specialized classes (e.g., subclasses).

You use a class to model objects of the same type. Different classes may have some common properties and behaviors, which can be generalized in a class that can be shared by other classes. You can define a specialized class that extends the generalized class. The specialized classes inherit the properties and methods from the general class.

VideoNote

Geometric class hierarchy

Consider geometric objects. Suppose you want to design the classes to model geometric objects such as circles and rectangles. Geometric objects have many common properties and behaviors. They can be drawn in a certain color and be filled or unfilled. Thus a general class `GeometricObject` can be used to model all geometric objects. This class contains the properties `color` and `filled` and their appropriate `get` and `set` methods. Assume that this class also contains the `dateCreated` property and the `getDateCreated()` and `toString()` methods. The `toString()` method returns a string representation of the object. Since a circle is a special type of geometric object, it shares common properties and methods with other geometric objects. Thus it makes sense to define the `Circle` class that extends the `GeometricObject` class. Likewise, `Rectangle` can also be defined as a subclass of `GeometricObject`. Figure 11.1 shows the relationship among these classes. A triangular arrow pointing to the superclass is used to denote the inheritance relationship between the two classes involved.

subclass
superclass

In Java terminology, a class `C1` extended from another class `C2` is called a *subclass*, and `C2` is called a *superclass*. A superclass is also referred to as a *parent class* or a *base class*, and a subclass as a *child class*, an *extended class*, or a *derived class*. A subclass inherits accessible data fields and methods from its superclass and may also add new data fields and methods.

The `Circle` class inherits all accessible data fields and methods from the `GeometricObject` class. In addition, it has a new data field, `radius`, and its associated `get` and `set` methods. The `Circle` class also contains the `getArea()`, `getPerimeter()`, and `getDiameter()` methods for returning the area, perimeter, and diameter of the circle.

The `Rectangle` class inherits all accessible data fields and methods from the `GeometricObject` class. In addition, it has the data fields `width` and `height` and their associated `get` and `set` methods. It also contains the `getArea()` and `getPerimeter()` methods for returning the area and perimeter of the rectangle.

The `GeometricObject`, `Circle`, and `Rectangle` classes are shown in Listings 11.1, 11.2, and 11.3.

avoid naming conflicts

Note

To avoid a naming conflict with the improved `GeometricObject`, `Circle`, and `Rectangle` classes introduced in Chapter 15, we'll name these classes

GeometricObject	
-color: String	The color of the object (default: white).
-filled: boolean	Indicates whether the object is filled with a color (default: false).
-dateCreated: java.util.Date	The date when the object was created.
+GeometricObject()	Creates a GeometricObject.
+GeometricObject(color: String, filled: boolean)	Creates a GeometricObject with the specified color and filled values.
+getColor(): String	Returns the color.
+setColor(color: String): void	Sets a new color.
+isFilled(): boolean	Returns the filled property.
+setFilled(filled: boolean): void	Sets a new filled property.
+getDateCreated(): java.util.Date	Returns the dateCreated.
+toString(): String	Returns a string representation of this object.

Circle
-radius: double
+Circle()
+Circle(radius: double)
+Circle(radius: double, color: String, filled: boolean)
+getRadius(): double
+setRadius(radius: double): void
+getArea(): double
+getPerimeter(): double
+getDiameter(): double
+printCircle(): void

Rectangle
-width: double
-height: double
+Rectangle()
+Rectangle(width: double, height: double)
+Rectangle(width: double, height: double color: String, filled: boolean)
+getWidth(): double
+setWidth(width: double): void
+getHeight(): double
+setHeight(height: double): void
+getArea(): double
+getPerimeter(): double

FIGURE 11.1 The GeometricObject class is the superclass for Circle and Rectangle.

SimpleGeometricObject, CircleFromSimpleGeometricObject, and RectangleFromSimpleGeometricObject in this chapter. For simplicity, we will still refer to them in the text as GeometricObject, Circle, and Rectangle classes. The best way to avoid naming conflicts is to place these classes in different packages. However, for simplicity and consistency, all classes in this book are placed in the default package.

LISTING 11.1 SimpleGeometricObject.java

```
public class SimpleGeometricObject {
  private String color = "white";
  private boolean filled;
  private java.util.Date dateCreated;

  /** Construct a default geometric object */
  public SimpleGeometricObject() {
    dateCreated = new java.util.Date();
```

data fields

constructor

date constructed

```java
  }

  /** Construct a geometric object with the specified color
    *  and filled value */
  public SimpleGeometricObject(String color, boolean filled) {
    dateCreated = new java.util.Date();
    this.color = color;
    this.filled = filled;
  }

  /** Return color */
  public String getColor() {
    return color;
  }

  /** Set a new color */
  public void setColor(String color) {
    this.color = color;
  }

  /** Return filled. Since filled is boolean,
     its get method is named isFilled */
  public boolean isFilled() {
    return filled;
  }

  /** Set a new filled */
  public void setFilled(boolean filled) {
    this.filled = filled;
  }

  /** Get dateCreated */
  public java.util.Date getDateCreated() {
    return dateCreated;
  }

  /** Return a string representation of this object */
  public String toString() {
    return "created on " + dateCreated + "\ncolor: " + color +
      " and filled: " + filled;
  }
}
```

LISTING 11.2 CircleFromSimpleGeometricObject.java

extends superclass
data fields
constructor

```java
public class CircleFromSimpleGeometricObject
    extends SimpleGeometricObject {
  private double radius;

  public CircleFromSimpleGeometricObject() {
  }

  public CircleFromSimpleGeometricObject(double radius) {
    this.radius = radius;
  }

  public CircleFromSimpleGeometricObject(double radius,
      String color, boolean filled) {
    this.radius = radius;
    setColor(color);
```

```
16       setFilled(filled);
17     }
18
19     /** Return radius */
20     public double getRadius() {
21       return radius;
22     }
23
24     /** Set a new radius */
25     public void setRadius(double radius) {
26       this.radius = radius;
27     }
28
29     /** Return area */
30     public double getArea() {
31       return radius * radius * Math.PI;
32     }
33
34     /** Return diameter */
35     public double getDiameter() {
36       return 2 * radius;
37     }
38
39     /** Return perimeter */
40     public double getPerimeter() {
41       return 2 * radius * Math.PI;
42     }
43
44     /** Print the circle info */
45     public void printCircle() {
46       System.out.println("The circle is created " + getDateCreated() +
47         " and the radius is " + radius);
48     }
49   }
```

methods

The Circle class (Listing 11.2) extends the GeometricObject class (Listing 11.1) using the following syntax:

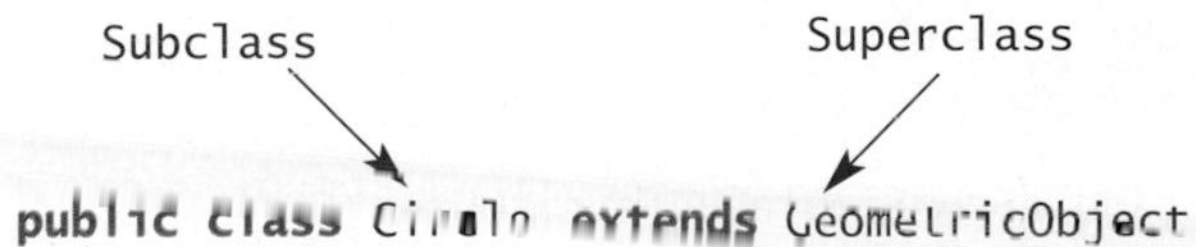

The keyword extends (lines 1–2) tells the compiler that the Circle class extends the GeometricObject class, thus inheriting the methods getColor, setColor, isFilled, setFilled, and toString.

The overloaded constructor Circle(double radius, String color, boolean filled) is implemented by invoking the setColor and setFilled methods to set the color and filled properties (lines 12–17). These two public methods are defined in the base class GeometricObject and are inherited in Circle, so they can be used in the derived class.

private member in base class

You might attempt to use the data fields color and filled directly in the constructor as follows:

```
public CircleFromSimpleGeometricObject(
    double radius, String color, boolean filled) {
```

```
    this.radius = radius;
    this.color = color; // Illegal
    this.filled = filled; // Illegal
  }
```

This is wrong, because the private data fields `color` and `filled` in the `GeometricObject` class cannot be accessed in any class other than in the `GeometricObject` class itself. The only way to read and modify `color` and `filled` is through their `get` and `set` methods.

The `Rectangle` class (Listing 11.3) extends the `GeometricObject` class (Listing 11.1) using the following syntax:

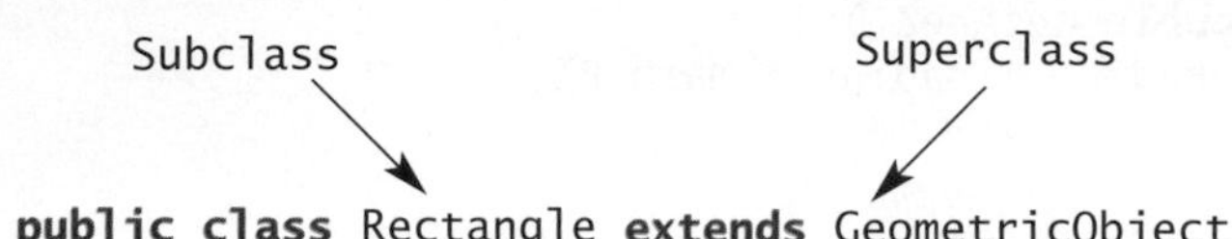

The keyword `extends` (lines 1–2) tells the compiler that the `Rectangle` class extends the `GeometricObject` class, thus inheriting the methods `getColor`, `setColor`, `isFilled`, `setFilled`, and `toString`.

Listing 11.3 RectangleFromSimpleGeometricObject.java

extends superclass (line 2); data fields (line 3); constructor (line 6); methods (line 24)

```
1  public class RectangleFromSimpleGeometricObject
2      extends SimpleGeometricObject {
3    private double width;
4    private double height;
5
6    public RectangleFromSimpleGeometricObject() {
7    }
8
9    public RectangleFromSimpleGeometricObject(
10       double width, double height) {
11     this.width = width;
12     this.height = height;
13   }
14
15   public RectangleFromSimpleGeometricObject(
16       double width, double height, String color, boolean filled) {
17     this.width = width;
18     this.height = height;
19     setColor(color);
20     setFilled(filled);
21   }
22
23   /** Return width */
24   public double getWidth() {
25     return width;
26   }
27
28   /** Set a new width */
29   public void setWidth(double width) {
30     this.width = width;
31   }
32
```

```
  /** Return height */
  public double getHeight() {
    return height;
  }

  /** Set a new height */
  public void setHeight(double height) {
    this.height = height;
  }

  /** Return area */
  public double getArea() {
    return width * height;
  }

  /** Return perimeter */
  public double getPerimeter() {
    return 2 * (width + height);
  }
}
```

The code in Listing 11.4 creates objects of `Circle` and `Rectangle` and invokes the methods on these objects. The `toString()` method is inherited from the `GeometricObject` class and is invoked from a `Circle` object (line 5) and a `Rectangle` object (line 13).

LISTING 11.4 TestCircleRectangle.java

```
1  public class TestCircleRectangle {
2    public static void main(String[] args) {
3      CircleFromSimpleGeometricObject circle =
4        new CircleFromSimpleGeometricObject(1);
5      System.out.println("A circle " + circle.toString());
6      System.out.println("The color is " + circle.getColor());
7      System.out.println("The radius is " + circle.getRadius());
8      System.out.println("The area is " + circle.getArea());
9      System.out.println("The diameter is " + circle.getDiameter());
10
11     RectangleFromSimpleGeometricObject rectangle =
12       new RectangleFromSimpleGeometricObject(2, 4);
13     System.out.println("\nA rectangle " + rectangle.toString());
14     System.out.println("The area is " + rectangle.getArea());
15     System.out.println("The perimeter is " +
16       rectangle.getPerimeter());
17   }
18 }
```

Circle object
invoke toString
invoke getColor

Rectangle object
invoke toString

```
A circle created on Thu Feb 10 19:54:25 EST 2011
color: white and filled: false
The color is white
The radius is 1.0
The area is 3.141592653589793
The diameter is 2.0
A rectangle created on Thu Feb 10 19:54:25 EST 2011
color: white and filled: false
The area is 8.0
The perimeter is 12.0
```

Note the following points regarding inheritance:

more in subclass

- Contrary to the conventional interpretation, a subclass is not a subset of its superclass. In fact, a subclass usually contains more information and methods than its superclass.

private data fields

- Private data fields in a superclass are not accessible outside the class. Therefore, they cannot be used directly in a subclass. They can, however, be accessed/mutated through public accessors/mutators if defined in the superclass.

nonextensible is-a

- Not all is-a relationships should be modeled using inheritance. For example, a square is a rectangle, but you should not extend a `Square` class from a `Rectangle` class, because the `width` and `height` properties are not appropriate for a square. Instead, you should define a `Square` class to extend the `GeometricObject` class and define the `side` property for the side of a square.

no blind extension

- Inheritance is used to model the is-a relationship. Do not blindly extend a class just for the sake of reusing methods. For example, it makes no sense for a `Tree` class to extend a `Person` class, even though they share common properties such as height and weight. A subclass and its superclass must have the is-a relationship.

multiple inheritance

single inheritance

- Some programming languages allow you to derive a subclass from several classes. This capability is known as *multiple inheritance*. Java, however, does not allow multiple inheritance. A Java class may inherit directly from only one superclass. This restriction is known as *single inheritance*. If you use the `extends` keyword to define a subclass, it allows only one parent class. Nevertheless, multiple inheritance can be achieved through interfaces, which will be introduced in Section 15.4.

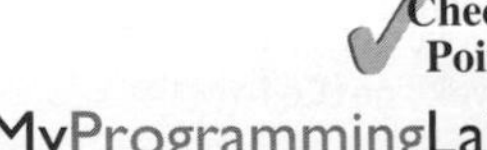

11.1 True or false? A subclass is a subset of a superclass.

11.2 What keyword do you use to define a subclass?

11.3 What is single inheritance? What is multiple inheritance? Does Java support multiple inheritance?

11.3 Using the **super** Keyword

The keyword `super` *refers to the superclass and can be used to invoke the superclass's methods and constructors.*

A subclass inherits accessible data fields and methods from its superclass. Does it inherit constructors? Can the superclass's constructors be invoked from a subclass? This section addresses these questions and their ramifications.

Section 10.4, The `this` Reference, introduced the use of the keyword `this` to reference the calling object. The keyword `super` refers to the superclass of the class in which `super` appears. It can be used in two ways:

- To call a superclass constructor.
- To call a superclass method.

11.3.1 Calling Superclass Constructors

A constructor is used to construct an instance of a class. Unlike properties and methods, the constructors of a superclass are not inherited by a subclass. They can only be invoked from the constructors of the subclasses using the keyword `super`.

The syntax to call a superclass's constructor is:

```
super(), or super(parameters);
```

The statement `super()` invokes the no-arg constructor of its superclass, and the statement `super(arguments)` invokes the superclass constructor that matches the `arguments`. The statement `super()` or `super(arguments)` must appear in the first line of the subclass's constructor; this is the only way to explicitly invoke a superclass constructor. For example, the constructor in lines 12–17 in Listing 11.2 can be replaced by the following code:

```
public CircleFromSimpleGeometricObject(
    double radius, String color, boolean filled) {
  super(color, filled);
  this.radius = radius;
}
```

Caution

You must use the keyword `super` to call the superclass constructor, and the call must be the first statement in the constructor. Invoking a superclass constructor's name in a subclass causes a syntax error.

11.3.2 Constructor Chaining

A constructor may invoke an overloaded constructor or its superclass constructor. If neither is invoked explicitly, the compiler automatically puts `super()` as the first statement in the constructor. For example:

```
public ClassName() {
  // some statements
}
```

Equivalent

```
public ClassName() {
  super();
  // some statements
}
```

```
public ClassName(double d) {
  // some statements
}
```

Equivalent

```
public ClassName(double d) {
  super();
  // some statements
}
```

In any case, constructing an instance of a class invokes the constructors of all the superclasses along the inheritance chain. When constructing an object of a subclass, the subclass constructor first invokes its superclass constructor before performing its own tasks. If the superclass is derived from another class, the superclass constructor invokes its parent-class constructor before performing its own tasks. This process continues until the last constructor along the inheritance hierarchy is called. This is called *constructor chaining*.

constructor chaining

Consider the following code:

```
public class Faculty extends Employee {
  public static void main(String[] args) {
    new Faculty();
  }

  public Faculty() {
```

invoke overloaded constructor

```
 7      System.out.println("(4) Performs Faculty's tasks");
 8    }
 9  }
10
11  class Employee extends Person {
12    public Employee() {
13      this("(2) Invoke Employee's overloaded constructor");
14      System.out.println("(3) Performs Employee's tasks ");
15    }
16
17    public Employee(String s) {
18      System.out.println(s);
19    }
20  }
21
22  class Person {
23    public Person() {
24      System.out.println("(1) Performs Person's tasks");
25    }
26  }
```

```
(1) Performs Person's tasks
(2) Invoke Employee's overloaded constructor
(3) Performs Employee's tasks
(4) Performs Faculty's tasks
```

The program produces the preceding output. Why? Let us discuss the reason. In line 3, **new Faculty()** invokes **Faculty**'s no-arg constructor. Since **Faculty** is a subclass of **Employee**, **Employee**'s no-arg constructor is invoked before any statements in **Faculty**'s constructor are executed. **Employee**'s no-arg constructor invokes **Employee**'s second constructor (line 12). Since **Employee** is a subclass of **Person**, **Person**'s no-arg constructor is invoked before any statements in **Employee**'s second constructor are executed. This process is illustrated in the following figure.

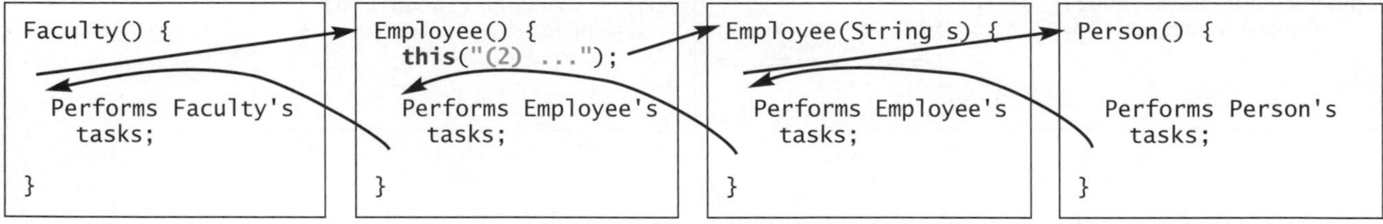

no-arg constructor

Caution

If a class is designed to be extended, it is better to provide a no-arg constructor to avoid programming errors. Consider the following code:

```
public class Apple extends Fruit {
}

class Fruit {
  public Fruit(String name) {
    System.out.println("Fruit's constructor is invoked");
  }
}
```

Since no constructor is explicitly defined in Apple, Apple's default no-arg constructor is defined implicitly. Since Apple is a subclass of Fruit, Apple's default constructor automatically invokes Fruit's no-arg constructor. However, Fruit does not have a no-arg constructor, because Fruit has an explicit constructor defined. Therefore, the program cannot be compiled.

Design Guide

If possible, you should provide a no-arg constructor for every class to make the class easy to extend and to avoid errors.

no-arg constructor

11.3.3 Calling Superclass Methods

The keyword super can also be used to reference a method other than the constructor in the superclass. The syntax is:

```
super.method(parameters);
```

You could rewrite the printCircle() method in the Circle class as follows:

```
public void printCircle() {
  System.out.println("The circle is created " +
    super.getDateCreated() + " and the radius is " + radius);
}
```

It is not necessary to put super before getDateCreated() in this case, however, because getDateCreated is a method in the GeometricObject class and is inherited by the Circle class. Nevertheless, in some cases, as shown in the next section, the keyword super is needed.

11.4 What is the printout of running the class C in (a)? What problem arises in compiling the program in (b)?

```
class A {
  public A() {
    System.out.println(
      "A's no-arg constructor is invoked");
  }
}

class B extends A {
}

public class C {
  public static void main(String[] args) {
    B b = new B();
  }
}
```

(a)

```
class A {
  public A(int x) {
  }
}

class B extends A {
  public B() {
  }
}

public class C {
  public static void main(String[] args) {
    B b = new B();
  }
}
```

(b)

11.5 How does a subclass invoke its superclass's constructor?

11.6 True or false? When invoking a constructor from a subclass, its superclass's no-arg constructor is always invoked.

11.4 Overriding Methods

To override a method, the method must be defined in the subclass using the same signature and the same return type as in its superclass.

A subclass inherits methods from a superclass. Sometimes it is necessary for the subclass to modify the implementation of a method defined in the superclass. This is referred to as *method overriding*.

method overriding

The `toString` method in the `GeometricObject` class (lines 46–49 in Listing 11.1) returns the string representation of a geometric object. This method can be overridden to return the string representation of a circle. To override it, add the following new method in the `Circle` class in Listing 11.2.

toString in superclass

```
1 public class CircleFromSimpleGeometricObject
2     extends SimpleGeometricObject {
3   // Other methods are omitted
4
5   // Override the toString method defined in the superclass
6   public String toString() {
7     return super.toString() + "\nradius is " + radius;
8   }
9 }
```

The `toString()` method is defined in the `GeometricObject` class and modified in the `Circle` class. Both methods can be used in the `Circle` class. To invoke the `toString` method defined in the `GeometricObject` class from the `Circle` class, use `super.toString()` (line 7).

no super.super.methodName()

Can a subclass of `Circle` access the `toString` method defined in the `GeometricObject` class using syntax such as `super.super.toString()`? No. This is a syntax error.

Several points are worth noting:

override accessible instance method

- An instance method can be overridden only if it is accessible. Thus a private method cannot be overridden, because it is not accessible outside its own class. If a method defined in a subclass is private in its superclass, the two methods are completely unrelated.

cannot override static method

- Like an instance method, a static method can be inherited. However, a static method cannot be overridden. If a static method defined in the superclass is redefined in a subclass, the method defined in the superclass is hidden. The hidden static methods can be invoked using the syntax `SuperClassName.staticMethodName`.

MyProgrammingLab™

11.7 True or false? You can override a private method defined in a superclass.

11.8 True or false? You can override a static method defined in a superclass.

11.9 How do you explicitly invoke a superclass's constructor from a subclass?

11.10 How do you invoke an overridden superclass method from a subclass?

11.5 Overriding vs. Overloading

Overloading *means to define multiple methods with the same name but different signatures.* Overriding *means to provide a new implementation for a method in the subclass.*

You learned about overloading methods in Section 5.8. To override a method, the method must be defined in the subclass using the same signature and the same return type.

Let us use an example to show the differences between overriding and overloading. In (a) below, the method `p(double i)` in class `A` overrides the same method defined in class `B`. In (b), however, the class `A` has two overloaded methods: `p(double i)` and `p(int i)`. The method `p(double i)` is inherited from `B`.

```
public class Test {
  public static void main(String[] args) {
    A a = new A();
    a.p(10);
    a.p(10.0);
  }
}

class B {
  public void p(double i) {
    System.out.println(i * 2);
  }
}

class A extends B {
  // This method overrides the method in B
  public void p(double i) {
    System.out.println(i);
  }
}
```

(a)

```
public class Test {
  public static void main(String[] args) {
    A a = new A();
    a.p(10);
    a.p(10.0);
  }
}

class B {
  public void p(double i) {
    System.out.println(i * 2);
  }
}

class A extends B {
  // This method overloads the method in B
  public void p(int i) {
    System.out.println(i);
  }
}
```

(b)

When you run the `Test` class in (a), both `a.p(10)` and `a.p(10.0)` invoke the `p(double i)` method defined in class `A` to display `10.0`. When you run the `Test` class in (b), `a.p(10)` invokes the `p(int i)` method defined in class `A` to display `10`, and `a.p(10.0)` invokes the `p(double i)` method defined in class `B` to display `20.0`.

Note the following:

- Overridden methods are in different classes related by inheritance; overloaded methods can be either in the same class or different classes related by inheritance.
- Overridden methods have the same signature and return type; overloaded methods have the same name but a different parameter list.

To avoid mistakes, you can use a special Java syntax, called *override annotation*, to place `@Override` before the method in the subclass. For example:

override annotation

```
public class CircleFromSimpleGeometricObject
    extends SimpleGeometricObject {
  // Other methods are omitted

  @Override
  public String toString() {
    return super.toString() + "\nradius is " + radius;
  }
}
```

`toString` in superclass

This annotation denotes that the annotated method is required to override a method in the superclass. If a method with this annotation does not override its superclass's method, the compiler will report an error. For example, if `toString` is mistyped as `tostring`, a compile error is reported. If the override annotation isn't used, the compile won't report an error. Using annotation avoids mistakes.

MyProgrammingLab™

11.11 Identify the problems in the following code:

```
public class Circle {
  private double radius;

  public Circle(double radius) {
    radius = radius;
  }

  public double getRadius() {
    return radius;
  }

  public double getArea() {
    return radius * radius * Math.PI;
  }
}

class B extends Circle {
  private double length;

  B(double radius, double length) {
    Circle(radius);
    length = length;
  }

  @Override
  public double getArea() {
    return getArea() * length;
  }
}
```

11.12 Explain the difference between method overloading and method overriding.

11.13 If a method in a subclass has the same signature as a method in its superclass with the same return type, is the method overridden or overloaded?

11.14 If a method in a subclass has the same signature as a method in its superclass with a different return type, will this be a problem?

11.15 If a method in a subclass has the same name as a method in its superclass with different parameter types, is the method overridden or overloaded?

11.16 What is the benefit of using the `@Override` annotation?

11.6 The `Object` Class and Its `toString()` Method

Every class in Java is descended from the `java.lang.Object` *class.*

If no inheritance is specified when a class is defined, the superclass of the class is `Object` by default. For example, the following two class definitions are the same:

```
public class ClassName {
  ...
}
```

Equivalent

```
public class ClassName extends Object {
  ...
}
```

Classes such as `String`, `StringBuilder`, `Loan`, and `GeometricObject` are implicitly subclasses of `Object` (as are all the main classes you have seen in this book so far). It is important to be familiar with the methods provided by the `Object` class so that you can use them in your classes. This section introduces the `toString` method in the `Object` class.

toString()

The signature of the `toString()` method is:

```
public String toString()
```

string representation

Invoking `toString()` on an object returns a string that describes the object. By default, it returns a string consisting of a class name of which the object is an instance, an at sign (`@`), and the object's memory address in hexadecimal. For example, consider the following code for the `Loan` class defined in Listing 10.2:

```
Loan loan = new Loan();
System.out.println(loan.toString());
```

The output for this code displays something like `Loan@15037e5`. This message is not very helpful or informative. Usually you should override the `toString` method so that it returns a descriptive string representation of the object. For example, the `toString` method in the `Object` class was overridden in the `GeometricObject` class in lines 46–49 in Listing 11.1 as follows:

```
public String toString() {
  return "created on " + dateCreated + "\ncolor: " + color +
    " and filled: " + filled;
}
```

Note

print object

You can also pass an object to invoke `System.out.println(object)` or `System.out.print(object)`. This is equivalent to invoking `System.out.println(object.toString())` or `System.out.print(object.toString())`. Thus, you could replace `System.out.println(loan.toString())` with `System.out.println(loan)`.

11.7 Polymorphism

Polymorphism means that a variable of a supertype can refer to a subtype object.

The three pillars of object-oriented programming are encapsulation, inheritance, and polymorphism. You have already learned the first two. This section introduces polymorphism.

subtype

supertype

First, let us define two useful terms: subtype and supertype. A class defines a type. A type defined by a subclass is called a *subtype*, and a type defined by its superclass is called a *supertype*. Therefore, you can say that `Circle` is a subtype of `GeometricObject` and `GeometricObject` is a supertype for `Circle`.

The inheritance relationship enables a subclass to inherit features from its superclass with additional new features. A subclass is a specialization of its superclass; every instance of a subclass is also an instance of its superclass, but not vice versa. For example, every circle is a geometric object, but not every geometric object is a circle. Therefore, you can always pass an instance of a subclass to a parameter of its superclass type. Consider the code in Listing 11.5.

LISTING 11.5 PolymorphismDemo.java

```
public class PolymorphismDemo {
  /** Main method */
  public static void main(String[] args) {
```

polymorphic call

polymorphic call

```
4      // Display circle and rectangle properties
5      displayObject(new CircleFromSimpleGeometricObject
6                       (1, "red", false));
7      displayObject(new RectangleFromSimpleGeometricObject
8                       (1, 1, "black", true));
9    }
10
11   /** Display geometric object properties */
12   public static void displayObject(SimpleGeometricObject object) {
13     System.out.println("Created on " + object.getDateCreated() +
14       ". Color is " + object.getColor());
15   }
16 }
```

```
Created on Mon Mar 09 19:25:20 EDT 2011. Color is red
Created on Mon Mar 09 19:25:20 EDT 2011. Color is black
```

The method `displayObject` (line 12) takes a parameter of the `GeometricObject` type. You can invoke `displayObject` by passing any instance of `GeometricObject` (e.g., `new CircleFromSimpleGeometricObject(1, "red", false)` and `new RectangleFromSimpleGeometricObject(1, 1, "black", false)` in lines 5–8). An object of a subclass can be used wherever its superclass object is used. This is commonly known as *polymorphism* (from a Greek word meaning "many forms"). In simple terms, polymorphism means that a variable of a supertype can refer to a subtype object.

what is polymorphism?

11.8 Dynamic Binding

A method can be implemented in several classes along the inheritance chain. The JVM decides which method is invoked at runtime.

A method can be defined in a superclass and overridden in its subclass. For example, the `toString()` method is defined in the `Object` class and overridden in `GeometricObject`. Consider the following code:

```
Object o = new GeometricObject();
System.out.println(o.toString());
```

Which `toString()` method is invoked by `o`? To answer this question, we first introduce two terms: declared type and actual type. A variable must be declared a type. The type that declares a variable is called the variable's *declared type*. Here `o`'s declared type is `Object`. A variable of a reference type can hold a `null` value or a reference to an instance of the declared type. The instance may be created using the constructor of the declared type or its subtype. The *actual type* of the variable is the actual class for the object referenced by the variable. Here `o`'s actual type is `GeometricObject`, because `o` references an object created using `new GeometricObject()`. Which `toString()` method is invoked by `o` is determined by `o`'s actual type. This is known as *dynamic binding*.

declared type

actual type

dynamic binding

Dynamic binding works as follows: Suppose an object `o` is an instance of classes C_1, C_2, . . ., C_{n-1}, and C_n, where C_1 is a subclass of C_2, C_2 is a subclass of C_3, . . ., and C_{n-1} is a subclass of C_n, as shown in Figure 11.2. That is, C_n is the most general class, and C_1 is the most specific class. In Java, C_n is the `Object` class. If `o` invokes a method `p`, the JVM searches for the implementation of the method `p` in C_1, C_2, . . ., C_{n-1}, and C_n, in this order, until it is found. Once an implementation is found, the search stops and the first-found implementation is invoked.

C_n ◁— C_{n-1} ◁— ..... ◁— C_2 ◁— C_1

java.lang.Object

If o is an instance of C_1, o is also an instance of C_2, C_3, …, C_{n-1}, and C_n

FIGURE 11.2 The method to be invoked is dynamically bound at runtime.

Listing 11.6 gives an example to demonstrate dynamic binding.

VideoNote

Polymorphism and dynamic binding demo

LISTING 11.6 DynamicBindingDemo.java

```
1  public class DynamicBindingDemo {
2    public static void main(String[] args) {
3      m(new GraduateStudent());
4      m(new Student());
5      m(new Person());
6      m(new Object());
7    }
8
9    public static void m(Object x) {
10     System.out.println(x.toString());
11   }
12 }
13
14 class GraduateStudent extends Student {
15 }
16
17 class Student extends Person {
18   @Override
19   public String toString() {
20     return "Student";
21   }
22 }
23
24 class Person extends Object {
25   @Override
26   public String toString() {
27     return "Person";
28   }
29 }
```

polymorphic call (line 3)

dynamic binding (line 10)

override toString() (line 19)

override toString() (line 26)

```
Student
Student
Person
java.lang.Object@130c19b
```

Method `m` (line 9) takes a parameter of the `Object` type. You can invoke `m` with any object (e.g., `new GraduateStudent()`, `new Student()`, `new Person()`, and `new Object()`) in lines 3–6).

When the method `m(Object x)` is executed, the argument `x`'s `toString` method is invoked. `x` may be an instance of `GraduateStudent`, `Student`, `Person`, or `Object`. The classes `GraduateStudent`, `Student`, `Person`, and `Object` have their own implementations of the `toString` method. Which implementation is used will be determined by `x`'s actual type at runtime. Invoking `m(new GraduateStudent())` (line 3) causes the `toString` method defined in the `Student` class to be invoked.

Invoking `m(new Student())` (line 4) causes the `toString` method defined in the `Student` class to be invoked; invoking `m(new Person())` (line 5) causes the `toString` method defined in the `Person` class to be invoked; and invoking `m(new Object())` (line 6) causes the `toString` method defined in the `Object` class to be invoked.

matching vs. binding

Matching a method signature and binding a method implementation are two separate issues. The *declared type* of the reference variable decides which method to match at compile time. The compiler finds a matching method according to the parameter type, number of parameters, and order of the parameters at compile time. A method may be implemented in several classes along the inheritance chain. The JVM dynamically binds the implementation of the method at runtime, decided by the actual type of the variable.

MyProgrammingLab™

11.17 What is polymorphism? What is dynamic binding?

11.18 Describe the difference between method matching and method binding.

11.19 Can you assign `new int[50]`, `new Integer[50]`, `new String[50]`, or `new Object[50]`, into a variable of `Object[]` type?

11.20 What is wrong in the following code?

```
public class Test {
  public static void main(String[] args) {
    Integer[] list1 = {12, 24, 55, 1};
    Double[] list2 = {12.4, 24.0, 55.2, 1.0};
    int[] list3 = {1, 2, 3};
    printArray(list1);
    printArray(list2);
    printArray(list3);
  }

  public static void printArray(Object[] list) {
    for (Object o: list)
      System.out.print(o + " ");
    System.out.println();
  }
}
```

11.21 Show the output of the following code:

```
public class Test {
  public static void main(String[] args) {
    new Person().printPerson();
    new Student().printPerson();
  }
}

class Student extends Person {
  @Override
  public String getInfo() {
    return "Student";
  }
}

class Person {
  public String getInfo() {
    return "Person";
  }

  public void printPerson() {
    System.out.println(getInfo());
  }
}
```

(a)

```
public class Test {
  public static void main(String[] args) {
    new Person().printPerson();
    new Student().printPerson();
  }
}

class Student extends Person {
  private String getInfo() {
    return "Student";
  }
}

class Person {
  private String getInfo() {
    return "Person";
  }

  public void printPerson() {
    System.out.println(getInfo());
  }
}
```

(b)

11.22 Show the output of following program:

```
public class Test {
  public static void main(String[] args) {
    A a = new A(3);
  }
}

class A extends B {
  public A(int t) {
    System.out.println("A's constructor is invoked");
  }
}

class B {
  public B() {
    System.out.println("B's constructor is invoked");
  }
}
```

Is the no-arg constructor of `Object` invoked when `new A(3)` is invoked?

11.9 Casting Objects and the `instanceof` Operator

One object reference can be typecast into another object reference. This is called casting object.

Key Point

In the preceding section, the statement

casting object

```
m(new Student());
```

assigns the object `new Student()` to a parameter of the `Object` type. This statement is equivalent to

```
Object o = new Student(); // Implicit casting
m(o);
```

The statement `Object o = new Student()`, known as *implicit casting*, is legal because an instance of `Student` is an instance of `Object`.

implicit casting

Suppose you want to assign the object reference `o` to a variable of the `Student` type using the following statement:

```
Student b = o;
```

In this case a compile error would occur. Why does the statement `Object o = new Student()` work but `Student b = o` doesn't? The reason is that a `Student` object is always an instance of `Object`, but an `Object` is not necessarily an instance of `Student`. Even though you can see that `o` is really a `Student` object, the compiler is not clever enough to know it. To tell the compiler that `o` is a `Student` object, use *explicit casting*. The syntax is similar to the one used for casting among primitive data types. Enclose the target object type in parentheses and place it before the object to be cast, as follows:

explicit casting

```
Student b = (Student)o; // Explicit casting
```

It is always possible to cast an instance of a subclass to a variable of a superclass (known as *upcasting*), because an instance of a subclass is *always* an instance of its superclass. When casting an instance of a superclass to a variable of its subclass (known as *downcasting*), explicit casting must be used to confirm your intention to the compiler with the

upcasting
downcasting

(SubclassName) cast notation. For the casting to be successful, you must make sure that the object to be cast is an instance of the subclass. If the superclass object is not an instance of the subclass, a runtime ***ClassCastException*** occurs. For example, if an object is not an instance of **Student**, it cannot be cast into a variable of **Student**. It is a good practice, therefore, to ensure that the object is an instance of another object before attempting a casting. This can be accomplished by using the ***instanceof*** operator. Consider the following code:

ClassCastException

instanceof

```
Object myObject = new Circle();
... // Some lines of code
/** Perform casting if myObject is an instance of Circle */
if (myObject instanceof Circle) {
  System.out.println("The circle diameter is " +
    ((Circle)myObject).getDiameter());
  ...
}
```

You may be wondering why casting is necessary. The variable **myObject** is declared **Object**. The *declared type* decides which method to match at compile time. Using **myObject.getDiameter()** would cause a compile error, because the **Object** class does not have the **getDiameter** method. The compiler cannot find a match for **myObject.getDiameter()**. Therefore, it is necessary to cast **myObject** into the **Circle** type to tell the compiler that **myObject** is also an instance of **Circle**.

Why not define **myObject** as a **Circle** type in the first place? To enable generic programming, it is a good practice to define a variable with a supertype, which can accept a value of any subtype.

lowercase keywords

Note

instanceof is a Java keyword. Every letter in a Java keyword is in lowercase.

casting analogy

Tip

To help understand casting, you may also consider the analogy of fruit, apple, and orange, with the **Fruit** class as the superclass for **Apple** and **Orange**. An apple is a fruit, so you can always safely assign an instance of **Apple** to a variable for **Fruit**. However, a fruit is not necessarily an apple, so you have to use explicit casting to assign an instance of **Fruit** to a variable of **Apple**.

Listing 11.7 demonstrates polymorphism and casting. The program creates two objects (lines 5–6), a circle and a rectangle, and invokes the **displayObject** method to display them (lines 9–10). The **displayObject** method displays the area and diameter if the object is a circle (line 15), and the area if the object is a rectangle (lines 21–22).

LISTING 11.7 CastingDemo.java

```
 1 public class CastingDemo {
 2   /** Main method */
 3   public static void main(String[] args) {
 4     // Create and initialize two objects
 5     Object object1 = new CircleFromSimpleGeometricObject(1);
 6     Object object2 = new RectangleFromSimpleGeometricObject(1, 1);
 7
 8     // Display circle and rectangle
 9     displayObject(object1);
10     displayObject(object2);
11   }
12
```

```
13   /** A method for displaying an object */
14   public static void displayObject(Object object) {
15     if (object instanceof CircleFromSimpleGeometricObject) {
16       System.out.println("The circle area is " +
17         ((CircleFromSimpleGeometricObject)object).getArea());
18       System.out.println("The circle diameter is " +
19         ((CircleFromSimpleGeometricObject)object).getDiameter());
20     }
21     else if (object instanceof
22                   RectangleFromSimpleGeometricObject) {
23       System.out.println("The rectangle area is " +
24         ((RectangleFromSimpleGeometricObject)object).getArea());
25     }
26   }
27 }
```

polymorphic call (line 17)

polymorphic call (line 24)

```
The circle area is 3.141592653589793
The circle diameter is 2.0
The rectangle area is 1.0
```

The **displayObject(Object object)** method is an example of generic programming. It can be invoked by passing any instance of **Object**.

The program uses implicit casting to assign a **Circle** object to **object1** and a **Rectangle** object to **object2** (lines 5–6), then invokes the **displayObject** method to display the information on these objects (lines 9–10).

In the **displayObject** method (lines 14–26), explicit casting is used to cast the object to **Circle** if the object is an instance of **Circle**, and the methods **getArea** and **getDiameter** are used to display the area and diameter of the circle.

Casting can be done only when the source object is an instance of the target class. The program uses the **instanceof** operator to ensure that the source object is an instance of the target class before performing a casting (line 15).

Explicit casting to **Circle** (lines 17, 19) and to **Rectangle** (line 24) is necessary because the **getArea** and **getDiameter** methods are not available in the **Object** class.

Caution

The object member access operator (**.**) precedes the casting operator. Use parentheses to ensure that casting is done before the **.** operator, as in

precedes casting

```
((Circle)object).getArea());
```

Casting a primitive type value is different from casting an object reference. Casting a primitive type value returns a new value. For example:

```
int age = 45;
byte newAge = (int)age; // A new value is assigned to newAge
```

However, casting an object reference does not create a new object. For example:

```
Object o = new Circle();
Circle c = (Circle)o; // No new object is created
```

Now reference variables **o** and **c** point to the same object.

MyProgrammingLab™

11.23 Indicate true or false for the following statements:

- You can always successfully cast an instance of a subclass to a superclass.
- You can always successfully cast an instance of a superclass to a subclass.

11.24 For the `GeometricObject` and `Circle` classes in Listings 11.1 and 11.2, answer the following questions:

a. Are the following Boolean expressions true or false?

```
Circle circle = new Circle(1);
GeometricObject object1 = new GeometricObject();
(circle instanceof GeometricObject)
(object1 instanceof GeometricObject)
(circle instanceof Circle)
(object1 instanceof Circle)
```

b. Can the following statements be compiled?

```
Circle circle = new Circle(5);
GeometricObject object = circle;
```

c. Can the following statements be compiled?

```
GeometricObject object = new GeometricObject();
Circle circle = (Circle)object;
```

11.25 Suppose that `Fruit`, `Apple`, `Orange`, `GoldenDelicious`, and `McIntosh` are defined in the following inheritance hierarchy:

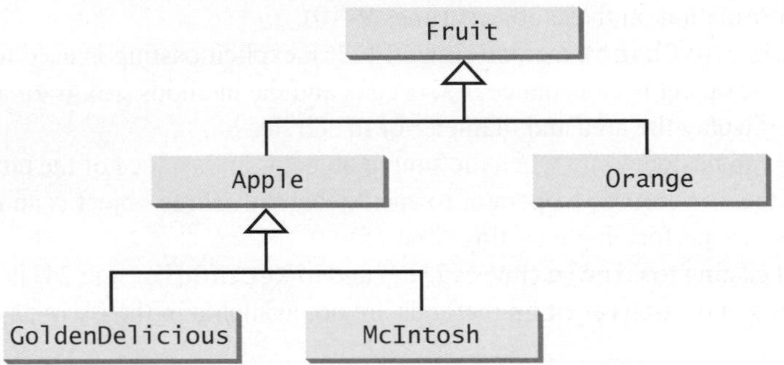

Assume that the following code is given:

```
Fruit fruit = new GoldenDelicious();
Orange orange = new Orange();
```

Answer the following questions:

a. Is `fruit instanceof Fruit`?

b. Is `fruit instanceof Orange`?

c. Is `fruit instanceof Apple`?

d. Is `fruit instanceof GoldenDelicious`?

e. Is `fruit instanceof McIntosh`?

f. Is `orange instanceof Orange`?

g. Is `orange instanceof Fruit`?

h. Is `orange instanceof Apple`?

i. Suppose the method `makeAppleCider` is defined in the `Apple` class. Can `fruit` invoke this method? Can `orange` invoke this method?

j. Suppose the method `makeOrangeJuice` is defined in the `Orange` class. Can `orange` invoke this method? Can `fruit` invoke this method?

k. Is the statement `Orange p = new Apple()` legal?

l. Is the statement `McIntosh p = new Apple()` legal?

m. Is the statement `Apple p = new McIntosh()` legal?

11.26 What is wrong in the following code?

```
public class Test {
  public static void main(String[] args) {
    Object fruit = new Fruit();
    Object apple = (Apple)fruit;
  }
}

class Apple extends Fruit {
}

class Fruit {
}
```

11.10 The **Object**'s **equals** Method

Like the `toString()` method, the `equals(Object)` method is another method defined in the `Object` class.

equals(Object)

Another method defined in the `Object` class that is often used is the `equals` method. Its signature is

```
public boolean equals(Object o)
```

This method tests whether two objects are equal. The syntax for invoking it is:

```
object1.equals(object2);
```

The default implementation of the `equals` method in the `Object` class is:

```
public boolean equals(Object obj) {
  return (this == obj);
}
```

This implementation checks whether two reference variables point to the same object using the == operator. You should override this method in your custom class to test whether two distinct objects have the same content.

The `equals` method is overridden in many classes in the Java API, such as `java.lang.String` and `java.util.Date`, to compare whether the contents of two objects are equal. You have already used the `equals` method to compare two strings in Section 9.2, The `String` Class. The `equals` method in the `String` class is inherited from the `Object` class and is overridden in the `String` class to test whether two strings are identical in content.

You can override the equals method in the Circle class to compare whether two circles are equal based on their radius as follows:

```
public boolean equals(Object o) {
  if (o instanceof Circle) {
    return radius == ((Circle)o).radius;
  }
  else
    return false;
}
```

== vs. equals

Note

The == comparison operator is used for comparing two primitive data type values or for determining whether two objects have the same references. The equals method is intended to test whether two objects have the same contents, provided that the method is overridden in the defining class of the objects. The == operator is stronger than the equals method, in that the == operator checks whether the two reference variables refer to the same object.

Caution

equals(Object)

Using the signature equals(SomeClassName obj) (e.g., equals(Circle c)) to override the equals method in a subclass is a common mistake. You should use equals(Object obj). See CheckPoint Question 11.28.

MyProgrammingLab™

11.27 Does every object have a toString method and an equals method? Where do they come from? How are they used? Is it appropriate to override these methods?

11.28 When overriding the equals method, a common mistake is mistyping its signature in the subclass. For example, the equals method is incorrectly written as equals(Circle circle), as shown in (a) in following the code; instead, it should be equals(Object circle), as shown in (b). Show the output of running class Test with the Circle class in (a) and in (b), respectively.

```
public class Test {
  public static void main(String[] args) {
    Object circle1 = new Circle();
    Object circle2 = new Circle();
    System.out.println(circle1.equals(circle2));
  }
}
```

```
class Circle {
  double radius;

  public boolean equals(Circle circle) {
    return this.radius == circle.radius;
  }
}
```

(a)

```
class Circle {
  double radius;

  public boolean equals(Object circle) {
    return this.radius ==
      ((Circle)circle).radius;
  }
}
```

(b)

11.11 The ArrayList Class

VideoNote

The ArrayList class

An ArrayList object can be used to store a list of objects.

Now we are ready to introduce a very useful class for storing objects. You can create an array to store objects. But, once the array is created, its size is fixed. Java provides the ArrayList class, which can be used to store an unlimited number of objects. Figure 11.3 shows some methods in `ArrayList`.

java.util.ArrayList<E>	
`+ArrayList()`	Creates an empty list.
`+add(o: E): void`	Appends a new element `o` at the end of this list.
`+add(index: int, o: E): void`	Adds a new element `o` at the specified index in this list.
`+clear(): void`	Removes all the elements from this list.
`+contains(o: Object): boolean`	Returns true if this list contains the element `o`.
`+get(index: int): E`	Returns the element from this list at the specified index.
`+indexOf(o: Object): int`	Returns the index of the first matching element in this list.
`+isEmpty(): boolean`	Returns true if this list contains no elements.
`+lastIndexOf(o: Object): int`	Returns the index of the last matching element in this list.
`+remove(o: Object): boolean`	Removes the element `o` from this list.
`+size(): int`	Returns the number of elements in this list.
`+remove(index: int): boolean`	Removes the element at the specified index.
`+set(index: int, o: E): E`	Sets the element at the specified index.

FIGURE 11.3 An `ArrayList` stores an unlimited number of objects.

`ArrayList` is known as a generic class with a generic type `E`. You can specify a concrete type to replace `E` when creating an `ArrayList`. For example, the following statement creates an `ArrayList` and assigns its reference to variable `cities`. This `ArrayList` object can be used to store strings.

```
ArrayList<String> cities = new ArrayList<String>();
```

The following statement creates an `ArrayList` and assigns its reference to variable `dates`. This `ArrayList` object can be used to store dates.

```
ArrayList<java.util.Date> dates = new ArrayList<java.util.Date> ();
```

Note

In JDK 7, the statement

```
ArrayList<AConcreteType> list = new ArrayList<AConcreteType> ();
```

can be simplified by

```
ArrayList<AConcreteType> list = new ArrayList<>();
```

The concrete type is no longer required in the constructor thanks to a feature called *type inference*. The compiler is able to infer the type from the variable declaration. More discussions on generics including how to define custom generic classes and methods will be introduced in Chapter 21, Generics.

type inference

Listing 11.8 gives an example of using `ArrayList` to store objects.

LISTING 11.8 TestArrayList.java

```
import java.util.ArrayList;

```

import ArrayList

create ArrayList
add element
list size
contains element?
element index
is empty?
remove element
remove element
toString()
get element
create ArrayList

```java
public class TestArrayList {
  public static void main(String[] args) {
    // Create a list to store cities
    ArrayList<String> cityList = new ArrayList<String>();

    // Add some cities in the list
    cityList.add("London");
    // cityList now contains [London]
    cityList.add("Denver");
    // cityList now contains [London, Denver]
    cityList.add("Paris");
    // cityList now contains [London, Denver, Paris]
    cityList.add("Miami");
    // cityList now contains [London, Denver, Paris, Miami]
    cityList.add("Seoul");
    // Contains [London, Denver, Paris, Miami, Seoul]
    cityList.add("Tokyo");
    // Contains [London, Denver, Paris, Miami, Seoul, Tokyo]

    System.out.println("List size? " + cityList.size());
    System.out.println("Is Miami in the list? " +
      cityList.contains("Miami"));
    System.out.println("The location of Denver in the list? "
      + cityList.indexOf("Denver"));
    System.out.println("Is the list empty? " +
      cityList.isEmpty()); // Print false

    // Insert a new city at index 2
    cityList.add(2, "Xian");
    // Contains [London, Denver, Xian, Paris, Miami, Seoul, Tokyo]

    // Remove a city from the list
    cityList.remove("Miami");
    // Contains [London, Denver, Xian, Paris, Seoul, Tokyo]

    // Remove a city at index 1
    cityList.remove(1);
    // Contains [London, Xian, Paris, Seoul, Tokyo]

    // Display the contents in the list
    System.out.println(cityList.toString());

    // Display the contents in the list in reverse order
    for (int i = cityList.size() - 1; i >= 0; i--)
      System.out.print(cityList.get(i) + " ");
    System.out.println();

    // Create a list to store two circles
    ArrayList<CircleFromSimpleGeometricObject> list
      = new ArrayList<CircleFromSimpleGeometricObject>();

    // Add two circles
    list.add(new CircleFromSimpleGeometricObject(2));
    list.add(new CircleFromSimpleGeometricObject(3));

    // Display the area of the first circle in the list
    System.out.println("The area of the circle? " +
      ((CircleFromSimpleGeometricObject)list.get(0)).getArea());
  }
}
```

```
List size? 6
Is Miami in the list? True
The location of Denver in the list? 1
Is the list empty? false
[London, Xian, Paris, Seoul, Tokyo]
Tokyo Seoul Paris Xian London
The area of the circle? 12.566370614359172
```

Since the `ArrayList` is in the `java.util` package, it is imported in line 1. The program creates an `ArrayList` of strings using its no-arg constructor and assigns the reference to `cityList` (line 6). The `add` method (lines 9–19) adds strings to the end of list. So, after `cityList.add("London")` (line 9), the list contains

add(Object)

```
[London]
```

After `cityList.add("Denver")` (line 11), the list contains

```
[London, Denver]
```

After adding `Paris`, `Miami`, `Seoul`, and `Tokyo` (lines 13–19), the list contains

```
[London, Denver, Paris, Miami, Seoul, Tokyo]
```

Invoking `size()` (line 22) returns the size of the list, which is currently `6`. Invoking `contains("Miami")` (line 24) checks whether the object is in the list. In this case, it returns `true`, since `Miami` is in the list. Invoking `indexOf("Denver")` (line 26) returns the index of `Denver` in the list, which is `1`. If `Denver` were not in the list, it would return `-1`. The `isEmpty()` method (line 28) checks whether the list is empty. It returns `false`, since the list is not empty.

size()

The statement `cityList.add(2, "Xian")` (line 31) inserts an object into the list at the specified index. After this statement, the list becomes

add(index, Object)

```
[London, Denver, Xian, Paris, Miami, Seoul, Tokyo]
```

The statement `cityList.remove("Miami")` (line 35) removes the object from the list. After this statement, the list becomes

remove(Object)

```
[London, Denver, Xian, Paris, Seoul, Tokyo]
```

The statement `cityList.remove(1)` (line 39) removes the object at the specified index from the list. After this statement, the list becomes

remove(index)

```
[London, Xian, Paris, Seoul, Tokyo]
```

The statement in line 43 is same as

```
System.out.println(cityList);
```

The `toString()` method returns a string representation of the list in the form of `[e0.toString(), e1.toString(), ..., ek.toString()]`, where `e0`, `e1`, . . . , and `ek` are the elements in the list.

toString()

The `get(index)` method (line 47) returns the object at the specified index.

getIndex()

`ArrayList` objects can be used like arrays, but there are many differences. Table 11.1 lists their similarities and differences.

array vs. ArrayList

Once an array is created, its size is fixed. You can access an array element using the square-bracket notation (e.g., `a[index]`). When an `ArrayList` is created, its size is `0`.

TABLE 11.1 Differences and Similarities between Arrays and `ArrayList`

Operation	*Array*	*ArrayList*
Creating an array/ArrayList	`String[] a = new String[10]`	`ArrayList<String> list = new ArrayList<>();`
Accessing an element	`a[index]`	`list.get(index);`
Updating an element	`a[index] = "London";`	`list.set(index, "London");`
Returning size	`a.length`	`list.size();`
Adding a new element		`list.add("London");`
Inserting a new element		`list.add(index, "London");`
Removing an element		`list.remove(index);`
Removing an element		`list.remove(Object);`
Removing all elements		`list.clear();`

You cannot use the `get` and `set` methods if the element is not in the list. It is easy to add, insert, and remove elements in a list, but it is rather complex to add, insert, and remove elements in an array. You have to write code to manipulate the array in order to perform these operations.

Suppose you want to create an `ArrayList` for storing integers. Can you use the following code to create a list?

```
ArrayList<int> list = new ArrayList<int>();
```

No. This will not work because the elements stored in an `ArrayList` must be of an object type. You cannot use a primitive data type such as `int` to replace a generic type. However, you can create an `ArrayList` for storing `Integer` objects as follows:

```
ArrayList<Integer> list = new ArrayList<Integer>();
```

Listing 11.9 gives a program that prompts the user to enter a sequence of numbers and displays the distinct numbers in the sequence. Assume that the input ends with `0` and `0` is not counted as a number in the sequence.

LISTING 11.9 DistinctNumbers.java

create an array list

contained in list?

add to list

```
import java.util.ArrayList;
import java.util.Scanner;

public class DistinctNumbers {
  public static void main(String[] args) {
    ArrayList<Integer> list = new ArrayList<Integer>();

    Scanner input = new Scanner(System.in);
    System.out.print("Enter integers (input ends with 0): ");
    int value;

    do {
      value = input.nextInt(); // Read a value from the input

      if (!list.contains(value) && value != 0)
        list.add(value); // Add the value if it is not in the list
    } while (value != 0);
```

```
18
19      // Display the distinct numbers
20      for (int i = 0; i < list.size(); i++)
21        System.out.print(list.get(i) + " ");
22    }
23  }
```

```
Enter numbers (input ends with 0): 1 2 3 2 1 6 3 4 5 4 5 1 2 3 0 ↵Enter
The distinct numbers are: 1 2 3 6 4 5
```

The program creates an `ArrayList` for `Integer` objects (line 6) and repeatedly reads a value in the loop (lines 12–17). For each value, if it is not in the list (line 15), add it to the list (line 16). You can rewrite this program using an array to store the elements rather than using an `ArrayList`. However, it is simpler to implement this program using an `ArrayList` for two reasons.

- First, the size of an `ArrayList` is flexible so you don't have to specify its size in advance. When creating an array, its size must be specified.
- Second, `ArrayList` contains many useful methods. For example, you can test whether an element is in the list using the `contains` method. If you use an array, you have to write additional code to implement this method.

Check Point
MyProgrammingLab™

11.29 How do you do the following?

a. Create an `ArrayList` for storing double values?

b. Append an object to a list?

c. Insert an object at the beginning of a list?

d. Find the number of objects in a list?

e. Remove a given object from a list?

f. Remove the last object from the list?

g. Check whether a given object is in a list?

h. Retrieve an object at a specified index from a list?

11.30 Identify the errors in the following code.

```
ArrayList<String> list = new ArrayList<String> ();
list.add("Denver");
list.add("Austin");
list.add(new java.util.Date());
String city = list.get(0);
list.set(3, "Dallas");
System.out.println(list.get(3));
```

11.31 Suppose the `ArrayList list` contains duplicate elements. Does the following code correctly remove the element from the array list? If not, correct the code.

```
for (int i = 0; i < list.size(); i++)
  list.remove(element);
```

11.32 Explain why the following code displays `[1, 3]` rather than `[2, 3]`.

```
ArrayList<Integer> list = new ArrayList<Integer>();
list.add(1);
```

```
list.add(2);
list.add(3);
list.remove(1);
System.out.println(list);
```

11.12 Case Study: A Custom Stack Class

This section designs a stack class for holding objects.

VideoNote
The MyStack class

Section 10.9 presented a stack class for storing `int` values. This section introduces a stack class to store objects. You can use an `ArrayList` to implement `Stack`, as shown in Listing 11.10. The UML diagram for the class is shown in Figure 11.4.

MyStack	
-list: ArrayList<Object>	A list to store elements.
+isEmpty(): boolean	Returns true if this stack is empty.
+getSize(): int	Returns the number of elements in this stack.
+peek(): Object	Returns the top element in this stack without removing it.
+pop(): Object	Returns and removes the top element in this stack.
+push(o: Object): void	Adds a new element to the top of this stack.

FIGURE 11.4 The `MyStack` class encapsulates the stack storage and provides the operations for manipulating the stack.

LISTING 11.10 MyStack.java

```
import java.util.ArrayList;

public class MyStack {
  private ArrayList<Object> list = new ArrayList<Object>();

  public boolean isEmpty() {
    return list.isEmpty();
  }

  public int getSize() {
    return list.size();
  }

  public Object peek() {
    return list.get(getSize() - 1);
  }

  public Object pop() {
    Object o = list.get(getSize() - 1);
    list.remove(getSize() - 1);
    return o;
  }

  public void push(Object o) {
    list.add(o);
  }

```

array list
stack empty?
get stack size
peek stack
remove
push

```
28     @Override
29     public String toString() {
30       return "stack: " + list.toString();
31     }
32   }
```

An array list is created to store the elements in the stack (line 4). The `isEmpty()` method (lines 6–8) returns `list.isEmpty()`. The `getSize()` method (lines 10–12) returns `list.size()`. The `peek()` method (lines 14–16) retrieves the element at the top of the stack without removing it. The end of the list is the top of the stack. The `pop()` method (lines 18–22) removes the top element from the stack and returns it. The `push(Object element)` method (lines 24–26) adds the specified element to the stack. The `toString()` method (lines 28–31) defined in the `Object` class is overridden to display the contents of the stack by invoking `list.toString()`. The `toString()` method implemented in `ArrayList` returns a string representation of all the elements in an array list.

Design Guide

In Listing 11.10, `MyStack` contains `ArrayList`. The relationship between `MyStack` and `ArrayList` is *composition*. While inheritance models an *is-a* relationship, composition models a *has-a* relationship. You could also implement `MyStack` as a subclass of `ArrayList` (see Programming Exercise 11.4). Using composition is better, however, because it enables you to define a completely new stack class without inheriting the unnecessary and inappropriate methods from `ArrayList`.

composition
is-a
has-a

11.13 The **protected** Data and Methods

A protected member of a class can be accessed from a subclass.

Key Point

So far you have used the `private` and `public` keywords to specify whether data fields and methods can be accessed from outside of the class. Private members can be accessed only from inside of the class, and public members can be accessed from any other classes.

Often it is desirable to allow subclasses to access data fields or methods defined in the superclass, but not to allow nonsubclasses to access these data fields and methods. To accomplish this, you can use the `protected` keyword. This way you can access protected data fields or methods in a superclass from its subclasses.

why `protected`?

The modifiers `private`, `protected`, and `public` are known as *visibility* or *accessibility modifiers* because they specify how classes and class members are accessed. The visibility of these modifiers increases in this order:

Visibility increases

private, default (no modifier), protected, public

Table 11.2 summarizes the accessibility of the members in a class. Figure 11.5 illustrates how a public, protected, default, and private datum or method in class `C1` can be accessed from a class `C2` in the same package, from a subclass `C3` in the same package, from a subclass `C4` in a different package, and from a class `C5` in a different package.

Use the `private` modifier to hide the members of the class completely so that they cannot be accessed directly from outside the class. Use no modifiers (the default) in order to allow the members of the class to be accessed directly from any class within the same package but not from other packages. Use the `protected` modifier to enable the members of the class to be accessed by the subclasses in any package or classes in the same package. Use the `public` modifier to enable the members of the class to be accessed by any class.

Your class can be used in two ways: (1) for creating instances of the class and (2) for defining subclasses by extending the class. Make the members `private` if they are not intended

TABLE 11.2 Data and Methods Visibility

Modifier on members in a class	*Accessed from the same class*	*Accessed from the same package*	*Accessed from a subclass in a different package*	*Accessed from a different package*
public	✓	✓	✓	✓
protected	✓	✓	✓	–
default (no modifier)	✓	✓	–	–
private	✓	–	–	–

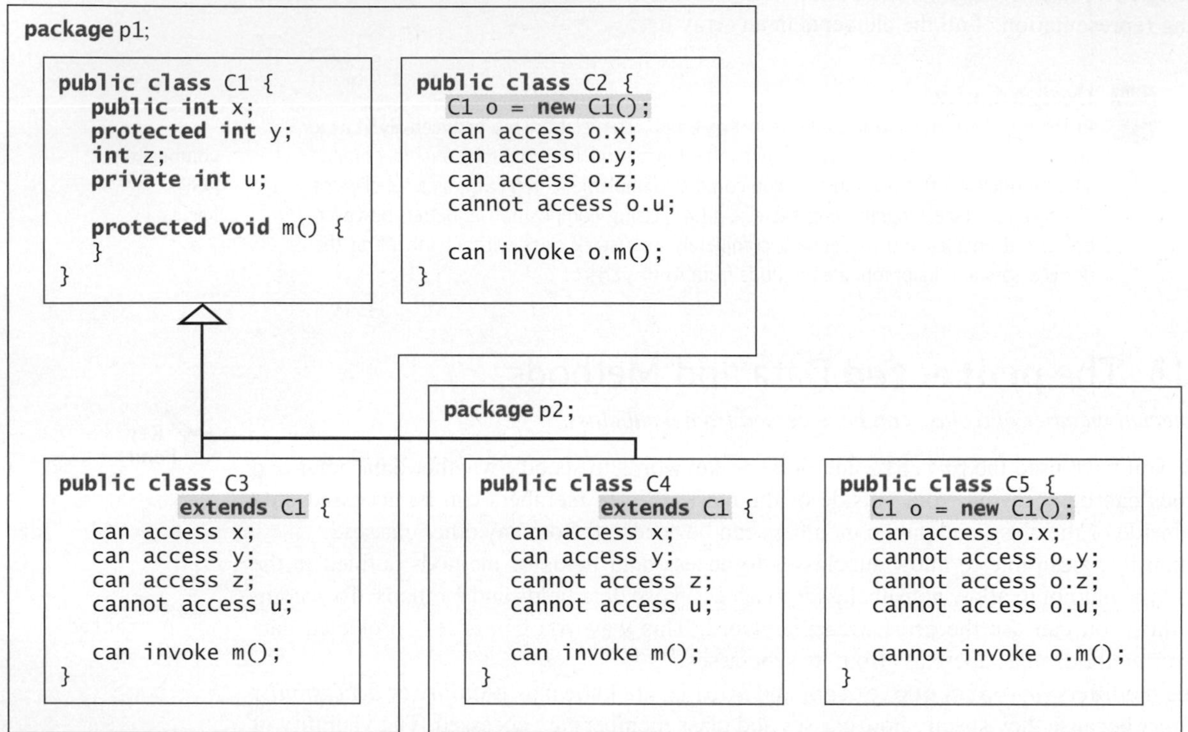

FIGURE 11.5 Visibility modifiers are used to control how data and methods are accessed.

for use from outside the class. Make the members `public` if they are intended for the users of the class. Make the fields or methods `protected` if they are intended for the extenders of the class but not for the users of the class.

The `private` and `protected` modifiers can be used only for members of the class. The `public` modifier and the default modifier (i.e., no modifier) can be used on members of the class as well as on the class. A class with no modifier (i.e., not a public class) is not accessible by classes from other packages.

change visibility

Note

A subclass may override a protected method defined in its superclass and change its visibility to public. However, a subclass cannot weaken the accessibility of a method defined in the superclass. For example, if a method is defined as public in the superclass, it must be defined as public in the subclass.

MyProgrammingLab™

11.33 What modifier should you use on a class so that a class in the same package can access it, but a class in a different package cannot access it?

11.34 What modifier should you use so that a class in a different package cannot access the class, but its subclasses in any package can access it?

11.35 In the following code, the classes A and B are in the same package. If the question marks in (a) are replaced by blanks, can class B be compiled? If the question marks are replaced by `private`, can class B be compiled? If the question marks are replaced by `protected`, can class B be compiled?

```
package p1;

public class A {
  ___?___ int i;

  ___?___ void m() {
    ...
  }
}
```

(a)

```
package p1;

public class B extends A {
  public void m1(String[] args) {
    System.out.println(i);
    m();
  }
}
```

(b)

11.36 In the following code, the classes A and B are in different packages. If the question marks in (a) are replaced by blanks, can class B be compiled? If the question marks are replaced by `private`, can class B be compiled? If the question marks are replaced by `protected`, can class B be compiled?

```
package p1;

public class A {
  ___?___ int i;

  ___?___ void m() {
    ...
  }
}
```

(a)

```
package p2;

public class B extends A {
  public void m1(String[] args) {
    System.out.println(i);
    m();
  }
}
```

(b)

11.14 Preventing Extending and Overriding

Neither a final class nor a final method can be extended. A final data field is a constant.

You may occasionally want to prevent classes from being extended. In such cases, use the `final` modifier to indicate that a class is final and cannot be a parent class. The `Math` class is a final class. The `String`, `StringBuilder`, and `StringBuffer` classes are also final classes. For example, the following class `A` is final and cannot be extended:

```
public final class A {
  // Data fields, constructors, and methods omitted
}
```

You also can define a method to be final; a final method cannot be overridden by its subclasses.

For example, the following method m is final and cannot be overridden:

```
public class Test {
  // Data fields, constructors, and methods omitted

  public final void m() {
    // Do something
  }
}
```

Note

The modifiers **public**, **protected**, **private**, **static**, **abstract**, and **final** are used on classes and class members (data and methods), except that the **final** modifier can also be used on local variables in a method. A **final** local variable is a constant inside a method.

MyProgrammingLab™

11.37 How do you prevent a class from being extended? How do you prevent a method from being overridden?

11.38 Indicate true or false for the following statements:

a. A protected datum or method can be accessed by any class in the same package.

b. A protected datum or method can be accessed by any class in different packages.

c. A protected datum or method can be accessed by its subclasses in any package.

d. A final class can have instances.

e. A final class can be extended.

f. A final method can be overridden.

Key Terms

actual type 422
casting objects 425
constructor chaining 415
declared type 422
dynamic binding 422
inheritance 408
`instanceof` 426
is-a relationship 437
method overriding 419
multiple inheritance 414
override 419
polymorphism 422
`protected` 437
single inheritance 414
subclass 408
subtype 421
superclass 408
supertype 421
type inference 431

Chapter Summary

1. You can define a new class from an existing class. This is known as class *inheritance*. The new class is called a *subclass*, *child class*, or *extended class*. The existing class is called a *superclass*, *parent class*, or *base class*.

2. A constructor is used to construct an instance of a class. Unlike properties and methods, the constructors of a superclass are not inherited in the subclass. They can be invoked only from the constructors of the subclasses, using the keyword `super`.

3. A constructor may invoke an overloaded constructor or its superclass's constructor. The call must be the first statement in the constructor. If none of them is invoked explicitly, the compiler puts `super()` as the first statement in the constructor, which invokes the superclass's no-arg constructor.

4. To *override* a method, the method must be defined in the subclass using the same signature and the same return type as in its superclass.

5. An instance method can be overridden only if it is accessible. Thus, a private method cannot be overridden because it is not accessible outside its own class. If a method defined in a subclass is private in its superclass, the two methods are completely unrelated.

6. Like an instance method, a static method can be inherited. However, a static method cannot be overridden. If a static method defined in the superclass is redefined in a subclass, the method defined in the superclass is hidden.

7. Every class in Java is descended from the `java.lang.Object` class. If no superclass is specified when a class is defined, its superclass is `Object`.

8. If a method's parameter type is a superclass (e.g., `Object`), you may pass an object to this method of any of the parameter's subclasses (e.g., `Circle` or `String`). This is known as polymorphism.

9. It is always possible to cast an instance of a subclass to a variable of a superclass, because an instance of a subclass is *always* an instance of its superclass. When casting an instance of a superclass to a variable of its subclass, explicit casting must be used to confirm your intention to the compiler with the (`SubclassName`) cast notation.

10. A class defines a type. A type defined by a subclass is called a *subtype* and a type defined by its superclass is called a *supertype*.

11. When invoking an instance method from a reference variable, the *actual type of* the variable decides which implementation of the method is used *at runtime*. This is known as dynamic binding.

12. You can use `obj instanceof AClass` to test whether an object is an instance of a class.

13. You can use the `ArrayList` class to create an object to store a list of objects.

14. You can use the `protected` modifier to prevent the data and methods from being accessed by nonsubclasses from a different package.

15. You can use the `final` modifier to indicate that a class is final and cannot be extended and to indicate that a method is final and cannot be overridden.

Test Questions

Do the test questions for this chapter online at www.cs.armstrong.edu/liang/intro9e/test.html.

MyProgrammingLab™

Programming Exercises

Sections 11.2–11.4

11.1 (*The `Triangle` class*) Design a class named `Triangle` that extends `GeometricObject`. The class contains:

- Three `double` data fields named `side1`, `side2`, and `side3` with default values `1.0` to denote three sides of the triangle.
- A no-arg constructor that creates a default triangle.
- A constructor that creates a triangle with the specified `side1`, `side2`, and `side3`.
- The accessor methods for all three data fields.
- A method named `getArea()` that returns the area of this triangle.
- A method named `getPerimeter()` that returns the perimeter of this triangle.
- A method named `toString()` that returns a string description for the triangle.

For the formula to compute the area of a triangle, see Programming Exercise 2.15. The `toString()` method is implemented as follows:

```
return "Triangle: side1 = " + side1 + " side2 = " + side2 +
  " side3 = " + side3;
```

Draw the UML diagrams for the classes `Triangle` and `GeometricObject` and implement the classes. Write a test program that prompts the user to enter three sides of the triangle, a color, and a Boolean value to indicate whether the triangle is filled. The program should create a `Triangle` object with these sides and set the `color` and `filled` properties using the input. The program should display the area, perimeter, color, and true or false to indicate whether it is filled or not.

Sections 11.5–11.14

11.2 (*The `Person`, `Student`, `Employee`, `Faculty`, and `Staff` classes*) Design a class named `Person` and its two subclasses named `Student` and `Employee`. Make `Faculty` and `Staff` subclasses of `Employee`. A person has a name, address, phone number, and email address. A student has a class status (freshman, sophomore, junior, or senior). Define the status as a constant. An employee has an office, salary, and date hired. Use the `MyDate` class defined in Programming Exercise 10.14 to create an object for date hired. A faculty member has office hours and a rank. A staff member has a title. Override the `toString` method in each class to display the class name and the person's name.

Draw the UML diagram for the classes and implement them. Write a test program that creates a `Person`, `Student`, `Employee`, `Faculty`, and `Staff`, and invokes their `toString()` methods.

11.3 (*Subclasses of `Account`*) In Programming Exercise 8.7, the `Account` class was defined to model a bank account. An account has the properties account number, balance, annual interest rate, and date created, and methods to deposit and withdraw funds. Create two subclasses for checking and saving accounts. A checking account has an overdraft limit, but a savings account cannot be overdrawn.

Draw the UML diagram for the classes and then implement them. Write a test program that creates objects of `Account`, `SavingsAccount`, and `CheckingAccount` and invokes their `toString()` methods.

11.4 (*Maximum element in* `ArrayList`) Write the following method that returns the maximum value in an `ArrayList` of integers. The method returns `null` if the list is `null` or the list size is `0`.

```
public static Integer max(ArrayList<Integer> list)
```

Write a test program that prompts the user to enter a sequence of numbers ending with `0`, and invokes this method to return the largest number in the input.

11.5 (*The* `Course` *class*) Rewrite the `Course` class in Listing 10.6. Use an `ArrayList` to replace an array to store students. You should not change the original contract of the `Course` class (i.e., the definition of the constructors and methods should not be changed).

11.6 (*Use* `ArrayList`) Write a program that creates an `ArrayList` and adds a `Loan` object, a `Date` object, a string, a `JFrame` object, and a `Circle` object to the list, and use a loop to display all the elements in the list by invoking the object's `toString()` method.

11.7 (*Shuffle* `ArrayList`) Write the following method that shuffles the elements in an `ArrayList` of integers.

```
public static void shuffle(ArrayList<Integer> list)
```

New `Account` class

****11.8** (*New* `Account` *class*) An `Account` class was specified in Programming Exercise 8.7. Design a new `Account` class as follows:

- Add a new data field `name` of the `String` type to store the name of the customer.
- Add a new constructor that constructs an account with the specified name, id, and balance.
- Add a new data field named `transactions` whose type is `ArrayList` that stores the transaction for the accounts. Each transaction is an instance of the `Transaction` class. The `Transaction` class is defined as shown in Figure 11.6.

The get and set methods for these data fields are provided in the class, but omitted in the UML diagram for brevity.

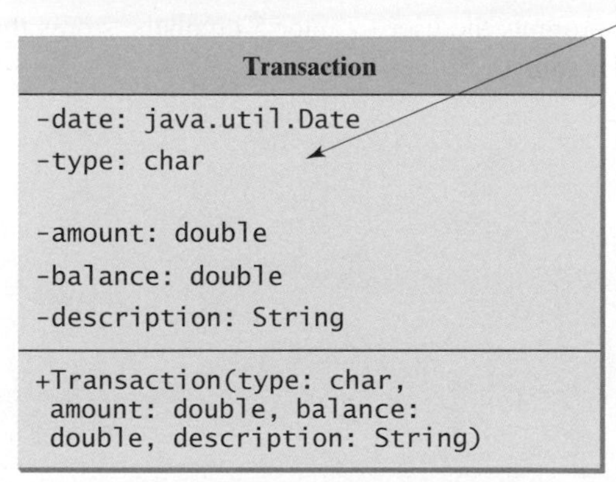

The date of this transaction.

The type of the transaction, such as 'W' for withdrawal, 'D' for deposit.

The amount of the transaction.

The new balance after this transaction.

The description of this transaction.

Construct a `Transaction` with the specified date, type, balance, and description.

FIGURE 11.6 The `Transaction` class describes a transaction for a bank account.

- Modify the `withdraw` and `deposit` methods to add a transaction to the `transactions` array list.
- All other properties and methods are the same as in Programming Exercise 8.7.

Write a test program that creates an `Account` with annual interest rate `1.5%`, balance `1000`, id `1122`, and name `George`. Deposit $30, $40, and $50 to the account and withdraw $5, $4, and $2 from the account. Print an account summary that shows account holder name, interest rate, balance, and all transactions.

***11.9** (*Largest rows and columns*) Write a program that randomly fills in `0`s and `1`s into an n-by-n matrix, prints the matrix, and finds the rows and columns with the most `1`s. (*Hint*: Use two `ArrayList`s to store the row and column indices with the most `1`s.) Here is a sample run of the program:

```
Enter the array size n: 4 ↵Enter
The random array is
0011
0011
1101
1010
The largest row index: 2
The largest column index: 2, 3
```

11.10 (*Implement `MyStack` using inheritance*) In Listing 11.10, `MyStack` is implemented using composition. Define a new stack class that extends `ArrayList`.

Draw the UML diagram for the classes and then implement `MyStack`. Write a test program that prompts the user to enter five strings and displays them in reverse order.

11.11 (*Sort `ArrayList`*) Write the following method that sorts an `ArrayList` of numbers:

```
public static void sort(ArrayList<Integer> list)
```

Write a test program that prompts the user to enter 5 numbers, stores them in an array list, and displays them in increasing order.

11.12 (*Sum `ArrayList`*) Write the following method that returns the sum of all numbers in an `ArrayList`:

```
public static double sum(ArrayList<Double> list)
```

Write a test program that prompts the user to enter 5 numbers, stores them in an array list, and displays their sum.

CHAPTER 12

GUI Basics

Objectives

- To distinguish between Swing and AWT (§12.2).
- To describe the Java GUI API hierarchy (§12.3).
- To create user interfaces using frames, panels, and simple GUI components (§12.4).
- To understand the role of layout managers and use the `FlowLayout`, `GridLayout`, and `BorderLayout` managers to lay out components in a container (§12.5).
- To use `JPanel` to group components in a subcontainer (§12.6).
- To create objects for colors using the `Color` class (§12.7).
- To create objects for fonts using the `Font` class (§12.8).
- To apply common features such as borders, tool tips, fonts, and colors on Swing components (§12.9).
- To decorate the border of GUI components (§12.9).
- To create image icons using the `ImageIcon` class (§12.10).
- To create and use buttons using the `JButton` class (§12.11).
- To create and use check boxes using the `JCheckBox` class (§12.12).
- To create and use radio buttons using the `JRadioButton` class (§12.13).
- To create and use labels using the `JLabel` class (§12.14).
- To create and use text fields using the `JTextField` class (§12.15).

12.1 Introduction

Java GUI is an excellent pedagogical tool for learning object-oriented programming.

The design of the API for Java GUI programming is an excellent example of how the object-oriented principle is applied. This chapter serves two purposes. First, it presents the basics of Java GUI programming. Second, it uses GUI to demonstrate OOP. Specifically, this chapter introduces the framework of the Java GUI API and discusses GUI components and their relationships, containers and layout managers, colors, fonts, borders, image icons, and tool tips. It also introduces some of the most frequently used GUI components.

12.2 Swing vs. AWT

AWT GUI components are replaced by more versatile and stable Swing GUI components.

We used simple GUI examples to demonstrate OOP in Section 8.6.3, Displaying GUI Components. We used the GUI components such as `JButton`, `JLabel`, `JTextField`, `JRadioButton`, and `JComboBox`. Why do the GUI component classes have the prefix *J*? Instead of `JButton`, why not name it simply `Button`? In fact, there is a class already named `Button` in the `java.awt` package.

AWT

When Java was introduced, the GUI classes were bundled in a library known as the *Abstract Windows Toolkit (AWT)*. AWT is fine for developing simple graphical user interfaces, but not for developing comprehensive GUI projects. In addition, AWT is prone to platform-specific bugs. The AWT user-interface components were replaced by a more robust, versatile, and flexible library known as *Swing components*. Swing components are painted directly on canvases using Java code, except for components that are subclasses of `java.awt.Window` or `java.awt.Panel`, which must be drawn using native GUI on a specific platform. Swing components depend less on the target platform and use less of the native GUI resource. For this reason, Swing components that don't rely on native GUI are referred to as *lightweight components*, and AWT components are referred to as *heavyweight components*.

Swing components

lightweight component

heavyweight component

why prefix J?

To distinguish new Swing component classes from their AWT counterparts, the Swing GUI component classes are named with a prefixed *J*. Although AWT components are still supported in Java, it is better to learn how to program using Swing components, because the AWT user-interface components will eventually fade away. This book uses Swing GUI components exclusively.

Check Point

MyProgrammingLab™

12.1 Why are the Swing GUI classes named with the prefix *J*?

12.2 Explain the difference between AWT GUI components and Swing GUI components.

12.3 The Java GUI API

The GUI API contains classes that can be classified into three groups: component classes, container classes, *and* helper classes.

The hierarchical relationships of the Java GUI API are shown in Figure 12.1. Recall that the triangular arrow denotes the inheritance relationship, the diamond denotes the composition relationship, and the filled diamond denotes the exclusive composition relationship. The object composition relationship was introduced in Section 10.7.

component class

container class

helper class

The subclasses of `Component` are called *component classes* for creating the user interface. The classes, such as `JFrame`, `JPanel`, and `JApplet`, are called *container classes* used to contain other components. The classes, such as `Graphics`, `Color`, `Font`, `FontMetrics`, and `Dimension`, are called *helper classes* used to support GUI components.

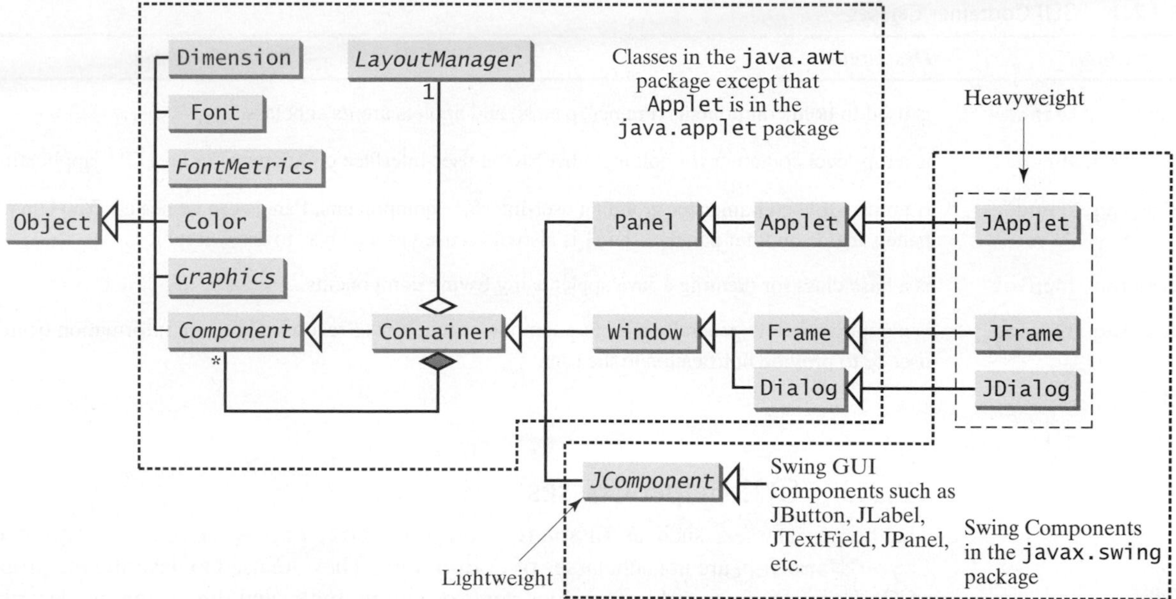

FIGURE 12.1 Java GUI programming utilizes the classes shown in this hierarchical diagram.

Note

The `JFrame`, `JApplet`, `JDialog`, and `JComponent` classes and their subclasses are grouped in the `javax.swing` package. `Applet` is in the `java.applet` class. All the other classes in Figure 12.1 are grouped in the `java.awt` package.

12.3.1 Component Classes

An instance of `Component` can be displayed on the screen. `Component` is the root class of all the user-interface classes including container classes, and `JComponent` is the root class of all the lightweight Swing components. Both `Component` and `JComponent` are abstract classes (abstract classes will be introduced in Chapter 15). For now, all you need to know is that abstract classes are the same as classes except that you cannot create instances using the `new` operator. For example, you cannot use `new JComponent()` to create an instance of `JComponent`. However, you can use the constructors of concrete subclasses of `JComponent` to create `JComponent` instances. It is important to become familiar with the class inheritance hierarchy. For example, the following statements all display true:

abstract class

```
JButton jbtOK = new JButton("OK");
System.out.println(jbtOK instanceof JButton);
System.out.println(jbtOK instanceof JComponent);
System.out.println(jbtOK instanceof Container);
System.out.println(jbtOK instanceof Component);
System.out.println(jbtOK instanceof Object);
```

12.3.2 Container Classes

An instance of `Container` can hold instances of `Component`. A container is called a *top-level container* if it can be displayed without being embedded in another container. `Window`, `Frame`, `Dialog`, `JFrame`, and `JDialog` are top-level containers. `Window`, `Panel`, `Applet`, `Frame`, and `Dialog` are the container classes for AWT components. To work with Swing components, use `Container`, `JFrame`, `JDialog`, `JApplet`, and `JPanel`, as described in Table 12.1.

top-level container

TABLE 12.1 GUI Container Classes

Container Class	*Description*
`java.awt.Container`	is used to hold components. Frames, panels, and applets are its subclasses.
`javax.swing.JFrame`	is a top-level container for holding other Swing user-interface components in Java GUI applications.
`javax.swing.JPanel`	is an invisible container for grouping user-interface components. Panels can be nested. You can place panels inside another panel. `JPanel` is also often used as a canvas to draw graphics.
`javax.swing.JApplet`	is a base class for creating a Java applet using Swing components.
`javax.swing.JDialog`	is a popup window generally used as a temporary window to receive additional information from the user or to provide notification to the user.

12.3.3 GUI Helper Classes

The helper classes, such as `Graphics`, `Color`, `Font`, `FontMetrics`, `Dimension`, and `LayoutManager`, are not subclasses of `Component`. They are used to describe the properties of GUI components, such as graphics context, colors, fonts, and dimension, as described in Table 12.2.

TABLE 12.2 GUI Helper Classes

Helper Class	*Description*
`java.awt.Graphics`	is an abstract class that provides the methods for drawing strings, lines, and simple shapes.
`java.awt.Color`	deals with the colors of GUI components. For example, you can specify background or foreground colors in components like `JFrame` and `JPanel`, or you can specify colors of lines, shapes, and strings in drawings.
`java.awt.Font`	specifies fonts for the text and drawings on GUI components. For example, you can specify the font type (e.g., SansSerif), style (e.g., bold), and size (e.g., 24 points) for the text on a button.
`java.awt.FontMetrics`	is an abstract class used to get the properties of the fonts.
`java.awt.Dimension`	encapsulates the width and height of a component (in integer precision) in a single object.
`java.awt.LayoutManager`	specifies how components are arranged in a container.

Note

The helper classes are in the `java.awt` package. The Swing components do not replace all the classes in the AWT, only the AWT GUI component classes (e.g., `Button`, `TextField`, `TextArea`). The AWT helper classes are still useful in GUI programming.

MyProgrammingLab™

12.3 Which class is the root of the Java GUI component classes? Is a container class a subclass of `Component`? Which class is the root of the Swing GUI component classes?

12.4 Which of the following statements have syntax errors?

```
Component c1 = new Component();
JComponent c2 = new JComponent();
Component c3 = new JButton();
JComponent c4 = new JButton();
```

12.4 Frames

A frame is a window for holding other GUI components.

To create a user interface, you need to create either a frame or an applet to hold the user-interface components. This section introduces frames. Creating Java applets will be introduced in Chapter 18.

12.4.1 Creating a Frame

To create a frame, use the `JFrame` class, as shown in Figure 12.2.

javax.swing.JFrame	
`+JFrame()`	Creates a default frame with no title.
`+JFrame(title: String)`	Creates a frame with the specified title.
`+setSize(width: int, height: int): void`	Sets the size of the frame.
`+setLocation(x: int, y: int): void`	Sets the upper-left-corner location of the frame.
`+setVisible(visible: boolean): void`	Sets true to display the frame.
`+setDefaultCloseOperation(mode: int): void`	Specifies the operation when the frame is closed.
`+setLocationRelativeTo(c: Component): void`	Sets the location of the frame relative to the specified component. If the component is null, the frame is centered on the screen.
`+pack(): void`	Automatically sets the frame size to hold the components in the frame.

FIGURE 12.2 The *`JFrame`* class is used to create a window for displaying GUI components.

The program in Listing 12.1 creates a frame.

LISTING 12.1 MyFrame.java

```
 1 import javax.swing.JFrame;
 2
 3 public class MyFrame {
 4   public static void main(String[] args) {
 5     JFrame frame = new JFrame("MyFrame"); // Create a frame
 6     frame.setSize(400, 300); // Set the frame size
 7     frame.setLocationRelativeTo(null); // Center a frame
 8     frame.setDefaultCloseOperation(JFrame.EXIT_ON_CLOSE);
 9     frame.setVisible(true); // Display the frame
10   }
11 }
```

import package
create frame
set size
center frame
close upon exit
display the frame

The frame is not displayed until the `frame.setVisible(true)` method is invoked. `frame.setSize(400, 300)` specifies that the frame is `400` pixels wide and `300` pixels high. If the `setSize` method is not used, the frame will be sized to display just the title bar. Since the `setSize` and `setVisible` methods are both defined in the `Component` class, they are inherited by the `JFrame` class. Later you will see that these methods are also useful in many other subclasses of `Component`.

When you run the `MyFrame` program, a window will be displayed on the screen (see Figure 12.3a).

Invoking `setLocationRelativeTo(null)` (line 7) centers the frame on the screen. Invoking `setDefaultCloseOperation(JFrame.EXIT_ON_CLOSE)` (line 8) tells the program to terminate when the frame is closed. If this statement is not used, the program does not terminate when the frame is closed. In that case, you have to stop the program by pressing *Ctrl+C* at the DOS prompt window in Windows or stop the process by using the kill command

Figure 12.3 (a) The program creates and displays a frame with the title `MyFrame`. (b) An OK button is added to the frame.

in UNIX. If you run the program from an IDE such as Eclipse or NetBeans, you need to click the red *Terminate* button in the Console pane to stop the program.

pixel and resolution

Note

Recall that a pixel is the smallest unit of space available for drawing on the screen. You can think of a pixel as a small rectangle and think of the screen as paved with pixels. The *resolution* specifies the number of pixels in horizontal and vertical dimensions of the screen. The more pixels the screen has, the higher the screen's resolution. The higher the resolution, the finer the detail you can see.

`setSize` before centering

Note

You should invoke the `setSize(w, h)` method before invoking `setLocationRelativeTo(null)` to center the frame.

12.4.2 Adding Components to a Frame

The frame shown in Figure 12.3a is empty. Using the `add` method, you can add components to the frame, as shown in Listing 12.2.

Listing 12.2 MyFrameWithComponents.java

```
import javax.swing.*;

public class MyFrameWithComponents {
  public static void main(String[] args) {
    JFrame frame = new JFrame("MyFrameWithComponents");

    // Add a button to the frame
    JButton jbtOK = new JButton("OK");            // create a button
    frame.add(jbtOK);                             // add to frame

    frame.setSize(400, 300);                      // set size
    frame.setDefaultCloseOperation(JFrame.EXIT_ON_CLOSE);  // exit upon closing window
    frame.setLocationRelativeTo(null); // Center the frame  // center the frame
    frame.setVisible(true);                       // set visible
  }
}
```

Each `JFrame` contains a *content pane*, which is an instance of `java.awt.Container`. The GUI components such as buttons are placed in the content pane in a frame. In earlier versions of Java, you had to use the `getContentPane` method in the `JFrame` class to return the content pane of the frame, then invoke the content pane's `add` method to place a component in the content pane, as follows:

```
java.awt.Container container = frame.getContentPane();
container.add(jbtOK);
```

This was cumbersome. Versions of Java since Java 5 allow you to place components in the content pane by invoking a frame's `add` method, as follows:

```
frame.add(jbtOK);
```

This feature is called *content-pane delegation*. Strictly speaking, a component is added to the content pane of a frame. For simplicity, we say that a component is added to a frame.

content-pane delegation

In Listing 12.2, an object of `JButton` was created using `new JButton("OK")`, and this object was added to the content pane of the frame (line 9).

The `add(Component comp)` method defined in the `Container` class adds an instance of `Component` to the container. Since `JButton` is a subclass of `Component`, an instance of `JButton` is also an instance of `Component`. To remove a component from a container, use the `remove` method. The following statement removes the button from the container:

```
container.remove(jbtOK);
```

When you run the program `MyFrameWithComponents`, the window will be displayed as in Figure 12.3b. The button is always centered in the frame and occupies the entire frame no matter how you resize it. This is because components are put in the frame by the content pane's layout manager, and the default layout manager for the content pane places the button in the center. In the next section, you will use several different layout managers to place components in the desired locations.

12.5 How do you create a frame? How do you set the size for a frame? How do you add components to a frame? What would happen if the statements `frame.setSize(400, 300)` and `frame.setVisible(true)` were swapped in Listing 12.2?

Check Point

12.5 Layout Managers

Key Point

Each container contains a layout manager, which is an object responsible for laying out the GUI components in the container.

In many other window systems, the user-interface components are arranged by using hard-coded pixel measurements. For example, when placing a button at location (`10, 10`) in a window using hard-coded pixel measurements, the user interface might look fine on one system but be unusable on another. Java's *layout managers* provide a level of abstraction that automatically maps your user interface on all window systems.

layout manager

The Java GUI components are placed in containers, where they are arranged by the container's layout manager. In the preceding program, you did not specify where to place the *OK* button in the frame, but Java knows where to place it, because the layout manager works behind the scenes to place components in the correct locations. A layout manager is created using a layout manager class.

Layout managers are set in containers using the `setLayout(aLayoutManager)` method. For example, you can use the following statements to create an instance of `XLayout` and set it in a container:

```
LayoutManager layoutManager = new XLayout();
container.setLayout(layoutManager);
```

This section introduces three basic layout managers: `FlowLayout`, `GridLayout`, and `BorderLayout`.

12.5.1 FlowLayout

VideoNote
Use FlowLayout

FlowLayout is the simplest layout manager. The components are arranged in the container from left to right in the order in which they were added. When one row is filled, a new row is started. You can specify the way the components are aligned by using one of three constants: FlowLayout.RIGHT, FlowLayout.CENTER, or FlowLayout.LEFT. You can also specify the gap between components in pixels. The class diagram for FlowLayout is shown in Figure 12.4.

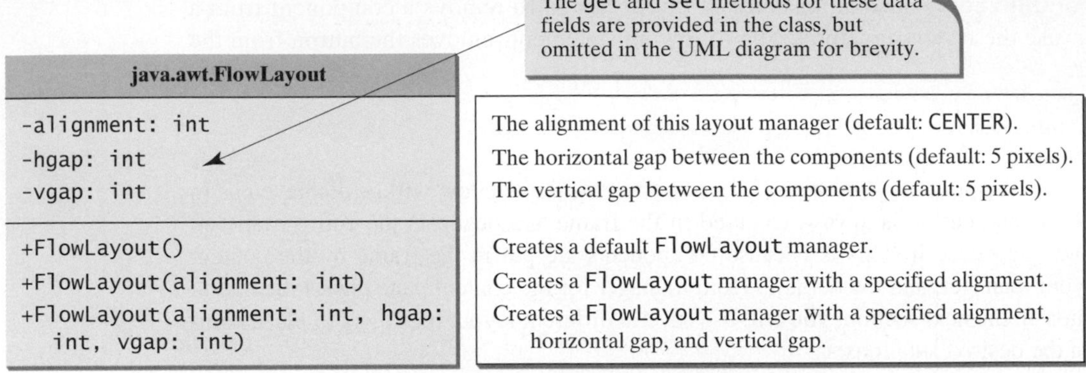

FIGURE 12.4 FlowLayout lays out components row by row.

Listing 12.3 gives a program that demonstrates flow layout. The program adds three labels and text fields to the frame with a FlowLayout manager, as shown in Figure 12.5.

LISTING 12.3 ShowFlowLayout.java

extends JFrame · set layout · add label · add text field

```
import javax.swing.JLabel;
import javax.swing.JTextField;
import javax.swing.JFrame;
import java.awt.FlowLayout;

public class ShowFlowLayout extends JFrame {
  public ShowFlowLayout() {
    // Set FlowLayout, aligned left with horizontal gap 10
    // and vertical gap 20 between components
    setLayout(new FlowLayout(FlowLayout.LEFT, 10, 20));

    // Add labels and text fields to the frame
    add(new JLabel("First Name"));
    add(new JTextField(8));
    add(new JLabel("MI"));
    add(new JTextField(1));
    add(new JLabel("Last Name"));
    add(new JTextField(8));
  }

  /** Main method */
  public static void main(String[] args) {
    ShowFlowLayout frame = new ShowFlowLayout();
    frame.setTitle("ShowFlowLayout");
    frame.setSize(200, 200);
```

```
26        frame.setLocationRelativeTo(null); // Center the frame
27        frame.setDefaultCloseOperation(JFrame.EXIT_ON_CLOSE);
28        frame.setVisible(true);
29    }
30 }
```

create frame

set visible

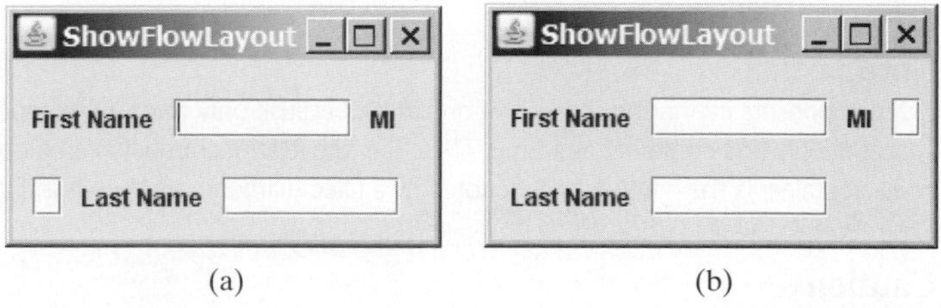

(a) (b)

FIGURE 12.5 The components are added by the `FlowLayout` manager to fill in the rows in the container one after another.

This example creates a program using a style different from the programs in the preceding section, where frames were created using the `JFrame` class. This example creates a class named `ShowFlowLayout` that extends the `JFrame` class (line 6). The `main` method in this program creates an instance of `ShowFlowLayout` (line 23). The constructor of `ShowFlowLayout` constructs and places the components in the frame. This is the preferred style of creating GUI applications—for three reasons:

- Creating a GUI application means creating a frame, so it is natural to define a frame to extend `JFrame`.
- The frame may be further extended to add new components or functions.
- The class can be easily reused. For example, you can create multiple frames by creating multiple instances of the class.

Using one style consistently makes programs easy to read. From now on, most of the GUI main classes will extend the `JFrame` class. The constructor of the main class constructs the user interface. The `main` method creates an instance of the main class and then displays the frame.

Will the program work if line 23 is replaced by the following code?

```
JFrame frame = new ShowFlowLayout();
```

Yes. The program will still work because `ShowFlowLayout` is a subclass of `JFrame` and the methods `setTitle`, `setSize`, `setLocationRelativeTo`, `setDefaultCloseOperation`, and `setVisible` (lines 24–28) are all available in the `JFrame` class.

In this example, the `FlowLayout` manager is used to place components in a frame. If you resize the frame, the components are automatically rearranged to fit. In Figure 12.5a, the first row has three components, but in Figure 12.5b, the first row has four components, because the width has been increased.

If you replace the `setLayout` statement (line 10) with `setLayout(new FlowLayout(FlowLayout.RIGHT, 0, 0))`, all the rows of buttons will be right aligned with no gaps.

An anonymous `FlowLayout` object was created in the statement (line 10):

```
setLayout(new FlowLayout(FlowLayout.LEFT, 10, 20));
```

which is equivalent to:

```
FlowLayout layout = new FlowLayout(FlowLayout.LEFT, 10, 20);
setLayout(layout);
```

This code creates an explicit reference to the object `layout` of the `FlowLayout` class. The explicit reference is not necessary, because the object is not directly referenced in the `ShowFlowLayout` class.

Suppose you add the same button to the frame ten times; will ten buttons appear in the frame? No, a GUI component such as a button can be added to only one container and only once in a container. Adding a button to a container multiple times is the same as adding it once.

Note

GUI components cannot be shared by containers, because only one GUI component can appear in only one container at a time. Therefore, the relationship between a component and a container is the composition denoted by a filled diamond, as shown in Figure 12.1.

Caution

Do not forget to put the `new` operator before a layout manager class when setting a layout style—for example, `setLayout(new FlowLayout())`.

Note

The constructor `ShowFlowLayout()` does not explicitly invoke the constructor `JFrame()`, but the constructor `JFrame()` is invoked implicitly. See Section 11.3.2, Constructor Chaining.

12.5.2 `GridLayout`

The `GridLayout` manager arranges components in a grid (matrix) formation. The components are placed in the grid from left to right, starting with the first row, then the second, and so on, in the order in which they are added. The class diagram for `GridLayout` is shown in Figure 12.6.

The `get` and `set` methods for these data fields are provided in the class, but omitted in the UML diagram for brevity.

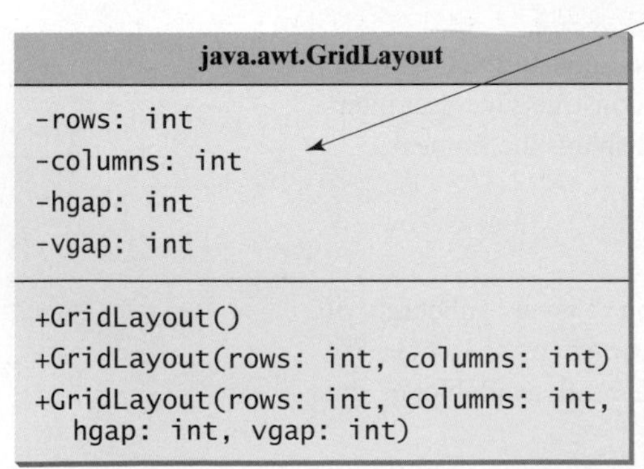

The number of rows in the grid (default: 1).
The number of columns in the grid (default: 1).
The horizontal gap between the components (default: 0).
The vertical gap between the components (default: 0).

Creates a default `GridLayout` manager.
Creates a `GridLayout` with a specified number of rows and columns.
Creates a `GridLayout` manager with a specified number of rows and columns, horizontal gap, and vertical gap.

FIGURE 12.6 `GridLayout` lays out components in equal-sized cells on a grid.

You can specify the number of rows and columns in the grid. The basic rules are as follows:

- The number of rows or the number of columns can be zero, but not for both. If one is zero and the other is nonzero, the nonzero dimension is fixed, while the zero dimension is determined dynamically by the layout manager. For example, if you specify zero rows and three columns for a grid that has ten components, `GridLayout` creates three fixed columns of four rows, with the last row containing one component. If you specify three rows and zero columns for a grid that has ten components, `GridLayout` creates three fixed rows of four columns, with the last row containing two components.

- If both the number of rows and the number of columns are nonzero, the number of rows is the dominating parameter; that is, the number of rows is fixed, and the layout manager dynamically calculates the number of columns. For example, if you specify three rows and three columns for a grid that has ten components, `GridLayout` creates three fixed rows of four columns, with the last row containing two components.

Listing 12.4 gives a program that demonstrates grid layout. The program is similar to the one in Listing 12.3, except that it adds three labels and three text fields to the frame of `GridLayout` instead of `FlowLayout`, as shown in Figure 12.7.

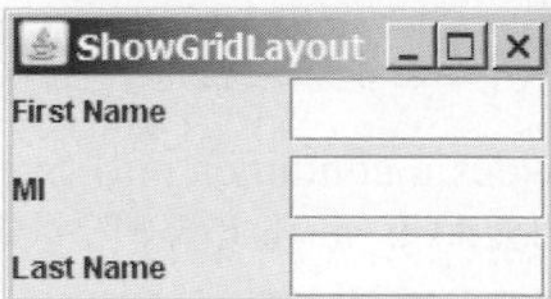

FIGURE 12.7 The `GridLayout` manager divides the container into grids; then the components are added to fill in the cells row by row.

LISTING 12.4 ShowGridLayout.java

```
 1 import javax.swing.JLabel;
 2 import javax.swing.JTextField;
 3 import javax.swing.JFrame;
 4 import java.awt.GridLayout;
 5
 6 public class ShowGridLayout extends JFrame {
 7   public ShowGridLayout() {
 8     // Set GridLayout, 3 rows, 2 columns, and gaps 5 between
 9     // components horizontally and vertically
10     setLayout(new GridLayout(3, 2, 5, 5));                      set layout
11
12     // Add labels and text fields to the frame
13     add(new JLabel("First Name"));                              add label
14     add(new JTextField(8));                                     add text field
15     add(new JLabel("MI"));
16     add(new JTextField(1));
17     add(new JLabel("Last Name"));
18     add(new JTextField(8));
19   }
20
21   /** Main method */
22   public static void main(String[] args) {
23     ShowGridLayout frame = new ShowGridLayout();
24     frame.setTitle("ShowGridLayout");
25     frame.setSize(200, 125);
26     frame.setLocationRelativeTo(null); // Center the frame      create the frame
27     frame.setDefaultCloseOperation(JFrame.EXIT_ON_CLOSE);
28     frame.setVisible(true);                                     set visible
29   }
30 }
```

If you resize the frame, the layout of the components remains unchanged (i.e., the number of rows and columns does not change, and the gaps don't change either).

All components are given equal size in the container of `GridLayout`.

Replacing the `setLayout` statement (line 10) with `setLayout(new GridLayout(3, 10))` would still yield three rows and *two* columns. The `columns` parameter is ignored because the **rows** parameter is nonzero. The actual number of columns is calculated by the layout manager.

What would happen if the **setLayout** statement (line 10) were replaced with **setLayout(new GridLayout(4, 2))** or with **setLayout(new GridLayout(2, 2))**? Please try it yourself.

Note

In **FlowLayout** and **GridLayout**, the order in which the components are added to the container is important. The order determines the location of the components in the container.

12.5.3 BorderLayout

The **BorderLayout** manager divides a container into five areas: East, South, West, North, and Center. Components are added to a **BorderLayout** by using **add(Component, index)**, where **index** is a constant **BorderLayout.EAST**, **BorderLayout.SOUTH**, **BorderLayout.WEST**, **BorderLayout.NORTH**, or **BorderLayout.CENTER**. The class diagram for **BorderLayout** is shown in Figure 12.8.

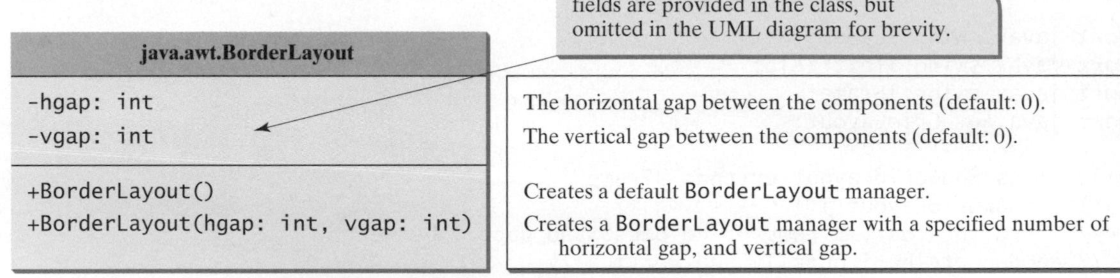

FIGURE 12.8 **BorderLayout** lays out components in five areas.

The components are laid out according to their preferred sizes and their placement in the container. The North and South components can stretch horizontally; the East and West components can stretch vertically; the Center component can stretch both horizontally and vertically to fill any empty space.

Listing 12.5 gives a program that demonstrates border layout. The program adds five buttons labeled **East**, **South**, **West**, **North**, and **Center** to the frame with a **BorderLayout** manager, as shown in Figure 12.9.

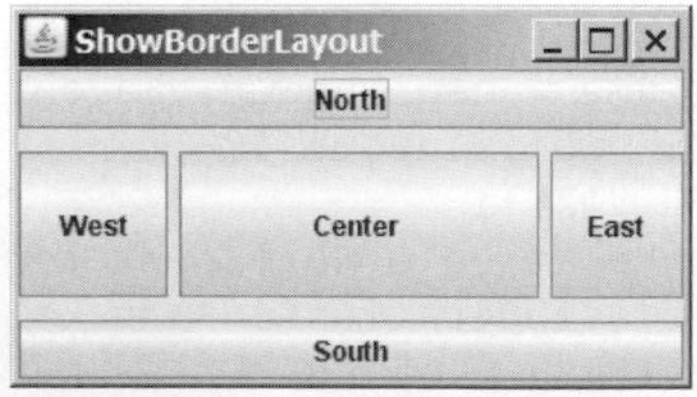

FIGURE 12.9 **BorderLayout** divides the container into five areas, each of which can hold a component.

LISTING 12.5 ShowBorderLayout.java

```
import javax.swing.JButton;
import javax.swing.JFrame;
import java.awt.BorderLayout;
```

```
4
5  public class ShowBorderLayout extends JFrame {
6    public ShowBorderLayout() {
7      // Set BorderLayout with horizontal gap 5 and vertical gap 10
8      setLayout(new BorderLayout(5, 10));
9
10     // Add buttons to the frame
11     add(new JButton("East"), BorderLayout.EAST);
12     add(new JButton("South"), BorderLayout.SOUTH);
13     add(new JButton("West"), BorderLayout.WEST);
14     add(new JButton("North"), BorderLayout.NORTH);
15     add(new JButton("Center"), BorderLayout.CENTER);
16   }
17
18   /** Main method */
19   public static void main(String[] args) {
20     ShowBorderLayout frame = new ShowBorderLayout();
21     frame.setTitle("ShowBorderLayout");
22     frame.setSize(300, 200);
23     frame.setLocationRelativeTo(null); // Center the frame
24     frame.setDefaultCloseOperation(JFrame.EXIT_ON_CLOSE);
25     frame.setVisible(true);
26   }
27 }
```

set layout

add buttons

create the frame

set visible

The buttons are added to the frame (lines 11–15). Note that the **add** method for **BorderLayout** is different from the one for **FlowLayout** and **GridLayout**. With **BorderLayout**, you specify where to put the components.

It is unnecessary to place components to occupy all the areas. If you remove the East button from the program and rerun it, you will see that the Center button stretches rightward to occupy the East area.

Note

BorderLayout interprets the absence of an index specification as **BorderLayout.CENTER**. For example, **add(component)** is the same as **add(Component, BorderLayout.CENTER)**. If you add two components to a container of **BorderLayout**, as follows,

```
container.add(component1);
container.add(component2);
```

only the last component is displayed.

12.5.4 Properties of Layout Managers

Layout managers have properties that can be changed dynamically.

- **FlowLayout** has **alignment**, **hgap**, and **vgap** properties. You can use the **setAlignment**, **setHgap**, and **setVgap** methods to specify the alignment and the horizontal and vertical gaps.
- **GridLayout** has the **rows**, **columns**, **hgap**, and **vgap** properties. You can use the **setRows**, **setColumns**, **setHgap**, and **setVgap** methods to specify the number of rows, the number of columns, and the horizontal and vertical gaps.
- **BorderLayout** has the **hgap** and **vgap** properties. You can use the **setHgap** and **setVgap** methods to specify the horizontal and vertical gaps.

In the preceding sections an anonymous layout manager is used because the properties of a layout manager do not change once it is created. If you have to change the properties of a layout manager dynamically, the layout manager must be explicitly referenced by a variable. You can then change the properties of the layout manager through the variable. For example, the following code creates a layout manager and sets its properties:

```
// Create a layout manager
FlowLayout flowLayout = new FlowLayout();

// Set layout properties
flowLayout.setAlignment(FlowLayout.RIGHT);
flowLayout.setHgap(10);
flowLayout.setVgap(20);
```

MyProgrammingLab™

12.6 Will the program work if ShowFlowLayout in line 23 in Listing 12.3 is replaced by JFrame?

Will the program work if ShowGridLayout in line 23 in Listing 12.4 is replaced by JFrame?

Will the program work if ShowBorderLayout line 20 in Listing 12.5 is replaced by JFrame?

12.7 Why do you need to use layout managers? What is the default layout manager for a frame? How do you add a component to a frame?

12.8 Describe FlowLayout. How do you create a FlowLayout manager? How do you add a component to a FlowLayout container? Is there a limit to the number of components that can be added to a FlowLayout container? What are the properties for setting the horizontal and vertical gaps between the components in the container? Can you specify alignment?

12.9 Describe GridLayout. How do you create a GridLayout manager? How do you add a component to a GridLayout container? Is there a limit to the number of components that can be added to a GridLayout container? What are the properties for setting the horizontal and vertical gaps between the components in the container?

12.10 Describe BorderLayout. How do you create a BorderLayout manager? How do you add a component to a BorderLayout container? What are the properties for setting the horizontal and vertical gaps between the components in the container?

12.11 The following program is supposed to display a button in a frame, but nothing is displayed. What is the problem?

```
public class Test extends javax.swing.JFrame {
  public Test() {
    add(new javax.swing.JButton("OK"));
  }

  public static void main(String[] args) {
    javax.swing.JFrame frame = new javax.swing.JFrame();
    frame.setSize(100, 200);
    frame.setVisible(true);
  }
}
```

12.6 Using Panels as Subcontainers

A container can be placed inside another container. Panels can be used as subcontainers to group GUI components to achieve the desired layout.

VideoNote
Use panels as subcontainers

Suppose that you want to place ten buttons and a text field in a frame. The buttons are placed in grid formation, but the text field is placed on a separate row. It is difficult to achieve the desired look by placing all the components in a single container. With Java GUI programming, you can divide a window into panels. Panels act as subcontainers to group user-interface components. You add the buttons in one panel, then add the panel to the frame.

The Swing version of panel is `JPanel`. You can use `new JPanel()` to create a panel with a default `FlowLayout` manager or `new JPanel(LayoutManager)` to create a panel with the specified layout manager. Use the `add(Component)` method to add a component to the panel. For example, the following code creates a panel and adds a button to it:

```
JPanel p = new JPanel();
p.add(new JButton("OK"));
```

Panels can be placed inside a frame or inside another panel. The following statement places panel `p` in frame `f`:

```
f.add(p);
```

Listing 12.6 gives an example that demonstrates using panels as subcontainers. The program creates a user interface for a microwave oven, as shown in Figure 12.10.

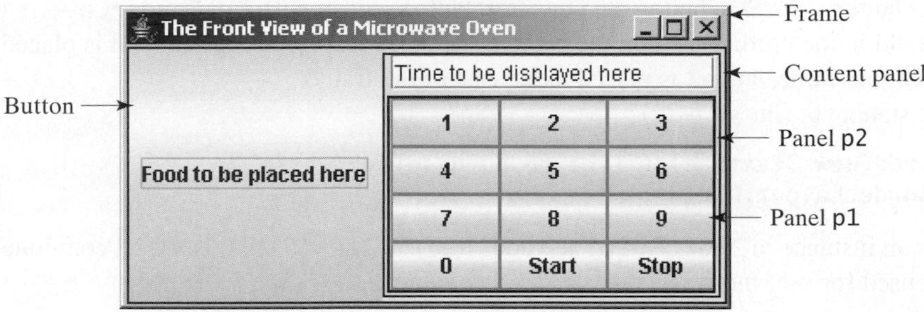

FIGURE 12.10 The program uses panels to organize components.

LISTING 12.6 TestPanels.java

```
import java.awt.*;
import javax.swing.*;

public class TestPanels extends JFrame {
  public TestPanels() {
    // Create panel p1 for the buttons and set GridLayout
    JPanel p1 = new JPanel();
    p1.setLayout(new GridLayout(4, 3));

    // Add buttons to the panel
    for (int i = 1; i <= 9; i++) {
      p1.add(new JButton("" + i));
    }

    p1.add(new JButton("" + 0));
    p1.add(new JButton("Start"));
    p1.add(new JButton("Stop"));

    // Create panel p2 to hold a text field and p1
    JPanel p2 = new JPanel(new BorderLayout());
    p2.add(new JTextField("Time to be displayed here"),
      BorderLayout.NORTH);
    p2.add(p1, BorderLayout.CENTER);

    // Add contents to the frame
    add(p2, BorderLayout.EAST);
    add(new JButton("Food to be placed here"),
      BorderLayout.CENTER);
  }

```

panel p1

panel p2

add p2 to frame

```
31   /** Main method */
32   public static void main(String[] args) {
33     TestPanels frame = new TestPanels();
34     frame.setTitle("The Front View of a Microwave Oven");
35     frame.setSize(400, 250);
36     frame.setLocationRelativeTo(null); // Center the frame
37     frame.setDefaultCloseOperation(JFrame.EXIT_ON_CLOSE);
38     frame.setVisible(true);
39   }
40 }
```

The `setLayout` method is defined in `java.awt.Container`. Since `JPanel` is a subclass of `Container`, you can use `setLayout` to set a new layout manager in the panel (line 8). Lines 7–8 can be replaced by `JPanel p1 = new JPanel(new GridLayout(4, 3))`.

To achieve the desired layout, the program uses panel `p1` of `GridLayout` to group the number buttons, the *Stop* button, and the *Start* button, and panel `p2` of `BorderLayout` to hold a text field in the north and `p1` in the center. The button representing the food is placed in the center of the frame, and `p2` is placed in the east of the frame.

The statement (lines 21–22)

```
p2.add(new JTextField("Time to be displayed here"),
  BorderLayout.NORTH);
```

creates an instance of `JTextField` and adds it to `p2`. `JTextField` is a GUI component that can be used for user input as well as to display values.

Note

superclass `Container`

It is worthwhile to note that the `Container` class is the superclass for GUI component classes, such as `JButton`. Every GUI component is a container. In theory, you could use the `setLayout` method to set the layout in a button and add components to a button, because all the public methods in the `Container` class are inherited by `JButton`, but for practical reasons you should not use buttons as containers.

MyProgrammingLab™

12.12 How do you create a panel with a specified layout manager?

12.13 What is the default layout manager for a `JPanel`? How do you add a component to a `JPanel`?

12.14 Can you use the `setTitle` method in a panel? What is the purpose of using a panel?

12.15 Since a GUI component class such as `JButton` is a subclass of `Container`, can you add components to a button?

12.7 The `Color` Class

Each GUI component has background and foreground colors. Colors are objects created from the `Color` class.

You can set colors for GUI components by using the `java.awt.Color` class. Colors are made of red, green, and blue components, each represented by an `int` value that describes its intensity, ranging from `0` (darkest shade) to `255` (lightest shade). This is known as the *RGB model*.

You can create a color using the following constructor:

```
public Color(int r, int g, int b);
```

in which `r`, `g`, and `b` specify a color by its red, green, and blue components. For example,

```
Color color = new Color(128, 100, 100);
```

Note

`IllegalArgumentException`

The arguments `r`, `g`, `b` are between `0` and `255`. If a value beyond this range is passed to the argument, an `IllegalArgumentException` will occur.

You can use the `setBackground(Color c)` and `setForeground(Color c)` methods defined in the `java.awt.Component` class to set a component's background and foreground colors. Here is an example of setting the background and foreground of a button:

```
JButton jbtOK = new JButton("OK");
jbtOK.setBackground(color);
jbtOK.setForeground(new Color(100, 1, 1));
```

Alternatively, you can use one of the 13 standard colors (`BLACK`, `BLUE`, `CYAN`, `DARK_GRAY`, `GRAY`, `GREEN`, `LIGHT_GRAY`, `MAGENTA`, `ORANGE`, `PINK`, `RED`, `WHITE`, and `YELLOW`) defined as constants in `java.awt.Color`. The following code, for instance, sets the foreground color of a button to red:

```
jbtOK.setForeground(Color.RED);
```

Check Point
MyProgrammingLab™

12.16 How do you create a color? What is wrong about creating a `Color` using `new Color(400, 200, 300)`? Which of two colors is darker, `new Color(10, 0, 0)` or `new Color(200, 0, 0)`?

12.17 How do you create a `Color` object with a random color?

12.18 How do you set a button object `jbtOK` with blue background?

12.8 The **Font** Class

Each GUI component has the font property. Fonts are objects created from the `Font` class.

You can create a font using the `java.awt.Font` class and set fonts for the components using the `setFont` method in the `Component` class.

The constructor for `Font` is:

```
public Font(String name, int style, int size);
```

You can choose a font name from `SansSerif`, `Serif`, `Monospaced`, `Dialog`, and `DialogInput`, choose a style from `Font.PLAIN` (0), `Font.BOLD` (1), `Font.ITALIC` (2), and `Font.BOLD + Font.ITALIC` (3), and specify a font size of any positive integer. For example, the following statements create two fonts and set one font to a button.

```
Font font1 = new Font("SansSerif", Font.BOLD, 16);
Font font2 = new Font("Serif", Font.BOLD + Font.ITALIC, 12);

JButton jbtOK = new JButton("OK");
jbtOK.setFont(font1);
```

Tip

find available fonts

If your system supports other fonts, such as "Times New Roman," you can use the font to create a `Font` object. To find the fonts available on your system, you need to obtain an instance of `java.awt.GraphicsEnvironment` using its static method `getLocalGraphicsEnvironment()`. `GraphicsEnvironment` is an abstract class that describes the graphics environment on a particular system. You can use its `getAllFonts()` method to obtain all the available fonts on the system and its `getAvailableFontFamilyNames()` method to obtain the names of all the available fonts. For example, the following statements print all the available font names in the system:

```
GraphicsEnvironment e =
  GraphicsEnvironment.getLocalGraphicsEnvironment();
String[] fontnames = e.getAvailableFontFamilyNames();

for (int i = 0; i < fontnames.length; i++)
  System.out.println(fontnames[i]);
```

MyProgrammingLab™

12.19 How do you create a **Font** object with font name **Courier**, size **20**, and style **bold**?

12.20 How do you find all available fonts on your system?

12.9 Common Features of Swing GUI Components

GUI components have common features. They are defined in the superclasses **Component**, **Container**, *and* **JComponent**.

VideoNote
Use Swing common properties

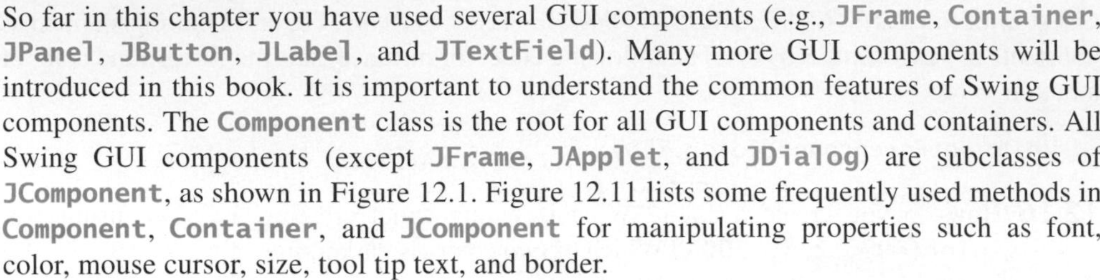

So far in this chapter you have used several GUI components (e.g., **JFrame**, **Container**, **JPanel**, **JButton**, **JLabel**, and **JTextField**). Many more GUI components will be introduced in this book. It is important to understand the common features of Swing GUI components. The **Component** class is the root for all GUI components and containers. All Swing GUI components (except **JFrame**, **JApplet**, and **JDialog**) are subclasses of **JComponent**, as shown in Figure 12.1. Figure 12.11 lists some frequently used methods in **Component**, **Container**, and **JComponent** for manipulating properties such as font, color, mouse cursor, size, tool tip text, and border.

Component
Container
JComponent
tool tip

A *tool tip* is text displayed on a component when you move the mouse onto the component. It is often used to describe the function of a component.

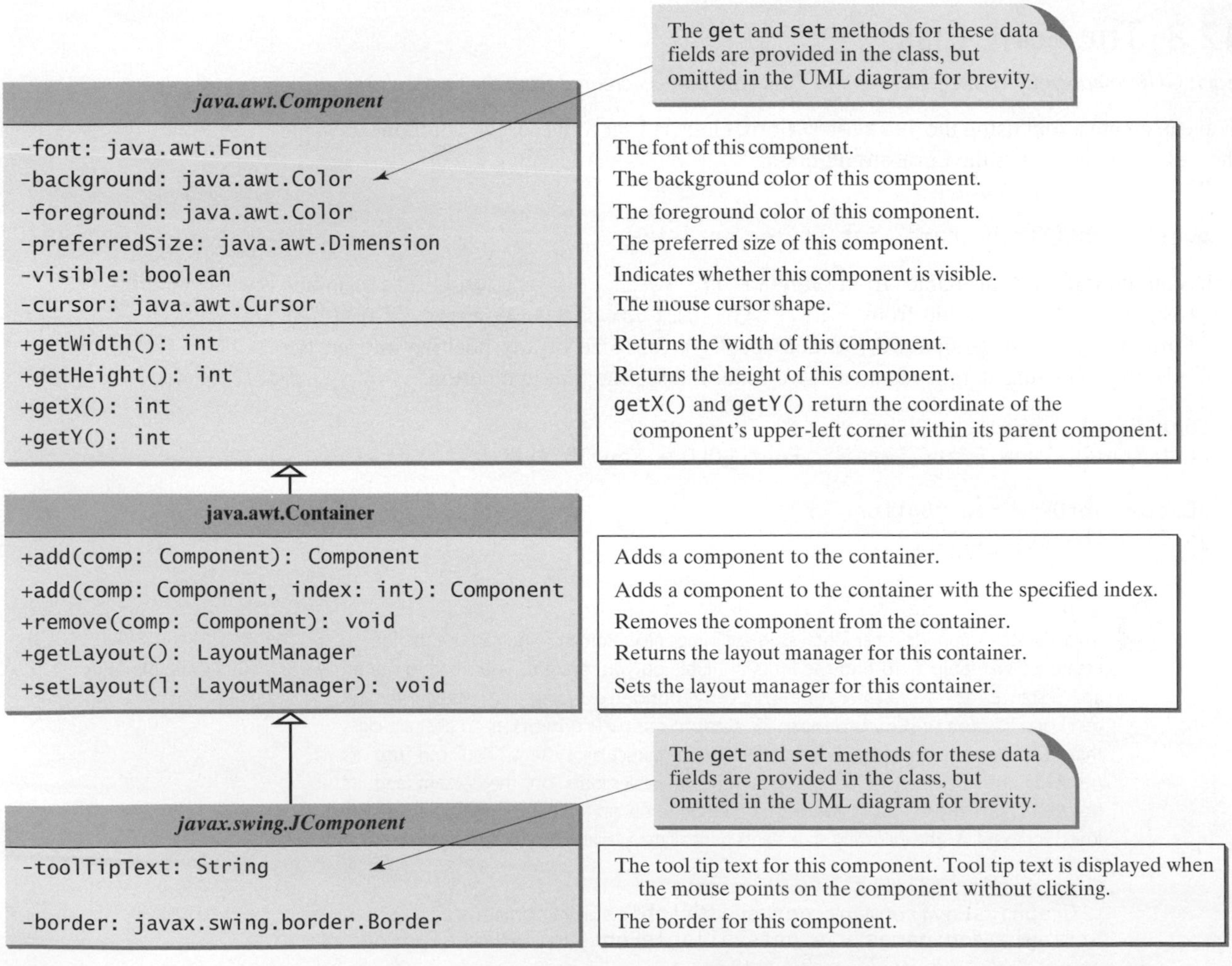

java.awt.Component

```
-font: java.awt.Font
-background: java.awt.Color
-foreground: java.awt.Color
-preferredSize: java.awt.Dimension
-visible: boolean
-cursor: java.awt.Cursor
+getWidth(): int
+getHeight(): int
+getX(): int
+getY(): int
```

The get and set methods for these data fields are provided in the class, but omitted in the UML diagram for brevity.

- The font of this component.
- The background color of this component.
- The foreground color of this component.
- The preferred size of this component.
- Indicates whether this component is visible.
- The mouse cursor shape.
- Returns the width of this component.
- Returns the height of this component.
- getX() and getY() return the coordinate of the component's upper-left corner within its parent component.

java.awt.Container

```
+add(comp: Component): Component
+add(comp: Component, index: int): Component
+remove(comp: Component): void
+getLayout(): LayoutManager
+setLayout(l: LayoutManager): void
```

- Adds a component to the container.
- Adds a component to the container with the specified index.
- Removes the component from the container.
- Returns the layout manager for this container.
- Sets the layout manager for this container.

javax.swing.JComponent

```
-toolTipText: String
-border: javax.swing.border.Border
```

The get and set methods for these data fields are provided in the class, but omitted in the UML diagram for brevity.

- The tool tip text for this component. Tool tip text is displayed when the mouse points on the component without clicking.
- The border for this component.

FIGURE 12.11 All the Swing GUI components inherit the public methods from **Component**, **Container**, and **JComponent**.

border

You can set a border for any object of the `JComponent` class. Swing has several types of borders. To create a titled border, use `new TitledBorder(String title)`. To create a line border, use `new LineBorder(Color color, int width)`, where `width` specifies the thickness of the line.

Listing 12.7 is an example to demonstrate Swing common features. The example creates a panel `p1` to hold three buttons (line 8) and a panel `p2` to hold two labels (line 26), as shown in Figure 12.12. The background of the button `jbtLeft` is set to white (line 12) and the foreground of the button `jbtCenter` is set to green (line 13). The tool tip of the button `jbtRight` is set in line 14. Titled borders are set on panels `p1` and `p2` (lines 18, 37) and line borders are set on the labels (lines 33–34).

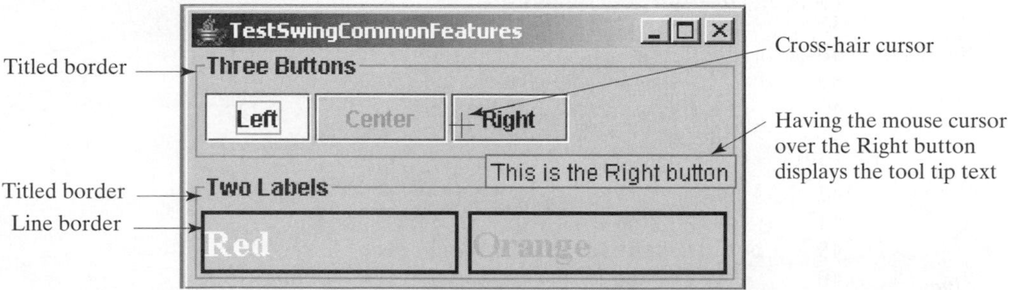

FIGURE 12.12 The font, color, border, and tool tip text are set in the message panel.

mouse cursor

The mouse cursor is set to the cross-hair shape in `p1` (line 19). The `Cursor` class contains the constants for specifying the cursor shape such as `DEFAULT_CURSOR`, `CROSSHAIR_CURSOR` (+), `HAND_CURSOR`, `MOVE_CURSOR`, `TEXT_CURSOR` (I), and so on. A `Cursor` object for the cross-hair cursor is created using `new Cursor(Cursor.CROSSHAIR_CURSOR)` (line 19) and this cursor is set for `p1`. Note that the default mouse cursor is still used in `p2`, because the program does not explicitly set a mouse cursor for `p2`.

LISTING 12.7 TestSwingCommonFeatures.java

```
1  import java.awt.*;
2  import javax.swing.*;
3  import javax.swing.border.*;
4
5  public class TestSwingCommonFeatures extends JFrame {
6    public TestSwingCommonFeatures() {
7      // Create a panel to group three buttons
8      JPanel p1 = new JPanel(new FlowLayout(FlowLayout.LEFT, 2, 2));
9      JButton jbtLeft = new JButton("Left");
10     JButton jbtCenter = new JButton("Center");
11     JButton jbtRight = new JButton("Right");
12     jbtLeft.setBackground(Color.WHITE);                    set background
13     jbtCenter.setForeground(Color.GREEN);                  set foreground
14     jbtRight.setToolTipText("This is the Right button");   set tool tip text
15     p1.add(jbtLeft);
16     p1.add(jbtCenter);
17     p1.add(jbtRight);
18     p1.setBorder(new TitledBorder("Three Buttons"));       set titled border
19     p1.setCursor(new Cursor(Cursor.CROSSHAIR_CURSOR));     set mouse cursor
20
21     // Create a font and a line border
22     Font largeFont = new Font("TimesRoman", Font.BOLD, 20);   create a font
23     Border lineBorder = new LineBorder(Color.BLACK, 2);       create a border
```

set foreground

set font

set line border

set titled border

```
24
25       // Create a panel to group two labels
26       JPanel p2 = new JPanel(new GridLayout(1, 2, 5, 5));
27       JLabel jlblRed = new JLabel("Red");
28       JLabel jlblOrange = new JLabel("Orange");
29       jlblRed.setForeground(Color.RED);
30       jlblOrange.setForeground(Color.ORANGE);
31       jlblRed.setFont(largeFont);
32       jlblOrange.setFont(largeFont);
33       jlblRed.setBorder(lineBorder);
34       jlblOrange.setBorder(lineBorder);
35       p2.add(jlblRed);
36       p2.add(jlblOrange);
37       p2.setBorder(new TitledBorder("Two Labels"));
38
39       // Add two panels to the frame
40       setLayout(new GridLayout(2, 1, 5, 5));
41       add(p1);
42       add(p2);
43     }
44
45     public static void main(String[] args) {
46       // Create a frame and set its properties
47       JFrame frame = new TestSwingCommonFeatures();
48       frame.setTitle("TestSwingCommonFeatures");
49       frame.setSize(300, 150);
50       frame.setLocationRelativeTo(null); // Center the frame
51       frame.setDefaultCloseOperation(JFrame.EXIT_ON_CLOSE);
52       frame.setVisible(true);
53     }
54   }
```

property default values

Note

The same property may have different default values in different components. For example, the `visible` property in `JFrame` is `false` by default, but it is `true` in every instance of `JComponent` (e.g., `JButton` and `JLabel`) by default. To display a `JFrame`, you have to invoke `setVisible(true)` to set the `visible` property `true`, but you don't have to set this property for a `JButton` or a `JLabel`, because it is already `true`. To make a `JButton` or a `JLabel` invisible, you can invoke `setVisible(false)`. Please run the program and see the effect after inserting the following two statements in line 38:

```
jbtLeft.setVisible(false);
jlblRed.setVisible(false);
```

MyProgrammingLab™

12.21 How do you set background color, foreground color, font, and tool tip text on a Swing GUI component?

12.22 Why is the tool tip text not displayed in the following code?

```
import javax.swing.*;

public class Test extends JFrame {
  private JButton jbtOK = new JButton("OK");

  public static void main(String[] args) {
    // Create a frame and set its properties
    JFrame frame = new Test();
    frame.setTitle("Logic Error");
    frame.setSize(200, 100);
    frame.setDefaultCloseOperation(JFrame.EXIT_ON_CLOSE);
```

```
    frame.setVisible(true);
  }

  public Test() {
    jbtOK.setToolTipText("This is a button");
    add(new JButton("OK"));
  }
}
```

12.23 Show the output of the following code:

```
import javax.swing.*;

public class Test {
  public static void main(String[] args) {
    JButton jbtOK = new JButton("OK");
    System.out.println(jbtOK.isVisible());

    JFrame frame = new JFrame();
    System.out.println(frame.isVisible());
  }
}
```

12.24 What happens if you add a button to a container several times, as shown below? Does it cause syntax errors? Does it cause runtime errors?

```
JButton jbt = new JButton();
JPanel panel = new JPanel();
panel.add(jbt);
panel.add(jbt);
panel.add(jbt);
```

12.10 Image Icons

Image icons can be displayed in many GUI components. Image icons are objects created using the `ImageIcon` *class.*

An icon is a fixed-size picture; typically it is small and used to decorate components. Images are normally stored in image files. Java currently supports three image formats: GIF (Graphics Interchange Format), JPEG (Joint Photographic Experts Group), and PNG (Portable Network Graphics). The image file names for these types end with **.gif**, **.jpg**, and **.png**, respectively. If you have a bitmap file or image files in other formats, you can use image-processing utilities to convert them into the GIF, JPEG, or PNG format for use in Java.

To display an image icon, first create an `ImageIcon` object using `new javax.swing.ImageIcon(filename)`. For example, the following statement creates an icon from an image file **us.gif** in the `image` directory under the current class path:

image-file format

```
ImageIcon icon = new ImageIcon("image/us.gif");
```

create ImageIcon

image/us.gif is located in **c:\book\image\us.gif**. The back slash (\) is the Windows file path notation. In UNIX, the forward slash (/) should be used. In Java, the forward slash (/) is used to denote a relative file path under the Java classpath (e.g., **image/us.gif**, as in this example).

file path character

Tip

File names are not case sensitive in Windows but are case sensitive in UNIX. To enable your programs to run on all platforms, name all the image files consistently, using lowercase.

naming files consistently

An image icon can be displayed in a label or a button using `new JLabel(imageIcon)` or `new JButton(imageIcon)`. Listing 12.8 demonstrates displaying icons in labels and buttons. The example creates two labels and two buttons with icons, as shown in Figure 12.13.

Figure 12.13 The image icons are displayed in labels and buttons.

Listing 12.8 TestImageIcon.java

create image icons

a label with image

a button with image

```
import javax.swing.*;
import java.awt.*;

public class TestImageIcon extends JFrame {
  private ImageIcon usIcon = new ImageIcon("image/us.gif");
  private ImageIcon myIcon = new ImageIcon("image/my.jpg");
  private ImageIcon frIcon = new ImageIcon("image/fr.gif");
  private ImageIcon ukIcon = new ImageIcon("image/uk.gif");

  public TestImageIcon() {
    setLayout(new GridLayout(1, 4, 5, 5));
    add(new JLabel(usIcon));
    add(new JLabel(myIcon));
    add(new JButton(frIcon));
    add(new JButton(ukIcon));
  }

  /** Main method */
  public static void main(String[] args) {
    TestImageIcon frame = new TestImageIcon();
    frame.setTitle("TestImageIcon");
    frame.setSize(200, 200);
    frame.setLocationRelativeTo(null); // Center the frame
    frame.setDefaultCloseOperation(JFrame.EXIT_ON_CLOSE);
    frame.setVisible(true);
  }
}
```

sharing borders and icons

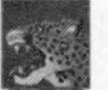

Note

Borders and icons can be shared. Thus, you can create a border or icon and use it to set the `border` or `icon` property for any GUI component. For example, the following statements set a border `b` for the panels `p1` and `p2`:

```
p1.setBorder(b);
p2.setBorder(b);
```

The following statements set an icon in the buttons `jbt1` and `jbt2`:

```
jbt1.setIcon(icon);
jbt2.setIcon(icon);
```

Tip

A *splash screen* is an image that is displayed while the application is starting up. If your program takes a long time to load, you may display a splash screen to alert the user. For example, the following command:

splash screen

```
java -splash:image/us.gif TestImageIcon
```

displays an image while the program `TestImageIcon` is being loaded.

12.25 How do you create an `ImageIcon` from the file **image/us.gif** in the class directory?

MyProgrammingLab™

12.26 Will the following code display three buttons? Will the buttons display the same icon?

```
import javax.swing.*;
import java.awt.*;

public class Test extends JFrame  {
  public static void main(String[] args) {
    // Create a frame and set its properties
    JFrame frame = new Test();
    frame.setTitle("ButtonIcons");
    frame.setSize(200, 100);
    frame.setDefaultCloseOperation(JFrame.EXIT_ON_CLOSE);
    frame.setVisible(true);
  }

  public Test() {
    ImageIcon usIcon = new ImageIcon("image/us.gif");
    JButton jbt1 = new JButton(usIcon);
    JButton jbt2 = new JButton(usIcon);

    JPanel p1 = new JPanel();
    p1.add(jbt1);

    JPanel p2 = new JPanel();
    p2.add(jbt2);

    JPanel p3 = new JPanel();
    p2.add(jbt1);

    add(p1, BorderLayout.NORTH);
    add(p2, BorderLayout.SOUTH);
    add(p3, BorderLayout.CENTER);
  }
}
```

12.27 Can a border or an icon be shared by GUI components?

12.11 JButton

To create a push button, use the `JButton` *class.*

We have used `JButton` in the examples to demonstrate the basics of GUI programming. This section will introduce more features of `JButton`. The following sections will introduce GUI components `JCheckBox`, `JRadioButton`, `JLabel`, `JTextField`, and `JPasswordField`. More GUI components such as `JTextArea`, `JComboBox`, `JList`, `JScrollBar`, and `JSlider` will be introduced in Chapter 17. The relationship of these classes is pictured in Figure 12.14.

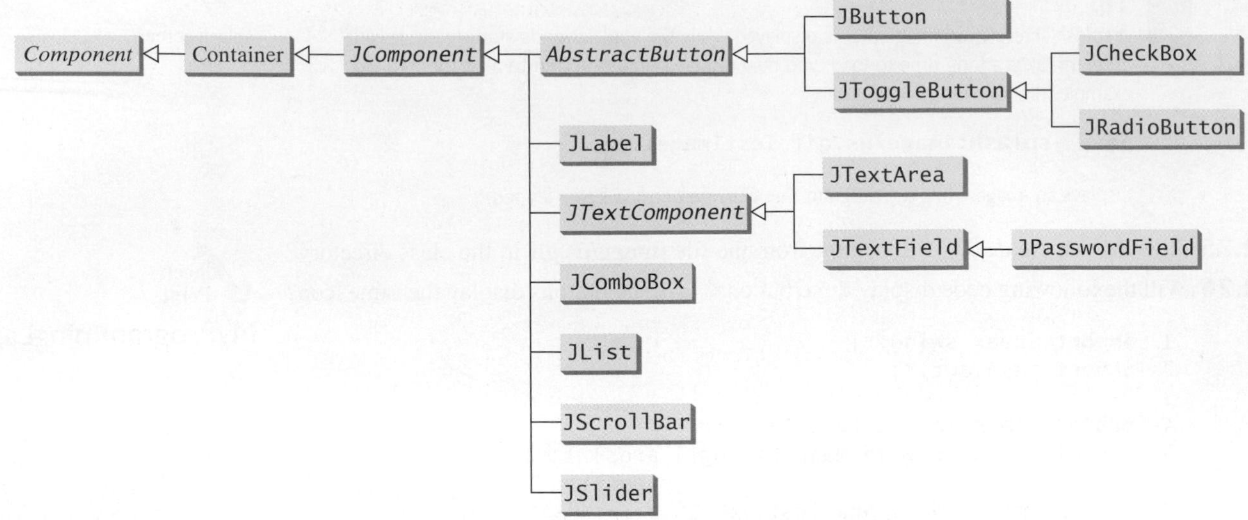

FIGURE 12.14 These Swing GUI components are frequently used to create user interfaces.

naming convention for components

> **Note**
>
> Throughout this book, the prefixes **jbt**, **jchk**, **jrb**, **jlbl**, **jtf**, **jpf**, **jta**, **jcbo**, **jlst**, **jscb**, and **jsld** are used to name reference variables for **JButton**, **JCheckBox**, **JRadioButton**, **JLabel**, **JTextField**, **JPasswordField**, **JTextArea**, **JComboBox**, **JList**, **JScrollBar**, and **JSlider**.

AbstractButton

A *button* is a component that triggers an action when clicked. Swing provides regular buttons, toggle buttons, check box buttons, and radio buttons. The common features of these buttons are defined in **javax.swing.AbstractButton**, as shown in Figure 12.15.

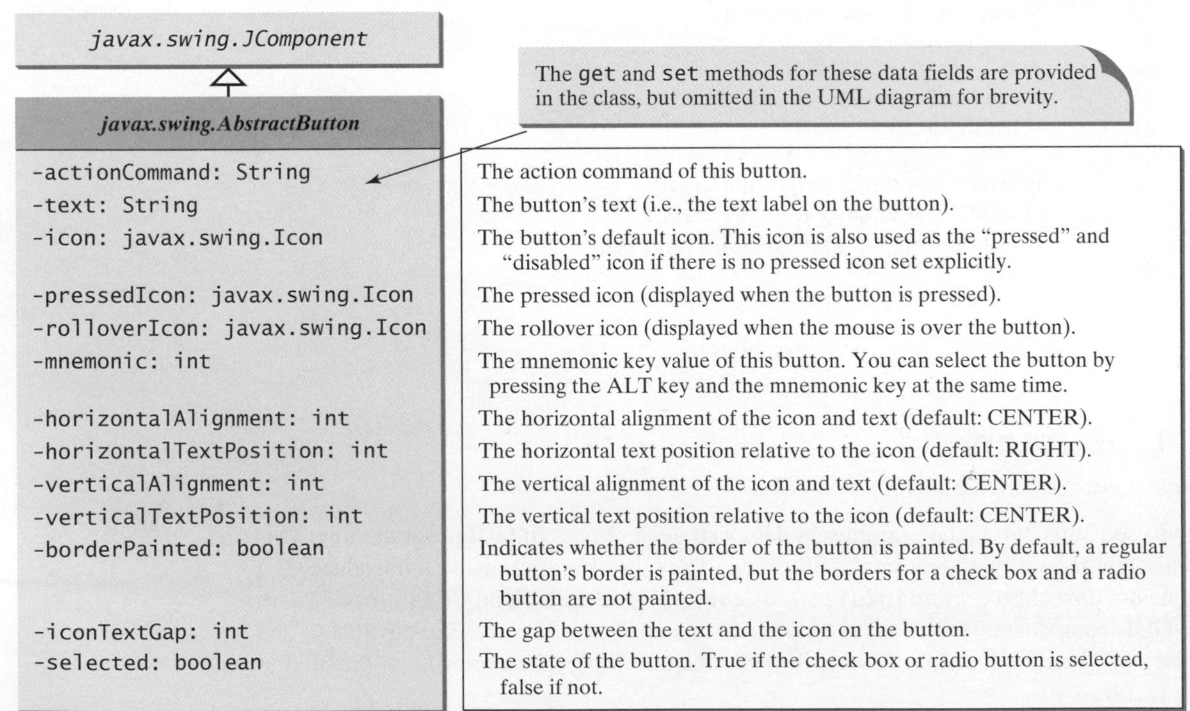

FIGURE 12.15 **AbstractButton** defines common features of different types of buttons.

JButton inherits **AbstractButton** and provides several constructors to create buttons, as shown in Figure 12.16.

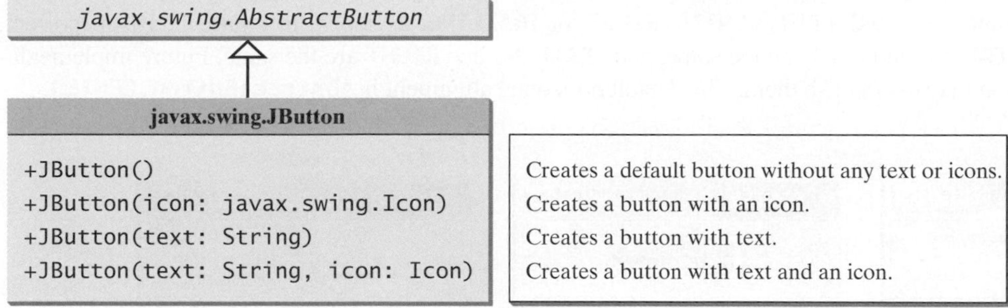

FIGURE 12.16 `JButton` defines a regular push button.

12.11.1 Icons, Pressed Icons, and Rollover Icons

A button has a default icon, a pressed icon, and a rollover icon. Normally you use the default icon, because the other icons are for special effects. A pressed icon is displayed when a button is pressed, and a rollover icon is displayed when the mouse is over the button but not pressed. For example, Listing 12.9 displays the U.S. flag as a regular icon, the Canadian flag as a pressed icon, and the British flag as a rollover icon, as shown in Figure 12.17.

LISTING 12.9 TestButtonIcons.java

```
import javax.swing.*;

public class TestButtonIcons extends JFrame  {
  public static void main(String[] args) {
    // Create a frame and set its properties
    JFrame frame = new TestButtonIcons();
    frame.setTitle("ButtonIcons");
    frame.setSize(200, 100);
    frame.setLocationRelativeTo(null); // Center the frame
    frame.setDefaultCloseOperation(JFrame.EXIT_ON_CLOSE);
    frame.setVisible(true);
  }

  public TestButtonIcons() {
    ImageIcon usIcon = new ImageIcon("image/usIcon.gif");
    ImageIcon caIcon = new ImageIcon("image/caIcon.gif");
    ImageIcon ukIcon = new ImageIcon("image/ukIcon.gif");

    JButton jbt = new JButton("Click it", usIcon);
    jbt.setPressedIcon(caIcon);
    jbt.setRolloverIcon(ukIcon);

    add(jbt);
  }
}
```

create icons

regular icon
pressed icon
rollover icon

add a button

ButtonIcons — Click it

(a) Default icon (b) Pressed icon (c) Rollover icon

FIGURE 12.17 A button can have several types of icons.

12.11.2 Alignments

horizontal alignment

Horizontal alignment specifies how the icon and text are placed horizontally on a button. You can set the horizontal alignment using `setHorizontalAlignment(int)` with one of the five constants `LEADING`, `LEFT`, `CENTER`, `RIGHT`, or `TRAILING`, as shown in Figure 12.18. At present, `LEADING` and `LEFT` are the same, and `TRAILING` and `RIGHT` are the same. Future implementation may distinguish them. The default horizontal alignment is `AbstractButton.CENTER`.

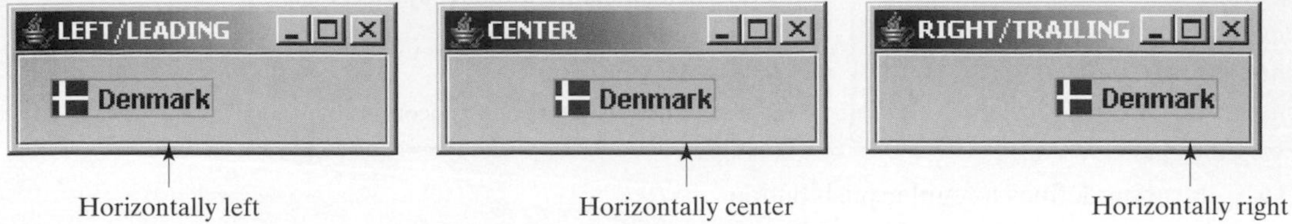

FIGURE 12.18 You can specify how the icon and text are placed on a button horizontally.

vertical alignment

Vertical alignment specifies how the icon and text are placed vertically on a button. You can set the vertical alignment using `setVerticalAlignment(int)` with one of the three constants `TOP`, `CENTER`, or `BOTTOM`, as shown in Figure 12.19. The default vertical alignment is `AbstractButton.CENTER`.

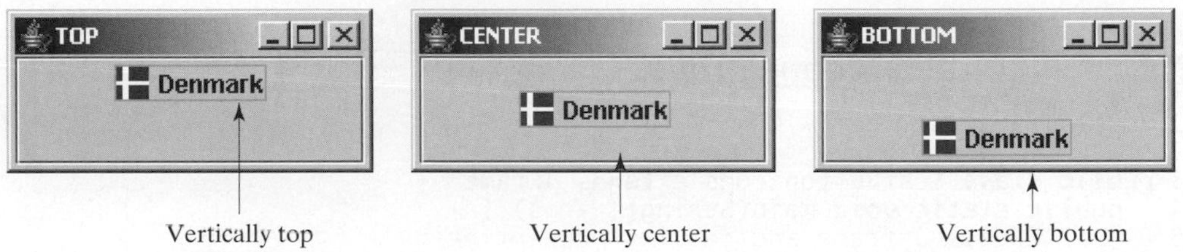

FIGURE 12.19 You can specify how the icon and text are placed on a button vertically.

12.11.3 Text Positions

horizontal text position

Horizontal text position specifies the horizontal position of the text relative to the icon. You can set the horizontal text position using `setHorizontalTextPosition(int)` with one of the five constants `LEADING`, `LEFT`, `CENTER`, `RIGHT`, or `TRAILING`, as shown in Figure 12.20. At present, `LEADING` and `LEFT` are the same, and `TRAILING` and `RIGHT` are the same. Future implementation may distinguish them. The default horizontal text position is `AbstractButton.RIGHT`.

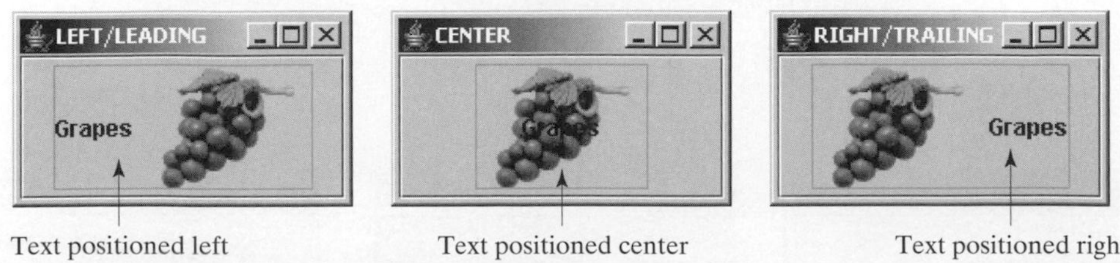

FIGURE 12.20 You can specify the horizontal position of the text relative to the icon.

vertical text position

Vertical text position specifies the vertical position of the text relative to the icon. You can set the vertical text position using `setVerticalTextPosition(int)` with one of the three constants TOP, CENTER, or BOTTOM, as shown in Figure 12.21. The default vertical text position is AbstractButton.CENTER.

FIGURE 12.21 You can specify the vertical position of the text relative to the icon.

12.28 How do you create a button with the text OK? How do you change text on a button? How do you set an icon, a pressed icon, and a rollover icon in a button?

12.29 Given a JButton object jbtOK, write statements to set the button's foreground to red, background to yellow, mnemonic to K, tool tip text to Click OK to proceed, horizontal alignment to RIGHT, vertical alignment to BOTTOM, horizontal text position to LEFT, vertical text position to TOP, and icon text gap to 5.

12.30 List at least five properties defined in the AbstractButton class.

12.12 JCheckBox

To create a check box button, use the JCheckBox *class.*

A *toggle button* is a two-state button like a light switch. JToggleButton *inherits* AbstractButton *and* implements a toggle button. Often JToggleButton's subclasses JCheckBox and JRadioButton are used to enable the user to toggle a choice on or off. This section introduces JCheckBox. JRadioButton will be introduced in the next section.

toggle button

JCheckBox inherits all the properties from AbstractButton, such as text, icon, mnemonic, verticalAlignment, horizontalAlignment, horizontalTextPosition, verticalTextPosition, and selected, and provides several constructors to create check boxes, as shown in Figure 12.22.

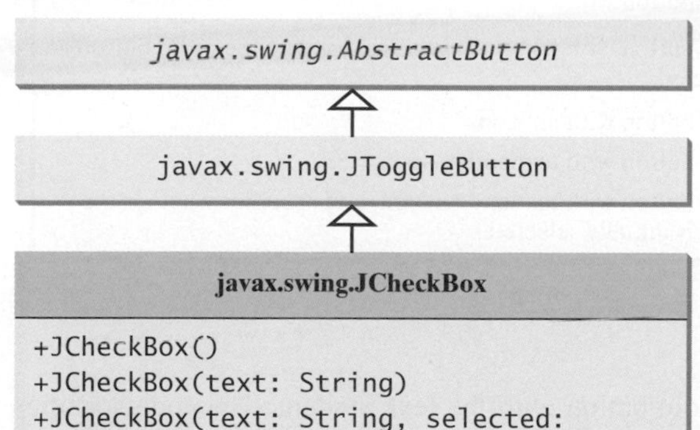

Creates a default check box without any text or icon.
Creates a check box with text.
Creates a check box with text and specifies whether the check box is initially selected.
Creates a check box with an icon.
Creates a check box with text and an icon.
Creates a check box with text and an icon, and specifies whether the check box is initially selected.

FIGURE 12.22 JCheckBox defines a check box button.

Here is an example for creating a check box with the text *Student*. Its foreground is `red`, the background is `white`, its mnemonic key is `S`, and it is initially selected.

```
JCheckBox jchk = new JCheckBox("Student", true);
jchk.setForeground(Color.RED);
jchk.setBackground(Color.WHITE);
jchk.setMnemonic('S');
```

Student

mnemonics

The button can also be accessed by using the keyboard mnemonics. Pressing *Alt+S* is equivalent to clicking the check box.

isSelected?

To see if a check box is selected, use the `isSelected()` method.

12.31 How do you create a check box? How do you create a check box with the box checked initially? How do you determine whether a check box is selected?

MyProgrammingLab™

12.13 JRadioButton

To create a radio button, use the `JRadioButton` class.

Radio buttons, also known as *option buttons*, enable you to choose a single item from a group of choices. In appearance radio buttons resemble check boxes, but check boxes display a square that is either checked or blank, whereas radio buttons display a circle that is either filled (if selected) or blank (if not selected).

`JRadioButton` inherits `AbstractButton` and provides several constructors to create radio buttons, as shown in Figure 12.23. These constructors are similar to the constructors for `JCheckBox`.

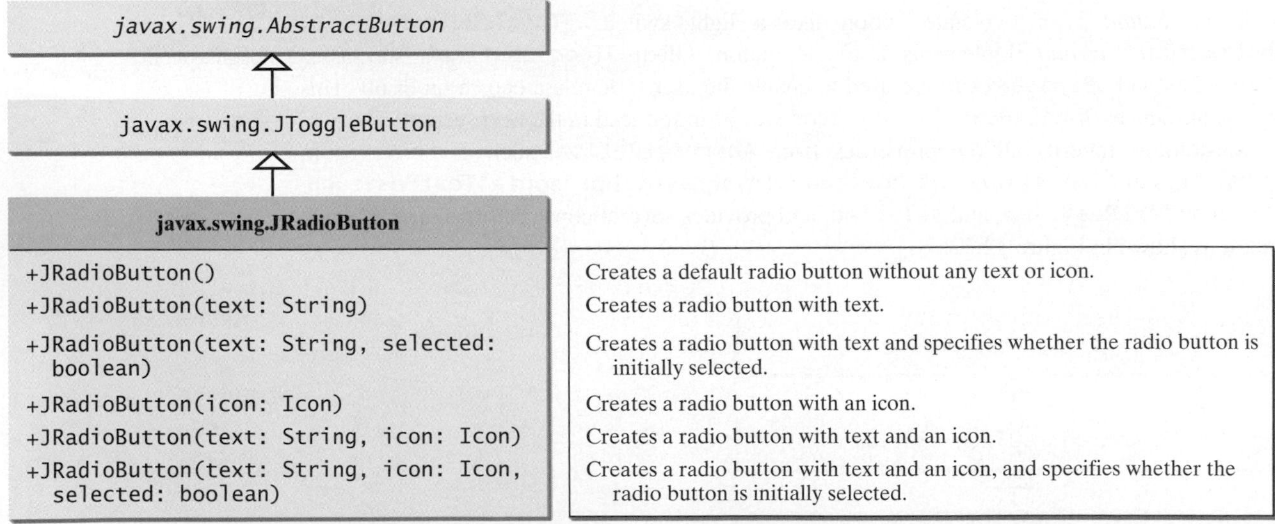

FIGURE 12.23 `JRadioButton` defines a radio button.

Here is an example for creating a radio button with the text Student. The code specifies `red` foreground, `white` background, mnemonic key `S`, and initially selected.

```
JRadioButton jrb = new JRadioButton("Student", true);
jrb.setForeground(Color.RED);
jrb.setBackground(Color.WHITE);
jrb.setMnemonic('S');
```

Student

To group radio buttons, you need to create an instance of `javax.swing.ButtonGroup` and use the `add` method to add them to it, as follows:

```
ButtonGroup group = new ButtonGroup();
group.add(jrb1);
group.add(jrb2);
```

This code creates a radio-button group for the radio buttons `jrb1` and `jrb2` so that they are selected mutually exclusively. Without grouping, `jrb1` and `jrb2` would be independent.

Note

`ButtonGroup` is not a subclass of `java.awt.Component`, so a `ButtonGroup` object cannot be added to a container. GUI helper class

To see if a radio button is selected, use the `isSelected()` method.

12.32 How do you create a radio button? How do you create a radio button with the button selected initially? How do you group radio buttons together? How do you determine whether a radio button is selected?

12.14 Labels

To create a label, use the `JLabel` class.

A *label* is a display area for a short text, an image, or both. It is often used to label other components (usually text fields). Figure 12.24 lists the constructors and methods in the `JLabel` class.

javax.swing.JComponent

▲

javax.swing.JLabel

The `get` and `set` methods for these data fields are provided in the class, but omitted in the UML diagram for brevity.

javax.swing.JLabel	
`-text: String`	The label's text.
`-icon: javax.swing.Icon`	The label's image icon.
`-horizontalAlignment: int`	The horizontal alignment of the text and icon on the label.
`-horizontalTextPosition: int`	The horizontal text position relative to the icon on the label.
`-verticalAlignment: int`	The vertical alignment of the text and icon on the label.
`-verticalTextPosition: int`	The vertical text position relative to the icon on the label.
`-iconTextGap: int`	The gap between the text and the icon on the label.
`+JLabel()`	Creates a default label without any text or icons.
`+JLabel(icon: javax.swing.Icon)`	Creates a label with an icon.
`+JLabel(icon: Icon, hAlignment: int)`	Creates a label with an icon and the specified horizontal alignment.
`+JLabel(text: String)`	Creates a label with text.
`+JLabel(text: String, icon: Icon, hAlignment: int)`	Creates a label with text, an icon, and the specified horizontal alignment.
`+JLabel(text: String, hAlignment: int)`	Creates a label with text and the specified horizontal alignment.

FIGURE 12.24 `JLabel` displays text or an icon, or both.

`JLabel` inherits all the properties from `JComponent` and has many properties similar to the ones in `JButton`, such as `text`, `icon`, `horizontalAlignment`, `verticalAlignment`, `horizontalTextPosition`, `verticalTextPosition`, and `iconTextGap`. For example, the following code displays a label with text and an icon:

```
// Create an image icon from an image file
ImageIcon icon = new ImageIcon("image/grapes.gif");

// Create a label with a text, an icon,
// with centered horizontal alignment
JLabel jlbl = new JLabel("Grapes", icon, JLabel.CENTER);

//Set label's text alignment and gap between text and icon
jlbl.setHorizontalTextPosition(JLabel.CENTER);
jlbl.setVerticalTextPosition(JLabel.BOTTOM);
jlbl.setIconTextGap(5);
```

Text and Icon Label

Grapes

MyProgrammingLab™

12.33 How do you create a label named `Address`? How do you change the name on a label? How do you set an icon in a label?

12.34 Given a `JLabel` object `jlblMap`, write statements to set the label's foreground to `red`, background to `yellow`, mnemonic to `M`, tool tip text to `Map image`, horizontal alignment to `RIGHT`, vertical alignment to `BOTTOM`, horizontal text position to `LEFT`, vertical text position to `TOP`, and icon text gap to `5`.

12.15 Text Fields

To create a text field, use the `JTextField` class.

A *text field* can be used to enter or display a string. `JTextField` is a subclass of `JTextComponent`. Figure 12.25 lists the constructors and methods in `JTextField`.

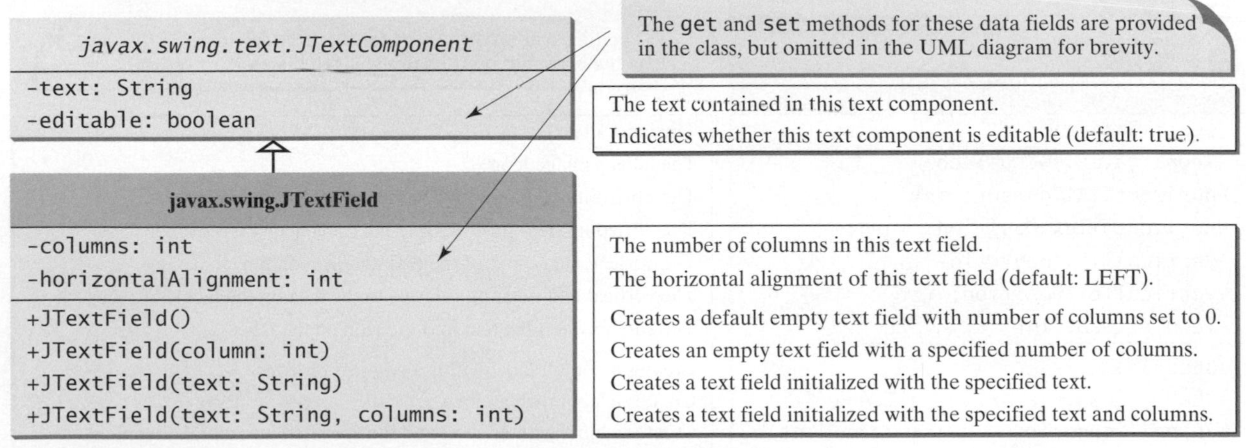

FIGURE 12.25 `JTextField` enables you to enter or display a string.

`JTextField` inherits `JTextComponent`, which inherits `JComponent`. Here is an example of creating a text field with red foreground color and right horizontal alignment:

```
JTextField jtfMessage = new JTextField("T-Storm");
jtfMessage.setForeground(Color.RED);
jtfMessage.setHorizontalAlignment(JTextField.RIGHT);
```

To set new text in a text field, use the `setText(newText)` method. To get the text from a text field, use the `getText()` method.

Note

If a text field is used for entering a password, use `JPasswordField` to replace `JTextField`. `JPasswordField extends JTextField` and hides the input text with echo characters (e.g., ******). By default, the echo character is *. You can specify a new echo character using the `setEchoChar(char)` method.

JPasswordField

Check Point
MyProgrammingLab™

12.35 How do you create a text field with `10` columns and the default text `Welcome to Java`? How do you write the code to check whether a text field is empty?

12.36 How do you create text field for entering passwords?

Key Terms

AWT 446
component class 446
container class 446
heavyweight component 446
helper class 446
layout manager 451
lightweight component 446
Swing components 446
splash screen 467
top-level container 447

Chapter Summary

1. Every container has a *layout manager* that is used to position and place components in the container in the desired locations. Three simple and frequently used layout managers are `FlowLayout`, `GridLayout`, and `BorderLayout`.

2. You can use a `JPanel` as a subcontainer to group components to achieve a desired layout.

3. Use the `add` method to place components in a `JFrame` or a `JPanel`. By default, the frame's layout is `BorderLayout`, and the `JPanel`'s layout is `FlowLayout`.

4. Colors are made of red, green, and blue components, each represented by an unsigned byte value that describes its intensity, ranging from `0` (darkest shade) to `255` (lightest shade). This is known as the *RGB model*.

5. To create a `Color` object, use `new Color(r, g, b)`, in which `r`, `g`, and `b` specify a color by its red, green, and blue components. Alternatively, you can use one of the 13 standard colors (`BLACK`, `BLUE`, `CYAN`, `DARK_GRAY`, `GRAY`, `GREEN`, `LIGHT_GRAY`, `MAGENTA`, `ORANGE`, `PINK`, `RED`, `WHITE`, `YELLOW`) defined as constants in `java.awt.Color`.

6. Every *Swing* GUI component is a subclass of `javax.swing.JComponent`, and `JComponent` is a subclass of `java.awt.Component`. The properties `font`, `background`, `foreground`, `height`, `width`, and `preferredSize` in `Component` are inherited in these subclasses, as are `toolTipText` and `border` in `JComponent`.

7. You can use borders on any Swing components. You can create an image icon using the `ImageIcon` class and display it in a label and a button. Icons and borders can be shared.

8. You can display a text and icon on buttons (`JButton`, `JCheckBox`, `JRadioButton`) and labels (`JLabel`).

9. You can specify the horizontal and vertical text alignment in `JButton`, `JCheckBox`, `JRadioButton`, and `JLabel`, and the horizontal text alignment in `JTextField`.

10. You can specify the horizontal and vertical text position relative to the icon in `JButton`, `JCheckBox`, `JRadioButton`, and `JLabel`.

Test Questions

Do the test questions for this chapter online at **www.cs.armstrong.edu/liang/intro9e/test.html**.

MyProgrammingLab™

Programming Exercises

download image files

Note

The image icons used in the exercises can be obtained from **www.cs.armstrong.edu/liang/intro9e/book.zip** under the image folder.

Sections 12.2–12.6

12.1 (*Use the* `FlowLayout` *manager*) Write a program that meets the following requirements (see Figure 12.26):

- Create a frame and set its layout to `FlowLayout`.
- Create two panels and add them to the frame.
- Each panel contains three buttons. The panel uses `FlowLayout`.

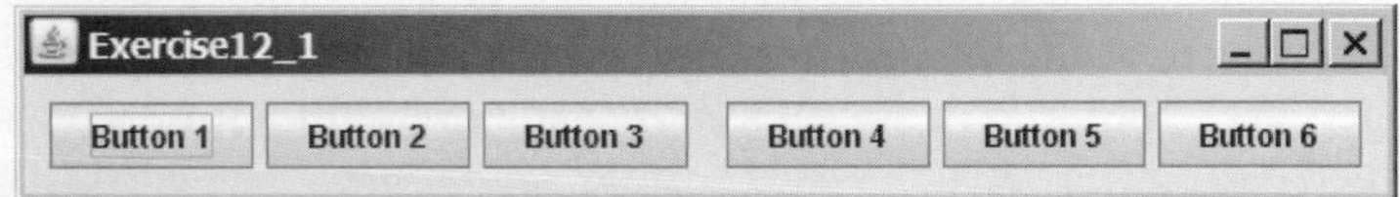

Figure 12.26 Exercise 12.1 places the first three buttons in one panel and the other three buttons in another panel.

12.2 (*Use the* `BorderLayout` *manager*) Rewrite the preceding program to create the same user interface, but instead of using `FlowLayout` for the frame, use `BorderLayout`. Place one panel in the south of the frame and the other in the center.

12.3 (*Use the* `GridLayout` *manager*) Rewrite Programming Exercise 12.1 to add six buttons into a frame. Use a `GridLayout` of two rows and three columns for the frame.

12.4 (*Use* `JPanel` *to group buttons*) Rewrite Programming Exercise 12.1 to create the same user interface. Instead of creating buttons and panels separately, define a class that extends the `JPanel` class. Place three buttons in your panel class, and create two panels from the user-defined panel class.

12.5 (*Display labels*) Write a program that displays four lines of text in four labels, as shown in Figure 12.27a. Add a line border around each label.

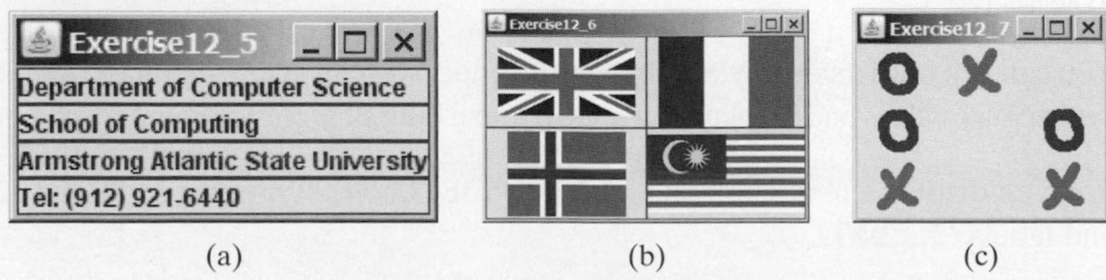

Figure 12.27 (a) Exercise 12.5 displays four labels. (b) Exercise 12.6 displays four icons. (c) Exercise 12.7 displays a tic-tac-toe board with image icons in labels.

Sections 12.7–12.15

12.6 (*Display icons*) Write a program that displays four icons in four labels, as shown in Figure 12.27b. Add a line border around each label.

****12.7** (*Game: display a tic-tac-toe board*) Display a frame that contains nine labels. A label may display an image icon for X or an image icon for O, as shown in Figure 12.27c. What to display is randomly decided. Use the `Math.random()` method to generate an integer `0` or `1`, which corresponds to displaying an X or O image icon. These images are in the files **x.gif** and **o.gif**.

***12.8** (*Swing common features*) Display a frame that contains six labels. Set the background of the labels to white. Set the foreground of the labels to black, blue, cyan, green, magenta, and orange, respectively, as shown in Figure 12.28a. Set the border of each label to a line border with the color yellow. Set the font of each label to Times Roman, bold, and 20 pixels. Set the text and tool tip text of each label to the name of its foreground color.

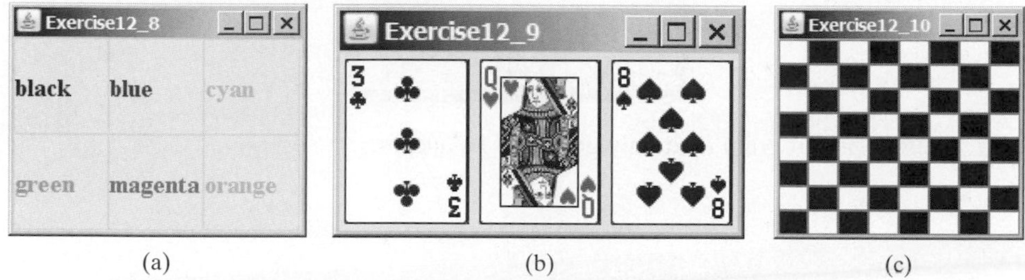

(a) (b) (c)

FIGURE 12.28 (a) Six labels are placed in the frame. (b) Three cards are randomly selected. (c) A checkerboard is displayed using buttons.

***12.9** (*Game: display three cards*) Display a frame that contains three labels. Each label displays a card, as shown in Figure 12.28b. The card image files are named **1.png**, **2.png**, . . ., **54.png** (including jokers) and stored in the **image/card** directory. All three cards are distinct and selected randomly.

***12.10** (*Game: display a checkerboard*) Write a program that displays a checkerboard in which each white and black cell is a `JButton` with a background black or white, as shown in Figure 12.28c.

VideoNote
Display a checkerboard

***12.11** (*Game: display four cards*) Use the same cards from Exercise 12.9 to display a frame that contains four buttons. All buttons have the same icon from **backCard.png**, as shown in Figure 12.29a. The pressed icons are four cards randomly selected from the 54 cards in a deck, as shown in Figure 12.29b.

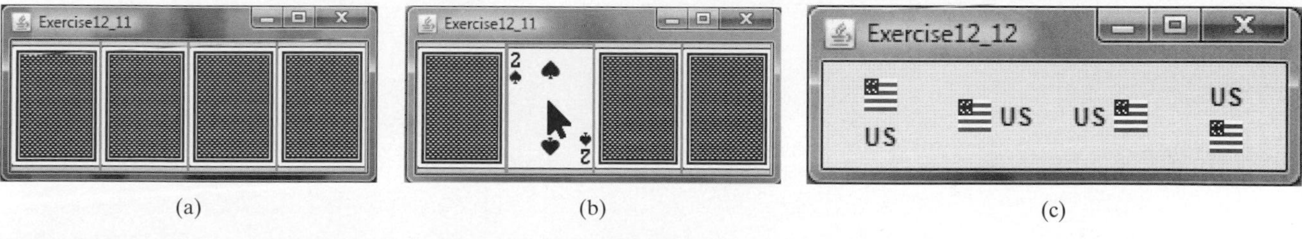

(a) (b) (c)

FIGURE 12.29 (a) The four buttons have the same icon. (b) Each button's pressed icon is randomly picked from the deck. (c) The image icons and texts are displayed in four labels.

12.12 (*Use labels*) Write a program that displays the image icon and the text in four labels, as shown Figure 12.29c.

12.13 (*Display 54 cards*) Expand Exercise 12.9 to display all 54 cards in 54 labels, nine per row.

VideoNote
Display a random matrix

***12.14** (*Display random 0 or 1*) Write a program that displays a 10-by-10 square matrix, as shown in Figure 12.30. Each element in the matrix is `0` or `1`, randomly generated. Display each number centered in a label.

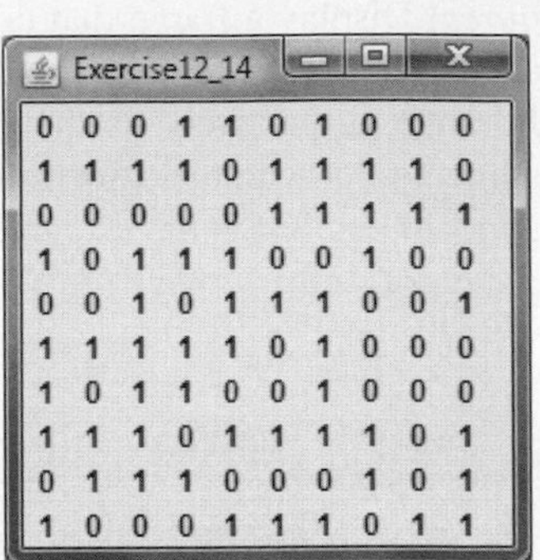

FIGURE 12.30 The program randomly generates 0s and 1s.

CHAPTER

13

GRAPHICS

Objectives

- To draw graphics using the methods in the `Graphics` class (§13.2).
- To override the `paintComponent` method to draw graphics on a GUI component (§13.2).
- To use a panel as a canvas to draw graphics (§13.2).
- To draw strings, lines, rectangles, ovals, arcs, and polygons (§§13.3, 13.5–13.6).
- To obtain font properties using `FontMetrics` and to display a text centered in a panel (§13.7).
- To display an image on a GUI component (§13.10).
- To develop the reusable GUI components `FigurePanel`, `MessagePanel`, `StillClock`, and `ImageViewer` (§§13.4, 13.8, 13.9, 13.11).

13.1 Introduction

You can draw custom shapes on a GUI component.

Problem

Suppose you want to draw shapes such as a bar chart, a clock, or a stop sign, as shown in Figure 13.1. How do you do so?

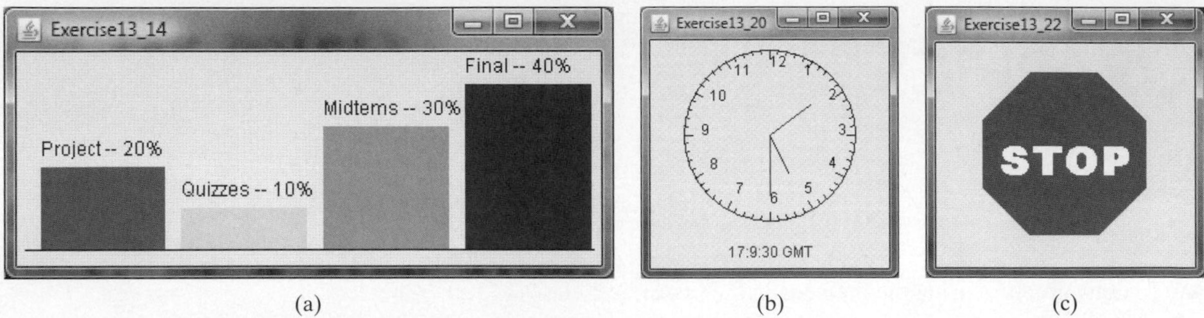

(a) (b) (c)

FIGURE 13.1 You can draw shapes using the drawing methods in the `Graphics` class.

This chapter describes how to use the methods in the `Graphics` class to draw strings, lines, rectangles, ovals, arcs, polygons, and images, and how to develop reusable GUI components.

13.2 The `Graphics` Class

Each GUI component has a graphics context, which is an object of the `Graphics` class. The `Graphics` class contains the methods for drawing various shapes.

The `Graphics` class provides the methods for drawing strings, lines, rectangles, ovals, arcs, polygons, and polylines, as shown in Figure 13.2.

Think of a GUI component as a piece of paper and the `Graphics` object as a pencil or paintbrush. You can apply the methods in the `Graphics` class to draw graphics on a GUI component.

To paint, you need to specify where to paint. Each component has its own coordinate system with the origin (`0`, `0`) at the upper-left corner. The *x*-coordinate increases to the right, and the *y*-coordinate increases downward. Note that the Java coordinate system differs from the conventional coordinate system, as shown in Figure 13.3.

The `Graphics` class–an abstract class—provides a device-independent graphics interface for displaying figures and images on the screen on different platforms. Whenever a component (e.g., a button, a label, or a panel) is displayed, the JVM automatically creates a `Graphics` object for the component on the native platform and passes this object to invoke the `paintComponent` method to display the drawings.

`paintComponent`

The signature of the `paintComponent` method is as follows:

```
protected void paintComponent(Graphics g)
```

This method, defined in the `JComponent` class, is invoked whenever a component is first displayed or redisplayed.

To draw on a component, you need to define a class that extends `JPanel` and overrides its `paintComponent` method to specify what to draw. Listing 13.1 gives an example that draws a line and a string on a panel, as shown in Figure 13.4.

java.awt.Graphics	
`+setColor(color: Color): void`	Sets a new color for subsequent drawings.
`+setFont(font: Font): void`	Sets a new font for subsequent drawings.
`+drawString(s: String, x: int, y: int): void`	Draws a string starting at point `(x, y)`.
`+drawLine(x1: int, y1: int, x2: int, y2: int): void`	Draws a line from `(x1, y1)` to `(x2, y2)`.
`+drawRect(x: int, y: int, w: int, h: int): void`	Draws a rectangle with specified upper-left corner point at `(x,y)` and width `w` and height `h`.
`+fillRect(x: int, y: int, w: int, h: int): void`	Draws a filled rectangle with specified upper-left corner point at `(x, y)` and width `w` and height `h`.
`+drawRoundRect(x: int, y: int, w: int, h: int, aw: int, ah: int): void`	Draws a round-cornered rectangle with specified arc width `aw` and arc height `ah`.
`+fillRoundRect(x: int, y: int, w: int, h: int, aw: int, ah: int): void`	Draws a filled round-cornered rectangle with specified arc width `aw` and arc height `ah`.
`+draw3DRect(x: int, y: int, w: int, h: int, raised: boolean): void`	Draws a 3-D rectangle raised above the surface or sunk into the surface.
`+fill3DRect(x: int, y: int, w: int, h: int, raised: boolean): void`	Draws a filled 3-D rectangle raised above the surface or sunk into the surface.
`+drawOval(x: int, y: int, w: int, h: int): void`	Draws an oval bounded by the rectangle specified by the parameters `x`, `y`, `w`, and `h`.
`+fillOval(x: int, y: int, w: int, h: int): void`	Draws a filled oval bounded by the rectangle specified by the parameters `x`, `y`, `w`, and `h`.
`+drawArc(x: int, y: int, w: int, h: int, startAngle: int, arcAngle: int): void`	Draws an arc conceived as part of an oval bounded by the rectangle specified by the parameters `x`, `y`, `w`, and `h`.
`+fillArc(x: int, y: int, w: int, h: int, startAngle: int, arcAngle: int): void`	Draws a filled arc conceived as part of an oval bounded by the rectangle specified by the parameters `x`, `y`, `w`, and `h`.
`+drawPolygon(xPoints: int[], yPoints: int[], nPoints: int): void`	Draws a closed polygon defined by arrays of `x`- and `y`-coordinates. Each pair of `(x[i], y[i])`-coordinates is a point.
`+fillPolygon(xPoints: int[], yPoints: int[], nPoints: int): void`	Draws a filled polygon defined by arrays of `x`- and `y`-coordinates. Each pair of `(x[i], y[i])`-coordinates is a point.
`+drawPolygon(g: Polygon): void`	Draws a closed polygon defined by a `Polygon` object.
`+fillPolygon(g: Polygon): void`	Draws a filled polygon defined by a `Polygon` object.
`+drawPolyline(xPoints: int[], yPoints: int[], nPoints: int): void`	Draws a polyline defined by arrays of `x`- and `y`-coordinates. Each pair of `(x[i], y[i])`-coordinates is a point.

FIGURE 13.2 The `Graphics` class contains the methods for drawing strings and shapes.

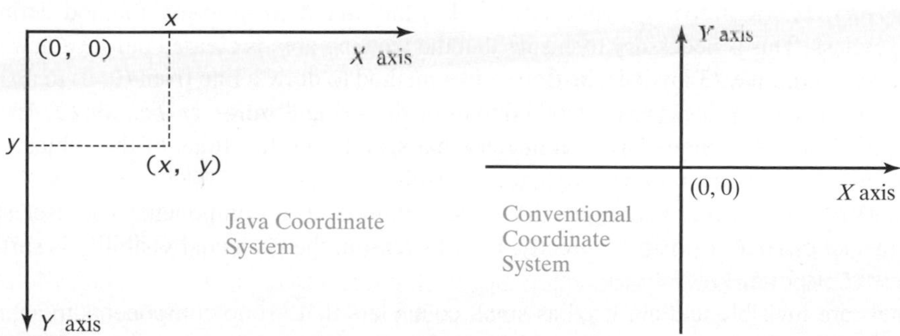

FIGURE 13.3 The Java coordinate system is measured in pixels, with `(0, 0)` at its upper-left corner.

LISTING 13.1 TestPaintComponent.java

```
import javax.swing.*;
import java.awt.Graphics;

```

create a panel

new panel class

override paintComponent

draw things in the superclass

draw line

draw string

```
4  public class TestPaintComponent extends JFrame {
5    public TestPaintComponent() {
6      add(new NewPanel());
7    }
8
9    public static void main(String[] args) {
10     TestPaintComponent frame = new TestPaintComponent();
11     frame.setTitle("TestPaintComponent");
12     frame.setSize(200, 100);
13     frame.setLocationRelativeTo(null); // Center the frame
14     frame.setDefaultCloseOperation(JFrame.EXIT_ON_CLOSE);
15     frame.setVisible(true);
16   }
17 }
18
19 class NewPanel extends JPanel {
20   @Override
21   protected void paintComponent(Graphics g) {
22     super.paintComponent(g);
23     g.drawLine(0, 0, 50, 50);
24     g.drawString("Banner", 0, 40);
25   }
26 }
```

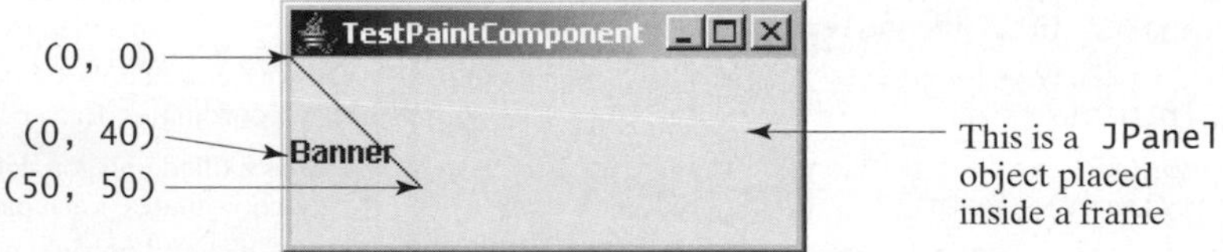

FIGURE 13.4 A line and a string are drawn on a panel.

The `paintComponent` method is automatically invoked to paint graphics when the component is first displayed or whenever the component needs to be redisplayed. Invoking `super.paintComponent(g)` (line 22) invokes the `paintComponent` method defined in the superclass. This is necessary to ensure that the viewing area is cleared before a new drawing is displayed. Line 23 invokes the `drawLine` method to draw a line from (`0`, `0`) to (`50`, `50`). Line 24 invokes the `drawString` method to draw the string `Banner` at location (`0`, `40`).

All the drawing methods have parameters that specify the locations of the subjects to be drawn. In Java, all measurements are made in pixels.

The JVM invokes `paintComponent` to draw things on a component. The user should never invoke `paintComponent` directly. For this reason, the protected visibility is sufficient for `paintComponent`.

Panels are invisible and are used as small containers that group components to achieve a desired layout. Another important use of `JPanel` is for drawing. You can draw things on any Swing GUI component, but normally you should use a `JPanel` as a canvas upon which to draw things. What happens if you replace `JPanel` with `JLabel` in line 19 as follows?

```
class NewPanel extends JLabel {
```

extends JPanel?

The program will work, but it is not preferred, because `JLabel` is designed for creating a label, not for drawing. For consistency, this book will define a canvas class by subclassing `JPanel`.

Tip

Some textbooks define a canvas class by subclassing `JComponent`. The problem with doing that is if you want to set a background in the canvas, you have to write the code to paint the background color. A simple `setBackground(Color color)` method will not set a background color in a `JComponent`.

extends JComponent?

13.1 Suppose that you want to draw a new message below an existing message. Should the *x*-coordinate, *y*-coordinate, or both increase or decrease?

Check Point

MyProgrammingLab™

13.2 How is a `Graphics` object created?

13.3 How is the `paintComponent` method invoked? How can a program invoke this method?

13.4 Why is the `paintComponent` method `protected`? What happens if you change it to `public` or `private` in a subclass? Why is `super.paintComponent(g)` invoked in line 22 in Listing 13.1?

13.5 Can you draw things on any Swing GUI component? Why should you use a panel as a canvas for drawings rather than a label or a button?

13.3 Drawing Strings, Lines, Rectangles, and Ovals

You can draw strings, lines, rectangles, and ovals in a graphics context.

Key Point

drawString

The `drawString(String s, int x, int y)` method draws a string starting at the point `(x, y)`, as shown in Figure 13.5a.

drawLine

The `drawLine(int x1, int y1, int x2, int y2)` method draws a straight line from point `(x1, y1)` to point `(x2, y2)`, as shown in Figure 13.5b.

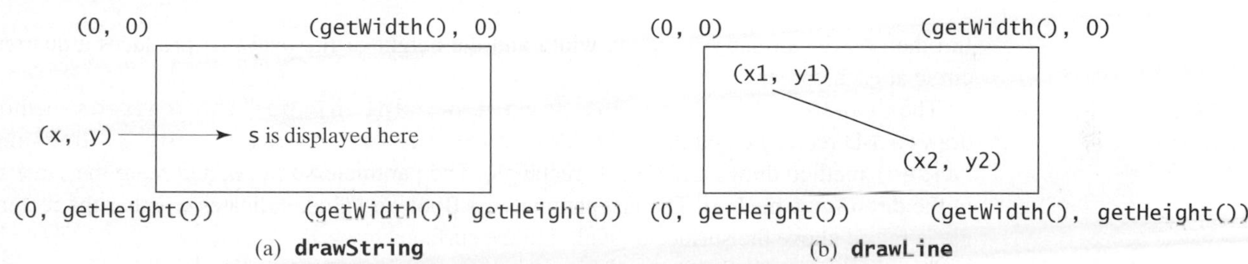

FIGURE 13.5 (a) The `drawString(s, x, y)` method draws a string starting at `(x, y)`. (b) The `drawLine(x1, y1, x2, y2)` method draws a line between two specified points.

Java provides six methods for drawing the outline of rectangles or rectangles filled with color. You can draw or fill plain rectangles, round-cornered rectangles, or three-dimensional rectangles.

drawRect
fillRect

The `drawRect(int x, int y, int w, int h)` method draws a plain rectangle, and the `fillRect(int x, int y, int w, int h)` method draws a filled rectangle. The parameters `x` and `y` represent the upper-left corner of the rectangle, and `w` and `h` are its width and height (see Figure 13.6).

drawRoundRect
fillRoundRect

The `drawRoundRect(int x, int y, int w, int h, int aw, int ah)` method draws a round-cornered rectangle, and the `fillRoundRect(int x, int y, int w, int h, int aw, int ah)` method draws a filled round-cornered rectangle. Parameters `x`, `y`, `w`, and `h` are the same as in the `drawRect` method, parameter `aw` is the horizontal diameter of the arcs at the corner, and `ah` is the vertical diameter of the arcs at the corner (see Figure 13.7a).

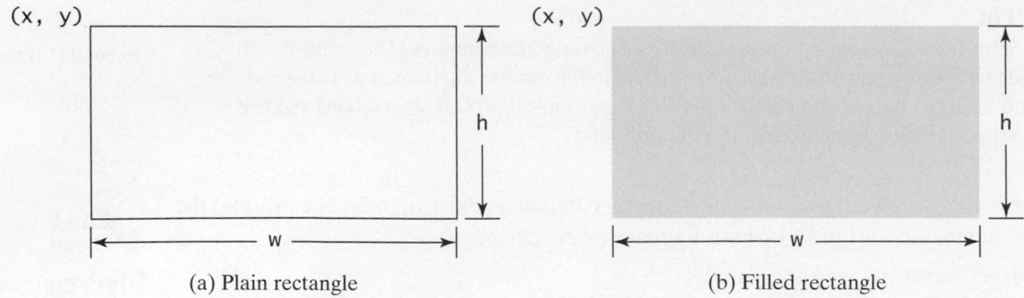

(a) Plain rectangle (b) Filled rectangle

FIGURE 13.6 (a) The `drawRect(x, y, w, h)` method draws a rectangle. (b) The `fillRect(x, y, w, h)` method draws a filled rectangle.

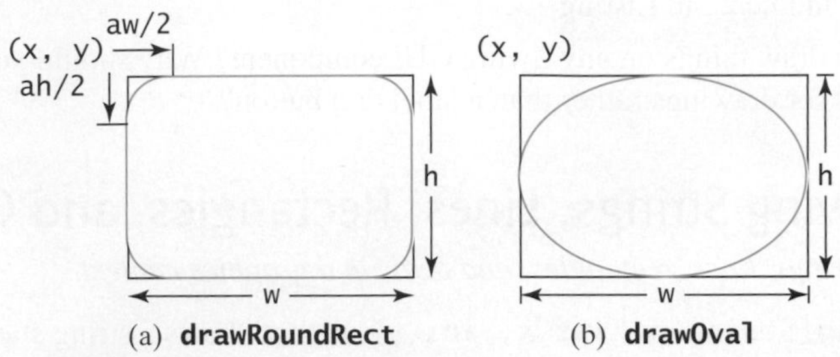

(a) **drawRoundRect** (b) **drawOval**

FIGURE 13.7 (a) The `drawRoundRect(x, y, w, h, aw, ah)` method draws a round-cornered rectangle. (b) The `drawOval(x, y, w, h)` method draws an oval based on its bounding rectangle.

In other words, `aw` and `ah` arc the width and the height of the oval that produces a quarter-circle at each corner.

draw3DRect
fill3DRect

The `draw3DRect(int x, int y, int w, int h, boolean raised)` method draws a 3-D rectangle and the `fill3DRect(int x, int y, int w, int h, boolean raised)` method draws a filled 3-D rectangle. The parameters `x`, `y`, `w`, and `h` are the same as in the `drawRect` method. The last parameter, a Boolean value, indicates whether the rectangle is raised above the surface or sunk into the surface.

drawOval
fillOval

Depending on whether you wish to draw an oval in outline or filled solid, you can use either the `drawOval(int x, int y, int w, int h)` method or the `fillOval(int x, int y, int w, int h)` method. An oval is drawn based on its bounding rectangle. Parameters `x` and `y` indicate the top-left corner of the bounding rectangle, and `w` and `h` indicate the width and height, respectively, of the bounding rectangle, as shown in Figure 13.7b.

MyProgrammingLab™

13.6 Describe the methods for drawing strings, lines, and the methods for drawing/filling rectangles, round-cornered rectangles, 3-D rectangles, and ovals.

13.7 Draw a thick line from (10, 10) to (70, 30). You can draw several lines next to each other to create the effect of one thick line.

13.8 Draw/fill a rectangle of width 100 and height 50 with the upper-left corner at (10, 10).

13.9 Draw/fill a round-cornered rectangle with width 100, height 200, corner horizontal diameter 40, and corner vertical diameter 20.

13.10 Draw/fill a circle with radius 30.

13.11 Draw/fill an oval with width 50 and height 100.

13.4 Case Study: The FigurePanel Class

This case study develops the `FigurePanel` *class for displaying various figures.*

Key Point

This example develops a useful class for displaying various figures. The class enables the user to set the figure type and specify whether the figure is filled, and it displays the figure on a panel. The UML diagram for the class is shown in Figure 13.8. The panel can display lines, rectangles, round-cornered rectangles, and ovals. Which figure to display is decided by the `type` property. If the `filled` property is `true`, the rectangle, round-cornered rectangle, and oval are filled in the panel.

VideoNote
The `FigurePanel` class

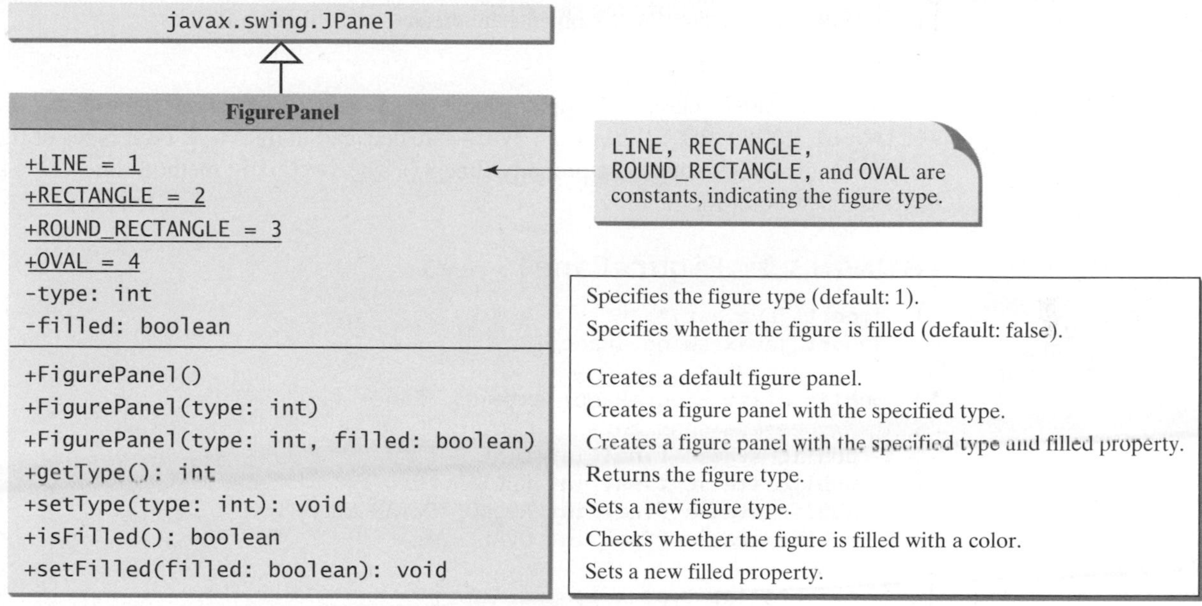

FIGURE 13.8 `FigurePanel` displays various types of figures on the panel.

The UML diagram serves as the contract for the `FigurePanel` class. The user can use the class without knowing how the class is implemented. Let us begin by writing a program in Listing 13.2 that uses the class to display six figure panels, as shown in Figure 13.9.

LISTING 13.2 `TestFigurePanel.java`

```
import java.awt.*;
import javax.swing.*;

public class TestFigurePanel extends JFrame {
  public TestFigurePanel() {
    setLayout(new GridLayout(2, 3, 5, 5));
    add(new FigurePanel(FigurePanel.LINE));
    add(new FigurePanel(FigurePanel.RECTANGLE));
    add(new FigurePanel(FigurePanel.ROUND_RECTANGLE));
    add(new FigurePanel(FigurePanel.OVAL));
    add(new FigurePanel(FigurePanel.RECTANGLE, true));
    add(new FigurePanel(FigurePanel.ROUND_RECTANGLE, true));
  }

  public static void main(String[] args) {
    TestFigurePanel frame = new TestFigurePanel();
    frame.setSize(400, 200);
    frame.setTitle("TestFigurePanel");
```

create figures

```
      frame.setLocationRelativeTo(null); // Center the frame
      frame.setDefaultCloseOperation(JFrame.EXIT_ON_CLOSE);
      frame.setVisible(true);
    }
  }
```

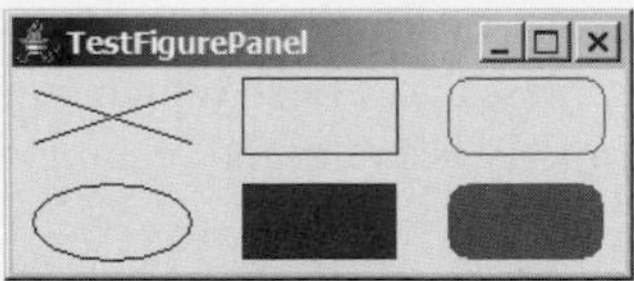

FIGURE 13.9 Six `FigurePanel` objects are created to display six figures.

The `FigurePanel` class is implemented in Listing 13.3. Four constants—`LINE`, `RECTANGLE`, `ROUND_RECTANGLE`, and `OVAL`—are declared in lines 6–9. Four types of figures are drawn according to the `type` property (line 37). The `setColor` method (lines 39, 44, 53, 62) sets a new color for the drawing.

LISTING 13.3 FigurePanel.java

```
 1  import java.awt.*;
 2  import javax.swing.JPanel;
 3
 4  public class FigurePanel extends JPanel {
 5    // Declare constants
 6    public static final int LINE = 1;                     constants
 7    public static final int RECTANGLE = 2;
 8    public static final int ROUND_RECTANGLE = 3;
 9    public static final int OVAL = 4;
10
11    private int type = 1;
12    private boolean filled = false;
13
14    /** Construct a default FigurePanel */
15    public FigurePanel() {
16    }
17
18    /** Construct a FigurePanel with the specified type */
19    public FigurePanel(int type) {
20      this.type = type;
21    }
22
23    /** Construct a FigurePanel with the specified type and filled */
24    public FigurePanel(int type, boolean filled) {
25      this.type = type;
26      this.filled = filled;
27    }
28
29    @Override // Draw a figure on the panel
30    protected void paintComponent(Graphics g) {           override paintComponent(g)
31      super.paintComponent(g);
32
33      // Get the appropriate size for the figure
34      int width = getWidth();
35      int height = getHeight();
36
37      switch (type) {                                     check type
38        case LINE: // Display two cross lines
```

```
        g.setColor(Color.BLACK);
        g.drawLine(10, 10, width - 10, height - 10);
        g.drawLine(width - 10, 10, 10, height - 10);
        break;
      case RECTANGLE: // Display a rectangle
        g.setColor(Color.BLUE);
        if (filled)
          g.fillRect((int)(0.1 * width), (int)(0.1 * height),
            (int)(0.8 * width), (int)(0.8 * height));
        else
          g.drawRect((int)(0.1 * width), (int)(0.1 * height),
            (int)(0.8 * width), (int)(0.8 * height));
        break;
      case ROUND_RECTANGLE: // Display a round-cornered rectangle
        g.setColor(Color.RED);
        if (filled)
          g.fillRoundRect((int)(0.1 * width), (int)(0.1 * height),
            (int)(0.8 * width), (int)(0.8 * height), 20, 20);
        else
          g.drawRoundRect((int)(0.1 * width), (int)(0.1 * height),
            (int)(0.8 * width), (int)(0.8 * height), 20, 20);
        break;
      case OVAL: // Display an oval
        g.setColor(Color.BLACK);
        if (filled)
          g.fillOval((int)(0.1 * width), (int)(0.1 * height),
            (int)(0.8 * width), (int)(0.8 * height));
        else
          g.drawOval((int)(0.1 * width), (int)(0.1 * height),
            (int)(0.8 * width), (int)(0.8 * height));
    }
  }

  /** Set a new figure type */
  public void setType(int type) {
    this.type = type;
    repaint();
  }

  /** Return figure type */
  public int getType() {
    return type;
  }

  /** Set a new filled property */
  public void setFilled(boolean filled) {
    this.filled = filled;
    repaint();
  }

  /** Check if the figure is filled */
  public boolean isFilled() {
    return filled;
  }

  @Override // Specify preferred size
  public Dimension getPreferredSize() {
    return new Dimension(80, 80);
  }
}
```

draw lines

fill a rectangle

draw a rectangle

fill round-cornered rect

draw round-cornered rect

fill an oval

draw an oval

repaint panel

repaint panel

override `getPreferredSize()`

The repaint method (lines 75, 86) is defined in the Component class. Invoking repaint causes the paintComponent method to be called. The repaint method is invoked to refresh the viewing area. Typically, you call it if you have new things to display.

don't invoke paintComponent

Caution

The paintComponent method should never be invoked directly. It is invoked either by the JVM whenever the viewing area changes or by the repaint method. You should override the paintComponent method to tell the system how to paint the viewing area, but never override the repaint method.

request repaint using repaint()

Note

The repaint method lodges a request to update the viewing area and returns immediately. Its effect is asynchronous, meaning that it is up to the JVM to execute the paintComponent method on a separate thread.

why override getPreferredSize()?

The getPreferredSize() method (lines 95–97), defined in Component, is overridden in FigurePanel to specify the preferred size for the layout manager to consider when laying out a FigurePanel object. This property may or may not be considered by the layout manager, depending on its rules. For example, a component uses its preferred size in a container with a FlowLayout manager, but its preferred size is ignored if it is placed in a container with a GridLayout manager. It is a good practice to override getPreferredSize() in a subclass of JPanel to specify a preferred size, because the default width and height for a JPanel is 0. You will see nothing if a JPanel component with a default 0 width and height is placed in a FlowLayout container.

13.12 Why should you override the preferredSize method in a subclass of JPanel?

13.13 How do you get and set colors and fonts in a Graphics object?

MyProgrammingLab™

13.5 Drawing Arcs

An arc is conceived as part of an oval bounded by a rectangle.

The methods to draw or fill an arc are as follows:

```
drawArc(int x, int y, int w, int h, int startAngle, int arcAngle)
fillArc(int x, int y, int w, int h, int startAngle, int arcAngle)
```

Parameters x, y, w, and h are the same as in the drawOval method; parameter startAngle is the starting angle; and arcAngle is the spanning angle (i.e., the angle covered by the arc). Angles are measured in degrees and follow the usual mathematical conventions (i.e., 0 degrees is in the easterly direction, and positive angles indicate counterclockwise rotation from the easterly direction); see Figure 13.10.

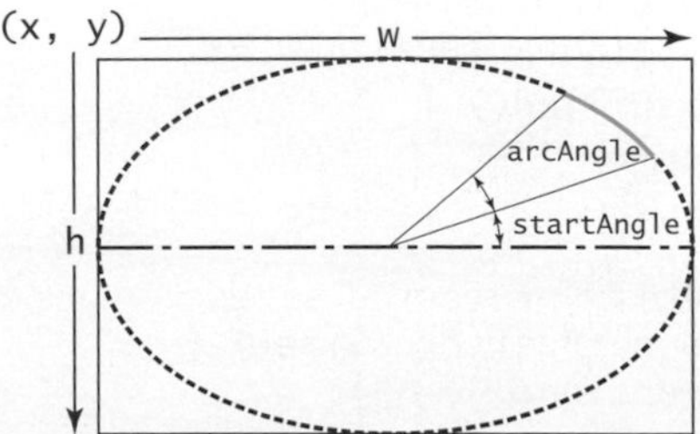

FIGURE 13.10 The drawArc method draws an arc based on an oval with specified angles.

Listing 13.4 is an example of how to draw arcs; the output is shown in Figure 13.11.

LISTING 13.4 DrawArcs.java

```
import javax.swing.JFrame;
import javax.swing.JPanel;
import java.awt.Graphics;

public class DrawArcs extends JFrame {
  public DrawArcs() {
    setTitle("DrawArcs");
    add(new ArcsPanel());
  }

  /** Main method */
  public static void main(String[] args) {
    DrawArcs frame = new DrawArcs();
    frame.setSize(250, 300);
    frame.setLocationRelativeTo(null); // Center the frame
    frame.setDefaultCloseOperation(JFrame.EXIT_ON_CLOSE);
    frame.setVisible(true);
  }
}

// The class for drawing arcs on a panel
class ArcsPanel extends JPanel {
  @Override // Draw four blades of a fan
  protected void paintComponent(Graphics g) {
    super.paintComponent(g);

    int xCenter = getWidth() / 2;
    int yCenter = getHeight() / 2;
    int radius = (int)(Math.min(getWidth(), getHeight()) * 0.4);

    int x = xCenter - radius;
    int y = yCenter - radius;

    g.fillArc(x, y, 2 * radius, 2 * radius, 0, 30);
    g.fillArc(x, y, 2 * radius, 2 * radius, 90, 30);
    g.fillArc(x, y, 2 * radius, 2 * radius, 180, 30);
    g.fillArc(x, y, 2 * radius, 2 * radius, 270, 30);
  }
}
```

add a panel

override paintComponent

30° arc from 0°

30° arc from 90°

30° arc from 180°

30° arc from 270°

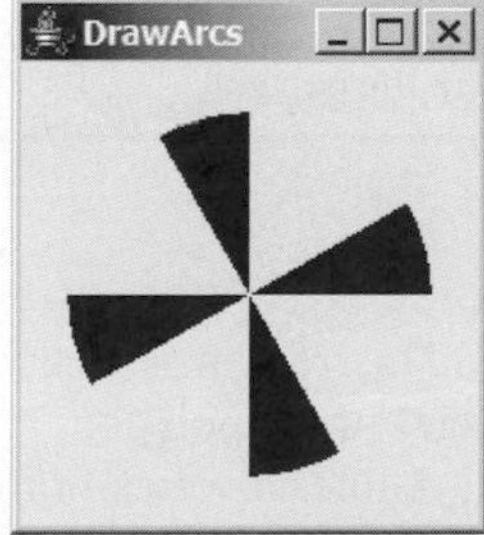

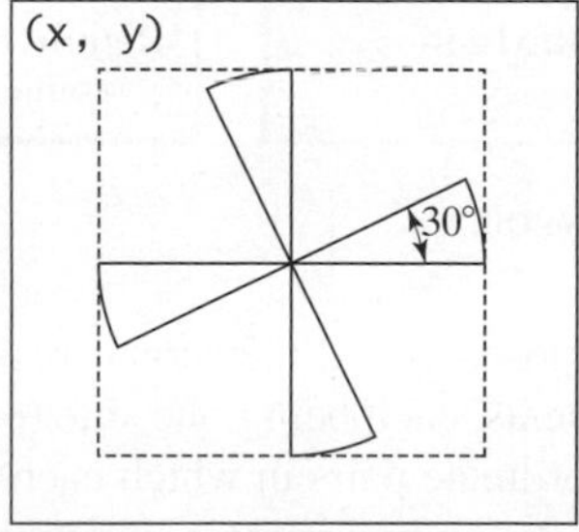

FIGURE 13.11 The program draws four filled arcs.

negative degrees

Angles may be negative. A negative starting angle sweeps clockwise from the easterly direction, as shown in Figure 13.12. A negative spanning angle sweeps clockwise from the starting angle. The following two statements draw the same arc:

```
g.fillArc(x, y, 2 * radius, 2 * radius, -30, -20);
g.fillArc(x, y, 2 * radius, 2 * radius, -50, 20);
```

The first statement uses negative starting angle `-30` and negative spanning angle `-20`, as shown in Figure 13.12a. The second statement uses negative starting angle `-50` and positive spanning angle `20`, as shown in Figure 13.12b.

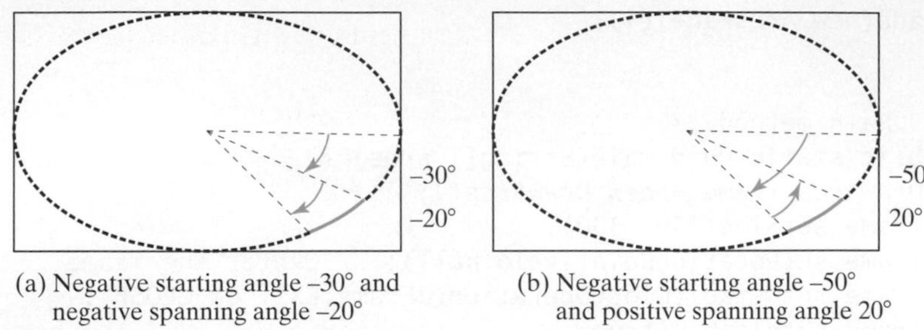

(a) Negative starting angle –30° and negative spanning angle –20°

(b) Negative starting angle –50° and positive spanning angle 20°

FIGURE 13.12 Angles may be negative.

Check Point

MyProgrammingLab™

13.14 Describe the methods for drawing/filling arcs.

13.15 Draw the upper half of a circle with radius `50`.

13.16 Fill the lower half of a circle with radius `50` using the red color.

13.6 Drawing Polygons and Polylines

Key Point

You can draw a polygon or a polyline that connects a set of points.

To draw a polygon, first create a `Polygon` object using the `Polygon` class, as shown in Figure 13.13.

java.awt.Polygon	
+xpoints: int[]	x-coordinates of all points in the polygon.
+ypoints: int[]	y-coordinates of all points in the polygon.
+npoints: int	The number of points in the polygon.
+Polygon()	Creates an empty polygon.
+Polygon(xpoints: int[], ypoints: int[], npoints: int)	Creates a polygon with the specified points.
+addPoint(x: int, y: int): void	Appends a point to the polygon.
+contains(x: int, y: int): boolean	Returns true if the specified point (x, y) is contained in the polygon.

FIGURE 13.13 The `Polygon` class models a polygon.

A polygon is a closed two-dimensional region. This region is bounded by an arbitrary number of line segments, each being one side (or edge) of the polygon. A polygon comprises a list of `(x, y)`-coordinate pairs in which each pair defines a vertex of the polygon, and two successive pairs are the endpoints of a line that is a side of the polygon. The first and final points are joined by a line segment that closes the polygon.

Here is an example of creating a polygon and adding points into it:

```
Polygon polygon = new Polygon();
polygon.addPoint(40, 20);
polygon.addPoint(70, 40);
polygon.addPoint(60, 80);
polygon.addPoint(45, 45);
polygon.addPoint(20, 60);
```

After these points are added, **xpoints** is {40, 70, 60, 45, 20}, **ypoints** is {20, 40, 80, 45, 60}, and **npoints** is 5. **xpoints**, **ypoints**, and **npoints** are public data fields in **Polygon**, which is a bad design. If the user changes a **Polygon**'s **npoints** data field without properly changing its **xpoints** and **ypoints** data fields, this will cause inconsistent data in the **Polygon** object.

To draw or fill a polygon, use one of the following methods in the **Graphics** class:

```
drawPolygon(Polygon polygon);
fillPolygon(Polygon polygon);

drawPolygon(int[] xpoints, int[] ypoints, int npoints);
fillPolygon(int[] xpoints, int[] ypoints, int npoints);
```

For example:

```
int x[] = {40, 70, 60, 45, 20};
int y[] = {20, 40, 80, 45, 60};
g.drawPolygon(x, y, x.length);
```

The drawing method opens the polygon by drawing lines between point **(x[i], y[i])** and point **(x[i+1], y[i+1])** for **i = 0, ... , x.length-1**; it closes the polygon by drawing a line between the first and last points (see Figure 13.14a).

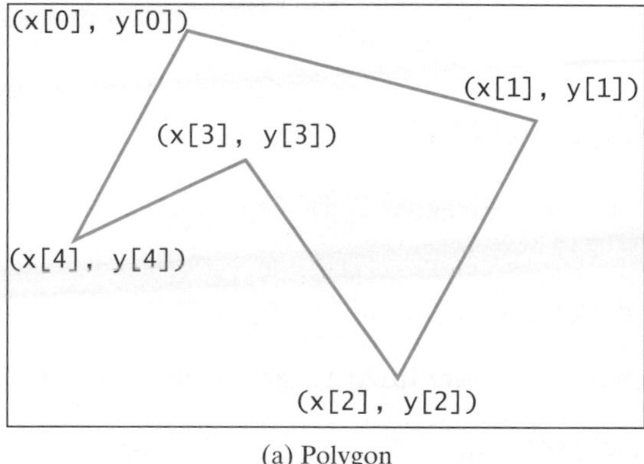

(a) Polygon

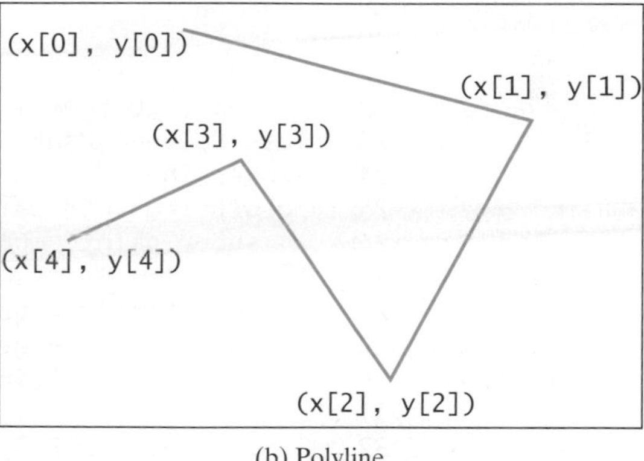

(b) Polyline

FIGURE 13.14 The **drawPolygon** method draws a polygon, and the **drawPolyLine** method draws a polyline.

To draw a polyline, use the **drawPolyline(int[] x, int[] y, int nPoints)** method, which draws a sequence of connected lines defined by arrays of *x*- and *y*-coordinates. For example, the following code draws the polyline like the one shown in Figure 13.14b.

```
int x[] = {40, 70, 60, 45, 20};
int y[] = {20, 40, 80, 45, 60};
g.drawPolyline(x, y, x.length);
```

Listing 13.5 is an example of how to draw a hexagon, with the output shown in Figure 13.15.

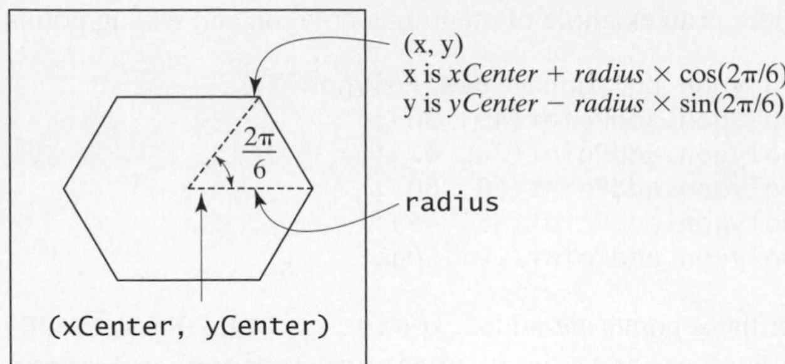

Figure 13.15 The program uses the **drawPolygon** method to draw a hexagon.

Listing 13.5 DrawPolygon.java

add a panel
paintComponent
add a point

```
import javax.swing.JFrame;
import javax.swing.JPanel;
import java.awt.Graphics;
import java.awt.Polygon;

public class DrawPolygon extends JFrame {
  public DrawPolygon() {
    setTitle("DrawPolygon");
    add(new PolygonsPanel());
  }

  /** Main method */
  public static void main(String[] args) {
    DrawPolygon frame = new DrawPolygon();
    frame.setSize(200, 250);
    frame.setLocationRelativeTo(null); // Center the frame
    frame.setDefaultCloseOperation(JFrame.EXIT_ON_CLOSE);
    frame.setVisible(true);
  }
}

// Draw a polygon in the panel
class PolygonsPanel extends JPanel {
  @Override
  protected void paintComponent(Graphics g) {
    super.paintComponent(g);

    int xCenter = getWidth() / 2;
    int yCenter = getHeight() / 2;
    int radius = (int)(Math.min(getWidth(), getHeight()) * 0.4);

    // Create a Polygon object
    Polygon polygon = new Polygon();

    // Add points to the polygon in this order
    polygon.addPoint(xCenter + radius, yCenter);
    polygon.addPoint ((int)(xCenter + radius *
      Math.cos(2 * Math.PI / 6)), (int)(yCenter - radius *
      Math.sin(2 * Math.PI / 6)));
    polygon.addPoint((int)(xCenter + radius *
      Math.cos(2 * 2 * Math.PI / 6)), (int)(yCenter - radius *
      Math.sin(2 * 2 * Math.PI / 6)));
    polygon.addPoint((int)(xCenter + radius *
      Math.cos(3 * 2 * Math.PI / 6)), (int)(yCenter - radius *
      Math.sin(3 * 2 * Math.PI / 6)));
```

```
      polygon.addPoint((int)(xCenter + radius *
        Math.cos(4 * 2 * Math.PI / 6)), (int)(yCenter - radius *
        Math.sin(4 * 2 * Math.PI / 6)));
      polygon.addPoint((int)(xCenter + radius *
        Math.cos(5 * 2 * Math.PI / 6)), (int)(yCenter - radius *
        Math.sin(5 * 2 * Math.PI / 6)));

      // Draw the polygon
      g.drawPolygon(polygon);
    }
  }
```

draw polygon

MyProgrammingLab™

13.17 Draw a polygon connecting the following points: (20, 40), (30, 50), (40, 90), (90, 10), (10, 30).

13.18 Create a `Polygon` object and add points (20, 40), (30, 50), (40, 90), (90, 10), (10, 30) in this order. Fill the polygon with the red color. Draw a polyline with a yellow color to connect all these points.

13.7 Centering a String Using the `FontMetrics` Class

You can use the `FontMetrics` class to measure the width and height of a string in the graphics context.

You can display a string at any location in a panel. Can you display it centered? Yes; to do so, you need to use the `FontMetrics` class to measure the exact width and height of the string for a particular font. `FontMetrics` can measure the following attributes for a given font (see Figure 13.16):

- **Leading,** pronounced *ledding*, is the amount of space between lines of text.
- **Ascent** is the distance from the baseline to the ascent line. The top of most characters in the font will be under the ascent line, but some may extend above the ascent line.
- **Descent** is the distance from the baseline to the descent line. The bottom of most descending characters (e.g., *j*, *y*, and *g*) in the font will be above the descent line, but some may extend below the descent line.
- **Height** is the sum of leading, ascent, and descent.

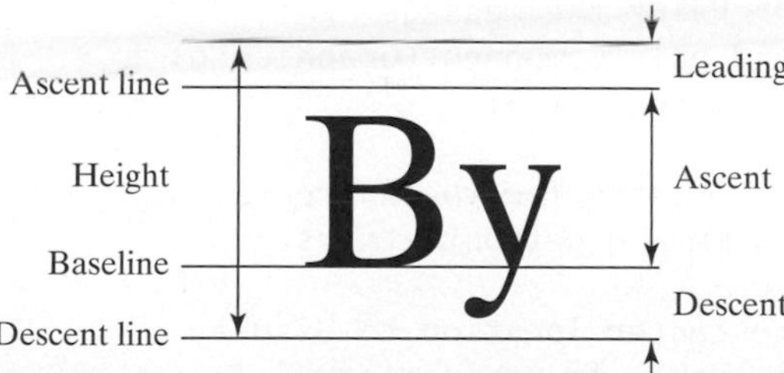

FIGURE 13.16 The `FontMetrics` class can be used to determine the font properties of characters for a given font.

`FontMetrics` is an abstract class. To get a `FontMetrics` object for a specific font, use the following `getFontMetrics` methods defined in the `Graphics` class:

- `public FontMetrics getFontMetrics(Font font)`

This method returns the font metrics of the specified font.

- `public FontMetrics getFontMetrics()`

This method returns the font metrics of the current font.

You can use the following instance methods in the **FontMetrics** class to obtain the attributes of a font and the width of a string when it is drawn using the font:

```
public int getAscent() // Return the ascent
public int getDescent() // Return the descent
public int getLeading() // Return the leading
public int getHeight() // Return the height
public int stringWidth(String str) // Return the width of the string
```

Listing 13.6 gives an example that displays a message in the center of the panel, as shown in Figure 13.17.

LISTING 13.6 TestCenterMessage.java

create a message panel
add a message panel
set background
set font
override paintComponent
get FontMetrics

```
import javax.swing.*;
import java.awt.*;

public class TestCenterMessage extends JFrame {
  public TestCenterMessage() {
    CenterMessage messagePanel = new CenterMessage();
    add(messagePanel);
    messagePanel.setBackground(Color.WHITE);
    messagePanel.setFont(new Font("Californian FB", Font.BOLD, 30));
  }

  /** Main method */
  public static void main(String[] args) {
    TestCenterMessage frame = new TestCenterMessage();
    frame.setSize(300, 150);
    frame.setTitle("CenterMessage");
    frame.setLocationRelativeTo(null); // Center the frame
    frame.setDefaultCloseOperation(JFrame.EXIT_ON_CLOSE);
    frame.setVisible(true);
  }
}

class CenterMessage extends JPanel {
  @Override /** Paint the message */
  protected void paintComponent(Graphics g) {
    super.paintComponent(g);

    // Get font metrics for the current font
    FontMetrics fm = g.getFontMetrics();

    // Find the center location to display
    int stringWidth = fm.stringWidth("Welcome to Java");
    int stringAscent = fm.getAscent();

    // Get the position of the leftmost character in the baseline
    int xCoordinate = getWidth() / 2 - stringWidth / 2;
    int yCoordinate = getHeight() / 2 + stringAscent / 2;

    g.drawString("Welcome to Java", xCoordinate, yCoordinate);
  }
}
```

FIGURE 13.17 The program uses the `FontMetrics` class to measure the string width and height and displays it at the center of the panel.

The methods `getWidth()` and `getHeight()` (lines 36–37) defined in the `Component` class return the component's width and height, respectively.

Since the message is `centered`, the first character of the string should be positioned at (`xCoordinate`, `yCoordinate`), as shown in Figure 13.17.

13.19 How do you find the leading, ascent, descent, and height of a font?

13.20 How do you find the exact length in pixels of a string in a `Graphics` object?

Check Point
MyProgrammingLab™

13.8 Case Study: The MessagePanel Class

Key Point

This case study develops a useful class that displays a message in a panel. The class enables the user to set the location of the message, center the message, and move the message a specified interval.

VideoNote
The MessagePanel class

The contract of the `MessagePanel` class is shown in Figure 13.18.

Let us first write a test program in Listing 13.7 that uses the `MessagePanel` class to display four message panels, as shown in Figure 13.19.

LISTING 13.7 TestMessagePanel.java

```
import java.awt.*;
import javax.swing.*;

public class TestMessagePanel extends JFrame {
  public TestMessagePanel() {
    MessagePanel messagePanel1 = new MessagePanel("Welcome to Java");
    MessagePanel messagePanel2 = new MessagePanel("Java is fun");
    MessagePanel messagePanel3 = new MessagePanel("Java is cool");
    MessagePanel messagePanel4 = new MessagePanel("I love Java");
    messagePanel1.setFont(new Font("SansSerif", Font.ITALIC, 20));
    messagePanel2.setFont(new Font("Courier", Font.BOLD, 20));
    messagePanel3.setFont(new Font("Times", Font.ITALIC, 20));
    messagePanel4.setFont(new Font("Californian FB", Font.PLAIN, 20));
    messagePanel1.setBackground(Color.RED);
    messagePanel2.setBackground(Color.CYAN);
    messagePanel3.setBackground(Color.GREEN);
    messagePanel4.setBackground(Color.WHITE);
```

create message panel
set font
set background

add message panel

```
    messagePanel1.setCentered(true);

    setLayout(new GridLayout(2, 2));
    add(messagePanel1);
    add(messagePanel2);
    add(messagePanel3);
    add(messagePanel4);
  }

  public static void main(String[] args) {
    TestMessagePanel frame = new TestMessagePanel();
    frame.setSize(300, 200);
    frame.setTitle("TestMessagePanel");
    frame.setLocationRelativeTo(null); // Center the frame
    frame.setDefaultCloseOperation(JFrame.EXIT_ON_CLOSE);
    frame.setVisible(true);
  }
}
```

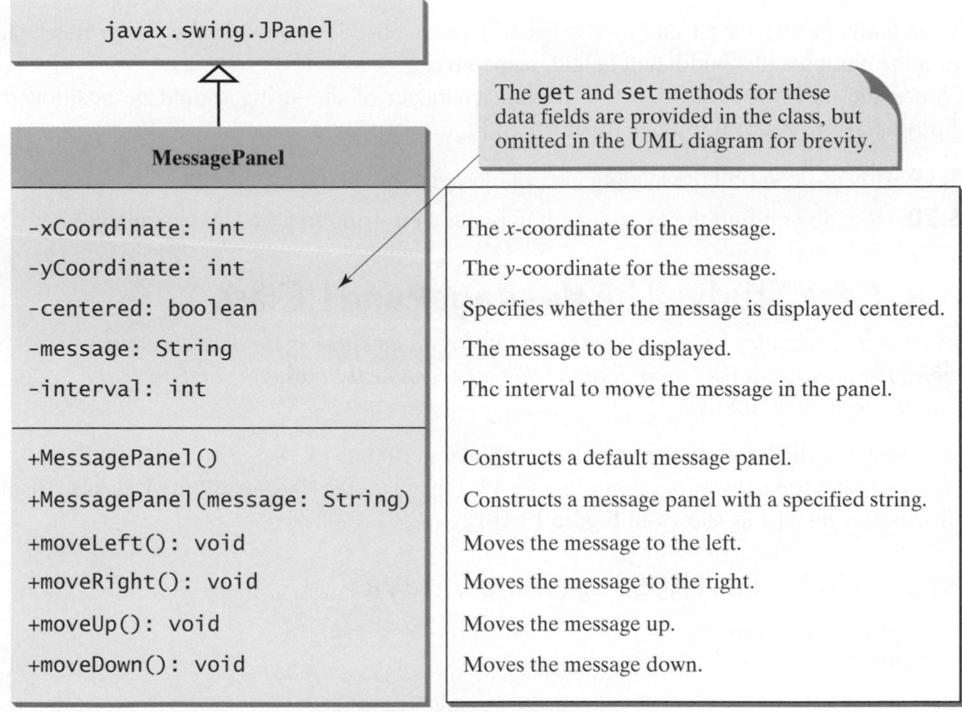

FIGURE 13.18 `MessagePanel` displays a message on the panel.

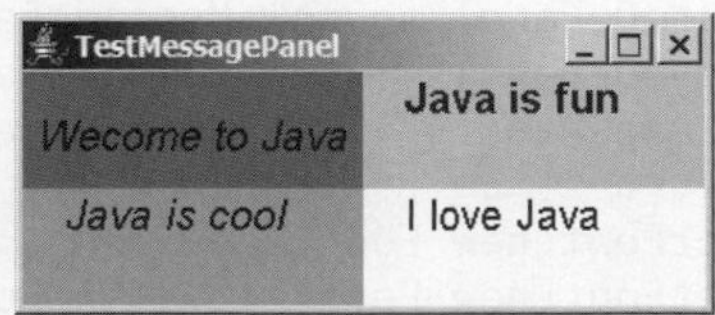

FIGURE 13.19 `TestMessagePanel` uses `MessagePanel` to display four message panels.

skip implementation?

The rest of this section explains how to implement the `MessagePanel` class. Since you can use the class without knowing how it is implemented, you may skip the implementation if you wish.

The `MessagePanel` class is implemented in Listing 13.8. The program seems long but is actually simple, because most of the methods are **get** and **set** methods, and each method is relatively short and easy to read.

LISTING 13.8 MessagePanel.java

```
import java.awt.FontMetrics;
import java.awt.Dimension;
import java.awt.Graphics;
import javax.swing.JPanel;

public class MessagePanel extends JPanel {
  /** The message to be displayed */
  private String message = "Welcome to Java";

  /** The x-coordinate where the message is displayed */
  private int xCoordinate = 20;

  /** The y-coordinate where the message is displayed */
  private int yCoordinate = 20;

  /** Indicate whether the message is displayed in the center */
  private boolean centered;

  /** The interval for moving the message horizontally
    * and vertically */
  private int interval = 10;

  /** Construct with default properties */
  public MessagePanel() {
  }

  /** Construct a message panel with a specified message */
  public MessagePanel(String message) {
    this.message = message;
  }

  /** Return message */
  public String getMessage() {
    return message;
  }

  /** Set a new message */
  public void setMessage(String message) {
    this.message = message;
    repaint();
  }

  /** Return xCoordinator */
  public int getXCoordinate() {
    return xCoordinate;
  }

  /** Set a new xCoordinator */
  public void setXCoordinate(int x) {
    this.xCoordinate = x;
    repaint();
  }

  /** Return yCoordinator */
```

repaint panel

repaint panel

```
  public int getYCoordinate() {
    return yCoordinate;
  }

  /** Set a new yCoordinator */
  public void setYCoordinate(int y) {
    this.yCoordinate = y;
```

repaint panel

```
    repaint();
  }

  /** Return centered */
  public boolean isCentered() {
    return centered;
  }

  /** Set true or false to tell whether the message is centered */
  public void setCentered(boolean centered) {
    this.centered = centered;
```

repaint panel

```
    repaint();
  }

  /** Return interval */
  public int getInterval() {
    return interval;
  }

  /** Set a new interval */
  public void setInterval(int interval) {
    this.interval = interval;
```

repaint panel

```
    repaint();
  }

```

override paintComponent

```
  @Override /** Paint the message */
  protected void paintComponent(Graphics g) {
    super.paintComponent(g);

```

check centered

```
    if (centered) {
      // Get font metrics for the current font
      FontMetrics fm = g.getFontMetrics();

      // Find the center location to display
      int stringWidth = fm.stringWidth(message);
      int stringAscent = fm.getAscent();
      // Get the position of the leftmost character in the baseline
      xCoordinate = getWidth() / 2 - stringWidth / 2;
      yCoordinate = getHeight() / 2 + stringAscent / 2;
    }

    g.drawString(message, xCoordinate, yCoordinate);
  }

  /** Move the message left */
  public void moveLeft() {
    xCoordinate -= interval;
    repaint();
  }

  /** Move the message right */
  public void moveRight() {
    xCoordinate += interval;
```

```
115      repaint();
116    }
117
118    /** Move the message up */
119    public void moveUp() {
120      yCoordinate -= interval;
121      repaint();
122    }
123
124    /** Move the message down */
125    public void moveDown() {
126      yCoordinate += interval;
127      repaint();
128    }
129
130    @Override /** Override get method for preferredSize */
131    public Dimension getPreferredSize() {
132      return new Dimension(200, 30);
133    }
134  }
```

override `getPreferredSize`

The `paintComponent` method displays the message centered, if the `centered` property is `true` (line 91). `message` is initialized to `Welcome to Java` in line 8. If it were not initialized, a `NullPointerException` runtime error would occur when you created a `MessagePanel` using the no-arg constructor, because `message` would be `null` in line 103.

Caution

The `MessagePanel` class uses the properties `xCoordinate` and `yCoordinate` to specify the position of the message displayed on the panel. Do not use the property names `x` and `y`, because they are already defined in the `Component` class to return the position of the component in the parent's coordinate system using `getX()` and `getY()`.

Note

The `Component` class has the `setBackground`, `setForeground`, and `setFont` methods. These methods are for setting colors and fonts for the entire component. If you wanted to draw several messages in a panel with different colors and fonts, you would have to use the `setColor` and `setFont` methods in the `Graphics` class to set the color and font for the current drawing.

Note

design classes for reuse

A key feature of Java programming is the reuse of classes. Throughout this book, reusable classes are developed and later reused. `MessagePanel` is an example, as are `Loan` in Listing 10.2 and `FigurePanel` in Listing 13.3. `MessagePanel` can be reused whenever you need to display a message on a panel. To make your class reusable in a wide range of applications, you should provide a variety of ways to use it. `MessagePanel` provides many properties and methods that will be used in several examples in the book.

13.21 If `message` is not initialized in line 8 in Listing 13.8, MessagePanel.java, what will happen when you create a `MessagePanel` using its no-arg constructor?

13.22 The following program is supposed to display a message on a panel, but nothing is displayed. There are problems in lines 2 and 15. Correct them.

```
public class TestDrawMessage extends javax.swing.JFrame {
  public void TestDrawMessage() {
    add(new DrawMessage());
  }

  public static void main(String[] args) {
    javax.swing.JFrame frame = new TestDrawMessage();
    frame.setSize(100, 200);
    frame.setVisible(true);
  }
}

class DrawMessage extends javax.swing.JPanel {
  @Override
  protected void PaintComponent(java.awt.Graphics g) {
    super.paintComponent(g);
    g.drawString("Welcome to Java", 20, 20);
  }
}
```

13.9 Case Study: The StillClock Class

This case study develops a class that displays a clock on a panel.

The StillClock class

The contract of the StillClock class is shown in Figure 13.20.

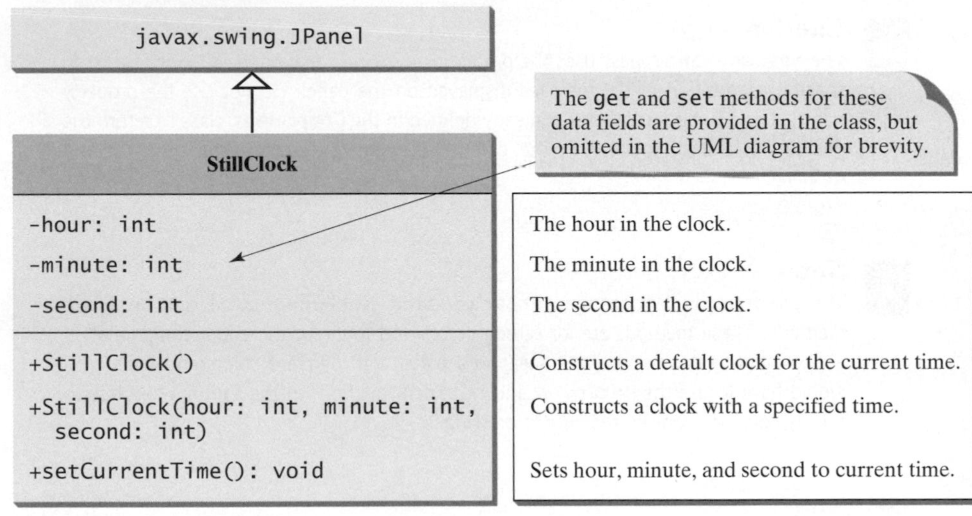

FIGURE 13.20 StillClock displays an analog clock.

Let us first write a test program in Listing 13.9 that uses the StillClock class to display an analog clock and uses the MessagePanel class to display the hour, minute, and second in a panel, as shown in Figure 13.21a.

LISTING 13.9 DisplayClock.java

```
import java.awt.*;
import javax.swing.*;

public class DisplayClock extends JFrame {
```

```
  public DisplayClock() {
    // Create an analog clock for the current time
    StillClock clock = new StillClock();

    // Display hour, minute, and second in the message panel
    MessagePanel messagePanel = new MessagePanel(clock.getHour() +
      ":" + clock.getMinute() + ":" + clock.getSecond());
    messagePanel.setCentered(true);
    messagePanel.setForeground(Color.blue);
    messagePanel.setFont(new Font("Courier", Font.BOLD, 16));

    // Add the clock and message panel to the frame
    add(clock);
    add(messagePanel, BorderLayout.SOUTH);
  }

  public static void main(String[] args) {
    DisplayClock frame = new DisplayClock();
    frame.setTitle("DisplayClock");
    frame.setSize(300, 350);
    frame.setLocationRelativeTo(null); // Center the frame
    frame.setDefaultCloseOperation(JFrame.EXIT_ON_CLOSE);
    frame.setVisible(true);
  }
}
```

create a clock

create a message panel

add a clock

add a message panel

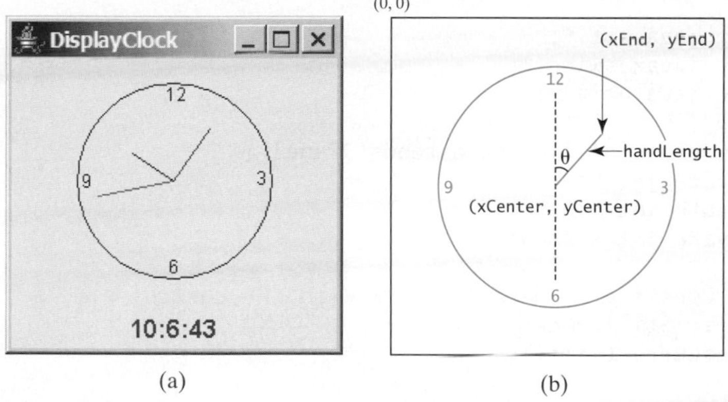

FIGURE 13.21 (a) The `DisplayClock` program displays a clock that shows the current time. (b) The endpoint of a clock hand can be determined, given the spanning angle, the hand length, and the center point.

The rest of this section explains how to implement the `StillClock` class. Since you can use the class without knowing how it is implemented, you may skip the implementation if you wish.

skip implementation?

To draw a clock, you need to draw a circle and three hands for the second, minute, and hour. To draw a hand, you need to specify the two ends of the line. As shown in Figure 13.21b, one end is the center of the clock at `(xCenter, yCenter)`; the other end, at `(xEnd, yEnd)`, is determined by the following formula:

implementation

```
xEnd = xCenter + handLength × sin(θ)
yEnd = yCenter - handLength × cos(θ)
```

Since there are 60 seconds in one minute, the angle for the second hand is

```
second × (2π/60)
```

The position of the minute hand is determined by the minute and second. The exact minute value combined with seconds is `minute + second/60`. For example, if the time is 3 minutes and 30 seconds, the total minutes are 3.5. Since there are 60 minutes in one hour, the angle for the minute hand is

```
(minute + second/60) × (2π/60)
```

Since one circle is divided into 12 hours, the angle for the hour hand is

```
(hour + minute/60 + second/(60 × 60)) × (2π/12)
```

For simplicity in computing the angles of the minute hand and hour hand, you can omit the seconds, because they are negligibly small. Therefore, the endpoints for the second hand, minute hand, and hour hand can be computed as:

```
xSecond = xCenter + secondHandLength × sin(second × (2π/60))
ySecond = yCenter - secondHandLength × cos(second × (2π/60))
xMinute = xCenter + minuteHandLength × sin(minute × (2π/60))
yMinute = yCenter - minuteHandLength × cos(minute × (2π/60))
xHour = xCenter + hourHandLength × sin((hour + minute/60) × (2π/12))
yHour = yCenter - hourHandLength × cos((hour + minute/60) × (2π/12))
```

The `StillClock` class is implemented in Listing 13.10.

LISTING 13.10 StillClock.java

```java
import java.awt.*;
import javax.swing.*;
import java.util.*;

public class StillClock extends JPanel {
  private int hour;
  private int minute;
  private int second;

  /** Construct a default clock with the current time*/
  public StillClock() {
    setCurrentTime();
  }

  /** Construct a clock with specified hour, minute, and second */
  public StillClock(int hour, int minute, int second) {
    this.hour = hour;
    this.minute = minute;
    this.second = second;
  }

  /** Return hour */
  public int getHour() {
    return hour;
  }

  /** Set a new hour */
  public void setHour(int hour) {
    this.hour = hour;
    repaint();
  }

  /** Return minute */
```

repaint panel

```
  public int getMinute() {
    return minute;
  }

  /** Set a new minute */
  public void setMinute(int minute) {
    this.minute = minute;
    repaint();
  }

  /** Return second */
  public int getSecond() {
    return second;
  }

  /** Set a new second */
  public void setSecond(int second) {
    this.second = second;
    repaint();
  }

  @Override /** Draw the clock */
  protected void paintComponent(Graphics g) {
    super.paintComponent(g);

    // Initialize clock parameters
    int clockRadius =
      (int)(Math.min(getWidth(), getHeight()) * 0.8 * 0.5);
    int xCenter = getWidth() / 2;
    int yCenter = getHeight() / 2;

    // Draw circle
    g.setColor(Color.BLACK);
    g.drawOval(xCenter - clockRadius, yCenter - clockRadius,
      2 * clockRadius, 2 * clockRadius);
    g.drawString("12", xCenter - 5, yCenter - clockRadius + 12);
    g.drawString("9", xCenter - clockRadius + 3, yCenter + 5);
    g.drawString("3", xCenter + clockRadius - 10, yCenter + 3);
    g.drawString("6", xCenter - 3, yCenter + clockRadius - 3);

    // Draw second hand
    int sLength = (int)(clockRadius * 0.8);
    int xSecond = (int)(xCenter + sLength *
      Math.sin(second * (2 * Math.PI / 60)));
    int ySecond = (int)(yCenter - sLength *
      Math.cos(second * (2 * Math.PI / 60)));
    g.setColor(Color.red);
    g.drawLine(xCenter, yCenter, xSecond, ySecond);

    // Draw minute hand
    int mLength = (int)(clockRadius * 0.65);
    int xMinute = (int)(xCenter + mLength *
      Math.sin(minute * (2 * Math.PI / 60)));
    int yMinute = (int)(yCenter - mLength *
      Math.cos(minute * (2 * Math.PI / 60)));
    g.setColor(Color.blue);
    g.drawLine(xCenter, yCenter, xMinute, yMinute);

    // Draw hour hand
    int hLength = (int)(clockRadius * 0.5);
```

repaint panel

repaint panel

override paintComponent

```
      int xHour = (int)(xCenter + hLength *
        Math.sin((hour % 12 + minute / 60.0) * (2 * Math.PI / 12)));
      int yHour = (int)(yCenter - hLength *
        Math.cos((hour % 12 + minute / 60.0) * (2 * Math.PI / 12)));
      g.setColor(Color.green);
      g.drawLine(xCenter, yCenter, xHour, yHour);
    }

    public void setCurrentTime() {
      // Construct a calendar for the current date and time
      Calendar calendar = new GregorianCalendar();

      // Set current hour, minute, and second
      this.hour = calendar.get(Calendar.HOUR_OF_DAY);
      this.minute = calendar.get(Calendar.MINUTE);
      this.second = calendar.get(Calendar.SECOND);
    }

    @Override
    public Dimension getPreferredSize() {
      return new Dimension(200, 200);
    }
  }
```

get current time

override getPreferredSize

The program enables the clock size to adjust as the frame resizes. Every time you resize the frame, the `paintComponent` method is automatically invoked to paint a new clock. The `paintComponent` method displays the clock in proportion to the panel width (`getWidth()`) and height (`getHeight()`) (lines 60–63 in `StillClock`).

13.10 Displaying Images

You can draw images in a graphics context.

You learned how to create image icons and display them in labels and buttons in Section 12.10, Image Icons. For example, the following statements create an image icon and display it in a label:

```
ImageIcon imageIcon = new ImageIcon("image/us.gif");
JLabel jlblImage = new JLabel(imageIcon);
```

An image icon displays a fixed-size image. To display an image in a flexible size, you need to use the `java.awt.Image` class. An image can be created from an image icon using the `getImage()` method as follows:

```
Image image = imageIcon.getImage();
```

Using a label as an area for displaying images is simple and convenient, but you don't have much control over how the image is displayed. A more flexible way to display images is to use the `drawImage` method of the `Graphics` class on a panel. Four versions of the `drawImage` method are shown in Figure 13.22.

`ImageObserver` specifies a GUI component for receiving notifications of image information as the image is constructed. To draw images using the `drawImage` method in a Swing component, such as `JPanel`, override the `paintComponent` method to tell the component how to display the image in the panel.

Listing 13.11 gives the code that displays an image from **image/us.gif**. The file **image/us.gif** (line 20) is under the class directory. An `Image` object is obtained in line 21. The `drawImage` method displays the image to fill in the whole panel, as shown in Figure 13.23.

java.awt.Graphics	
`+drawImage(image: Image, x: int, y: int, bgcolor: Color, observer: ImageObserver): void`	Draws the image in a specified location. The image's top-left corner is at (*x*, *y*) in the graphics context's coordinate space. Transparent pixels in the image are drawn in the specified color `bgcolor`. The observer is the object on which the image is displayed. The image is cut off if it is larger than the area it is being drawn on.
`+drawImage(image: Image, x: int, y: int, observer: ImageObserver): void`	Same as the preceding method except that it does not specify a background color.
`+drawImage(image: Image, x: int, y: int, width: int, height: int, observer: ImageObserver): void`	Draws a scaled version of the image that can fill all of the available space in the specified rectangle.
`+drawImage(image: Image, x: int, y: int, width: int, height: int, bgcolor: Color, observer: ImageObserver): void`	Same as the preceding method except that it provides a solid background color behind the image being drawn.

FIGURE 13.22 You can apply the `drawImage` method on a `Graphics` object to display an image on a GUI component.

LISTING 13.11 DisplayImage.java

```
import java.awt.*;
import javax.swing.*;

public class DisplayImage extends JFrame {
  public DisplayImage() {
    add(new ImagePanel());                                    // add panel
  }

  public static void main(String[] args) {
    JFrame frame = new DisplayImage();
    frame.setTitle("DisplayImage");
    frame.setSize(300, 300);
    frame.setLocationRelativeTo(null); // Center the frame
    frame.setDefaultCloseOperation(JFrame.EXIT_ON_CLOSE);
    frame.setVisible(true);
  }
}

class ImagePanel extends JPanel {                             // panel class
  private ImageIcon imageIcon = new ImageIcon("image/us.gif"); // create image icon
  private Image image = imageIcon.getImage();                 // get image

  @Override /** Draw image on the panel */
  protected void paintComponent(Graphics g) {                 // override paintComponent
    super.paintComponent(g);

    if (image != null)
      g.drawImage(image, 0, 0, getWidth(), getHeight(), this); // draw image
  }
}
```

FIGURE 13.23 An image is displayed in a panel.

13.11 Case Study: The **ImageViewer** Class

This case study develops the `ImageViewer` class for displaying an image in a panel.

Displaying an image is a common task in Java programming. This case study develops a reusable component named `ImageViewer` that displays an image on a panel. The class contains the properties `image`, `stretched`, `xCoordinate`, and `yCoordinate`, with associated accessor and mutator methods, as shown in Figure 13.24.

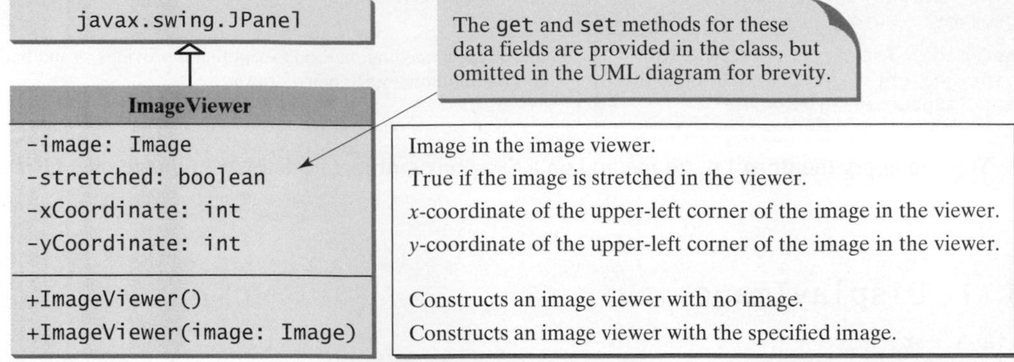

FIGURE 13.24 The `ImageViewer` class displays an image on a panel.

stretchable image

You can use images in Swing components such as `JLabel` and `JButton`, but these images are not stretchable. The image in an `ImageViewer` can be stretched.

Let us write a test program in Listing 13.12 that displays six images using the `ImageViewer` class. Figure 13.25 shows a sample run of the program.

LISTING 13.12 SixFlags.java

create image

create image viewer

```
import javax.swing.*;
import java.awt.*;

public class SixFlags extends JFrame {
  public SixFlags() {
    Image image1 = new ImageIcon("image/us.gif").getImage();
    Image image2 = new ImageIcon("image/ca.gif").getImage();
    Image image3 = new ImageIcon("image/india.gif").getImage();
    Image image4 = new ImageIcon("image/uk.gif").getImage();
    Image image5 = new ImageIcon("image/china.gif").getImage();
    Image image6 = new ImageIcon("image/norway.gif").getImage();

    setLayout(new GridLayout(2, 0, 5, 5));
    add(new ImageViewer(image1));
    add(new ImageViewer(image2));
    add(new ImageViewer(image3));
    add(new ImageViewer(image4));
    add(new ImageViewer(image5));
    add(new ImageViewer(image6));
  }

  public static void main(String[] args) {
    SixFlags frame = new SixFlags();
    frame.setTitle("SixFlags");
    frame.setSize(400, 320);
    frame.setLocationRelativeTo(null); // Center the frame
```

```
    frame.setDefaultCloseOperation(JFrame.EXIT_ON_CLOSE);
    frame.setVisible(true);
  }
}
```

FIGURE 13.25 Six images are displayed in six `ImageViewer` components.

The `ImageViewer` class is implemented in Listing 13.13. (*Note: You may skip the implementation.*) The accessor and mutator methods for the properties `image`, `stretched`, `xCoordinate`, and `yCoordinate` are easy to implement. The `paintComponent` method (lines 27–36) displays the image on the panel. Line 30 ensures that the image is not `null` before displaying it. Line 31 checks whether the image is stretched or not.

implementation
skip implementation?

LISTING 13.13 ImageViewer.java

```
1  import java.awt.*;
2  import javax.swing.*;
3
4  public class ImageViewer extends JPanel {
5    /** Hold value of property image */
6    private java.awt.Image image;
7
8    /** Hold value of property stretched */
9    private boolean stretched = true;
10
11   /** Hold value of property xCoordinate */
12   private int xCoordinate;
13
14   /** Hold value of property yCoordinate */
15   private int yCoordinate;
16
17   /** Construct an empty image viewer */
18   public ImageViewer() {
19   }
20
21   /** Construct an image viewer for a specified Image object */
22   public ImageViewer(Image image) {
23     this.image = image;
24   }
25
26   @Override
27   protected void paintComponent(Graphics g) {
28     super.paintComponent(g);
29
30     if (image != null)
31       if (isStretched())
32         g.drawImage(image, xCoordinate, yCoordinate,
33           getWidth(), getHeight(), this);
34       else
35         g.drawImage(image, xCoordinate, yCoordinate, this);
36   }
```

properties
constructor
constructor
image null?
stretched
nonstretched

```java

  /** Return value of property image */
  public java.awt.Image getImage() {
    return image;
  }

  /** Set a new value for property image */
  public void setImage(java.awt.Image image) {
    this.image = image;
    repaint();
  }

  /** Return value of property stretched */
  public boolean isStretched() {
    return stretched;
  }

  /** Set a new value for property stretched */
  public void setStretched(boolean stretched) {
    this.stretched = stretched;
    repaint();
  }

  /** Return value of property xCoordinate */
  public int getXCoordinate() {
    return xCoordinate;
  }

  /** Set a new value for property xCoordinate */
  public void setXCoordinate(int xCoordinate) {
    this.xCoordinate = xCoordinate;
    repaint();
  }

  /** Return value of property yCoordinate */
  public int getYCoordinate() {
    return yCoordinate;
  }

  /** Set a new value for property yCoordinate */
  public void setYCoordinate(int yCoordinate) {
    this.yCoordinate = yCoordinate;
    repaint();
  }
}
```

MyProgrammingLab™

13.23 How do you create an `Image` object from the `ImageIcon` object?

13.24 How do you create an `ImageIcon` object from an `Image` object?

13.25 Describe the `drawImage` method in the `Graphics` class.

13.26 Explain the differences between displaying images in a `JLabel` and in a `JPanel`.

13.27 Which package contains `ImageIcon`, and which contains `Image`?

Chapter Summary

1. Each component has its own coordinate system with the origin (`0, 0`) at the upper-left corner of the window. In Java, the *x*-coordinate increases to the right, and the *y*-coordinate increases downward.

2. Whenever a component (e.g., a button, a label, or a panel) is displayed, the JVM automatically creates a `Graphics` object for the component on the native platform and passes this object to invoke the `paintComponent` method to display the drawings.

3. Normally you use `JPanel` as a canvas. To draw on a `JPanel`, you create a new class that extends `JPanel` and overrides the `paintComponent` method to tell the panel how to draw graphics.

4. Invoking `super.paintComponent(g)` is necessary to ensure that the viewing area is cleared before a new drawing is displayed. The user can request the component to be redisplayed by invoking the `repaint()` method defined in the `Component` class. Invoking `repaint()` causes `paintComponent` to be invoked by the JVM. The user should never invoke `paintComponent` directly. For this reason, the protected visibility is sufficient for `paintComponent`.

5. The `Component` class has the `setBackground`, `setForeground`, and `setFont` methods. These methods are used to set colors and fonts for the entire component. If you want to draw several messages in a panel with different colors and fonts, you have to use the `setColor` and `setFont` methods in the `Graphics` class to set the color and font for the current drawing.

6. `FontMetrics` can be used to compute the exact length and width of a string, which is helpful for measuring the size of a string in order to display it in the right position.

7. To display an image, first create an image icon. You can then use `ImageIcon`'s `getImage()` method to get an `Image` object for the image and draw the image using the `drawImage` method in the `java.awt.Graphics` class.

Test Questions

Do the test questions for this chapter online at www.cs.armstrong.edu/liang/intro9e/test.html.

Programming Exercises

MyProgrammingLab™

Sections 13.2–13.7

*13.1 (*Display a 3 × 3 grid*) Write a program that displays a 3 × 3 grid, as shown in Figure 13.26a. Use red color for vertical lines and blue for horizontals.

**13.2 (*Create a custom button class*) Develop a custom button class named `OvalButton` that extends `JButton` and displays the button text inside an oval. Figure 13.26b shows two buttons created using the `OvalButton` class.

*13.3 (*Display a checkerboard*) Programming Exercise 12.10 displays a checkerboard in which each white and black cell is a `JButton`. Rewrite a program that draws a checkerboard on a `JPanel` using the drawing methods in the `Graphics` class, as shown in Figure 13.26c. Use the `drawRect` method to draw each cell in the checkerboard.

*13.4 (*Display a multiplication table*) Write a program that displays a multiplication table in a panel using the drawing methods, as shown in Figure 13.27a.

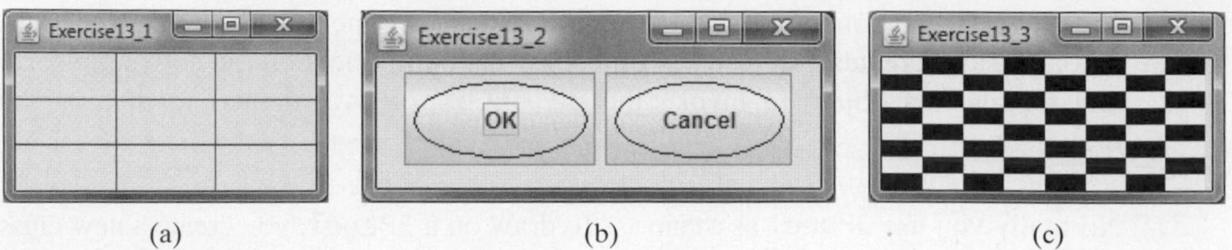

(a) (b) (c)

FIGURE 13.26 (a) Exercise 13.1 displays a grid. (b) Exercise 13.2 displays two objects of `OvalButton`. (c) Exercise 13.3 displays a checkerboard.

****13.5** (*Display numbers in a triangular pattern*) Write a program that displays numbers in a triangular pattern, as shown in Figure 13.27b. The number of lines in the display changes to fit the window as the window resizes.

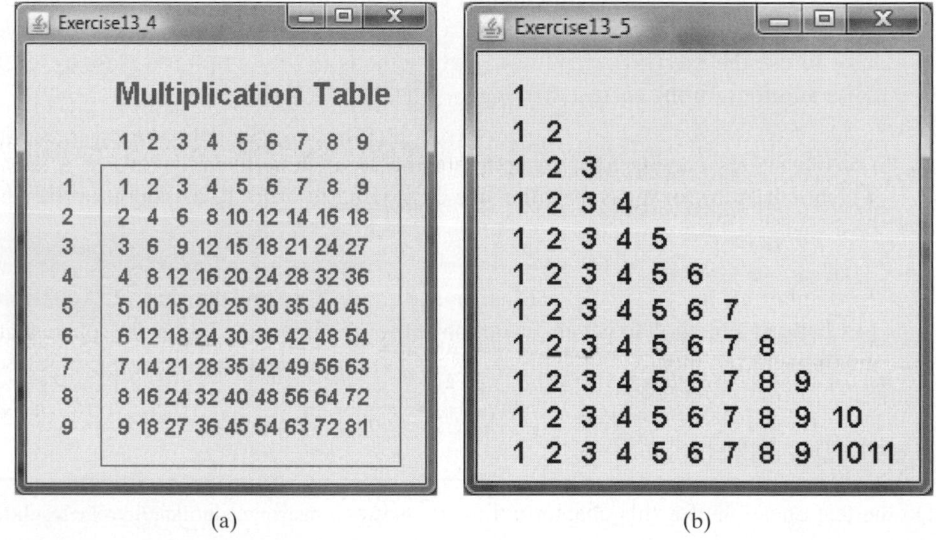

(a) (b)

FIGURE 13.27 (a) Exercise 13.4 displays a multiplication table. (b) Exercise 13.5 displays numbers in a triangle formation.

****13.6** (*Improve `FigurePanel`*) The `FigurePanel` class in Listing 13.3 can display lines, rectangles, round-cornered rectangles, and ovals. Add appropriate new code in the class to display arcs and polygons. Write a test program to display the shapes as shown in Figure 13.28a using the new `FigurePanel` class.

****13.7** (*Display a tic-tac-toe board*) Create a custom panel that displays `X`, `O`, or nothing. What to display is randomly decided whenever a panel is repainted. Use the `Math.random()` method to generate an integer `0`, `1`, or `2`, which corresponds to displaying `X`, `O`, or nothing. Create a frame that contains nine custom panels, as shown in Figure 13.28b.

****13.8** (*Draw an octagon*) Write a program that draws an octagon, as shown in Figure 13.28c.

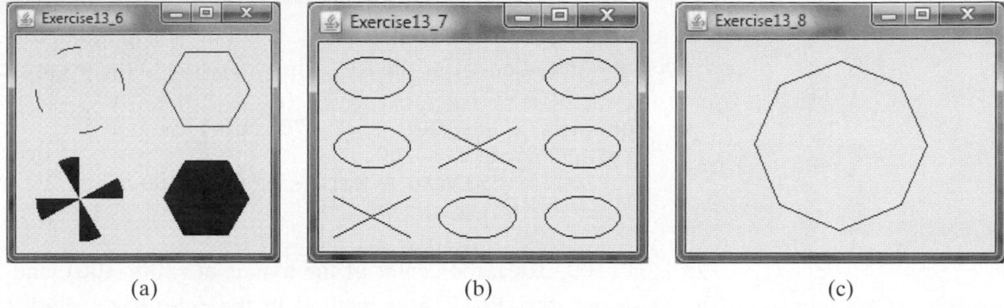

(a) (b) (c)

FIGURE 13.28 (a) Four panels of geometric figures are displayed in a frame of `GridLayout`. (b) `TicTacToe` cells randomly display X, O, or nothing. (c) Exercise 13.8 draws an octagon.

***13.9** (*Create four fans*) Write a program that places four fans in a frame of `GridLayout` with two rows and two columns, as shown in Figure 13.29a.

***13.10** (*Display a cylinder*) Write a program that draws a cylinder, as shown in Figure 13.29b.

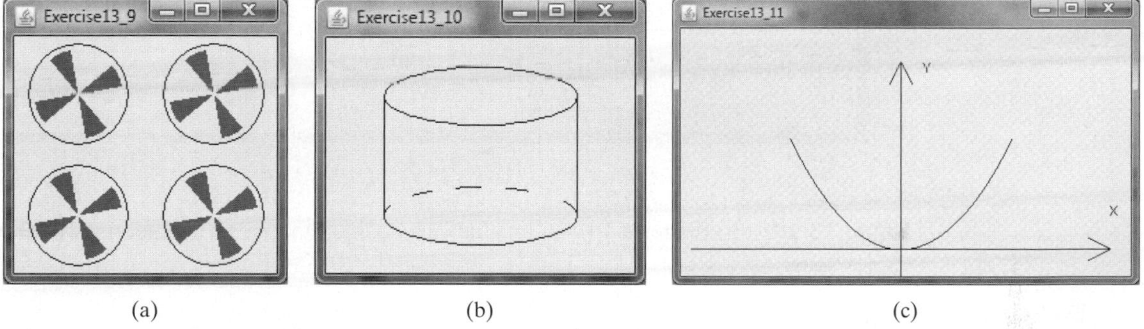

(a) (b) (c)

FIGURE 13.29 (a) Exercise 13.9 draws four fans. (b) Exercise 13.10 draws a cylinder. (c) Exercise 13.11 draws a diagram for function $f(x) = x^2$.

***13.11** (*Plot the square function*) Write a program that draws a diagram for the function $f(x) = x^2$ (see Figure 13.29c).

Hint: Add points to a polygon `p` using the following loop:

```
double scaleFactor = 0.1;

for (int x = -100; x <= 100; x++) {
  p.addPoint(x + 200, 200 - (int)(scaleFactor * x * x));
}
```

Connect the points using `g.drawPolyline(p.xpoints, p.ypoints, p.npoints)` for a `Graphics` object `g`. `p.xpoints` returns an array of x-coordinates, `p.ypoints` an array of y-coordinates, and `p.npoints` the number of points in `Polygon` object `p`.

VideoNote
Plot a function

****13.12** (*Plot the sine and cosine functions*) Write a program that plots the sine function in red and cosine in blue, as shown in Figure 13.30a.

Hint: The Unicode for π is `\u03c0`. To display -2π, use `g.drawString("-2\u03c0", x, y)`. For a trigonometric function like `sin(x)`, `x` is in radians. Use the following loop to add the points to a polygon `p`:

```
for (int x = -170; x <= 170; x++) {
  p.addPoint(x + 200,
    100 - (int)(50 * Math.sin((x / 100.0) * 2 * Math.PI)));
}
```

-2π is at (100, 100), the center of the axis is at (200, 100), and 2π is at (300, 100). Use the `drawPolyline` method in the `Graphics` class to connect the points.

****13.13** (*Paint a smiley face*) Write a program that paints a smiley face, as shown in Figure 13.30b.

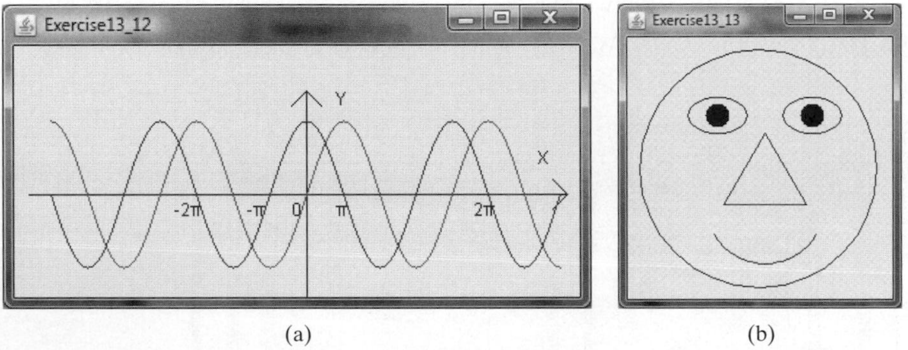

(a) (b)

FIGURE 13.30 (a) Exercise 13.12 plots the sine/cosine functions. (b) Exercise 13.13 paints a smiley face.

****13.14** (*Display a bar chart*) Write a program that uses a bar chart to display the percentages of the overall grade represented by projects, quizzes, midterm exams, and the final exam, as shown in Figure 13.1a. Suppose that projects take 20 percent and are displayed in red, quizzes take 10 percent and are displayed in blue, midterm exams take 30 percent and are displayed in green, and the final exam takes 40 percent and is displayed in orange.

VideoNote

Plot a bar chart

****13.15** (*Display a pie chart*) Write a program that uses a pie chart to display the percentages of the overall grade represented by projects, quizzes, midterm exams, and the final exam, as shown in Figure 13.31a. Suppose that projects take 20 percent and are displayed in red, quizzes take 10 percent and are displayed in blue, midterm exams take 30 percent and are displayed in green, and the final exam takes 40 percent and is displayed in orange.

13.16 (*Obtain font information*) Write a program that displays the message `Java is fun` in a panel. Set the panel's font to `TimesRoman`, `bold`, and `20` pixel. Display the font's leading, ascent, descent, height, and the string width as a tool tip text for the panel, as shown in Figure 13.31b.

13.17 (*Game: hangman*) Write a program that displays a drawing for the popular hangman game, as shown in Figure 13.31c.

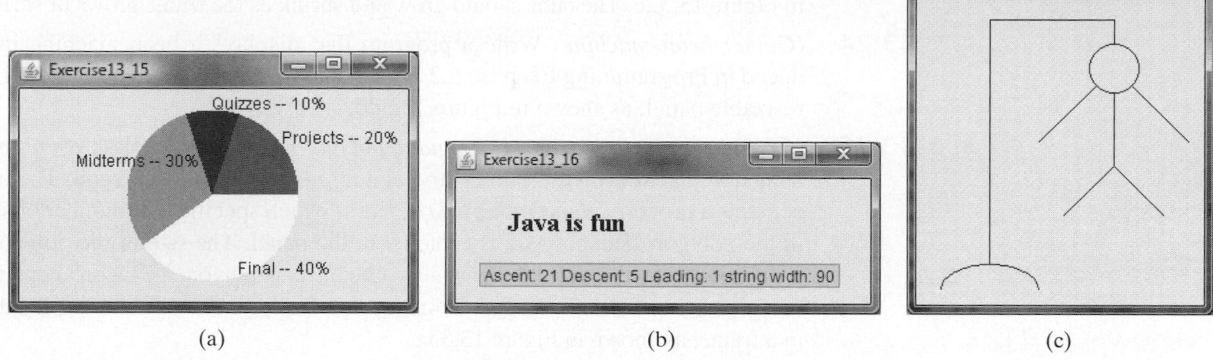

(a) (b) (c)

FIGURE 13.31 (a) Exercise 13.15 uses a pie chart to show the percentages of projects, quizzes, midterm exams, and final exam in the overall grade. (b) Exercise 13.16 displays font properties in a tool tip text. (c) Exercise 13.17 draws a sketch for the hangman game.

13.18 (*Use the* `StillClock` *class*) Write a program that displays two clocks. The hour, minute, and second values are `4`, `20`, `45` for the first clock and `22`, `46`, `15` for the second clock, as shown in Figure 13.32a.

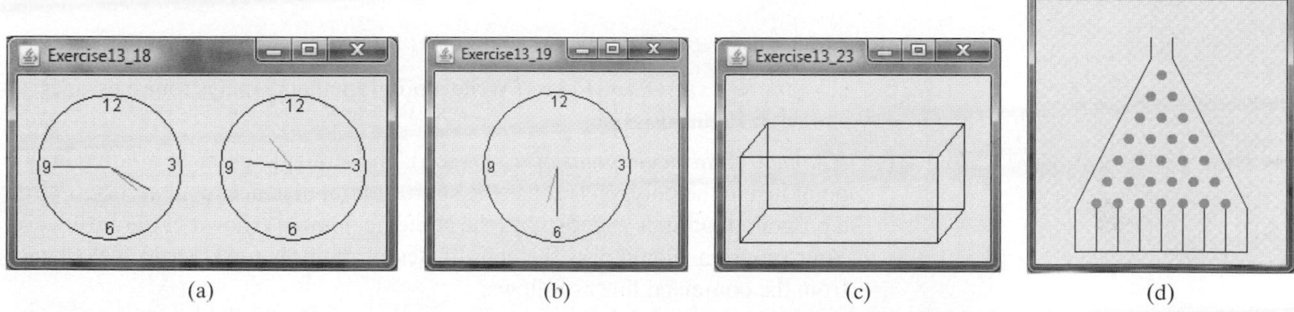

(a) (b) (c) (d)

FIGURE 13.32 (a) Exercise 13.18 displays two clocks. (b) Exercise 13.19 displays a clock with random hour and minute values. (c) Exercise 13.23 displays a rectanguloid. (d) Exercise 13.24 simulates a bean machine.

***13.19** (*Random time*) Modify the `StillClock` class with three new Boolean properties—`hourHandVisible`, `minuteHandVisible`, and `secondHandVisible`—and their associated accessor and mutator methods. You can use the `set` methods to make a hand visible or invisible. Write a test program that displays only the hour and minute hands. The hour and minute values are randomly generated. The hour is between `0` and `11`, and the minute is either `0` or `30`, as shown in Figure 13.32b.

****13.20** (*Draw a detailed clock*) Modify the `StillClock` class in Section 13.9 to draw the clock with more details on the hours and minutes, as shown in Figure 13.1b.

****13.21** (*Display a tic-tac-toe board with images*) Rewrite Programming Exercise 12.7 to display an image in a `JPanel` instead of displaying an image icon in a `JLabel`.

***13.22** (*Display a STOP sign*) Write a program that displays a STOP sign, as shown in Figure 13.1c. The octagon is in red and the sign is in white. (*Hint*: See Listing 13.5, DrawPolygon.java, and Listing 13.6, TestCenterMessage.java.)

13.23 (*Display a rectanguloid*) Write a program that displays a rectanguloid, as shown in Figure 13.32c. The cube should grow and shrink as the frame grows or shrinks.

****13.24** (*Game: bean machine*) Write a program that displays a bean machine introduced in Programming Exercise 6.21. The bean machine should be centered in a resizable panel, as shown in Figure 13.32d.

****13.25** (*Geometry: display an n-sided regular polygon*) Define a subclass of `JPanel`, named `RegularPolygonPanel`, to paint an *n*-sided regular polygon. The class contains a property named `numberOfSides`, which specifies the number of sides in the polygon. The polygon is centered in the panel. The size of the polygon is proportional to the size of the panel. Create a pentagon, hexagon, heptagon, octagon, nonagon, and decagon from `RegularPolygonPanel` and display them in a frame, as shown in Figure 13.33a.

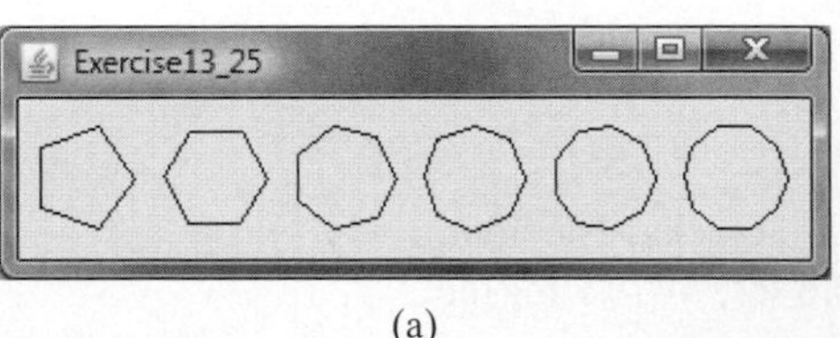

(a)

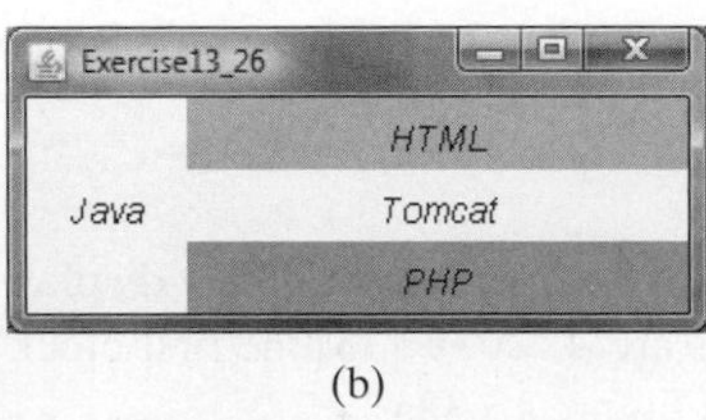

(b)

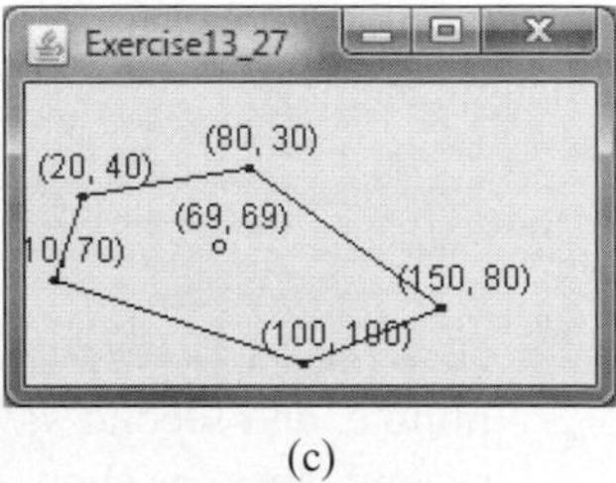

(c)

FIGURE 13.33 (a) Exercise 13.25 displays several n-sided polygons. (b) Exercise 13.26 uses `MessagePanel` to display four strings. (c) The polygon and its strategic point are displayed.

Sections 13.8–13.11

13.26 (*Use the `MessagePanel` class*) Write a program that displays four messages, as shown in Figure 13.33b.

****13.27** (*Geometry: strategic point of a polygon*) The strategic point of a polygon is a point inside the polygon that has the shortest total distance to all vertices. Write a program that finds and displays the strategic point, as shown in Figure 13.33c. Your program should pass the coordinates of the polygon's vertices clockwise from the command line as follows:

```
java Exercise13_27 x1 y1 x2 y2 x3 y3 . . .
```

The program displays the polygon and its strategic point in the frame. (*Hint*: To find the strategic point, consider every pixel point inside the polygon to see if it is a strategic point. Use the `contains` method to check whether a point is inside the polygon.)

****13.28** (*Draw an arrow line*) Write a static method that draws an arrow line from a starting point to an ending point using the following method header:

```
public static void drawArrowLine(int x1, int y1,
  int x2, int y2, Graphics g)
```

Write a test program that randomly draws an arrow line, as shown in Figure 13.34a. Whenever you resize the frame, a new arrow line is drawn.

***13.29** (*Two circles and their distance*) Write a program that draws two filled circles with radius `15` pixels, centered at random locations, with a line connecting the two circles. The distance between the two centers is displayed on the line, as shown in Figure 13.34b-c. Whenever you resize the frame, the circles are redisplayed in new random locations.

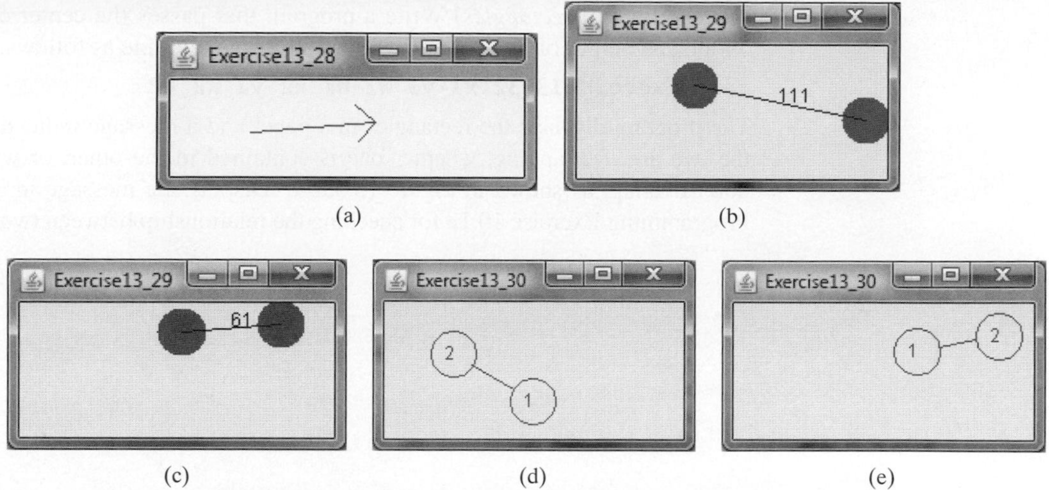

FIGURE 13.34 (a) The program displays an arrow line. (b-c) Exercise13.29 connects the centers of two filled circles. (d-e) Exercise13.30 connects two circles from their perimeter.

***13.30** (*Connect two circles*) Write a program that draws two filled circles with radius 15 pixels, centered at random locations, with a line connecting the two circles. The line should not cross inside the circles, as shown in Figure 13.34d-e. When you resize the frame, the circles are redisplayed in new random locations.

***13.31** (*Geometry: Inside a polygon?*) Write a program that passes the coordinates of five points from the command line as follows:

```
java Exercise13_31 x1 y1 x2 y2 x3 y3 x4 y4 x5 y5
```

The first four points form a polygon, and the program displays the polygon in a panel and a message in a label that indicates whether the fifth point is inside the polygon, as shown in Figure 13.35a.

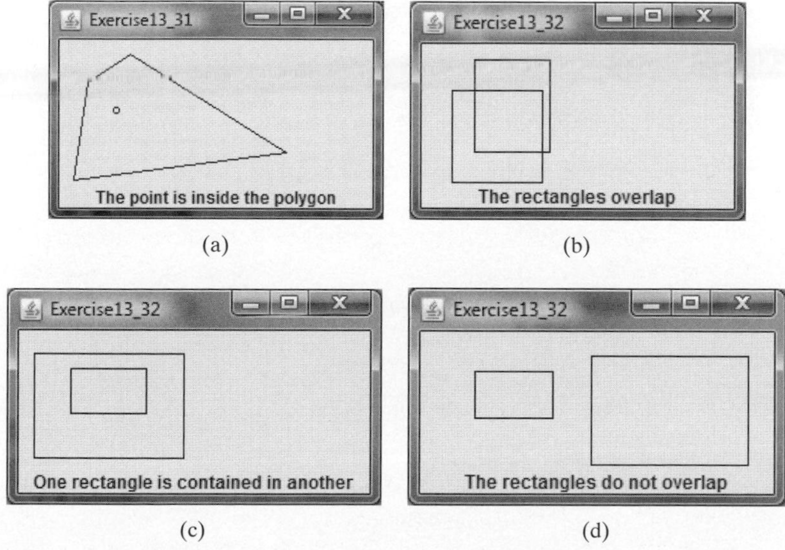

FIGURE 13.35 (a) The polygon and a point are displayed. (b-d) Two rectangles are displayed.

***13.32** (*Geometry: two rectangles*) Write a program that passes the center coordinates, width, and height of two rectangles from the command line as follows:

```
java Exercise13_32 x1 y1 w1 h1 x2 y2 w2 h2
```

The program displays the rectangles in a panel and a message indicating whether the two are overlapping, whether one is contained in the other, or whether they don't overlap, as shown in Figure 13.35b-d. Display the message in a label. See Programming Exercise 10.13 for checking the relationship between two rectangles.

CHAPTER

14

EXCEPTION HANDLING AND TEXT I/O

Objectives

- To get an overview of exceptions and exception handling (§14.2).
- To explore the advantages of using exception handling (§14.2).
- To distinguish exception types: `Error` (fatal) vs. `Exception` (nonfatal) and checked vs. unchecked (§14.3).
- To declare exceptions in a method header (§14.4.1).
- To throw exceptions in a method (§14.4.2).
- To write a `try-catch` block to handle exceptions (§14.4.3).
- To explain how an exception is propagated (§14.4.3).
- To obtain information from an exception object (§14.4.4).
- To develop applications with exception handling (§14.4.5).
- To use the `finally` clause in a `try-catch` block (§14.5).
- To use exceptions only for unexpected errors (§14.6).
- To rethrow exceptions in a `catch` block (§14.7).
- To create chained exceptions (§14.8).
- To define custom exception classes (§14.9).
- To discover file/directory properties, to delete and rename files/directories, and to create directories using the `File` class (§14.10).
- To write data to a file using the `PrintWriter` class (§14.11.1).
- To read data from a file using the `Scanner` class (§14.11.2).
- To understand how data is read using a `Scanner` (§14.11.3).
- To develop a program that replaces text in a file (§14.11.4).
- To open files using a file dialog box (§14.12).
- To read data from the Web (§14.13).

14.1 Introduction

Exception handling *enables a program to deal with exceptional situations and continue its normal execution.*

Runtime errors occur while a program is running if the JVM detects an operation that is impossible to carry out. For example, if you access an array using an index that is out of bounds, you will get a runtime error with an `ArrayIndexOutOfBoundsException`. If you enter a `double` value when your program expects an integer, you will get a runtime error with an `InputMismatchException`.

exception

In Java, runtime errors are thrown as exceptions. An *exception* is an object that represents an error or a condition that prevents execution from proceeding normally. If the exception is not handled, the program will terminate abnormally. How can you handle the exception so that the program can continue to run or else terminate gracefully? This chapter introduces this subject and text input and output.

14.2 Exception-Handling Overview

Exceptions are thrown from a method. The caller of the method can catch and handle the exception.

VideoNote
Exception-handling advantages

To demonstrate exception handling, including how an exception object is created and thrown, let's begin with the example in Listing 14.1, which reads in two integers and displays their quotient.

Listing 14.1 Quotient.java

reads two integers

integer division

```
import java.util.Scanner;

public class Quotient {
  public static void main(String[] args) {
    Scanner input = new Scanner(System.in);

    // Prompt the user to enter two integers
    System.out.print("Enter two integers: ");
    int number1 = input.nextInt();
    int number2 = input.nextInt();

    System.out.println(number1 + " / " + number2 + " is " +
      (number1 / number2));
  }
}
```

```
Enter two integers: 5 2 ↵Enter
5 / 2 is 2
```

```
Enter two integers: 3 0 ↵Enter
Exception in thread "main" java.lang.ArithmeticException: / by zero
at Quotient.main(Quotient.java:11)
```

If you entered `0` for the second number, a runtime error would occur, because you cannot divide an integer by `0`. (*Recall that a floating-point number divided by* `0` *does not raise an exception.*) A simple way to fix this error is to add an `if` statement to test the second number, as shown in Listing 14.2.

Listing 14.2 QuotientWithIf.java

```
import java.util.Scanner;

public class QuotientWithIf {
  public static void main(String[] args) {
    Scanner input = new Scanner(System.in);

    // Prompt the user to enter two integers
    System.out.print("Enter two integers: ");
    int number1 = input.nextInt();
    int number2 = input.nextInt();

    if (number2 != 0)
      System.out.println(number1 + " / " + number2
        + " is " + (number1 / number2));
    else
      System.out.println("Divisor cannot be zero ");
  }
}
```

reads two integers

test number2

```
Enter two integers: 5 0 ↵Enter
Divisor cannot be zero
```

To demonstrate the concept of exception handling, we can rewrite Listing 14.2 to compute a quotient using a method, as shown in Listing 14.3.

Listing 14.3 QuotientWithMethod.java

```
import java.util.Scanner;

public class QuotientWithMethod {
  public static int quotient(int number1, int number2) {
    if (number2 == 0) {
      System.out.println("Divisor cannot be zero");
      System.exit(1);
    }

    return number1 / number2;
  }

  public static void main(String[] args) {
    Scanner input = new Scanner(System.in);

    // Prompt the user to enter two integers
    System.out.print("Enter two integers: ");
    int number1 = input.nextInt();
    int number2 = input.nextInt();

    int result = quotient(number1, number2);
    System.out.println(number1 + " / " + number2 + " is "
      + result);
  }
}
```

quotient method

terminate the program

reads two integers

invoke method

```
Enter two integers: 5 3 ↵Enter
5 / 3 is 1
```

```
Enter two integers: 5 0 ↵Enter
Divisor cannot be zero
```

The method `quotient` (lines 4–11) returns the quotient of two integers. If `number2` is `0`, it cannot return a value, so the program is terminated in line 7. This is clearly a problem. You should not let the method terminate the program—the *caller* should decide whether to terminate the program.

How can a method notify its caller an exception has occurred? Java enables a method to throw an exception that can be caught and handled by the caller. Listing 14.3 can be rewritten, as shown in Listing 14.4.

Listing 14.4 QuotientWithException.java

quotient method (line 4) · throw exception (line 6) · reads two integers (line 16) · `try` block (line 19) · invoke method (line 20) · `catch` block (line 24)

```
import java.util.Scanner;

public class QuotientWithException {
  public static int quotient(int number1, int number2) {
    if (number2 == 0)
      throw new ArithmeticException("Divisor cannot be zero");

    return number1 / number2;
  }

  public static void main(String[] args) {
    Scanner input = new Scanner(System.in);

    // Prompt the user to enter two integers
    System.out.print("Enter two integers: ");
    int number1 = input.nextInt();
    int number2 = input.nextInt();

    try {
      int result = quotient(number1, number2);
      System.out.println(number1 + " / " + number2 + " is "
        + result);
    }
    catch (ArithmeticException ex) {
      System.out.println("Exception: an integer " +
        "cannot be divided by zero ");
    }

    System.out.println("Execution continues ...");
  }
}
```

If an ArithmeticException occurs

```
Enter two integers: 5 3 ↵Enter
5 / 3 is 1
Execution continues ...
```

```
Enter two integers: 5 0 ↵Enter
Exception: an integer cannot be divided by zero
Execution continues ...
```

If number2 is 0, the method throws an exception (line 6) by executing

throw statement

```
throw new ArithmeticException("Divisor cannot be zero");
```

exception
throwing exception

The value thrown, in this case new ArithmeticException("Divisor cannot be zero"), is called an *exception*. The execution of a throw statement is called *throwing an exception*. The exception is an object created from an exception class. In this case, the exception class is java.lang.ArithmeticException. The constructor ArithmeticException(str) is invoked to construct an exception object, where str is a message that describes the exception.

When an exception is thrown, the normal execution flow is interrupted. As the name suggests, to "throw an exception" is to pass the exception from one place to another. The statement for invoking the method is contained in a try block and a catch block. The try block (lines 19–23) contains the code that is executed in normal circumstances. The exception is caught by the catch block. The code in the catch block is executed to *handle the exception*. Afterward, the statement (line 29) after the catch block is executed.

handle exception

The throw statement is analogous to a method call, but instead of calling a method, it calls a catch block. In this sense, a catch block is like a method definition with a parameter that matches the type of the value being thrown. Unlike a method, however, after the catch block is executed, the program control does not return to the throw statement; instead, it executes the next statement after the catch block.

The identifier ex in the catch–block header

```
catch (ArithmeticException ex)
```

catch–block parameter

acts very much like a parameter in a method. Thus, this parameter is referred to as a catch–block parameter. The type (e.g., ArithmeticException) preceding ex specifies what kind of exception the catch block can catch. Once the exception is caught, you can access the thrown value from this parameter in the body of a catch block.

In summary, a template for a try-throw-catch block may look like this:

```
try {
  Code to run;
  A statement or a method that may throw an exception;
  More code to run;
}
catch (type ex) {
  Code to process the exception;
}
```

An exception may be thrown directly by using a throw statement in a try block, or by invoking a method that may throw an exception.

The main method invokes quotient (line 20). If the quotient method executes normally, it returns a value to the caller. If the quotient method encounters an exception, it throws the exception back to its caller. The caller's catch block handles the exception.

advantage

Now you can see the *advantage* of using exception handling: It enables a method to throw an exception to its caller, enabling the caller to handle the exception. Without this capability, the called method itself must handle the exception or terminate the program. Often the called method does not know what to do in case of error. This is typically the case for the library methods. The library method can detect the error, but only the caller knows what needs to be done when an error occurs. The key benefit of exception handling is separating the detection of an error (done in a called method) from the handling of an error (done in the calling method).

Many library methods throw exceptions. Listing 14.5 gives an example that handles an `InputMismatchException` when reading an input.

LISTING 14.5 InputMismatchExceptionDemo.java

create a Scanner

try block

catch block

```
1  import java.util.*;
2
3  public class InputMismatchExceptionDemo {
4    public static void main(String[] args) {
5      Scanner input = new Scanner(System.in);
6      boolean continueInput = true;
7
8      do {
9        try {
10         System.out.print("Enter an integer: ");
11         int number = input.nextInt();
12
13         // Display the result
14         System.out.println(
15           "The number entered is " + number);
16
17         continueInput = false;
18       }
19       catch (InputMismatchException ex) {
20         System.out.println("Try again. (" +
21           "Incorrect input: an integer is required)");
22         input.nextLine(); // Discard input
23       }
24     } while (continueInput);
25   }
26 }
```

If an InputMismatchException occurs

```
Enter an integer: 3.5 ↵Enter
Try again. (Incorrect input: an integer is required)
Enter an integer: 4 ↵Enter
The number entered is 4
```

When executing `input.nextInt()` (line 11), an `InputMismatchException` occurs if the input entered is not an integer. Suppose `3.5` is entered. An `InputMismatchException` occurs and the control is transferred to the `catch` block. The statements in the `catch` block are now executed. The statement `input.nextLine()` in line 22 discards the current input line so that the user can enter a new line of input. The variable `continueInput` controls the loop. Its initial value is `true` (line 6), and it is changed to `false` (line 17) when a valid input is received. Once a valid input is received, there is no need to continue the input.

MyProgrammingLab™

14.1 What is the advantage of using exception handling?

14.2 Which of the following statements will throw an exception?

```
System.out.println(1 / 0);
System.out.println(1.0 / 0);
```

14.3 Point out the problem in the following code. Does the code throw any exceptions?

```
long value = Long.MAX_VALUE + 1;
System.out.println(value);
```

14.4 What does the JVM do when an exception occurs? How do you catch an exception?

14.5 What is the printout of the following code?

```
public class Test {
  public static void main(String[] args) {
    try {
      int value = 30;
      if (value < 40)
        throw new Exception("value is too small");
    }
    catch (Exception ex) {
      System.out.println(ex.getMessage());
    }
    System.out.println("Continue after the catch block");
  }
}
```

What would be the printout if the line

```
int value = 30;
```

were changed to

```
int value = 50;
```

14.6 Show the output of the following code.

```
public class Test {
  public static void main(String[] args) {
    for (int i = 0; i < 2; i++) {
      System.out.print(i + " ");
      try {
        System.out.println(1 / 0);
      }
      catch (Exception ex) {
      }
    }
  }
}
```

(a)

```
public class Test {
  public static void main(String[] args) {
    try {
      for (int i = 0; i < 2; i++) {
        System.out.print(i + " ");
        System.out.println(1 / 0);
      }
    }
    catch (Exception ex) {
    }
  }
}
```

(b)

14.3 Exception Types

Exceptions are objects, and objects are defined using classes. The root class for exceptions is `java.lang.Throwable`.

The preceding section used the classes `ArithmeticException` and `InputMismatchException`. Are there any other types of exceptions you can use? Can you define your own exception classes? Yes. There are many predefined exception classes in the Java API. Figure 14.1 shows some of them, and in Section 14.9 you will learn how to define your own exception classes.

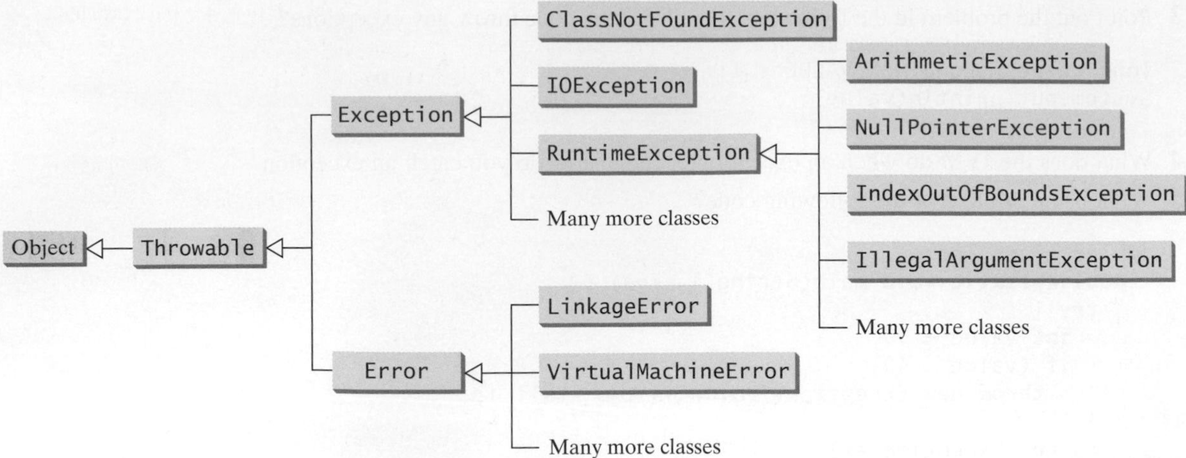

FIGURE 14.1 Exceptions thrown are instances of the classes shown in this diagram, or of subclasses of one of these classes.

Note

The class names `Error`, `Exception`, and `RuntimeException` are somewhat confusing. All three of these classes are exceptions, and all of the errors occur at runtime.

The `Throwable` class is the root of exception classes. All Java exception classes inherit directly or indirectly from `Throwable`. You can create your own exception classes by extending `Exception` or a subclass of `Exception`.

The exception classes can be classified into three major types: system errors, exceptions, and runtime exceptions.

system error

- *System errors* are thrown by the JVM and are represented in the `Error` class. The `Error` class describes internal system errors, though such errors rarely occur. If one does, there is little you can do beyond notifying the user and trying to terminate the program gracefully. Examples of subclasses of `Error` are listed in Table 14.1.

TABLE 14.1 Examples of Subclasses of `Error`

Class	*Reasons for Exception*
`LinkageError`	A class has some dependency on another class, but the latter class has changed incompatibly after the compilation of the former class.
`VirtualMachineError`	The JVM is broken or has run out of the resources it needs in order to continue operating.

exception

- *Exceptions* are represented in the `Exception` class, which describes errors caused by your program and by external circumstances. These errors can be caught and handled by your program. Examples of subclasses of `Exception` are listed in Table 14.2.

TABLE 14.2 Examples of Subclasses of `Exception`

Class	*Reasons for Exception*
`ClassNotFoundException`	Attempt to use a class that does not exist. This exception would occur, for example, if you tried to run a nonexistent class using the **java** command, or if your program were composed of, say, three class files, only two of which could be found.
`IOException`	Related to input/output operations, such as invalid input, reading past the end of a file, and opening a nonexistent file. Examples of subclasses of `IOException` are `InterruptedIOException`, `EOFException` (EOF is short for End of File), and `FileNotFoundException`.

- *Runtime exceptions* are represented in the `RuntimeException` class, which describes programming errors, such as bad casting, accessing an out-of-bounds array, and numeric errors. Runtime exceptions are generally thrown by the JVM. Examples of subclasses are listed in Table 14.3.

runtime exception

TABLE 14.3 Examples of Subclasses of `RuntimeException`

Class	*Reasons for Exception*
`ArithmeticException`	Dividing an integer by zero. Note that floating-point arithmetic does not throw exceptions (see Appendix E, Special Floating-Point Values).
`NullPointerException`	Attempt to access an object through a `null` reference variable.
`IndexOutOfBoundsException`	Index to an array is out of range.
`IllegalArgumentException`	A method is passed an argument that is illegal or inappropriate.

`RuntimeException`, `Error`, and their subclasses are known as *unchecked exceptions*. All other exceptions are known as *checked exceptions*, meaning that the compiler forces the programmer to check and deal with them in a `try-catch` block or declare it in the method header. Declaring an exception in the method header will be covered in Section 14.4.

unchecked exception
checked exception

In most cases, unchecked exceptions reflect programming logic errors that are unrecoverable. For example, a `NullPointerException` is thrown if you access an object through a reference variable before an object is assigned to it; an `IndexOutOfBoundsException` is thrown if you access an element in an array outside the bounds of the array. These are logic errors that should be corrected in the program. Unchecked exceptions can occur anywhere in a program. To avoid cumbersome overuse of `try-catch` blocks, Java does not mandate that you write code to catch or declare unchecked exceptions.

Check Point
MyProgrammingLab™

14.7 Describe the Java `Throwable` class, its subclasses, and the types of exceptions.

14.8 What `RuntimeException` will the following programs throw, if any?

```
public class Test {
  public static void main(String[] args) {
    System.out.println(1 / 0);
  }
}
```

(a)

```
public class Test {
  public static void main(String[] args) {
    int[] list = new int[5];
    System.out.println(list[5]);
  }
}
```

(b)

```
public class Test {
  public static void main(String[] args) {
    String s = "abc";
    System.out.println(s.charAt(3));
  }
}
```

(c)

```
public class Test {
  public static void main(String[] args) {
    Object o = new Object();
    String d = (String)o;
  }
}
```

(d)

```
public class Test {
  public static void main(String[] args) {
    Object o = null;
    System.out.println(o.toString());
  }
}
```

(e)

```
public class Test {
  public static void main(String[] args) {
    System.out.println(1.0 / 0);
  }
}
```

(f)

14.4 More on Exception Handling

A handler for an exception is found by propagating the exception backward through a chain of method calls, starting from the current method.

The preceding sections gave you an overview of exception handling and introduced several predefined exception types. This section provides an in-depth discussion of exception handling.

Java's exception-handling model is based on three operations: *declaring an exception*, *throwing an exception*, and *catching an exception*, as shown in Figure 14.2.

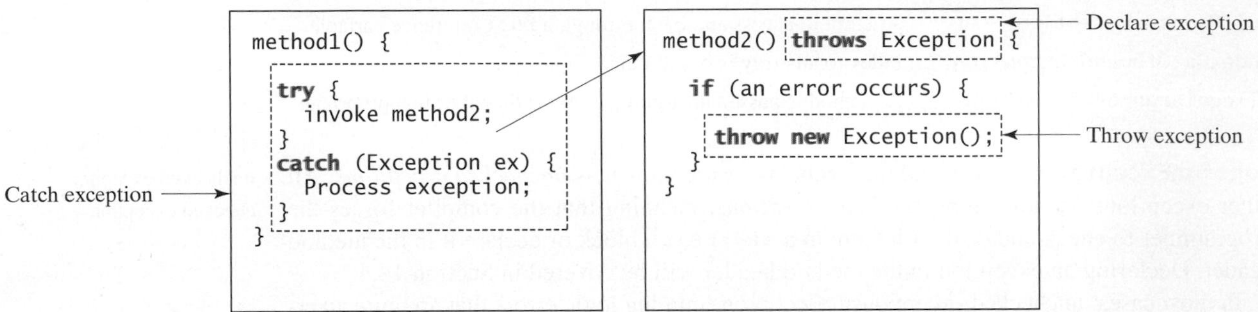

FIGURE 14.2 Exception handling in Java consists of declaring exceptions, throwing exceptions, and catching and processing exceptions.

14.4.1 Declaring Exceptions

In Java, the statement currently being executed belongs to a method. The Java interpreter invokes the `main` method to start executing a program. Every method must state the types of checked exceptions it might throw. This is known as *declaring exceptions*. Because system errors and runtime errors can happen to any code, Java does not require that you declare `Error` and `RuntimeException` (unchecked exceptions) explicitly in the method. However, all other exceptions thrown by the method must be explicitly declared in the method header so that the caller of the method is informed of the exception.

declare exception

To declare an exception in a method, use the `throws` keyword in the method header, as in this example:

```
public void myMethod() throws IOException
```

The `throws` keyword indicates that `myMethod` might throw an `IOException`. If the method might throw multiple exceptions, add a list of the exceptions, separated by commas, after `throws`:

```
public void myMethod()
  throws Exception1, Exception2, ..., ExceptionN
```

Note

If a method does not declare exceptions in the superclass, you cannot override it to declare exceptions in the subclass.

14.4.2 Throwing Exceptions

A program that detects an error can create an instance of an appropriate exception type and throw it. This is known as *throwing an exception*. Here is an example: Suppose the program detects that an argument passed to the method violates the method contract (e.g., the argument

throw exception

must be nonnegative, but a negative argument is passed); the program can create an instance of `IllegalArgumentException` and throw it, as follows:

```
IllegalArgumentException ex =
  new IllegalArgumentException("Wrong Argument");
throw ex;
```

Or, if you prefer, you can use the following:

```
throw new IllegalArgumentException("Wrong Argument");
```

Note

`IllegalArgumentException` is an exception class in the Java API. In general, each exception class in the Java API has at least two constructors: a no-arg constructor, and a constructor with a `String` argument that describes the exception. This argument is called the *exception message*, which can be obtained using `getMessage()`.

exception message

Tip

The keyword to declare an exception is `throws`, and the keyword to throw an exception is `throw`.

`throws` vs. `throw`

14.4.3 Catching Exceptions

You now know how to declare an exception and how to throw an exception. When an exception is thrown, it can be caught and handled in a `try-catch` block, as follows:

catch exception

```
try {
  statements; // Statements that may throw exceptions
}
catch (Exception1 exVar1) {
  handler for exception1;
}
catch (Exception2 exVar2) {
  handler for exception2;
}
...
catch (ExceptionN exVar3) {
  handler for exceptionN;
}
```

If no exceptions arise during the execution of the `try` block, the `catch` blocks are skipped.

If one of the statements inside the `try` block throws an exception, Java skips the remaining statements in the `try` block and starts the process of finding the code to handle the exception. The code that handles the exception is called the *exception handler*; it is found by *propagating the exception* backward through a chain of method calls, starting from the current method. Each `catch` block is examined in turn, from first to last, to see whether the type of the exception object is an instance of the exception class in the `catch` block. If so, the exception object is assigned to the variable declared, and the code in the `catch` block is executed. If no handler is found, Java exits this method, passes the exception to the method that invoked the method, and continues the same process to find a handler. If no handler is found in the chain of methods being invoked, the program terminates and prints an error message on the console. The process of finding a handler is called *catching an exception*.

exception handler

exception propagation

Suppose the `main` method invokes `method1`, `method1` invokes `method2`, `method2` invokes `method3`, and `method3` throws an exception, as shown in Figure 14.3. Consider the following scenario:

- If the exception type is `Exception3`, it is caught by the `catch` block for handling exception `ex3` in `method2`. `statement5` is skipped, and `statement6` is executed.
- If the exception type is `Exception2`, `method2` is aborted, the control is returned to `method1`, and the exception is caught by the `catch` block for handling exception `ex2` in `method1`. `statement3` is skipped, and `statement4` is executed.
- If the exception type is `Exception1`, `method1` is aborted, the control is returned to the `main` method, and the exception is caught by the `catch` block for handling exception `ex1` in the `main` method. `statement1` is skipped, and `statement2` is executed.
- If the exception type is not caught in `method2`, `method1`, or `main`, the program terminates, and `statement1` and `statement2` are not executed.

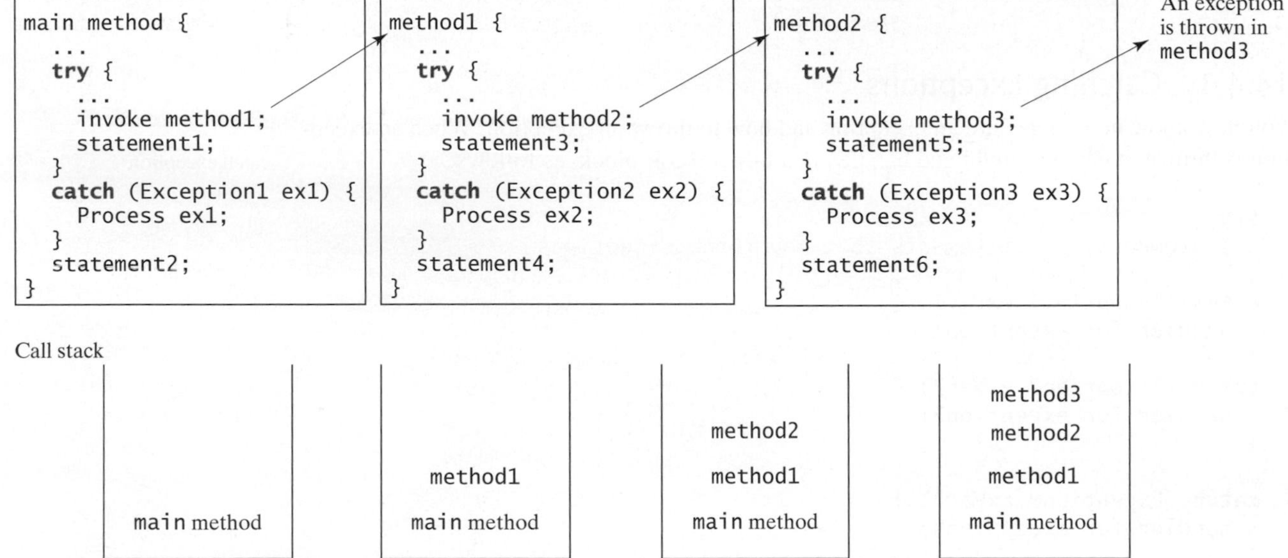

FIGURE 14.3 If an exception is not caught in the current method, it is passed to its caller. The process is repeated until the exception is caught or passed to the `main` method.

catch block

Note

Various exception classes can be derived from a common superclass. If a `catch` block catches exception objects of a superclass, it can catch all the exception objects of the subclasses of that superclass.

order of exception handlers

Note

The order in which exceptions are specified in `catch` blocks is important. A compile error will result if a catch block for a superclass type appears before a catch block for a subclass type. For example, the ordering in (a) on the next page is erroneous, because `RuntimeException` is a subclass of `Exception`. The correct ordering should be as shown in (b).

```
try {
  ...
}
catch (Exception ex) {
  ...
}
catch (RuntimeException ex) {
  ...
}
```

(a) Wrong order

```
try {
  ...
}
catch (RuntimeException ex) {
  ...
}
catch (Exception ex) {
  ...
}
```

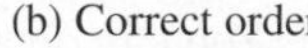

(b) Correct order

Note

catch or declare checked exceptions

Java forces you to deal with checked exceptions. If a method declares a checked exception (i.e., an exception other than `Error` or `RuntimeException`), you must invoke it in a `try-catch` block or declare to throw the exception in the calling method. For example, suppose that method `p1` invokes method `p2`, and `p2` may throw a checked exception (e.g., `IOException`); you have to write the code as shown in (a) or (b) below.

```
void p1() {
  try {
    p2();
  }
  catch (IOException ex) {
    ...
  }
}
```

(a) Catch exception

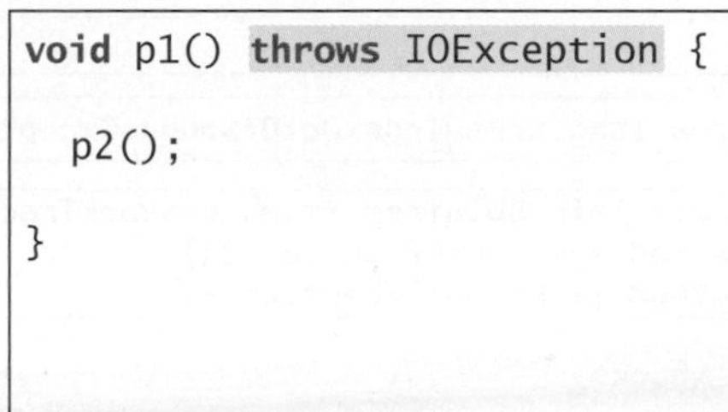

```
void p1() throws IOException {

  p2();

}
```

(b) Throw exception

Note

JDK 7 multi-catch

You can use the new JDK 7 multi-catch feature to simplify coding for the exceptions with the same handling code. The syntax is:

```
catch (Exception1 | Exception2 | ... | Exceptionk ex) {
  // Code to handle exceptions
}
```

Each exception type is separated from the next with a vertical bar (`|`). If one of the exceptions is caught, the handling code is executed.

14.4.4 Getting Information from Exceptions

methods in `Throwable`

An exception object contains valuable information about the exception. You may use the following instance methods in the `java.lang.Throwable` class to get information regarding the exception, as shown in Figure 14.4. The `printStackTrace()` method prints stack trace

java.lang.Throwable	
`+getMessage(): String`	Returns the message that describes this exception object.
`+toString(): String`	Returns the concatenation of three strings: (1) the full name of the exception class; (2) `": "` (a colon and a space); (3) the `getMessage()` method.
`+printStackTrace(): void`	Prints the `Throwable` object and its call stack trace information on the console.
`+getStackTrace(): StackTraceElement[]`	Returns an array of stack trace elements representing the stack trace pertaining to this exception object.

FIGURE 14.4 `Throwable` is the root class for all exception objects.

information on the console. The `getStackTrace()` method provides programmatic access to the stack trace information printed by `printStackTrace()`.

Listing 14.6 gives an example that uses the methods in `Throwable` to display exception information. Line 4 invokes the `sum` method to return the sum of all the elements in the array. There is an error in line 23 that causes the `ArrayIndexOutOfBoundsException`, a subclass of `IndexOutOfBoundsException`. This exception is caught in the `try-catch` block. Lines 7, 8, and 9 display the stack trace, exception message, and exception object and message using the `printStackTrace()`, `getMessage()`, and `toString()` methods, as shown in Figure 14.5. Line 12 brings stack trace elements into an array. Each element represents a method call. You can obtain the method (line 14), class name (line 15), and exception line number (line 16) for each element.

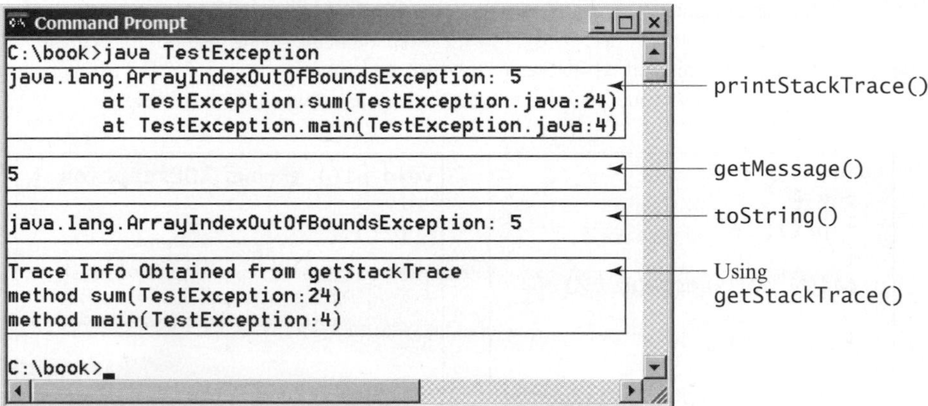

Figure 14.5 You can use the `printStackTrace()`, `getMessage()`, `toString()`, and `getStackTrace()` methods to obtain information from exception objects.

Listing 14.6 TestException.java

invoke sum
printStackTrace()
getMessage()
toString()

```
1  public class TestException  {
2    public static void main(String[] args) {
3      try {
4        System.out.println(sum(new int[] {1, 2, 3, 4, 5}));
5      }
6      catch (Exception ex) {
7        ex.printStackTrace();
8        System.out.println("\n" + ex.getMessage());
9        System.out.println("\n" + ex.toString());
10
11       System.out.println("\nTrace Info Obtained from getStackTrace");
12       StackTraceElement[] traceElements = ex.getStackTrace();
13       for (int i = 0; i < traceElements.length; i++) {
14         System.out.print("method " + traceElements[i].getMethodName());
15         System.out.print("(" + traceElements[i].getClassName() + ":");
16         System.out.println(traceElements[i].getLineNumber() + ")");
17       }
18     }
19   }
20
21   private static int sum(int[] list) {
22     int result = 0;
23     for (int i = 0; i <= list.length; i++)
```

```
      result += list[i];
    return result;
  }
}
```

14.4.5 Example: Declaring, Throwing, and Catching Exceptions

This example demonstrates declaring, throwing, and catching exceptions by modifying the `setRadius` method in the `Circle` class in Listing 8.9, CircleWithPrivateDataFields.java. The new `setRadius` method throws an exception if the radius is negative.

Listing 14.7 defines a new circle class named `CircleWithException`, which is the same as `CircleWithPrivateDataFields` except that the `setRadius(double newRadius)` method throws an `IllegalArgumentException` if the argument `newRadius` is negative.

LISTING 14.7 CircleWithException.java

```
public class CircleWithException {
  /** The radius of the circle */
  private double radius;

  /** The number of the objects created */
  private static int numberOfObjects = 0;

  /** Construct a circle with radius 1 */
  public CircleWithException() {
    this(1.0);
  }

  /** Construct a circle with a specified radius */
  public CircleWithException(double newRadius) {
    setRadius(newRadius);
    numberOfObjects++;
  }

  /** Return radius */
  public double getRadius() {
    return radius;
  }

  /** Set a new radius */
  public void setRadius(double newRadius)
      throws IllegalArgumentException {                declare exception
    if (newRadius >= 0)
      radius = newRadius;
    else
      throw new IllegalArgumentException(              throw exception
        "Radius cannot be negative");
  }

  /** Return numberOfObjects */
  public static int getNumberOfObjects() {
    return numberOfObjects;
  }

  /** Return the area of this circle */
  public double findArea() {
    return radius * radius * 3.14159;
  }
}
```

A test program that uses the new `Circle` class is given in Listing 14.8.

LISTING 14.8 TestCircleWithException.java

```
 1 public class TestCircleWithException {
 2   public static void main(String[] args) {
 3     try {
 4       CircleWithException c1 = new CircleWithException(5);
 5       CircleWithException c2 = new CircleWithException(-5);
 6       CircleWithException c3 = new CircleWithException(0);
 7     }
 8     catch (IllegalArgumentException ex) {
 9       System.out.println(ex);
10     }
11 
12     System.out.println("Number of objects created: " +
13       CircleWithException.getNumberOfObjects());
14   }
15 }
```

try

catch

```
java.lang.IllegalArgumentException: Radius cannot be negative
Number of objects created: 1
```

The original `Circle` class remains intact except that the class name is changed to `CircleWithException`, a new constructor `CircleWithException(newRadius)` is added, and the `setRadius` method now declares an exception and throws it if the radius is negative.

The `setRadius` method declares to throw `IllegalArgumentException` in the method header (lines 25–32 in CircleWithException.java). The `CircleWithException` class would still compile if the `throws IllegalArgumentException` clause were removed from the method declaration, since it is a subclass of `RuntimeException` and every method can throw `RuntimeException` (an unchecked exception) regardless of whether it is declared in the method header.

The test program creates three `CircleWithException` objects—`c1`, `c2`, and `c3`—to test how to handle exceptions. Invoking `new CircleWithException(-5)` (line 5 in Listing 14.8) causes the `setRadius` method to be invoked, which throws an `IllegalArgumentException`, because the radius is negative. In the `catch` block, the type of the object `ex` is `IllegalArgumentException`, which matches the exception object thrown by the `setRadius` method, so this exception is caught by the `catch` block.

The exception handler prints a short message, `ex.toString()` (line 9 in Listing 14.8), about the exception, using `System.out.println(ex)`.

Note that the execution continues in the event of the exception. If the handlers had not caught the exception, the program would have abruptly terminated.

The test program would still compile if the `try` statement were not used, because the method throws an instance of `IllegalArgumentException`, a subclass of `RuntimeException` (an unchecked exception). If a method throws an exception other than `RuntimeException` or `Error`, the method must be invoked within a `try-catch` block.

MyProgrammingLab™

14.9 What is the purpose of declaring exceptions? How do you declare an exception, and where? Can you declare multiple exceptions in a method header?

14.10 What is a checked exception, and what is an unchecked exception?

14.11 How do you throw an exception? Can you throw multiple exceptions in one `throw` statement?

14.12 What is the keyword `throw` used for? What is the keyword `throws` used for?

14.13 Suppose that `statement2` causes an exception in the following `try-catch` block:

```
try {
  statement1;
  statement2;
  statement3;
}
catch (Exception1 ex1) {
}
catch (Exception2 ex2) {
}

statement4;
```

Answer the following questions:

- Will `statement3` be executed?
- If the exception is not caught, will `statement4` be executed?
- If the exception is caught in the `catch` block, will `statement4` be executed?

14.14 What is displayed when the following program is run?

```
public class Test {
  public static void main(String[] args) {
    try {
      int[] list = new int[10];
      System.out.println("list[10] is " + list[10]);
    }
    catch (ArithmeticException ex) {
      System.out.println("ArithmeticException");
    }
    catch (RuntimeException ex) {
      System.out.println("RuntimeException");
    }
    catch (Exception ex) {
      System.out.println("Exception");
    }
  }
}
```

14.15 What is displayed when the following program is run?

```
public class Test {
  public static void main(String[] args) {
    try {
      method();
      System.out.println("After the method call");
    }
    catch (ArithmeticException ex) {
      System.out.println("ArithmeticException");
    }
    catch (RuntimeException ex) {
      System.out.println("RuntimeException");
    }
    catch (Exception e) {
      System.out.println("Exception");
    }
  }

  static void method() throws Exception {
```

```
      System.out.println(1 / 0);
    }
  }
```

14.16 What is displayed when the following program is run?

```
public class Test {
  public static void main(String[] args) {
    try {
      method();
      System.out.println("After the method call");
    }
    catch (RuntimeException ex) {
      System.out.println("RuntimeException in main");
    }
    catch (Exception ex) {
      System.out.println("Exception in main");
    }
  }

  static void method() throws Exception {
    try {
      String s ="abc";
      System.out.println(s.charAt(3));
    }
    catch (RuntimeException ex) {
      System.out.println("RuntimeException in method()");
    }
    catch (Exception ex) {
      System.out.println("Exception in method()");
    }
  }
}
```

14.17 What does the method `getMessage()` do?

14.18 What does the method `printStackTrace` do?

14.19 Does the presence of a `try-catch` block impose overhead when no exception occurs?

14.20 Correct a compile error in the following code:

```
public void m(int value) {
  if (value < 40)
    throw new Exception("value is too small");
}
```

14.5 The `finally` Clause

The `finally` clause is always executed regardless whether an exception occurred or not.

Occasionally, you may want some code to be executed regardless of whether an exception occurs or is caught. Java has a `finally` clause that can be used to accomplish this objective. The syntax for the `finally` clause might look like this:

```
try {
  statements;
}
catch (TheException ex) {
  handling ex;
}
```

```
finally {
  finalStatements;
}
```

The code in the finally block is executed under all circumstances, regardless of whether an exception occurs in the try block or is caught. Consider three possible cases:

- If no exception arises in the try block, finalStatements is executed, and the next statement after the try statement is executed.
- If a statement causes an exception in the try block that is caught in a catch block, the rest of the statements in the try block are skipped, the catch block is executed, and the finally clause is executed. The next statement after the try statement is executed.
- If one of the statements causes an exception that is not caught in any catch block, the other statements in the try block are skipped, the finally clause is executed, and the exception is passed to the caller of this method.

The finally block executes even if there is a return statement prior to reaching the finally block.

Note

omitting catch block

The catch block may be omitted when the finally clause is used.

A common use of the finally clause is in I/O programming. To ensure that a file is closed under all circumstances, you may place a file closing statement in the finally block. Text I/O will be introduced later in this chapter.

Check Point

MyProgrammingLab™

14.21 Suppose that statement2 causes an exception in the following statement:

```
try {
  statement1;
  statement2;
  statement3;
}
catch (Exception1 ex1) {
}
finally {
  statement4;
}
statement5;
```

Answer the following questions:

- If no exception occurs, will statement4 be executed, and will statement5 be executed?
- If the exception is of type Exception1, will statement4 be executed, and will statement5 be executed?
- If the exception is not of type Exception1, will statement4 be executed, and will statement5 be executed?

14.6 When to Use Exceptions

A method should throw an exception if the error needs to be handled by its caller.

The try block contains the code that is executed in normal circumstances. The catch block contains the code that is executed in exceptional circumstances. Exception handling separates error-handling code from normal programming tasks, thus making programs easier to read and to modify. Be aware, however, that exception handling usually requires more time and resources, because it requires instantiating a new exception object, rolling back the call stack, and propagating the exception through the chain of methods invoked to search for the handler.

An exception occurs in a method. If you want the exception to be processed by its caller, you should create an exception object and throw it. If you can handle the exception in the method where it occurs, there is no need to throw or use exceptions.

In general, common exceptions that may occur in multiple classes in a project are candidates for exception classes. Simple errors that may occur in individual methods are best handled without throwing exceptions. This can be done by using `if` statements to check for errors.

When should you use a `try-catch` block in the code? Use it when you have to deal with unexpected error conditions. Do not use a `try-catch` block to deal with simple, expected situations. For example, the following code

```
try {
  System.out.println(refVar.toString());
}
catch (NullPointerException ex) {
  System.out.println("refVar is null");
}
```

is better replaced by

```
if (refVar != null)
  System.out.println(refVar.toString());
else
  System.out.println("refVar is null");
```

Which situations are exceptional and which are expected is sometimes difficult to decide. The point is not to abuse exception handling as a way to deal with a simple logic test.

14.22 The following method checks whether a string is a numeric string:

```
public static boolean isNumeric(String token) {
  try {
    Double.parseDouble(token);
    return true;
  }
  catch (java.lang.NumberFormatException ex) {
    return false;
  }
}
```

Is it correct? Rewrite it without using exceptions.

14.7 Rethrowing Exceptions

Java allows an exception handler to rethrow the exception if the handler cannot process the exception or simply wants to let its caller be notified of the exception.

The syntax for rethrowing an exception may look like this:

```
try {
  statements;
}
catch (TheException ex) {
```

```
    perform operations before exits;
    throw ex;
  }
```

The statement `throw ex` rethrows the exception to the caller so that other handlers in the caller get a chance to process the exception `ex`.

Check Point

MyProgrammingLab™

14.23 Suppose that `statement2` causes an exception in the following statement:

```
try {
  statement1;
  statement2;
  statement3;
}
catch (Exception1 ex1) {
}
catch (Exception2 ex2) {
  throw ex2;
}
finally {
  statement4;
}
statement5;
```

Answer the following questions:

- If no exception occurs, will `statement4` be executed, and will `statement5` be executed?
- If the exception is of type `Exception1`, will `statement4` be executed, and will `statement5` be executed?
- If the exception is of type `Exception2`, will `statement4` be executed, and will `statement5` be executed?
- If the exception is not `Exception1` nor `Exception2`, will `statement4` be executed, and will `statement5` be executed?

14.8 Chained Exceptions

Throwing an exception along with another exception forms a chained exception.

Key Point

In the preceding section, the `catch` block rethrows the original exception. Sometimes, you may need to throw a new exception (with additional information) along with the original exception. This is called *chained exceptions*. Listing 14.9 illustrates how to create and throw chained exceptions.

chained exception

Listing 14.9 `ChainedExceptionDemo.java`

```
public class ChainedExceptionDemo {
  public static void main(String[] args) {
    try {
      method1();
    }
    catch (Exception ex) {
      ex.printStackTrace();
    }
  }

```

stack trace

chained exception

throw exception

```
11   public static void method1() throws Exception {
12     try {
13       method2();
14     }
15     catch (Exception ex) {
16       throw new Exception("New info from method1", ex);
17     }
18   }
19
20   public static void method2() throws Exception {
21     throw new Exception("New info from method2");
22   }
23 }
```

```
java.lang.Exception: New info from method1
  at ChainedExceptionDemo.method1(ChainedExceptionDemo.java:16)
  at ChainedExceptionDemo.main(ChainedExceptionDemo.java:4)
Caused by: java.lang.Exception: New info from method2
  at ChainedExceptionDemo.method2(ChainedExceptionDemo.java:21)
  at ChainedExceptionDemo.method1(ChainedExceptionDemo.java:13)
  ... 1 more
```

The `main` method invokes `method1` (line 4), `method1` invokes `method2` (line 13), and `method2` throws an exception (line 21). This exception is caught in the `catch` block in `method1` and is wrapped in a new exception in line 16. The new exception is thrown and caught in the catch block in the `main` method in line 6. The sample output shows the output from the `printStackTrace()` method in line 7. The new exception thrown from `method1` is displayed first, followed by the original exception thrown from `method2`.

14.9 Defining Custom Exception Classes

You can define a custom exception class by extending the `java.lang.Exception` class.

VideoNote
Create custom exception classes

Java provides quite a few exception classes. Use them whenever possible instead of defining your own exception classes. However, if you run into a problem that cannot be adequately described by the predefined exception classes, you can create your own exception class, derived from `Exception` or from a subclass of `Exception`, such as `IOException`.

In Listing 14.7, CircleWithException.java, the `setRadius` method throws an exception if the radius is negative. Suppose you wish to pass the radius to the handler. In that case, you can define a custom exception class, as shown in Listing 14.10.

Listing 14.10 InvalidRadiusException.java

extends Exception

```
public class InvalidRadiusException extends Exception {
  private double radius;

  /** Construct an exception */
  public InvalidRadiusException(double radius) {
    super("Invalid radius " + radius);
    this.radius = radius;
  }

  /** Return the radius */
  public double getRadius() {
    return radius;
  }
}
```

This custom exception class extends `java.lang.Exception` (line 1). The `Exception` class extends `java.lang.Throwable`. All the methods (e.g., `getMessage()`, `toString()`, and `printStackTrace()`) in `Exception` are inherited from `Throwable`. The `Exception` class contains four constructors. Among them, the following two constructors are often used:

java.lang.Exception	
+Exception()	Constructs an exception with no message.
+Exception(message: String)	Constructs an exception with the specified message.

Line 6 invokes the superclass's constructor with a message. This message will be set in the exception object and can be obtained by invoking `getMessage()` on the object.

Tip

Most exception classes in the Java API contain two constructors: a no-arg constructor and a constructor with a message parameter.

To create an `InvalidRadiusException`, you have to pass a radius. Therefore, the `setRadius` method in Listing 14.7 can be modified as shown in Listing 14.11.

LISTING 14.11 TestCircleWithCustomException.java

```
public class TestCircleWithCustomException {
  public static void main(String[] args) {
    try {
      new CircleWithCustomException(5);
      new CircleWithCustomException(-5);
      new CircleWithCustomException(0);
    }
    catch (InvalidRadiusException ex) {
      System.out.println(ex);
    }

    System.out.println("Number of objects created: " +
      CircleWithCustomException.getNumberOfObjects());
  }
}

class CircleWithCustomException {
  /** The radius of the circle */
  private double radius;

  /** The number of objects created */
  private static int numberOfObjects = 0;

  /** Construct a circle with radius 1 */
  public CircleWithCustomException() throws InvalidRadiusException {   // declare exception
    this(1.0);
  }

  /** Construct a circle with a specified radius */
  public CircleWithCustomException(double newRadius)   // throw exception
      throws InvalidRadiusException {
    setRadius(newRadius);
    numberOfObjects++;
  }

  /** Return radius */
```

```
37   public double getRadius() {
38     return radius;
39   }
40
41   /** Set a new radius */
42   public void setRadius(double newRadius)
43       throws InvalidRadiusException {
44     if (newRadius >= 0)
45       radius = newRadius;
46     else
47       throw new InvalidRadiusException(newRadius);
48   }
49
50   /** Return numberOfObjects */
51   public static int getNumberOfObjects() {
52     return numberOfObjects;
53   }
54
55   /** Return the area of this circle */
56   public double findArea() {
57     return radius * radius * 3.14159;
58   }
59 }
```

```
InvalidRadiusException: Invalid radius -5.0
Number of objects created: 1
```

The `setRadius` method in `CircleWithCustomException` throws an `InvalidRadiusException` when radius is negative (line 47). Since `InvalidRadiusException` is a checked exception, the `setRadius` method must declare it in the method header (line 42). Since the constructors for `CircleWithCustomException` invoke the `setRadius` method to a set a new radius and it may throw an `InvalidRadiusException`, the constructors are declared to throw `InvalidRadiusException` (lines 25, 31).

Invoking `new CircleWithCustomException(-5)` throws an `InvalidRadiusException`, which is caught by the handler. The handler displays the radius in the exception object `ex`.

checked custom exception

Tip

Can you define a custom exception class by extending `RuntimeException`? Yes, but it is not a good way to go, because it makes your custom exception unchecked. It is better to make a custom exception checked, so that the compiler can force these exceptions to be caught in your program.

MyProgrammingLab™

14.24 How do you define a custom exception class?

14.25 Suppose the `setRadius` method throws the `InValidRadiusException` defined in Listing 14.10. What is displayed when the following program is run?

```
public class Test {
  public static void main(String[] args) {
    try {
      method();
      System.out.println("After the method call");
    }
    catch (RuntimeException ex) {
      System.out.println("RuntimeException in main");
```

```
    }
    catch (Exception ex) {
      System.out.println("Exception in main");
    }
  }

  static void method() throws Exception {
    try {
      Circle c1 = new Circle(1);
      c1.setRadius(-1);
      System.out.println(c1.getRadius());
    }
    catch (RuntimeException ex) {
      System.out.println("RuntimeException in method()");
    }
    catch (Exception ex) {
      System.out.println("Exception in method()");
      throw ex;
    }
  }
}
```

14.10 The **File** Class

The `File` *class contains the methods for obtaining the properties of a file/directory and for renaming and deleting a file/directory.*

Having learned exception handling, you are ready to step into file processing. Data stored in the program are temporary; they are lost when the program terminates. To permanently store the data created in a program, you need to save them in a file on a disk or other permanent storage device. The file can then be transported and read later by other programs. Since data are stored in files, this section introduces how to use the `File` class to obtain file/directory properties, to delete and rename files/directories, and to create directories. The next section introduces how to read/write data from/to text files.

why file?

Every file is placed in a directory in the file system. An *absolute file name* (or *full name*) contains a file name with its complete path and drive letter. For example, **c:\book\Welcome.java** is the absolute file name for the file **Welcome.java** on the Windows operating system. Here **c:\book** is referred to as the *directory path* for the file. Absolute file names are machine dependent. On the UNIX platform, the absolute file name may be **/home/liang/book/Welcome.java**, where **/home/liang/book** is the directory path for the file **Welcome.java**.

absolute file name

directory path

A *relative file name* is in relation to the current working directory. The complete directory path for a relative file name is omitted. For example, **Welcome.java** is a relative file name. If the current working directory is **c:\book**, the absolute file name would be **c:\book\Welcome.java**.

relative file name

The `File` class is intended to provide an abstraction that deals with most of the machine-dependent complexities of files and path names in a machine-independent fashion. The `File` class contains the methods for obtaining file and directory properties and for renaming and deleting files and directories, as shown in Figure 14.6. However, *the* `File` *class does not contain the methods for reading and writing file contents.*

The file name is a string. The `File` class is a wrapper class for the file name and its directory path. For example, `new File("c:\\book")` creates a `File` object for the directory **c:\book**, and `new File("c:\\book\\test.dat")` creates a `File` object for the file **c:\book\test.dat**, both on Windows. You can use the `File` class's `isDirectory()` method to check whether the object represents a directory, and the `isFile()` method to check whether the object represents a file.

java.io.File	
+File(pathname: String)	Creates a File object for the specified path name. The path name may be a directory or a file.
+File(parent: String, child: String)	Creates a File object for the child under the directory parent. The child may be a file name or a subdirectory.
+File(parent: File, child: String)	Creates a File object for the child under the directory parent. The parent is a File object. In the preceding constructor, the parent is a string.
+exists(): boolean	Returns true if the file or the directory represented by the File object exists.
+canRead(): boolean	Returns true if the file represented by the File object exists and can be read.
+canWrite(): boolean	Returns true if the file represented by the File object exists and can be written.
+isDirectory(): boolean	Returns true if the File object represents a directory.
+isFile(): boolean	Returns true if the File object represents a file.
+isAbsolute(): boolean	Returns true if the File object is created using an absolute path name.
+isHidden(): boolean	Returns true if the file represented in the File object is hidden. The exact definition of *hidden* is system-dependent. On Windows, you can mark a file hidden in the File Properties dialog box. On Unix systems, a file is hidden if its name begins with a period(.) character.
+getAbsolutePath(): String	Returns the complete absolute file or directory name represented by the File object.
+getCanonicalPath(): String	Returns the same as getAbsolutePath() except that it removes redundant names, such as "." and "..", from the path name, resolves symbolic links (on Unix), and converts drive letters to standard uppercase (on Windows).
+getName(): String	Returns the last name of the complete directory and file name represented by the File object. For example, new File("c:\\book\\test.dat").getName() returns test.dat.
+getPath(): String	Returns the complete directory and file name represented by the File object. For example, new File("c:\\book\\test.dat").getPath() returns c:\book\test.dat.
+getParent(): String	Returns the complete parent directory of the current directory or the file represented by the File object. For example, new File("c:\\book\\test.dat").getParent() returns c:\book.
+lastModified(): long	Returns the time that the file was last modified.
+length(): long	Returns the size of the file, or 0 if it does not exist or if it is a directory.
+listFile(): File[]	Returns the files under the directory for a directory File object.
+delete(): boolean	Deletes the file or directory represented by this File object.The method returns true if the deletion succeeds.
+renameTo(dest: File): boolean	Renames the file or directory represented by this File object to the specified name represented in dest. The method returns true if the operation succeeds.
+mkdir(): boolean	Creates a directory represented in this File object. Returns true if the the directory is created successfully.
+mkdirs(): boolean	Same as mkdir() except that it creates directory along with its parent directories if the parent directories do not exist.

FIGURE 14.6 The File class can be used to obtain file and directory properties, to delete and rename files and directories, and to create directories.

\ in file names

Caution

The directory separator for Windows is a backslash (\). The backslash is a special character in Java and should be written as \\ in a string literal (see Table 2.6).

Note

*Constructing a **File** instance does not create a file on the machine.* You can create a **File** instance for any file name regardless whether it exists or not. You can invoke the **exists()** method on a **File** instance to check whether the file exists.

relative file name

Java directory separator (/)

Do not use absolute file names in your program. If you use a file name such as **c:\\book\\Welcome.java**, it will work on Windows but not on other platforms. You should use a file name relative to the current directory. For example, you may create a **File** object using **new File("Welcome.java")** for the file **Welcome.java** in the current directory. You may create a **File** object using **new File("image/us.gif")** for the file **us.gif** under the **image** directory in the current directory. The forward slash (/) is the Java directory separator, which is the same as on UNIX. The statement `new File("image/us.gif")` works on Windows, UNIX, and any other platform.

Listing 14.12 demonstrates how to create a `File` object and use the methods in the `File` class to obtain its properties. The program creates a `File` object for the file **us.gif**. This file is stored under the **image** directory in the current directory.

Listing 14.12 TestFileClass.java

```
1  public class TestFileClass {
2    public static void main(String[] args) {
3      java.io.File file = new java.io.File("image/us.gif");
4      System.out.println("Does it exist? " + file.exists());
5      System.out.println("The file has " + file.length() + " bytes");
6      System.out.println("Can it be read? " + file.canRead());
7      System.out.println("Can it be written? " + file.canWrite());
8      System.out.println("Is it a directory? " + file.isDirectory());
9      System.out.println("Is it a file? " + file.isFile());
10     System.out.println("Is it absolute? " + file.isAbsolute());
11     System.out.println("Is it hidden? " + file.isHidden());
12     System.out.println("Absolute path is " +
13       file.getAbsolutePath());
14     System.out.println("Last modified on " +
15       new java.util.Date(file.lastModified()));
16   }
17 }
```

create a `File` object
`exists()`
`length()`
`canRead()`
`canWrite()`
`isDirectory()`
`isFile()`
`isAbsolute()`
`isHidden()`
`getAbsolutePath()`
`lastModified()`

The `lastModified()` method returns the date and time when the file was last modified, measured in milliseconds since the beginning of UNIX time (00:00:00 GMT, January 1, 1970). The `Date` class is used to display it in a readable format in lines 14–15.

Figure 14.7a shows a sample run of the program on Windows, and Figure 14.7b, a sample run on UNIX. As shown in the figures, the path-naming conventions on Windows are different from those on UNIX.

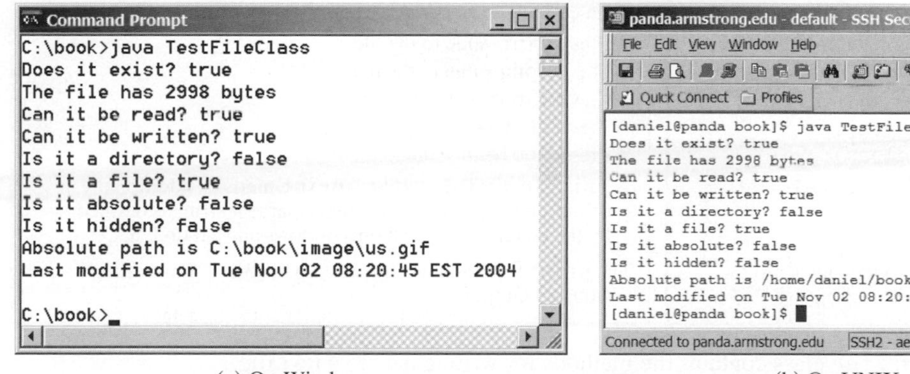

Figure 14.7 The program creates a `File` object and displays file properties.

14.26 What is wrong about creating a `File` object using the following statement?

```
new File("c:\book\test.dat");
```

14.27 How do you check whether a file already exists? How do you delete a file? How do you rename a file? Can you find the file size (the number of bytes) using the `File` class? How do you create a directory?

14.28 Can you use the `File` class for I/O? Does creating a `File` object create a file on the disk?

14.11 File Input and Output

Key Point

Use the `Scanner` class for reading text data from a file and the `PrintWriter` class for writing text data to a file.

VideoNote
Write and read data

A `File` object encapsulates the properties of a file or a path, but it does not contain the methods for creating a file or for writing/reading data to/from a file (referred to as data *input* and *output*, or *I/O* for short). In order to perform I/O, you need to create objects using appropriate Java I/O classes. The objects contain the methods for reading/writing data from/to a file. There are two types of files: text and binary. Text files are essentially strings on disk. This section introduces how to read/write strings and numeric values from/to a text file using the `Scanner` and `PrintWriter` classes. Binary files will be introduced in Chapter 19.

14.11.1 Writing Data Using `PrintWriter`

The `java.io.PrintWriter` class can be used to create a file and write data to a text file. First, you have to create a `PrintWriter` object for a text file as follows:

```
PrintWriter output = new PrintWriter(filename);
```

Then, you can invoke the `print`, `println`, and `printf` methods on the `PrintWriter` object to write data to a file. Figure 14.8 summarizes frequently used methods in `PrintWriter`.

java.io.PrintWriter	
`+PrintWriter(file: File)`	Creates a `PrintWriter` object for the specified file object.
`+PrintWriter(filename: String)`	Creates a `PrintWriter` object for the specified file-name string.
`+print(s: String): void`	Writes a string to the file.
`+print(c: char): void`	Writes a character to the file.
`+print(cArray: char[]): void`	Writes an array of characters to the file.
`+print(i: int): void`	Writes an `int` value to the file.
`+print(l: long): void`	Writes a `long` value to the file.
`+print(f: float): void`	Writes a `float` value to the file.
`+print(d: double): void`	Writes a `double` value to the file.
`+print(b: boolean): void`	Writes a `boolean` value to the file.
Also contains the overloaded `println` methods.	A `println` method acts like a `print` method; additionally, it prints a line separator. The line-separator string is defined by the system. It is `\r\n` on Windows and `\n` on Unix.
Also contains the overloaded `printf` methods.	The `printf` method was introduced in §3.16, "Formatting Console Output."

FIGURE 14.8 The `PrintWriter` class contains the methods for writing data to a text file.

Listing 14.13 gives an example that creates an instance of `PrintWriter` and writes two lines to the file **scores.txt**. Each line consists of a first name (a string), a middle-name initial (a character), a last name (a string), and a score (an integer).

LISTING 14.13 `WriteData.java`

throws an exception
create `File` object
file exist?

```
public class WriteData {
  public static void main(String[] args) throws IoException {
    java.io.File file = new java.io.File("scores.txt");
    if (file.exists()) {
```

```
5       System.out.println("File already exists");
6       System.exit(1);
7     }
8
9     // Create a file
10    java.io.PrintWriter output = new java.io.PrintWriter(file);
11
12    // Write formatted output to the file
13    output.print("John T Smith ");
14    output.println(90);
15    output.print("Eric K Jones ");
16    output.println(85);
17
18    // Close the file
19    output.close();
20  }
21 }
```

create PrintWriter

print data

```
John T Smith 90
Eric K Jones 85
```

scores.txt

close file

Lines 4–7 check whether the file scores.txt exists. If so, exit the program (line 6).

create a file

Invoking the constructor of **PrintWriter** will create a new file if the file does not exist. If the file already exists, the current content in the file will be discarded without verifying with the user.

throws IOException

Invoking the constructor of **PrintWriter** may throw an I/O exception. Java forces you to write the code to deal with this type of exception. For simplicity, we declare **throws** ***IOException*** in the main method header (line 2).

print method

You have used the **System.out.print**, **System.out.println**, and **System.out.printf** methods to write text to the console. **System.out** is a standard Java object for the console. You can create **PrintWriter** objects for writing text to any file using **print**, **println**, and **printf** (lines 13–16).

close file

The **close()** method must be used to close the file. If this method is not invoked, the data may not be saved properly in the file.

14.11.2 Reading Data Using Scanner

The **java.util.Scanner** class was used to read strings and primitive values from the console in Section 2.3, Reading Input from the Console. A **Scanner** breaks its input into tokens delimited by whitespace characters. To read from the keyboard, you create a **Scanner** for **System.in**, as follows:

```
Scanner input = new Scanner(System.in);
```

To read from a file, create a **Scanner** for a file, as follows:

```
Scanner input = new Scanner(new File(filename));
```

Figure 14.9 summarizes frequently used methods in **Scanner**.

Listing 14.14 gives an example that creates an instance of **Scanner** and reads data from the file **scores.txt**.

LISTING 14.14 ReadData.java

```
import java.util.Scanner;

public class ReadData {
  public static void main(String[] args) throws Exception {
    // Create a File instance
    java.io.File file = new java.io.File("scores.txt");

    // Create a Scanner for the file
```

create a file

create a Scanner
has next?
read items
close file

```
 9    Scanner input = new Scanner(file);
10
11    // Read data from a file
12    while (input.hasNext()) {
13      String firstName = input.next();
14      String mi = input.next();
15      String lastName = input.next();
16      int score = input.nextInt();
17      System.out.println(
18        firstName + " " + mi + " " + lastName + " " + score);
19    }
20
21    // Close the file
22    input.close();
23  }
24 }
```

scores.txt

```
John T Smith 90
Eric K Jones 85
```

java.util.Scanner	
+Scanner(source: File)	Creates a Scanner that produces values scanned from the specified file.
+Scanner(source: String)	Creates a Scanner that produces values scanned from the specified string.
+close()	Closes this scanner.
+hasNext(): boolean	Returns true if this scanner has more data to be read.
+next(): String	Returns next token as a string from this scanner.
+nextLine(): String	Returns a line ending with the line separator from this scanner.
+nextByte(): byte	Returns next token as a byte from this scanner.
+nextShort(): short	Returns next token as a short from this scanner.
+nextInt(): int	Returns next token as an int from this scanner.
+nextLong(): long	Returns next token as a long from this scanner.
+nextFloat(): float	Returns next token as a float from this scanner.
+nextDouble(): double	Returns next token as a double from this scanner.
+useDelimiter(pattern: String): Scanner	Sets this scanner's delimiting pattern and returns this scanner.

Figure 14.9 The Scanner class contains the methods for scanning data.

File class

Note that `new Scanner(String)` creates a `Scanner` for a given string. To create a `Scanner` to read data from a file, you have to use the `java.io.File` class to create an instance of the `File` using the constructor `new File(filename)` (line 6), and use `new Scanner(File)` to create a `Scanner` for the file (line 9).

throws Exception

Invoking the constructor `new Scanner(File)` may throw an I/O exception, so the `main` method declares `throws Exception` in line 4.

Each iteration in the `while` loop reads the first name, middle initial, last name, and score from the text file (lines 12–19). The file is closed in line 22.

close file

It is not necessary to close the input file (line 22), but it is a good practice to do so to release the resources occupied by the file.

14.11.3 How Does Scanner Work?

token-reading method
change delimiter

The `nextByte()`, `nextShort()`, `nextInt()`, `nextLong()`, `nextFloat()`, `nextDouble()`, and `next()` methods are known as *token-reading methods*, because they read tokens separated by delimiters. By default, the delimiters are whitespace. You can use the `useDelimiter(String regex)` method to set a new pattern for delimiters.

How does an input method work? A token-reading method first skips any delimiters (whitespace by default), then reads a token ending at a delimiter. The token is then automatically converted into a value of the **byte**, **short**, **int**, **long**, **float**, or **double** type for **nextByte()**, **nextShort()**, **nextInt()**, **nextLong()**, **nextFloat()**, and **nextDouble()**, respectively. For the **next()** method, no conversion is performed. If the token does not match the expected type, a runtime exception **java.util.InputMismatchException** will be thrown.

InputMismatchException

Both methods **next()** and **nextLine()** read a string. The **next()** method reads a string delimited by delimiters, and **nextLine()** reads a line ending with a line separator.

next() vs. nextLine()

Note

The line-separator string is defined by the system. It is \r\n on Windows and \n on UNIX. To get the line separator on a particular platform, use

line separator

```
String lineSeparator = System.getProperty("line.separator");
```

If you enter input from a keyboard, a line ends with the *Enter* key, which corresponds to the \n character.

The token-reading method does not read the delimiter after the token. If the **nextLine()** method is invoked after a token-reading method, this method reads characters that start from this delimiter and end with the line separator. The line separator is read, but it is not part of the string returned by **nextLine()**.

behavior of nextLine()

Suppose a text file named **test.txt** contains a line

input from file

```
34 567
```

After the following code is executed,

```
Scanner input = new Scanner(new File("test.txt"));
int intValue = input.nextInt();
String line = input.nextLine();
```

intValue contains **34** and **line** contains the characters **' '**, **5**, **6**, and **7**.

What happens if the input is *entered from the keyboard*? Suppose you enter **34**, press the *Enter* key, then enter **567** and press the *Enter* key for the following code:

input from keyboard

```
Scanner input = new Scanner(System.in);
int intValue = input.nextInt();
String line = input.nextLine();
```

You will get **34** in **intValue** and an empty string in **line**. Why? Here is the reason. The token-reading method **nextInt()** reads in **34** and stops at the delimiter, which in this case is a line separator (the *Enter* key). The **nextLine()** method ends after reading the line separator and returns the string read before the line separator. Since there are no characters before the line separator, **line** is empty.

You can read data from a file or from the keyboard using the **Scanner** class. You can also scan data from a string using the **Scanner** class. For example, the following code

scan a string

```
Scanner input = new Scanner("13 14");
int sum = input.nextInt() + input.nextInt();
System.out.println("Sum is " + sum);
```

displays

```
The sum is 27
```

14.11.4 Case Study: Replacing Text

Suppose you are to write a program named `ReplaceText` that replaces all occurrences of a string in a text file with a new string. The file name and strings are passed as command-line arguments as follows:

```
java ReplaceText sourceFile targetFile oldString newString
```

For example, invoking

```
java ReplaceText FormatString.java t.txt StringBuilder StringBuffer
```

replaces all the occurrences of `StringBuilder` by `StringBuffer` in the file **FormatString.java** and saves the new file in **t.txt**.

Listing 14.15 gives the program. The program checks the number of arguments passed to the `main` method (lines 7–11), checks whether the source and target files exist (lines 14–25), creates a `Scanner` for the source file (line 28), creates a `PrintWriter` for the target file, and repeatedly reads a line from the source file (line 32), replaces the text (line 33), and writes a new line to the target file (line 34). You must close the output file (line 38) to ensure that data are saved to the file properly.

LISTING 14.15 ReplaceText.java

check command usage (line 7)
source file exists? (line 15)
target file exists? (line 22)
create a `Scanner` (line 28)
create a `PrintWriter` (line 29)
has next? (line 31)
read a line (line 32)

```
1  import java.io.*;
2  import java.util.*;
3
4  public class ReplaceText {
5    public static void main(String[] args) throws Exception {
6      // Check command-line parameter usage
7      if (args.length != 4) {
8        System.out.println(
9          "Usage: java ReplaceText sourceFile targetFile oldStr newStr");
10       System.exit(1);
11     }
12
13     // Check if source file exists
14     File sourceFile = new File(args[0]);
15     if (!sourceFile.exists()) {
16       System.out.println("Source file " + args[0] + " does not exist");
17       System.exit(2);
18     }
19
20     // Check if target file exists
21     File targetFile = new File(args[1]);
22     if (targetFile.exists()) {
23       System.out.println("Target file " + args[1] + " already exists");
24       System.exit(3);
25     }
26
27     // Create a Scanner for input and a PrintWriter for output
28     Scanner input = new Scanner(sourceFile);
29     PrintWriter output = new PrintWriter(targetFile);
30
31     while (input.hasNext()) {
32       String s1 = input.nextLine();
33       String s2 = s1.replaceAll(args[2], args[3]);
34       output.println(s2);
35     }
36
```

```
37       input.close();
38       output.close();
39     }
40   }
```

close file

In a normal situation, the program is terminated after a file is copied. The program is terminated abnormally if the command-line arguments are not used properly (lines 7–11), if the source file does not exist (lines 14–18), or if the target file already exists (lines 22–25). The exit status code 1, 2, and 3 are used to indicate these abnormal terminations (lines 10, 17, 24).

14.29 How do you create a `PrintWriter` to write data to a file? What is the reason to declare `throws Exception` in the main method in Listing 14.13, WriteData.java? What would happen if the `close()` method were not invoked in Listing 14.13?

14.30 Show the contents of the file **temp.txt** after the following program is executed.

```
public class Test {
  public static void main(String[] args) throws Exception {
    java.io.PrintWriter output = new
      java.io.PrintWriter("temp.txt");
    output.printf("amount is %f %e\r\n", 32.32, 32.32);
    output.printf("amount is %5.4f %5.4e\r\n", 32.32, 32.32);
    output.printf("%6b\r\n", (1 > 2));
    output.printf("%6s\r\n", "Java");
    output.close();
  }
}
```

14.31 How do you create a `Scanner` to read data from a file? What is the reason to define `throws Exception` in the main method in Listing 14.14, ReadData.java? What would happen if the `close()` method were not invoked in Listing 14.14?

14.32 What will happen if you attempt to create a `Scanner` for a nonexistent file? What will happen if you attempt to create a `PrintWriter` for an existing file?

14.33 Is the line separator the same on all platforms? What is the line separator on Windows?

14.34 Suppose you enter `45 57.8 789`, then press the *Enter* key. Show the contents of the variables after the following code is executed.

```
Scanner input = new Scanner(System.in);
int intValue = input.nextInt();
double doubleValue = input.nextDouble();
String line = input.nextLine();
```

14.35 Suppose you enter `45`, press the *Enter* key, `57.8`, press the *Enter* key, `789`, and press the *Enter* key. Show the contents of the variables after the following code is executed.

```
Scanner input = new Scanner(System.in);
int intValue = input.nextInt();
double doubleValue = input.nextDouble();
String line = input.nextLine();
```

14.12 File Dialogs

`JFileChooser` *is a GUI component for displaying a file dialog.*

Java provides the `javax.swing.JFileChooser` class for displaying a file dialog, as shown in Figure 14.10. From this dialog box, the user can choose a file.

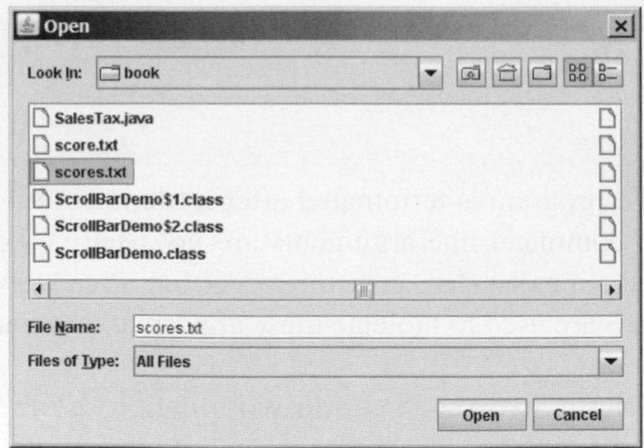

FIGURE 14.10 `JFileChooser` can be used to display a file dialog for opening a file.

Listing 14.16 gives a program that prompts the user to choose a file and displays its contents on the console.

LISTING 14.16 ReadFileUsingJFileChooser.java

create a JFileChooser
display file chooser
check status
getSelectedFile

```
1  import java.util.Scanner;
2  import javax.swing.JFileChooser;
3
4  public class ReadFileUsingJFileChooser {
5    public static void main(String[] args) throws Exception {
6      JFileChooser fileChooser = new JFileChooser();
7      if (fileChooser.showOpenDialog(null)
8          == JFileChooser.APPROVE_OPTION) {
9        // Get the selected file
10       java.io.File file = fileChooser.getSelectedFile();
11
12       // Create a Scanner for the file
13       Scanner input = new Scanner(file);
14
15       // Read text from the file
16       while (input.hasNext()) {
17         System.out.println(input.nextLine());
18       }
19
20       // Close the file
21       input.close();
22     }
23     else {
24       System.out.println("No file selected");
25     }
26   }
27 }
```

showOpenDialog

APPROVE_OPTION

The program creates a `JFileChooser` in line 6. The `showOpenDialog(null)` method displays a dialog box, as shown in Figure 14.10. The method returns an `int` value, either `APPROVE_OPTION` or `CANCEL_OPTION`, which indicates whether the *Open* button or the *Cancel* button was clicked.

getSelectedFile

The `getSelectedFile()` method (line 10) returns the selected file from the file dialog box. Line 13 creates a scanner for the file. The program continuously reads the lines from the file and displays them to the console (lines 16–18).

Check Point

MyProgrammingLab™

14.36 How do you create a File Open dialog box? What is returned from invoking `getSelectFile()` on a `JFileChooser` object?

14.13 Reading Data from the Web

Just like you can read data from a file on your computer, you can read data from a file on the Web.

In addition to reading data from a local file on a computer or file server, you can also access data from a file that is on the Web if you know the file's URL (Uniform Resource Locator—the unique address for a file on the Web). For example, www.google.com/index.html is the URL for the file **index.html** located on the Google Web server. When you enter the URL in a Web browser, the Web server sends the data to your browser, which renders the data graphically. Figure 14.11 illustrates how this process works.

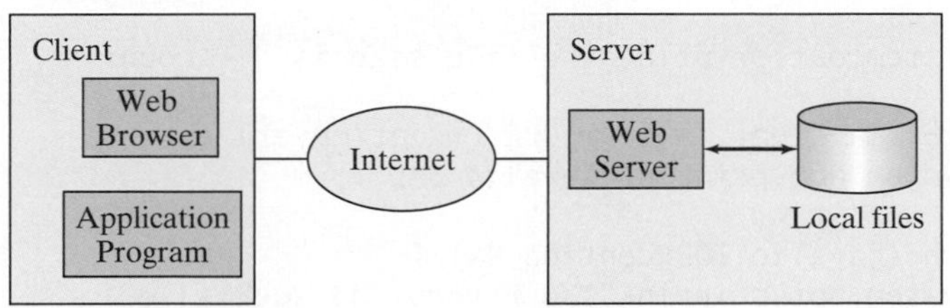

FIGURE 14.11 The client retrieves files from a Web server.

For an application program to read data from a URL, you first need to create a `URL` object using the `java.net.URL` class with this constructor:

```
public URL(String spec) throws MalformedURLException
```

For example, the following statement creates a URL object for http://www.google.com/index.html.

```
1 try {
2   URL url = new URL("http://www.google.com/index.html");
3 }
4 catch (MalformedURLException ex) {
5   ex.printStackTrace();
6 }
```

A `MalformedURLException` is thrown if the URL string has a syntax error. For example, the URL string "http:/www.google.com/index.html" would cause a `MalformedURLException` runtime error because two slashes (`//`) are required after the colon (`:`). Note that the `http://` prefix is required for the `URL` class to recognize a valid URL. It would be wrong if you replace line 2 with the following code:

```
URL url = new URL("www.google.com/index.html");
```

After a `URL` object is created, you can use the `openStream()` method defined in the `URL` class to open an input stream and use this stream to create a `Scanner` object as follows:

```
Scanner input = new Scanner(url.openStream());
```

Now you can read the data from the input stream just like from a local file. The example in Listing 14.17 prompts the user to enter a URL and displays the size of the file.

LISTING 14.17 `ReadFileFromURL.java`

```
import java.util.Scanner;

```

enter a URL

create a URL object

create a Scanner object

more to read?

read a line

MalformedURLException

IOException

```
3  public class ReadFileFromURL {
4    public static void main(String[] args) {
5      System.out.print("Enter a URL: ");
6      String URLString = new Scanner(System.in).next();
7
8      try {
9        java.net.URL url = new java.net.URL(URLString);
10       int count = 0;
11       Scanner input = new Scanner(url.openStream());
12       while (input.hasNext()) {
13         String line = input.nextLine();
14         count += line.length();
15       }
16
17       System.out.println("The file size is " + count + " bytes");
18     }
19     catch (java.net.MalformedURLException ex) {
20       System.out.println("Invalid URL");
21     }
22     catch (java.io.IOException ex) {
23       System.out.println("I/O Errors: no such file");
24     }
25   }
26 }
```

```
Enter a URL: http://cs.armstrong.edu/liang/data/Lincoln.txt ↵Enter
The file size is 1469 bytes
```

```
Enter a URL: http://www.yahoo.com ↵Enter
The file size is 190006 bytes
```

MalformedURLException

The program prompts the user to enter a URL string (line 6) and creates a **URL** object (line 9). The constructor will throw a **java.net.MalformedURLException** (line 19) if the URL isn't formed correctly.

The program creates a **Scanner** object from the input stream for the URL (line 11). If the URL is formed correctly but does not exist, an **IOException** will be thrown (line 22). For example, http://google.com/index1.html uses the appropriate form, but the URL itself does not exist. An **IOException** would be thrown if this URL was used for this program.

14.37 How do you create a **Scanner** object for reading text from a URL?

MyProgrammingLab™

Key Terms

Chapter Summary

1. Exception handling enables a method to throw an exception to its caller.

2. A Java *exception* is an instance of a class derived from `java.lang.Throwable`. Java provides a number of predefined exception classes, such as `Error`, `Exception`, `RuntimeException`, `ClassNotFoundException`, `NullPointerException`, and `ArithmeticException`. You can also define your own exception class by extending `Exception`.

3. Exceptions occur during the execution of a method. `RuntimeException` and `Error` are *unchecked exceptions*; all other exceptions are *checked*.

4. When *declaring a method*, you have to declare a checked exception if the method might throw it, thus telling the compiler what can go wrong.

5. The keyword for declaring an exception is `throws`, and the keyword for throwing an exception is `throw`.

6. To invoke the method that declares checked exceptions, enclose it in a `try` statement. When an exception occurs during the execution of the method, the `catch` block catches and handles the exception.

7. If an exception is not caught in the current method, it is passed to its caller. The process is repeated until the exception is caught or passed to the `main` method.

8. Various exception classes can be derived from a common superclass. If a `catch` block catches the exception objects of a superclass, it can also catch all the exception objects of the subclasses of that superclass.

9. The order in which exceptions are specified in a `catch` block is important. A compile error will result if you specify an exception object of a class after an exception object of the superclass of that class.

10. When an exception occurs in a method, the method exits immediately if it does not catch the exception. If the method is required to perform some task before exiting, you can catch the exception in the method and then rethrow it to its caller.

11. The code in the `finally` block is executed under all circumstances, regardless of whether an exception occurs in the `try` block or whether an exception is caught if it occurs.

12. Exception handling separates error-handling code from normal programming tasks, thus making programs easier to read and to modify.

13. Exception handling should not be used to replace simple tests. You should perform simple test using `if` statements whenever possible, and reserve exception handling for dealing with situations that cannot be handled with `if` statements.

14. The `File` class is used to obtain file properties and manipulate files. It does not contain the methods for creating a file or for reading/writing data from/to a file.

15. You can use Scanner to read string and primitive data values from a text file and use PrintWriter to create a file and write data to a text file.

16. The JFileChooser class can be used to display file dialogs for choosing files.

17. You can read from a file on the Web using the URL class.

Test Questions

Do the test questions for this chapter online at www.cs.armstrong.edu/liang/intro9e/test.html.

MyProgrammingLab™

Programming Exercises

Sections 14.2–14.9

*14.1 (*NumberFormatException*) Listing 9.5, Calculator.java, is a simple command-line calculator. Note that the program terminates if any operand is nonnumeric. Write a program with an exception handler that deals with nonnumeric operands; then write another program without using an exception handler to achieve the same objective. Your program should display a message that informs the user of the wrong operand type before exiting (see Figure 14.12).

```
Administrator: Command Prompt

c:\exercise>java Exercise14_01 "4 + 5"
4 + 5 = 9

c:\exercise>java Exercise14_01 "4 - 5"
4 - 5 = -1

c:\exercise>java Exercise14_01 "4x - 5"
Wrong Input: 4x

c:\exercise>_
```

Figure 14.12 The program performs arithmetic operations and detects input errors.

*14.2 (*InputMismatchException*) Write a program that prompts the user to read two integers and displays their sum. Your program should prompt the user to read the number again if the input is incorrect.

*14.3 (*ArrayIndexOutOfBoundsException*) Write a program that meets the following requirements:

- Creates an array with 100 randomly chosen integers.
- Prompts the user to enter the index of the array, then displays the corresponding element value. If the specified index is out of bounds, display the message **Out of Bounds**.

*14.4 (*IllegalArgumentException*) Modify the Loan class in Listing 10.2 to throw IllegalArgumentException if the loan amount, interest rate, or number of years is less than or equal to zero.

*14.5 (*IllegalTriangleException*) Programming Exercise 11.1 defined the Triangle class with three sides. In a triangle, the sum of any two sides is greater than the other side. The Triangle class must adhere to this rule. Create the IllegalTriangleException class, and modify the constructor of the

`Triangle` class to throw an `IllegalTriangleException` object if a triangle is created with sides that violate the rule, as follows:

```
/** Construct a triangle with the specified sides */
public Triangle(double side1, double side2, double side3)
  throws IllegalTriangleException {
  // Implement it
}
```

***14.6** (*NumberFormatException*) Listing 9.2 implements the `hexToDecimal(String hexString)` method, which converts a hex string into a decimal number. Implement the `hexToDecimal` method to throw a `NumberFormatException` if the string is not a hex string.

***14.7** (*NumberFormatException*) Programming Exercise 9.8 specifies the `binaryToDecimal(String binaryString)` method, which converts a binary string into a decimal number. Implement the `binaryToDecimal` method to throw a `NumberFormatException` if the string is not a binary string.

***14.8** (*HexFormatException*) Exercise 14.6 implements the `hexToDecimal` method to throw a `NumberFormatException` if the string is not a hex string. Define a custom exception called `HexFormatException`. Implement the `hexToDecimal` method to throw a `HexFormatException` if the string is not a hex string.

***14.9** (*BinaryFormatException*) Exercise 14.7 implements the `binaryToDecimal` method to throw a `BinaryFormatException` if the string is not a binary string. Define a custom exception called `BinaryFormatException`. Implement the `binaryToDecimal` method to throw a `BinaryFormatException` if the string is not a binary string.

***14.10** (*OutOfMemoryError*) Write a program that causes the JVM to throw an `OutOfMemoryError` and catches and handles this error.

Sections 14.10–14.12

****14.11** (*Remove text*) Write a program that removes all the occurrences of a specified string from a text file. For example, invoking

```
java Exercise14_11 John filename
```

removes the string `John` from the specified file. Your program should get the arguments from the command line.

****14.12** (*Reformat Java source code*) Write a program that converts the Java source code from the next-line brace style to the end-of-line brace style. For example, the following Java source in (a) uses the next-line brace style. Your program converts it to the end-of-line brace style in (b).

```
public class Test
{
  public static void main(String[] args)
  {
    // Some statements
  }
}
```

(a) Next-line brace style

```
public class Test {
  public static void main(String[] args) {
    // Some statements
  }
}
```

(b) End-of-line brace style

Your program can be invoked from the command line with the Java source-code file as the argument. It converts the Java source code to a new format. For example, the following command converts the Java source-code file **Test.java** to the end-of-line brace style.

```
java Exercise14_12 Test.java
```

*14.13 (*Count characters, words, and lines in a file*) Write a program that will count the number of characters, words, and lines in a file. Words are separated by whitespace characters. The file name should be passed as a command-line argument, as shown in Figure 14.13.

FIGURE 14.13 The program displays the number of characters, words, and lines in the given file.

*14.14 (*Process scores in a text file*) Suppose that a text file contains an unspecified number of scores separated by blanks. Write a program that prompts the user to enter the file, reads the scores from the file, and displays their total and average. Scores are separated by blanks.

*14.15 (*Write/read data*) Write a program to create a file named **Exercise14_15.txt** if it does not exist. Write `100` integers created randomly into the file using text I/O. Integers are separated by spaces in the file. Read the data back from the file and display the sorted data.

**14.16 (*Replace text*) Listing 14.15, ReplaceText.java, gives a program that replaces text in a source file and saves the change into a new file. Revise the program to save the change into the original file. For example, invoking

```
java Exercise14_16 file oldString newString
```

replaces `oldString` in the source file with `newString`.

***14.17 (*Game: hangman*) Rewrite Exercise 9.25. The program reads the words stored in a text file named **hangman.txt**. Words are delimited by spaces.

**14.18 (*Add package statement*) Suppose you have Java source files under the directories `chapter1`, `chapter2`, . . . , `chapter34`. Write a program to insert the statement `package chapteri;` as the first line for each Java source file under the directory `chapteri`. Suppose `chapter1`, `chapter2`, . . . , `chapter34` are under the root directory `srcRootDirectory`. The root directory and `chapteri` directory may contain other folders and files. Use the following command to run the program:

```
java Exercise14_18 srcRootDirectory
```

*14.19 (*Count words*) Write a program that counts the number of words in President Abraham Lincoln's Gettysburg address from http://cs.armstrong.edu/liang/data/Lincoln.txt.

****14.20** (*Remove package statement*) Suppose you have Java source files under the directories `chapter1`, `chapter2`, . . . , `chapter34`. Write a program to remove the statement `package chapteri;` in the first line for each Java source file under the directory `chapteri`. Suppose `chapter1`, `chapter2`, . . . , `chapter34` are under the root directory `srcRootDirectory`. The root directory and `chapteri` directory may contain other folders and files. Use the following command to run the program:

```
java Exercise14_20 srcRootDirectory
```

****14.21** (*Display a graph*) A graph consists of vertices and edges that connect vertices. Write a program that reads a graph from a file and displays it on a panel. The first line in the file contains a number that indicates the number of vertices (`n`). The vertices are labeled as `0`, `1`, . . . , `n-1`. Each subsequent line, with the format `u x y v1 v2 ...`, describes that the vertex `u` is located at position (`x`, `y`) with edges (`u`, `v1`), (`u`, `v2`), and so on. Figure 14.14a gives an example of the file for a graph. Your program prompts the user to enter the name of the file, reads data from the file, and displays the graph on a panel, as shown in Figure 14.14b. Write another program that reads data from a Web URL such as http://cs.armstrong.edu/liang/data/graph.txt. This program should prompt the user to enter the URL for the file.

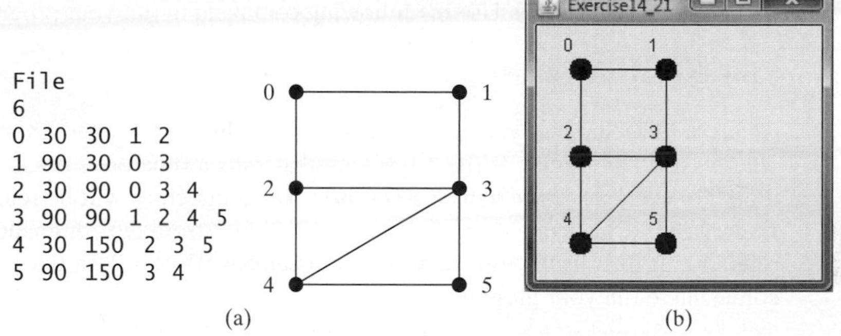

FIGURE 14.14 Exercise 14.21 reads the information about the graph and displays it visually.

****14.22** (*Replace text*) Revise Exercise 14.16 to replace a string in a file with a new string for all files in the specified directory using the command:

```
java Exercise14_22 dir oldString newString
```

****14.23** (*Process scores in a text file on the Web*) Suppose that the text file on the Web http://cs.armstrong.edu/liang/data/Scores.txt contains an unspecified number of scores. Write a program that reads the scores from the file and displays their total and average. Scores are separated by blanks.

***14.24** (*Create large dataset*) Create a data file with 1,000 lines. Each line in the file consists of a faculty member's first name, last name, rank, and salary. The faculty member's first name and last name for the *i*th line are FirstName*i* and LastName*i*. The rank is randomly generated as assistant, associate, and full. The salary is randomly generated as a number with two digits after the decimal point. The salary for an assistant professor should be in the range from 50,000 to

80,000, for associate professor from 60,000 to 110,000, and for full professor from 75,000 to 130,000. Save the file in **Salary.txt**. Here are some sample data:

FirstName1 LastName1 assistant 60055.95

FirstName2 LastName2 associate 81112.45

. . .

FirstName1000 LastName1000 full 92255.21

***14.25** (*Process large dataset*) A university posts its employees' salaries at http://cs.armstrong.edu/liang/data/Salary.txt. Each line in the file consists of a faculty member's first name, last name, rank, and salary (see Exercise 14.24). Write a program to display the total salary for assistant professors, associate professors, full professors, and all faculty, respectively, and display the average salary for assistant professors, associate professors, full professors, and all faculty, respectively.

****14.26** (*Create a directory*) Write a program that prompts the user to enter a directory name and creates a directory using the `File`'s `mkdirs` method. The program displays the message "Directory created successfully" if a directory is created or "Directory already exists" if the directory already exists.

****14.27** (*Replace words*) Suppose you have a lot of files in a directory that contain words **Exercise*i*_*j***, where *i* and *j* are digits. Write a program that pads a 0 before *i* if *i* is a single digit and 0 before *j* if *j* is a single digit. For example, the word **Exercise2_1** in a file will be replaced by **Exercise02_01**. In Java, when you pass the symbol * from the command line, it refers to all files in the directory (see Supplement III.AC). Use the following command to run your program.

```
java Exercise14_27 *
```

****14.28** (*Rename files*) Suppose you have a lot of files in a directory named **Exercise*i*_*j***, where *i* and *j* are digits. Write a program that pads a 0 before *i* if *i* is a single digit. For example, a file named **Exercise2_1** in a directory will be renamed to **Exercise02_1**. In Java, when you pass the symbol * from the command line, it refers to all files in the directory (see Supplement III.AC). Use the following command to run your program.

```
java Exercise14_28 *
```

****14.29** (*Rename files*) Suppose you have a lot of files in a directory named **Exercise*i*_*j***, where *i* and *j* are digits. Write a program that pads a 0 before *j* if *j* is a single digit. For example, a file named **Exercise2_1** in a directory will be renamed to **Exercise2_01**. In Java, when you pass the symbol * from the command line, it refers to all files in the directory (see Supplement III.AC). Use the following command to run your program.

```
java Exercise14_29 *
```

CHAPTER

15

Abstract Classes and Interfaces

Objectives

- To design and use abstract classes (§15.2).
- To generalize numeric wrapper classes, `BigInteger`, and `BigDecimal` using the abstract `Number` class (§15.3).
- To process a calendar using the `Calendar` and `GregorianCalendar` classes (§15.4).
- To specify common behavior for objects using interfaces (§15.5).
- To define interfaces and define classes that implement interfaces (§15.5).
- To define a natural order using the `Comparable` interface (§15.6).
- To make objects cloneable using the `Cloneable` interface (§15.7).
- To explore the similarities and differences among concrete classes, abstract classes, and interfaces (§15.8).
- To design the `Rational` class for processing rational numbers (§15.9).

15.1 Introduction

A superclass defines common behavior for related subclasses. An interface *can be used to define common behavior for classes (including unrelated classes).*

problem

interface

You have learned how to write simple programs to create and display GUI components. Can you write the code to respond to user actions, such as clicking a button to perform an action?

In order to write such code, you have to know about interfaces. An *interface* is for defining common behavior for classes (including unrelated classes). Before discussing interfaces, we introduce a closely related subject: abstract classes.

15.2 Abstract Classes

An abstract class cannot be used to create objects. An abstract class can contain abstract methods, which are implemented in concrete subclasses.

VideoNote

Abstract `GeometricObject` class

abstract class

In the inheritance hierarchy, classes become more specific and concrete *with each new subclass*. If you move from a subclass back up to a superclass, the classes become more general and less specific. Class design should ensure that a superclass contains common features of its subclasses. Sometimes a superclass is so abstract that it cannot have any specific instances. Such a class is referred to as an *abstract class*.

abstract method

abstract modifier

In Chapter 11, `GeometricObject` was defined as the superclass for `Circle` and `Rectangle`. `GeometricObject` models common features of geometric objects. Both `Circle` and `Rectangle` contain the `getArea()` and `getPerimeter()` methods for computing the area and perimeter of a circle and a rectangle. Since you can compute areas and perimeters for all geometric objects, it is better to define the `getArea()` and `getPerimeter()` methods in the `GeometricObject` class. However, these methods cannot be implemented in the `GeometricObject` class, because their implementation depends on the specific type of geometric object. Such methods are referred to as *abstract methods* and are denoted using the `abstract` modifier in the method header. After you define the methods in `GeometricObject`, it becomes an abstract class. Abstract classes are denoted using the `abstract` modifier in the class header. In UML graphic notation, the names of abstract classes and their abstract methods are italicized, as shown in Figure 15.1. Listing 15.1 gives the source code for the new `GeometricObject` class.

LISTING 15.1 GeometricObject.java

abstract class

```
public abstract class GeometricObject {
  private String color = "white";
  private boolean filled;
  private java.util.Date dateCreated;

  /** Construct a default geometric object */
  protected GeometricObject() {
    dateCreated = new java.util.Date();
  }

  /** Construct a geometric object with color and filled value */
  protected GeometricObject(String color, boolean filled) {
    dateCreated = new java.util.Date();
    this.color = color;
    this.filled = filled;
  }

  /** Return color */
  public String getColor() {
    return color;
```

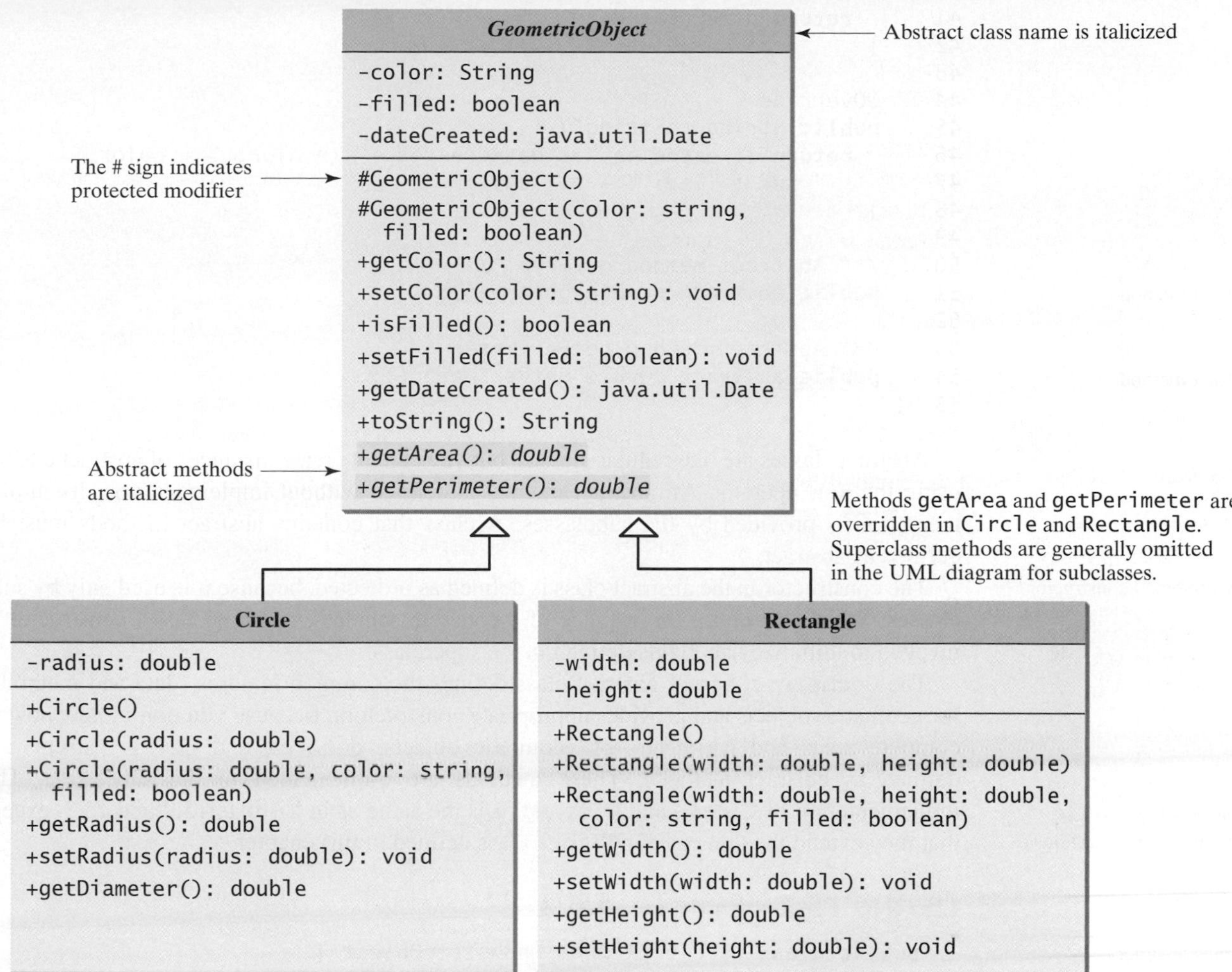

FIGURE 15.1 The new `GeometricObject` class contains abstract methods.

```
  }

  /** Set a new color */
  public void setColor(String color) {
    this.color = color;
  }

  /** Return filled. Since filled is boolean,
   * the get method is named isFilled */
  public boolean isFilled() {
    return filled;
  }

  /** Set a new filled */
  public void setFilled(boolean filled) {
    this.filled = filled;
  }

  /** Get dateCreated */
  public java.util.Date getDateCreated() {
```

```
    return dateCreated;
  }

  @Override
  public String toString() {
    return "created on " + dateCreated + "\ncolor: " + color +
      " and filled: " + filled;
  }

  /** Abstract method getArea */
  public abstract double getArea();

  /** Abstract method getPerimeter */
  public abstract double getPerimeter();
}
```

abstract method
abstract method

Abstract classes are like regular classes, but you cannot create instances of abstract classes using the `new` operator. An abstract method is defined without implementation. Its implementation is provided by the subclasses. A class that contains abstract methods must be defined as abstract.

why protected constructor?

The constructor in the abstract class is defined as protected, because it is used only by subclasses. When you create an instance of a concrete subclass, its superclass's constructor is invoked to initialize data fields defined in the superclass.

implementing `Circle`
implementing `Rectangle`

The `GeometricObject` abstract class defines the common features (data and methods) for geometric objects and provides appropriate constructors. Because you don't know how to compute areas and perimeters of geometric objects, `getArea` and `getPerimeter` are defined as abstract methods. These methods are implemented in the subclasses. The implementation of `Circle` and `Rectangle` is the same as in Listings 15.2 and 15.3, except that they extend the `GeometricObject` class defined in this chapter.

LISTING 15.2 Circle.java

extends abstract `GeometricObject`

```
public class Circle extends GeometricObject {
  // Same as lines 3-48 in Listing 11.2, so omitted
}
```

LISTING 15.3 Rectangle.java

extends abstract `GeometricObject`

```
public class Rectangle extends GeometricObject {
  // Same as lines 3-51 in Listing 11.3, so omitted
}
```

15.2.1 Why Abstract Methods?

You may be wondering what advantage is gained by defining the methods `getArea` and `getPerimeter` as abstract in the `GeometricObject` class. The example in Listing 15.4 shows the benefits of defining them in the `GeometricObject` class. The program creates two geometric objects, a circle and a rectangle, invokes the `equalArea` method to check whether they have equal areas, and invokes the `displayGeometricObject` method to display them.

LISTING 15.4 TestGeometricObject.java

create a circle
create a rectangle

```
public class TestGeometricObject {
  /** Main method */
  public static void main(String[] args) {
    // Create two geometric objects
    GeometricObject geoObject1 = new Circle(5);
    GeometricObject geoObject2 = new Rectangle(5, 3);
```

```
 7
 8     System.out.println("The two objects have the same area? " +
 9       equalArea(geoObject1, geoObject2));
10
11     // Display circle
12     displayGeometricObject(geoObject1);
13
14     // Display rectangle
15     displayGeometricObject(geoObject2);
16   }
17
18   /** A method for comparing the areas of two geometric objects */
19   public static boolean equalArea(GeometricObject object1,
20       GeometricObject object2) {
21     return object1.getArea() == object2.getArea();
22   }
23
24   /** A method for displaying a geometric object */
25   public static void displayGeometricObject(GeometricObject object) {
26     System.out.println();
27     System.out.println("The area is " + object.getArea());
28     System.out.println("The perimeter is " + object.getPerimeter());
29   }
30 }
```

equalArea

displayGeometricObject

```
The two objects have the same area? false

The area is 78.53981633974483
The perimeter is 31.41592653589793

The area is 15.0
The perimeter is 16.0
```

The methods getArea() and getPerimeter() defined in the GeometricObject class are overridden in the Circle class and the Rectangle class. The statements (lines 5–6)

```
GeometricObject geoObject1 = new Circle(5);
GeometricObject geoObject2 = new Rectangle(5, 3);
```

create a new circle and rectangle and assign them to the variables geoObject1 and geoObject2. These two variables are of the GeometricObject type.

When invoking equalArea(geoObject1, geoObject2) (line 9), the getArea() method defined in the Circle class is used for object1.getArea(), since geoObject1 is a circle, and the getArea() method defined in the Rectangle class is used for object2.getArea(), since geoObject2 is a rectangle.

Similarly, when invoking displayGeometricObject(geoObject1) (line 12), the methods getArea() and getPerimeter() defined in the Circle class are used, and when invoking displayGeometricObject(geoObject2) (line 15), the methods getArea and getPerimeter defined in the Rectangle class are used. The JVM dynamically determines which of these methods to invoke at runtime, depending on the actual object that invokes the method.

Note that you could not define the equalArea method for comparing whether two geometric objects have the same area if the getArea method were not defined in GeometricObject. Now you have seen the benefits of defining the abstract methods in GeometricObject.

why abstract methods?

15.2.2 Interesting Points about Abstract Classes

The following points about abstract classes are worth noting:

abstract method in abstract class

- An abstract method cannot be contained in a nonabstract class. If a subclass of an abstract superclass does not implement all the abstract methods, the subclass must be defined as abstract. In other words, in a nonabstract subclass extended from an abstract class, all the abstract methods must be implemented. Also note that abstract methods are nonstatic.

object cannot be created from abstract class

- An abstract class cannot be instantiated using the **new** operator, but you can still define its constructors, which are invoked in the constructors of its subclasses. For instance, the constructors of **GeometricObject** are invoked in the **Circle** class and the **Rectangle** class.

abstract class without abstract method

- A class that contains abstract methods must be abstract. However, it is possible to define an abstract class that doesn't contain any abstract methods. In this case, you cannot create instances of the class using the **new** operator. This class is used as a base class for defining subclasses.

superclass of abstract class may be concrete

- A subclass can be abstract even if its superclass is concrete. For example, the **Object** class is concrete, but its subclasses, such as **GeometricObject**, may be abstract.

concrete method overridden to be abstract

- A subclass can override a method from its superclass to define it as abstract. This is *very unusual*, but it is useful when the implementation of the method in the superclass becomes invalid in the subclass. In this case, the subclass must be defined as abstract.

abstract class as type

- You cannot create an instance from an abstract class using the **new** operator, but an abstract class can be used as a data type. Therefore, the following statement, which creates an array whose elements are of the **GeometricObject** type, is correct.

```
GeometricObject[] objects = new GeometricObject[10];
```

You can then create an instance of **GeometricObject** and assign its reference to the array like this:

```
objects[0] = new Circle();
```

MyProgrammingLab™

15.1 Which of the following classes defines a legal abstract class?

```
class A {
  abstract void unfinished() {
  }
}
```

(a)

```
public class abstract A {
  abstract void unfinished();
}
```

(b)

```
class A {
  abstract void unfinished();
}
```

(c)

```
abstract class A {
  protected void unfinished();
}
```

(d)

```
abstract class A {
  abstract void unfinished();
}
```

(e)

```
abstract class A {
  abstract int unfinished();
}
```

(f)

15.2 The `getArea` and `getPerimeter` methods may be removed from the `GeometricObject` class. What are the benefits of defining `getArea` and `getPerimeter` as abstract methods in the `GeometricObject` class?

15.3 True or false?

a. An abstract class can be used just like a nonabstract class except that you cannot use the `new` operator to create an instance from the abstract class.

b. An abstract class can be extended.

c. A subclass of a nonabstract superclass cannot be abstract.

d. A subclass cannot override a concrete method in a superclass to define it as abstract.

e. An abstract method must be nonstatic.

15.3 Case Study: the Abstract **Number** Class

`Number` is an abstract superclass for numeric wrapper classes, `BigInteger`, and `BigDecimal`.

Section 10.12 introduced numeric wrapper classes and Section 10.14 introduced the `BigInteger` and `BigDecimal` classes. These classes have common methods `byteValue()`, `shortValue()`, `intValue()`, `longValue()`, `floatValue()`, and `doubleValue()` for returning a `byte`, `short`, `int`, `long`, `float`, and `double` value from an object of these classes. These common methods are actually defined in the `Number` class, which is a superclass for the numeric wrapper classes, `BigInteger`, and `BigDecimal`, as shown in Figure 15.2.

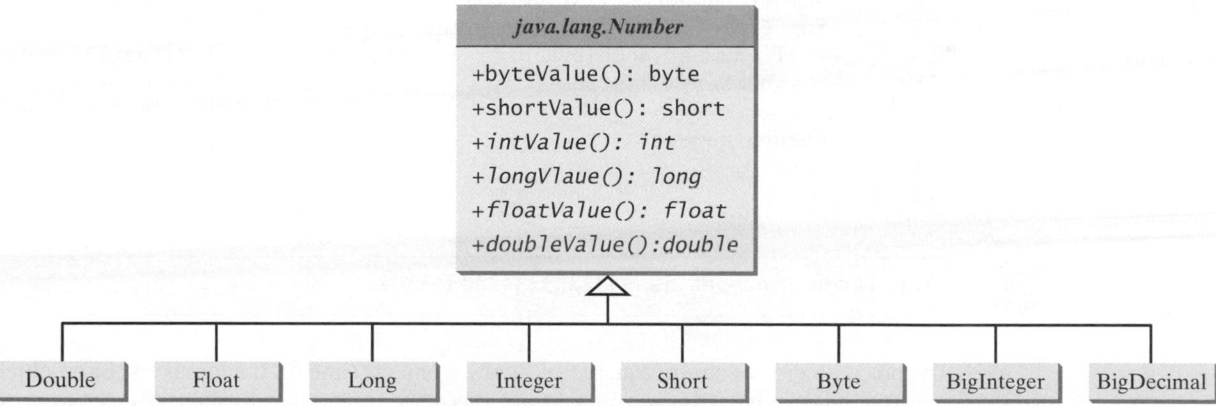

FIGURE 15.2 The `Number` class is an abstract superclass for `Double`, `Float`, `Long`, `Integer`, `Short`, `Byte`, `BigInteger` and `BigDecimal`.

Since the `intValue()`, `longValue()`, `floatValue()`, and `doubleValue()` methods cannot be implemented in the `Number` class, they are defined as abstract methods in the `Number` class. The `Number` class is therefore an abstract class. The `byteValue()` and `shortValue()` method are implemented from the `intValue()` method as follows:

```
public byte byteValue() {
  return (byte)intValue();
}
```

```
public short shortValue() {
  return (short)intValue();
}
```

With **Number** defined as the superclass for the numeric classes, we can define methods to perform common operations for numbers. Listing 15.5 gives a program that finds the largest number in a list of **Number** objects.

LISTING 15.5 LargestNumbers.java

create an array list

add number to list

invoke getLargestNumber

doubleValue

```
1  import java.util.ArrayList;
2  import java.math.*;
3
4  public class LargestNumbers {
5    public static void main(String[] args) {
6      ArrayList<Number> list = new ArrayList<Number>();
7      list.add(45); // Add an integer
8      list.add(3445.53); // Add a double
9      // Add a BigInteger
10     list.add(new BigInteger("3432323234344343101"));
11     // Add a BigDecimal
12     list.add(new BigDecimal("2.0909090989091343433344343"));
13
14     System.out.println("The largest number is " +
15       getLargestNumber(list));
16   }
17
18   public static Number getLargestNumber(ArrayList<Number> list) {
19     if (list == null || list.size() == 0)
20       return null;
21
22     Number number = list.get(0);
23     for (int i = 1; i < list.size(); i++)
24       if (number.doubleValue() < list.get(i).doubleValue())
25         number = list.get(i);
26
27     return number;
28   }
29 }
```

```
The largest number is 3432323234344343101
```

The program creates an **ArrayList** of **Number** objects (line 6). It adds an **Integer** object, a **Double** object, a **BigInteger** object, and a **BigDecimal** object to the list (lines 7–12). Note that **45** is automatically converted into an **Integer** object and added to the list in line 7 and that **3445.53** is automatically converted into a **Double** object and added to the list in line 8 using autoboxing.

Invoking the **getLargestNumber** method returns the largest number in the list (line 15). The **getLargestNumber** method returns **null** if the list is **null** or the list size is **0** (lines 19–20). To find the largest number in the list, the numbers are compared by invoking their **doubleValue()** method (line 24). The **doubleValue()** method is defined in the **Number** class and implemented in the concrete subclass of **Number**. If a number is an **Integer** object, the **Integer**'s **doubleValue()** is invoked. If a number is a **BigDecimal** object, the **BigDecimal**'s **doubleValue()** is invoked.

If the **doubleValue()** method were not defined in the **Number** class, you will not be able to find the largest number among different types of numbers using the **Number** class.

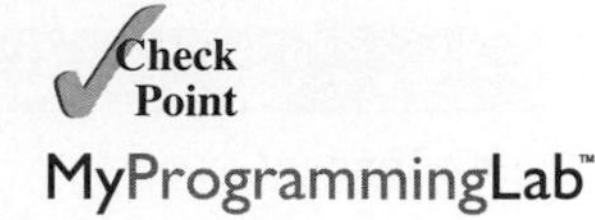

15.4 Why do the following two lines of code compile but cause a runtime error?

```
Number numberRef = new Integer(0);
Double doubleRef = (Double)numberRef;
```

15.5 Why do the following two lines of code compile but cause a runtime error?

```
Number[] numberArray = new Integer[2];
numberArray[0] = new Double(1.5);
```

15.6 Show the output of the following code.

```
public class Test {
  public static void main(String[] args) {
    Number x = 3;
    System.out.println(x.intValue());
    System.out.println(x.doubleValue());
  }
}
```

15.7 What is wrong in the following code? (Note that the `compareTo` method for the `Integer` and `Double` classes was introduced in Section 10.12.)

```
public class Test {
  public static void main(String[] args) {
    Number x = new Integer(3);
    System.out.println(x.intValue());
    System.out.println(x.compareTo(new Integer(4)));
  }
}
```

15.8 What is wrong in the following code?

```
public class Test {
  public static void main(String[] args) {
    Number x = new Integer(3);
    System.out.println(x.intValue());
    System.out.println((Integer)x.compareTo(new Integer(4)));
  }
}
```

15.4 Case Study: **Calendar** and **GregorianCalendar**

`GregorianCalendar` is a concrete subclass of the abstract class `Calendar`.

VideoNote

`Calendar` and `GregorianCalendar` classes

An instance of `java.util.Date` represents a specific instant in time with millisecond precision. `java.util.Calendar` is an abstract base class for extracting detailed calendar information, such as the year, month, date, hour, minute, and second. Subclasses of `Calendar` can implement specific calendar systems, such as the Gregorian calendar, the lunar calendar, and the Jewish calendar. Currently, `java.util.GregorianCalendar` for the Gregorian calendar is supported in Java, as shown in Figure 15.3. The `add` method is abstract in the `Calendar` class, because its implementation is dependent on a concrete calendar system.

abstract add method

You can use `new GregorianCalendar()` to construct a default `GregorianCalendar` with the current time and `new GregorianCalendar(year, month, date)` to construct a `GregorianCalendar` with the specified `year`, `month`, and `date`. The `month` parameter is `0` based—that is, `0` is for January.

constructing calendar

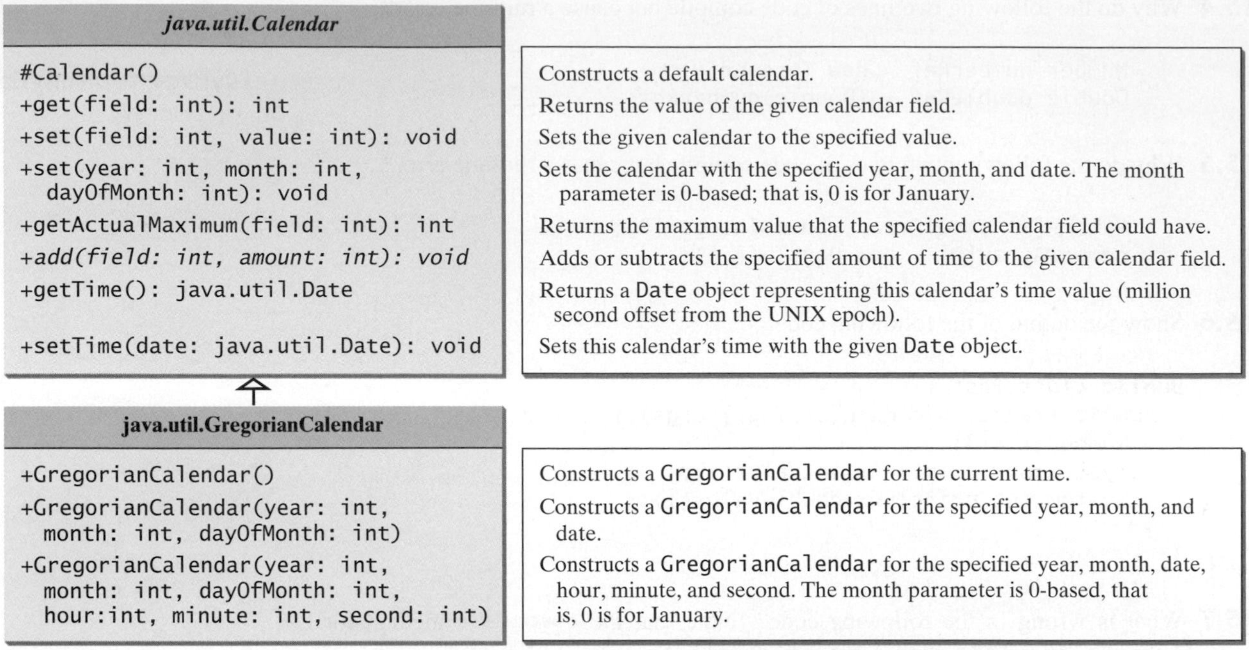

java.util.Calendar	
`#Calendar()`	Constructs a default calendar.
`+get(field: int): int`	Returns the value of the given calendar field.
`+set(field: int, value: int): void`	Sets the given calendar to the specified value.
`+set(year: int, month: int, dayOfMonth: int): void`	Sets the calendar with the specified year, month, and date. The month parameter is 0-based; that is, 0 is for January.
`+getActualMaximum(field: int): int`	Returns the maximum value that the specified calendar field could have.
`+add(field: int, amount: int): void`	Adds or subtracts the specified amount of time to the given calendar field.
`+getTime(): java.util.Date`	Returns a `Date` object representing this calendar's time value (million second offset from the UNIX epoch).
`+setTime(date: java.util.Date): void`	Sets this calendar's time with the given `Date` object.

java.util.GregorianCalendar	
`+GregorianCalendar()`	Constructs a `GregorianCalendar` for the current time.
`+GregorianCalendar(year: int, month: int, dayOfMonth: int)`	Constructs a `GregorianCalendar` for the specified year, month, and date.
`+GregorianCalendar(year: int, month: int, dayOfMonth: int, hour:int, minute: int, second: int)`	Constructs a `GregorianCalendar` for the specified year, month, date, hour, minute, and second. The month parameter is 0-based, that is, 0 is for January.

Figure 15.3 The abstract `Calendar` class defines common features of various calendars.

`get(field)`

The `get(int field)` method defined in the `Calendar` class is useful for extracting the date and time information from a `Calendar` object. The fields are defined as constants, as shown in Table 15.1.

Table 15.1 Field Constants in the `Calendar` Class

Constant	*Description*
`YEAR`	The year of the calendar.
`MONTH`	The month of the calendar, with 0 for January.
`DATE`	The day of the calendar.
`HOUR`	The hour of the calendar (12-hour notation).
`HOUR_OF_DAY`	The hour of the calendar (24-hour notation).
`MINUTE`	The minute of the calendar.
`SECOND`	The second of the calendar.
`DAY_OF_WEEK`	The day number within the week, with 1 for Sunday.
`DAY_OF_MONTH`	Same as DATE.
`DAY_OF_YEAR`	The day number in the year, with 1 for the first day of the year.
`WEEK_OF_MONTH`	The week number within the month, with 1 for the first week.
`WEEK_OF_YEAR`	The week number within the year, with 1 for the first week.
`AM_PM`	Indicator for AM or PM (0 for AM and 1 for PM).

Listing 15.6 gives an example that displays the date and time information for the current time.

Listing 15.6 TestCalendar.java

```
import java.util.*;

```

```
public class TestCalendar {
  public static void main(String[] args) {
    // Construct a Gregorian calendar for the current date and time
    Calendar calendar = new GregorianCalendar();
    System.out.println("Current time is " + new Date());
    System.out.println("YEAR: " + calendar.get(Calendar.YEAR));
    System.out.println("MONTH: " + calendar.get(Calendar.MONTH));
    System.out.println("DATE: " + calendar.get(Calendar.DATE));
    System.out.println("HOUR: " + calendar.get(Calendar.HOUR));
    System.out.println("HOUR_OF_DAY: " +
      calendar.get(Calendar.HOUR_OF_DAY));
    System.out.println("MINUTE: " + calendar.get(Calendar.MINUTE));
    System.out.println("SECOND: " + calendar.get(Calendar.SECOND));
    System.out.println("DAY_OF_WEEK: " +
      calendar.get(Calendar.DAY_OF_WEEK));
    System.out.println("DAY_OF_MONTH: " +
      calendar.get(Calendar.DAY_OF_MONTH));
    System.out.println("DAY_OF_YEAR: " +
      calendar.get(Calendar.DAY_OF_YEAR));
    System.out.println("WEEK_OF_MONTH: " +
      calendar.get(Calendar.WEEK_OF_MONTH));
    System.out.println("WEEK_OF_YEAR: " +
      calendar.get(Calendar.WEEK_OF_YEAR));
    System.out.println("AM_PM: " + calendar.get(Calendar.AM_PM));

    // Construct a calendar for September 11, 2001
    Calendar calendar1 = new GregorianCalendar(2001, 8, 11);
    String[] dayNameOfWeek = {"Sunday", "Monday", "Tuesday", "Wednesday",
      "Thursday", "Friday", "Saturday"};
    System.out.println("September 11, 2001 is a " +
      dayNameOfWeek[calendar1.get(Calendar.DAY_OF_WEEK) - 1]);
  }
}
```

calendar for current time

extract fields in calendar

create a calendar

```
Current time is Sun Nov 27 17:48:15 EST 2011
YEAR: 2011
MONTH: 10
DATE: 27
HOUR: 5
HOUR_OF_DAY: 17
MINUTE: 48
SECOND: 15
DAY_OF_WEEK: 1
DAY_OF_MONTH: 27
DAY_OF_YEAR: 331
WEEK_OF_MONTH: 5
WEEK_OF_YEAR: 49
AM_PM: 1
September 11, 2001 is a Tuesday
```

The `set(int field, value)` method defined in the `Calendar` class can be used to set a field. For example, you can use `calendar.set(Calendar.DAY_OF_MONTH, 1)` to set the `calendar` to the first day of the month.

`set(field, value)`

The `add(field, value)` method adds the specified amount to a given field. For example, `add(Calendar.DAY_OF_MONTH, 5)` adds five days to the current time of the calendar. `add(Calendar.DAY_OF_MONTH, -5)` subtracts five days from the current time of the calendar.

`add(field, amount)`

getActualMaximum(field)

To obtain the number of days in a month, use `calendar.getActualMaximum(Calendar.DAY_OF_MONTH)`. For example, if the `calendar` were for March, this method would return `31`.

setTime(date)
getTime()

You can set a time represented in a `Date` object for the `calendar` by invoking `calendar.setTime(date)` and retrieve the time by invoking `calendar.getTime()`.

Check Point
MyProgrammingLab™

15.9 Can you create a `Calendar` object using the `Calendar` class?

15.10 Which method in the `Calendar` class is abstract?

15.11 How do you create a `Calendar` object for the current time?

15.12 For a `Calendar` object `c`, how do you get its year, month, date, hour, minute, and second?

15.5 Interfaces

Key Point

An interface is a class-like construct that contains only constants and abstract methods.

VideoNote
The concept of interface

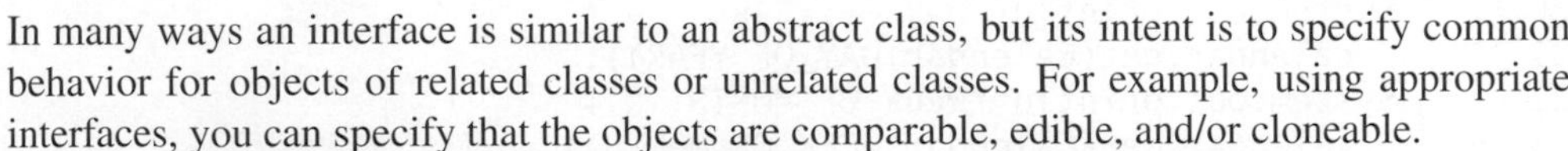

In many ways an interface is similar to an abstract class, but its intent is to specify common behavior for objects of related classes or unrelated classes. For example, using appropriate interfaces, you can specify that the objects are comparable, edible, and/or cloneable.

To distinguish an interface from a class, Java uses the following syntax to define an interface:

```
modifier interface InterfaceName {
  /** Constant declarations */
  /** Abstract method signatures */
}
```

Here is an example of an interface:

```
public interface Edible {
  /** Describe how to eat */
  public abstract String howToEat();
}
```

An interface is treated like a special class in Java. Each interface is compiled into a separate bytecode file, just like a regular class. You can use an interface more or less the same way you use an abstract class. For example, you can use an interface as a data type for a reference variable, as the result of casting, and so on. As with an abstract class, you cannot create an instance from an interface using the `new` operator.

You can use the `Edible` interface to specify whether an object is edible. This is accomplished by letting the class for the object implement this interface using the `implements` keyword. For example, the classes `Chicken` and `Fruit` in Listing 15.7 (lines 20, 39) implement the `Edible` interface. The relationship between the class and the interface is known as *interface inheritance*. Since interface inheritance and class inheritance are essentially the same, we will simply refer to both as *inheritance*.

interface inheritance

LISTING 15.7 TestEdible.java

```
1  public class TestEdible {
2    public static void main(String[] args) {
3      Object[] objects = {new Tiger(), new Chicken(), new Apple()};
4      for (int i = 0; i < objects.length; i++) {
5        if (objects[i] instanceof Edible)
6          System.out.println(((Edible)objects[i]).howToEat());
7
8        if (objects[i] instanceof Animal) {
9          System.out.println(((Animal)objects[i]).sound());
10       }
```

```
11      }
12    }
13  }
14
15  abstract class Animal {
16    /** Return animal sound */
17    public abstract String sound();
18  }
19
20  class Chicken extends Animal implements Edible {
21    @Override
22    public String howToEat() {
23      return "Chicken: Fry it";
24    }
25
26    @Override
27    public String sound() {
28      return "Chicken: cock-a-doodle-doo";
29    }
30  }
31
32  class Tiger extends Animal {
33    @Override
34    public String sound() {
35      return "Tiger: RROOAARR";
36    }
37  }
38
39  abstract class Fruit implements Edible {
40    // Data fields, constructors, and methods omitted here
41  }
42
43  class Apple extends Fruit {
44    @Override
45    public String howToEat() {
46      return "Apple: Make apple cider";
47    }
48  }
49
50  class Orange extends Fruit {
51    @Override
52    public String howToEat() {
53      return "Orange: Make orange juice";
54    }
55  }
```

Animal class

implements Edible

howToEat()

Tiger class

implements Edible

Apple class

Orange class

```
Tiger: RROOAARR
Chicken: Fry it
Chicken: cock-a-doodle-doo
Apple: Make apple cider
```

This example uses several classes and interfaces. Their inheritance relationship is shown in Figure 15.4.

The **Animal** class defines the **sound** method (line 17). It is an abstract method and will be implemented by a concrete animal class.

The **Chicken** class implements **Edible** to specify that chickens are edible. When a class implements an interface, it implements all the methods defined in the interface with the exact

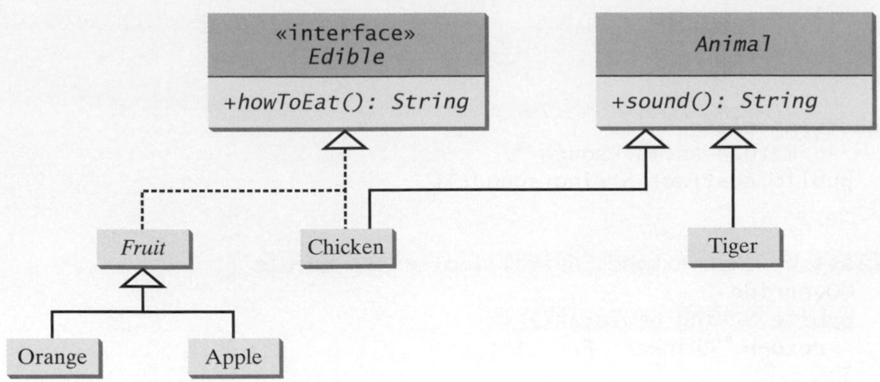

Figure 15.4 Edible is a supertype for Chicken and Fruit. Animal is a supertype for Chicken and Tiger. Fruit is a supertype for Orange and Apple.

signature and return type. The Chicken class implements the howToEat method (lines 22–24). Chicken also extends Animal to implement the sound method (lines 27–29).

The Fruit class implements Edible. Since it does not implement the howToEat method, Fruit must be denoted as abstract (line 39). The concrete subclasses of Fruit must implement the howToEat method. The Apple and Orange classes implement the howToEat method (lines 45, 52).

The main method creates an array with three objects for Tiger, Chicken, and Apple (line 3), and invokes the howToEat method if the element is edible (line 6) and the sound method if the element is an animal (line 9).

common behavior

In essence, the Edible interface defines common behavior for edible objects. All edible objects have the howToEat method.

Note

omitting modifiers

Since all data fields are *public static final* and all methods are *public abstract* in an interface, Java allows these modifiers to be omitted. Therefore the following interface definitions are equivalent:

```
public interface T {
  public static final int K = 1;

  public abstract void p();
}
```

Equivalent

```
public interface T {
  int K = 1;

  void p();
}
```

Tip

accessing constants

A constant defined in an interface can be accessed using the syntax InterfaceName.CONSTANT_NAME (e.g., T.K). It is a good practice to define common constants that are shared by many classes in an interface. For example, the constants LEFT, CENTER, RIGHT, LEADING, TRAILING, TOP, and BOTTOM used in AbstractButton are also used in many other Swing components. These constants are centrally defined in the javax.swing.SwingConstants interface. All Swing GUI components implement SwingConstants. You can reference the constants through SwingConstants or a GUI component. For example, SwingConstants.CENTER is the same as JButton.CENTER.

SwingConstants

Check Point

MyProgrammingLab™

15.13 Suppose A is an interface. Can you create an instance using new A()?

15.14 Suppose A is an interface. Can you declare a reference variable x with type A like this?

```
A x;
```

15.15 Which of the following is a correct interface?

```
interface A {
  void print() { };
}
```

(a)

```
abstract interface A extends I1, I2 {
  abstract void print() { };
}
```

(b)

```
abstract interface A {
  print();
}
```

(c)

```
interface A {
  void print();
}
```

(d)

15.16 Explain why SwingConstants.LEFT, AbstractButton.LEFT, JButton.LEFT, JCheckBox.LEFT, JRadioButton.LEFT, and JLabel.LEFT all have the same value.

15.6 The **Comparable** Interface

The Comparable interface defines the compareTo method for comparing objects.

Suppose you want to design a generic method to find the larger of two objects of the same type, such as two students, two dates, two circles, two rectangles, or two squares. In order to accomplish this, the two objects must be comparable, so the common behavior for the objects must be comparable. Java provides the Comparable interface for this purpose. The interface is defined as follows:

java.lang.Comparable

```
// Interface for comparing objects, defined in java.lang
package java.lang;

public interface Comparable<E> {
  public int compareTo(E o);
}
```

The compareTo method determines the order of this object with the specified object o and returns a negative integer, zero, or a positive integer if this object is less than, equal to, or greater than o.

The Comparable interface is a generic interface. The generic type E is replaced by a concrete type when implementing this interface. Many classes in the Java library implement Comparable to define a natural order for objects. The classes Byte, Short, Integer, Long, Float, Double, Character, BigInteger, BigDecimal, Calendar, String, and Date all implement the Comparable interface. For example, the Integer, BigInteger, String, and Date classes are defined as follows in the Java API:

```
public class Integer extends Number
    implements Comparable<Integer> {
  // class body omitted

  @Override
  public int compareTo(Integer o) {
    // Implementation omitted
  }
}
```

```
public class BigInteger extends Number
    implements Comparable<BigInteger> {
  // class body omitted

  @Override
  public int compareTo(BigInteger o) {
    // Implementation omitted
  }
}
```

```
public class String extends Object
    implements Comparable<String> {
  // class body omitted

  @Override
  public int compareTo(String o) {
    // Implementation omitted
  }
}
```

```
public class Date extends Object
    implements Comparable<Date> {
  // class body omitted

  @Override
  public int compareTo(Date o) {
    // Implementation omitted
  }
}
```

Thus, numbers are comparable, strings are comparable, and so are dates. You can use the **compareTo** method to compare two numbers, two strings, and two dates. For example, the following code

```
1  System.out.println(new Integer(3).compareTo(new Integer(5)));
2  System.out.println("ABC".compareTo("ABE"));
3  java.util.Date date1 = new java.util.Date(2013, 1, 1);
4  java.util.Date date2 = new java.util.Date(2012, 1, 1);
5  System.out.println(date1.compareTo(date2));
```

displays

```
-1
-2
1
```

Line 1 displays a negative value since 3 is less than 5. Line 2 displays a negative value since ABC is less than ABE. Line 5 displays a positive value since **date1** is greater than **date2**.

Let **n** be an **Integer** object, **s** be a **String** object, and **d** be a **Date** object. All the following expressions are **true**.

```
n instanceof Integer
n instanceof Object
n instanceof Comparable
```

```
s instanceof String
s instanceof Object
s instanceof Comparable
```

```
d instanceof java.util.Date
d instanceof Object
d instanceof Comparable
```

Since all **Comparable** objects have the **compareTo** method, the **java.util.Arrays.sort(Object[])** method in the Java API uses the **compareTo** method to compare and sorts the objects in an array, provided that the objects are instances of the **Comparable** interface. Listing 15.8 gives an example of sorting an array of strings and an array of **BigInteger** objects.

Listing 15.8 SortComparableObjects.java

create an array
sort the array
create an array

```
import java.math.*;

public class SortComparableObjects {
  public static void main(String[] args) {
    String[] cities = {"Savannah", "Boston", "Atlanta", "Tampa"};
    java.util.Arrays.sort(cities);
    for (String city: cities)
      System.out.print(city + " ");
    System.out.println();

    BigInteger[] hugeNumbers = {new BigInteger("2323231092923992"),
```

```
12          new BigInteger("432232323239292"),
13          new BigInteger("54623239292")};
14        java.util.Arrays.sort(hugeNumbers);
15        for (BigInteger number: hugeNumbers)
16          System.out.print(number + " ");
17      }
18    }
```

sort the array

```
Atlanta Boston Savannah Tampa
54623239292 432232323239292 2323231092923992
```

The program creates an array of strings (line 5) and invokes the `sort` method to sort the strings (line 6). The program creates an array of `BigInteger` objects (lines 11–13) and invokes the `sort` method to sort the `BigInteger` objects (line 14).

You cannot use the `sort` method to sort an array of `Rectangle` objects, because `Rectangle` does not implement `Comparable`. However, you can define a new rectangle class that implements `Comparable`. The instances of this new class are comparable. Let this new class be named `ComparableRectangle`, as shown in Listing 15.9.

Listing 15.9 ComparableRectangle.java

```
public class ComparableRectangle extends Rectangle
    implements Comparable<ComparableRectangle> {
  /** Construct a ComparableRectangle with specified properties */
  public ComparableRectangle(double width, double height) {
    super(width, height);
  }

  @Override // Implement the compareTo method defined in Comparable
  public int compareTo(ComparableRectangle o) {
    if (getArea() > o.getArea())
      return 1;
    else if (getArea() < o.getArea())
      return -1;
    else
      return 0;
  }

  @Override // Implement the toString method in GeometricObject
  public String toString() {
    return super.toString() + " Area: " + getArea();
  }
}
```

implements `Comparable`

implement `compareTo`

implement `toString`

`ComparableRectangle` extends `Rectangle` and implements `Comparable`, as shown in Figure 15.5. The keyword `implements` indicates that `ComparableRectangle` inherits all the constants from the `Comparable` interface and implements the methods in the interface. The `compareTo` method compares the areas of two rectangles. An instance of `ComparableRectangle` is also an instance of `Rectangle`, `GeometricObject`, `Object`, and `Comparable`.

You can now use the `sort` method to sort an array of `ComparableRectangle` objects, as in Listing 15.10.

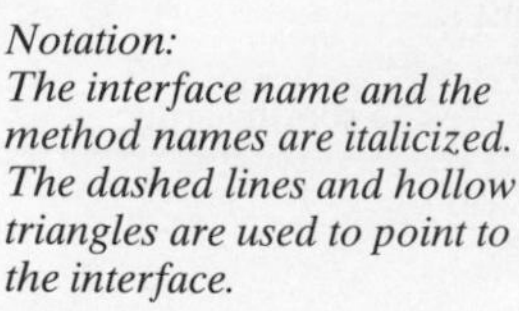

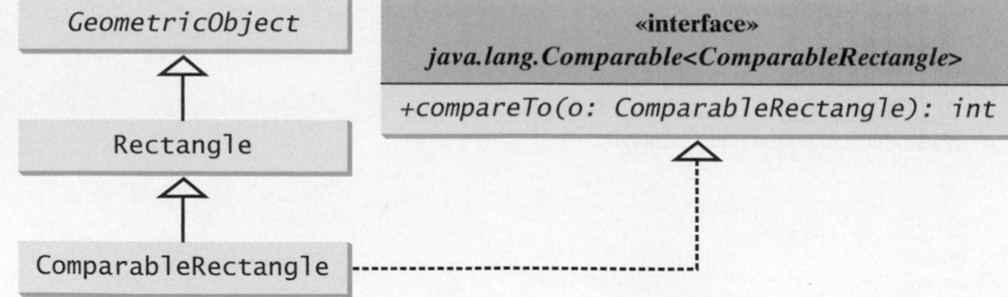

FIGURE 15.5 ComparableRectangle extends Rectangle and implements Comparable.

LISTING 15.10 SortRectangles.java

create an array

sort the array

```
public class SortRectangles {
  public static void main(String[] args) {
    ComparableRectangle[] rectangles = {
      new ComparableRectangle(3.4, 5.4),
      new ComparableRectangle(13.24, 55.4),
      new ComparableRectangle(7.4, 35.4),
      new ComparableRectangle(1.4, 25.4)};
    java.util.Arrays.sort(rectangles);
    for (Rectangle rectangle: rectangles) {
      System.out.print(rectangle + " ");
      System.out.println();
    }
  }
}
```

```
Width: 3.4 Height: 5.4 Area: 18.36
Width: 1.4 Height: 25.4 Area: 35.559999999999995
Width: 7.4 Height: 35.4 Area: 261.96
Width: 13.24 Height: 55.4 Area: 733.496
```

benefits of interface

An interface provides another form of generic programming. It would be difficult to use a generic sort method to sort the objects without using an interface in this example, because multiple inheritance would be necessary to inherit Comparable and another class, such as Rectangle, at the same time.

The Object class contains the equals method, which is intended for the subclasses of the Object class to override in order to compare whether the contents of the objects are the same. Suppose that the Object class contains the compareTo method, as defined in the Comparable interface; the sort method can be used to compare a list of *any* objects. Whether a compareTo method should be included in the Object class is debatable. Since the compareTo method is not defined in the Object class, the Comparable interface is defined in Java to enable objects to be compared if they are instances of the Comparable interface. It is strongly recommended (though not required) that compareTo should be consistent with equals. That is, for two objects o1 and o2, o1.compareTo(o2) == 0 if and only if o1.equals(o2) is true.

15.17 True or false? If a class implements Comparable, the object of the class can invoke the compareTo method.

15.18 Which of the following is the correct method header for the `compareTo` method in the `String` class?

```
public int compareTo(String o)
public int compareTo(Object o)
```

15.19 Can the following code be compiled? Why?

```
Integer n1 = new Integer(3);
Object n2 = new Integer(4);
System.out.println(n1.compareTo(n2));
```

15.20 You can define the `compareTo` method in a class without implementing the `Comparable` interface. What are the benefits of implementing the `Comparable` interface?

15.21 True or false? If a class implements `Comparable`, the object of the class can invoke the `compareTo` method.

15.7 The **Cloneable** Interface

The `Cloneable` interface specifies that an object can be cloned.

Key Point

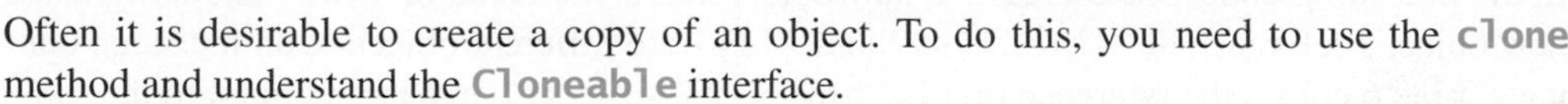

Often it is desirable to create a copy of an object. To do this, you need to use the `clone` method and understand the `Cloneable` interface.

An interface contains constants and abstract methods, but the `Cloneable` interface is a special case. The `Cloneable` interface in the `java.lang` package is defined as follows:

java.lang.Cloneable

```
package java.lang;

public interface Cloneable {
}
```

marker interface

This interface is empty. An interface with an empty body is referred to as a *marker interface*. A marker interface does not contain constants or methods. It is used to denote that a class possesses certain desirable properties. A class that implements the `Cloneable` interface is marked cloneable, and its objects can be cloned using the `clone()` method defined in the `Object` class.

Many classes in the Java library (e.g., `Date`, `Calendar`, and `ArrayList`) implement `Cloneable`. Thus, the instances of these classes can be cloned. For example, the following code

```
1 Calendar calendar = new GregorianCalendar(2013, 2, 1);
2 Calendar calendar1 = calendar;
3 Calendar calendar2 = (Calendar)calendar.clone();
4 System.out.println("calendar == calendar1 is " +
5   (calendar == calendar1));
6 System.out.println("calendar == calendar2 is " +
7   (calendar == calendar2));
8 System.out.println("calendar.equals(calendar2) is " +
9   calendar.equals(calendar2));
```

displays

```
calendar == calendar1 is true
calendar == calendar2 is false
calendar.equals(calendar2) is true
```

In the preceding code, line 2 copies the reference of `calendar` to `calendar1`, so `calendar` and `calendar1` point to the same `Calendar` object. Line 3 creates a new object that is the clone of calendar and assigns the new object's reference to calendar2. calendar2 and calendar are different objects with the same contents.

The following code

```
1  ArrayList<Double> list1 = new ArrayList<Double>();
2  list1.add(1.5);
3  list1.add(2.5);
4  list1.add(3.5);
5  ArrayList<Double> list2 = (ArrayList<Double>)list1.clone();
6  ArrayList<Double> list3 = list1;
7  list2.add(4.5);
8  list3.remove(1.5);
9  System.out.println("list1 is " + list1);
10 System.out.println("list2 is " + list2);
11 System.out.println("list3 is " + list3);
```

displays

```
list1 is [2.5, 3.5]
list2 is [1.5, 2.5, 3.5, 4.5]
list3 is [2.5, 3.5]
```

In the preceding code, line 5 creates a new object that is the clone of list1 and assigns the new object's reference to list2. list2 and list1 are different objects with the same contents. Line 6 copies the reference of list1 to list3, so list1 and list3 point to the same ArrayList object. Line 7 adds 4.5 into list2. Line 8 removes 1.5 from list3. Since list1 and list3 point to the same ArrayList, line 9 and 11 display the same content.

clone arrays

You can clone an array using the clone method. For example, the following code

```
int[] list1 = {1, 2};
int[] list2 = list1.clone();
list1[0] = 7;
list2[1] = 8;
System.out.println("list1 is " + list1[0] + ", " + list1[1]);
System.out.println("list2 is " + list2[0] + ", " + list2[1]);
```

displays

```
list1 is 7, 2
list2 is 1, 8
```

how to implement Cloneable

To define a custom class that implements the Cloneable interface, the class must override the clone() method in the Object class. Listing 15.11 defines a class named House that implements Cloneable and Comparable.

LISTING 15.11 House.java

```
public class House implements Cloneable, Comparable<House> {
  private int id;
  private double area;
  private java.util.Date whenBuilt;

  public House(int id, double area) {
    this.id = id;
    this.area = area;
    whenBuilt = new java.util.Date();
  }

  public int getId() {
```

```
13       return id;
14     }
15
16     public double getArea() {
17       return area;
18     }
19
20     public java.util.Date getWhenBuilt() {
21       return whenBuilt;
22     }
23
24     @Override /** Override the protected clone method defined in
25       the Object class, and strengthen its accessibility */
26     public Object clone() throws CloneNotSupportedException {
27       return super.clone();
28     }
29
30     @Override // Implement the compareTo method defined in Comparable
31     public int compareTo(House o) {
32       if (area > o.area)
33         return 1;
34       else if (area < o.area)
35         return -1;
36       else
37         return 0;
38     }
39   }
```

This exception is thrown if `House` does not implement `Cloneable`

The `House` class implements the `clone` method (lines 26–28) defined in the `Object` class. The header is:

```
protected native Object clone() throws CloneNotSupportedException;
```

The keyword `native` indicates that this method is not written in Java but is implemented in the JVM for the native platform. The keyword `protected` restricts the method to be accessed in the same package or in a subclass. For this reason, the `House` class must override the method and change the visibility modifier to `public` so that the method can be used in any package. Since the `clone` method implemented for the native platform in the `Object` class performs the task of cloning objects, the `clone` method in the `House` class simply invokes `super.clone()`. The `clone` method defined in the `Object` class may throw `CloneNotSupportedException`.

`CloneNotSupportedException`

The `House` class implements the `compareTo` method (lines 31–38) defined in the `Comparable` interface. The method compares the areas of two houses.

You can now create an object of the `House` class and create an identical copy from it, as follows:

```
House house1 = new House(1, 1750.50);
House house2 = (House)house1.clone();
```

`house1` and `house2` are two different objects with identical contents. The `clone` method in the `Object` class copies each field from the original object to the target object. If the field is of a primitive type, its value is copied. For example, the value of `area` (`double` type) is copied from `house1` to `house2`. If the field is of an object, the reference of the field is copied. For example, the field `whenBuilt` is of the `Date` class, so its reference is copied into `house2`, as shown in Figure 15.6. Therefore, `house1.whenBuilt == house2.whenBuilt` is true, although `house1 == house2` is false. This is referred to as a *shallow copy* rather than a *deep copy*, meaning that if the field is of an object type, the object's reference is copied rather than its contents.

shallow copy

deep copy

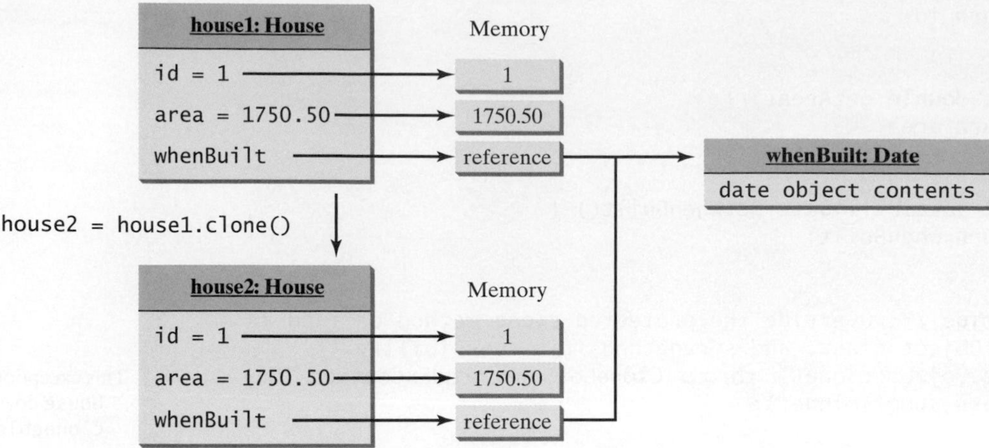

FIGURE 15.6 The default clone method performs a shallow copy.

deep copy

To perform a deep copy for a House object, replace the clone() method in lines 26–27 with the following code:

```
public Object clone() throws CloneNotSupportedException {
  // Perform a shallow copy
  House houseClone = (House)super.clone();
  // Deep copy on whenBuilt
  houseClone.whenBuilt = (java.util.Date)(whenBuilt.clone());
  return houseClone;
}
```

or

```
public Object clone() {
  try {
    // Perform a shallow copy
    House houseClone = (House)super.clone();
    // Deep copy on whenBuilt
    houseClone.whenBuilt = (java.util.Date)(whenBuilt.clone());
    return houseClone;
  }
  catch (CloneNotSupportedException ex) {
    return null;
  }
}
```

Now if you clone a House object in the following code:

```
House house1 = new House(1, 1750.50);
House house2 = (House)house1.clone();
```

house1.whenBuilt == house2.whenBuilt will be false. house1 and house2 reference two different Date objects.

MyProgrammingLab™

15.22 Can you invoke the clone() method to clone an object if the class for the object does not implement the java.lang.Cloneable? Does the Date class implement Cloneable?

15.23 What would happen if the House class (defined in Listing 15.9) did not override the clone() method or if House did not implement java.lang.Cloneable?

15.24 Show the printout of the following code:

```
java.util.Date date = new java.util.Date();
java.util.Date date1 = date;
java.util.Date date2 = (java.util.Date)(date.clone());
System.out.println(date == date1);
System.out.println(date == date2);
System.out.println(date.equals(date2));
```

15.25 Show the printout of the following code:

```
ArrayList<String> list = new ArrayList<String>();
list.add("New York");
ArrayList<String> list1 = list;
ArrayList<String> list2 = (ArrayList<String>)(list.clone());
list.add("Atlanta");
System.out.println(list == list1);
System.out.println(list == list2);
System.out.println("list is " + list);
System.out.println("list1 is " + list1);
System.out.println("list2.get(0) is " + list2.get(0));
System.out.println("list2.size() is " + list2.size());
```

15.26 What is wrong in the following code?

```
public class Test {
  public static void main(String[] args) {
    GeometricObject x = new Circle(3);
    GeometricObject y = x.clone();
    System.out.println(x == y);
  }
}
```

15.8 Interfaces vs. Abstract Classes

A class can implement multiple interfaces, but it can only extend one superclass.

An interface can be used more or less the same way as an abstract class, but defining an interface is different from defining an abstract class. Table 15.2 summarizes the differences.

TABLE 15.2 Interfaces vs. Abstract Classes

	Variables	*Constructors*	*Methods*
Abstract class	No restrictions.	Constructors are invoked by subclasses through constructor chaining. An abstract class cannot be instantiated using the new operator.	No restrictions.
Interface	All variables must be `public static final`.	No constructors. An interface cannot be instantiated using the new operator.	All methods must be public abstract instance methods

Java allows only *single inheritance* for class extension but allows *multiple extensions* for interfaces. For example,

single inheritance

multiple inheritance

```
public class NewClass extends BaseClass
    implements Interface1, . . ., InterfaceN {
  . . .
}
```

An interface can inherit other interfaces using the `extends` keyword. Such an interface is called a *subinterface*. For example, `NewInterface` in the following code is a subinterface of `Interface1`, . . . , and `InterfaceN`.

subinterface

```
public interface NewInterface extends Interface1, . . . , InterfaceN {
  // constants and abstract methods
}
```

A class implementing `NewInterface` must implement the abstract methods defined in `NewInterface`, `Interface1`, . . . , and `InterfaceN`. An interface can extend other interfaces but not classes. A class can extend its superclass and implement multiple interfaces.

All classes share a single root, the `Object` class, but there is no single root for interfaces. Like a class, an interface also defines a type. A variable of an interface type can reference any instance of the class that implements the interface. If a class implements an interface, the interface is like a superclass for the class. You can use an interface as a data type and cast a variable of an interface type to its subclass, and vice versa. For example, suppose that `c` is an instance of `Class2` in Figure 15.7. `c` is also an instance of `Object`, `Class1`, `Interface1`, `Interface1_1`, `Interface1_2`, `Interface2_1`, and `Interface2_2`.

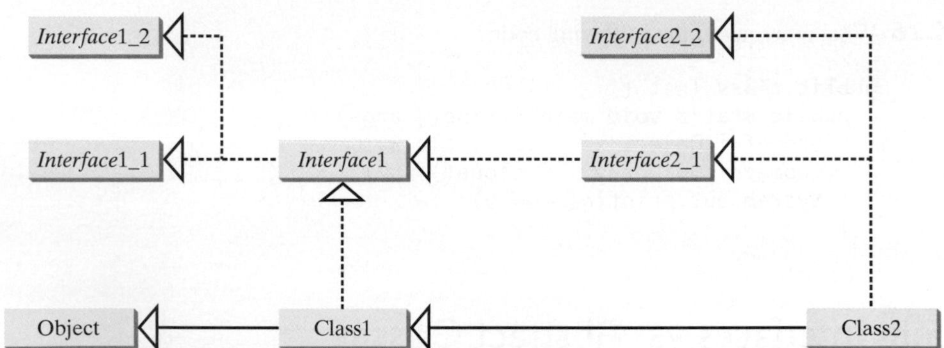

Figure 15.7 `Class1` implements `Interface1`; `Interface1` extends `Interface1_1` and `Interface1_2`. `Class2` extends `Class1` and implements `Interface2_1` and `Interface2_2`.

naming convention

Note

Class names are nouns. Interface names may be adjectives or nouns.

Design Guide

Abstract classes and interfaces can both be used to specify common behavior of objects. How do you decide whether to use an interface or a class? In general, a *strong is-a relationship* that clearly describes a parent-child relationship should be modeled using classes. For example, Gregorian calendar is a calendar, so the relationship between the class `java.util.GregorianCalendar` and `java.util.Calendar` is modeled using class inheritance. A *weak is-a relationship*, also known as an *is-kind-of relationship*, indicates that an object possesses a certain property. A weak is-a relationship can be modeled using interfaces. For example, all strings are comparable, so the `String` class implements the `Comparable` interface.

is-a relationship
is-kind-of relationship

interface preferred

In general, interfaces are preferred over abstract classes because an interface can define a common supertype for unrelated classes. Interfaces are more flexible than classes. Consider the Animal class. Suppose the howToEat method is defined in the Animal class, as follows:

```
abstract class Animal {
  public abstract String howToEat();
}
```

Animal class

Two subclasses of Animal are defined as follows:

```
class Chicken extends Animal {
  @Override
  public String howToEat() {
    return "Fry it";
  }
}
```

Chicken class

```
class Duck extends Animal {
  @Override
  public String howToEat() {
    return "Roast it";
  }
}
```

Duck class

Given this inheritance hierarchy, polymorphism enables you to hold a reference to a Chicken object or a Duck object in a variable of type Animal, as in the following code:

```
public static void main(String[] args) {
  Animal animal = new Chicken();
  eat(animal);

  animal = new Duck();
  eat(animal);
}

public static void eat(Animal animal) {
  animal.howToEat();
}
```

The JVM dynamically decides which howToEat method to invoke based on the actual object that invokes the method.

You can define a subclass of Animal. However, there is a restriction: The subclass must be for another animal (e.g., Turkey).

Interfaces don't have this restriction. Interfaces give you more flexibility than classes, because you don't have to make everything fit into one type of class. You may define the howToEat() method in an interface and let it serve as a common supertype for other classes. For example,

```
public static void main(String[] args) {
  Edible stuff = new Chicken();
  eat(stuff);

  stuff = new Duck();
  eat(stuff);

  stuff = new Broccoli();
  eat(stuff);
}
```

```
public static void eat(Edible stuff) {
  stuff.howToEat();
}
```

Edible interface

```
interface Edible {
  public String howToEat();
}
```

Chicken class

```
class Chicken implements Edible {
  @Override
  public String howToEat() {
    return "Fry it";
  }
}
```

Duck class

```
class Duck implements Edible {
  @Override
  public String howToEat() {
    return "Roast it";
  }
}
```

Broccoli class

```
class Broccoli implements Edible {
  @Override
  public String howToEat() {
    return "Stir-fry it";
  }
}
```

To define a class that represents edible objects, simply let the class implement the `Edible` interface. The class is now a subtype of the `Edible` type, and any `Edible` object can be passed to invoke the `eat` method.

MyProgrammingLab™

15.27 Give an example to show why interfaces are preferred over abstract classes.

15.28 Define the terms abstract classes and interfaces. What are the similarities and differences between abstract classes and interfaces?

15.28 True or false?

a. An interface is compiled into a separate bytecode file.

b. An interface can have static methods.

c. An interface can extend one or more interfaces.

d. An interface can extend an abstract class.

e. An abstract class can extend an interface.

15.9 Case Study: The `Rational` Class

This section shows how to design the `Rational` class for representing and processing rational numbers.

A rational number has a numerator and a denominator in the form `a/b`, where `a` is the numerator and `b` the denominator. For example, `1/3`, `3/4`, and `10/4` are rational numbers.

A rational number cannot have a denominator of `0`, but a numerator of `0` is fine. Every integer `i` is equivalent to a rational number `i/1`. Rational numbers are used in exact computations involving fractions—for example, `1/3 = 0.33333`. . . . This number cannot be precisely represented in floating-point format using either the data type `double` or `float`. To obtain the exact result, we must use rational numbers.

Java provides data types for integers and floating-point numbers, but not for rational numbers. This section shows how to design a class to represent rational numbers.

Since rational numbers share many common features with integers and floating-point numbers, and `Number` is the root class for numeric wrapper classes, it is appropriate to define `Rational` as a subclass of `Number`. Since rational numbers are comparable, the `Rational` class should also implement the `Comparable` interface. Figure 15.8 illustrates the `Rational` class and its relationship to the `Number` class and the `Comparable` interface.

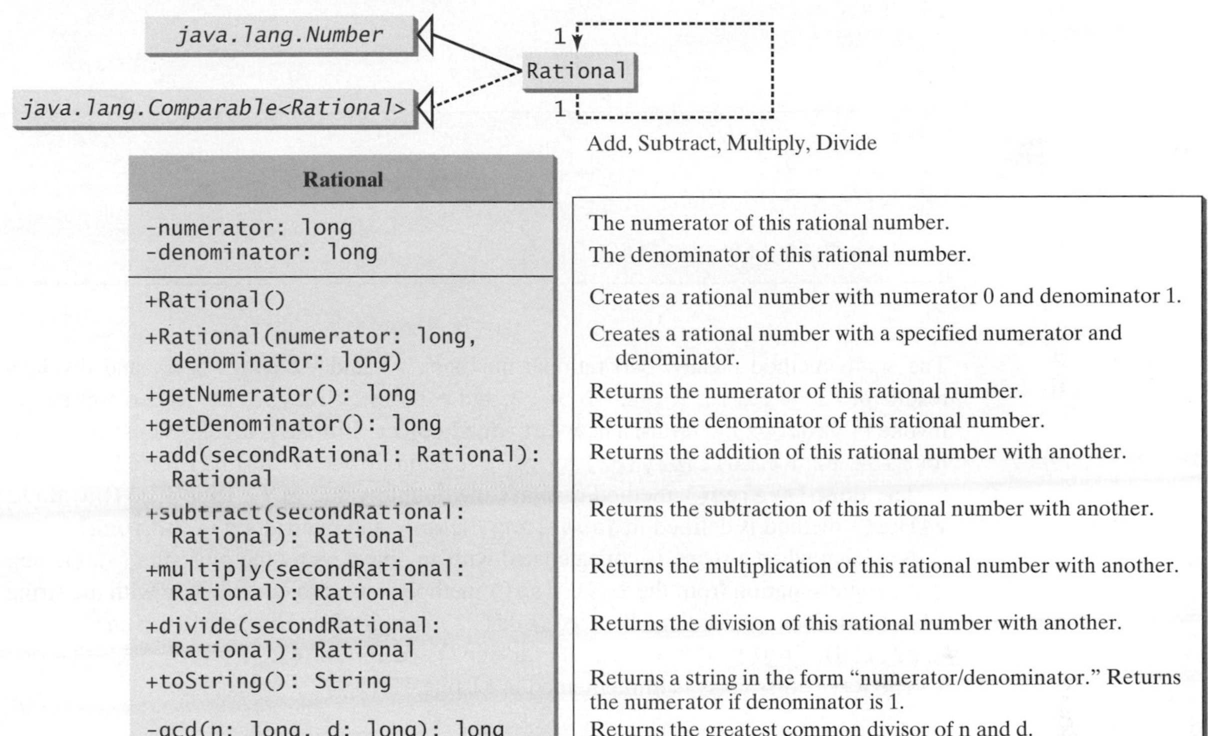

FIGURE 15.8 The properties, constructors, and methods of the `Rational` class are illustrated in UML.

A rational number consists of a numerator and a denominator. There are many equivalent rational numbers—for example, `1/3 = 2/6 = 3/9 = 4/12`. The numerator and the denominator of `1/3` have no common divisor except `1`, so `1/3` is said to be in *lowest terms*.

To reduce a rational number to its lowest terms, you need to find the greatest common divisor (GCD) of the absolute values of its numerator and denominator, then divide both the numerator and denominator by this value. You can use the method for computing the GCD of two integers `n` and `d`, as suggested in Listing 4.9, GreatestCommonDivisor.java. The numerator and denominator in a `Rational` object are reduced to their lowest terms.

As usual, let us first write a test program to create two `Rational` objects and test its methods. Listing 15.12 is a test program.

LISTING 15.12 TestRationalClass.java

```
public class TestRationalClass {
  /** Main method */
  public static void main(String[] args) {
    // Create and initialize two rational numbers r1 and r2
```

create a Rational
create a Rational
add

```
5      Rational r1 = new Rational(4, 2);
6      Rational r2 = new Rational(2, 3);
7
8      // Display results
9      System.out.println(r1 + " + " + r2 + " = " + r1.add(r2));
10     System.out.println(r1 + " - " + r2 + " = " + r1.subtract(r2));
11     System.out.println(r1 + " * " + r2 + " = " + r1.multiply(r2));
12     System.out.println(r1 + " / " + r2 + " = " + r1.divide(r2));
13     System.out.println(r2 + " is " + r2.doubleValue());
14   }
15 }
```

```
2 + 2/3 = 8/3
2 - 2/3 = 4/3
2 * 2/3 = 4/3
2 / 2/3 = 3
2/3 is 0.6666666666666666
```

The `main` method creates two rational numbers, `r1` and `r2` (lines 5–6), and displays the results of `r1 + r2`, `r1 - r2`, `r1 x r2`, and `r1 / r2` (lines 9–12). To perform `r1 + r2`, invoke `r1.add(r2)` to return a new `Rational` object. Similarly, invoke `r1.subtract(r2)` for `r1 - r2`, `r1.multiply(r2)` for `r1 x r2` , and `r1.divide(r2)` for `r1 / r2`.

The `doubleValue()` method displays the double value of `r2` (line 13). The `doubleValue()` method is defined in `java.lang.Number` and overridden in `Rational`.

Note that when a string is concatenated with an object using the plus sign (+), the object's string representation from the `toString()` method is used to concatenate with the string. So `r1 + " + " + r2 + " = " + r1.add(r2)` is equivalent to `r1.toString() + " + " + r2.toString() + " = " + r1.add(r2).toString()`.

The `Rational` class is implemented in Listing 15.13.

LISTING 15.13 Rational.java

```
public class Rational extends Number implements Comparable<Rational> {
  // Data fields for numerator and denominator
  private long numerator = 0;
  private long denominator = 1;

  /** Construct a rational with default properties */
  public Rational() {
    this(0, 1);
  }

  /** Construct a rational with specified numerator and denominator */
  public Rational(long numerator, long denominator) {
    long gcd = gcd(numerator, denominator);
    this.numerator = ((denominator > 0) ? 1 : -1) * numerator / gcd;
    this.denominator = Math.abs(denominator) / gcd;
  }

  /** Find GCD of two numbers */
  private static long gcd(long n, long d) {
    long n1 = Math.abs(n);
    long n2 = Math.abs(d);
    int gcd = 1;
```

```java

    for (int k = 1; k <= n1 && k <= n2; k++) {
      if (n1 % k == 0 && n2 % k == 0)
        gcd = k;
    }

    return gcd;
  }

  /** Return numerator */
  public long getNumerator() {
    return numerator;
  }

  /** Return denominator */
  public long getDenominator() {
    return denominator;
  }

  /** Add a rational number to this rational */
  public Rational add(Rational secondRational) {
    long n = numerator * secondRational.getDenominator() +
      denominator * secondRational.getNumerator();
    long d = denominator * secondRational.getDenominator();
    return new Rational(n, d);
  }
```

$\frac{a}{b} + \frac{c}{d} = \frac{ad + bc}{bd}$

```java

  /** Subtract a rational number from this rational */
  public Rational subtract(Rational secondRational) {
    long n = numerator * secondRational.getDenominator()
      - denominator * secondRational.getNumerator();
    long d = denominator * secondRational.getDenominator();
    return new Rational(n, d);
  }
```

$\frac{a}{b} - \frac{c}{d} = \frac{ad - bc}{bd}$

```java

  /** Multiply a rational number by this rational */
  public Rational multiply(Rational secondRational) {
    long n = numerator * secondRational.getNumerator();
    long d = denominator * secondRational.getDenominator();
    return new Rational(n, d);
  }
```

$\frac{a}{b} \times \frac{c}{d} = \frac{ac}{bd}$

```java

  /** Divide a rational number by this rational */
  public Rational divide(Rational secondRational) {
    long n = numerator * secondRational.getDenominator();
    long d = denominator * secondRational.numerator;
    return new Rational(n, d);
  }
```

$\frac{a}{b} \div \frac{c}{d} = \frac{ad}{bc}$

```java

  @Override
  public String toString() {
    if (denominator == 1)
      return numerator + "";
    else
      return numerator + "/" + denominator;
  }

  @Override // Override the equals method in the Object class
  public boolean equals(Object other) {
    if ((this.subtract((Rational)(other))).getNumerator() == 0)
```

```
83         return true;
84       else
85         return false;
86     }
87
88     @Override // Implement the abstract intValue method in Number
89     public int intValue() {
90       return (int)doubleValue();
91     }
92
93     @Override // Implement the abstract floatValue method in Number
94     public float floatValue() {
95       return (float)doubleValue();
96     }
97
98     @Override // Implement the doubleValue method in Number
99     public double doubleValue() {
100      return numerator * 1.0 / denominator;
101    }
102
103    @Override // Implement the abstract longValue method in Number
104    public long longValue() {
105      return (long)doubleValue();
106    }
107
108    @Override // Implement the compareTo method in Comparable
109    public int compareTo(Rational o) {
110      if (this.subtract(o).getNumerator() > 0)
111        return 1;
112      else if (this.subtract(o).getNumerator() < 0)
113        return -1;
114      else
115        return 0;
116    }
117  }
```

The rational number is encapsulated in a Rational object. Internally, a rational number is represented in its lowest terms (line 13), and the numerator determines its sign (line 14). The denominator is always positive (line 15).

The gcd method (lines 19–30 in the Rational class) is private; it is not intended for use by clients. The gcd method is only for internal use by the Rational class. The gcd method is also static, since it is not dependent on any particular Rational object.

The abs(x) method (lines 20–21 in the Rational class) is defined in the Math class and returns the absolute value of x.

Two Rational objects can interact with each other to perform add, subtract, multiply, and divide operations. These methods return a new Rational object (lines 43–70).

The methods toString and equals in the Object class are overridden in the Rational class (lines 72–86). The toString() method returns a string representation of a Rational object in the form numerator/denominator, or simply numerator if denominator is 1. The equals(Object other) method returns true if this rational number is equal to the other rational number.

The abstract methods intValue, longValue, floatValue, and doubleValue in the Number class are implemented in the Rational class (lines 88–106). These methods return the int, long, float, and double value for this rational number.

The compareTo(Rational other) method in the Comparable interface is implemented in the Rational class (lines 108–116) to compare this rational number to the other rational number.

Tip

The `get` methods for the properties `numerator` and `denominator` are provided in the `Rational` class, but the `set` methods are not provided, so, once a `Rational` object is created, its contents cannot be changed. The `Rational` class is immutable. The `String` class and the wrapper classes for primitive type values are also immutable.

immutable

Tip

The numerator and denominator are represented using two variables. It is possible to use an array of two integers to represent the numerator and denominator (see Programming Exercise 15.16). The signatures of the public methods in the `Rational` class are not changed, although the internal representation of a rational number is changed. This is a good example to illustrate the idea that the data fields of a class should be kept private so as to encapsulate the implementation of the class from the use of the class.

encapsulation

The `Rational` class has serious limitations and can easily overflow. For example, the following code will display an incorrect result, because the denominator is too large.

overflow

```
public class Test {
  public static void main(String[] args) {
    Rational r1 = new Rational(1, 123456789);
    Rational r2 = new Rational(1, 123456789);
    Rational r3 = new Rational(1, 123456789);
    System.out.println("r1 * r2 * r3 is " +
      r1.multiply(r2.multiply(r3)));
  }
}
```

```
r1 * r2 * r3 is -1/2204193661661244627
```

To fix it, you can implement the `Rational` class using the `BigInteger` for numerator and denominator (see Programming Exercise 15.21).

Check Point
MyProgrammingLab™

15.30 Show the printout of the following code?

```
Rational r1 = new Rational(-2, 6);
System.out.println(r1.getNumerator());
System.out.println(r1.getDenominator());
System.out.println(r1.intValue());
System.out.println(r1.doubleValue());
```

15.31 Why is the following code wrong?

```
Rational r1 = new Rational(-2, 6);
Object r2 = new Rational(1, 45);
System.out.println(r2.compareTo(r1));
```

15.32 Why is the following code wrong?

```
Object r1 = new Rational(-2, 6);
Rational r2 = new Rational(1, 45);
System.out.println(r2.compareTo(r1));
```

Key Terms

abstract class 560
abstract method 560
deep copy 579
interface 560
marker interface 577
shallow copy 579
subinterface 582

Chapter Summary

1. *Abstract classes* are like regular classes with data and methods, but you cannot create instances of abstract classes using the `new` operator.

2. An *abstract method* cannot be contained in a nonabstract class. If a subclass of an abstract superclass does not implement all the inherited abstract methods of the superclass, the subclass must be defined as abstract.

3. A class that contains abstract methods must be abstract. However, it is possible to define an abstract class that doesn't contain any abstract methods.

4. A subclass can be abstract even if its superclass is concrete.

5. An *interface* is a class-like construct that contains only constants and abstract methods. In many ways, an interface is similar to an abstract class, but an abstract class can contain constants and abstract methods as well as variables and concrete methods.

6. An interface is treated like a special class in Java. Each interface is compiled into a separate bytecode file, just like a regular class.

7. The `java.lang.Comparable` interface defines the `compareTo` method. Many classes in the Java library implement `Comparable`.

8. The `java.lang.Cloneable` interface is a *marker interface*. An object of the class that implements the `Cloneable` interface is cloneable.

9. A class can extend only one superclass but can implement one or more interfaces.

10. An interface can extend one or more interfaces.

Test Questions

Do the test questions for this chapter online at www.cs.armstrong.edu/liang/intro9e/test.html.

MyProgrammingLab™

Programming Exercises

Sections 15.2–15.3

**15.1 (*Plot functions using abstract methods*) Write an abstract class that draws the diagram for a function. The class is defined as follows:

```
public abstract class AbstractDrawFunction extends JPanel {
  /** Polygon to hold the points */
  private Polygon p = new Polygon();
```

```
    protected AbstractDrawFunction () {
      drawFunction();
    }

    /** Return the y-coordinate */
    abstract double f(double x);

    /** Obtain points for x-coordinates 100, 101, . . ., 300 */
    public void drawFunction() {
      for (int x = -100; x <= 100; x++) {
        p.addPoint(x + 200, 200 - (int)f(x));
      }
    }

    @Override /** Draw axes, labels, and connect points */
    protected void paintComponent(Graphics g) {
      // To be completed by you
    }
  }
```

Test the class with the following functions:

a. `f(x) = x`^{2}`;`
b. `f(x) = sin(x);`
c. `f(x) = cos(x);`
d. `f(x) = tan(x);`
e. `f(x) = cos(x) + 5sin(x);`
f. `f(x) = 5cos(x) + sin(x);`
g. `f(x) = log(x) + x`^{2}`;`

For each function, create a class that extends the `AbstractDrawFunction` class and implements the `f` method. Figure 15.9 displays the drawings for the first three functions.

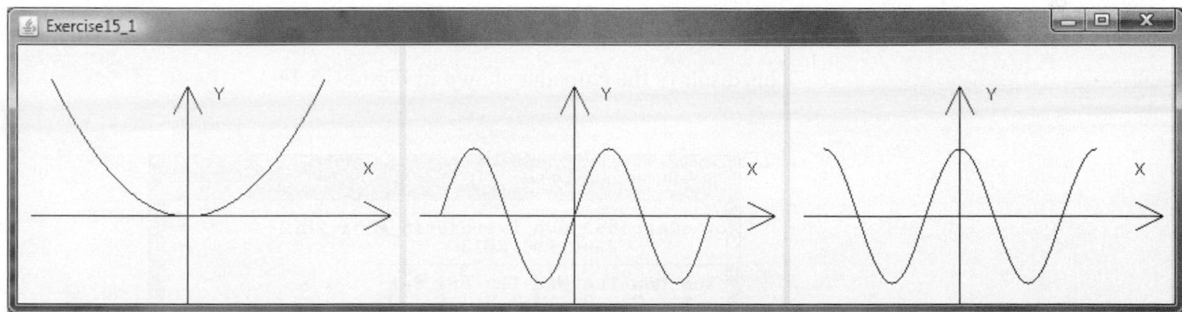

FIGURE 15.9 Exercise 15.1 draws the square, sine, and cosine functions.

****15.2** (*Triangle class*) Design a new `Triangle` class that extends the abstract `GeometricObject` class. Draw the UML diagram for the classes `Triangle` and `GeometricObject` and then implement the `Triangle` class. Write a test program that prompts the user to enter three sides of the triangle, a color, and a Boolean value to indicate whether the triangle is filled. The program should create a `Triangle` object with these sides and set the color and filled properties using the input. The program should display the area, perimeter, color, and true or false to indicate whether it is filled or not.

***15.3** (*Shuffle ArrayList*) Write the following method that shuffles an `ArrayList` of numbers:

```
public static void shuffle(ArrayList<Number> list)
```

***15.4** (*Sort ArrayList*) Write the following method that sorts an `ArrayList` of numbers.

```
public static void sort(ArrayList<Number> list)
```

****15.5** (*Display a calendar*) Write a program that displays the calendar for the current month, as shown in Figure 15.10. Use labels, and set text on the labels to display the calendar. Use the `GregorianCalendar` class to obtain the information for the month, year, first day of the month, and number of days in the month.

Exercise15_5

11/2011

Sunday	Monday	Tuesday	Wednesday	Thursday	Friday	Saturday
		1	2	3	4	5
6	7	8	9	10	11	12
13	14	15	16	17	18	19
20	21	22	23	24	25	26
27	28	29	30			

JLabel

JPanel with GridLayout

Each cell is a JLabel

FIGURE 15.10 The program displays the calendar for the current month.

****15.6** (*Display calendars*) Rewrite the `PrintCalendar` class in Listing 5.12 to display a calendar for a specified month using the `Calendar` and `GregorianCalendar` classes. Your program receives the month and year from the command line. For example:

```
java Exercise15_06 1 2012
```

This displays the calendar shown in Figure 15.11.

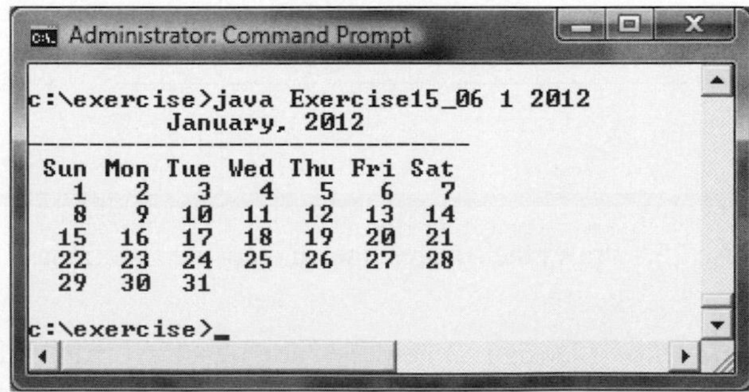

FIGURE 15.11 The program displays a calendar for January 2012.

You also can run the program without the year. In this case, the year is the current year. If you run the program without specifying a month and a year, the month is the current month.

Sections 15.4–15.8

***15.7** (*Enable `GeometricObject` comparable*) Modify the `GeometricObject` class to implement the `Comparable` interface, and define a static `max` method in the `GeometricObject` class for finding the larger of two `GeometricObject` objects. Draw the UML diagram and implement the new `GeometricObject` class. Write a test program that uses the `max` method to find the larger of two circles and the larger of two rectangles.

***15.8** (*The `ComparableCircle` class*) Define a class named `ComparableCircle` that extends `Circle` and implements `Comparable`. Draw the UML diagram and implement the `compareTo` method to compare the circles on the basis of area. Write a test class to find the larger of two instances of `ComparableCircle` objects.

***15.9** (*The `Colorable` interface*) Design an interface named `Colorable` with a `void` method named `howToColor()`. Every class of a colorable object must implement the `Colorable` interface. Design a class named `Square` that extends `GeometricObject` and implements `Colorable`. Implement `howToColor` to display the message `Color all four sides`.

Draw a UML diagram that involves `Colorable`, `Square`, and `GeometricObject`. Write a test program that creates an array of five `GeometricObjects`. For each object in the array, invoke its `howToColor` method if it is colorable.

***15.10** (*Revise the `MyStack` class*) Rewrite the `MyStack` class in Listing 11.9 to perform a deep copy of the `list` field.

***15.11** (*Enable `Circle` comparable*) Rewrite the `Circle` class in Listing 15.2 to extend `GeometricObject` and implement the `Comparable` interface. Override the `equals` method in the `Object` class. Two `Circle` objects are equal if their radii are the same. Draw the UML diagram that involves `Circle`, `GeometricObject`, and `Comparable`.

***15.12** (*Enable `Rectangle` comparable*) Rewrite the `Rectangle` class in Listing 15.3 to extend `GeometricObject` and implement the `Comparable` interface. Override the `equals` method in the `Object` class. Two `Rectangle` objects are equal if their areas are the same. Draw the UML diagram that involves `Rectangle`, `GeometricObject`, and `Comparable`.

Redesign the `Rectangle` class

***15.13** (*The `Octagon` class*) Write a class named `Octagon` that extends `GeometricObject` and implements the `Comparable` and `Cloneable` interfaces. Assume that all eight sides of the octagon are of equal size. The area can be computed using the following formula:

$$area = (2 + 4/\sqrt{2}) * side * side$$

Draw the UML diagram that involves `Octagon`, `GeometricObject`, `Comparable`, and `Cloneable`. Write a test program that creates an `Octagon` object with side value `5` and displays its area and perimeter. Create a new object using the `clone` method and compare the two objects using the `compareTo` method.

***15.14** (*Sum the areas of geometric objects*) Write a method that sums the areas of all the geometric objects in an array. The method signature is:

```
public static double sumArea(GeometricObject[] a)
```

Write a test program that creates an array of four objects (two circles and two rectangles) and computes their total area using the `sumArea` method.

***15.15** (*Enable the* `Course` *class cloneable*) Rewrite the `Course` class in Listing 10.6 to add a `clone` method to perform a deep copy on the `students` field.

Section 15.9

***15.16** (*Demonstrate the benefits of encapsulation*) Rewrite the `Rational` class in Listing 15.13 using a new internal representation for the numerator and denominator. Create an array of two integers as follows:

```
private long[] r = new long[2];
```

Use `r[0]` to represent the numerator and `r[1]` to represent the denominator. The signatures of the methods in the `Rational` class are not changed, so a client application that uses the previous `Rational` class can continue to use this new `Rational` class without being recompiled.

***15.17** (*Use* `BigInteger` *for the* `Rational` *class*) Redesign and implement the `Rational` class in Listing 15.11 using `BigInteger` for the numerator and denominator.

***15.18** (*Create a rational-number calculator*) Write a program similar to Listing 9.5, Calculator.java. Instead of using integers, use rationals, as shown in Figure 15.12a. You will need to use the `split` method in the `String` class, introduced in Section 9.2.6, Converting, Replacing, and Splitting Strings, to retrieve the numerator string and denominator string, and convert strings into integers using the `Integer.parseInt` method.

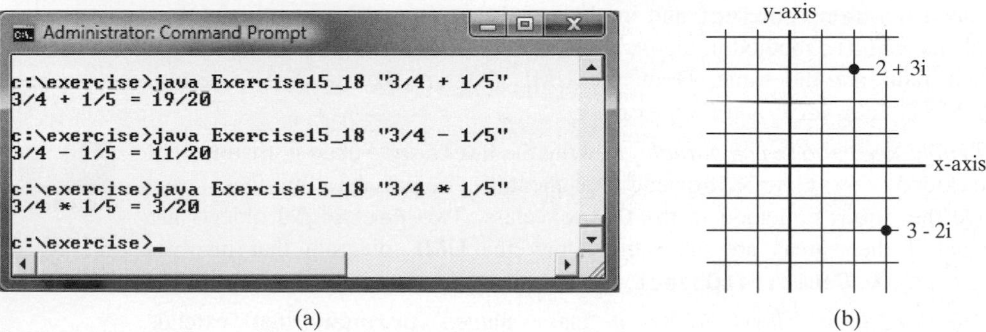

FIGURE 15.12 (a) The program takes three arguments (operand1, operator, and operand2) from the command line and displays the expression and the result of the arithmetic operation. (b) A complex number can be interpreted as a point in a plane.

***15.19** (*Math: The* `Complex` *class*) A complex number is a number in the form $a + bi$, where a and b are real numbers and i is $\sqrt{-1}$. The numbers `a` and `b` are known as the real part and imaginary part of the complex number, respectively. You can perform addition, subtraction, multiplication, and division for complex numbers using the following formulas:

$$a + bi + c + di = (a + c) + (b + d)i$$

$$a + bi - (c + di) = (a - c) + (b - d)i$$

$$(a + bi)*(c + di) = (ac - bd) + (bc + ad)i$$

$$(a + bi)/(c + di) = (ac + bd)/(c^2 + d^2) + (bc - ad)i/(c^2 + d^2)$$

You can also obtain the absolute value for a complex number using the following formula:

$$|a + bi| = \sqrt{a^2 + b^2}$$

(A complex number can be interpreted as a point on a plane by identifying the (a,b) values as the coordinates of the point. The absolute value of the complex number corresponds to the distance of the point to the origin, as shown in Figure 15.12b.)

Design a class named `Complex` for representing complex numbers and the methods `add`, `subtract`, `multiply`, `divide`, and `abs` for performing complex-number operations, and override `toString` method for returning a string representation for a complex number. The `toString` method returns `(a + bi)` as a string. If `b` is `0`, it simply returns `a`.

Provide three constructors `Complex(a, b)`, `Complex(a)`, and `Complex()`. `Complex()` creates a `Complex` object for number `0` and `Complex(a)` creates a `Complex` object with `0` for `b`. Also provide the `getRealPart()` and `getImaginaryPart()` methods for returning the real and imaginary part of the complex number, respectively.

Write a test program that prompts the user to enter two complex numbers and displays the result of their addition, subtraction, multiplication, and division. Here is a sample run:

```
Enter the first complex number: 3.5 5.5 ↵Enter
Enter the second complex number: -3.5 1 ↵Enter
(3.5 + 5.5i) + (-3.5 + 1.0i) = 0.0 + 6.5i
(3.5 + 5.5i) - (-3.5 + 1.0i) = 7.0 + 4.5i
(3.5 + 5.5i) * (-3.5 + 1.0i) = -17.75 + -15.75i
(3.5 + 5.5i) / (-3.5 + 1.0i) = -0.5094 + -1.7i
|(3.5 + 5.5i)| = 6.519202405202649
```

****15.20** (*Mandelbrot fractal*) Mandelbrot fractal is a well-known image created from a Mandelbrot set (see Figure 15.13a). A Mandelbrot set is defined using the following iteration:

$$z_{n+1} = z_n^2 + c$$

c is a complex number and the starting point of iteration is $z_0 = 0$. For a given c, the iteration will produce a sequence of complex numbers: $\{z_0, z_1, \ldots, z_n, \ldots\}$. It can be shown that the sequence either tends to infinity or stays bounded, depending on the value of c. For example, if c is `0`, the sequence is $\{0, 0, \ldots\}$, which is bounded. If c is i, the sequence is $\{0, i, -1 + i, -i, -1 + i, i, \ldots\}$, which is bounded. If c is $1 + i$, the sequence is $\{0, 1 + i, 1 + 3i, \ldots\}$, which is unbounded. It is known that if the absolute value of a complex value z_i in the sequence is greater than 2, then the sequence is unbounded. The Mandelbrot set consists of the c value such that the sequence is bounded. For example, 0 and i are in the Mandelbrot set. A Mandelbrot image can be created using the following code:

```
class MandelbrotCanvas extends JPanel {
  final static int COUNT_LIMIT = 60;
```

```
3
4    @Override /** Paint a Mandelbrot image */
5    protected void paintComponent(Graphics g) {
6      super.paintComponent(g);
7
8      for (double x = -2.0; x < 2.0; x += 0.01)
9        for (double y = -2.0; y < 2.0; y += 0.01) {
10         int c = count(new Complex(x, y));
11         if (c == COUNT_LIMIT)
12           g.setColor(Color.BLACK); // c is in a Mandelbrot set
13         else
14           g.setColor(new Color(
15             c * 77 % 256, c * 58 % 256, c * 159 % 256));
16
17         g.drawRect((int)(x * 100) + 200, (int)(y * 100) + 200,
18           1, 1); // Fill a tiny rectangle with the specified color
19       }
20   }
21
22   /** Return the iteration count */
23   static int count(Complex c) {
24     Complex z = new Complex(0, 0); // z0
25
26     for (int i = 0; i < COUNT_LIMIT; i++) {
27       z = z.multiply(z).add(c); // Get z1, z2, . . .
28       if (z.abs() > 2) return i; // The sequence is unbounded
29     }
30
31     return COUNT_LIMIT; // Indicate a bounded sequence
32   }
33 }
```

The `count(Complex c)` method (lines 23–32) computes z1, z2, . . ., z60. If none of their absolute values exceeds `2`, we assume *c* is in the Mandelbrot set. Of course, there could always be an error, but `60 (COUNT_LIMIT)` iterations usually are enough. Once we find that the sequence is unbounded, the method returns the

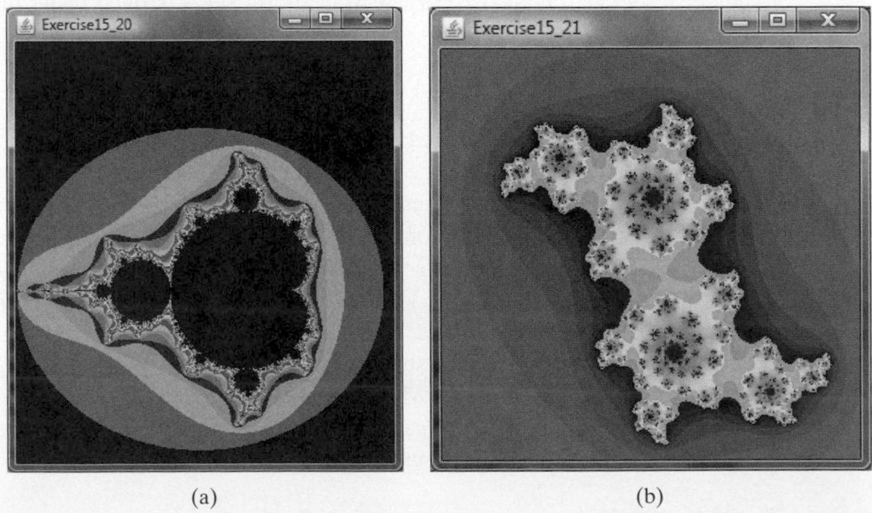

(a) (b)

FIGURE 15.13 A Mandelbrot image is shown in (a) and a Julia set image is shown in (b).

iteration count (line 28). The method returns `COUNT_LIMIT` if the sequence is bounded (line 31).

The loop in lines 8–9 examines each point (x, y) for $-2 < x < 2$ and $-2 < y < 2$ with interval 0.01 to see if its corresponding complex number $c = x + yi$ is in the Mandelbrot set (line 10). If so, paint the point black (line 12). If not, set a color that is dependent on its iteration count (line 15). Note that the point is painted in a square with width u and height `1`. All the points are scaled and mapped to a grid of 400-by-400 pixels (lines 14–15). Note that the values `77`, `58`, and `159` are set arbitrarily. You may set different numbers to get new colors.

Complete the program to draw a Mandelbrot image, as shown in Figure 15.13a.

****15.21** (*Julia set*) The preceding exercise describes Mandelbrot sets. The Mandelbrot set consists of the complex c value such that the sequence $z_{n+1} = z_n^2 + c$ is bounded with z_0 fixed and c varying. If we fix c and vary z_0 $(= x + yi)$, the point (x, y) is said to be in a Julia set for a fixed complex value c, if the function $z_{n+1} = z_n^2 + c$ stays bounded. Revise Exercise 15.20 to draw a Julia set as shown in Figure 15.13b. Note that you only need to revise the `count` method by using a fixed c value $(-0.3 + 0.6i)$.

15.22 (*Use the `Rational` class*) Write a program that computes the following summation series using the `Rational` class:

$$\frac{1}{2} + \frac{2}{3} + \frac{3}{4} + \ldots + \frac{98}{99} + \frac{99}{100}$$

You will discover that the output is incorrect because of integer overflow (too large). To fix this problem, see Programming Exercise 15.17.

CHAPTER

16

Event-Driven Programming

Objectives

- To get a taste of event-driven programming (§16.1).
- To describe events, event sources, and event classes (§16.2).
- To define listener classes, register listener objects with the source object, and write the code to handle events (§16.3).
- To define listener classes using inner classes (§16.4).
- To define listener classes using anonymous inner classes (§16.5).
- To explore various coding styles for creating and registering listener classes (§16.6).
- To develop a GUI application for a loan calculator (§16.7).
- To write programs to deal with `MouseEvent`s (§16.8).
- To simplify coding for listener classes using listener interface adapters (§16.9).
- To write programs to deal with `KeyEvent`s (§16.10).
- To use the `javax.swing.Timer` class to control animations (§16.11).

16.1 Introduction

You can write code to process events such as a button click or a timer.

problem

Suppose you want to write a GUI program that lets the user enter a loan amount, annual interest rate, and number of years and click the *Compute Payment* button to obtain the monthly payment and total payment, as shown in Figure 16.1a. How do you accomplish the task? You have to use *event-driven programming* to write the code to respond to the button-clicking event.

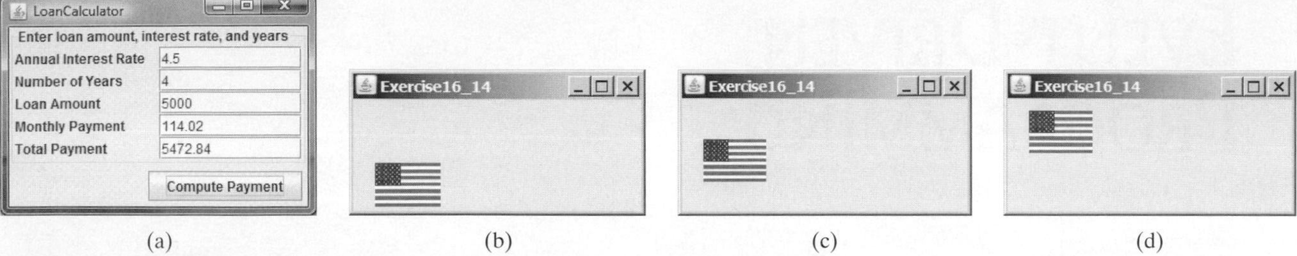

FIGURE 16.1 (a) The program computes loan payments. (b)–(d) A flag is rising upward.

Suppose you want to write a program that animates a rising flag, as shown in Figure 16.1b–d. How do you accomplish the task? There are several ways to program this. An effective one is to use a timer in event-driven programming, which is the subject of this chapter.

problem

Before delving into event-driven programming, it is helpful to get a taste using a simple example. The example displays two buttons in a frame, as shown in Figure 16.2.

FIGURE 16.2 (a) The program displays two buttons. (b) A message is displayed in the console when a button is clicked.

To respond to a button click, you need to write the code to process the button-clicking action. The button is an *event source object*—where the action originates. You need to create an object capable of handling the action event on a button. This object is called an *event listener*, as shown in Figure 16.3.

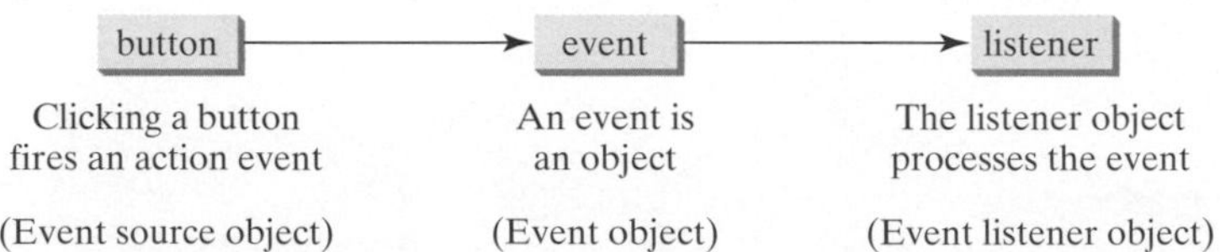

FIGURE 16.3 A listener object processes the event fired from the source object.

Not all objects can be listeners for an action event. To be a listener of an action event, two requirements must be met:

`ActionListener` interface

1. The object must be an instance of the **`ActionListener`** interface. This interface defines the common behavior for all action listeners.

`addActionListener(listener)`

2. The **`ActionListener`** object **`listener`** must be registered with the event source object using the method **`source.addActionListener(listener)`**.

The `ActionListener` interface contains the `actionPerformed` method for processing the event. Your listener class must override this method to respond to the event. Listing 16.1 gives the code that processes the `ActionEvent` on the two buttons. When you click the *OK* button, the message "OK button clicked" is displayed. When you click the *Cancel* button, the message "Cancel button clicked" is displayed, as shown in Figure 16.2.

LISTING 16.1 HandleEvent.java

```
1  import javax.swing.*;
2  import java.awt.event.*;
3
4  public class HandleEvent extends JFrame {
5    public HandleEvent() {
6      // Create two buttons
7      JButton jbtOK = new JButton("OK");
8      JButton jbtCancel = new JButton("Cancel");
9
10     // Create a panel to hold buttons
11     JPanel panel = new JPanel();
12     panel.add(jbtOK);
13     panel.add(jbtCancel);
14
15     add(panel); // Add panel to the frame
16
17     // Register listeners
18     OKListenerClass listener1 = new OKListenerClass();
19     CancelListenerClass listener2 = new CancelListenerClass();
20     jbtOK.addActionListener(listener1);
21     jbtCancel.addActionListener(listener2);
22   }
23
24   public static void main(String[] args) {
25     JFrame frame = new HandleEvent();
26     frame.setTitle("Handle Event");
27     frame.setSize(200, 150);
28     frame.setLocation(200, 100);
29     frame.setDefaultCloseOperation(JFrame.EXIT_ON_CLOSE);
30     frame.setVisible(true);
31   }
32 }
33
34 class OKListenerClass implements ActionListener {
35   @Override
36   public void actionPerformed(ActionEvent e) {
37     System.out.println("OK button clicked");
38   }
39 }
40
41 class CancelListenerClass implements ActionListener {
42   @Override
43   public void actionPerformed(ActionEvent e) {
44     System.out.println("Cancel button clicked");
45   }
46 }
```

create listener (line 18)
register listener (line 20)
listener class (line 34)
process event (line 36)
listener class (line 41)
process event (line 43)

Two listener classes are defined in lines 34–46. Each listener class implements `ActionListener` to process `ActionEvent`. The object `listener1` is an instance of `OKListenerClass` (line 18), which is registered with the button `jbtOK` (line 20). When the *OK* button is clicked, the `actionPerformed(ActionEvent)` method (line 36) in

OKListenerClass is invoked to process the event. The object listener2 is an instance of CancelListenerClass (line 19), which is registered with the button jbtCancel in line 21. When the *Cancel* button is clicked, the actionPerformed(ActionEvent) method (line 43) in CancelListenerClass is invoked to process the event.

You now have seen a glimpse of event-driven programming in Java. You probably have many questions, such as why a listener class is defined to implement the ActionListener. The following sections will give you all the answers.

16.2 Events and Event Sources

An event is an object created from an event source. **Firing an event** *means to create an event and delegate the listener to handle the event.*

event-driven programming
event

When you run a Java GUI program, the program interacts with the user, and the events drive its execution. This is called *event-driven programming.* An *event* can be defined as a signal to the program that something has happened. Events are triggered either by external user actions, such as mouse movements, button clicks, and keystrokes, or by internal program activities, such as a timer. The program can choose to respond to or ignore an event. The example in the preceding section gave you a taste of event-driven programming.

fire event
event source object
source object

The component that creates an event and fires it is called the *event source object*, or simply *source object* or *source component*. For example, a button is the source object for a button-clicking action event. An event is an instance of an event class. The root class of the event classes is java.util.EventObject. The hierarchical relationships of some event classes are shown in Figure 16.4.

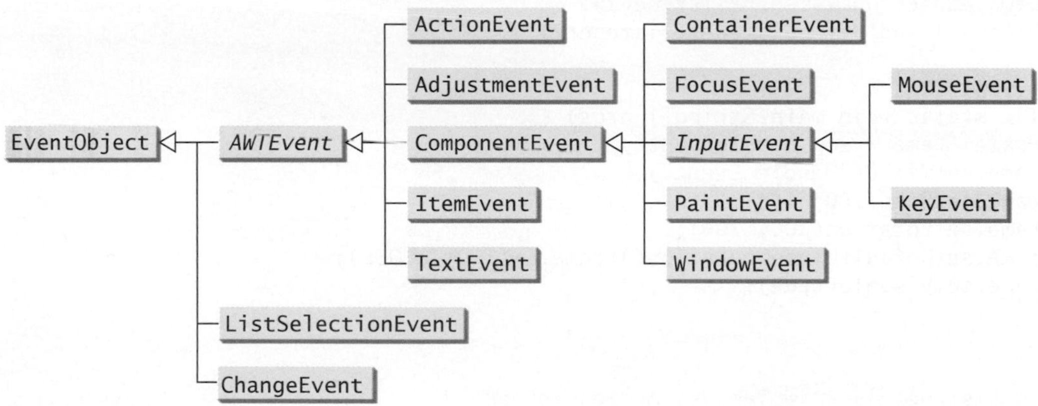

FIGURE 16.4 An event is an object of the EventObject class.

event object
getSource()

An *event object* contains whatever properties are pertinent to the event. You can identify the source object of an event using the getSource() instance method in the EventObject class. The subclasses of EventObject deal with specific types of events, such as action events, window events, component events, mouse events, and key events. The first three columns in Table 16.1 list some external user actions, source objects, and event types fired. For example, when clicking a button, the button creates and fires an ActionEvent, as indicated in the first line of this table. Here the button is an event source object and an ActionEvent is the event object fired by the source object, as shown in Figure 16.2.

Note

If a component can fire an event, any subclass of the component can fire the same type of event. For example, every GUI component can fire MouseEvent and KeyEvent, since Component is the superclass of all GUI components.

Table 16.1 User Action, Source Object, Event Type, Listener Interface, and Handler

User Action	*Source Object*	*Event Type Fired*	*Listener Interface*	*Listener Interface Methods*
Click a button	`JButton`	`ActionEvent`	`ActionListener`	`actionPerformed(ActionEvent e)`
Press Enter in a text field	`JTextField`	`ActionEvent`	`ActionListener`	`actionPerformed(ActionEvent e)`
Check or uncheck	`JRadioButton`	`ActionEvent` `ItemEvent`	`ActionListener` `ItemListener`	`actionPerformed(ActionEvent e)` `itemStateChanged(ItemEvent e)`
Check or uncheck	`JCheckBox`	`ActionEvent` `ItemEvent`	`ActionListener` `ItemListener`	`actionPerformed(ActionEvent e)` `itemStateChanged(ItemEvent e)`
Select a new item	`JComboBox`	`ActionEvent` `ItemEvent`	`ActionListener` `ItemListener`	`actionPerformed(ActionEvent e)` `itemStateChanged(ItemEvent e)`
Mouse pressed	`Component`	`MouseEvent`	`MouseListener`	`mousePressed(MouseEvent e)`
Mouse released				`mouseReleased(MouseEvent e)`
Mouse clicked				`mouseClicked(MouseEvent e)`
Mouse entered				`mouseEntered(MouseEvent e)`
Mouse exited				`mouseExited(MouseEvent e)`
Mouse moved			`MouseMotionListener`	`mouseMoved(MouseEvent e)`
Mouse dragged				`mouseDragged(MouseEvent e)`
Key pressed	`Component`	`KeyEvent`	`KeyListener`	`keyPressed(KeyEvent e)`
Key released				`keyReleased(KeyEvent e)`
Key typed				`keyTyped(KeyEvent e)`

Note

All the event classes in Figure 16.4 are included in the `java.awt.event` package except `ListSelectionEvent` and `ChangeEvent`, which are in the `javax.swing.event` package. AWT events were originally designed for AWT components, but many Swing components fire them.

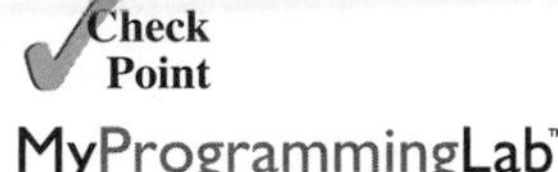

16.1 What is an event source object? What is an event object? Describe the relationship between an event source object and an event object.

16.2 Can a button fire a `MouseEvent`? Can a button fire a `KeyEvent`? Can a button fire an `ActionEvent`?

16.3 Listeners, Registrations, and Handling Events

Key Point

***A listener** is an object that must be registered with an event source object, and it must be an instance of an appropriate event-handling interface.*

Java uses a delegation-based model for event handling: a source object fires an event, and an object interested in the event handles it. The latter object is called an *event listener* or simply *listener*. For an object to be a listener for an event on a source object, two things are needed, as shown in Figure 16.5.

event delegation
event listener

1. *The listener object must be an instance of the corresponding event-listener interface* to ensure that the listener has the correct method for processing the event. Java provides a listener interface for every type of event. The listener interface is usually named `XListener` for `XEvent`, with the exception of `MouseMotionListener`. The last

event-listener interface

`XListener/XEvent`

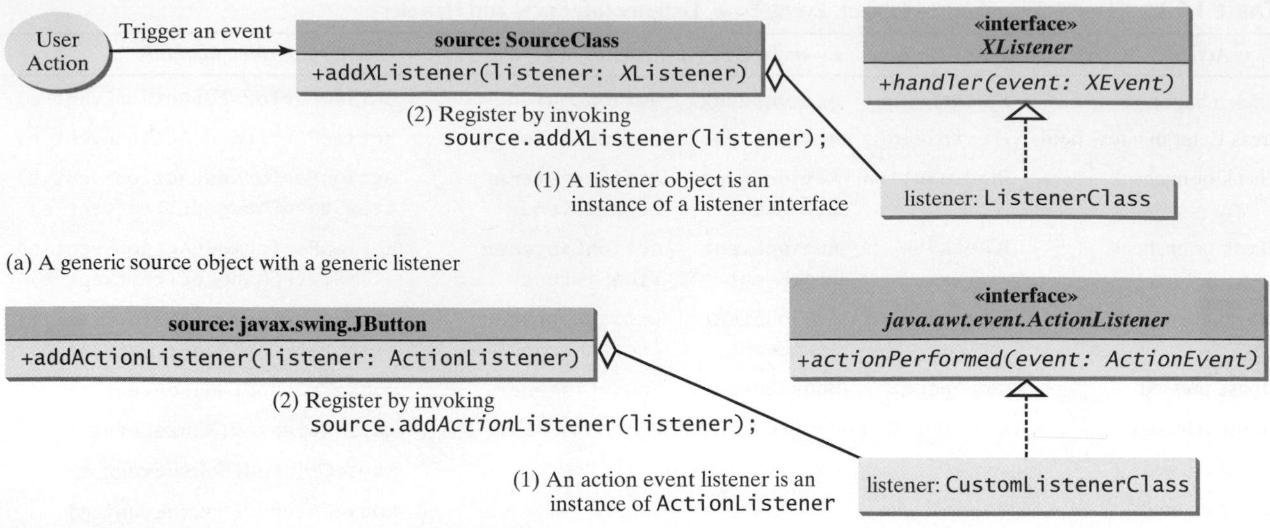

FIGURE 16.5 A listener must be an instance of a listener interface and must be registered with a source object.

three columns in Table 16.1 list event types, the corresponding listener interfaces, and the methods defined in the listener interfaces. The listener interface contains the method(s), known as the *event handler(s)*, for processing the event. For example, as shown in the first line of this table, the corresponding listener interface for `ActionEvent` is `ActionListener`; each listener for `ActionEvent` should implement the `ActionListener` interface; the `ActionListener` interface contains the handler `actionPerformed(ActionEvent)` for processing an `ActionEvent`.

event handler

register listener

2. *The listener object must be registered by the source object.* Registration methods depend on the event type. For `ActionEvent`, the method is `addActionListener`. In general, the method is named `addXListener` for `XEvent`. A source object may fire several types of events, and for each event the source object maintains a list of registered listeners and notifies them by invoking the *handler* of the listener object to respond to the event, as shown in Figure 16.6. (Note that this figure shows the internal implementation of a source class. You don't have to know how a source class such as `JButton` is implemented in order to use it, but this knowledge will help you understand the Java event-driven programming framework.)

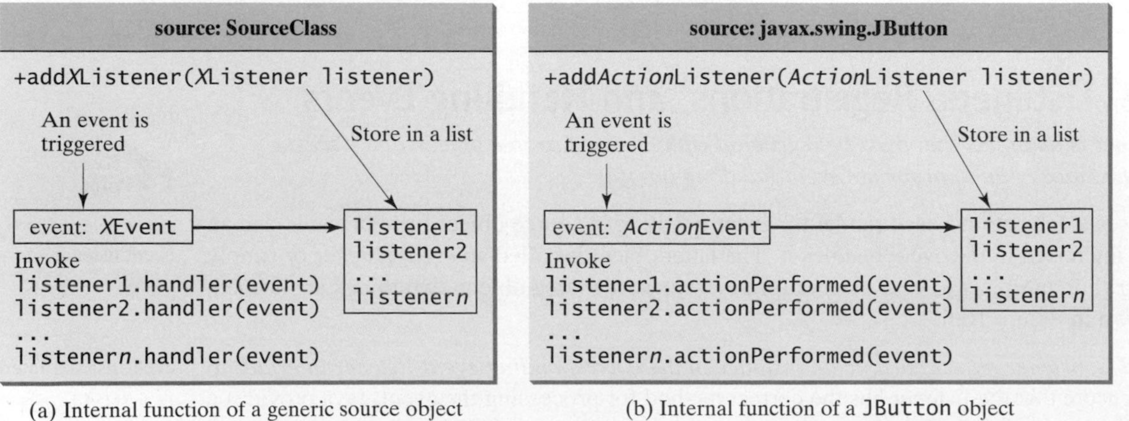

FIGURE 16.6 The source object notifies the listeners of the event by invoking the listener object's handler.

Let's revisit Listing 16.1, HandleEvent.java. Since a `JButton` object fires `ActionEvent`, a listener object for `ActionEvent` must be an instance of `ActionListener`, so the listener class implements `ActionListener` in line 34. The source object invokes `addActionListener(listener)` to register a listener, as follows:

```
JButton jbtOK = new JButton("OK"); // Line 7 in Listing 16.1

OKListenerClass listener1
  = new OKListenerClass(); // Line 18 in Listing 16.1

jbtOK.addActionListener(listener1); // Line 20 in Listing 16.1
```

create source object

create listener object

register listener

When you click the button, the `JButton` object fires an `ActionEvent` and passes it to invoke the listener's `actionPerformed` method to handle the event.

The event object contains information pertinent to the event, which can be obtained using the methods, as shown in Figure 16.7. For example, you can use `e.getSource()` to obtain the source object that fired the event. For an action event, you can use `e.getWhen()` to obtain the time when the event occurred.

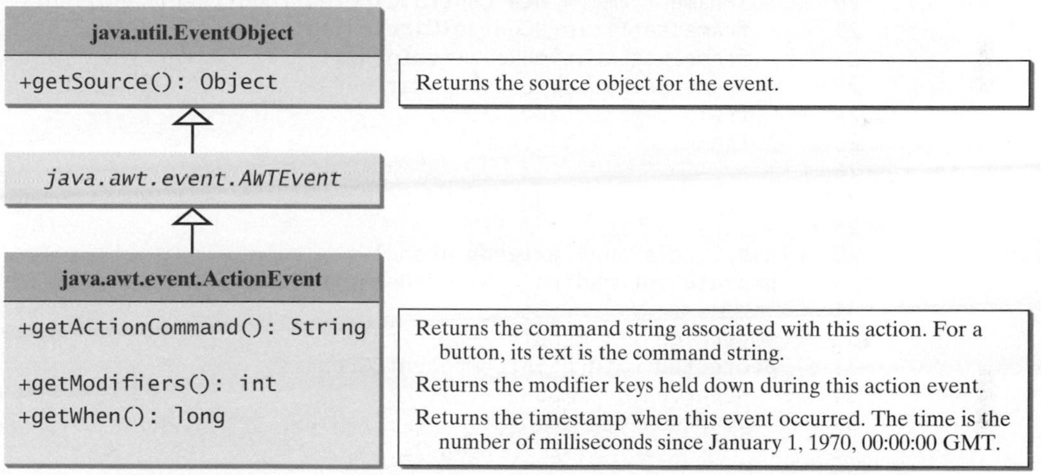

FIGURE 16.7 You can obtain useful information from an event object.

We now write a program that uses two buttons to control the size of a circle, as shown in Figure 16.8.

FIGURE 16.8 The user clicks the *Enlarge* and *Shrink* buttons to enlarge and shrink the size of the circle.

We will develop this program incrementally. First we will write the program in Listing 16.2 that displays the user interface with a circle in the center (line 14) and two buttons on the bottom (line 15).

first version

LISTING 16.2 ControlCircleWithoutEventHandling.java

buttons

circle canvas

CirclePanel class

paint the circle

```
import javax.swing.*;
import java.awt.*;

public class ControlCircleWithoutEventHandling extends JFrame {
  private JButton jbtEnlarge = new JButton("Enlarge");
  private JButton jbtShrink = new JButton("Shrink");
  private CirclePanel canvas = new CirclePanel();

  public ControlCircleWithoutEventHandling() {
    JPanel panel = new JPanel(); // Use the panel to group buttons
    panel.add(jbtEnlarge);
    panel.add(jbtShrink);

    this.add(canvas, BorderLayout.CENTER); // Add canvas to center
    this.add(panel, BorderLayout.SOUTH); // Add buttons to the frame
  }

  /** Main method */
  public static void main(String[] args) {
    JFrame frame = new ControlCircleWithoutEventHandling();
    frame.setTitle("ControlCircleWithoutEventHandling");
    frame.setLocationRelativeTo(null); // Center the frame
    frame.setDefaultCloseOperation(JFrame.EXIT_ON_CLOSE);
    frame.setSize(200, 200);
    frame.setVisible(true);
  }
}

class CirclePanel extends JPanel {
  private int radius = 5; // Default circle radius

  @Override /** Repaint the circle */
  protected void paintComponent(Graphics g) {
    super.paintComponent(g);
    g.drawOval(getWidth() / 2 - radius, getHeight() / 2 - radius,
      2 * radius, 2 * radius);
  }
}
```

second version

How do you use the buttons to enlarge or shrink the circle? When the *Enlarge* button is clicked, you want the circle to be repainted with a larger radius. How can you accomplish this? You can expand the program in Listing 16.2 into Listing 16.3 with the following features:

1. Define a listener class named `EnlargeListener` that implements `ActionListener` (lines 31–36).
2. Create a listener and register it with `jbtEnlarge` (line 18).
3. Add a method named `enlarge()` in `CirclePanel` to increase the radius, then repaint the panel (lines 42–45).
4. Implement the `actionPerformed` method in `EnlargeListener` to invoke `canvas.enlarge()` (line 34).
5. To make the reference variable `canvas` accessible from the `actionPerformed` method, define `EnlargeListener` as an inner class of the `ControlCircle` class (lines 31–36). (*Inner classes* are defined inside another class. We will introduce inner classes in the next section.)

inner class

6. To avoid compile errors, the `CirclePanel` class (lines 38–53) now is also defined as an inner class in `ControlCircle`, since another `CirclePanel` class is already defined in Listing 16.2.

LISTING 16.3 ControlCircle.java

VideoNote
Listener and its registration

```
1  import javax.swing.*;
2  import java.awt.*;
3  import java.awt.event.*;
4
5  public class ControlCircle extends JFrame {
6    private JButton jbtEnlarge = new JButton("Enlarge");
7    private JButton jbtShrink = new JButton("Shrink");
8    private CirclePanel canvas = new CirclePanel();
9
10   public ControlCircle() {
11     JPanel panel = new JPanel(); // Use the panel to group buttons
12     panel.add(jbtEnlarge);
13     panel.add(jbtShrink);
14
15     this.add(canvas, BorderLayout.CENTER); // Add canvas to center
16     this.add(panel, BorderLayout.SOUTH); // Add buttons to the frame
17
18     jbtEnlarge.addActionListener(new EnlargeListener());
19   }
20
21   /** Main method */
22   public static void main(String[] args) {
23     JFrame frame = new ControlCircle();
24     frame.setTitle("ControlCircle");
25     frame.setLocationRelativeTo(null); // Center the frame
26     frame.setDefaultCloseOperation(JFrame.EXIT_ON_CLOSE);
27     frame.setSize(200, 200);
28     frame.setVisible(true);
29   }
30
31   class EnlargeListener implements ActionListener { // Inner class
32     @Override
33     public void actionPerformed(ActionEvent e) {
34       canvas.enlarge();
35     }
36   }
37
38   class CirclePanel extends JPanel { // Inner class
39     private int radius = 5; // Default circle radius
40
41     /** Enlarge the circle */
42     public void enlarge() {
43       radius++;
44       repaint();
45     }
46
47     @Override
48     protected void paintComponent(Graphics g) {
49       super.paintComponent(g);
50       g.drawOval(getWidth() / 2 - radius, getHeight() / 2 - radius,
51         2 * radius, 2 * radius);
52     }
53   }
54 }
```

create/register listener (line 18)

listener class (line 31)

`CirclePanel` class (line 38)

`enlarge` method (line 42)

the *Shrink* button

Similarly, you can add the code for the *Shrink* button to display a smaller circle when the *Shrink* button is clicked.

MyProgrammingLab™

16.3 Why must a listener be an instance of an appropriate listener interface? Explain how to register a listener object and how to implement a listener interface.

16.4 Can a source have multiple listeners? Can a listener listen to multiple sources? Can a source be a listener for itself?

16.5 How do you implement a method defined in the listener interface? Do you need to implement all the methods defined in the listener interface?

16.6 What method do you use to get the timestamp for an action event?

16.4 Inner Classes

An inner class, or nested class, is a class defined within the scope of another class. Inner classes are useful for defining listener classes.

We now introduce inner classes in this section and anonymous inner classes in the next section and use them to define listener classes. First let us see the code in Figure 16.9. The code in Figure 16.9a defines two separate classes, `Test` and `A`. The code in Figure 16.9b defines `A` as an inner class in `Test`.

```
public class Test {
  ...
}

public class A {
  ...
}
```

(a)

```
public class Test {
  ...

  // Inner class
  public class A {
    ...
  }
}
```

(b)

```
// OuterClass.java: inner class demo
public class OuterClass {
  private int data;

  /** A method in the outer class */
  public void m() {
    // Do something
  }

  // An inner class
  class InnerClass {
    /** A method in the inner class */
    public void mi() {
      // Directly reference data and method
      // defined in its outer class
      data++;
      m();
    }
  }
}
```

(c)

FIGURE 16.9 Inner classes combine dependent classes into the primary class.

The class `InnerClass` defined inside `OuterClass` in Figure 16.9c is another example of an inner class. An inner class may be used just like a regular class. Normally, you define a class as an inner class if it is used only by its outer class. An inner class has the following features:

- An inner class is compiled into a class named `OuterClassName$InnerClassName.class`. For example, the inner class `A` in `Test` is compiled into `Test$A.class` in Figure 16.9b.
- An inner class can reference the data and methods defined in the outer class in which it nests, so you need not pass the reference of an object of the outer class to the constructor of the inner class. For this reason, inner classes can make programs simple and concise.

For example, `canvas` is defined in `ControlCircle` in Listing 16.3 (line 8). It can be referenced in the inner class `EnlargeListener` in line 34.

- An inner class can be defined with a visibility modifier subject to the same visibility rules applied to a member of the class.
- An inner class can be defined as `static`. A `static` inner class can be accessed using the outer class name. A `static` inner class cannot access nonstatic members of the outer class.
- Objects of an inner class are often created in the outer class. But you can also create an object of an inner class from another class. If the inner class is nonstatic, you must first create an instance of the outer class, then use the following syntax to create an object for the inner class:

```
OuterClass.InnerClass innerObject = outerObject.new InnerClass();
```

- If the inner class is static, use the following syntax to create an object for it:

```
OuterClass.InnerClass innerObject = new OuterClass.InnerClass();
```

A simple use of inner classes is to combine dependent classes into a primary class. This reduces the number of source files. It also makes class files easy to organize, since they are all named with the primary class as the prefix. For example, rather than creating the two source files **Test.java** and **A.java** in Figure 16.9a, you can merge class `A` into class `Test` and create just one source file, **Test.java** in Figure 16.9b. The resulting class files are **Test.class** and **Test$A.class**.

Another practical use of inner classes is to avoid class-naming conflicts. Two versions of `CirclePanel` are defined in Listings 16.2 and 16.3. You can define them as inner classes to avoid a conflict.

A listener class is designed specifically to create a listener object for a GUI component (e.g., a button). The listener class will not be shared by other applications and therefore is appropriate to be defined inside the frame class as an inner class.

16.7 Can an inner class be used in a class other than the class in which it nests?

16.8 Can the modifiers `public`, `private`, and `static` be used for inner classes?

16.5 Anonymous Class Listeners

An anonymous inner class is an inner class without a name. It combines defining an inner class and creating an instance of the class into one step.

anonymous inner class

Inner-class listeners can be shortened using *anonymous inner classes*. The inner class in Listing 16.3 can be replaced by an anonymous inner class as shown below.

```
public ControlCircle() {
  // Omitted

  jbtEnlarge.addActionListener(
    new EnlargeListener());
}

class EnlargeListener
    implements ActionListener {
  @Override
  public void actionPerformed(ActionEvent e) {
    canvas.enlarge();
  }
}
```

(a) Inner class `EnlargeListener`

```
public ControlCircle() {
  // Omitted

  jbtEnlarge.addActionListener(
    new class EnlargeListener
        implements ActionListener() {
      @Override
      public void actionPerformed(ActionEvent e) {
        canvas.enlarge();
      }
    });
}
```

(b) Anonymous inner class

The syntax for an anonymous inner class is:

```
new SuperClassName/InterfaceName() {
  // Implement or override methods in superclass or interface

  // Other methods if necessary
}
```

Since an anonymous inner class is a special kind of inner class, it is treated like an inner class with the following features:

- An anonymous inner class must always extend a superclass or implement an interface, but it cannot have an explicit `extends` or `implements` clause.
- An anonymous inner class must implement all the abstract methods in the superclass or in the interface.
- An anonymous inner class always uses the no-arg constructor from its superclass to create an instance. If an anonymous inner class implements an interface, the constructor is `Object()`.
- An anonymous inner class is compiled into a class named `OuterClassName$n.class`. For example, if the outer class `Test` has two anonymous inner classes, they are compiled into `Test$1.class` and `Test$2.class`.

Listing 16.4 gives an example that handles the events from four buttons, as shown in Figure 16.10.

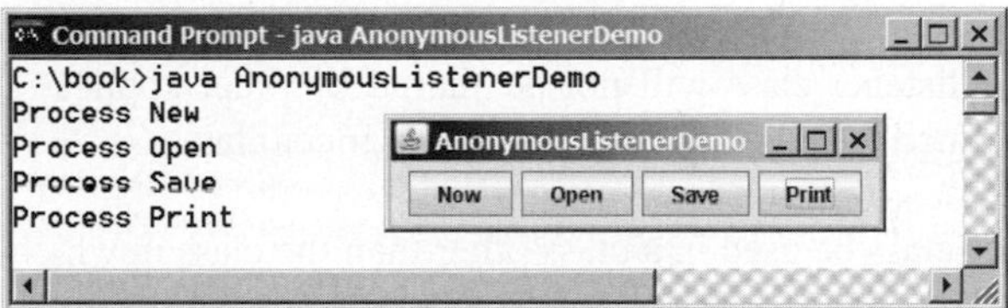

FIGURE 16.10 The program handles the events from four buttons.

VideoNote
Anonymous listener

LISTING 16.4 AnonymousListenerDemo.java

```
import javax.swing.*;
import java.awt.event.*;

public class AnonymousListenerDemo extends JFrame {
  public AnonymousListenerDemo() {
    // Create four buttons
    JButton jbtNew = new JButton("New");
    JButton jbtOpen = new JButton("Open");
    JButton jbtSave = new JButton("Save");
    JButton jbtPrint = new JButton("Print");

    // Create a panel to hold buttons
    JPanel panel = new JPanel();
    panel.add(jbtNew);
    panel.add(jbtOpen);
    panel.add(jbtSave);
    panel.add(jbtPrint);

    add(panel);
```

```
20
21       // Create and register anonymous inner-class listener
22       jbtNew.addActionListener(new ActionListener() {
23           @Override
24           public void actionPerformed(ActionEvent e) {
25             System.out.println("Process New");
26           }
27         }
28       );
29
30       jbtOpen.addActionListener(new ActionListener() {
31           @Override
32           public void actionPerformed(ActionEvent e) {
33             System.out.println("Process Open");
34           }
35         }
36       );
37
38       jbtSave.addActionListener(new ActionListener() {
39           @Override
40           public void actionPerformed(ActionEvent e) {
41             System.out.println("Process Save");
42           }
43         }
44       );
45
46       jbtPrint.addActionListener(new ActionListener() {
47           @Override
48           public void actionPerformed(ActionEvent e) {
49             System.out.println("Process Print");
50           }
51         }
52       );
53     }
54
55     /** Main method */
56     public static void main(String[] args) {
57       JFrame frame = new AnonymousListenerDemo();
58       frame.setTitle("AnonymousListenerDemo");
59       frame.setLocationRelativeTo(null); // Center the frame
60       frame.setDefaultCloseOperation(JFrame.EXIT_ON_CLOSE);
61       frame.pack();
62       frame.setVisible(true);
63     }
64   }
```

anonymous listener
handle event

The program creates four listeners using anonymous inner classes (lines 22–52). Without using anonymous inner classes, you would have to create four separate classes. An anonymous listener works the same way as an inner class listener. The program is condensed using an anonymous inner class.

Anonymous inner classes are compiled into `OuterClassName$#.class`, where `#` starts at `1` and is incremented for each anonymous class the compiler encounters. In this example, the anonymous inner classes are compiled into `AnonymousListenerDemo$1.class`, `AnonymousListenerDemo$2.class`, `AnonymousListenerDemo$3.class`, and `AnonymousListenerDemo$4.class`.

Instead of using the `setSize` method to set the size for the frame, the program uses the `pack()` method (line 61), which automatically sizes the frame according to the size of the components placed in it.

pack()

MyProgrammingLab™

16.9 If class A is an inner class in class B, what is the .class file for A? If class B contains two anonymous inner classes, what are the .class file names for these two classes?

16.10 What is wrong in the following code?

```
import java.swing.*;
import java.awt.*;

public class Test extends JFrame {
  public Test() {
    JButton jbtOK = new JButton("OK");
    add(jbtOK);
  }

  private class Listener
      implements ActionListener {
    public void actionPerform
        (ActionEvent e) {
      System.out.println
        (jbtOK.getActionCommand());
    }
  }

  /** Main method omitted */
}
```

(a)

```
import java.awt.event.*;
import javax.swing.*;

public class Test extends JFrame {
  public Test() {
    JButton jbtOK = new JButton("OK");
    add(jbtOK);
    jbtOK.addActionListener(
      new ActionListener() {
        public void actionPerformed
            (ActionEvent e) {
          System.out.println
            (jbtOK.getActionCommand());
        }
      } // Something missing here
  }

  /** Main method omitted */
}
```

(b)

16.11 What is the difference between the `setSize(width, height)` method and the `pack()` method in `JFrame`?

16.6 Alternative Ways of Defining Listener Classes

Using an inner class or an anonymous inner class is preferred for defining listener classes.

There are many other ways to define the listener classes. For example, you can rewrite Listing 16.4 by creating just one listener, register the listener with the buttons, and let the listener detect the event source—that is, which button fires the event—as shown in Listing 16.5.

LISTING 16.5 DetectSourceDemo.java

```
import javax.swing.*;
import java.awt.event.*;

public class DetectSourceDemo extends JFrame {
  // Create four buttons
  private JButton jbtNew = new JButton("New");
  private JButton jbtOpen = new JButton("Open");
  private JButton jbtSave = new JButton("Save");
  private JButton jbtPrint = new JButton("Print");

  public DetectSourceDemo() {
    // Create a panel to hold buttons
    JPanel panel = new JPanel();
    panel.add(jbtNew);
    panel.add(jbtOpen);
    panel.add(jbtSave);
    panel.add(jbtPrint);

```

```
19      add(panel);
20
21      // Create a listener
22      ButtonListener listener = new ButtonListener();
23
24      // Register listener with buttons
25      jbtNew.addActionListener(listener);
26      jbtOpen.addActionListener(listener);
27      jbtSave.addActionListener(listener);
28      jbtPrint.addActionListener(listener);
29    }
30
31    class ButtonListener implements ActionListener {
32      @Override
33      public void actionPerformed(ActionEvent e) {
34        if (e.getSource() == jbtNew)
35          System.out.println("Process New");
36        else if (e.getSource() == jbtOpen)
37          System.out.println("Process Open");
38        else if (e.getSource() == jbtSave)
39          System.out.println("Process Save");
40        else if (e.getSource() == jbtPrint)
41          System.out.println("Process Print");
42      }
43    }
44
45    /** Main method */
46    public static void main(String[] args) {
47      JFrame frame = new DetectSourceDemo();
48      frame.setTitle("DetectSourceDemo");
49      frame.setLocationRelativeTo(null); // Center the frame
50      frame.setDefaultCloseOperation(JFrame.EXIT_ON_CLOSE);
51      frame.pack();
52      frame.setVisible(true);
53    }
54  }
```

create listener

register listener

listener class

handle event

This program defines just one inner listener class (lines 31–43), creates a listener from the class (line 22), and registers it to four buttons (lines 25–28). When a button is clicked, the button fires an **ActionEvent** and invokes the listener's **actionPerformed** method. The **actionPerformed** method checks the source of the event using the **getSource()** method for the event (lines 34, 36, 38, 40) and determines which button fired the event.

Defining one listener class for handling a large number of events is efficient. In this case, you create just one listener object. Using anonymous inner classes, you would create four listener objects.

You could also rewrite Listing 16.4 by defining the custom frame class that implements **ActionListener**, as shown in Listing 16.6.

LISTING 16.6 FrameAsListenerDemo.java

```
import javax.swing.*;
import java.awt.event.*;

public class FrameAsListenerDemo extends JFrame
    implements ActionListener {
  // Create four buttons
  private JButton jbtNew = new JButton("New");
  private JButton jbtOpen = new JButton("Open");
  private JButton jbtSave = new JButton("Save");
```

implement ActionListener

```
10     private JButton jbtPrint = new JButton("Print");
11
12     public FrameAsListenerDemo() {
13       // Create a panel to hold buttons
14       JPanel panel = new JPanel();
15       panel.add(jbtNew);
16       panel.add(jbtOpen);
17       panel.add(jbtSave);
18       panel.add(jbtPrint);
19
20       add(panel);
21
22       // Register listener with buttons
23       jbtNew.addActionListener(this);
24       jbtOpen.addActionListener(this);
25       jbtSave.addActionListener(this);
26       jbtPrint.addActionListener(this);
27     }
28
29     @Override /** Implement actionPerformed */
30     public void actionPerformed(ActionEvent e) {
31       if (e.getSource() == jbtNew)
32         System.out.println("Process New");
33       else if (e.getSource() == jbtOpen)
34         System.out.println("Process Open");
35       else if (e.getSource() == jbtSave)
36         System.out.println("Process Save");
37       else if (e.getSource() == jbtPrint)
38         System.out.println("Process Print");
39     }
40
41     /** Main method */
42     public static void main(String[] args) {
43       JFrame frame = new FrameAsListenerDemo();
44       frame.setTitle("FrameAsListenerDemo");
45       frame.setLocationRelativeTo(null); // Center the frame
46       frame.setDefaultCloseOperation(JFrame.EXIT_ON_CLOSE);
47       frame.pack();
48       frame.setVisible(true);
49     }
50   }
```

register listeners

handle event

The frame class extends `JFrame` and implements `ActionListener` (line 5), so the class is a listener class for action events. The listener is registered to four buttons (lines 23–26). When a button is clicked, the button fires an `ActionEvent` and invokes the listener's `actionPerformed` method. The `actionPerformed` method checks the source of the event using the `getSource()` method for the event (lines 31, 33, 35, 37) and determines which button fired the event.

This design is not desirable, however, because it puts too many responsibilities into one class. It is better to design a listener class that is solely responsible for handling events, which makes the code easy to read and easy to maintain.

Which way is preferred?

You should define listener classes using either inner classes or anonymous inner classes—choose whichever produces shorter, clearer, and cleaner code. In general, use anonymous inner classes if the code in the listener is short and the listener is registered for one event source. Use inner classes if the code in the listener is long or the listener is registered for multiple event sources.

MyProgrammingLab™

16.12 Why should you avoid defining the custom frame class that implements `ActionListener`?

16.13 What method do you use to get the source object from an event object `e`?

16.7 Case Study: Loan Calculator

This case study uses GUI components and events.

Now we will write the program for the loan-calculator problem presented at the beginning of this chapter. Here are the major steps in the program:

1. Create the user interface, as shown in Figure 16.11.

   a. Create a panel of a `GridLayout` with `5` rows and `2` columns. Add labels and text fields to the panel. Set the title "Enter loan amount, interest rate, and years" for the panel.

   b. Create another panel with a `FlowLayout(FlowLayout.RIGHT)` and add a button to the panel.

   c. Add the first panel to the center of the frame and the second panel on the south side of the frame.

2. Process the event.

   Create and register the listener for processing the button-clicking action event. The handler obtains the user input on the loan amount, interest rate, and number of years, computes the monthly and total payments, and displays the values in the text fields.

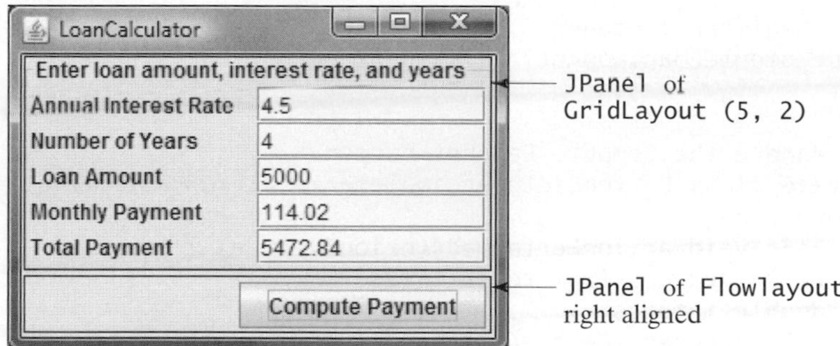

FIGURE 16.11 The program computes loan payments.

The complete program is given in Listing 16.7.

LISTING 16.7 LoanCalculator.java

```
import java.awt.*;
import java.awt.event.*;
import javax.swing.*;
import javax.swing.border.TitledBorder;

public class LoanCalculator extends JFrame {
  // Create text fields for interest rate, years,
  // loan amount, monthly payment, and total payment
  private JTextField jtfAnnualInterestRate = new JTextField();
  private JTextField jtfNumberOfYears = new JTextField();
  private JTextField jtfLoanAmount = new JTextField();
  private JTextField jtfMonthlyPayment = new JTextField();
  private JTextField jtfTotalPayment = new JTextField();

  // Create a Compute Payment button
  private JButton jbtComputeLoan = new JButton("Compute Payment");
```

text fields

button

create UI

add to frame

register listener

get input

create loan

set result

```

  public LoanCalculator() {
    // Panel p1 to hold labels and text fields
    JPanel p1 = new JPanel(new GridLayout(5, 2));
    p1.add(new JLabel("Annual Interest Rate"));
    p1.add(jtfAnnualInterestRate);
    p1.add(new JLabel("Number of Years"));
    p1.add(jtfNumberOfYears);
    p1.add(new JLabel("Loan Amount"));
    p1.add(jtfLoanAmount);
    p1.add(new JLabel("Monthly Payment"));
    p1.add(jtfMonthlyPayment);
    p1.add(new JLabel("Total Payment"));
    p1.add(jtfTotalPayment);
    p1.setBorder(new
      TitledBorder("Enter loan amount, interest rate, and years"));

    // Panel p2 to hold the button
    JPanel p2 = new JPanel(new FlowLayout(FlowLayout.RIGHT));
    p2.add(jbtComputeLoan);

    // Add the panels to the frame
    add(p1, BorderLayout.CENTER);
    add(p2, BorderLayout.SOUTH);

    // Register listener
    jbtComputeLoan.addActionListener(new ButtonListener());
  }

  /** Handle the Compute Payment button */
  private class ButtonListener implements ActionListener {
    @Override
    public void actionPerformed(ActionEvent e) {
      // Get values from text fields
      double interest =
        Double.parseDouble(jtfAnnualInterestRate.getText());
      int year = Integer.parseInt(jtfNumberOfYears.getText());
      double loanAmount =
        Double.parseDouble(jtfLoanAmount.getText());

      // Create a loan object. Loan defined in Listing 10.2
      Loan loan = new Loan(interest, year, loanAmount);

      // Display monthly payment and total payment
      jtfMonthlyPayment.setText(String.format("%.2f",
        loan.getMonthlyPayment()));
      jtfTotalPayment.setText(String.format("%.2f",
        loan.getTotalPayment()));
    }
  }

  public static void main(String[] args) {
    LoanCalculator frame = new LoanCalculator();
    frame.pack();
    frame.setTitle("LoanCalculator");
    frame.setLocationRelativeTo(null); // Center the frame
    frame.setDefaultCloseOperation(JFrame.EXIT_ON_CLOSE);
    frame.setVisible(true);
  }
}
```

The user interface is created in the constructor (lines 18–44). The button is the source of the event. A listener is created and registered with the button (line 43).

The `ButtonListener` class (lines 47–66) implements the `actionPerformed` method. When the button is clicked, the `actionPerformed` method is invoked to get the interest rate (line 51), number of years (line 53), and loan amount (line 54). Invoking `jtfAnnualInterestRate.getText()` returns the string text in the `jtfAnnualInterestRate` text field. The `Loan` class is used for computing the loan payments. This class was introduced in Listing 10.2, Loan.java. Invoking `loan.getMonthlyPayment()` returns the monthly payment for the loan (line 62). The `String.format` method, introduced in Section 9.2.11, is used to format a number into a desirable format and returns it as a string (lines 61, 63). Invoking the `setText` method on a text field sets a string value in the text field (line 61).

16.8 Mouse Events

A mouse event is fired whenever a mouse button is pressed, released, or clicked, the mouse is moved, or the mouse is dragged onto a component.

The `MouseEvent` object captures the event, such as the number of clicks associated with it, the location (the *x*- and *y*-coordinates) of the mouse, or which button was pressed, as shown in Figure 16.12.

java.awt.event.InputEvent	
`+getWhen(): long`	Returns the timestamp when this event occurred.
`+isAltDown(): boolean`	Returns true if the `Alt` key is pressed on this event.
`+isControlDown(): boolean`	Returns true if the `Control` key is pressed on this event.
`+isMetaDown(): boolean`	Returns true if the `Meta` mouse button is pressed on this event.
`+isShiftDown(): boolean`	Returns true if the `Shift` key is pressed on this event.

java.awt.event.MouseEvent	
`+getButton(): int`	Indicates which mouse button has been clicked.
`+getClickCount(): int`	Returns the number of mouse clicks associated with this event.
`+getPoint(): java.awt.Point`	Returns a `Point` object containing the *x*- and *y*-coordinates.
`+getX(): int`	Returns the *x*-coordinate of the mouse point.
`+getY(): int`	Returns the *y*-coordinate of the mouse point.

FIGURE 16.12 The `MouseEvent` class encapsulates information for mouse events.

Since the `MouseEvent` class inherits `InputEvent`, you can use the methods defined in the `InputEvent` class on a `MouseEvent` object. For example, the `isControlDown()` method detects whether the *CTRL* key was pressed when a `MouseEvent` is fired.

Three `int` constants—`BUTTON1`, `BUTTON2`, and `BUTTON3`—are defined in `MouseEvent` to indicate the left, middle, and right mouse buttons. You can use the `getButton()` method to detect which button is pressed. For example, `getButton() == MouseEvent.BUTTON3` indicates that the right button was pressed. detect mouse buttons

The `java.awt.Point` class represents a point on a component. The class contains two public variables, `x` and `y`, for coordinates. To create a `Point`, use the following constructor: `Point` class

```
Point(int x, int y)
```

This constructs a **Point** object with the specified *x*- and *y*-coordinates. Normally, the data fields in a class should be private, but this class has two public data fields.

Java provides two listener interfaces, **MouseListener** and **MouseMotionListener**, to handle mouse events, as shown in Figure 16.13. Implement the **MouseListener** interface to listen for such actions as pressing, releasing, entering, exiting, or clicking the mouse, and implement the **MouseMotionListener** interface to listen for such actions as dragging or moving the mouse.

«interface» *java.awt.event.MouseListener*	
+mousePressed(e: MouseEvent): void	Invoked after the mouse button has been pressed on the source component.
+mouseReleased(e: MouseEvent): void	Invoked after the mouse button has been released on the source component.
+mouseClicked(e: MouseEvent): void	Invoked after the mouse button has been clicked (pressed and released) on the source component.
+mouseEntered(e: MouseEvent): void	Invoked after the mouse enters the source component.
+mouseExited(e: MouseEvent): void	Invoked after the mouse exits the source component.

«interface» *java.awt.event.MouseMotionListener*	
+mouseDragged(e: MouseEvent): void	Invoked after a mouse button is moved with a button pressed.
+mouseMoved(e: MouseEvent): void	Invoked after a mouse button is moved without a button pressed.

FIGURE 16.13 The **MouseListener** interface handles mouse pressed, released, clicked, entered, and exited events. The **MouseMotionListener** interface handles mouse dragged and moved events.

To demonstrate using mouse events, we give an example that displays a message in a panel and enables the message to be moved using a mouse. The message moves as the mouse is dragged, and it is always displayed at the mouse point. Listing 16.8 gives the program. A sample run of the program is shown in Figure 16.14.

FIGURE 16.14 You can move the message by dragging the mouse.

VideoNote
Move message using the mouse

LISTING 16.8 MoveMessageDemo.java

```
import java.awt.*;
import java.awt.event.*;
import javax.swing.*;

public class MoveMessageDemo extends JFrame {
  public MoveMessageDemo() {
```

```
7      // Create a MovableMessagePanel instance for moving a message
8      MovableMessagePanel p = new MovableMessagePanel
9        ("Welcome to Java");
10
11     // Place the message panel in the frame
12     add(p);
13   }
14
15   /** Main method */
16   public static void main(String[] args) {
17     MoveMessageDemo frame = new MoveMessageDemo();
18     frame.setTitle("MoveMessageDemo");
19     frame.setSize(200, 100);
20     frame.setLocationRelativeTo(null); // Center the frame
21     frame.setDefaultCloseOperation(JFrame.EXIT_ON_CLOSE);
22     frame.setVisible(true);
23   }
24
25   // Inner class: MovableMessagePanel draws a message
26   static class MovableMessagePanel extends JPanel {
27     private String message = "Welcome to Java";
28     private int x = 20;
29     private int y = 20;
30
31     /** Construct a panel to draw string s */
32     public MovableMessagePanel(String s) {
33       message = s;
34       addMouseMotionListener(new MouseMotionListener() {
35         @Override /** Handle mouse-dragged event */
36         public void mouseDragged(MouseEvent e) {
37           // Get the new location and repaint the screen
38           x = e.getX();
39           y = e.getY();
40           repaint();
41         }
42
43         @Override /** Handle mouse-moved event */
44         public void mouseMoved(MouseEvent e) {
45         }
46       });
47     }
48
49     @Override
50     protected void paintComponent(Graphics g) {
51       super.paintComponent(g);
52       g.drawString(message, x, y);
53     }
54   }
55 }
```

create a panel (line 8)
inner class (line 26)
set a new message (line 33)
anonymous listener (line 34)
override handler (line 36)
new location (line 38)
repaint (line 40)
paint message (line 50)

The **MovableMessagePanel** class extends **JPanel** to draw a message (line 26). Additionally, it handles redisplaying the message when the mouse is dragged. This class is defined as an inner class inside the main class because it is used only in this class. Furthermore, the inner class is defined as static because it does not reference any instance members of the main class.

The **MouseMotionListener** interface contains two handlers, **mouseMoved** and **mouseDragged**, for handling mouse-motion events. When you move the mouse with a button pressed, the **mouseDragged** method is invoked to repaint the viewing area and display the message at the mouse point. When you move the mouse without pressing a button, the mouseMoved method is invoked. Because the listener is interested only in the mouse-dragged event, the mouseDragged method is implemented (lines 36–41).

The mouseDragged method is invoked when you move the mouse with a button pressed. This method obtains the mouse location using the getX and getY methods (lines 38–39) in the MouseEvent class. This becomes the new location for the message. Invoking the repaint() method (line 40) causes paintComponent to be invoked (line 50), which displays the message in a new location.

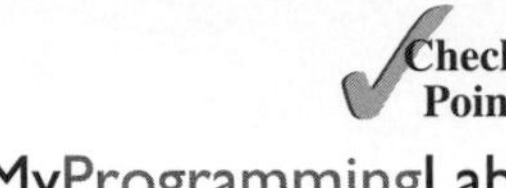

16.14 What method do you use to get the mouse-point position for a mouse event?

16.15 What is the listener interface for mouse pressed, released, clicked, entered, and exited? What is the listener interface for mouse moved and dragged?

16.9 Listener Interface Adapters

A listener interface adapter *is a class that provides the default implementation for all the methods in the listener interface.*

listener interface adapter

Because the methods in the MouseMotionListener interface are abstract, you must implement all of them even if your program does not care about some of the events. Java provides support classes, called *listener interface adapters*, that provide default implementations for all the methods in the listener interface. The default implementation is simply an empty body. Java provides listener interface adapters for every AWT listener interface with multiple handlers. A listener interface adapter is named *X*Adapter for *X*Listener. For example, MouseMotionAdapter is a listener interface adapter for MouseMotionListener. Table 16.2 lists some listener interface adapters used in this book.

Table 16.2 Listener Interface Adapters

Adapter	*Interface*
MouseAdapter	MouseListener
MouseMotionAdapter	MouseMotionListener
KeyAdapter	KeyListener
WindowAdapter	WindowListener

Using MouseMotionAdapter, the code in lines 34–46 in Listing 16.8 (shown in (a)) can be replaced by the following code, as shown in (b).

```
addMouseMotionListener(
    new MouseMotionListener() {
  @Override /** Handle mouse-dragged event */
  public void mouseDragged(MouseEvent e){
    x = e.getX();
    y = e.getY();
    repaint();
  }

  @Override /** Handle mouse-moved event */
  public void mouseMoved(MouseEvent e) {
  }
});
```

(a) Using a listener interface

```
addMouseMotionListener(
    new MouseMotionAdapter() {
  @Override /** Handle mouse-dragged event */
  public void mouseDragged(MouseEvent e){
    x = e.getX();
    y = e.getY();
    repaint();
  }
});
```

(b) Using a listener interface adapter

16.16 Why does the `ActionListener` interface have no listener interface adapter?

16.17 What is the advantage of using a listener interface adapter rather than a listener interface?

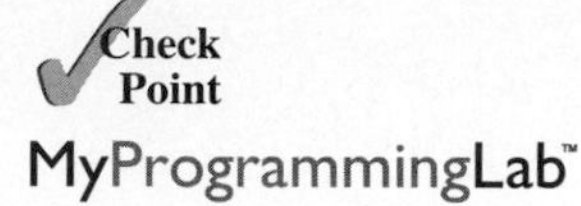

16.10 Key Events

A key event is fired whenever a key is pressed, released, or typed on a component.

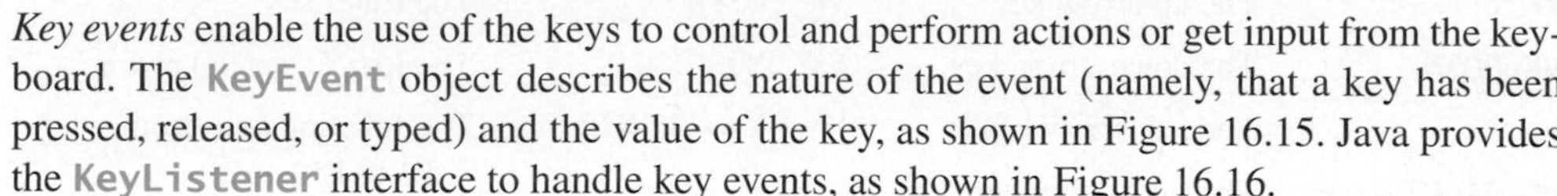

Key events enable the use of the keys to control and perform actions or get input from the keyboard. The `KeyEvent` object describes the nature of the event (namely, that a key has been pressed, released, or typed) and the value of the key, as shown in Figure 16.15. Java provides the `KeyListener` interface to handle key events, as shown in Figure 16.16.

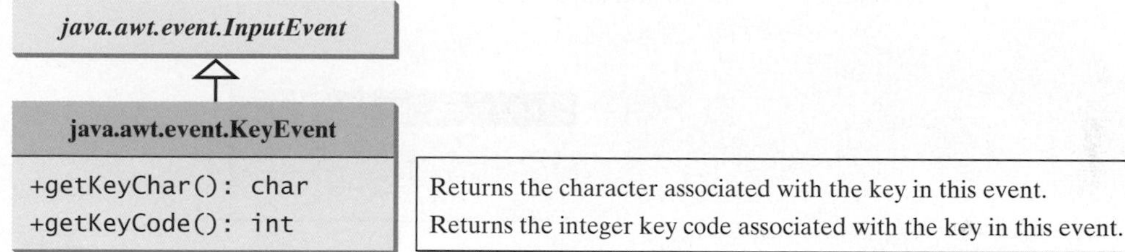

FIGURE 16.15 The `KeyEvent` class encapsulates information about key events.

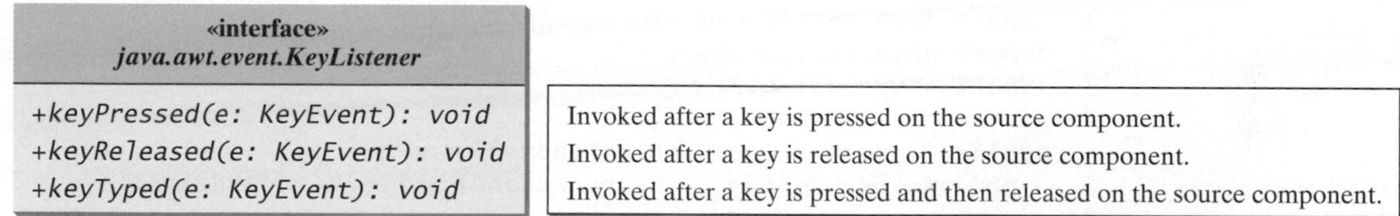

FIGURE 16.16 The `KeyListener` interface handles key pressed, released, and typed events.

The `keyPressed` handler is invoked when a key is pressed, the `keyReleased` handler is invoked when a key is released, and the `keyTyped` handler is invoked when a Unicode character is entered. If a key does not have a Unicode (e.g., function keys, modifier keys, action keys, and control keys), the `keyTyped` handler will not be invoked.

Every key event has an associated key character or key code that is returned by the `getKeyChar()` or `getKeyCode()` method in `KeyEvent`. The key codes are constants defined in the `KeyEvent` class. Table 16.3 lists some constants. See the Java API for a complete list of the constants. For a key of the Unicode character, the key code is the same as the Unicode value. For the key-pressed and key-released events, `getKeyCode()` returns the value as defined in the table. For the key-typed event, `getKeyCode()` returns `VK_UNDEFINED` (0), and `getKeyChar()` returns the character entered.

The program in Listing 16.9 displays a user-input character. The user can move the character up, down, left, and right, using the arrow keys `VK_UP`, `VK_DOWN`, `VK_LEFT`, and `VK_RIGHT`. Figure 16.17 contains a sample run of the program.

TABLE 16.3 Key Constants

Constant	*Description*	*Constant*	*Description*
VK_HOME	The Home key	VK_SHIFT	The Shift key
VK_END	The End key	VK_BACK_SPACE	The Backspace key
VK_PGUP	The Page Up key	VK_CAPS_LOCK	The Caps Lock key
VK_PGDN	The Page Down key	VK_NUM_LOCK	The Num Lock key
VK_UP	The up-arrow key	VK_ENTER	The Enter key
VK_DOWN	The down-arrow key	VK_UNDEFINED	The keyCode unknown
VK_LEFT	The left-arrow key	VK_F1 to VK_F12	The function keys from F1 to F12
VK_RIGHT	The right-arrow key		
VK_ESCAPE	The Esc key	VK_0 to VK_9	The number keys from 0 to 9
VK_TAB	The Tab key	VK_A to VK_Z	The letter keys from A to Z
VK_CONTROL	The Control key		

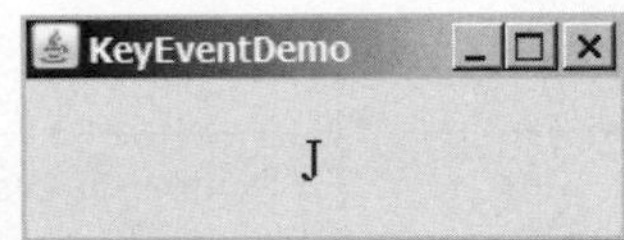

FIGURE 16.17 The program responds to key events by displaying a character and moving it up, down, left, or right.

LISTING 16.9 KeyEventDemo.java

create a panel

focusable

inner class

```
import java.awt.*;
import java.awt.event.*;
import javax.swing.*;

public class KeyEventDemo extends JFrame {
  private KeyboardPanel keyboardPanel = new KeyboardPanel();

  /** Initialize UI */
  public KeyEventDemo() {
    // Add the keyboard panel to accept and display user input
    add(keyboardPanel);

    // Set focus
    keyboardPanel.setFocusable(true);
  }

  /** Main method */
  public static void main(String[] args) {
    KeyEventDemo frame = new KeyEventDemo();
    frame.setTitle("KeyEventDemo");
    frame.setSize(300, 300);
    frame.setLocationRelativeTo(null); // Center the frame
    frame.setDefaultCloseOperation(JFrame.EXIT_ON_CLOSE);
    frame.setVisible(true);
  }

  // Inner class: KeyboardPanel for receiving key input
  static class KeyboardPanel extends JPanel {
```

```
29     private int x = 100;
30     private int y = 100;
31     private char keyChar = 'A'; // Default key
32
33     public KeyboardPanel() {
34       addKeyListener(new KeyAdapter() {
35         @Override
36         public void keyPressed(KeyEvent e) {
37           switch (e.getKeyCode()) {
38             case KeyEvent.VK_DOWN: y += 10; break;
39             case KeyEvent.VK_UP: y -= 10; break;
40             case KeyEvent.VK_LEFT: x -= 10; break;
41             case KeyEvent.VK_RIGHT: x += 10; break;
42             default: keyChar = e.getKeyChar();
43           }
44
45           repaint();
46         }
47       });
48     }
49
50     @Override /** Draw the character */
51     protected void paintComponent(Graphics g) {
52       super.paintComponent(g);
53
54       g.setFont(new Font("TimesRoman", Font.PLAIN, 24));
55       g.drawString(String.valueOf(keyChar), x, y);
56     }
57   }
58 }
```

register listener

override handler

get the key pressed

repaint

redraw character

The **KeyboardPanel** class extends **JPanel** to display a character (line 28). This class is defined as an inner class inside the main class, because it is used only in this class. Furthermore, the inner class is defined as static, because it does not reference any instance members of the main class.

Because the program gets input from the keyboard, it listens for **KeyEvent** and extends **KeyAdapter** to handle key input (line 34).

When a key is pressed, the **keyPressed** handler is invoked. The program uses **e.getKeyCode()** to obtain the key code and **e.getKeyChar()** to get the character for the key. When a nonarrow key is pressed, the character is displayed (line 42). When an arrow key is pressed, the character moves in the direction indicated by the arrow key (lines 38–41).

Only a focused component can receive **KeyEvent**. To make a component focusable, set its **focusable** property to **true** (line 14).

focusable

Every time the component is repainted, a new font is created for the **Graphics** object in line 54. This is not efficient—it would be better to create the font once as a data field.

efficient?

We can now add more control for our **ControlCircle** example in Listing 16.3 to increase/decrease the circle radius by clicking the left/right mouse button or by pressing the UP and DOWN arrow keys. The new program is given in Listing 16.10.

LISTING 16.10 ControlCircleWithMouseAndKey.java

```
import javax.swing.*;
import java.awt.*;
import java.awt.event.*;

public class ControlCircleWithMouseAndKey extends JFrame {
  private JButton jbtEnlarge = new JButton("Enlarge");
  private JButton jbtShrink = new JButton("Shrink");
```

create/register listener
request focus
request focus
left button?
right button?
UP pressed?
DOWN pressed?

```
  private CirclePanel canvas = new CirclePanel();

  public ControlCircleWithMouseAndKey() {
    JPanel panel = new JPanel(); // Use the panel to group buttons
    panel.add(jbtEnlarge);
    panel.add(jbtShrink);

    this.add(canvas, BorderLayout.CENTER); // Add canvas to center
    this.add(panel, BorderLayout.SOUTH); // Add buttons to the frame

    jbtEnlarge.addActionListener(new ActionListener() {
      @Override
      public void actionPerformed(ActionEvent e) {
        canvas.enlarge();
        canvas.requestFocusInWindow();
      }
    });

    jbtShrink.addActionListener(new ActionListener() {
      @Override
      public void actionPerformed(ActionEvent e) {
        canvas.shrink();
        canvas.requestFocusInWindow();
      }
    });

    canvas.addMouseListener(new MouseAdapter() {
      @Override
      public void mouseClicked(MouseEvent e) {
        if (e.getButton() == MouseEvent.BUTTON1)
          canvas.enlarge();
        else if (e.getButton() == MouseEvent.BUTTON3)
          canvas.shrink();
      }
    });

    canvas.setFocusable(true);
    canvas.addKeyListener(new KeyAdapter() {
      @Override
      public void keyPressed(KeyEvent e) {
        if (e.getKeyCode() == KeyEvent.VK_UP)
          canvas.enlarge();
        else if (e.getKeyCode() == KeyEvent.VK_DOWN)
          canvas.shrink();
      }
    });
  }

  /** Main method */
  public static void main(String[] args) {
    JFrame frame = new ControlCircleWithMouseAndKey();
    frame.setTitle("ControlCircle");
    frame.setLocationRelativeTo(null); // Center the frame
    frame.setDefaultCloseOperation(JFrame.EXIT_ON_CLOSE);
    frame.setSize(200, 200);
    frame.setVisible(true);
  }

  class CirclePanel extends JPanel { // Inner class
    private int radius = 5; // Default circle radius
```

```
68
69     /** Enlarge the circle */
70     public void enlarge() {
71       radius++;
72       repaint();
73     }
74
75     /** Shrink the circle */
76     public void shrink() {
77       if (radius >= 1) radius--;
78       repaint();
79     }
80
81     @Override
82     protected void paintComponent(Graphics g) {
83       super.paintComponent(g);
84       g.drawOval(getWidth() / 2 - radius, getHeight() / 2 - radius,
85         2 * radius, 2 * radius);
86     }
87   }
88 }
```

MouseEvent

A listener for `MouseEvent` is created to handle mouse-clicked events in lines 34–42. If the left mouse button is clicked, the circle is enlarged (lines 37–38); if the right mouse button is clicked, the circle is shrunk (lines 39–40).

KeyEvent

A listener for `KeyEvent` is created to handle key-pressed events in lines 45–53. If the UP arrow key is pressed, the circle is enlarged (lines 48–49); if the DOWN arrow key is pressed, the circle is shrunk (lines 50–51).

setFocusable

requestFocusInWindow()

Invoking `setFocusable` on `canvas` makes `canvas` focusable. However, once a button is clicked, the canvas is no longer focused. Invoking `canvas.requestFocusInWindow()` (lines 22, 30) resets the focus on `canvas` so that `canvas` can listen for key events.

MyProgrammingLab™

16.18 What method do you use to get the timestamp for an action event, a mouse event, or a key event?

16.19 What method do you use to get the key character for a key event?

16.20 How do you set focus on a component so it can listen for key events?

16.21 Does every key in the keyboard have a Unicode? Is a key code in the `KeyEvent` class equivalent to a Unicode?

16.22 Is the `keyPressed` handler invoked after a key is pressed? Is the `keyReleased` handler invoked after a key is released? Is the `keyTyped` handler invoked after *any* key is typed?

16.11 Animation Using the **Timer** Class

A `Timer` is a source object that fires `ActionEvent` at a fixed rate.

Not all source objects are GUI components. The `javax.swing.Timer` class is a source component that fires an `ActionEvent` at a predefined rate. Figure 16.18 lists some of the methods in the class.

A `Timer` object serves as the source of an `ActionEvent`. The listeners must be instances of `ActionListener` and registered with a `Timer` object. You create a `Timer` object using its sole constructor with a delay and a listener, where `delay` specifies the number of milliseconds between two action events. You can add additional listeners using the `addActionListener` method and adjust the `delay` using the `setDelay` method. To start the timer, invoke the `start()` method; to stop the timer, invoke the `stop()` method.

javax.swing.Timer	
+Timer(delay: int, listener: ActionListener)	Creates a `Timer` object with a specified delay in milliseconds and an `ActionListener`.
+addActionListener(listener: ActionListener): void	Adds an `ActionListener` to the timer.
+start(): void	Starts this timer.
+stop(): void	Stops this timer.
+setDelay(delay: int): void	Sets a new delay value for this timer.

FIGURE 16.18 A `Timer` object fires an `ActionEvent` at a fixed rate.

The `Timer` class can be used to control animations. Listing 16.11 gives a program that displays two messages in separate panels (see Figure 16.19). You can use the mouse button to control the animation speed for each message. The speed increases when the left mouse button is clicked and decreases when the right button is clicked.

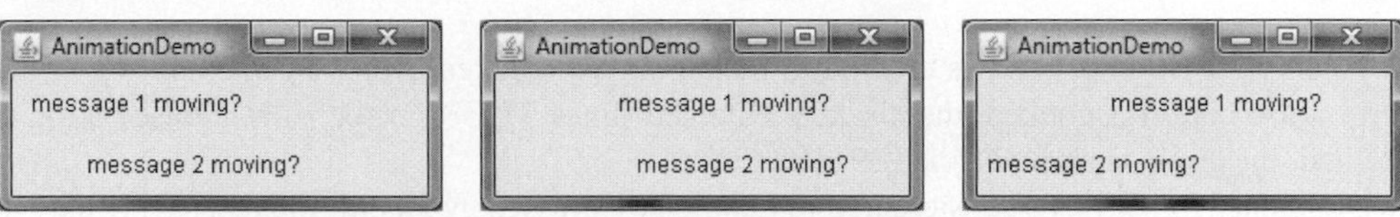

FIGURE 16.19 Two messages move in the panels.

LISTING 16.11 AnimationDemo.java

```java
import java.awt.*;
import java.awt.event.*;
import javax.swing.*;

public class AnimationDemo extends JFrame {
  public AnimationDemo() {
    // Create two MovingMessagePanel for displaying two moving messages
    this.setLayout(new GridLayout(2, 1));
```

create message panel

```java
    add(new MovingMessagePanel("message 1 moving?"));
    add(new MovingMessagePanel("message 2 moving?"));
  }

  /** Main method */
  public static void main(String[] args) {
    AnimationDemo frame = new AnimationDemo();
    frame.setTitle("AnimationDemo");
    frame.setLocationRelativeTo(null); // Center the frame
    frame.setDefaultCloseOperation(JFrame.EXIT_ON_CLOSE);
    frame.setSize(280, 100);
    frame.setVisible(true);
  }

  // Inner class: Displaying a moving message
  static class MovingMessagePanel extends JPanel {
    private String message = "Welcome to Java";
    private int xCoordinate = 0;
    private int yCoordinate = 20;
```

create timer

```java
    private Timer timer = new Timer(1000, new TimerListener());
```

```
29
30       public MovingMessagePanel(String message) {
31         this.message = message;
32
33         // Start timer for animation
34         timer.start();
35
36         // Control animation speed using mouse buttons
37         this.addMouseListener(new MouseAdapter() {
38           @Override
39           public void mouseClicked(MouseEvent e) {
40             int delay = timer.getDelay();
41             if (e.getButton() == MouseEvent.BUTTON1)
42               timer.setDelay(delay > 10 ? delay - 10 : 0);
43             else if (e.getButton() == MouseEvent.BUTTON3)
44               timer.setDelay(delay < 50000 ? delay + 10 : 50000);
45           }
46         });
47       }
48
49       @Override /** Paint the message */
50       protected void paintComponent(Graphics g) {
51         super.paintComponent(g);
52
53         if (xCoordinate > getWidth()) {
54           xCoordinate = -20;
55         }
56         xCoordinate += 5;
57         g.drawString(message, xCoordinate, yCoordinate);
58       }
59
60       class TimerListener implements ActionListener {
61         @Override
62         public void actionPerformed(ActionEvent e) {
63           repaint();
64         }
65       }
66     }
67   }
```

set message (line 31)
start timer (line 34)
mouse listener (line 37)
reset *x*-coordinate (line 54)
move message (line 56)
listener class (line 60)
event handler (line 61)
repaint (line 62)

Two instances of **MovingMessagePanel** are created to display two messages (lines 9–10). The **MovingMessagePanel** class extends **JPanel** to display a message (line 24). This class is defined as an inner class inside the main class, because it is used only in this class. Furthermore, the inner class is defined as static, because it does not reference any instance members of the main class.

An inner class listener is defined in line 60 to listen for **ActionEvent** from a timer. Line 28 creates a **Timer** for the listener, and the timer is started in line 34. The timer fires an **ActionEvent** every 1 second initially, and the listener responds in line 62 to repaint the panel. When a panel is painted, its *x*-coordinate is increased (line 56), so the message is displayed to the right. When the *x*-coordinate exceeds the bound of the panel, it is reset to **-20** (line 54), so the message continues moving from left to right circularly.

A mouse listener is registered with the panel to listen for the mouse click event (lines 37–46). When the left mouse button is clicked, a new reduced delay time is set for the timer (lines 41–42). When the right mouse button is clicked, a new increased delay time is set for the timer (lines 43–44). The minimum delay time is **0** and the maximum can be **Integer.MAX_VALUE**, but it is set to **50000** in this program (line 44).

In Section 13.9, Case Study: The **StillClock** Class, you drew a **StillClock** to show the current time. The clock does not tick after it is displayed. What can you do to make the clock display a new current time every second? The key to making the clock tick is to repaint it every second with a new current time. You can use a timer to control the repainting of the clock with the code in Listing 16.12.

VideoNote
Animate a clock

LISTING 16.12 ClockAnimation.java

create a clock
create a timer
start timer
listener class
implement handler
set new time
repaint

```
1  import java.awt.event.*;
2  import javax.swing.*;
3
4  public class ClockAnimation extends JFrame {
5    private StillClock clock = new StillClock();
6
7    public ClockAnimation() {
8      add(clock);
9
10     // Create a timer with delay 1000 ms
11     Timer timer = new Timer(1000, new TimerListener());
12     timer.start();
13   }
14
15   private class TimerListener implements ActionListener {
16     @Override /** Handle the action event */
17     public void actionPerformed(ActionEvent e) {
18       // Set new time and repaint the clock to display current time
19       clock.setCurrentTime();
20       clock.repaint();
21     }
22   }
23
24   /** Main method */
25   public static void main(String[] args) {
26     JFrame frame = new ClockAnimation();
27     frame.setTitle("ClockAnimation");
28     frame.setSize(200, 200);
29     frame.setLocationRelativeTo(null); // Center the frame
30     frame.setDefaultCloseOperation(JFrame.EXIT_ON_CLOSE);
31     frame.setVisible(true);
32   }
33 }
```

The program displays a running clock, as shown in Figure 16.20. `ClockAnimation` creates a `StillClock` (line 5). Line 11 creates a `Timer` for a `ClockAnimation`. The timer is started in line 12. The timer fires an `ActionEvent` every second, and the listener responds to set a new time (line 19) and repaint the clock (line 20). The `setCurrentTime()` method defined in `StillClock` sets the current time in the clock.

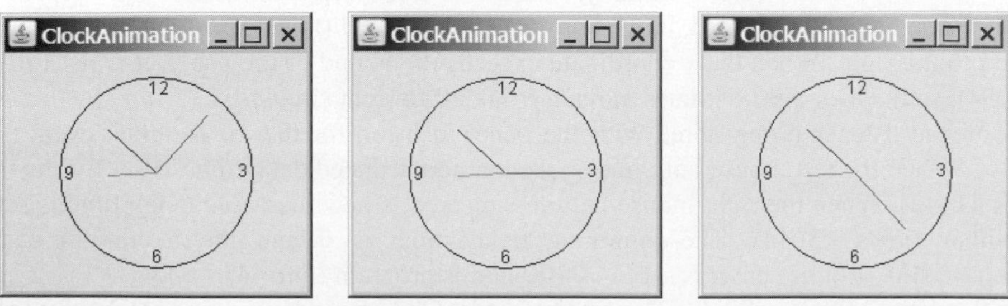

FIGURE 16.20 A live clock is displayed in the panel.

16.23 How do you create a timer? How do you start a timer? How do you stop a timer?

16.24 Does the `Timer` class have a no-arg constructor? Can you add multiple listeners to a timer?

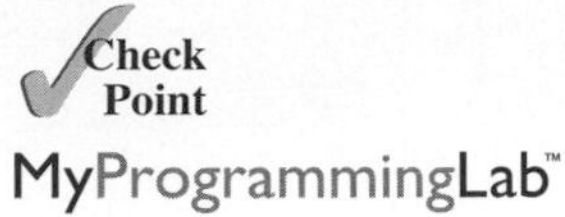

Key Terms

anonymous inner class 609
event 602
event-driven programming 602
event handler 604
event-listener interface 603
event object 602
event source object 602
event listener object 603
inner class 606
listener interface adapter 620
source object 602

Chapter Summary

1. The root class of the event classes is `java.util.EventObject`. The subclasses of `EventObject` deal with special types of events, such as action events, window events, component events, mouse events, and key events. You can identify the source object of an event by using the `getSource()` instance method in the `EventObject` class. If a component can fire an event, any subclass of the component can fire the same type of event.

2. The listener object's class must implement the corresponding *event-listener interface*. Java provides a listener interface for every event class. The listener interface is usually named *X*`Listener` for *X*`Event`, with the exception of `MouseMotionListener`. For example, the corresponding listener interface for `ActionEvent` is `ActionListener`; each listener for `ActionEvent` should implement the `ActionListener` interface. The listener interface contains the method(s), known as the *handler(s)*, which process the events.

3. The listener object must be registered by the *source object*. Registration methods depend on the event type. For `ActionEvent`, the method is `addActionListener`. In general, the method is named `add`*X*`Listener` for *X*`Event`.

4. An *inner class*, or *nested class*, is defined within the scope of another class. An inner class can reference the data and methods defined in the outer class in which it nests, so you need not pass the reference of the outer class to the constructor of the inner class.

5. *Listener interface adapters* are support classes that provide default implementations for all the methods in the listener interface. Java provides listener interface adapters for every AWT listener interface with multiple handlers. A listener interface adapter is named *X*`Adapter` for *X*`Listener`.

6. A source object may fire several types of events. For each event, the source object maintains a list of registered listeners and notifies them by invoking the *handler* on the listener object to process the event.

7. A `MouseEvent` is fired whenever a mouse is pressed, released, clicked, entered, exited, moved, or dragged on a component. The mouse-event object captures the event, such as the number of clicks associated with it or the location (*x*- and *y*-coordinates) of the mouse point.

8. Java provides two listener interfaces, MouseListener and MouseMotionListener, to handle mouse events. Java implements the MouseListener interface to listen for such actions as mouse pressed, released, clicked, entered, or exited, and the MouseMotionListener interface to listen for such actions as mouse dragged or moved.

9. A KeyEvent is fired when a key is pressed, released, or typed. The key value and key character can be obtained from the key-event object.

10. A listener's keyPressed handler is invoked when a key is pressed, its keyReleased handler is invoked when a key is released, and its keyTyped handler is invoked when a Unicode character key is entered. If a key does not have a Unicode (e.g., function keys, modifier keys, action keys, and control keys), a listener's keyTyped handler will be not be invoked.

11. You can use the Timer class to control Java animations. A timer fires an ActionEvent at a fixed rate. The listener updates the painting to simulate an animation.

Test Questions

Do the test questions for this chapter online at www.cs.armstrong.edu/liang/intro9e/test.html.

MyProgrammingLab™

Programming Exercises

Sections 16.2–16.7

*16.1 (*Pick four cards*) Write a program that lets the user click the *Refresh* button to display four cards from a deck of 52 cards, as shown in Figure 16.21a. (*Hint*: See Listing 6.2 on how to draw four cards randomly.)

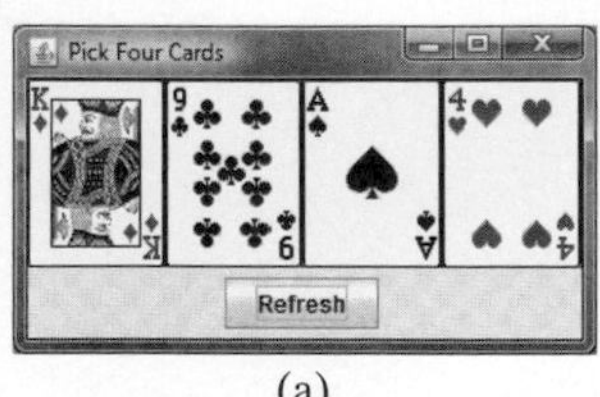

(a)

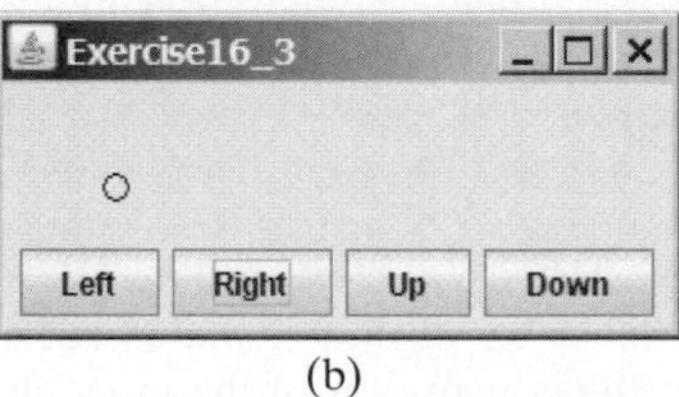

(b)

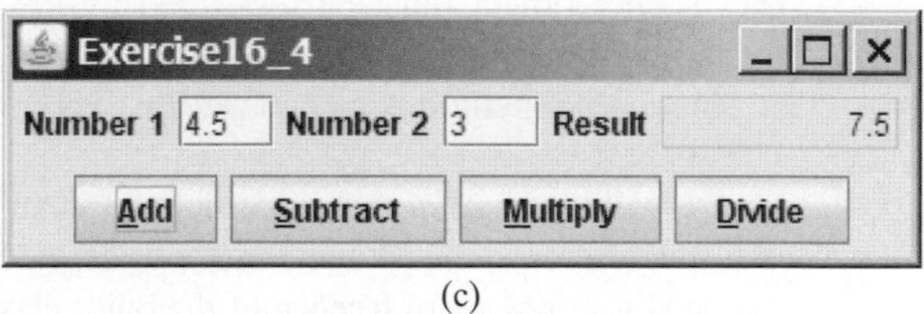

(c)

Figure 16.21 (a) Exercise 16.1 displays four cards randomly. (b) Exercise 16.3 uses the buttons to move the ball. (c) Exercise 16.4 performs addition, subtraction, multiplication, and division on double numbers.

16.2 (*Find which button has been clicked on the console*) Add the code to Programming Exercise 12.1 that will display a message on the console indicating which button has been clicked.

*16.3 (*Move the ball*) Write a program that moves the ball in a panel. You should define a panel class for displaying the ball and provide the methods for moving the ball left, right, up, and down, as shown in Figure 16.21b. Check the boundary to prevent the ball from moving out of sight completely.

*16.4 (*Create a simple calculator*) Write a program to perform addition, subtraction, multiplication, and division, as shown in Figure 16.21c.

*16.5 (*Create an investment-value calculator*) Write a program that calculates the future value of an investment at a given interest rate for a specified number of years. The formula for the calculation is:

```
futureValue = investmentAmount * (1 + monthlyInterestRate)^(years*12)
```

Use text fields for the investment amount, number of years, and annual interest rate. Display the future amount in a text field when the user clicks the *Calculate* button, as shown in Figure 16.22a.

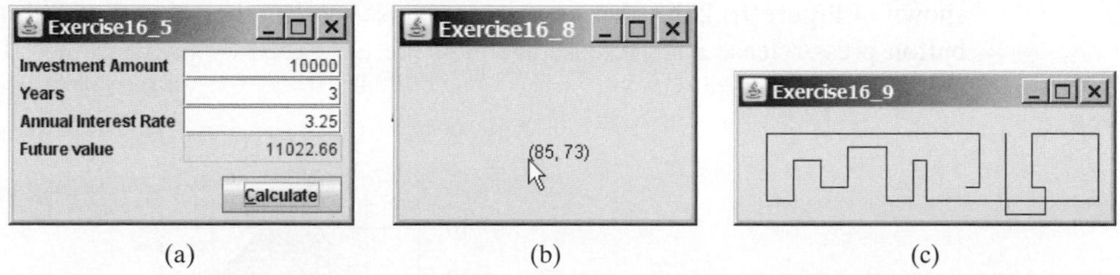

(a) (b) (c)

FIGURE 16.22 (a) The user enters the investment amount, years, and interest rate to compute future value. (b) Exercise 16.8 displays the mouse position. (c) Exercise 16.9 uses the arrow keys to draw the lines.

Sections 16.8–16.9

**16.6 (*Alternate two messages*) Write a program to rotate with a mouse click the two messages `Java is fun` and `Java is powerful` displayed on a panel.

*16.7 (*Set background color using a mouse*) Write a program that displays the background color of a panel as black when the mouse button is pressed and as white when the mouse button is released.

*16.8 (*Display the mouse position*) Write two programs, such that one displays the mouse position when the mouse button is clicked (see Figure 16.22b) and the other displays the mouse position when the mouse button is pressed and ceases to display it when the mouse button is released.

Section 16.10

*16.9 (*Draw lines using the arrow keys*) Write a program that draws line segments using the arrow keys. The line starts from the center of the frame and draws toward east, north, west, or south when the right-arrow key, up-arrow key, left-arrow key, or down-arrow key is pressed, as shown in Figure 16.22c.

**16.10 (*Enter and display a string*) Write a program that receives a string from the keyboard and displays it on a panel. The *Enter* key signals the end of a string. Whenever a new string is entered, it is displayed on the panel.

*16.11 (*Display a character*) Write a program to get a character input from the keyboard and display the character where the mouse points.

Section 16.11

**16.12 (*Display a running fan*) Listing 13.4, DrawArcs.java, displays a motionless fan. Write a program that displays a running fan.

16.13 (*Slide show*) Twenty-five slides are stored as image files (slide0.jpg**, **slide1.jpg**, . . ., **slide24.jpg**) in the **image** directory downloadable along with the source code in the book. The size of each image is 800 × 600. Write a Java application that automatically displays the slides repeatedly. Each slide is shown for a second. The slides are displayed in order. When the last slide finishes, the first slide is redisplayed, and so on. (*Hint*: Place a label in the frame and set a slide as an image icon in the label.)

**16.14 (*Raise flag*) Write a Java program that animates raising a flag, as shown in Figure 16.1. (See Section 13.10, Displaying Images, for how to display images.)

VideoNote
Animate a rising flag

**16.15 (*Racing car*) Write a Java program that simulates car racing, as shown in Figure 16.23a. The car moves from left to right. When it hits the right end, it restarts from the left and continues the same process. You can use a timer to control animation. Redraw the car with a new base coordinates (x, y), as shown in Figure 16.23b. Also let the user pause/resume the animation with a button press/release and increase/decrease the car speed by pressing the UP and DOWN arrow keys.

(a) (b)

FIGURE 16.23 (a) Exercise 16.15 displays a moving car. (b) You can redraw a car with a new base point.

*16.16 (*Display a flashing label*) Write a program that displays a flashing label. (*Hint*: To make the label flash, you need to repaint the panel alternately with the label and without it (a blank screen) at a fixed rate. Use a `boolean` variable to control the alternation.)

*16.17 (*Control a moving label*) Modify Listing 16.11, AnimationDemo.java, to control a moving label using the mouse. The label freezes when the mouse is pressed, and moves again when the button is released.

Comprehensive

*16.18 (*Move a circle using keys*) Write a program that moves a circle up, down, left, or right using the arrow keys.

VideoNote
Check mouse point location

**16.19 (*Geometry: inside a circle?*) Write a program that draws a fixed circle centered at (`100`, `60`) with radius `50`. Whenever the mouse is moved, display a message indicating whether the mouse point is inside the circle at the mouse point or outside of it, as shown in Figure 16.24a.

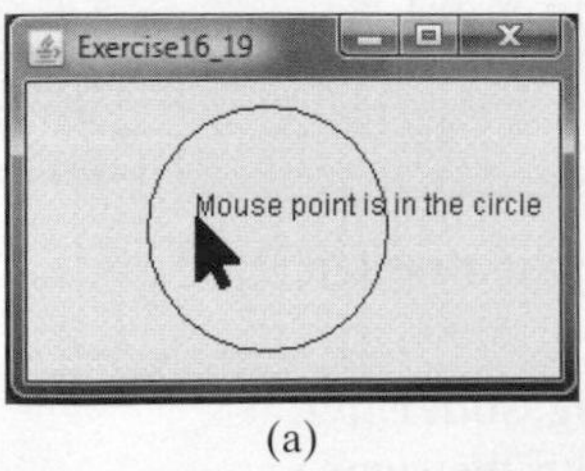

(a)

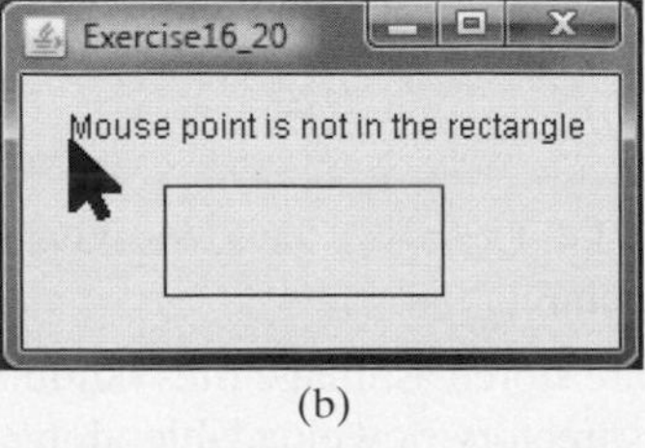

(b)

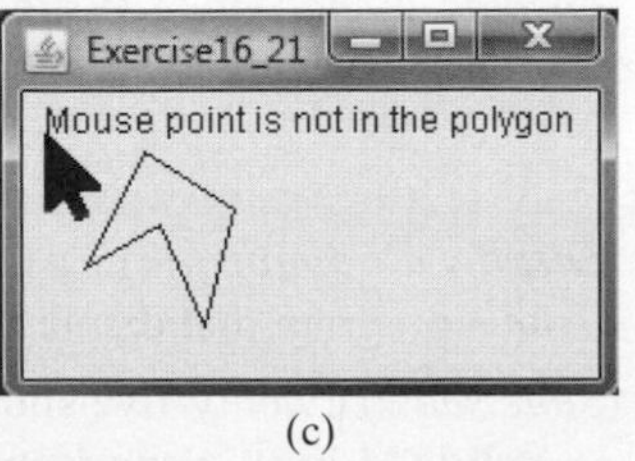

(c)

FIGURE 16.24 Detect whether a point is inside a circle, a rectangle, or a polygon.

**16.20 (*Geometry: inside a rectangle?*) Write a program that draws a fixed rectangle centered at (100, 60) with width 100 and height 40. Whenever the mouse is moved, display a message indicating whether the mouse point is inside the rectangle at the mouse point or outside of it, as shown in Figure 16.24b. To detect whether a point is inside a rectangle, use the `MyRectangle2D` class defined in Programming Exercise 10.13.

**16.21 (*Geometry: inside a polygon?*) Write a program that draws a fixed polygon with points at (40, 20), (70, 40), (60, 80), (45, 45), and (20, 60). Whenever the mouse is moved, display a message indicating whether the mouse point is inside the polygon at the mouse point or outside of it, as shown in Figure 16.24c. To detect whether a point is inside a polygon, use the `contains` method defined in the `Polygon` class (see Figure 13.13).

***16.22 (*Game: bean-machine animation*) Write a program that animates the bean machine introduced in Programming Exercise 6.21. The animation terminates after ten balls are dropped, as shown in Figure 16.25.

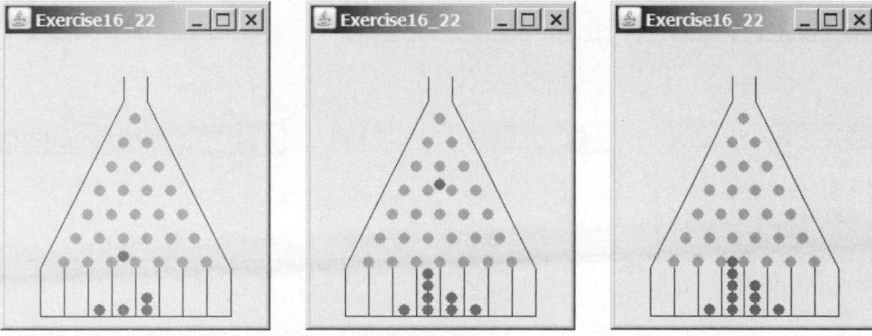

FIGURE 16.25 The balls are dropped into the bean machine.

***16.23 (*Geometry: closest pair of points*) Write a program that lets the user click on the panel to dynamically create points. Initially, the panel is empty. When a panel has two or more points, highlight the pair of closest points. Whenever a new point is created, a new pair of closest points is highlighted. Display the points using small circles and highlight the points using filled circles, as shown in Figure 16.26a–c. (*Hint*: store the points in an `ArrayList`.)

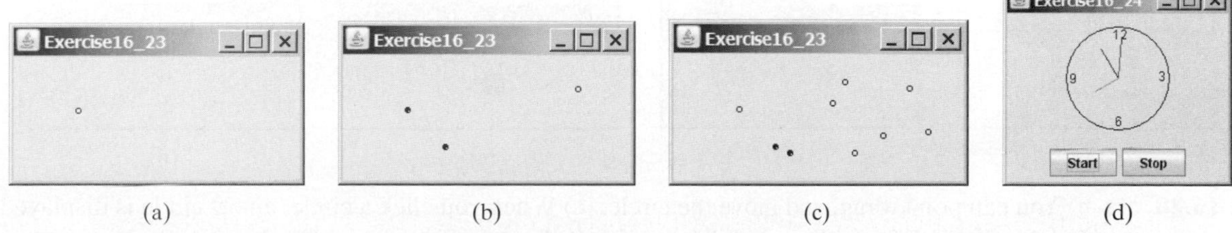

FIGURE 16.26 Exercise 16.23 allows the user to create new points with a mouse click and highlights the pair of the closest points. Exercise 16.24 allows the user to start and stop a clock.

*16.24 (*Control a clock*) Modify Listing 16.12, ClockAnimation.java, to add the two methods `start()` and `stop()` to start and stop the clock. Write a program that lets the user control the clock with the *Start* and *Stop* buttons, as shown in Figure 16.26d.

***16.25 (*Game: hit balloons*) Write a program that displays a balloon in a random position in a panel (Figure 16.27a). Use the left- and right-arrow keys to point the gun left or right to aim at the balloon (Figure 16.27b). Press the up-arrow key to fire a small ball from the gun (Figure 16.27c–d). Once the ball hits the balloon, the debris is displayed (Figure 16.27e) and a new balloon is displayed in a random location (Figure 16.27f). If the ball misses the balloon, the ball disappears once it hits the boundary of the panel. You can then press the up-arrow key to fire another ball. Whenever you press the left- or the right-arrow key, the gun turns 5 degrees left or right. (Instructors may modify the game as follows: 1. Display the number of the balloons destroyed; 2. display a countdown timer (e.g., 60 seconds) and terminate the game once the time expires; and/or 3. allow the balloon to rise dynamically.)

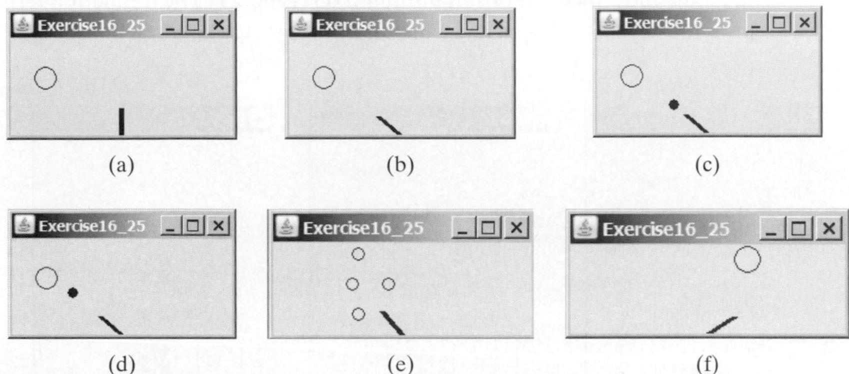

FIGURE 16.27 (a) A balloon is displayed in a random location. (b) Press the left-/right-arrow keys to aim at the balloon. (c) Press the up-arrow key to fire a ball. (d) The ball moves straight toward the balloon. (e) The ball hits the balloon. (f) A new balloon is displayed in a random position.

**16.26 (*Move a circle using mouse*) Write a program that displays a circle with radius 10 pixels. You can point the mouse inside the circle and drag (i.e., move with mouse pressed) the circle wherever the mouse goes, as shown in Figure 16.28a–b.

FIGURE 16.28 (a–b) You can point, drag, and move the circle. (c) When you click a circle, a new circle is displayed at a random location. (d) After 20 circles are clicked, the time spent is displayed in the panel.

***16.27 (*Game: eye-hand coordination*) Write a program that displays a circle of radius 10 pixels filled with a random color at a random location on a panel, as shown in Figure 16.28c. When you click the circle, it disappears and a new random-color circle is displayed at another random location. After twenty circles are clicked, display the time spent in the panel, as shown in Figure 16.28d.

***16.28 (*Simulation: self-avoiding random walk*) A self-avoiding walk in a lattice is a path from one point to another that does not visit the same point twice. Self-avoiding walks have applications in physics, chemistry, and mathematics. They can be used to model chain-like entities such as solvents and polymers. Write a program that displays a random path that starts from the center and ends at a point on the boundary, as shown in Figure 16.29a, or ends at a dead-end point (i.e., surrounded by four points that have already been visited), as shown in Figure 16.29b. Assume the size of the lattice is **16** by **16**.

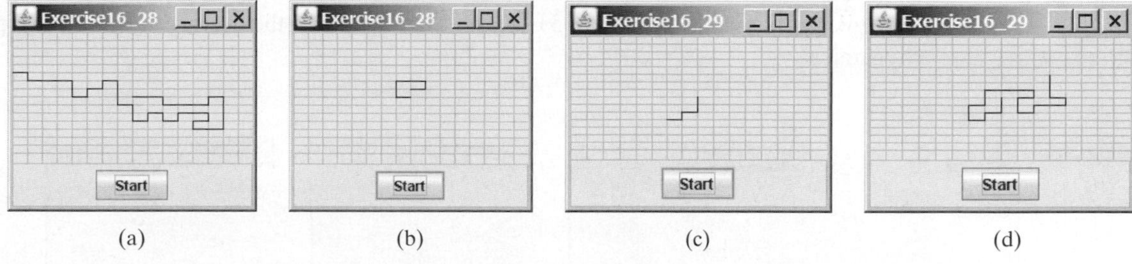

(a) (b) (c) (d)

FIGURE 16.29 (a) A path ends at a boundary point. (b) A path ends at dead-end point. (c–d) Animation shows the progress of a path step by step.

***16.29 (*Animation: self-avoiding random walk*) Revise the preceding exercise to display the walk step by step in an animation, as shown in Figure 16.29c–d.

**16.30 (*Simulation: self-avoiding random walk*) Write a simulation program to show that the chance of getting dead-end paths increases as the grid size increases. Your program simulates lattices with size from 10 to 80. For each lattice size, simulate a self-avoiding random walk 10,000 times and display the probability of the dead-end paths, as shown in the following sample output:

```
For a lattice of size 10, the probability of dead-end paths is 10.6%
For a lattice of size 11, the probability of dead-end paths is 14.0%
. . .
For a lattice of size 80, the probability of dead-end paths is 99.5%
```

*16.31 (*Geometry: display an n-sided regular polygon*) Programming Exercise 13.25 created the **RegularPolygonPanel** for displaying an *n*-sided regular polygon. Write a program that displays a regular polygon and uses two buttons named *+1* and *−1* to increase or decrease the size of the polygon, as shown in Figure 16.30a–b. Also enable the user to increase or decrease the size by clicking the right or left mouse button and by pressing the UP and DOWN arrow keys.

**16.32 (*Geometry: add and remove points*) Write a program that lets the user click on a panel to dynamically create and remove points (see Figure 16.30c). When the user right-clicks the mouse, a point is created and displayed at the mouse point. The user can remove a point by pointing to it and left-clicking the mouse.

**16.33 (*Geometry: pendulum*) Write a program that animates a pendulum swinging, as shown in Figure 16.31. Press the UP arrow key to increase the speed and the DOWN key to decrease it. Press the *S* key to stop animation and the *R* key to resume it.

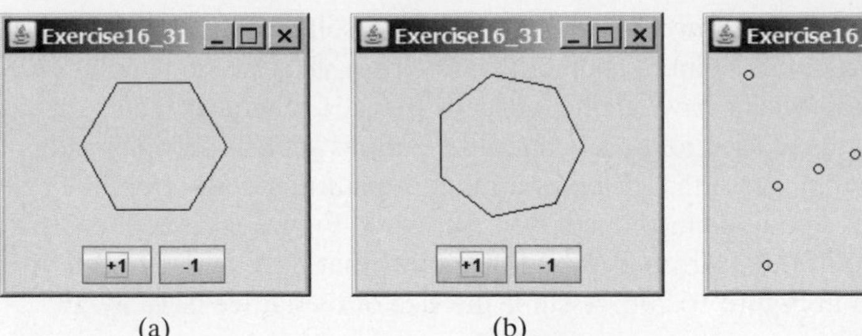

FIGURE 16.30 Clicking the +1 or −1 button increases or decreases the number of sides of a regular polygon in Exercise 16.31. Exercise 16.32 allows the user to create/remove points dynamically.

FIGURE 16.31 Exercise 16.33 animates a pendulum swinging.

**16.34 (Game: hangman) Write a program that animates a hangman game swinging, as shown in Figure 16.32. Press the UP arrow key to increase the speed and the DOWN arrow key to decrease it. Press the *S* key to stop animation and the *R* key to resume it.

FIGURE 16.32 The program animates a hangman game swinging.

***16.35 (*Animation: ball on curve*) Write a program that animates a ball moving along a sine curve, as shown in Figure 16.33. When the ball gets to the right border, it starts over from the left. Enable the user to resume/pause the animation with a click on the left/right mouse button.

*16.36 (*Flip coins*) Write a program that displays heads (`H`) or tails (`T`) for each of nine coins, as shown in Figure 16.34a–b. When a cell is clicked, the coin is flipped. A cell is a `JLabel`. Write a custom cell class that extends `JLabel`

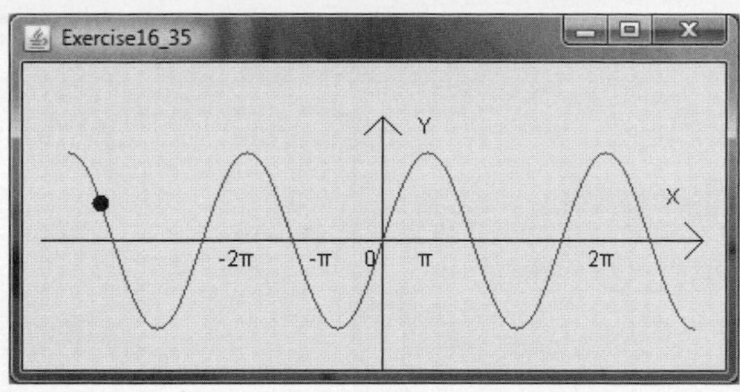

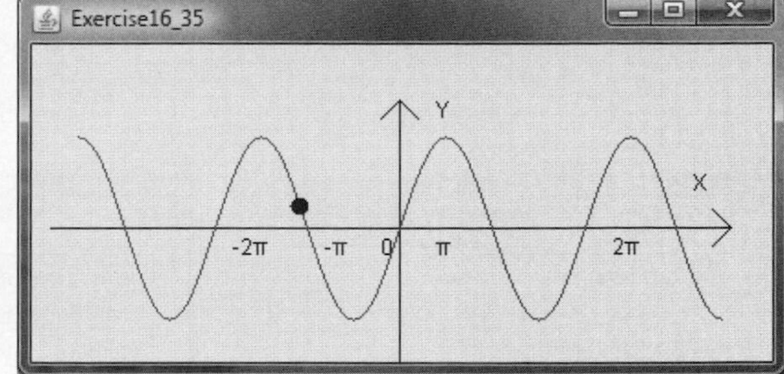

FIGURE 16.33 The program animates a ball travelling along a sine curve.

Exercise16_36

H	H	H
H	H	H
H	H	H

(a)

Exercise16_36

H	H	H
T	T	T
H	H	H

(b)

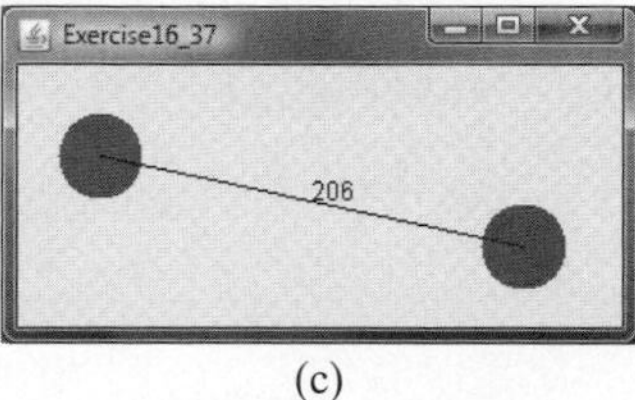

(c)

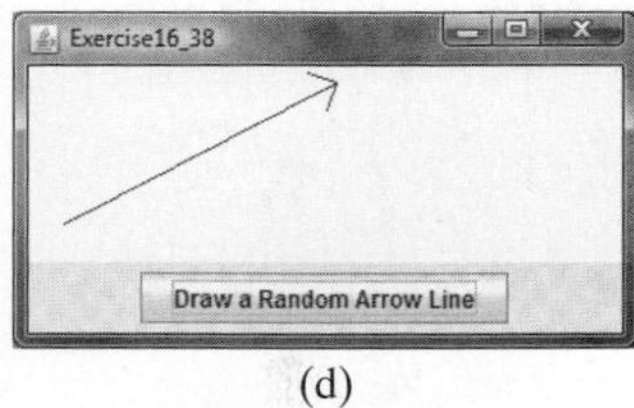

(d)

FIGURE 16.34 (a–b) Exercise 16.36 enables the user to click a cell to flip a coin. (c) The user can drag the circles. (d) Exercise 16.38 draws an arrow line randomly.

with the mouse listener for handling the clicks. When the program starts, all cells initially display H.

***16.37** (*Two movable vertices and their distances*) Write a program that displays two circles with radius 20 at location (20, 20) and (120, 50) with a line connecting the two circles, as shown in Figure 16.34c. The distance between the circles is displayed along the line. The user can drag a circle. When that happens, the circle and its line are moved and the distance between the circles is updated. Your program should not allow the circles to get too close. Keep them at least 70 pixels apart between the two circles' centers.

****16.38** (*Draw an arrow line*) Write a static method that draws an arrow line from a starting point to an ending point using the following method header:

```
public static void drawArrowLine(int x1, int y1,
  int x2, int y2, Graphics g)
```

Write a test program that randomly draws an arrow line when the *Draw a Random Arrow Line* button is clicked, as shown in Figure 16.34d.

****16.39** (*Geometry: find the bounding rectangle*) Write a program that enables the user to add and remove points in a two-dimensional plane dynamically, as shown in Figure 16.35a–b. A minimum bounding rectangle is updated as the points are added and removed. Assume the radius of each point is 10 pixels.

***16.40** (*Display random 0 or 1*) Write a program that displays a 10-by-10 square matrix, as shown in Figure 16.35c. Each element in the matrix is 0 or 1, randomly generated with a click of the *Refresh* button. Display each number centered in a label.

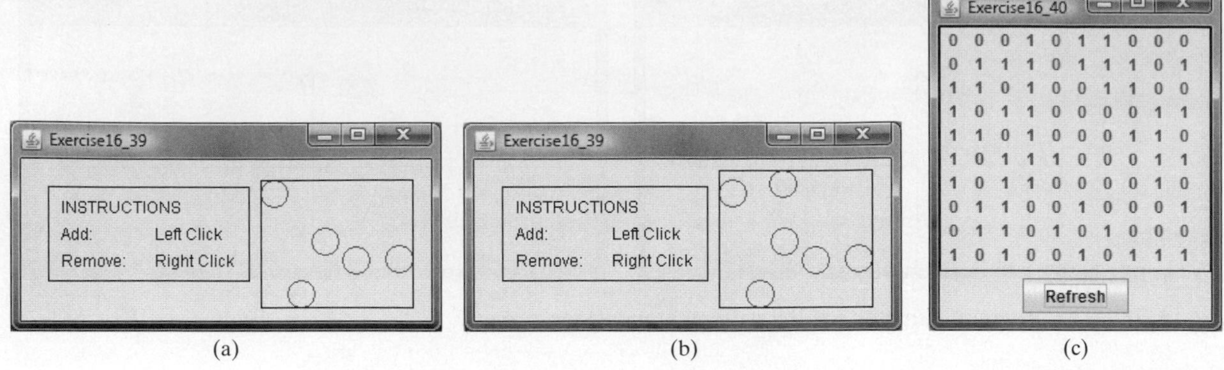

Figure 16.35 (a–b) Exercise 16.39 enables the user to add/remove points dynamically and displays the bounding rectangle. (c) Exercise 16.40 displays 0s and 1s randomly with a click of the *Refresh* button.

CHAPTER 17

GUI Components

Objectives

- To create graphical user interfaces with various user-interface components (§§17.2–17.8).
- To create listeners for `JCheckBox`, `JRadioButton`, and `JTextField` (§17.2).
- To enter multiple-line texts using `JTextArea` (§17.3).
- To select a single item using `JComboBox` (§17.4).
- To select a single or multiple items using `JList` (§17.5).
- To select a range of values using `JScrollBar` (§17.6).
- To select a range of values using `JSlider` and explore differences between `JScrollBar` and `JSlider` (§17.7).
- To display multiple windows in an application (§17.8).

17.1 Introduction

Swing provides many GUI components for developing a comprehensive user interface.

Previous chapters briefly introduced `JButton`, `JCheckBox`, `JRadioButton`, `JLabel`, `JTextField`, and `JPasswordField`. This chapter introduces in detail how the events are processed for these components. We will also introduce `JTextArea`, `JComboBox`, `JList`, `JScrollBar`, and `JSlider`. More GUI components such as `JMenu`, `JToolBar`, `JTabbedPane`, `JSplitPane`, `JSpinner`, `JTree`, and `JTable` will be introduced in bonus Web Chapters 36–40.

17.2 Events for JCheckBox, JRadioButton, and JTextField

A GUI component may fire many types of events. `ActionEvent` is commonly processed for `JCheckBox`, `JRadioButton`, and `JTextField`, and `ItemEvent` can be used for `JCheckBox` and `JRadioButton`.

In the previous chapter, you learned how to handle an action event for `JButton`. This section introduces handling events for check boxes, radio buttons, and text fields.

When a `JCheckBox` or a `JRadioButton` is clicked (that is, checked or unchecked), it fires an `ItemEvent` and then an `ActionEvent`. When you press the *Enter* key on a `JTextField`, it fires an `ActionEvent`.

Listing 17.1 gives a program that demonstrates how to handle events from check boxes, radio buttons, and text fields. The program displays a label and allows the user to set the colors of the text in the label using radio buttons, set fonts using check boxes, and set new text entered from a text field, as shown in Figure 17.1.

FIGURE 17.1 The program demonstrates check boxes, radio buttons, and text fields.

LISTING 17.1 GUIEventDemo.java

create label
create check boxes
create radio buttons

```
import java.awt.*;
import java.awt.event.*;
import javax.swing.*;
import javax.swing.border.*;

public class GUIEventDemo extends JFrame {
  private JLabel jlblMessage = new JLabel("Hello", JLabel.CENTER);

  // Create check boxes to set the font for the message
  private JCheckBox jchkBold = new JCheckBox("Bold");
  private JCheckBox jchkItalic = new JCheckBox("Italic");

  // Create three radio buttons to set message colors
  private JRadioButton jrbRed = new JRadioButton("Red");
  private JRadioButton jrbGreen = new JRadioButton("Green");
  private JRadioButton jrbBlue = new JRadioButton("Blue");

  // Create a text field for setting a new message
```

```
  private JTextField jtfMessage = new JTextField(10);

  public static void main(String[] args) {
    GUIEventDemo frame = new GUIEventDemo();
    frame.pack();
    frame.setTitle("GUIEventDemo");
    frame.setLocationRelativeTo(null); // Center the frame
    frame.setDefaultCloseOperation(JFrame.EXIT_ON_CLOSE);
    frame.setVisible(true);
  }

  public GUIEventDemo() {
    jlblMessage.setBorder(new LineBorder(Color.BLACK, 2));
    add(jlblMessage, BorderLayout.CENTER);

    // Create a panel to hold check boxes
    JPanel jpCheckBoxes = new JPanel();
    jpCheckBoxes.setLayout(new GridLayout(2, 1));
    jpCheckBoxes.add(jchkBold);
    jpCheckBoxes.add(jchkItalic);
    add(jpCheckBoxes, BorderLayout.EAST);

    // Create a panel to hold radio buttons
    JPanel jpRadioButtons = new JPanel();
    jpRadioButtons.setLayout(new GridLayout(3, 1));
    jpRadioButtons.add(jrbRed);
    jpRadioButtons.add(jrbGreen);
    jpRadioButtons.add(jrbBlue);
    add(jpRadioButtons, BorderLayout.WEST);

    // Create a radio-button group to group three buttons
    ButtonGroup group = new ButtonGroup();
    group.add(jrbRed);
    group.add(jrbGreen);
    group.add(jrbBlue);

    // Set initial message color to blue
    jrbBlue.setSelected(true);
    jlblMessage.setForeground(Color.blue);

    // Create a panel to hold label and text field
    JPanel jpTextField = new JPanel();
    jpTextField.setLayout(new BorderLayout(5, 0));
    jpTextField.add(
      new JLabel("Enter a new message"), BorderLayout.WEST);
    jpTextField.add(jtfMessage, BorderLayout.CENTER);
    jtfMessage.setHorizontalAlignment(JTextField.RIGHT);
    add(jpTextField, BorderLayout.NORTH);

    // Set mnemonic keys for check boxes and radio buttons
    jchkBold.setMnemonic('B');
    jchkItalic.setMnemonic('I');
    jrbRed.setMnemonic('E');
    jrbGreen.setMnemonic('G');
    jrbBlue.setMnemonic('U');

    // Register listeners with check boxes
    jchkBold.addActionListener(new ActionListener() {
      @Override
      public void actionPerformed(ActionEvent e) {
```

create text field
create frame
pack frame
create UI
place label
panel for check boxes
panel for radio buttons
group buttons
panel for text field
set mnemonics
register listener

```
 79           setNewFont();
 80         }
 81       });
```

register listener

```
 82       jchkItalic.addActionListener(new ActionListener() {
 83         @Override
 84         public void actionPerformed(ActionEvent e) {
 85           setNewFont();
 86         }
 87       });
 88
 89       // Register listeners for radio buttons
```

register listener

```
 90       jrbRed.addActionListener(new ActionListener() {
 91         @Override
 92         public void actionPerformed(ActionEvent e) {
 93           jlblMessage.setForeground(Color.red);
 94         }
 95       });
```

register listener

```
 96       jrbGreen.addActionListener(new ActionListener() {
 97         @Override
 98         public void actionPerformed(ActionEvent e) {
 99           jlblMessage.setForeground(Color.green);
100         }
101       });
```

register listener

```
102       jrbBlue.addActionListener(new ActionListener() {
103         @Override
104         public void actionPerformed(ActionEvent e) {
105           jlblMessage.setForeground(Color.blue);
106         }
107       });
108
109       // Register listener for text field
```

register listener

```
110       jtfMessage.addActionListener(new ActionListener() {
111         @Override
112         public void actionPerformed(ActionEvent e) {
113           jlblMessage.setText(jtfMessage.getText());
114           jtfMessage.requestFocusInWindow();
115         }
116       });
117     }
118
119     private void setNewFont() {
120       // Determine a font style
121       int fontStyle = Font.PLAIN;
122       fontStyle += (jchkBold.isSelected() ? Font.BOLD : Font.PLAIN);
123       fontStyle += (jchkItalic.isSelected() ? Font.ITALIC : Font.PLAIN);
124
125       // Set font for the message
126       Font font = jlblMessage.getFont();
```

set a new font

```
127       jlblMessage.setFont(
128         new Font(font.getName(), fontStyle, font.getSize()));
129     }
130   }
```

The program creates a label, check boxes, radio buttons, and a text field (lines 7–19). It places a label in the center of the frame (lines 31–32), check boxes in the east (lines 35–39), radio buttons in the west (lines 42–47), and a text field in the north (lines 60–66).

mnemonic keys

The program also sets mnemonics for check boxes and radio buttons (lines 69–73). You can use a mouse click or a shortcut key to select a check box or a radio button.

The program registers action listeners for check boxes, radio buttons, and the text field (lines 76–116). register listeners

When a check box is checked or unchecked, the listener's actionPerformed method is invoked to process the event (lines 79, 85). The current font name and size used in JLabel are obtained from jlblMessage.getFont() using the getName() and getSize() methods (line 128). The font styles (Font.BOLD and Font.ITALIC) are specified in the check boxes. If no font style is selected, the default font style is Font.PLAIN (line 121). The font style is an integer 0 for Font.PLAIN, 1 for Font.BOLD, and 2 for Font.ITALIC. The font style can be combined by adding together the integers that represent the fonts (lines 122–123). For example, Font.BOLD + Font.ITALIC is 3, which represents a combined font of bold and italic. check boxes

The setFont method (line 127) defined in the Component class is inherited in the JLabel class. This method automatically invokes the repaint method. Invoking setFont on jlblMessage automatically repaints jlblMessage.

A check box fires an ItemEvent and then an ActionEvent when it is clicked. You could process either the ItemEvent or the ActionEvent to redisplay the message. The program in this example processes the ActionEvent. If you want to process the ItemEvent, create a listener for ItemEvent and register it with a check box. The listener must implement the itemStateChanged handler to process an ItemEvent. For example, the following code registers an ItemListener with jchkBold:

```
// To listen for ItemEvent
jchkBold.addItemListener(new ItemListener() {
  @Override /** Handle ItemEvent */
  public void itemStateChanged(ItemEvent e) {
    setNewFont();
  }
});
```

When a radio button is clicked, its action event listener sets the corresponding foreground color in jlblMessage (lines 93, 99, 105). radio buttons

The program creates a ButtonGroup and puts three JRadioButton instances (jrbRed, jrbGreen, and jrbBlue) in the group (lines 50–53) so they can only be selected exclusively—the text will be either red *or* green *or* blue. radio button group

A radio button fires an ItemEvent and then an ActionEvent when it is selected or deselected. You could process either the ItemEvent or the ActionEvent to choose a color. This program processes the ActionEvent. As an exercise, rewrite the code using the ItemEvent.

After you type a new message in the text field and press the *Enter* key, a new message is displayed. Pressing the *Enter* key on the text field triggers an action event. The listener sets a new message in jlblMessage (line 113). ActionEvent for JTextField

The requestFocusInWindow() method (line 114) defined in the Component class requests the component to receive input focus. Thus, jtfMessage.requestFocusInWindow() requests the input focus on jtfMessage. You will see the cursor on jtfMessage after the actionPerformed method is invoked. requestFocusInWindow()

The pack() method (line 23) automatically sizes the frame according to the size of the components placed in it. pack()

Check Point
MyProgrammingLab™

17.1 Can a JButton, JLabel, JCheckBox, JRadioButton, and JTextField fire an ActionEvent?

17.2 Can a JButton, JLabel, JCheckBox, JRadioButton, and JTextField fire an ItemEvent?

17.3 What happens after invoking jtfMessage.requestFocusInWindow()?

17.3 Text Areas

A `JTextArea` enables the user to enter multiple lines of text.

If you want to let the user enter multiple lines of text, you may create several instances of `JTextField`. A better alternative is to use `JTextArea`, which enables the user to enter multiple lines of text. Figure 17.2 lists the constructors and methods in `JTextArea`.

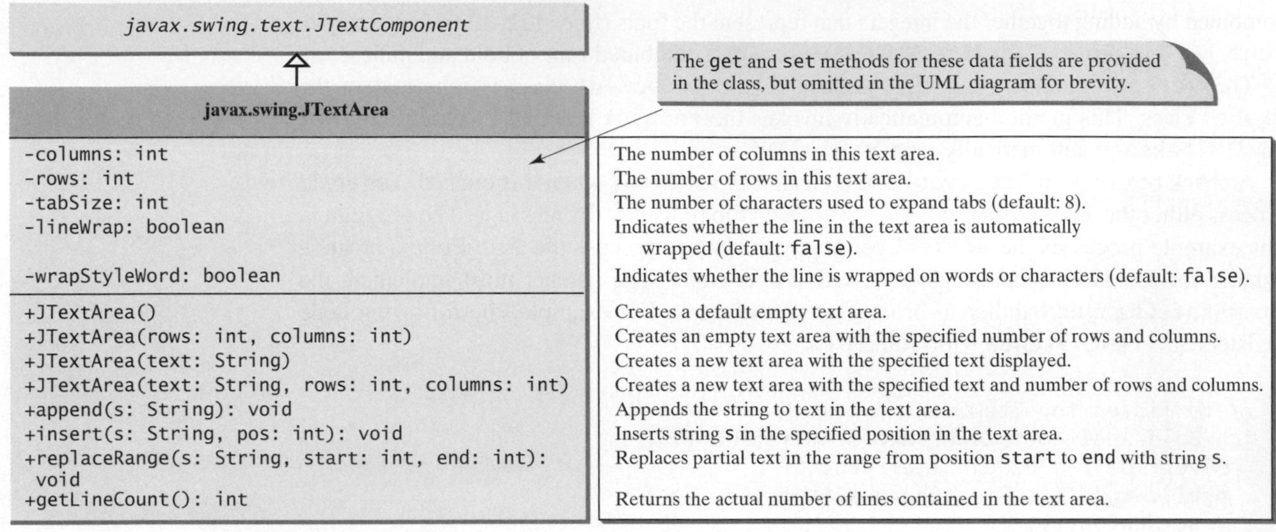

FIGURE 17.2 `JTextArea` enables you to enter or display multiple lines of characters.

Like `JTextField`, `JTextArea` inherits `JTextComponent`, which contains the methods `getText`, `setText`, `isEditable`, and `setEditable`. You can specify whether a line is wrapped in the `lineWrap` property. If `lineWrap` is true, you can specify how line is wrapped in the `wrapStyleWord` property. If `wrapStyleWord` is true, line is wrapped on words. If it is false, line is wrapped on characters. The following example creates a text area with `5` rows and `20` columns, line-wrapped on words, `red` foreground color, and `Courier` font, `bold`, `20` pixels.

wrap line
wrap word

```
JTextArea jtaNote = new JTextArea("This is a text area", 5, 20);
jtaNote.setLineWrap(true);
jtaNote.setWrapStyleWord(true);
jtaNote.setForeground(Color.red);
jtaNote.setFont(new Font("Courier", Font.BOLD, 20));
```

`JTextArea` does not handle scrolling, but you can create a `JScrollPane` object to hold an instance of `JTextArea` and let `JScrollPane` handle scrolling for `JTextArea`, as follows:

```
// Create a scroll pane to hold text area
JScrollPane scrollPane = new JScrollPane(jtaNote);
add(scrollPane, BorderLayout.CENTER);
```

`JScrollPane`

Tip

You can place any swing GUI component in a `JScrollPane`. `JScrollPane` provides vertical and horizontal scrolling automatically if the component is too large to fit in the viewing area.

Listing 17.3 gives a program that displays an image and a text in a label, and a text in a text area, as shown in Figure 17.3.

FIGURE 17.3 The program displays an image in a label, a title in a label, and text in the text area.

Here are the major steps in the program:

1. Define a class named **DescriptionPanel** that extends **JPanel**, as shown in Listing 17.2. This class contains a text area inside a scroll pane, and a label for displaying an image icon and a title. The class **DescriptionPanel** will be reused in later examples.
2. Define a class named **TextAreaDemo** that extends **JFrame**, as shown in Listing 17.3. Create an instance of **DescriptionPanel** and add it to the center of the frame. The relationship between **DescriptionPanel** and **TextAreaDemo** is shown in Figure 17.4.

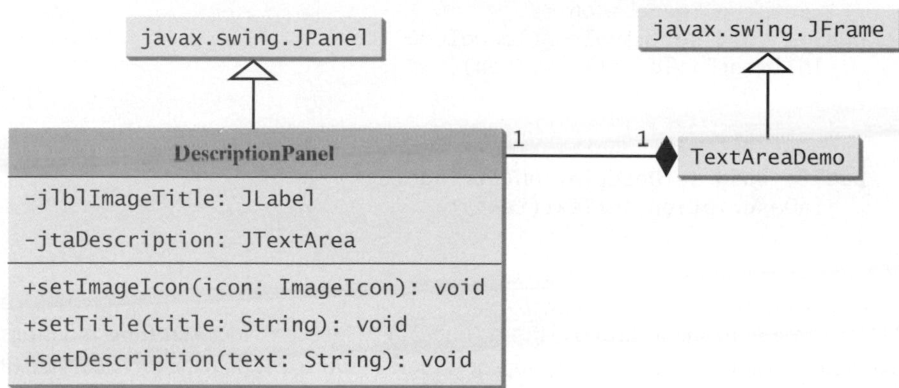

FIGURE 17.4 **TextAreaDemo** uses **DescriptionPanel** to display an image, title, and text description of a national flag.

LISTING 17.2 DescriptionPanel.java

```
import javax.swing.*;
import java.awt.*;

public class DescriptionPanel extends JPanel {
  /** Label for displaying an image icon and a title */
  private JLabel jlblImageTitle = new JLabel();

  /** Text area for displaying text */
  private JTextArea jtaDescription = new JTextArea();

  public DescriptionPanel() {
    // Center the icon and text and place the text under the icon
    jlblImageTitle.setHorizontalAlignment(JLabel.CENTER);
    jlblImageTitle.setHorizontalTextPosition(JLabel.CENTER);
    jlblImageTitle.setVerticalTextPosition(JLabel.BOTTOM);

```

label

text area

label properties

wrap line; wrap word; read only; scroll pane

```
17       // Set the font in the label and the text field
18       jlblImageTitle.setFont(new Font("SansSerif", Font.BOLD, 16));
19       jtaDescription.setFont(new Font("Serif", Font.PLAIN, 14));
20
21       // Set lineWrap and wrapStyleWord true for the text area
22       jtaDescription.setLineWrap(true);
23       jtaDescription.setWrapStyleWord(true);
24       jtaDescription.setEditable(false);
25
26       // Create a scroll pane to hold the text area
27       JScrollPane scrollPane = new JScrollPane(jtaDescription);
28
29       // Set BorderLayout for the panel, add label and scroll pane
30       setLayout(new BorderLayout(5, 5));
31       add(scrollPane, BorderLayout.CENTER);
32       add(jlblImageTitle, BorderLayout.WEST);
33     }
34
35     /** Set the title */
36     public void setTitle(String title) {
37       jlblImageTitle.setText(title);
38     }
39
40     /** Set the image icon */
41     public void setImageIcon(ImageIcon icon) {
42       jlblImageTitle.setIcon(icon);
43     }
44
45     /** Set the text description */
46     public void setDescription(String text) {
47       jtaDescription.setText(text);
48     }
49   }
```

The text area is inside a **JScrollPane** (line 27), which provides scrolling functions for the text area. Scroll bars automatically appear if there is more text than the physical size of the text area.

The **lineWrap** property is set to **true** (line 22) so that the line is automatically wrapped when the text cannot fit in one line. The **wrapStyleWord** property is set to **true** (line 23) so that the line is wrapped on words rather than characters. The text area is set as noneditable (line 24), so you cannot edit the description in the text area.

It is not necessary to create a separate class for **DescriptionPanel** in this example. However, this class was created for reuse in the next section, where you will use it to display a description panel for various images.

LISTING 17.3 TextAreaDemo.java

create descriptionPanel; create frame

```
import java.awt.*;
import javax.swing.*;

public class TextAreaDemo extends JFrame {
  // Declare and create a description panel
  private DescriptionPanel descriptionPanel = new DescriptionPanel();

  public static void main(String[] args) {
    TextAreaDemo frame = new TextAreaDemo();
    frame.pack();
    frame.setLocationRelativeTo(null); // Center the frame
```

```
12       frame.setDefaultCloseOperation(JFrame.EXIT_ON_CLOSE);
13       frame.setTitle("TextAreaDemo");
14       frame.setVisible(true);
15     }
16
17     public TextAreaDemo() {
18       // Set title, text, and image in the description panel
19       descriptionPanel.setTitle("Canada");
20       String description = "The Canadian national flag...";
21       descriptionPanel.setImageIcon(new ImageIcon("image/ca.gif"));
22       descriptionPanel.setDescription(description);
23
24       // Add the description panel to the frame
25       setLayout(new BorderLayout());
26       add(descriptionPanel, BorderLayout.CENTER);
27     }
28   }
```

create UI

add descriptionPanel

The program in Listing 17.3 creates an instance of `DescriptionPanel` (line 6) and sets the title (line 19), image (line 21), and text in the description panel (line 22). `DescriptionPanel` is a subclass of `JPanel`. `DescriptionPanel` contains a label for displaying an image icon and a text title, and a text area for displaying a description of the image.

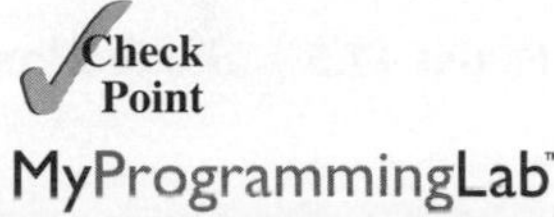

17.4 How do you create a text area with `10` rows and `20` columns?

17.5 How do you insert or append three lines into the text area?

17.6 How do you create a scrollable text area?

17.7 What method do you use to get the text from a text area? How do you get the line count in the text area?

17.8 How do you specify a line wrap? How do you specify wrapping on characters? How do you specify wrapping on words?

17.4 Combo Boxes

A combo box, also known as a choice list *or* drop-down list, *contains a list of items from which the user can choose.*

A combo box is useful for limiting a user's range of choices and avoids the cumbersome validation of data input. Figure 17.5 lists several frequently used constructors and methods in `JComboBox`.

The following statements create a combo box with four items, red foreground, white background, and the second item selected.

```
JComboBox jcb = new JComboBox(new Object[]
  {"Item 1", "Item 2", "Item3", "Item 4"});
jcb.setForeground(Color.red);
jcb.setBackground(Color.white);
jcb.setSelectedItem("Item 2");
```

`JComboBox` can fire `ItemEvent` and `ActionEvent` among many other events. Whenever an item is selected, an `ActionEvent` is fired. Whenever a new item is selected, `JComboBox` fires `ItemEvent` twice: once for deselecting the previously selected item, and the other for selecting the currently selected item. Note that no `ItemEvent` is fired if the current item is reselected. To respond to an `ItemEvent`, you need to implement the `itemStateChanged(ItemEvent e)` handler for processing a choice. To get data from a `JComboBox` menu, you can use `getSelectedItem()` to return the currently selected item, or the `e.getItem()` method to get the item from the `itemStateChanged(ItemEvent e)` handler.

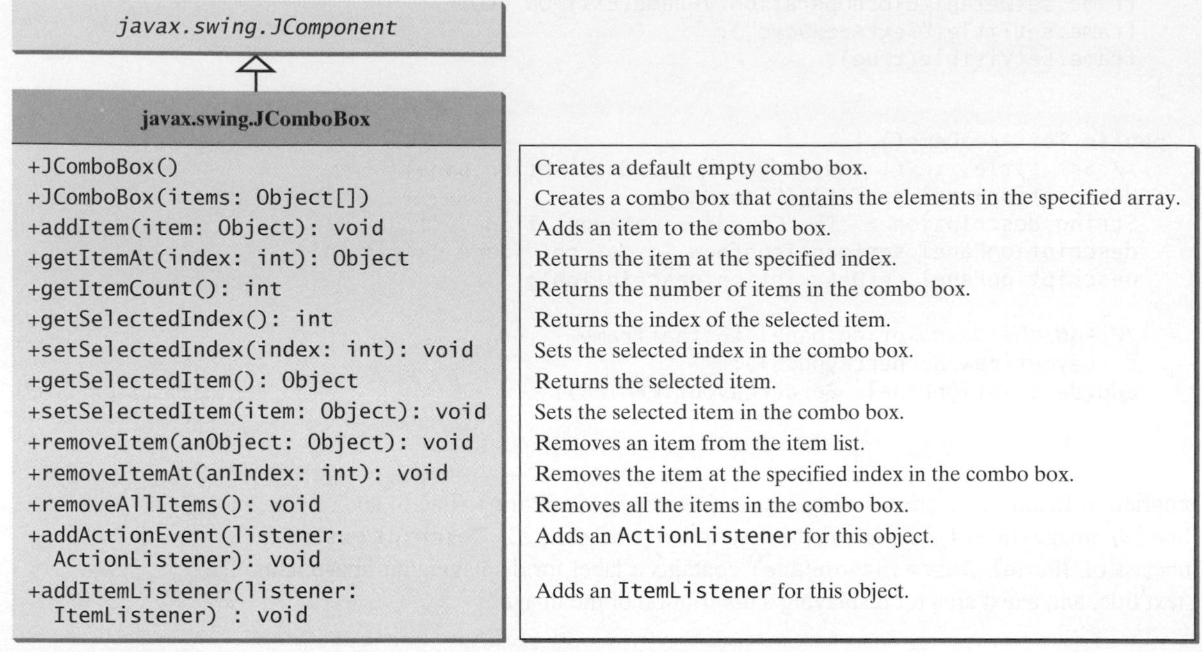

FIGURE 17.5 `JComboBox` enables you to select an item from a set of items.

Listing 17.4 gives a program that lets users view an image and a description of a country's flag by selecting the country from a combo box, as shown in Figure 17.6.

FIGURE 17.6 Information about a country, including an image and a description of its flag, is displayed when the country is selected in the combo box.

Here are the major steps in the program:

1. Create the user interface.
   Create a combo box with country names as its selection values. Create a **`DescriptionPanel`** object (the **`DescriptionPanel`** class was introduced in the preceding section). Place the combo box in the north of the frame and the description panel in the center of the frame.

2. Process the event.
   Create a listener to implement the **`itemStateChanged`** handler to set the flag title, image, and text in the description panel for the selected country name.

LISTING 17.4 ComboBoxDemo.java

```
import java.awt.*;
import java.awt.event.*;
import javax.swing.*;

public class ComboBoxDemo extends JFrame {
  // Create an array of Strings for flag titles
  private String[] flagTitles = {"Canada", "China", "Denmark",
    "France", "Germany", "India", "Norway", "United Kingdom",
    "United States of America"};

  // Declare an ImageIcon array for the national flags of 9 countries
  private ImageIcon[] flagImage = {
    new ImageIcon("image/ca.gif"),
    new ImageIcon("image/china.gif"),
    new ImageIcon("image/denmark.gif"),
    new ImageIcon("image/fr.gif"),
    new ImageIcon("image/germany.gif"),
    new ImageIcon("image/india.gif"),
    new ImageIcon("image/norway.gif"),
    new ImageIcon("image/uk.gif"),
    new ImageIcon("image/us.gif")
  };

  // Declare an array of strings for flag descriptions
  private String[] flagDescription = new String[9];

  // Declare and create a description panel
  private DescriptionPanel descriptionPanel = new DescriptionPanel();

  // Create a combo box for selecting countries
  private JComboBox jcbo = new JComboBox(flagTitles);

  public static void main(String[] args) {
    ComboBoxDemo frame = new ComboBoxDemo();
    frame.pack();
    frame.setTitle("ComboBoxDemo");
    frame.setLocationRelativeTo(null); // Center the frame
    frame.setDefaultCloseOperation(JFrame.EXIT_ON_CLOSE);
    frame.setVisible(true);
  }

  public ComboBoxDemo() {
    // Set text description
    flagDescription[0] = "The Canadian national flag...";
    flagDescription[1] = "Description for China ... ";
    flagDescription[2] = "Description for Denmark ... ";
    flagDescription[3] = "Description for France ... ";
    flagDescription[4] = "Description for Germany ... ";
    flagDescription[5] = "Description for India ... ";
    flagDescription[6] = "Description for Norway ... ";
    flagDescription[7] = "Description for UK ... ";
    flagDescription[8] = "Description for US ... ";

    // Set the first country (Canada) for display
    setDisplay(0);

    // Add combo box and description panel to the frame
    add(jcbo, BorderLayout.NORTH);
```

country

image icon

description

combo box

create UI

```
59      add(descriptionPanel, BorderLayout.CENTER);
60
61      // Register listener
62      jcbo.addItemListener(new ItemListener() {
63        @Override /** Handle item selection */
64        public void itemStateChanged(ItemEvent e) {
65          setDisplay(jcbo.getSelectedIndex());
66        }
67      });
68    }
69
70    /** Set display information on the description panel */
71    public void setDisplay(int index) {
72      descriptionPanel.setTitle(flagTitles[index]);
73      descriptionPanel.setImageIcon(flagImage[index]);
74      descriptionPanel.setDescription(flagDescription[index]);
75    }
76  }
```

listener

The listener listens to **ItemEvent** from the combo box and implements **ItemListener** (lines 62–67). Instead of using **ItemEvent**, you could rewrite the program to use **ActionEvent** for handling combo-box item selection.

The program stores the flag information in three arrays: **flagTitles**, **flagImage**, and **flagDescription** (lines 7–25). The array **flagTitles** contains the names of nine countries, the array **flagImage** contains images of the nine countries' flags, and the array **flagDescription** contains descriptions of the flags.

The program creates an instance of **DescriptionPanel** (line 28), which was presented in Listing 17.2, DescriptionPanel.java. The program creates a combo box with initial values from **flagTitles** (line 31). When the user selects an item in the combo box, the **itemStateChanged** handler is executed. The handler finds the selected index and sets its corresponding flag title, flag image, and flag description on the panel.

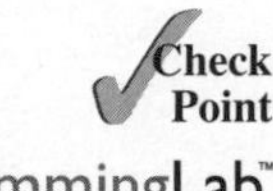

MyProgrammingLab™

17.9 How do you create a combo box and add three items to it?

17.10 How do you retrieve an item from a combo box? How do you retrieve a selected item from a combo box?

17.11 How do you get the number of items in a combo box? How do you retrieve an item at a specified index in a combo box?

17.12 What events would a **JComboBox** fire upon selecting a new item?

17.5 Lists

A list *is a component that basically performs the same function as a combo box, but it enables the user to choose a single value or multiple values.*

The Swing **JList** is very versatile. Figure 17.7 lists several frequently used constructors and methods in **JList**.

selectionMode is one of the three values (**SINGLE_SELECTION**, **SINGLE_INTERVAL_SELECTION**, and **MULTIPLE_INTERVAL_SELECTION**) defined in **javax.swing.ListSelectionModel** that indicate whether a single item, single-interval item, or multiple-interval item can be selected. Single selection allows only one item to be selected. Single-interval selection allows multiple selections, but the selected items must be contiguous. Multiple-interval selection allows selections of multiple contiguous items without restrictions, as shown in Figure 17.8. The default value is **MULTIPLE_INTERVAL_SELECTION**.

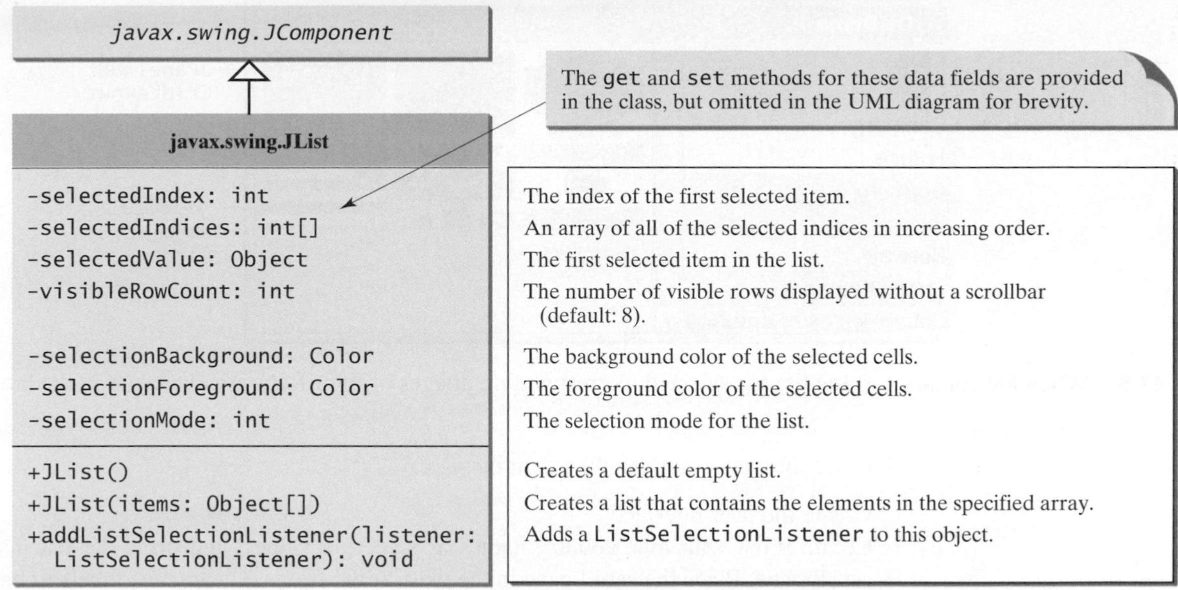

FIGURE 17.7 `JList` enables you to select multiple items from a set of items.

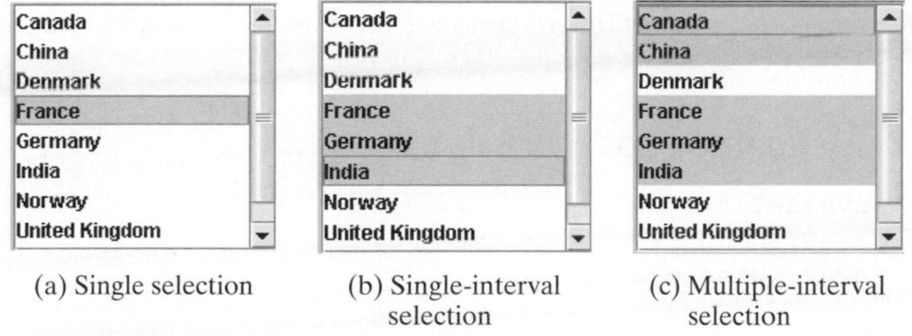

FIGURE 17.8 `JList` has three selection modes: single selection, single-interval selection, and multiple-interval selection.

The following statements create a list with six items, `red` foreground, `white` background, `pink` selection foreground, `black` selection background, and visible row count `4`.

```
JList jlst = new JList(new String[]
  {"Item 1", "Item 2", "Item 3", "Item 4", "Item 5", "Item 6"});
jlst.setForeground(Color.RED);
jlst.setBackground(Color.WHITE);
jlst.setSelectionForeground(Color.PINK);
jlst.setSelectionBackground(Color.BLACK);
jlst.setVisibleRowCount(4);
```

Lists do not scroll automatically. To make a list scrollable, create a scroll pane and add the list to it.

`JList` fires `javax.swing.event.ListSelectionEvent` to notify the listeners of the selections. The listener must implement the `valueChanged` handler in the `javax.swing.event.ListSelectionListener` interface to process the event.

Listing 17.5 gives a program that lets users select countries in a list and displays the flags of the selected countries in the labels. Figure 17.9 shows a sample run of the program.

FIGURE 17.9 When the countries in the list are selected, corresponding images of their flags are displayed in the labels.

Here are the major steps in the program:

1. Create the user interface.
   Create a list with nine country names as selection values, and place the list inside a scroll pane. Place the scroll pane in the west of the frame. Create nine labels to be used to display the countries' flag images. Place the labels in the panel, and place the panel in the center of the frame.

2. Process the event.
   Create a listener to implement the `valueChanged` method in the `ListSelectionListener` interface to set the selected countries' flag images in the labels.

LISTING 17.5 `ListDemo.java`

```
import java.awt.*;
import javax.swing.*;
import javax.swing.event.*;

public class ListDemo extends JFrame {
  final int NUMBER_OF_FLAGS = 9;

  // Declare an array of Strings for flag titles
  private String[] flagTitles = {"Canada", "China", "Denmark",
    "France", "Germany", "India", "Norway", "United Kingdom",
    "United States of America"};

  // The list for selecting countries
  private JList jlst = new JList(flagTitles);

  // Declare an ImageIcon array for the national flags of 9 countries
  private ImageIcon[] imageIcons = {
    new ImageIcon("image/ca.gif"),
    new ImageIcon("image/china.gif"),
    new ImageIcon("image/denmark.gif"),
    new ImageIcon("image/fr.gif"),
    new ImageIcon("image/germany.gif"),
    new ImageIcon("image/india.gif"),
    new ImageIcon("image/norway.gif"),
    new ImageIcon("image/uk.gif"),
    new ImageIcon("image/us.gif")
  };

```

```
29    // Arrays of labels for displaying images
30    private JLabel[] jlblImageViewer = new JLabel[NUMBER_OF_FLAGS];
31
32    public static void main(String[] args) {
33      ListDemo frame = new ListDemo();
34      frame.setSize(650, 500);
35      frame.setTitle("ListDemo");
36      frame.setLocationRelativeTo(null); // Center the frame
37      frame.setDefaultCloseOperation(JFrame.EXIT_ON_CLOSE);
38      frame.setVisible(true);
39    }
40
41    public ListDemo() {
42      // Create a panel to hold nine labels
43      JPanel p = new JPanel(new GridLayout(3, 3, 5, 5));
44
45      for (int i = 0; i < NUMBER_OF_FLAGS; i++) {
46        p.add(jlblImageViewer[i] = new JLabel());
47        jlblImageViewer[i].setHorizontalAlignment
48          (SwingConstants.CENTER);
49      }
50
51      // Add p and the list to the frame
52      add(p, BorderLayout.CENTER);
53      add(new JScrollPane(jlst), BorderLayout.WEST);
54
55      // Register listeners
56      jlst.addListSelectionListener(new ListSelectionListener() {
57        @Override /** Handle list selection */
58        public void valueChanged(ListSelectionEvent e) {
59          // Get selected indices
60          int[] indices = jlst.getSelectedIndices();
61
62          int i;
63          // Set icons in the labels
64          for (i = 0; i < indices.length; i++) {
65            jlblImageViewer[i].setIcon(imageIcons[indices[i]]);
66          }
67
68          // Remove icons from the rest of the labels
69          for (; i < NUMBER_OF_FLAGS; i++) {
70            jlblImageViewer[i].setIcon(null);
71          }
72        }
73      });
74    }
75  }
```

create frame

create UI

event handler

The anonymous inner-class listener listens to **ListSelectionEvent** for handling the selection of country names in the list (lines 56–73). **ListSelectionEvent** and **ListSelectionListener** are defined in the **javax.swing.event** package, so this package is imported into the program (line 3).

The program creates an array of nine labels for displaying flag images for nine countries. The program loads the images of the nine countries into an image array (lines 17–27) and creates a list of the nine countries in the same order as in the title array (lines 9–11). Thus, the index **0** of the image array corresponds to the first country in the list.

The list is placed in a scroll pane (line 53) so that it can be scrolled when the number of items in the list extends beyond the viewing area.

By default, the selection mode of the list is multiple-interval, which allows the user to select multiple items from different blocks in the list. When the user selects countries in the list, the `valueChanged` handler (lines 58–72) is executed, which gets the indices of the selected items and sets their corresponding image icons in the label to display the flags.

Check Point
MyProgrammingLab™

17.13 How do you create a list with an array of strings?

17.14 How do you set the visible row count in a list?

17.15 What selection modes are available for a list? How do you set a selection mode?

17.16 How do you set the foreground and background color of a list? How do you set the foreground and background color of the selected items?

17.6 Scroll Bars

Key Point

`JScrollBar` *is a component that enables the user to select from a range of values.*

Figure 17.10 shows a scroll bar. Normally, the user changes the value of the scroll bar by making a gesture with the mouse. For example, the user can drag the scroll bar's bubble up and down, or click in the scroll bar's unit-increment or block-increment areas. Keyboard gestures can also be mapped to the scroll bar. By convention, the *Page Up* and *Page Down* keys are equivalent to clicking in the scroll bar's block-increment and block-decrement areas.

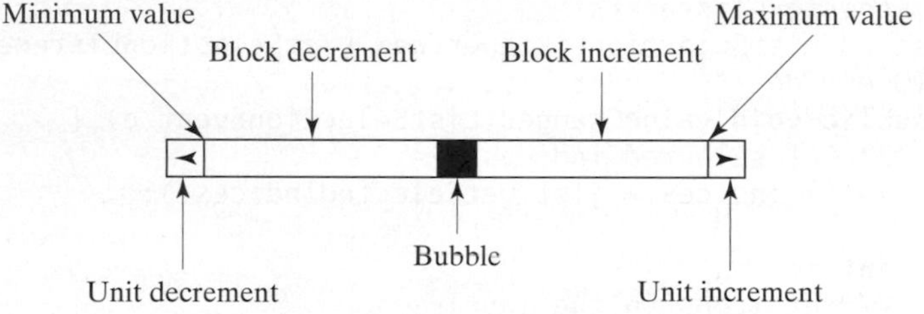

FIGURE 17.10 A scroll bar represents a range of values graphically.

Note

The width of the scroll bar's track corresponds to `maximum + visibleAmount`. When a scroll bar is set to its maximum value, the left side of the bubble is at `maximum`, and the right side is at `maximum + visibleAmount`.

`JScrollBar` has the following properties, as shown in Figure 17.11.

When the user changes the value of the scroll bar, the scroll bar fires an `AdjustmentEvent`. A listener class for this event must implement the `adjustmentValueChanged` handler in the `java.awt.event.AdjustmentListener` interface.

Listing 17.6 gives a program that uses horizontal and vertical scroll bars to control a message displayed on a panel. The horizontal scroll bar is used to move the message to the left and the right, and the vertical scroll bar to move it up and down. A sample run of the program is shown in Figure 17.12.

Here are the major steps in the program:

1. Create the user interface.
   Create a `MessagePanel` object and place it in the center of the frame. Create a vertical scroll bar and place it in the east of the frame. Create a horizontal scroll bar and place it in the south of the frame.

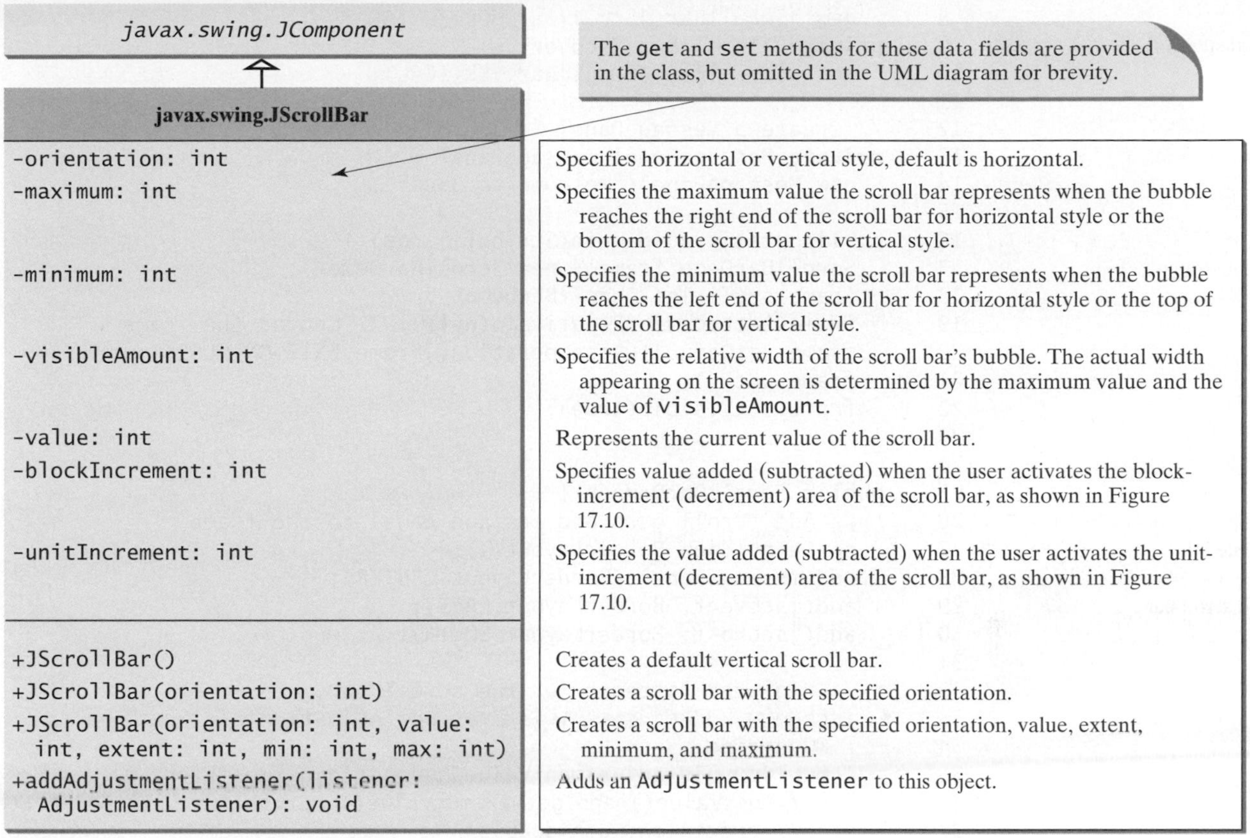

javax.swing.JComponent	
javax.swing.JScrollBar	The `get` and `set` methods for these data fields are provided in the class, but omitted in the UML diagram for brevity.
`-orientation: int`	Specifies horizontal or vertical style, default is horizontal.
`-maximum: int`	Specifies the maximum value the scroll bar represents when the bubble reaches the right end of the scroll bar for horizontal style or the bottom of the scroll bar for vertical style.
`-minimum: int`	Specifies the minimum value the scroll bar represents when the bubble reaches the left end of the scroll bar for horizontal style or the top of the scroll bar for vertical style.
`-visibleAmount: int`	Specifies the relative width of the scroll bar's bubble. The actual width appearing on the screen is determined by the maximum value and the value of `visibleAmount`.
`-value: int`	Represents the current value of the scroll bar.
`-blockIncrement: int`	Specifies value added (subtracted) when the user activates the block-increment (decrement) area of the scroll bar, as shown in Figure 17.10.
`-unitIncrement: int`	Specifies the value added (subtracted) when the user activates the unit-increment (decrement) area of the scroll bar, as shown in Figure 17.10.
`+JScrollBar()`	Creates a default vertical scroll bar.
`+JScrollBar(orientation: int)`	Creates a scroll bar with the specified orientation.
`+JScrollBar(orientation: int, value: int, extent: int, min: int, max: int)`	Creates a scroll bar with the specified orientation, value, extent, minimum, and maximum.
`+addAdjustmentListener(listener: AdjustmentListener): void`	Adds an `AdjustmentListener` to this object.

FIGURE 17.11 `JScrollBar` enables you to select from a range of values.

FIGURE 17.12 The scroll bars move the message on a panel horizontally and vertically.

2. Process the event.
   Create listeners to implement the **`adjustmentValueChanged`** handler to move the message according to the bar movement in the scroll bars.

LISTING 17.6 ScrollBarDemo.java

```
import java.awt.*;
import java.awt.event.*;
import javax.swing.*;

public class ScrollBarDemo extends JFrame {
  // Create horizontal and vertical scroll bars
  private JScrollBar jscbHort =
```

horizontal scroll bar

vertical scroll bar

create frame

create UI

add scroll bar

adjustment listener

adjustment listener

```
8       new JScrollBar(JScrollBar.HORIZONTAL);
9     private JScrollBar jscbVert =
10      new JScrollBar(JScrollBar.VERTICAL);
11
12    // Create a MessagePanel
13    private MessagePanel messagePanel =
14      new MessagePanel("Welcome to Java");
15
16    public static void main(String[] args) {
17      ScrollBarDemo frame = new ScrollBarDemo();
18      frame.setTitle("ScrollBarDemo");
19      frame.setLocationRelativeTo(null); // Center the frame
20      frame.setDefaultCloseOperation(JFrame.EXIT_ON_CLOSE);
21      frame.pack();
22      frame.setVisible(true);
23    }
24
25    public ScrollBarDemo() {
26      // Add scroll bars and message panel to the frame
27      setLayout(new BorderLayout());
28      add(messagePanel, BorderLayout.CENTER);
29      add(jscbVert, BorderLayout.EAST);
30      add(jscbHort, BorderLayout.SOUTH);
31
32      // Register listener for the scroll bars
33      jscbHort.addAdjustmentListener(new AdjustmentListener() {
34        @Override
35        public void adjustmentValueChanged(AdjustmentEvent e) {
36          // getValue() and getMaximumValue() return int, but for better
37          // precision, use double
38          double value = jscbHort.getValue();
39          double maximumValue = jscbHort.getMaximum();
40          double newX = (value * messagePanel.getWidth() /
41            maximumValue);
42          messagePanel.setXCoordinate((int)newX);
43        }
44      });
45      jscbVert.addAdjustmentListener(new AdjustmentListener() {
46        @Override
47        public void adjustmentValueChanged(AdjustmentEvent e) {
48          // getValue() and getMaximum() return int, but for better
49          // precision, use double
50          double value = jscbVert.getValue();
51          double maximumValue = jscbVert.getMaximum();
52          double newY = (value * messagePanel.getHeight() /
53            maximumValue);
54          messagePanel.setYCoordinate((int)newY);
55        }
56      });
57    }
58  }
```

The program creates two scroll bars (**jscbVert** and **jscbHort**) (lines 7–10) and an instance of **MessagePanel** (**messagePanel**) (lines 13–14). **messagePanel** is placed in the center of the frame (line 28); **jscbVert** and **jscbHort** are placed in the east and south sections of the frame (lines 29–30), respectively.

You can specify the orientation of the scroll bar in the constructor or use the **setOrientation** method. By default, the property value is **100** for **maximum**, **0** for **minimum**, **10** for **blockIncrement**, and **10** for **visibleAmount**.

When the user drags the bubble, or clicks the increment or decrement unit, the value of the scroll bar changes. An instance of `AdjustmentEvent` is fired and passed to the listener by invoking the `adjustmentValueChanged` handler. The listener for the vertical scroll bar moves the message up and down (lines 33–44), and the listener for the horizontal bar moves the message to the right and left (lines 45–56).

The maximum value of the vertical scroll bar corresponds to the height of the panel, and the maximum value of the horizontal scroll bar corresponds to the width of the panel. The ratio between the current and maximum values of the horizontal scroll bar is the same as the ratio between the `x` value and the width of the message panel. Similarly, the ratio between the current and maximum values of the vertical scroll bar is the same as the ratio between the `y` value and the height of the message panel. The *x*-coordinate and *y*-coordinate are set in response to the scroll bar adjustments (lines 39, 50).

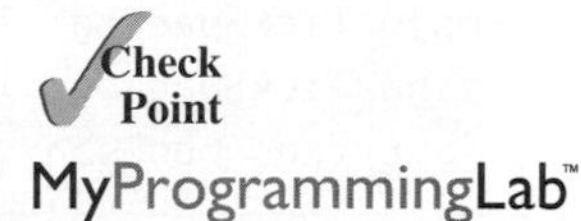

17.17 How do you create a horizontal scroll bar? How do you create a vertical scroll bar?

17.18 What event can a scroll bar fire when the user changes the value on a scroll bar? What is the corresponding interface for the event? What is the handler defined in the interface?

17.19 How do you get the value from a scroll bar? How do you get the maximum value from a scroll bar?

17.7 Sliders

`JSlider` is similar to `JScrollBar`, but `JSlider` has more properties and can appear in many forms.

Figure 17.13 shows two sliders. `JSlider` lets the user graphically select a value by sliding a knob within a bounded interval. The slider can show both major tick marks and minor tick marks between them. The number of pixels between the tick marks is controlled by the `majorTickSpacing` and `minorTickSpacing` properties. Sliders can be displayed horizontally and/or vertically, with or without ticks, and with or without labels.

FIGURE 17.13 The sliders move the message on a panel horizontally and vertically.

The frequently used constructors and properties in `JSlider` are shown in Figure 17.14.

Note

The values of a vertical scroll bar increase from top to bottom, but the values of a vertical slider decrease from top to bottom by default.

Note

All the properties listed in Figure 17.14 have the associated `get` and `set` methods, but they are omitted for brevity. By convention, the `get` method for a Boolean property is named *`is<PropertyName>()`*. In the `JSlider` class, the `get` methods for

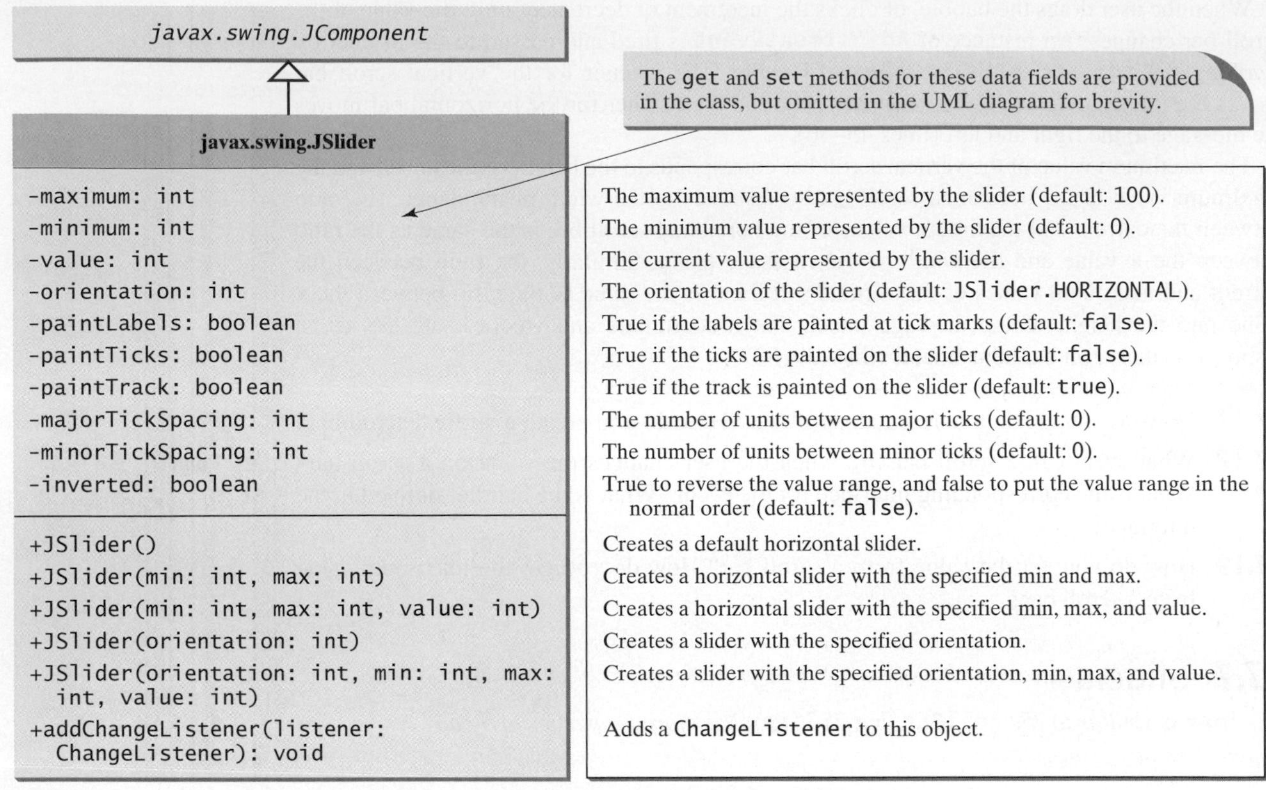

FIGURE 17.14 `JSlider` enables you to select from a range of values.

`paintLabels`, `paintTicks`, `paintTrack`, and `inverted` are `getPaintLabels()`, `getPaintTicks()`, `getPaintTrack()`, and `getInverted()`, which violate the naming convention.

When the user changes the value of the slider, the slider fires an instance of `javax.swing.event.ChangeEvent`, which is passed to any registered listeners. Any object that should be notified of changes to the slider's value must implement the `stateChanged` method in the `ChangeListener` interface defined in the package `javax.swing.event`.

The program in Listing 17.7 uses the sliders to control a message displayed on a panel, as shown in Figure 17.14. Here are the major steps in the program:

1. Create the user interface.
   Create a `MessagePanel` object and place it in the center of the frame. Create a vertical slider and place it in the east of the frame. Create a horizontal slider and place it in the south of the frame.

2. Process the event.
   Create listeners to implement the `stateChanged` handler in the `ChangeListener` interface to move the message according to the knot movement in the slider.

LISTING 17.7 `SliderDemo.java`

```
import java.awt.*;
import javax.swing.*;
import javax.swing.event.*;
```

```
public class SliderDemo extends JFrame {
  // Create horizontal and vertical sliders
  private JSlider jsldHort = new JSlider(JSlider.HORIZONTAL);
  private JSlider jsldVert = new JSlider(JSlider.VERTICAL);

  // Create a MessagePanel
  private MessagePanel messagePanel =
    new MessagePanel("Welcome to Java");

  public static void main(String[] args) {
    SliderDemo frame = new SliderDemo();
    frame.setTitle("SliderDemo");
    frame.setLocationRelativeTo(null); // Center the frame
    frame.setDefaultCloseOperation(JFrame.EXIT_ON_CLOSE);
    frame.pack();
    frame.setVisible(true);
  }

  public SliderDemo() {
    // Add sliders and message panel to the frame
    setLayout(new BorderLayout(5, 5));
    add(messagePanel, BorderLayout.CENTER);
    add(jsldVert, BorderLayout.EAST);
    add(jsldHort, BorderLayout.SOUTH);

    // Set properties for sliders
    jsldHort.setMaximum(50);
    jsldHort.setPaintLabels(true);
    jsldHort.setPaintTicks(true);
    jsldHort.setMajorTickSpacing(10);
    jsldHort.setMinorTickSpacing(1);
    jsldHort.setPaintTrack(false);
    jsldVert.setInverted(true);
    jsldVert.setMaximum(10);
    jsldVert.setPaintLabels(true);
    jsldVert.setPaintTicks(true);
    jsldVert.setMajorTickSpacing(10);
    jsldVert.setMinorTickSpacing(1);

    // Register listener for the sliders
    jsldHort.addChangeListener(new ChangeListener() {
      @Override /** Handle scroll-bar adjustment actions */
      public void stateChanged(ChangeEvent e) {
        // getValue() and getMaximumValue() return int, but for better
        // precision, use double
        double value = jsldHort.getValue();
        double maximumValue = jsldHort.getMaximum();
        double newX = (value * messagePanel.getWidth() /
          maximumValue);
        messagePanel.setXCoordinate((int)newX);
      }
    });
    jsldVert.addChangeListener(new ChangeListener() {
      @Override /** Handle scroll-bar adjustment actions */
      public void stateChanged(ChangeEvent e) {
        // getValue() and getMaximum() return int, but for better
        // precision, use double
        double value = jsldVert.getValue();
        double maximumValue = jsldVert.getMaximum();
```

horizontal slider
vertical slider
create frame
create UI
slider properties
listener
listener

```
64          double newY = (value * messagePanel.getHeight() /
65            maximumValue);
66          messagePanel.setYCoordinate((int)newY);
67        }
68      });
69    }
70  }
```

JSlider is similar to JScrollBar but has more features. As shown in this example, you can specify maximum, labels, major ticks, and minor ticks on a JSlider (lines 31–35). You can also choose to hide the track (line 36). Since the default values of a vertical slider decrease from top to bottom, the setInverted method reverses the order (line 37).

JSlider fires ChangeEvent when the slider is changed. The listener needs to implement the stateChanged handler in ChangeListener (lines 45–68). Note that JScrollBar fires AdjustmentEvent when the scroll bar is adjusted.

17.20 How do you create a horizontal slider? How do you create a vertical slider?

17.21 What event can a slider fire when the user changes the value on a slider? What is the corresponding interface for the event? What is the handler defined in the interface?

17.22 How do you get the value from a slider? How do you get the maximum value from a slider?

17.8 Creating Multiple Windows

Multiple windows can be created in one program.

Occasionally, you may want to create multiple windows in an application so that the application can open a new window to perform a specified task. The new windows are called *subwindows*, and the main frame is called the *main window*.

Listing 17.8 gives a program that creates a main window with a text area in the scroll pane and a button named *Show Histogram*. When the user clicks the button, a new window appears that displays a histogram to show the occurrences of the letters in the text area. Figure 17.15 contains a sample run of the program.

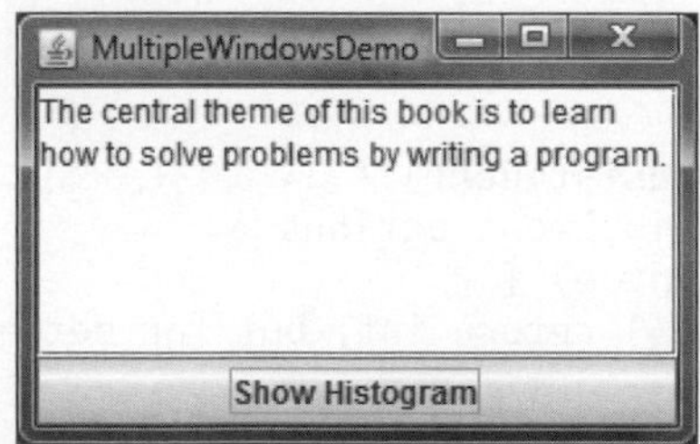

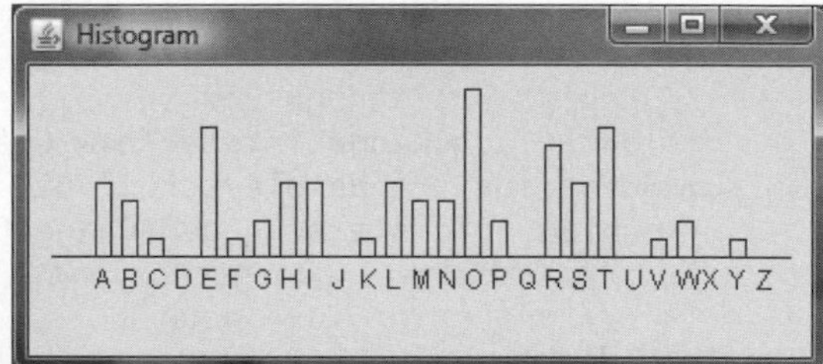

Figure 17.15 The histogram is displayed in a separate frame.

Here are the major steps in the program:

1. Define a main class for the frame named MultipleWindowsDemo in Listing 17.8. Add a text area inside a scroll pane, and place the scroll pane in the center of the frame. Create a button *Show Histogram* and place it in the south of the frame.

2. Define a subclass of JPanel named Histogram in Listing 17.9. The class contains a data field named count of the int[] type, which counts the occurrences of 26 letters. The values in count are displayed in the histogram.

3. Implement the `actionPerformed` handler in `MultipleWindowsDemo`, as follows:

   a. Create an instance of `Histogram`. Count the letters in the text area and set the count in the `Histogram` object.

   b. Create a new frame and place the `Histogram` object in the center of frame. Display the frame.

LISTING 17.8 `MultipleWindowsDemo.java`

```java
import java.awt.*;
import java.awt.event.*;
import javax.swing.*;

public class MultipleWindowsDemo extends JFrame {
  private JTextArea jta;
  private JButton jbtShowHistogram = new JButton("Show Histogram");
  private Histogram histogram = new Histogram();

  // Create a new frame to hold the histogram panel
  private JFrame histogramFrame = new JFrame();

  public MultipleWindowsDemo() {
    // Store text area in a scroll pane
    JScrollPane scrollPane = new JScrollPane(jta = new JTextArea());
    scrollPane.setPreferredSize(new Dimension(300, 200));
    jta.setWrapStyleWord(true);
    jta.setLineWrap(true);

    // Place scroll pane and button in the frame
    add(scrollPane, BorderLayout.CENTER);
    add(jbtShowHistogram, BorderLayout.SOUTH);

    // Register listener
    jbtShowHistogram.addActionListener(new ActionListener() {
      @Override /** Handle the button action */
      public void actionPerformed(ActionEvent e) {
        // Count the letters in the text area
        int[] count = countLetters();

        // Set the letter count to histogram for display
        histogram.showHistogram(count);

        // Show the frame
        histogramFrame.setVisible(true);
      }
    });

    // Add the histogram panel to the frame
    histogramFrame.add(histogram);
    histogramFrame.pack();
    histogramFrame.setTitle("Histogram");
  }

  /** Count the letters in the text area */
  private int[] countLetters() {
    // Count for 26 letters
    int[] count = new int[26];

    // Get contents from the text area
```

create subframe

create UI

display subframe

```
    String text = jta.getText();

    // Count occurrences of each letter (case insensitive)
    for (int i = 0; i < text.length(); i++) {
      char character = text.charAt(i);

      if (character >= 'A' && character <= 'Z') {
        count[character - 'A']++;
      }
      else if (character >= 'a' && character <= 'z') {
        count[character - 'a']++;
      }
    }

    return count; // Return the count array
  }

  public static void main(String[] args) {
    MultipleWindowsDemo frame = new MultipleWindowsDemo();
    frame.setLocationRelativeTo(null); // Center the frame
    frame.setDefaultCloseOperation(JFrame.EXIT_ON_CLOSE);
    frame.setTitle("MultipleWindowsDemo");
    frame.pack();
    frame.setVisible(true);
  }
}
```

create main frame

Listing 17.9 Histogram.java

```
import javax.swing.*;
import java.awt.*;

public class Histogram extends JPanel {
  // Count the occurrences of 26 letters
  private int[] count;

  /** Set the count and display histogram */
  public void showHistogram(int[] count) {
    this.count = count;
    repaint();
  }

  @Override /** Paint the histogram */
  protected void paintComponent(Graphics g) {
    if (count == null) return; // No display if count is null

    super.paintComponent(g);

    // Find the panel size and bar width and interval dynamically
    int width = getWidth();
    int height = getHeight();
    int interval = (width - 40) / count.length;
    int individualWidth = (int)(((width - 40) / 24) * 0.60);

    // Find the maximum count. The maximum count has the highest bar
    int maxCount = 0;
    for (int i = 0; i < count.length; i++) {
      if (maxCount < count[i])
        maxCount = count[i];
    }
```

paint histogram

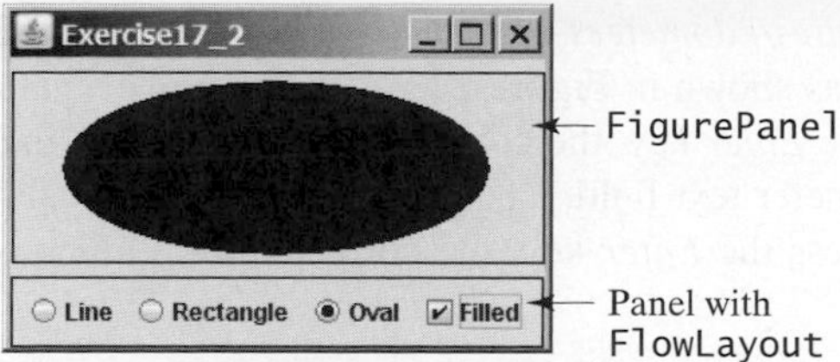

FIGURE 17.18 The program displays lines, rectangles, and ovals when you select a shape type.

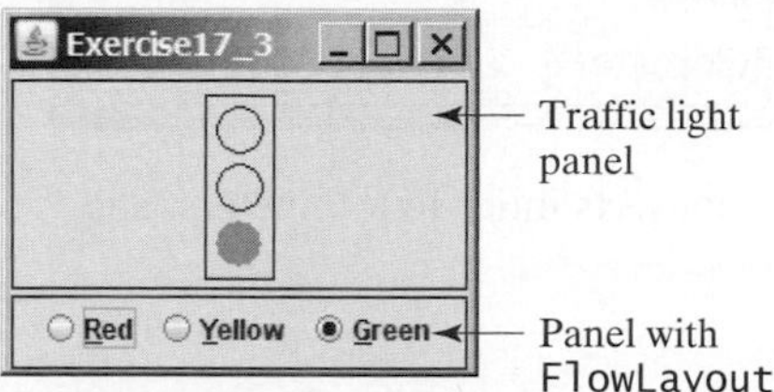

FIGURE 17.19 The radio buttons are grouped to let you select only one color in the group to control a traffic light.

Sections 17.6–17.8

****17.4** (*Text viewer*) Write a program that displays a text file in a text area, as shown in Figure 17.20a. The user enters a file name in a text field and clicks the *View* button; the file is then displayed in a text area.

FIGURE 17.20 (a) The program displays the text from a file in a text area. (b) The program displays a histogram that shows the occurrences of each letter in the file.

****17.5** (*Create a histogram* for *occurrences of letters*) The program in Listing 17.8, MultipleWindowsDemo.java, displays a histogram to show the occurrences of each letter in a text area. Reuse the `Histogram` class created in Listing 17.9 to write a program that will display a histogram on a panel. The histogram should show the occurrences of each letter in a text file, as shown in Figure 17.20b. Assume that the letters are not case sensitive.

- Place the panel that will display the histogram in the center of the frame.
- Place a label and a text field in a panel, and put the panel in the south side of the frame. The text file will be entered from this text field.
- Pressing the *Enter* key on the text field causes the program to count the occurrences of each letter and display the count in a histogram.

*17.6 (*Create a miles/kilometers converter*) Write a program that converts miles and kilometers, as shown in Figure 17.21. If you enter a value in the Mile text field and press the *Enter* key, the corresponding kilometer measurement is displayed in the Kilometer text field. Likewise, if you enter a value in the Kilometer text field and press the *Enter* key, the corresponding miles is displayed in the Mile text field.

FIGURE 17.21 The program converts miles to kilometers, and vice versa.

*17.7 (*Set clock time*) Write a program that displays a clock and sets the time with the input from three text fields, as shown in Figure 17.22. Use the `StillClock` in Listing 13.10.

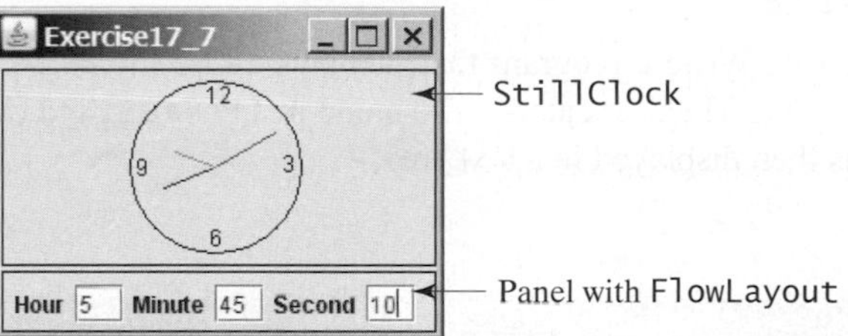

FIGURE 17.22 The program displays the time specified in the text fields.

**17.8 (*Select a font*) Write a program that can dynamically change the font of a message to be displayed on a panel. The message can be displayed in bold and italic at the same time, and/or it can be displayed in the center of the panel. You can select the font name or font size from combo boxes, as shown in Figure 17.23. The available font names can be obtained using `getAvailableFontFamilyNames()` in `GraphicsEnvironment` (see Section 12.8, The `Font` Class). The combo box for the font size is initialized with numbers from `1` to `100`.

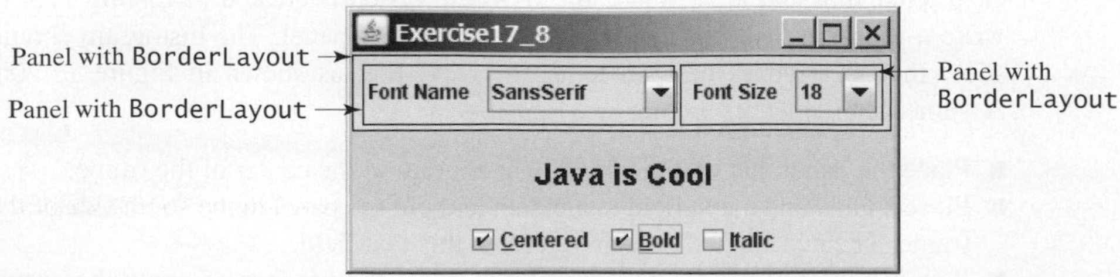

FIGURE 17.23 You can dynamically set the font for the message.

****17.9** (*Demonstrate `JLabel` properties*) Write a program to let the user dynamically set the properties `horizontalAlignment`, `verticalAlignment`, `horizontalTextAlignment`, and `verticalTextAlignment`, as shown in Figure 17.24.

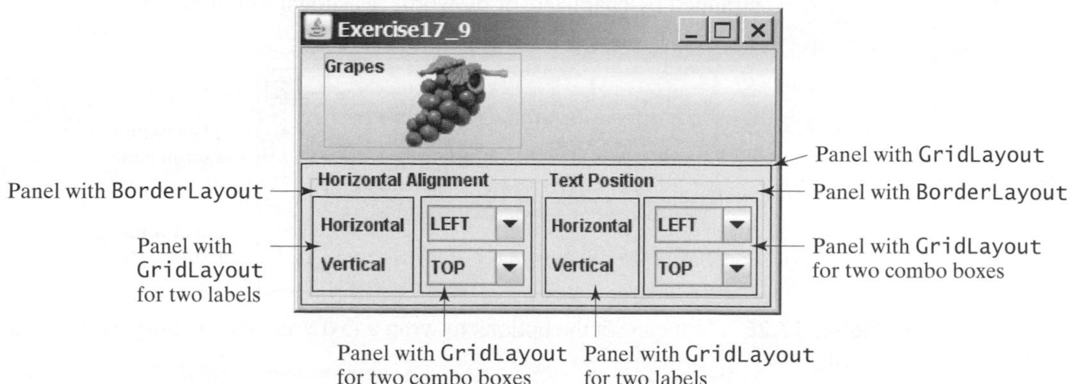

FIGURE 17.24 You can set the alignment and text-position properties of a label dynamically.

***17.10** (*Mandelbrot fractal*) Programming Exercise 15.20 displays Mandelbrot fractal. Note that the values `77`, `58`, and `159` in line 15 in the `MandelbrotCanvas` class in Programming Exercise 15.20 impact the color of the image. Revise the program to let the user enter these values from text fields dynamically, as shown in Figure 17.25a.

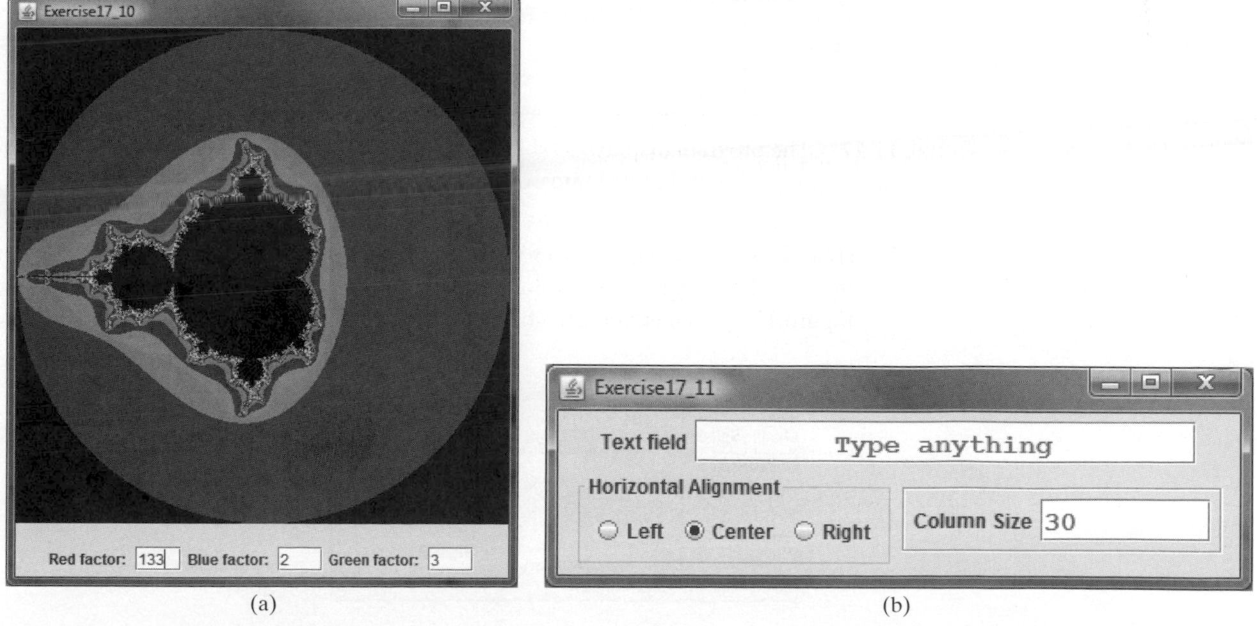

FIGURE 17.25 (a) The program enables the user to set the colors dynamically. (b) You can set a text field's properties for the horizontal alignment and column size dynamically.

***17.11** (*Demonstrate `JTextField` properties*) Write a program that sets the horizontal-alignment and column-size properties of a text field dynamically, as shown in Figure 17.25b.

VideoNote
Use text areas

***17.12** (*Demonstrate `JTextArea` properties*) Write a program that demonstrates the wrapping styles of the text area. The program uses a check box to indicate whether the text area is wrapped. If the text area is wrapped, you can specify whether it is wrapped by characters or by words, as shown in Figure 17.26.

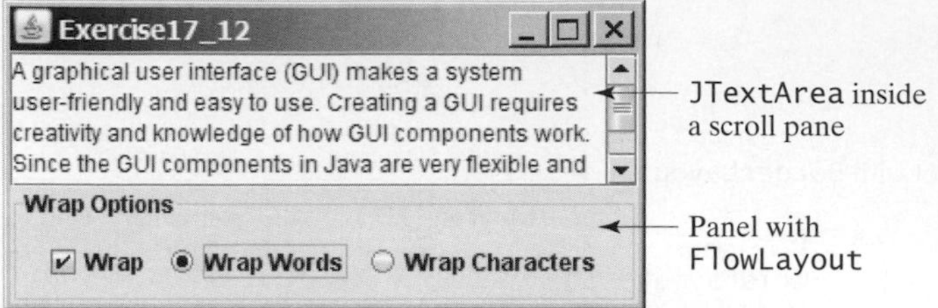

FIGURE 17.26 You can set the options to wrap a text area dynamically by characters or by words.

***17.13** (*Compare loans with various interest rates*) Rewrite Programming Exercise 4.21 to create a user interface, as shown in Figure 17.27. Your program should let the user enter the loan amount and loan period in the number of years from a text field, and it should display the monthly and total payments for each interest rate starting from 5 percent to 8 percent, with increments of one-eighth, in a text area.

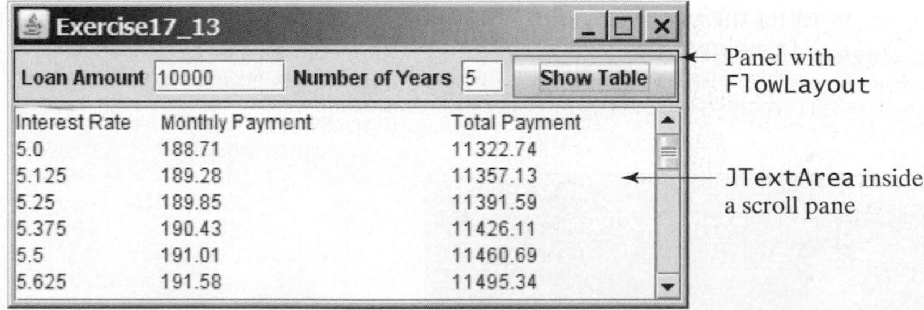

FIGURE 17.27 The program displays a table for monthly payments and total payments on a given loan based on various interest rates.

***17.14** (*Use `JComboBox` and `JList`*) Write a program that demonstrates selecting items in a list. The program uses a combo box to specify a selection mode, as shown in Figure 17.28. When you select items, they are displayed in a label below the list.

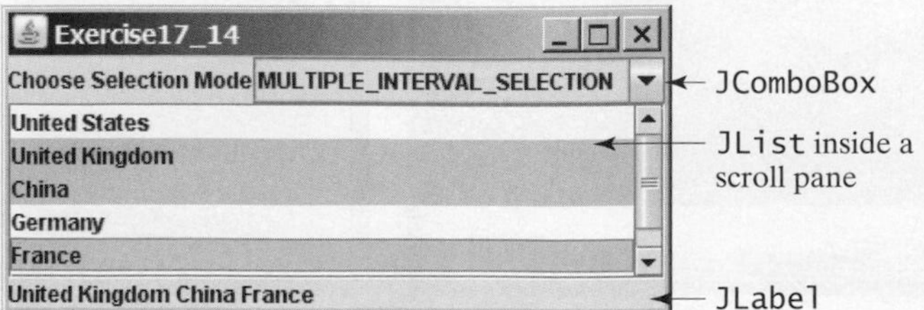

FIGURE 17.28 You can choose single selection, single-interval selection, or multiple-interval selection in a list.

Sections 17.6–17.8

****17.15** (*Use `JScrollBar`*) Write a program that uses scroll bars to select the foreground color for a label, as shown in Figure 17.29. Three horizontal scroll bars are used for selecting the color's red, green, and blue components. Use a title border on the panel that holds the scroll bars.

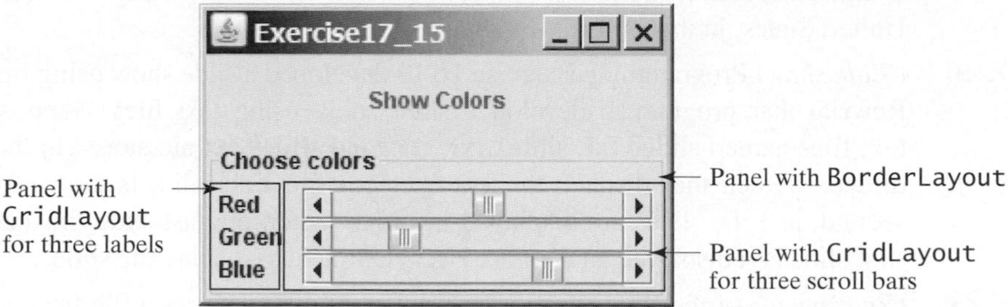

FIGURE 17.29 The foreground color changes in the label as you adjust the scroll bars.

****17.16** (*Use `JSlider`*) Revise the preceding exercise using sliders.

*****17.17** (*Display a calendar*) Write a program that displays the calendar for the current month. You can use the *Prior* and *Next* buttons to show the calendar of the previous or next month. Display the dates in the current month in black and display the dates in the previous month and next month in gray, as shown in Figure 17.30.

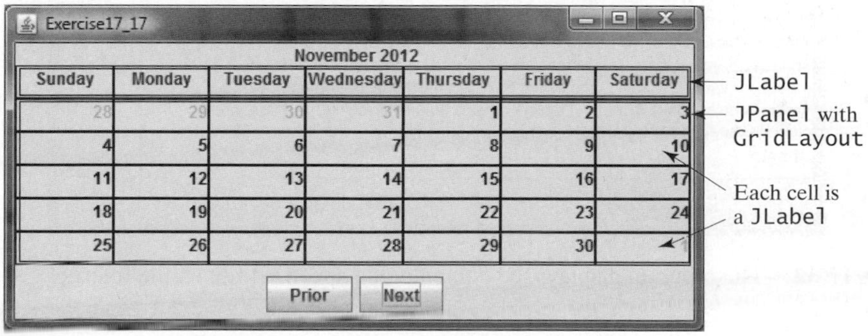

FIGURE 17.30 The program displays the calendar for the current month.

***17.18** (*Revise Listing 17.8, MultipleWindowsDemo.java*) Instead of displaying the occurrences of the letters using the `Histogram` component in Listing 17.8, use a bar chart, so that the display is as shown in Figure 17.31.

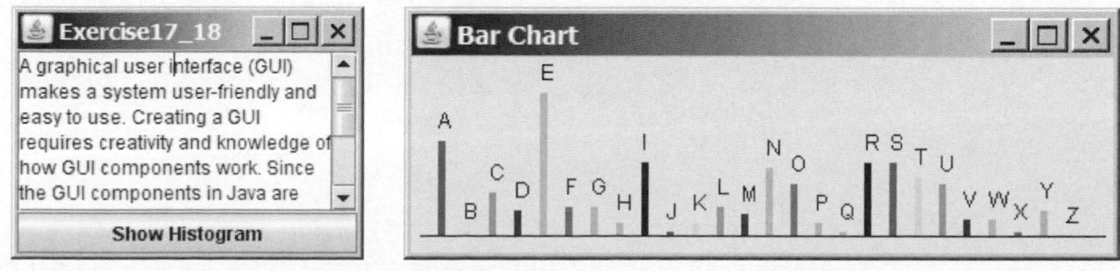

FIGURE 17.31 The number of occurrences of each letter is displayed in a bar chart.

17.19 (*Display country flag and flag description*) Listing 17.4, ComboBoxDemo.java, gives a program that lets users view a country's flag image and description by selecting the country from a combo box. The description is a string coded in the program. Rewrite the program to read the text description from a file. Suppose that the descriptions are stored in the files **description0.txt, . . ., and **description8.txt** under the **text** directory for the nine countries Canada, China, Denmark, France, Germany, India, Norway, the United Kingdom, and the United States, in this order.

17.20 (*Slide show*) Programming Exercise 16.13 developed a slide show using images. Rewrite that program to develop a slide show using text files. Suppose ten text files named **slide0.txt, **slide1.txt**, . . ., and **slide9.txt** are stored in the **text** directory. Each slide displays the text from one file. Each slide is shown for one second, and the slides are displayed in order. When the last slide finishes, the first slide is redisplayed, and so on. Use a text area to display the slide.

**17.21 (*Retrieve files from Web*) Write a Java program that retrieves a file from a Web server, as shown in Figure 17.32. The user interface includes a text field in which to enter the URL of the file name, a text area in which to show the file, and a button that can be used to submit an action. A label is added at the bottom of the applet to indicate the status, such as *File loaded successfully* or *Network connection problem*.

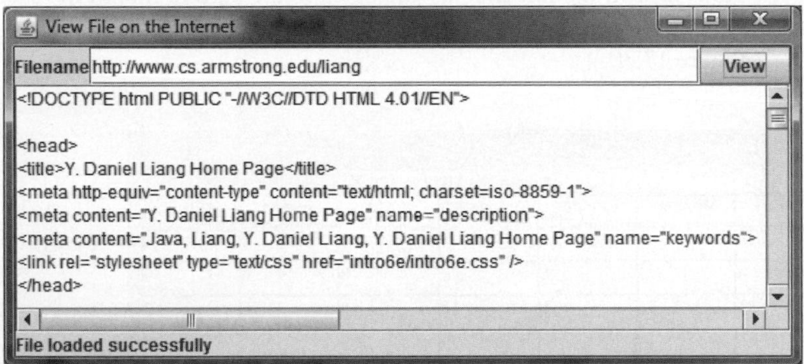

FIGURE 17.32 The program displays the contents of a specified file on the Internet.

CHAPTER

18

APPLETS AND MULTIMEDIA

Objectives

- To convert GUI applications into applets (§18.2).
- To embed applets in Web pages (§18.3).
- To run applets from Web browsers and from the **appletviewer** command (§§18.3.1–18.3.2).
- To understand the applet security sandbox model (§18.4).
- To write a Java program that can run both as an application and as an applet (§18.5).
- To override the applet life-cycle methods `init`, `start`, `stop`, and `destroy` (§18.6).
- To pass string values to applets from HTML (§18.7).
- To develop an animation for a bouncing ball (§18.8).
- To develop an applet for the tic-tac-toe game (§18.9).
- To locate resources (images and audio) using the `URL` class (§18.10).
- To play audio in any Java program (§18.11).

18.1 Introduction

Java applets are Java programs running from a Web browser.

When browsing the Web, often the graphical user interface and animation you see have been developed using Java. The Java programs that run from a Web browser are called *Java applets*. How do you write Java applets with graphics, images, and audio? This chapter will show you how.

18.2 Developing Applets

Java applets are instances of the `Applet` *class.* `JApplet` *is a subclass of* `Applet`, *and it is suitable for developing applets using Swing components.*

VideoNote
First applet

So far, you have used and written Java applications. Everything you have learned about writing applications, however, applies also to writing applets. Applications and applets share many common programming features, although they differ slightly in some aspects. For example, every application must have a `main` method, which is invoked by the Java interpreter. Java applets, on the other hand, do not need a `main` method. They run in the Web browser environment. Because applets are embedded in a Web page, Java provides special features that enable applets to run from a Web browser.

The `Applet` class provides the essential framework that enables applets to be run from a Web browser. While every Java application has a `main` method that is executed when the application starts, applets, because they don't have a `main` method, depend on the browser to run them. Every applet is an instance of `java.applet.Applet`. The `Applet` class is an AWT class and is not designed to work with Swing components. To use Swing components in Java applets, you need to define a Java applet that extends `javax.swing.JApplet`, which is a subclass of `java.applet.Applet`.

Every Java GUI program you have developed can be converted into an applet by replacing `JFrame` with `JApplet` and deleting the `main` method. Figure 18.1a shows a Java GUI application program, which can be converted into a Java applet as shown in Figure 18.1b.

```
import javax.swing.*;

public class DisplayLabel extends JFrame {
  public DisplayLabel() {
    add(new JLabel("Great!", JLabel.CENTER));
  }

  public static void main(String[] args) {
    JFrame frame = new DisplayLabel();
    frame.setTitle("DisplayLabel");
    frame.setSize(200, 100);
    frame.setLocationRelativeTo(null);
    frame.setDefaultCloseOperation(
      JFrame.EXIT_ON_CLOSE);
    frame.setVisible(true);
  }
}
```

(a) GUI application

```
import javax.swing.*;
                                     JApplet
public class DisplayLabel extends JFrame {
  public DisplayLabel() {
    add(new JLabel("Great!", JLabel.CENTER));
  }

  public static void main(String[] args) {
    JFrame frame = new DisplayLabel();
    frame.setTitle("DisplayLabel");
    frame.setSize(200, 100);
    frame.setLocationRelativeTo(null);
    frame.setDefaultCloseOperation(
      JFrame.EXIT_ON_CLOSE);
    frame.setVisible(true);
  }
}
```

(b) Applet

FIGURE 18.1 You can convert a GUI application into an applet.

Listing 18.1 gives the complete code for the applet.

LISTING 18.1 `DisplayLabel.java`

extend Japplet

```
import javax.swing.*;

public class DisplayLabel extends JApplet {
```

```
4   public DisplayLabel() {
5     add(new JLabel("Great!", JLabel.CENTER));
6   }
7 }
```

Like JFrame, JApplet is a container that can contain other GUI components (see the GUI class diagrams in Figure 12.1). The default layout manager for JApplet is BorderLayout. So, the label is placed in the center of the applet (line 5).

Check Point

MyProgrammingLab™

18.1 Is every applet an instance of java.applet.Applet?

18.2 Is javax.swing.JApplet a subclass of java.applet.Applet?

18.3 The HTML File and the <applet> Tag

Key Point

To run an applet, you need to create an HTML file with an <applet> tag for embedding the applet.

HTML

HTML is a markup language that presents static documents on the Web. It uses *tags* to instruct the Web browser how to render a Web page and contains a tag called <applet> that incorporates applets into a Web page.

The HTML file in Listing 18.2 embeds the applet **DisplayLabel.class**.

LISTING 18.2 DisplayLabel.html

```
<html>
  <head>
    <title>Java Applet Demo</title>
  </head>
  <body>
    <applet
      code = "DisplayLabel.class"
      width = 250
      height = 50>
    </applet>
  </body>
</html>
```

applet class

tag

An HTML *tag* is an instruction to the Web browser. The browser interprets the tag and decides how to display or otherwise treat the subsequent contents of the HTML document. Tags are enclosed inside brackets (< >). The first word in a tag, called the *tag name*, describes tag functions. A tag can have additional attributes, sometimes with values after an equals sign, which further define the tag's action. For example, in the preceding HTML file, <applet> is the tag name, and code, width, and height are attributes. The width and height attributes specify the rectangular viewing area of the applet.

<applet> tag

Most tags have a *start tag* and a corresponding *end tag*. The tag has a specific effect on the region between the start tag and the end tag. For example, <applet...>...</applet> tells the browser to display an applet. An end tag is always the start tag's name preceded by a slash.

An HTML document begins with the <html> tag, which declares that the document is written in HTML. Each document has two parts, a *head* and a *body*, defined by <head> and <body> tags, respectively. The head part contains the document title, including the <title> tag and other information the browser can use when rendering the document, and the body part holds the actual contents of the document. The header is optional. For more information, refer to Supplement V.A, HTML and XHTML Tutorial.

The complete syntax of the <applet> tag is as follows:

```
<applet
  [codebase = applet_url]
```

```
    code = classfilename.class
    width = applet_viewing_width_in_pixels
    height = applet_viewing_height_in_pixels
    [archive = archivefile]
    [vspace = vertical_margin]
    [hspace = horizontal_margin]
    [align = applet_alignment]
    [alt = alternative_text]
  >
  <param name = param_name1 value = param_value1>
  <param name = param_name2 value = param_value2>
  ...
  <param name = param_namei value = param_valuei>
  </applet>
```

<param> tag

The `code`, `width`, and `height` attributes are required; all the others are optional. The `<param>` tag will be introduced in Section 18.7, Passing Strings to Applets. The other attributes are explained below.

codebase attribute

- `codebase` specifies the base from which your classes are loaded. If this attribute is not used, the Web browser loads the applet from the directory in which the HTML page is located. If your applet is located in a different directory from the HTML page, you must specify the `applet_url` for the browser to load the applet. This attribute enables you to load the class from anywhere on the Internet. The classes used by the applet are dynamically loaded when needed.

archive attribute

- `archive` instructs the browser to load an archive file that contains all the class files needed to run the applet. Archiving allows the Web browser to load all the classes from a single compressed file at one time, thus reducing loading time and improving performance. To create archives, see Supplement III.Q, Packaging and Deploying Java Projects.
- `vspace` and `hspace` specify the size, in pixels, of the blank margin to pad around the applet vertically and horizontally.
- `align` specifies how the applet will be aligned in the browser. One of nine values is used: `left`, `right`, `top`, `texttop`, `middle`, `absmiddle`, `baseline`, `bottom`, or `absbottom`.
- `alt` specifies the text to be displayed in case the browser cannot run Java.

18.3.1 Viewing Applets from a Web Browser

To display an applet from a Web browser, open the applet's HTML file (e.g., **DisplayLabel.html**). Its output is shown in Figure 18.2a.

To make your applet accessible on the Web, you need to store the **DisplayLabel.class** and **DisplayLabel.html** files on a Web server, as shown in Figure 18.3. You can view the applet

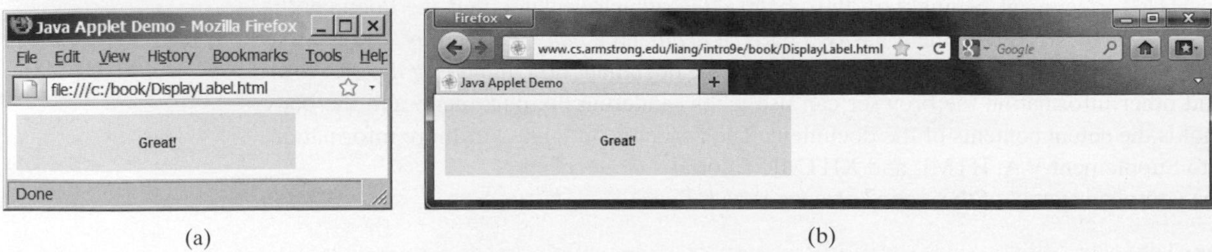

(a) (b)

FIGURE 18.2 The DisplayLabel program is loaded from a local host in (a) and from a Web server in (b).

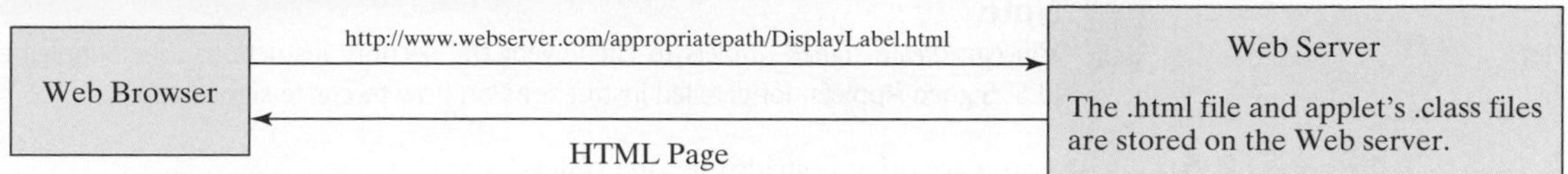

FIGURE 18.3 A Web browser requests an HTML file from a Web server.

from an appropriate URL. For example, I have uploaded these two files on Web server www.cs.armstrong.edu/. As shown in Figure 18.2b, you can access the applet from www.cs.armstrong.edu/liang/intro9e/book/DisplayLabel.html.

18.3.2 Viewing Applets Using the Applet Viewer Utility

You can test the applet using the applet viewer utility, which can be launched from the DOS prompt using the **appletviewer** command, as shown in Figure 18.4a. Its output is shown in Figure 18.4b. appletviewer

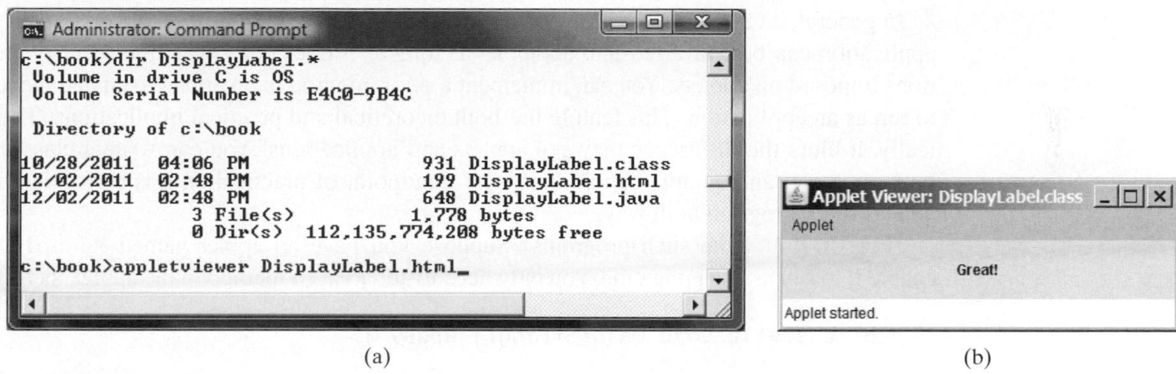

(a) (b)

FIGURE 18.4 The **appletviewer** command runs a Java applet in the applet viewer utility.

The applet viewer functions as a browser. It is convenient for testing applets during development without launching a Web browser.

18.3 Describe the `<applet>` HTML tag. How do you embed an applet in a web page?

18.4 How do you test an applet using the **appletviewer** command?

Check Point
MyProgrammingLab™

18.4 Applet Security Restrictions

Applet security restrictions ensure that safety is maintained when running applets.

Key Point

Java uses the so-called "sandbox security model" for executing applets to prevent destructive programs from damaging the system on which the browser is running. Applets are not allowed to use resources outside the "sandbox." Specifically, the sandbox restricts the following activities:

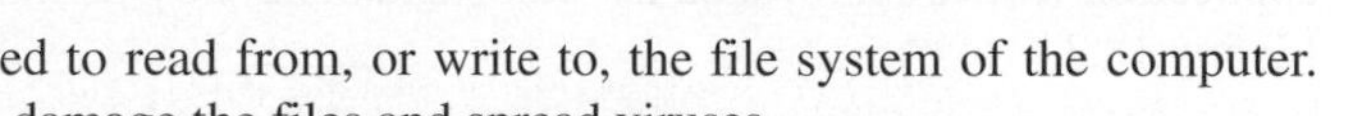

- Applets are not allowed to read from, or write to, the file system of the computer. Otherwise, they could damage the files and spread viruses.
- Applets are not allowed to run programs on the browser's computer. Otherwise, they might call destructive local programs and damage the local system on the user's computer.
- Applets are not allowed to establish connections between the user's computer and any other computer, except for the server where the applets are stored. This restriction prevents the applet from connecting the user's computer to another computer without the user's knowledge.

signed applet

Note

You can create *signed applets* to circumvent the security restrictions. See Supplement III.S, Signed Applets, for detailed instructions on how to create signed applets.

Check Point

18.5 List some security restrictions on applets.

MyProgrammingLab™

18.5 Enabling Applets to Run as Applications

Key Point

You can add a main method in the applet to enable the applet to run as a standalone application.

VideoNote

Run applets standalone

Despite some differences, the **JFrame** class and the **JApplet** class have a lot in common. Since they both are subclasses of the **Container** class, all their user-interface components, layout managers, and event-handling features are the same. Applications, however, are invoked from the static **main** method by the Java interpreter, and applets are run by the Web browser. The Web browser creates an instance of the applet using the applet's no-arg constructor and controls and executes the applet.

In general, an applet can be converted into an application without loss of functionality. An application can be converted into an applet as long as it does not violate the security restrictions imposed on applets. You can implement a **main** method in an applet to enable the applet to run as an application. This feature has both theoretical and practical implications. Theoretically, it blurs the difference between applets and applications: You can write a class that is both an applet and an application. From the standpoint of practicality, it is convenient to be able to run a program both ways.

How do you write such programs? Suppose you have an applet named **MyApplet**. To enable it to run as an application, you only need to add a **main** method in the applet, as follows:

create framc

create applet

add applet

show frame

```
public static void main(String[] args) {
  // Create a frame
  JFrame frame = new JFrame("Applet is in the frame");

  // Create an instance of the applet
  MyApplet applet = new MyApplet();

  // Add the applet to the frame
  frame.add(applet, BorderLayout.CENTER);

  // Display the frame
  frame.setSize(300, 300);
  frame.setLocationRelativeTo(null); // Center the frame
  frame.setDefaultCloseOperation(JFrame.EXIT_ON_CLOSE);
  frame.setVisible(true);
}
```

run standalone

You can revise the **DisplayLabel** class in Listing 18.1 to enable it to run as a standalone application (often abbreviated as "run standalone") by adding a **main** method, as shown in Listing 18.3.

LISTING 18.3 New DisplayLabel.java with a main Method

```
import javax.swing.*;

public class DisplayLabel extends JApplet {
  public DisplayLabel() {
    add(new JLabel("Great!", JLabel.CENTER));
  }

```

new main method

```
8     public static void main(String[] args) {
9       // Create a frame
10      JFrame frame = new JFrame("Applet is in the frame");
11
12      // Create an instance of the applet
13      DisplayLabel applet = new DisplayLabel();
14
15      // Add the applet to the frame
16      frame.add(applet);
17
18      // Display the frame
19      frame.setSize(300, 100);
20      frame.setLocationRelativeTo(null); // Center the frame
21      frame.setDefaultCloseOperation(JFrame.EXIT_ON_CLOSE);
22      frame.setVisible(true);
23    }
24  }
```

When the applet is run from a Web browser, the browser creates an instance of the applet and displays it. When the applet is run standalone, the main method is invoked to create a frame (line 10) to hold the applet. The applet is created (line 13) and added to the frame (line 16). The frame is displayed in line 22.

Note that you can add an applet to a container, but not a frame to a container. A frame is a top-level container that cannot be embedded in another container.

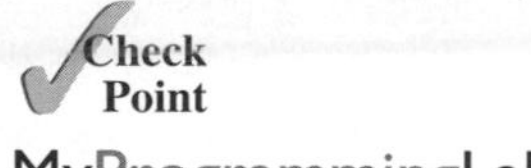

18.6 How do you add components to a `JApplet`? What is the default layout manager of `JApplet`?

18.7 Can you place a frame in an applet?

18.8 Can you place an applet in a frame?

18.9 What are the differences between applications and applets? How do you run an application, and how do you run an applet? Is the compilation process different for applications and applets?

18.6 Applet Life-Cycle Methods

The Web browser controls and executes applets using the applet life-cycle methods.

applet container

Applets are actually run from the *applet container*, which is a plug-in of a Web browser. A plug-in is a software component that can be added into a larger software to provide additional functions. The `Applet` class contains the `init()`, `start()`, `stop()`, and `destroy()` methods, known as the *life-cycle methods*. These methods are called by the applet container to control the execution of an applet. They are implemented with an empty body in the `Applet` class, so they do nothing by default. You may override them in a subclass of `Applet` to perform desired operations. Figure 18.5 shows how the applet container calls these methods.

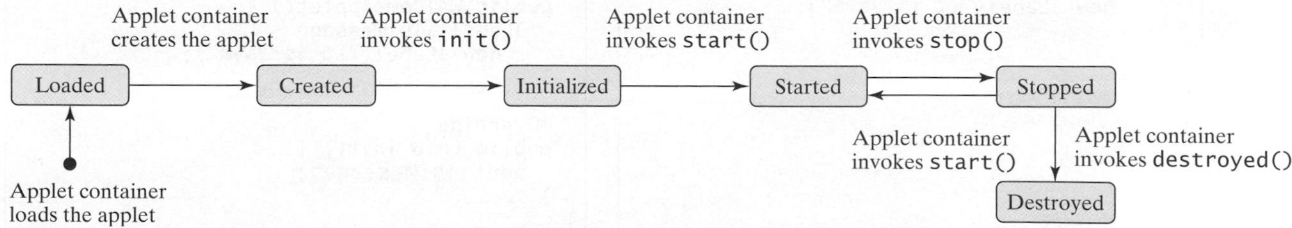

Figure 18.5 The applet container uses the `init`, `start`, `stop`, and `destroy` methods to control the applet.

18.6.1 The `init` Method

init()

The `init` method is invoked after the applet is created. If a subclass of `Applet` has an initialization to perform, it should override this method. The functions usually implemented in this method include getting string parameter values from the `<applet>` tag in the HTML page.

18.6.2 The `start` Method

start()

The `start` method is invoked after the `init` method. It is also called when the user returns to the Web page containing the applet after surfing other pages.

A subclass of `Applet` overrides this method if it has any operation that needs to be performed whenever the Web page containing the applet is visited. An applet with animation, for example, might start the timer to resume animation.

18.6.3 The `stop` Method

stop()

The `stop` method is the opposite of the `start` method. The `start` method is called when the user moves back to the page that contains the applet. The `stop` method is invoked when the user leaves the page.

A subclass of `Applet` overrides this method if it has any operation to be performed each time the Web page containing the applet is no longer visible. An applet with animation, for example, might stop the timer to pause animation.

18.6.4 The `destroy` Method

destroy()

The `destroy` method is invoked when the browser exits normally to inform the applet that it is no longer needed and should release any resources it has allocated. The `stop` method is always called before the `destroy` method.

A subclass of `Applet` overrides this method if it has any operation to be performed before it is destroyed. Usually, you won't need to override this method unless you want to release specific resources that the applet created.

MyProgrammingLab™

18.10 Describe the `init()`, `start()`, `stop()`, and `destroy()` methods in the `Applet` class.

18.11 Why does the applet in (a) below display nothing? Why does the applet in (b) have a runtime `NullPointerException` on the highlighted line?

```
import javax.swing.*;

public class WelcomeApplet extends JApplet {
  public void WelcomeApplet() {
    JLabel jlblMessage =
      new JLabel("It is Java");
  }
}
```

(a)

```
import javax.swing.*;

public class WelcomeApplet extends JApplet {
  private JLabel jlblMessage;

  public WelcomeApplet() {
    JLabel jlblMessage =
      new JLabel("It is Java");
  }

  @Override
  public void init() {
    add(jlblMessage);
  }
}
```

(b)

18.7 Passing Strings to Applets

Key Point

You can pass string parameters from an HTML file to an applet.

In Section 9.7, Command-Line Arguments, you learned how to pass strings to Java applications from a command line. Strings are passed to the `main` method as an array of strings. When the application starts, the `main` method can use these strings. There is no `main` method in an applet, however, and applets are not run from the command line by the Java interpreter.

How, then, can applets accept arguments? In this section, you will learn how to pass strings to Java applets. To be passed to an applet, a parameter must be defined in the HTML file and must be read by the applet when it is initialized. Parameters are defined using the `<param>` tag. The `<param>` tag must be embedded in the `<applet>` tag. Its syntax is:

```
<param name = parametername value = stringvalue />
```

The `<param>` tag defines a parameter and its corresponding string value.

Note

No comma separates the parameter name from the parameter value in the HTML code. The HTML parameter names are not case sensitive.

Suppose you want to write an applet to display a message. The message is passed as a parameter. In addition, you want the message to be displayed at a specific location with *x*-coordinate and *y*-coordinate, which are passed as two parameters. The parameters and their values are listed in Table 18.1.

TABLE 18.1 Parameter Names and Values for the `DisplayMessage` Applet

Parameter Name	*Parameter Value*
MESSAGE	"Welcome to Java"
X	20
Y	30

The HTML source file is given in Listing 18.4.

LISTING 18.4 DisplayMessage.html

```
<html>
  <head>
    <title>Passing Strings to Java Applets</title>
  </head>
  <body>
    <p>This applet gets a message from the HTML
      page and displays it.</p>
    <applet
      code = "DisplayMessage.class"
      width = 200
      height = 50
      alt = "You must have a Java-enabled browser to view the applet"
    >
      <param name = MESSAGE value = "Welcome to Java" />
      <param name = X value = 20 />
```

```
    <param name = Y value = 30 />
  </applet>
 </body>
</html>
```

To read the parameter from the applet, use the following method defined in the **Applet** class:

```
public String getParameter(String parametername);
```

This returns the value of the specified parameter.

The applet is given in Listing 18.5. A sample run of the applet is shown in Figure 18.6.

LISTING 18.5 DisplayMessage.java

getParameter

add to applet

```
1  import javax.swing.*;
2
3  public class DisplayMessage extends JApplet {
4    @Override /** Initialize the applet */
5    public void init() {
6      // Get parameter values from the HTML file
7      String message = getParameter("MESSAGE");
8      int x = Integer.parseInt(getParameter("X"));
9      int y = Integer.parseInt(getParameter("Y"));
10
11     // Create a message panel
12     MessagePanel messagePanel = new MessagePanel(message);
13     messagePanel.setXCoordinate(x);
14     messagePanel.setYCoordinate(y);
15
16     // Add the message panel to the applet
17     add(messagePanel);
18   }
19 }
```

FIGURE 18.6 The applet displays the message **Welcome to Java** passed from the HTML page.

The program gets the parameter values from the HTML file in the **init** method. The values are strings obtained using the **getParameter** method (lines 7–9). Because **x** and **y** are **int**s, the program uses **Integer.parseInt(string)** to parse a digital string into an **int** value.

If you change *Welcome to Java* in the HTML file to *Welcome to HTML*, and reload the HTML file in the Web browser, you should see *Welcome to HTML* displayed. Similarly, the **x** and **y** values can be changed to display the message in a desired location.

Caution

The **Applet**'s **getParameter** method can be invoked only after an instance of the applet is created. Therefore, this method cannot be invoked in the constructor of the applet class. You should invoke it from the **init** method.

You can add a main method to enable this applet to run as a standalone application. The applet takes the parameters from the HTML file when it runs as an applet and takes the parameters from the command line when it runs standalone. The program, as shown in Listing 18.6, is identical to `DisplayMessage` except for the addition of a new `main` method and of a variable named `isStandalone` to indicate whether it is running as an applet or as an application.

LISTING 18.6 DisplayMessageApp.java

```
import javax.swing.*;
import java.awt.Font;
import java.awt.BorderLayout;

public class DisplayMessageApp extends JApplet {
  private String message = "A default message"; // Message to display
  private int x = 20; // Default x-coordinate
  private int y = 20; // Default y-coordinate

  /** Determine whether it is an application */
  private boolean isStandalone = false;

  @Override /** Initialize the applet */
  public void init() {
    if (!isStandalone) {
      // Get parameter values from the HTML file
      message = getParameter("MESSAGE");
      x = Integer.parseInt(getParameter("X"));
      y = Integer.parseInt(getParameter("Y"));
    }

    // Create a message panel
    MessagePanel messagePanel = new MessagePanel(message);
    messagePanel.setFont(new Font("SansSerif", Font.BOLD, 20));
    messagePanel.setXCoordinate(x);
    messagePanel.setYCoordinate(y);

    // Add the message panel to the applet
    add(messagePanel);
  }

  /** Main method to display a message
     @param args[0] x-coordinate
     @param args[1] y-coordinate
     @param args[2] message
    */
  public static void main(String[] args) {
    // Create a frame
    JFrame frame = new JFrame("DisplayMessageApp");

    // Create an instance of the applet
    DisplayMessageApp applet = new DisplayMessageApp();

    // It runs as an application
    applet.isStandalone = true;

    // Get parameters from the command line
    applet.getCommandLineParameters(args);

    // Add the applet instance to the frame
    frame.add(applet, BorderLayout.CENTER);
```

isStandalone

applet params

standalone

command params

```
52
53       // Invoke applet's init method
54       applet.init();
55       applet.start();
56
57       // Display the frame
58       frame.setSize(300, 300);
59       frame.setLocationRelativeTo(null); // Center the frame
60       frame.setDefaultCloseOperation(JFrame.EXIT_ON_CLOSE);
61       frame.setVisible(true);
62     }
63
64     /** Get command-line parameters */
65     private void getCommandLineParameters(String[] args) {
66       // Check usage and get x, y and message
67       if (args.length != 3) {
68         System.out.println(
69           "Usage: java DisplayMessageApp x y message");
70         System.exit(1);
71       }
72       else {
73         x = Integer.parseInt(args[0]);
74         y = Integer.parseInt(args[1]);
75         message = args[2];
76       }
77     }
78   }
```

When you run the program as an applet, the `main` method is ignored. When you run it as an application, the `main` method is invoked. Sample runs of the program as an application and as an applet are shown in Figure 18.7.

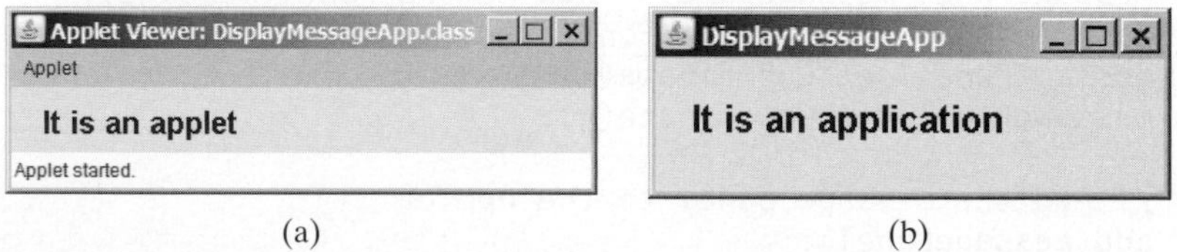

(a) (b)

FIGURE 18.7 The `DisplayMessageApp` class can run as an applet in (a) and as an application in (b).

The `main` method creates a `JFrame` object `frame` and creates a `JApplet` object `applet`, then places the applet `applet` into the frame `frame` and invokes its `init` method. The application runs just like an applet.

The `main` method sets `isStandalone` as `true` (line 45) so that it does not attempt to retrieve HTML parameters when the `init` method is invoked.

The `setVisible(true)` method (line 61) is invoked *after* the components are added to the applet, and the applet is added to the frame to ensure that the components will be visible. Otherwise, the components are not shown when the frame starts.

omitting `main` method

Important Pedagogical Note

From now on, all the GUI examples will be created as applets with a `main` method. Thus, you will be able to run the program either as an applet or as an application. For brevity, the `main` method is not listed in the text.

MyProgrammingLab™

18.12 How do you pass parameters to an applet?

18.13 Where is the `getParameter` method defined?

18.14 What is wrong if the `DisplayMessage` applet is revised as follows?

```
public class DisplayMessage extends JApplet {
  /** Initialize the applet */
  public DisplayMessage() {
    // Get parameter values from the HTML file
    String message = getParameter("MESSAGE");
    int x =
      Integer.parseInt(getParameter("X"));
    int y =
      Integer.parseInt(getParameter("Y"));

    // Create a message panel
    MessagePanel messagePanel =
      new MessagePanel(message);
    messagePanel.setXCoordinate(x);
    messagePanel.setYCoordinate(y);

    // Add the message panel to the applet
    add(messagePanel);
  }
}
```

(a) Revision 1

```
public class DisplayMessage extends JApplet {
  private String message;
  private int x;
  private int y;

  @Override /** Initialize the applet */
  public void init() {
    // Get parameter values from the HTML file
    message = getParameter("MESSAGE");
    x = Integer.parseInt(getParameter("X"));
    y = Integer.parseInt(getParameter("Y"));
  }

  public DisplayMessage() {
    // Create a message panel
    MessagePanel messagePanel =
      new  MessagePanel(message);
    messagePanel.setXCoordinate(x);
    messagePanel.setYCoordinate(y);

    // Add the message panel to the applet
    add(messagePanel);
  }
}
```

(b) Revision 2

18.8 Case Study: Bouncing Ball

This section presents an applet that displays a ball bouncing in a panel.

The applet uses two buttons to suspend and resume the bouncing movement, and uses a scroll bar to control the bouncing speed, as shown in Figure 18.8.

FIGURE 18.8 The ball's movement is controlled by the *Suspend* and *Resume* buttons and the scroll bar.

Here are the major steps to write this program:

1. Define a subclass of `JPanel` named `Ball` to display a ball bouncing, as shown in Listing 18.7.
2. Define a subclass of `JPanel` named `BallControl` to set the ball speed with a scroll bar, and two control buttons *Suspend* and *Resume*, as shown in Listing 18.8.
3. Define an applet named `BounceBallApp` to contain an instance of `BallControl` and enable the applet to run as a standalone application, as shown in Listing 18.9.

The relationship among these classes is shown in Figure 18.9.

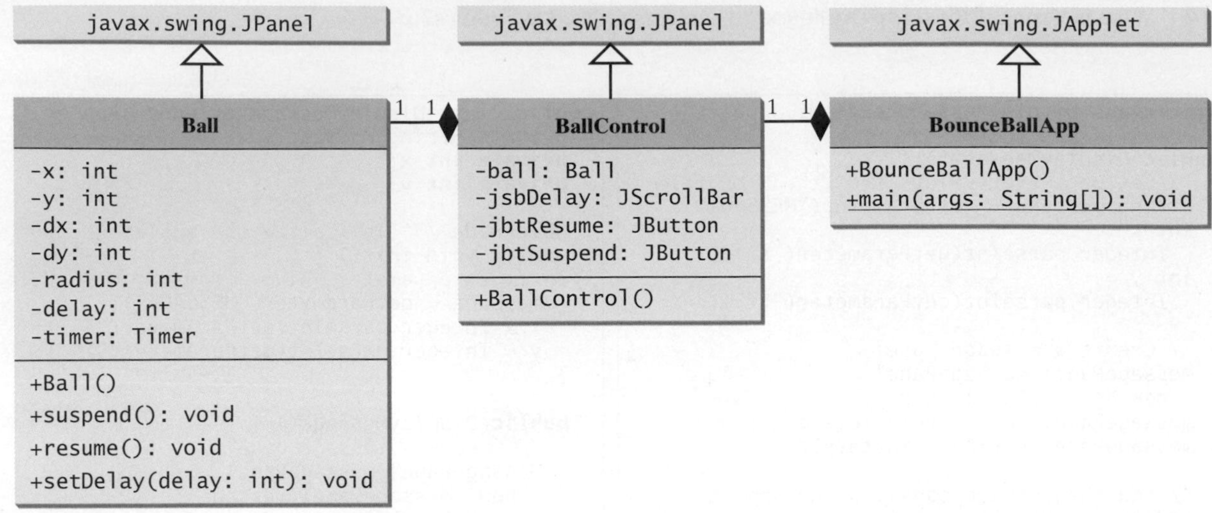

FIGURE 18.9 BounceBallApp contains BallControl, and BallControl contains Ball.

LISTING 18.7 Ball.java

timer delay

create timer

start timer

timer listener

repaint ball

paint ball

```
import javax.swing.Timer;
import java.awt.*;
import javax.swing.*;
import java.awt.event.*;

public class Ball extends JPanel {
  private int delay = 10;

  // Create a timer with the specified delay in milliseconds
  private Timer timer = new Timer(delay, new TimerListener());

  private int x = 0; private int y = 0; // Current ball position
  private int radius = 5; // Ball radius
  private int dx = 2; // Increment on ball's x-coordinate
  private int dy = 2; // Increment on ball's y-coordinate

  public Ball() {
    timer.start();
  }

  private class TimerListener implements ActionListener {
    @Override /** Handle the action event */
    public void actionPerformed(ActionEvent e) {
      repaint();
    }
  }

  @Override
  protected void paintComponent(Graphics g) {
    super.paintComponent(g);

    g.setColor(Color.red);

    // Check boundaries
    if (x < 0 || x > getWidth())
      dx *= -1;
```

```
37       if (y < 0 || y > getHeight())
38         dy *= -1;
39
40       // Adjust ball position
41       x += dx;
42       y += dy;
43       g.fillOval(x - radius, y - radius, radius * 2, radius * 2);
44     }
45
46     public void suspend() {
47       timer.stop(); // Suspend timer
48     }
49
50     public void resume() {
51       timer.start(); // Resume timer
52     }
53
54     public void setDelay(int delay) {
55       this.delay = delay;
56       timer.setDelay(delay);
57     }
58   }
```

The use of `Timer` to control animation was introduced in Section 16.11, Animation Using the `Timer` Class. `Ball` extends `JPanel` to display a moving ball. The timer listener implements `ActionListener` to listen for `ActionEvent` (line 21). Line 10 creates a `Timer` for a `Ball`. The timer is started in line 18 when a `Ball` is constructed. The timer fires an `ActionEvent` at a fixed rate. The listener responds in line 24 to repaint the ball to animate ball movement. The center of the ball is at (`x`, `y`), which changes to (`x + dx`, `y + dy`) on the next display (lines 41–42). When the ball is out of the horizontal boundary, the sign of `dx` is changed (from positive to negative, or vice versa) (lines 35–36). This causes the ball to change its horizontal movement direction. When the ball is out of the vertical boundary, the sign of `dy` is changed (from positive to negative, or vice versa) (lines 37–38). This causes the ball to change its vertical movement direction. The `suspend` and `resume` methods (lines 46–52) can be used to stop and start the timer. The `setDelay(int)` method (lines 54–57) sets a new delay.

LISTING 18.8 BallControl.java

```
import javax.swing.*;
import java.awt.event.*;
import java.awt.*;

public class BallControl extends JPanel {
  private Ball ball = new Ball();
  private JButton jbtSuspend = new JButton("Suspend");
  private JButton jbtResume = new JButton("Resume");
  private JScrollBar jsbDelay = new JScrollBar();

  public BallControl() {
    // Group buttons in a panel
    JPanel panel = new JPanel();
    panel.add(jbtSuspend);
    panel.add(jbtResume);

    // Add ball and buttons to the panel
    ball.setBorder(new javax.swing.border.LineBorder(Color.red));
    jsbDelay.setOrientation(JScrollBar.HORIZONTAL);
    ball.setDelay(jsbDelay.getMaximum());
    setLayout(new BorderLayout());
```

button

scroll bar

create UI

register listener
suspend
register listener
resume
register listener
new delay

```
22      add(jsbDelay, BorderLayout.NORTH);
23      add(ball, BorderLayout.CENTER);
24      add(panel, BorderLayout.SOUTH);
25
26      // Register listeners
27      jbtSuspend.addActionListener(new ActionListener() {
28        @Override
29        public void actionPerformed(ActionEvent e) {
30          ball.suspend();
31        }
32      });
33      jbtResume.addActionListener(new ActionListener() {
34        @Override
35        public void actionPerformed(ActionEvent e) {
36          ball.resume();
37        }
38      });
39      jsbDelay.addAdjustmentListener(new AdjustmentListener() {
40        @Override
41        public void adjustmentValueChanged(AdjustmentEvent e) {
42          ball.setDelay(jsbDelay.getMaximum() - e.getValue());
43        }
44      });
45    }
46  }
```

The `BallControl` class extends `JPanel` to display the ball with a scroll bar and two control buttons. When the *Suspend* button is clicked, the ball's `suspend()` method is invoked to suspend the ball's movement (line 30). When the *Resume* button is clicked, the ball's `resume()` method is invoked to resume the ball's movement (line 36). The bouncing speed can be changed using the scroll bar.

Listing 18.9 BounceBallApp.java

add `BallControl`
`main` method omitted

```
import java.awt.*;
import javax.swing.*;

public class BounceBallApp extends JApplet {
  public BounceBallApp() {
    add(new BallControl());
  }
}
```

The `BounceBallApp` class simply places an instance of `BallControl` in the applet. The `main` method is provided in the applet (not displayed in the listing for brevity) so that you can also run it standalone.

Check Point

MyProgrammingLab™

18.15 How does the program make the ball moving?

18.16 How does the code in Listing 18.7 Ball.java change the direction of the ball movement?

18.17 What does the program do when the *Suspend* button is clicked? What does the program do when the *Resume* button is clicked?

18.9 Case Study: Developing a Tic-Tac-Toe Game

VideoNote
TicTacToe

Key Point

This section develops an applet for playing tic-tac-toe.

From the many examples in this and earlier chapters you have learned about objects, classes, arrays, class inheritance, GUI, event-driven programming, and applets. Now it is time to put what you have learned to work in developing comprehensive projects. In this section, we will develop a Java applet with which to play the popular game of tic-tac-toe.

Two players take turns marking an available cell in a 3 × 3 grid with their respective tokens (either X or O). When one player has placed three tokens in a horizontal, vertical, or diagonal row on the grid, the game is over and that player has won. A draw (no winner) occurs when all the cells on the grid have been filled with tokens and neither player has achieved a win. Figure 18.10 shows the representative sample runs of the example.

(a) The X player won the game

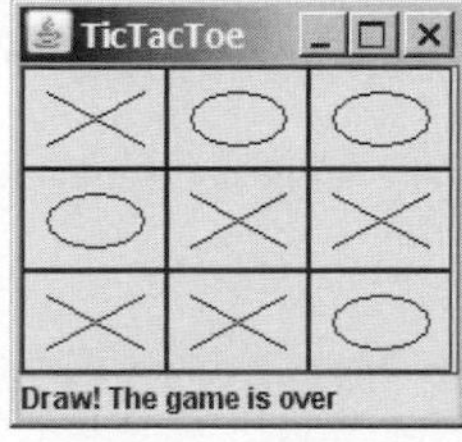

(b) Draw—no winners

(c) The O player won the game

FIGURE 18.10 Two players play a tic-tac-toe game.

All the examples you have seen so far show simple behaviors that are easy to model with classes. The behavior of the tic-tac-toe game is somewhat more complex. To create classes that model the behavior, you need to study and understand the game.

Assume that all the cells are initially empty, and that the first player takes the X token and the second player the O token. To mark a cell, the player points the mouse to the cell and clicks it. If the cell is empty, the token (X or O) is displayed. If the cell is already filled, the player's action is ignored.

From the preceding description, it is obvious that a cell is a GUI object that handles the mouse-click event and displays tokens. Such an object could be either a button or a panel. Drawing on panels is more flexible than drawing on buttons, because on a panel the token (X or O) can be drawn in any size, but on a button it can be displayed only as a text label. Therefore, a panel should be used to model a cell. How do you know the state of the cell (empty, X, or O)? You use a property named `token` of the `char` type in the `Cell` class. The `Cell` class is responsible for drawing the token when an empty cell is clicked, so you need to write the code for listening to the `MouseEvent` and for painting the shapes for tokens X and O. The `Cell` class can be defined as shown in Figure 18.11.

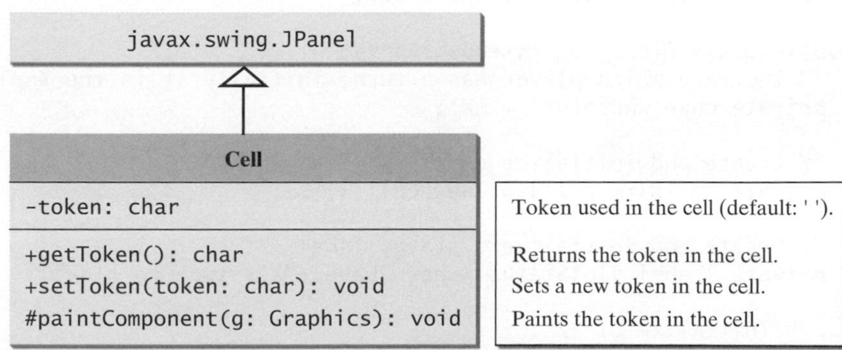

FIGURE 18.11 The `Cell` class paints the token in a cell.

The tic-tac-toe board consists of nine cells, created using `new Cell[3][3]`. To determine which player's turn it is, you can introduce a variable named `whoseTurn` of the `char` type. `whoseTurn` is initially `'X'`, then changes to `'O'`, and subsequently changes between `'X'` and `'O'` whenever a new cell is occupied. When the game is over, set `whoseTurn` to `' '`.

How do you know whether the game is over, whether there is a winner, and who the winner, if any, is? You can define a method named `isWon(char token)` to check whether a specified token has won and a method named `isFull()` to check whether all the cells are occupied.

Clearly, two classes emerge from the foregoing analysis. One is the `Cell` class, which handles operations for a single cell; the other is the `TicTacToe` class, which plays the whole game and deals with all the cells. The relationship between these two classes is shown in Figure 18.12.

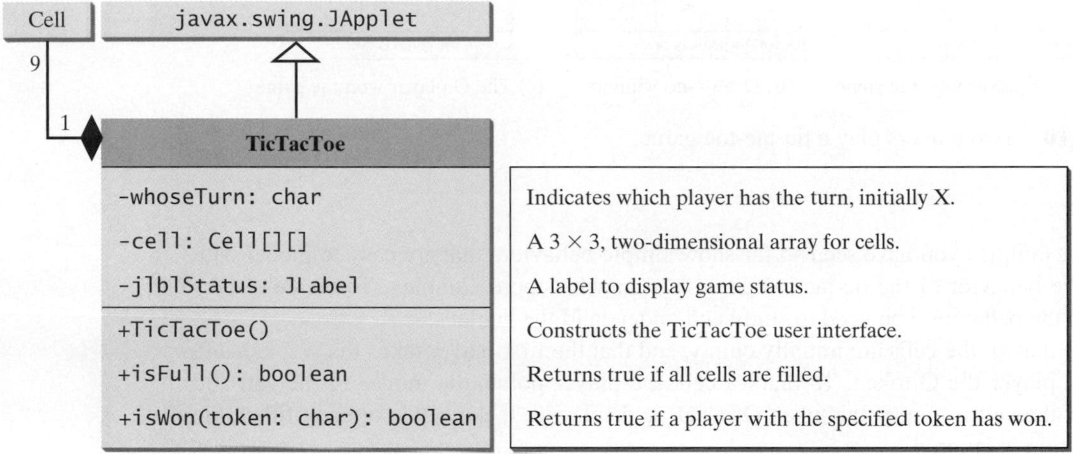

FIGURE 18.12 The `TicTacToe` class contains nine cells.

Since the `Cell` class is only to support the `TicTacToe` class, it can be defined as an inner class in `TicTacToe`. The complete program is given in Listing 18.10.

LISTING 18.10 TicTacToe.java

main class TicTacToe

```
import java.awt.*;
import java.awt.event.*;
import javax.swing.*;
import javax.swing.border.LineBorder;

public class TicTacToe extends JApplet {
  // Indicate which player has a turn; initially it is the X player
  private char whoseTurn = 'X';

  // Create and initialize cells
  private Cell[][] cells =  new Cell[3][3];

  // Create and initialize a status label
  private JLabel jlblStatus = new JLabel("X's turn to play");

  /** Initialize UI */
  public TicTacToe() {
    // Panel p to hold cells
```

```
    JPanel p = new JPanel(new GridLayout(3, 3, 0, 0));
    for (int i = 0; i < 3; i++)
      for (int j = 0; j < 3; j++)
        p.add(cells[i][j] = new Cell());

    // Set line borders on the cells' panel and the status label
    p.setBorder(new LineBorder(Color.red, 1));
    jlblStatus.setBorder(new LineBorder(Color.yellow, 1));

    // Place the panel and the label for the applet
    add(p, BorderLayout.CENTER);
    add(jlblStatus, BorderLayout.SOUTH);
  }

  /** Determine whether the cells are all occupied */
```

check `isFull`

```
  public boolean isFull() {
    for (int i = 0; i < 3; i++)
      for (int j = 0; j < 3; j++)
        if (cells[i][j].getToken() == ' ')
          return false;

    return true;
  }

  /** Determine whether the player with the specified token wins */
  public boolean isWon(char token) {
```

check rows

```
    for (int i = 0; i < 3; i++)
      if ((cells[i][0].getToken() == token)
          && (cells[i][1].getToken() == token)
          && (cells[i][2].getToken() == token)) {
        return true;
      }

```

check columns

```
    for (int j = 0; j < 3; j++)
      if ((cells[0][j].getToken() ==  token)
          && (cells[1][j].getToken() == token)
          && (cells[2][j].getToken() == token)) {
        return true;
      }

```

check major diagonal

```
    if ((cells[0][0].getToken() == token)
        && (cells[1][1].getToken() == token)
        && (cells[2][2].getToken() == token)) {
      return true;
    }

```

check subdiagonal

```
    if ((cells[0][2].getToken() == token)
        && (cells[1][1].getToken() == token)
        && (cells[2][0].getToken() == token)) {
      return true;
    }

    return false;
  }

  // An inner class for a cell
```

inner class `Cell`

```
  public class Cell extends JPanel {
    // Token used for this cell
    private char token = ' ';

```

```
79     public Cell() {
80       setBorder(new LineBorder(Color.black, 1)); // Set cell's border
81       addMouseListener(new MyMouseListener());  // Register listener
82     }
83 
84     /** Return token */
85     public char getToken() {
86       return token;
87     }
88 
89     /** Set a new token */
90     public void setToken(char c) {
91       token = c;
92       repaint();
93     }
94 
95     @Override /** Paint the cell */
96     protected void paintComponent(Graphics g) {
97       super.paintComponent(g);
98 
99       if (token == 'X') {
100        g.drawLine(10, 10, getWidth() - 10, getHeight() - 10);
101        g.drawLine(getWidth() - 10, 10, 10, getHeight() - 10);
102      }
103      else if (token == 'O') {
104        g.drawOval(10, 10, getWidth() - 20, getHeight() - 20);
105      }
106    }
107 
108    private class MyMouseListener extends MouseAdapter {
109      @Override /** Handle mouse click on a cell */
110      public void mouseClicked(MouseEvent e) {
111        // If cell is empty and game is not over
112        if (token == ' ' && whoseTurn != ' ') {
113          setToken(whoseTurn); // Set token in the cell
114 
115          // Check game status
116          if (isWon(whoseTurn)) {
117            jlblStatus.setText(whoseTurn + " won! The game is over");
118            whoseTurn = ' '; // Game is over
119          }
120          else if (isFull()) {
121            jlblStatus.setText("Draw! The game is over");
122            whoseTurn = ' '; // Game is over
123          }
124          else {
125            // Change the turn
126            whoseTurn = (whoseTurn == 'X') ? 'O' : 'X';
127            // Display whose turn
128            jlblStatus.setText(whoseTurn + "'s turn");
129          }
130        }
131      }
132    }
133  }
134 }
```

register listener

paint cell

listener class

`main` method omitted

The **TicTacToe** class initializes the user interface with nine cells placed in a panel of **GridLayout** (lines 19–22). A label named **jlblStatus** is used to show the status of the game (line 14). The variable **whoseTurn** (line 8) is used to track the next type of token to be placed in a cell. The methods `isFull` (lines 34–41) and `isWon` (lines 44–72) are for checking the status of the game.

Since `Cell` is an inner class in `TicTacToe`, the variable (`whoseTurn`) and methods (`isFull` and `isWon`) defined in `TicTacToe` can be referenced from the `Cell` class. The inner class makes programs simple and concise. If `Cell` were not defined as an inner class of `TicTacToe`, you would have to pass an object of `TicTacToe` to `Cell` in order for the variables and methods in `TicTacToe` to be used in `Cell`. You will rewrite the program without using an inner class in Programming Exercise 18.6.

The listener for `MouseEvent` is registered for the cell (line 81). If an empty cell is clicked and the game is not over, a token is set in the cell (line 113). If the game is over, `whoseTurn` is set to `' '` (lines 118, 122). Otherwise, `whoseTurn` is alternated to a new turn (line 126).

Tip

Use an incremental approach in developing and testing a Java project of this kind. For example, this program can be divided into five steps:

incremental development and testing

1. Lay out the user interface and display a fixed token X on a cell.
2. Enable the cell to display a fixed token X upon a mouse click.
3. Coordinate between the two players so as to display tokens X and O alternately.
4. Check whether a player wins, or whether all the cells are occupied without a winner.
5. Implement displaying a message on the label upon each move by a player.

Check Point

MyProgrammingLab™

18.18 When the game starts, what value is in `whoseTurn`? When the game is over, what value is in `whoseTurn`?

18.19 What happens when the user clicks on an empty cell if the game is not over? What happens when the user clicks on an empty cell if the game is over?

18.20 How does the program check whether a player wins? How does the program check whether all cells are filled?

18.21 Delete `super.paintComponent(g)` on line 97 in TicTacToe.java in Listing 18.10 and run the program to see what happens.

18.10 Locating Resources Using the URL Class

Key Point

You can use the `URL` class to load a resource file for an applet, as long as the resource file is located in the applet's class directory.

You have used the `ImageIcon` class to create an icon from an image file and used the `setIcon` method or the constructor to place the icon in a GUI component, such as a button or a label. For example, the following statements create an `ImageIcon` and set it on a `JLabel` object `jlbl`:

```
ImageIcon imageIcon = new ImageIcon("c:\\book\\image\\us.gif");
jlbl.setIcon(imageIcon);
```

This approach presents a problem. The file location is fixed, because it uses the absolute file path on the Windows platform. As a result, the program cannot run on other platforms and cannot run as an applet. Assume that **image/us.gif** is under the class directory. You can circumvent this problem by using a relative path as follows:

```
ImageIcon imageIcon = new ImageIcon("image/us.gif");
```

This works fine with Java applications on all platforms but not with Java applets, because applets cannot load local files. To enable it to work with both applications and applets, you need to locate the file's *URL* (Uniform Resource Locator).

why URL class?

The **java.net.URL** class was used to locate a text file on the Internet in Section 14.13. It can also be used to locate image files and audio files on the Internet. In general, a **URL** object is a pointer to a "resource" on a local machine or a remote host. A resource can be a file or a directory.

The **URL** class can be used to locate a resource file from a class in a way that is independent of the file's location, as long as the resource file is located in the class directory. Recall that the class directory is where the class is stored. To obtain the **URL** object for a file from a class, use the following statement in the applet or application:

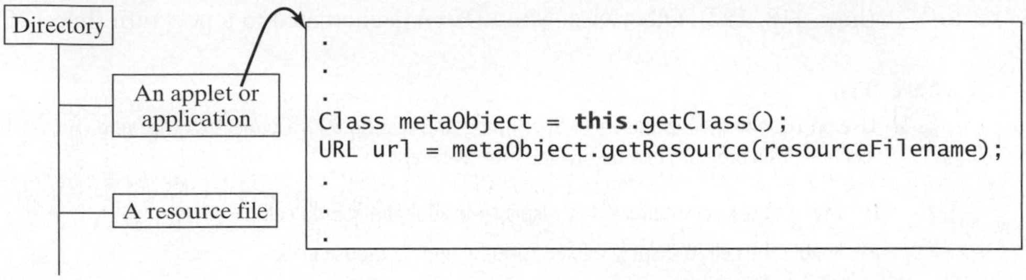

Directory

An applet or application

A resource file

```
.
.
.
Class metaObject = this.getClass();
URL url = metaObject.getResource(resourceFilename);
.
.
.
```

meta object

The **getClass()** method returns an instance of the **java.lang.Class** class for the current class. This instance is automatically created by the JVM for every class loaded into the memory. This instance, also known as a *meta object*, contains the information about the class file such as class name, constructors, and methods. You can obtain a **URL** object for a file in the class path by invoking the **getResource(filename)** method on the meta object. For example, if the class file is in **c:\book**, the following statements obtain a **URL** object for **c:\book\image\us.gif**.

C:\book

An applet or application

image

us.gif

```
.
.
.
Class metaObject = this.getClass();
URL url = metaObject.getResource("image/us.gif");
.
.
.
```

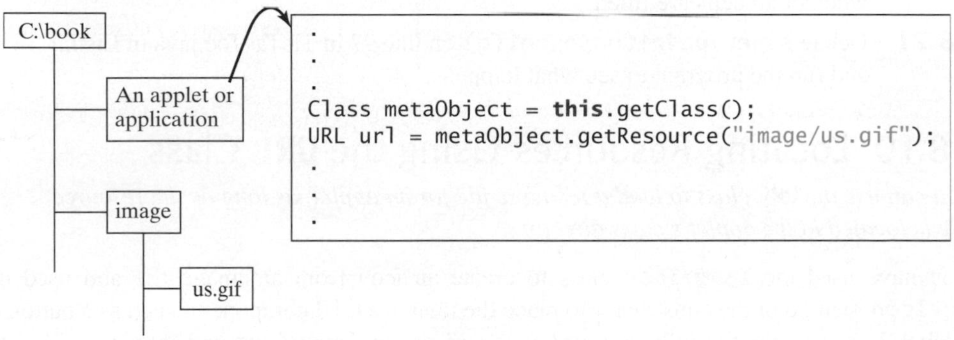

You can now create an **ImageIcon** using

```
ImageIcon imageIcon = new ImageIcon(url);
```

Listing 18.11 gives the code that displays an image from **image/us.gif** in the class directory. The file **image/us.gif** is under the class directory, and its **URL** object is obtained using the **getResource** method (line 5). A label with an image icon is created in line 6. The image icon is obtained from the **URL** object.

Listing 18.11 DisplayImageWithURL.java

```
1  import javax.swing.*;
2
3  public class DisplayImageWithURL extends JApplet {
```

```
4   public DisplayImageWithURL() {
5     java.net.URL url = this.getClass().getResource("image/us.gif");
6     add(new JLabel(new ImageIcon(url)));
7   }
8 }
```

get image URL
create a label
main method omitted

If you replace the code in lines 5–6 with the following code,

```
add(new JLabel(new ImageIcon("image/us.gif")));
```

you can still run the program as a standalone application, but not as an applet from a browser, as shown in Figure 18.13.

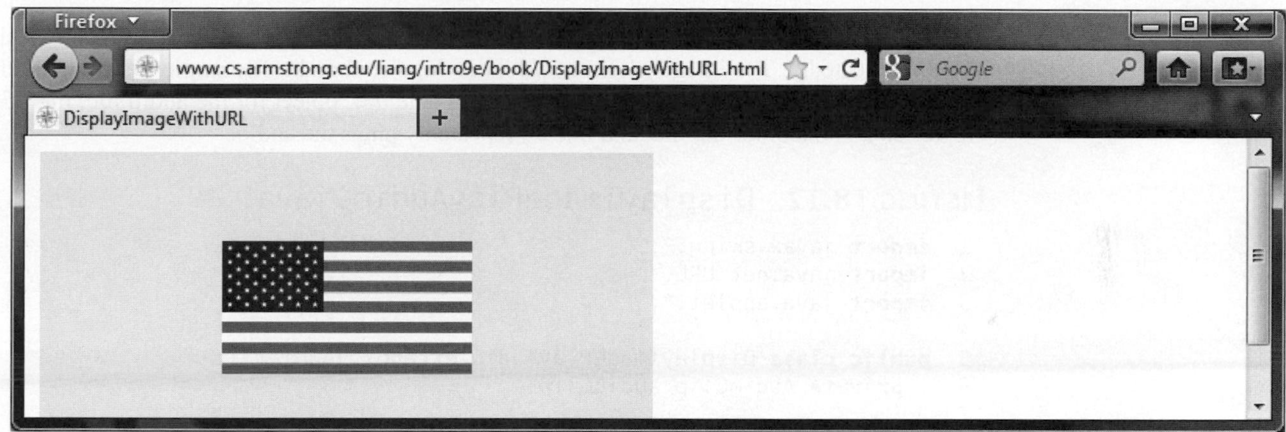

FIGURE 18.13 The applet loads an image from an image file located in the same directory as the applet.

18.22 How do you create a `URL` object for the file **image/us.gif** in the class directory?

18.23 How do you create an `ImageIcon` from the file **image/us.gif** in the class directory?

18.11 Playing Audio in Any Java Program

The `Applet` class contains the methods for obtaining an `AudioClip` object for an audio file. The `AudioClip` object contains the methods for playing audio files.

There are several formats for audio files. Java programs can play audio files in the WAV, AIFF, MIDI, AU, and RMF formats.

To play an audio file in Java (application or applet), first create an *audio clip object* for the file. The audio clip is created once and can be played repeatedly without reloading the file. To create an audio clip, use the static method `newAudioClip()` in the `java.applet.Applet` class:

```
AudioClip audioClip = Applet.newAudioClip(url);
```

Audio originally could be played only from Java applets. For this reason, the `AudioClip` interface is in the `java.applet` package. Since JDK 1.2, audio can be played in any Java program.

The following statements, for example, create an `AudioClip` for the `beep.au` audio file in the class directory:

```
Class metaObject = this.getClass();
URL url = metaObject.getResource("beep.au");
AudioClip audioClip = Applet.newAudioClip(url);
```

To manipulate a sound for an audio clip, use the `play()`, `loop()`, and `stop()` methods in `java.applet.AudioClip`, as shown in Figure 18.14.

«interface» *java.applet.AudioClip*	
+play()	Starts playing this audio clip. Each time this method is called, the clip is restarted from the beginning.
+loop()	Plays the clip repeatedly.
+stop()	Stops playing the clip.

FIGURE 18.14 The `AudioClip` interface provides the methods for playing sound.

Listing 18.12 gives the code that displays the Danish flag and plays the Danish national anthem repeatedly. The image file **image/denmark.gif** and audio file **audio/denmark.mid** are stored under the class directory. Line 12 obtains the `URL` object for the audio file, line 13 creates an audio clip for the file, and line 14 repeatedly plays the audio.

LISTING 18.12 DisplayImagePlayAudio.java

```
 1 import javax.swing.*;
 2 import java.net.URL;
 3 import java.applet.*;
 4
 5 public class DisplayImagePlayAudio extends JApplet {
 6   private AudioClip audioClip;
 7
 8   public DisplayImagePlayAudio() {
 9     URL urlForImage = getClass().getResource("image/denmark.gif");
10     add(new JLabel(new ImageIcon(urlForImage)));
11
12     URL urlForAudio = getClass().getResource("audio/denmark.mid");
13     audioClip = Applet.newAudioClip(urlForAudio);
14     audioClip.loop();
15   }
16
17   @Override
18   public void start() {
19     if (audioClip != null) audioClip.loop();
20   }
21
22   @Override
23   public void stop() {
24     if (audioClip != null) audioClip.stop();
25   }
26 }
```

get image URL (line 9)
create a label (line 10)
get audio URL (line 12)
create an audio clip (line 13)
play audio repeatedly (line 14)
start audio (line 19)
stop audio (line 24)
main method omitted (line 26)

The `stop` method (lines 23–25) stops the audio when the applet is not displayed, and the `start` method (lines 18–20) restarts the audio when the applet is redisplayed. Try to run this applet without the `stop` and `start` methods from a browser and observe the effect.

Run this program as a standalone application from the main method and from a Web browser to test it. Recall that, for brevity, the `main` method in all applets is not printed in the text.

MyProgrammingLab™

18.24 What types of audio files are used in Java?

18.25 How do you create an audio clip from the file **anthem/us.mid** in the class directory?

18.26 How do you play, repeatedly play, and stop an audio clip?

18.12 Case Study: National Flags and Anthems

This case study presents an applet that displays a nation's flag and plays its anthem.

The images in the applet are for seven national flags, named **flag0.gif**, **flag1.gif**, . . ., **flag6.gif** for Denmark, Germany, China, India, Norway, the U.K., and the U.S. They are stored under the **image** directory in the class path. The audio consists of national anthems for these seven nations, named **anthem0.mid**, **anthem1.mid**, . . ., and **anthem6.mid**. They are stored under the **audio** directory in the class path.

The program enables the user to select a nation from a combo box and then displays its flag and plays its anthem. The user can suspend the audio by clicking the *Suspend* button and resume it by clicking the *Resume* button, as shown in Figure 18.15.

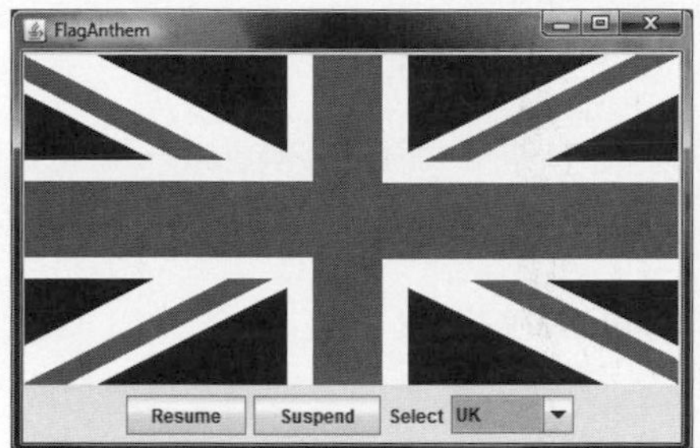

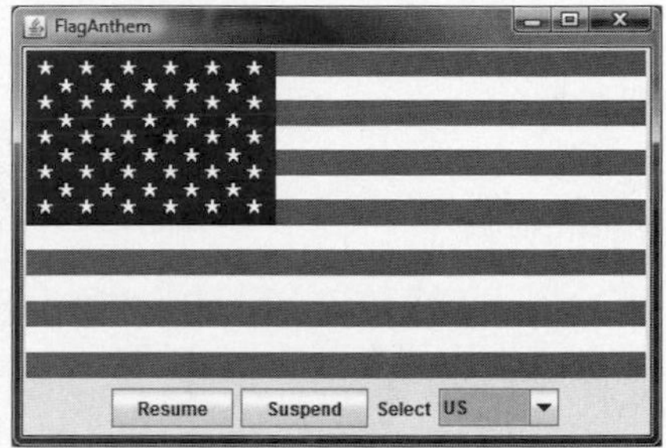

FIGURE 18.15 The applet displays a sequence of images and plays audio.

The program is given in Listing 18.13.

VideoNote
Audio and image

LISTING 18.13 FlagAnthem.java

```
import java.awt.*;
import java.awt.event.*;
import javax.swing.*;
import java.applet.*;

public class FlagAnthem extends JApplet {
  private final static int NUMBER_OF_NATIONS = 7;
  private int current = 0;
  private ImageIcon[] icons = new ImageIcon[NUMBER_OF_NATIONS];
  private AudioClip[] audioClips = new AudioClip[NUMBER_OF_NATIONS];
  private AudioClip currentAudioClip;

  private JLabel jlblImageLabel = new JLabel();
  private JButton jbtResume = new JButton("Resume");
  private JButton jbtSuspend = new JButton("Suspend");
  private JComboBox jcboNations = new JComboBox(new Object[]
    {"Denmark", "Germany", "China", "India", "Norway", "UK", "US"});

  public FlagAnthem() {
    // Load image icons and audio clips
    for (int i = 0; i < NUMBER_OF_NATIONS; i++) {
      icons[i] = new ImageIcon(getClass().getResource(
        "image/flag" + i + ".gif"));
      audioClips[i] = Applet.newAudioClip(
        getClass().getResource("audio/anthem" + i + ".mid"));
    }

    JPanel panel = new JPanel();
```

image icons
audio clips
current audio clip
GUI components
create icons
create audio clips
create UI

```
29      panel.add(jbtResume);
30      panel.add(jbtSuspend);
31      panel.add(new JLabel("Select"));
32      panel.add(jcboNations);
33      add(jlblImageLabel, BorderLayout.CENTER);
34      add(panel, BorderLayout.SOUTH);
35
36      jbtResume.addActionListener(new ActionListener() {        // register listener
37        @Override
38        public void actionPerformed(ActionEvent e) {
39          start();                                               // start audio
40        }
41      });
42      jbtSuspend.addActionListener(new ActionListener() {       // register listener
43        @Override
44        public void actionPerformed(ActionEvent e) {
45          stop();                                                // stop audio
46        }
47      });
48      jcboNations.addActionListener(new ActionListener() {      // register listener
49        @Override
50        public void actionPerformed(ActionEvent e) {
51          stop();
52          current = jcboNations.getSelectedIndex();              // select a nation
53          presentNation(current);                                // present a nation
54        }
55      });
56
57      jlblImageLabel.setIcon(icons[0]);
58      jlblImageLabel.setHorizontalAlignment(JLabel.CENTER);
59      currentAudioClip = audioClips[0];
60      currentAudioClip.play();
61    }
62
63    private void presentNation(int index) {
64      jlblImageLabel.setIcon(icons[index]);
65      jcboNations.setSelectedIndex(index);
66      currentAudioClip = audioClips[index];
67      currentAudioClip.play();
68    }
69
70    @Override
71    public void start() {
72      currentAudioClip.play();                                   // play a clip
73    }
74
75    @Override
76    public void stop() {
77      currentAudioClip.stop();                                   // stop audio clip
78    }
79  }                                                              // main method omitted
```

A label is created in line 13 to display a flag image. An array of flag images for seven nations is created in lines 22–23. An array of audio clips is created in lines 24–25. The image files and audio files are stored in the same directory as the applet class file so these files can be located using the **getResource** method.

The combo box for country names is created in lines 16–17. When a new country name in the combo box is selected, the current presentation is stopped and a new selected nation is presented (lines 51–53).

The **presentNation(index)** method (lines 63–68) presents a nation with the specified index. It sets a new image in the label (line 64), synchronizes with the combo box by setting the selected index (line 65), and plays the new audio (line 67).

The applet's **start** and **stop** methods are overridden to resume and suspend the audio (lines 70–78).

18.27 Which code sets the initial image icon? Which code plays the initial audio clip?

18.28 What does the program do when the *Suspend* button is clicked? What does the program do when the *Resume* button is clicked?

Key Terms

applet 673
applet container 677
archive 674
HTML 673
signed applet 676
tag 673

Chapter Summary

1. **JApplet** is a subclass of **Applet**. It is used for developing Java applets with Swing components.

2. The applet class file must be specified, using the **<applet>** *tag* in an *HTML file* to tell the Web browser where to find the applet. The applet can accept string parameters from HTML using the **<param>** tag.

3. The *applet container* controls and executes applets through the **init**, **start**, **stop**, and **destroy** methods in the **Applet** class.

4. When an applet is loaded, the applet container creates an instance of it by invoking its no-arg constructor. The **init** method is invoked after the applet is created. The **start** method is invoked after the **init** method. It is also called whenever the applet becomes active again after the page containing the applet is revisited. The **stop** method is invoked when the applet becomes inactive.

5. The **destroy** method is invoked when the browser exits normally to inform the applet that it is no longer needed and should release any resources it has allocated. The **stop** method is always called before the **destroy** method.

6. Applications and applets are very similar. An applet can easily be converted into an application, and vice versa. Moreover, an applet can be written with a **main** method to run standalone.

7. You can pass arguments to an applet using the **param** attribute in the applet's tag in HTML. To retrieve the value of the parameter, invoke the **getParameter(paramName)** method.

8. The **Applet**'s **getParameter** method can be invoked only after an instance of the applet is created. Therefore, this method cannot be invoked in the constructor of the applet class. You should invoke this method from the **init** method.

9. You learned how to incorporate images and audio in Java applications and applets. To load audio and images for Java applications and applets, you have to create a **URL** object for the audio and image file. The resource files must be stored in the class directory.

10. To play an audio, create an audio clip from the `URL` object for the audio source. You can use the `AudioClip`'s `play()` method to play it once, the `loop()` method to play it repeatedly, and the `stop()` method to stop it.

Test Questions

Do the test questions for this chapter online at www.cs.armstrong.edu/liang/intro9e/test.html.

MyProgrammingLab™

Programming Exercises

Pedagogical Note

For every applet in the exercise, add a main method to enable it to run as a standalone application.

Sections 18.2–18.6

18.1 (*Loan calculator*) Revise Listing 16.7, LoanCalculator.java, to be an applet for computing loan payment.

18.2 (*Convert applications to applets*) Rewrite `ClockAnimation` in Listing 16.12 as an applet and enable it to run standalone.

***18.3** (*Guess capitals and states*) Revise Programming Exercise 9.17 to write an applet that repeatedly prompts the user to enter a capital for a state or vice versa, as shown in Figure 18.16a. Upon clicking the *Answer* button, the program gets the user input from the text field, reports whether the answer is correct in a message dialog box (Figure 18.16b–c), shows the correct count and total count, and then displays the next question. The user can specify whether to let the program generate a question randomly or sequentially, and whether to generate questions for a capital or a state.

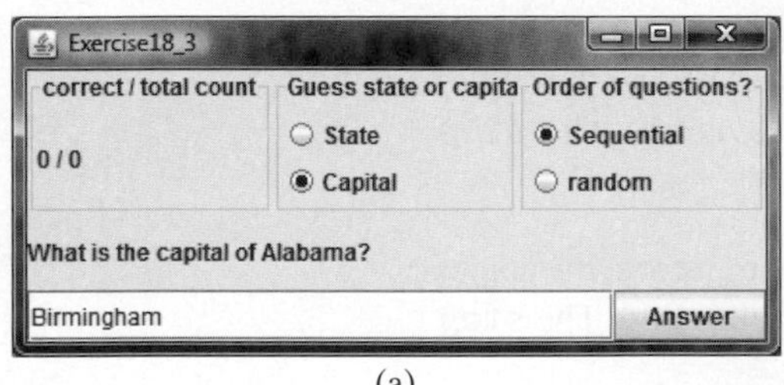

(a)

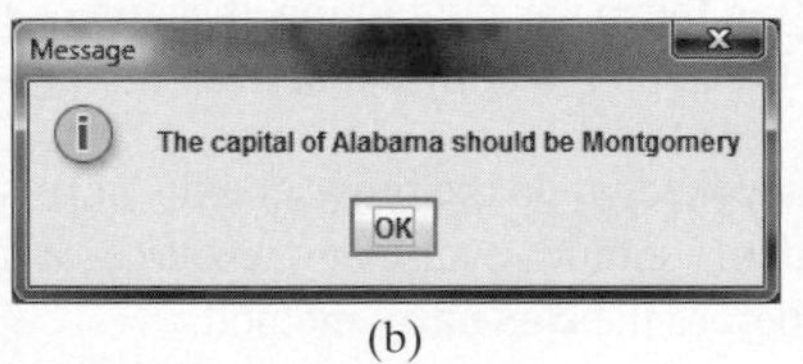

(b)

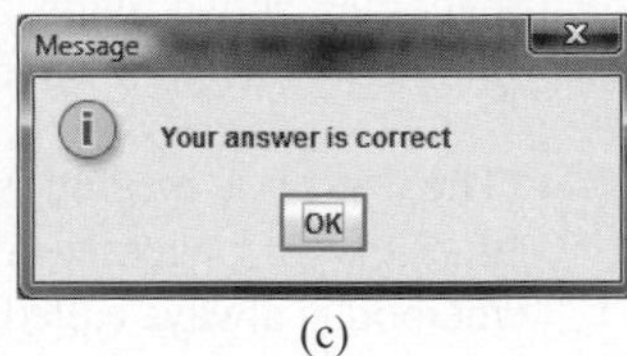

(c)

Figure 18.16 The applet tests the user knowledge on states and capitals.

***18.4** (*Pass strings to applets*) Rewrite Listing 18.5, DisplayMessage.java, to display a message with a standard color, font, and size. The `message`, `x`, `y`, `color`, `fontname`, and `fontsize` are parameters in the `<applet>` tag, as shown below:

```
<applet
  code = "Exercise18_04.class"
  width = 200
  height = 50
  alt = "You must have a Java-enabled browser to view the applet"
>
  <param name = MESSAGE value = "Welcome to Java" />
  <param name = X value = 40 />
  <param name = Y value = 50 />
  <param name = COLOR value = "red" />
```

```
<param name = FONTNAME value = "Monospaced" />
<param name = FONTSIZE value = 20 />
</applet>
```

****18.5** (*Game: a clock learning tool*) Develop a clock applet to show a first-grade student how to read a clock. Modify Programming Exercise 13.19 to display a detailed clock with an hour hand and a minute hand in an applet, as shown in Figure 18.17a. The hour and minute values are randomly generated. The hour is between `0` and `11`, and the minute is `0`, `15`, `30`, or `45`. Upon a mouse click, a new random time is displayed on the clock.

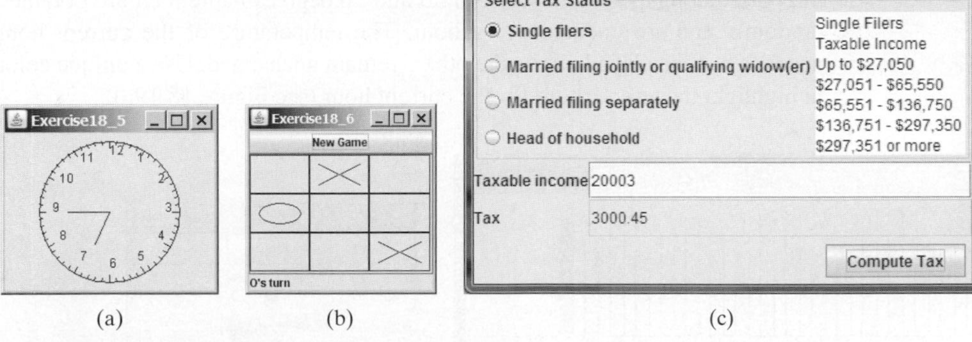

FIGURE 18.17 (a) Upon a mouse click on the clock, the clock time is randomly displayed. (b) Clicking the *New Game* button starts a new game. (c) The tax calculator computes the tax for the specified taxable income and tax status.

****18.6** (*Game: tic-tac-toe*) Rewrite the program in Listing 18.10 TicTacToe.java with the following modifications:

- Define `Cell` as a separate class rather than an inner class.
- Add a button named *New Game*, as shown in Figure 18.17b. Clicking the *New Game* button starts a new game.

****18.7** (*Financial application: tax calculator*) Create an applet to compute tax, as shown in Figure 18.17c. The applet lets the user select the tax status and enter the taxable income to compute the tax based on the 2001 federal tax rates, as shown in Programming Exercise 10.8.

*****18.8** (*Create a calculator*) Use various panels of `FlowLayout`, `GridLayout`, and `BorderLayout` to lay out the following calculator and to implement addition (+), subtraction (-), division (/), square root (`sqrt`), and modulus (%) functions (see Figure 18.18a).

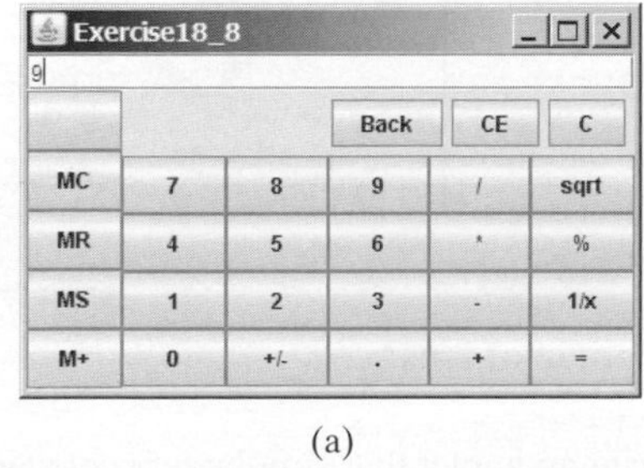

(a)

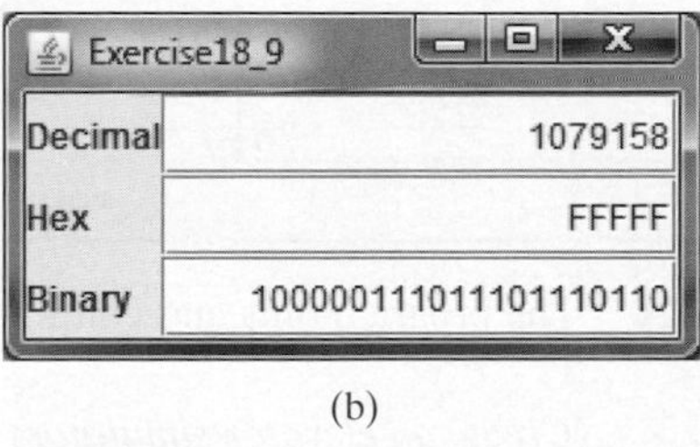

(b)

FIGURE 18.18 (a) Exercise 18.8 is a Java implementation of a popular calculator. (b) Exercise 18.9 converts between decimal, hex, and binary numbers.

*18.9 (*Convert numbers*) Write an applet that converts between decimal, hex, and binary numbers, as shown in Figure 18.18b. When you enter a decimal value in the decimal-value text field and press the *Enter* key, its corresponding hex and binary numbers are displayed in the other two text fields. Likewise, you can enter values in the other fields and convert them accordingly.

**18.10 (*Repaint a partial area*) When you repaint the entire viewing area of a panel, sometimes only a tiny portion of the viewing area is changed. You can improve the performance by repainting only the affected area, but do not invoke `super.paintComponent(g)` when repainting the panel, because this will cause the entire viewing area to be cleared. Use this approach to write an applet to display the temperatures of each hour during the last 24 hours in a histogram. Suppose that temperatures between 50 and 90 degrees Fahrenheit are obtained randomly and are updated every hour. The temperature of the current hour needs to be redisplayed, while the others remain unchanged. Use a unique color to highlight the temperature for the current hour (see Figure 18.19a).

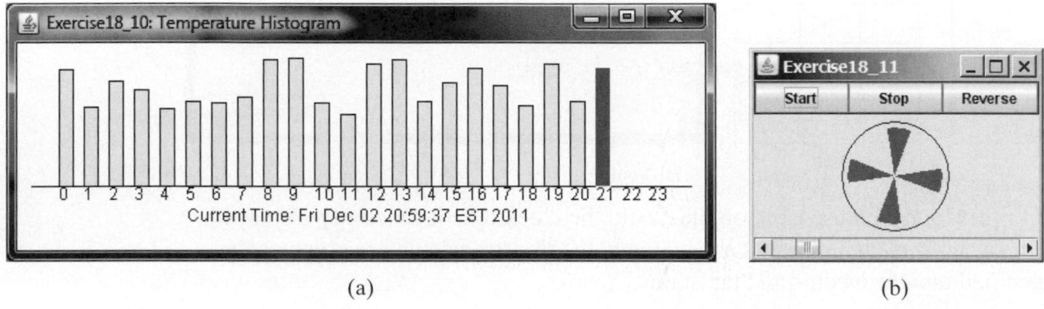

FIGURE 18.19 (a) The histogram displays the average temperature of every hour in the last 24 hours. (b) The program simulates a running fan.

**18.11 (*Simulation: a running fan*) Write a Java applet that simulates a running fan, as shown in Figure 18.19b. The buttons *Start*, *Stop*, and *Reverse* control the fan. The scrollbar controls the fan's speed. Create a class named `Fan`, a subclass of `JPanel`, to display the fan. This class also contains the methods to suspend and resume the fan, set its speed, and reverse its direction. Create a class named `FanControl` that contains a fan, and three buttons and a scroll bar to control the fan. Create a Java applet that contains an instance of `FanControl`.

**18.12 (*Control a group of fans*) Write a Java applet that displays three fans in a group, with control buttons to start and stop all of them, as shown in Figure 18.20.

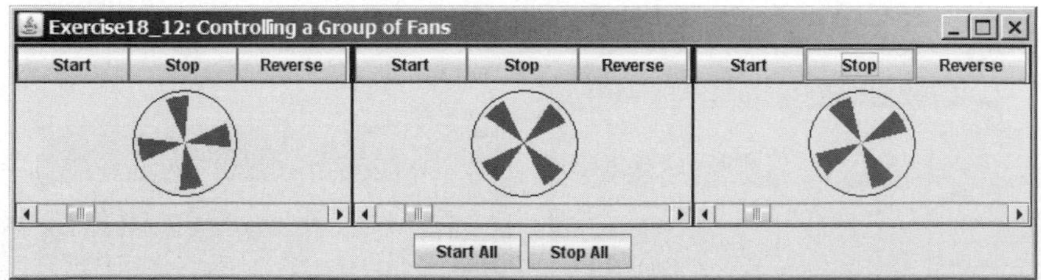

FIGURE 18.20 The program runs and controls a group of fans.

***18.13 (*Create an elevator simulator*) Write an applet that simulates an elevator going up and down (see Figure 18.21). The buttons on the left indicate the floor where the passenger is now located. The passenger must click a button on the left to request that the elevator come to his or her floor. On entering the elevator, the passenger clicks a button on the right to request that it go to the specified floor.

FIGURE 18.21 The program simulates elevator operations.

VideoNote
Control a group of clocks

***18.14** (*Control a group of clocks*) Write a Java applet that displays three clocks in a group, with control buttons to start and stop all of them, as shown in Figure 18.22.

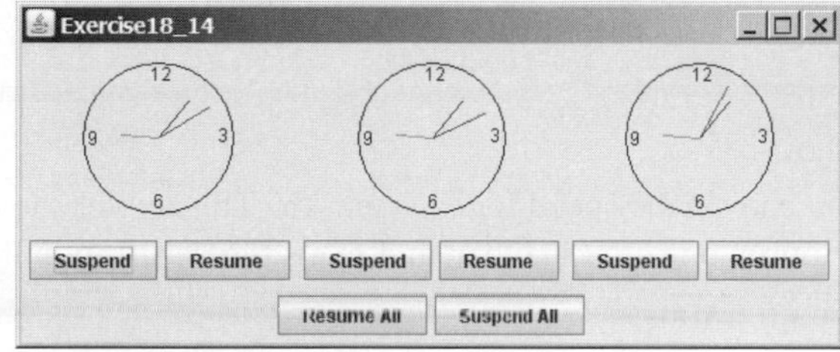

FIGURE 18.22 Three clocks run independently with individual control and group control.

Sections 18.10–18.12

***18.15** (*Enlarge and shrink an image*) Write an applet that will display a sequence of images from a single image file in different sizes. Initially, the viewing area for this image has a width of 300 and a height of 300. Your program should continuously shrink the viewing area by 1 in width and 1 in height until it reaches a width of 50 and a height of 50. At that point, the viewing area should continuously enlarge by 1 in width and 1 in height until it reaches a width of 300 and a height of 300. The viewing area should shrink and enlarge (alternately) to create animation for the single image.

*****18.16** (*Simulate a stock ticker*) Write a Java applet that displays a stock-index ticker (see Figure 18.23). The stock-index information is passed from the `<param>` tag in the HTML file. Each index has four parameters: Index Name (e.g., S&P

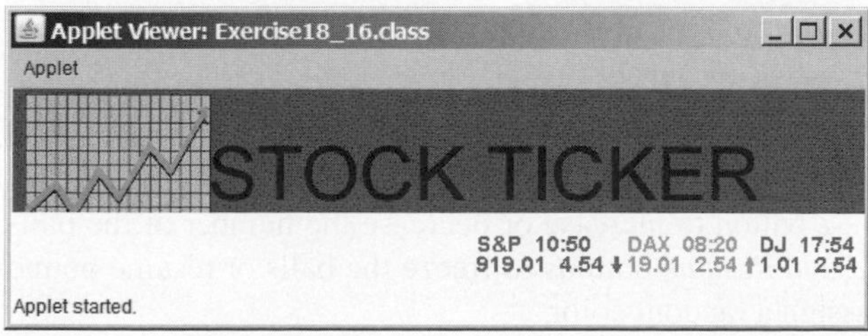

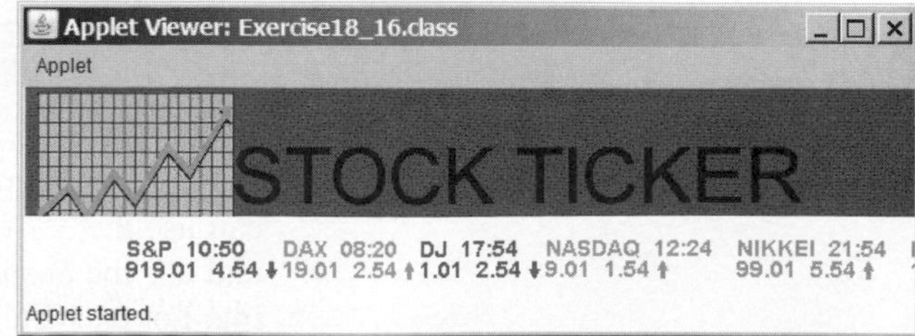

FIGURE 18.23 The program displays a stock-index ticker.

500), Current Time (e.g., 15:54), the index from the previous day (e.g., 919.01), and Change (e.g., 4.54). Use at least five indexes, such as Dow Jones, S&P 500, NASDAQ, NIKKEI, and Gold & Silver Index. Display positive changes in green and negative changes in red. The indexes move from right to left in the applet's viewing area. The applet freezes the ticker when the mouse button is pressed; it moves again when the mouse button is released.

**18.17 (*Racing cars*) Write an applet that simulates four cars racing, as shown in Figure 18.24a. You can set the speed for each car, with maximum 100.

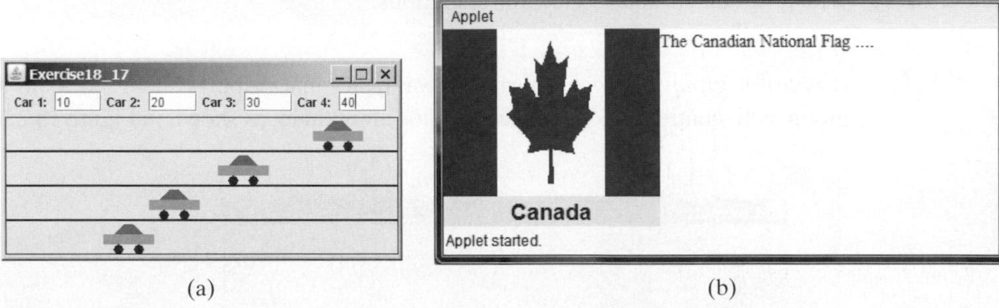

Figure 18.24 (a) You can set the speed for each car. (b) This applet shows each country's flag, name, and description, one after another, and reads the description that is currently shown.

18.18 (*Show national flags*) Write an applet that introduces national flags, one after the other, by presenting each one's photo, name, and description (see Figure 18.24b) along with audio that reads the description. Suppose your applet displays the flags of eight countries. Assume that the photo image files, named **flag0.gif, **flag1.gif**, and so on, up to **flag7.gif**, are stored in a subdirectory named **image** in the applet's directory. The length of each audio is less than 10 seconds. Assume that the name and description of each country's flag are passed from the HTML using the parameters `name0`, `name1`, . . . , `name7`, and `description0`, `description1`, . . . , and `description7`. Pass the number of countries as an HTML parameter using `numberOfCountries`. Here is an example:

```
<param name = "numberOfCountries" value = 8>
<param name = "name0" value = "Canada">
<param name = "description0" value = "The Canadian ... ">
```

Hint
Use the `DescriptionPanel` class to display the image, name, and the text. The `DescriptionPanel` class was introduced in Listing 17.2.

***18.19 (*Bouncing balls*) The example in Section 18.8 simulates a bouncing ball. Extend the example to allow multiple balls, as shown in Figure 18.25a. You can use the *+1* or *−1* button to increase or decrease the number of the balls, and use the *Suspend* and *Resume* buttons to freeze the balls or resume bouncing. For each ball, assign a random color.

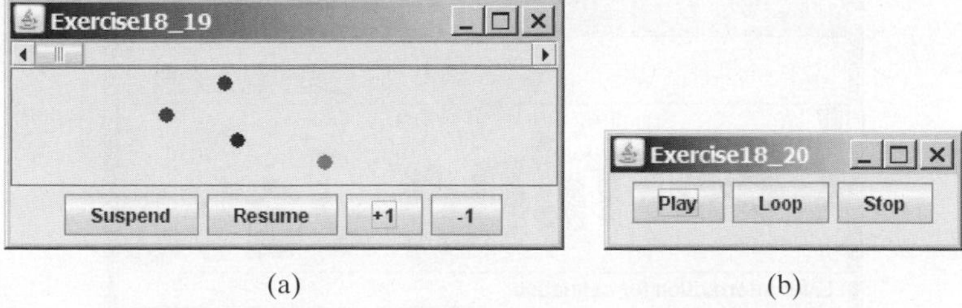

FIGURE 18.25 (a) The applet allows you to add or remove bouncing balls. (b) Click *Play* to play an audio clip once, click *Loop* to play an audio repeatedly, and click *Stop* to terminate playing.

***18.20** (*Play, loop, and stop a sound clip*) Write an applet that meets the following requirements:

- Get an audio file from the class directory.
- Place three buttons labeled *Play*, *Loop*, and *Stop*, as shown in Figure 18.25b.
- If you click the *Play* button, the audio file is played once. If you click the *Loop* button, the audio file keeps playing repeatedly. If you click the *Stop* button, the playing stops.
- The applet can run as an application.

****18.21** (*Create an alarm clock*) Write an applet that will display a digital clock with a large display panel that shows the hour, minute, and second. This clock should allow the user to set an alarm. Figure 18.26a shows an example of such a clock. To turn on the alarm, check the *Alarm* check box. To specify the alarm time, click the *Set alarm* button to display a new frame, as shown in Figure 18.26b. You can set the alarm time in the frame.

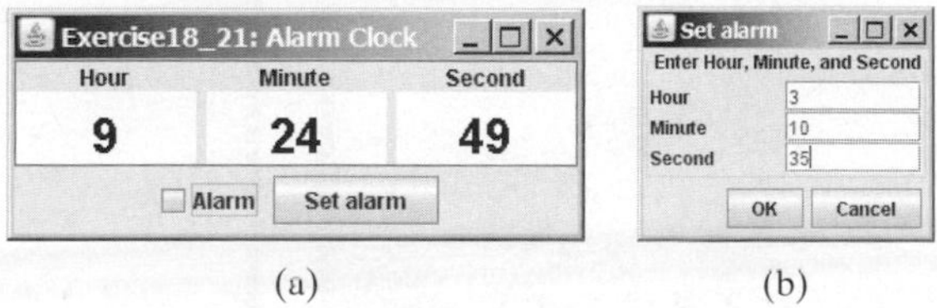

FIGURE 18.26 The program displays the current hour, minute, and second and enables you to set an alarm.

****18.22** (*Create an image animator with audio*) Create animation using the applet shown in Figure 18.27 to meet the following requirements:

- Allow the user to specify the animation speed in a text field.
- Get the number of frames and the image's file-name prefix from the user. For example, if the user enters **n** for the number of frames and **L** for the image prefix, then the files are **L1**, **L2**, and so on, to **L*n***. Assume that the images are stored in the **image** directory, a subdirectory of the applet's directory.
- Allow the user to specify an audio file name. The audio file is stored in the same directory as the applet. The sound is played while the animation runs.

FIGURE 18.27 This applet lets the user select image files, an audio file, and the animation speed.

****18.23** (*Simulation: raise flag and play anthem*) Create an applet that displays a flag rising up, as shown in Figure 16.1b–d. As the national flag rises, play the national anthem. (You may use a flag image and anthem audio file from Listing 18.13.)

Comprehensive

*****18.24** (*Game: bean-machine animation*) Write an applet that enhances the bean machine animation in Programming Exercise 16.22. The applet lets you set the number of slots, as shown in Figure 18.28. Click *Start* to start or restart the animation and click *Stop* to stop.

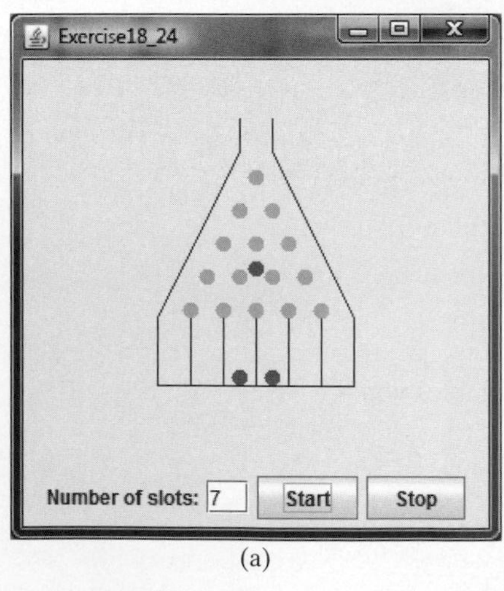

(a)

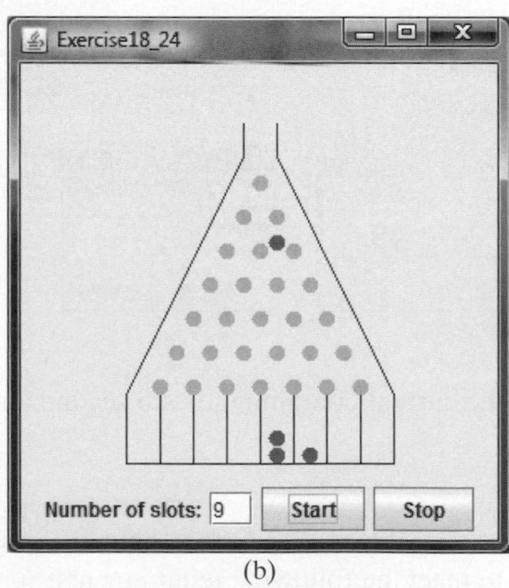

(b)

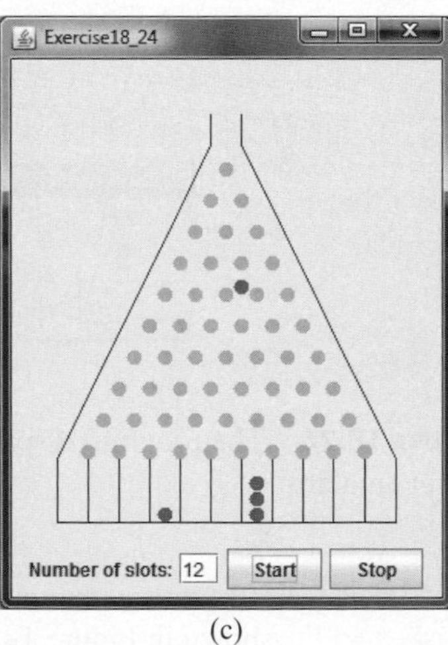

(c)

FIGURE 18.28 The applet controls a bean-machine animation.

****18.25** (*Game: guess birthdays*) Listing 3.3, GuessBirthday.java, gives a program for guessing a birthday. Create an applet for guessing birthdays as shown in Figure 18.29. The applet prompts the user to check whether the date is in any of the five sets. The date is displayed in the text field upon clicking the *Guess Birthday* button.

*****18.26** (*Game: math quiz*) Listing 3.1, AdditionQuiz.java, and Listing 3.4, SubtractionQuiz.java, generate and grade math quizzes. Write an applet that allows

FIGURE 18.29 This applet guesses the birthday.

the user to select a question type and difficulty level, as shown in Figure 18.30a. When the user clicks the *Start* button, the program begins to generate a question. After the user enters an answer with the *Enter* key, a new question is displayed. When the user clicks the *Start* button, the elapsed time is displayed. The time is updated every second until the *Stop* button is clicked. The correct count is updated whenever a correct answer is made.

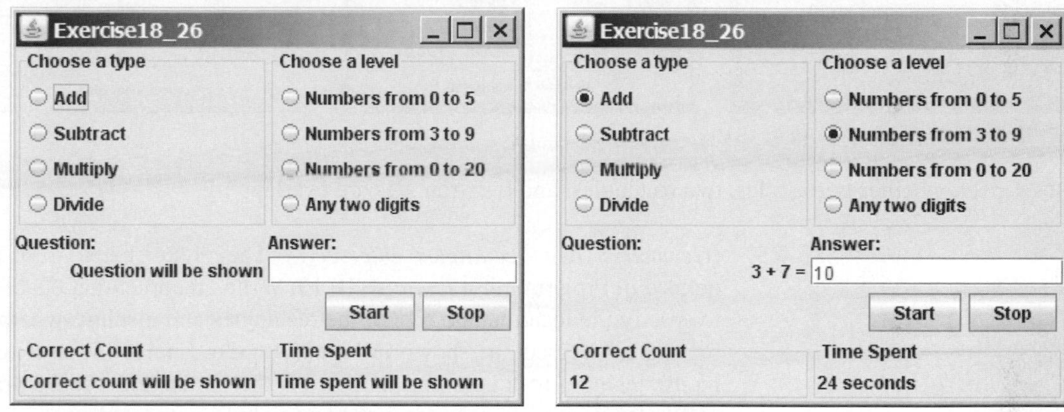

(a) Before a session starts (b) After a session is started

FIGURE 18.30 The applet tests math skills.

*****18.27** (*Graphs*) A graph consists of vertices and edges that connect vertices. Write a program that enables the user to draw vertices and edges dynamically, as shown in Figure 18.31. The radius of each vertex is **20** pixels. Implement the following functions: (1) The user clicks the left-mouse button to place a vertex centered at the mouse point, provided that the mouse point is not inside or too

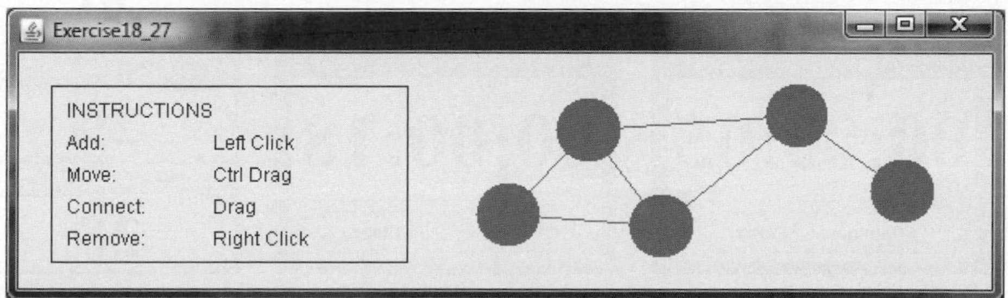

FIGURE 18.31 The applet enables users to draw a graph dynamically.

close to an existing vertex. (2) The user clicks the right-mouse button inside an existing vertex to remove the vertex. (3) The user presses a mouse button inside a vertex and drags to another vertex and then releases the button to create an edge. (4) The user drags a vertex while pressing the *CTRL* key to move a vertex.

**18.28 (*Geometry: two circles intersect?*) The `Circle2D` class was defined in Programming Exercise 10.11. Write an applet that enables the user to specify the location and size of the circles and displays whether the two circles intersect, as shown in Figure 18.32a. Enable the user to point the mouse inside a circle and drag it. As the circle is being dragged, the circle's center coordinates in the text fields are updated.

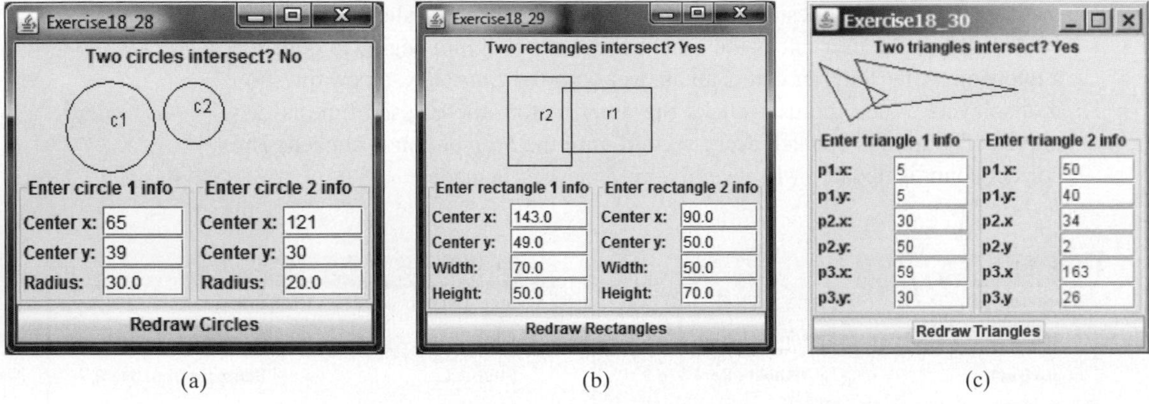

FIGURE 18.32 Check whether two circles, two rectangles, and two triangles are overlapping.

**18.29 (*Geometry: two rectangles intersect?*) The `MyRectangle2D` class was defined in Programming Exercise 10.13. Write an applet that enables the user to specify the location and size of the rectangles and displays whether the two rectangles intersect, as shown in Figure 18.32b. Enable the user to point the mouse inside a rectangle and drag it. As the rectangle is being dragged, the rectangle's center coordinates in the text fields are updated.

**18.30 (*Geometry: two triangles intersect?*) The `Triangle2D` class was defined in Programming Exercise 10.12. Write an applet that enables the user to specify the location of the two triangles and displays whether the two triangles intersect, as shown in Figure 18.32c.

*18.31 (*Count-up stopwatch*) Write an applet that simulates a stopwatch, as shown in Figure 18.33a. When the user clicks the *Start* button, the button's label

FIGURE 18.33 (a)–(c) The applet counts up the time. (d) The applet counts down the time.

is changed to *Pause*, as shown in Figure 18.33b. When the user clicks the *Pause* button, the button's label is changed to *Resume*, as shown in Figure 18.33c. The *Clear* button resets the count to 0 and resets the button's label to *Start*.

***18.32** (*Count-down stopwatch*) Write an applet that allows the user to enter time in seconds in the text field and press the *Enter* key to count down the minutes, as shown in Figure 18.33(d). The remaining seconds are redisplayed every one second. When the minutes are expired, the program starts to play music continuously.

****18.33** (*Pattern recognition: consecutive four equal numbers*) Write an applet for Programming Exercise 7.19, as shown in Figure 18.34a–b. Let the user enter the numbers in the text fields in a grid of 6 rows and 7 columns. The user can click the *Solve* button to highlight a sequence of four equal numbers, if it exists.

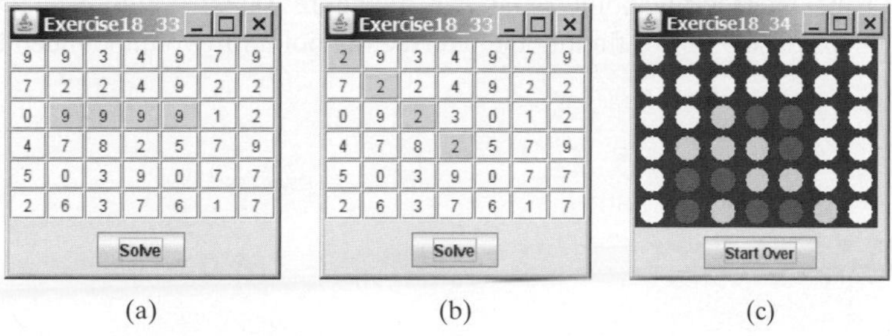

FIGURE 18.34 (a)–(b) Clicking the *Solve* button to highlight the four consecutive numbers in a row, a column, or a diagonal. (c) The applet enables two players to play the connect-four game.

*****18.34** (*Game: connect four*) Programming Exercise 7.20 enables two players to play the connect-four game on the console. Rewrite the program using an applet, as shown in Figure 18.34c. The applet enables two players to place red and yellow discs in turn. To place a disk, the player needs to click on an available cell. An *available cell* is unoccupied and its downward neighbor is occupied. The applet flashes the four winning cells if a player wins and reports no winners if all cells are occupied with no winners.

*****18.35** (*Game: play connect four with computer*) Revise Exercise 18.34 to play the game with the computer. The program lets the user make a move first, followed by a move by the computer. The minimum requirement is for the computer to make a legal move. You are encouraged to design good strategies for the computer to make intelligent moves.

****18.36** (*Geometry: display angles*) Write a program that enables the user to drag the vertices of a triangle and displays the angles dynamically as the triangle shape changes, as shown in Figure 18.35a. Change the mouse cursor to the cross-hair shape when the mouse is moved close to a vertex. The formula to compute angles A, B, and C are as follows (see Figure 18.35b):

```
A = Math.acos((a * a - b * b - c * c) / (-2 * b * c))
B = Math.acos((b * b - a * a - c * c) / (-2 * a * c))
C = Math.acos((c * c - b * b - a * a) / (-2 * a * b))
```

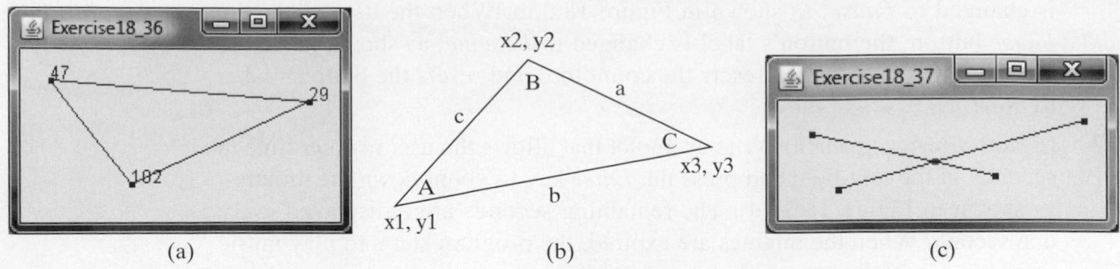

FIGURE 18.35 (a–b) Exercise18.36 enables the user to drag vertices and display the angles dynamically. (c) Exercise18.37 enables the user to drag vertices and display the lines and their intersecting point dynamically.

****18.37** (*Geometry: intersecting point*) Write a program that displays two line segments with their end points, and their intersecting point. Initially, the end points are at (20, 20) and (56, 130) for line 1 and at (100, 20) and (16, 130) for line 2. The user can use the mouse to drag a point and dynamically display the intersecting point, as shown in Figure 18.35c. *Hint*: See Programming Exercise 3.25 for finding the intersecting point of two unbounded lines.

CHAPTER 19

BINARY I/O

Objectives

- To discover how I/O is processed in Java (§19.2).
- To distinguish between text I/O and binary I/O (§19.3).
- To read and write bytes using `FileInputStream` and `FileOutputStream` (§19.4.1).
- To filter data using the base classes `FilterInputStream` and `FilterOutputStream` (§19.4.2).
- To read and write primitive values and strings using `DataInputStream` and `DataOutputStream` (§19.4.3).
- To improve I/O performance by using `BufferedInputStream` and `BufferedOutputStream` (§19.4.4).
- To write a program that copies a file (§19.5).
- To store and restore objects using `ObjectOutputStream` and `ObjectInputStream` (§19.6).
- To implement the `Serializable` interface to make objects serializable (§19.6.1).
- To serialize arrays (§19.6.2).
- To read and write files using the `RandomAccessFile` class (§19.7).

19.1 Introduction

Java provides many classes for performing text I/O and binary I/O.

text file
binary file

Files can be classified as either text or binary. A file that can be processed (read, created, or modified) using a text editor such as Notepad on Windows or vi on UNIX is called a *text file*. All the other files are called *binary files*. You cannot read binary files using a text editor—they are designed to be read by programs. For example, Java source programs are stored in text files and can be read by a text editor, but Java class files are stored in binary files and are read by the JVM.

why binary I/O?

Although it is not technically precise and correct, you can envision a text file as consisting of a sequence of characters and a binary file as consisting of a sequence of bits. Characters in a text file are encoded using a character encoding scheme such as ASCII or Unicode. For example, the decimal integer **199** is stored as the sequence of the three characters **1**, **9**, **9** in a text file, and the same integer is stored as a byte-type value **C7** in a binary file, because decimal **199** equals hex **C7** ($199 = 12 \times 16^1 + 7$). The advantage of binary files is that they are more efficient to process than text files.

text I/O
binary I/O

Java offers many classes for performing file input and output. These can be categorized as *text I/O classes* and *binary I/O classes.* In Section 14.11, File Input and Output, you learned how to read and write strings and numeric values from/to a text file using **Scanner** and **PrintWriter**. This chapter introduces the classes for performing binary I/O.

19.2 How Is Text I/O Handled in Java?

*Text data is read using the **Scanner** class and written using the **PrintWriter** class.*

Recall that a **File** object encapsulates the properties of a file or a path but does not contain the methods for reading/writing data from/to a file. In order to perform I/O, you need to create objects using appropriate Java I/O classes. The objects contain the methods for reading/writing data from/to a file. For example, to write text to a file named **temp.txt**, you can create an object using the **PrintWriter** class as follows:

```
PrintWriter output = new PrintWriter("temp.txt");
```

You can now invoke the **print** method on the object to write a string to the file. For example, the following statement writes **Java 101** to the file.

```
output.print("Java 101");
```

The next statement closes the file.

```
output.close();
```

There are many I/O classes for various purposes. In general, these can be classified as input classes and output classes. An *input class* contains the methods to read data, and an *output class* contains the methods to write data. **PrintWriter** is an example of an output class, and **Scanner** is an example of an input class. The following code creates an input object for the file **temp.txt** and reads data from the file.

```
Scanner input = new Scanner(new File("temp.txt"));
System.out.println(input.nextLine());
```

If **temp.txt** contains the text **Java 101**, **input.nextLine()** returns the string **"Java 101"**.

stream
input stream
output stream

Figure 19.1 illustrates Java I/O programming. An input object reads a *stream* of data from a file, and an output object writes a stream of data to a file. An input object is also called an *input stream* and an output object an *output stream.*

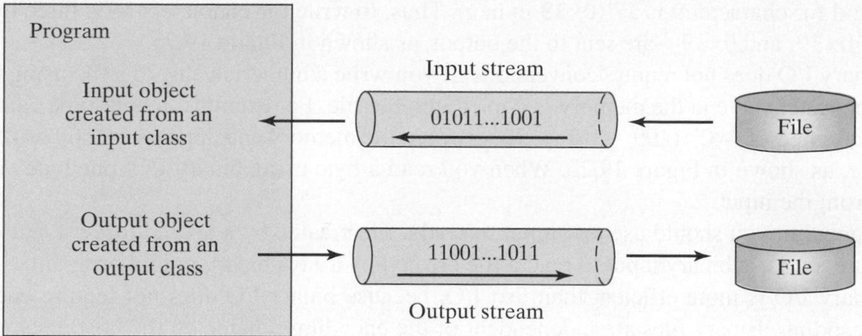

FIGURE 19.1 The program receives data through an input object and sends data through an output object.

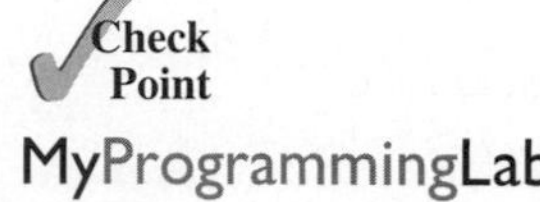

19.1 What is a text file, and what is a binary file? Can you view a text file or a binary file using a text editor?

19.2 How do you read or write text data in Java? What is a stream?

19.3 Text I/O vs. Binary I/O

Binary I/O does not involve encoding or decoding and thus is more efficient than text I/O.

Computers do not differentiate between binary files and text files. All files are stored in binary format, and thus all files are essentially binary files. Text I/O is built upon binary I/O to provide a level of abstraction for character encoding and decoding, as shown in Figure 19.2a. Encoding and decoding are automatically performed for text I/O. The JVM converts Unicode to a file-specific encoding when writing a character, and it converts a file-specific encoding to Unicode when reading a character. For example, suppose you write the string `"199"` using text I/O to a file. Each character is written to the file. Since the Unicode for character `1` is `0x0031`, the Unicode `0x0031` is converted to a code that depends on the encoding scheme for the file. (Note that the prefix `0x` denotes a hex number.) In the United States, the default encoding for text files on Windows is ASCII. The ASCII code for character `1` is `49` (`0x31` in

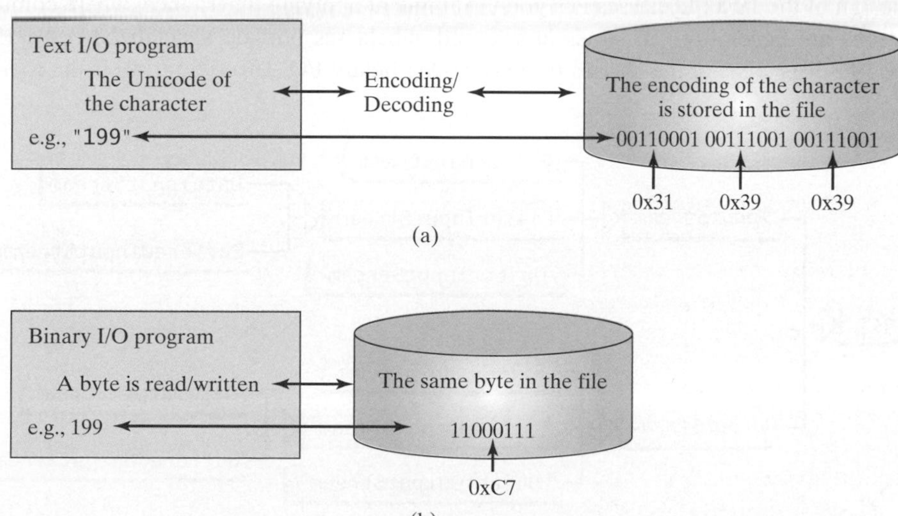

FIGURE 19.2 Text I/O requires encoding and decoding, whereas binary I/O does not.

hex) and for character 9 is 57 (0x39 in hex). Thus, to write the characters 199, three bytes—0x31, 0x39, and 0x39—are sent to the output, as shown in Figure 19.2a.

Binary I/O does not require conversions. If you write a numeric value to a file using binary I/O, the exact value in the memory is copied into the file. For example, a byte-type value 199 is represented as 0xC7 ($199 = 12 \times 16^1 + 7$) in the memory and appears exactly as 0xC7 in the file, as shown in Figure 19.2b. When you read a byte using binary I/O, one byte value is read from the input.

In general, you should use text input to read a file created by a text editor or a text output program, and use binary input to read a file created by a Java binary output program.

Binary I/O is more efficient than text I/O, because binary I/O does not require encoding and decoding. Binary files are independent of the encoding scheme on the host machine and thus are portable. Java programs on any machine can read a binary file created by a Java program. This is why Java class files are binary files. Java class files can run on a JVM on any machine.

.txt and .dat

Note

For consistency, this book uses the extension **.txt** to name text files and **.dat** to name binary files.

MyProgrammingLab™

19.3 What are the differences between text I/O and binary I/O?

19.4 How is a Java character represented in the memory, and how is a character represented in a text file?

19.5 If you write the string "ABC" to an ASCII text file, what values are stored in the file?

19.6 If you write the string "100" to an ASCII text file, what values are stored in the file? If you write a numeric byte-type value 100 using binary I/O, what values are stored in the file?

19.7 What is the encoding scheme for representing a character in a Java program? By default, what is the encoding scheme for a text file on Windows?

19.4 Binary I/O Classes

The abstract `InputStream` *is the root class for reading binary data and the abstract* `OutputStream` *is the root class for writing binary data.*

The design of the Java I/O classes is a good example of applying inheritance, where common operations are generalized in superclasses, and subclasses provide specialized operations. Figure 19.3 lists some of the classes for performing binary I/O. `InputStream` is the root for

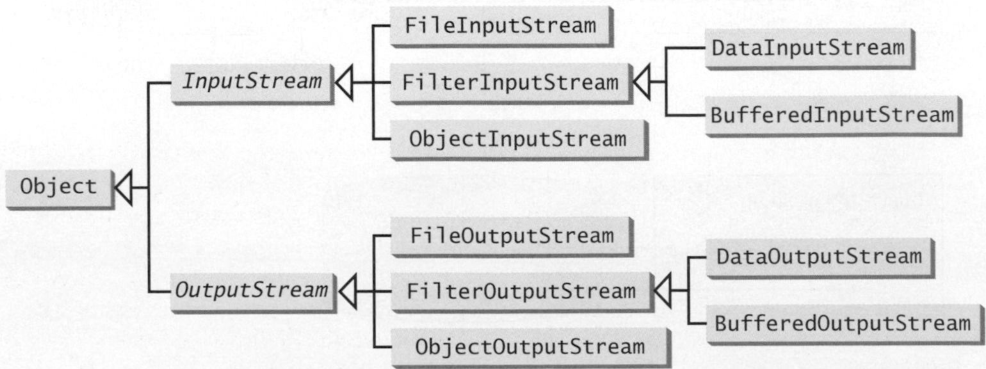

FIGURE 19.3 `InputStream`, `OutputStream`, and their subclasses are for performing binary I/O.

java.io.InputStream	
+read(): int	Reads the next byte of data from the input stream. The value byte is returned as an `int` value in the range `0` to `255`. If no byte is available because the end of the stream has been reached, the value –1 is returned.
+read(b: byte[]): int	Reads up to `b.length` bytes into array `b` from the input stream and returns the actual number of bytes read. Returns –1 at the end of the stream.
+read(b: byte[], off: int, len: int): int	Reads bytes from the input stream and stores them in `b[off]`, `b[off+1]`, . . ., `b[off+len-1]`. The actual number of bytes read is returned. Returns –1 at the end of the stream.
+available(): int	Returns an estimate of the number of bytes that can be read from the input stream.
+close(): void	Closes this input stream and releases any system resources occupied by it.
+skip(n: long): long	Skips over and discards `n` bytes of data from this input stream. The actual number of bytes skipped is returned.
+markSupported(): boolean	Tests whether this input stream supports the `mark` and `reset` methods.
+mark(readlimit: int): void	Marks the current position in this input stream.
+reset(): void	Repositions this stream to the position at the time the `mark` method was last called on this input stream.

FIGURE 19.4 The abstract `InputStream` class defines the methods for the input stream of bytes.

binary input classes, and `OutputStream` is the root for binary output classes. Figures 19.4 and 19.5 list all the methods in the classes `InputStream` and `OutputStream`.

Note

All the methods in the binary I/O classes are declared to throw `java.io.IOException` or a subclass of `java.io.IOException`.

throws IOException

java.io.OutputStream	
+write(int b): void	Writes the specified byte to this output stream. The parameter `b` is an `int` value. `(byte)b` is written to the output stream.
+write(b: byte[]): void	Writes all the bytes in array `b` to the output stream.
+write(b: byte[], off: int, len: int): void	Writes `b[off]`, `b[off+1]`,. . ., `b[off+len-1]` into the output stream.
+close(): void	Closes this output stream and releases any system resources occupied by it.
+flush(): void	Flushes this output stream and forces any buffered output bytes to be written out.

FIGURE 19.5 The abstract `OutputStream` class defines the methods for the output stream of bytes.

19.4.1 FileInputStream/FileOutputStream

`FileInputStream`/`FileOutputStream` is for reading/writing bytes from/to files. All the methods in these classes are inherited from `InputStream` and `OutputStream`. `FileInputStream`/`FileOutputStream` does not introduce new methods. To construct a `FileInputStream`, use the constructors shown in Figure 19.6.

A `java.io.FileNotFoundException` will occur if you attempt to create a `FileInputStream` with a nonexistent file.

FileNotFoundException

To construct a `FileOutputStream`, use the constructors shown in Figure 19.7.

If the file does not exist, a new file will be created. If the file already exists, the first two constructors will delete the current content of the file. To retain the current content and append new data into the file, use the last two constructors and pass `true` to the `append` parameter.

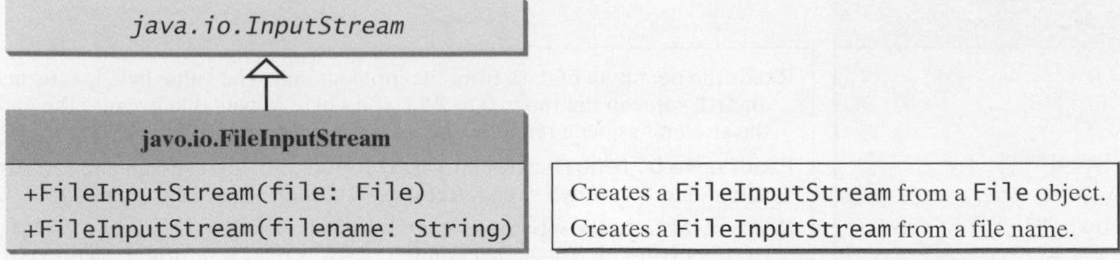

FIGURE 19.6 `FileInputStream` inputs a stream of bytes from a file.

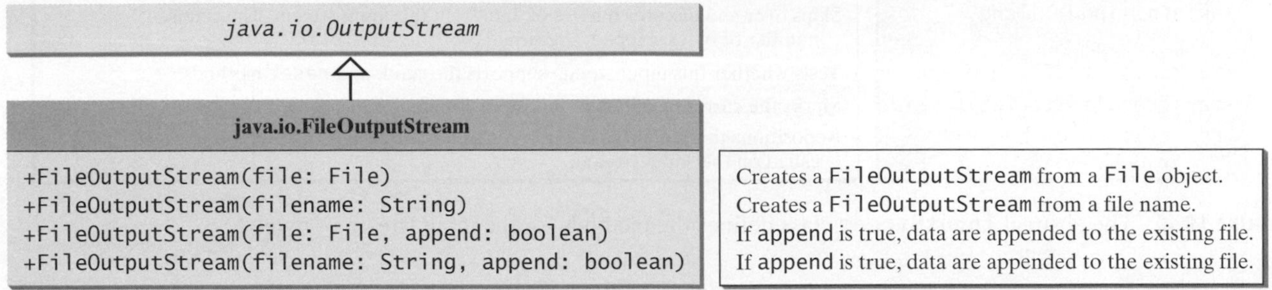

FIGURE 19.7 `FileOutputStream` outputs a stream of bytes to a file.

IOException

Almost all the methods in the I/O classes throw **java.io.IOException**. Therefore, you have to declare **java.io.IOException** to throw in the method or place the code in a try-catch block, as shown below:

Declaring exception in the method

```
public static void main(String[] args)
    throws IOException {
  // Perform I/O operations
}
```

Using try-catch block

```
public static void main(String[] args) {
  try {
    // Perform I/O operations
  }
  catch (IOException ex) {
    ex.printStackTrace();
  }
}
```

Listing 19.1 uses binary I/O to write ten byte values from **1** to **10** to a file named **temp.dat** and reads them back from the file.

LISTING 19.1 TestFileStream.java

import · output stream · output

```
import java.io.*;

public class TestFileStream {
  public static void main(String[] args) throws IOException {
    // Create an output stream to the file
    FileOutputStream output = new FileOutputStream("temp.dat");

    // Output values to the file
    for (int i = 1; i <= 10; i++)
      output.write(i);

    // Close the output stream
    output.close();

```

```
15      // Create an input stream for the file
16      FileInputStream input = new FileInputStream("temp.dat");
17
18      // Read values from the file
19      int value;
20      while ((value = input.read()) != -1)
21        System.out.print(value + " ");
22
23      // Close the input stream
24      input.close();
25    }
26  }
```

input stream

input

```
1 2 3 4 5 6 7 8 9 10
```

A **FileOutputStream** is created for the file **temp.dat** in line 6. The **for** loop writes ten byte values into the file (lines 9–10). Invoking **write(i)** is the same as invoking **write((byte)i)**. Line 13 closes the output stream. Line 16 creates a **FileInputStream** for the file **temp.dat**. Values are read from the file and displayed on the console in lines 19–21. The expression **((value = input.read()) != -1)** (line 20) reads a byte from **input.read()**, assigns it to **value**, and checks whether it is **-1**. The input value of **-1** signifies the end of a file.

end of a file

The file **temp.dat** created in this example is a binary file. It can be read from a Java program but not from a text editor, as shown in Figure 19.8.

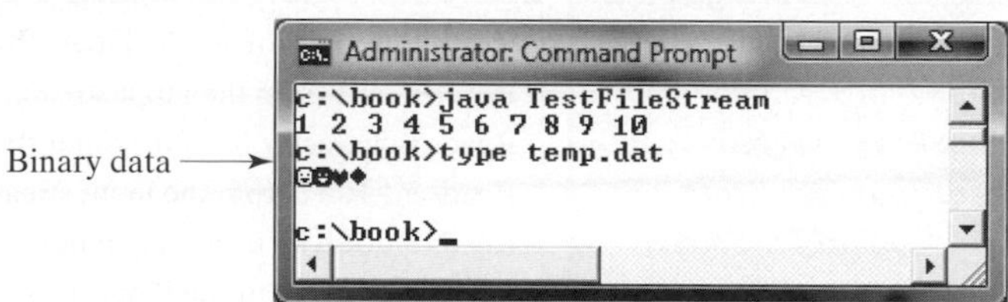

FIGURE 19.8 A binary file cannot be displayed in text mode.

Tip

When a stream is no longer needed, always close it using the **close()** method. Not closing streams may cause data corruption in the output file, or other programming errors.

close stream

Note

The root directory for the file is the classpath directory. For the example in this book, the root directory is **c:\book**, so the file **temp.dat** is located at **c:\book**. If you wish to place **temp.dat** in a specific directory, replace line 6 with

where is the file?

```
FileOutputStream output =
  new FileOutputStream ("directory/temp.dat");
```

Note

An instance of **FileInputStream** can be used as an argument to construct a **Scanner**, and an instance of **FileOutputStream** can be used as an argument to construct a **PrintWriter**. You can create a **PrintWriter** to append text into a file using

appending to text file

```
new PrintWriter(new FileOutputStream("temp.txt", true));
```

If **temp.txt** does not exist, it is created. If **temp.txt** already exists, new data are appended to the file.

19.4.2 `FilterInputStream`/`FilterOutputStream`

Filter streams are streams that filter bytes for some purpose. The basic byte input stream provides a `read` method that can be used only for reading bytes. If you want to read integers, doubles, or strings, you need a filter class to wrap the byte input stream. Using a filter class enables you to read integers, doubles, and strings instead of bytes and characters. `FilterInputStream` and `FilterOutputStream` are the base classes for filtering data. When you need to process primitive numeric types, use `DataInputStream` and `DataOutputStream` to filter bytes.

19.4.3 `DataInputStream`/`DataOutputStream`

`DataInputStream` reads bytes from the stream and converts them into appropriate primitive type values or strings. `DataOutputStream` converts primitive type values or strings into bytes and outputs the bytes to the stream.

`DataInputStream` extends `FilterInputStream` and implements the `DataInput` interface, as shown in Figure 19.9. `DataOutputStream` extends `FilterOutputStream` and implements the `DataOutput` interface, as shown in Figure 19.10.

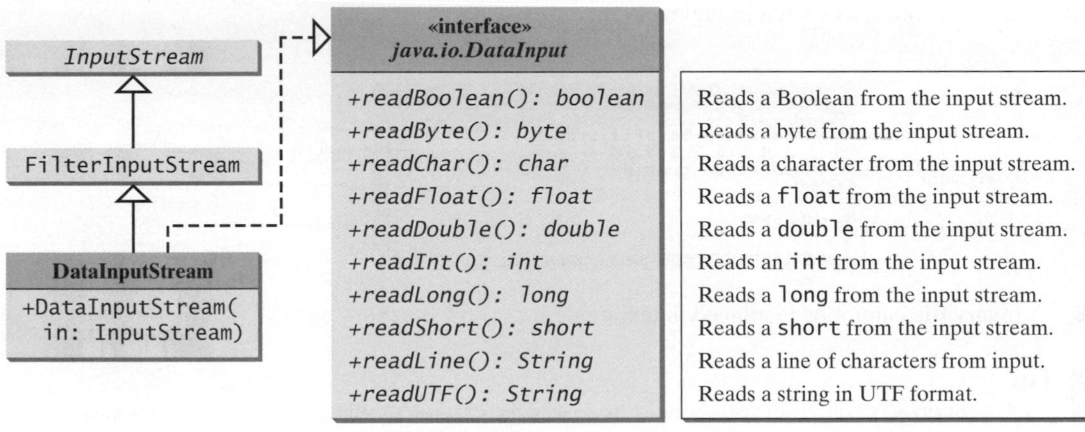

FIGURE 19.9 `DataInputStream` filters an input stream of bytes into primitive data type values and strings.

`DataInputStream` implements the methods defined in the `DataInput` interface to read primitive data type values and strings. `DataOutputStream` implements the methods defined in the `DataOutput` interface to write primitive data type values and strings. Primitive values are copied from memory to the output without any conversions. Characters in a string may be written in several ways, as discussed in the next section.

Characters and Strings in Binary I/O

A Unicode character consists of two bytes. The `writeChar(char c)` method writes the Unicode of character `c` to the output. The `writeChars(String s)` method writes the Unicode for each character in the string `s` to the output. The `writeBytes(String s)` method writes the lower byte of the Unicode for each character in the string `s` to the output. The high byte of the Unicode is discarded. The `writeBytes` method is suitable for strings that consist

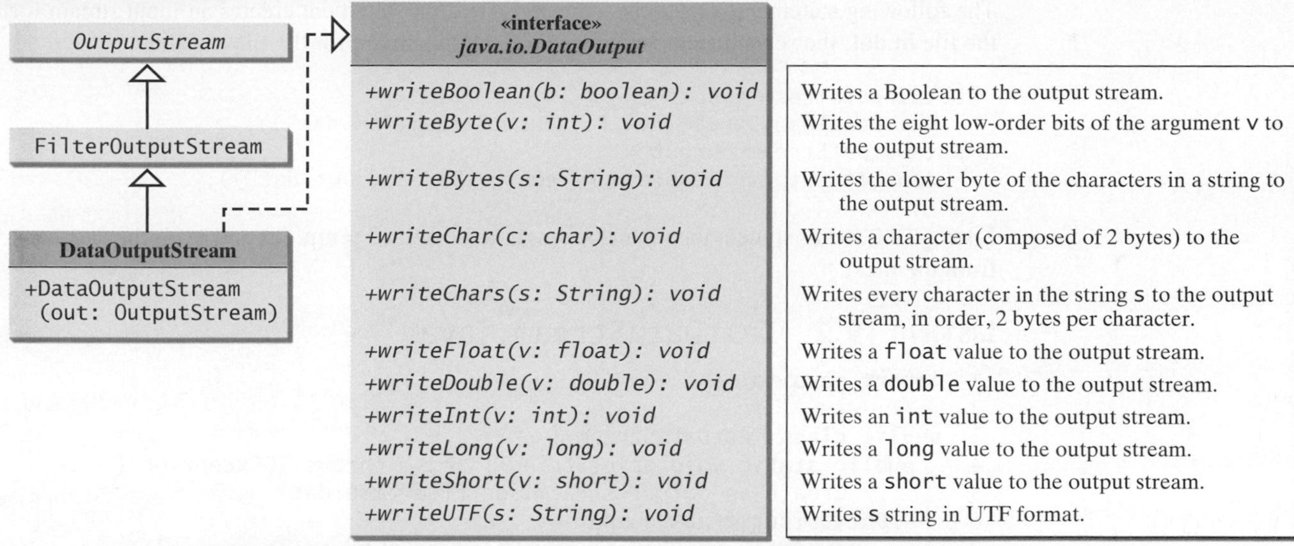

FIGURE 19.10 `DataOutputStream` enables you to write primitive data type values and strings into an output stream.

of ASCII characters, since an ASCII code is stored only in the lower byte of a Unicode. If a string consists of non-ASCII characters, you have to use the `writeChars` method to write the string.

The `writeUTF(String s)` method writes two bytes of length information to the output stream, followed by the modified UTF-8 representation of every character in the string `s`. UTF-8 is a coding scheme that allows systems to operate with both ASCII and Unicode. Most operating systems use ASCII. Java uses Unicode. The ASCII character set is a subset of the Unicode character set. Since most applications need only the ASCII character set, it is a waste to represent an 8-bit ASCII character as a 16-bit Unicode character. The modified UTF-8 scheme stores a character using one, two, or three bytes. Characters are coded in one byte if their code is less than or equal to `0x7F`, in two bytes if their code is greater than `0x7F` and less than or equal to `0x7FF`, or in three bytes if their code is greater than `0x7FF`.

UTF-8 scheme

The initial bits of a UTF-8 character indicate whether a character is stored in one byte, two bytes, or three bytes. If the first bit is `0`, it is a one-byte character. If the first bits are `110`, it is the first byte of a two-byte sequence. If the first bits are `1110`, it is the first byte of a three-byte sequence. The information that indicates the number of characters in a string is stored in the first two bytes preceding the UTF-8 characters. For example, `writeUTF("ABCDEF")` actually writes eight bytes (i.e., `00 06 41 42 43 44 45 46`) to the file, because the first two bytes store the number of characters in the string.

The `writeUTF(String s)` method converts a string into a series of bytes in the UTF-8 format and writes them into an output stream. The `readUTF()` method reads a string that has been written using the `writeUTF` method.

The UTF-8 format has the advantage of saving a byte for each ASCII character, because a Unicode character takes up two bytes and an ASCII character in UTF-8 only one byte. If most of the characters in a long string are regular ASCII characters, using UTF-8 is more efficient.

Creating DataInputStream/DataOutputStream

`DataInputStream`/`DataOutputStream` are created using the following constructors (see Figures 19.9 and 19.10):

```
public DataInputStream(InputStream instream)
public DataOutputStream(OutputStream outstream)
```

The following statements create data streams. The first statement creates an input stream for the file **in.dat**; the second statement creates an output stream for the file **out.dat**.

```
DataInputStream input =
  new DataInputStream(new FileInputStream("in.dat"));
DataOutputStream output =
  new DataOutputStream(new FileOutputStream("out.dat"));
```

Listing 19.2 writes student names and scores to a file named **temp.dat** and reads the data back from the file.

LISTING 19.2 TestDataStream.java

output stream

output

close stream

input stream

input

```
1  import java.io.*;
2
3  public class TestDataStream {
4    public static void main(String[] args) throws IOException {
5      // Create an output stream for file temp.dat
6      DataOutputStream output =
7        new DataOutputStream(new FileOutputStream("temp.dat"));
8
9      // Write student test scores to the file
10     output.writeUTF("John");
11     output.writeDouble(85.5);
12     output.writeUTF("Susan");
13     output.writeDouble(185.5);
14     output.writeUTF("Kim");
15     output.writeDouble(105.25);
16
17     // Close output stream
18     output.close();
19
20     // Create an input stream for file temp.dat
21     DataInputStream input =
22       new DataInputStream(new FileInputStream("temp.dat"));
23
24     // Read student test scores from the file
25     System.out.println(input.readUTF() + " " + input.readDouble());
26     System.out.println(input.readUTF() + " " + input.readDouble());
27     System.out.println(input.readUTF() + " " + input.readDouble());
28   }
29 }
```

```
John 85.5
Susan 185.5
Kim 105.25
```

A `DataOutputStream` is created for file **temp.dat** in lines 6–7. Student names and scores are written to the file in lines 10–15. Line 18 closes the output stream. A `DataInputStream` is created for the same file in lines 21–22. Student names and scores are read back from the file and displayed on the console in lines 25–27.

`DataInputStream` and `DataOutputStream` read and write Java primitive type values and strings in a machine-independent fashion, thereby enabling you to write a data file on one machine and read it on another machine that has a different operating system or file structure. An application uses a data output stream to write data that can later be read by a program using a data input stream.

Caution

You have to read data in the same order and format in which they are stored. For example, since names are written in UTF-8 using **writeUTF**, you must read names using **readUTF**.

Detecting the End of a File

If you keep reading data at the end of an **InputStream**, an **EOFException** will occur. This exception can be used to detect the end of a file, as shown in Listing 19.3.

EOFException

LISTING 19.3 DetectEndOfFile.java

```
1  import java.io.*;
2
3  public class DetectEndOfFile {
4    public static void main(String[] args) {
5      try {
6        DataOutputStream output =
7          new DataOutputStream(new FileOutputStream("test.dat"));
8        output.writeDouble(4.5);
9        output.writeDouble(43.25);
10       output.writeDouble(3.2);
11       output.close();
12
13       DataInputStream input =
14         new DataInputStream(new FileInputStream("test.dat"));
15       while (true) {
16         System.out.println(input.readDouble());
17       }
18     }
19     catch (EOFException ex) {
20       System.out.println("All data were read");
21     }
22     catch (IOException ex) {
23       ex.printStackTrace();
24     }
25   }
26 }
```

output stream
output
close stream
input stream
input
EOFException

```
4.5
43.25
3.2
All data were read
```

The program writes three double values to the file using **DataOutputStream** (lines 6–10), and reads the data using **DataInputStream** (lines 13–14). When reading past the end of the file, an **EOFException** is thrown. The exception is caught in line 19.

19.4.4 BufferedInputStream/BufferedOutputStream

BufferedInputStream/BufferedOutputStream can be used to speed up input and output by reducing the number of disk reads and writes. Using **BufferedInputStream**, the whole block of data on the disk is read into the buffer in the memory once. The individual data are then delivered to your program from the buffer, as shown in Figure 19.11a. Using **BufferedOutputStream**, the individual data are first written to the buffer in the memory. When the buffer is full, all data in the buffer is written to the disk once, as shown in Figure 19.11b.

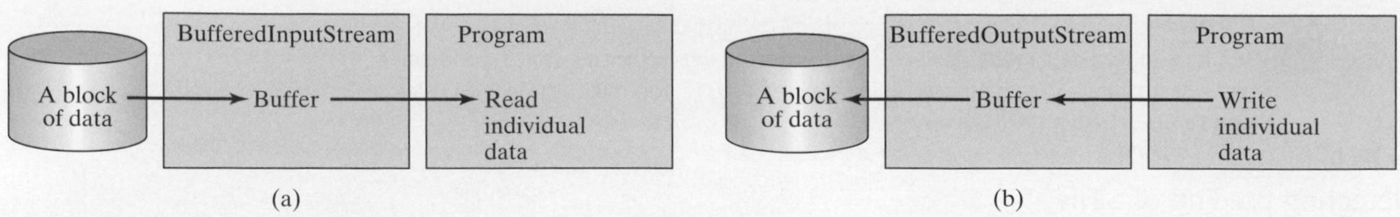

Figure 19.11 Buffer I/O places data in a buffer for fast processing.

`BufferedInputStream`/`BufferedOutputStream` does not contain new methods. All the methods in `BufferedInputStream`/`BufferedOutputStream` are inherited from the `InputStream`/`OutputStream` classes. `BufferedInputStream`/`BufferedOutputStream` manages a buffer behind the scene and automatically reads/writes data from/to disk on demand.

You can wrap a `BufferedInputStream`/`BufferedOutputStream` on any `InputStream`/`OutputStream` using the constructors shown in Figures 19.12 and 19.13.

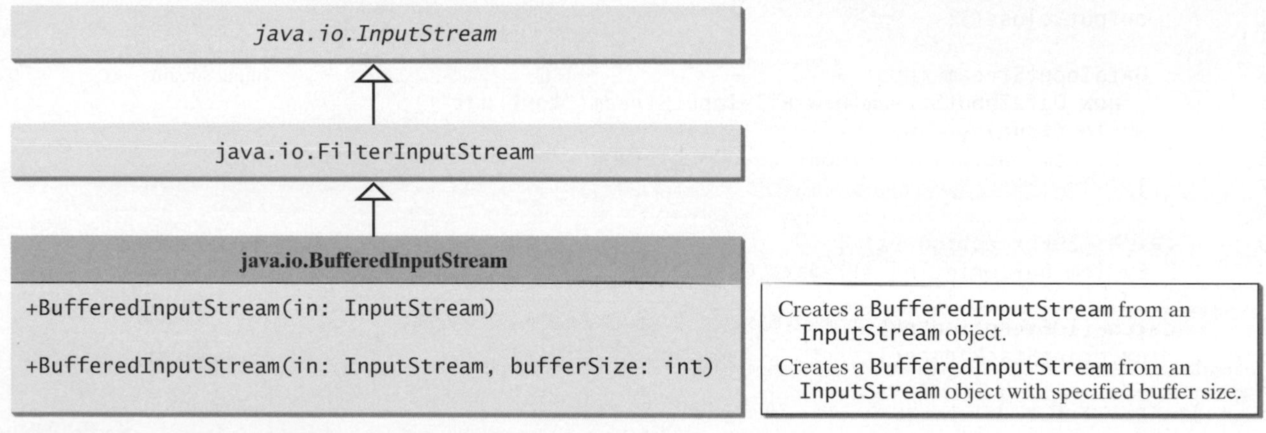

Figure 19.12 `BufferedInputStream` buffers an input stream.

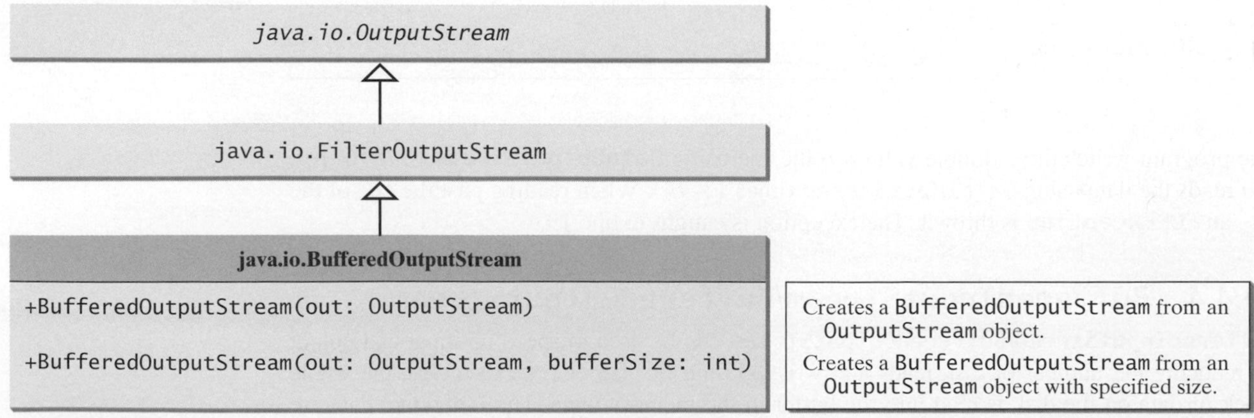

Figure 19.13 `BufferedOutputStream` buffers an output stream.

If no buffer size is specified, the default size is `512` bytes. You can improve the performance of the `TestDataStream` program in Listing 19.2 by adding buffers in the stream in lines 6–7 and 21–22, as follows:

```
DataOutputStream output = new DataOutputStream(
  new BufferedOutputStream(new FileOutputStream("temp.dat")));
DataInputStream input = new DataInputStream(
  new BufferedInputStream(new FileInputStream("temp.dat")));
```

Tip

You should always use buffered I/O to speed up input and output. For small files, you may not notice performance improvements. However, for large files—over 100 MB—you will see substantial improvements using buffered I/O.

19.8 Why do you have to declare to throw `IOException` in the method or use a try-catch block to handle `IOException` for Java I/O programs?

19.9 Why should you always close streams?

19.10 The `read()` method in `InputStream` reads a byte. Why does it return an `int` instead of a `byte`? Find the abstract methods in `InputStream` and `OutputStream`.

19.11 Does `FileInputStream`/`FileOutputStream` introduce any new methods beyond the methods inherited from `InputStream`/`OutputStream`? How do you create a `FileInputStream`/`FileOutputStream`?

19.12 What will happen if you attempt to create an input stream on a nonexistent file? What will happen if you attempt to create an output stream on an existing file? Can you append data to an existing file?

19.13 How do you append data to an existing text file using `java.io.PrintWriter`?

19.14 Suppose a file contains an unspecified number of `double` values. Theses values were written to the file using the `writeDouble` method using a `DataOutputStream`. How do you write a program to read all these values? How do you detect the end of a file?

19.15 What is written to a file using `writeByte(91)` on a `FileOutputStream`?

19.16 How do you check the end of a file in an input stream (`FileInputStream`, `DataInputStream`)?

19.17 What is wrong in the following code?

```
import java.io.*;

public class Test {
  public static void main(String[] args) {
    try {
      FileInputStream fis = new FileInputStream("test.dat");
    }
    catch (IOException ex) {
      ex.printStackTrace();
    }
    catch (FileNotFoundException ex) {
      ex.printStackTrace();
    }
  }
}
```

19.18 Suppose you run the program on Windows using the default ASCII encoding. After the program is finished, how many bytes are in the file **t.txt**? Show the contents of each byte.

```
public class Test {
  public static void main(String[] args)
      throws java.io.IOException {
    java.io.PrintWriter output =
      new java.io.PrintWriter("t.txt");
    output.printf("%s", "1234");
    output.printf("%s", "5678");
    output.close();
  }
}
```

19.19 After the program is finished, how many bytes are in the file **t.dat**? Show the contents of each byte.

```
import java.io.*;

public class Test {
  public static void main(String[] args) throws IOException {
    DataOutputStream output = new DataOutputStream(
      new FileOutputStream("t.dat"));
    output.writeInt(1234);
    output.writeInt(5678);
    output.close();
  }
}
```

19.20 For each of the following statements on a **DataOutputStream output**, how many bytes are sent to the output?

```
output.writeChar('A');
output.writeChars("BC");
output.writeUTF("DEF");
```

19.21 What are the advantages of using buffered streams? Are the following statements correct?

```
BufferedInputStream input1 =
  new BufferedInputStream(new FileInputStream("t.dat"));

DataInputStream input2 = new DataInputStream(
  new BufferedInputStream(new FileInputStream("t.dat")));

ObjectInputStream input3 = new ObjectInputStream(
  new BufferedInputStream(new FileInputStream("t.dat")));
```

19.5 Case Study: Copying Files

This section develops a useful utility for copying files.

In this section, you will learn how to write a program that lets users copy files. The user needs to provide a source file and a target file as command-line arguments using the command:

VideoNote
Copy file

```
java Copy source target
```

The program copies the source file to the target file and displays the number of bytes in the file. The program should alert the user if the source file does not exist or if the target file already exists. A sample run of the program is shown in Figure 19.14.

FIGURE 19.14 The program copies a file.

To copy the contents from a source file to a target file, it is appropriate to use an input stream to read bytes from the source file and an output stream to send bytes to the target file, regardless of the file's contents. The source file and the target file are specified from the command line. Create an `InputFileStream` for the source file and an `OutputFileStream` for the target file. Use the `read()` method to read a byte from the input stream, and then use the `write(b)` method to write the byte to the output stream. Use `BufferedInputStream` and `BufferedOutputStream` to improve the performance. Listing 19.4 gives the solution to the problem.

LISTING 19.4 Copy.java

```
import java.io.*;

public class Copy {
  /** Main method
     @param args[0] for source file
     @param args[1] for target file
   */
  public static void main(String[] args) throws IOException {
    // Check command-line parameter usage
    if (args.length != 2) {
      System.out.println(
        "Usage: java Copy sourceFile targetFile");
      System.exit(1);
    }

    // Check whether source file exists
    File sourceFile = new File(args[0]);
    if (!sourceFile.exists()) {
      System.out.println("Source file " + args[0]
        + " does not exist");
      System.exit(2);
    }

    // Check whether target file exists
    File targetFile = new File(args[1]);
    if (targetFile.exists()) {
      System.out.println("Target file " + args[1]
        + " already exists");
      System.exit(3);
    }

    // Create an input stream
    BufferedInputStream input =
```

check usage

source file

target file

input stream

output stream
read
write
close stream

```
34       new BufferedInputStream(new FileInputStream(sourceFile));
35
36     // Create an output stream
37     BufferedOutputStream output =
38       new BufferedOutputStream(new FileOutputStream(targetFile));
39
40     // Continuously read a byte from input and write it to output
41     int r, numberOfBytesCopied = 0;
42     while ((r = input.read()) != -1) {
43       output.write((byte)r);
44       numberOfBytesCopied++;
45     }
46
47     // Close streams
48     input.close();
49     output.close();
50
51     // Display the file size
52     System.out.println(numberOfBytesCopied + " bytes copied");
53   }
54 }
```

The program first checks whether the user has passed the two required arguments from the command line in lines 10–14.

The program uses the **File** class to check whether the source file and target file exist. If the source file does not exist (lines 18–22) or if the target file already exists (lines 25–30), the program ends.

An input stream is created using **BufferedInputStream** wrapped on **FileInputStream** in lines 33–34, and an output stream is created using **BufferedOutputStream** wrapped on **FileOutputStream** in lines 37–38.

The expression **((r = input.read()) != -1)** (line 42) reads a byte from **input.read()**, assigns it to **r**, and checks whether it is **-1**. The input value of **-1** signifies the end of a file. The program continuously reads bytes from the input stream and sends them to the output stream until all of the bytes have been read.

MyProgrammingLab™

19.22 How does the program check if a file already exists?

19.23 How does the program detect the end of the file while reading data?

19.24 How does the program count the number of bytes read from the file?

19.6 Object I/O

ObjectInputStream/ObjectOutputStream classes can be used to read/write serializable objects.

VideoNote
Object I/O

DataInputStream/DataOutputStream enables you to perform I/O for primitive type values and strings. **ObjectInputStream/ObjectOutputStream** enables you to perform I/O for objects in addition to primitive type values and strings. Since **ObjectInputStream/ObjectOutputStream** contains all the functions of **DataInputStream/DataOutputStream**, you can replace **DataInputStream/DataOutputStream** completely with **ObjectInputStream/ObjectOutputStream**.

ObjectInputStream extends **InputStream** and implements **ObjectInput** and **ObjectStreamConstants**, as shown in Figure 19.15. **ObjectInput** is a subinterface of **DataInput** (**DataInput** is shown in Figure 19.9). **ObjectStreamConstants** contains the constants to support **ObjectInputStream/ObjectOutputStream**.

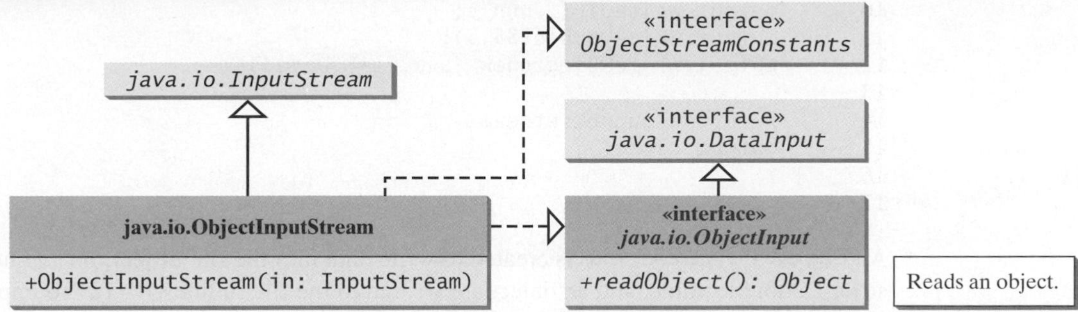

FIGURE 19.15 `ObjectInputStream` can read objects, primitive type values, and strings.

`ObjectOutputStream` extends `OutputStream` and implements `ObjectOutput` and `ObjectStreamConstants`, as shown in Figure 19.16. `ObjectOutput` is a subinterface of `DataOutput` (`DataOutput` is shown in Figure 19.10).

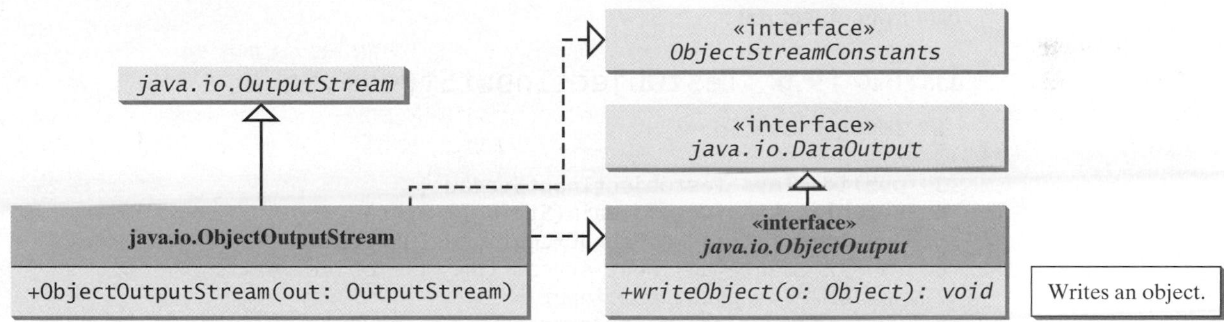

FIGURE 19.16 `ObjectOutputStream` can write objects, primitive type values, and strings.

You can wrap an `ObjectInputStream`/`ObjectOutputStream` on any `InputStream`/`OutputStream` using the following constructors:

```
// Create an ObjectInputStream
public ObjectInputStream(InputStream in)

// Create an ObjectOutputStream
public ObjectOutputStream(OutputStream out)
```

Listing 19.5 writes student names, scores, and the current date to a file named **object.dat**.

LISTING 19.5 TestObjectOutputStream.java

```
import java.io.*;

public class TestObjectOutputStream {
  public static void main(String[] args) throws IOException {
    // Create an output stream for file object.dat
    ObjectOutputStream output =
      new ObjectOutputStream(new FileOutputStream("object.dat"));

    // Write a string, double value, and object to the file
```

output stream

output

```
10      output.writeUTF("John");
11      output.writeDouble(85.5);
12      output.writeObject(new java.util.Date());
13
14      // Close output stream
15      output.close();
16    }
17  }
```

An **ObjectOutputStream** is created to write data into the file **object.dat** in lines 6–7. A string, a double value, and an object are written to the file in lines 10–12. To improve performance, you may add a buffer in the stream using the following statement to replace lines 6–7:

```
ObjectOutputStream output = new ObjectOutputStream(
  new BufferedOutputStream(new FileOutputStream("object.dat")));
```

Multiple objects or primitives can be written to the stream. The objects must be read back from the corresponding **ObjectInputStream** with the same types and in the same order as they were written. Java's safe casting should be used to get the desired type. Listing 19.6 reads data from **object.dat**.

Listing 19.6 TestObjectInputStream.java

input stream

input

```
1  import java.io.*;
2
3  public class TestObjectInputStream {
4    public static void main(String[] args)
5      throws ClassNotFoundException, IOException {
6      // Create an input stream for file object.dat
7      ObjectInputStream input =
8        new ObjectInputStream(new FileInputStream("object.dat"));
9
10     // Read a string, double value, and object from the file
11     String name = input.readUTF();
12     double score = input.readDouble();
13     java.util.Date date = (java.util.Date)(input.readObject());
14     System.out.println(name + " " + score + " " + date);
15
16     // Close input stream
17     input.close();
18   }
19 }
```

```
John 85.5 Sun Dec 04 10:35:31 EST 2011
```

ClassNotFoundException

The **readObject()** method may throw **java.lang.ClassNotFoundException**, because when the JVM restores an object, it first loads the class for the object if the class has not been loaded. Since **ClassNotFoundException** is a checked exception, the **main** method declares to throw it in line 5. An **ObjectInputStream** is created to read input from **object.dat** in lines 7–8. You have to read the data from the file in the same order and format as they were written to the file. A string, a double value, and an object are read in lines 11–13. Since **readObject()** returns an **Object**, it is cast into **Date** and assigned to a **Date** variable in line 13.

19.6.1 The Serializable Interface

Not every object can be written to an output stream. Objects that can be so written are said to be *serializable*. A serializable object is an instance of the `java.io.Serializable` interface, so the object's class must implement `Serializable`. serializable

The `Serializable` interface is a marker interface. Since it has no methods, you don't need to add additional code in your class that implements `Serializable`. Implementing this interface enables the Java serialization mechanism to automate the process of storing objects and arrays.

To appreciate this automation feature, consider what you otherwise need to do in order to store an object. Suppose you want to store a `JButton` object. To do this you need to store all the current values of the properties (e.g., color, font, text, alignment) in the object. Since `JButton` is a subclass of `AbstractButton`, the property values of `AbstractButton` have to be stored as well as the properties of all the superclasses of `AbstractButton`. If a property is of an object type (e.g., `background` of the `Color` type), storing it requires storing all the property values inside this object. As you can see, this would be a very tedious process. Fortunately, you don't have to go through it manually. Java provides a built-in mechanism to automate the process of writing objects. This process is referred to as *object serialization*, which is implemented in `ObjectOutputStream`. In contrast, the process of reading objects is referred to as *object deserialization*, which is implemented in `ObjectInputStream`. serialization deserialization

Many classes in the Java API implement `Serializable`. The utility classes, such as `java.util.Date`, and all the Swing GUI component classes implement `Serializable`. Attempting to store an object that does not support the `Serializable` interface would cause a `NotSerializableException`. NotSerializableException

When a serializable object is stored, the class of the object is encoded; this includes the class name and the signature of the class, the values of the object's instance variables, and the closure of any other objects referenced by the object. The values of the object's static variables are not stored.

Note

nonserializable fields

If an object is an instance of `Serializable` but contains nonserializable instance data fields, can it be serialized? The answer is no. To enable the object to be serialized, mark these data fields with the `transient` keyword to tell the JVM to ignore them when writing the object to an object stream. Consider the following class: transient

```
public class C implements java.io.Serializable {
  private int v1;
  private static double v2;
  private transient A v3 = new A();
}

class A { } // A is not serializable
```

When an object of the `C` class is serialized, only variable `v1` is serialized. Variable `v2` is not serialized because it is a static variable, and variable `v3` is not serialized because it is marked `transient`. If `v3` were not marked `transient`, a `java.io.NotSerializableException` would occur.

Note

duplicate objects

If an object is written to an object stream more than once, will it be stored in multiple copies? No, it will not. When an object is written for the first time, a serial number is created for it. The JVM writes the complete contents of the object along with the serial number into the object stream. After the first time, only the serial number is stored if the same object is written again. When the objects are read back, their references are the same, since only one object is actually created in the memory.

19.6.2 Serializing Arrays

An array is serializable if all its elements are serializable. An entire array can be saved into a file using **writeObject** and later can be restored using **readObject**. Listing 19.7 stores an array of five **int** values and an array of three strings and reads them back to display on the console.

LISTING 19.7 TestObjectStreamForArray.java

output stream
store array
input stream
restore array

```
1  import java.io.*;
2
3  public class TestObjectStreamForArray {
4    public static void main(String[] args)
5        throws ClassNotFoundException, IOException {
6      int[] numbers = {1, 2, 3, 4, 5};
7      String[] strings = {"John", "Susan", "Kim"};
8
9      // Create an output stream for file array.dat
10     ObjectOutputStream output = new ObjectOutputStream(new
11       FileOutputStream("array.dat", true));
12
13     // Write arrays to the object output stream
14     output.writeObject(numbers);
15     output.writeObject(strings);
16
17     // Close the stream
18     output.close();
19
20     // Create an input stream for file array.dat
21     ObjectInputStream input =
22       new ObjectInputStream(new FileInputStream("array.dat"));
23
24     int[] newNumbers = (int[])(input.readObject());
25     String[] newStrings = (String[])(input.readObject());
26
27     // Display arrays
28     for (int i = 0; i < newNumbers.length; i++)
29       System.out.print(newNumbers[i] + " ");
30     System.out.println();
31
32     for (int i = 0; i < newStrings.length; i++)
33       System.out.print(newStrings[i] + " ");
34
35     // Close the stream
36     input.close();
37   }
38 }
```

```
1 2 3 4 5
John Susan Kim
```

Lines 14–15 write two arrays into file **array.dat**. Lines 24–25 read two arrays back in the same order they were written. Since **readObject()** returns **Object**, casting is used to cast the objects into **int[]** and **String[]**.

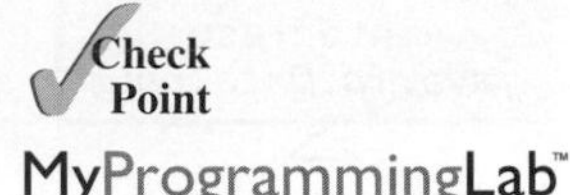

19.25 What types of objects can be stored using the `ObjectOutputStream`? What is the method for writing an object? What is the method for reading an object? What is the return type of the method that reads an object from `ObjectInputStream`?

19.26 If you serialize two objects of the same type, will they take the same amount of space? If not, give an example.

19.27 Is it true that any instance of `java.io.Serializable` can be successfully serialized? Are the static variables in an object serialized? How do you mark an instance variable not to be serialized?

19.28 Can you write an array to an `ObjectOutputStream`?

19.29 Is it true that `DataInputStream`/`DataOutputStream` can always be replaced by `ObjectInputStream`/`ObjectOutputStream`?

19.30 What will happen when you attempt to run the following code?

```
import java.io.*;

public class Test {
  public static void main(String[] args) throws IOException {
    ObjectOutputStream output =
      new ObjectOutputStream(new FileOutputStream("object.dat"));

    output.writeObject(new A());
  }
}

class A implements Serializable {
  B b = new B();
}

class B {
}
```

19.7 Random-Access Files

Java provides the `RandomAccessFile` *class to allow a file to be read from and written to at random locations.*

read-only
write-only
sequential
random-access file

All of the streams you have used so far are known as *read-only* or *write-only* streams. The external files of these streams are *sequential* files that cannot be updated without creating a new file. However, it is often necessary to modify files. Java provides the `RandomAccessFile` class to allow a file to be read from and written to at *random* locations.

The `RandomAccessFile` class implements the `DataInput` and `DataOutput` interfaces, as shown in Figure 19.17. The `DataInput` interface (see Figure 19.9) defines the methods for reading primitive type values and strings (e.g., `readInt`, `readDouble`, `readChar`, `readBoolean`, `readUTF`), and the `DataOutput` interface (see Figure 19.10) defines the methods for writing primitive type values and strings (e.g., `writeInt`, `writeDouble`, `writeChar`, `writeBoolean`, `writeUTF`).

When creating a `RandomAccessFile`, you can specify one of two modes: `r` or `rw`. Mode `r` means that the stream is read-only, and mode `rw` indicates that the stream allows both read and write. For example, the following statement creates a new stream, `raf`, that allows the program to read from and write to the file **test.dat**:

```
RandomAccessFile raf = new RandomAccessFile("test.dat", "rw");
```

If **test.dat** already exists, `raf` is created to access it; if **test.dat** does not exist, a new file named **test.dat** is created, and `raf` is created to access the new file. The method `raf.length()` returns the number of bytes in **test.dat** at any given time. If you append new data into the file, `raf.length()` increases.

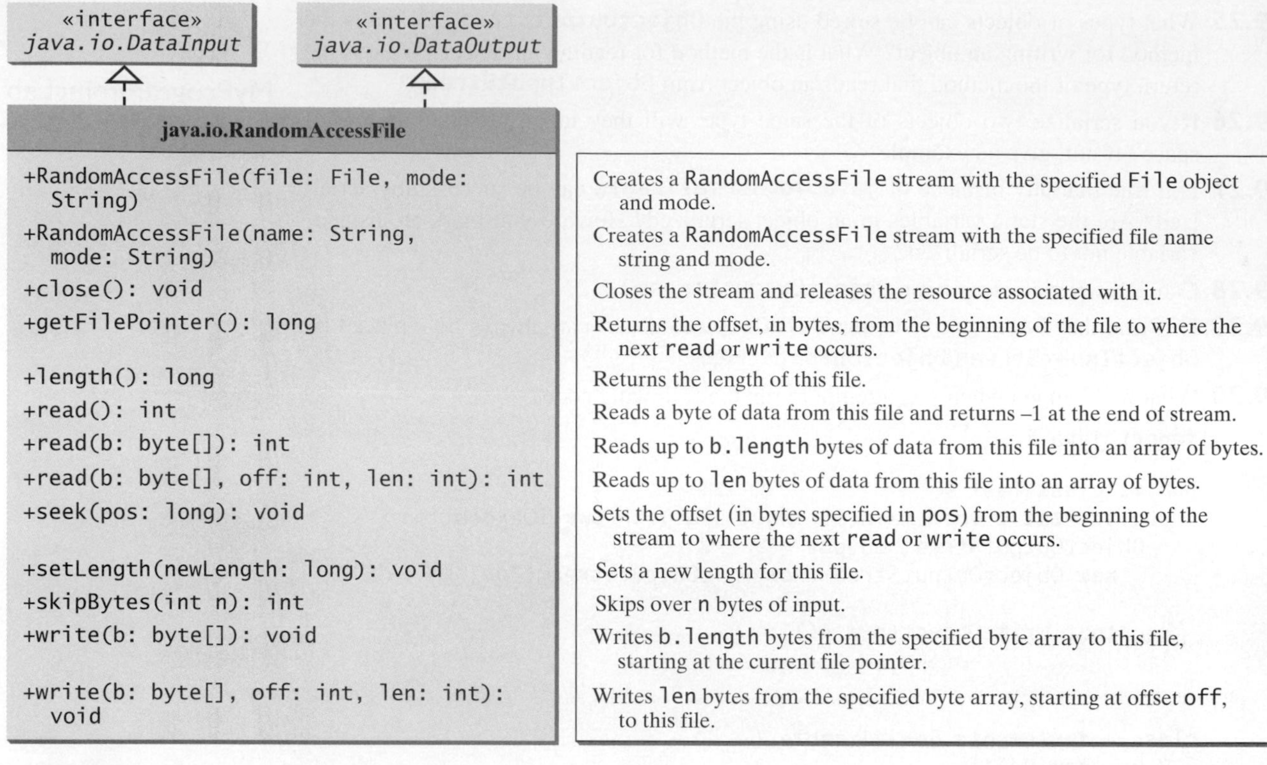

FIGURE 19.17 `RandomAccessFile` implements the `DataInput` and `DataOutput` interfaces with additional methods to support random access.

Tip

If the file is not intended to be modified, open it with the `r` mode. This prevents unintentional modification of the file.

file pointer

A random-access file consists of a sequence of bytes. A special marker called a *file pointer* is positioned at one of these bytes. A read or write operation takes place at the location of the file pointer. When a file is opened, the file pointer is set at the beginning of the file. When you read or write data to the file, the file pointer moves forward to the next data item. For example, if you read an `int` value using `readInt()`, the JVM reads `4` bytes from the file pointer, and now the file pointer is `4` bytes ahead of the previous location, as shown in Figure 19.18.

For a `RandomAccessFile raf`, you can use the `raf.seek(position)` method to move the file pointer to a specified position. `raf.seek(0)` moves it to the beginning of the file, and `raf.seek(raf.length())` moves it to the end of the file. Listing 19.8 demonstrates

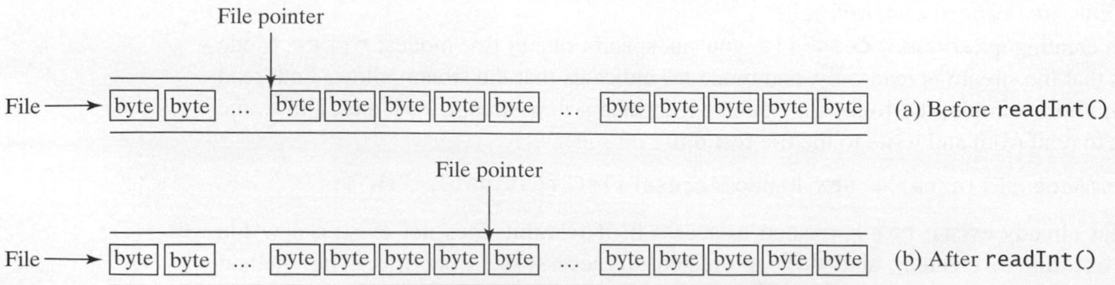

FIGURE 19.18 After an `int` value is read, the file pointer is moved 4 bytes ahead.

Chapter Summary

1. I/O can be classified into *text I/O* and *binary I/O*. Text I/O interprets data in sequences of characters. Binary I/O interprets data as raw binary values. How text is stored in a file depends on the encoding scheme for the file. Java automatically performs encoding and decoding for text I/O.

2. The `InputStream` and `OutputStream` classes are the roots of all binary I/O classes. `FileInputStream/FileOutputStream` associates a file for input/output. `BufferedInputStream/BufferedOutputStream` can be used to wrap any binary I/O stream to improve performance. `DataInputStream/DataOutputStream` can be used to read/write primitive values and strings.

3. `ObjectInputStream/ObjectOutputStream` can be used to read/write objects in addition to primitive values and strings. To enable object *serialization*, the object's defining class must implement the `java.io.Serializable` marker interface.

4. The `RandomAccessFile` class enables you to read and write data to a file. You can open a file with the `r` mode to indicate that it is read-only, or with the `rw` mode to indicate that it is updateable. Since the `RandomAccessFile` class implements `DataInput` and `DataOutput` interfaces, many methods in `RandomAccessFile` are the same as those in `DataInputStream` and `DataOutputStream`.

Test Questions

Do the test questions for this chapter online at www.cs.armstrong.edu/liang/intro9e/test.html.

Programming Exercises

MyProgrammingLab™

Section 19.3

***19.1** (*Create a text file*) Write a program to create a file named **Exercise19_01.txt** if it does not exist. Append new data to it if it already exists. Write 100 integers created randomly into the file using text I/O. Integers are separated by a space.

Section 19.4

***19.2** (*Create a binary data file*) Write a program to create a file named **Exercise19_02.dat** if it does not exist. Append new data to it if it already exists. Write 100 integers created randomly into the file using binary I/O.

***19.3** (*Sum all the integers in a binary data file*) Suppose a binary data file named **Exercise19_03.dat** has been created and its data are created using `writeInt(int)` in `DataOutputStream`. The file contains an unspecified number of integers. Write a program to find the sum of the integers.

***19.4** (*Convert a text file into UTF*) Write a program that reads lines of characters from a text file and writes each line as a UTF-8 string into a binary file. Display the sizes of the text file and the binary file. Use the following command to run the program:

```
java Exercise19_04 Welcome.java Welcome.utf
```

Section 19.6

***19.5** (*Store objects and arrays in a file*) Write a program that stores an array of the five `int` values `1`, `2`, `3`, `4` and `5`, a `Date` object for the current time, and the `double` value `5.5` into the file named **Exercise19_05.dat**.

***19.6** (*Store `Loan` objects*) The `Loan` class in Listing 10.2 does not implement `Serializable`. Rewrite the `Loan` class to implement `Serializable`. Write a program that creates five `Loan` objects and stores them in a file named **Exercise19_06.dat**.

***19.7** (*Restore objects from a file*) Suppose a file named **Exercise19_07.dat** has been created using the `ObjectOutputStream`. The file contains `Loan` objects. The `Loan` class in Listing 10.2 does not implement `Serializable`. Rewrite the `Loan` class to implement `Serializable`. Write a program that reads the `Loan` objects from the file and computes the total loan amount. Suppose you don't know how many `Loan` objects are in the file. Use `EOFException` to end the loop.

Section 19.7

***19.8** (*Update count*) Suppose you want to track how many times a program has been executed. You can store an `int` to count the file. Increase the count by `1` each time this program is executed. Let the program be **Exercise19_08** and store the count in **Exercise19_08.dat**.

*****19.9** (*Address book*) Supplement VI.B has a case study of using random-access files for creating and manipulating an address book. Modify the case study by adding an *Update* button, as shown in Figure 19.19, to enable the user to modify the address that is being displayed.

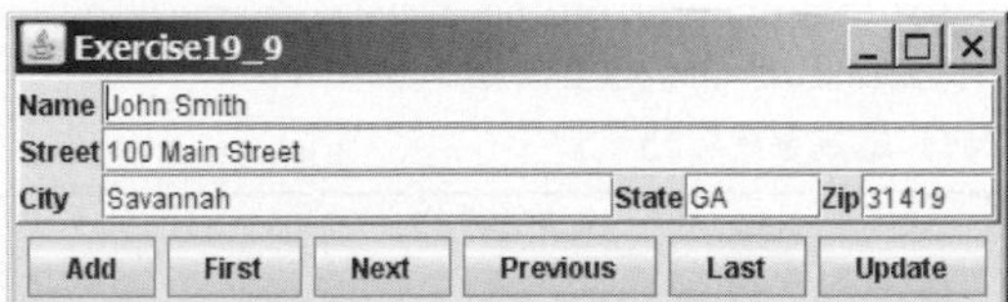

FIGURE 19.19 The application can store, retrieve, and update addresses from a file.

Comprehensive

Split a large file

***19.10** (*Split files*) Suppose you want to back up a huge file (e.g., a 10-GB AVI file) to a CD-R. You can achieve it by splitting the file into smaller pieces and backing up these pieces separately. Write a utility program that splits a large file into smaller ones using the following command:

```
java Exercise19_10 SourceFile numberOfPieces
```

The command creates the files **SourceFile.1**, **SourceFile.2**, . . . , **SourceFile.n**, where **n** is `numberOfPieces` and the output files are about the same size.

****19.11** (*Split files GUI*) Rewrite Exercise 19.10 with a GUI, as shown in Figure 19.20a.

***19.12** (*Combine files*) Write a utility program that combines the files together into a new file using the following command:

```
java Exercise19_12 SourceFile1 . . . SourceFilen TargetFile
```

The command combines SourceFile1, . . . , and SourceFilen into TargetFile.

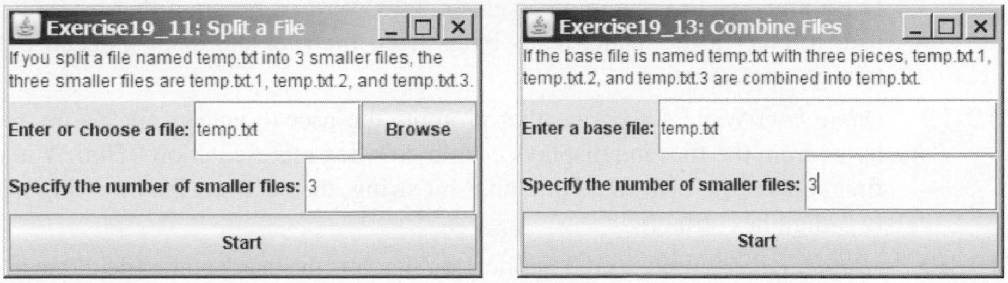

(a) (b)

FIGURE 19.20 (a) The program splits a file. (b) The program combines files into a new file.

***19.13** (*Combine files GUI*) Rewrite Exercise 19.12 with a GUI, as shown in Figure 19.20b.

19.14 (*Encrypt files*) Encode the file by adding `5` to every byte in the file. Write a program that prompts the user to enter an input file name and an output file name and saves the encrypted version of the input file to the output file.

19.15 (*Decrypt files*) Suppose a file is encrypted using the scheme in Programming Exercise 19.14. Write a program to decode an encrypted file. Your program should prompt the user to enter an input file name for the encrypted file and an output file name for the unencrypted version of the input file.

19.16 (*Frequency of characters*) Write a program that prompts the user to enter the name of an ASCII text file and displays the frequency of the characters in the file.

****19.17** (*`BitOutputStream`*) Implement a class named `BitOutputStream`, as shown in Figure 19.21, for writing bits to an output stream. The `writeBit(char bit)` method stores the bit in a byte variable. When you create a `BitOutputStream`, the byte is empty. After invoking `writeBit('1')`, the byte becomes `00000001`. After invoking `writeBit("0101")`, the byte becomes `00010101`. The first three bits are not filled yet. When a byte is full, it is sent to the output stream. Now the byte is reset to empty. You must close the stream by invoking the `close()` method. If the byte is neither empty nor full, the `close()` method first fills the zeros to make a full `8` bits in the byte, and then outputs the byte and closes the stream. For a hint, see Programming Exercise 4.46. Write a test program that sends the bits `010000100100001001101` to the file named **Exercise19_17.dat**.

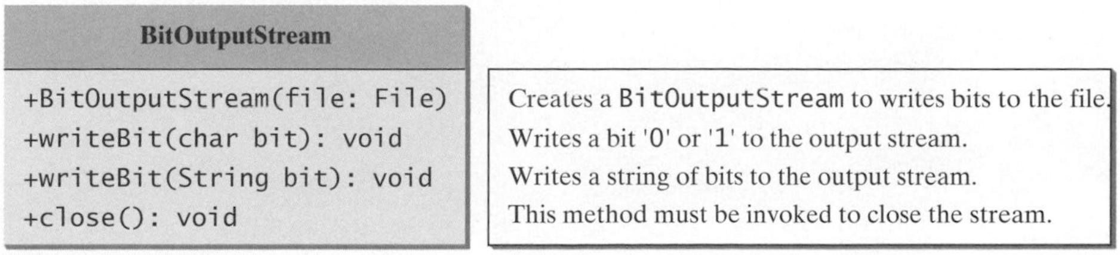

BitOutputStream	
`+BitOutputStream(file: File)`	Creates a `BitOutputStream` to writes bits to the file.
`+writeBit(char bit): void`	Writes a bit '0' or '1' to the output stream.
`+writeBit(String bit): void`	Writes a string of bits to the output stream.
`+close(): void`	This method must be invoked to close the stream.

FIGURE 19.21 `BitOutputStream` outputs a stream of bits to a file.

***19.18** (*View bits*) Write the following method that displays the bit representation for the last byte in an integer:

```
public static String getBits(int value)
```

For a hint, see Programming Exercise 4.46. Write a program that prompts the user to enter a file name, reads bytes from the file, and displays each byte's binary representation.

***19.19** (*View hex*) Write a program that prompts the user to enter a file name, reads bytes from the file, and displays each byte's hex representation. (*Hint*: You can first convert the byte value into an 8-bit string, then convert the bit string into a two-digit hex string.)

****19.20** (*Binary editor*) Write a GUI application that lets the user enter a file name in the text field and press the *Enter* key to display its binary representation in a text area. The user can also modify the binary code and save it back to the file, as shown in Figure 19.22a.

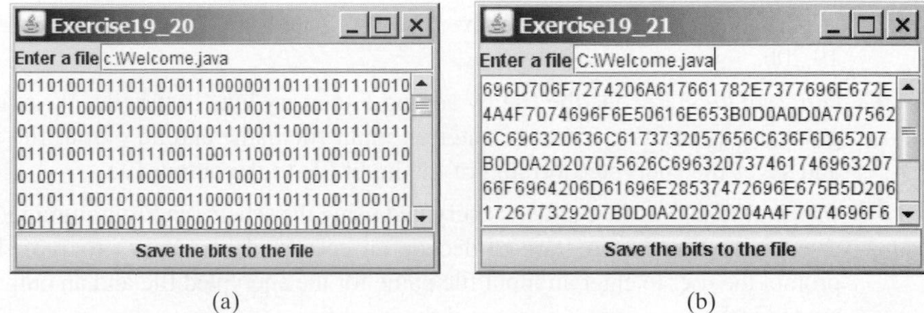

FIGURE 19.22 The programs enable the user to manipulate the contents of the file in (a) binary and (b) hex.

****19.21** (*Hex editor*) Write a GUI application that lets the user enter a file name in the text field and press the *Enter* key to display its hex representation in a text area. The user can also modify the hex code and save it back to the file, as shown in Figure 19.22b.

CHAPTER

20

RECURSION

Objectives

- To describe what a recursive method is and the benefits of using recursion (§20.1).
- To develop recursive methods for recursive mathematical functions (§§20.2–20.3).
- To explain how recursive method calls are handled in a call stack (§§20.2–20.3).
- To solve problems using recursion (§20.4).
- To use an overloaded helper method to design a recursive method (§20.5).
- To implement a selection sort using recursion (§20.5.1).
- To implement a binary search using recursion (§20.5.2).
- To get the directory size using recursion (§20.6).
- To solve the Towers of Hanoi problem using recursion (§20.7).
- To draw fractals using recursion (§20.8).
- To discover the relationship and difference between recursion and iteration (§20.9).
- To know tail-recursive methods and why they are desirable (§20.10).

20.1 Introduction

Recursion is a technique that leads to elegant solutions to problems that are difficult to program using simple loops.

search word problem

Suppose you want to find all the files under a directory that contain a particular word. How do you solve this problem? There are several ways to do so. An intuitive and effective solution is to use recursion by searching the files in the subdirectories recursively.

H-tree problem

H-trees, depicted in Figure 20.1, are used in a very large-scale integration (VLSI) design as a clock distribution network for routing timing signals to all parts of a chip with equal propagation delays. How do you write a program to display H-trees? A good approach is to use recursion.

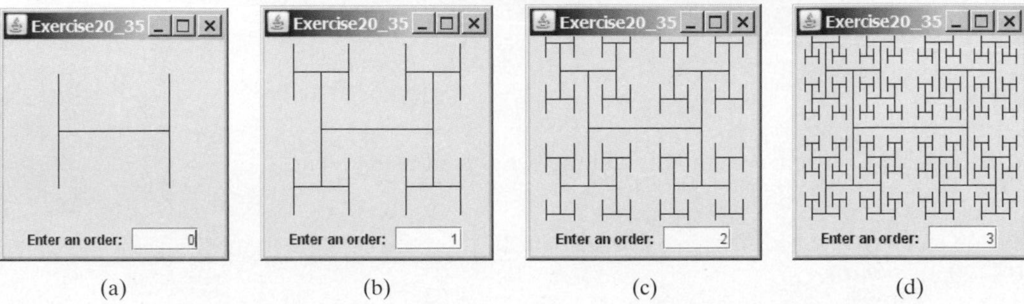

FIGURE 20.1 An H-tree can be displayed using recursion.

recursive method

To use recursion is to program using *recursive methods*—that is, to use methods that invoke themselves. Recursion is a useful programming technique. In some cases, it enables you to develop a natural, straightforward, simple solution to an otherwise difficult problem. This chapter introduces the concepts and techniques of recursive programming and illustrates with examples of how to "think recursively."

20.2 Case Study: Computing Factorials

A recursive method is one that invokes itself.

Many mathematical functions are defined using recursion. Let's begin with a simple example. The factorial of a number `n` can be recursively defined as follows:

```
0! = 1;
n! = n × (n - 1)!; n > 0
```

How do you find `n!` for a given `n`? To find `1!` is easy, because you know that `0!` is `1`, and `1!` is `1 × 0!`. Assuming that you know `(n - 1)!`, you can obtain `n!` immediately by using `n × (n - 1)!`. Thus, the problem of computing `n!` is reduced to computing `(n - 1)!`. When computing `(n - 1)!`, you can apply the same idea recursively until `n` is reduced to `0`.

Let `factorial(n)` be the method for computing `n!`. If you call the method with `n = 0`, it immediately returns the result. The method knows how to solve the simplest case, which is referred to as the *base case* or the *stopping condition*. If you call the method with `n > 0`, it reduces the problem into a subproblem for computing the factorial of `n - 1`. The *subproblem* is essentially the same as the original problem, but it is simpler or smaller. Because the subproblem has the same property as the original problem, you can call the method with a different argument, which is referred to as a *recursive call*.

base case or stopping condition

recursive call

The recursive algorithm for computing `factorial(n)` can be simply described as follows:

```
if (n == 0)
  return 1;
```

```
else
  return n * factorial(n - 1);
```

A recursive call can result in many more recursive calls, because the method keeps on dividing a subproblem into new subproblems. For a recursive method to terminate, the problem must eventually be reduced to a stopping case, at which point the method returns a result to its caller. The caller then performs a computation and returns the result to its own caller. This process continues until the result is passed back to the original caller. The original problem can now be solved by multiplying `n` by the result of `factorial(n - 1)`.

Listing 20.1 gives a complete program that prompts the user to enter a nonnegative integer and displays the factorial for the number.

LISTING 20.1 ComputeFactorial.java

```
1  import java.util.Scanner;
2
3  public class ComputeFactorial {
4    /** Main method */
5    public static void main(String[] args) {
6      // Create a Scanner
7      Scanner input = new Scanner(System.in);
8      System.out.print("Enter a nonnegative integer: ");
9      int n = input.nextInt();
10
11     // Display factorial
12     System.out.println("Factorial of " + n + " is " + factorial(n));
13   }
14
15   /** Return the factorial for the specified number */
16   public static long factorial(int n) {
17     if (n == 0) // Base case
18       return 1;
19     else
20       return n * factorial(n - 1); // Recursive call
21   }
22 }
```

base case

recursion

```
Enter a nonnegative integer: 4 ↵Enter
Factorial of 4 is 24
```

```
Enter a nonnegative integer: 10 ↵Enter
Factorial of 10 is 3628800
```

The `factorial` method (lines 16–21) is essentially a direct translation of the recursive mathematical definition for the factorial into Java code. The call to `factorial` is recursive because it calls itself. The parameter passed to `factorial` is decremented until it reaches the base case of `0`.

You see how to write a recursive method. How does recursion work? Figure 20.2 illustrates the execution of the recursive calls, starting with `n = 4`. The use of stack space for recursive calls is shown in Figure 20.3.

how does it work?

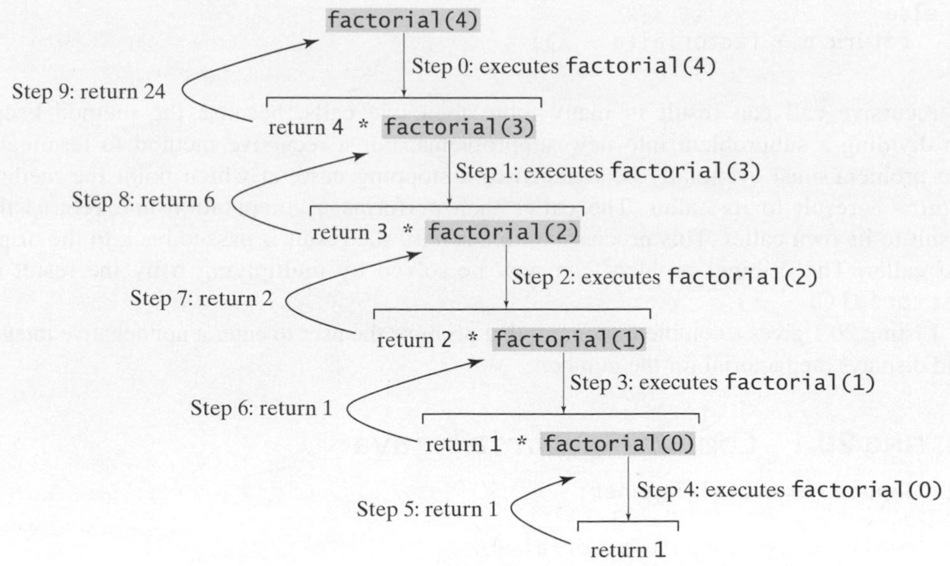

FIGURE 20.2 Invoking `factorial(4)` spawns recursive calls to `factorial`.

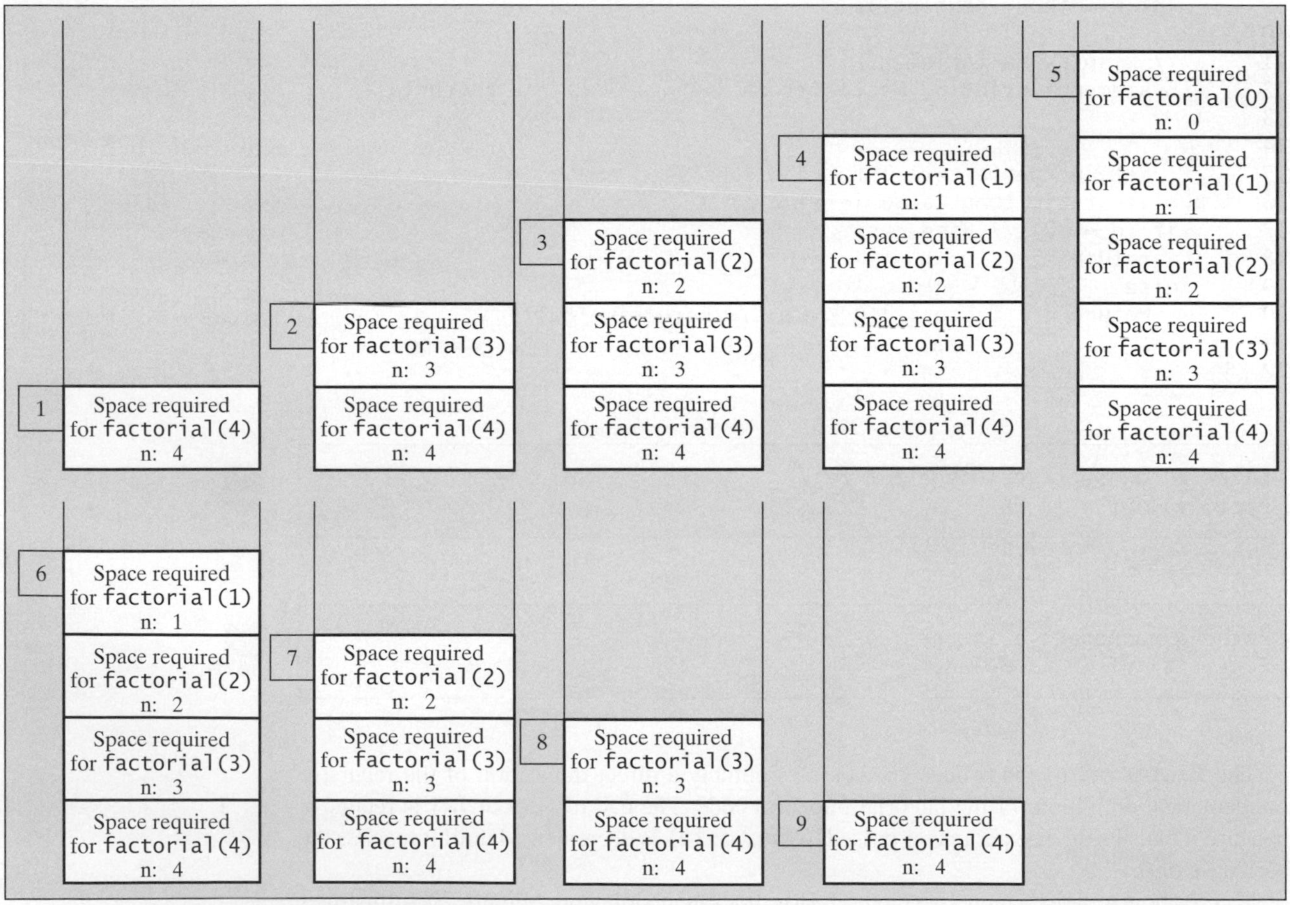

1
Space required for factorial(4) n: 4

2
Space required for factorial(3) n: 3
Space required for factorial(4) n: 4

3
Space required for factorial(2) n: 2
Space required for factorial(3) n: 3
Space required for factorial(4) n: 4

4
Space required for factorial(1) n: 1
Space required for factorial(2) n: 2
Space required for factorial(3) n: 3
Space required for factorial(4) n: 4

5
Space required for factorial(0) n: 0
Space required for factorial(1) n: 1
Space required for factorial(2) n: 2
Space required for factorial(3) n: 3
Space required for factorial(4) n: 4

6
Space required for factorial(1) n: 1
Space required for factorial(2) n: 2
Space required for factorial(3) n: 3
Space required for factorial(4) n: 4

7
Space required for factorial(2) n: 2
Space required for factorial(3) n: 3
Space required for factorial(4) n: 4

8
Space required for factorial(3) n: 3
Space required for factorial(4) n: 4

9
Space required for factorial(4) n: 4

FIGURE 20.3 When `factorial(4)` is being executed, the `factorial` method is called recursively, causing stack space to dynamically change.

Pedagogical Note

It is simpler and more efficient to implement the `factorial` method using a loop. However, we use the recursive `factorial` method here to demonstrate the concept of recursion. Later in this chapter, we will present some problems that are inherently recursive and are difficult to solve without using recursion.

If recursion does not reduce the problem in a manner that allows it to eventually converge into the base case, *infinite recursion* can occur. For example, suppose you mistakenly write the `factorial` method as follows:

infinite recursion

```
public static long factorial(int n) {
  return n * factorial(n - 1);
}
```

The method runs infinitely and causes a `StackOverflowError`.

The example discussed in this section shows a recursive method that invokes itself. This is known as *direct recursion*. It is also possible to create *indirect recursion*. This occurs when method A invokes method B, which in turn invokes method A. There can even be several more methods involved in the recursion. For example, method A invokes method B, which invokes method C, which invokes method A.

direct recursion
indirect recursion

Check Point
MyProgrammingLab™

20.1 What is a recursive method? What is an infinite recursion?

20.2 How many times is the `factorial` method in Listing 20.1 invoked for `factorial(6)`?

20.3 Show the output of the following programs and identify base cases and recursive calls.

```
public class Test {
  public static void main(String[] args) {
    System.out.println(
      "Sum is " + xMethod(5));
  }

  public static int xMethod(int n) {
    if (n == 1)
      return 1;
    else
      return n + xMethod(n - 1);
  }
}
```

```
public class Test {
  public static void main(String[] args) {
    xMethod(1234567);
  }

  public static void xMethod(int n) {
    if (n > 0) {
      System.out.print(n % 10);
      xMethod(n / 10);
    }
  }
}
```

20.4 Write a recursive mathematical definition for computing 2^n for a positive integer n.

20.5 Write a recursive mathematical definition for computing x^n for a positive integer n and a real number x.

20.6 Write a recursive mathematical definition for computing $1 + 2 + 3 + \ldots + n$ for a positive integer.

20.3 Case Study: Computing Fibonacci Numbers

In some cases, recursion enables you to create an intuitive, straightforward, simple solution to a problem.

The `factorial` method in the preceding section could easily be rewritten without using recursion. In this section, we show an example for creating an intuitive solution to a problem using recursion. Consider the well-known Fibonacci-series problem:

The series:	0	1	1	2	3	5	8	13	21	34	55	89	. . .
indices:	0	1	2	3	4	5	6	7	8	9	10	11	

The Fibonacci series begins with `0` and `1`, and each subsequent number is the sum of the preceding two. The series can be recursively defined as:

```
fib(0) = 0;
fib(1) = 1;
fib(index) = fib(index - 2) + fib(index - 1); index >= 2
```

The Fibonacci series was named for Leonardo Fibonacci, a medieval mathematician, who originated it to model the growth of the rabbit population. It can be applied in numeric optimization and in various other areas.

How do you find `fib(index)` for a given `index`? It is easy to find `fib(2)`, because you know `fib(0)` and `fib(1)`. Assuming that you know `fib(index - 2)` and `fib(index - 1)`, you can obtain `fib(index)` immediately. Thus, the problem of computing `fib(index)` is reduced to computing `fib(index - 2)` and `fib(index - 1)`. When doing so, you apply the idea recursively until `index` is reduced to `0` or `1`.

The base case is `index = 0` or `index = 1`. If you call the method with `index = 0` or `index = 1`, it immediately returns the result. If you call the method with `index >= 2`, it divides the problem into two subproblems for computing `fib(index - 1)` and `fib(index - 2)` using recursive calls. The recursive algorithm for computing `fib(index)` can be simply described as follows:

```
if (index == 0)
  return 0;
else if (index == 1)
  return 1;
else
  return fib(index - 1) + fib(index - 2);
```

Listing 20.2 gives a complete program that prompts the user to enter an index and computes the Fibonacci number for that index.

LISTING 20.2 ComputeFibonacci.java

```
import java.util.Scanner;

public class ComputeFibonacci {
  /** Main method */
  public static void main(String[] args) {
    // Create a Scanner
    Scanner input = new Scanner(System.in);
    System.out.print("Enter an index for a Fibonacci number: ");
    int index = input.nextInt();

    // Find and display the Fibonacci number
    System.out.println("The Fibonacci number at index "
      + index + " is " + fib(index));
  }

  /** The method for finding the Fibonacci number */
  public static long fib(long index) {
    if (index == 0) // Base case
      return 0;
```

base case

```
    else if (index == 1) // Base case
      return 1;
    else  // Reduction and recursive calls
      return fib(index - 1) + fib(index - 2);
  }
}
```

base case

recursion

```
Enter an index for a Fibonacci number: 1 ↵Enter
The Fibonacci number at index 1 is 1
```

```
Enter an index for a Fibonacci number: 6 ↵Enter
The Fibonacci number at index 6 is 8
```

```
Enter an index for a Fibonacci number: 7 ↵Enter
The Fibonacci number at index 7 is 13
```

The program does not show the considerable amount of work done behind the scenes by the computer. Figure 20.4, however, shows the successive recursive calls for evaluating `fib(4)`. The original method, `fib(4)`, makes two recursive calls, `fib(3)` and `fib(2)`, and then returns `fib(3) + fib(2)`. But in what order are these methods called? In Java, operands are evaluated from left to right, so `fib(2)` is called after `fib(3)` is completely evaluated. The labels in Figure 20.4 show the order in which the methods are called.

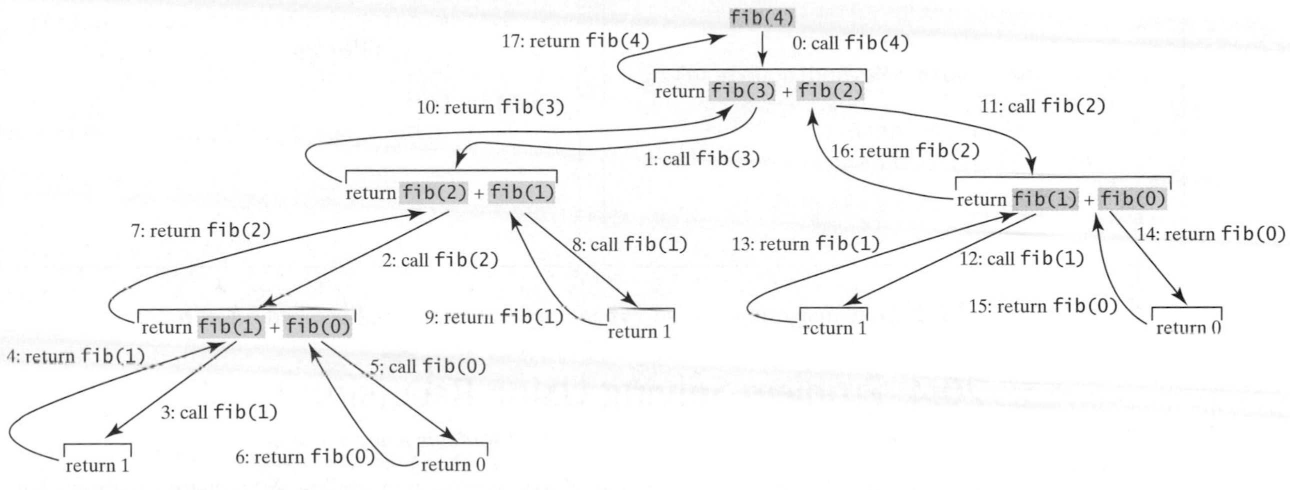

FIGURE 20.4 Invoking `fib(4)` spawns recursive calls to `fib`.

As shown in Figure 20.4, there are many duplicated recursive calls. For instance, `fib(2)` is called twice, `fib(1)` three times, and `fib(0)` twice. In general, computing `fib(index)` requires roughly twice as many recursive calls as does computing `fib(index - 1)`. As you try larger index values, the number of calls substantially increases, as shown in Table 20.1.

TABLE 20.1 Number of Recursive Calls in `fib(index)`

`index`	2	3	4	10	20	30	40	50
# of calls	3	5	9	177	21891	2,692,537	331,160,281	2,075,316,483

Pedagogical Note

The recursive implementation of the `fib` method is very simple and straightforward, but it isn't efficient, since it requires more time and memory to run recursive methods. See Programming Exercise 20.2 for an efficient solution using loops. Though it is not practical, the recursive `fib` method is a good example of how to write recursive methods.

MyProgrammingLab™

20.7 Show the output of the following two programs:

```
public class Test {
  public static void main(String[] args) {
    xMethod(5);
  }

  public static void xMethod(int n) {
    if (n > 0) {
      System.out.print(n + " ");
      xMethod(n - 1);
    }
  }
}
```

```
public class Test {
  public static void main(String[] args) {
    xMethod(5);
  }

  public static void xMethod(int n) {
    if (n > 0) {
      xMethod(n - 1);
      System.out.print(n + " ");
    }
  }
}
```

20.8 What is wrong in the following method?

```
public class Test {
  public static void main(String[] args) {
    xMethod(1234567);
  }

  public static void xMethod(double n) {
    if (n != 0) {
      System.out.print(n);
      xMethod(n / 10);
    }
  }
}
```

```
public class Test {
  public static void main(String[] args) {
    Test test = new Test();
    System.out.println(test.toString());
  }

  public Test() {
    Test test = new Test();
  }
}
```

20.9 How many times is the `fib` method in Listing 20.2 invoked for `fib(6)`?

20.4 Problem Solving Using Recursion

If you think recursively, you can solve many problems using recursion.

recursion characteristics

The preceding sections presented two classic recursion examples. All recursive methods have the following characteristics:

- `if-else` — The method is implemented using an `if-else` or a `switch` statement that leads to different cases.
- base cases — One or more base cases (the simplest case) are used to stop recursion.
- reduction — Every recursive call reduces the original problem, bringing it increasingly closer to a base case until it becomes that case.

In general, to solve a problem using recursion, you break it into subproblems. Each subproblem is the same as the original problem but smaller in size. You can apply the same approach to each subproblem to solve it recursively.

think recursively

Recursion is everywhere. It is fun to *think recursively*. Consider drinking coffee. You may describe the procedure recursively as follows:

```
public static void drinkCoffee(Cup cup) {
  if (!cup.isEmpty()) {
    cup.takeOneSip(); // Take one sip
    drinkCoffee(cup);
  }
}
```

Assume `cup` is an object for a cup of coffee with the instance methods `isEmpty()` and `takeOneSip()`. You can break the problem into two subproblems: one is to drink one sip of coffee and the other is to drink the rest of the coffee in the cup. The second problem is the same as the original problem but smaller in size. The base case for the problem is when the cup is empty.

Consider the problem of printing a message `n` times. You can break the problem into two subproblems: one is to print the message one time and the other is to print it `n - 1` times. The second problem is the same as the original problem but it is smaller in size. The base case for the problem is `n == 0`. You can solve this problem using recursion as follows:

recursive call

```
public static void nPrintln(String message, int times) {
  if (times >= 1) {
    System.out.println(message);
    nPrintln(message, times - 1);
  } // The base case is times == 0
}
```

Note that the `fib` method in the preceding section returns a value to its caller, but the `drinkCoffee` and `nPrintln` methods are `void` and they do not return a value.

think recursively

If you *think recursively*, you can use recursion to solve many of the problems presented in earlier chapters of this book. Consider the palindrome problem in Listing 9.1. Recall that a string is a palindrome if it reads the same from the left and from the right. For example, "mom" and "dad" are palindromes, but "uncle" and "aunt" are not. The problem of checking whether a string is a palindrome can be divided into two subproblems:

- Check whether the first character and the last character of the string are equal.
- Ignore the two end characters and check whether the rest of the substring is a palindrome.

The second subproblem is the same as the original problem but smaller in size. There are two base cases: (1) the two end characters are not the same, and (2) the string size is `0` or `1`. In case 1, the string is not a palindrome; in case 2, the string is a palindrome. The recursive method for this problem can be implemented as shown in Listing 20.3.

LISTING 20.3 RecursivePalindromeUsingSubstring.java

method header · base case · base case · recursive call

```
public class RecursivePalindromeUsingSubstring {
  public static boolean isPalindrome(String s) {
    if (s.length() <= 1) // Base case
      return true;
    else if (s.charAt(0) != s.charAt(s.length() - 1)) // Base case
      return false;
    else
      return isPalindrome(s.substring(1, s.length() - 1));
  }

  public static void main(String[] args) {
```

```
12        System.out.println("Is moon a palindrome? "
13          + isPalindrome("moon"));
14        System.out.println("Is noon a palindrome? "
15          + isPalindrome("noon"));
16        System.out.println("Is a a palindrome? " + isPalindrome("a"));
17        System.out.println("Is aba a palindrome? " +
18          isPalindrome("aba"));
19        System.out.println("Is ab a palindrome? " + isPalindrome("ab"));
20      }
21    }
```

```
Is moon a palindrome? false
Is noon a palindrome? true
Is a a palindrome? true
Is aba a palindrome? true
Is ab a palindrome? false
```

The **substring** method in line 8 creates a new string that is the same as the original string except without the first and last characters. Checking whether a string is a palindrome is equivalent to checking whether the substring is a palindrome if the two end characters in the original string are the same.

MyProgrammingLab™

20.10 Describe the characteristics of recursive methods.

20.11 For the **isPalindrome** method in Listing 20.3, what are the base cases? How many times is this method called when invoking **isPalindrome("abdxcxdba")**?

20.12 Show the call stack for **isPalindrome("abcba")** using the method defined in Listing 20.3.

20.5 Recursive Helper Methods

Sometimes you can find a recursive solution by slightly changing the original problem. This new method is called a recursive helper method.

The recursive **isPalindrome** method in Listing 20.3 is not efficient, because it creates a new string for every recursive call. To avoid creating new strings, you can use the low and high indices to indicate the range of the substring. These two indices must be passed to the recursive method. Since the original method is **isPalindrome(String s)**, you have to create the new method **isPalindrome(String s, int low, int high)** to accept additional information on the string, as shown in Listing 20.4.

Listing 20.4 RecursivePalindrome.java

helper method (line 6), base case (line 7), base case (line 9)

```
public class RecursivePalindrome {
  public static boolean isPalindrome(String s) {
    return isPalindrome(s, 0, s.length() - 1);
  }

  private static boolean isPalindrome(String s, int low, int high) {
    if (high <= low) // Base case
      return true;
    else if (s.charAt(low) != s.charAt(high)) // Base case
      return false;
    else
      return isPalindrome(s, low + 1, high - 1);
  }

```

```
    public static void main(String[] args) {
      System.out.println("Is moon a palindrome? "
        + isPalindrome("moon"));
      System.out.println("Is noon a palindrome? "
        + isPalindrome("noon"));
      System.out.println("Is a a palindrome? " + isPalindrome("a"));
      System.out.println("Is aba a palindrome? " + isPalindrome("aba"));
      System.out.println("Is ab a palindrome? " + isPalindrome("ab"));
    }
}
```

Two overloaded `isPalindrome` methods are defined. The first, `isPalindrome(String s)`, checks whether a string is a palindrome, and the second, `isPalindrome(String s, int low, int high)`, checks whether a substring `s(low..high)` is a palindrome. The first method passes the string `s` with `low = 0` and `high = s.length() - 1` to the second method. The second method can be invoked recursively to check a palindrome in an ever-shrinking substring. It is a common design technique in recursive programming to define a second method that receives additional parameters. Such a method is known as a *recursive helper method*.

recursive helper method

Helper methods are very useful in designing recursive solutions for problems involving strings and arrays. The sections that follow give two more examples.

20.5.1 Recursive Selection Sort

Selection sort was introduced in Section 6.11.1. Recall that it finds the smallest element in the list and swaps it with the first element. It then finds the smallest element remaining and swaps it with the first element in the remaining list, and so on until the remaining list contains only a single element. The problem can be divided into two subproblems:

- Find the smallest element in the list and swap it with the first element.
- Ignore the first element and sort the remaining smaller list recursively.

The base case is that the list contains only one element. Listing 20.5 gives the recursive sort method.

LISTING 20.5 RecursiveSelectionSort.java

helper method
base case

```
public class RecursiveSelectionSort {
  public static void sort(double[] list) {
    sort(list, 0, list.length - 1); // Sort the entire list
  }

  private static void sort(double[] list, int low, int high) {
    if (low < high) {
      // Find the smallest number and its index in list[low .. high]
      int indexOfMin = low;
      double min = list[low];
      for (int i = low + 1; i <= high; i++) {
        if (list[i] < min) {
          min = list[i];
          indexOfMin = i;
        }
      }

      // Swap the smallest in list[low .. high] with list[low]
      list[indexOfMin] = list[low];
      list[low] = min;

```

recursive call

```
        // Sort the remaining list[low+1 .. high]
        sort(list, low + 1, high);
      }
    }
  }
```

Two overloaded `sort` methods are defined. The first method, `sort(double[] list)`, sorts an array in `list[0..list.length - 1]` and the second method, `sort(double[] list, int low, int high)`, sorts an array in `list[low..high]`. The second method can be invoked recursively to sort an ever-shrinking subarray.

20.5.2 Recursive Binary Search

VideoNote
Binary search

Binary search was introduced in Section 6.10.2. For binary search to work, the elements in the array must be in an increasing order. The binary search first compares the key with the element in the middle of the array. Consider the following three cases:

- Case 1: If the key is less than the middle element, recursively search for the key in the first half of the array.
- Case 2: If the key is equal to the middle element, the search ends with a match.
- Case 3: If the key is greater than the middle element, recursively search for the key in the second half of the array.

Case 1 and Case 3 reduce the search to a smaller list. Case 2 is a base case when there is a match. Another base case is that the search is exhausted without a match. Listing 20.6 gives a clear, simple solution for the binary search problem using recursion.

Listing 20.6 Recursive Binary Search Method

helper method, base case, recursive call, base case, recursive call

```
public class RecursiveBinarySearch {
  public static int recursiveBinarySearch(int[] list, int key) {
    int low = 0;
    int high = list.length - 1;
    return recursiveBinarySearch(list, key, low, high);
  }

  private static int recursiveBinarySearch(int[] list, int key,
      int low, int high) {
    if (low > high)  // The list has been exhausted without a match
      return -low - 1;

    int mid = (low + high) / 2;
    if (key < list[mid])
      return recursiveBinarySearch(list, key, low, mid - 1);
    else if (key == list[mid])
      return mid;
    else
      return recursiveBinarySearch(list, key, mid + 1, high);
  }
}
```

The first method finds a key in the whole list. The second method finds a key in the list with index from `low` to `high`.

The first `binarySearch` method passes the initial array with `low = 0` and `high = list.length - 1` to the second `binarySearch` method. The second method is invoked recursively to find the key in an ever-shrinking subarray.

Check Point
MyProgrammingLab™

20.13 Show the call stack for `isPalindrome("abcba")` using the method defined in Listing 20.4.

20.14 Show the call stack for `selectionSort(new double[]{2, 3, 5, 1})` using the method defined in Listing 20.5.

20.15 What is a recursive helper method?

20.6 Case Study: Finding the Directory Size

Key Point

Recursive methods are efficient for solving problems with recursive structures.

VideoNote
Directory size

The preceding examples can easily be solved without using recursion. This section presents a problem that is difficult to solve without using recursion. The problem is to find the size of a directory. The size of a directory is the sum of the sizes of all files in the directory. A directory d may contain subdirectories. Suppose a directory contains files $f_1, f_2, \ldots, f_m$ and subdirectories $d_1, d_2, \ldots, d_n$, as shown in Figure 20.5.

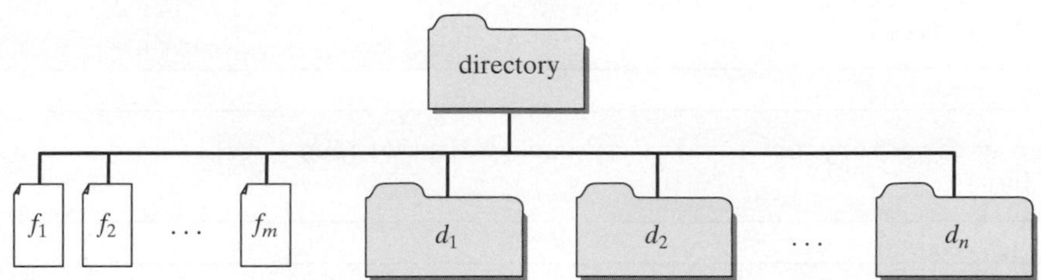

FIGURE 20.5 A directory contains files and subdirectories.

The size of the directory can be defined recursively as follows:

$$size(d) = size(f_1) + size(f_2) + \ldots + size(f_m) + size(d_1) + size(d_2) + \ldots + size(d_n)$$

The `File` class, introduced in Section 14.10, can be used to represent a file or a directory and obtain the properties for files and directories. Two methods in the `File` class are useful for this problem:

- The `length()` method returns the size of a file.
- The `listFiles()` method returns an array of `File` objects under a directory.

Listing 20.7 gives a program that prompts the user to enter a directory or a file and displays its size.

LISTING 20.7 DirectorySize.java

```
import java.io.File;
import java.util.Scanner;

public class DirectorySize {
  public static void main(String[] args) {
    // Prompt the user to enter a directory or a file
    System.out.print("Enter a directory or a file: ");
    Scanner input = new Scanner(System.in);
    String directory = input.nextLine();

    // Display the size
    System.out.println(getSize(new File(directory)) + " bytes");
  }

```

invoke method

getSize method
is directory?
all subitems
recursive call
base case

```
15   public static long getSize(File file) {
16     long size = 0; // Store the total size of all files
17
18     if (file.isDirectory()) {
19       File[] files = file.listFiles(); // All files and subdirectories
20       for (int i = 0; files != null && i < files.length; i++) {
21         size += getSize(files[i]); // Recursive call
22       }
23     }
24     else { // Base case
25       size += file.length();
26     }
27
28     return size;
29   }
30 }
```

```
Enter a directory or a file: c:\book ↵Enter
48619631 bytes
```

```
Enter a directory or a file: c:\book\Welcome.java ↵Enter
172 bytes
```

```
Enter a directory or a file: c:\book\NonExistentFile ↵Enter
0 bytes
```

If the **file** object represents a directory (line 18), each subitem (file or subdirectory) in the directory is recursively invoked to obtain its size (line 21). If the **file** object represents a file (line 24), the file size is obtained (line 25).

What happens if an incorrect or a nonexistent directory is entered? The program will detect that it is not a directory and invoke **file.length()** (line 25), which returns **0**. Thus, in this case, the **getSize** method will return **0**.

testing all cases

Tip

To avoid mistakes, it is a good practice to test all cases. For example, you should test the program for an input of file, an empty directory, a nonexistent directory, and a nonexistent file.

MyProgrammingLab™

20.16 What is the base case for the **getSize** method?

20.17 How does the program get all files and directories under a given directory?

20.18 How many times will the **getSize** method be invoked for a directory if the directory has three subdirectories and each subdirectory has four files?

20.7 Case Study: Towers of Hanoi

The Towers of Hanoi problem is a classic problem that can be solved easily using recursion, but it is difficult to solve otherwise.

The problem involves moving a specified number of disks of distinct sizes from one tower to another while observing the following rules:

- There are n disks labeled 1, 2, 3, . . . , n and three towers labeled A, B, and C.
- No disk can be on top of a smaller disk at any time.

- All the disks are initially placed on tower A.
- Only one disk can be moved at a time, and it must be the smallest disk on a tower.

The objective of the problem is to move all the disks from A to B with the assistance of C. For example, if you have three disks, the steps to move all of the disks from A to B are shown in Figure 20.6.

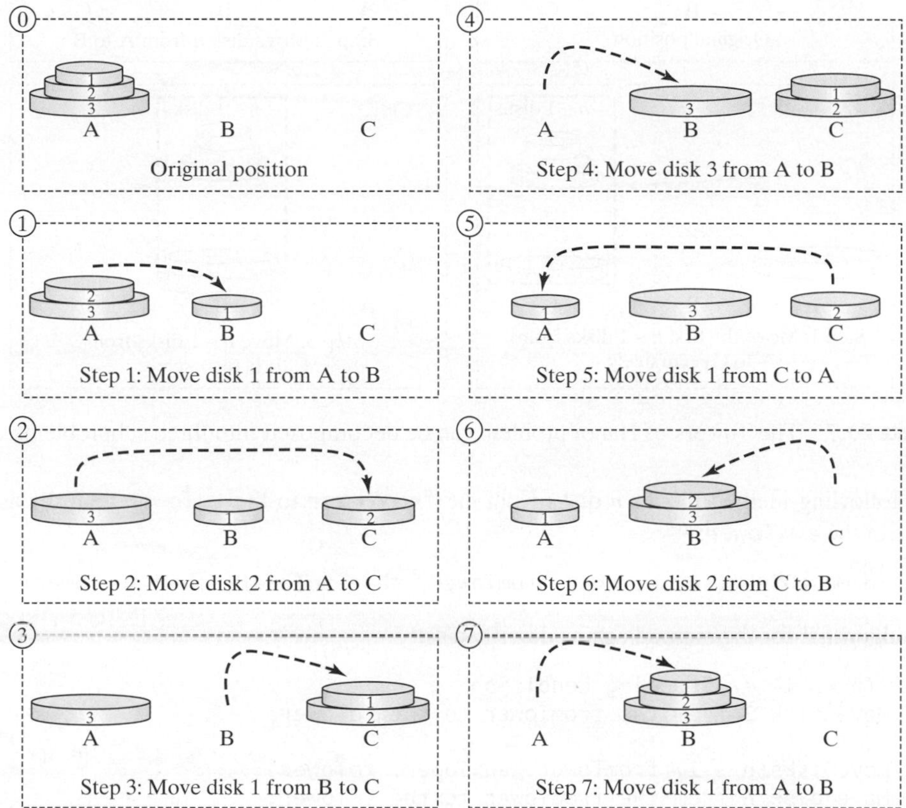

FIGURE 20.6 The goal of the Towers of Hanoi problem is to move disks from tower A to tower B without breaking the rules.

Note

The Towers of Hanoi is a classic computer-science problem, to which many websites are devoted. One of them worth looking at is www.cut-the-knot.com/recurrence/hanoi.html.

In the case of three disks, you can find the solution manually. For a larger number of disks, however—even for four—the problem is quite complex. Fortunately, the problem has an inherently recursive nature, which leads to a straightforward recursive solution.

The base case for the problem is `n = 1`. If `n == 1`, you could simply move the disk from A to B. When `n > 1`, you could split the original problem into the following three subproblems and solve them sequentially.

1. Move the first `n - 1` disks from A to C with the assistance of tower B, as shown in Step 1 in Figure 20.7.
2. Move disk `n` from A to B, as shown in Step 2 in Figure 20.7.
3. Move `n - 1` disks from C to B with the assistance of tower A, as shown in Step 3 in Figure 20.7.

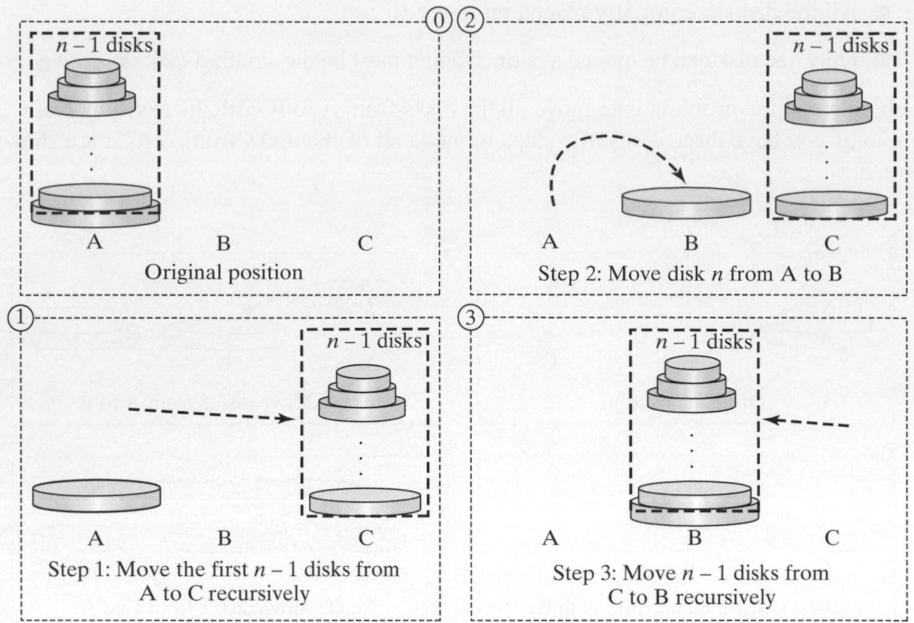

FIGURE 20.7 The Towers of Hanoi problem can be decomposed into three subproblems.

The following method moves *n* disks from the **fromTower** to the **toTower** with the assistance of the **auxTower**:

```
void moveDisks(int n, char fromTower, char toTower, char auxTower)
```

The algorithm for the method can be described as:

```
if (n == 1) // Stopping condition
  Move disk 1 from the fromTower to the toTower;
else {
  moveDisks(n - 1, fromTower, auxTower, toTower);
  Move disk n from the fromTower to the toTower;
  moveDisks(n - 1, auxTower, toTower, fromTower);
}
```

Listing 20.8 gives a program that prompts the user to enter the number of disks and invokes the recursive method **moveDisks** to display the solution for moving the disks.

LISTING 20.8 TowersOfHanoi.java

```
import java.util.Scanner;

public class TowersOfHanoi {
  /** Main method */
  public static void main(String[] args) {
    // Create a Scanner
    Scanner input = new Scanner(System.in);
    System.out.print("Enter number of disks: ");
    int n = input.nextInt();

    // Find the solution recursively
    System.out.println("The moves are:");
    moveDisks(n, 'A', 'B', 'C');
  }

```

```
  /** The method for finding the solution to move n disks
      from fromTower to toTower with auxTower */
  public static void moveDisks(int n, char fromTower,
      char toTower, char auxTower) {
    if (n == 1) // Stopping condition
      System.out.println("Move disk " + n + " from " +
        fromTower + " to " + toTower);
    else {
      moveDisks(n - 1, fromTower, auxTower, toTower);
      System.out.println("Move disk " + n + " from " +
        fromTower + " to " + toTower);
      moveDisks(n - 1, auxTower, toTower, fromTower);
    }
  }
}
```

base case

recursion

recursion

```
Enter number of disks: 4 ↵Enter
The moves are:
Move disk 1 from A to C
Move disk 2 from A to B
Move disk 1 from C to B
Move disk 3 from A to C
Move disk 1 from B to A
Move disk 2 from B to C
Move disk 1 from A to C
Move disk 4 from A to B
Move disk 1 from C to B
Move disk 2 from C to A
Move disk 1 from B to A
Move disk 3 from C to B
Move disk 1 from A to C
Move disk 2 from A to B
Move disk 1 from C to B
```

This problem is inherently recursive. Using recursion makes it possible to find a natural, simple solution. It would be difficult to solve the problem without using recursion.

Consider tracing the program for `n = 3`. The successive recursive calls are shown in Figure 20.8. As you can see, writing the program is easier than tracing the recursive calls. The

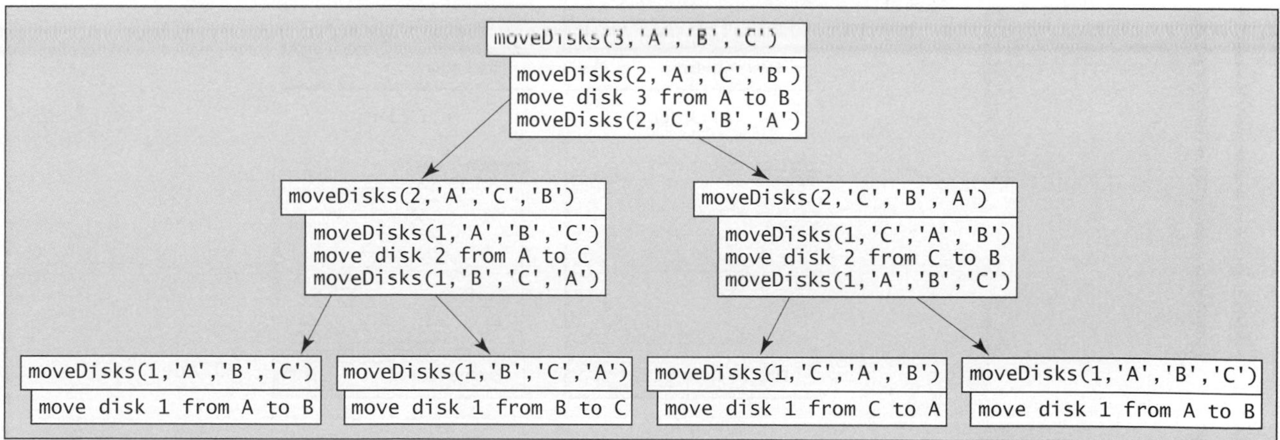

FIGURE 20.8 Invoking `moveDisks(3, 'A', 'B', 'C')` spawns calls to `moveDisks` recursively.

system uses stacks to manage the calls behind the scenes. To some extent, recursion provides a level of abstraction that hides iterations and other details from the user.

20.19 How many times is the `moveDisks` method in Listing 20.8 invoked for `moveDisks(5, 'A', 'B', 'C')`?

20.8 Case Study: Fractals

Using recursion is ideal for displaying fractals, because fractals are inherently recursive.

A *fractal* is a geometrical figure, but unlike triangles, circles, and rectangles, fractals can be divided into parts, each of which is a reduced-size copy of the whole. There are many interesting examples of fractals. This section introduces a simple fractal, the *Sierpinski triangle*, named after a famous Polish mathematician.

A Sierpinski triangle is created as follows:

1. Begin with an equilateral triangle, which is considered to be a Sierpinski fractal of order (or level) 0, as shown in Figure 20.9a.
2. Connect the midpoints of the sides of the triangle of order 0 to create a Sierpinski triangle of order 1 (Figure 20.9b).
3. Leave the center triangle intact. Connect the midpoints of the sides of the three other triangles to create a Sierpinski triangle of order 2 (Figure 20.9c).
4. You can repeat the same process recursively to create a Sierpinski triangle of order 3, 4, . . . , and so on (Figure 20.9d).

The problem is inherently recursive. How do you develop a recursive solution for it? Consider the base case when the order is 0. It is easy to draw a Sierpinski triangle of order 0.

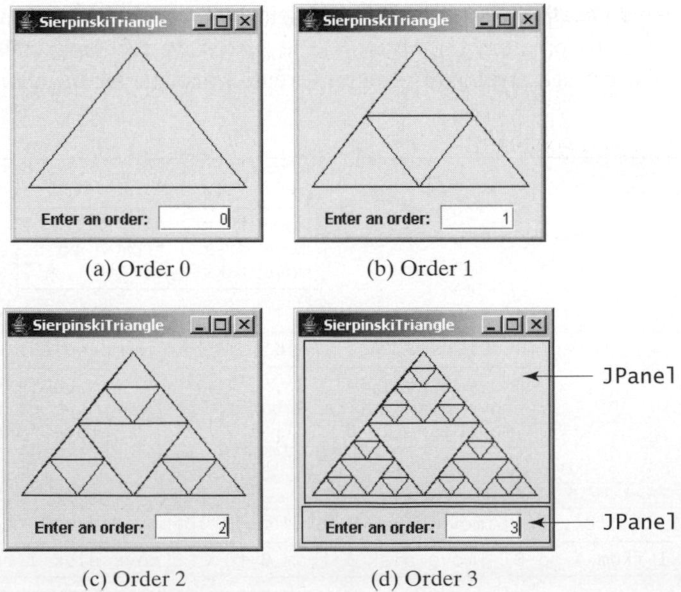

(a) Order 0 (b) Order 1

(c) Order 2 (d) Order 3

FIGURE 20.9 A Sierpinski triangle is a pattern of recursive triangles.

How do you draw a Sierpinski triangle of order 1? The problem can be reduced to drawing three Sierpinski triangles of order 0. How do you draw a Sierpinski triangle of order 2? The problem can be reduced to drawing three Sierpinski triangles of order 1, so the problem of drawing a Sierpinski triangle of order *n* can be reduced to drawing three Sierpinski triangles of order *n* - 1.

Listing 20.9 gives a Java applet that displays a Sierpinski triangle of any order, as shown in Figure 20.9. You can enter an order in a text field to display a Sierpinski triangle of the specified order.

LISTING 20.9 SierpinskiTriangle.java

```
import javax.swing.*;
import java.awt.*;
import java.awt.event.*;

public class SierpinskiTriangle extends JApplet {
  private JTextField jtfOrder = new JTextField("0", 5); // Order
  private SierpinskiTrianglePanel trianglePanel =
    new SierpinskiTrianglePanel(); // To display the pattern

  public SierpinskiTriangle() {
    // Panel to hold label, text field, and a button
    JPanel panel = new JPanel();
    panel.add(new JLabel("Enter an order: "));
    panel.add(jtfOrder);
    jtfOrder.setHorizontalAlignment(SwingConstants.RIGHT);

    // Add a Sierpinski triangle panel to the applet
    add(trianglePanel);
    add(panel, BorderLayout.SOUTH);

    // Register a listener
    jtfOrder.addActionListener(new ActionListener() {
      @Override
      public void actionPerformed(ActionEvent e) {
        trianglePanel.setOrder(Integer.parseInt(jtfOrder.getText()));
      }
    });
  }

  static class SierpinskiTrianglePanel extends JPanel {
    private int order = 0;

    /** Set a new order */
    public void setOrder(int order) {
      this.order = order;
      repaint();
    }

    @Override
    protected void paintComponent(Graphics g) {
      super.paintComponent(g);

      // Select three points in proportion to the panel size
      Point p1 = new Point(getWidth() / 2, 10);
      Point p2 = new Point(10, getHeight() - 10);
      Point p3 = new Point(getWidth() - 10, getHeight() - 10);

```

listener

set a new order

three initial points

draw a triangle

top subtriangle

left subtriangle

right subtriangle

main method omitted

```
48      displayTriangles(g, order, p1, p2, p3);
49    }
50
51    private static void displayTriangles(Graphics g, int order,
52        Point p1, Point p2, Point p3) {
53      if (order == 0) {
54        // Draw a triangle to connect three points
55        g.drawLine(p1.x, p1.y, p2.x, p2.y);
56        g.drawLine(p1.x, p1.y, p3.x, p3.y);
57        g.drawLine(p2.x, p2.y, p3.x, p3.y);
58      }
59      else {
60        // Get the midpoint on each edge of the triangle
61        Point p12 = midpoint(p1, p2);
62        Point p23 = midpoint(p2, p3);
63        Point p31 = midpoint(p3, p1);
64
65        // Recursively display three triangles
66        displayTriangles(g, order - 1, p1, p12, p31);
67        displayTriangles(g, order - 1, p12, p2, p23);
68        displayTriangles(g, order - 1, p31, p23, p3);
69      }
70    }
71
72    private static Point midpoint(Point p1, Point p2) {
73      return new Point((p1.x + p2.x) / 2, (p1.y + p2.y) / 2);
74    }
75  }
76 }
```

`displayTriangle` method

The initial triangle has three points set in proportion to the panel size (lines 44–46). If `order == 0`, the `displayTriangles(g, order, p1, p2, p3)` method displays a triangle that connects the three points `p1`, `p2`, and `p3` in lines 55–57, as shown in Figure 20.10a. Otherwise, it performs the following tasks:

1. Obtain the midpoint between `p1` and `p2` (line 61), the midpoint between `p2` and `p3` (line 62), and the midpoint between `p3` and `p1` (line 63), as shown in Figure 20.10b.
2. Recursively invoke `displayTriangles` with a reduced order to display three smaller Sierpinski triangles (lines 66–68). Note that each small Sierpinski triangle is structurally identical to the original big Sierpinski triangle except that the order of a small triangle is one less, as shown in Figure 20.10b.

A Sierpinski triangle is displayed in a `SierpinskiTrianglePanel`. The `order` property in the inner class `SierpinskiTrianglePanel` specifies the order for the Sierpinski triangle. The `Point` class, introduced in Section 16.8, Mouse Events, represents a point on a component. The `midpoint(Point p1, Point p2)` method returns the midpoint between `p1` and `p2` (lines 72–74).

MyProgrammingLab™

20.20 How do you obtain the midpoint between two points?

20.21 What is the base case for the `displayTriangles` method?

20.22 How many times is the `displayTriangles` method invoked for a Sierpinski triangle of order 0, order 1, order 2, and order n?

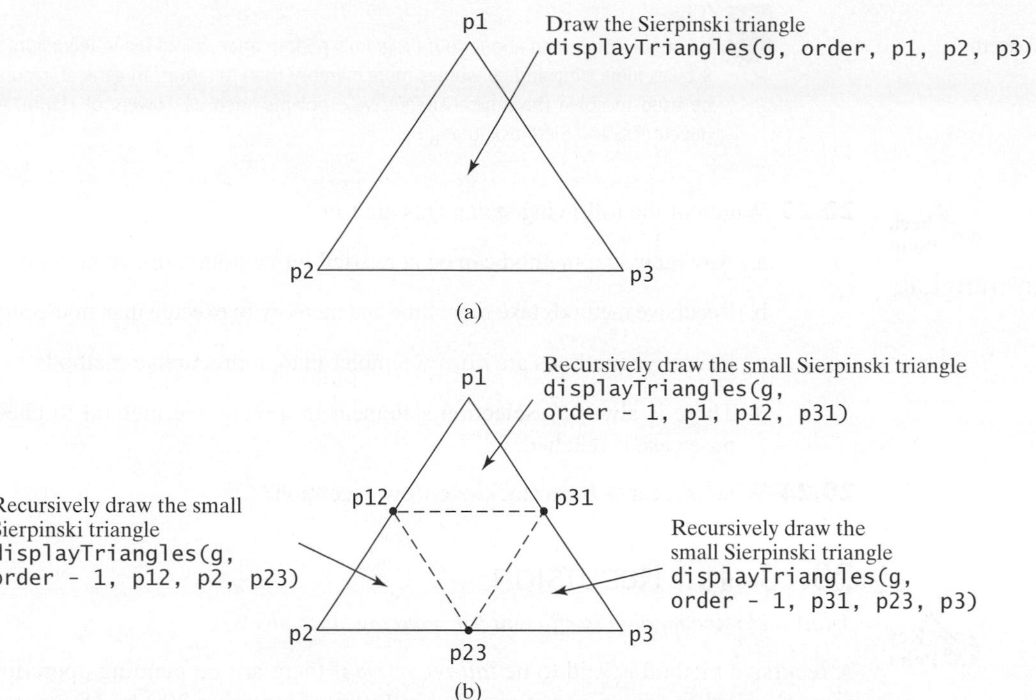

FIGURE 20.10 Drawing a Sierpinski triangle spawns calls to draw three small Sierpinski triangles recursively.

20.9 Recursion vs. Iteration

Recursion is an alternative form of program control. It is essentially repetition without a loop.

When you use loops, you specify a loop body. The repetition of the loop body is controlled by the loop control structure. In recursion, the method itself is called repeatedly. A selection statement must be used to control whether to call the method recursively or not.

Recursion bears substantial overhead. Each time the program calls a method, the system must allocate memory for all of the method's local variables and parameters. This can consume considerable memory and requires extra time to manage the memory. recursion overhead

Any problem that can be solved recursively can be solved nonrecursively with iterations. Recursion has some negative aspects: it uses up too much time and too much memory. Why, then, should you use it? In some cases, using recursion enables you to specify a clear, simple solution for an inherently recursive problem that would otherwise be difficult to obtain. Examples are the directory-size problem, the Towers of Hanoi problem, and the fractal problem, which are rather difficult to solve without using recursion. recursion advantages

The decision whether to use recursion or iteration should be based on the nature of, and your understanding of, the problem you are trying to solve. The rule of thumb is to use whichever approach can best develop an intuitive solution that naturally mirrors the problem. If an iterative solution is obvious, use it. It will generally be more efficient than the recursive option. recursion or iteration?

Note

Recursive programs can run out of memory, causing a `StackOverflowError`. `StackOverflowError`

performance concern

Tip

If you are concerned about your program's performance, avoid using recursion, because it takes more time and consumes more memory than iteration. In general, recursion can be used to solve the inherent recursive problems such as Towers of Hanoi, recursive directories, and Sierpinski triangles.

MyProgrammingLab™

20.23 Which of the following statements are true?

a. Any recursive method can be converted into a nonrecursive method.

b. Recursive methods take more time and memory to execute than nonrecursive methods.

c. Recursive methods are *always* simpler than nonrecursive methods.

d. There is always a selection statement in a recursive method to check whether a base case is reached.

20.24 What is a cause for a stack-overflow exception?

20.10 Tail Recursion

A tail recursive method is efficient for reducing stack size.

tail recursion

A recursive method is said to be *tail recursive* if there are no pending operations to be performed on return from a recursive call, as illustrated in Figure 20.11a. However, method **B** in Figure 20.11b is not tail recursive because there are pending operations after a method call is returned.

```
Recursive method A
    ...
    ...
    ...
    Invoke method A recursively
```

(a) Tail recursion

```
Recursive method B
    ...
    ...
    Invoke method B recursively
    ...
    ...
```

(b) Nontail recursion

FIGURE 20.11 A tail-recursive method has no pending operations after a recursive call.

For example, the recursive **isPalindrome** method (lines 6–13) in Listing 20.4 is tail recursive because there are no pending operations after recursively invoking **isPalindrome** in line 12. However, the recursive **factorial** method (lines 16–21) in Listing 20.1 is not tail recursive, because there is a pending operation, namely multiplication, to be performed on return from each recursive call.

Tail recursion may be desirable: because the method ends when the last recursive call ends, there is no need to store the intermediate calls in the stack. Some compilers can optimize tail recursion to reduce stack size.

A nontail-recursive method can often be converted to a tail-recursive method by using auxiliary parameters. These parameters are used to contain the result. The idea is to incorporate the pending operations into the auxiliary parameters in such a way that the recursive call no longer has a pending operation. You can define a new auxiliary recursive method with the auxiliary parameters. This method may overload the original method with the same name but a different signature. For example, the **factorial** method in Listing 20.1 is written in a tail-recursive way in Listing 20.10.

LISTING 20.10 ComputeFactorialTailRecursion.java

```
1  public class ComputeFactorialTailRecursion {
2    /** Return the factorial for a specified number */
3    public static long factorial(int n) {
4      return factorial(n, 1); // Call auxiliary method
5    }
6
7    /** Auxiliary tail-recursive method for factorial */
8    private static long factorial(int n, int result) {
9      if (n == 0)
10       return result;
11     else
12       return factorial(n - 1, n * result); // Recursive call
13   }
14 }
```

original method
invoke auxiliary method
auxiliary method
recursive call

The first `factorial` method (line 3) simply invokes the second auxiliary method (line 4). The second method contains an auxiliary parameter `result` that stores the result for the factorial of `n`. This method is invoked recursively in line 12. There is no pending operation after a call is returned. The final result is returned in line 10, which is also the return value from invoking `factorial(n, 1)` in line 4.

MyProgrammingLab™

20.25 Identify tail-recursive methods in this chapter.

20.26 Rewrite the `fib` method in Listing 20.2 using tail recursion.

Key Terms

base case 738
direct recursion 741
indirect recursion 741
infinite recursion 741
recursive helper method 747
recursive method 738
stopping condition 738
tail recursion 758

Chapter Summary

1. A *recursive method* is one that directly or indirectly invokes itself. For a recursive method to terminate, there must be one or more *base cases*.

2. *Recursion* is an alternative form of program control. It is essentially repetition without a loop control. It can be used to specify simple, clear solutions for inherently recursive problems that would otherwise be difficult to solve.

3. Sometimes the original method needs to be modified to receive additional parameters in order to be invoked recursively. A *recursive helper method* can be defined for this purpose.

4. Recursion bears substantial overhead. Each time the program calls a method, the system must allocate memory for all of the method's local variables and parameters. This can consume considerable memory and requires extra time to manage the memory.

5. A recursive method is said to be *tail recursive* if there are no pending operations to be performed on return from a recursive call. Some compilers can optimize tail recursion to reduce stack size.

Test Questions

Do the test questions for this chapter online at www.cs.armstrong.edu/liang/intro9e/test.html.

MyProgrammingLab™

Programming Exercises

Sections 20.2–20.3

***20.1** (*Factorial*) Using the `BigInteger` class introduced in Section 10.14, you can find the factorial for a large number (e.g., `100!`). Implement the `factorial` method using recursion. Write a program that prompts the user to enter an integer and displays its factorial.

***20.2** (*Fibonacci numbers*) Rewrite the `fib` method in Listing 20.2 using iterations.

Hint: To compute `fib(n)` without recursion, you need to obtain `fib(n - 2)` and `fib(n - 1)` first. Let `f0` and `f1` denote the two previous Fibonacci numbers. The current Fibonacci number would then be `f0 + f1`. The algorithm can be described as follows:

```
f0 = 0; // For fib(0)
f1 = 1; // For fib(1)

for (int i = 1; i <= n; i++) {
  currentFib = f0 + f1;
  f0 = f1;
  f1 = currentFib;
}
// After the loop, currentFib is fib(n)
```

Write a test program that prompts the user to enter an index and displays its Fibonacci number.

***20.3** (*Compute greatest common divisor using recursion*) The `gcd(m, n)` can also be defined recursively as follows:

- If `m % n` is `0`, `gcd(m, n)` is `n`.
- Otherwise, `gcd(m, n)` is `gcd(n, m % n)`.

Write a recursive method to find the GCD. Write a test program that prompts the user to enter two integers and displays their GCD.

20.4 (*Sum series*) Write a recursive method to compute the following series:

$$m(i) = 1 + \frac{1}{2} + \frac{1}{3} + \ldots + \frac{1}{i}$$

Write a test program that displays `m(i)` for `i` = `1, 2, . . . , 10`.

20.5 (*Sum series*) Write a recursive method to compute the following series:

$$m(i) = \frac{1}{3} + \frac{2}{5} + \frac{3}{7} + \frac{4}{9} + \frac{5}{11} + \frac{6}{13} + \ldots + \frac{i}{2i + 1}$$

Write a test program that displays `m(i)` for `i` = `1, 2, . . . , 10`.

***20.6** (*Sum series*) Write a recursive method to compute the following series:

$$m(i) = \frac{1}{2} + \frac{2}{3} + \ldots + \frac{i}{i + 1}$$

Write a test program that displays `m(i)` for `i` = `1, 2, . . . , 10`.

***20.7** (*Fibonacci series*) Modify Listing 20.2, ComputeFibonacci.java, so that the program finds the number of times the `fib` method is called. (*Hint*: Use a static variable and increment it every time the method is called.)

Section 20.4

***20.8** (*Print the digits in an integer reversely*) Write a recursive method that displays an `int` value reversely on the console using the following header:

```
public static void reverseDisplay(int value)
```

For example, `reverseDisplay(12345)` displays `54321`. Write a test program that prompts the user to enter an integer and displays its reversal.

***20.9** (*Print the characters in a string reversely*) Write a recursive method that displays a string reversely on the console using the following header:

```
public static void reverseDisplay(String value)
```

For example, `reverseDisplay("abcd")` displays `dcba`. Write a test program that prompts the user to enter a string and displays its reversal.

***20.10** (*Occurrences of a specified character in a string*) Write a recursive method that finds the number of occurrences of a specified letter in a string using the following method header:

```
public static int count(String str, char a)
```

For example, `count("Welcome", 'e')` returns `2`. Write a test program that prompts the user to enter a string and a character, and displays the number of occurrences for the character in the string.

***20.11** (*Sum the digits in an integer using recursion*) Write a recursive method that computes the sum of the digits in an integer. Use the following method header:

```
public static int sumDigits(long n)
```

For example, `sumDigits(234)` returns $2 + 3 + 4 = 9$. Write a test program that prompts the user to enter an integer and displays its sum.

Section 20.5

****20.12** (*Print the characters in a string reversely*) Rewrite Exercise 20.9 using a helper method to pass the substring `high` index to the method. The helper method header is:

```
public static void reverseDisplay(String value, int high)
```

***20.13** (*Find the largest number in an array*) Write a recursive method that returns the largest integer in an array. Write a test program that prompts the user to enter a list of eight integers and displays the largest element.

***20.14** (*Find the number of uppercase letters in a string*) Write a recursive method to return the number of uppercase letters in a string. Write a test program that prompts the user to enter a string and displays the number of uppercase letters in the string.

***20.15** (*Occurrences of a specified character in a string*) Rewrite Exercise 20.10 using a helper method to pass the substring `high` index to the method. The helper method header is:

```
public static int count(String str, char a, int high)
```

***20.16** (*Find the number of uppercase letters in an array*) Write a recursive method to return the number of uppercase letters in an array of characters. You need to define the following two methods. The second one is a recursive helper method.

```
public static int count(char[] chars)
public static int count(char[] chars, int high)
```

Write a test program that prompts the user to enter a list of characters in one line and displays the number of uppercase letters in the list.

***20.17** (*Occurrences of a specified character in an array*) Write a recursive method that finds the number of occurrences of a specified character in an array. You need to define the following two methods. The second one is a recursive helper method.

```
public static int count(char[] chars, char ch)
public static int count(char[] chars, char ch, int high)
```

Write a test program that prompts the user to enter a list of characters in one line, and a character, and displays the number of occurrences of the character in the list.

Sections 20.6–20.10

***20.18** (*Towers of Hanoi*) Modify Listing 20.8, TowersOfHanoi.java, so that the program finds the number of moves needed to move *n* disks from tower A to tower B. (*Hint*: Use a static variable and increment it every time the method is called.)

***20.19** (*Sierpinski triangle*) Revise Listing 20.9 to develop an applet that lets the user use the + and − buttons to increase or decrease the current order by `1`, as shown in Figure 20.12a. The initial order is `0`. If the current order is `0`, the *Decrease* button is ignored.

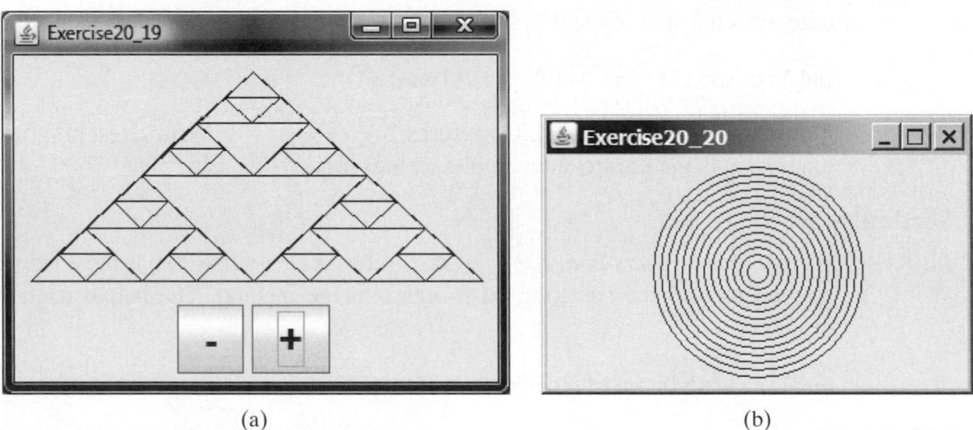

FIGURE 20.12 (a) Exercise 20.19 uses the + and − buttons to increase or decrease the current order by `1`. (b) Exercise 20.20 draws ovals using a recursive method.

***20.20** (*Display circles*) Write a Java applet that displays ovals, as shown in Figure 20.12b. The ovals are centered in the panel. The gap between two adjacent ovals is `10` pixels, and the gap between the border of the panel and the largest oval is also `10`.

***20.21** (*Decimal to binary*) Write a recursive method that converts a decimal number into a binary number as a string. The method header is:

```
public static String decimalToBinary(int value)
```

Write a test program that prompts the user to enter a decimal number and displays its binary equivalent.

***20.22** (*Decimal to hex*) Write a recursive method that converts a decimal number into a hex number as a string. The method header is:

```
public static String decimalToHex(int value)
```

Write a test program that prompts the user to enter a decimal number and displays its hex equivalent.

***20.23** (*Binary to decimal*) Write a recursive method that parses a binary number as a string into a decimal integer. The method header is:

```
public static int binaryToDecimal(String binaryString)
```

Write a test program that prompts the user to enter a binary string and displays its decimal equivalent.

***20.24** (*Hex to decimal*) Write a recursive method that parses a hex number as a string into a decimal integer. The method header is:

```
public static int hexToDecimal(String hexString)
```

Write a test program that prompts the user to enter a hex string and displays its decimal equivalent.

****20.25** (*String permutation*) Write a recursive method to print all the permutations of a string. For example, for the string `abc`, the printout is

```
abc
acb
bac
bca
cab
cba
```

(*Hint*: Define the following two methods. The second is a helper method.)

```
public static void displayPermutation(String s)
public static void displayPermutation(String s1, String s2)
```

The first method simply invokes `displayPermutation(" ", s)`. The second method uses a loop to move a character from `s2` to `s1` and recursively invokes it with a new `s1` and `s2`. The base case is that `s2` is empty and prints `s1` to the console.

Write a test program that prompts the user to enter a string and displays all its permutations.

****20.26** (*Create a maze*) Write an applet that will find a path in a maze, as shown in Figure 20.13a. The maze is represented by an 8×8 board. The path must meet the following conditions:

- The path is between the upper-left corner cell and the lower-right corner cell in the maze.
- The applet enables the user to place or remove a mark on a cell. A path consists of adjacent unmarked cells. Two cells are said to be adjacent if they are horizontal or vertical neighbors, but not if they are diagonal neighbors.
- The path does not contain cells that form a square. The path in Figure 20.13b, for example, does not meet this condition. (The condition makes a path easy to identify on the board.)

(a) Correct path (b) Illegal path

FIGURE 20.13 The program finds a path from the upper-left corner to the bottom-right corner.

****20.27** (*Koch snowflake fractal*) The text presented the Sierpinski triangle fractal. In this exercise, you will write an applet to display another fractal, called the *Koch snowflake*, named after a famous Swedish mathematician. A Koch snowflake is created as follows:

1. Begin with an equilateral triangle, which is considered to be the Koch fractal of order (or level) 0, as shown in Figure 20.14a.
2. Divide each line in the shape into three equal line segments and draw an outward equilateral triangle with the middle line segment as the base to create a Koch fractal of order 1, as shown in Figure 20.14b.
3. Repeat Step 2 to create a Koch fractal of order 2, 3, . . . , and so on, as shown in Figure 20.14c–d.

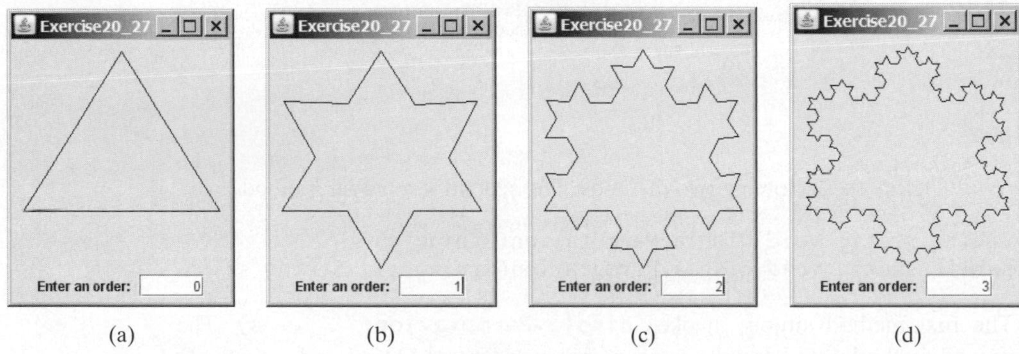

(a) (b) (c) (d)

FIGURE 20.14 A Koch snowflake is a fractal starting with a triangle.

****20.28** (*Nonrecursive directory size*) Rewrite Listing 20.7, DirectorySize.java, without using recursion.

***20.29** (*Number of files in a directory*) Write a program that prompts the user to enter a directory and displays the number of the files in the directory.

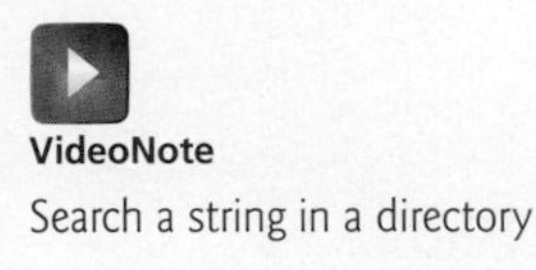

VideoNote
Search a string in a directory

****20.30** (*Find words*) Write a program that finds all occurrences of a word in all the files under a directory, recursively. Pass the parameters from the command line as follows:

```
java Exercise20_30 dirName word
```

****20.31** (*Replace words*) Write a program that replaces all occurrences of a word with a new word in all the files under a directory, recursively. Pass the parameters from the command line as follows:

```
java Exercise20_31 dirName oldWord newWord
```

***20.32 (*Game: Knight's Tour*) The Knight's Tour is an ancient puzzle. The objective is to move a knight, starting from any square on a chessboard, to every other square once, as shown in Figure 20.15a. Note that the knight makes only L-shaped moves (two spaces in one direction and one space in a perpendicular direction). As shown in Figure 20.15b, the knight can move to eight squares. Write a program that displays the moves for the knight in an applet, as shown in Figure 20.15c.

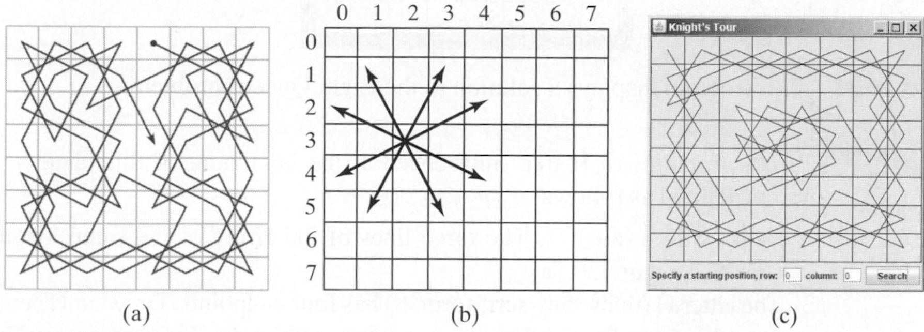

FIGURE 20.15 (a) A knight traverses all squares once. (b) A knight makes an L-shaped move. (c) An applet displays a Knight's Tour path.

(*Hint*: A brute-force approach for this problem is to move the knight from one square to another available square arbitrarily. Using such an approach, your program will take a long time to finish. A better approach is to employ some heuristics. A knight has two, three, four, six, or eight possible moves, depending on its location. Intuitively, you should attempt to move the knight to the least accessible squares first and leave those more accessible squares open, so there will be a better chance of success at the end of the search.)

***20.33 (*Game: Knight's Tour animation*) Write an applet for the Knight's Tour problem. Your applet should let the user move a knight to any starting square and click the *Solve* button to animate a knight moving along the path, as shown in Figure 20.16.

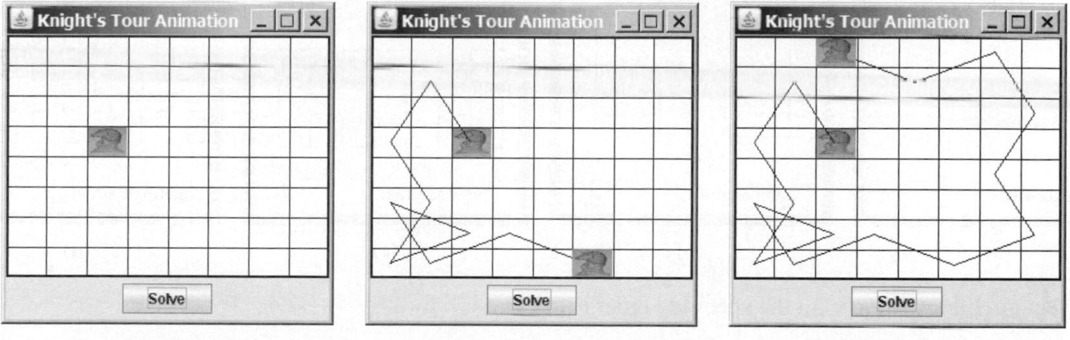

FIGURE 20.16 A knight traverses along the path.

**20.34 (*Game: Eight Queens*) The Eight Queens problem is to find a solution to place a queen in each row on a chessboard such that no two queens can attack each other. Write a program to solve the Eight Queens problem using recursion and display the result as shown in Figure 20.17.

FIGURE 20.17 The program displays a solution to the Eight Queens problem.

****20.35** (*H-tree fractal*) An H-tree (introduced at the beginning of this chapter) is a fractal defined as follows:

1. Begin with a letter H. The three lines of the H are of the same length, as shown in Figure 20.1a.
2. The letter H (in its sans-serif form, H) has four endpoints. Draw an H centered at each of the four endpoints to an H-tree of order 1, as shown in Figure 20.1b. These Hs are half the size of the H that contains the four endpoints.
3. Repeat Step 2 to create an H-tree of order 2, 3, . . . , and so on, as shown in Figure 20.1c–d.

Write an applet that draws an H-tree, as shown in Figure 20.1.

****20.36** (*Hilbert curve*) The Hilbert curve, first described by German mathematician David Hilbert in 1891, is a space-filling curve that visits every point in a square grid with a size of 2×2, 4×4, 8×8, 16×16, or any other power of 2. Write a Java applet that displays a Hilbert curve for the specified order, as shown in Figure 20.18.

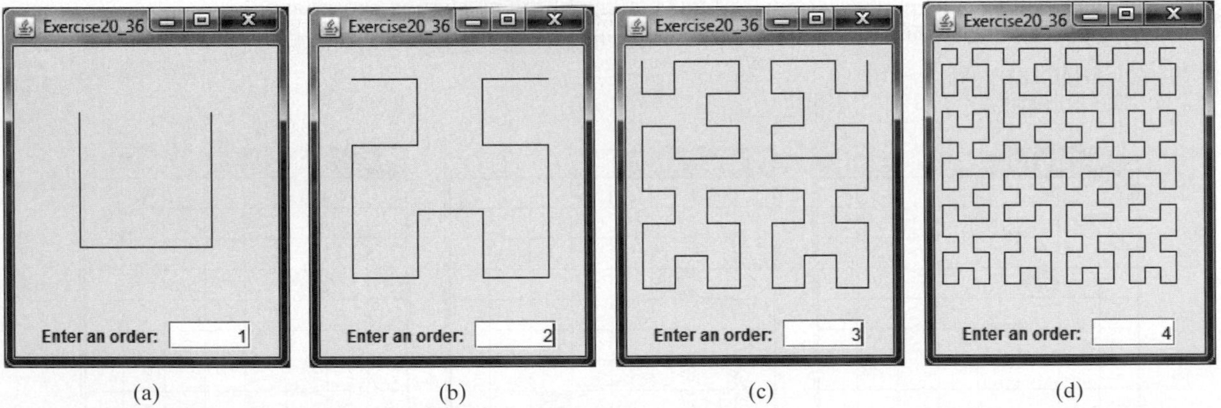

FIGURE 20.18 A Hilbert curve with the specified order is drawn.

20.37 (*Sierpinski triangle*) Write a program that prompts the user to enter the order and display the filled Sierpinski triangles as shown in Figure 20.19.

****20.38** (*Recursive tree*) Write an applet to display a recursive tree as shown in Figure 20.20.

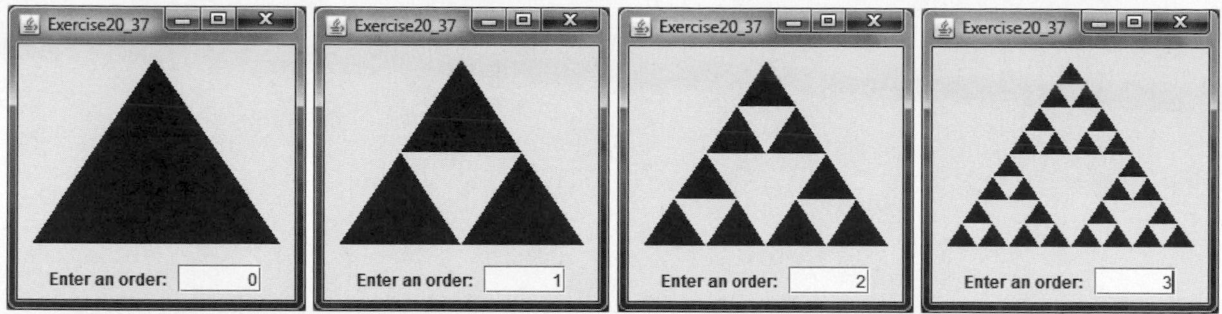

FIGURE 20.19 A filled Sierpinski triangle is displayed.

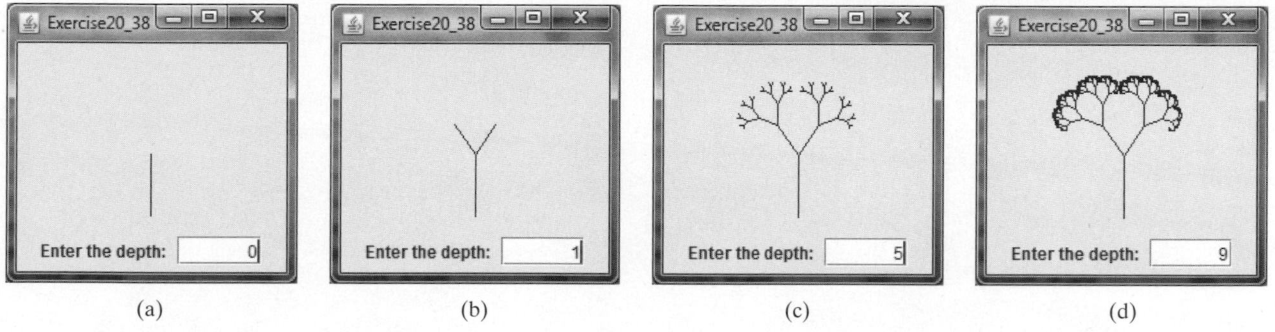

FIGURE 20.20 A recursive tree with the specified depth is drawn.

****20.39** (*Dragging the tree*) Revise Exercise 20.38 to move the tree to where the mouse is dragged.

CHAPTER 21

GENERICS

Objectives

- To describe the benefits of generics (§21.2).
- To use generic classes and interfaces (§21.2).
- To define generic classes and interfaces (§21.3).
- To explain why generic types can improve reliability and readability (§21.3).
- To define and use generic methods and bounded generic types (§21.4).
- To develop a generic sort method to sort an array of `Comparable` objects (§21.5).
- To use raw types for backward compatibility (§21.6).
- To explain why wildcard generic types are necessary (§21.7).
- To describe generic type erasure and list certain restrictions and limitations on generic types caused by type erasure (§21.8).
- To design and implement generic matrix classes (§21.9).

21.1 Introduction

Generics enable you to detect errors at compile time rather than at runtime.

what is generics?

You have used a generic class `ArrayList` in Chapter 11 and generic interface `Comparable` in Chapter 15. *Generics* let you parameterize types. With this capability, you can define a class or a method with generic types that the compiler can replace with concrete types. For example, Java defines a generic `ArrayList` class for storing the elements of a generic type. From this generic class, you can create an `ArrayList` object for holding strings and an `ArrayList` object for holding numbers. Here, strings and numbers are concrete types that replace the generic type.

why generics?

The key benefit of generics is to enable errors to be detected at compile time rather than at runtime. A generic class or method permits you to specify allowable types of objects that the class or method can work with. If you attempt to use an incompatible object, the compiler will detect that error.

This chapter explains how to define and use generic classes, interfaces, and methods and demonstrates how generics can be used to improve software reliability and readability. It can be intertwined with Chapter 15, Abstract Classes and Interfaces.

21.2 Motivations and Benefits

The motivation for using Java generics is to detect errors at compile time.

Java has allowed you to define generic classes, interfaces, and methods since JDK 1.5. Several interfaces and classes in the Java API are modified using generics. For example, prior to JDK 1.5 the `java.lang.Comparable` interface was defined as shown in Figure 21.1a, but since JDK 1.5 it is modified as shown in Figure 21.1b.

```
package java.lang;

public interface Comparable {
  public int compareTo(Object o)
}
```

(a) Prior to JDK 1.5

```
package java.lang;

public interface Comparable<T> {
  public int compareTo(T o)
}
```

(b) Since JDK 1.5

FIGURE 21.1 The `java.lang.Comparable` interface was modified in JDK 1.5 with a generic type.

formal generic type
actual concrete type
generic instantiation

Here, `<T>` represents a *formal generic type*, which can be replaced later with an *actual concrete type*. Replacing a generic type is called a *generic instantiation*. By convention, a single capital letter such as `E` or `T` is used to denote a formal generic type.

To see the benefits of using generics, let us examine the code in Figure 21.2. The statement in Figure 21.2a declares that `c` is a reference variable whose type is `Comparable` and invokes the `compareTo` method to compare a `Date` object with a string. The code compiles fine, but it has a runtime error because a string cannot be compared with a date.

```
Comparable c = new Date();
System.out.println(c.compareTo("red"));
```

(a) Prior to JDK 1.5

```
Comparable<Date> c = new Date();
System.out.println(c.compareTo("red"));
```

(b) Since JDK 1.5

FIGURE 21.2 The new generic type detects possible errors at compile time.

The statement in Figure 21.2b declares that `c` is a reference variable whose type is `Comparable<Date>` and invokes the `compareTo` method to compare a `Date` object with a string. This code generates a compile error, because the argument passed to the `compareTo` method must be of the `Date` type. Since the errors can be detected at compile time rather than at runtime, the generic type makes the program more reliable.

reliable

`ArrayList` was introduced in Section 11.11, The `ArrayList` Class. This class has been a generic class since JDK 1.5. Figure 21.3 shows the class diagram for `ArrayList` before and since JDK 1.5, respectively.

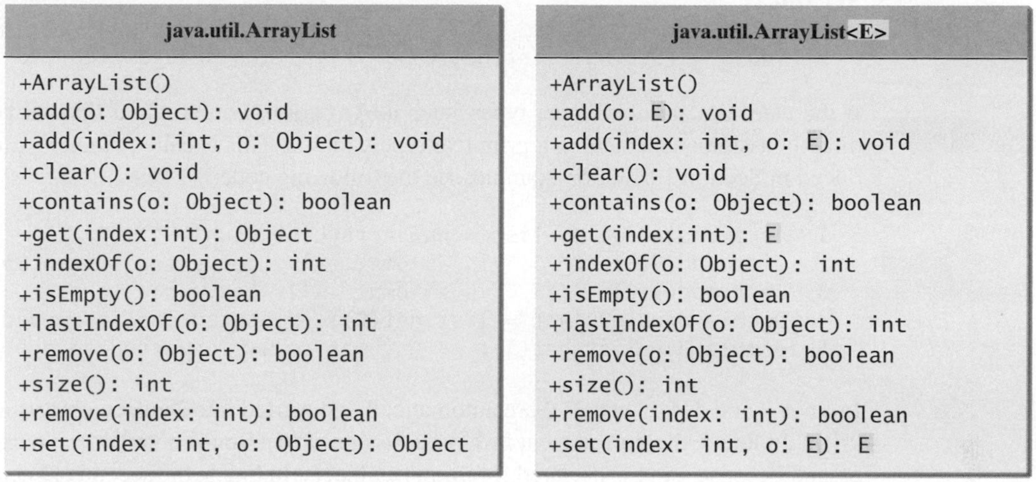

java.util.ArrayList
+ArrayList() +add(o: Object): void +add(index: int, o: Object): void +clear(): void +contains(o: Object): boolean +get(index:int): Object +indexOf(o: Object): int +isEmpty(): boolean +lastIndexOf(o: Object): int +remove(o: Object): boolean +size(): int +remove(index: int): boolean +set(index: int, o: Object): Object

(a) `ArrayList` before JDK 1.5

java.util.ArrayList<E>
+ArrayList() +add(o: E): void +add(index: int, o: E): void +clear(): void +contains(o: Object): boolean +get(index:int): E +indexOf(o: Object): int +isEmpty(): boolean +lastIndexOf(o: Object): int +remove(o: Object): boolean +size(): int +remove(index: int): boolean +set(index: int, o: E): E

(b) `ArrayList` since JDK 1.5

FIGURE 21.3 `ArrayList` is a generic class since JDK 1.5.

For example, the following statement creates a list for strings:

```
ArrayList<String> list = new ArrayList<String>();
```

You can now add *only strings* into the list. For instance,

only strings allowed

```
list.add("Red");
```

If you attempt to add a nonstring, a compile error will occur. For example, the following statement is now illegal, because `list` can contain only strings.

```
list.add(new Integer(1));
```

Generic types must be reference types. You cannot replace a generic type with a primitive type such as `int`, `double`, or `char`. For example, the following statement is wrong:

generic reference type

```
ArrayList<int> intList = new ArrayList<int>();
```

To create an `ArrayList` object for `int` values, you have to use:

```
ArrayList<Integer> intList = new ArrayList<Integer>();
```

You can add an `int` value to `intList`. For example,

```
intList.add(5);
```

Java automatically wraps `5` into `new Integer(5)`. This is called *autoboxing*, as introduced in Section 10.13, Automatic Conversion between Primitive Types and Wrapper Class Types.

autoboxing

no casting needed

Casting is not needed to retrieve a value from a list with a specified element type, because the compiler already knows the element type. For example, the following statements create a list that contains strings, add strings to the list, and retrieve strings from the list.

```
ArrayList<String> list = new ArrayList<String>();
list.add("Red");
list.add("White");
String s = list.get(0); // No casting is needed
```

Prior to JDK 1.5, without using generics, you would have had to cast the return value to **String** as:

```
String s = (String)(list.get(0)); // Casting needed prior to JDK 1.5
```

autounboxing

If the elements are of wrapper types, such as **Integer**, **Double**, and **Character**, you can directly assign an element to a primitive type variable. This is called *autounboxing*, as introduced in Section 10.13. For example, see the following code:

```
1 ArrayList<Double> list = new ArrayList<Double>();
2 list.add(5.5); // 5.5 is automatically converted to new Double(5.5)
3 list.add(3.0); // 3.0 is automatically converted to new Double(3.0)
4 Double doubleObject = list.get(0); // No casting is needed
5 double d = list.get(1); // Automatically converted to double
```

In lines 2 and 3, **5.5** and **3.0** are automatically converted into **Double** objects and added to **list**. In line 4, the first element in **list** is assigned to a **Double** variable. No casting is necessary, because **list** is declared for **Double** objects. In line 5, the second element in **list** is assigned to a **double** variable. The object in **list.get(1)** is automatically converted into a primitive type value.

MyProgrammingLab™

21.1 Are there any compile errors in (a) and (b)?

```
ArrayList dates = new ArrayList();
dates.add(new Date());
dates.add(new String());
```

(a) Prior to JDK 1.5

```
ArrayList<Date> dates =
  new ArrayList<Date>();
dates.add(new Date());
dates.add(new String());
```

(b) Since JDK 1.5

21.2 What is wrong in (a)? Is the code in (b) correct?

```
ArrayList dates = new ArrayList();
dates.add(new Date());
Date date = dates.get(0);
```

(a) Prior to JDK 1.5

```
ArrayList<Date> dates =
  new  ArrayList<Date>();
dates.add(new Date());
Date date = dates.get(0);
```

(b) Since JDK 1.5

21.3 What are the benefits of using generic types?

21.3 Defining Generic Classes and Interfaces

A generic type can be defined for a class or interface. A concrete type must be specified when using the class to create an object or using the class or interface to declare a reference variable.

Let us revise the stack class in Section 11.12, Case Study: A Custom Stack Class, to generalize the element type with a generic type. The new stack class, named `GenericStack`, is shown in Figure 21.4 and is implemented in Listing 21.1.

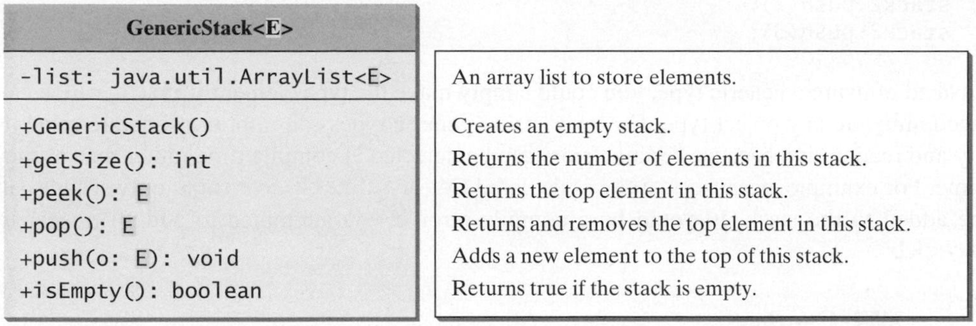

GenericStack<E>	
-list: java.util.ArrayList<E>	An array list to store elements.
+GenericStack()	Creates an empty stack.
+getSize(): int	Returns the number of elements in this stack.
+peek(): E	Returns the top element in this stack.
+pop(): E	Returns and removes the top element in this stack.
+push(o: E): void	Adds a new element to the top of this stack.
+isEmpty(): boolean	Returns true if the stack is empty.

FIGURE 21.4 The `GenericStack` class encapsulates the stack storage and provides the operations for manipulating the stack.

LISTING 21.1 GenericStack.java

generic type E declared
generic array list
getSize
peek
push
pop
isEmpty

```
public class GenericStack<E> {
  private java.util.ArrayList<E> list = new java.util.ArrayList<E>();

  public int getSize() {
    return list.size();
  }

  public E peek() {
    return list.get(getSize() - 1);
  }

  public void push(E o) {
    list.add(o);
  }

  public E pop() {
    E o = list.get(getSize() - 1);
    list.remove(getSize() - 1);
    return o;
  }

  public boolean isEmpty() {
    return list.isEmpty();
  }

  @Override
  public String toString() {
    return "stack: " + list.toString();
  }
}
```

The following example creates a stack to hold strings and adds three strings to the stack:

```
GenericStack<String> stack1 = new GenericStack<String>();
stack1.push("London");
stack1.push("Paris");
stack1.push("Berlin");
```

This example creates a stack to hold integers and adds three integers to the stack:

```
GenericStack<Integer> stack2 = new GenericStack<Integer>();
stack2.push(1); // autoboxing 1 to new Integer(1)
stack2.push(2);
stack2.push(3);
```

benefits of using generic types

Instead of using a generic type, you could simply make the type element `Object`, which can accommodate any object type. However, using generic types can improve software reliability and readability, because certain errors can be detected at compile time rather than at runtime. For example, because `stack1` is declared `GenericStack<String>`, only strings can be added to the stack. It would be a compile error if you attempted to add an integer to `stack1`.

generic class constructor

Caution

To create a stack of strings, you use `new GenericStack<String>()`. This could mislead you into thinking that the constructor of `GenericStack` should be defined as

```
public GenericStack<E>()
```

This is wrong. It should be defined as

```
public GenericStack()
```

multiple generic parameters

Note

Occasionally, a generic class may have more than one parameter. In this case, place the parameters together inside the brackets, separated by commas—for example, `<E1, E2, E3>`.

inheritance with generics

Note

You can define a class or an interface as a subtype of a generic class or interface. For example, the `java.lang.String` class is defined to implement the `Comparable` interface in the Java API as follows:

```
public class String implements Comparable<String>
```

MyProgrammingLab™

21.4 What is the generic definition for `java.lang.Comparable` in the Java API?

21.5 Since you create an instance of `ArrayList` of strings using `new ArrayList<String>()`, should the constructor in the `ArrayList` class be defined as

```
public ArrayList<E>()
```

21.6 Can a generic class have multiple generic parameters?

21.7 How do you declare a generic type in a class?

21.4 Generic Methods

A generic type can be defined for a static method.

generic method

You can define generic interfaces (e.g., the `Comparable` interface in Figure 21.1b) and classes (e.g., the `GenericStack` class in Listing 21.1). You can also use generic types to define generic methods. For example, Listing 21.2 defines a generic method `print` (lines 10–14) to print an array of objects. Line 6 passes an array of integer objects to invoke the generic `print` method. Line 7 invokes `print` with an array of strings.

LISTING 21.2 GenericMethodDemo.java

```
public class GenericMethodDemo {
  public static void main(String[] args ) {
    Integer[] integers = {1, 2, 3, 4, 5};
    String[] strings = {"London", "Paris", "New York", "Austin"};

    GenericMethodDemo.<Integer>print(integers);
    GenericMethodDemo.<String>print(strings);
  }

  public static <E> void print(E[] list) {
    for (int i = 0; i < list.length; i++)
      System.out.print(list[i] + " ");
    System.out.println();
  }
}
```

generic method

To declare a generic method, you place the generic type <E> immediately after the keyword `static` in the method header. For example,

declare a generic method

```
public static <E> void print(E[] list)
```

To invoke a generic method, prefix the method name with the actual type in angle brackets. For example,

invoke generic method

```
GenericMethodDemo.<Integer>print(integers);
GenericMethodDemo.<String>print(strings);
```

or simply invoke it as follows:

```
print(integers);
print(strings);
```

In the latter case, the actual type is not explicitly specified. The compiler automatically discovers the actual type.

A generic type can be specified as a subtype of another type. Such a generic type is called *bounded*. For example, Listing 21.3 revises the `equalArea` method in Listing 15.4, TestGeometricObject.java, to test whether two geometric objects have the same area. The bounded generic type `<E extends GeometricObject>` (line 7) specifies that `E` is a generic subtype of `GeometricObject`. You must invoke `equalArea` by passing two instances of `GeometricObject`.

bounded generic type

LISTING 21.3 BoundedTypeDemo.java

```
 1 public class BoundedTypeDemo {
 2   public static void main(String[] args ) {
 3     Rectangle rectangle = new Rectangle(2, 2);
 4     Circle circle = new Circle(2);
 5
 6     System.out.println("Same area? " +
 7       equalArea(rectangle, circle));
 8   }
 9
10   public static <E extends GeometricObject> boolean equalArea(
11       E object1, E object2) {
12     return object1.getArea() == object2.getArea();
13   }
14 }
```

`Rectangle` in Listing 15.3
`Circle` in Listing 15.2
bounded generic type

Note

An unbounded generic type <E> is the same as <E extends Object>.

generic class parameter vs. generic method parameter

Note

To define a generic type for a class, place it after the class name, such as `GenericStack<E>`. To define a generic type for a method, place the generic type before the method return type, such as `<E> void max(E o1, E o2)`.

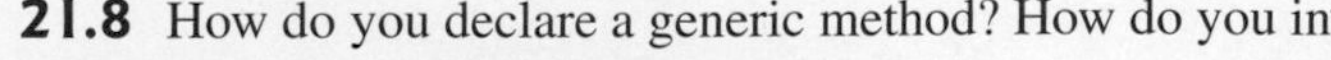

Check Point

21.8 How do you declare a generic method? How do you invoke a generic method?

21.9 What is a bounded generic type?

21.5 Case Study: Sorting an Array of Objects

You can develop a generic method for sorting an array of **Comparable** *objects.*

This section presents a generic method for sorting an array of `comparable` objects. The objects are instances of the `Comparable` interface, and they are compared using the `compareTo` method. To test the method, the program sorts an array of integers, an array of double numbers, an array of characters, and an array of strings. The program is shown in Listing 21.4.

LISTING 21.4 GenericSort.java

sort Integer objects
sort Double objects
sort Character objects
sort String objects

```
public class GenericSort {
  public static void main(String[] args) {
    // Create an Integer array
    Integer[] intArray = {new Integer(2), new Integer(4),
      new Integer(3)};

    // Create a Double array
    Double[] doubleArray = {new Double(3.4), new Double(1.3),
      new Double(-22.1)};

    // Create a Character array
    Character[] charArray = {new Character('a'),
      new Character('J'), new Character('r')};

    // Create a String array
    String[] stringArray = {"Tom", "Susan", "Kim"};

    // Sort the arrays
    sort(intArray);
    sort(doubleArray);
    sort(charArray);
    sort(stringArray);

    // Display the sorted arrays
    System.out.print("Sorted Integer objects: ");
    printList(intArray);
    System.out.print("Sorted Double objects: ");
    printList(doubleArray);
    System.out.print("Sorted Character objects: ");
    printList(charArray);
    System.out.print("Sorted String objects: ");
    printList(stringArray);
  }

```

```
35    /** Sort an array of comparable objects */
36    public static <E extends Comparable<E>> void sort(E[] list) {
37      E currentMin;
38      int currentMinIndex;
39
40      for (int i = 0; i < list.length - 1; i++) {
41        // Find the minimum in the list[i...list.length-1]
42        currentMin = list[i];
43        currentMinIndex = i;
44
45        for (int j = i + 1; j < list.length; j++) {
46          if (currentMin.compareTo(list[j]) > 0) {
47            currentMin = list[j];
48            currentMinIndex = j;
49          }
50        }
51
52        // Swap list[i] with list[currentMinIndex] if necessary;
53        if (currentMinIndex != i) {
54          list[currentMinIndex] = list[i];
55          list[i] = currentMin;
56        }
57      }
58    }
59
60    /** Print an array of objects */
61    public static void printList(Object[] list) {
62      for (int i = 0; i < list.length; i++)
63        System.out.print(list[i] + " ");
64      System.out.println();
65    }
66  }
```

generic sort method

compareTo

```
Sorted Integer objects: 2 3 4
Sorted Double objects: -22.1 1.3 3.4
Sorted Character objects: J a r
Sorted String objects: Kim Susan Tom
```

The algorithm for the **sort** method is the same as in Listing 6.8, SelectionSort.java The **sort** method in that program sorts an array of **double** values. The **sort** method in this example can sort an array of any object type, provided that the objects are also instances of the **Comparable** interface. The generic type is defined as **<E extends Comparable<E>>** (line 36). This has two meanings. First, it specifies that **E** is a subtype of **Comparable**. Second, it specifies that the elements to be compared are of the **E** type as well.

The **sort** method uses the **compareTo** method to determine the order of the objects in the array (line 46). **Integer**, **Double**, **Character**, and **String** implement **Comparable**, so the objects of these classes can be compared using the **compareTo** method. The program creates arrays of **Integer** objects, **Double** objects, **Character** objects, and **String** objects (lines 4–16) and invoke the **sort** method to sort these arrays (lines 19–22).

21.10 Given **int[] list = {1, 2, -1}**, can you invoke **sort(list)** using the **sort** method in Listing 21.4?

21.11 Given **int[] list = {new Integer(1), new Integer(2), new Integer(-1)}**, can you invoke **sort(list)** using the **sort** method in Listing 21.4?

21.6 Raw Types and Backward Compatibility

A generic class or interface used without specifying a concrete type, called a raw type, *enables backward compatibility with earlier versions of Java.*

You can use a generic class without specifying a concrete type like this:

```
GenericStack stack = new GenericStack(); // raw type
```

This is roughly equivalent to

```
GenericStack<Object> stack = new GenericStack<Object>();
```

raw type

backward compatibility

A generic class such as **GenericStack** and **ArrayList** used without a type parameter is called a *raw type*. Using raw types allows for backward compatibility with earlier versions of Java. For example, a generic type has been used in **java.lang.Comparable** since JDK 1.5, but a lot of code still uses the raw type **Comparable**, as shown in Listing 21.5:

LISTING 21.5 Max.java

raw type

```
1 public class Max {
2   /** Return the maximum of two objects */
3   public static Comparable max(Comparable o1, Comparable o2) {
4     if (o1.compareTo(o2) > 0)
5       return o1;
6     else
7       return o2;
8   }
9 }
```

Comparable o1 and **Comparable o2** are raw type declarations. Be careful: *raw types are unsafe*. For example, you might invoke the **max** method using

```
Max.max("Welcome", 23); // 23 is autoboxed into new Integer(23)
```

Xlint:unchecked

This would cause a runtime error, because you cannot compare a string with an integer object. The Java compiler displays a warning on line 3 when compiled with the option ***-Xlint:unchecked***, as shown in Figure 21.5.

```
Command Prompt
C:\book>javac -Xlint:unchecked Max.java
Max.java:6: warning: [unchecked] unchecked call to compareTo(T) as a member of the raw type java.lang.Comparable
    if (o1.compareTo(o2) > 0)
                    ^
1 warning

C:\book>
```

FIGURE 21.5 The unchecked warnings are displayed using the compiler option **-Xlint:unchecked**.

A better way to write the **max** method is to use a generic type, as shown in Listing 21.6.

LISTING 21.6 MaxUsingGenericType.java

bounded type

```
public class MaxUsingGenericType {
  /** Return the maximum of two objects */
  public static <E extends Comparable<E>> E max(E o1, E o2) {
    if (o1.compareTo(o2) > 0)
      return o1;
    else
```

```
        return o2;
    }
}
```

If you invoke the max method using

```
// 23 is autoboxed into new Integer(23)
MaxUsingGenericType.max("Welcome", 23);
```

a compile error will be displayed, because the two arguments of the max method in MaxUsingGenericType must have the same type (e.g., two strings or two integer objects). Furthermore, the type E must be a subtype of Comparable<E>.

As another example, in the following code you can declare a raw type stack in line 1, assign new GenericStack<String> to it in line 2, and push a string and an integer object to the stack in lines 3 and 4.

```
1  GenericStack stack;
2  stack = new GenericStack<String>();
3  stack.push("Welcome to Java");
4  stack.push(new Integer(2));
```

However, line 4 is unsafe because the stack is intended to store strings, but an Integer object is added into the stack. Line 3 should be okay, but the compiler will show warnings for both line 3 and line 4, because it cannot follow the semantic meaning of the program. All the compiler knows is that stack is a raw type, and performing certain operations is unsafe. Therefore, warnings are displayed to alert potential problems.

Tip

Since raw types are unsafe, this book will not use them from here on.

21.12 What is a raw type? Why is a raw type unsafe? Why is the raw type allowed in Java?

21.13 What is the syntax to declare an ArrayList reference variable using the raw type and assign a raw type ArrayList object to it?

21.7 Wildcard Generic Types

You can use unbounded wildcards, bounded wildcards, or lower-bound wildcards to specify a range for a generic type.

What are wildcard generic types and why are they needed? Listing 21.7 gives an example to demonstrate the needs. The example defines a generic max method for finding the maximum in a stack of numbers (lines 12–22). The main method creates a stack of integer objects, adds three integers to the stack, and invokes the max method to find the maximum number in the stack.

LISTING 21.7 WildCardNeedDemo.java

```
1  public class WildCardNeedDemo {
2    public static void main(String[] args ) {
3      GenericStack<Integer> intStack = new GenericStack<Integer>();
4      intStack.push(1); // 1 is autoboxed into new Integer(1)
5      intStack.push(2);
6      intStack.push(-2);
7
8      System.out.print("The max number is " + max(intStack));
9    }
10
```

GenericStack<Integer> type

GenericStack<Number> type

```
11   /** Find the maximum in a stack of numbers */
12   public static double max(GenericStack<Number> stack) {
13     double max = stack.pop().doubleValue(); // Initialize max
14
15     while (!stack.isEmpty()) {
16       double value = stack.pop().doubleValue();
17       if (value > max)
18         max = value;
19     }
20
21     return max;
22   }
23 }
```

The program in Listing 21.7 has a compile error in line 8 because **intStack** is not an instance of **GenericStack<Number>**. Thus, you cannot invoke **max(intStack)**.

The fact is that **Integer** is a subtype of **Number**, but **GenericStack<Integer>** is not a subtype of **GenericStack<Number>**. To circumvent this problem, use wildcard generic types. A wildcard generic type has three forms: **?** and **? extends T**, as well as **? super T**, where **T** is a generic type.

unbounded wildcard
bounded wildcard
lower-bound wildcard

The first form, **?**, called an *unbounded wildcard*, is the same as **? extends Object**. The second form, **? extends T**, called a *bounded wildcard*, represents **T** or an unknown subtype of **T**. The third form, **? super T**, called a *lower-bound wildcard*, denotes **T** or an unknown supertype of **T**.

You can fix the error by replacing line 12 in Listing 21.7 as follows:

```
public static double max(GenericStack<? extends Number> stack) {
```

<? extends Number> is a wildcard type that represents **Number** or a subtype of **Number**, so it is legal to invoke **max(new GenericStack<Integer>())** or **max(new GenericStack<Double>())**.

Listing 21.8 shows an example of using the **?** wildcard in the **print** method that prints objects in a stack and empties the stack. **<?>** is a wildcard that represents any object type. It is equivalent to **<? extends Object>**. What happens if you replace **GenericStack<?>** with **GenericStack<Object>**? It would be wrong to invokc **print(intStack)**, because **intStack** is not an instance of **GenericStack<Object>**. Please note that **GenericStack<Integer>** is not a subtype of **GenericStack<Object>**, even though **Integer** is a subtype of **Object**.

LISTING 21.8 AnyWildCardDemo.java

GenericStack<Integer> type

wildcard type

```
public class AnyWildCardDemo {
  public static void main(String[] args ) {
    GenericStack<Integer> intStack = new GenericStack<Integer>();
    intStack.push(1); // 1 is autoboxed into new Integer(1)
    intStack.push(2);
    intStack.push(-2);

    print(intStack);
  }

  /** Prints objects and empties the stack */
  public static void print(GenericStack<?> stack) {
    while (!stack.isEmpty()) {
      System.out.print(stack.pop() + " ");
    }
  }
}
```

When is the wildcard `<? super T>` needed? Consider the example in Listing 21.9. The example creates a stack of strings in **stack1** (line 3) and a stack of objects in **stack2** (line 4), and invokes **add(stack1, stack2)** (line 8) to add the strings in **stack1** into **stack2**. `GenericStack<? super T>` is used to declare **stack2** in line 13. If `<? super T>` is replaced by `<T>`, a compile error will occur on **add(stack1, stack2)** in line 8, because **stack1**'s type is `GenericStack<String>` and **stack2**'s type is `GenericStack<Object>`. `<? super T>` represents type **T** or a supertype of **T**. **Object** is a supertype of **String**.

why <? Super T>

LISTING 21.9 SuperWildCardDemo.java

```
 1 public class SuperWildCardDemo {
 2   public static void main(String[] args) {
 3     GenericStack<String> stack1 = new GenericStack<String>();
 4     GenericStack<Object> stack2 = new GenericStack<Object>();
 5     stack2.push("Java");
 6     stack2.push(2);
 7     stack1.push("Sun");
 8     add(stack1, stack2);
 9     AnyWildCardDemo.print(stack2);
10   }
11
12   public static <T> void add(GenericStack<T> stack1,
13       GenericStack<? super T> stack2) {
14     while (!stack1.isEmpty())
15       stack2.push(stack1.pop());
16   }
17 }
```

GenericStack<String> type

<? Super T> type

This program will also work if the method header in lines 12–13 is modified as follows:

```
public static <T> void add(GenericStack<? extends T> stack1,
    GenericStack<T> stack2)
```

The inheritance relationship involving generic types and wildcard types is summarized in Figure 21.6. In this figure, **A** and **B** represent classes or interfaces, and **E** is a generic type parameter.

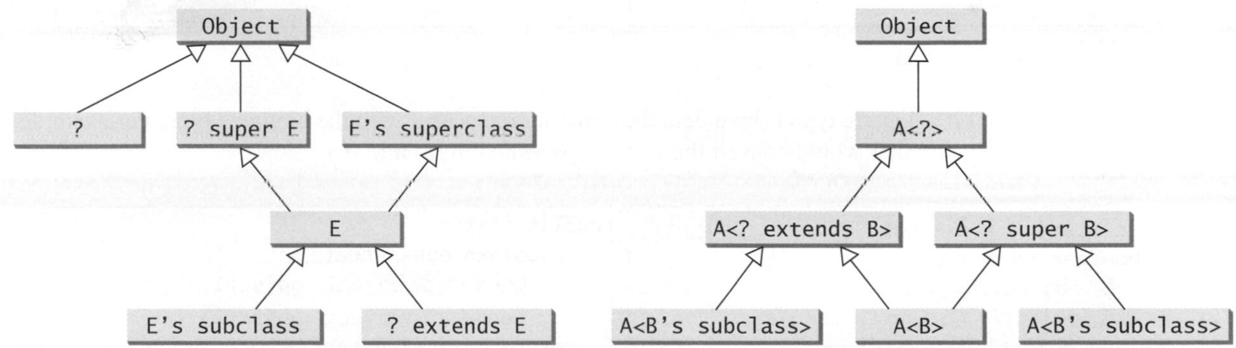

FIGURE 21.6 The relationship between generic types and wildcard types.

21.14 Is **GenericStack** the same as `GenericStack<Object>`?

21.15 What are an unbounded wildcard, a bounded wildcard, and a lower-bound wildcard?

21.16 What happens if lines 12–13 in Listing 21.9 are changed to

```
public static <T> void add(GenericStack<T> stack1,
    GenericStack<T> stack2)
```

MyProgrammingLab™

21.17 What happens if lines 12–13 in Listing 21.9 are changed to

```
public static <T> void add(GenericStack<? extends T> stack1,
    GenericStack<T> stack2)
```

21.8 Erasure and Restrictions on Generics

The information on generics is used by the compiler but is not available at runtime. This is called type erasure.

type erasure

Generics are implemented using an approach called *type erasure*: The compiler uses the generic type information to compile the code, but erases it afterward. Thus, the generic information is not available at runtime. This approach enables the generic code to be backward compatible with the legacy code that uses raw types.

erase generics

The generics are present at compile time. Once the compiler confirms that a generic type is used safely, it converts the generic type to a raw type. For example, the compiler checks whether the following code in (a) uses generics correctly and then translates it into the equivalent code in (b) for runtime use. The code in (b) uses the raw type.

```
ArrayList<String> list = new ArrayList<String>();
list.add("Oklahoma");
String state = list.get(0);
```

(a)

```
ArrayList list = new ArrayList();
list.add("Oklahoma");
String state = (String)(list.get(0));
```

(b)

replace generic type

When generic classes, interfaces, and methods are compiled, the compiler replaces the generic type with the `Object` type. For example, the compiler would convert the following method in (a) into (b).

```
public static <E> void print(E[] list) {
  for (int i = 0; i < list.length; i++)
    System.out.print(list[i] + " ");
  System.out.println();
}
```

(a)

```
public static void print(Object[] list) {
  for (int i = 0; i < list.length; i++)
    System.out.print(list[i] + " ");
  System.out.println();
}
```

(b)

replace bounded type

If a generic type is bounded, the compiler replaces it with the bounded type. For example, the compiler would convert the following method in (a) into (b).

```
public static <E extends GeometricObject>
    boolean equalArea(
      E object1,
      E object2) {
  return object1.getArea() ==
    object2.getArea();
}
```

(a)

```
public static
    boolean equalArea(
      GeometricObject object1,
      GeometricObject object2) {
  return object1.getArea() ==
    object2.getArea();
}
```

(b)

important fact

It is important to note that a generic class is shared by all its instances regardless of its actual concrete type. Suppose `list1` and `list2` are created as follows:

```
ArrayList<String> list1 = new ArrayList<String>();
ArrayList<Integer> list2 = new ArrayList<Integer>();
```

Although ArrayList<String> and ArrayList<Integer> are two types at compile time, only one ArrayList class is loaded into the JVM at runtime. list1 and list2 are both instances of ArrayList, so the following statements display true:

```
System.out.println(list1 instanceof ArrayList);
System.out.println(list2 instanceof ArrayList);
```

However, the expression list1 instanceof ArrayList<String> is wrong. Since ArrayList<String> is not stored as a separate class in the JVM, using it at runtime makes no sense.

Because generic types are erased at runtime, there are certain restrictions on how generic types can be used. Here are some of the restrictions:

Restriction 1: Cannot Use *new E()*

You cannot create an instance using a generic type parameter. For example, the following statement is wrong:

```
E object = new E();
```

no new E()

The reason is that new E() is executed at runtime, but the generic type E is not available at runtime.

Restriction 2: Cannot Use *new E[]*

You cannot create an array using a generic type parameter. For example, the following statement is wrong:

```
E[] elements = new E[capacity];
```

no new E[capacity]

You can circumvent this limitation by creating an array of the Object type and then casting it to E[], as follows:

```
E[] elements = (E[])new Object[capacity];
```

unavoidable compile warning

However, casting to (E[]) causes an unchecked compile warning. The warning occurs because the compiler is not certain that casting will succeed at runtime. For example, if E is String and new Object[] is an array of Integer objects, (String[])(new Object[]) will cause a ClassCastException. This type of compile warning is a limitation of Java generics and is unavoidable.

Generic array creation using a generic class is not allowed, either. For example, the following code is wrong:

```
ArrayList<String>[] list = new ArrayList<String>[10];
```

You can use the following code to circumvent this restriction:

```
ArrayList<String>[] list = (ArrayList<String>[])new
  ArrayList[10];
```

However, you will still get a compile warning.

Restriction 3: A Generic Type Parameter of a Class Is Not Allowed in a Static Context

Since all instances of a generic class have the same runtime class, the static variables and methods of a generic class are shared by all its instances. Therefore, it is illegal to refer to a generic type parameter for a class in a static method, field, or initializer. For example, the following code is illegal:

```
public class Test<E> {
  public static void m(E o1) { // Illegal
  }

  public static E o1; // Illegal

  static {
    E o2; // Illegal
  }
}
```

Restriction 4: Exception Classes Cannot Be Generic

A generic class may not extend `java.lang.Throwable`, so the following class declaration would be illegal:

```
public class MyException<T> extends Exception {
}
```

Why? If it were allowed, you would have a `catch` clause for `MyException<T>` as follows:

```
try {
  ...
}
catch (MyException<T> ex) {
  ...
}
```

The JVM has to check the exception thrown from the `try` clause to see if it matches the type specified in a `catch` clause. This is impossible, because the type information is not present at runtime.

MyProgrammingLab™

21.18 What is erasure? Why are Java generics implemented using erasure?

21.19 If your program uses `ArrayList<String>` and `ArrayList<Date>`, does the JVM load both of them?

21.20 Can you create an instance using `new E()` for a generic type `E`? Why?

21.21 Can a method that uses a generic class parameter be static? Why?

21.22 Can you define a custom generic exception class? Why?

21.9 Case Study: Generic Matrix Class

This section presents a case study on designing classes for matrix operations using generic types.

The addition and multiplication operations for all matrices are similar except that their element types differ. Therefore, you can design a superclass that describes the common operations shared by matrices of all types regardless of their element types, and you can create subclasses tailored to specific types of matrices. This case study gives implementations for two types: `int` and `Rational`. For the `int` type, the wrapper class `Integer` should be used to wrap an `int` value into an object, so that the object is passed in the methods for operations.

The class diagram is shown in Figure 21.7. The methods `addMatrix` and `multiplyMatrix` add and multiply two matrices of a generic type `E[][]`. The static method `printResult` displays the matrices, the operator, and their result. The methods `add`, `multiply`, and `zero` are abstract, because their implementations depend on the specific type of the array elements. For example, the `zero()` method returns `0` for the `Integer` type and

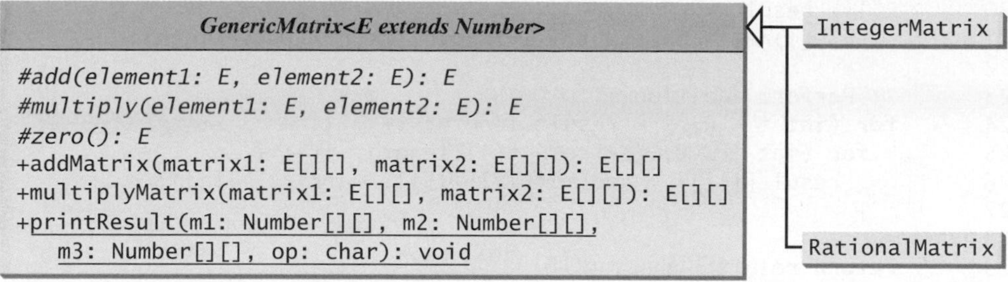

FIGURE 21.7 The `GenericMatrix` class is an abstract superclass for `IntegerMatrix` and `RationalMatrix`.

`0/1` for the `Rational` type. These methods will be implemented in the subclasses in which the matrix element type is specified.

`IntegerMatrix` and `RationalMatrix` are concrete subclasses of `GenericMatrix`. These two classes implement the `add`, `multiply`, and `zero` methods defined in the `GenericMatrix` class.

Listing 21.10 implements the `GenericMatrix` class. `<E extends Number>` in line 1 specifies that the generic type is a subtype of `Number`. Three abstract methods—`add`, `multiply`, and `zero`—are defined in lines 3, 6, and 9. These methods are abstract because we cannot implement them without knowing the exact type of the elements. The `addMaxtrix` (lines 12–30) and `multiplyMatrix` (lines 33–57) methods implement the methods for adding and multiplying two matrices. All these methods must be nonstatic, because they use generic type `E` for the class. The `printResult` method (lines 60–84) is static because it is not tied to specific instances.

The matrix element type is a generic subtype of `Number`. This enables you to use an object of any subclass of `Number` as long as you can implement the abstract `add`, `multiply`, and `zero` methods in subclasses.

The `addMatrix` and `multiplyMatrix` methods (lines 12–57) are concrete methods. They are ready to use as long as the `add`, `multiply`, and `zero` methods are implemented in the subclasses.

The `addMatrix` and `multiplyMatrix` methods check the bounds of the matrices before performing operations. If the two matrices have incompatible bounds, the program throws an exception (lines 16, 36).

LISTING 21.10 GenericMatrix.java

```
 1 public abstract class GenericMatrix<E extends Number> {         // bounded generic type
 2   /** Abstract method for adding two elements of the matrices */
 3   protected abstract E add(E o1, E o2);                         // abstract method
 4
 5   /** Abstract method for multiplying two elements of the matrices */
 6   protected abstract E multiply(E o1, E o2);                    // abstract method
 7
 8   /** Abstract method for defining zero for the matrix element */
 9   protected abstract E zero();                                  // abstract method
10
11   /** Add two matrices */
12   public E[][] addMatrix(E[][] matrix1, E[][] matrix2) {        // add two matrices
13     // Check bounds of the two matrices
14     if ((matrix1.length != matrix2.length) ||
15         (matrix1[0].length != matrix2[0].length)) {
16       throw new RuntimeException(
17         "The matrices do not have the same size");
18     }
19
```

```
    E[][] result =
      (E[][])new Number[matrix1.length][matrix1[0].length];

    // Perform addition
    for (int i = 0; i < result.length; i++)
      for (int j = 0; j < result[i].length; j++) {
        result[i][j] = add(matrix1[i][j], matrix2[i][j]);
      }

    return result;
  }

  /** Multiply two matrices */
  public E[][] multiplyMatrix(E[][] matrix1, E[][] matrix2) {
    // Check bounds
    if (matrix1[0].length != matrix2.length) {
      throw new RuntimeException(
        "The matrices do not have compatible size");
    }

    // Create result matrix
    E[][] result =
      (E[][])new Number[matrix1.length][matrix2[0].length];

    // Perform multiplication of two matrices
    for (int i = 0; i < result.length; i++) {
      for (int j = 0; j < result[0].length; j++) {
        result[i][j] = zero();

        for (int k = 0; k < matrix1[0].length; k++) {
          result[i][j] = add(result[i][j],
            multiply(matrix1[i][k], matrix2[k][j]));
        }
      }
    }

    return result;
  }

  /** Print matrices, the operator, and their operation result */
  public static void printResult(
      Number[][] m1, Number[][] m2, Number[][] m3, char op) {
    for (int i = 0; i < m1.length; i++) {
      for (int j = 0; j < m1[0].length; j++)
        System.out.print(" " + m1[i][j]);

      if (i == m1.length / 2)
        System.out.print("  " + op + "  ");
      else
        System.out.print("     ");

      for (int j = 0; j < m2.length; j++)
        System.out.print(" " + m2[i][j]);

      if (i == m1.length / 2)
        System.out.print(" = ");
      else
        System.out.print("     ");

      for (int j = 0; j < m3.length; j++)
```

multiply two matrices

display result

```
          System.out.print(m3[i][j] + " ");

        System.out.println();
      }
    }
  }
```

Listing 21.11 implements the **IntegerMatrix** class. The class extends **GenericMatrix<Integer>** in line 1. After the generic instantiation, the **add** method in **GenericMatrix<Integer>** is now **Integer add(Integer o1, Integer o2)**. The **add**, **multiply**, and **zero** methods are implemented for **Integer** objects. These methods are still protected, because they are invoked only by the **addMatrix** and **multiplyMatrix** methods.

LISTING 21.11 IntegerMatrix.java

```
 1  public class IntegerMatrix extends GenericMatrix<Integer> {
 2    @Override /** Add two integers */
 3    protected Integer add(Integer o1, Integer o2) {
 4      return o1 + o2;
 5    }
 6
 7    @Override /** Multiply two integers */
 8    protected Integer multiply(Integer o1, Integer o2) {
 9      return o1 * o2;
10    }
11
12    @Override /** Specify zero for an integer */
13    protected Integer zero() {
14      return 0;
15    }
16  }
```

extends generic type
implement add
implement multiply
implement zero

Listing 21.12 implements the **RationalMatrix** class. The **Rational** class was introduced in Listing 15.13 Rational.java. **Rational** is a subtype of **Number**. The **RationalMatrix** class extends **GenericMatrix<Rational>** in line 1. After the generic instantiation, the **add** method in **GenericMatrix<Rational>** is now **Rational add(Rational r1, Rational r2)**. The **add**, **multiply**, and **zero** methods are implemented for **Rational** objects. These methods are still protected, because they are invoked only by the **addMatrix** and **multiplyMatrix** methods.

LISTING 21.12 RationalMatrix.java

```
 1  public class RationalMatrix extends GenericMatrix<Rational> {
 2    @Override /** Add two rational numbers */
 3    protected Rational add(Rational r1, Rational r2) {
 4      return r1.add(r2);
 5    }
 6
 7    @Override /** Multiply two rational numbers */
 8    protected Rational multiply(Rational r1, Rational r2) {
 9      return r1.multiply(r2);
10    }
11
12    @Override /** Specify zero for a Rational number */
13    protected Rational zero() {
14      return new Rational(0, 1);
15    }
16  }
```

extends generic type
implement add
implement multiply
implement zero

Listing 21.13 gives a program that creates two `Integer` matrices (lines 4–5) and an `IntegerMatrix` object (line 8), and adds and multiplies two matrices in lines 12 and 16.

Listing 21.13 TestIntegerMatrix.java

create matrices

create `IntegerMatrix`

add two matrices

multiply two matrices

```
 1 public class TestIntegerMatrix {
 2   public static void main(String[] args) {
 3     // Create Integer arrays m1, m2
 4     Integer[][] m1 = new Integer[][]{{1, 2, 3}, {4, 5, 6}, {1, 1, 1}};
 5     Integer[][] m2 = new Integer[][]{{1, 1, 1}, {2, 2, 2}, {0, 0, 0}};
 6
 7     // Create an instance of IntegerMatrix
 8     IntegerMatrix integerMatrix = new IntegerMatrix();
 9
10     System.out.println("\nm1 + m2 is ");
11     GenericMatrix.printResult(
12       m1, m2, integerMatrix.addMatrix(m1, m2), '+');
13
14     System.out.println("\nm1 * m2 is ");
15     GenericMatrix.printResult(
16       m1, m2, integerMatrix.multiplyMatrix(m1, m2), '*');
17   }
18 }
```

```
m1 + m2 is
 1 2 3     1 1 1     2 3 4
 4 5 6  +  2 2 2  =  6 7 8
 1 1 1     0 0 0     1 1 1

m1 * m2 is
 1 2 3     1 1 1     5  5  5
 4 5 6  *  2 2 2  =  14 14 14
 1 1 1     0 0 0     3  3  3
```

Listing 21.14 gives a program that creates two `Rational` matrices (lines 4–10) and a `RationalMatrix` object (line 13) and adds and multiplies two matrices in lines 17 and 21.

Listing 21.14 TestRationalMatrix.java

create matrices

create `RationalMatrix`

add two matrices

```
 1 public class TestRationalMatrix {
 2   public static void main(String[] args) {
 3     // Create two Rational arrays m1 and m2
 4     Rational[][] m1 = new Rational[3][3];
 5     Rational[][] m2 = new Rational[3][3];
 6     for (int i = 0; i < m1.length; i++)
 7       for (int j = 0; j < m1[0].length; j++) {
 8         m1[i][j] = new Rational(i + 1, j + 5);
 9         m2[i][j] = new Rational(i + 1, j + 6);
10       }
11
12     // Create an instance of RationalMatrix
13     RationalMatrix rationalMatrix = new RationalMatrix();
14
15     System.out.println("\nm1 + m2 is ");
16     GenericMatrix.printResult(
17       m1, m2, rationalMatrix.addMatrix(m1, m2), '+');
18
19     System.out.println("\nm1 * m2 is ");
```

```
      GenericMatrix.printResult(
        m1, m2, rationalMatrix.multiplyMatrix(m1, m2), '*');
    }
  }
```

multiply two matrices

```
m1 + m2 is
 1/5 1/6 1/7      1/6 1/7 1/8      11/30 13/42 15/56
 2/5 1/3 2/7  +   1/3 2/7 1/4  =   11/15 13/21 15/28
 3/5 1/2 3/7      1/2 3/7 3/8      11/10 13/14 45/56

m1 * m2 is
 1/5 1/6 1/7      1/6 1/7 1/8      101/630 101/735 101/840
 2/5 1/3 2/7  *   1/3 2/7 1/4  =   101/315 202/735 101/420
 3/5 1/2 3/7      1/2 3/7 3/8      101/210 101/245 101/280
```

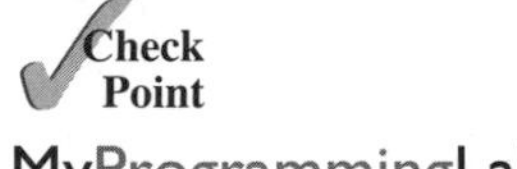

21.23 Why are the `add`, `multiple`, and `zero` methods defined abstract in the `GenericMatrix` class?

21.24 How are the `add`, `multiple`, and `zero` methods implemented in the `IntegerMatrix` class?

21.25 How are the `add`, `multiple`, and `zero` methods implemented in the `RationalMatrix` class?

21.26 What would be wrong if the `printResult` method defined as follows?

```
public static void printResult(
  E[][] m1, E[][] m2, E[][] m3, char op)
```

Key Terms

actual concrete type 770
bounded generic type 775
bounded wildcard (`<? extends E>`) 780
formal generic type 770
generic instantiation 770
lower-bound wildcard (`<? super E>`) 780
raw type 778
unbounded wildcard (`<?>`) 780

Chapter Summary

1. *Generics* give you the capability to parameterize types. You can define a class or a method with generic types, which the compiler replaces with concrete types.

2. The key benefit of generics is to enable errors to be detected at compile time rather than at runtime.

3. A generic class or method permits you to specify allowable types of objects that the class or method can work with. If you attempt to use a class or method with an incompatible object, the compiler will detect the error.

4. A generic type defined in a class, interface, or a static method is called a *formal generic type*, which can be replaced later with an *actual concrete type*. Replacing a generic type is called a *generic instantiation*.

5. A generic class such as `ArrayList` used without a type parameter is called a *raw type*. Use of raw types is allowed for backward compatibility with the earlier versions of Java.

6. A wildcard generic type has three forms: `?` and `? extends T`, and `? super T`, where `T` is a generic type. The first form, `?`, called an *unbounded wildcard*, is the same as `? extends Object`. The second form, `? extends T`, called a *bounded wildcard*, represents `T` or an unknown subtype of `T`. The third form, `? super T`, called a *lower-bound wildcard*, denotes `T` or an unknown supertype of `T`.

7. Generics are implemented using an approach called *type erasure*. The compiler uses the generic type information to compile the code but erases it afterward, so the generic information is not available at runtime. This approach enables the generic code to be backward compatible with the legacy code that uses raw types.

8. You cannot create an instance using a generic type parameter.

9. You cannot create an array using a generic type parameter.

10. You cannot use a generic type parameter of a class in a static context.

11. Generic type parameters cannot be used in exception classes.

Test Questions

Do the test questions for this chapter online at www.cs.armstrong.edu/liang/intro9e/test.html.

MyProgrammingLab™

Programming Exercises

21.1 (*Revising Listing 21.1*) Revise the `GenericStack` class in Listing 21.1 to implement it using an array rather than an `ArrayList`. You should check the array size before adding a new element to the stack. If the array is full, create a new array that doubles the current array size and copy the elements from the current array to the new array.

21.2 (*Implement* `GenericStack` *using inheritance*) In Listing 21.1, `GenericStack` is implemented using composition. Create a new stack class that extends `ArrayList`.
Draw the UML diagram for the classes and then implement `GenericStack`. Write a test program that prompts the user to enter five strings and displays them in reverse order.

21.3 (*Distinct elements in* `ArrayList`) Write the following method that returns a new `ArrayList`. The new list contains the non-duplicate elements from the original list.

```
public static <E> ArrayList<E> removeDuplicates(ArrayList<E> list)
```

21.4 (*Generic insertion sort*) Implement the following method using insertion sort.

```
public static <E extends Comparable<E>>
  void insertionSort(E[] list)
```

21.5 (*Maximum element in an array*) Implement the following method that returns the maximum element in an array.

```
public static <E extends Comparable<E>> E max(E[] list)
```

21.6 (*Maximum element in a two-dimensional array*) Write a generic method that returns the maximum element in a two-dimensional array.

```
public static <E extends Comparable<E>> E max(E[][] list)
```

21.7 (*Generic binary search*) Implement the following method using binary search.

```
public static <E extends Comparable<E>>
  int binarySearch(E[] list, E key)
```

21.8 (*Shuffle* `ArrayList`) Write the following method that shuffles an `ArrayList`:

```
public static <E> void shuffle(ArrayList<E> list)
```

21.9 (*Sort* `ArrayList`) Write the following method that sorts an `ArrayList`:

```
public static <E extends Comparable<E>>
  void sort(ArrayList<E> list)
```

21.10 (*Largest element in* `ArrayList`) Write the following method that returns the largest element in an `ArrayList`:

```
public static <E extends Comparable<E>> E max(ArrayList<E> list)
```

CHAPTER 22

Lists, Stacks, Queues, and Priority Queues

Objectives

- To explore the relationship between interfaces and classes in the Java Collections Framework hierarchy (§22.2).
- To use the common methods defined in the `Collection` interface for operating collections (§22.2).
- To use the `Iterator` interface to traverse the elements in a collection (§22.3).
- To use a for-each loop to traverse the elements in a collection (§22.3).
- To explore how and when to use `ArrayList` or `LinkedList` to store a list of elements (§22.4).
- To compare elements using the `Comparable` interface and the `Comparator` interface (§22.5).
- To use the static utility methods in the `Collections` class for sorting, searching, shuffling lists, and finding the largest and smallest element in collections (§22.6).
- To develop a multiple bouncing balls application using `ArrayList` (§22.7).
- To distinguish between `Vector` and `ArrayList` and to use the `Stack` class for creating stacks (§22.8).
- To explore the relationships among `Collection`, `Queue`, `LinkedList`, and `PriorityQueue` and to create priority queues using the `PriorityQueue` class (§22.9).
- To use stacks to write a program to evaluate expressions (§22.10).

22.1 Introduction

Choosing the best data structures and algorithms for a particular task is one of the keys to developing high-performance software.

data structure

A *data structure* is a collection of data organized in some fashion. The structure not only stores data but also supports operations for accessing and manipulating the data.

container

In object-oriented thinking, a data structure, also known as a *container* or *container object*, is an object that stores other objects, referred to as data or elements. To define a data structure is essentially to define a class. The class for a data structure should use data fields to store data and provide methods to support such operations as search, insertion, and deletion. To create a data structure is therefore to create an instance from the class. You can then apply the methods on the instance to manipulate the data structure, such as inserting an element into or deleting an element from the data structure.

Java Collections Framework

Section 11.11 introduced the `ArrayList` class, which is a data structure to store elements in a list. Java provides several more data structures that can be used to organize and manipulate data efficiently. These are commonly known as *Java Collections Framework*. We will introduce the applications of lists, vectors, stacks, queues, and priority queues in this chapter and sets and maps in the next chapter. The implementation of these data structures will be discussed in Chapters 26–29.

22.2 Collections

The `Collection` interface defines the common operations for lists, vectors, stacks, queues, priority queues, and sets.

The Java Collections Framework supports two types of containers:

collection

map

- One for storing a collection of elements is simply called a *collection*.
- The other, for storing key/value pairs, is called a *map*.

Maps are efficient data structures for quickly searching an element using a key. We will introduce maps in the next chapter. Now we turn our attention to collections.

There are different kinds of collections.

`Set`

`List`

`Queue`

- `Set`s store a group of nonduplicate elements.
- `List`s store an ordered collection of elements.
- `Queue`s store objects that are processed in first-in, first-out fashion.

The common features of these collections are defined in the interfaces, and implementations are provided in concrete classes, as shown in Figure 22.1.

Note

All the interfaces and classes defined in the Java Collections Framework are grouped in the `java.util` package.

Design Guide

convenience abstract class

The design of the Java Collections Framework is an excellent example of using interfaces, abstract classes, and concrete classes. The interfaces define the framework. The abstract classes provide partial implementation. The concrete classes implement the interfaces with concrete data structures. Providing an abstract class that partially implements an interface makes it convenient for the user to write the code. The user can simply define a concrete class that extends the abstract class rather implements all the methods in the interface. The abstract classes such as `AbstractCollection` are provided for convenience. For this reason, they are called *convenience abstract classes*.

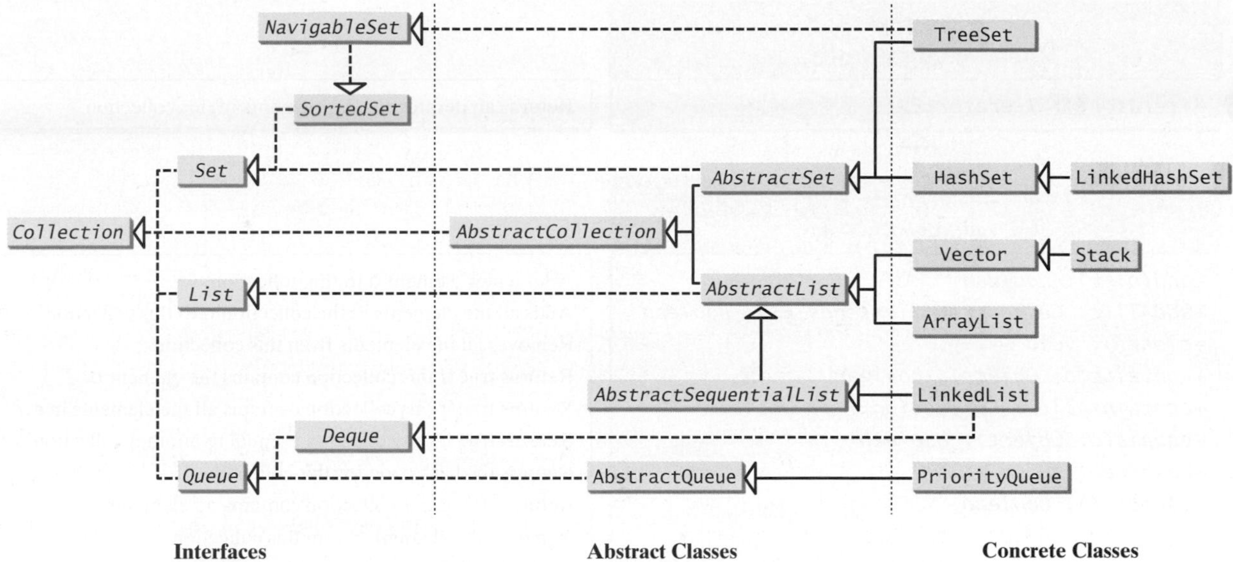

FIGURE 22.1 A collection is a container that stores objects.

The `Collection` interface is the root interface for manipulating a collection of objects. Its public methods are listed in Figure 22.2. The `AbstractCollection` class provides partial implementation for the `Collection` interface. It implements all the methods in `Collection` except the `size` and `iterator` methods. These are implemented in appropriate concrete subclasses.

The `Collection` interface provides the basic operations for adding and removing elements in a collection. The `add` method adds an element to the collection. The `addAll` method adds all the elements in the specified collection to this collection. The `remove` method removes an element from the collection. The `removeAll` method removes the elements from this collection that are present in the specified collection. The `retainAll` method retains the elements in this collection that are also present in the specified collection. All these methods return `boolean`. The return value is `true` if the collection is changed as a result of the method execution. The `clear()` method simply removes all the elements from the collection. basic operations

Note

The methods `addAll`, `removeAll`, and `retainAll` are similar to the set union, difference, and intersection operations. set operations

The `Collection` interface provides various query operations. The `size` method returns the number of elements in the collection. The `contains` method checks whether the collection contains the specified element. The `containsAll` method checks whether the collection contains all the elements in the specified collection. The `isEmpty` method returns `true` if the collection is empty. query operations

The `Collection` interface provides the `toArray()` method, which returns an array representation for the collection.

Design Guide

Some of the methods in the `Collection` interface cannot be implemented in the concrete subclass. In this case, the method would throw `java.lang.UnsupportedOperationException`, a subclass of `RuntimeException`. unsupported operations

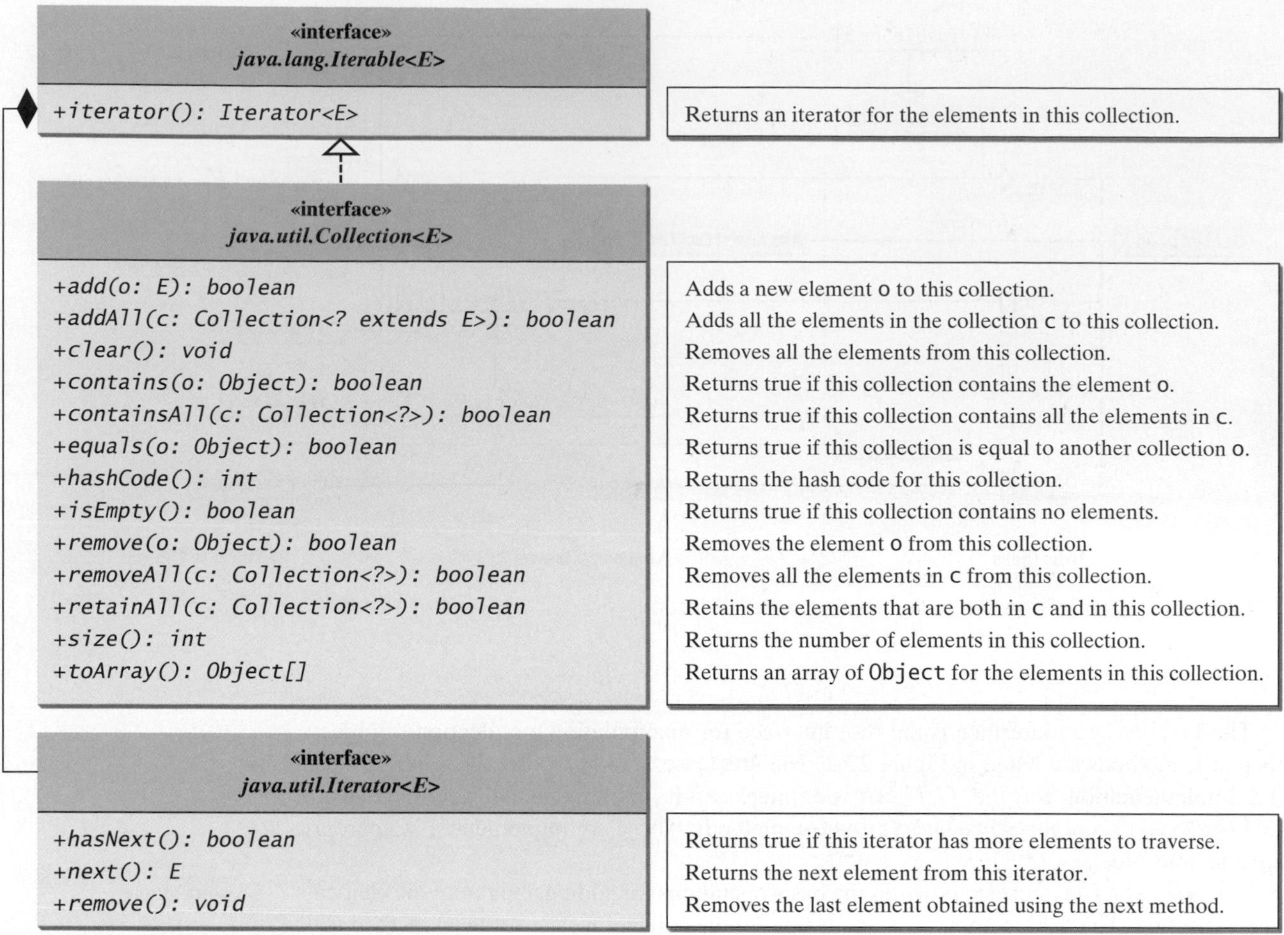

FIGURE 22.2 The `Collection` interface contains the methods for manipulating the elements in a collection, and you can obtain an iterator object for traversing elements in the collection.

This is a good design that you can use in your project. If a method has no meaning in the subclass, you can implement it as follows:

```
public void someMethod() {
  throw new UnsupportedOperationException
    ("Method not supported");
}
```

Listing 22.1 gives an example to use the methods defined in the `Collection` interface.

LISTING 22.1 TestCollection.java

create an array list
add elements

```
import java.util.*;

public class TestCollection {
  public static void main(String[] args) {
    ArrayList<String> collection1 = new ArrayList<String>();
    collection1.add("New York");
    collection1.add("Atlanta");
    collection1.add("Dallas");
    collection1.add("Madison");

```

```
11         System.out.println("A list of cities in collection1:");
12         System.out.println(collection1);
13
14         System.out.println("\nIs Dallas in collection1? "
15           + collection1.contains("Dallas"));
16
17         collection1.remove("Dallas");
18         System.out.println("\n" + collection1.size() +
19           " cities are in collection1 now");
20
21         Collection<String> collection2 = new ArrayList<String>();
22         collection2.add("Seattle");
23         collection2.add("Portland");
24         collection2.add("Los Angeles");
25         collection2.add("Atlanta");
26
27         System.out.println("\nA list of cities in collection2:");
28         System.out.println(collection2);
29
30         ArrayList<String> c1 = (ArrayList<String>)(collection1.clone());
31         c1.addAll(collection2);
32         System.out.println("\nCities in collection1 or collection2: ");
33         System.out.println(c1);
34
35         c1 = (ArrayList<String>)(collection1.clone());
36         c1.retainAll(collection2);
37         System.out.print("\nCities in collection1 and collection2: ");
38         System.out.println(c1);
39
40         c1 = (ArrayList<String>)(collection1.clone());
41         c1.removeAll(collection2);
42         System.out.print("\nCities in collection1, but not in 2: ");
43         System.out.println(c1);
44     }
45   }
```

contains?

size?

clone

addAll

retainAll

removeAll

```
A list of cities in collection1:
[New York, Atlanta, Dallas, Madison]
Is Dallas in collection1? true
3 cities are in collection1 now
A list of cities in collection2:
[Seattle, Portland, Los Angeles, Atlanta]
Cities in collection1 or collection2:
[New York, Atlanta, Madison, Seattle, Portland, Los Angeles, Atlanta]
Cities in collection1 and collection2: [Atlanta]
Cities in collection1, but not in 2: [New York, Madison]
```

The program creates a concrete collection object using `ArrayList` (line 5), and invokes the `Collection` interface's `contains` method (line 15), `remove` method (line 17), `size` method (line 18), `addAll` method (line 31), `retainAll` method (line 36), and `removeAll` method (line 41).

For this example, we use `ArrayList`. You can use any concrete class of `Collection` such as `HashSet`, `LinkedList`, `Vector`, and `Stack` to replace `ArrayList` to test these methods defined in the `Collection` interface.

Every concrete class except `java.util.PriorityQueue` in the Java Collections Framework implements the `clone()` method. The program creates a copy of an array list (lines 30,

35, 40). The purpose of this is to keep the original array list intact and use its copy to perform **addAll**, **retainAll**, and **removeAll** operations.

Note

Cloneable
Serializable

All the concrete classes in the Java Collections Framework implement the **java.lang.Cloneable** and **java.io.Serializable** interfaces except that **java.util.PriorityQueue** does not implement the **Cloneable** interface. Thus, all instances except priority queues can be cloned and all instances can be serialized.

MyProgrammingLab™

22.1 What is a data structure?

22.2 Describe the Java Collections Framework. List the interfaces, convenience abstract classes, and concrete classes under the **Collection** interface.

22.3 Can a collection object be cloned and serialized?

22.4 What method do you use to add all the elements from one collection to another collection?

22.5 When should a method throw an **UnsupportedOperationException**?

22.3 Iterators

*Each collection has an **Iterator** object that can be used to traverse all the elements in the collection.*

Iterator is a classic design pattern for walking through a data structure without having to expose the details of how data is stored in the data structure.

The **Collection** interface extends the **Iterable** interface. The **Iterable** interface defines the **iterator** method, which returns an iterator. The **Iterator** interface provides a uniform way for traversing elements in various types of collections. The **iterator** method in the **Collection** interface returns an instance of the **Iterator** interface, as shown in Figure 22.2, which provides sequential access to the elements in the collection using the **next()** method. You can also use the **hasNext()** method to check whether there are more elements in the iterator, and the **remove()** method to remove the last element returned by the iterator.

Listing 22.2 gives an example that uses the iterator to traverse all the elements in an array list.

LISTING 22.2 TestIterator.java

create an array list
add elements
iterator
hasNext()
next()

```
import java.util.*;

public class TestIterator {
  public static void main(String[] args) {
    Collection<String> collection = new ArrayList<String>();
    collection.add("New York");
    collection.add("Atlanta");
    collection.add("Dallas");
    collection.add("Madison");

    Iterator<String> iterator = collection.iterator();
    while (iterator.hasNext()) {
      System.out.print(iterator.next().toUpperCase() + " ");
    }
    System.out.println();
  }
}
```

```
NEW YORK ATLANTA DALLAS MADISON
```

The program creates a concrete collection object using **`ArrayList`** (line 5) and adds four strings into the list (lines 6–9). The program then obtains an iterator for the collection (line 11) and uses the iterator to traverse all the strings in the list and displays the strings in uppercase (lines 12–14).

Tip

You can simplify the code in lines 11–14 using a for-each loop without using an iterator, as follows:

for-each loop

```
for (String element: collection)
  System.out.print(element.toUpperCase() + " ");
```

This loop is read as "for each element in the collection, do the following." The for-each loop can be used for arrays (see Section 6.2.7) as well as any instance of **`Iterable`**.

MyProgrammingLab™

22.6 How do you obtain an iterator from a collection object?

22.7 What method do you use to obtain an element in the collection from an iterator?

22.8 Can you use a for-each loop to traverse the elements in any instance of **`Collection`**?

22.9 When using a for-each loop to traverse all elements in a collection, do you need to use the **`next()`** or **`hasNext()`** methods in an iterator?

22.4 Lists

*The **`List`** interface extends the **`Collection`** interface and defines a collection for storing elements in a sequential order. To create a list, use one of its two concrete classes: **`ArrayList`** or **`LinkedList`**.*

We used **`ArrayList`** to test the methods in the **`Collection`** interface in the preceding sections. Now we will examine **`ArrayList`** in more depth. We will also introduce another useful list, **`LinkedList`**, in this section.

22.4.1 The Common Methods in the `List` Interface

`ArrayList` and **`LinkedList`** are defined under the **`List`** interface. The **`List`** interface extends **`Collection`** to define an ordered collection with duplicates allowed. The **`List`** interface adds

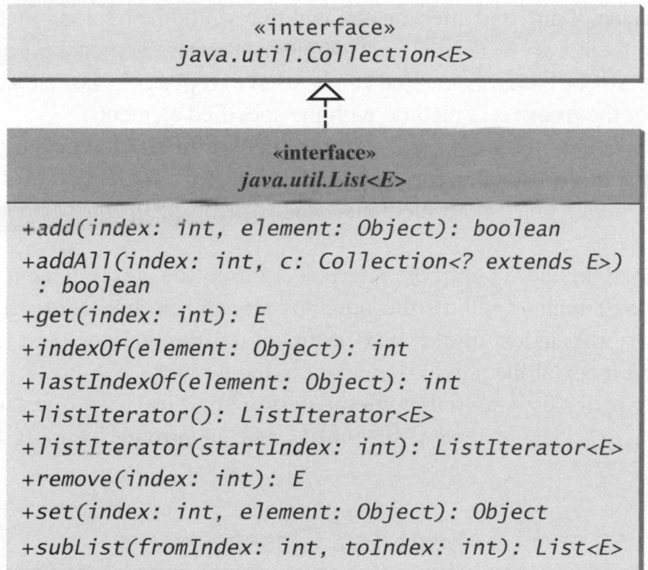

Adds a new element at the specified index.
Adds all the elements in `c` to this list at the specified index.
Returns the element in this list at the specified index.
Returns the index of the first matching element.
Returns the index of the last matching element.
Returns the list iterator for the elements in this list.
Returns the iterator for the elements from `startIndex`.
Removes the element at the specified index.
Sets the element at the specified index.
Returns a sublist from `fromIndex` to `toIndex-1`.

FIGURE 22.3 The **`List`** interface stores elements in sequence and permits duplicates.

position-oriented operations, as well as a new list iterator that enables the user to traverse the list bidirectionally. The methods introduced in the `List` interface are shown in Figure 22.3.

The `add(index, element)` method is used to insert an element at a specified index, and the `addAll(index, collection)` method to insert a collection of elements at a specified index. The `remove(index)` method is used to remove an element at the specified index from the list. A new element can be set at the specified index using the `set(index, element)` method.

The `indexOf(element)` method is used to obtain the index of the specified element's first occurrence in the list, and the `lastIndexOf(element)` method to obtain the index of its last occurrence. A sublist can be obtained by using the `subList(fromIndex, toIndex)` method.

The `listIterator()` or `listIterator(startIndex)` method returns an instance of `ListIterator`. The `ListIterator` interface extends the `Iterator` interface to add bidirectional traversal of the list. The methods in `ListIterator` are listed in Figure 22.4.

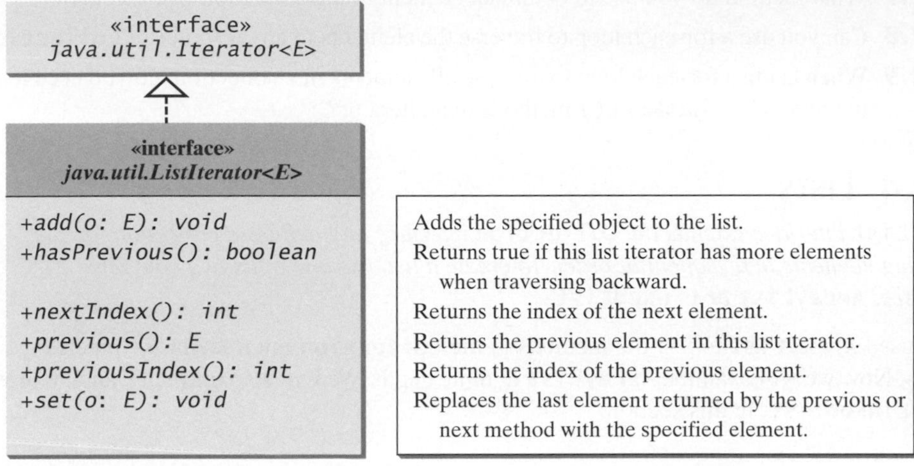

FIGURE 22.4 `ListIterator` enables traversal of a list bidirectionally.

The `add(element)` method inserts the specified element into the list. The element is inserted immediately before the next element that would be returned by the `next()` method defined in the `Iterator` interface, if any, and after the element that would be returned by the `previous()` method, if any. If the list doesn't contain any elements, the new element becomes the sole element in the list. The `set(element)` method can be used to replace the last element returned by the `next` method or the `previous` method with the specified element.

The `hasNext()` method defined in the `Iterator` interface is used to check whether the iterator has more elements when traversed in the forward direction, and the `hasPrevious()` method to check whether the iterator has more elements when traversed in the backward direction.

The `next()` method defined in the `Iterator` interface returns the next element in the iterator, and the `previous()` method returns the previous element in the iterator. The `nextIndex()` method returns the index of the next element in the iterator, and the `previousIndex()` returns the index of the previous element in the iterator.

The `AbstractList` class provides a partial implementation for the `List` interface. The `AbstractSequentialList` class extends `AbstractList` to provide support for linked lists.

22.4.2 The `ArrayList` and `LinkedList` Classes

`ArrayList` vs. `LinkedList`

The `ArrayList` class and the `LinkedList` class are two concrete implementations of the `List` interface. `ArrayList` stores elements in an array. The array is dynamically created. If the capacity of the array is exceeded, a larger new array is created and all the elements from the current array are copied to the new array. `LinkedList` stores elements in a *linked list*. Which of the two classes you use depends on your specific needs. If you need to support random access through an index without inserting or removing elements at the beginning of the list, `ArrayList` offers the most efficient collection. If, however, your application requires the insertion or deletion of elements at the beginning of the list, you should choose `LinkedList`. A list can grow or shrink dynamically. Once it is created, an array is fixed. If your application does not require the insertion or deletion of elements, an array is the most efficient data structure.

linked list

`ArrayList` is a resizable-array implementation of the `List` interface. It also provides methods for manipulating the size of the array used internally to store the list, as shown in Figure 22.5. Each `ArrayList` instance has a capacity, which is the size of the array used to store the elements in the list. It is always at least as large as the list size. As elements are added to an `ArrayList`, its capacity grows automatically. An `ArrayList` does not automatically shrink. You can use the `trimToSize()` method to reduce the array capacity to the size of the list. An `ArrayList` can be constructed using its no-arg constructor, `ArrayList(Collection)`, or `ArrayList(initialCapacity)`.

trimToSize()

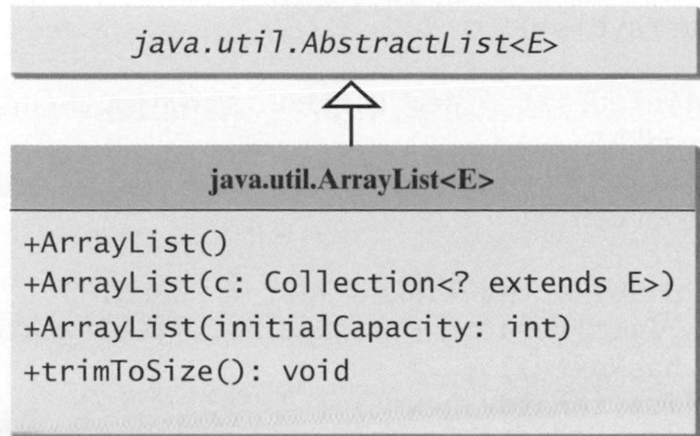

FIGURE 22.5 `ArrayList` implements `List` using an array.

`LinkedList` is a linked list implementation of the `List` interface. In addition to implementing the `List` interface, this class provides the methods for retrieving, inserting, and removing elements from both ends of the list, as shown in Figure 22.6. A `LinkedList` can be constructed using its no-arg constructor or `LinkedList(Collection)`.

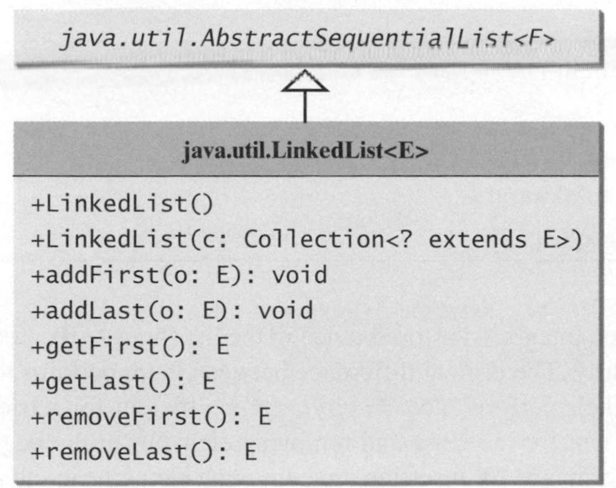

FIGURE 22.6 `LinkedList` provides methods for adding and inserting elements at both ends of the list.

Listing 22.3 gives a program that creates an array list filled with numbers and inserts new elements into specified locations in the list. The example also creates a linked list from the array list and inserts and removes elements from the list. Finally, the example traverses the list forward and backward.

LISTING 22.3 TestArrayAndLinkedList.java

array list

linked list

list iterator

list iterator

```
 1 import java.util.*;
 2
 3 public class TestArrayAndLinkedList {
 4   public static void main(String[] args) {
 5     List<Integer> arrayList = new ArrayList<Integer>();
 6     arrayList.add(1); // 1 is autoboxed to new Integer(1)
 7     arrayList.add(2);
 8     arrayList.add(3);
 9     arrayList.add(1);
10     arrayList.add(4);
11     arrayList.add(0, 10);
12     arrayList.add(3, 30);
13
14     System.out.println("A list of integers in the array list:");
15     System.out.println(arrayList);
16
17     LinkedList<Object> linkedList = new LinkedList<Object>(arrayList);
18     linkedList.add(1, "red");
19     linkedList.removeLast();
20     linkedList.addFirst("green");
21
22     System.out.println("Display the linked list forward:");
23     ListIterator<Object> listIterator = linkedList.listIterator();
24     while (listIterator.hasNext()) {
25       System.out.print(listIterator.next() + " ");
26     }
27     System.out.println();
28
29     System.out.println("Display the linked list backward:");
30     listIterator = linkedList.listIterator(linkedList.size());
31     while (listIterator.hasPrevious()) {
32       System.out.print(listIterator.previous() + " ");
33     }
34   }
35 }
```

```
A list of integers in the array list:
[10, 1, 2, 30, 3, 1, 4]
Display the linked list forward:
green 10 red 1 2 30 3 1
Display the linked list backward:
1 3 30 2 1 red 10 green
```

A list can hold identical elements. Integer `1` is stored twice in the list (lines 6, 9). `ArrayList` and `LinkedList` operate similarly. The critical difference between them pertains to internal implementation, which affects their performance. `ArrayList` is efficient for retrieving elements and `LinkedList` is efficient for inserting and removing elements at the beginning of the list. Both have the same performance for inserting and removing elements in the middle or at the end of the list.

The `get(i)` method is available for a linked list, but it is a time-consuming operation. Do not use it to traverse all the elements in a list as shown in (a). Instead you should use an iterator as shown in (b). Note that a for-each loop uses an iterator implicitly. You will know the reason when you learn how to implement a linked list in Chapter 26.

```
for (int i = 0; i < linkedList.size(); i++) {
  process linkedList.get(i);
}
```

(a) Very inefficient

```
for (listElementType s: linkedList) {
  process s;
}
```

(b) Efficient

Tip

Java provides the static `asList` method for creating a list from a variable-length argument list of a generic type. Thus you can use the following code to create a list of strings and a list of integers:

`Arrays.asList(T... a)` method

```
List<String> list1 = Arrays.asList("red", "green", "blue");
List<Integer> list2 = Arrays.asList(10, 20, 30, 40, 50);
```

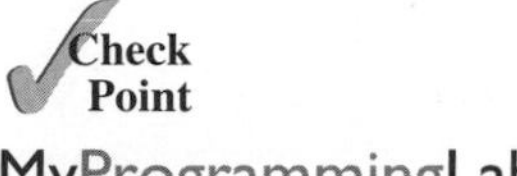

22.10 How do you add and remove elements from a list? How do you traverse a list in both directions?

22.11 Suppose that `list1` is a list that contains the strings `red`, `yellow`, and `green`, and that `list2` is another list that contains the strings `red`, `yellow`, and `blue`. Answer the following questions:

a. What are `list1` and `list2` after executing `list1.addAll(list2)`?

b. What are `list1` and `list2` after executing `list1.add(list2)`?

c. What are `list1` and `list2` after executing `list1.removeAll(list2)`?

d. What are `list1` and `list2` after executing `list1.remove(list2)`?

e. What are `list1` and `list2` after executing `list1.retainAll(list2)`?

f. What is `list1` after executing `list1.clear()`?

22.12 What are the differences between `ArrayList` and `LinkedList`? Which list should you use to insert and delete elements at the beginning of a list?

22.13 Are all the methods in `ArrayList` also in `LinkedList`? What methods are in `LinkedList` but not in `ArrayList`?

22.14 How do you create a list from an array of objects?

22.5 The **Comparator** Interface

`Comparator` can be used to compare the objects of a class that doesn't implement `Comparable`.

You have learned how to compare elements using the `Comparable` interface (introduced in Section 15.6). Several classes in the Java API, such as `String`, `Date`, `Calendar`, `BigInteger`, `BigDecimal`, and all the numeric wrapper classes for the primitive types, implement the `Comparable` interface. The `Comparable` interface defines the `compareTo` method, which is used to compare two elements of the same class that implement the `Comparable` interface.

What if the elements' classes do not implement the `Comparable` interface or the elements have different types? Can these elements be compared? You can define a *comparator* to

comparator

compare the elements of different classes. To do so, define a class that implements the **java.util.Comparator<T>** interface. The **Comparator<T>** interface has two methods, **compare** and **equals**.

- **public int** compare(T element1, T element2)
  Returns a negative value if **element1** is less than **element2**, a positive value if **element1** is greater than **element2**, and zero if they are equal.
- **public boolean** equals(Object element)
  Returns **true** if the specified object is also a comparator and imposes the same ordering as this comparator.

The **equals** method is also defined in the **Object** class. Therefore, you will not get a compile error even if you don't implement the **equals** method in your custom comparator class. However, in some cases implementing this method may improve performance by allowing programs to determine quickly whether two distinct comparators impose the same order.

The **GeometricObject** class was introduced in Section 15.2, Abstract Classes. The **GeometricObject** class does not implement the **Comparable** interface. To compare the objects of the **GeometricObject** class, you can define a comparator class, as shown in Listing 22.4.

LISTING 22.4 GeometricObjectComparator.java

implements Comparator
implements compare

```
1  import java.util.Comparator;
2
3  public class GeometricObjectComparator
4      implements Comparator<GeometricObject>, java.io.Serializable {
5    public int compare(GeometricObject o1, GeometricObject o2) {
6      double area1 = o1.getArea();
7      double area2 = o2.getArea();
8
9      if (area1 < area2)
10       return -1;
11     else if (area1 == area2)
12       return 0;
13     else
14       return 1;
15   }
16 }
```

Line 4 implements **Comparator<GeometricObject>**. Line 5 overrides the **compare** method to compare two geometric objects. The class also implements **Serializable**. It is generally a good idea for comparators to implement **Serializable**, as they may be used as ordering methods in serializable data structures. In order for the data structure to serialize successfully, the comparator (if provided) must implement **Serializable**.

Listing 22.5 gives a method that returns a larger object between two geometric objects. The objects are compared using the **GeometricObjectComparator**.

LISTING 22.5 TestComparator.java

```
import java.util.Comparator;

public class TestComparator {
  public static void main(String[] args) {
    GeometricObject g1 = new Rectangle(5, 5);
    GeometricObject g2 = new Circle(5);

    GeometricObject g =
```

```
 9         max(g1, g2, new GeometricObjectComparator());
10
11       System.out.println("The area of the larger object is " +
12         g.getArea());
13     }
14
15     public static GeometricObject max(GeometricObject g1,
16         GeometricObject g2, Comparator<GeometricObject> c) {
17       if (c.compare(g1, g2) > 0)
18         return g1;
19       else
20         return g2;
21     }
22   }
```

invoke max

the max method

invoke compare

```
The area of the larger object is 78.53981633974483
```

The program creates a **Rectangle** and a **Circle** object in lines 5–6 (the **Rectangle** and **Circle** classes were defined in Section 15.2, Abstract Classes). They are all subclasses of **GeometricObject**. The program invokes the **max** method to obtain the geometric object with the larger area (lines 8–9).

The **GeometricObjectComparator** is created and passed to the **max** method (line 9) and this comparator is used in the **max** method to compare the geometric objects in line 17.

Note

Comparable is used to compare the objects of the class that implement **Comparable**. **Comparator** can be used to compare the objects of a class that doesn't implement **Comparable**.

Comparable vs. Comparator

Comparing elements using the **Comparable** interface is referred to as comparing using *natural order*, and comparing elements using the **Comparator** interface is referred to as comparing using *comparator*.

natural order
using Comparator

22.15 What are the differences between the **Comparable** interface and the **Comparator** interface? In which package is **Comparable**, and in which package is **Comparator**?

22.16 The **Comparator** interface contains the **equals** method. Why is the method not implemented in the **GeometricObjectComparator** class in this section?

22.6 Static Methods for Lists and Collections

The **Collections** *class contains static methods to perform common operations in a collection and a list.*

Often you need to sort a list. The Java Collections Framework provides static methods in the **Collections** class that can be used to sort a list. The **Collections** class also contains the **binarySearch**, **reverse**, **shuffle**, **copy**, and **fill** methods for lists, and **max**, **min**, **disjoint**, and **frequency** methods for collections, as shown in Figure 22.7.

You can sort the comparable elements in a list in its natural order with the **compareTo** method in the **Comparable** interface. You may also specify a comparator to sort elements. For example, the following code sorts strings in a list.

sort list

```
List<String> list = Arrays.asList("red", "green", "blue");
Collections.sort(list);
System.out.println(list);
```

	java.util.Collections	
List	+sort(list: List): void	Sorts the specified list.
	+sort(list: List, c: Comparator): void	Sorts the specified list with the comparator.
	+binarySearch(list: List, key: Object): int	Searches the key in the sorted list using binary search.
	+binarySearch(list: List, key: Object, c: Comparator): int	Searches the key in the sorted list using binary search with the comparator.
	+reverse(list: List): void	Reverses the specified list.
	+reverseOrder(): Comparator	Returns a comparator with the reverse ordering.
	+shuffle(list: List): void	Shuffles the specified list randomly.
	+shuffle(list: List, rmd: Random): void	Shuffles the specified list with a random object.
	+copy(des: List, src: List): void	Copies from the source list to the destination list.
	+nCopies(n: int, o: Object): List	Returns a list consisting of *n* copies of the object.
	+fill(list: List, o: Object): void	Fills the list with the object.
Collection	+max(c: Collection): Object	Returns the `max` object in the collection.
	+max(c: Collection, c: Comparator): Object	Returns the `max` object using the comparator.
	+min(c: Collection): Object	Returns the `min` object in the collection.
	+min(c: Collection, c: Comparator): Object	Returns the `min` object using the comparator.
	+disjoint(c1: Collection, c2: Collection): boolean	Returns true if `c1` and `c2` have no elements in common.
	+frequency(c: Collection, o: Object): int	Returns the number of occurrences of the specified element in the collection.

FIGURE 22.7 The `Collections` class contains static methods for manipulating lists and collections.

The output is `[blue, green, red]`.

ascending order
descending order

The preceding code sorts a list in ascending order. To sort it in descending order, you can simply use the `Collections.reverseOrder()` method to return a `Comparator` object that orders the elements in reverse order. For example, the following code sorts a list of strings in descending order.

```
List<String> list = Arrays.asList("yellow", "red",
  "green", "blue");
Collections.sort(list, Collections.reverseOrder());
System.out.println(list);
```

The output is `[yellow, red, green, blue]`.

`binarySearch`

You can use the `binarySearch` method to search for a key in a list. To use this method, the list must be sorted in increasing order. If the key is not in the list, the method returns −(*insertion point* + *1*). Recall that the insertion point is where the item would fall in the list if it were present. For example, the following code searches the keys in a list of integers and a list of strings.

```
List<Integer> list1 =
  Arrays.asList(2, 4, 7, 10, 11, 45, 50, 59, 60, 66);
System.out.println("(1) Index: " + Collections.binarySearch(list1, 7));
System.out.println("(2) Index: " + Collections.binarySearch(list1, 9));

List<String> list2 = Arrays.asList("blue", "green", "red");
System.out.println("(3) Index: " +
  Collections.binarySearch(list2, "red"));
System.out.println("(4) Index: " +
  Collections.binarySearch(list2, "cyan"));
```

The output of the preceding code is:

```
(1) Index: 2
(2) Index: -4
(3) Index: 2
(4) Index: -2
```

You can use the `reverse` method to reverse the elements in a list. For example, the following code displays `[blue, green, red, yellow]`.

reverse

```
List<String> list = Arrays.asList("yellow", "red", "green", "blue");
Collections.reverse(list);
System.out.println(list);
```

You can use the `shuffle(List)` method to randomly reorder the elements in a list. For example, the following code shuffles the elements in `list`.

shuffle

```
List<String> list = Arrays.asList("yellow", "red", "green", "blue");
Collections.shuffle(list);
System.out.println(list);
```

You can also use the `shuffle(List, Random)` method to randomly reorder the elements in a list with a specified `Random` object. Using a specified `Random` object is useful to generate a list with identical sequences of elements for the same original list. For example, the following code shuffles the elements in `list`.

```
List<String> list1 = Arrays.asList("yellow", "red", "green", "blue");
List<String> list2 = Arrays.asList("yellow", "red", "green", "blue");
Collections.shuffle(list1, new Random(20));
Collections.shuffle(list2, new Random(20));
System.out.println(list1);
System.out.println(list2);
```

You will see that `list1` and `list2` have the same sequence of elements before and after the shuffling.

You can use the `copy(det, src)` method to copy all the elements from a source list to a destination list on the same index. The destination list must be as long as the source list. If it is longer, the remaining elements in the source list are not affected. For example, the following code copies `list2` to `list1`.

copy

```
List<String> list1 = Arrays.asList("yellow", "red", "green", "blue");
List<String> list2 = Arrays.asList("white", "black");
Collections.copy(list1, list2);
System.out.println(list1);
```

The output for `list1` is `[white, black, green, blue]`. The `copy` method performs a shallow copy: only the references of the elements from the source list are copied.

You can use the `nCopies(int n, Object o)` method to create an immutable list that consists of `n` copies of the specified object. For example, the following code creates a list with five `Calendar` objects.

nCopies

```
List<GregorianCalendar> list1 = Collections.nCopies
  (5, new GregorianCalendar(2005, 0, 1));
```

The list created from the `nCopies` method is immutable, so you cannot add, remove, or update elements in the list. All the elements have the same references.

fill

You can use the fill(List list, Object o) method to replace all the elements in the list with the specified element. For example, the following code displays [black, black, black].

```
List<String> list = Arrays.asList("red", "green", "blue");
Collections.fill(list, "black");
System.out.println(list);
```

max and min methods

You can use the max and min methods for finding the maximum and minimum elements in a collection. The elements must be comparable using the Comparable interface or the Comparator interface. For example, the following code displays the largest and smallest strings in a collection.

```
Collection<String> collection = Arrays.asList("red", "green", "blue");
System.out.println(Collections.max(collection));
System.out.println(Collections.min(collection));
```

disjoint method

The disjoint(collection1, collection2) method returns true if the two collections have no elements in common. For example, in the following code, disjoint(collection1, collection2) returns false, but disjoint(collection1, collection3) returns true.

```
Collection<String> collection1 = Arrays.asList("red", "cyan");
Collection<String> collection2 = Arrays.asList("red", "blue");
Collection<String> collection3 = Arrays.asList("pink", "tan");
System.out.println(Collections.disjoint(collection1, collection2));
System.out.println(Collections.disjoint(collection1, collection3));
```

frequency method

The frequency(collection, element) method finds the number of occurrences of the element in the collection. For example, frequency(collection, "red") returns 2 in the following code.

```
Collection<String> collection = Arrays.asList("red", "cyan", "red");
System.out.println(Collections.frequency(collection, "red"));
```

22.17 Are all the methods in the Collections class static?

22.18 Which of the following static methods in the Collections class are for lists, and which are for collections?

```
sort, binarySearch, reverse, shuffle, max, min, disjoint, frequency
```

22.19 Show the printout of the following code:

```
import java.util.*;

public class Test {
  public static void main(String[] args) {
    List<String> list =
      Arrays.asList("yellow", "red", "green", "blue");
    Collections.reverse(list);
    System.out.println(list);

    List<String> list1 =
      Arrays.asList("yellow", "red", "green", "blue");
    List<String> list2 = Arrays.asList("white", "black");
    Collections.copy(list1, list2);
    System.out.println(list1);
```

```
    Collection<String> c1 = Arrays.asList("red", "cyan");
    Collection<String> c2 = Arrays.asList("red", "blue");
    Collection<String> c3 = Arrays.asList("pink", "tan");
    System.out.println(Collections.disjoint(c1, c2));
    System.out.println(Collections.disjoint(c1, c3));

    Collection<String> collection =
      Arrays.asList("red", "cyan", "red");
    System.out.println(Collections.frequency(collection, "red"));
  }
}
```

22.20 Which method can you use to sort the elements in an `ArrayList` or a `LinkedList`? Which method can you use to sort an array of strings?

22.21 Which method can you use to perform binary search for elements in an `ArrayList` or a `LinkedList`? Which method can you use to perform binary search for an array of strings?

22.22 Write a statement to find the largest element in an array of comparable objects.

22.7 Case Study: Bouncing Balls

This section presents an applet that displays bouncing balls and enables the user to add, remove balls.

Section 18.8 presents an applet that displays one bouncing ball. This section presents an applet that displays multiple bouncing balls. You can use two buttons to suspend and resume the movement of the balls, a scroll bar to control the ball speed, and the *+1* or *−1* button add or remove a ball, as shown in Figure 22.8.

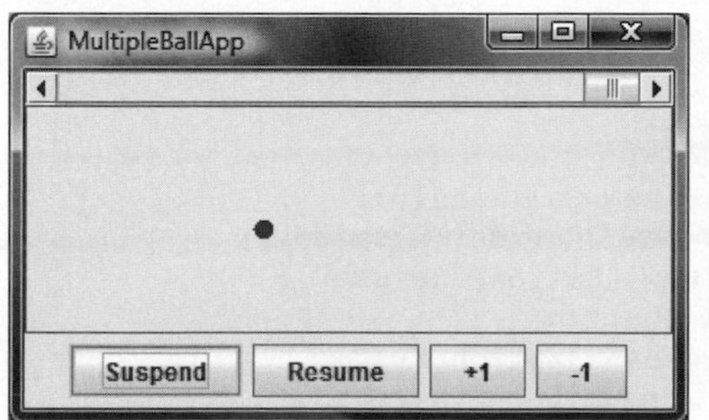

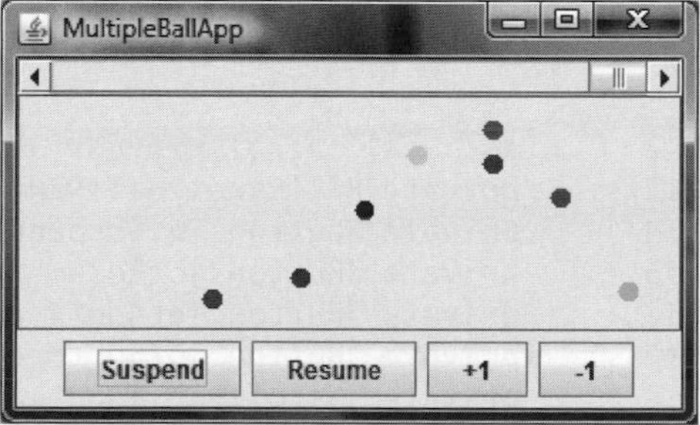

FIGURE 22.8 Pressing the + or − button adds or removes a ball.

The example in Section 18.8 only had to store one ball. How do you store the multiple balls in this example? An array list is a good data structure for storing the balls. Initially, the array list is empty. When a new ball is created, add it to the end of the list. To remove a ball, simply remove the last one in the array list.

Each ball has its state: the location, color, and direction to move. You can define a class named `Ball` with appropriate data fields to store this information. When a ball is created, it starts from the upper-left corner and moves downward to the right. A random color is assigned to a new ball.

The `BallPanel` class is responsible for displaying the ball and the `BallControl` class places the control components and implements the control. The `MultipleBallApp` places the `BallControl` in an applet. The relationship of these classes is shown in Figure 22.9. Listing 22.6 gives the program.

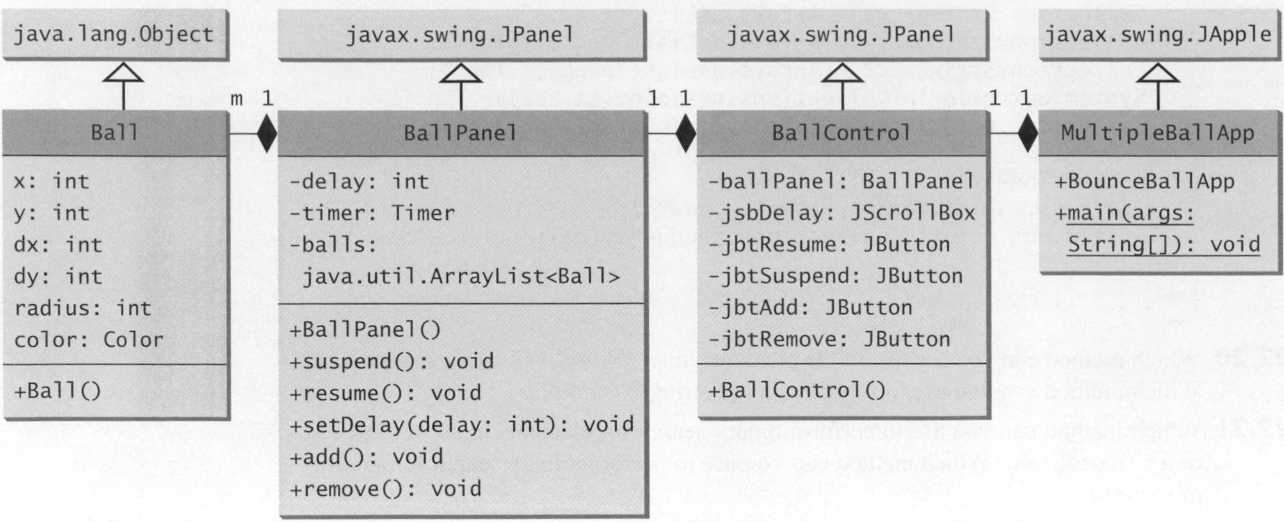

FIGURE 22.9 `MultipleBallApp` contains `BallControl`, `BallControl` contains `BallPanel`, and `BallPanel` contains `Ball`.

LISTING 22.6 MultipleBallApp.java

create a ball control

BallControl class

```
import javax.swing.Timer;
import java.util.ArrayList;
import java.awt.*;
import javax.swing.*;
import java.awt.event.*;

public class MultipleBallApp extends JApplet {
  public MultipleBallApp() {
    add(new BallControl());
  }

  class BallControl extends JPanel {
    private BallPanel ballPanel = new BallPanel();
    private JButton jbtSuspend = new JButton("Suspend");
    private JButton jbtResume = new JButton("Resume");
    private JButton jbtAdd = new JButton("+1");
    private JButton jbtSubtract = new JButton("-1");
    private JScrollBar jsbDelay = new JScrollBar();

    public BallControl() {
      // Group buttons in a panel
      JPanel panel = new JPanel();
      panel.add(jbtSuspend);
      panel.add(jbtResume);
      panel.add(jbtAdd);
      panel.add(jbtSubtract);

      // Add ball and buttons to the panel
      ballPanel.setBorder(
        new javax.swing.border.LineBorder(Color.red));
      jsbDelay.setOrientation(JScrollBar.HORIZONTAL);
      ballPanel.setDelay(jsbDelay.getMaximum());
      setLayout(new BorderLayout());
      add(jsbDelay, BorderLayout.NORTH);
      add(ballPanel, BorderLayout.CENTER);
```

```
    add(panel, BorderLayout.SOUTH);

    // Register listeners
    jbtSuspend.addActionListener(new Listener());
    jbtResume.addActionListener(new Listener());
    jbtAdd.addActionListener(new Listener());
    jbtSubtract.addActionListener(new Listener());
    jsbDelay.addAdjustmentListener(new AdjustmentListener() {
      @Override
      public void adjustmentValueChanged(AdjustmentEvent e) {
        ballPanel.setDelay(jsbDelay.getMaximum() - e.getValue());
      }
    });
  }

  class Listener implements ActionListener {
    @Override
    public void actionPerformed(ActionEvent e) {
      if (e.getSource() == jbtSuspend)
        ballPanel.suspend();
      else if (e.getSource() == jbtResume)
        ballPanel.resume();
      else if (e.getSource() == jbtAdd)
        ballPanel.add();
      else if (e.getSource() == jbtSubtract)
        ballPanel.subtract();
    }
  }
}

```

BallPanel class

```
class BallPanel extends JPanel {
  private int delay = 10;
  private ArrayList<Ball> list = new ArrayList<Ball>();

  // Create a timer with the initial delay
  protected Timer timer = new Timer(delay, new ActionListener() {
    @Override /** Handle the action event */
    public void actionPerformed(ActionEvent e) {
      repaint();
    }
  });

  public BallPanel() {
    timer.start();
  }

```

add a ball

```
  public void add() {
    list.add(new Ball());
  }

```

remove a ball

```
  public void subtract() {
    if (list.size() > 0)
      list.remove(list.size() - 1); // Remove the last ball
  }

  @Override
  protected void paintComponent(Graphics g) {
    super.paintComponent(g);

```

paint all balls

```
    for (int i = 0; i < list.size(); i++) {
```

Ball class

main method omitted

```
96          Ball ball = (Ball)list.get(i); // Get a ball
97          g.setColor(ball.color); // Set ball color
98
99          // Check boundaries
100         if (ball.x < 0 || ball.x > getWidth())
101           ball.dx = -ball.dx;
102
103         if (ball.y < 0 || ball.y > getHeight())
104           ball.dy = -ball.dy;
105
106         // Adjust ball position
107         ball.x += ball.dx;
108         ball.y += ball.dy;
109         g.fillOval(ball.x - ball.radius, ball.y - ball.radius,
110           ball.radius * 2, ball.radius * 2);
111       }
112     }
113
114     public void suspend() {
115       timer.stop();
116     }
117
118     public void resume() {
119       timer.start();
120     }
121
122     public void setDelay(int delay) {
123       this.delay = delay;
124       timer.setDelay(delay);
125     }
126   }
127
128   class Ball {
129     int x = 0;
130     int y = 0; // Current ball position
131     int dx = 2; // Increment on ball's x-coordinate
132     int dy = 2; // Increment on ball's y-coordinate
133     int radius = 5; // Ball radius
134     Color color = new Color((int)(Math.random() * 256),
135        (int)(Math.random() * 256), (int)(Math.random() * 256));
136   }
137 }
```

An array list is created to store the balls (line 68). When the user clicks the *+1* button, a new ball is created and added to the array list (line 83). When the user clicks the *−1* button, the last ball in the array list is removed (line 88).

The **paintComponent** method in the **BallPanel** class gets every ball in the array list, adjusts the balls' positions (lines 107–108), and paints them (lines 109–110).

This program uses an **ArrayList** to store balls. The program will work fine if **ArrayList** is replaced by **LinkedList**, but it is more efficient to use **ArrayList** in this example.

MyProgrammingLab™

22.23 Will the **MutilpleBallApp** program work if **ArrayList** is replaced by **LinkedList**? Why is the **ArrayList** a better choice than the **LinkedList** for this program?

22.24 If you change the **MutilpleBallApp** program to remove the first ball in the list when the *−1* button is clicked, should you use **ArrayList** or **LinkedList** to store the balls in this program?

22.25 How do you modify the code in the `MutilpleBallApp` program so that each ball will get a random radius between 10 and 20?

22.8 The Vector and Stack Classes

`Vector` is a subclass of `AbstractList`, and `Stack` is a subclass of `Vector` in the Java API.

The Java Collections Framework was introduced in Java 2. Several data structures were supported earlier, among them the `Vector` and `Stack` classes. These classes were redesigned to fit into the Java Collections Framework, but all their old-style methods are retained for compatibility.

`Vector` is the same as `ArrayList`, except that it contains synchronized methods for accessing and modifying the vector. Synchronized methods can prevent data corruption when a vector is accessed and modified by two or more threads concurrently. We will discuss synchronization in Chapter 32, Multithreading and Parallel Programming. For the many applications that do not require synchronization, using `ArrayList` is more efficient than using `Vector`.

The `Vector` class extends the `AbstractList` class. It also has the methods contained in the original `Vector` class defined prior to Java 2, as shown in Figure 22.10.

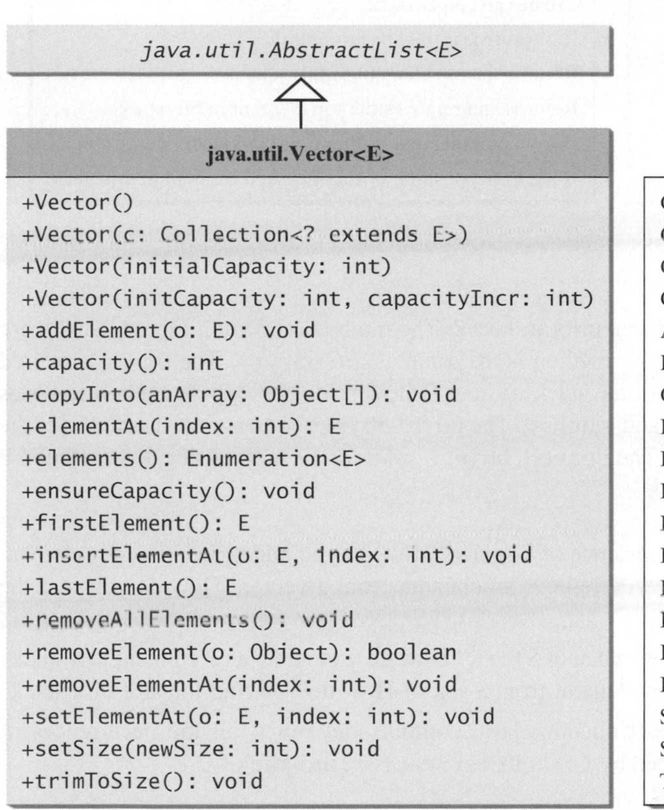

Creates a default empty vector with initial capacity 10.
Creates a vector from an existing collection.
Creates a vector with the specified initial capacity.
Creates a vector with the specified initial capacity and increment.
Appends the element to the end of this vector.
Returns the current capacity of this vector.
Copies the elements in this vector to the array.
Returns the object at the specified index.
Returns an enumeration of this vector.
Increases the capacity of this vector.
Returns the first element in this vector.
Inserts `o` into this vector at the specified index.
Returns the last element in this vector.
Removes all the elements in this vector.
Removes the first matching element in this vector.
Removes the element at the specified index.
Sets a new element at the specified index.
Sets a new size in this vector.
Trims the capacity of this vector to its size.

FIGURE 22.10 Starting in Java 2, the `Vector` class extends `AbstractList` and also retains all the methods in the original `Vector` class.

Most of the methods in the `Vector` class listed in the UML diagram in Figure 22.10 are similar to the methods in the `List` interface. These methods were introduced before the Java Collections Framework. For example, **`addElement(Object element)`** is the same as the add(Object element) method, except that the addElement method is synchronized. Use the ArrayList class if you don't need synchronization. It works much faster than Vector.

Note

The elements() method returns an Enumeration. The Enumeration interface was introduced prior to Java 2 and was superseded by the Iterator interface.

Note

Vector is widely used in Java programming because it was the Java resizable array implementation before Java 2. Many of the Swing data models use vectors.

In the Java Collections Framework, Stack is implemented as an extension of Vector, as illustrated in Figure 22.11.

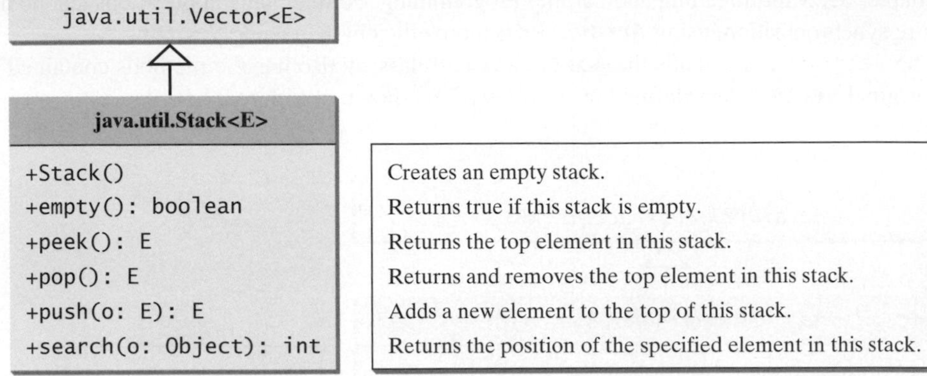

FIGURE 22.11 The Stack class extends Vector to provide a last-in, first-out data structure.

The Stack class was introduced prior to Java 2. The methods shown in Figure 22.11 were used before Java 2. The empty() method is the same as isEmpty(). The peek() method looks at the element at the top of the stack without removing it. The pop() method removes the top element from the stack and returns it. The push(Object element) method adds the specified element to the stack. The search(Object element) method checks whether the specified element is in the stack.

22.26 How do you create an instance of Vector? How do you add or insert a new element into a vector? How do you remove an element from a vector? How do you find the size of a vector?

22.27 How do you create an instance of Stack? How do you add a new element to a stack? How do you remove an element from a stack? How do you find the size of a stack?

22.28 Does Listing 22.1, TestCollection.java, compile and run if all the occurrences of ArrayList are replaced by LinkedList, Vector, or Stack?

22.9 Queues and Priority Queues

In a priority queue, the element with the highest priority is removed first.

queue
priority queue

A *queue* is a first-in, first-out data structure. Elements are appended to the end of the queue and are removed from the beginning of the queue. In a *priority queue*, elements are assigned priorities. When accessing elements, the element with the highest priority is removed first. This section introduces queues and priority queues in the Java API.

22.9.1 The Queue Interface

Queue interface

The **Queue** interface extends `java.util.Collection` with additional insertion, extraction, and inspection operations, as shown in Figure 22.12.

queue operations

The `offer` method is used to add an element to the queue. This method is similar to the `add` method in the `Collection` interface, but the `offer` method is preferred for queues. The `poll` and `remove` methods are similar, except that `poll()` returns `null` if the queue is empty, whereas `remove()` throws an exception. The `peek` and `element` methods are similar, except that `peek()` returns `null` if the queue is empty, whereas `element()` throws an exception.

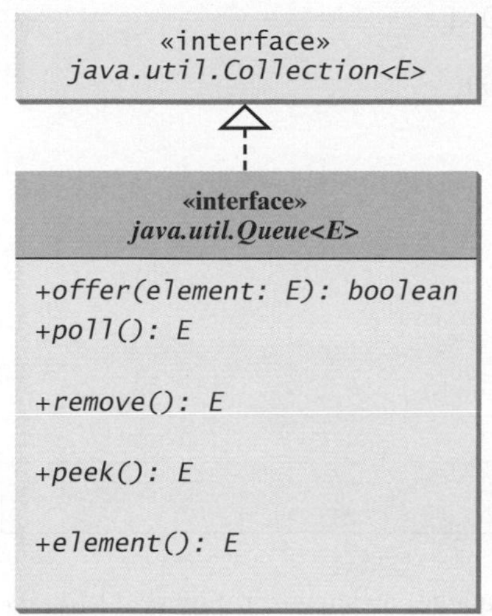

Inserts an element into the queue.

Retrieves and removes the head of this queue, or `null` if this queue is empty.

Retrieves and removes the head of this queue and throws an exception if this queue is empty.

Retrieves, but does not remove, the head of this queue, returning `null` if this queue is empty.

Retrieves, but does not remove, the head of this queue, throwing an exception if this queue is empty.

FIGURE 22.12 The **Queue** interface extends `Collection` to provide additional insertion, extraction, and inspection operations.

22.9.2 Deque and LinkedList

The `LinkedList` class implements the **Deque** interface, which extends the **Queue** interface, as shown in Figure 22.13. Therefore, you can use `LinkedList` to create a queue. `LinkedList` is ideal for queue operations because it is efficient for inserting and removing elements from both ends of a list.

Deque supports element insertion and removal at both ends. The name *deque* is short for "double-ended queue" and is usually pronounced "deck." The **Deque** interface extends **Queue** with additional methods for inserting and removing elements from both ends of the

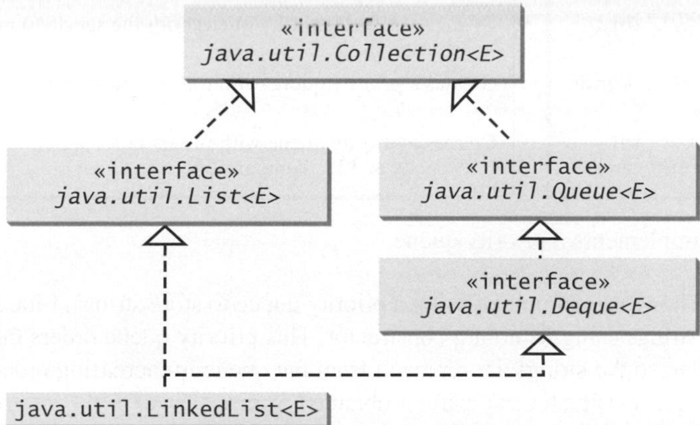

FIGURE 22.13 `LinkedList` implements `List` and **Deque**.

queue. The methods `addFirst(e)`, `removeFirst()`, `addLast(e)`, `removeLast()`, `getFirst()`, and `getLast()` are defined in the `Deque` interface.

Listing 22.7 shows an example of using a queue to store strings. Line 4 creates a queue using `LinkedList`. Four strings are added to the queue in lines 5–8. The `size()` method defined in the `Collection` interface returns the number of elements in the queue (line 10). The `remove()` method retrieves and removes the element at the head of the queue (line 11).

LISTING 22.7 TestQueue.java

creates a queue
inserts an element
queue size
remove element

```
 1 public class TestQueue {
 2   public static void main(String[] args) {
 3     java.util.Queue<String> queue =
 4       new java.util.LinkedList<String>();
 5     queue.offer("Oklahoma");
 6     queue.offer("Indiana");
 7     queue.offer("Georgia");
 8     queue.offer("Texas");
 9
10     while (queue.size() > 0)
11       System.out.print(queue.remove() + " ");
12   }
13 }
```

```
Oklahoma Indiana Georgia Texas
```

PriorityQueue class

The `PriorityQueue` class implements a priority queue, as shown in Figure 22.14. By default, the priority queue orders its elements according to their natural ordering using `Comparable`. The element with the least value is assigned the highest priority and thus is removed from the queue first. If there are several elements with the same highest priority, the tie is broken arbitrarily. You can also specify an ordering using `Comparator` in the constructor `PriorityQueue(initialCapacity, comparator)`.

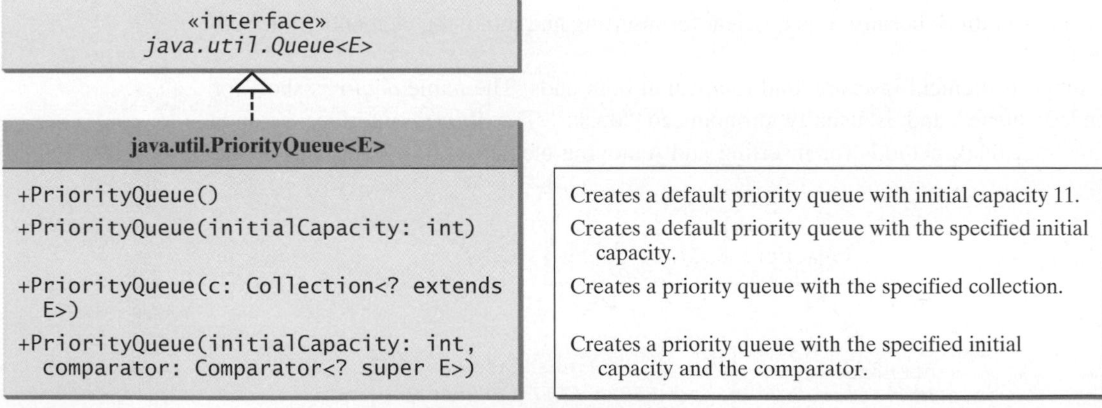

FIGURE 22.14 The `PriorityQueue` class implements a priority queue.

Listing 22.8 shows an example of using a priority queue to store strings. Line 5 creates a priority queue for strings using its no-arg constructor. This priority queue orders the strings using their natural order, so the strings are removed from the queue in increasing order. Lines 16–17 create a priority queue using the comparator obtained from `Collections.reverseOrder()`, which orders the elements in reverse order, so the strings are removed from the queue in decreasing order.

LISTING 22.8 PriorityQueueDemo.java

```
import java.util.*;

public class PriorityQueueDemo {
  public static void main(String[] args) {
    PriorityQueue<String> queue1 = new PriorityQueue<String>();
    queue1.offer("Oklahoma");
    queue1.offer("Indiana");
    queue1.offer("Georgia");
    queue1.offer("Texas");

    System.out.println("Priority queue using Comparable:");
    while (queue1.size() > 0) {
      System.out.print(queue1.remove() + " ");
    }

    PriorityQueue<String> queue2 = new PriorityQueue<String>(
      4, Collections.reverseOrder());
    queue2.offer("Oklahoma");
    queue2.offer("Indiana");
    queue2.offer("Georgia");
    queue2.offer("Texas");

    System.out.println("\nPriority queue using Comparator:");
    while (queue2.size() > 0) {
      System.out.print(queue2.remove() + " ");
    }
  }
}
```

a default queue

inserts an element

a queue with comparator

comparator

```
Priority queue using Comparable:
Georgia Indiana Oklahoma Texas
Priority queue using Comparator:
Texas Oklahoma Indiana Georgia
```

22.29 Is `java.util.Queue` a subinterface of `java.util.Collection`, `java.util.Set`, or `java.util.List`? Does `LinkedList` implement `Queue`?

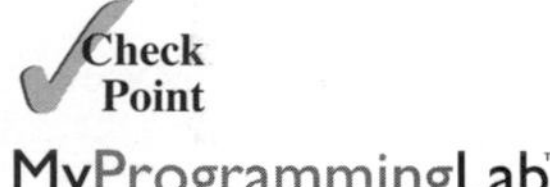

22.30 How do you create a priority queue for integers? By default, how are elements ordered in a priority queue? Is the element with the least value assigned the highest priority in a priority queue?

22.31 How do you create a priority queue that reverses the natural order of the elements?

22.10 Case Study: Evaluating Expressions

Stacks can be used to evaluate expressions.

Stacks and queues have many applications. This section gives an application that uses stacks to evaluate expressions. You can enter an arithmetic expression from Google to evaluate the expression, as shown in Figure 22.15.

How does Google evaluate an expression? This section presents a program that evaluates a *compound expression* with multiple operators and parentheses (e.g., `(15 + 2) * 34 - 2`). For simplicity, assume that the operands are integers and the operators are of four types: `+`, `-`, `*`, and `/`.

compound expression

The problem can be solved using two stacks, named `operandStack` and `operatorStack`, for storing operands and operators, respectively. Operands and operators are pushed into the

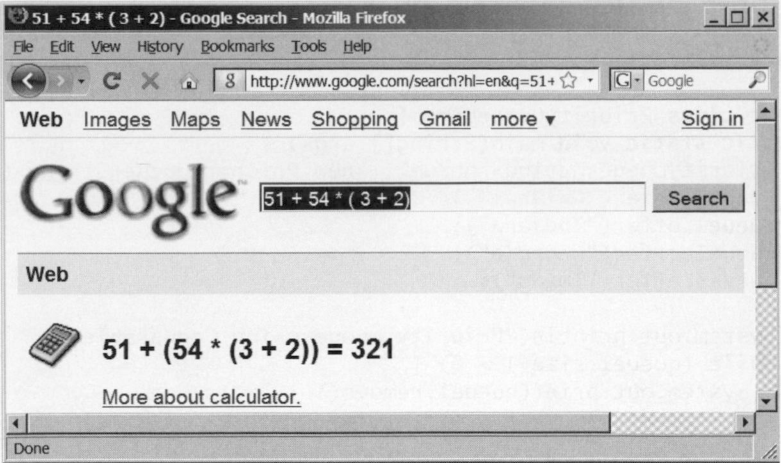

FIGURE 22.15 You can evaluate an arithmetic expression using a Google search engine.

process an operator

stacks before they are processed. When an *operator is processed*, it is popped from `operatorStack` and applied to the first two operands from `operandStack` (the two operands are popped from `operandStack`). The resultant value is pushed back to `operandStack`.

The algorithm proceeds in two phases:

Phase 1: Scanning the expression

The program scans the expression from left to right to extract operands, operators, and the parentheses.

1.1. If the extracted item is an operand, push it to `operandStack`.

1.2. If the extracted item is a `+` or `-` operator, process all the operators at the top of `operatorStack` and push the extracted operator to `operatorStack`.

1.3. If the extracted item is a `*` or `/` operator, process the `*` or `/` operators at the top of `operatorStack` and push the extracted operator to `operatorStack`.

1.4. If the extracted item is a `(` symbol, push it to `operatorStack`.

1.5. If the extracted item is a `)` symbol, repeatedly process the operators from the top of `operatorStack` until seeing the `(` symbol on the stack.

Phase 2: Clearing the stack

Repeatedly process the operators from the top of `operatorStack` until `operatorStack` is empty.

Table 22.1 shows how the algorithm is applied to evaluate the expression `(1 + 2) * 4 - 3`. Listing 22.9 gives the program, and Figure 22.16 shows some sample output.

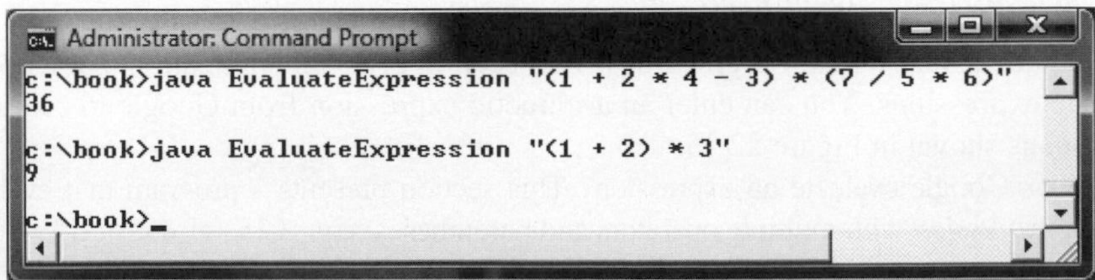

FIGURE 22.16 The program takes an expression as command-line arguments.

TABLE 22.1 Evaluating an expression

Expression	*Scan*	*Action*	operandStack	operatorStack
(1 + 2) * 4 − 3 ↑	(	Phase 1.4		(
(1 + 2) * 4 − 3 ↑	1	Phase 1.1	1	(
(1 + 2) * 4 − 3 ↑	+	Phase 1.2	1	+ (
(1 + 2) * 4 − 3 ↑	2	Phase 1.1	2 1	+ (
(1 + 2) * 4 − 3 ↑	)	Phase 1.5	3	
(1 + 2) * 4 − 3 ↑	*	Phase 1.3	3	*
(1 + 2) * 4 − 3 ↑	4	Phase 1.1	4 3	*
(1 + 2) * 4 − 3 ↑	−	Phase 1.2	12	−
(1 + 2) * 4 − 3 ↑	3	Phase 1.1	3 12	−
(1 + 2) * 4 − 3 ↑	none	Phase 2	9	

LISTING 22.9 EvaluateExpression.java

```
import java.util.Stack;

public class EvaluateExpression {
  public static void main(String[] args) {
    // Check number of arguments passed
    if (args.length != 1) {
      System.out.println(
        "Usage: java EvaluateExpression \"expression\"");
      System.exit(1);
    }

    try {
      System.out.println(evaluateExpression(args[0]));
    }
    catch (Exception ex) {
      System.out.println("Wrong expression: " + args[0]);
    }
  }

  /** Evaluate an expression */
  public static int evaluateExpression(String expression) {
    // Create operandStack to store operands
    Stack<Integer> operandStack = new Stack<Integer>();

```

check usage

evaluate expression

exception

operandStack

operatorStack
prepare for extraction
extract tokens
process tokens
+ or - scanned
* or / scanned
(scanned
) scanned
an operand scanned
clear operatorStack

```
    // Create operatorStack to store operators
    Stack<Character> operatorStack = new Stack<Character>();

    // Insert blanks around (, ), +, -, /, and *
    expression = insertBlanks(expression);

    // Extract operands and operators
    String[] tokens = expression.split(" ");

    // Phase 1: Scan tokens
    for (String token: tokens) {
      if (token.length() == 0) // Blank space
        continue; // Back to the while loop to extract the next token
      else if (token.charAt(0) == '+' || token.charAt(0) == '-') {
        // Process all +, -, *, / in the top of the operator stack
        while (!operatorStack.isEmpty() &&
          (operatorStack.peek() == '+' ||
           operatorStack.peek() == '-' ||
           operatorStack.peek() == '*' ||
           operatorStack.peek() == '/')) {
          processAnOperator(operandStack, operatorStack);
        }

        // Push the + or - operator into the operator stack
        operatorStack.push(token.charAt(0));
      }
      else if (token.charAt(0) == '*' || token.charAt(0) == '/') {
        // Process all *, / in the top of the operator stack
        while (!operatorStack.isEmpty() &&
          (operatorStack.peek() == '*' ||
          operatorStack.peek() == '/')) {
          processAnOperator(operandStack, operatorStack);
        }

        // Push the * or / operator into the operator stack
        operatorStack.push(token.charAt(0));
      }
      else if (token.trim().charAt(0) == '(') {
        operatorStack.push('('); // Push '(' to stack
      }
      else if (token.trim().charAt(0) == ')') {
        // Process all the operators in the stack until seeing '('
        while (operatorStack.peek() != '(') {
          processAnOperator(operandStack, operatorStack);
        }

        operatorStack.pop(); // Pop the '(' symbol from the stack
      }
      else { // An operand scanned
        // Push an operand to the stack
        operandStack.push(new Integer(token));
      }
    }

    // Phase 2: Process all the remaining operators in the stack
    while (!operatorStack.isEmpty()) {
      processAnOperator(operandStack, operatorStack);
    }

    // Return the result
```

```
85      return operandStack.pop();                                          return result
86    }
87
88    /** Process one operator: Take an operator from operatorStack and
89     *  apply it on the operands in the operandStack */
90    public static void processAnOperator(
91        Stack<Integer> operandStack, Stack<Character> operatorStack) {
92      char op = operatorStack.pop();
93      int op1 = operandStack.pop();
94      int op2 = operandStack.pop();
95      if (op == '+')                                                      process +
96        operandStack.push(op2 + op1);
97      else if (op == '-')                                                 process -
98        operandStack.push(op2 - op1);
99      else if (op == '*')                                                 process *
100       operandStack.push(op2 * op1);
101     else if (op == '/')                                                 process /
102       operandStack.push(op2 / op1);
103   }
104
105   public static String insertBlanks(String s) {                         insert blanks
106     String result = "";
107
108     for (int i = 0; i < s.length(); i++) {
109       if (s.charAt(i) == '(' || s.charAt(i) == ')' ||
110           s.charAt(i) == '+' || s.charAt(i) == '-' ||
111           s.charAt(i) == '*' || s.charAt(i) == '/')
112         result += " " + s.charAt(i) + " ";
113       else
114         result += s.charAt(i);
115     }
116
117     return result;
118   }
119 }
```

You can use the **GenericStack** class provided by the book or the **java.util.Stack** class defined in the Java API for creating stacks. This example uses the **java.util.Stack** class. The program will work if it is replaced by **GenericStack**.

The program takes an expression as a command-line argument in one string.

The **evaluateExpression** method creates two stacks, **operandStack** and **operatorStack** (lines 23, 26), and extracts operands, operators, and parentheses delimited by space (lines 29–32). The **insertBlanks** method is used to ensure that operands, operators, and parentheses are separated by at least one blank (line 29).

The program scans each token in the **for** loop (lines 35–77). If a token is empty, skip it (line 37). If a token is an operand, push it to **operandStack** (line 75). If a token is a **+** or **–** operator (line 38), process all the operators from the top of **operatorStack**, if any (lines 40–46), and push the newly scanned operator into the stack (line 49). If a token is a ***** or **/** operator (line 51), process all the ***** and **/** operators from the top of **operatorStack**, if any (lines 53–57), and push the newly scanned operator to the stack (line 60). If a token is a **(** symbol (line 62), push it into **operatorStack**. If a token is a **)** symbol (line 65), process all the operators from the top of **operatorStack** until seeing the **)** symbol (lines 67–69) and pop the **)** symbol from the stack.

After all tokens are considered, the program processes the remaining operators in **operatorStack** (lines 80–82).

The **processAnOperator** method (lines 90–103) processes an operator. The method pops the operator from **operatorStack** (line 92) and pops two operands from **operandStack** (lines 93–94). Depending on the operator, the method performs an operation and pushes the result of the operation back to `operandStack` (lines 96, 98, 100, 102).

MyProgrammingLab™

22.32 Can the `EvaluateExpression` program evaluate the following expressions `"1+2"`, `"1 +    2"`, `"(1) +    2"`, `"((1)) +    2"`, and `"(1 +    2)"`?

22.33 Show the change of the contents in the stacks when evaluating `"3 + (4 + 5) * (3 + 5) + 4 * 5"` using the `EvaluateExpression` program.

Key Terms

collection 794
comparator 803
convenience abstract class 794
data structure 794
linked list 801
`list` 794
priority queue 814
`queue` 794

Chapter Summary

1. The Java Collections Framework supports *sets*, *lists*, *queues*, and *maps*. They are defined in the interfaces `Set`, `List`, `Queue`, and `Map`.

2. A *list* stores an ordered *collection* of elements.

3. All the concrete classes in the Java Collections Framework implement the `Cloneable` and `Serializable` interfaces. Thus, their instances can be cloned and serialized.

4. To allow duplicate elements to be stored in a collection, you need to use a list. A list not only can store duplicate elements but also allows the user to specify where they are stored. The user can access elements by an index.

5. Two types of lists are supported: `ArrayList` and `LinkedList`. `ArrayList` is a resizable-array implementation of the `List` interface. All the methods in `ArrayList` are defined in `List`. `LinkedList` is a *linked-list* implementation of the `List` interface. In addition to implementing the `List` interface, this class provides the methods for retrieving, inserting, and removing elements from both ends of the list.

6. `Comparator` can be used to compare the objects of a class that doesn't implement `Comparable`.

7. The `Vector` class extends the `AbstractList` class. Starting with Java 2, `Vector` has been the same as `ArrayList`, except that the methods for accessing and modifying the vector are synchronized. The `Stack` class extends the `Vector` class and provides several methods for manipulating the stack.

8. The `Queue` interface represents a queue. The `PriorityQueue` class implements `Queue` for a *priority queue*.

Test Questions

Do the test questions for this chapter online at www.cs.armstrong.edu/liang/intro9e/test.html.

Programming Exercises

MyProgrammingLab™

Sections 22.2–22.7

*22.1 (*Display words in ascending alphabetical order*) Write a program that reads words from a text file and displays all the words (duplicates allowed) in ascending alphabetical order. The words must start with a letter. The text file is passed as a command-line argument.

*22.2 (*Store numbers in a linked list*) Write a program that lets the user enter numbers from a graphical user interface and displays them in a text area, as shown in Figure 22.17a. Use a linked list to store the numbers. Do not store duplicate numbers. Add the buttons *Sort*, *Shuffle*, and *Reverse* to sort, shuffle, and reverse the list.

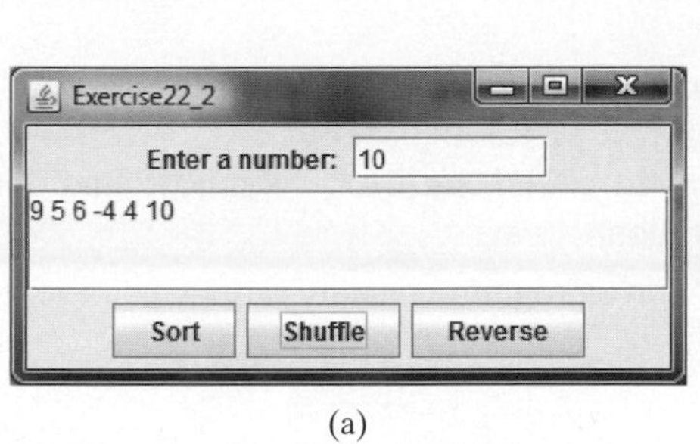

(a)

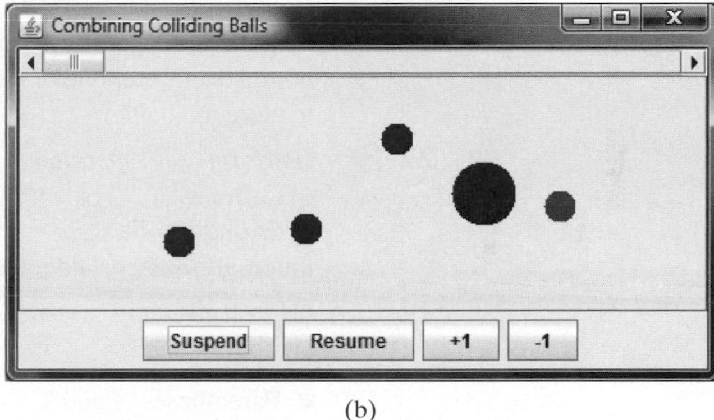

(b)

Figure 22.17 (a) The numbers are stored in a list and displayed in the text area. (b) The colliding balls are combined.

*22.3 (*Guessing the capitals*) Rewrite Programming Exercise 9.17 to store the pairs of states and capitals so that the questions are displayed randomly.

*22.4 (*Sort points in a plane*) Write a program that meets the following requirements:

- Define a class named `Point` with two data fields `x` and `y` to represent a point's *x*- and *y*-coordinates. Implement the `Comparable` interface for comparing the points on *x*-coordinates. If two points have the same *x*-coordinates, compare their *y*-coordinates.
- Define a class named `CompareY` that implements `Comparator<Point>`. Implement the `compare` method to compare two points on their *y*-coordinates. If two points have the same *y*-coordinates, compare their *x*-coordinates.
- Randomly create `100` points and apply the `Arrays.sort` method to display the points in increasing order of their *x*-coordinates and in increasing order of their *y*-coordinates, respectively.

***22.5 (*Combine colliding bouncing balls*) The example in Section 22.7 displays multiple bouncing balls. Extend the example to detect collisions. Once two balls collide, remove the later ball that was added to the panel and add its radius to the other ball, as shown in Figure 22.17b. Add a mouse listener that removes a ball when the mouse clicks on the ball.

22.6 (*Use iterators on linked lists*) Write a test program that stores 5 million integers in a linked list and test the time to traverse the list using an `iterator` vs. using the `get(index)` method.

*****22.7** (*Game: hangman*) Programming Exercise 9.25 presents a console version of the popular hangman game. Write a GUI program that lets a user play the game. The user guesses a word by entering one letter at a time, as shown in Figure 22.18. If the user misses seven times, a hanging man swings. Once a word is finished, the user can press the *Enter* key to continue to guess another word.

****22.8** (*Game: lottery*) Revise Programming Exercise 3.15 to add an additional $2,000 award if two digits from the user input are in the lottery number. (*Hint*: Sort the three digits in the lottery number and three digits in the user input into two lists, and use the `Collection`'s `containsAll` method to check whether the two digits in the user input are in the lottery number.)

Sections 22.8–22.10

*****22.9** (*Remove the largest ball first*) Modify Listing 22.6, MultipleBallApp.java to assign a random radius between 2 and 20 when a ball is created. When the *−1* button is clicked, one of largest balls is removed. (*Hint*: Use a `PriorityQueue` to store the balls.)

22.10 (*Perform set operations on priority queues*) Create two priority queues, {`"George"`, `"Jim"`, `"John"`, `"Blake"`, `"Kevin"`, `"Michael"`} and {`"George"`, `"Katie"`, `"Kevin"`, `"Michelle"`, `"Ryan"`}, and find their union, difference, and intersection.

***22.11** (*Match grouping symbols*) A Java program contains various pairs of grouping symbols, such as:

- Parentheses: `(` and `)`
- Braces: `{` and `}`
- Brackets: `[` and `]`

Note that the grouping symbols cannot overlap. For example, `(a{b)}` is illegal. Write a program to check whether a Java source-code file has correct pairs of grouping symbols. Pass the source-code file name as a command-line argument.

22.12 (*Clone* `PriorityQueue`) Define `MyPriorityQueue` class that extends `PriorityQueue` to implement the `Cloneable` interface and implement the `clone()` method to clone a priority queue.

****22.13** (*Game: the 24-point card game*) The 24-point game is to pick any 4 cards from 52 cards, as shown in Figure 22.19. Note that the Jokers are excluded. Each card represents a number. An Ace, King, Queen, and Jack represent `1`, `13`, `12`, and `11`, respectively. You can click the *Refresh* button to get four cards. Enter an expression that uses the four numbers from the four selected cards. Each number must be used once and only once. You can use the operators (addition, subtraction, multiplication, and division) and parentheses in the expression. The expression must evaluate to `24`. After entering the expression, click the *Verify* button to check whether the numbers in the expression are currently selected and whether the result of the expression is correct. Display the verification in a dialog box. Assume that images are stored in files named **1.png**, **2.png**, . . . , **52.png**, in the order of spades, hearts, diamonds, and clubs. So, the first 13 images are for spades 1, 2, 3, . . . , and 13.

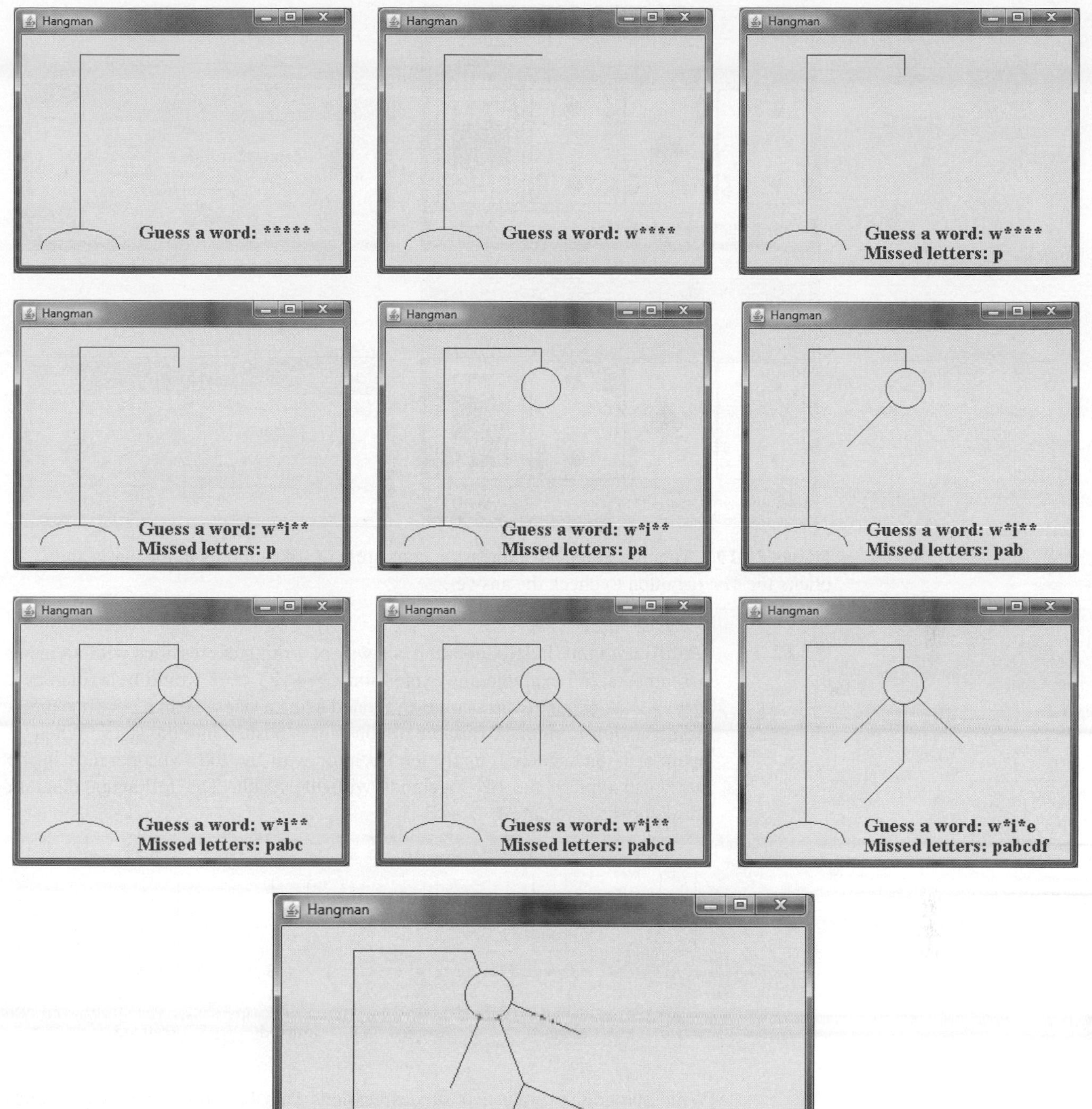

FIGURE 22.18 The program displays a hangman game.

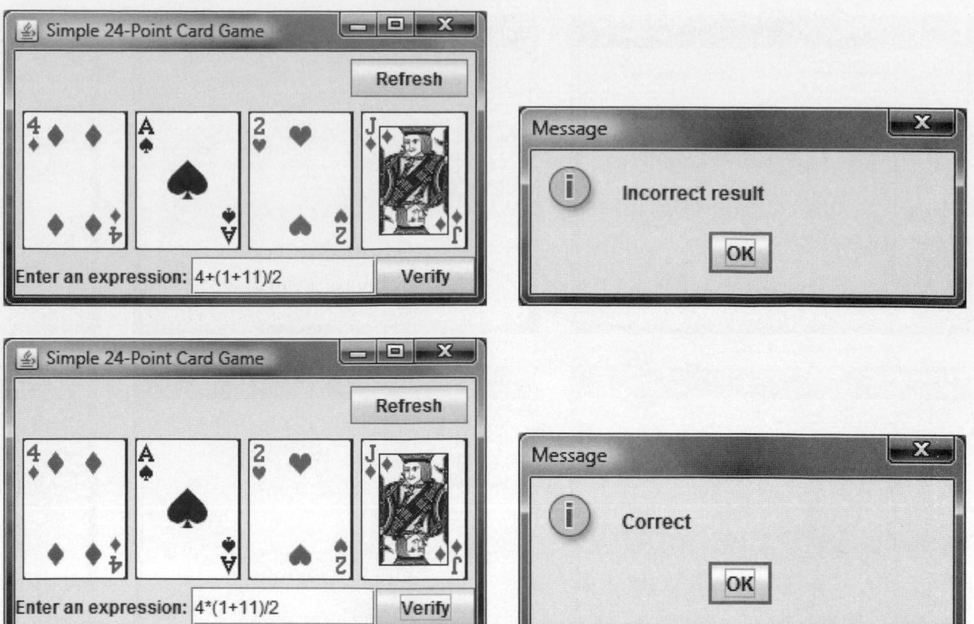

Figure 22.19 The user enters an expression consisting of the numbers in the cards and clicks the *Verify* button to check the answer.

****22.14** (*Postfix notation*) Postfix notation is a way of writing expressions without using parentheses. For example, the expression `(1 + 2) * 3` would be written as `1 2 + 3 *`. A postfix expression is evaluated using a stack. Scan a postfix expression from left to right. A variable or constant is pushed into the stack. When an operator is encountered, apply the operator with the top two operands in the stack and replace the two operands with the result. The following diagram shows how to evaluate `1 2 + 3 *`.

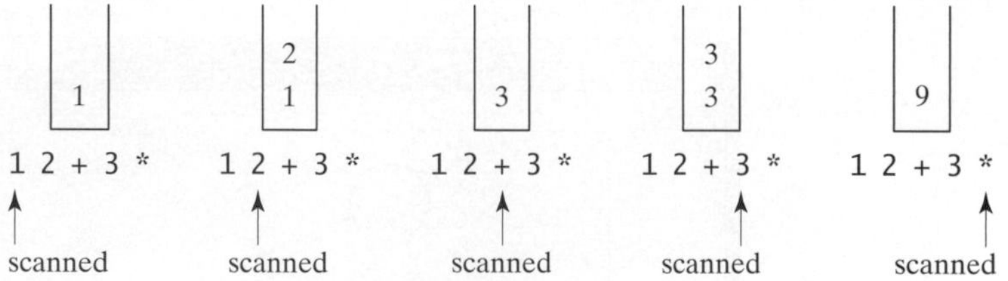

Write a program to evaluate postfix expressions. Pass the expression as a command-line argument in one string.

*****22.15** (*Game: the 24-point card game*) Improve Exercise 22.13 to enable the computer to display the expression if one exists, as shown in Figure 22.20. Otherwise, report that the expression does not exist.

****22.16** (*Convert infix to postfix*) Write a method that converts an infix expression into a postfix expression using the following header:

```
public static String infixToPostfix(String expression)
```

For example, the method should convert the infix expression `(1 + 2) * 3` to `1 2 + 3 *` and `2 * (1 + 3)` to `2 1 3 + *`.

FIGURE 22.20 The program can automatically find a solution if one exists.

*****22.17** (*Game: the 24-point card game*) This exercise is a variation of the 24-point card game described in Exercise 22.13. Write an applet to check whether there is a 24-point solution for the four specified numbers. The applet lets the user enter four values, each between `1` and `13`, as shown in Figure 22.21. The user can then click the *Solve* button to display the solution or display "No solution" if none exist.

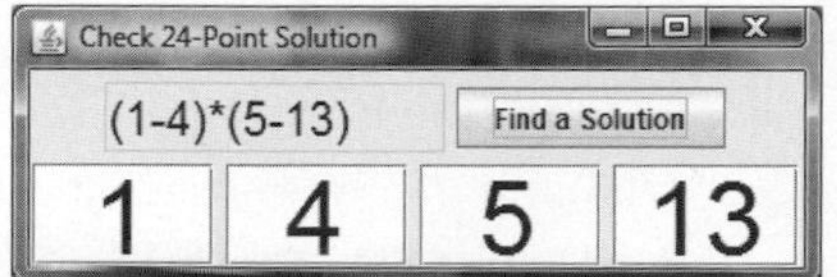

FIGURE 22.21 The user enters four numbers and the program finds a solution.

***22.18** (*Directory size*) Listing 20.7, DirectorySize.java, gives a recursive method for finding a directory size. Rewrite this method without using recursion. Your program should use a queue to store the subdirectories under a directory. The algorithm can be described as follows:

```
long getSize(File directory) {
  long size = 0;
  add directory to the queue;

  while (queue is not empty) {
    Remove an item from the queue into t;
    if (t is a file)
      size += t.length();
    else
      add all the files and subdirectories under t into the
        queue;
  }

  return size;
}
```

*****22.19** (*Game: solution ratio for 24-point game*) When you pick four cards from a deck of 52 cards for the 24-point game introduced in Exercise 22.13, the four cards may not have a 24-point solution. What is the number of all possible picks of four cards from 52 cards? Among all possible picks, how many of them have 24-point solutions? What is the success ratio—that is, (number of picks with solutions)/(number of all possible picks of four cards)? Write a program to find these answers.

***22.20** (*Directory size*) Rewrite Exercise 22.18 using a stack instead of a queue.

***22.21** (*Use* `Comparator`) Write the following generic method using selection sort and a comparator.

```
public static <E> void selectionSort(E[] list,
  Comparator<? super E> comparator)
```

Write a test program that creates an array of 10 `GeometricObject`s and invokes this method using the `GeometricObjectComparator` introduced in Listing 22.4 to sort the elements. Display the sorted elements. Use the following statement to create the array.

```
GeometricObject[] list = {new Circle(5), new Rectangle(4, 5),
  new Circle(5.5), new Rectangle(2.4, 5), new Circle(0.5),
  new Rectangle(4, 65), new Circle(4.5), new Rectangle(4.4, 1),
  new Circle(6.5), new Rectangle(4, 5)};
```

***22.22** (*Nonrecursive Tower of Hanoi*) Implement the `moveDisks` method in Listing 20.8 using a stack instead of using recursion.

CHAPTER

23

Sets and Maps

Objectives

- To store unordered, nonduplicate elements using a set (§23.2).
- To explore how and when to use `HashSet` (§23.2.1), `LinkedHashSet` (§23.2.2), or `TreeSet` (§23.2.3) to store a set of elements.
- To compare the performance of sets and lists (§23.3).
- To use sets to develop a program that counts the keywords in a Java source file (§23.4).
- To tell the differences between `Collection` and `Map` and describe when and how to use `HashMap`, `LinkedHashMap`, or `TreeMap` to store values associated with keys (§23.5).
- To use maps to develop a program that counts the occurrence of the words in a text (§23.6).
- To obtain singleton sets, lists, and maps, and unmodifiable sets, lists, and maps, using the static methods in the `Collections` class (§23.7).

23.1 Introduction

A set *is an efficient data structure for storing and processing nonduplicate elements. A* map *is like a dictionary that provides a quick lookup to retrieve a value using a key.*

The "**No-Fly**" **list** is a list, created and maintained by the U.S. government's Terrorist Screening Center, of people who are not permitted to board a commercial aircraft for travel in or out of the United States. Suppose we need to write a program that checks whether a person is on the No-Fly list. You can use a list to store names in the No-Fly list. However, a more efficient data structure for this application is a *set*.

why set?

Suppose your program also needs to store detailed information about terrorists in the No-Fly list. The detailed information such as gender, height, weight, and nationality can be retrieved using the name as the key. A *map* is an efficient data structure for such a task.

why map?

This chapter introduces sets and maps in the Java Collections Framework.

23.2 Sets

You can create a set using one of its three concrete classes: `HashSet`*,* `LinkedHashSet`*, or* `TreeSet`.

set

no duplicates

The `Set` interface extends the `Collection` interface, as shown in Figure 22.1. It does not introduce new methods or constants, but it stipulates that an instance of `Set` contains no duplicate elements. The concrete classes that implement `Set` must ensure that no duplicate elements can be added to the set. That is, no two elements `e1` and `e2` can be in the set such that `e1.equals(e2)` is `true`.

`AbstractSet`

The `AbstractSet` class extends `AbstractCollection` and partially implements `Set`. The `AbstractSet` class provides concrete implementations for the `equals` method and the `hashCode` method. The hash code of a set is the sum of the hash codes of all the elements in the set. Since the `size` method and `iterator` method are not implemented in the `AbstractSet` class, `AbstractSet` is an abstract class.

Three concrete classes of `Set` are `HashSet`, `LinkedHashSet`, and `TreeSet`, as shown in Figure 23.1.

23.2.1 `HashSet`

hash set

The `HashSet` class is a concrete class that implements `Set`. You can create an empty *hash set* using its no-arg constructor or create a hash set from an existing collection. By default, the initial capacity is `16` and the load factor is `0.75`. If you know the size of your set, you can specify the initial capacity and load factor in the constructor. Otherwise, use the default setting. The load factor is a value between `0.0` and `1.0`.

load factor

The load factor measures how full the set is allowed to be before its capacity is increased. When the number of elements exceeds the product of the capacity and load factor, the capacity is automatically doubled. For example, if the capacity is `16` and load factor is `0.75`, the capacity will be doubled to `32` when the size reaches `12` (16 * 0.75 = 12). A higher load factor decreases the space costs but increases the search time. Generally, the default load factor `0.75` is a good trade-off between time and space costs. We will discuss more on the load factor in Chapter 28, Hashing.

`hashCode()`

A `HashSet` can be used to store *duplicate-free* elements. For efficiency, objects added to a hash set need to implement the `hashCode` method in a manner that properly disperses the hash code. Recall that `hashCode` is defined in the `Object` class. The hash codes of two objects must be the same if the two objects are equal. Two unequal objects may have the same hash code, but you should implement the `hashCode` method to avoid too many such cases. Most of the classes in the Java API implement the `hashCode` method. For example, the `hashCode` in the `Integer` class returns its `int` value. The `hashCode` in the `Character` class returns the Unicode of the character. The `hashCode` in the `String` class returns $s_0*31^{(n-1)} + s_1*31^{(n-2)} + \ldots + s_{n-1}$, where s_i is `s.charAt(i)`.

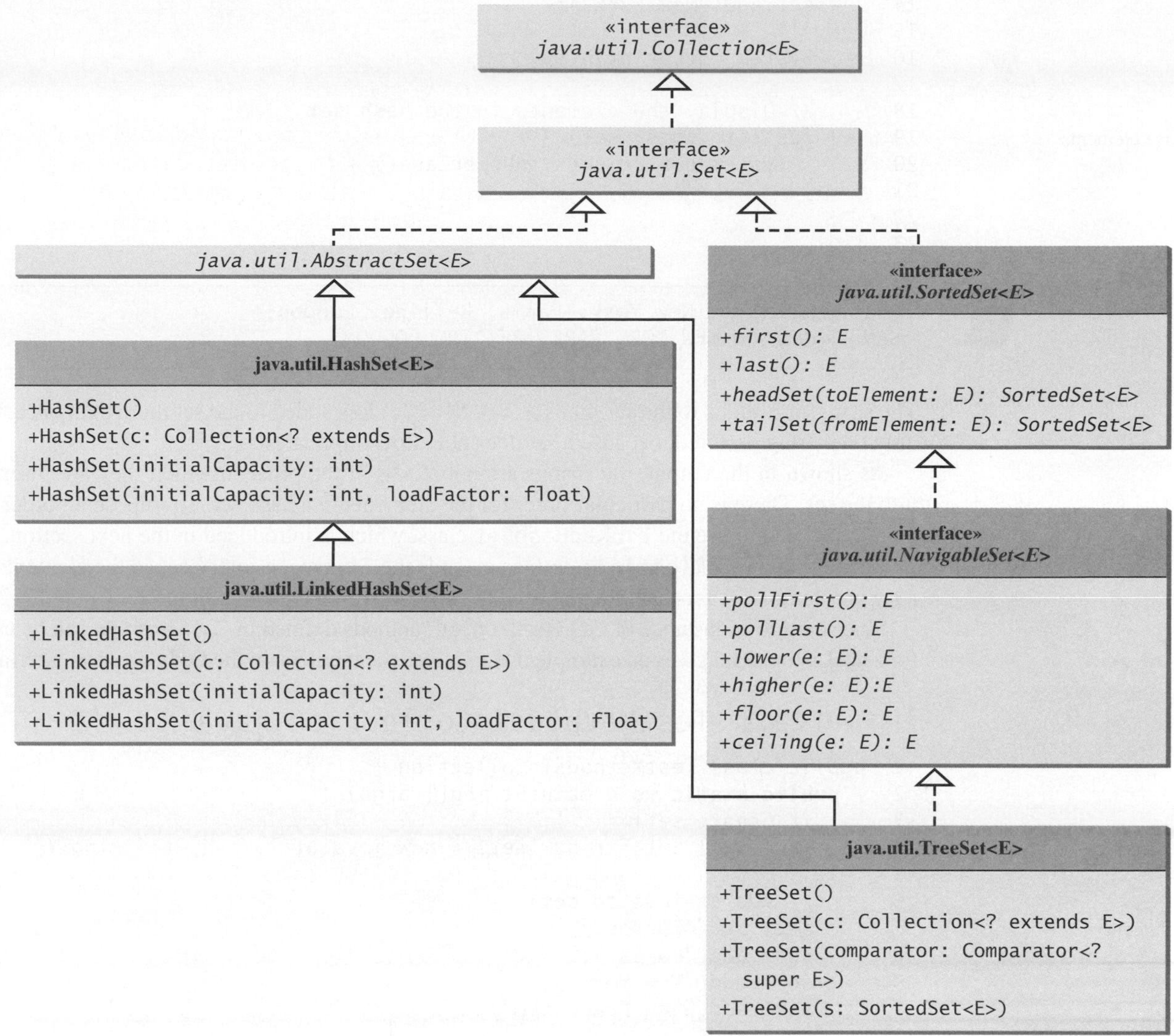

FIGURE 23.1 The Java Collections Framework provides three concrete set classes.

Listing 23.1 gives a program that creates a hash set to store strings and uses an iterator to traverse the elements in the set.

LISTING 23.1 TestHashSet.java

```
import java.util.*;

public class TestHashSet {
  public static void main(String[] args) {
    // Create a hash set
    Set<String> set = new HashSet<String>();

    // Add strings to the set
    set.add("London");
    set.add("Paris");
    set.add("New York");
    set.add("San Francisco");
    set.add("Beijing");
```

create set

add element

traverse elements

```
14       set.add("New York");
15
16       System.out.println(set);
17
18       // Display the elements in the hash set
19       for (String s: set) {
20         System.out.print(s.toUpperCase() + " ");
21       }
22     }
23   }
```

```
[San Francisco, New York, Paris, Beijing, London]
SAN FRANCISCO NEW YORK PARIS BEIJING LONDON
```

The strings are added to the set (lines 9–14). **New York** is added to the set more than once, but only one string is stored, because a set does not allow duplicates.

As shown in the output, the strings are not stored in the order in which they are inserted into the set. There is no particular order for the elements in a hash set. To impose an order on them, you need to use the **LinkedHashSet** class, which is introduced in the next section.

Recall that the **Collection** interface extends the **Iterable** interface, so the elements in a set are iterable. A for-each loop is used to traverse all the elements in the set (lines 19–21).

Since a set is an instance of **Collection**, all methods defined in **Collection** can be used for sets. Listing 23.2 gives an example that explores the methods in the **Collection** interface.

LISTING 23.2 TestMethodsInCollection.java

create a set · add element · get size · remove element · create a set · add element · contains element?

```
public class TestMethodsInCollection {
  public static void main(String[] args) {
    // Create set1
    java.util.Set<String> set1 = new java.util.HashSet<String>();

    // Add strings to set1
    set1.add("London");
    set1.add("Paris");
    set1.add("New York");
    set1.add("San Francisco");
    set1.add("Beijing");

    System.out.println("set1 is " + set1);
    System.out.println(set1.size() + " elements in set1");

    // Delete a string from set1
    set1.remove("London");
    System.out.println("\nset1 is " + set1);
    System.out.println(set1.size() + " elements in set1");

    // Create set2
    java.util.Set<String> set2 = new java.util.HashSet<String>();

    // Add strings to set2
    set2.add("London");
    set2.add("Shanghai");
    set2.add("Paris");
    System.out.println("\nset2 is " + set2);
    System.out.println(set2.size() + " elements in set2");

    System.out.println("\nIs Taipei in set2? "
      + set2.contains("Taipei"));
```

```
33
34         set1.addAll(set2);
35         System.out.println("\nAfter adding set2 to set1, set1 is "
36           + set1);
37
38         set1.removeAll(set2);
39         System.out.println("After removing set2 from set1, set1 is "
40           + set1);
41
42         set1.retainAll(set2);
43         System.out.println("After removing common elements in set2 "
44           + "from set1, set1 is " + set1);
45     }
46   }
```

addAll

removeAll

retainAll

```
set1 is [San Francisco, New York, Paris, Beijing, London]
5 elements in set1

set1 is [San Francisco, New York, Paris, Beijing]
4 elements in set1

set2 is [Shanghai, Paris, London]
3 elements in set2

Is Taipei in set2? false

After adding set2 to set1, set1 is
  [San Francisco, New York, Shanghai, Paris, Beijing, London]

After removing set2 from set1, set1 is
  [San Francisco, New York, Beijing]

After removing common elements in set2 from set1, set1 is []
```

The program creates two sets (lines 4, 22). The `size()` method returns the number of the elements in a set (line 14). Line 17

```
set1.remove("London");
```

removes `London` from `set1`.

The `contains` method (line 32) checks whether an element is in the set.

Line 34

```
set1.addAll(set2);
```

adds `set2` to `set1`. Therefore, `set1` becomes `[San Francisco, New York, Shanghai, Paris, Beijing, London]`.

Line 38

```
set1.removeAll(set2);
```

removes `set2` from `set1`. Thus, `set1` becomes `[San Francisco, New York, Beijing]`.

Line 42

```
set1.retainAll(set2);
```

retains the common elements in `set1`. Since `set1` and `set2` have no common elements, `set1` becomes empty.

23.2.2 LinkedHashSet

LinkedHashSet extends **HashSet** with a linked-list implementation that supports an ordering of the elements in the set. The elements in a **HashSet** are not ordered, but the elements in a **LinkedHashSet** can be retrieved in the order in which they were inserted into the set. A **LinkedHashSet** can be created by using one of its four constructors, as shown in Figure 23.1. These constructors are similar to the constructors for **HashSet**.

linked hash set

Listing 23.3 gives a test program for **LinkedHashSet**. The program simply replaces **HashSet** by **LinkedHashSet** in Listing 23.1.

LISTING 23.3 TestLinkedHashSet.java

create linked hash set
add element
display elements

```
 1 import java.util.*;
 2
 3 public class TestLinkedHashSet {
 4   public static void main(String[] args) {
 5     // Create a hash set
 6     Set<String> set = new LinkedHashSet<String>();
 7
 8     // Add strings to the set
 9     set.add("London");
10     set.add("Paris");
11     set.add("New York");
12     set.add("San Francisco");
13     set.add("Beijing");
14     set.add("New York");
15
16     System.out.println(set);
17
18     // Display the elements in the hash set
19     for (String element: set)
20       System.out.print(element.toLowerCase() + " ");
21   }
22 }
```

```
[London, Paris, New York, San Francisco, Beijing]
london paris new york san francisco beijing
```

A **LinkedHashSet** is created in line 6. As shown in the output, the strings are stored in the order in which they are inserted. Since **LinkedHashSet** is a set, it does not store duplicate elements.

The **LinkedHashSet** maintains the order in which the elements are inserted. To impose a different order (e.g., increasing or decreasing order), you can use the **TreeSet** class, which is introduced in the next section.

> **Tip**
>
> If you don't need to maintain the order in which the elements are inserted, use **HashSet**, which is more efficient than **LinkedHashSet**.

23.2.3 TreeSet

SortedSet is a subinterface of **Set**, which guarantees that the elements in the set are sorted. Additionally, it provides the methods **first()** and **last()** for returning the first and last elements in the set, and **headSet(toElement)** and **tailSet(fromElement)** for returning a portion of the set whose elements are less than **toElement** and greater than or equal to **fromElement**.

NavigableSet extends **SortedSet** to provide navigation methods **lower(e)**, **floor(e)**, **ceiling(e)**, and **higher(e)** that return elements respectively less than, less than or equal, greater than or equal, and greater than a given element and return **null** if there is no such element. The **pollFirst()** and **pollLast()** methods remove and return the first and last element in the tree set, respectively.

TreeSet implements the **SortedSet** interface. To create a **TreeSet**, use a constructor, as shown in Figure 23.1. You can add objects into a *tree set* as long as they can be compared with each other.

tree set

As discussed in Section 22.5, the elements can be compared in two ways: using the **Comparable** interface or the **Comparator** interface.

Listing 23.4 gives an example of ordering elements using the **Comparable** interface. The preceding example in Listing 23.3 displays all the strings in their insertion order. This example rewrites the preceding example to display the strings in alphabetical order using the **TreeSet** class.

LISTING 23.4 TestTreeSet.java

```
import java.util.*;

public class TestTreeSet {
  public static void main(String[] args) {
    // Create a hash set
    Set<String> set = new HashSet<String>();

    // Add strings to the set
    set.add("London");
    set.add("Paris");
    set.add("New York");
    set.add("San Francisco");
    set.add("Beijing");
    set.add("New York");

    TreeSet<String> treeSet = new TreeSet<String>(set);
    System.out.println("Sorted tree set: " + treeSet);

    // Use the methods in SortedSet interface
    System.out.println("first(): " + treeSet.first());
    System.out.println("last(): " + treeSet.last());
    System.out.println("headSet(\"New York\"): " +
      treeSet.headSet("New York"));
    System.out.println("tailSet(\"New York\"): " +
      treeSet.tailSet("New York"));

    // Use the methods in NavigableSet interface
    System.out.println("lower(\"P\"): " + treeSet.lower("P"));
    System.out.println("higher(\"P\"): " + treeSet.higher("P"));
    System.out.println("floor(\"P\"): " + treeSet.floor("P"));
    System.out.println("ceiling(\"P\"): " + treeSet.ceiling("P"));
    System.out.println("pollFirst(): " + treeSet.pollFirst());
    System.out.println("pollLast(): " + treeSet.pollLast());
    System.out.println("New tree set: " + treeSet);
  }
}
```

create hash set

create tree set

display elements

```
Sorted tree set: [Beijing, London, New York, Paris, San Francisco]
first(): Beijing
last(): San Francisco
```

```
headSet("New York"): [Beijing, London]
tailSet("New York"): [New York, Paris, San Francisco]
lower("P"): New York
higher("P"): Paris
floor("P"): New York
ceiling("P"): Paris
pollFirst(): Beijing
pollLast(): San Francisco
New tree set: [London, New York, Paris]
```

The example creates a hash set filled with strings, then creates a tree set for the same strings. The strings are sorted in the tree set using the `compareTo` method in the `Comparable` interface.

The elements in the set are sorted once you create a `TreeSet` object from a `HashSet` object using `new TreeSet<String>(set)` (line 16). You may rewrite the program to create an instance of `TreeSet` using its no-arg constructor, and add the strings into the `TreeSet` object.

`treeSet.first()` returns the first element in `treeSet` (line 20), and `treeSet.last()` returns the last element in `treeSet` (line 21). `treeSet.headSet("New York")` returns the elements in `treeSet` before New York (lines 22–23). `treeSet.tailSet("New York")` returns the elements in `treeSet` after New York, including New York (lines 24–25).

`treeSet.lower("P")` returns the largest element less than `P` in `treeSet` (line 28). `treeSet.higher("P")` returns the smallest element greater than `P` in `treeSet` (line 29). `treeSet.floor("P")` returns the largest element less than or equal to `P` in `treeSet` (line 30). `treeSet.ceiling("P")` returns the smallest element greater than or equal to `P` in `treeSet` (line 31). `treeSet.pollFirst()` removes the first element in `treeSet` and returns the removed element (line 32). `treeSet.pollLast()` removes the last element in `treeSet` and returns the removed element (line 33).

Note

All the concrete classes in Java Collections Framework (see Figure 22.1) have at least two constructors. One is the no-arg constructor that constructs an empty collection. The other constructs instances from a collection. Thus the `TreeSet` class has the constructor `TreeSet(Collection c)` for constructing a `TreeSet` from a collection `c`. In this example, `new TreeSet<String>(set)` creates an instance of `TreeSet` from the collection `set`.

Tip

If you don't need to maintain a sorted set when updating a set, you should use a hash set, because it takes less time to insert and remove elements in a hash set. When you need a sorted set, you can create a tree set from the hash set.

If you create a `TreeSet` using its no-arg constructor, the `compareTo` method is used to compare the elements in the set, assuming that the class of the elements implements the `Comparable` interface. To use a comparator, you have to use the constructor `TreeSet(Comparator comparator)` to create a sorted set that uses the `compare` method in the comparator to order the elements in the set.

Listing 23.5 gives a program that demonstrates how to sort elements in a tree set using the `Comparator` interface.

LISTING 23.5 TestTreeSetWithComparator.java

```
import java.util.*;

public class TestTreeSetWithComparator {
```

```
 4   public static void main(String[] args) {
 5     // Create a tree set for geometric objects using a comparator
 6     Set<GeometricObject> set =
 7       new TreeSet<GeometricObject>(new GeometricObjectComparator());
 8     set.add(new Rectangle(4, 5));
 9     set.add(new Circle(40));
10     set.add(new Circle(40));
11     set.add(new Rectangle(4, 1));
12
13     // Display geometric objects in the tree set
14     System.out.println("A sorted set of geometric objects");
15     for (GeometricObject element: set)
16       System.out.println("area = " + element.getArea());
17   }
18 }
```

tree set

display elements

```
A sorted set of geometric objects
area = 4.0
area = 20.0
area = 5023.548245743669
```

The **GeometricObjectComparator** class is defined in Listing 22.4. The program creates a tree set of geometric objects using the **GeometricObjectComparator** for comparing the elements in the set (lines 6–7).

The **Circle** and **Rectangle** classes were defined in Section 15.2, Abstract Classes. They are all subclasses of **GeometricObject**. They are added to the set (lines 8–11).

Two circles of the same radius are added to the tree set (lines 9–10), but only one is stored, because the two circles are equal and the set does not allow duplicates.

23.1 How do you create an instance of **Set**? How do you insert a new element in a set? How do you remove an element from a set? How do you find the size of a set?

23.2 If the two objects **o1** and **o2** are equal, what is **o1.equals(o2)** and **o1.hashCode() == o2.hashCode()**?

23.3 What are the differences between **HashSet**, **LinkedHashSet**, and **TreeSet**?

23.4 How do you traverse the elements in a set?

23.5 How do you sort the elements in a set using the **compareTo** method in the **Comparable** interface? How do you sort the elements in a set using the **Comparator** interface? What would happen if you added an element that could not be compared with the existing elements in a tree set?

23.6 Suppose that **set1** is a set that contains the strings **red**, **yellow**, and **green**, and that **set2** is another set that contains the strings **red**, **yellow**, and **blue**. Answer the following questions:

- What are in **set1** and **set2** after executing **set1.addAll(set2)**?
- What are in **set1** and **set2** after executing **set1.add(set2)**?
- What are in **set1** and **set2** after executing **set1.removeAll(set2)**?
- What are in **set1** and **set2** after executing **set1.remove(set2)**?
- What are in **set1** and **set2** after executing **set1.retainAll(set2)**?
- What is in **set1** after executing **set1.clear()**?

23.7 Show the output of the following code:

```
import java.util.*;

public class Test {
  public static void main(String[] args) {
    LinkedHashSet<String> set1 = new LinkedHashSet<String>();
    set1.add("New York");
    LinkedHashSet<String> set2 = set1;
    LinkedHashSet<String> set3 =
      (LinkedHashSet<String>)(set1.clone());
    set1.add("Atlanta");
    System.out.println("set1 is " + set1);
    System.out.println("set2 is " + set2);
    System.out.println("set3 is " + set3);
  }
}
```

23.8 Show the output of the following code:

```
import java.util.*;
import java.io.*;

public class Test {
  public static void main(String[] args) throws Exception {
    ObjectOutputStream output = new ObjectOutputStream(
      new FileOutputStream("c:\\test.dat"));
    LinkedHashSet<String> set1 = new LinkedHashSet<String>();
    set1.add("New York");
    LinkedHashSet<String> set2 =
      (LinkedHashSet<String>)set1.clone();
    set1.add("Atlanta");
    output.writeObject(set1);
    output.writeObject(set2);
    output.close();

    ObjectInputStream input = new ObjectInputStream(
      new FileInputStream("c:\\test.dat"));
    set1 = (LinkedHashSet<String>)input.readObject();
    set2 = (LinkedHashSet<String>)input.readObject();
    System.out.println(set1);
    System.out.println(set2);
    output.close();
  }
}
```

23.3 Comparing the Performance of Sets and Lists

Sets are more efficient than lists for storing nonduplicate elements. Lists are useful for accessing elements through the index.

The elements in a list can be accessed through the index. However, sets do not support indexing, because the elements in a set are unordered. To traverse all elements in a set, use a foreach loop. We now conduct an interesting experiment to test the performance of sets and lists. Listing 23.6 gives a program that shows the execution time of (1) testing whether an element is in a hash set, linked hash set, tree set, array list, and linked list, and (2) removing elements from a hash set, linked hash set, tree set, array list, and linked list.

LISTING 23.6 SetListPerformanceTest.java

```
import java.util.*;

public class SetListPerformanceTest {
  static final int N = 50000;

  public static void main(String[] args) {
    // Add numbers 0, 1, 2, ..., N - 1 to the array list
    List<Integer> list = new ArrayList<Integer>();
    for (int i = 0; i < N; i++)
      list.add(i);
    Collections.shuffle(list); // Shuffle the array list

    // Create a hash set, and test its performance
    Collection<Integer> set1 = new HashSet<Integer>(list);
    System.out.println("Member test time for hash set is " +
      getTestTime(set1) + " milliseconds");
    System.out.println("Remove element time for hash set is " +
      getRemoveTime(set1) + " milliseconds");

    // Create a linked hash set, and test its performance
    Collection<Integer> set2 = new LinkedHashSet<Integer>(list);
    System.out.println("Member test time for linked hash set is " +
      getTestTime(set2) + " milliseconds");
    System.out.println("Remove element time for linked hash set is "
      + getRemoveTime(set2) + " milliseconds");

    // Create a tree set, and test its performance
    Collection<Integer> set3 = new TreeSet<Integer>(list);
    System.out.println("Member test time for tree set is " +
      getTestTime(set3) + " milliseconds");
    System.out.println("Remove element time for tree set is " +
      getRemoveTime(set3) + " milliseconds");

    // Create an array list, and test its performance
    Collection<Integer> list1 = new ArrayList<Integer>(list);
    System.out.println("Member test time for array list is " +
      getTestTime(list1) + " milliseconds");
    System.out.println("Remove element time for array list is " +
      getRemoveTime(list1) + " milliseconds");

    // Create a linked list, and test its performance
    Collection<Integer> list2 = new LinkedList<Integer>(list);
    System.out.println("Member test time for linked list is " +
      getTestTime(list2) + " milliseconds");
    System.out.println("Remove element time for linked list is " +
      getRemoveTime(list2) + " milliseconds");
  }

  public static long getTestTime(Collection<Integer> c) {
    long startTime = System.currentTimeMillis();

    // Test if a number is in the collection
    for (int i = 0; i < N; i++)
      c.contains((int)(Math.random() * 2 * N));

    return System.currentTimeMillis() - startTime;
  }

```

create test data

shuffle

a hash set

a linked hash set

a tree set

an array list

a linked list

start time

test membership

return execution time

```
59   public static long getRemoveTime(Collection<Integer> c) {
60     long startTime = System.currentTimeMillis();
61
62     for (int i = 0; i < N; i++)
63       c.remove(i);                                    // remove from container
64
65     return System.currentTimeMillis() - startTime;    // return execution time
66   }
67 }
```

```
Member test time for hash set is 20 milliseconds
Remove element time for hash set is 27 milliseconds
Member test time for linked hash set is 27 milliseconds
Remove element time for linked hash set is 26 milliseconds
Member test time for tree set is 47 milliseconds
Remove element time for tree set is 34 milliseconds
Member test time for array list is 39802 milliseconds
Remove element time for array list is 16196 milliseconds
Member test time for linked list is 52197 milliseconds
Remove element time for linked list is 14870 milliseconds
```

The program creates a list for numbers from `0` to `N-1` (for `N` = `50000`) (lines 8–10) and shuffles the list (line 11). From this list, the program creates a hash set (line 14), a linked hash set (line 21), a tree set (line 28), an array list (line 35), and a linked list (line 42). The program obtains the execution time for testing whether a number is in the hash set (line 16), linked hash set (line 23), tree set (line 30), array list (line 37), and linked list (line 44), and obtains the execution time for removing the elements from the hash set (line 18), linked hash set (line 25), tree set (line 32), array list (line 39), and linked list (line 46).

The `getTestTime` method invokes the `contains` method to test whether a number is in the container (line 54) and the `getRemoveTime` method invokes the `remove` method to remove an element from the container (line 63).

sets are better

As these runtimes illustrate, sets are much more efficient than lists for testing whether an element is in a set or a list. Therefore, the No-Fly list should be implemented using a set instead of a list, because it is much faster to test whether an element is in a set than in a list.

You may wonder why sets are more efficient than lists. The questions will be answered in Chapters 26 and 28 when we introduce the implementations of lists and sets.

MyProgrammingLab™

23.9 Suppose you need to write a program that stores non-duplicate elements, what data structure should you use?

23.10 Suppose you need to write a program that stores non-duplicate elements in the order of insertion, what data structure should you use?

23.11 Suppose you need to write a program that stores non-duplicate elements in increasing order of the element values, what data structure should you use?

23.12 Suppose you need to write a program that stores a fixed number of the elements (possibly duplicates), what data structure should you use?

23.13 Suppose you need to write a program that stores the elements in a list with frequent operations to add and insert elements at the end of the list, what data structure should you use?

23.14 Suppose you need to write a program that stores the elements in a list with frequent operations to add and insert elements at the beginning of the list, what data structure should you use?

23.4 Case Study: Counting Keywords

This section presents an application that counts the number of the keywords in a Java source file.

For each word in a Java source file, we need to determine whether the word is a keyword. To handle this efficiently, store all the keywords in a **HashSet** and use the **contains** method to test if a word is in the keyword set. Listing 23.7 gives this program.

LISTING 23.7 CountKeywords.java

```
import java.util.*;
import java.io.*;

public class CountKeywords {
  public static void main(String[] args) throws Exception {
    Scanner input = new Scanner(System.in);
    System.out.print("Enter a Java source file: ");
    String filename = input.nextLine();

    File file = new File(filename);
    if (file.exists()) {
      System.out.println("The number of keywords in " + filename
        + " is " + countKeywords(file));
    }
    else {
      System.out.println("File " + filename + " does not exist");
    }
  }

  public static int countKeywords(File file) throws Exception {
    // Array of all Java keywords + true, false and null
    String[] keywordString = {"abstract", "assert", "boolean",
        "break", "byte", "case", "catch", "char", "class", "const",
        "continue", "default", "do", "double", "else", "enum",
        "extends", "for", "final", "finally", "float", "goto",
        "if", "implements", "import", "instanceof", "int",
        "interface", "long", "native", "new", "package", "private",
        "protected", "public", "return", "short", "static",
        "strictfp", "super", "switch", "synchronized", "this",
        "throw", "throws", "transient", "try", "void", "volatile",
        "while", "true", "false", "null"};

    Set<String> keywordSet =
      new HashSet<String>(Arrays.asList(keywordString));
    int count = 0;

    Scanner input = new Scanner(file);

    while (input.hasNext()) {
      String word = input.next();
      if (keywordSet.contains(word))
        count++;
    }

    return count;
  }
}
```

enter a filename

file exists?

count keywords

keywords

keyword set

is a keyword?

```
Enter a Java source file: c:\Welcome.java ↵Enter
The number of keywords in c:\Welcome.java is 5
```

```
Enter a Java source file: c:\TTT.java ↵Enter
File c:\TTT.java does not exist
```

The program prompts the user to enter a Java source filename (line 7) and reads the filename (line 8). If the file exists, the **countKeywords** method is invoked to count the keywords in the file (line 13).

The **countKeywords** method creates an array of strings for the keywords (lines 22–31) and creates a hash set from this array (lines 33–34). It then reads each word from the file and tests if the word is in the set (line 41). If so, the program increases the count by **1** (line 42).

You may rewrite the program to use a **LinkedHashSet**, **TreeSet**, **ArrayList**, or **LinkedList** to store the keywords. However, using a **HashSet** is the most efficient for this program.

23.15 Will the **CountKeywords** program work if lines 33–34 are changed to

```
Set<String> keywordSet =
  new LinkedHashSet<String>(Arrays.asList(keywordString));
```

23.16 Will the **CountKeywords** program work if lines 33–34 are changed to

```
List<String> keywordSet =
  new ArrayList<String>(Arrays.asList(keywordString));
```

23.5 Maps

You can create a map using one of its three concrete classes: **HashMap**, **LinkedHashMap**, *or* **TreeMap**.

map

A *map* is a container object that stores a collection of key/value pairs. It enables fast retrieval, deletion, and updating of the pair through the key. A map stores the values along with the keys. The keys are like indexes. In **List**, the indexes are integers. In **Map**, the keys can be any objects. A map cannot contain duplicate keys. Each key maps to one value. A key and its corresponding value form an entry stored in a map, as shown in Figure 23.2a. Figure 23.2b shows a map in which each entry consists of a Social Security number as the key and a name as the value.

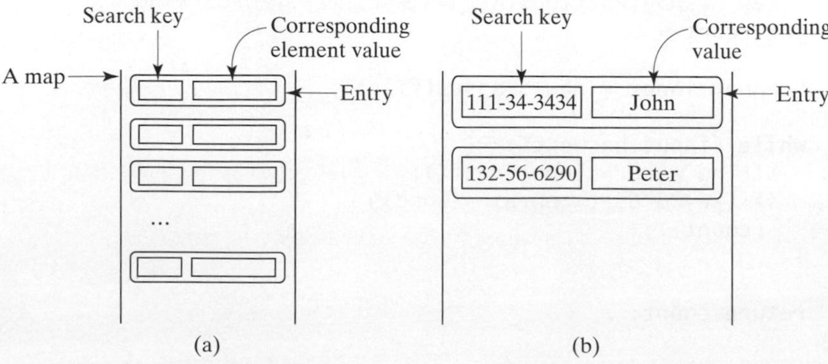

FIGURE 23.2 The entries consisting of key/value pairs are stored in a map.

There are three types of maps: `HashMap`, `LinkedHashMap`, and `TreeMap`. The common features of these maps are defined in the `Map` interface. Their relationship is shown in Figure 23.3.

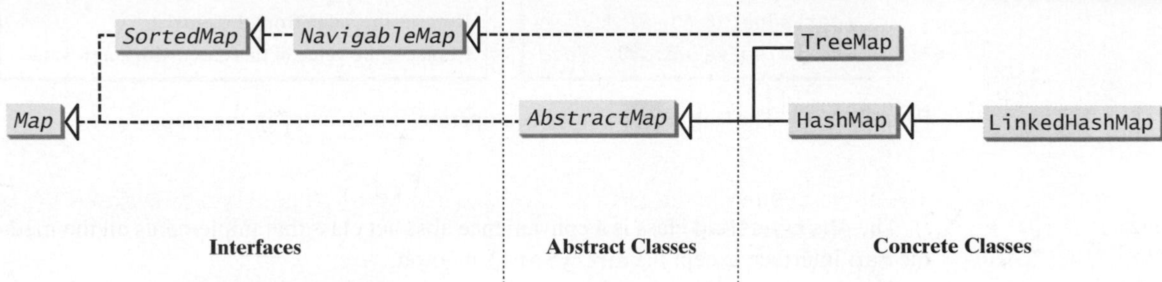

FIGURE 23.3 A map stores key/value pairs.

The `Map` interface provides the methods for querying, updating, and obtaining a collection of values and a set of keys, as shown in Figure 23.4.

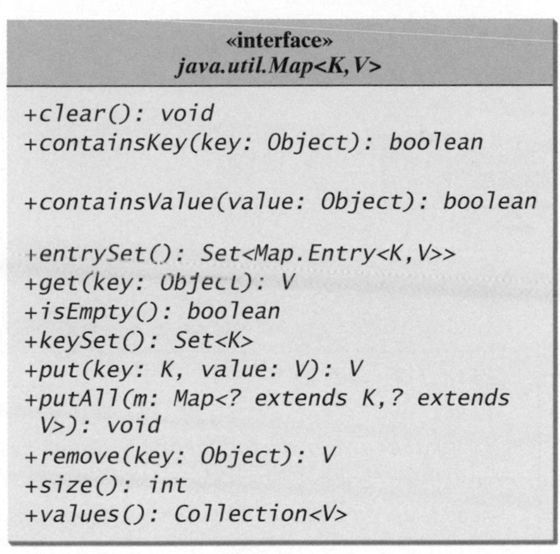

Removes all entries from this map.
Returns true if this map contains an entry for the specified key.
Returns true if this map maps one or more keys to the specified value.
Returns a set consisting of the entries in this map.
Returns the value for the specified key in this map.
Returns true if this map contains no entries.
Returns a set consisting of the keys in this map.
Puts an entry into this map.
Adds all the entries from `m` to this map.
Removes the entries for the specified key.
Returns the number of entries in this map.
Returns a collection consisting of the values in this map.

FIGURE 23.4 The `Map` interface maps keys to values.

update methods

The *update methods* include `clear`, `put`, `putAll`, and `remove`. The `clear()` method removes all entries from the map. The `put(K key, V value)` method associates a value with a key in the map. If the map formerly contained an entry for this key, the old value is replaced by the new value and the old value associated with the key is returned. The `putAll(Map m)` method adds all entries in `m` to this map. The `remove(Object key)` method removes the entry for the specified key from the map.

query methods

The *query methods* include `containsKey`, `containsValue`, `isEmpty`, and `size`. The `containsKey(Object key)` method checks whether the map contains an entry for the specified key. The `containsValue(Object value)` method checks whether the map contains an entry for this value. The `isEmpty()` method checks whether the map contains any entries. The `size()` method returns the number of entries in the map.

`keySet()`
`values()`
`entrySet()`

You can obtain a set of the keys in the map using the `keySet()` method, and a collection of the values in the map using the `values()` method. The `entrySet()` method returns a set of objects that implement the `Map.Entry<K, V>` interface, where `Entry` is an inner interface for the `Map` interface, as shown in Figure 23.5. Each object in the set is a specific key/value pair in the underlying map.

«interface» *java.util.Map.Entry<K,V>*	
`+getKey(): K`	Returns the key from this entry.
`+getValue(): V`	Returns the value from this entry.
`+setValue(value: V): void`	Replaces the value in this entry with a new value.

FIGURE 23.5 The `Map.Entry` interface operates on an entry in the map.

`AbstractMap`

The `AbstractMap` class is a convenience abstract class that implements all the methods in the `Map` interface except the `entrySet()` method.

The `SortedMap` interface extends the `Map` interface to maintain the entries in ascending order of keys with the additional methods `firstKey()` and `lastKey()` for returning the lowest and highest key, `headMap(toKey)` for returning the portion of the map whose keys are less than `toKey`, and `tailMap(fromKey)` for returning the portion of the map whose keys are greater than or equal to `fromKey`.

concrete implementation

The `HashMap`, `LinkedHashMap`, and `TreeMap` classes are three *concrete implementations* of the `Map` interface, as shown in Figure 23.6.

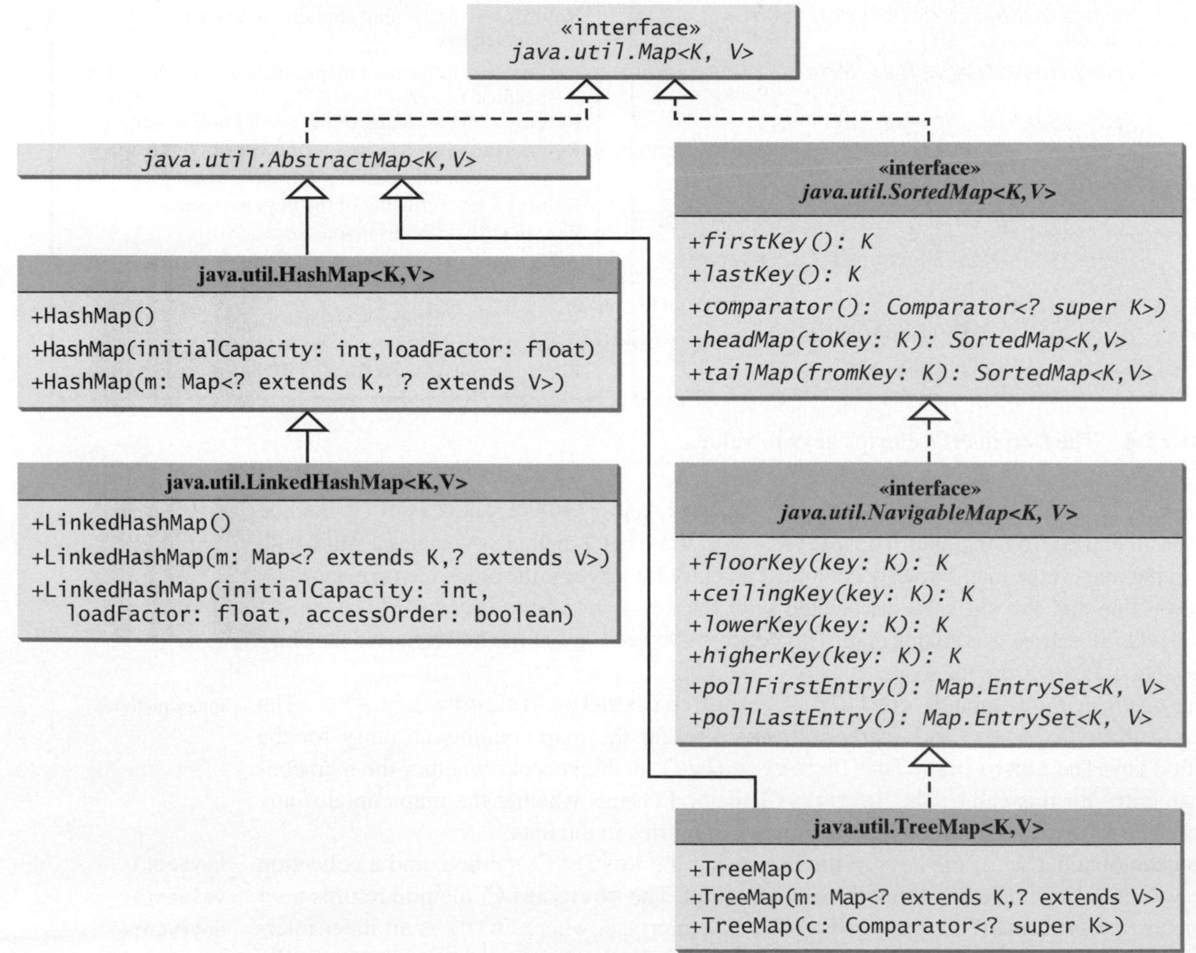

FIGURE 23.6 The Java Collections Framework provides three concrete map classes.

HashMap
LinkedHashMap
insertion order
access order

The `HashMap` class is efficient for locating a value, inserting an entry, and deleting an entry. `LinkedHashMap` extends `HashMap` with a linked-list implementation that supports an ordering of the entries in the map. The entries in a `HashMap` are not ordered, but the entries in a `LinkedHashMap` can be retrieved either in the order in which they were inserted into the map (known as the *insertion order*) or in the order in which they were last accessed, from least recently to most recently accessed (*access order*). The no-arg constructor constructs a `LinkedHashMap` with the insertion order. To construct a `LinkedHashMap` with the access order, use `LinkedHashMap(initialCapacity, loadFactor, true)`.

TreeMap

The `TreeMap` class is efficient for traversing the keys in a sorted order. The keys can be sorted using the `Comparable` interface or the `Comparator` interface. If you create a `TreeMap` using its no-arg constructor, the `compareTo` method in the `Comparable` interface is used to compare the keys in the map, assuming that the class for the keys implements the `Comparable` interface. To use a comparator, you have to use the `TreeMap(Comparator comparator)` constructor to create a sorted map that uses the `compare` method in the comparator to order the entries in the map based on the keys.

SortedMap

`SortedMap` is a subinterface of `Map`, which guarantees that the entries in the map are sorted. Additionally, it provides the methods `firstKey()` and `lastKey()` for returning the first and last keys in the map, and `headMap(toKey)` and `tailMap(fromKey)` for returning a portion of the map whose keys are less than `toKey` and greater than or equal to `fromKey`.

NavigableMap

`NavigableMap` extends `SortedMap` to provide the navigation methods `lowerKey(key)`, `floorKey(key)`, `ceilingKey(key)`, and `higherKey(key)` that return keys respectively less than, less than or equal, greater than or equal, and greater than a given key and return `null` if there is no such key. The `pollFirstEntry()` and `pollLastEntry()` methods remove and return the first and last entry in the tree map, respectively.

Note

Hashtable

Prior to Java 2, `java.util.Hashtable` was used for mapping keys with values. `Hashtable` was redesigned to fit into the Java Collections Framework with all its methods retained for compatibility. `Hashtable` implements the `Map` interface and is used in the same way as `HashMap`, except that `Hashtable` is synchronized.

hash map
linked hash map
tree map

Listing 23.8 gives an example that creates a *hash map*, a *linked hash map*, and a *tree map* for mapping students to ages. The program first creates a hash map with the student's name as its key and the age as its value. The program then creates a tree map from the hash map and displays the entries in ascending order of the keys. Finally, the program creates a linked hash map, adds the same entries to the map, and displays the entries.

Listing 23.8 TestMap.java

create map
add entry
tree map

```
import java.util.*;

public class TestMap {
  public static void main(String[] args) {
    // Create a HashMap
    Map<String, Integer> hashMap = new HashMap<String, Integer>();
    hashMap.put("Smith", 30);
    hashMap.put("Anderson", 31);
    hashMap.put("Lewis", 29);
    hashMap.put("Cook", 29);

    System.out.println("Display entries in HashMap");
    System.out.println(hashMap + "\n");

    // Create a TreeMap from the preceding HashMap
    Map<String, Integer> treeMap =
      new TreeMap<String, Integer>(hashMap);
```

linked hash map

```
18     System.out.println("Display entries in ascending order of key");
19     System.out.println(treeMap);
20 
21     // Create a LinkedHashMap
22     Map<String, Integer> linkedHashMap =
23       new LinkedHashMap<String, Integer>(16, 0.75f, true);
24     linkedHashMap.put("Smith", 30);
25     linkedHashMap.put("Anderson", 31);
26     linkedHashMap.put("Lewis", 29);
27     linkedHashMap.put("Cook", 29);
28 
29     // Display the age for Lewis
30     System.out.println("\nThe age for " + "Lewis is " +
31       linkedHashMap.get("Lewis"));
32 
33     System.out.println("Display entries in LinkedHashMap");
34     System.out.println(linkedHashMap);
35   }
36 }
```

```
Display entries in HashMap
{Cook=29, Smith=30, Lewis=29, Anderson=31}

Display entries in ascending order of key
{Anderson=31, Cook=29, Lewis=29, Smith=30}

The age for Lewis is 29
Display entries in LinkedHashMap
{Smith=30, Anderson=31, Cook=29, Lewis=29}
```

As shown in the output, the entries in the **HashMap** are in random order. The entries in the **TreeMap** are in increasing order of the keys. The entries in the **LinkedHashMap** are in the order of their access, from least recently accessed to most recently.

All the concrete classes that implement the **Map** interface have at least two constructors. One is the no-arg constructor that constructs an empty map, and the other constructs a map from an instance of **Map**. Thus, **new TreeMap<String, Integer>(hashMap)** (lines 16–17) constructs a tree map from a hash map.

You can create an insertion-ordered or access-ordered linked hash map. An access-ordered linked hash map is created in lines 22–23. The most recently accessed entry is placed at the end of the map. The entry with the key **Lewis** is last accessed in line 31, so it is displayed last in line 34.

Tip

If you don't need to maintain an order in a map when updating it, use a **HashMap**. When you need to maintain the insertion order or access order in the map, use a **LinkedHashMap**. When you need the map to be sorted on keys, use a **TreeMap**.

MyProgrammingLab™

23.17 How do you create an instance of **Map**? How do you add an entry to a map consisting of a key and a value? How do you remove an entry from a map? How do you find the size of a map? How do you traverse entries in a map?

23.18 Describe and compare **HashMap**, **LinkedHashMap**, and **TreeMap**.

23.19 Show the printout of the following code:

```
public class Test {
  public static void main(String[] args) {
```

```
        Map map = new LinkedHashMap();
        map.put("123", "John Smith");
        map.put("111", "George Smith");
        map.put("123", "Steve Yao");
        map.put("222", "Steve Yao");
        System.out.println("(1) " + map);
        System.out.println("(2) " + new TreeMap(map));
      }
    }
```

23.6 Case Study: Occurrences of Words

This case study writes a program that counts the occurrences of words in a text and displays the words and their occurrences in alphabetical order of the words.

The program uses a **TreeMap** to store an entry consisting of a word and its count. For each word, check whether it is already a key in the map. If not, add an entry to the map with the word as the key and value **1**. Otherwise, increase the value for the word (key) by **1** in the map. Assume the words are case insensitive; e.g., **Good** is treated the same as **good**.

Listing 23.9 gives the solution to the problem.

LISTING 23.9 CountOccurrenceOfWords.java

```
import java.util.*;

public class CountOccurrenceOfWords {
  public static void main(String[] args) {
    // Set text in a string
    String text = "Good morning. Have a good class. " +
      "Have a good visit. Have fun!";

    // Create a TreeMap to hold words as key and count as value
    Map<String, Integer> map = new TreeMap<String, Integer>();      tree map

    String[] words = text.split("[ \n\t\r.,;:!?(){}]");              split string
    for (int i = 0; i < words.length; i++) {
      String key = words[i].toLowerCase();

      if (key.length() > 0) {
        if (!map.containsKey(key)) {
          map.put(key, 1);                                           add entry
        }
        else {
          int value = map.get(key);
          value++;
          map.put(key, value);                                       add entry
        }
      }
    }

    // Get all entries into a set
    Set<Map.Entry<String, Integer>> entrySet = map.entrySet();      entry set

    // Get key and value from each entry
    for (Map.Entry<String, Integer> entry: entrySet)
      System.out.println(entry.getKey() + "\t" + entry.getValue()); display entry
  }
}
```

```
a           2
class       1
fun         1
good        3
have        3
morning     1
visit       1
```

The program creates a **TreeMap** (line 10) to store pairs of words and their occurrence counts. The words serve as the keys. Since all values in the map must be stored as objects, the count is wrapped in an **Integer** object.

The program extracts a word from a text using the **split** method (line 12) in the **String** class (see Section 9.2.7). For each word extracted, the program checks whether it is already stored as a key in the map (line 17). If not, a new pair consisting of the word and its initial count (**1**) is stored in the map (line 18). Otherwise, the count for the word is incremented by **1** (lines 21–23).

The program obtains the entries of the map in a set (line 29), and traverses the set to display the count and the key in each entry (lines 32–33).

Since the map is a tree map, the entries are displayed in increasing order of words. To display them in ascending order of the occurrence counts, see Programming Exercise 23.8.

Now sit back and think how you would write this program without using map. Your new program would be longer and more complex. You will find that map is a very efficient and powerful data structure for solving problems such as this.

23.20 Will the **CountOccurrenceOfWords** program work if line 10 is changed to

```
Map<String, int> map = new TreeMap<String, int>();
```

23.21 Will the **CountOccurrenceOfWords** program work if line 17 is changed to

```
if (map.get(key) == null) {
```

23.22 Will the **CountOccurrenceOfWords** program work if lines 32–33 are changed to

```
for (String key: map)
  System.out.println(key + "\t" + map.getValue(key));
```

23.7 Singleton and Unmodifiable Collections and Maps

You can create singleton sets, lists, and maps and unmodifiable sets, lists, and maps using the static methods in the **Collections** *class.*

The **Collections** class contains the static methods for lists and collections. It also contains the methods for creating immutable singleton sets, lists, and maps, and for creating read-only sets, lists, and maps, as shown in Figure 23.7.

The **Collections** class defines three constants—**EMPTY_SET**, **EMPTY_LIST**, and **EMPTY_MAP**—for an empty set, an empty list, and an empty map. These collections are immutable. The class also provides the **singleton(Object o)** method for creating an immutable set containing only a single item, the **singletonList(Object o)** method for creating an immutable list containing only a single item, and the **singletonMap(Object key, Object value)** method for creating an immutable map containing only a single entry.

read-only view

The **Collections** class also provides six static methods for returning *read-only views for collections*: **unmodifiableCollection(Collection c)**, **unmodifiableList(List list)**, **unmodifiableMap(Map m)**, **unmodifiableSet(Set set)**, **unmodifiableSortedMap(SortedMap m)**, and **unmodifiableSortedSet(SortedSet s)**. This type of view is like a reference to the actual collection. But you cannot modify the

java.util.Collections	
+singleton(o: Object): Set	Returns an immutable set containing the specified object.
+singletonList(o: Object): List	Returns an immutable list containing the specified object.
+singletonMap(key: Object, value: Object): Map	Returns an immutable map with the key and value pair.
+unmodifiableCollection(c: Collection): Collection	Returns a read-only view of the collection.
+unmodifiableList(list: List): List	Returns a read-only view of the list.
+unmodifiableMap(m: Map): Map	Returns a read-only view of the map.
+unmodifiableSet(s: Set): Set	Returns a read-only view of the set.
+unmodifiableSortedMap(s: SortedMap): SortedMap	Returns a read-only view of the sorted map.
+unmodifiableSortedSet(s: SortedSet): SortedSet	Returns a read-only view of the sorted set.

FIGURE 23.7 The `Collections` class contains the static methods for creating singleton and read-only sets, lists, and maps.

collection through a read-only view. Attempting to modify a collection through a read-only view will cause an `UnsupportedOperationException`.

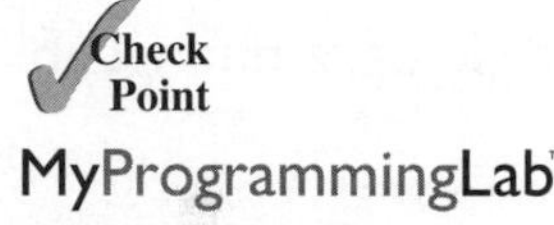

23.23 What is wrong in the following code?

```
Set<String> set = Collections.singleton("Chicago");
set.add("Dallas");
```

23.24 What happens when you run the following code?

```
List list = Collections.unmodifiableList(Arrays.asList("Chicago",
  "Boston"));
list.remove("Dallas");
```

KEY TERMS

CHAPTER SUMMARY

1. A set stores nonduplicate elements. To allow duplicate elements to be stored in a collection, you need to use a list.

2. A *map* stores key/value pairs. It provides a quick lookup for a value using a key.

3. Three types of sets are supported: `HashSet`, `LinkedHashSet`, and `TreeSet`. `HashSet` stores elements in an unpredictable order. `LinkedHashSet` stores elements in the order they were inserted. `TreeSet` stores elements sorted. All the methods in `HashSet`, `LinkedHashSet`, and `TreeSet` are inherited from the `Collection` interface.

4. The `Map` interface maps keys to the elements. The keys are like indexes. In `List`, the indexes are integers. In `Map`, the keys can be any objects. A map cannot contain duplicate keys. Each key can map to at most one value. The `Map` interface provides the methods for querying, updating, and obtaining a collection of values and a set of keys.

5. Three types of maps are supported: `HashMap`, `LinkedHashMap`, and `TreeMap`. `HashMap` is efficient for locating a value, inserting an entry, and deleting an entry. `LinkedHashMap` supports ordering of the entries in the map. The entries in a `HashMap` are not ordered, but the entries in a `LinkedHashMap` can be retrieved either in the order in which they were inserted into the map (known as the *insertion order*) or in the order in which they were last accessed, from least recently accessed to most recently (*access order*). `TreeMap` is efficient for traversing the keys in a sorted order. The keys can be sorted using the `Comparable` interface or the `Comparator` interface.

Test Questions

Do the test questions for this chapter online at www.cs.armstrong.edu/liang/intro9e/test.html.

MyProgrammingLab™

Programming Exercises

Sections 23.2–23.4

23.1 (*Perform set operations on hash sets*) Create two hash sets {`"George"`, `"Jim"`, `"John"`, `"Blake"`, `"Kevin"`, `"Michael"`} and {`"George"`, `"Katie"`, `"Kevin"`, `"Michelle"`, `"Ryan"`} and find their union, difference, and intersection. (You can clone the sets to preserve the original sets from being changed by these set methods.)

23.2 (*Display nonduplicate words in ascending order*) Write a program that reads words from a text file and displays all the nonduplicate words in ascending order. The text file is passed as a command-line argument.

****23.3** (*Count the keywords in Java source code*) Revise the program in Listing 23.7. If a keyword is in a comment or in a string, don't count it. Pass the Java file name from the command line. Assume that the Java source code is correct and line comments and paragraph comments do not overlap.

***23.4** (*Count consonants and vowels*) Write a program that prompts the user to enter a text file name and displays the number of vowels and consonants in the file. Use a set to store the vowels `A`, `E`, `I`, `O`, and `U`.

*****23.5** (*Syntax highlighting*) Write a program that converts a Java file into an HTML file. In the HTML file, the keywords, comments, and literals are displayed in bold navy, green, and blue, respectively. Use the command line to pass a Java file and an HTML file. For example, the following command

```
java Exercise23_05 Welcome.java Welcome.html
```

converts **Welcome.java** into **Welcome.html**. Figure 23.8a shows a Java file. The corresponding HTML file is shown in Figure 23.8b.

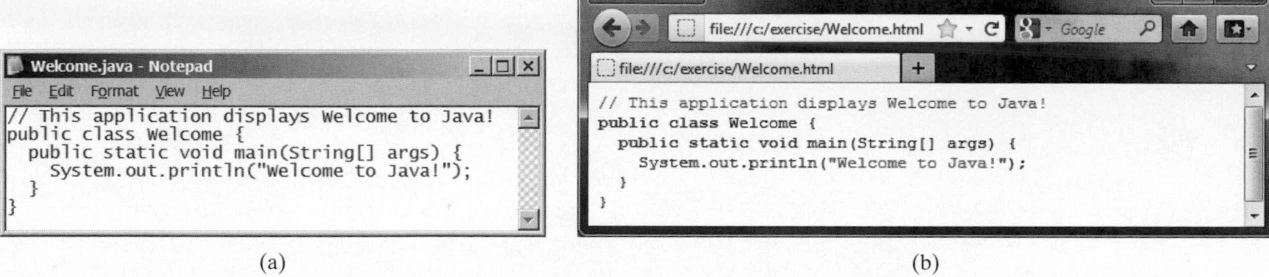

FIGURE 23.8 The Java code in plain text in (a) is displayed in HTML with syntax highlighted in (b).

Sections 23.5–23.7

***23.6** (*Count the occurrences of numbers entered*) Write a program that reads an unspecified number of integers and finds the one that has the most occurrences. The input ends when the input is `0`. For example, if you entered `2 3 40 3 5 4 -3 3 3 2 0`, the number `3` occurred most often. If not one but several numbers have the most occurrences, all of them should be reported. For example, since `9` and `3` appear twice in the list `9 30 3 9 3 2 4`, both occurrences should be reported.

****23.7** (*Revise Listing 23.9, CountOccurrenceOfWords.java*) Rewrite Listing 23.9 to display the words in ascending order of occurrence counts.

(*Hint*: Create a class named `WordOccurrence` that implements the `Comparable` interface. The class contains two fields, `word` and `count`. The `compareTo` method compares the counts. For each pair in the hash set in Listing 23.9, create an instance of `WordOccurrence` and store it in an array list. Sort the array list using the `Collections.sort` method. What would be wrong if you stored the instances of `WordOccurrence` in a tree set?)

****23.8** (*Count the occurrences of words in a text file*) Rewrite Listing 23.9 to read the text from a text file. The text file is passed as a command-line argument. Words are delimited by whitespace, punctuation marks (`, ; . : ?`), quotation marks (`' "`), and parentheses. Count words in case-insensitive fashion (e.g., consider `Good` and `good` to be the same word). The words must start with a letter. Display the output in alphabetical order of words, with each word preceded by its occurrence count.

****23.9** (*Guess the capitals using maps*) Rewrite Programming Exercise 9.17 to store pairs of each state and its capital in a map. Your program should prompt the user to enter a state and should display the capital for the state.

***23.10** (*Count the occurrences of each keyword*) Rewrite Listing 23.7 CountKeywords.java to read in a Java source code file and count the occurrence of each keyword in the file, but don't count the keyword if it is in a comment or in a string literal.

CHAPTER

24

Developing Efficient Algorithms

Objectives

- To estimate algorithm efficiency using the Big *O* notation (§24.2).
- To explain growth rates and why constants and nondominating terms can be ignored in the estimation (§24.2).
- To determine the complexity of various types of algorithms (§24.3).
- To analyze the binary search algorithm (§24.4.1).
- To analyze the selection sort algorithm (§24.4.2).
- To analyze the insertion sort algorithm (§24.4.3).
- To analyze the Towers of Hanoi algorithm (§24.4.4).
- To describe common growth functions (constant, logarithmic, log-linear, quadratic, cubic, exponential) (§24.4.5).
- To design efficient algorithms for finding Fibonacci numbers using dynamic programming (§24.5).
- To find the GCD using Euclid's algorithm (§24.6).
- To find prime numbers using the sieve of Eratosthenes (§24.7).
- To design efficient algorithms for finding the closest pair of points using the divide-and-conquer approach (§24.8).
- To solve the Eight Queens problem using the backtracking approach (§24.9).
- To design efficient algorithms for finding a convex hull for a set of points (§24.10).

24.1 Introduction

Algorithm design is to develop a mathematical process for solving a program. Algorithm analysis is to predict the performance of an algorithm.

The preceding two chapters introduced classic data structures (lists, stacks, queues, priority queues, sets, and maps) and applied them to solve problems. This chapter will use a variety of examples to introduce common algorithmic techniques (dynamic programming, divide-and-conquer, and backtracking) for developing efficient algorithms. Later in the book, we will introduce efficient algorithms for trees and graphs in Chapters 27, 29, 30, and 31. Before introducing developing efficient algorithms, we need to address the question on how to measure algorithm efficiency.

24.2 Measuring Algorithm Efficiency Using Big *O* Notation

The Big O *notation obtains a function for measuring algorithm time complexity based on the input size. You can ignore multiplicative constants and nondominating terms in the function.*

Suppose two algorithms perform the same task, such as search (linear search vs. binary search) or sort (selection sort vs. insertion sort). Which one is better? To answer this question, you might implement these algorithms and run the programs to get execution time. But there are two problems with this approach:

what is algorithm efficiency?

- First, many tasks run concurrently on a computer. The execution time of a particular program depends on the system load.
- Second, the execution time depends on specific input. Consider, for example, linear search and binary search. If an element to be searched happens to be the first in the list, linear search will find the element quicker than binary search.

It is very difficult to compare algorithms by measuring their execution time. To overcome these problems, a theoretical approach was developed to analyze algorithms independent of computers and specific input. This approach approximates the effect of a change on the size of the input. In this way, you can see how fast an algorithm's execution time increases as the input size increases, so you can compare two algorithms by examining their *growth rates*.

growth rates

Consider linear search. The linear search algorithm compares the key with the elements in the array sequentially until the key is found or the array is exhausted. If the key is not in the array, it requires n comparisons for an array of size n. If the key is in the array, it requires $n/2$ comparisons on average. The algorithm's execution time is proportional to the size of the array. If you double the size of the array, you will expect the number of comparisons to double. The algorithm grows at a linear rate. The growth rate has an order of magnitude of n. Computer scientists use the Big O notation to represent the "order of magnitude." Using this notation, the complexity of the linear search algorithm is $O(n)$, pronounced as "*order of n*."

Big *O* notation

For the same input size, an algorithm's execution time may vary, depending on the input. An input that results in the shortest execution time is called the *best-case input*, and an input that results in the longest execution time is the *worst-case input*. Best-case analysis and worst-case analysis are to analyze the algorithms for their best-case input and worst-case input. Best-case and worst-case analysis are not representative, but worst-case analysis is very useful. You can be assured that the algorithm will never be slower than the worst case. An *average-case analysis* attempts to determine the average amount of time among all possible inputs of the same size. Average-case analysis is ideal, but difficult to perform, because for many problems it is hard to determine the relative probabilities and distributions of various

best-case input

worst-case input

average-case analysis

TABLE 24.1 Growth Rates

n \ $f(n)$	n	$n/2$	$100n$	
100	100	50	10000	
200	200	100	20000	
	2	2	2	$f(200) / f(100)$

input instances. Worst-case analysis is easier to perform, so the analysis is generally conducted for the worst case.

The linear search algorithm requires n comparisons in the worst case and $n/2$ comparisons in the average case if you are nearly always looking for something known to be in the list. Using the Big O notation, both cases require $O(n)$ time. The multiplicative constant (1/2) can be omitted. Algorithm analysis is focused on growth rate. The multiplicative constants have no impact on growth rates. The growth rate for $n/2$ or $100n$ is the same as for n, as illustrated in Table 24.1. Therefore, $O(n) = O(n/2) = O(100n)$.

ignoring multiplicative constants

Consider the algorithm for finding the maximum number in an array of n elements. To find the maximum number if n is 2, it takes one comparison; if n is 3, two comparisons. In general, it takes $n - 1$ comparisons to find the maximum number in a list of n elements. Algorithm analysis is for large input size. If the input size is small, there is no significance in estimating an algorithm's efficiency. As n grows larger, the n part in the expression $n - 1$ dominates the complexity. The Big O notation allows you to ignore the nondominating part (e.g., -1 in the expression $n - 1$) and highlight the important part (e.g., n in the expression $n - 1$). Therefore, the complexity of this algorithm is $O(n)$.

large input size

ignoring nondominating terms

The Big O notation estimates the execution time of an algorithm in relation to the input size. If the time is not related to the input size, the algorithm is said to take *constant time* with the notation $O(1)$. For example, a method that retrieves an element at a given index in an array takes constant time, because the time does not grow as the size of the array increases.

constant time

The following mathematical summations are often useful in algorithm analysis:

useful summations

$$1 + 2 + 3 + \ldots. + (n - 2) + (n - 1) = \frac{n(n-1)}{2} = O(n^2)$$

$$1 + 2 + 3 + \ldots. + (n - 1) + n = \frac{n(n+1)}{2} = O(n^2)$$

$$a^0 + a^1 + a^2 + a^3 + \ldots. + a^{(n-1)} + a^n = \frac{a^{n+1} - 1}{a - 1} = O(a^n)$$

$$2^0 + 2^1 + 2^2 + 2^3 + \ldots. + 2^{(n-1)} + 2^n = \frac{2^{n+1} - 1}{2 - 1} = 2^{n+1} - 1 = O(2^n)$$

24.1 Why is a constant factor ignored in the Big O notation? Why is a nondominating term ignored in the Big O notation?

Check Point

24.2 What is the order of each of the following functions?

MyProgrammingLab™

$$\frac{(n^2 + 1)^2}{n}, \frac{(n^2 + \log^2 n)^2}{n}, n^3 + 100n^2 + n, 2^n + 100n^2 + 45n, n2^n + n^2 2^n$$

24.3 Examples: Determining Big O

Key Point

This section gives several examples of determining Big O for repetition, sequence, and selection statements.

Example 1

Consider the time complexity for the following loop:

```
for (i = 1; i <= n; i++) {
  k = k + 5;
}
```

It is a constant time, *c*, for executing

```
k = k + 5;
```

Since the loop is executed *n* times, the time complexity for the loop is

$$T(n) = (\text{a constant } c) * n = O(n).$$

Example 2

What is the time complexity for the following loop?

```
for (i = 1; i <= n; i++) {
  for (j = 1; j <= n; j++) {
    k = k + i + j;
  }
}
```

It is a constant time, *c*, for executing

```
k = k + i + j;
```

The outer loop executes *n* times. For each iteration in the outer loop, the inner loop is executed *n* times. Thus, the time complexity for the loop is

$$T(n) = (\text{a constant } c) * n * n = O(n^2)$$

quadratic time

An algorithm with the $O(n^2)$ time complexity is called a *quadratic algorithm*. The quadratic algorithm grows quickly as the problem size increases. If you double the input size, the time for the algorithm is quadrupled. Algorithms with a nested loop are often quadratic.

Example 3

Consider the following loop:

```
for (i = 1; i <= n; i++) {
  for (j = 1; j <= i; j++) {
    k = k + i + j;
  }
}
```

The outer loop executes *n* times. For $i = 1, 2, \ldots,$ the inner loop is executed one time, two times, and *n* times. Thus, the time complexity for the loop is

$$\begin{aligned} T(n) &= c + 2c + 3c + 4c + \ldots + nc \\ &= cn(n + 1)/2 \\ &= (c/2)\, n^2 + (c/2)n \\ &= O(n^2) \end{aligned}$$

Example 4

Consider the following loop:

```
for (i = 1; i <= n; i++) {
  for (j = 1; j <= 20; j++) {
    k = k + i + j;
  }
}
```

The inner loop executes 20 times, and the outer loop *n* times. Therefore, the time complexity for the loop is

$$T(n) = 20 * c * n = O(n)$$

Example 5

Consider the following sequences:

```
for (j = 1; j <= 10; j++) {
  k = k + 4;
}

for (i = 1; i <= n; i++) {
  for (j = 1; j <= 20; j++) {
    k = k + i + j;
  }
}
```

The first loop executes 10 times, and the second loop 20 * *n* times. Thus, the time complexity for the loop is

$$T(n) = 10 * c + 20 * c * n = O(n)$$

Example 6

Consider the following selection statement:

```
if (list.contains(e)) {
  System.out.println(e);
}
else
  for (Object t: list) {
    System.out.println(t);
  }
```

Suppose the list contains *n* elements. The execution time for `list.contains(e)` is $O(n)$. The loop in the `else` clause takes $O(n)$ time. Hence, the time complexity for the entire statement is

$$\begin{aligned} T(n) &= \text{if test time} + \text{worst-case time(if clause, else clause)} \\ &= O(n) + O(n) = O(n) \end{aligned}$$

Example 7

Consider the computation of a^n for an integer *n*. A simple algorithm would multiply *a* *n* times, as follows:

```
result = 1;
for (int i = 1; i <= n; i++)
  result *= a;
```

The algorithm takes $O(n)$ time. Without loss of generality, assume $n = 2^k$. You can improve the algorithm using the following scheme:

```
result = a;
for (int i = 1; i <= k; i++)
  result = result * result;
```

The algorithm takes $O(\log n)$ time. For an arbitrary n, you can revise the algorithm and prove that the complexity is still $O(\log n)$. (See Checkpoint Question 24.7.)

omitting base

Note

For simplicity, since $O(\log n) = O(\log_2 n) = O(\log_a n)$, the constant base is omitted.

Check Point

MyProgrammingLab™

24.3 Count the number of iterations in the following loops.

```
int count = 1;
while (count < 30) {
  count = count * 2;
}
```

(a)

```
int count = 15;
while (count < 30) {
  count = count * 3;
}
```

(b)

```
int count = 1;
while (count < n) {
  count = count * 2;
}
```

(c)

```
int count = 15;
while (count < n) {
  count = count * 3;
}
```

(d)

24.4 How many stars are displayed in the following code if **n** is 10? How many if **n** is 20? Use the Big O notation to estimate the time complexity.

```
for (int i = 0; i < n; i++) {
  System.out.print('*');
}
```

(a)

```
for (int i = 0; i < n; i++) {
  for (int j = 0; j < n; j++) {
    System.out.print('*');
  }
}
```

(b)

```
for (int k = 0; k < n; k++) {
  for (int i = 0; i < n; i++) {
    for (int j = 0; j < n; j++) {
      System.out.print('*');
    }
  }
}
```

(c)

```
for (int k = 0; k < 10; k++) {
  for (int i = 0; i < n; i++) {
    for (int j = 0; j < n; j++) {
      System.out.print('*');
    }
  }
}
```

(d)

24.5 Use the Big *O* notation to estimate the time complexity of the following methods:

```
public static void mA(int n) {
  for (int i = 0; i < n; i++) {
    System.out.print(Math.random());
  }
}
```

(a)

```
public static void mB(int n) {
  for (int i = 0; i < n; i++) {
    for (int j = 0; j < i; j++)
      System.out.print(Math.random());
  }
}
```

(b)

```
public static void mC(int[] m) {
  for (int i = 0; i < m.length; i++) {
    System.out.print(m[i]);
  }

  for (int i = m.length - 1; i >= 0; )
  {
    System.out.print(m[i]);
    i--;
  }
}
```

(c)

```
public static void mD(int[] m) {
  for (int i = 0; i < m.length; i++) {
    for (int j = 0; j < i; j++)
      System.out.print(m[i] * m[j]);
  }
}
```

(d)

24.6 Design an $O(n)$ time algorithm for computing the sum of numbers from n1 to n2 for (n1 $<$ n2). Can you design an $O(1)$ for performing the same task?

24.7 Example 7 in Section 24.3 assumes $n = 2^k$. Revise the algorithm for an arbitrary n and prove that the complexity is still $O(\log n)$.

24.4 Analyzing Algorithm Time Complexity

This section analyzes the complexity of several well-known algorithms: binary search, selection sort, insertion sort, and Towers of Hanoi.

24.4.1 Analyzing Binary Search

binary search animation on the Companion Website

The binary search algorithm presented in Listing 6.7, BinarySearch.java, searches for a key in a sorted array. Each iteration in the algorithm contains a fixed number of operations, denoted by *c*. Let $T(n)$ denote the time complexity for a binary search on a list of n elements. Without loss of generality, assume n is a power of 2 and $k = \log n$. Since a binary search eliminates half of the input after two comparisons,

$$
\begin{aligned}
T(n) &= T\left(\frac{n}{2}\right) + c = T\left(\frac{n}{2^2}\right) + c + c = T\left(\frac{n}{2^k}\right) + kc \\
&= T(1) + c\log n = 1 + (\log n)c \\
&= O(\log n)
\end{aligned}
$$

logarithmic time

Ignoring constants and nondominating terms, the complexity of the binary search algorithm is $O(\log n)$. An algorithm with the $O(\log n)$ time complexity is called a *logarithmic algorithm*. The base of the log is 2, but the base does not affect a logarithmic growth rate, so it can be omitted. The logarithmic algorithm grows slowly as the problem size increases. In the case of binary search, each time you double the array size, at most one more comparison will be required. If you square the input size of any logarithmic time algorithm, you only double the time of execution. So a logarithmic-time algorithm is very efficient.

selection sort animation on the Companion Website

24.4.2 Analyzing Selection Sort

The selection sort algorithm presented in Listing 6.8, SelectionSort.java, finds the smallest element in the list and swaps it with the first element. It then finds the smallest element remaining and swaps it with the first element in the remaning list, and so on until the remaining list contains only one element left to be sorted. The number of comparisons is $n - 1$ for the first iteration, $n - 2$ for the second iteration, and so on. Let $T(n)$ denote the complexity for selection sort and c denote the total number of other operations such as assignments and additional comparisons in each iteration. Thus,

$$\begin{aligned} T(n) &= (n - 1) + c + (n - 2) + c + \ldots + 2 + c + 1 + c \\ &= \frac{(n - 1)(n - 1 + 1)}{2} + c(n - 1) = \frac{n^2}{2} - \frac{n}{2} + cn - c \\ &= O(n^2) \end{aligned}$$

Therefore, the complexity of the selection sort algorithm is $O(n^2)$.

insertion search animation on the Companion Website

24.4.3 Analyzing Insertion Sort

The insertion sort algorithm presented in Listing 6.9, InsertionSort.java, sorts a list of elements by repeatedly inserting a new element into a sorted partial array until the whole array is sorted. At the kth iteration, to insert an element into an array of size k, it may take k comparisons to find the insertion position, and k moves to insert the element. Let $T(n)$ denote the complexity for insertion sort and c denote the total number of other operations such as assignments and additional comparisons in each iteration. Thus,

$$\begin{aligned} T(n) &= (2 + c) + (2 \times 2 + c) + \ldots + (2 \times (n - 1) + c) \\ &= 2(1 + 2 + \ldots + n - 1) + c(n - 1) \\ &= 2\frac{(n - 1)n}{2} + cn - c = n^2 - n + cn - c \\ &= O(n^2) \end{aligned}$$

Therefore, the complexity of the insertion sort algorithm is $O(n^2)$. Hence, the selection sort and insertion sort are of the same time complexity.

24.4.4 Analyzing the Towers of Hanoi Problem

The Towers of Hanoi problem presented in Listing 20.8, TowersOfHanoi.java, recursively moves n disks from tower A to tower B with the assistance of tower C as follows:

1. Move the first $n - 1$ disks from A to C with the assistance of tower B.
2. Move disk n from A to B.
3. Move $n - 1$ disks from C to B with the assistance of tower A.

The complexity of this algorithm is measured by the number of moves. Let $T(n)$ denote the number of moves for the algorithm to move n disks from tower A to tower B. Thus $T(1)$ is 1. Thus,

$$\begin{aligned} T(n) &= T(n - 1) + 1 + T(n - 1) \\ &= 2T(n - 1) + 1 \\ &= 2(2T(n - 2) + 1) + 1 \end{aligned}$$

$$= 2(2(2T(n - 3) + 1) + 1) + 1$$

$$= 2^{n-1}T(1) + 2^{n-2} + \ldots + 2 + 1$$

$$= 2^{n-1} + 2^{n-2} + \ldots + 2 + 1 = (2^n - 1) = O(2^n)$$

An algorithm with $O(2^n)$ time complexity is called an *exponential algorithm*. As the input size increases, the time for the exponential algorithm grows exponentially. Exponential algorithms are not practical for large input size. Suppose the disk is moved at a rate of 1 per second. It would take $2^{32}/(365 * 24 * 60 * 60) = 136$ years to move 32 disks and $2^{64}/(365 * 24 * 60 * 60) = 585$ billion years to move 64 disks.

$O(2^n)$
exponential time

24.4.5 Common Recurrence Relations

Recurrence relations are a useful tool for analyzing algorithm complexity. As shown in the preceding examples, the complexity for binary search, selection sort and insertion sort, and the Towers of Hanoi is $T(n) = T\left(\frac{n}{2}\right) + c$, $T(n) = T(n - 1) + O(n)$, and $T(n) = 2T(n - 1) + O(1)$, respectively. Table 24.2 summarizes the common recurrence relations.

TABLE 24.2 Common Recurrence Functions

Recurrence Relation	*Result*	*Example*
$T(n) = T(n/2) + O(1)$	$T(n) = O(\log n)$	Binary search, Euclid's GCD
$T(n) = T(n - 1) + O(1)$	$T(n) = O(n)$	Linear search
$T(n) = 2T(n/2) + O(1)$	$T(n) = O(n)$	Checkpoint Question 24.20
$T(n) = 2T(n/2) + O(n)$	$T(n) = O(n \log n)$	Merge sort (Chapter 25)
$T(n) = T(n - 1) + O(n)$	$T(n) = O(n^2)$	Selection sort, insertion sort
$T(n) = 2T(n - 1) + O(1)$	$T(n) = O(2^n)$	Towers of Hanoi
$T(n) = T(n - 1) + T(n - 2) + O(1)$	$T(n) = O(2^n)$	Recursive Fibonacci algorithm

24.4.6 Comparing Common Growth Functions

The preceding sections analyzed the complexity of several algorithms. Table 24.3 lists some common growth functions and shows how growth rates change as the input size doubles from $n = 25$ to $n = 50$.

TABLE 24.3 Change of Growth Rates

Function	*Name*	$n = 25$	$n = 50$	$f(50)/f(25)$
$O(1)$	Constant time	1	1	1
$O(\log n)$	Logarithmic time	4.64	5.64	1.21
$O(n)$	Linear time	25	50	2
$O(n \log n)$	Log-linear time	116	282	2.43
$O(n^2)$	Quadratic time	625	2,500	4
$O(n^3)$	Cubic time	15,625	125,000	8
$O(2^n)$	Exponential time	3.36×10^7	1.27×10^{15}	3.35×10^7

These functions are ordered as follows, as illustrated in Figure 24.1.

$$O(1) < O(\log n) < O(n) < O(n \log n) < O(n^2) < O(n^3) < O(2^n)$$

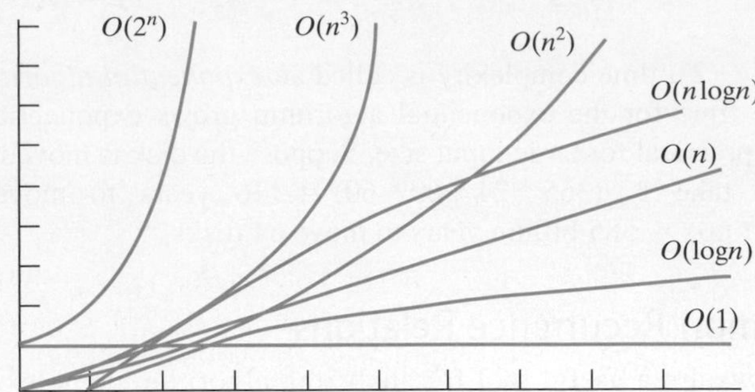

FIGURE 24.1 As the size n increases, the function grows.

24.8 Put the following growth functions in order:

$$\frac{5n^3}{4032}, 44 \log n, 10n \log n, 500, 2n^2, \frac{2^n}{45}, 3n$$

24.9 Estimate the time complexity for adding two $n \times m$ matrices, and for multiplying an $n \times m$ matrix by an $m \times k$ matrix.

24.10 Describe an algorithm for finding the occurrence of the max element in an array. Analyze the complexity of the algorithm.

24.11 Describe an algorithm for removing duplicates from an array. Analyze the complexity of the algorithm.

24.12 Analyze the following sorting algorithm:

```
for (int i = 0; i < list.length - 1; i++) {
  if (list[i] > list[i + 1]) {
    swap list[i] with list[i + 1];
    i = -1;
  }
}
```

24.5 Finding Fibonacci Numbers Using Dynamic Programming

This section analyzes and designs an efficient algorithm for finding Fibonacci numbers using dynamic programming.

Section 20.3, Case Study: Computing Fibonacci Numbers, gave a recursive method for finding the Fibonacci number, as follows:

```
/** The method for finding the Fibonacci number */
public static long fib(long index) {
  if (index == 0) // Base case
    return 0;
  else if (index == 1) // Base case
    return 1;
  else  // Reduction and recursive calls
    return fib(index - 1) + fib(index - 2);
}
```

We can now prove that the complexity of this algorithm is $O(2^n)$. For convenience, let the index be n. Let $T(n)$ denote the complexity for the algorithm that finds fib(n) and c denote the constant time for comparing the index with `0` and `1`; that is, $T(1)$ is c. Thus,

$$\begin{aligned} T(n) &= T(n-1) + T(n-2) + c \\ &\le 2T(n-1) + c \\ &\le 2(2T(n-2) + c) + c \\ &= 2^2T(n-2) + 2c + c \end{aligned}$$

Similar to the analysis of the Towers of Hanoi problem, we can show that $T(n)$ is $O(2^n)$.

However, this algorithm is not efficient. Is there an efficient algorithm for finding a Fibonacci number? The trouble with the recursive `fib` method is that the method is invoked redundantly with the same arguments. For example, to compute `fib(4)`, `fib(3)` and `fib(2)` are invoked. To compute `fib(3)`, `fib(2)` and `fib(1)` are invoked. Note that `fib(2)` is redundantly invoked. We can improve it by avoiding repeated calling of the `fib` method with the same argument. Note that a new Fibonacci number is obtained by adding the preceding two numbers in the sequence. If you use the two variables `f0` and `f1` to store the two preceding numbers, the new number, `f2`, can be immediately obtained by adding `f0` with `f1`. Now you should update `f0` and `f1` by assigning `f1` to `f0` and assigning `f2` to `f1`, as shown in Figure 24.2.

```
                   f0 f1 f2
Fibonacci series:  0  1  1  2  3  5  8  13  21  34  55  89 ...
         indices:  0  1  2  3  4  5  6  7   8   9   10  11

                      f0 f1 f2
Fibonacci series:  0  1  1  2  3  5  8  13  21  34  55  89 ...
         indices:  0  1  2  3  4  5  6  7   8   9   10  11

                                                f0  f1  f2
Fibonacci series:  0  1  1  2  3  5  8  13  21  34  55  89 ...
         indices:  0  1  2  3  4  5  6  7   8   9   10  11
```

FIGURE 24.2 Variables `f0`, `f1`, and `f2` store three consecutive Fibonacci numbers in the series.

The new method is implemented in Listing 24.1.

LISTING 24.1 ImprovedFibonacci.java

```
import java.util.Scanner;

public class ImprovedFibonacci {
  /** Main method */
  public static void main(String args[]) {
    // Create a Scanner
    Scanner input = new Scanner(System.in);
    System.out.print("Enter an index for the Fibonacci number: ");
    int index = input.nextInt();                                        input

    // Find and display the Fibonacci number
    System.out.println(
      "Fibonacci number at index " + index + " is " + fib(index));      invoke fib
  }

  /** The method for finding the Fibonacci number */
```

f0
f1
f2
update f0, f1, f2

```
  public static long fib(long n) {
    long f0 = 0; // For fib(0)
    long f1 = 1; // For fib(1)
    long f2 = 1; // For fib(2)

    if (n == 0)
      return f0;
    else if (n == 1)
      return f1;
    else if (n == 2)
      return f2;

    for (int i = 3; i <= n; i++) {
      f0 = f1;
      f1 = f2;
      f2 = f0 + f1;
    }

    return f2;
  }
}
```

```
Enter an index for the Fibonacci number: 6 ↵Enter
Fibonacci number at index 6 is 8
```

```
Enter an index for the Fibonacci number: 7 ↵Enter
Fibonacci number at index 7 is 13
```

$O(n)$

Obviously, the complexity of this new algorithm is $O(n)$. This is a tremendous improvement over the recursive $O(2^n)$ algorithm.

dynamic programming

The algorithm for computing Fibonacci numbers presented here uses an approach known as *dynamic programming*. Dynamic programming is the process of solving subproblems, then combining the solutions of the subproblems to obtain an overall solution. This naturally leads to a recursive solution. However, it would be inefficient to use recursion, because the subproblems overlap. The key idea behind dynamic programming is to solve each subproblem only once and store the results for subproblems for later use to avoid redundant computing of the subproblems.

MyProgrammingLab™

24.13 What is dynamic programming? Give an example of dynamic programming.

24.14 Why is the recursive Fibonacci algorithm inefficient, but the nonrecursive Fibonacci algorithm efficient?

24.6 Finding Greatest Common Divisors Using Euclid's Algorithm

This section presents several algorithms in the search for an efficient algorithm for finding the greatest common divisor of two integers.

GCD

brute force

The greatest common divisor (GCD) of two integers is the largest number that can evenly divide both integers. Listing 4.9, GreatestCommonDivisor.java, presented a brute-force algorithm for finding the greatest common divisor of two integers `m` and `n`. *Brute force* refers to an algorithmic approach that solves a problem in the simplest or most direct or obvious way. As a result, such an algorithm can end up doing far more work to solve a given problem than a cleverer or more sophisticated algorithm might do. On the other hand, a brute-force algorithm is often easier to implement than a more sophisticated one and, because of this simplicity, sometimes it can be more efficient.

The brute-force algorithm checks whether `k` (for `k` = `2`, `3`, `4`, and so on) is a common divisor for `n1` and `n2`, until `k` is greater than `n1` or `n2`. The algorithm can be described as follows:

```
public static int gcd(int m, int n) {
  int gcd = 1;

  for (int k = 2; k <= m && k <= n; k++) {
    if (m % k == 0 && n % k == 0)
      gcd = k;
  }

  return gcd;
}
```

Assuming $m \geq n$, the complexity of this algorithm is obviously $O(n)$.

assume $m \geq n$

$O(n)$

Is there a better algorithm for finding the GCD? Rather than searching a possible divisor from `1` up, it is more efficient to search from `n` down. Once a divisor is found, the divisor is the GCD. Therefore, you can improve the algorithm using the following loop:

improved solutions

```
for (int k = n; k >= 1; k--) {
  if (m % k == 0 && n % k == 0) {
    gcd = k;
    break;
  }
}
```

This algorithm is better than the preceding one, but its worst-case time complexity is still $O(n)$.

A divisor for a number `n` cannot be greater than `n / 2`, so you can further improve the algorithm using the following loop:

```
for (int k = m / 2; k >= 1; k--) {
  if (m % k == 0 && n % k == 0) {
    gcd = k;
    break;
  }
}
```

However, this algorithm is incorrect, because `n` can be a divisor for `m`. This case must be considered. The correct algorithm is shown in Listing 24.2.

LISTING 24.2 GCD.java

```
import java.util.Scanner;

public class GCD {
  /** Find GCD for integers m and n */
  public static int gcd(int m, int n) {
    int gcd = 1;

    if (m % n == 0) return n;

    for (int k = n / 2; k >= 1; k--) {
      if (m % k == 0 && n % k == 0) {
        gcd = k;
        break;
      }
    }
```

check divisor

GCD found

```java

    return gcd;
  }

  /** Main method */
  public static void main(String[] args) {
    // Create a Scanner
    Scanner input = new Scanner(System.in);

    // Prompt the user to enter two integers
    System.out.print("Enter first integer: ");
    int m = input.nextInt();
    System.out.print("Enter second integer: ");
    int n = input.nextInt();

    System.out.println("The greatest common divisor for " + m +
      " and " + n + " is " + gcd(m, n));
  }
}
```

```
Enter first integer: 2525 ↵Enter
Enter second integer: 125 ↵Enter
The greatest common divisor for 2525 and 125 is 25
```

```
Enter first integer: 3 ↵Enter
Enter second integer: 3 ↵Enter
The greatest common divisor for 3 and 3 is 3
```

O(n)

Assuming $m \geq n$, the **for** loop is executed at most n/2 times, which cuts the time by half from the previous algorithm. The time complexity of this algorithm is still $O(n)$, but practically, it is much faster than the algorithm in Listing 4.8.

Note

The Big *O* notation provides a good theoretical estimate of algorithm efficiency. However, two algorithms of the same time complexity are not necessarily equally efficient. As shown in the preceding example, both algorithms in Listings 4.9 and 24.2 have the same complexity, but in practice the one in Listing 24.2 is obviously better.

practical consideration

Euclid's algorithm

A more efficient algorithm for finding the GCD was discovered by Euclid around 300 B.C. This is one of the oldest known algorithms. It can be defined recursively as follows:

Let `gcd(m, n)` denote the GCD for integers `m` and `n`:

- If `m % n` is `0`, `gcd (m, n)` is `n`.
- Otherwise, `gcd(m, n)` is `gcd(n, m % n)`.

It is not difficult to prove the correctness of this algorithm. Suppose `m % n = r`. Thus, `m = qn + r`, where `q` is the quotient of `m / n`. Any number that is divisible by `m` and `n` must also be divisible by `r`. Therefore, `gcd(m, n)` is the same as `gcd(n, r)`, where `r = m % n`. The algorithm can be implemented as in Listing 24.3.

Listing 24.3 GCDEuclid.java

```java
import java.util.Scanner;

public class GCDEuclid {
```

```
  /** Find GCD for integers m and n */
  public static int gcd(int m, int n) {
    if (m % n == 0)
      return n;
    else
      return gcd(n, m % n);
  }

  /** Main method */
  public static void main(String[] args) {
    // Create a Scanner
    Scanner input = new Scanner(System.in);

    // Prompt the user to enter two integers
    System.out.print("Enter first integer: ");
    int m = input.nextInt();
    System.out.print("Enter second integer: ");
    int n = input.nextInt();

    System.out.println("The greatest common divisor for " + m +
      " and " + n + " is " + gcd(m, n));
  }
}
```

base case

reduction

input

input

```
Enter first integer: 2525 ↵Enter
Enter second integer: 125 ↵Enter
The greatest common divisor for 2525 and 125 is 25
```

```
Enter first integer: 3 ↵Enter
Enter second integer: 3 ↵Enter
The greatest common divisor for 3 and 3 is 3
```

best case

average case

worst case

In the best case when `m % n` is `0`, the algorithm takes just one step to find the GCD. It is difficult to analyze the average case. However, we can prove that the worst-case time complexity is $O(\log n)$.

Assuming $m \geq n$, we can show that `m % n < m / 2`, as follows:

- If `n <= m / 2`, `m % n < m / 2`, since the remainder of m divided by n is always less than n.
- If `n > m / 2`, `m % n = m - n < m / 2`. Therefore, `m % n < m / 2`.

Euclid's algorithm recursively invokes the **gcd** method. It first calls **gcd(m, n)**, then calls **gcd(n, m % n)**, and **gcd(m % n, n % (m % n))**, and so on, as follows:

```
  gcd(m, n)
= gcd(n, m % n)
= gcd(m % n, n % (m % n))
= ...
```

Since `m % n < m / 2` and `n % (m % n) < n / 2`, the argument passed to the **gcd** method is reduced by half after every two iterations. After invoking **gcd** two times, the second parameter is less than $n/2$. After invoking **gcd** four times, the second parameter is less than $n/4$. After invoking **gcd** six times, the second parameter is less than $\frac{n}{2^3}$. Let k be the number of times the **gcd** method is invoked. After invoking **gcd** k times, the second parameter is less than $\frac{n}{2^{(k/2)}}$, which is greater than or equal to 1. That is,

$$\frac{n}{2^{(k/2)}} \geq 1 \quad => \quad n \geq 2^{(k/2)} \quad => \quad \log n \geq k/2 \quad => \quad k \leq 2 \log n$$

Therefore, $k \leq 2 \log n$. So the time complexity of the **gcd** method is $O(\log n)$.

The worst case occurs when the two numbers result in the most divisions. It turns out that two successive Fibonacci numbers will result in the most divisions. Recall that the Fibonacci series begins with 0 and 1, and each subsequent number is the sum of the preceding two numbers in the series, such as:

0 1 1 2 3 5 8 13 21 34 55 89 . . .

The series can be recursively defined as

```
fib(0) = 0;
fib(1) = 1;
fib(index) = fib(index - 2) + fib(index - 1); index >= 2
```

For two successive Fibonacci numbers **fib(index)** and **fib(index - 1)**,

```
gcd(fib(index), fib(index - 1))
= gcd(fib(index - 1), fib(index - 2))
= gcd(fib(index - 2), fib(index - 3))
= gcd(fib(index - 3), fib(index - 4))
= ...
= gcd(fib(2), fib(1))
= 1
```

For example,

```
gcd(21, 13)
= gcd(13, 8)
= gcd(8, 5)
= gcd(5, 3)
= gcd(3, 2)
= gcd(2, 1)
= 1
```

Therefore, the number of times the **gcd** method is invoked is the same as the index. We can prove that $index \leq 1.44 \log n$, where $n = \text{fib}(\text{index} - 1)$. This is a tighter bound than $index \leq 2 \log n$.

Table 24.4 summarizes the complexity of three algorithms for finding the GCD.

TABLE 24.4 Comparisons of GCD Algorithms

Algorithm	*Complexity*	*Description*
Listing 4.9	$O(n)$	Brute-force, checking all possible divisors
Listing 24.2	$O(n)$	Checking half of all possible divisors
Listing 24.3	$O(\log n)$	Euclid's algorithm

MyProgrammingLab™

24.15 Prove that the following algorithm for finding the GCD of the two integers **m** and **n** is incorrect.

```
int gcd = 1;
for (int k = Math.min(Math.sqrt(n), Math.sqrt(m)); k >= 1; k--) {
```

```
        if (m % k == 0 && n % k == 0) {
          gcd = k;
          break;
        }
      }
```

24.7 Efficient Algorithms for Finding Prime Numbers

Key Point

This section presents several algorithms in the search for an efficient algorithm for finding prime numbers.

A \$150,000 award awaits the first individual or group who discovers a prime number with at least 100,000,000 decimal digits (w2.eff.org/awards/coop-prime-rules.php).

Can you design a fast algorithm for finding prime numbers?

what is prime?

An integer greater than `1` is *prime* if its only positive divisor is `1` or itself. For example, `2`, `3`, `5`, and `7` are prime numbers, but `4`, `6`, `8`, and `9` are not.

How do you determine whether a number `n` is prime? Listing 4.14 presented a brute-force algorithm for finding prime numbers. The algorithm checks whether `2, 3, 4, 5, . . .`, or `n - 1` is divisible by `n`. If not, `n` is prime. This algorithm takes $O(n)$ time to check whether `n` is prime. Note that you need to check only whether `2, 3, 4, 5, . . .`, and `n/2` is divisible by `n`. If not, `n` is prime. This algorithm is slightly improved, but it is still of $O(n)$.

In fact, we can prove that if `n` is not a prime, `n` must have a factor that is greater than `1` and less than or equal to $\sqrt{n}$. Here is the proof. Since `n` is not a prime, there exist two numbers `p` and `q` such that `n = pq` with $1 < p \leq q$. Note that $n = \sqrt{n}\sqrt{n}$. `p` must be less than or equal to $\sqrt{n}$. Hence, you need to check only whether `2, 3, 4, 5, . . .`, or $\sqrt{n}$ is divisible by `n`. If not, `n` is prime. This significantly reduces the time complexity of the algorithm to $O(\sqrt{n})$.

Now consider the algorithm for finding all the prime numbers up to `n`. A straightforward implementation is to check whether `i` is prime for $i =$ `2, 3, 4, . . . , n`. The program is given in Listing 24.4.

Listing 24.4 PrimeNumbers.java

check prime

```
import java.util.Scanner;

public class PrimeNumbers {
  public static void main(String[] args) {
    Scanner input = new Scanner(System.in);
    System.out.print("Find all prime numbers <= n, enter n: ");
    int n = input.nextInt();

    final int NUMBER_PER_LINE = 10; // Display 10 per line
    int count = 0; // Count the number of prime numbers
    int number = 2; // A number to be tested for primeness

    System.out.println("The prime numbers are:");

    // Repeatedly find prime numbers
    while (number <= n) {
      // Assume the number is prime
      boolean isPrime = true; // Is the current number prime?

      // Test if number is prime
      for (int divisor = 2; divisor <= (int)(Math.sqrt(number));
          divisor++) {
        if (number % divisor == 0) { // If true, number is not prime
          isPrime = false; // Set isPrime to false
          break; // Exit the for loop
```

increase count

check next number

```
26         }
27       }
28
29       // Print the prime number and increase the count
30       if (isPrime) {
31         count++; // Increase the count
32
33         if (count % NUMBER_PER_LINE == 0) {
34           // Print the number and advance to the new line
35           System.out.printf("%7d\n", number);
36         }
37         else
38           System.out.printf("%7d", number);
39       }
40
41       // Check if the next number is prime
42       number++;
43     }
44
45     System.out.println("\n" + count +
46       " prime(s) less than or equal to " + n);
47   }
48 }
```

```
Find all prime numbers <= n, enter n: 1000 ↵Enter
The prime numbers are:
      2      3      5      7     11     13     17     19     23     29
     31     37     41     43     47     53     59     61     67     71
...
...
168 prime(s) less than or equal to 1000
```

The program is not efficient if you have to compute `Math.sqrt(number)` for every iteration of the `for` loop (line 21). A good compiler should evaluate `Math.sqrt(number)` only once for the entire `for` loop. To ensure this happens, you can explicitly replace line 21 with the following two lines:

```
int squareRoot = (int)(Math.sqrt(number));
for (int divisor = 2; divisor <= squareRoot; divisor++) {
```

In fact, there is no need to actually compute `Math.sqrt(number)` for every `number`. You need look only for the perfect squares such as 4, 9, 16, 25, 36, 49, and so on. Note that for all the numbers between 36 and 48, inclusively, their `(int)(Math.sqrt(number))` is 6. With this insight, you can replace the code in lines 16–26 with the following:

```
...
int squareRoot = 1;

// Repeatedly find prime numbers
while (number <= n) {
  // Assume the number is prime
  boolean isPrime = true; // Is the current number prime?

  if (squareRoot * squareRoot < number) squareRoot++;

  // Test if number is prime
```

```
    for (int divisor = 2; divisor <= squareRoot; divisor++) {
      if (number % divisor == 0) { // If true, number is not prime
        isPrime = false; // Set isPrime to false
        break; // Exit the for loop
      }
    }
  ...
```

Now we turn our attention to analyzing the complexity of this program. Since it takes $\sqrt{i}$ steps in the `for` loop (lines 21–27) to check whether number i is prime, the algorithm takes $\sqrt{2} + \sqrt{3} + \sqrt{4} + \ldots + \sqrt{n}$ steps to find all the prime numbers less than or equal to n. Observe that

$$\sqrt{2} + \sqrt{3} + \sqrt{4} + \ldots + \sqrt{n} \leq n\sqrt{n}$$

Therefore, the time complexity for this algorithm is $O(n\sqrt{n})$.

To determine whether i is prime, the algorithm checks whether 2, 3, 4, 5, . . . , and $\sqrt{i}$ are divisible by i. This algorithm can be further improved. In fact, you need to check only whether the prime numbers from 2 to $\sqrt{i}$ are possible divisors for i.

We can prove that if i is not prime, there must exist a prime number p such that $i = pq$ and $p \leq q$. Here is the proof. Assume that i is not prime; let p be the smallest factor of i. p must be prime, otherwise, p has a factor k with $2 \leq k < p$. k is also a factor of i, which contradicts that p be the smallest factor of i. Therefore, if i is not prime, you can find a prime number from `2` to $\sqrt{i}$ that is divisible by i. This leads to a more efficient algorithm for finding all prime numbers up to `n`, as shown in Listing 24.5.

LISTING 24.5 EfficientPrimeNumbers.java

```
import java.util.Scanner;

public class EfficientPrimeNumbers {
  public static void main(String[] args) {
    Scanner input = new Scanner(System.in);
    System.out.print("Find all prime numbers <= n, enter n: ");
    int n = input.nextInt();

    // A list to hold prime numbers
    java.util.List<Integer> list =
      new java.util.ArrayList<Integer>();

    final int NUMBER_PER_LINE = 10; // Display 10 per line
    int count = 0; // Count the number of prime numbers
    int number = 2; // A number to be tested for primeness
    int squareRoot = 1; // Check whether number <= squareRoot

    System.out.println("The prime numbers are \n");

    // Repeatedly find prime numbers
    while (number <= n) {
      // Assume the number is prime
      boolean isPrime = true; // Is the current number prime?

      if (squareRoot * squareRoot < number) squareRoot++;

      // Test whether number is prime
      for (int k = 0; k < list.size()
                    && list.get(k) <= squareRoot; k++) {
        if (number % list.get(k) == 0) { // If true, not prime
```

check prime

increase count

check next number

```
          isPrime = false; // Set isPrime to false
          break; // Exit the for loop
        }
      }

      // Print the prime number and increase the count
      if (isPrime) {
        count++; // Increase the count
        list.add(number); // Add a new prime to the list
        if (count % NUMBER_PER_LINE == 0) {
          // Print the number and advance to the new line
          System.out.println(number);
        }
        else
          System.out.print(number + " ");
      }

      // Check whether the next number is prime
      number++;
    }

    System.out.println("\n" + count +
      " prime(s) less than or equal to " + n);
  }
}
```

```
Find all prime numbers <= n, enter n: 1000 ↵Enter
The prime numbers are:
     2     3     5     7    11    13    17    19    23    29
    31    37    41    43    47    53    59    61    67    71
...
...
168 prime(s) less than or equal to 1000
```

Let π (i) denote the number of prime numbers less than or equal to i. The primes under **20** are **2**, **3**, **5**, **7**, **11**, **13**, **17**, and **19**. Therefore, π (2) is **1**, π (3) is **2**, π (6) is **3**, and π (20) is **8**. It has been proved that π (i) is approximately $\frac{i}{\log i}$ (see primes.utm.edu/howmany.shtml).

For each number **i**, the algorithm checks whether a prime number less than or equal to $\sqrt{i}$ is divisible by i. The number of the prime numbers less than or equal to $\sqrt{i}$ is

$$\frac{\sqrt{i}}{\log\sqrt{i}} = \frac{2\sqrt{i}}{\log i}$$

Thus, the complexity for finding all prime numbers up to **n** is

$$\frac{2\sqrt{2}}{\log 2} + \frac{2\sqrt{3}}{\log 3} + \frac{2\sqrt{4}}{\log 4} + \frac{2\sqrt{5}}{\log 5} + \frac{2\sqrt{6}}{\log 6} + \frac{2\sqrt{7}}{\log 7} + \frac{2\sqrt{8}}{\log 8} + \ldots + \frac{2\sqrt{n}}{\log n}$$

Since $\frac{\sqrt{i}}{\log i} < \frac{\sqrt{n}}{\log n}$ for $i < n$ and $n \geq 16$,

$$\frac{2\sqrt{2}}{\log 2} + \frac{2\sqrt{3}}{\log 3} + \frac{2\sqrt{4}}{\log 4} + \frac{2\sqrt{5}}{\log 5} + \frac{2\sqrt{6}}{\log 6} + \frac{2\sqrt{7}}{\log 7} + \frac{2\sqrt{8}}{\log 8} + \ldots + \frac{2\sqrt{n}}{\log n} < \frac{2n\sqrt{n}}{\log n}$$

Therefore, the complexity of this algorithm is $O\left(\frac{n\sqrt{n}}{\log n}\right)$.

This algorithm is another example of dynamic programming. The algorithm stores the results of the subproblems in the array list and uses them later to check whether a new number is prime.

dynamic programming

Is there any algorithm better than $O\left(\frac{n\sqrt{n}}{\log n}\right)$? Let us examine the well-known Eratosthenes algorithm for finding prime numbers. Eratosthenes (276–194 B.C.) was a Greek mathematician who devised a clever algorithm, known as the *Sieve of Eratosthenes*, for finding all prime numbers $\leq n$. His algorithm is to use an array named **primes** of n Boolean values. Initially, all elements in **primes** are set **true**. Since the multiples of **2** are not prime, set **primes[2 * i]** to **false** for all $2 \leq i \leq n/2$, as shown in Figure 24.3. Since we don't care about **primes[0]** and **primes[1]**, these values are marked $\times$ in the figure.

Sieve of Eratosthenes

primes array

index	0	1	2	3	4	5	6	7	8	9	10	11	12	13	14	15	16	17	18	19	20	21	22	23	24	25	26	27
initial	×	×	T	T	T	T	T	T	T	T	T	T	T	T	T	T	T	T	T	T	T	T	T	T	T	T	T	T
$k = 2$	×	×	T	T	F	T	F	T	F	T	F	T	F	T	F	T	F	T	F	T	F	T	F	T	F	T	F	T
$k = 3$	×	×	T	T	F	T	F	T	F	F	F	T	F	T	F	F	F	T	F	T	F	F	F	T	F	T	F	F
$k = 5$	×	×	(T)	(T)	F	(T)	F	(T)	F	F	F	(T)	F	(T)	F	F	F	(T)	F	(T)	F	F	F	(T)	F	F	F	F

Figure 24.3 The values in **primes** are changed with each prime number **k**.

Since the multiples of **3** are not prime, set **primes[3 * i]** to **false** for all $3 \leq i \leq n/3$. Because the multiples of **5** are not prime, set **primes[5 * i]** to **false** for all $5 \leq i \leq n/5$. Note that you don't need to consider the multiples of **4**, because the multiples of **4** are also the multiples of **2**, which have already been considered. Similarly, multiples of **6**, **8**, and **9** need not be considered. You only need to consider the multiples of a prime number **k = 2, 3, 5, 7, 11**, . . . , and set the corresponding element in **primes** to **false**. Afterward, if **primes[i]** is still true, then **i** is a prime number. As shown in Figure 24.3, **2**, **3**, **5**, **7**, **11**, **13**, **17**, **19**, and **23** are prime numbers. Listing 24.6 gives the program for finding the prime numbers using the Sieve of Eratosthenes algorithm.

Listing 24.6 SieveOfEratosthenes.java

```
import java.util.Scanner;

public class SieveOfEratosthenes {
  public static void main(String[] args) {
    Scanner input = new Scanner(System.in);
    System.out.print("Find all prime numbers <= n, enter n: ");
    int n = input.nextInt();

    boolean[] primes = new boolean[n + 1]; // Prime number sieve

    // Initialize primes[i] to true
    for (int i = 0; i < primes.length; i++) {
      primes[i] = true;
    }

    for (int k = 2; k <= n / k; k++) {
      if (primes[k]) {
        for (int i = k; i <= n / k; i++) {
          primes[k * i] = false; // k * i is not prime
```

sieve

initialize sieve

nonprime

```
20          }
21        }
22      }
23
24      int count = 0; // Count the number of prime numbers found so far
25      // Print prime numbers
26      for (int i = 2; i < primes.length; i++) {
27        if (primes[i]) {
28          count++;
29          if (count % 10 == 0)
30            System.out.printf("%7d\n", i);
31          else
32            System.out.printf("%7d", i);
33        }
34      }
35
36      System.out.println("\n" + count +
37        " prime(s) less than or equal to " + n);
38    }
39  }
```

```
Find all prime numbers <= n, enter n: 1000 ↵Enter
The prime numbers are:
      2      3      5      7     11     13     17     19     23     29
     31     37     41     43     47     53     59     61     67     71
...
...
168 prime(s) less than or equal to 1000
```

Note that **k <= n / k** (line 16). Otherwise, **k * i** would be greater than **n** (line 19). What is the time complexity of this algorithm?

For each prime number **k** (line 17), the algorithm sets **primes[k * i]** to **false** (line 19). This is performed **n / k - k + 1** times in the **for** loop (line 18). Thus, the complexity for finding all prime numbers up to **n** is

$$\frac{n}{2} - 2 + 1 + \frac{n}{3} - 3 + 1 + \frac{n}{5} - 5 + 1 + \frac{n}{7} - 7 + 1 + \frac{n}{11} - 11 + 1 \ldots$$

$$= O\left(\frac{n}{2} + \frac{n}{3} + \frac{n}{5} + \frac{n}{7} + \frac{n}{11} + \ldots\right) < O(n\pi(n))$$

$$= O\left(n\frac{\sqrt{n}}{\log n}\right)$$

This upper bound $O\left(\frac{n\sqrt{n}}{\log n}\right)$ is very loose. The actual time complexity is much better than $O\left(\frac{n\sqrt{n}}{\log n}\right)$. The Sieve of Eratosthenes algorithm is good for a small **n** such that the array **primes** can fit in the memory.

Table 24.5 summarizes the complexity of these three algorithms for finding all prime numbers up to n.

TABLE 24.5 Comparisons of Prime-Number Algorithms

Algorithm	*Complexity*	*Description*
Listing 4.14	$O(n^2)$	Brute-force, checking all possible divisors
Listing 24.4	$O(n\sqrt{n})$	Checking divisors up to $\sqrt{n}$
Listing 24.5	$O\left(\frac{n\sqrt{n}}{\log n}\right)$	Checking prime divisors up to $\sqrt{n}$
Listing 24.6	$O\left(\frac{n\sqrt{n}}{\log n}\right)$	Sieve of Eratosthenes

24.16 Prove that if n is not prime, there must exist a prime number p such that $p <= \sqrt{n}$ and p is a factor of n.

24.17 Describe how the sieve of Eratosthenes is used to find the prime numbers.

24.8 Finding the Closest Pair of Points Using Divide-and-Conquer

This section presents efficient algorithms for finding the closest pair of points using divide-and-conquer.

closest-pair animation on Companion Website

Given a set of points, the closest-pair problem is to find the two points that are nearest to each other. As shown in Figure 24.4, a line is drawn to connect the two nearest points in the closest-pair animation.

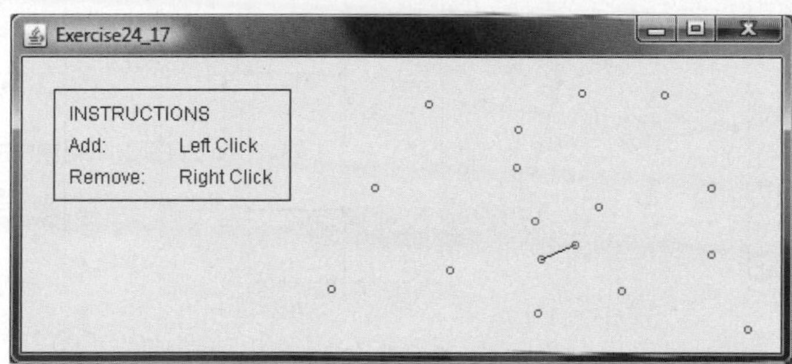

FIGURE 24.4 The closet-pair animation draws a line to connect the closest pair of points dynamically as points are added and removed interactively.

Section 7.6, Case Study: Finding the Closest Pair, presented a brute-force algorithm for finding the closest pair of points. The algorithm computes the distances between all pairs of points and finds the one with the minimum distance. Clearly, the algorithm takes $O(n^2)$ time. Can we design a more efficient algorithm?

divide-and-conquer

We will use an approach called *divide-and-conquer* to solve this problem. The approach divides the problem into subproblems, solves the subproblems, then combines the solutions of the subproblems to obtain the solution for the entire problem. Unlike the dynamic programming approach, the subproblems in the divide-and-conquer approach don't overlap. A subproblem is like the original problem with a smaller size, so you can apply recursion to solve the problem. In fact, all the solutions for recursive problems follow the divide-and-conquer approach.

Listing 24.7 describes how to solve the closest pair problem using the divide-and-conquer approach.

Listing 24.7 Algorithm for Finding the Closest Pair

Step 1: Sort the points in increasing order of *x*-coordinates. For the points with the same *x*-coordinates, sort on *y*-coordinates. This results in a sorted list *S* of points.

Step 2: Divide *S* into two subsets, S_1 and S_2, of equal size using the midpoint in the sorted list. Let the midpoint be in S_1. Recursively find the closest pair in S_1 and S_2. Let d_1 and d_2 denote the distance of the closest pairs in the two subsets, respectively.

Step 3: Find the closest pair between a point in S_1 and a point in S_2 and denote their distance as d_3. The closest pair is the one with the distance $\min(d_1, d_2, d_3)$.

Selection sort and insertion sort take $O(n^2)$ time. In Chapter 25 we will introduce merge sort and heap sort. These sorting algorithms take $O(n \log n)$ time. Step 1 can be done in $O(n \log n)$ time.

Step 3 can be done in $O(n)$ time. Let $d = \min(d_1, d_2)$. We already know that the closest-pair distance cannot be larger than *d*. For a point in S_1 and a point in S_2 to form the closest pair in *S*, the left point must be in **stripL** and the right point in **stripR**, as illustrated in Figure 24.5a.

For a point *p* in **stripL**, you need only consider a right point within the $d \times 2d$ rectangle, as shown in 24.5b. Any right point outside the rectangle cannot form the closest pair with *p*. Since the closest-pair distance in S_2 is greater than or equal to *d*, there can be at most six points in the rectangle. Thus, for each point in **stripL**, at most six points in **stripR** need to be considered.

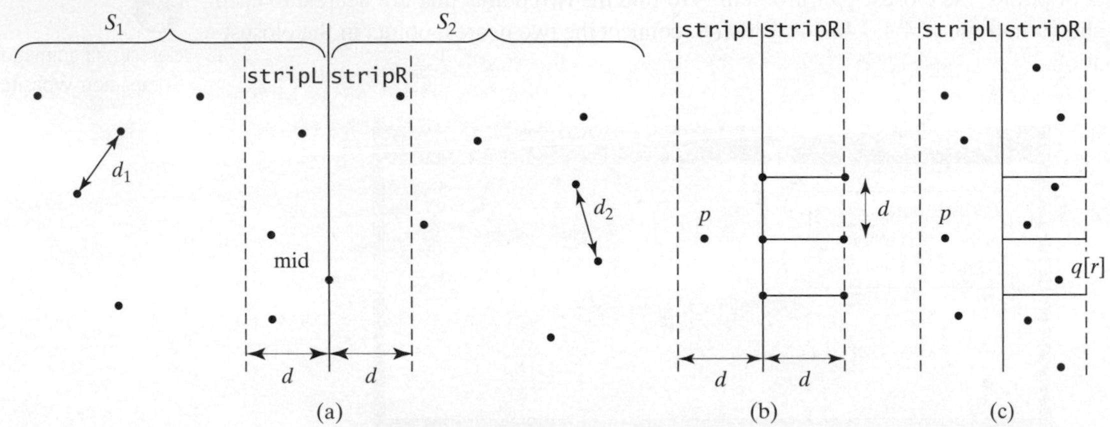

Figure 24.5 The midpoint divides the points into two sets of equal size.

For each point *p* in **stripL**, how do you locate the points in the corresponding $d \times 2d$ rectangle area in **stripR**? This can be done efficiently if the points in **stripL** and **stripR** are sorted in increasing order of their *y*-coordinates. Let **pointsOrderedOnY** be the list of the points sorted in increasing order of *y*-coordinates. **pointsOrderedOnY** can be obtained beforehand in the algorithm. **stripL** and **stripR** can be obtained from **pointsOrderedOnY** in Step 3 as shown in Listing 24.8.

Listing 24.8 Algorithm for Obtaining stripL and stripR

```
for each point p in pointsOrderedOnY
  if (p is in S1 and mid.x - p.x <= d)
    append p to stripL;
  else if (p is in S2 and p.x - mid.x <= d)
    append p to stripR;
```

stripL

stripR

Let the points in `stripL` and `stripR` be $\{p_0, p_1, \ldots, p_k\}$ and $\{q_0, q_1, \ldots, q_t\}$, as shown in Figure 24.5c. The closest pair between a point in `stripL` and a point in `stripR` can be found using the algorithm described in Listing 24.9.

LISTING 24.9 Algorithm for Finding the Closest Pair in Step 3

```
1  d = min(d1, d2);
2  r = 0; // r is the index in stripR
3  for (each point p in stripL) {
4    // Skip the points below the rectangle area
5    while (r < stripR.length && q[r].y <= p.y - d)
6      r++;
7
8    let r1 = r;
9    while (r1 < stripR.length && |q[r1].y - p.y| <= d) {
10     // Check if (p, q[r1]) is a possible closest pair
11     if (distance(p, q[r1]) < d) {
12       d = distance(p, q[r1]);
13       (p, q[r1]) is now the current closest pair;
14     }
15
16     r1 = r1 + 1;
17   }
18 }
```

update closest pair

The points in `stripL` are considered from $p_0, p_1, \ldots, p_k$ in this order. For a point `p` in `stripL`, skip the points in `stripR` that are below `p.y - d` (lines 5–6). Once a point is skipped, it will no longer be considered. The `while` loop (lines 9–17) checks whether `(p, q[r1])` is a possible closest pair. There are at most six such `q[r1]` pairs, so the complexity for finding the closest pair in Step 3 is $O(n)$.

Let $T(n)$ denote the time complexity for this algorithm. Thus,

$$T(n) = 2T(n/2) + O(n) = O(n \log n)$$

Therefore, the closest pair of points can be found in $O(n \log n)$ time. The complete implementation of this algorithm is left as an exercise (see Programming Exercise 24.7).

24.18 What is the divide-and-conquer approach? Give an example.

24.19 What is the difference between divide-and-conquer and dynamic programming?

24.20 Can you design an algorithm for finding the minimum element in a list using divide-and-conquer? What is the complexity of this algorithm?

24.9 Solving the Eight Queens Problem Using Backtracking

This section solves the Eight Queens problem using the backtracking approach.

The Eight Queens problem, introduced in Programming Exercise 20.34, is to find a solution to place a queen in each row on a chessboard such that no two queens can attack each other. The problem was solved using recursion. In this section, we will introduce a common algorithm design technique called *backtracking* for solving this problem. The backtracking approach searches for a candidate solution incrementally, abandoning that option as soon as it determines that the candidate cannot possibly be a valid solution, and then looks for a new candidate.

backtracking

You can use a two-dimensional array to represent a chessboard. However, since each row can have only one queen, it is sufficient to use a one-dimensional array to denote the position of the queen in the row. Thus, you can define the **queens** array as:

```
int[] queens = new int[8];
```

Assign **j** to **queens[i]** to denote that a queen is placed in row **i** and column **j**. Figure 24.6a shows the contents of the **queens** array for the chessboard in Figure 24.6b.

queens[0]	0
queens[1]	4
queens[2]	7
queens[3]	5
queens[4]	2
queens[5]	6
queens[6]	1
queens[7]	3

(a)

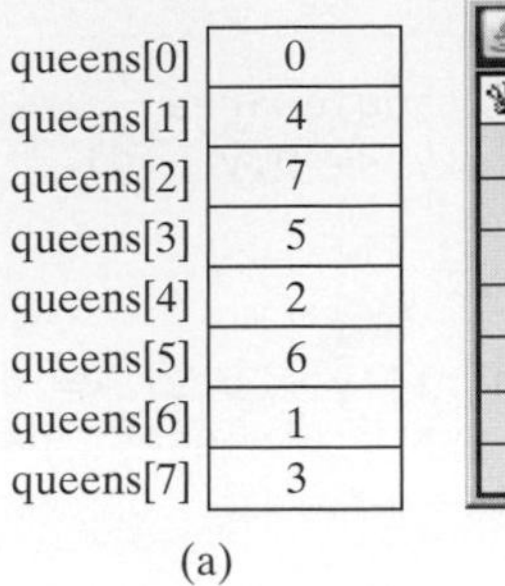

(b)

Figure 24.6 **queens[i]** denotes the position of the queen in row **i**.

search algorithm

The search starts from the first row with k = 0, where *k* is the index of the current row being considered. The algorithm checks whether a queen can be possibly placed in the *j*th column in the row for j = 0, 1, . . . , 7, in this order. The search is implemented as follows:

- If successful, it continues to search for a placement for a queen in the next row. If the current row is the last row, a solution is found.
- If not successful, it backtracks to the previous row and continues to search for a new placement in the next column in the previous row.
- If the algorithm backtracks to the first row and cannot find a new placement for a queen in this row, no solution can be found.

Eight Queens animation on the Companion Website

To see how the algorithm works, go to www.cs.armstrong.edu/liang/animation/EightQueensAnimation.html.

Listing 24.10 gives the program that displays a solution for the Eight Queens problem.

LISTING 24.10 EightQueens.java

initialize the board

search for solution

```
import java.awt.*;
import javax.swing.*;

public class EightQueens extends JApplet {
  public static final int SIZE = 8; // The size of the chessboard
  // queens are placed at (i, queens[i])
  // -1 indicates that no queen is currently placed in the ith row
  // Initially, place a queen at (0, 0) in the 0th row
  private int[] queens = {-1, -1, -1, -1, -1, -1, -1, -1};

  public EightQueens() {
    if (search()) // Search for a solution
      add(new ChessBoard(), BorderLayout.CENTER);
    else
      JOptionPane.showMessageDialog(null, "No solution found");
  }

  /** Search for a solution */
```

```java
  private boolean search() {
    // k - 1 indicates the number of queens placed so far
    // We are looking for a position in the kth row to place a queen
    int k = 0;
    while (k >= 0 && k <= 7) {
      // Find a position to place a queen in the kth row
      int j = findPosition(k);
      if (j < 0) {
        queens[k] = -1;
        k--; // back track to the previous row
      } else {
        queens[k] = j;
        k++;
      }
    }

    if (k == -1)
      return false; // No solution
    else
      return true; // A solution is found
  }

  public int findPosition(int k) {
    int start = queens[k] + 1; // Search for a new placement

    for (int j = start; j < 8; j++) {
      if (isValid(k, j))
        return j; // (k, j) is the place to put the queen now
    }

    return -1;
  }

  /** Return true if a queen can be placed at (row, column) */
  public boolean isValid(int row, int column) {
    for (int i = 1; i <= row; i++)
      if (queens[row - i] == column // Check column
        || queens[row - i] == column - i // Check up-left diagonal
        || queens[row - i] == column + i) // Check up-right diagonal
        return false; // There is a conflict
    return true; // No conflict
  }

  class ChessBoard extends JPanel {
    private java.net.URL url
      = getClass().getResource("image/queen.jpg");
    private Image queenImage = new ImageIcon(url).getImage();

    ChessBoard() {
      setBorder(BorderFactory.createLineBorder(Color.BLACK, 2));
    }

    @Override
    protected void paintComponent(Graphics g) {
      super.paintComponent(g);

      // Paint the queens
      for (int i = 0; i < SIZE; i++) {
        int j = queens[i]; // The position of the queen in row i
        g.drawImage(queenImage, j * getWidth() / SIZE,
```

find a column

backtrack

place a queen

search the next row

```
79            i * getHeight() / SIZE, getWidth() / SIZE,
80            getHeight() / SIZE, this);
81        }
82
83        // Draw the horizontal and vertical lines
84        for (int i = 1; i < SIZE; i++) {
85          g.drawLine(0, i * getHeight() / SIZE,
86            getWidth(), i * getHeight() / SIZE);
87          g.drawLine(i * getWidth() / SIZE, 0,
88            i * getWidth() / SIZE, getHeight());
89        }
90      }
91    }
92  }
```

main method omitted

The program invokes **search()** (line 12) to search for a solution. Initially, no queens are placed in any rows (line 9). The search now starts from the first row with **k = 0** (line 22) and finds a place for the queen (line 25). If successful, place it in the row (line 30) and consider the next row (line 31). If not successful, backtrack to the previous row (lines 27–28).

The **findPosition(k)** method searches for a possible position to place a queen in row **k** starting from **queen[k] + 1** (line 42). It checks whether a queen can be placed at **start**, **start + 1**, . . . , and **7**, in this order (lines 44–47). If possible, return the column index (line 46); otherwise, return **-1** (line 49).

The **isValid(row, column)** method is called to check whether placing a queen at the specified position causes a conflict with the queens placed earlier (line 45). It ensures that no queen is placed in the same column (line 55), in the upper-left diagonal (line 56), or in the upper-right diagonal (line 57), as shown in Figure 24.7.

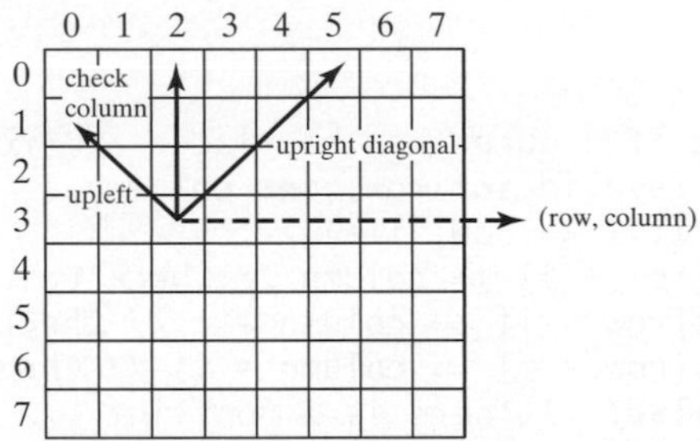

Figure 24.7 Invoking **isValid(row, column)** checks whether a queen can be placed at (row, column).

MyProgrammingLab™

24.21 What is backtracking? Give an example.

24.22 If you generalize the Eight Queens problem to the *n*-Queens problem in an *n*-by-*n* chessboard, what will be the complexity of the algorithm?

24.10 Computational Geometry: Finding a Convex Hull

This section presents efficient geometric algorithms for finding a convex hull for a set of points.

Computational geometry is to study the algorithms for geometrical problems. It has applications in computer graphics, games, pattern recognition, image processing, robotics, geographical information systems, and computer-aided design and manufacturing. Section 24.8 presented a geometrical algorithm for finding the closest pair of points. This section introduces geometrical algorithms for finding a convex hull.

Given a set of points, a *convex hull* is the smallest convex polygon that encloses all these points, as shown in Figure 24.8a. A polygon is convex if every line connecting two vertices is inside the polygon. For example, the vertices v0, v1, v2, v3, v4, and v5 in Figure 24.8a form a convex polygon, but not in Figure 24.8b, because the line that connects v3 and v1 is not inside the polygon.

convex hull

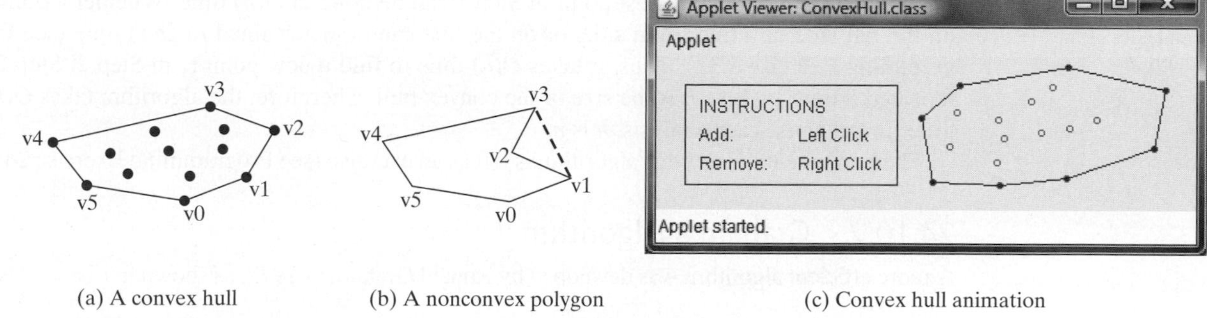

(a) A convex hull (b) A nonconvex polygon (c) Convex hull animation

FIGURE 24.8 A convex hull is the smallest convex polygon that contains a set of points.

A convex hull has many applications in game programming, pattern recognition, and image processing. Before we introduce the algorithms, it is helpful to get acquainted with the concept using an interactive tool from www.cs.armstrong.edu/liang/animation/ConvexHull.html, as shown in Figure 24.8c. This tool allows you to add and remove points and displays the convex hull dynamically.

convex hull animation on the Companion Website

Many algorithms have been developed to find a convex hull. This section introduces two popular algorithms: the gift-wrapping algorithm and Graham's algorithm.

24.10.1 Gift-Wrapping Algorithm

An intuitive approach, called the *gift-wrapping algorithm*, works as shown in Listing 24.11:

LISTING 24.11 Finding a Convex Hull Using Gift-Wrapping Algorithm

Step 1: Given a list of points *S*, let the points in *S* be labeled s_0, s_1, ..., s_k. Select the rightmost lowest point *S*. As shown in Figure 24.9a, h_0 is such a point. Add h_0 to list *H*. (*H* is initially empty. *H* will hold all points in the convex hull after the algorithm is finished.) Let t_0 be h_0.

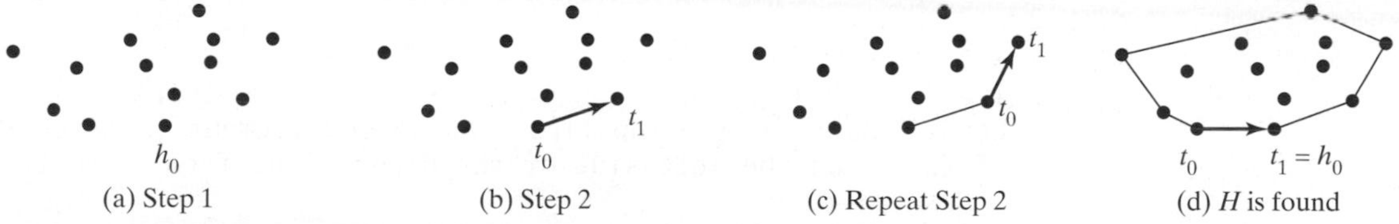

(a) Step 1 (b) Step 2 (c) Repeat Step 2 (d) *H* is found

FIGURE 24.9 (a) h_0 is the rightmost lowest point in S. (b) Step 2 finds point t_1. (c) A convex hull is expanded repeatedly. (d) A convex hull is found when t_1 becomes h_0.

Step 2: Let t_1 be s_0.
        For every point p in *S*,
          if *p* is on the right side of the direct line from t_0 to t_1, then
            let t_1 be *p*.
(After Step 2, no points lie on the right side of the direct line from t_0 to t_1, as shown in Figure 24.9b.)

```
Step 3: If t1 is h0 (see Figure 24.9d), the points in H form a convex
hull for S. Otherwise, add t1 to H, let t0 be t1, and go back to Step 2
(see Figure 24.9c).
```

correctness of the algorithm

The convex hull is expanded incrementally. The correctness is supported by the fact that no points lie on the right side of the direct line from t_0 to t_1 after Step 2. This ensures that every line segment with two points in *S* falls inside the polygon.

time complexity of the algorithm

Finding the rightmost lowest point in Step 1 can be done in *O*(*n*) time. Whether a point is on the left side of a line, right side, or on the line can be determined in *O*(1) time (see Programming Exercise 3.32). Thus, it takes *O*(*n*) time to find a new point t_1 in Step 2. Step 2 is repeated *h* times, where *h* is the size of the convex hull. Therefore, the algorithm takes *O*(*hn*) time. In the worst-case analysis, *h* is *n*.

The implementation of this algorithm is left as an exercise (see Programming Exercise 24.9).

24.10.2 Graham's Algorithm

A more efficient algorithm was developed by Ronald Graham in 1972, as shown in Listing 24.12.

LISTING 24.12 Finding a Convex Hull Using Graham's Algorithm

```
Step 1: Given a list of points S, select the rightmost lowest point and
name it p0. As shown in Figure 24.10a, p0 is such a point.
```

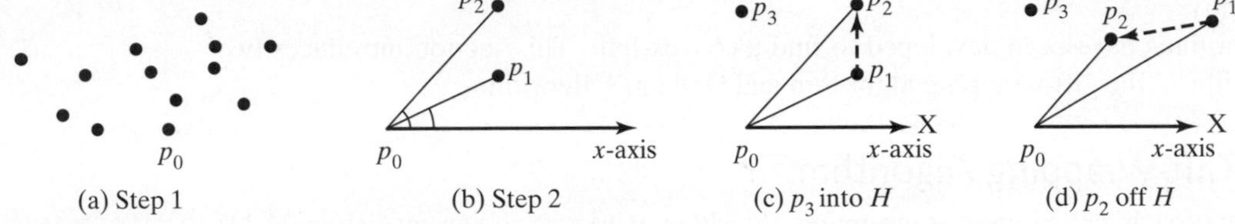

FIGURE 24.10 (a) p_0 is the rightmost lowest point in S. (b) Points are sorted by their angles. (c–d) A convex hull is discovered incrementally.

```
Step 2: Sort the points in S angularly along the x-axis with p0 as the
center, as shown in Figure 24.10b. If there is a tie and two points have
the same angle, discard the one that is closer to p0. The points in S are
now sorted as p0, p1, p2, ..., pn-1.
Step 3: Push p0, p1, and p2 into stack H. (After the algorithm finishes,
H contains all the points in the convex hull.)
Step 4:
    i = 3;
    while (i < n) {
      Let t1 and t2 be the top first and second element in stack H;
      if (pi is on the left side of the direct line from t2 to t1) {
        Push pi to H;
        i++; // Consider the next point in S.
      }
      else
        Pop the top element off stack H.
    }
Step 5: The points in H form a convex hull.
```

The convex hull is discovered incrementally. Initially, p_0, p_1,and p_2 form a convex hull. Consider p_3. p_3 is outside of the current convex hull since points are sorted in increasing order of their angles. If p_3 is strictly on the left side of the line from p_1 to p_2 (see Figure 24.10c), push p_3 into *H*. Now p_0, p_1, p_2, and p_3 form a convex hull. If p_3 is on the right side of the line from p_1 to p_2 (see Figure 24.10d), pop p_2 out of *H* and push p_3 into *H*. Now p_0, p_1, and p_3 form a convex hull and p_2 is inside of this convex hull. You can prove by induction that all the points in *H* in Step 5 form a convex hull for all the points in the input list *S*.

correctness of the algorithm

Finding the rightmost lowest point in Step 1 can be done in $O(n)$ time. The angles can be computed using trigonometry functions. However, you can sort the points without actually computing their angles. Observe that p_2 would make a greater angle than p_1 if and only if p_2 lies on the left side of the line from p_0 to p_1. Whether a point is on the left side of a line can be determined in $O(1)$ time, as shown in Programming Exercise 3.32. Sorting in Step 2 can be done in $O(n \log n)$ time using the merge-sort or heap-sort algorithms that will be introduced in Chapter 25. Step 4 can be done in $O(n)$ time. Therefore, the algorithm takes $O(n \log n)$ time.

time complexity of the algorithm

The implementation of this algorithm is left as an exercise (see Programming Exercise 24.11).

24.23 What is a convex hull?

24.24 Describe the gift-wrapping algorithm for finding a convex hull. Should list `H` be implemented using an `ArrayList` or a `LinkedList`?

24.25 Describe Graham's algorithm for finding a convex hull. Why does the algorithm use a stack to store the points in a convex hull?

Check Point

MyProgrammingLab™

Key Terms

average-case analysis 854
backtracking approach 877
best-case input 854
Big *O* notation 854
constant time 855
convex hull 881
divide-and-conquer approach 875
dynamic programming approach 864
exponential time 861
growth rate 854
logarithmic time 859
quadratic time 856
worst-case input 854

Chapter Summary

1. The *Big O notation* is a theoretical approach for analyzing the performance of an algorithm. It estimates how fast an algorithm's execution time increases as the input size increases, which enables you to compare two algorithms by examining their *growth rates*.

2. An input that results in the shortest execution time is called the *best-case* input and one that results in the longest execution time is called the *worst-case* input. Best case and worst case are not representative, but worst-case analysis is very useful. You can be assured that the algorithm will never be slower than the worst case.

3. An *average-case analysis* attempts to determine the average amount of time among all possible input of the same size. Average-case analysis is ideal, but difficult to perform, because for many problems it is hard to determine the relative probabilities and distributions of various input instances.

4. If the time is not related to the input size, the algorithm is said to take *constant time* with the notation $O(1)$.

5. Linear search takes $O(n)$ time. An algorithm with the $O(n)$ time complexity is called a *linear algorithm*. Binary search takes $O(\log n)$ time. An algorithm with the $O(\log n)$ time complexity is called a *logarithmic algorithm*.

6. The worst-time complexity for selection sort and insertion sort is $O(n^2)$. An algorithm with the $O(n^2)$ time complexity is called a *quadratic algorithm*.

7. The time complexity for the Towers of Hanoi problem is $O(2^n)$. An algorithm with the $O(2^n)$ time complexity is called an *exponential algorithm*.

8. A Fibonacci number at a given index can be found in $O(n)$ time using dynamic programming.

9. Dynamic programming is the process of solving subproblems, then combining the solutions of the subproblems to obtain an overall solution. The key idea behind dynamic programming is to solve each subproblem only once and store the results for subproblems for later use to avoid redundant computing of the subproblems.

10. Euclid's GCD algorithm takes $O(\log n)$ time.

11. All prime numbers less than or equal to n can be found in $O\left(\frac{n\sqrt{n}}{\log n}\right)$ time.

12. The closest pair can be found in $O(n \log n)$ time using the *divide-and-conquer approach.*

13. The divide-and-conquer approach divides the problem into subproblems, solves the subproblems, then combines the solutions of the subproblems to obtain the solution for the entire problem. Unlike the dynamic programming approach, the subproblems in the divide-and-conquer approach don't overlap. A subproblem is like the original problem with a smaller size, so you can apply recursion to solve the problem.

14. The Eight Queens problem can be solved using backtracking.

15. The backtracking approach searches for a candidate solution incrementally, abandoning that option as soon as it determines that the candidate cannot possibly be a valid solution, and then looks for a new candidate.

16. A *convex hull* for a set of points can be found in $O(n^2)$ time using the gift-wrapping algorithm and in $O(n \log n)$ time using the Graham's algorithm.

Test Questions

Do the test questions for this chapter online at www.cs.armstrong.edu/liang/intro9e/test.html.

MyProgrammingLab™

Programming Exercises

*24.1 (*Maximum consecutive increasingly ordered substring*) Write a program that prompts the user to enter a string and displays the maximum consecutive increasingly ordered substring. Analyze the time complexity of your program. Here is a sample run:

```
Enter a string: Welcome ↵Enter
Wel
```

****24.2** (*Maximum increasingly ordered subsequence*) Write a program that prompts the user to enter a string and displays the maximum increasingly ordered subsequence of characters. Analyze the time complexity of your program. Here is a sample run:

```
Enter a string: Welcome ↵Enter
Welo
```

***24.3** (*Pattern matching*) Write a program that prompts the user to enter two strings and tests whether the second string is a substring of the first string. *Suppose the neighboring characters in the string are distinct.* (Don't use the `indexOf` method in the `String` class.) Analyze the time complexity of your algorithm. Your algorithm needs to be at least `O(n)` time. Here is a sample run of the program:

```
Enter a string s1: Welcome to Java ↵Enter
Enter a string s2: come ↵Enter
matched at index 3
```

***24.4** (*Pattern matching*) Write a program that prompts the user to enter two strings and tests whether the second string is a substring of the first string. (Don't use the `indexOf` method in the `String` class.) Analyze the time complexity of your algorithm. Here is a sample run of the program:

```
Enter a string s1: Mississippi ↵Enter
Enter a string s2: sip ↵Enter
matched at index 6
```

***24.5** (*Same-number subsequence*) Write an $O(n)$ program that prompts the user to enter a sequence of integers ending with `0` and finds the longest subsequence with the same number. Here is a sample run of the program:

```
Enter a series of numbers ending with 0:
  2 4 4 8 8 8 8 2 4 4 0 ↵Enter
The longest same number sequence starts at index 3 with 4
values of 8
```

***24.6** (*Execution time for GCD*) Write a program that obtains the execution time for finding the GCD of every two consecutive Fibonacci numbers from the index 40 to index 45 using the algorithms in Listings 24.2 and 24.3. Your program should print a table like this:

	40	41	42	43	44	45
Listing 24.2 GCD						
Listing 24.3 GCDEuclid						

(*Hint*: You can use the following code template to obtain the execution time.)

```
long startTime = System.currentTimeMillis();
perform the task;
long endTime = System.currentTimeMillis();
long executionTime = endTime - startTime;
```

****24.7** (*Closest pair of points*) Section 24.8 introduced an algorithm for finding the closest pair of points using a divide-and-conquer approach. Implement the algorithm to meet the following requirements:

- Define the classes `Point` and `CompareY` in the same way as in Programming Exercise 22.4.
- Define a class named `Pair` with the data fields `p1` and `p2` to represent two points, and a method named `getDistance()` that returns the distance between the two points.
- Implement the following methods:

```
/** Return the distance of the closest pair of points */
public static Pair getClosestPair(double[][] points)

/** Return the distance of the closest pair of points */
public static Pair getClosestPair(Point[] points)

/** Return the distance of the closest pair of points
 * in pointsOrderedOnX[low..high]. This is a recursive
 * method. pointsOrderedOnX and pointsOrderedOnY are
 * not changed in the subsequent recursive calls.
 */
public static Pair distance(Point[] pointsOrderedOnX,
    int low, int high, Point[] pointsOrderedOnY)

/** Compute the distance between two points p1 and p2 */
public static double distance(Point p1, Point p2)

/** Compute the distance between points (x1, y1) and (x2, y2) */
public static double distance(double x1, double y1,
    double x2, double y2)
```

****24.8** (*All prime numbers up to* `10,000,000,000`) Write a program that finds all prime numbers up to `10,000,000,000`. There are approximately `455,052,511` such prime numbers. Your program should meet the following requirements:

- Your program should store the prime numbers in a binary data file, named **PrimeNumbers.dat**. When a new prime number is found, the number is appended to the file.
- To find whether a new number is prime, your program should load the prime numbers from the file to an array of the `long` type of size `10000`. If no number in the array is a divisor for the new number, continue to read the next `10000` prime numbers from the data file, until a divisor is found or all numbers in the file are read. If no divisor is found, the new number is prime.
- Since this program takes a long time to finish, you should run it as a batch job from a UNIX machine. If the machine is shut down and rebooted, your program should resume by using the prime numbers stored in the binary data file rather than start over from scratch.

****24.9** (*Geometry: gift-wrapping algorithm for finding a convex hull*) Section 24.10.1 introduced the gift-wrapping algorithm for finding a convex hull for a set of points. Assume that the Java's coordinate system is used for the points. Implement the algorithm using the following method:

```
/** Return the points that form a convex hull */
public static ArrayList<MyPoint> getConvexHull(double[][] s)
```

MyPoint is a static inner class defined as follows:

```
static class MyPoint {
  double x, y;

  MyPoint(double x, double y) {
    this.x = x; this.y = y;
  }
}
```

Write a test program that prompts the user to enter the set size and the points and displays the points that form a convex hull. Here is a sample run:

```
How many points are in the set? 6 [Enter]
Enter 6 points: 1 2.4 2.5 2 1.5 34.5 5.5 6 6 2.4 5.5 9 [Enter]
The convex hull is
  (1.5, 34.5) (5.5, 9.0) (6.0, 2.4) (2.5, 2.0) (1.0, 2.4)
```

24.10 (*Number of prime numbers*) Exercise 24.8 stores the prime numbers in a file named **PrimeNumbers.dat**. Write a program that finds the number of prime numbers that are less than or equal to 10, 100, 1,000, 10,000, 100,000, 1,000,000, 10,000,000, 100,000,000, 1,000,000,000, and 10,000,000,000. Your program should read the data from **PrimeNumbers.dat**. Note that the data file may continue to grow as more prime numbers are stored in the file.

****24.11** (*Geometry: Graham's algorithm for finding a convex hull*) Section 24.10.2 introduced Graham's algorithm for finding a convex hull for a set of points. Assume that the Java's coordinate system is used for the points. Implement the algorithm using the following method:

```
/** Return the points that form a convex hull */
public static ArrayList<MyPoint> getConvexHull(double[][] s)
```

MyPoint is a static inner class defined as follows:

```
private static class MyPoint implements Comparable<MyPoint> {
  double x, y;

  MyPoint rightMostLowestPoint;

  MyPoint(double x, double y) {
    this.x = x; this.y = y;
  }

  public void setRightMostLowestPoint(MyPoint p) {
    rightMostLowestPoint = p;
  }

  @Override
  public int compareTo(MyPoint o) {
    // Implement it to compare this point with point o
    // angularly along the x-axis with rightMostLowestPoint
    // as the center, as shown in Figure 24.10b. By implementing
    // the Comparable interface, you can use the Array.sort
    // method to sort the points to simplify coding.
  }
```

Write a test program that prompts the user to enter the set size and the points and displays the points that form a convex hull. Here is a sample run:

```
How many points are in the set? 6 ↵Enter
Enter 6 points: 1 2.4 2.5 2 1.5 34.5 5.5 6 6 2.4 5.5 9 ↵Enter
The convex hull is
  (1.5, 34.5) (5.5, 9.0) (6.0, 2.4) (2.5, 2.0) (1.0, 2.4)
```

***24.12** (*Last 100 prime numbers*) Exercise 24.8 stores the prime numbers in a file named **PrimeNumbers.dat**. Write an efficient program that reads the last `100` numbers in the file. (*Hint*: Don't read all numbers from the file. Skip all numbers before the last 100 numbers in the file.)

****24.13** (*Geometry: convex hull applet*) Exercise 24.11 finds a convex hull for a set of points entered from the console. Write an applet that enables the user to add/remove points by clicking the left/right mouse button, and displays a convex hull, as shown in Figure 24.8c.

***24.14** (*Execution time for prime numbers*) Write a program that obtains the execution time for finding all the prime numbers less than 8,000,000, 10,000,000, 12,000,000, 14,000,000, 16,000,000, and 18,000,000 using the algorithms in Listings 24.4–24.6. Your program should print a table like this:

	8000000	10000000	12000000	14000000	16000000	18000000
Listing 24.4						
Listing 24.5						
Listing 24.6						

****24.15** (*Geometry: non-cross polygon*) Write an applet that enables the user to add/remove points by clicking the left/right mouse button, and displays a non-crossed polygon that links all the points, as shown in Figure 24.11a. A polygon is crossed if two or more sides intersect, as shown in Figure 24.11b. Use the following algorithm to construct a polygon from a set of points.

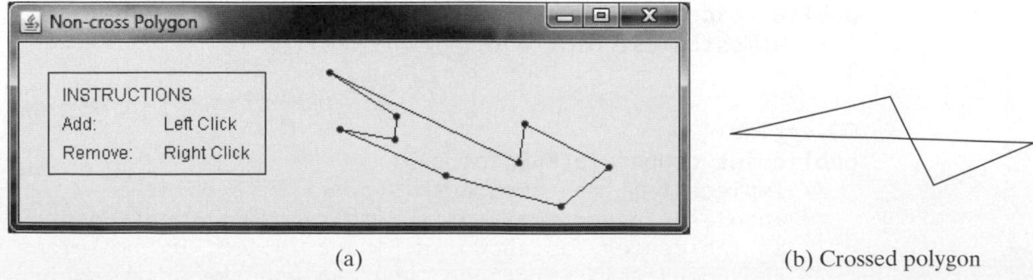

(a) (b) Crossed polygon

FIGURE 24.11 (a) Exercise24.15 displays a non-crossed polygon for a set of points. (b) Two or more sides intersect in a crossed polygon.

Step 1: Given a set of points *S*, select the rightmost lowest point p_0 in the set *S*.

Step 2: Sort the points in *S* angularly along the *x*-axis with p_0 as the center. If there is a tie and two points have the same angle, the one that is closer to p_0 is considered greater. The points in *S* are now sorted as p_0, p_1, p_2, ..., p_{n-1}.

Step 3: The sorted points form a non-cross polygon.

****24.16** (*Linear search animation*) Write an applet that animates the linear search algorithm. Create an array that consists of 20 distinct numbers from 1 to 20 in a random order. The array elements are displayed in a histogram, as shown in Figure 24.12. You need to enter a search key in the text field. Clicking the *Step* button causes the program to perform one comparison in the algorithm and repaints the histogram with a bar indicating the search position. This button also freezes the text field to prevent its value from being changed. When the algorithm is finished, display a dialog box to inform the user. Clicking the *Reset* button creates a new random array for a new start. This button also makes the text field editable.

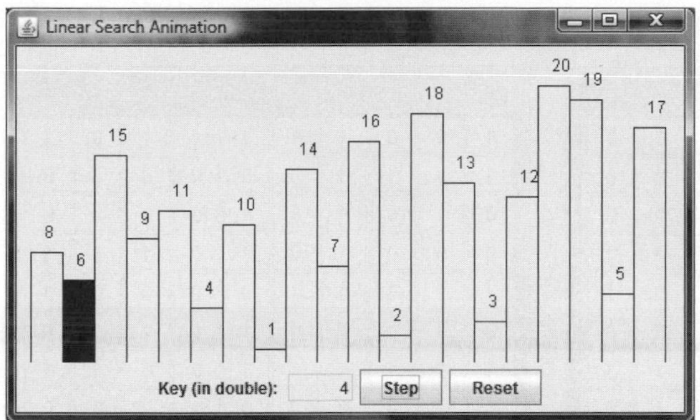

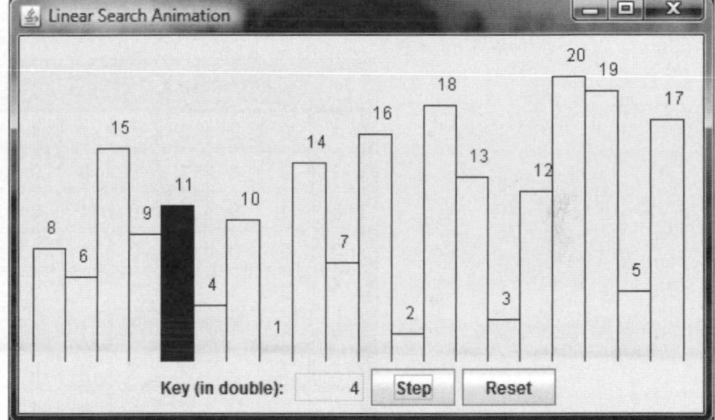

FIGURE 24.12 The program animates a linear search.

****24.17** (*Closest-pair animation*) Write an applet that enables the user to add/remove points by clicking the left/right mouse button, and displays a line that connects the pair of nearest points, as shown in Figure 24.4.

****24.18** (*Binary search animation*) Write an applet that animates the binary search algorithm. Create an array with numbers from 1 to 20 in this order. The array elements are displayed in a histogram, as shown in Figure 24.13. You need to

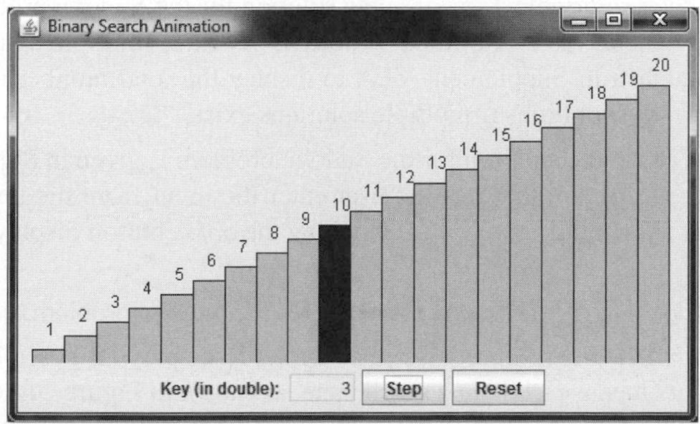

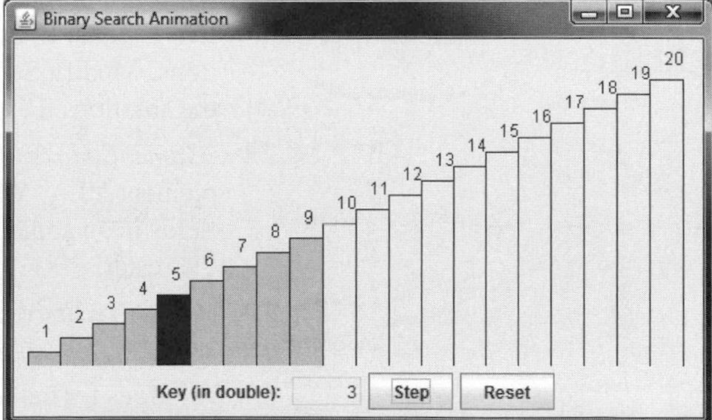

FIGURE 24.13 The program animates a binary search.

enter a search key in the text field. Clicking the *Step* button causes the program to perform one comparison in the algorithm. Use a light-gray color to paint the bars for the numbers in the current search range and use a black color to paint the a bar indicating the middle number in the search range. The *Step* button also freezes the text field to prevent its value from being changed. When the algorithm is finished, display a dialog box to inform the user. Clicking the *Reset* button enables a new search to start. This button also makes the text field editable.

***24.19** (*Largest block*) The problem for finding a largest block is described in Programming Exercise 7.35. Design a dynamic programming algorithm for solving this problem in $O(n^2)$ time. Write a test program that displays a 10-by-10 square matrix, as shown in Figure 24.14. Each element in the matrix is 0 or 1, randomly generated with a click of the *Refresh* button. Display each number centered in a text field. *Use a text field for each entry. Allow the user to change the entry value.* Click the *Find Largest Block* button to find a largest square submatrix that consists of 1s. Highlight the numbers in the block, as shown in Figure 24.14b. See www.cs.armstrong.edu/liang/animation/FindLargestBlock.html for an interactive test.

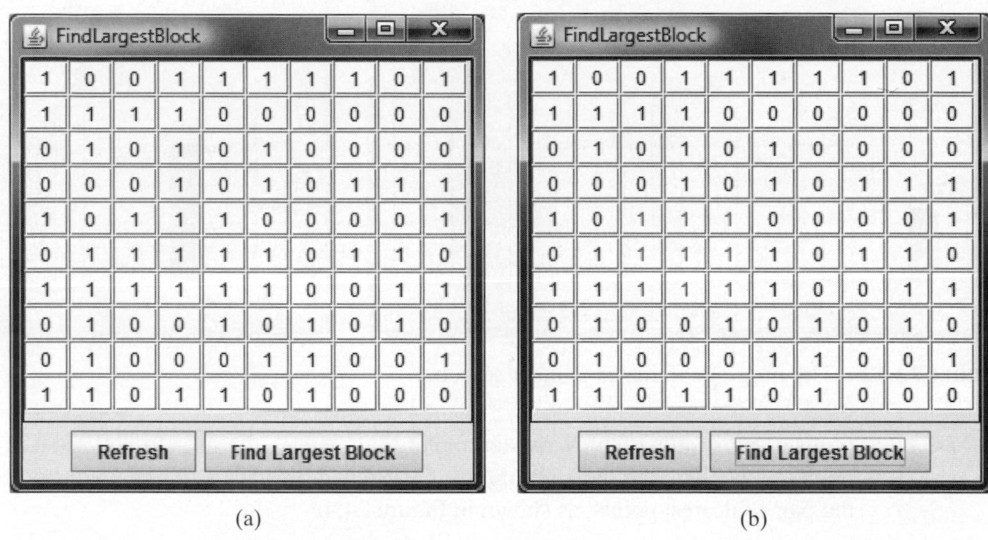

FIGURE 24.14 The program finds the largest block of 1s.

*****24.20** (*Game: multiple Sudoku solutions*) The complete solution for the Sudoku problem is given in Supplement VI.A. A Sudoku problem may have multiple solutions. Modify Sudoku.java in Supplement VI.A to display the total number of the solutions. Display two solutions if multiple solutions exist.

*****24.21** (*Game: Sudoku*) The complete solution for the Sudoku problem is given in Supplement VI.A. Write a program that lets the user enter the input from the text fields in an applet, as shown in Figure 24.15. Clicking the *Solve* button displays the result.

*****24.22** (*Game: recursive Sudoku*) Write a recursive solution for the Sudoku problem.

*****24.23** (*Game: multiple Eight Queens solution*) Write an applet to display all possible solutions for the Eight Queens puzzle in a scroll pane, as shown in Figure 24.16. For each solution, put a label to denote the solution number. (*Hint*: Place all solution panels into one panel and place this one panel into a `JScrollPane`.)

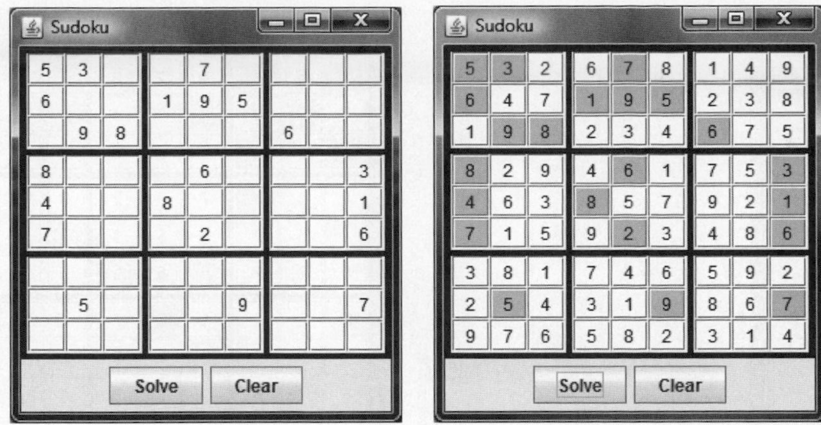

FIGURE 24.15 The program solves the Sudoku problem.

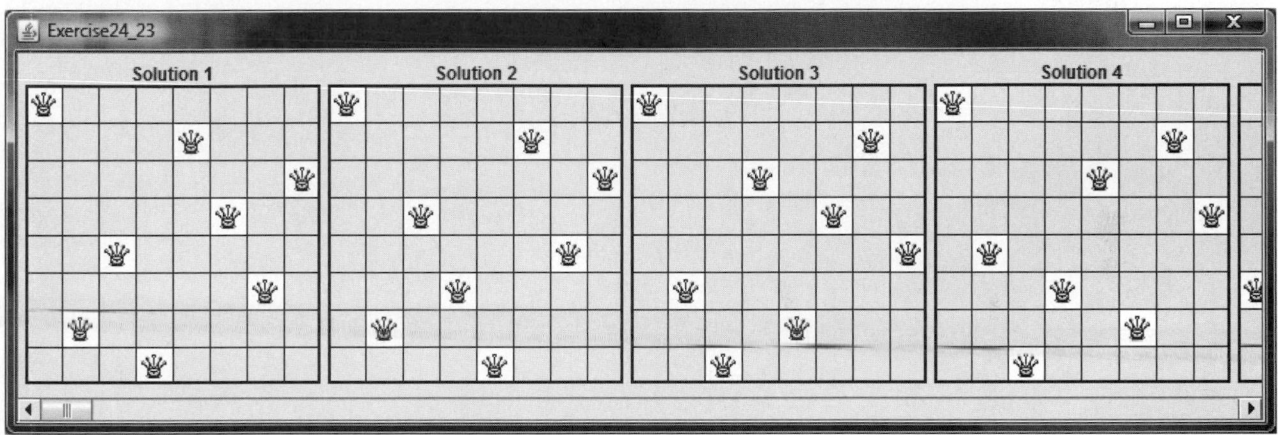

FIGURE 24.16 All solutions are placed in a scroll pane.

The solution panel class should override the `getPreferredSize()` method to ensure that a solution panel is displayed properly. See Listing 13.3, FigurePanel.java, for how to override `getPreferredSize()`.

****24.24** (*Find the smallest number*) Write a method that uses the divide-and-conquer approach to find the smallest number in a list.

*****24.25** (*Game: Sudoku*) Revise Exercise 24.21 to display all solutions for the Sudoku game, as shown in Figure 24.17a. When you click the *Solve* button, the program stores all solutions in an `ArrayList`. Each element in the list is a two-dimensional 9-by-9 grid. If the program has multiple solutions, the *OK* button appears as shown in Figure 24.17b. You can click the *Next* button to display the next solution, as shown in Figure 24.17c. When the *Clear* button is clicked, the cells are cleared and the *Next* button is hidden.

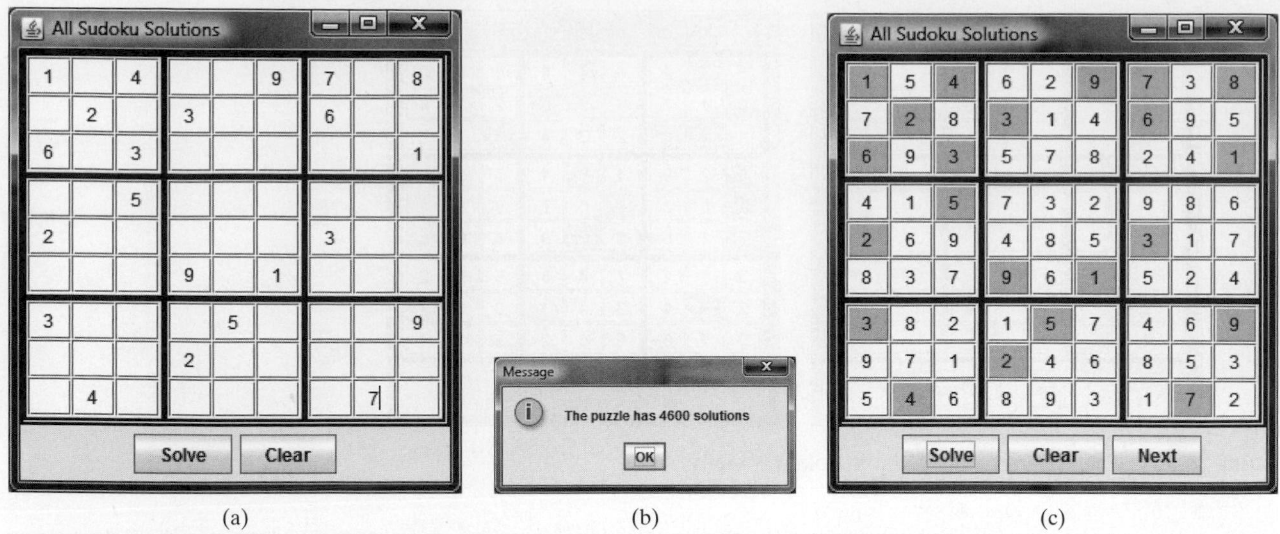

FIGURE 24.17 The program can display multiple Sudoku solutions.

CHAPTER

25

SORTING

Objectives

- To study and analyze time complexity of various sorting algorithms (§§25.2–25.7).
- To design, implement, and analyze bubble sort (§25.2).
- To design, implement, and analyze merge sort (§25.3).
- To design, implement, and analyze quick sort (§25.4).
- To design and implement a binary heap (§25.5).
- To design, implement, and analyze heap sort (§25.5).
- To design, implement, and analyze bucket sort and radix sort (§25.6).
- To design, implement, and analyze external sort for files that have a large amount of data (§25.7).

25.1 Introduction

Sorting algorithms are good examples for studying algorithm design and analysis.

When presidential candidate Barack Obama visited Google in 2007, Google CEO Eric Schmidt asked Obama the most efficient way to sort a million 32-bit integers (www.youtube.com/watch?v=k4RRi_ntQc8). Obama answered that the bubble sort would be the wrong way to go. Was he right? We will examine different sorting algorithms in this chapter and see if he was correct.

why study sorting?

Sorting is a classic subject in computer science. There are three reasons to study sorting algorithms.

- First, sorting algorithms illustrate many creative approaches to problem solving, and these approaches can be applied to solve other problems.
- Second, sorting algorithms are good for practicing fundamental programming techniques using selection statements, loops, methods, and arrays.
- Third, sorting algorithms are excellent examples to demonstrate algorithm performance.

what data to sort?

The data to be sorted might be integers, doubles, characters, or objects. Section 6.11, Sorting Arrays, presented selection sort and insertion sort for numeric values. The selection sort algorithm was extended to sort an array of objects in Section 21.5, Case Study: Sorting an Array of Objects. The Java API contains several overloaded sort methods for sorting primitive type values and objects in the `java.util.Arrays` and `java.util.Collections` classes. For simplicity, this chapter assumes:

1. data to be sorted are integers,
2. data are stored in an array, and
3. data are sorted in ascending order.

The programs can be easily modified to sort other types of data, to sort in descending order, or to sort data in an `ArrayList` or a `LinkedList`.

There are many algorithms for sorting. You have already learned selection sort and insertion sort. This chapter introduces bubble sort, merge sort, quick sort, bucket sort, radix sort, and external sort.

25.2 Bubble Sort

A bubble sort sorts the array in multiple phases. Each pass successively swaps the neighboring elements if the elements are not in order.

bubble sort

The bubble sort algorithm makes several passes through the array. On each pass, successive neighboring pairs are compared. If a pair is in decreasing order, its values are swapped; otherwise, the values remain unchanged. The technique is called a *bubble sort* or *sinking sort*, because the smaller values gradually "bubble" their way to the top and the larger values sink to the bottom. After the first pass, the last element becomes the largest in the array. After the second pass, the second-to-last element becomes the second largest in the array. This process is continued until all elements are sorted.

bubble sort illustration

bubble sort on the Companion Website

Figure 25.1a shows the first pass of a bubble sort on an array of six elements (2 9 5 4 8 1). Compare the elements in the first pair (2 and 9), and no swap is needed because they are already in order. Compare the elements in the second pair (9 and 5), and swap 9 with 5 because 9 is greater than 5. Compare the elements in the third pair (9 and 4), and swap 9 with 4. Compare the elements in the fourth pair (9 and 8), and swap 9 with 8. Compare the

(a) 1st pass	(b) 2nd pass	(c) 3rd pass	(d) 4th pass	(e) 5th pass
2 9 5 4 8 1	2 5 4 8 1 9	2 4 5 1 8 9	2 4 1 5 8 9	1 2 4 5 8 9
2 5 9 4 8 1	2 4 5 8 1 9	2 4 5 1 8 9	2 1 4 5 8 9	
2 5 4 9 8 1	2 4 5 8 1 9	2 4 1 5 8 9		
2 5 4 8 9 1	2 4 5 1 8 9			
2 5 4 8 1 9				

FIGURE 25.1 Each pass compares and orders the pairs of elements sequentially.

elements in the fifth pair (9 and 1), and swap 9 with 1. The pairs being compared are highlighted and the numbers already sorted are italicized in Figure 25.1.

The first pass places the largest number (9) as the last in the array. In the second pass, as shown in Figure 25.1b, you compare and order pairs of elements sequentially. There is no need to consider the last pair, because the last element in the array is already the largest. In the third pass, as shown in Figure 25.1c, you compare and order pairs of elements sequentially except the last two elements, because they are already in order. So in the *k*th pass, you don't need to consider the last $k - 1$ elements, because they are already ordered.

The algorithm for a bubble sort is described in Listing 25.1.

algorithm

LISTING 25.1 Bubble Sort Algorithm

```
for (int k = 1; k < list.length; k++) {
  // Perform the kth pass
  for (int i = 0; i < list.length - k; i++) {
    if (list[i] > list[i + 1])
      swap list[i] with list[i + 1];
  }
}
```

Note that if no swap takes place in a pass, there is no need to perform the next pass, because all the elements are already sorted. You can use this property to improve the algorithm in Listing 25.1 as in Listing 25.2.

LISTING 25.2 Improved Bubble Sort Algorithm

```
boolean needNextPass = true;
for (int k = 1; k < list.length && needNextPass; k++) {
  // Array may be sorted and next pass not needed
  needNextPass = false;
  // Perform the kth pass
  for (int i = 0; i < list.length - k; i++) {
    if (list[i] > list[i + 1]) {
      swap list[i] with list[i + 1];
      needNextPass = true; // Next pass still needed
    }
  }
}
```

The algorithm can be implemented in Listing 25.3.

LISTING 25.3 BubbleSort.java

```
public class BubbleSort {
  /** Bubble sort method */
  public static void bubbleSort(int[] list) {
    boolean needNextPass = true;

```

perform one pass

```
    for (int k = 1; k < list.length && needNextPass; k++) {
      // Array may be sorted and next pass not needed
      needNextPass = false;
      for (int i = 0; i < list.length - k; i++) {
        if (list[i] > list[i + 1]) {
          // Swap list[i] with list[i + 1]
          int temp = list[i];
          list[i] = list[i + 1];
          list[i + 1] = temp;

          needNextPass = true; // Next pass still needed
        }
      }
    }
  }

  /** A test method */
  public static void main(String[] args) {
    int[] list = {2, 3, 2, 5, 6, 1, -2, 3, 14, 12};
    bubbleSort(list);
    for (int i = 0; i < list.length; i++)
      System.out.print(list[i] + " ");
  }
}
```

```
-2 1 2 2 3 3 5 6 12 14
```

bubble sort time complexity

In the best-case analysis, the bubble sort algorithm needs just the first pass to find that the array is already sorted—no next pass is needed. Since the number of comparisons is $n - 1$ in the first pass, the best-case time for a bubble sort is $O(n)$.

In the worst-case analysis, the bubble sort algorithm requires $n - 1$ passes. The first pass makes $n - 1$ comparisons; the second pass makes $n - 2$ comparisons; and so on; the last pass makes 1 comparison. Thus, the total number of comparisons is:

$$(n - 1) + (n - 2) + \ldots + 2 + 1$$

$$= \frac{(n - 1)n}{2} = \frac{n^2}{2} - \frac{n}{2} = O(n^2)$$

Therefore, the worst-case time for a bubble sort is $O(n^2)$.

MyProgrammingLab™

25.1 Describe how a bubble sort works. What is the time complexity for a bubble sort?

25.2 Use Figure 25.1 as an example to show how to apply a bubble sort on {45, 11, 50, 59, 60, 2, 4, 7, 10}.

25.3 If a list is already sorted, how many comparisons will the `bubbleSort` method perform?

25.3 Merge Sort

merge sort

The merge sort *algorithm can be described recursively as follows: The algorithm divides the array into two halves and applies a merge sort on each half recursively. After the two halves are sorted, merge them.*

The algorithm for a merge sort is given in Listing 25.4.

LISTING 25.4 Merge Sort Algorithm

```
public static void mergeSort(int[] list) {
  if (list.length > 1) {
    mergeSort(list[0 ... list.length / 2]);
    mergeSort(list[list.length / 2 + 1 ... list.length]);
    merge list[0 ... list.length / 2] with
      list[list.length / 2 + 1 ... list.length];
  }
}
```

base condition
sort first half
sort second half
merge two halves

merge sort illustration

Figure 25.2 illustrates a merge sort of an array of eight elements (2 9 5 4 8 1 6 7). The original array is split into (2 9 5 4) and (8 1 6 7). Apply a merge sort on these two subarrays recursively to split (2 9 5 4) into (2 9) and (5 4) and (8 1 6 7) into (8 1) and (6 7). This process continues until the subarray contains only one element. For example, array (2 9) is split into the subarrays (2) and (9). Since array (2) contains a single element, it cannot be further split. Now merge (2) with (9) into a new sorted array (2 9); merge (5) with (4) into a new sorted array (4 5). Merge (2 9) with (4 5) into a new sorted array (2 4 5 9), and finally merge (2 4 5 9) with (1 6 7 8) into a new sorted array (1 2 4 5 6 7 8 9).

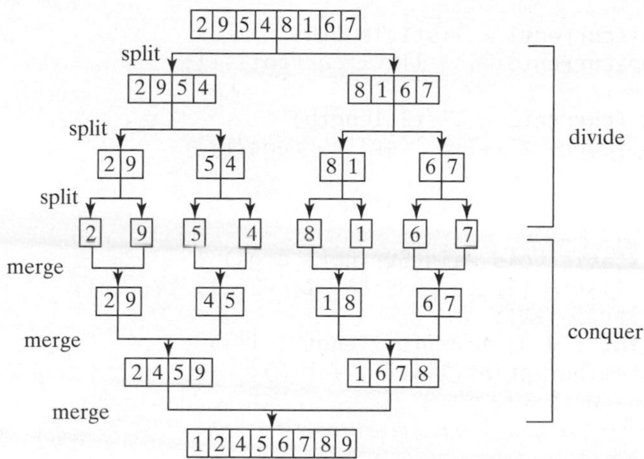

FIGURE 25.2 Merge sort employs a divide-and-conquer approach to sort the array.

The recursive call continues dividing the array into subarrays until each subarray contains only one element. The algorithm then merges these small subarrays into larger sorted subarrays until one sorted array results.

The merge sort algorithm is implemented in Listing 25.5.

LISTING 25.5 MergeSort.java

```
public class MergeSort {
  /** The method for sorting the numbers */
  public static void mergeSort(int[] list) {
    if (list.length > 1) {
      // Merge sort the first half
      int[] firstHalf = new int[list.length / 2];
      System.arraycopy(list, 0, firstHalf, 0, list.length / 2);
      mergeSort(firstHalf);

      // Merge sort the second half
      int secondHalfLength = list.length - list.length / 2;
      int[] secondHalf = new int[secondHalfLength];
```

base case
sort first half

sort second half

merge two halves

list1 to temp

list2 to temp

rest of list1 to temp

rest of list2 to temp

```
13       System.arraycopy(list, list.length / 2,
14         secondHalf, 0, secondHalfLength);
15       mergeSort(secondHalf);
16 
17       // Merge firstHalf with secondHalf into list
18       merge(firstHalf, secondHalf, list);
19     }
20   }
21 
22   /** Merge two sorted lists */
23   public static void merge(int[] list1, int[] list2, int[] temp) {
24     int current1 = 0; // Current index in list1
25     int current2 = 0; // Current index in list2
26     int current3 = 0; // Current index in temp
27 
28     while (current1 < list1.length && current2 < list2.length) {
29       if (list1[current1] < list2[current2])
30         temp[current3++] = list1[current1++];
31       else
32         temp[current3++] = list2[current2++];
33     }
34 
35     while (current1 < list1.length)
36       temp[current3++] = list1[current1++];
37 
38     while (current2 < list2.length)
39       temp[current3++] = list2[current2++];
40   }
41 
42   /** A test method */
43   public static void main(String[] args) {
44     int[] list = {2, 3, 2, 5, 6, 1, -2, 3, 14, 12};
45     mergeSort(list);
46     for (int i = 0; i < list.length; i++)
47       System.out.print(list[i] + " ");
48   }
49 }
```

The `mergeSort` method (lines 3–20) creates a new array `firstHalf`, which is a copy of the first half of `list` (line 7). The algorithm invokes `mergeSort` recursively on `firstHalf` (line 8). The length of the `firstHalf` is `list.length / 2` and the length of the `secondHalf` is `list.length - list.length / 2`. The new array `secondHalf` was created to contain the second part of the original array `list`. The algorithm invokes `mergeSort` recursively on `secondHalf` (line 15). After `firstHalf` and `secondHalf` are sorted, they are merged to `list` (line 18). Thus, array `list` is now sorted.

The `merge` method (lines 23–40) merges two sorted arrays `list1` and `list2` into array `temp`. `current1` and `current2` point to the current element to be considered in `list1` and `list2` (lines 24–26). The method repeatedly compares the current elements from `list1` and `list2` and moves the smaller one to `temp`. `current1` is increased by `1` (line 30) if the smaller one is in `list1` and `current2` is increased by `1` (line 32) if the smaller one is in `list2`. Finally, all the elements in one of the lists are moved to `temp`. If there are still unmoved elements in `list1`, copy them to `temp` (lines 35–36). If there are still unmoved elements in `list2`, copy them to `temp` (lines 38–39).

merge animation on Companion Website

Figure 25.3 illustrates how to merge the two arrays `list1` (2 4 5 9) and `list2` (1 6 7 8). Initially the current elements to be considered in the arrays are 2 and 1. Compare them and move the smaller element 1 to `temp`, as shown in Figure 25.3a. `current2` and `current3` are increased by 1. Continue to compare the current elements in the two arrays and move the

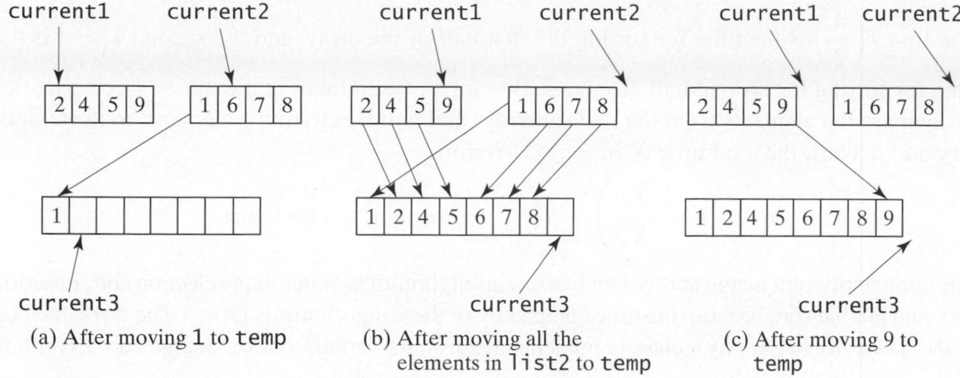

FIGURE 25.3 Two sorted arrays are merged into one sorted array.

smaller one to **temp** until one of the arrays is completely moved. As shown in Figure 25.3b, all the elements in **list2** are moved to **temp** and **current1** points to element 9 in **list1**. Copy 9 to **temp**, as shown in Figure 25.3c.

The **mergeSort** method creates two temporary arrays (lines 6, 12) during the dividing process, copies the first half and the second half of the array into the temporary arrays (lines 7, 13), sorts the temporary arrays (lines 8, 15), and then merges them into the original array (line 18), as shown in Figure 25.4a. You can rewrite the code to recursively sort the first half of the array and the second half of the array without creating new temporary arrays, and then merge the two arrays into a temporary array and copy its contents to the original array, as shown in Figure 25.4b. This is left for you to do in Programming Exercise 25.20.

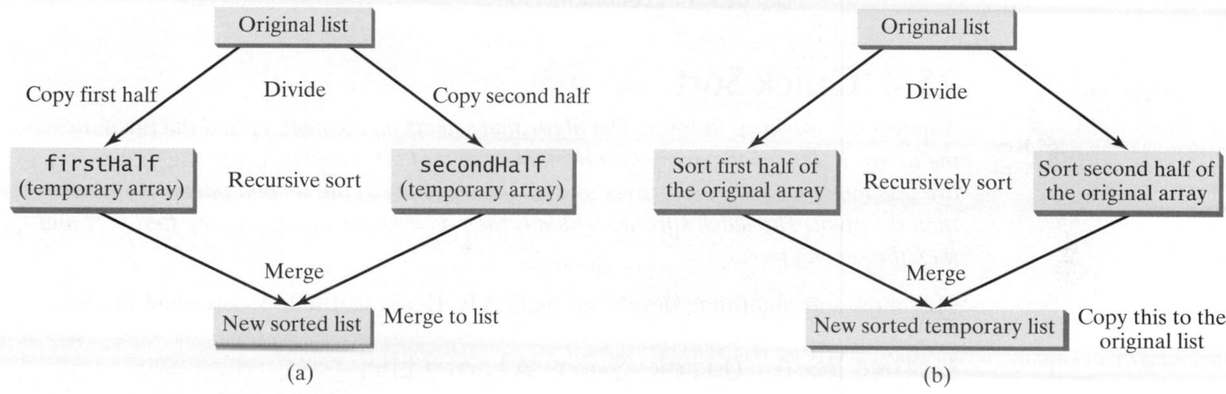

FIGURE 25.4 Temporary arrays are created to support a merge sort.

Note

A merge sort can be implemented efficiently using parallel processing. See Section 32.18, Parallel Programming, for a parallel implementation of a merge sort.

merge sort time complexity

Let $T(n)$ denote the time required for sorting an array of n elements using a merge sort. Without loss of generality, assume n is a power of 2. The merge sort algorithm splits the array into two subarrays, sorts the subarrays using the same algorithm recursively, and then merges the subarrays. Therefore,

$$T(n) = T\left(\frac{n}{2}\right) + T\left(\frac{n}{2}\right) + mergetime$$

The first $T\left(\frac{n}{2}\right)$ is the time for sorting the first half of the array, and the second $T\left(\frac{n}{2}\right)$ is the time for sorting the second half. To merge two subarrays, it takes at most $n - 1$ comparisons to compare the elements from the two subarrays and n moves to move elements to the temporary array. Thus, the total time is $2n - 1$. Therefore,

$$T(n) = T\left(\frac{n}{2}\right) + T\left(\frac{n}{2}\right) + 2n - 1 = O(n \log n)$$

$O(n \log n)$ merge sort

The complexity of a merge sort is $O(n \log n)$. This algorithm is better than selection sort, insertion sort, and bubble sort, because the time complexity of these algorithms is $O(n^2)$. The **sort** method in the **java.util.Arrays** class is implemented using a variation of the merge sort algorithm.

MyProgrammingLab™

25.4 Describe how a merge sort works. What is the time complexity for a merge sort?

25.5 Use Figure 25.2 as an example to show how to apply a merge sort on {45, 11, 50, 59, 60, 2, 4, 7, 10}.

25.6 What is wrong if lines 6–15 in Listing 25.5, MergeSort.java, are replaced by the following code?

```
int[] firstHalf = new int[list.length / 2 + 1];
System.arraycopy(list, 0, firstHalf, 0, list.length / 2 + 1);
mergeSort(firstHalf);

// Merge sort the second half
int secondHalfLength = list.length - list.length / 2 - 1;
int[] secondHalf = new int[secondHalfLength];
System.arraycopy(list, list.length / 2 + 1,
  secondHalf, 0, secondHalfLength);
mergeSort(secondHalf);
```

25.4 Quick Sort

quick sort

A quick sort works as follows: The algorithm selects an element, called the pivot, in the array. It divides the array into two parts, so that all the elements in the first part are less than or equal to the pivot and all the elements in the second part are greater than the pivot. The quick sort algorithm is then recursively applied to the first part and then the second part.

The quick sort algorithm, developed by C.A.R. Hoare in 1962, is described in Listing 25.6.

Listing 25.6 Quick Sort Algorithm

base condition
select the pivot
partition the list
sort first part
sort second part

```
public static void quickSort(int[] list) {
  if (list.length > 1) {
    select a pivot;
    partition list into list1 and list2 such that
      all elements in list1 <= pivot and
      all elements in list2 > pivot;
    quickSort(list1);
    quickSort(list2);
  }
}
```

pivot
| list1 | | list2 |

how to partition

Each partition places the pivot in the right place. The selection of the pivot affects the performance of the algorithm. Ideally, the algorithm should choose the pivot that divides the two parts evenly. For simplicity, assume the first element in the array is chosen as the pivot. (Programming Exercise 25.4 proposes an alternative strategy for selecting the pivot.)

quick sort illustration

Figure 25.5 illustrates how to sort an array (5 2 9 3 8 4 0 1 6 7) using quick sort. Choose the first element, 5, as the pivot. The array is partitioned into two parts, as shown in Figure 25.5b. The highlighted pivot is placed in the right place in the array. Apply quick sort on two partial arrays (4 2 1 3 0) and then (8 9 6 7). The pivot 4 partitions (4 2 1 3 0) into just one partial array (0 2 1 3), as shown in Figure 25.5c. Apply quick sort on (0 2 1 3). The pivot 0 partitions it into just one partial array (2 1 3), as shown in Figure 25.5d. Apply quick sort on (2 1 3). The pivot 2 partitions it into (1) and (3), as shown in Figure 25.5e. Apply quick sort on (1). Since the array contains just one element, no further partition is needed.

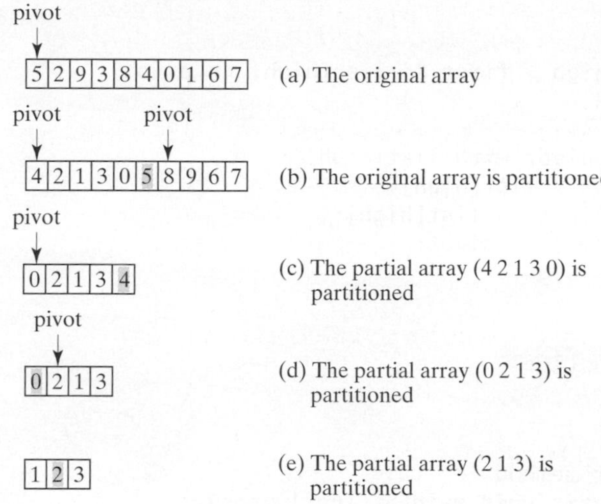

FIGURE 25.5 The quick sort algorithm is recursively applied to partial arrays.

The quick sort algorithm is implemented in Listing 25.7. There are two overloaded `quickSort` methods in the class. The first method (line 2) is used to sort an array. The second is a helper method (line 6) that sorts a partial array with a specified range.

LISTING 25.7 QuickSort.java

```
 1 public class QuickSort {
 2   public static void quickSort(int[] list) {
 3     quickSort(list, 0, list.length - 1);
 4   }
 5
 6   public static void quickSort(int[] list, int first, int last) {
 7     if (last > first) {
 8       int pivotIndex = partition(list, first, last);
 9       quickSort(list, first, pivotIndex - 1);
10       quickSort(list, pivotIndex + 1, last);
11     }
12   }
13
14   /** Partition the array list[first..last] */
15   public static int partition(int[] list, int first, int last) {
16     int pivot = list[first]; // Choose the first element as the pivot
17     int low = first + 1; // Index for forward search
18     int high = last; // Index for backward search
19
20     while (high > low) {
21       // Search forward from left
22       while (low <= high && list[low] <= pivot)
23         low++;
24
```

sort method

helper method

recursive call

forward

backward

swap

place pivot

pivot's new index

pivot's original index

```
25       // Search backward from right
26       while (low <= high && list[high] > pivot)
27         high--;
28 
29       // Swap two elements in the list
30       if (high > low) {
31         int temp = list[high];
32         list[high] = list[low];
33         list[low] = temp;
34       }
35     }
36 
37     while (high > first && list[high] >= pivot)
38       high--;
39 
40     // Swap pivot with list[high]
41     if (pivot > list[high]) {
42       list[first] = list[high];
43       list[high] = pivot;
44       return high;
45     }
46     else {
47       return first;
48     }
49   }
50 
51   /** A test method */
52   public static void main(String[] args) {
53     int[] list = {2, 3, 2, 5, 6, 1, -2, 3, 14, 12};
54     quickSort(list);
55     for (int i = 0; i < list.length; i++)
56       System.out.print(list[i] + " ");
57   }
58 }
```

```
-2 1 2 2 3 3 5 6 12 14
```

The **partition** method (lines 15–49) partitions the array **list[first..last]** using the pivot. The first element in the partial array is chosen as the pivot (line 16). Initially **low** points to the second element in the partial array (line 17) and **high** points to the last element in the partial array (line 18).

Starting from the left, the method searches forward in the array for the first element that is greater than the pivot (lines 22–23), then searches from the right backward for the first element in the array that is less than or equal to the pivot (lines 26–27). It then swaps these two elements and repeats the same search and swap operations until all the elements are searched in a **while** loop (lines 20–35).

The method returns the new index for the pivot that divides the partial array into two parts if the pivot has been moved (line 44). Otherwise, it returns the original index for the pivot (line 47).

partition illustration

partition animation on Companion Website

Figure 25.6 illustrates how to partition an array (5 2 9 3 8 4 0 1 6 7). Choose the first element, 5, as the pivot. Initially **low** is the index that points to element 2 and **high** points to element 7, as shown in Figure 25.6a. Advance index **low** forward to search for the first element (9) that is greater than the pivot and move index **high** backward to search for the first element (1) that is less than or equal to the pivot, as shown in Figure 25.6b. Swap 9 with 1, as shown in Figure 25.6c. Continue the search and move **low** to point to element 8 and **high** to point to element 0, as shown in Figure 25.6d. Swap element 8 with 0, as shown in Figure 25.6e.

Continue to move `low` until it passes `high`, as shown in Figure 25.6f. Now all the elements are examined. Swap the pivot with element 4 at index `high`. The final partition is shown in Figure 25.6g. The index of the pivot is returned when the method is finished.

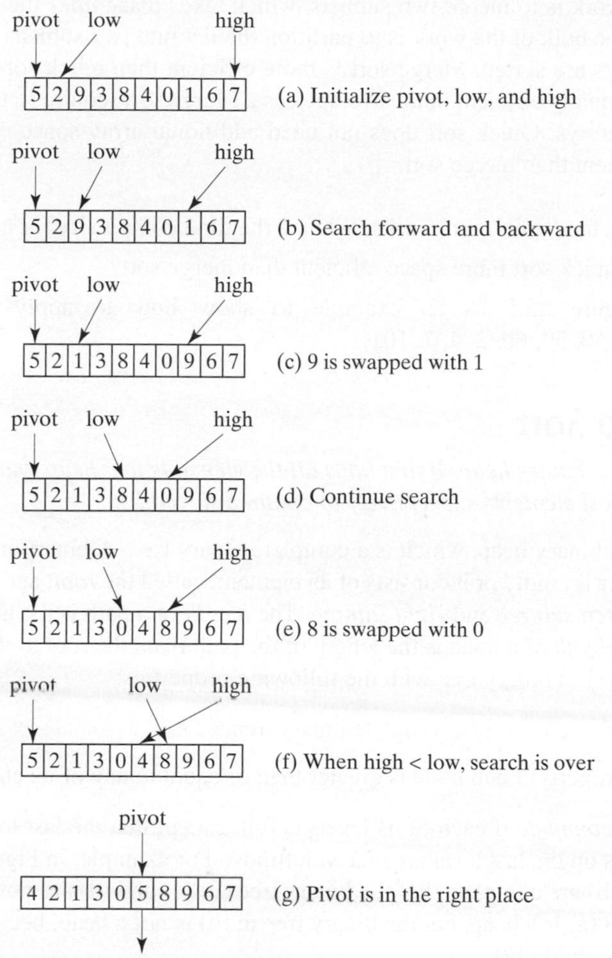

FIGURE 25.6 The `partition` method returns the index of the pivot after it is put in the correct place.

To partition an array of n elements, it takes n comparisons and n moves in the worst-case analysis. Thus, the time required for partition is $O(n)$. $O(n)$ partition time

In the worst case, the pivot divides the array each time into one big subarray with the other array empty. The size of the big subarray is one less than the one before divided. The algorithm requires $(n - 1) + (n - 2) + \ldots + 2 + 1 = O(n^2)$ time. $O(n^2)$ worst-case time

In the best case, the pivot divides the array each time into two parts of about the same size. Let $T(n)$ denote the time required for sorting an array of n elements using quick sort. Thus, $O(n \log n)$ best-case time

recursive quick sort on two subarrays — partition time

$$T(n) = T\left(\frac{n}{2}\right) + T\left(\frac{n}{2}\right) + n.$$

Similar to the merge sort analysis, $T(n) = O(n \log n)$.

O(n logn) average-case time

On the average, the pivot will not divide the array into two parts of the same size or one empty part each time. Statistically, the sizes of the two parts are very close. Therefore, the average time is $O(n \log n)$. The exact average-case analysis is beyond the scope of this book.

quick sort vs. merge sort

Both merge sort and quick sort employ the divide-and-conquer approach. For merge sort, the bulk of the work is to merge two sublists, which takes place *after* the sublists are sorted. For quick sort, the bulk of the work is to partition the list into two sublists, which takes place *before* the sublists are sorted. Merge sort is more efficient than quick sort in the worst case, but the two are equally efficient in the average case. Merge sort requires a temporary array for sorting two subarrays. Quick sort does not need additional array space. Thus, quick sort is more space efficient than merge sort.

MyProgrammingLab™

25.7 Describe how quick sort works. What is the time complexity for a quick sort?

25.8 Why is quick sort more space efficient than merge sort?

25.9 Use Figure 25.5 as an example to show how to apply a quick sort on {45, 11, 50, 59, 60, 2, 4, 7, 10}.

25.5 Heap Sort

A heap sort uses a binary heap. It first adds all the elements to a heap and then removes the largest elements successively to obtain a sorted list.

heap sort
root
left subtree
right subtree
length
depth

Heap sorts use a binary heap, which is a complete binary tree. A binary tree is a hierarchical structure. It either is empty or it consists of an element, called the *root*, and two distinct binary trees, called the *left subtree* and *right subtree*. The *length* of a path is the number of the edges in the path. The *depth* of a node is the length of the path from the root to the node.

A *binary heap* is a binary tree with the following properties:

- Shape property: It is a complete binary tree.
- Heap property: Each node is greater than or equal to any of its children.

complete binary tree

A binary tree is *complete* if each of its levels is full, except that the last level may not be full and all the leaves on the last level are placed leftmost. For example, in Figure 25.7, the binary trees in (a) and (b) are complete, but the binary trees in (c) and (d) are not complete. Further, the binary tree in (a) is a heap, but the binary tree in (b) is not a heap, because the root (39) is less than its right child (42).

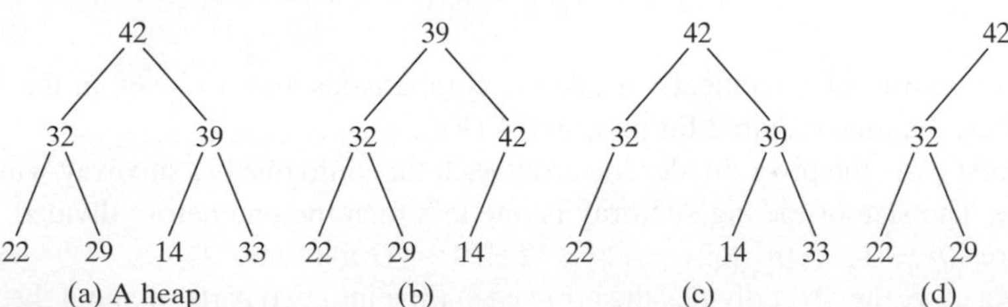

Figure 25.7 A binary heap is a special complete binary tree.

heap

Note
Heap is a term with many meanings in computer science. In this chapter, heap means a binary heap.

Pedagogical Note

A heap can be implemented efficiently for inserting keys and for deleting the root. For an interactive demo on how a heap works, go to www.cs.armstrong.edu/liang/animation/HeapAnimation.html, as shown in Figure 25.8.

heap animation on Companion Website

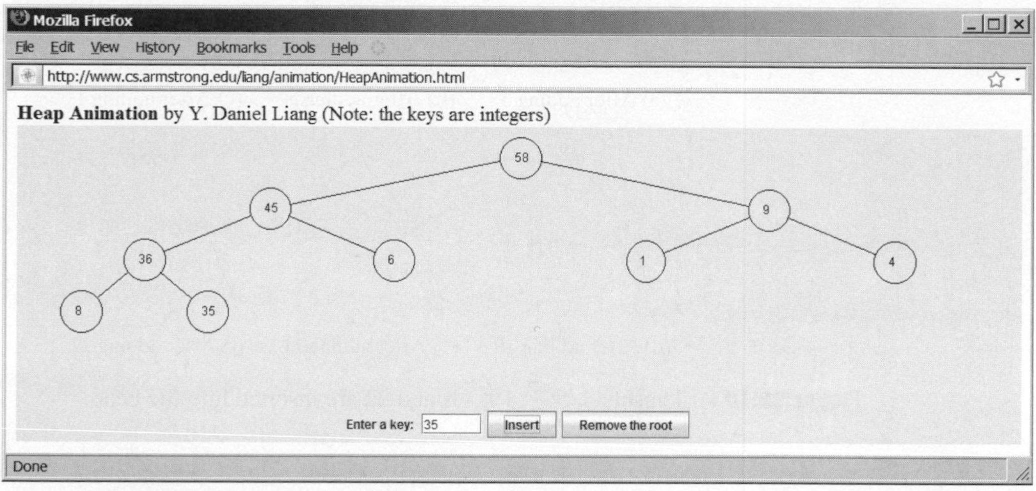

FIGURE 25.8 The heap animation tool enables you to insert a key and delete the root visually.

25.5.1 Storing a Heap

A heap can be stored in an `ArrayList` or an array if the heap size is known in advance. The heap in Figure 25.9a can be stored using the array in Figure 25.9b. The root is at position 0, and its two children are at positions 1 and 2. For a node at position i, its left child is at position $2i + 1$, its right child is at position $2i + 2$, and its parent is $(i - 1)/2$. For example, the node for element 39 is at position 4, so its left child (element 14) is at 9 ($2 \times 4 + 1$), its right child (element 33) is at 10 ($2 \times 4 + 2$), and its parent (element 42) is at 1 ($(4 - 1)/2$).

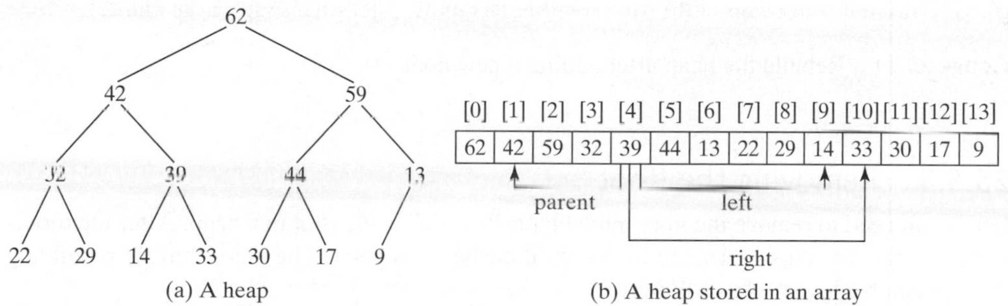

FIGURE 25.9 A binary heap can be implemented using an array.

25.5.2 Adding a New Node

To add a new node to the heap, first add it to the end of the heap and then rebuild the tree as follows:

```
Let the last node be the current node;
while (the current node is greater than its parent) {
  Swap the current node with its parent;
  Now the current node is one level up;
}
```

Suppose a heap is initially empty. That heap is shown in Figure 25.10, after adding numbers 3, 5, 1, 19, 11, and 22 in this order.

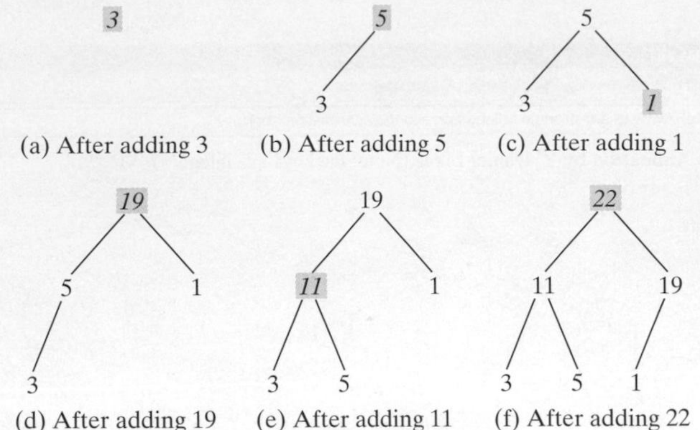

FIGURE 25.10 Elements 3, 5, 1, 19, 11, and 22 are inserted into the heap.

Now consider adding 88 into the heap. Place the new node 88 at the end of the tree, as shown in Figure 25.11a. Swap 88 with 19, as shown in Figure 25.18b. Swap 88 with 22, as shown in Figure 25.11c.

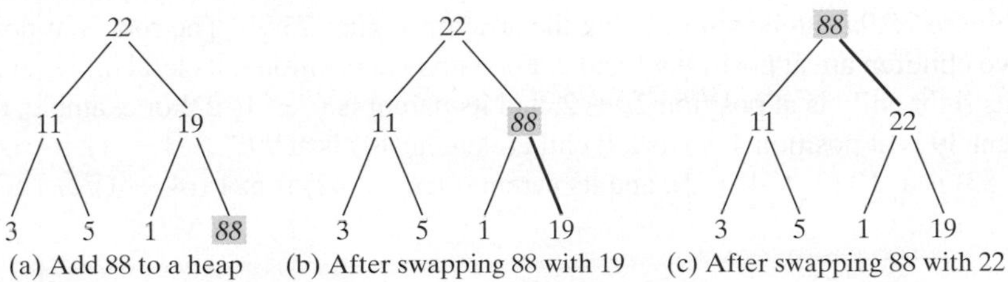

FIGURE 25.11 Rebuild the heap after adding a new node.

25.5.3 Removing the Root

Often you need to remove the maximum element, which is the root in a heap. After the root is removed, the tree must be rebuilt to maintain the heap property. The algorithm for rebuilding the tree can be described as follows:

```
Move the last node to replace the root;
Let the root be the current node;
while (the current node has children and the current node is
        smaller than one of its children) {
  Swap the current node with the larger of its children;
  Now the current node is one level down;
}
```

Figure 25.12 shows the process of rebuilding a heap after the root 62 is removed from Figure 25.9a. Move the last node, 9, to the root, as shown in Figure 25.12a. Swap 9 with 59, as shown in Figure 25.12b; swap 9 with 44, as shown in Figure 25.12c; and swap 9 with 30, as shown in Figure 25.12d.

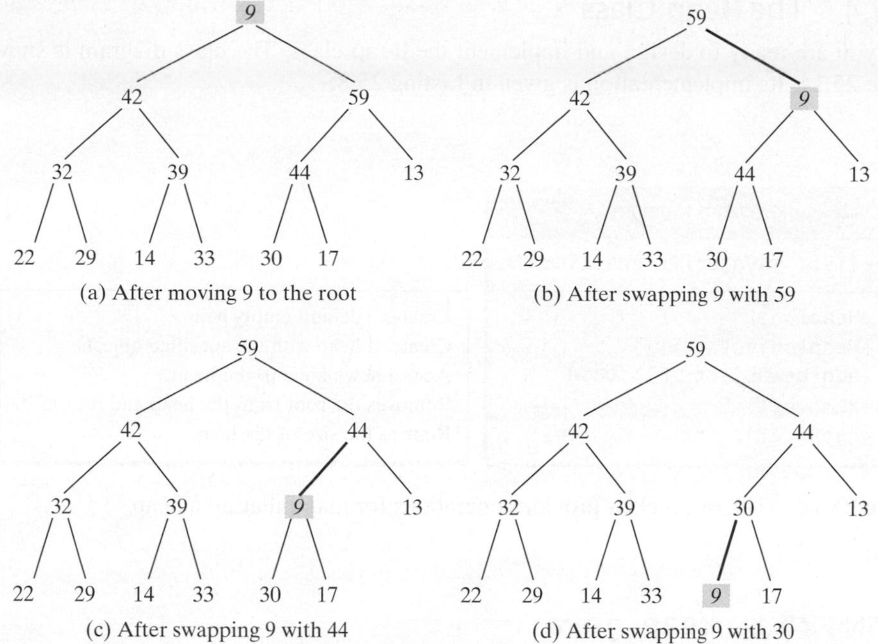

FIGURE 25.12 Rebuild the heap after the root 62 is removed.

Figure 25.13 shows the process of rebuilding a heap after the root, 59, is removed from Figure 25.12d. Move the last node, 17, to the root, as shown in Figure 25.13a. Swap 17 with 44, as shown in Figure 25.13b, and then swap 17 with 30, as shown in Figure 25.13c.

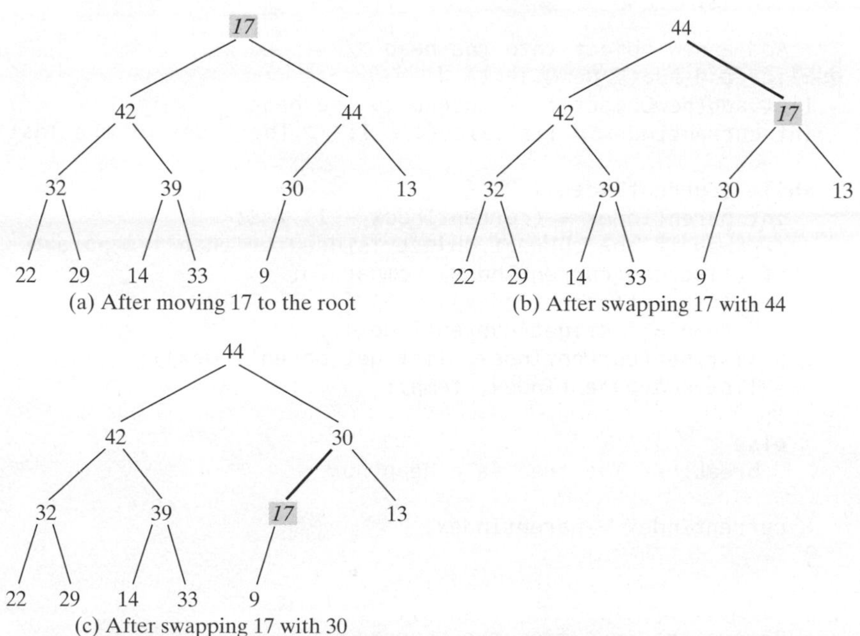

FIGURE 25.13 Rebuild the heap after the root, 59, is removed.

25.5.4 The Heap Class

Now you are ready to design and implement the **Heap** class. The class diagram is shown in Figure 25.14. Its implementation is given in Listing 25.8.

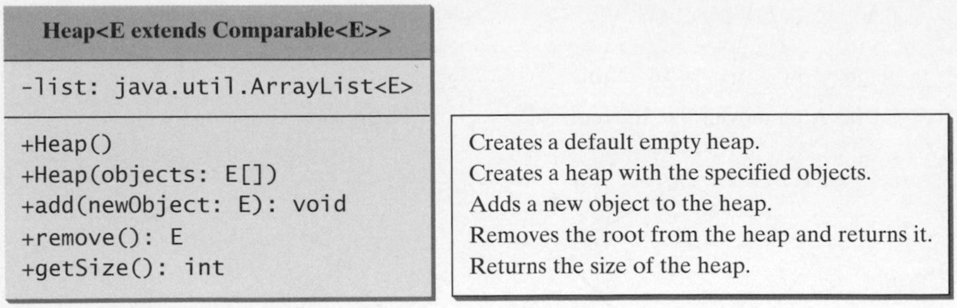

Heap<E extends Comparable<E>>	
-list: java.util.ArrayList<E>	
+Heap()	Creates a default empty heap.
+Heap(objects: E[])	Creates a heap with the specified objects.
+add(newObject: E): void	Adds a new object to the heap.
+remove(): E	Removes the root from the heap and returns it.
+getSize(): int	Returns the size of the heap.

Figure 25.14 The **Heap** class provides operations for manipulating a heap.

LISTING 25.8 Heap.java

```
public class Heap<E extends Comparable<E>> {
  private java.util.ArrayList<E> list = new java.util.ArrayList<E>();

  /** Create a default heap */
  public Heap() {
  }

  /** Create a heap from an array of objects */
  public Heap(E[] objects) {
    for (int i = 0; i < objects.length; i++)
      add(objects[i]);
  }

  /** Add a new object into the heap */
  public void add(E newObject) {
    list.add(newObject); // Append to the heap
    int currentIndex = list.size() - 1; // The index of the last node

    while (currentIndex > 0) {
      int parentIndex = (currentIndex - 1) / 2;
      // Swap if the current object is greater than its parent
      if (list.get(currentIndex).compareTo(
          list.get(parentIndex)) > 0) {
        E temp = list.get(currentIndex);
        list.set(currentIndex, list.get(parentIndex));
        list.set(parentIndex, temp);
      }
      else
        break; // The tree is a heap now

      currentIndex = parentIndex;
    }
  }

  /** Remove the root from the heap */
  public E remove() {
```

internal heap representation
no-arg constructor
constructor
add a new object
append the object
swap with parent
heap now
remove the root

```
37      if (list.size() == 0) return null;
38
39      E removedObject = list.get(0);
40      list.set(0, list.get(list.size() - 1));
41      list.remove(list.size() - 1);
42
43      int currentIndex = 0;
44      while (currentIndex < list.size()) {
45        int leftChildIndex = 2 * currentIndex + 1;
46        int rightChildIndex = 2 * currentIndex + 2;
47
48        // Find the maximum between two children
49        if (leftChildIndex >= list.size()) break; // The tree is a heap
50        int maxIndex = leftChildIndex;
51        if (rightChildIndex < list.size()) {
52          if (list.get(maxIndex).compareTo(
53              list.get(rightChildIndex)) < 0) {
54            maxIndex = rightChildIndex;
55          }
56        }
57
58        // Swap if the current node is less than the maximum
59        if (list.get(currentIndex).compareTo(
60            list.get(maxIndex)) < 0) {
61          E temp = list.get(maxIndex);
62          list.set(maxIndex, list.get(currentIndex));
63          list.set(currentIndex, temp);
64          currentIndex = maxIndex;
65        }
66        else
67          break; // The tree is a heap
68      }
69
70      return removedObject;
71    }
72
73    /** Get the number of nodes in the tree */
74    public int getSize() {
75      return list.size();
76    }
77  }
```

empty heap

root

new root

remove the last

adjust the tree

compare two children

swap with the larger child

A heap is represented using an array list internally (line 2). You can change the array list to other data structures, but the **Heap** class contract will remain unchanged.

The **add(E newObject)** method (lines 15–33) appends the object to the tree and then swaps the object with its parent if the object is greater than its parent. This process continues until the new object becomes the root or is not greater than its parent.

The **remove()** method (lines 36–71) removes and returns the root. To maintain the heap property, the method moves the last object to the root position and swaps it with its larger child if it is less than the larger child. This process continues until the last object becomes a leaf or is not less than its children.

25.5.5 Sorting Using the Heap Class

To sort an array using a heap, first create an object using the **Heap** class, add all the elements to the heap using the **add** method, and remove all the elements from the heap using the **remove** method. The elements are removed in descending order. Listing 25.9 gives a program for sorting an array using a heap.

LISTING 25.9 HeapSort.java

```java
public class HeapSort {
  /** Heap sort method */
  public static <E extends Comparable> void heapSort(E[] list) {
    // Create a Heap of integers
    Heap<E> heap = new Heap<E>();

    // Add elements to the heap
    for (int i = 0; i < list.length; i++)
      heap.add(list[i]);

    // Remove elements from the heap
    for (int i = list.length - 1; i >= 0; i--)
      list[i] = heap.remove();
  }

  /** A test method */
  public static void main(String[] args) {
    Integer[] list = {-44, -5, -3, 3, 3, 1, -4, 0, 1, 2, 4, 5, 53};
    heapSort(list);
    for (int i = 0; i < list.length; i++)
      System.out.print(list[i] + " ");
  }
}
```

create a Heap

add element

remove element

invoke sort method

```
-44 -5 -4 -3 0 1 1 2 3 3 4 5 53
```

25.5.6 Heap Sort Time Complexity

height of a heap

Let us turn our attention to analyzing the time complexity for the heap sort. Let h denote the height for a heap of n elements. The height of a heap is the number of nodes in the longest path from the root to a leaf node. Since a heap is a complete binary tree, the first level has 1 node, the second level has 2 nodes, the kth level has 2^{k-1} nodes, the $(h - 1)$ level has 2^{h-2} nodes, and the hth level has at least 1 and at most 2^{h-1} nodes. Therefore,

$$1 + 2 + \ldots + 2^{h-2} < n \leq 1 + 2 + \ldots + 2^{h-2} + 2^{h-1}$$

That is,

$$2^{h-1} - 1 < n \leq 2^h - 1$$
$$2^{h-1} < n + 1 \leq 2^h$$
$$h - 1 < \log(n + 1) \leq h$$

Thus, $h < \log(n + 1) + 1$ and $\log(n + 1) \leq h$. Therefore, $\log(n + 1) \leq h < \log(n + 1) + 1$. Hence, the height of the heap is $O(\log n)$.

O(n logn) worst-case time

Since the `add` method traces a path from a leaf to a root, it takes at most h steps to add a new element to the heap. Thus, the total time for constructing an initial heap is $O(n \log n)$ for an array of n elements. Since the `remove` method traces a path from a root to a leaf, it takes at most h steps to rebuild a heap after removing the root from the heap. Since the `remove` method is invoked n times, the total time for producing a sorted array from a heap is $O(n \log n)$.

heap sort vs. merge sort

Both merge sorts and heap sorts require $O(n \log n)$ time. A merge sort requires a temporary array for merging two subarrays; a heap sort does not need additional array space. Therefore, a heap sort is more space efficient than a merge sort.

25.10 What is a complete binary tree? What is a heap? Describe how to remove the root from a heap and how to add a new object to a heap.

25.11 What is the return value from invoking the `remove` method if the heap is empty?

25.12 Add the elements `4`, `5`, `1`, `2`, `9`, and `3` into a heap in this order. Draw the diagrams to show the heap after each element is added.

25.13 Show the heap after the root in the heap in Figure 25.13c is removed.

25.14 What is the time complexity of inserting a new element into a heap and what is the time complexity of deleting an element from a heap?

25.15 Show the steps of creating a heap using {45, 11, 50, 59, 60, 2, 4, 7, 10}.

25.16 Given the following heap, show the steps of removing all nodes from the heap.

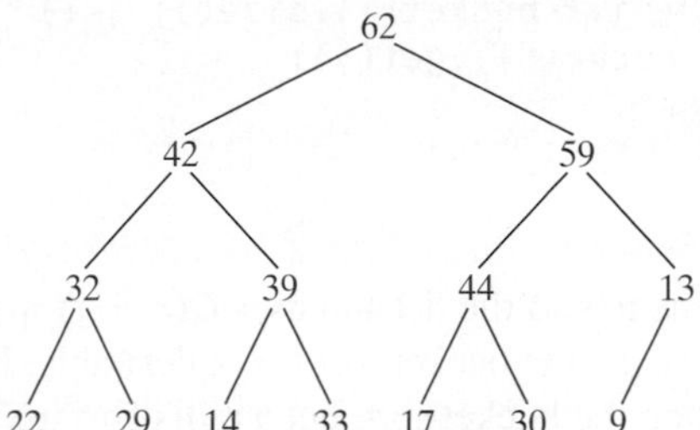

25.17 Which of the following statements are wrong?

```
Heap<Object> heap1 = new Heap<Object>();
Heap<Number> heap2 = new Heap<Number>();
Heap<BigInteger> heap3 = new Heap<BigInteger>();
Heap<Calendar> heap4 = new Heap<Calendar>();
Heap<String> heap5 = new Heap<String>();
```

25.6 Bucket Sort and Radix Sort

Bucket sorts and radix sorts are efficient for sorting integers.

All sort algorithms discussed so far are general sorting algorithms that work for any types of keys (e.g., integers, strings, and any comparable objects). These algorithms sort the elements by comparing their keys. The lower bound for general sorting algorithms is $O(n \log n)$, so no sorting algorithms based on comparisons can perform better than $O(n \log n)$. However, if the keys are small integers, you can use a bucket sort without having to compare the keys.

The bucket sort algorithm works as follows. Assume the keys are in the range from `0` to `t`. We need `t + 1` buckets labeled `0`, `1`, . . . , and `t`. If an element's key is `i`, the element is put into the bucket `i`. Each bucket holds the elements with the same key value.

bucket sort

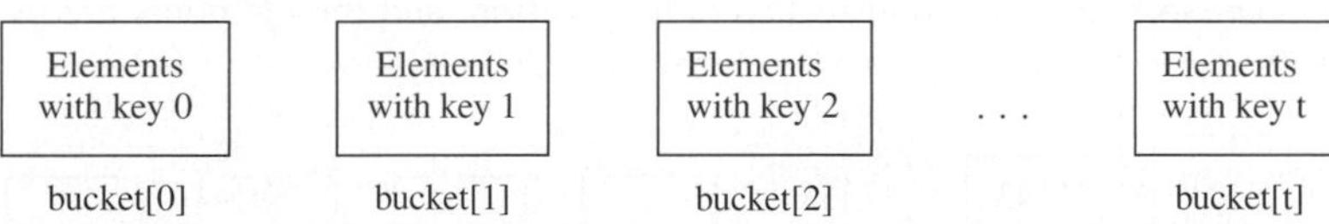

You can use an `ArrayList` to implement a bucket. The bucket sort algorithm for sorting a list of elements can be described as follows:

```
void bucketSort(E[] list) {
  E[] bucket = (E[])new java.util.ArrayList[t+1];

  // Distribute the elements from list to buckets
  for (int i = 0; i < list.length; i++) {
```

```
            int key = list[i].getKey();

            if (bucket[key] == null)
              bucket[key] = new java.util.ArrayList();

            bucket[key].add(list[i]);
          }

          // Now move the elements from the buckets back to list
          int k = 0; // k is an index for list
          for (int i = 0; i < bucket.length; i++) {
            if (bucket[i] != null) {
              for (int j = 0; j < bucket[i].size(); j++)
                list[k++] = bucket[i].get(j);
            }
          }
        }
```

Clearly, it takes $O(n + t)$ time to sort the list and uses $O(n + t)$ space, where n is the list size.

Note that if t is too large, using the bucket sort is not desirable. Instead, you can use a radix sort. The radix sort is based on the bucket sort, but a radix sort uses only ten buckets.

stable

It is worthwhile to note that a bucket sort is *stable*, meaning that if two elements in the original list have the same key value, their order is not changed in the sorted list. That is, if element e_1 and element e_2 have the same key and e_1 precedes e_2 in the original list, e_1 still precedes e_2 in the sorted list.

radix sort

Assume that the keys are positive integers. The idea for the *radix sort* is to divide the keys into subgroups based on their radix positions. It applies a bucket sort repeatedly for the key values on radix positions, starting from the least-significant position.

radix sort on Companion Website

Consider sorting the elements with the following keys:

331, 454, 230, 34, 343, 45, 59, 453, 345, 231, 9

queue

Apply the bucket sort on the last radix position, and the elements are put into the buckets as follows:

bucket[0]	bucket[1]	bucket[2]	bucket[3]	bucket[4]	bucket[5]	bucket[6]	bucket[7]	bucket[8]	bucket[9]
230	331 231		343 453	454 34	45 345				59 9

After being removed from the buckets, the elements are in the following order:

230, 331, 231, 343, 453, 454, 34, 45, 345, 59, 9

queue

Apply the bucket sort on the second-to-last radix position, and the elements are put into the buckets as follows:

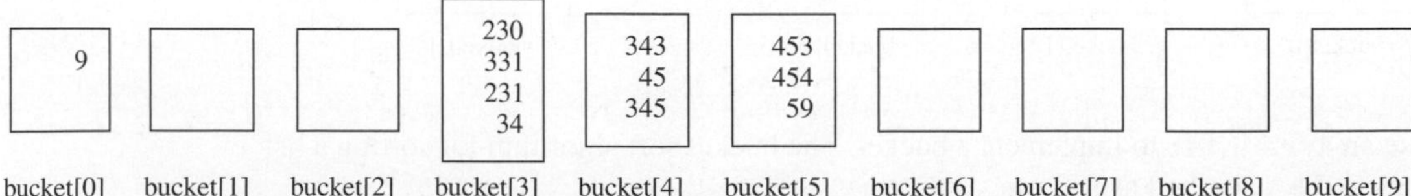

After being removed from the buckets, the elements are in the following order:

9, 230, 331, 231, 34, 343, 45, 345, 453, 454, 59

(Note that 9 is 009.)

Apply the bucket sort on the third-to-last radix position, and the elements are put into the buckets as follows:

queue

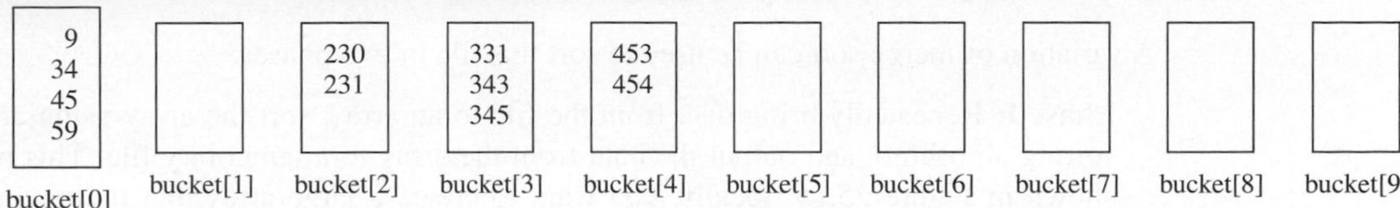

After being removed from the buckets, the elements are in the following order:

```
9, 34, 45, 59, 230, 231, 331, 343, 345, 453, 454
```

The elements are now sorted.

Radix sort takes $O(dn)$ time to sort n elements with integer keys, where d is the maximum number of the radix positions among all keys.

25.18 Can you sort a list of strings using a bucket sort?

25.19 Show how the radix sort works using the numbers 454, 34, 23, 43, 74, 86, and 76.

25.7 External Sort

You can sort a large amount data using an external sort.

All the sort algorithms discussed in the preceding sections assume that all the data to be sorted are available at one time in internal memory, such as in an array. To sort data stored in an external file, you must first bring the data to the memory and then sort it internally. However, if the file is too large, all the data in the file cannot be brought to memory at one time. This section discusses how to sort data in a large external file. This is called an *external sort*.

external sort

For simplicity, assume that two million `int` values are stored in a binary file named **largedata.dat**. This file was created using the program in Listing 25.10.

LISTING 25.10 CreateLargeFile.java

```
import java.io.*;

public class CreateLargeFile {
  public static void main(String[] args) throws Exception {
    DataOutputStream output = new DataOutputStream(
      new BufferedOutputStream(
      new FileOutputStream("largedata.dat")));

    for (int i = 0; i < 800004; i++)
      output.writeInt((int)(Math.random() * 1000000));

    output.close();

    // Display first 100 numbers
    DataInputStream input =
      new DataInputStream(new FileInputStream("largedata.dat"));
    for (int i = 0; i < 100; i++)
      System.out.print(input.readInt() + " ");

    input.close();
  }
}
```

a binary output stream

output an `int` value

close output file

read an `int` value

close input file

```
569193 131317 608695 776266 767910 624915 458599 5010 ... (omitted)
```

A variation of merge sort can be used to sort this file in two phases:

Phase I: Repeatedly bring data from the file to an array, sort the array using an internal sorting algorithm, and output the data from the array to a temporary file. This process is shown in Figure 25.15. Ideally, you want to create a large array, but its maximum size depends on how much memory is allocated to the JVM by the operating system. Assume that the maximum array size is 100,000 `int` values. In the temporary file, every 100,000 `int` values are sorted. They are denoted as S_1, S_2, . . . , and S_k, where the last segment, S_k, may contain less than 100000 values.

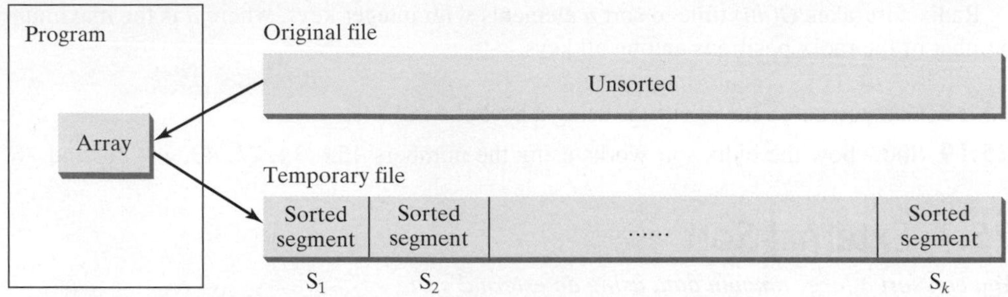

FIGURE 25.15 The original file is sorted in segments.

Phase II: Merge a pair of sorted segments (e.g., S_1 with S_2, S_3 with S_4, . . . , and so on) into a larger sorted segment and save the new segment into a new temporary file. Continue the same process until only one sorted segment results. Figure 25.16 shows how to merge eight segments.

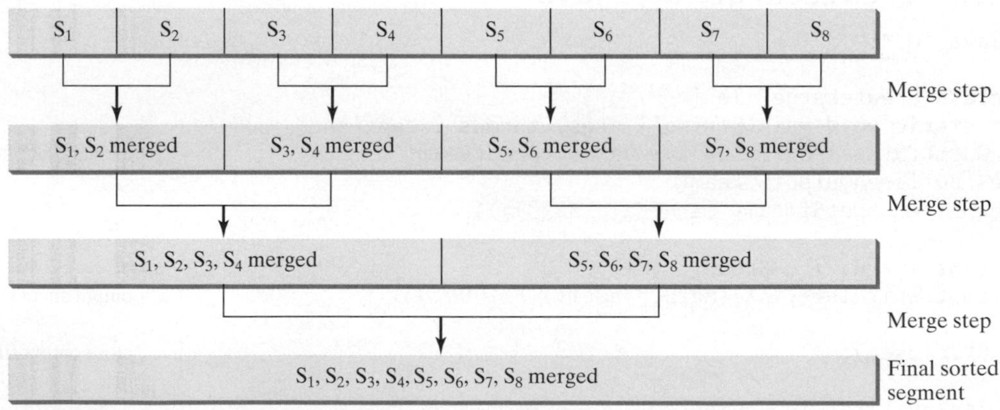

FIGURE 25.16 Sorted segments are merged iteratively.

Note

It is not necessary to merge two successive segments. For example, you can merge S_1 with S_5, S_2 with S_6, S_3 with S_7, and S_4 with S_8, in the first merge step. This observation is useful in implementing Phase II efficiently.

25.7.1 Implementing Phase I

Listing 25.11 gives the method that reads each segment of data from a file, sorts the segment, and stores the sorted segments into a new file. The method returns the number of segments.

LISTING 25.11 Creating Initial Sorted Segments

```
1  /** Sort original file into sorted segments */
2  private static int initializeSegments
3      (int segmentSize, String originalFile, String f1)
4      throws Exception {
5    int[] list = new int[segmentSize];
6    DataInputStream input = new DataInputStream(
7      new BufferedInputStream(new FileInputStream(originalFile)));
8    DataOutputStream output = new DataOutputStream(
9      new BufferedOutputStream(new FileOutputStream(f1)));
10
11   int numberOfSegments = 0;
12   while (input.available() > 0) {
13     numberOfSegments++;
14     int i = 0;
15     for ( ; input.available() > 0 && i < segmentSize; i++) {
16       list[i] = input.readInt();
17     }
18
19     // Sort an array list[0..i-1]
20     java.util.Arrays.sort(list, 0, i);
21
22     // Write the array to f1.dat
23     for (int j = 0; j < i; j++) {
24       output.writeInt(list[j]);
25     }
26   }
27
28   input.close();
29   output.close();
30
31   return numberOfSegments;
32 }
```

Margin notes: original file (line 7); file with sorted segments (line 9); sort a segment (line 20); output to file (line 24); close file (line 28); return # of segments (line 31).

The method creates an array with the maximum size in line 5, a data input stream for the original file in line 6, and a data output stream for a temporary file in line 8. Buffered streams are used to improve performance.

Lines 14–17 read a segment of data from the file into the array. Line 20 sorts the array. Lines 23–25 write the data in the array to the temporary file.

The number of segments is returned in line 31. Note that every segment has `MAX_ARRAY_SIZE` number of elements except the last segment, which may have fewer elements.

25.7.2 Implementing Phase II

In each merge step, two sorted segments are merged to form a new segment. The size of the new segment is doubled. The number of segments is reduced by half after each merge step. A segment is too large to be brought to an array in memory. To implement a merge step, copy half the number of segments from the file **f1.dat** to a temporary file **f2.dat**. Then merge the first remaining segment in **f1.dat** with the first segment in **f2.dat** into a temporary file named **f3.dat**, as shown in Figure 25.17.

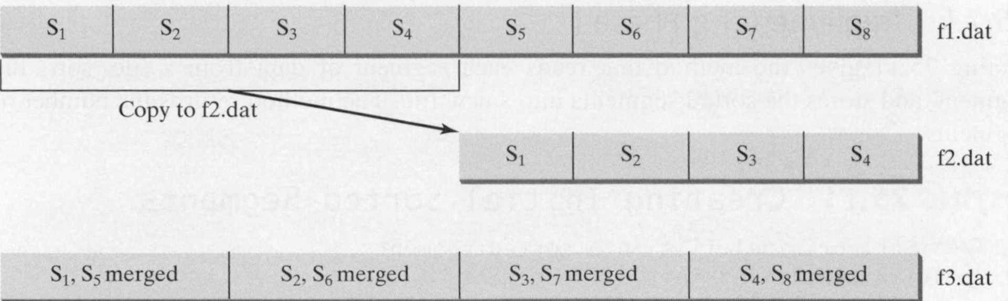

FIGURE 25.17 Sorted segments are merged iteratively.

Note

f1.dat may have one segment more than **f2.dat**. If so, move the last segment into **f3.dat** after the merge.

Listing 25.12 gives a method that copies the first half of the segments in f1.dat to f2.dat. Listing 25.13 gives a method that merges a pair of segments in f1.dat and f2.dat. Listing 25.14 gives a method that merges two segments.

LISTING 25.12 Copying First Half Segments

input stream f1 · output stream f2 · segments copied

```
private static void copyHalfToF2(int numberOfSegments,
    int segmentSize, DataInputStream f1, DataOutputStream f2)
    throws Exception {
  for (int i = 0; i < (numberOfSegments / 2) * segmentSize; i++) {
    f2.writeInt(f1.readInt());
  }
}
```

LISTING 25.13 Merging All Segments

input stream f1 and f2 · output stream f3 · merge two segments · extra segment in f1?

```
private static void mergeSegments(int numberOfSegments,
    int segmentSize, DataInputStream f1, DataInputStream f2,
    DataOutputStream f3) throws Exception {
  for (int i = 0; i < numberOfSegments; i++) {
    mergeTwoSegments(segmentSize, f1, f2, f3);
  }

  // If f1 has one extra segment, copy it to f3
  while (f1.available() > 0) {
    f3.writeInt(f1.readInt());
  }
}
```

LISTING 25.14 Merging Two Segments

input stream f1 and f2 · output stream f3 · read from f1 · read from f2 · write to f3

```
private static void mergeTwoSegments(int segmentSize,
    DataInputStream f1, DataInputStream f2,
    DataOutputStream f3) throws Exception {
  int intFromF1 = f1.readInt();
  int intFromF2 = f2.readInt();
  int f1Count = 1;
  int f2Count = 1;

  while (true) {
    if (intFromF1 < intFromF2) {
      f3.writeInt(intFromF1);
```

```
        if (f1.available() == 0 || f1Count++ >= segmentSize) {
          f3.writeInt(intFromF2);
          break;
        }
        else {
          intFromF1 = f1.readInt();
        }
      }
      else {
        f3.writeInt(intFromF2);
        if (f2.available() == 0 || f2Count++ >= segmentSize) {
          f3.writeInt(intFromF1);
          break;
        }
        else {
          intFromF2 = f2.readInt();
        }
      }
    }

    while (f1.available() > 0 && f1Count++ < segmentSize) {
      f3.writeInt(f1.readInt());
    }

    while (f2.available() > 0 && f2Count++ < segmentSize) {
      f3.writeInt(f2.readInt());
    }
  }
```

segment in f1 finished

write to f3

segment in f2 finished

remaining f1 segment

remaining f2 segment

25.7.3 Combining Two Phases

Listing 25.15 gives the complete program for sorting `int` values in **largedata.dat** and storing the sorted data in **sortedfile.dat**.

LISTING 25.15 SortLargeFile.java

```
import java.io.*;

public class SortLargeFile {
  public static final int MAX_ARRAY_SIZE = 100000;
  public static final int BUFFER_SIZE = 100000;

  public static void main(String[] args) throws Exception {
    // Sort largedata.dat to sortedfile.dat
    sort("largedata.dat", "sortedfile.dat");

    // Display the first 100 numbers in the sorted file
    displayFile("sortedfile.dat");
  }

  /** Sort data in source file and into target file */
  public static void sort(String sourcefile, String targetfile)
      throws Exception {
    // Implement Phase 1: Create initial segments
    int numberOfSegments =
      initializeSegments(MAX_ARRAY_SIZE, sourcefile, "f1.dat");

    // Implement Phase 2: Merge segments recursively
    merge(numberOfSegments, MAX_ARRAY_SIZE,
      "f1.dat", "f2.dat", "f3.dat", targetfile);
```

max array size

I/O stream buffer size

create initial segments

merge recursively

merge one step
merge recursively
final sorted file
input stream `f1Input`
output stream `f2Output`
copy half segments to `f2`
close `f2Output`
input stream `f2Input`
output stream `f3Output`
merge two segments
close streams

```
  }

  /** Sort original file into sorted segments */
  private static int initializeSegments
      (int segmentSize, String originalFile, String f1)
      throws Exception {
    // Same as Listing 25.11, so omitted
  }

  private static void merge(int numberOfSegments, int segmentSize,
      String f1, String f2, String f3, String targetfile)
      throws Exception {
    if (numberOfSegments > 1) {
      mergeOneStep(numberOfSegments, segmentSize, f1, f2, f3);
      merge((numberOfSegments + 1) / 2, segmentSize * 2,
        f3, f1, f2, targetfile);
    }
    else { // Rename f1 as the final sorted file
      File sortedFile = new File(targetfile);
      if (sortedFile.exists()) sortedFile.delete();
      new File(f1).renameTo(sortedFile);
    }
  }

  private static void mergeOneStep(int numberOfSegments,
      int segmentSize, String f1, String f2, String f3)
      throws Exception {
    DataInputStream f1Input = new DataInputStream(
      new BufferedInputStream(new FileInputStream(f1), BUFFER_SIZE));
    DataOutputStream f2Output = new DataOutputStream(
      new BufferedOutputStream(new FileOutputStream(f2), BUFFER_SIZE));

    // Copy half number of segments from f1.dat to f2.dat
    copyHalfToF2(numberOfSegments, segmentSize, f1Input, f2Output);
    f2Output.close();

    // Merge remaining segments in f1 with segments in f2 into f3
    DataInputStream f2Input = new DataInputStream(
      new BufferedInputStream(new FileInputStream(f2), BUFFER_SIZE));
    DataOutputStream f3Output = new DataOutputStream(
      new BufferedOutputStream(new FileOutputStream(f3), BUFFER_SIZE));

    mergeSegments(numberOfSegments / 2,
      segmentSize, f1Input, f2Input, f3Output);

    f1Input.close();
    f2Input.close();
    f3Output.close();
  }

  /** Copy first half number of segments from f1.dat to f2.dat */
  private static void copyHalfToF2(int numberOfSegments,
      int segmentSize, DataInputStream f1, DataOutputStream f2)
      throws Exception {
    // Same as Listing 25.12, so omitted
  }

  /** Merge all segments */
  private static void mergeSegments(int numberOfSegments,
      int segmentSize, DataInputStream f1, DataInputStream f2,
```

```
85        DataOutputStream f3) throws Exception {
86      // Same as Listing 25.13, so omitted
87    }
88
89    /** Merges two segments */
90    private static void mergeTwoSegments(int segmentSize,
91      DataInputStream f1, DataInputStream f2,
92      DataOutputStream f3) throws Exception {
93      // Same as Listing 25.14, so omitted
94    }
95
96    /** Display the first 100 numbers in the specified file */
97    public static void displayFile(String filename) {
98      try {
99        DataInputStream input =
100         new DataInputStream(new FileInputStream(filename));
101       for (int i = 0; i < 100; i++)
102         System.out.print(input.readInt() + " ");
103       input.close();
104     }
105     catch (IOException ex) {
106       ex.printStackTrace();
107     }
108   }
109 }
```

display file

```
0 1 1 1 2 2 2 3 3 4 5 6 8 8 9 9 9 10 10 11 . . . (omitted)
```

Before you run this program, first run Listing 25.10, CreateLargeFile.java, to create the file largedata.dat. Invoking `sort("largedata.dat", "sortedfile.dat")` (line 9) reads data from `largedata.dat` and writes sorted data to `sortedfile.dat`. Invoking `displayFile("sortedfile.dat")` (line 12) displays the first `100` numbers in the specified file. Note that the files are created using binary I/O. You cannot view them using a text editor such as Notepad.

The `sort` method first creates initial segments from the original array and stores the sorted segments in a new file, f1.dat (lines 19–20), then produces a sorted file in `targetfile` (lines 23–24).

The `merge` method

```
merge(int numberOfSegments, int segmentSize,
  String f1, String f2, String f3, String targetfile)
```

merges the segments in `f1` into `f3` using `f2` to assist the merge. The `merge` method is invoked recursively with many merge steps. Each merge step reduces the `numberOfSegments` by half and doubles the sorted segment size. After the completion of one merge step, the next merge step merges the new segments in `f3` to `f2` using `f1` to assist the merge. The statement to invoke the new merge method is

```
merge((numberOfSegments + 1) / 2, segmentSize * 2,
  f3, f1, f2, targetfile);
```

The `numberOfSegments` for the next merge step is `(numberOfSegments + 1) / 2`. For example, if `numberOfSegments` is `5`, `numberOfSegments` is `3` for the next merge step, because every two segments are merged but one is left unmerged.

The recursive `merge` method ends when `numberOfSegments` is `1`. In this case, `f1` contains sorted data. File `f1` is renamed to `targetfile` (line 45).

25.7.4 External Sort Complexity

In the external sort, the dominating cost is that of I/O. Assume n is the number of elements to be sorted in the file. In Phase I, n number of elements are read from the original file and output to a temporary file. Therefore, the I/O for Phase I is $O(n)$.

In Phase II, before the first merge step, the number of sorted segments is $\frac{n}{c}$, where c is `MAX_ARRAY_SIZE`. Each merge step reduces the number of segments by half. Thus, after the first merge step, the number of segments is $\frac{n}{2c}$. After the second merge step, the number of segments is $\frac{n}{2^2c}$, and after the third merge step the number of segments is $\frac{n}{2^3c}$. After $\log\left(\frac{n}{c}\right)$ merge steps, the number of segments has been reduced to 1. Therefore, the total number of merge steps is $\log\left(\frac{n}{c}\right)$.

In each merge step, half the number of segments are read from file `f1` and then written into a temporary file `f2`. The remaining segments in `f1` are merged with the segments in `f2`. The number of I/Os in each merge step is $O(n)$. Since the total number of merge steps is $\log\left(\frac{n}{c}\right)$, the total number of I/Os is

$$O(n) \times \log\left(\frac{n}{c}\right) = O(n \log n)$$

Therefore, the complexity of the external sort is $O(n \log n)$.

25.20 Describe how external sort works. What is the complexity of the external sort algorithm?

25.21 Ten numbers {2, 3, 4, 0, 5, 6, 7, 9, 8, 1} are stored in the external file **largedata.dat**. Trace the `SortLargeFile` program by hand with `MAX_ARRAY_SIZE` 2.

Key Terms

bubble sort 894
bucket sort 911
complete binary tree 904
external sort 913
heap 904
heap sort 904
height of a heap 910
merge sort 896
quick sort 900
radix sort 912

Chapter Summary

1. The worst-case complexity for a selection sort, insertion sort, *bubble sort*, and *quick sort* is $O(n^2)$.

2. The average-case and worst-case complexity for a *merge sort* is $O(n \log n)$. The average time for a quick sort is also $O(n \log n)$.

3. *Heaps* are a useful data structure for designing efficient algorithms such as sorting. You learned how to define and implement a heap class, and how to insert and delete elements to/from a heap.

4. The time complexity for a *heap sort* is $O(n \log n)$.

5. *Bucket sorts* and *radix sorts* are specialized sorting algorithms for integer keys. These algorithms sort keys using buckets rather than by comparing keys. They are more efficient than general sorting algorithms.

6. A variation of the merge sort—called an *external sort*—can be applied to sort large amounts of data from external files.

Test Questions

Do the test questions for this chapter online at www.cs.armstrong.edu/liang/intro9e/test.html.

Programming Exercises

MyProgrammingLab™

Sections 25.2–25.4

25.1 (*Generic bubble sort*) Write the following two generic methods using bubble sort. The first method sorts the elements using the **Comparable** interface and the second uses the **Comparator** interface.

```
public static <E extends Comparable<E>>
  void bubbleSort(E[] list)
public static <E> void bubbleSort(E[] list,
  Comparator<? super E> comparator)
```

25.2 (*Generic merge sort*) Write the following two generic methods using merge sort. The first method sorts the elements using the **Comparable** interface and the second uses the **Comparator** interface.

```
public static <E extends Comparable<E>>
  void mergeSort(E[] list)
public static <E> void mergeSort(E[] list,
  Comparator<? super E> comparator)
```

25.3 (*Generic quick sort*) Write the following two generic methods using quick sort. The first method sorts the elements using the **Comparable** interface and the second uses the **Comparator** interface.

```
public static <E extends Comparable<E>>
  void quickSort(E[] list)
public static <E> void quickSort(E[] list,
  Comparator<? super E> comparator)
```

25.4 (*Improve quick sort*) The quick sort algorithm presented in the book selects the first element in the list as the pivot. Revise it by selecting the median among the first, middle, and last elements in the list.

***25.5** (*Generic heap sort*) Write the following two generic methods using heap sort. The first method sorts the elements using the **Comparable** interface and the second uses the **Comparator** interface.

```
public static <E extends Comparable<E>>
  void heapSort(E[] list)
public static <E> void heapSort(E[] list,
  Comparator<? super E> comparator)
```

25.6 (*Check order*) Write the following overloaded methods that check whether an array is ordered in ascending order or descending order. By default, the method checks ascending order. To check descending order, pass **false** to the ascending argument in the method.

```
public static boolean ordered(int[] list)
public static boolean ordered(int[] list, boolean ascending)
public static boolean ordered(double[] list)
public static boolean ordered
  (double[] list, boolean descending)
public static <E extends Comparable<E>>
  boolean ordered(E[] list)
public static <E extends Comparable<E>> boolean ordered
  (E[] list, boolean ascending)
public static <E> boolean ordered(E[] list,
  Comparator<? super E> comparator)
public static <E> boolean ordered(E[] list,
  Comparator<? super E> comparator, boolean ascending)
```

Section 25.5

max-heap
min-heap

25.7 (*Min-heap*) The heap presented in the text is also known as a *max-heap*, in which each node is greater than or equal to any of its children. A *min-heap* is a heap in which each node is less than or equal to any of its children. Min-heaps are often used to implement priority queues. Revise the **Heap** class in Listing 25.8 to implement a min-heap.

***25.8** (*Sort using a heap*) Implement the following **sort** method using a heap.

```
public static <E extends Comparable<E>> void sort(E[] list)
```

25.9** (*Generic* ***Heap *using* ***Comparator***) Revise **Heap** in Listing 25.8, using a generic parameter and a **Comparator** for comparing objects. Define a new constructor with a **Comparator** as its argument as follows:

```
Heap(Comparator<? super E> comparator)
```

****25.10** (*Heap visualization*) Write a Java applet that displays a heap graphically, as shown in Figure 25.8. The applet lets you insert and delete an element from the heap.

25.11 (*Heap* ***clone*** *and* ***equals***) Implement the **clone** and **equals** method in the **Heap** class.

Section 25.6

***25.12** (*Radix sort*) Write a program that randomly generates 1,000,000 integers and sorts them using radix sort.

***25.13** (*Execution time for sorting*) Write a program that obtains the execution time of selection sort, bubble sort, merge sort, quick sort, heap sort, and radix sort for input size 50,000, 100,000, 150,000, 200,000, 250,000, and 300,000. Your program should create data randomly and print a table like this:

Array size	Selection Sort	Bubble Sort	Merge Sort	Quick Sort	Heap Sort	Radix Sort
50,000						
100,000						
150,000						
200,000						
250,000						
300,000						

(*Hint*: You can use the following code template to obtain the execution time.)

```
long startTime = System.currentTimeMillis();
perform the task;
long endTime = System.currentTimeMillis();
long executionTime = endTime - startTime;
```

The text gives a recursive quick sort. Write a nonrecursive version in this exercise.

Section 25.7

***25.14** (*Execution time for external sorting*) Write a program that obtains the execution time of external sorts for integers of size 5,000,000, 10,000,000, 15,000,000, 20,000,000, 25,000,000, and 30,000,000. Your program should print a table like this:

File size	5,000,000	10,000,000	15,000,000	20,000,000	25,000,000	30,000,000
Time						

Comprehensive

***25.15** (*Selection sort animation*) Write a Java applet that animates the selection sort algorithm. Create an array that consists of 20 distinct numbers from 1 to 20 in a random order. The array elements are displayed in a histogram, as shown in Figure 25.18a. Clicking the *Step* button causes the program to perform an iteration of the outer loop in the algorithm and repaints the histogram for the new array. Color the last bar in the sorted subarray. When the algorithm is finished, display a dialog box to inform the user. Clicking the *Reset* button creates a new random array for a new start. (You can easily modify the program to animate the insertion algorithm.)

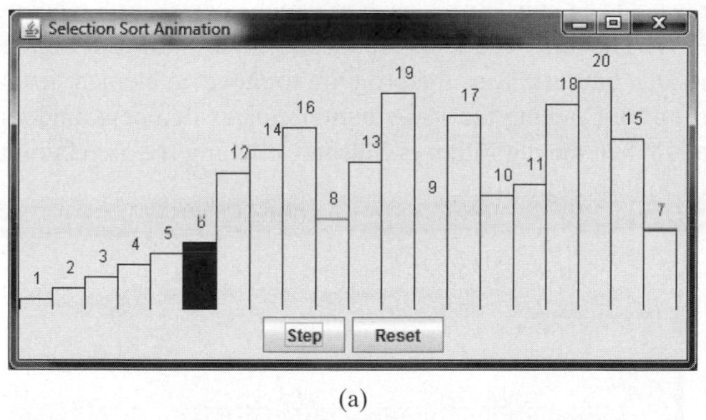

(a)

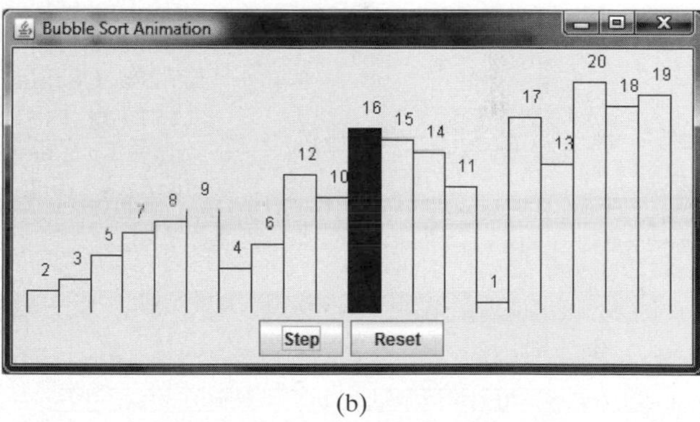

(b)

FIGURE 25.18 (a) The program animates selection sort. (b) The program animates bubble sort.

***25.16** (*Bubble sort animation*) Write a Java applet that animates the bubble sort algorithm. Create an array that consists of 20 distinct numbers from 1 to 20 in a random order. The array elements are displayed in a histogram, as shown in Figure 25.18b. Clicking the *Step* button causes the program to perform one comparison in the algorithm and repaints the histogram for the new array.

Color the bar that represents the number being considered in the swap. When the algorithm is finished, display a dialog box to inform the user. Clicking the *Reset* button creates a new random array for a new start.

***25.17** (*Radix sort animation*) Write a Java applet that animates the radix sort algorithm. Create an array that consists of 20 random numbers from 0 to 1,000. The array elements are displayed, as shown in Figure 25.19. Clicking the *Step* button causes the program to place a number in a bucket. The number that has just been placed is displayed in red. Once all the numbers are placed in the buckets, clicking the *Step* button collects all the numbers from the buckets and moves them back to the array. When the algorithm is finished, clicking the *Step* button displays a dialog box to inform the user. Clicking the *Reset* button creates a new random array for a new start.

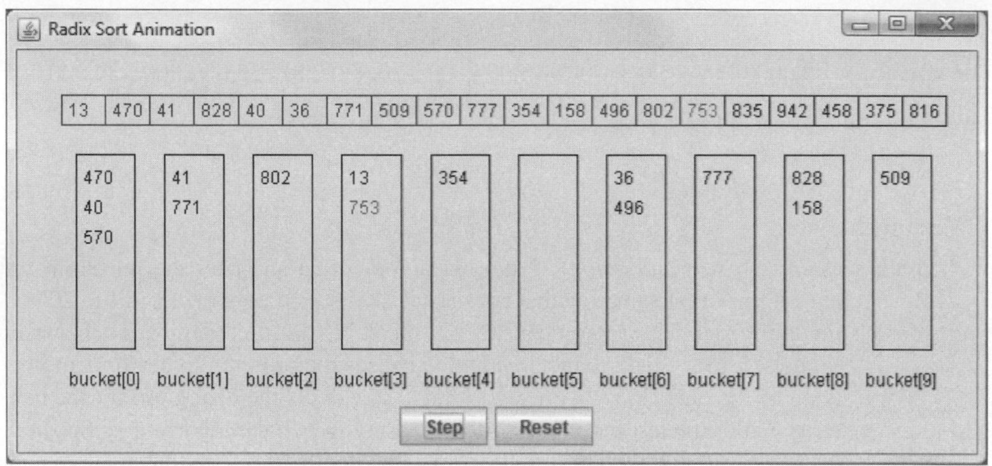

FIGURE 25.19 The program animates radix sort.

***25.18** (*Merge animation*) Write a Java applet that animates the merge of two sorted lists. Create two arrays, `list1` and `list2`, each of which consists of 8 random numbers from 1 to 999. The array elements are displayed, as shown in Figure 25.20a. Clicking the *Step* button causes the program to move an element from `list1` or `list2` to `temp`. Clicking the *Reset* button creates two new random arrays for a new start. When the algorithm is finished, clicking the *Step* button displays a dialog box to inform the user.

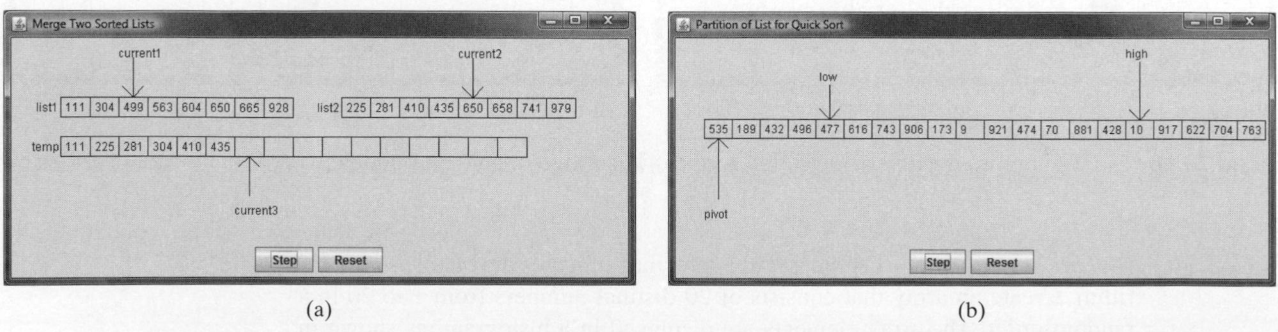

FIGURE 25.20 The program animates a merge of two sorted lists. (b) The program animates a partition for quick sort.

***25.19** (*Quick sort partition animation*) Write a Java applet that animates the partition for a quick sort. The applet creates a list that consists of 20 random numbers from 1 to 999. The list is displayed, as shown in Figure 25.20b. Clicking the *Step* button causes the program to move `low` to the right or `high` to the left, or swap the elements at `low` and `high`. Clicking the *Reset* button creates a new list of random numbers for a new start. When the algorithm is finished, clicking the *Step* button displays a dialog box to inform the user.

***25.20** (*Modify merge sort*) Rewrite the `mergeSort` method to recursively sort the first half of the array and the second half of the array without creating new temporary arrays, and then merge the two into a temporary array and copy its contents to the original array, as shown in Figure 25.4b.

CHAPTER 26

IMPLEMENTING LISTS, STACKS, QUEUES, AND PRIORITY QUEUES

Objectives

- To design common features of lists in an interface and provide skeleton implementation in a convenience abstract class (§26.2).
- To design and implement an array list using an array (§26.3).
- To design and implement a linked list using a linked structure (§26.4).
- To design and implement a stack class using an array list and a queue class using a linked list (§26.5).
- To design and implement a priority queue using a heap (§26.6).

26.1 Introduction

This chapter focuses on implementing data structures.

Lists, stacks, queues, and priority queues are classic data structures typically covered in a data structures course. They are supported in the Java API, and their uses were presented in Chapter 22, Lists, Stacks, Queues, and Priority Queues. This chapter will examine how these data structures are implemented under the hood. Implementation of sets and maps is covered in Chapter 28. Through these examples, you will learn how to design and implement custom data structures.

26.2 Common Features for Lists

Common features of lists are defined in the `List` interface.

A list is a popular data structure for storing data in sequential order—for example, a list of students, a list of available rooms, a list of cities, a list of books. You can perform the following operations on most lists:

- Retrieve an element from the list.
- Insert a new element into the list.
- Delete an element from the list.
- Find out how many elements are in the list.
- Determine whether an element is in the list.
- Check whether the list is empty.

There are two ways to implement a list. One is to use an *array* to store the elements. Array size is fixed. If the capacity of the array is exceeded, you need to create a new, larger array and copy all the elements from the current array to the new array. The other approach is to use a *linked structure*. A linked structure consists of nodes. Each node is dynamically created to hold an element. All the nodes are linked together to form a list. Thus you can define two classes for lists. For convenience, let's name these two classes `MyArrayList` and `MyLinkedList`. These two classes have common operations but different implementations.

Design Guide

convenience abstract class for interface

The common operations can be generalized in an interface or an abstract class. A good strategy is to combine the virtues of interfaces and abstract classes by providing both an interface and a convenience abstract class in the design so that the user can use either of them, whichever is convenient. The abstract class provides a skeletal implementation of the interface, which minimizes the effort required to implement the interface.

list animation on Companion Website

Pedagogical Note

For an interactive demo on how array lists and linked lists work, go to www.cs.armstrong.edu/liang/animation/ArrayListAnimation.html and www.cs.armstrong.edu/liang/animation/LinkedListAnimation.html, as shown in Figure 26.1.

Let us name the interface `MyList` and the convenience abstract class `MyAbstractList`. Figure 26.2 shows the relationship of `MyList`, `MyAbstractList`, `MyArrayList`, and `MyLinkedList`. The methods in `MyList` and the methods implemented in `MyAbstractList` are shown in Figure 26.3. Listing 26.1 gives the source code for `MyList`.

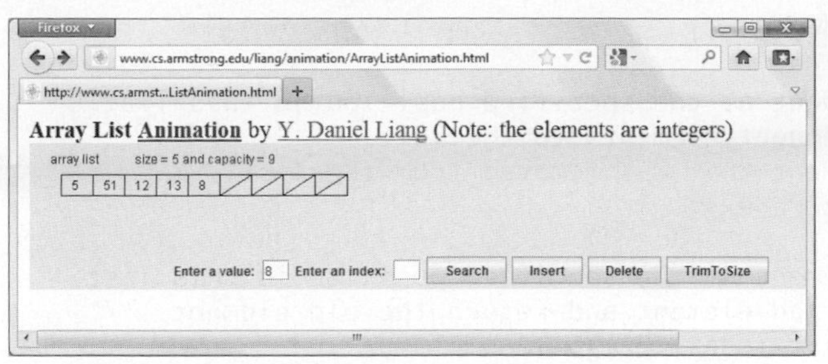

(a) Array list animation

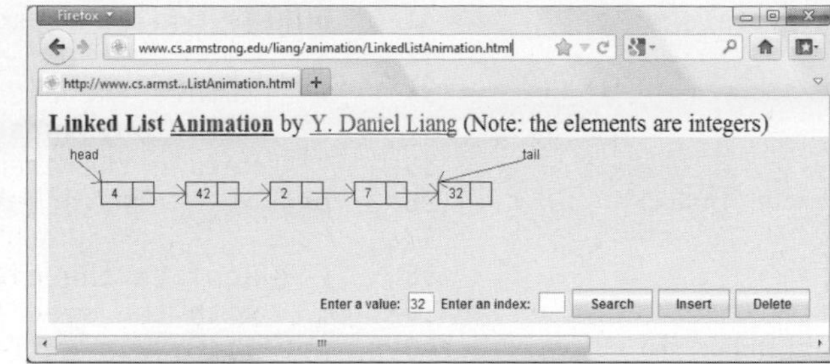

(b) Linked list animation

FIGURE 26.1 The animation tool enables you to see how array lists and linked lists work.

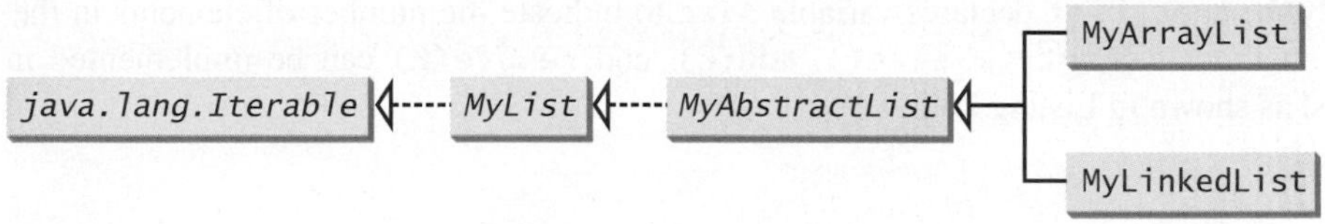

Figure 26.2 `MyList` defines a common interface for `MyAbstractList`, `MyArrayList`, and `MyLinkedList`.

LISTING 26.1 MyList.java

```
public interface MyList<E> extends java.lang.Iterable<E> {
  /** Add a new element at the end of this list */
  public void add(E e);

  /** Add a new element at the specified index in this list */
  public void add(int index, E e);

  /** Clear the list */
  public void clear();

  /** Return true if this list contains the element */
  public boolean contains(E e);

  /** Return the element from this list at the specified index */
  public E get(int index);

  /** Return the index of the first matching element in this list.
   *  Return -1 if no match. */
  public int indexOf(E e);

  /** Return true if this list doesn't contain any elements */
  public boolean isEmpty();

  /** Return the index of the last matching element in this list
   *  Return -1 if no match. */
  public int lastIndexOf(E e);

  /** Remove the first occurrence of the element e from this list.
   *  Shift any subsequent elements to the left.
   *  Return true if the element is removed. */
```

add(e)
add(index, e)
clear()
contains(e)
get(index)
indexOf(e)
isEmpty(e)
lastIndexOf(e)

remove(e)

remove(index)

set(index, e)

size(e)

```
  public boolean remove(E e);

  /** Remove the element at the specified position in this list.
   *  Shift any subsequent elements to the left.
   *  Return the element that was removed from the list. */
  public E remove(int index);

  /** Replace the element at the specified position in this list
   *  with the specified element and return the old element. */
  public Object set(int index, E e);

  /** Return the number of elements in this list */
  public int size();
}
```

MyAbstractList declares variable **size** to indicate the number of elements in the list. The methods **isEmpty()**, **size()**, **add(E)**, and **remove(E)** can be implemented in the class, as shown in Listing 26.2.

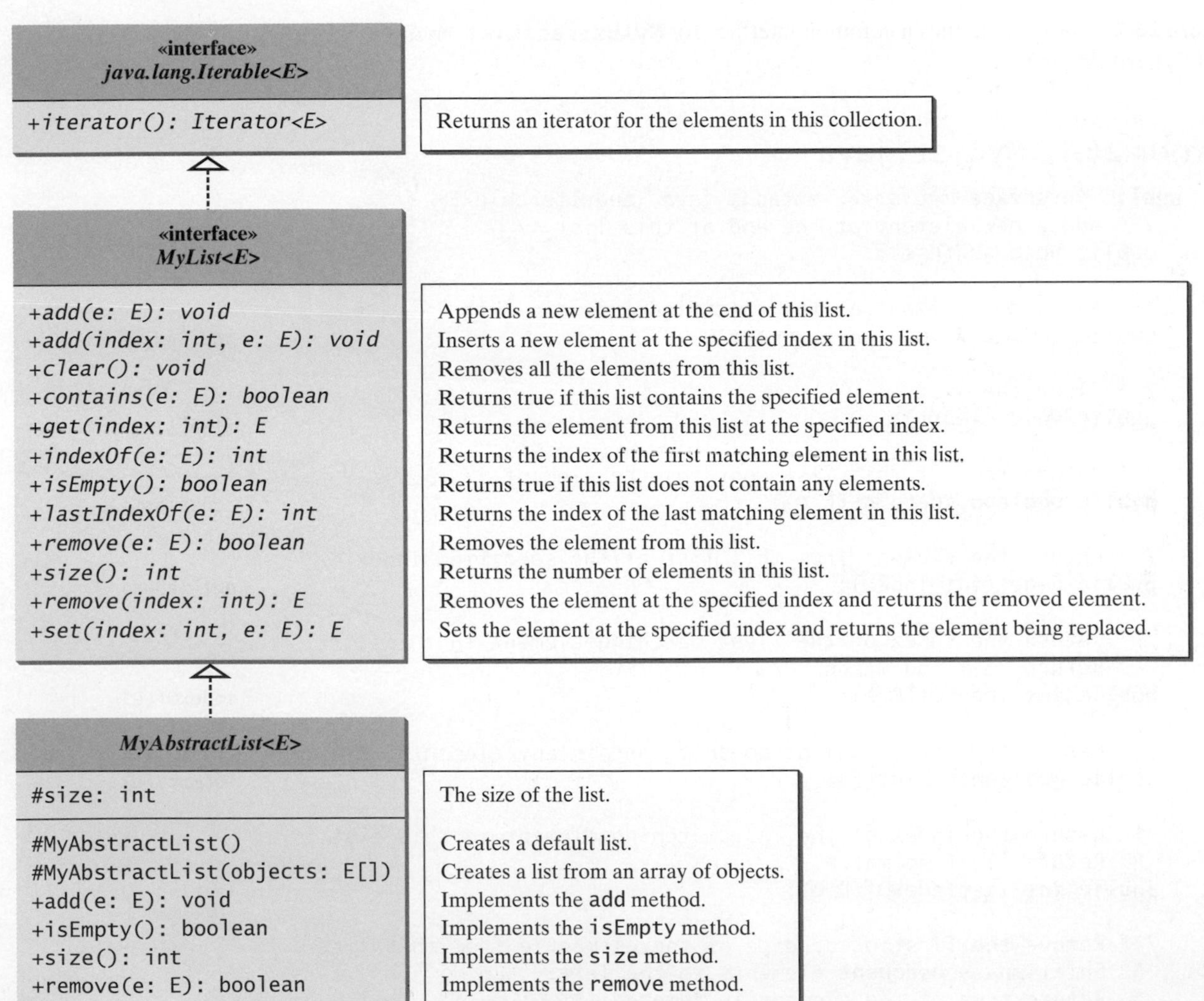

Figure 26.3 **MyList** defines the methods for manipulating a list. **MyAbstractList** provides a partial implementation of the **MyList** interface.

LISTING 26.2 MyAbstractList.java

```
public abstract class MyAbstractList<E> implements MyList<E> {
  protected int size = 0; // The size of the list

  /** Create a default list */
  protected MyAbstractList() {
  }

  /** Create a list from an array of objects */
  protected MyAbstractList(E[] objects) {
    for (int i = 0; i < objects.length; i++)
      add(objects[i]);
  }

  @Override /** Add a new element at the end of this list */
  public void add(E e) {
    add(size, e);
  }

  @Override /** Return true if this list doesn't contain any elements */
  public boolean isEmpty() {
    return size == 0;
  }

  @Override /** Return the number of elements in this list */
  public int size() {
    return size;
  }

  @Override /** Remove the first occurrence of the element e
   *  from this list. Shift any subsequent elements to the left.
   *  Return true if the element is removed. */
  public boolean remove(E e) {
    if (indexOf(e) >= 0) {
      remove(indexOf(e));
      return true;
    }
    else
      return false;
  }
}
```

size · no-arg constructor · constructor · implement add(E e) · implement isEmpty() · implement size() · implement remove(E e)

The following sections give the implementation for **MyArrayList** and **MyLinkedList**, respectively.

Design Guide

Protected data fields are rarely used. However, making **size** a protected data field in the **MyAbstractList** class is a good choice. The subclass of **MyAbstractList** can access **size**, but nonsubclasses of **MyAbstractList** in different packages cannot access it. As a general rule, you can declare protected data fields in abstract classes.

protected data field

26.1 Suppose **list** is an instance of **MyList**, can you get an iterator for **list** using **list.iterator()**?

26.2 Can you create a list using **new MyAbstractList()** ?

26.3 What methods in **MyList** are overridden in **MyAbstractList**?

26.4 What are the benefits of defining both the **MyList** interface and the **MyAbstractList** class?

Check Point

MyProgrammingLab™

26.3 Array Lists

An array list is implemented using an array.

An array is a fixed-size data structure. Once an array is created, its size cannot be changed. Nevertheless, you can still use arrays to implement dynamic data structures. The trick is to create a larger new array to replace the current array, if the current array cannot hold new elements in the list.

Initially, an array, say **data** of **E[]** type, is created with a default size. When inserting a new element into the array, first make sure that there is enough room in the array. If not, create a new array twice as large as the current one. Copy the elements from the current array to the new array. The new array now becomes the current array. Before inserting a new element at a specified index, shift all the elements after the index to the right and increase the list size by **1**, as shown in Figure 26.4.

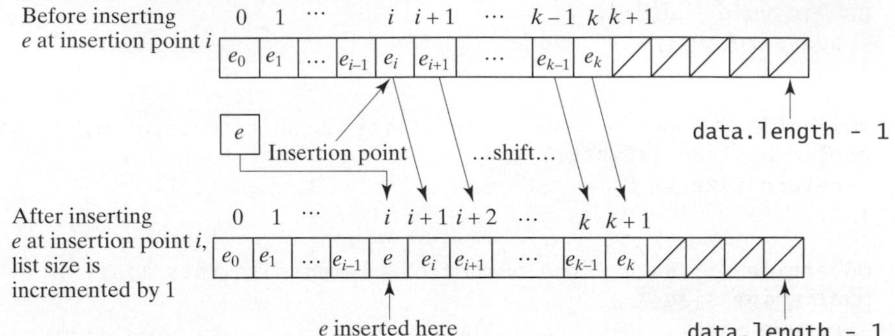

FIGURE 26.4 Inserting a new element into the array requires that all the elements after the insertion point be shifted one position to the right, so that the new element can be inserted at the insertion point.

Note

The data array is of type **E[]**. Each cell in the array actually stores the reference of an object.

To remove an element at a specified index, shift all the elements after the index to the left by one position and decrease the list size by **1**, as shown in Figure 26.5.

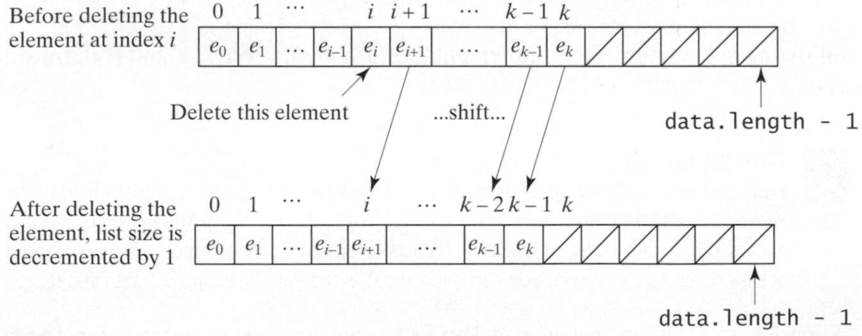

FIGURE 26.5 Deleting an element from the array requires that all the elements after the deletion point be shifted one position to the left.

MyArrayList uses an array to implement **MyAbstractList**, as shown in Figure 26.6. Its implementation is given in Listing 26.3.

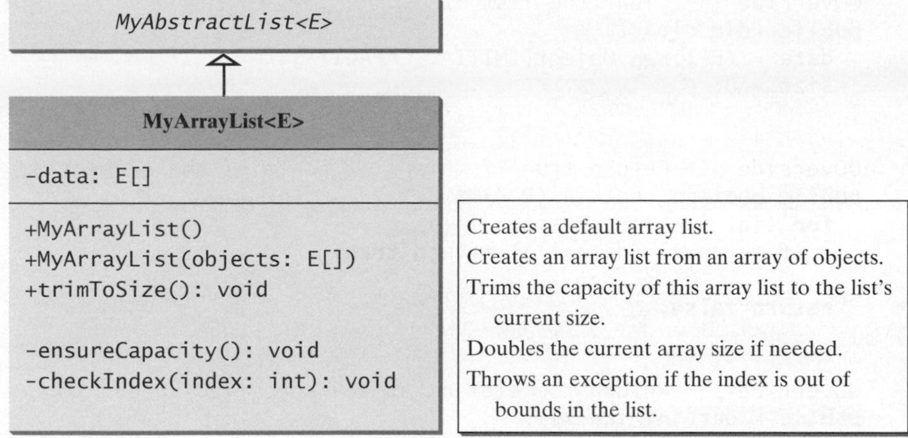

Figure 26.6 `MyArrayList` implements a list using an array.

Listing 26.3 MyArrayList.java

```java
public class MyArrayList<E> extends MyAbstractList<E> {
  public static final int INITIAL_CAPACITY = 16;
  private E[] data = (E[])new Object[INITIAL_CAPACITY];

  /** Create a default list */
  public MyArrayList() {
  }

  /** Create a list from an array of objects */
  public MyArrayList(E[] objects) {
    for (int i = 0; i < objects.length; i++)
      add(objects[i]); // Warning: don't use super(objects)!
  }

  @Override /** Add a new element at the specified index */
  public void add(int index, E e) {
    ensureCapacity();

    // Move the elements to the right after the specified index
    for (int i = size - 1; i >= index; i--)
      data[i + 1] = data[i];

    // Insert new element to data[index]
    data[index] = e;

    // Increase size by 1
    size++;
  }

  /** Create a new larger array, double the current size + 1 */
  private void ensureCapacity() {
    if (size >= data.length) {
      E[] newData = (E[])(new Object[size * 2 + 1]);
      System.arraycopy(data, 0, newData, 0, size);
      data = newData;
    }
  }

```

Margin notes: initial capacity; create an array; no-arg constructor; constructor; add; `ensureCapacity`; double capacity + 1

```java
  @Override /** Clear the list */
  public void clear() {
    data = (E[])new Object[INITIAL_CAPACITY];
    size = 0;
  }

  @Override /** Return true if this list contains the element */
  public boolean contains(E e) {
    for (int i = 0; i < size; i++)
      if (e.equals(data[i])) return true;

    return false;
  }

  @Override /** Return the element at the specified index */
  public E get(int index) {
    checkIndex(index);
    return data[index];
  }

  private void checkIndex(int index) {
    if (index < 0 || index >= size)
      throw new IndexOutOfBoundsException
        ("index " + index + " out of bounds");
  }

  @Override /** Return the index of the first matching element
   *  in this list. Return -1 if no match. */
  public int indexOf(E e) {
    for (int i = 0; i < size; i++)
      if (e.equals(data[i])) return i;

    return -1;
  }

  @Override /** Return the index of the last matching element
   *  in this list. Return -1 if no match. */
  public int lastIndexOf(E e) {
    for (int i = size - 1; i >= 0; i--)
      if (e.equals(data[i])) return i;

    return -1;
  }

  @Override /** Remove the element at the specified position
   *  in this list. Shift any subsequent elements to the left.
   *  Return the element that was removed from the list. */
  public E remove(int index) {
    checkIndex(index);

    E e = data[index];

    // Shift data to the left
    for (int j = index; j < size - 1; j++)
      data[j] = data[j + 1];

    data[size - 1] = null; // This element is now null

    // Decrement size
    size--;
```

```

    return e;
  }

  @Override /** Replace the element at the specified position
   *  in this list with the specified element. */
  public E set(int index, E e) {
    checkIndex(index);
    E old = data[index];
    data[index] = e;
    return old;
  }

  @Override
  public String toString() {
    StringBuilder result = new StringBuilder("[");

    for (int i = 0; i < size; i++) {
      result.append(data[i]);
      if (i < size - 1) result.append(", ");
    }

    return result.toString() + "]";
  }

  /** Trims the capacity to current size */
  public void trimToSize() {
    if (size != data.length) {
      E[] newData = (E[])(new Object[size]);
      System.arraycopy(data, 0, newData, 0, size);
      data = newData;
    } // If size == capacity, no need to trim
  }

  @Override /** Override iterator() defined in Iterable */
  public java.util.Iterator<E> iterator() {
    return new ArrayListIterator();
  }

  private class ArrayListIterator
      implements java.util.Iterator<E> {
    private int current = 0; // Current index

    @Override
    public boolean hasNext() {
      return (current < size);
    }

    @Override
    public E next() {
      return data[current++];
    }

    @Override
    public void remove() {
      MyArrayList.this.remove(current);
    }
  }
}
```

set

toString

trimToSize

iterator

The constant **INITIAL_CAPACITY** (line 2) is used to create an initial array **data** (line 3). Owing to generics type erasure, you cannot create a generic array using the syntax **new e[INITIAL_CAPACITY]**. To circumvent this limitation, an array of the **Object** type is created in line 3 and cast into **E[]**.

Note that the implementation of the second constructor in **MyArrayList** is the same as for **MyAbstractList**. Can you replace lines 11–12 with **super(objects)**? See Checkpoint Question 26.8 for answers.

add

The **add(int index, E e)** method (lines 16–28) inserts element **e** at the specified **index** in the array. This method first invokes **ensureCapacity()** (line 17), which ensures that there is a space in the array for the new element. It then shifts all the elements after the index one position to the right before inserting the element (lines 20–21). After the element is added, **size** is incremented by **1** (line 27). Note that the variable **size** is defined as **protected** in **MyAbstractList**, so it can be accessed in **MyArrayList**.

ensureCapacity

The **ensureCapacity()** method (lines 31–37) checks whether the array is full. If so, the program creates a new array that doubles the current array size + 1, copies the current array to the new array using the **System.arraycopy** method, and sets the new array as the current array.

clear

The **clear()** method (lines 40–43) creates a new array using the size as **INITIAL_CAPACITY** and resets the variable **size** to **0**. The class will work if line 41 is deleted. However, the class will have a memory leak, because the elements are still in the array, although they are no longer needed. By creating a new array and assigning it to **data**, the old array and the elements stored in the old array become garbage, which will be automatically collected by the JVM.

contains

The **contains(E e)** method (lines 46–51) checks whether element **e** is contained in the array by comparing **e** with each element in the array using the **equals** method.

The **get(int index)** method (lines 54–57) checks if **index** is within the range and returns **data[index]** if **index** is in the range.

checkIndex

The **checkIndex(int index)** method (lines 59–63) checks if **index** is within the range. If not, the method throws an **IndexOutOfBoundsException** (line 61).

indexOf

The **indexOf(E e)** method (lines 67–72) compares element **e** with the elements in the array, starting from the first one. If a match is found, the index of the element is returned; otherwise, **-1** is returned.

lastIndexOf

The **lastIndexOf(E e)** method (lines 76–81) compares element **e** with the elements in the array, starting from the last one. If a match is found, the index of the element is returned; otherwise, **-1** is returned.

remove

The **remove(int index)** method (lines 86–101) shifts all the elements after the index one position to the left (lines 92–93) and decrements **size** by **1** (line 98). The last element is not used anymore and is set to **null** (line 95).

set

The **set(int index, E e)** method (lines 105–110) simply assigns **e** to **data[index]** to replace the element at the specified index with element **e**.

toString

The **toString()** method (lines 113–122) overrides the **toString** method in the **Object** class to return a string representing all the elements in the list.

trimToSize

The **trimToSize()** method creates a new array whose size matches the current array-list size (line 127), copies the current array to the new array using the **System.arraycopy** method (line 128), and sets the new array as the current array (line 129). Note that if **size == capacity**, there is no need to trim the size of the array.

iterator

The **iterator()** method defined in the **java.lang.Iterable** interface is implemented to return an instance on **java.util.Iterator** (lines 134–136). The **ArrayListIterator** class implements **Iterator** with concrete methods for **hasNext**, **next**, and **remove** (lines 143–155). It uses **current** to denote the current position of the element being traversed (line 140).

Listing 26.4 gives an example that creates a list using **MyArrayList**. It uses the **add** method to add strings to the list and the **remove** method to remove strings. Since

`MyArrayList` implements `Iterable`, the elements can be traversed using a for-each loop (lines 35–36).

LISTING 26.4 TestMyArrayList.java

```
1  public class TestMyArrayList {
2    public static void main(String[] args) {
3      // Create a list
4      MyList<String> list = new MyArrayList<String>();
5
6      // Add elements to the list
7      list.add("America"); // Add it to the list
8      System.out.println("(1) " + list);
9
10     list.add(0, "Canada"); // Add it to the beginning of the list
11     System.out.println("(2) " + list);
12
13     list.add("Russia"); // Add it to the end of the list
14     System.out.println("(3) " + list);
15
16     list.add("France"); // Add it to the end of the list
17     System.out.println("(4) " + list);
18
19     list.add(2, "Germany"); // Add it to the list at index 2
20     System.out.println("(5) " + list);
21
22     list.add(5, "Norway"); // Add it to the list at index 5
23     System.out.println("(6) " + list);
24
25     // Remove elements from the list
26     list.remove("Canada"); // Same as list.remove(0) in this case
27     System.out.println("(7) " + list);
28
29     list.remove(2); // Remove the element at index 2
30     System.out.println("(8) " + list);
31
32     list.remove(list.size() - 1); // Remove the last element
33     System.out.print("(9) " + list + "\n(10) ");
34
35     for (String s: list)
36       System.out.print(s.toUpperCase() + " ");
37   }
38 }
```

create a list

add to list

remove from list

using iterator

```
(1) [America]
(2) [Canada, America]
(3) [Canada, America, Russia]
(4) [Canada, America, Russia, France]
(5) [Canada, America, Germany, Russia, France]
(6) [Canada, America, Germany, Russia, France, Norway]
(7) [America, Germany, Russia, France, Norway]
(8) [America, Germany, France, Norway]
(9) [America, Germany, France]
(10) AMERICA GERMANY FRANCE
```

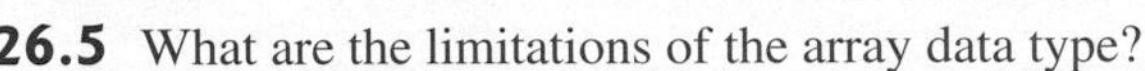

26.5 What are the limitations of the array data type?

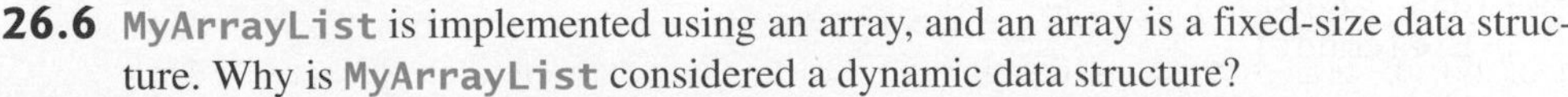

26.6 `MyArrayList` is implemented using an array, and an array is a fixed-size data structure. Why is `MyArrayList` considered a dynamic data structure?

26.7 Show the length of the array in `MyArrayList` after each of the following statements is executed.

```
MyArrayList<Double> list = new MyArrayList<Double>();
list.add(1.5);
list.trimToSize();
list.add(3.4);
list.add(7.4);
list.add(17.4);
```

26.8 What is wrong if lines 11–12 in Listing 26.3, MyArrayList.java,

```
for (int i = 0; i < objects.length; i++)
  add(objects[i]);
```

are replaced by

```
super(objects);
```

or

```
data = objects;
size = objects.length;
```

26.9 If you change the code in line 33 in Listing 26.3, MyArrayList.java, from

```
E[] newData = (E[])(new Object[size * 2 + 1]);
```

to

```
E[] newData = (E[])(new Object[size * 2]);
```

the program is incorrect. Can you find the reason?

26.10 Will the `MyArrayList` class have memory leak if the following code in line 41 is deleted?

```
data = (E[])new Object[INITIAL_CAPACITY];
```

26.4 Linked Lists

A linked list is implemented using a linked structure.

Since `MyArrayList` is implemented using an array, the methods `get(int index)` and `set(int index, E e)` for accessing and modifying an element through an index and the `add(E e)` method for adding an element at the end of the list are efficient. However, the methods `add(int index, E e)` and `remove(int index)` are inefficient, because they require shifting a potentially large number of elements. You can use a linked structure to implement a list to improve efficiency for adding and removing an element at the beginning of a list.

26.4.1 Nodes

In a linked list, each element is contained in an object, called the *node*. When a new element is added to the list, a node is created to contain it. Each node is linked to its next neighbor, as shown in Figure 26.7.

A node can be created from a class defined as follows:

```
class Node<E> {
  E element;
```

```
    Node<E> next;

    public Node(E e) {
      element = e;
    }
  }
```

```
                                                   tail
                  Node 1          Node 2                 Node n
head ──────► element 1 ──► element 2 ──► ...  ──► element n
                  next            next                   null
```

FIGURE 26.7 A linked list consists of any number of nodes chained together.

We use the variable **head** to refer to the first node in the list, and the variable **tail** to the last node. If the list is empty, both **head** and **tail** are **null**. Here is an example that creates a linked list to hold three nodes. Each node stores a string element.

Step 1: Declare **head** and **tail**.

```
Node<String> head = null;     The list is empty now
Node<String> tail = null;
```

head and **tail** are both **null**. The list is empty.

Step 2: Create the first node and append it to the list, as shown in Figure 26.8. After the first node is inserted in the list, **head** and **tail** point to this node.

```
head - new Node<String>("Chicago");     After the first node is inserted
tail = head;
                                         head ──► "Chicago"
                                         tail ──► next: null
```

FIGURE 26.8 Append the first node to the list.

Step 3: Create the second node and append it into the list, as shown in Figure 26.9a. To append the second node to the list, link the first node with the new node. The new node is now the tail node, so you should move **tail** to point to this new node, as shown in Figure 26.9b.

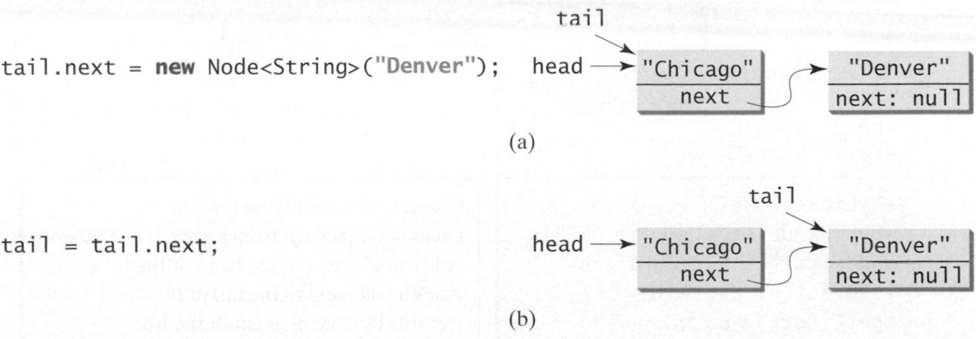

FIGURE 26.9 Append the second node to the list.

Step 4: Create the third node and append it to the list, as shown in Figure 26.10a. To append the new node to the list, link the last node in the list with the new node. The

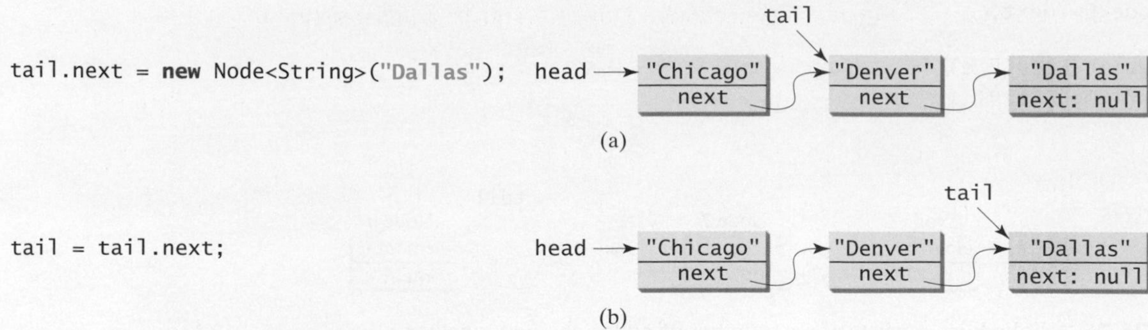

FIGURE 26.10 Append the third node to the list.

new node is now the tail node, so you should move `tail` to point to this new node, as shown in Figure 26.10b.

Each node contains the element and a data field named `next` that points to the next element. If the node is the last in the list, its pointer data field `next` contains the value `null`. You can use this property to detect the last node. For example, you can write the following loop to traverse all the nodes in the list.

current pointer
check last node
next node

```
1 Node current = head;
2 while (current != null) {
3   System.out.println(current.element);
4   current = current.next;
5 }
```

The variable `current` points initially to the first node in the list (line 1). In the loop, the element of the current node is retrieved (line 3), and then `current` points to the next node (line 4). The loop continues until the current node is `null`.

26.4.2 The `MyLinkedList` Class

The `MyLinkedList` class uses a linked structure to implement a dynamic list. It extends `MyAbstractList`. In addition, it provides the methods `addFirst`, `addLast`, `removeFirst`, `removeLast`, `getFirst`, and `getLast`, as shown in Figure 26.11.

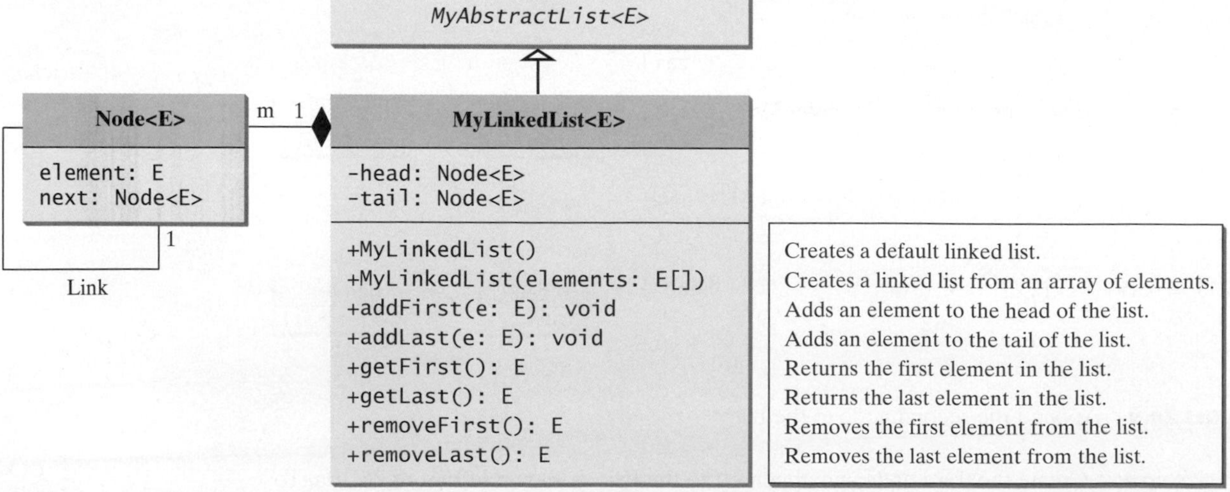

Figure 26.11 `MyLinkedList` implements a list using a linked list of nodes.

Assuming that the class has been implemented, Listing 26.5 gives a test program that uses the class.

LISTING 26.5 TestMyLinkedList.java

```
public class TestMyLinkedList {
  /** Main method */
  public static void main(String[] args) {
    // Create a list for strings
    MyLinkedList<String> list = new MyLinkedList<String>();

    // Add elements to the list
    list.add("America"); // Add it to the list
    System.out.println("(1) " + list);

    list.add(0, "Canada"); // Add it to the beginning of the list
    System.out.println("(2) " + list);

    list.add("Russia"); // Add it to the end of the list
    System.out.println("(3) " + list);

    list.addLast("France"); // Add it to the end of  the list
    System.out.println("(4) " + list);

    list.add(2, "Germany"); // Add it to the list at index 2
    System.out.println("(5) " + list);

    list.add(5, "Norway"); // Add it to the list at index 5
    System.out.println("(6) " + list);

    list.add(0, "Poland"); // Same as list.addFirst("Poland")
    System.out.println("(7) " + list);

    // Remove elements from the list
    list.remove(0); // Same as list.remove("Poland") in this case
    System.out.println("(8) " + list);

    list.remove(2); // Remove the element at index 2
    System.out.println("(9) " + list);

    list.remove(list.size() - 1); // Remove the last element
    System.out.print("(10) " + list + "\n(11) ");

    for (String s: list)
      System.out.print(s.toUpperCase() + " ");
  }
}
```

create list
append element
print list
insert element
append element
append element
insert element
insert element
insert element
remove element
remove element
remove element
traverse using iterator

```
(1) [America]
(2) [Canada, America]
(3) [Canada, America, Russia]
(4) [Canada, America, Russia, France]
(5) [Canada, America, Germany, Russia, France]
(6) [Canada, America, Germany, Russia, France, Norway]
(7) [Poland, Canada, America, Germany, Russia, France, Norway]
(8) [Canada, America, Germany, Russia, France, Norway]
(9) [Canada, America, Russia, France, Norway]
(10) [Canada, America, Russia, France]
(11) CANADA AMERICA RUSSIA FRANCE
```

26.4.3 Implementing MyLinkedList

Now let us turn our attention to implementing the **MyLinkedList** class. We will discuss how to implement the methods **addFirst**, **addLast**, **add(index, e)**, **removeFirst**, **removeLast**, and **remove(index)** and leave the other methods in the **MyLinkedList** class as exercises.

26.4.3.1 Implementing addFirst(e)

The **addFirst(e)** method creates a new node for holding element **e**. The new node becomes the first node in the list. It can be implemented as follows:

create a node
link with head
head to new node
increase size
was empty?

```
1 public void addFirst(E e) {
2   Node<E> newNode = new Node<E>(e); // Create a new node
3   newNode.next = head; // link the new node with the head
4   head = newNode; // head points to the new node
5   size++; // Increase list size
6
7   if (tail == null) // The new node is the only node in list
8     tail = head;
9 }
```

The **addFirst(e)** method creates a new node to store the element (line 2) and inserts the node at the beginning of the list (line 3), as shown in Figure 26.12a. After the insertion, **head** should point to this new element node (line 4), as shown in Figure 26.12b.

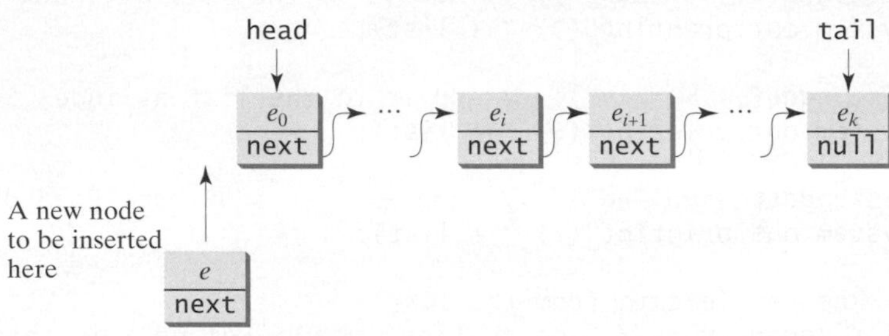

(a) Before a new node is inserted.

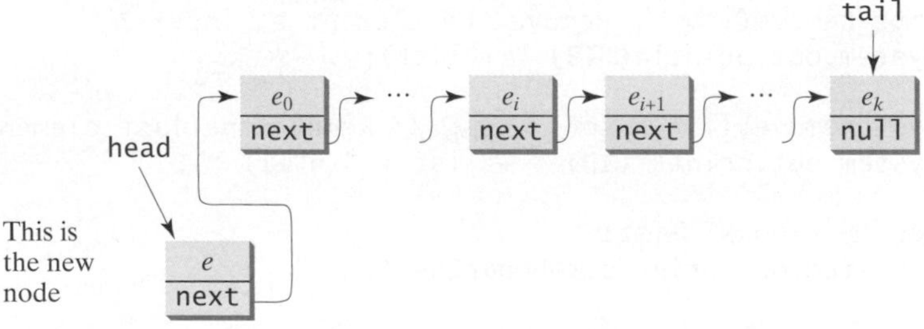

(b) After a new node is inserted.

FIGURE 26.12 A new element is added to the beginning of the list.

If the list is empty (line 7), both **head** and **tail** will point to this new node (line 8). After the node is created, **size** should be increased by **1** (line 5).

26.4.3.2 Implementing addLast(e)

The **addLast(e)** method creates a node to hold the element and appends the node at the end of the list. It can be implemented as follows:

create a node

```
1 public void addLast(E e) {
2   Node<E> newNode = new Node<E>(e); // Create a new node for e
3
```

```
4     if (tail == null) {
5       head = tail = newNode; // The only node in list
6     }
7     else {
8       tail.next = newNode; // Link the new with the last node
9       tail = tail.next; // tail now points to the last node
10    }
11
12    size++; // Increase size
13  }
```

increase size

The **addLast(e)** method creates a new node to store the element (line 2) and appends it to the end of the list. Consider two cases:

1. If the list is empty (line 4), both **head** and **tail** will point to this new node (line 5);
2. Otherwise, link the node with the last node in the list (line 8). **tail** should now point to this new node (line 9). Figure 26.13a and Figure 26.13b show the new node for element **e** before and after the insertion.

In any case, after the node is created, the size should be increased by **1** (line 12).

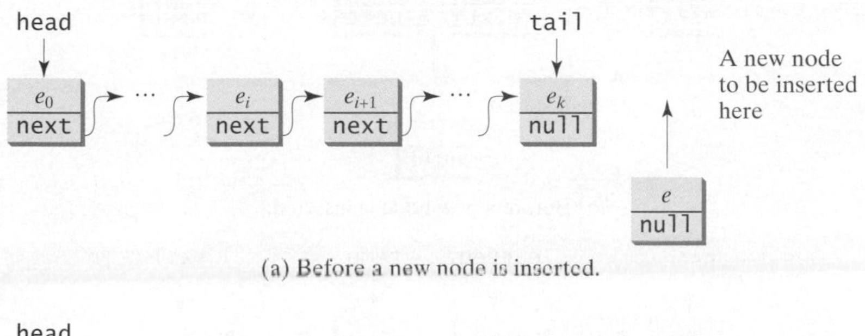

(a) Before a new node is inserted.

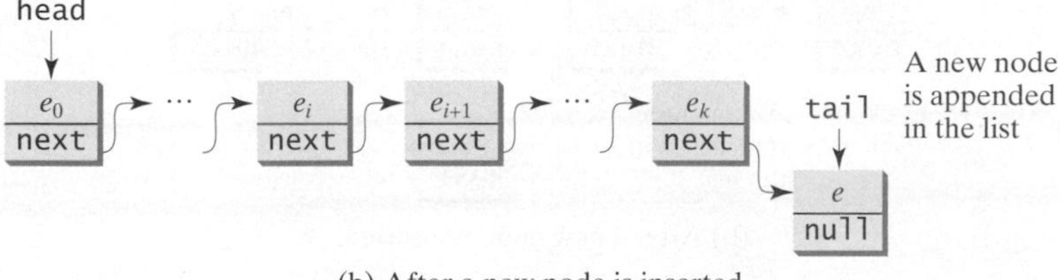

(b) After a new node is inserted.

FIGURE 26.13 A new element is added at the end of the list.

26.4.3.3 Implementing **add(index, e)**

The **add(index, e)** method inserts an element into the list at the specified index. It can be implemented as follows:

```
public void add(int index, E e) {
  if (index == 0) addFirst(e); // Insert first
  else if (index >= size) addLast(e); // Insert last
  else { // Insert in the middle
    Node<E> current = head;
    for (int i = 1; i < index; i++)
      current = current.next;
    Node<E> temp = current.next;
    current.next = new Node<E>(e);
    (current.next).next = temp;
```

insert first

insert last

create a node

increase size

```
11        size++;
12      }
13    }
```

There are three cases when inserting an element into the list:

1. If **index** is **0**, invoke **addFirst(e)** (line 2) to insert the element at the beginning of the list.
2. If **index** is greater than or equal to **size**, invoke **addLast(e)** (line 3) to insert the element at the end of the list.
3. Otherwise, create a new node to store the new element and locate where to insert it. As shown in Figure 26.14a, the new node is to be inserted between the nodes **current** and **temp**. The method assigns the new node to **current.next** and assigns **temp** to the new node's **next**, as shown in Figure 26.14b. The size is now increased by **1** (line 11).

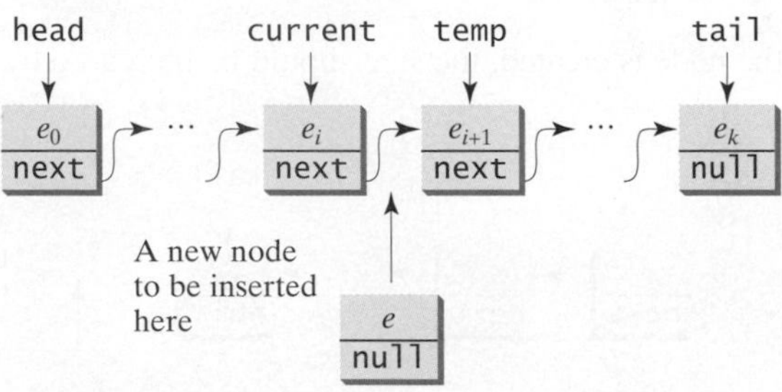

(a) Before a new node is inserted.

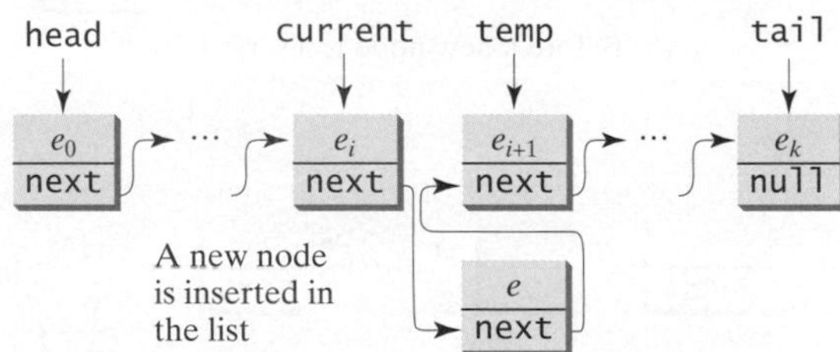

(b) After a new node is inserted.

FIGURE 26.14 A new element is inserted in the middle of the list.

26.4.3.4 Implementing removeFirst()

The **removeFirst()** method removes the first element from the list. It can be implemented as follows:

nothing to remove
keep old head
new head
decrease size
destroy the node

```
public E removeFirst() {
  if (size == 0) return null; // Nothing to delete
  else {
    Node<E> temp = head; // Keep the first node temporarily
    head = head.next; // Move head to point to next node
    size--; // Reduce size by 1
    if (head == null) tail = null; // List becomes empty
    return temp.element; // Return the deleted element
  }
}
```

Consider two cases:

1. If the list is empty, there is nothing to delete, so return **null** (line 2).
2. Otherwise, remove the first node from the list by pointing **head** to the second node. Figure 26.15a and Figure 26.15b show the linked list before and after the deletion. The size is reduced by **1** after the deletion (line 6). If the list becomes empty, after removing the element, **tail** should be set to **null** (line 7).

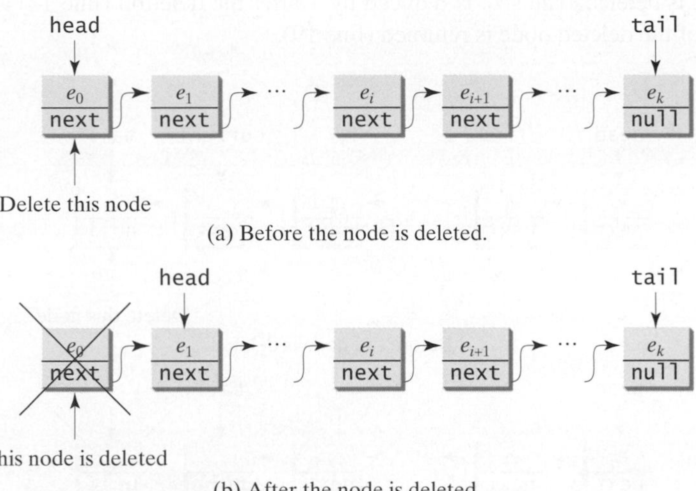

(a) Before the node is deleted.

(b) After the node is deleted.

FIGURE 26.15 The first node is deleted from the list.

26.4.3.5 Implementing **removeLast()**

The **removeLast()** method removes the last element from the list. It can be implemented as follows:

```
public E removeLast() {
  if (size == 0) return null; // Nothing to remove
  else if (size == 1) { // Only one element in the list
    Node<E> temp = head;
    head = tail = null; // list becomes empty
    size = 0;
    return temp.element;
  }
  else {
    Node<E> current = head;

    for (int i = 0; i < size - 2; i++)
      current = current.next;

    Node<E> temp = tail;
    tail = current;
    tail.next = null;
    size--;
    return temp.element;
  }
}
```

empty?
size 1?
head and tail null
size is 0
return element
size > 1
move tail
reduce size
return element

Consider three cases:

1. If the list is empty, return `null` (line 2).
2. If the list contains only one node, this node is destroyed; `head` and `tail` both become `null` (line 5). The size becomes `0` after the deletion (line 6) and the element value of the deleted node is returned (line 7).
3. Otherwise, the last node is destroyed (line 17) and the `tail` is repositioned to point to the second-to-last node. Figure 26.16a and Figure 26.16b show the last node before and after it is deleted. The size is reduced by `1` after the deletion (line 18) and the element value of the deleted node is returned (line 19).

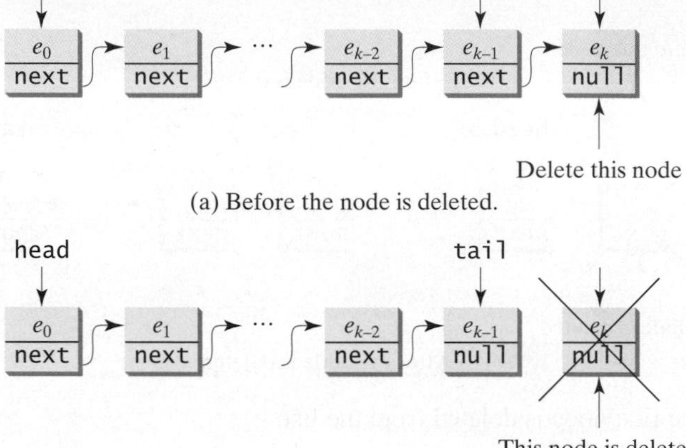

(a) Before the node is deleted.

(b) After the node is deleted.

FIGURE 26.16 The last node is deleted from the list.

26.4.3.6 Implementing `remove(index)`

The `remove(index)` method finds the node at the specified index and then removes it. It can be implemented as follows:

```
public E remove(int index) {
  if (index < 0 || index >= size) return null; // Out of range
  else if (index == 0) return removeFirst(); // Remove first
  else if (index == size - 1) return removeLast(); // Remove last
  else {
    Node<E> previous = head;

    for (int i = 1; i < index; i++) {
      previous = previous.next;
    }

    Node<E> current = previous.next;
    previous.next = current.next;
    size--;
    return current.element;
  }
}
```

out of range
remove first
remove last
locate previous
locate current
remove from list
reduce size
return element

Consider four cases:

1. If **index** is beyond the range of the list (i.e., **index < 0 || index >= size**), return **null** (line 2).
2. If **index** is **0**, invoke **removeFirst()** to remove the first node (line 3).
3. If **index** is **size - 1**, invoke **removeLast()** to remove the last node (line 4).
4. Otherwise, locate the node at the specified **index**. Let **current** denote this node and **previous** denote the node before this node, as shown in Figure 26.17a. Assign **current.next** to **previous.next** to eliminate the current node, as shown in Figure 26.17b.

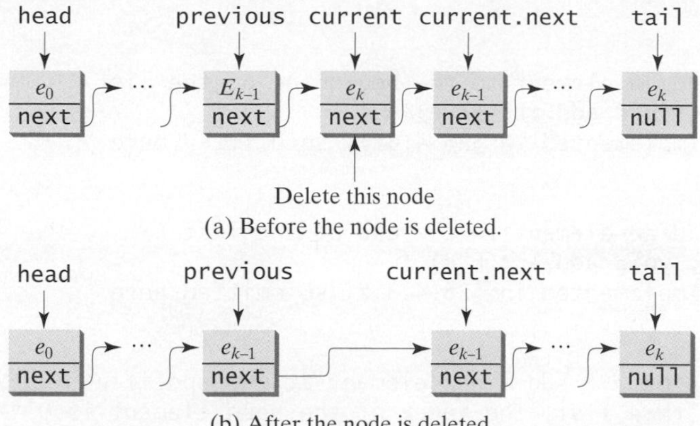

FIGURE 26.17 A node is deleted from the list.

Listing 26.6 gives the implementation of **MyLinkedList**. The implementation of **get(index)**, **indexOf(e)**, **lastIndexOf(e)**, **contains(e)**, and **set(index, e)** is omitted and left as an exercise. The **iterator()** method defined in the **java.lang.Iterable** interface is implemented to return an instance on **java.util.Iterator** (lines 126–128). The **LinkedListIterator** class implements **Iterator** with concrete methods for **hasNext**, **next**, and **remove** (lines 134–149). This implementation uses **current** to point to the current position of the element being traversed (line 132). Initially, **current** points to the head of the list.

iterator

LISTING 26.6 MyLinkedList.java

```
 1 public class MyLinkedList<E> extends MyAbstractList<E> {
 2   private Node<E> head, tail;                              // head, tail
 3
 4   /** Create a default list */
 5   public MyLinkedList() {                                  // no-arg constructor
 6   }
 7
 8   /** Create a list from an array of objects */
 9   public MyLinkedList(E[] objects) {                       // constructor
10     super(objects);
11   }
12
13   /** Return the head element in the list */
14   public E getFirst() {                                    // getFirst
15     if (size == 0) {
16       return null;
```

getLast
addFirst
addLast
add
removeFirst
removeLast
remove
toString

```
    }
    else {
      return head.element;
    }
  }

  /** Return the last element in the list */
  public E getLast() {
    if (size == 0) {
      return null;
    }
    else {
      return tail.element;
    }
  }

  /** Add an element to the beginning of the list */
  public void addFirst(E e) {
    // Implemented in §26.4.3.1, so omitted here
  }

  /** Add an element to the end of the list */
  public void addLast(E e) {
    // Implemented in §26.4.3.2, so omitted here
  }

  @Override /** Add a new element at the specified index
   * in this list. The index of the head element is 0 */
  public void add(int index, E e) {
    // Implemented in §26.4.3.3, so omitted here
  }

  /** Remove the head node and
   *  return the object that is contained in the removed node. */
  public E removeFirst() {
    // Implemented in §26.4.3.4, so omitted here
  }

  /** Remove the last node and
   * return the object that is contained in the removed node. */
  public E removeLast() {
    // Implemented in §26.4.3.5, so omitted here
  }

  @Override /** Remove the element at the specified position in this
   *  list. Return the element that was removed from the list. */
  public E remove(int index) {
    // Implemented earlier in §26.4.3.6, so omitted here
  }

  @Override
  public String toString() {
    StringBuilder result = new StringBuilder("[");

    Node<E> current = head;
    for (int i = 0; i < size; i++) {
      result.append(current.element);
      current = current.next;
      if (current != null) {
        result.append(", "); // Separate two elements with a comma
```

```
      }
      else {
        result.append("]"); // Insert the closing ] in the string
      }
    }

    return result.toString();
  }

```

clear

```
  @Override /** Clear the list */
  public void clear() {
    size = 0;
    head = tail = null;
  }

```

contains

```
  @Override /** Return true if this list contains the element e */
  public boolean contains(E e) {
    System.out.println("Implementation left as an exercise");
    return true;
  }

```

get

```
  @Override /** Return the element at the specified index */
  public E get(int index) {
    System.out.println("Implementation left as an exercise");
    return null;
  }

```

indexOf

```
  @Override /** Return the index of the head matching element
   *  in this list. Return -1 if no match. */
  public int indexOf(E e) {
    System.out.println("Implementation left as an exercise");
    return 0;
  }

```

lastIndexOf

```
  @Override /** Return the index of the last matching element
   *  in this list. Return -1 if no match. */
  public int lastIndexOf(E e) {
    System.out.println("Implementation left as an exercise");
    return 0;
  }

```

set

```
  @Override /** Replace the element at the specified position
   * in this list with the specified element. */
  public E set(int index, E e) {
    System.out.println("Implementation left as an exercise");
    return null;
  }

```

iterator

```
  @Override /** Override iterator() defined in Iterable */
  public java.util.Iterator<E> iterator() {
    return new LinkedListIterator();
  }

```

LinkedListIterator class

```
  private class LinkedListIterator
      implements java.util.Iterator<E> {
    private Node<E> current = head; // Current index

    @Override
    public boolean hasNext() {
      return (current != null);
```

Node inner class

```
      }

      @Override
      public E next() {
        E e = current.element;
        current = current.next;
        return e;
      }

      @Override
      public void remove() {
        System.out.println("Implementation left as an exercise");
      }
    }

    // This class is only used in LinkedList, so it is private.
    // This class does not need to access any
    // instance members of LinkedList, so it is defined static.
    private static class Node<E> {
      E element;
      Node<E> next;

      public Node(E element) {
        this.element = element;
      }
    }
  }
```

26.6.4 MyArrayList vs. MyLinkedList

Both MyArrayList and MyLinkedList can be used to store a list. MyArrayList is implemented using an array and MyLinkedList is implemented using a linked list. The overhead of MyArrayList is smaller than that of MyLinkedList. However, MyLinkedList is more efficient if you need to insert elements into and delete elements from the beginning of the list. Table 26.1 summarizes the complexity of the methods in MyArrayList and MyLinkedList.

TABLE 26.1 Time Complexities for Methods in MyArrayList and MyLinkedList

Methods	*MyArrayList/ArrayList*	*MyLinkedList/LinkedList*
add(e: E)	$O(1)$	$O(1)$
add(index: int, e: E)	$O(n)$	$O(n)$
clear()	$O(1)$	$O(1)$
contains(e: E)	$O(n)$	$O(n)$
get(index: int)	$O(1)$	$O(n)$
indexOf(e: E)	$O(n)$	$O(n)$
isEmpty()	$O(1)$	$O(1)$
lastIndexOf(e: E)	$O(n)$	$O(n)$
remove(e: E)	$O(n)$	$O(n)$
size()	$O(1)$	$O(1)$
remove(index: int)	$O(n)$	$O(n)$
set(index: int, e: E)	$O(n)$	$O(n)$
addFirst(e: E)	$O(n)$	$O(1)$
removeFirst()	$O(n)$	$O(1)$

Note that `MyArrayList` is the same as `java.util.ArrayList` and `MyLinkedList` is the same as `java.util.LinkedList`.

26.4.5 Variations of Linked Lists

The linked list introduced in the preceding sections is known as a *singly linked list*. It contains a pointer to the list's first node, and each node contains a pointer to the next node sequentially. Several variations of the linked list are useful in certain applications.

A *circular, singly linked list* is like a singly linked list, except that the pointer of the last node points back to the first node, as shown in Figure 26.18a. Note that `tail` is not needed for circular linked lists. `head` points to the current node in the list. Insertion and deletion take place at the current node. A good application of a circular linked list is in the operating system that serves multiple users in a timesharing fashion. The system picks a user from a circular list and grants a small amount of CPU time, then moves on to the next user in the list.

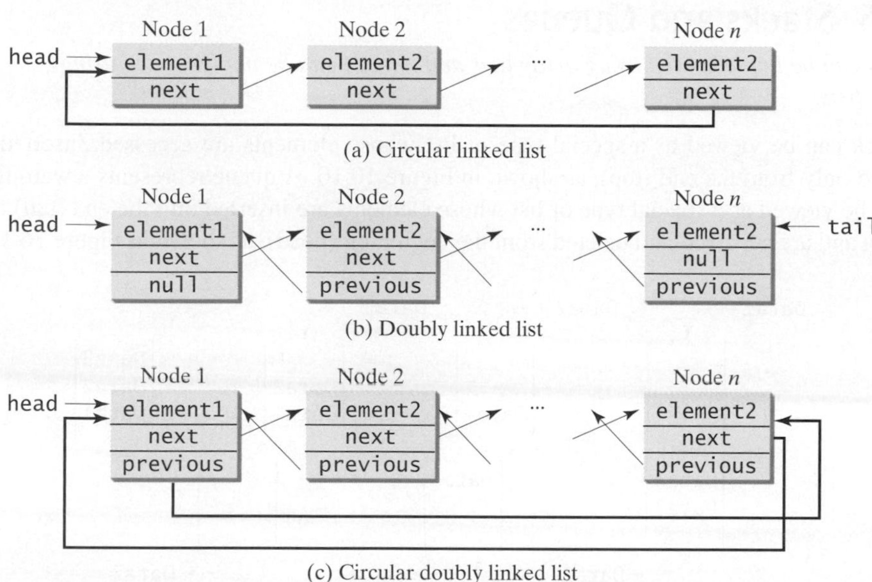

FIGURE 26.18 Linked lists may appear in various forms.

A *doubly linked list* contains nodes with two pointers. One points to the next node and the other to the previous node, as shown in Figure 26.18b. These two pointers are conveniently called *a forward pointer* and *a backward pointer*. Thus, a doubly linked list can be traversed forward and backward. The `java.util.LinkedList` class is implemented using a doubly linked list, and it supports traversing of the list forward and backward using the `ListIterator`.

A *circular, doubly linked list* is like a doubly linked list, except that the forward pointer of the last node points to the first node and the backward pointer of the first pointer points to the last node, as shown in Figure 26.18c.

The implementations of these linked lists are left as exercises.

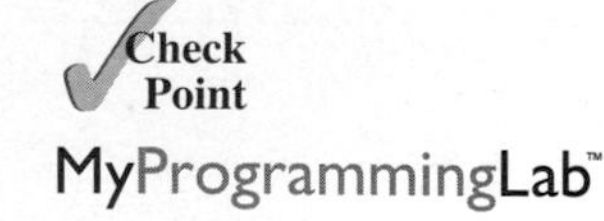

26.11 Both `MyArrayList` and `MyLinkedList` are used to store a list of objects. Why do we need both types of lists?

26.12 Draw a diagram to show the linked list after each of the following statements is executed.

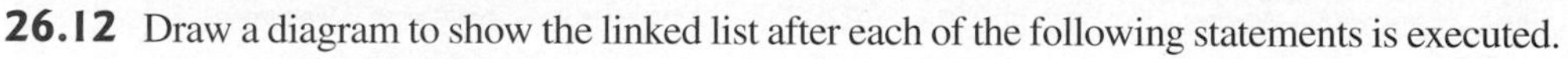

```
MyLinkedList<Double> list = new MyLinkedList<Double>();
list.add(1.5);
list.add(6.2);
```

```
list.add(3.4);
list.add(7.4);
list.remove(1.5);
list.remove(2);
```

26.13 What is the time complexity of the `addFirst(e)` and `removeFirst()` methods in `MyLinkedList`?

26.14 Suppose you need to store a list of elements. If the number of elements in the program is fixed, what data structure should you use? If the number of elements in the program changes, what data structure should you use?

26.15 If you have to add or delete the elements at the beginning of a list, should you use `MyArrayList` or `MyLinkedList`? If most of the operations on a list involve retrieving an element at a given index, should you use `MyArrayList` or `MyLinkedList`?

26.5 Stacks and Queues

Stacks can be implemented using array lists and queues can be implemented using linked lists.

A stack can be viewed as a special type of list whose elements are accessed, inserted, and deleted only from the end (top), as shown in Figure 10.10. A queue represents a waiting list. It can be viewed as a special type of list whose elements are inserted into the end (tail) of the queue, and are accessed and deleted from the beginning (head), as shown in Figure 26.19.

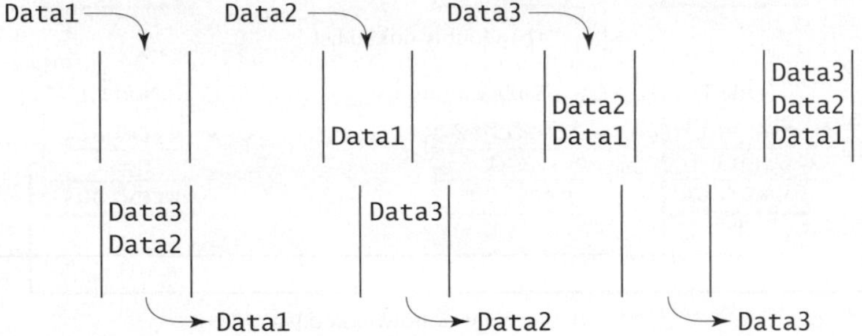

FIGURE 26.19 A queue holds objects in a first-in, first-out fashion.

stack and queue animation on Companion Website

Pedagogical Note

For an interactive demo on how stacks and queues work, go to www.cs.armstrong.edu/liang/animation/StackAnimation.html, and www.cs.armstrong.edu/liang/animation/QueueAnimation.html, as shown in Figure 26.20.

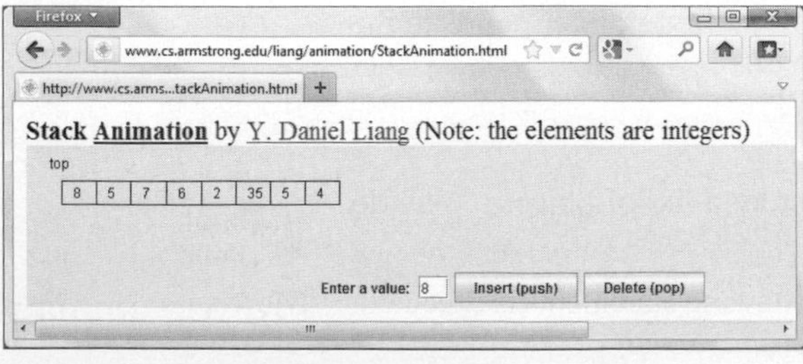

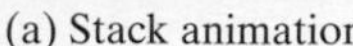
(a) Stack animation

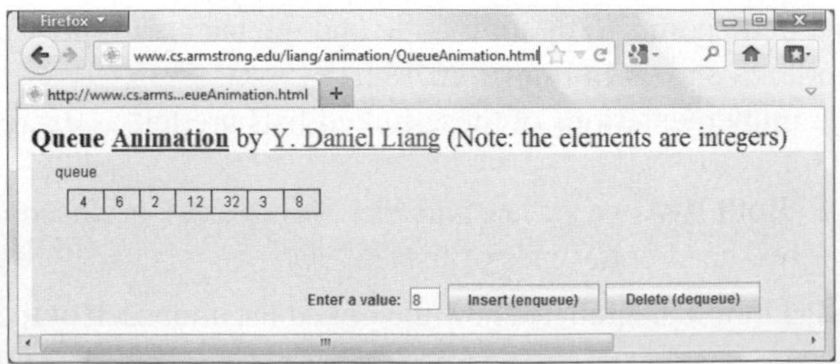

(b) Queue animation

FIGURE 26.20 The animation tool enables you to see how stacks and queues work.

Since the insertion and deletion operations on a stack are made only at the end of the stack, it is more efficient to implement a stack with an array list than with a linked list. Since deletions are made at the beginning of the list, it is more efficient to implement a queue using a linked list than an array list. This section implements a stack class using an array list and a queue class using a linked list.

There are two ways to design the stack and queue classes:

- Using inheritance: You can define a stack class by extending `ArrayList`, and a queue class by extending `LinkedList`, as shown in Figure 26.21a. (inheritance)
- Using composition: You can define an array list as a data field in the stack class, and a linked list as a data field in the queue class, as shown in Figure 26.21b. (composition)

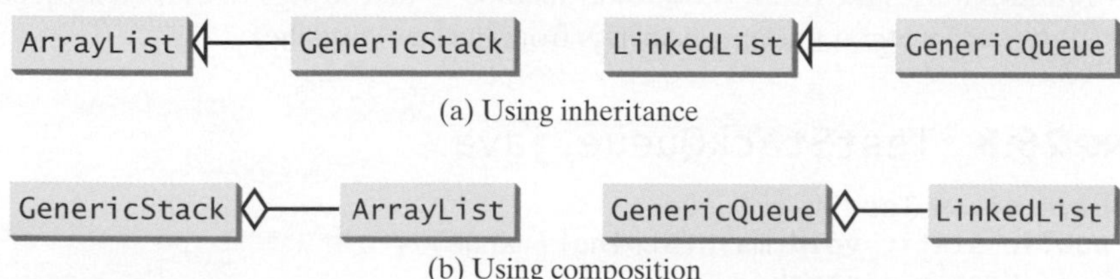

Figure 26.21 `GenericStack` and `GenericQueue` may be implemented using inheritance or composition.

Both designs are fine, but using composition is better because it enables you to define a completely new stack class and queue class without inheriting the unnecessary and inappropriate methods from the array list and linked list. The implementation of the stack class using the composition approach was given in Listing 21.1, GenericStack.java. Listing 26.7 implements the `GenericQueue` class using the composition approach. Figure 26.22 shows the UML of the class.

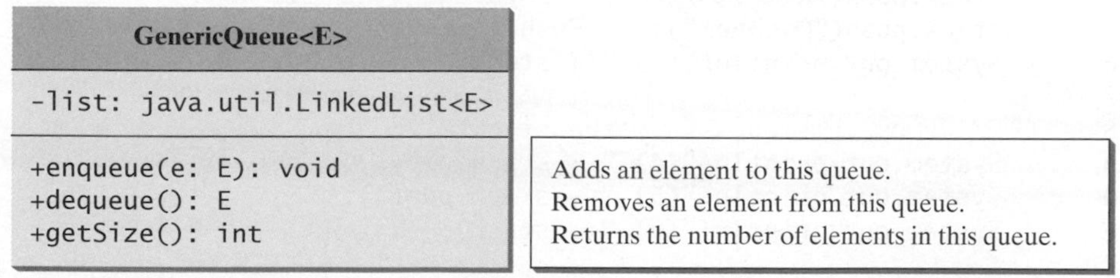

Figure 26.22 `GenericQueue` uses a linked list to provide a first-in, first-out data structure.

Listing 26.7 GenericQueue.java

```
public class GenericQueue<E> {
  private java.util.LinkedList<E> list
    = new java.util.LinkedList<E>();

  public void enqueue(E e) {
    list.addLast(e);
  }

  public E dequeue() {
    return list.removeFirst();
  }

  public int getSize() {
    return list.size();
  }
```

linked list · enqueue · dequeue · getSize

toString

```
16
17   @Override
18   public String toString() {
19     return "Queue: " + list.toString();
20   }
21 }
```

A linked list is created to store the elements in a queue (lines 2–3). The **enqueue(e)** method (lines 5–7) adds element **e** into the tail of the queue. The **dequeue()** method (lines 9–11) removes an element from the head of the queue and returns the removed element. The **getSize()** method (lines 13–15) returns the number of elements in the queue.

Listing 26.8 gives an example that creates a stack using **GenericStack** and a queue using **GenericQueue**. It uses the **push** (**enqueue**) method to add strings to the stack (queue) and the **pop** (**dequeue**) method to remove strings from the stack (queue).

LISTING 26.8 TestStackQueue.java

```
public class TestStackQueue {
  public static void main(String[] args) {
    // Create a stack
    GenericStack<String> stack =
      new GenericStack<String>();

    // Add elements to the stack
    stack.push("Tom"); // Push it to the stack
    System.out.println("(1) " + stack);

    stack.push("Susan"); // Push it to the the stack
    System.out.println("(2) " + stack);

    stack.push("Kim"); // Push it to the stack
    stack.push("Michael"); // Push it to the stack
    System.out.println("(3) " + stack);

    // Remove elements from the stack
    System.out.println("(4) " + stack.pop());
    System.out.println("(5) " + stack.pop());
    System.out.println("(6) " + stack);

    // Create a queue
    GenericQueue<String> queue = new GenericQueue<String>();

    // Add elements to the queue
    queue.enqueue("Tom"); // Add it to the queue
    System.out.println("(7) " + queue);

    queue.enqueue("Susan"); // Add it to the queue
    System.out.println("(8) " + queue);

    queue.enqueue("Kim"); // Add it to the queue
    queue.enqueue("Michael"); // Add it to the queue
    System.out.println("(9) " + queue);

    // Remove elements from the queue
    System.out.println("(10) " + queue.dequeue());
    System.out.println("(11) " + queue.dequeue());
    System.out.println("(12) " + queue);
  }
}
```

```
(1) stack: [Tom]
(2) stack: [Tom, Susan]
(3) stack: [Tom, Susan, Kim, Michael]
(4) Michael
(5) Kim
(6) stack: [Tom, Susan]
(7) Queue: [Tom]
(8) Queue: [Tom, Susan]
(9) Queue: [Tom, Susan, Kim, Michael]
(10) Tom
(11) Susan
(12) Queue: [Kim, Michael]
```

stack time complexity

For a stack, the **push(e)** method adds an element to the top of the stack, and the **pop()** method removes the top element from the stack and returns the removed element. It is easy to see that the time complexity for the **push** and **pop** methods is $O(1)$.

queue time complexity

For a queue, the **enqueue(e)** method adds an element to the tail of the queue, and the **dequeue()** method removes the element from the head of the queue. It is easy to see that the time complexity for the **enqueue** and **dequeue** methods is $O(1)$.

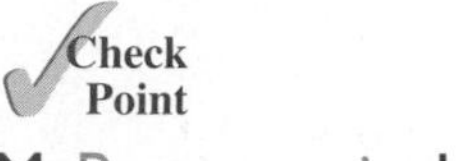

Check Point

MyProgrammingLab™

26.16 You can use inheritance or composition to design the data structures for stacks and queues. Discuss the pros and cons of these two approaches.

26.17 If **LinkedList** is replaced by **ArrayList** in lines 2–3 in Listing 26.7 GenericQueue.java, what will be the time complexity for the **enqueue** and **dequeue** methods?

26.18 Which lines of the following code are wrong?

```
1 List<String> list = new ArrayList<String>();
2 list.add("Tom");
3 list = new LinkedList<String>();
4 list.add("Tom");
5 list = new GenericStack<String>();
6 list.add("Tom");
```

26.6 Priority Queues

Priority queues can be implemented using heaps.

Key Point

An ordinary queue is a first-in, first out data structure. Elements are appended to the end of the queue and removed from the beginning. In a *priority queue*, elements are assigned with priorities. When accessing elements, the element with the highest priority is removed first. For example, the emergency room in a hospital assigns priority numbers to patients; the patient with the highest priority is treated first.

A priority queue can be implemented using a heap, in which the root is the object with the highest priority in the queue. Heaps were introduced in Section 25.5, Heap Sort. The class diagram for the priority queue is shown in Figure 26.23. Its implementation is given in Listing 26.9.

MyPriorityQueue <E extends Comparable<E>>	
-heap: Heap<E>	
+enqueue(element: E): void	Adds an element to this queue.
+dequeue(): E	Removes an element from this queue.
+getSize(): int	Returns the number of elements in this queue.

Figure 26.23 **MyPriorityQueue** uses a heap to provide a largest-in, first-out data structure.

LISTING 26.9 MyPriorityQueue.java

heap for priority queue · enqueue · dequeue · getsize

```
public class MyPriorityQueue<E extends Comparable<E>> {
  private Heap<E> heap = new Heap<E>();

  public void enqueue(E newObject) {
    heap.add(newObject);
  }

  public E dequeue() {
    return heap.remove();
  }

  public int getSize() {
    return heap.getSize();
  }
}
```

Listing 26.10 gives an example of using a priority queue for patients. The **Patient** class is defined in lines 19–37. Four patients are created with associated priority values in lines 3–6. Line 8 creates a priority queue. The patients are enqueued in lines 10–13. Line 16 dequeues a patient from the queue.

LISTING 26.10 TestPriorityQueue.java

create a patient · create a priority queue · add to queue · remove from queue · inner class Patient · compareTo

```
1  public class TestPriorityQueue {
2    public static void main(String[] args) {
3      Patient patient1 = new Patient("John", 2);
4      Patient patient2 = new Patient("Jim", 1);
5      Patient patient3 = new Patient("Tim", 5);
6      Patient patient4 = new Patient("Cindy", 7);
7
8      MyPriorityQueue<Patient> priorityQueue
9        = new MyPriorityQueue<Patient>();
10     priorityQueue.enqueue(patient1);
11     priorityQueue.enqueue(patient2);
12     priorityQueue.enqueue(patient3);
13     priorityQueue.enqueue(patient4);
14
15     while (priorityQueue.getSize() > 0)
16       System.out.print(priorityQueue.dequeue() + " ");
17   }
18
19   static class Patient implements Comparable<Patient> {
20     private String name;
21     private int priority;
22
23     public Patient(String name, int priority) {
24       this.name = name;
25       this.priority = priority;
26     }
27
28     @Override
29     public String toString() {
30       return name + "(priority:" + priority + ")";
31     }
32
33     @Override
34     public int compareTo(Patient patient) {
```

```
        return this.priority - patient.priority;
      }
    }
  }
```

```
Cindy(priority:7) Tim(priority:5) John(priority:2) Jim(priority:1)
```

Check Point
MyProgrammingLab™

26.19 What is a priority queue?

26.20 What are the time complexity of the **enqueue**, **dequeue** , and **getSize** methods in **MyProrityQueue**?

26.21 Which of the following statements are wrong?

```
MyPriorityQueue<Object> q1 = new MyPriorityQueue<Object>();
MyPriorityQueue<Number> q2 = new MyPriorityQueue<Number>();
MyPriorityQueue<Integer> q3 = new MyPriorityQueue<Integer>();
MyPriorityQueue<Date> q4 = new MyPriorityQueue<Date>();
MyPriorityQueue<String> q5 = new MyPriorityQueue<String>();
```

Chapter Summary

1. You learned how to implement array lists, linked lists, stacks, and queues.

2. To define a data structure is essentially to define a class. The class for a data structure should use data fields to store data and provide methods to support operations such as insertion and deletion.

3. To create a data structure is to create an instance from the class. You can then apply the methods on the instance to manipulate the data structure, such as inserting an element into the data structure or deleting an element from the data structure.

4. You learned how to implement a priority queue using a heap.

Test Questions

Do the test questions for this chapter online at **www.cs.armstrong.edu/liang/intro9e/test.html**.

Programming Exercises

MyProgrammingLab™

26.1 (*Add set operations in* **MyList**) Define the following methods in **MyList** and implement them in **MyAbstractList**:

```
/** Adds the elements in otherList to this list.
  * Returns true if this list changed as a result of the call */
public boolean addAll(MyList<E> otherList);

/** Removes all the elements in otherList from this list
  * Returns true if this list changed as a result of the call */
public boolean removeAll(MyList<E> otherList);

/** Retains the elements in this list that are also in otherList
  * Returns true if this list changed as a result of the call */
public boolean retainAll(MyList<E> otherList);
```

Write a test program that creates two MyArrayLists, list1 and list2, with the initial values {"Tom", "George", "Peter", "Jean", "Jane"} and {"Tom", "George", "Michael", "Michelle", "Daniel"}, then perform the following operations:

- Invokes list1.addAll(list2), and displays list1 and list2.
- Recreates list1 and list2 with the same initial values, invokes list1.removeAll(list2), and displays list1 and list2.
- Recreates list1 and list2 with the same initial values, invokes list1.retainAll(list2), and displays list1 and list2.

***26.2** (*Implement MyLinkedList*) The implementations of the methods contains(E e), get(int index), indexOf(E e), lastIndexOf(E e), and set(int index, E e) are omitted in the text. Implement these methods.

***26.3** (*Implement a doubly linked list*) The MyLinkedList class used in Listing 26.6 is a one-way directional linked list that enables one-way traversal of the list. Modify the Node class to add the new field name previous to refer to the previous node in the list, as follows:

```
public class Node<E> {
  E element;
  Node<E> next;
  Node<E> previous;

  public Node(E e) {
    element = e;
  }
}
```

Implement a new class named MyTwoWayLinkedList that uses a doubly linked list to store elements. The MyLinkedList class in the text extends MyAbstractList. Define MyTwoWayLinkedList to extend the java.util.AbstractSequentialList class. You need to implement the methods listIterator() and listIterator(int index). Both return an instance of java.util.ListIterator<E>. The former sets the cursor to the head of the list and the latter to the element at the specified index.

26.4 (*Use the GenericStack class*) Write a program that displays the first 50 prime numbers in descending order. Use a stack to store the prime numbers.

26.5 (*Implement GenericQueue using inheritance*) In Section 26.5, Stacks and Queues, GenericQueue is implemented using composition. Define a new queue class that extends java.util.LinkedList.

***26.6** (*Generic PriorityQueue using Comparator*) Revise MyPriorityQueue in Listing 26.9, using a generic parameter for comparing objects. Define a new constructor with a Comparator as its argument as follows:

```
PriorityQueue(Comparator<? super E> comparator)
```

****26.7** (*Animation: linked list*) Write an applet to animate search, insertion, and deletion in a linked list, as shown in Figure 26.1b. The *Search* button searches to determine whether the specified value is in the list. The *Delete* button deletes the specified value from the list. The *Insert* button inserts the value into the specified index in the list.

***26.8** (*Animation: array list*) Write an applet to animate search, insertion, and deletion in an array list, as shown in Figure 26.1a. The *Search* button searches to determine whether the specified value is in the list. The *Delete* button deletes the specified value from the list. The *Insert* button inserts the value into the specified index in the list.

***26.9** (*Animation: queue*) Write an applet to animate the **enqueue** and **dequeue** operations on a queue, as shown in Figure 26.20b.

***26.10** (*Animation: stack*) Write an applet to animate push and pop in a stack, as shown in Figure 26.20a.

***26.11** (*Animation: doubly linked list*) Write an applet to animate search, insertion, and deletion in a doubly linked list, as shown in Figure 26.24a. The *Search* button searches to determine whether the specified value is in the list. The *Delete* button deletes the specified value from the list. The *Insert* button inserts the value into the specified index in the list. Also add two buttons named *Forward Traversal* and *Backward Traversal* for displaying the elements in a message dialog box forward and backward order, respectively, using iterators, as shown in Figure 26.24b.

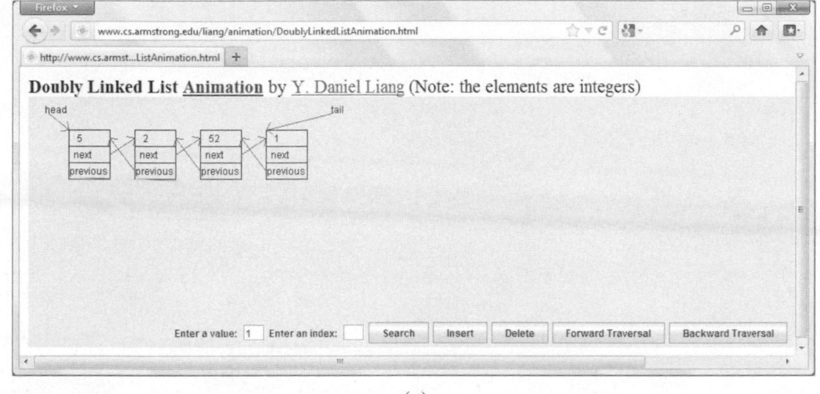

(a)

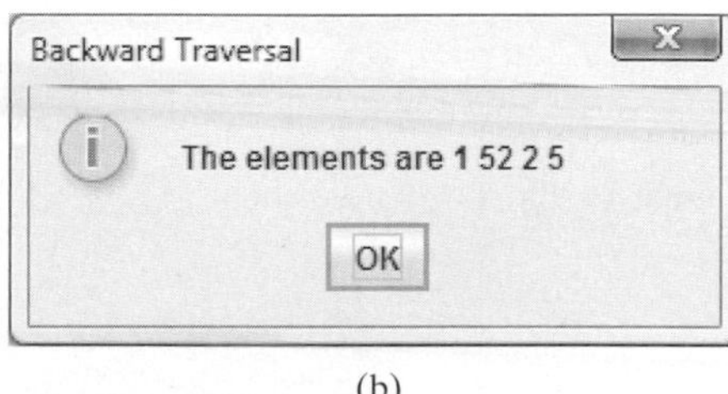

(b)

FIGURE 26.24 The applet animates the work of a doubly linked list.

CHAPTER

27

Binary Search Trees

Objectives

- To design and implement a binary search tree (§27.2).
- To represent binary trees using linked data structures (§27.2.1).
- To search an element in a binary search tree (§27.2.2).
- To insert an element into a binary search tree (§27.2.3).
- To traverse elements in a binary tree (§27.2.4).
- To design and implement the `Tree` interface, `AbstractTree` class, and the `BST` class (§27.2.5).
- To delete elements from a binary search tree (§27.3).
- To display a binary tree graphically (§27.4).
- To create iterators for traversing a binary tree (§27.5).
- To implement Huffman coding for compressing data using a binary tree (§27.6).

27.1 Introduction

A tree is a classic data structure with many important applications.

A *tree* provides a hierarchical organization in which data are stored in the nodes. This chapter introduces binary search trees. You will learn how to construct a binary search tree, how to search an element, insert an element, delete an element, and traverse elements in a binary search tree.

27.2 Binary Search Trees

A binary search tree can be implemented using a linked structure.

binary tree
root
left subtree
right subtree

Recall that lists, stacks, and queues are linear structures that consist of a sequence of elements. A *binary tree* is a hierarchical structure. It either is empty or consists of an element, called the *root*, and two distinct binary trees, called the *left subtree* and *right subtree*, either or both of which may be empty. Examples of binary trees are shown in Figure 27.1.

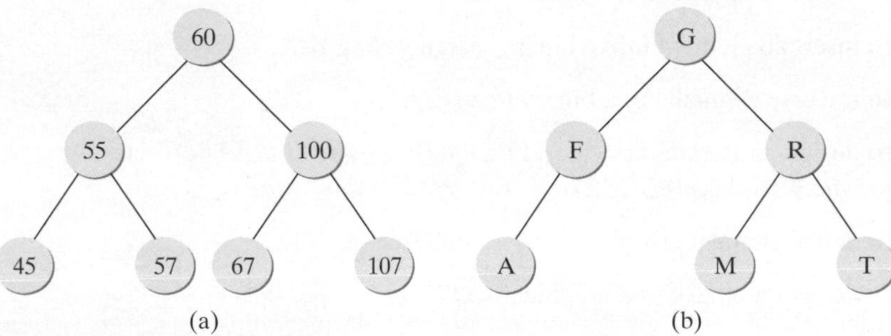

FIGURE 27.1 Each node in a binary tree has zero, one, or two subtrees.

length
depth
level
sibling
leaf
height

The *length* of a path is the number of the edges in the path. The *depth* of a node is the length of the path from the root to the node. The set of all nodes at a given depth is sometimes called a *level* of the tree. *Siblings* are nodes that share the same parent node. The root of a left (right) subtree of a node is called a *left (right) child* of the node. A node without children is called a *leaf*. The *height* of an empty tree is 0. The height of a nonempty tree is the length of the path from the root node to its furthest leaf + 1. Consider the tree in Figure 27.1a. The length of the path from node 60 to 45 is 2. The depth of node 60 is 0, the depth of node 55 is 1, and the depth of node 45 is 2. The height of the tree is 3. Nodes 45 and 57 are siblings. Nodes 45, 57, 67, and 107 are at the same level.

binary search tree

A special type of binary tree called a *binary search tree* (BST) is often useful. A BST (with no duplicate elements) has the property that for every node in the tree, the value of any node in its left subtree is less than the value of the node, and the value of any node in its right subtree is greater than the value of the node. The binary trees in Figure 27.1 are all BSTs.

BST animation on Companion Website

Pedagogical Note

For an interactive GUI demo to see how a BST works, go to www.cs.armstrong.edu/liang/animation/BSTAnimation.html, as shown in Figure 27.2.

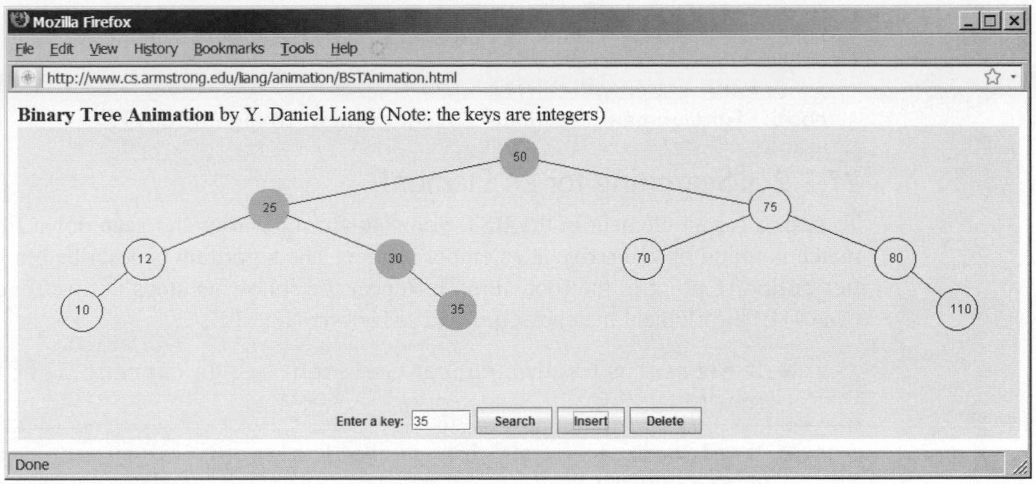

FIGURE 27.2 The animation tool enables you to insert, delete, and search elements.

27.2.1 Representing Binary Search Trees

A binary tree can be represented using a set of linked nodes. Each node contains a value and two links named *left* and *right* that reference the left child and right child, respectively, as shown in Figure 27.3.

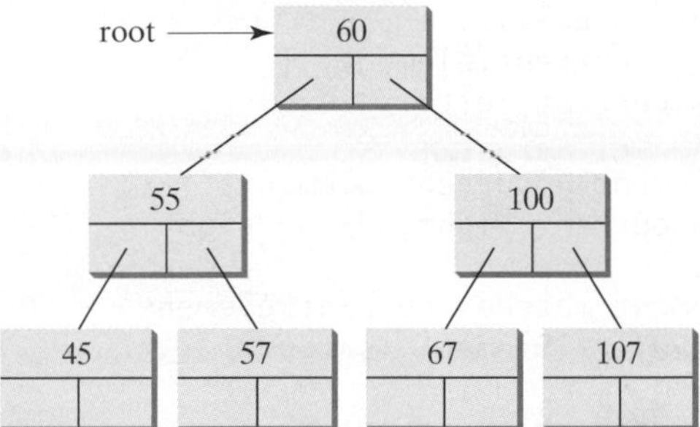

FIGURE 27.3 A binary tree can be represented using a set of linked nodes.

A node can be defined as a class, as follows:

```
class TreeNode<E> {
  protected E element;
  protected TreeNode<E> left;
  protected TreeNode<E> right;

  public TreeNode(E e) {
    element = e;
  }
}
```

The variable `root` refers to the root node of the tree. If the tree is empty, `root` is `null`. The following code creates the first three nodes of the tree in Figure 27.3.

```
// Create the root node
TreeNode<Integer> root = new TreeNode<Integer>(new Integer(60));
```

```
// Create the left child node
root.left = new TreeNode<Integer>(new Integer(55));

// Create the right child node
root.right = new TreeNode<Integer>(new Integer(100));
```

27.2.2 Searching for an Element

To search for an element in the BST, you start from the root and scan down from it until a match is found or you arrive at an empty subtree. The algorithm is described in Listing 27.1. Let `current` point to the root (line 2). Repeat the following steps until `current` is `null` (line 4) or the element matches `current.element` (line 12).

- If `element` is less than `current.element`, assign `current.left` to `current` (line 6).
- If `element` is greater than `current.element`, assign `current.right` to `current` (line 9).
- If `element` is equal to `current.element`, return `true` (line 12).

If `current` is `null`, the subtree is empty and the element is not in the tree (line 14).

LISTING 27.1 Searching for an Element in a BST

```
1  public boolean search(E element) {
2    TreeNode<E> current = root; // Start from the root
3
4    while (current != null)
5      if (element < current.element) {
6        current = current.left; // Go left
7      }
8      else if (element > current.element) {
9        current = current.right; // Go right
10     }
11     else // Element matches current.element
12       return true; // Element is found
13
14   return false; // Element is not in the tree
15 }
```

start from root
left subtree
right subtree
found
not found

27.2.3 Inserting an Element into a BST

To insert an element into a BST, you need to locate where to insert it in the tree. The key idea is to locate the parent for the new node. Listing 27.2 gives the algorithm.

LISTING 27.2 Inserting an Element into a BST

```
boolean insert(E e) {
  if (tree is empty)
    // Create the node for e as the root;
  else {
    // Locate the parent node
    parent = current = root;
    while (current != null)
      if (e < the value in current.element) {
        parent = current;  // Keep the parent
        current = current.left; // Go left
      }
      else if (e > the value in current.element) {
        parent = current; // Keep the parent
```

create a new node
locate parent
left child

```
14            current = current.right; // Go right
15          }
16          else
17            return false; // Duplicate node not inserted
18
19        // Create a new node for e and attach it to parent
20
21        return true; // Element inserted
22      }
23    }
```

right child

If the tree is empty, create a root node with the new element (lines 2–3). Otherwise, locate the parent node for the new element node (lines 6–17). Create a new node for the element and link this node to its parent node. If the new element is less than the parent element, the node for the new element will be the left child of the parent. If the new element is greater than the parent element, the node for the new element will be the right child of the parent.

For example, to insert `101` into the tree in Figure 27.3, after the `while` loop finishes in the algorithm, `parent` points to the node for `107`, as shown in Figure 27.4a. The new node for `101` becomes the left child of the parent. To insert `59` into the tree, after the `while` loop finishes in the algorithm, the parent points to the node for `57`, as shown in Figure 27.4b. The new node for `59` becomes the right child of the parent.

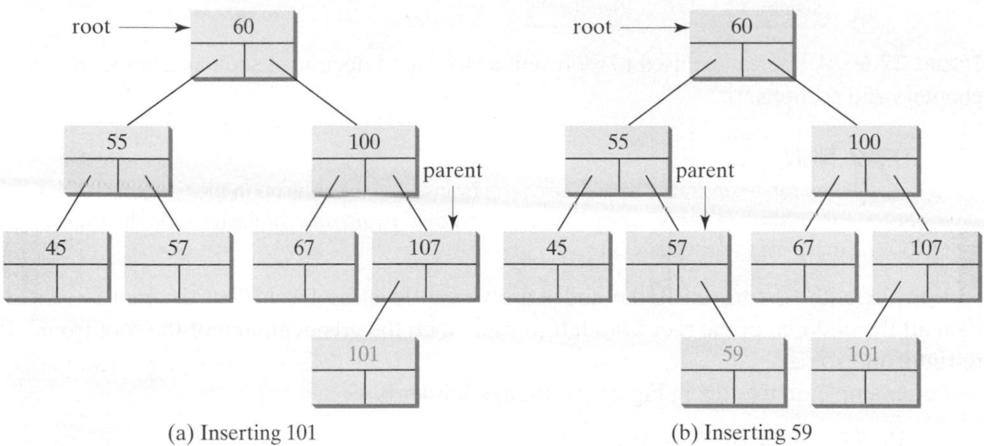

(a) Inserting 101 (b) Inserting 59

FIGURE 27.4 Two new elements are inserted into the tree.

27.2.4 Tree Traversal

tree traversal

Tree traversal is the process of visiting each node in the tree exactly once. There are several ways to traverse a tree. This section presents *inorder*, *postorder, preorder*, *depth-first,* and *breadth-first* traversals.

inorder traversal

With *inorder traversal*, the left subtree of the current node is visited first recursively, then the current node, and finally the right subtree of the current node recursively. The inorder traversal displays all the nodes in a BST in increasing order.

postorder traversal

With *postorder traversal*, the left subtree of the current node is visited recursively first, then recursively the right subtree of the current node, and finally the current node itself. An application of postorder is to find the size of the directory in a file system. As shown in Figure 27.5, each directory is an internal node and a file is a leaf node. You can apply postorder to get the size of each file and subdirectory before finding the size of the root directory.

preorder traversal

depth-first traversal

With *preorder traversal*, the current node is visited first, then recursively the left subtree of the current node, and finally the right subtree of the current node recursively. Depth-first traversal is the same as preorder traversal. An application of preorder is to print a structured document. As shown in Figure 27.6, you can print a book's table of contents using preorder traversal.

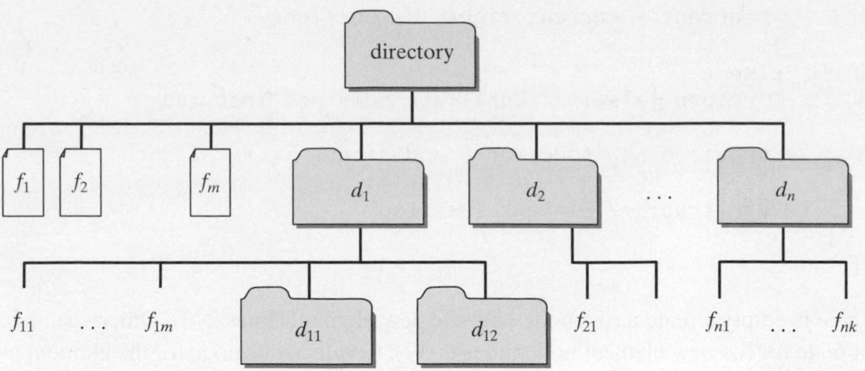

FIGURE 27.5 A directory contains files and subdirectories.

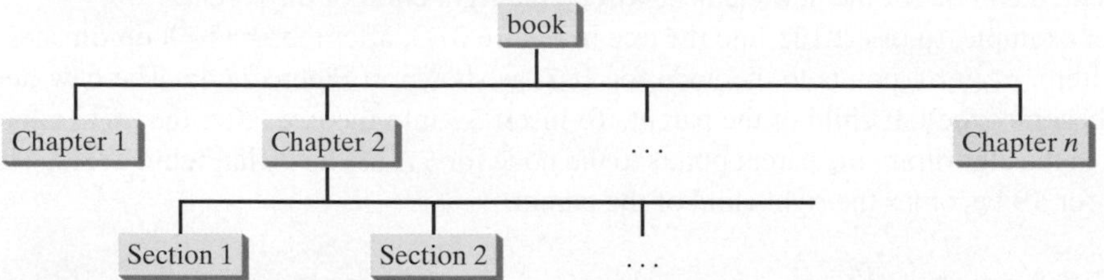

FIGURE 27.6 A tree can be used to represent a structured document such as a book and its chapters and sections.

Note

You can reconstruct a binary search tree by inserting the elements in their preorder. The reconstructed tree preserves the parent and child relationship for the nodes in the original binary search tree.

breadth-first traversal

With breadth-first traversal, the nodes are visited level by level. First the root is visited, then all the children of the root from left to right, then the grandchildren of the root from left to right, and so on.

For example, in the tree in Figure 27.4b, the inorder is

```
45 55 57 59 60 67 100 101 107
```

The postorder is

```
45 59 57 55 67 101 107 100 60
```

The preorder is

```
60 55 45 57 59 100 67 107 101
```

The breadth-first traversal is

```
60 55 100 45 57 67 107 59 101
```

You can use the following tree to help remember inorder, postorder, and preorder.

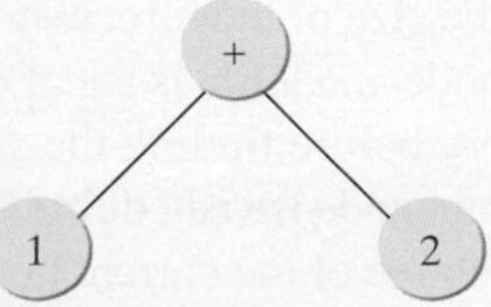

The inorder is `1 + 2`, the postorder is `1 2 +`, and the preorder is `+ 1 2`.

27.2.5 The BST Class

Following the design pattern of the Java Collections Framework API, we use an interface named **Tree** to define all common operations for trees and provide an abstract class named **AbstractTree** that partially implements **Tree**, as shown in Figure 27.7. A concrete **BST** class can be defined to extend **AbstractTree**, as shown in Figure 27.8.

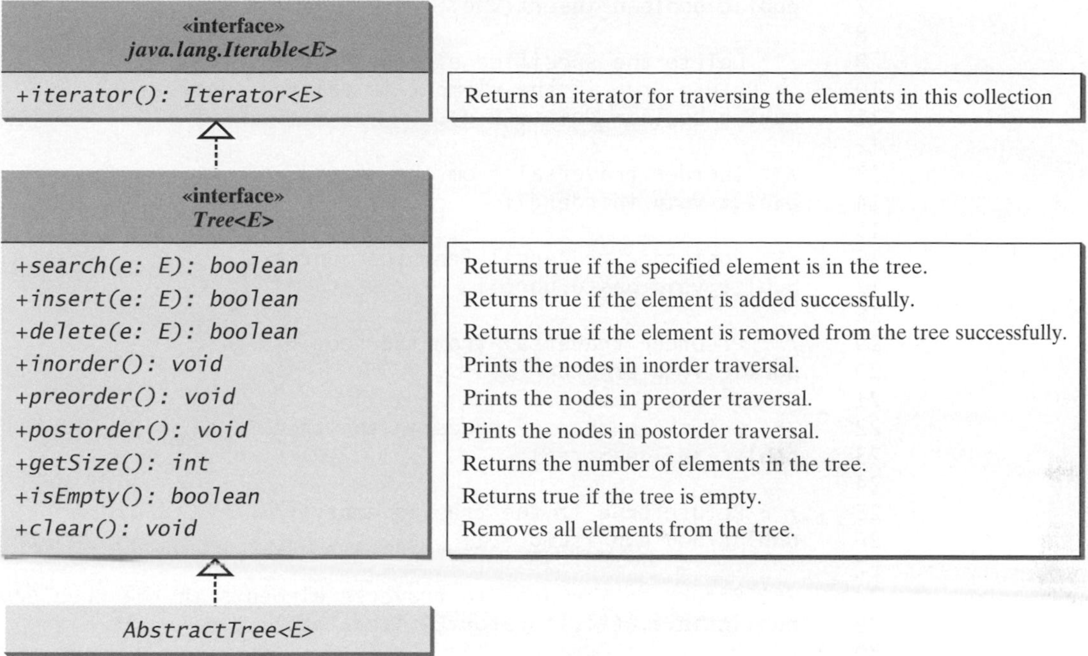

FIGURE 27.7 The **Tree** interface defines common operations for trees, and the **AbstractTree** class partially implements **Tree**.

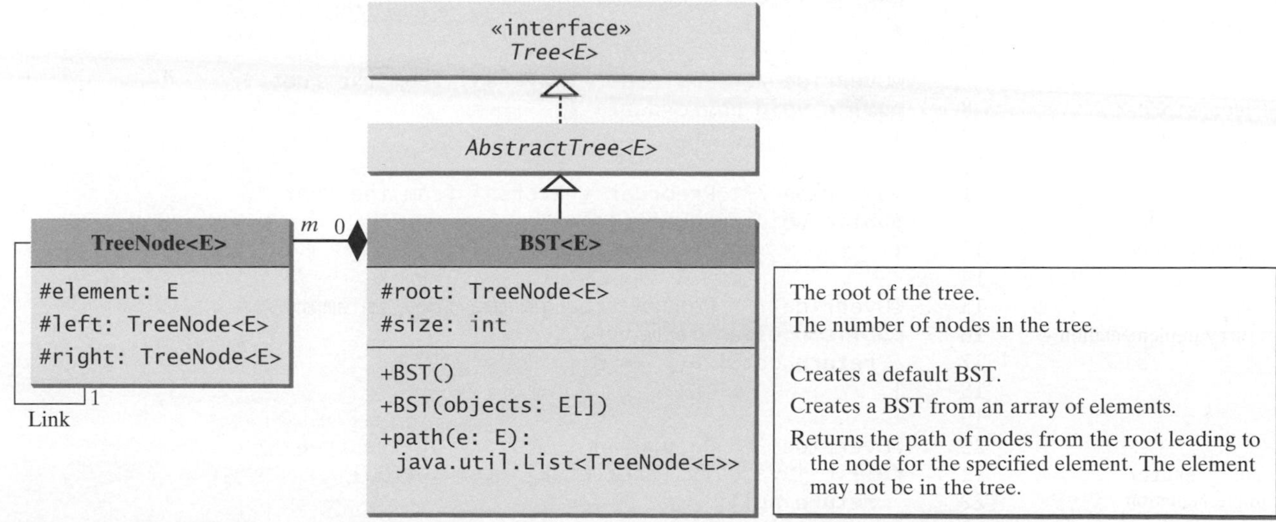

FIGURE 27.8 The **BST** class defines a concrete BST.

Listings 27.3, 27.4, and 27.5 give the implementations for **Tree**, **AbstractTree**, and **BST**.

LISTING 27.3 Tree.java

interface; search; insert; delete; inorder; postorder; preorder; getSize; isEmpty; iterator

```
public interface Tree<E extends Comparable<E>> extends Iterable<E> {
  /** Return true if the element is in the tree */
  public boolean search(E e);

  /** Insert element e into the binary search tree.
   * Return true if the element is inserted successfully. */
  public boolean insert(E e);

  /** Delete the specified element from the tree.
   * Return true if the element is deleted successfully. */
  public boolean delete(E e);

  /** Inorder traversal from the root*/
  public void inorder();

  /** Postorder traversal from the root */
  public void postorder();

  /** Preorder traversal from the root */
  public void preorder();

  /** Get the number of nodes in the tree */
  public int getSize();

  /** Return true if the tree is empty */
  public boolean isEmpty();

  /** Return an iterator to traverse elements in the tree */
  public java.util.Iterator<E> iterator();
}
```

LISTING 27.4 AbstractTree.java

abstract class; default inorder implementation; default postorder implementation; default preorder implementation; isEmpty implementation; default iterator implementation

```
public abstract class AbstractTree<E extends Comparable<E>>
    implements Tree<E> {
  @Override /** Inorder traversal from the root*/
  public void inorder() {
  }

  @Override /** Postorder traversal from the root */
  public void postorder() {
  }

  @Override /** Preorder traversal from the root */
  public void preorder() {
  }

  @Override /** Return true if the tree is empty */
  public boolean isEmpty() {
    return getSize() == 0;
  }

  @Override /** Return an iterator for the tree */
  public java.util.Iterator<E> iterator() {
    return null;
  }
}
```

LISTING 27.5 BST.java

```
public class BST<E extends Comparable<E>>
    extends AbstractTree<E> {
  protected TreeNode<E> root;
  protected int size = 0;

  /** Create a default binary search tree */
  public BST() {
  }

  /** Create a binary search tree from an array of objects */
  public BST(E[] objects) {
    for (int i = 0; i < objects.length; i++)
      insert(objects[i]);
  }

  @Override /** Return true if the element is in the tree */
  public boolean search(E e) {
    TreeNode<E> current = root; // Start from the root

    while (current != null) {
      if (e.compareTo(current.element) < 0) {
        current = current.left;
      }
      else if (e.compareTo(current.element) > 0) {
        current = current.right;
      }
      else // element matches current.element
        return true; // Element is found
    }

    return false;
  }

  @Override /** Insert element e into the binary search tree.
   * Return true if the element is inserted successfully. */
  public boolean insert(E e) {
    if (root == null)
      root = createNewNode(e); // Create a new root
    else {
      // Locate the parent node
      TreeNode<E> parent = null;
      TreeNode<E> current = root;
      while (current != null)
        if (e.compareTo(current.element) < 0) {
          parent = current;
          current = current.left;
        }
        else if (e.compareTo(current.element) > 0) {
          parent = current;
          current = current.right;
        }
        else
          return false; // Duplicate node not inserted

      // Create the new node and attach it to the parent node
      if (e.compareTo(parent.element) < 0)
        parent.left = createNewNode(e);
      else
```

BST class
root
size
no-arg constructor
constructor
search
compare objects
insert
new root
compare objects
link to parent

```
        parent.right = createNewNode(e);
    }

```

increase size

```
    size++;
    return true; // Element inserted
  }

```

create new node

```
  protected TreeNode<E> createNewNode(E e) {
    return new TreeNode<E>(e);
  }

  @Override /** Inorder traversal from the root*/
```

inorder

```
  public void inorder() {
    inorder(root);
  }

  /** Inorder traversal from a subtree */
```

recursive helper method

```
  protected void inorder(TreeNode<E> root) {
    if (root == null) return;
    inorder(root.left);
    System.out.print(root.element + " ");
    inorder(root.right);
  }

  @Override /** Postorder traversal from the root */
```

postorder

```
  public void postorder() {
    postorder(root);
  }

  /** Postorder traversal from a subtree */
```

recursive helper method

```
  protected void postorder(TreeNode<E> root) {
    if (root == null) return;
    postorder(root.left);
    postorder(root.right);
    System.out.print(root.element + " ");
  }

  @Override /** Preorder traversal from the root */
```

preorder

```
  public void preorder() {
    preorder(root);
  }

  /** Preorder traversal from a subtree */
```

recursive helper method

```
  protected void preorder(TreeNode<E> root) {
    if (root == null) return;
    System.out.print(root.element + " ");
    preorder(root.left);
    preorder(root.right);
  }

  /** This inner class is static, because it does not access
     any instance members defined in its outer class */
```

inner class

```
  public static class TreeNode<E extends Comparable<E>> {
    protected E element;
    protected TreeNode<E> left;
    protected TreeNode<E> right;

    public TreeNode(E e) {
      element = e;
    }
```

```
  }

  @Override /** Get the number of nodes in the tree */
  public int getSize() {
    return size;
  }

  /** Returns the root of the tree */
  public TreeNode<E> getRoot() {
    return root;
  }

  /** Returns a path from the root leading to the specified element */
  public java.util.ArrayList<TreeNode<E>> path(E e) {
    java.util.ArrayList<TreeNode<E>> list =
      new java.util.ArrayList<TreeNode<E>>();
    TreeNode<E> current = root; // Start from the root

    while (current != null) {
      list.add(current); // Add the node to the list
      if (e.compareTo(current.element) < 0) {
        current = current.left;
      }
      else if (e.compareTo(current.element) > 0) {
        current = current.right;
      }
      else
        break;
    }

    return list; // Return an array of nodes
  }

  @Override /** Delete an element from the binary search tree.
   * Return true if the element is deleted successfully.
   * Return false if the element is not in the tree. */
  public boolean delete(E e) {
    // Locate the node to be deleted and also locate its parent node
    TreeNode<E> parent = null;
    TreeNode<E> current = root;
    while (current != null) {
      if (e.compareTo(current.element) < 0) {
        parent = current;
        current = current.lell;
      }
      else if (e.compareTo(current.element) > 0) {
        parent = current;
        current = current.right;
      }
      else
        break; // Element is in the tree pointed at by current
    }

    if (current == null)
      return false; // Element is not in the tree

    // Case 1: current has no left children
    if (current.left == null) {
      // Connect the parent with the right child of the current node
      if (parent == null) {
```

getSize
getRoot
path
delete
locate parent
locate current
current found
not found
Case 1

reconnect parent
reconnect parent
Case 2
locate parentOfRightMost
locate rightMost
replace current
reconnect parentOfRightMost
reduce size
successful deletion
iterator
iterator class
internal list
current position
obtain inorder list

```
      root = current.right;
    }
    else {
      if (e.compareTo(parent.element) < 0)
        parent.left = current.right;
      else
        parent.right = current.right;
    }
  }
  else {
    // Case 2: The current node has a left child.
    // Locate the rightmost node in the left subtree of
    // the current node and also its parent.
    TreeNode<E> parentOfRightMost = current;
    TreeNode<E> rightMost = current.left;

    while (rightMost.right != null) {
      parentOfRightMost = rightMost;
      rightMost = rightMost.right; // Keep going to the right
    }

    // Replace the element in current by the element in rightMost
    current.element = rightMost.element;

    // Eliminate rightmost node
    if (parentOfRightMost.right == rightMost)
      parentOfRightMost.right = rightMost.left;
    else
      // Special case: parentOfRightMost == current
      parentOfRightMost.left = rightMost.left;
  }

  size--;
  return true; // Element deleted
}

@Override /** Obtain an iterator. Use inorder. */
public java.util.Iterator<E> iterator() {
  return new InorderIterator();
}

// Inner class InorderIterator
private class InorderIterator implements java.util.Iterator<E> {
  // Store the elements in a list
  private java.util.ArrayList<E> list =
    new java.util.ArrayList<E>();
  private int current = 0; // Point to the current element in list

  public InorderIterator() {
    inorder(); // Traverse binary tree and store elements in list
  }

  /** Inorder traversal from the root*/
  private void inorder() {
    inorder(root);
  }

  /** Inorder traversal from a subtree */
```

```
237      private void inorder(TreeNode<E> root) {
238        if (root == null) return;
239        inorder(root.left);
240        list.add(root.element);
241        inorder(root.right);
242      }
243
244      @Override /** More elements for traversing? */
245      public boolean hasNext() {
246        if (current < list.size())
247          return true;
248
249        return false;
250      }
251
252      @Override /** Get the current element and move to the next */
253      public E next() {
254        return list.get(current++);
255      }
256
257      @Override /** Remove the current element */
258      public void remove() {
259        delete(list.get(current)); // Delete the current element
260        list.clear(); // Clear the list
261        inorder(); // Rebuild the list
262      }
263    }
264
265    /** Remove all elements from the tree */
266    public void clear() {
267      root = null;
268      size = 0;
269    }
270  }
```

hasNext in iterator?

get next element

remove the current

refresh list

clear

The **insert(E e)** method (lines 36–64) creates a node for element **e** and inserts it into the tree. If the tree is empty, the node becomes the root. Otherwise, the method finds an appropriate parent for the node to maintain the order of the tree. If the element is already in the tree, the method returns **false**; otherwise it returns **true**.

The **inorder()** method (lines 71–81) invokes **inorder(root)** to traverse the entire tree. The method **inorder(TreeNode root)** traverses the tree with the specified root. This is a recursive method. It recursively traverses the left subtree, then the root, and finally the right subtree. The traversal ends when the tree is empty.

The **postorder()** method (lines 84–94) and the **preorder()** method (lines 97–107) are implemented similarly using recursion.

The **path(E e)** method (lines 132–150) returns a path of the nodes as an array list. The path starts from the root leading to the element. The element may not be in the tree. For example, in Figure 27.4a, **path(45)** contains the nodes for elements **60**, **55**, and **45**, and **path(58)** contains the nodes for elements **60**, **55**, and **57**.

The implementation of **delete()** and **iterator()** (lines 155–269) will be discussed in Sections 27.3 and 27.5.

Listing 27.6 gives an example that creates a binary search tree using **BST** (line 4). The program adds strings into the tree (lines 5–11), traverses the tree in inorder, postorder, and preorder (lines 14–20), searches for an element (line 24), and obtains a path from the node containing **Peter** to the root (lines 28–31).

LISTING 27.6 TestBST.java

create tree · insert · inorder · postorder · preorder · getSize · search

```
 1 public class TestBST {
 2   public static void main(String[] args) {
 3     // Create a BST
 4     BST<String> tree = new BST<String>();
 5     tree.insert("George");
 6     tree.insert("Michael");
 7     tree.insert("Tom");
 8     tree.insert("Adam");
 9     tree.insert("Jones");
10     tree.insert("Peter");
11     tree.insert("Daniel");
12
13     // Traverse tree
14     System.out.print("Inorder (sorted): ");
15     tree.inorder();
16     System.out.print("\nPostorder: ");
17     tree.postorder();
18     System.out.print("\nPreorder: ");
19     tree.preorder();
20     System.out.print("\nThe number of nodes is " + tree.getSize());
21
22     // Search for an element
23     System.out.print("\nIs Peter in the tree? " +
24       tree.search("Peter"));
25
26     // Get a path from the root to Peter
27     System.out.print("\nA path from the root to Peter is: ");
28     java.util.ArrayList<BST.TreeNode<String>>  path
29       = tree.path("Peter");
30     for (int i = 0; path != null && i < path.size(); i++)
31       System.out.print(path.get(i).element + " ");
32
33     Integer[] numbers = {2, 4, 3, 1, 8, 5, 6, 7};
34     BST<Integer> intTree = new BST<Integer>(numbers);
35     System.out.print("\nInorder (sorted): ");
36     intTree.inorder();
37   }
38 }
```

```
Inorder (sorted): Adam Daniel George Jones Michael Peter Tom
Postorder: Daniel Adam Jones Peter Tom Michael George
Preorder: George Adam Daniel Michael Jones Tom Peter
The number of nodes is 7
Is Peter in the tree? true
A path from the root to Peter is: George Michael Tom Peter
Inorder (sorted): 1 2 3 4 5 6 7 8
```

The program checks `path != null` in line 30 to ensure that the path is not `null` before invoking `path.get(i)`. This is an example of defensive programming to avoid potential runtime errors.

The program creates another tree for storing `int` values (line 34). After all the elements are inserted in the trees, the trees should appear as shown in Figure 27.9.

If the elements are inserted in a different order (e.g., Daniel, Adam, Jones, Peter, Tom, Michael, George), the tree will look different. However, the inorder traversal prints elements in the same order as long as the set of elements is the same. The inorder traversal displays a sorted list.

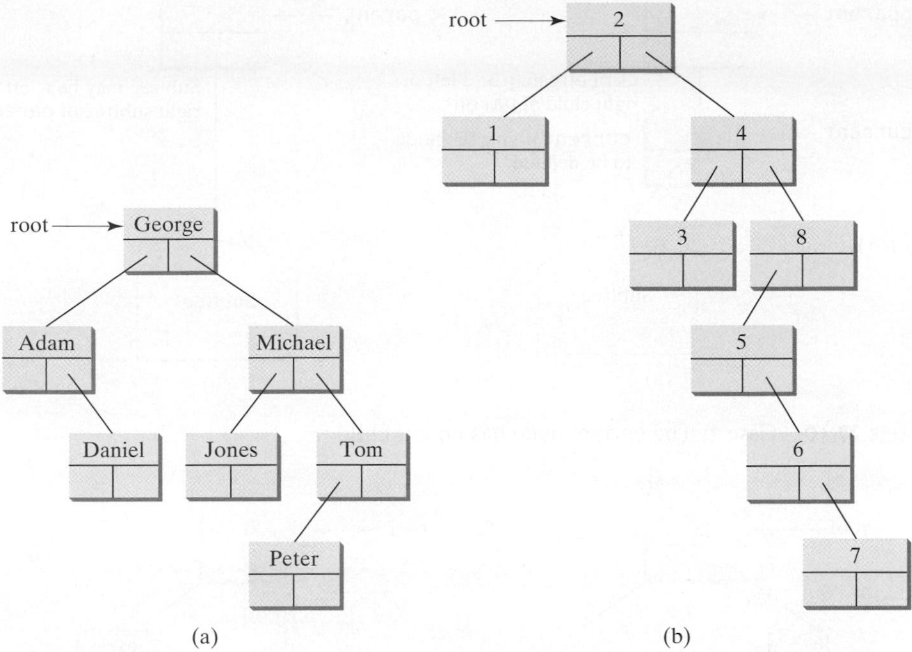

FIGURE 27.9 The BSTs in Listing 27.6 are pictured here after they are created.

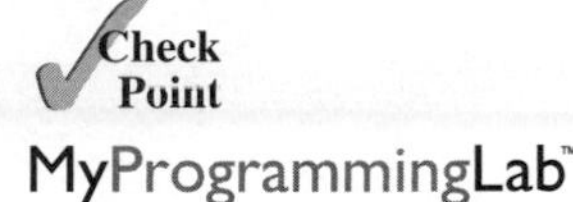

27.1 Show the result of inserting `44` into Figure 27.4b.

27.2 Show the inorder, preorder, and postorder of traversing the elements in the binary tree shown in Figure 27.1b.

27.3 If a set of elements is inserted into a BST in two different orders, will the two corresponding BSTs look the same? Will the inorder traversal be the same? Will the postorder traversal be the same? Will the preorder traversal be the same?

27.4 What is the time complexity of inserting an element into a BST?

27.3 Deleting Elements from a BST

To delete an element from a BST, first locate it in the tree and then consider two cases—whether or not the node has a left child—before deleting the element and reconnecting the tree.

The `insert(element)` method was presented in Section 27.2.3. Often you need to delete an element from a binary search tree. Doing so is far more complex than adding an element into a binary search tree.

locating element

To delete an element from a binary search tree, you need to first locate the node that contains the element and also its parent node. Let `current` point to the node that contains the element in the binary search tree and `parent` point to the parent of the `current` node. The `current` node may be a left child or a right child of the `parent` node. There are two cases to consider.

Case 1: The current node does not have a left child, as shown in Figure 27.10a. In this case, simply connect the parent with the right child of the current node, as shown in Figure 27.10b.

For example, to delete node `10` in Figure 27.11a, you would connect the parent of node `10` with the right child of node `10`, as shown in Figure 27.11b.

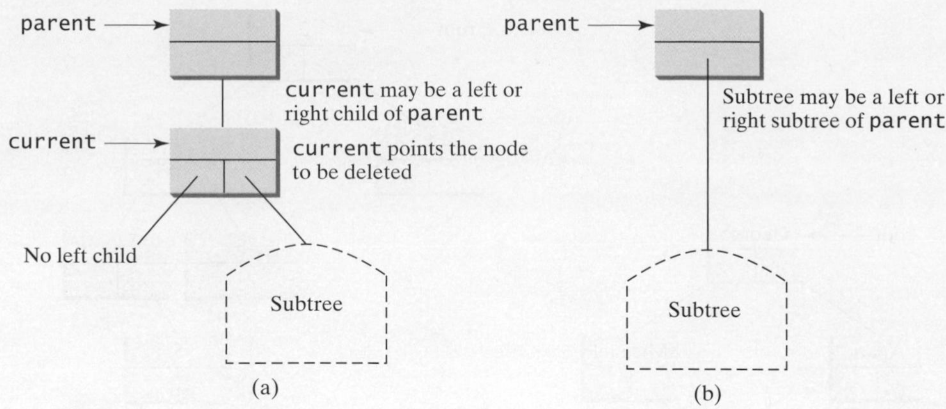

FIGURE 27.10 Case 1: The current node has no left child.

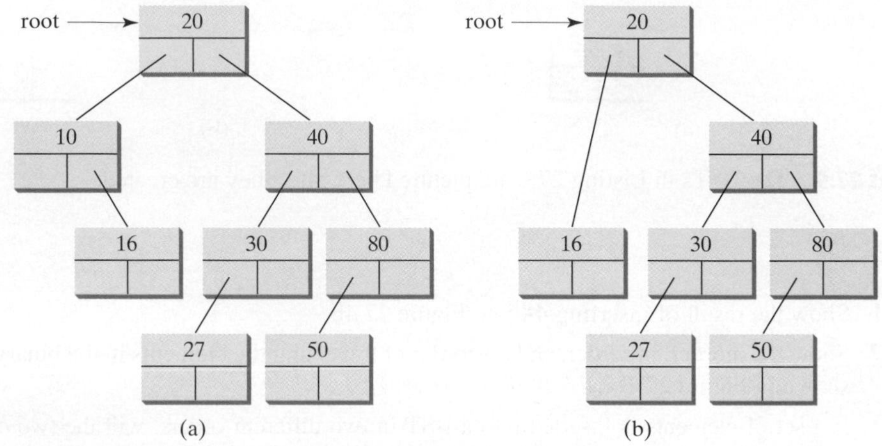

FIGURE 27.11 Case 1: Deleting node **10** from (a) results in (b).

delete a leaf

Note

If the current node is a leaf, it falls into Case 1. For example, to delete element **16** in Figure 27.11a, connect its right child (in this case, it is **null**) to the parent of node **16**. In this case, the right child of node **16** is **null**.

Case 2: The **current** node has a left child. Let **rightMost** point to the node that contains the largest element in the left subtree of the **current** node and **parentOfRightMost** point to the parent node of the **rightMost** node, as shown in Figure 27.12a. Note that the **rightMost** node cannot have a right child but may have a left child. Replace the element value in the **current** node with the one in the **rightMost** node, connect the **parentOfRightMost** node with the left child of the **rightMost** node, and delete the **rightMost** node, as shown in Figure 27.12b.

For example, consider deleting node **20** in Figure 27.13a. The **rightMost** node has the element value **16**. Replace the element value **20** with **16** in the **current** node and make node **10** the parent for node **14**, as shown in Figure 27.13b.

Note

If the left child of **current** does not have a right child, **current.left** points to the large element in the left subtree of **current**. In this case, **rightMost** is **current.left** and **parentOfRightMost** is **current**. You have to take care of this special case to reconnect the right child of **rightMost** with **parentOfRightMost**.

special case

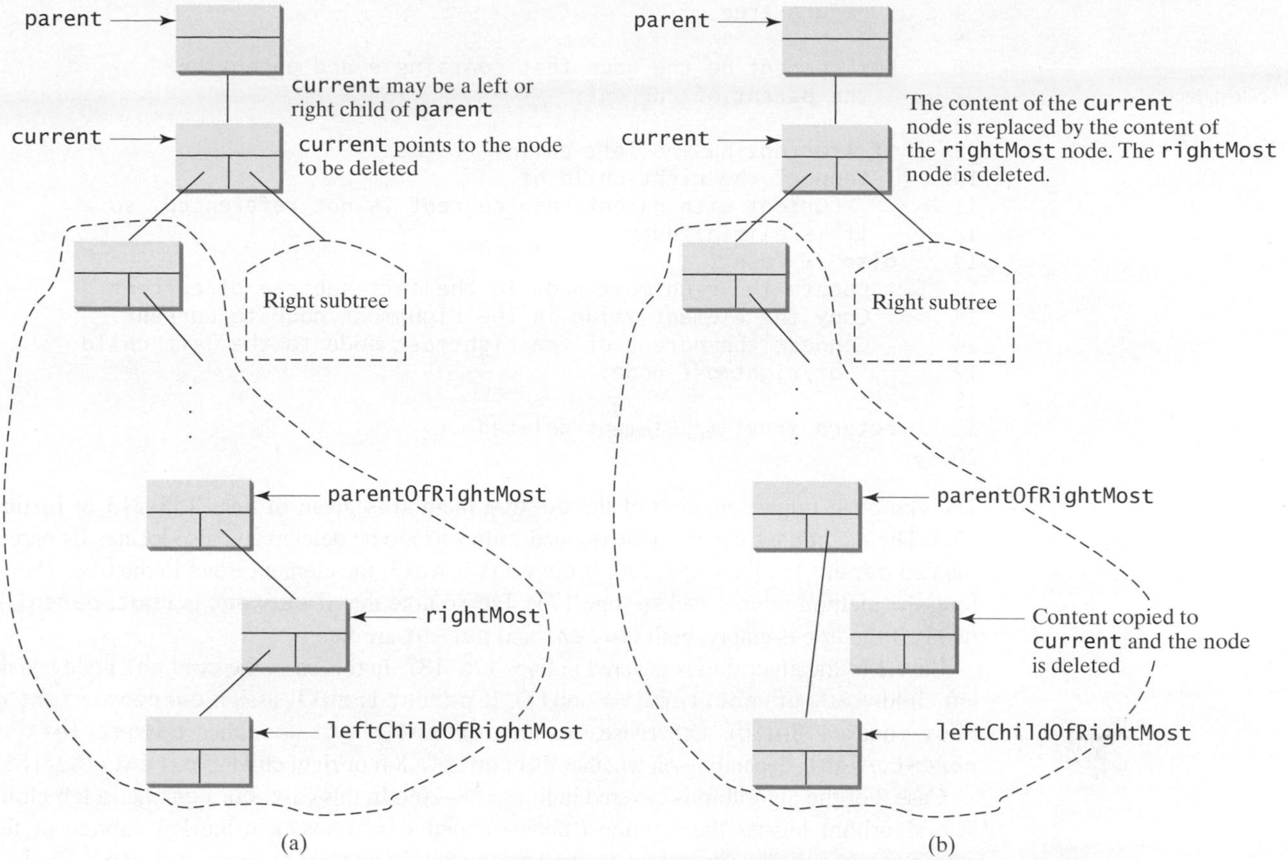

parent
current may be a left or right child of parent
current
current points to the node to be deleted
Right subtree
parentOfRightMost
rightMost
leftChildOfRightMost
(a)
parent
The content of the current node is replaced by the content of the rightMost node. The rightMost node is deleted.
current
Right subtree
parentOfRightMost
Content copied to current and the node is deleted
leftChildOfRightMost
(b)

FIGURE 27.12 Case 2: The current node has a left child.

root
20
10
40
rightMost
16
30
80
14
27
50
(a)
root
16
10
40
30
80
14
27
50
(b)

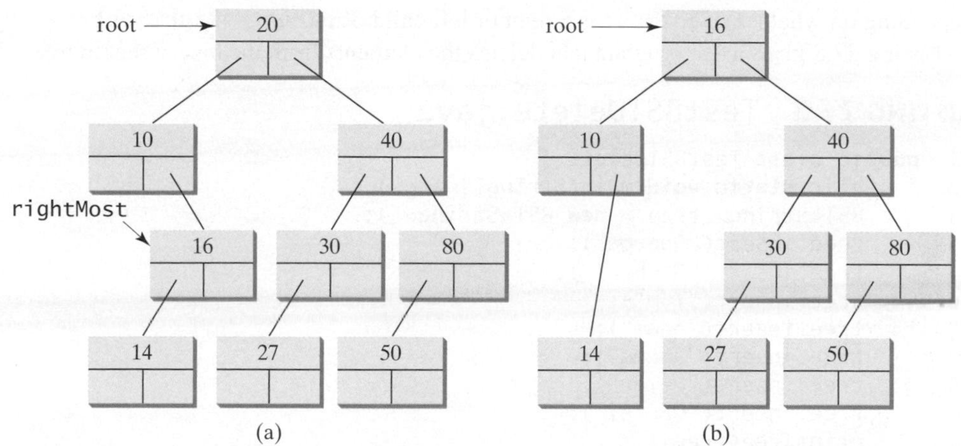

FIGURE 27.13 Case 2: Deleting node 20 from (a) results in (b).

The algorithm for deleting an element from a binary search tree can be described in Listing 27.7. delete method

LISTING 27.7 Deleting an Element from a BST

```
boolean delete(E e) {
  Locate element e in the tree;
  if element e is not found
```

not in the tree

locate parent · Case 1 · Case 2

```
    return true;

  Let current be the node that contains e and parent be
    the parent of current;

  if (current has no left child) // Case 1
    Connect the right child of
      current with parent; now current is not referenced, so
    it is eliminated;
  else // Case 2
    Locate the rightmost node in the left subtree of current.
    Copy the element value in the rightmost node to current.
    Connect the parent of the rightmost node to the left child
      of rightmost node;

  return true; // Element deleted
}
```

The complete implementation of the **delete** method is given in lines 155–213 in Listing 27.5. The method locates the node (named **current**) to be deleted and also locates its parent (named **parent**) in lines 157–170. If **current** is **null**, the element is not in the tree. Therefore, the method returns **false** (line 173). Please note that if **current** is **root**, **parent** is **null**. If the tree is empty, both **current** and **parent** are **null**.

Case 1 of the algorithm is covered in lines 176–187. In this case, the **current** node has no left child (i.e., **current.left == null**). If **parent** is **null**, assign **current.right** to **root** (lines 178–180). Otherwise, assign **current.right** to either **parent.left** or **parent.right**, depending on whether **current** is a left or right child of **parent** (182–185).

Case 2 of the algorithm is covered in lines 188–209. In this case, **current** has a left child. The algorithm locates the rightmost node (named **rightMost**) in the left subtree of the current node and also its parent (named **parentOfRightMost**) (lines 195–198). Replace the element in **current** by the element in **rightMost** (line 201); assign **rightMost.left** to either **parentOfRightMost.right** or **parentOfRightMost.left** (lines 204–208), depending on whether **rightMost** is a right or left child of **parentOfRightMost**.

Listing 27.8 gives a test program that deletes the elements from the binary search tree.

LISTING 27.8 TestBSTDelete.java

delete an element · delete an element · delete an element

```
public class TestBSTDelete {
  public static void main(String[] args) {
    BST<String> tree = new BST<String>();
    tree.insert("George");
    tree.insert("Michael");
    tree.insert("Tom");
    tree.insert("Adam");
    tree.insert("Jones");
    tree.insert("Peter");
    tree.insert("Daniel");
    printTree(tree);

    System.out.println("\nAfter delete George:");
    tree.delete("George");
    printTree(tree);

    System.out.println("\nAfter delete Adam:");
    tree.delete("Adam");
    printTree(tree);

    System.out.println("\nAfter delete Michael:");
    tree.delete("Michael");
```

```
      printTree(tree);
    }

    public static void printTree(BST tree) {
      // Traverse tree
      System.out.print("Inorder (sorted): ");
      tree.inorder();
      System.out.print("\nPostorder: ");
      tree.postorder();
      System.out.print("\nPreorder: ");
      tree.preorder();
      System.out.print("\nThe number of nodes is " + tree.getSize());
      System.out.println();
    }
  }
```

```
Inorder (sorted): Adam Daniel George Jones Michael Peter Tom
Postorder: Daniel Adam Jones Peter Tom Michael George
Preorder: George Adam Daniel Michael Jones Tom Peter
The number of nodes is 7

After delete George:
Inorder (sorted): Adam Daniel Jones Michael Peter Tom
Postorder: Adam Jones Peter Tom Michael Daniel
Preorder: Daniel Adam Michael Jones Tom Peter
The number of nodes is 6

After delete Adam:
Inorder (sorted): Daniel Jones Michael Peter Tom
Postorder: Jones Peter Tom Michael Daniel
Preorder: Daniel Michael Jones Tom Peter
The number of nodes is 5

After delete Michael:
Inorder (sorted): Daniel Jones Peter Tom
Postorder: Peter Tom Jones Daniel
Preorder: Daniel Jones Tom Peter
The number of nodes is 4
```

Figures 27.14–27.16 show how the tree evolves as the elements are deleted from it.

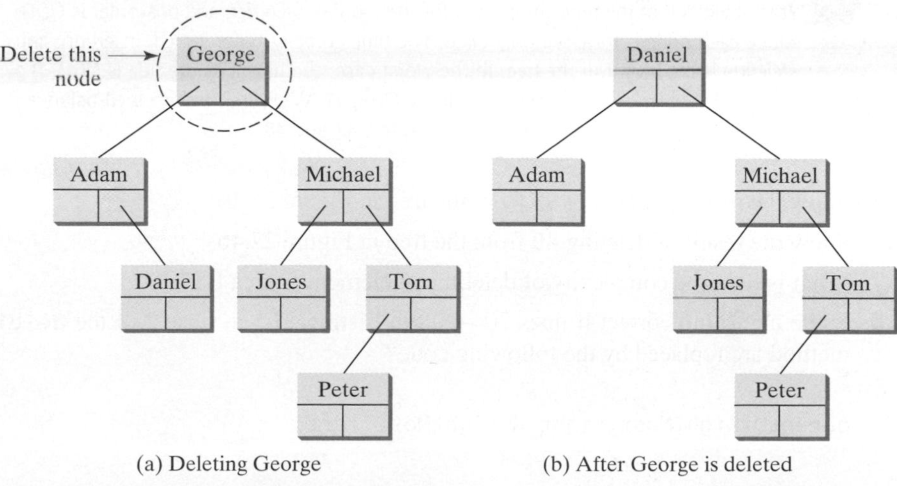

(a) Deleting George (b) After George is deleted

FIGURE 27.14 Deleting George falls into Case 2.

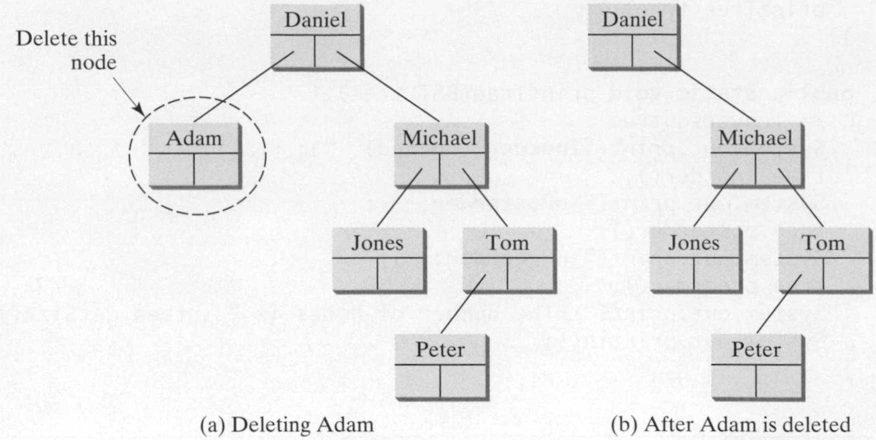

FIGURE 27.15 Deleting Adam falls into Case 1.

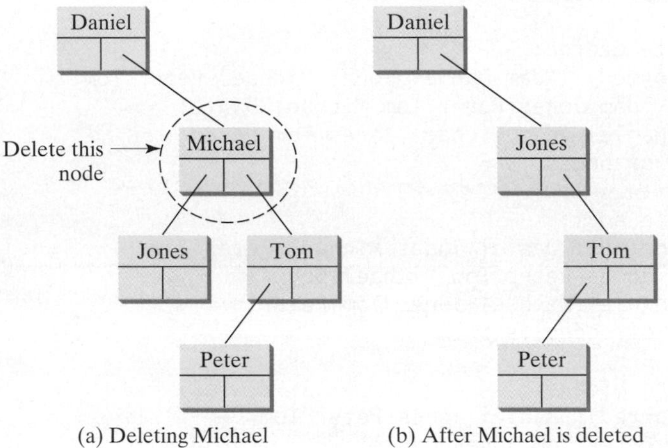

FIGURE 27.16 Deleting Michael falls into Case 2.

BST time complexity

Note

It is obvious that the time complexity for the inorder, preorder, and postorder is $O(n)$, since each node is traversed only once. The time complexity for search, insertion, and deletion is the height of the tree. In the worst case, the height of the tree is $O(n)$. If a tree is well-balanced, the height would be $O(\log n)$. We will introduce well-balanced binary trees in Chapter 29 and bonus Chapters 47 and 48.

MyProgrammingLab™

27.5 Show the result of deleting `55` from the tree in Figure 27.4b.

27.6 Show the result of deleting `60` from the tree in Figure 27.4b.

27.7 What is the time complexity of deleting an element from a BST?

27.8 Is the algorithm correct if lines 204–208 in Listing 27.5 in Case 2 of the `delete()` method are replaced by the following code?

```
parentOfRightMost.right = rightMost.left;
```

27.4 Tree Visualization

You can use recursion to display a binary tree.

Pedagogical Note

One challenge facing the data-structure course is to motivate students. Displaying a binary tree graphically will not only help you understand the working of a binary tree but perhaps also stimulate your interest in programming. You can apply visualization techniques to other projects.

How do you display a binary tree? It is a recursive structure, so you can display a binary tree using recursion. You can simply display the root, then display the two subtrees recursively. The techniques for displaying the Sierpinski triangle (Listing 20.9, SierpinskiTriangle.java) can be applied to displaying a binary tree. For simplicity, we assume the keys are positive integers less than **100**. Listings 27.9 and 27.10 give the program, and Figure 27.17 shows some sample runs of the program.

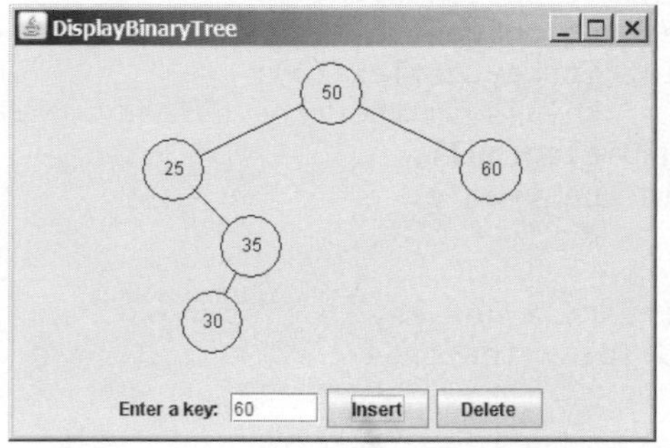

(a) Inserting 50, 25, 35, 30, and 60

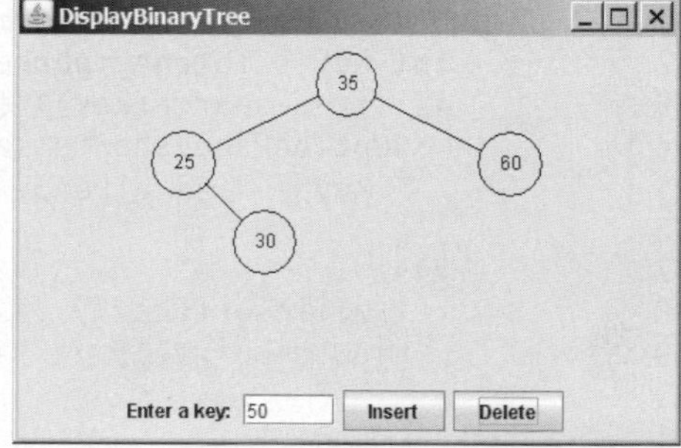

(b) After 50 is deleted

FIGURE 27.17 A binary tree is displayed graphically.

LISTING 27.9 DisplayBST.java

```
import javax.swing.*;

public class DisplayBST extends JApplet {
  public DisplayBST() {
    add(new TreeControl(new BST<Integer>()));
  }
}
```

create a view

main method omitted

LISTING 27.10 TreeControl.java

```
import java.awt.*;
import java.awt.event.*;
import javax.swing.*;

public class TreeControl extends JPanel {
  private BST<Integer> tree; // A binary tree to be displayed
  private JTextField jtfKey = new JTextField(5);
  private TreeView view = new TreeView();
  private JButton jbtInsert = new JButton("Insert");
  private JButton jbtDelete = new JButton("Delete");

```

binary tree

paint tree

```
  /** Construct a view for a binary tree */
  public TreeControl(BST<Integer> tree) {
    this.tree = tree; // Set a binary tree to be displayed
    setUI();
  }

  /** Initialize UI for binary tree */
  private void setUI() {
    this.setLayout(new BorderLayout());
    add(view, BorderLayout.CENTER);
    JPanel panel = new JPanel();
    panel.add(new JLabel("Enter a key: "));
    panel.add(jtfKey);
    panel.add(jbtInsert);
    panel.add(jbtDelete);
    add(panel, BorderLayout.SOUTH);

    jbtInsert.addActionListener(new ActionListener() {
      @Override // Process the Insert button event
      public void actionPerformed(ActionEvent e) {
        int key = Integer.parseInt(jtfKey.getText());
        if (tree.search(key)) { // key is in the tree already
          JOptionPane.showMessageDialog(null,
            key + " is already in the tree");
        }
        else {
          tree.insert(key); // Insert a new key
          view.repaint(); // Redisplay the tree
        }
      }
    });

    jbtDelete.addActionListener(new ActionListener() {
      @Override  // Process the Delete button event
      public void actionPerformed(ActionEvent e) {
        int key = Integer.parseInt(jtfKey.getText());
        if (!tree.search(key)) { // key is not in the tree
          JOptionPane.showMessageDialog(null,
            key + " is not in the tree");
        }
        else {
          tree.delete(key); // Delete a key
          view.repaint(); // Redisplay the tree
        }
      }
    });
  }

  // Inner class TreeView for displaying a tree on a panel
  class TreeView extends JPanel {
    private int radius = 20; // Tree node radius
    private int vGap = 50; // Gap between two levels in a tree

    @Override
    protected void paintComponent(Graphics g) {
      super.paintComponent(g);

      if (tree.getRoot() != null) {
        // Display tree recursively
        displayTree(g, tree.getRoot(), getWidth() / 2, 30,
```

create UI
insert button listener
insert key
repaint the tree
delete button listener
delete key
repaint the tree
TreeView class
display tree

```
72              getWidth() / 4);
73        }
74      }
75
76      /** Display a subtree rooted at position (x, y) */
77      private void displayTree(Graphics g,
78          BST.TreeNode<Integer> root, int x, int y, int hGap) {
79        // Display the root
80        g.drawOval(x - radius, y - radius, 2 * radius, 2 * radius);
81        g.drawString(root.element + "", x - 6, y + 4);
82
83        if (root.left != null) {
84          // Draw a line to the left node
85          connectTwoCircles(g, x - hGap, y + vGap, x, y);
86          // Draw the left subtree recursively
87          displayTree(g, root.left, x - hGap, y + vGap, hGap / 2);
88        }
89
90        if (root.right != null) {
91          // Draw a line to the right node
92          connectTwoCircles(g, x + hGap, y + vGap, x, y);
93          // Draw the right subtree recursively
94          displayTree(g, root.right, x + hGap, y + vGap, hGap / 2);
95        }
96      }
97
98      /** Connect two circles centered at (x1, y1) and (x2, y2) */
99      private void connectTwoCircles(Graphics g,
100         int x1, int y1, int x2, int y2) {
101       double d = Math.sqrt(vGap * vGap + (x2 - x1) * (x2 - x1));
102       int x11 = (int)(x1 - radius * (x1 - x2) / d);
103       int y11 = (int)(y1 - radius * (y1 - y2) / d);
104       int x21 = (int)(x2 + radius * (x1 - x2) / d);
105       int y21 = (int)(y2 + radius * (y1 - y2) / d);
106       g.drawLine(x11, y11, x21, y21);
107     }
108   }
109 }
```

paint a node (line 80)
connect two nodes (line 85)
draw left subtree (line 87)
connect two nodes (line 92)
draw right subtree (line 94)

After a new key is inserted into the tree (line 38), the tree is repainted (line 39) to reflect the change. After a key is deleted (line 53), the tree is repainted (line 54) to reflect the change.

The node is displayed as a circle with **radius 20** (line 62). The distance between two levels in the tree is defined in **vGap 50** (line 63). **hGap** (line 77) defines the distance between two nodes horizontally. This value is reduced by half (**hGap / 2**) in the next level when the **displayTree** method is called recursively (lines 87, 94). Note that **vGap** is not changed in the tree.

Invoking **connectTwoCircles** connects a parent with a left or right child. You need to find the two endpoints (**x11**, **y11**) and (**x21**, **y21**) in order to connect the two nodes, as shown in Figure 27.18. The mathematical calculation for finding the two ends is illustrated in Figure 27.18. Note that

$$d = \sqrt{vGap^2 + (x_2 - x_1)^2}$$

$$\frac{x_{11} - x_1}{radius} = \frac{x_2 - x_1}{d}, \text{ so } x_{11} = x_1 + radius \times \frac{x_2 - x_1}{d},$$

$$\frac{y_{11} - y_1}{radius} = \frac{y_2 - y_1}{d}, \text{ so } y_{11} = y_1 + radius \times \frac{y_2 - y_1}{d}$$

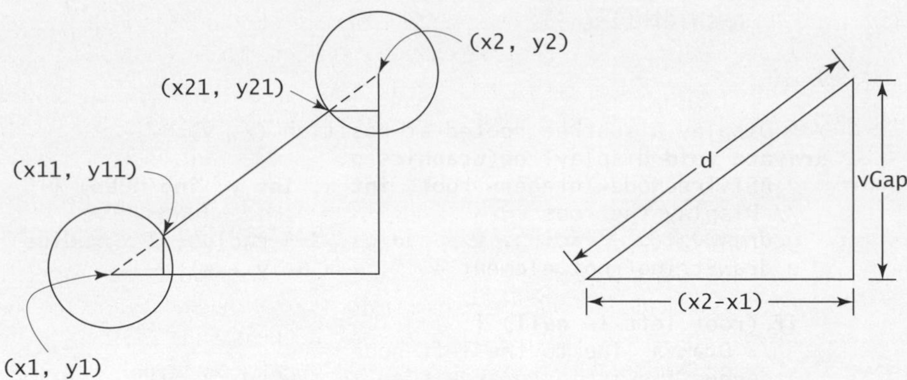

FIGURE 27.18 You need to find the position of the endpoints to connect two nodes.

The program assumes that the keys are integers. You can easily modify the program with a generic type to display keys of characters or short strings.

MyProgrammingLab™

27.9 How many times will the `displayTree` method be invoked if the tree is empty? How many times will the `displayTree` method be invoked if the tree has `100` nodes?

27.10 In what order are the nodes in the tree visited by the `displayTree` method: inorder, preorder, or postorder?

27.5 Iterators

`BST` is iterable because it is defined as a subtype of the `java.lang.Iterable` interface.

The methods `inorder()`, `preorder()`, and `postorder()` display the elements in `inorder`, `preorder`, and `postorder` in a binary tree. These methods are limited to displaying the elements in a tree. If you wish to process the elements in a binary tree rather than display them, these methods cannot be used. Recall that an iterator is provided for traversing the elements in a set or list. You can apply the same approach in a binary tree to provide a uniform way of traversing the elements in a binary tree.

iterator

The `java.lang.Iterable` interface defines the `iterator` method, which returns an instance of the `java.util.Iterator` interface. The `java.util.Iterator` interface (see Figure 27.19) defines the common features of iterators.

«interface» *java.util.Iterator*	
+hasNext(): boolean	Returns true if the iterator has more elements.
+next(): Object	Returns the next element in the iterator.
+remove(): void	Removes from the underlying container the last element returned by the iterator (optional operation).

FIGURE 27.19 The `Iterator` interface defines a uniform way of traversing the elements in a container.

The `Tree` interface extends `java.lang.Iterable`. Since `BST` is a subclass of `AbstractTree` and `AbstractTree` implements `Tree`, `BST` is a subtype of `Iterable`. The `Iterable` interface contains the `iterator()` method that returns an instance of `java.util.Iterator`.

You can traverse a binary tree in inorder, preorder, or postorder. Since inorder is used frequently, we will use inorder for traversing the elements in a binary tree. We define an iterator class named **InorderIterator** to implement the **java.util.Iterator** interface in Listing 27.5 (lines 221–263). The **iterator** method simply returns an instance of **InorderIterator** (line 217).

how to create an iterator

The **InorderIterator** constructor invokes the **inorder** method (line 228). The **inorder(root)** method (lines 237–242) stores all the elements from the tree in **list**. The elements are traversed in **inorder**.

Once an **Iterator** object is created, its **current** value is initialized to **0** (line 225), which points to the first element in the list. Invoking the **next()** method returns the current element and moves **current** to point to the next element in the list (line 253).

The **hasNext()** method checks whether **current** is still in the range of **list** (line 246).

The **remove()** method removes the current element from the tree (line 259). Afterward, a new list is created (lines 260–261). Note that **current** does not need to be changed.

Listing 27.11 gives a test program that stores the strings in a BST and displays all strings in uppercase.

LISTING 27.11 TestBSTWithIterator.java

```
 1 public class TestBSTWithIterator {
 2   public static void main(String[] args) {
 3     BST<String> tree = new BST<String>();
 4     tree.insert("George");
 5     tree.insert("Michael");
 6     tree.insert("Tom");
 7     tree.insert("Adam");
 8     tree.insert("Jones");
 9     tree.insert("Peter");
10     tree.insert("Daniel");
11
12     for (String s: tree)
13       System.out.print(s.toUpperCase() + " ");
14   }
15 }
```

using an iterator
get uppercase letters

```
ADAM DANIEL GEORGE JONES MICHAEL PETER TOM
```

The for-each loop (lines 12–13) uses an iterator to traverse all elements in the tree.

Design Guide

Iterator is an important software design pattern. It provides a uniform way of traversing the elements in a container, while hiding the container's structural details. By implementing the same interface **java.util.Iterator**, you can write a program that traverses the elements of all containers in the same way.

iterator pattern
advantages of iterators

Note

java.util.Iterator defines a forward iterator, which traverses the element in the iterator in a forward direction, and each element can be traversed only once. The Java API also provides the **java.util.ListIterator**, which supports traversing in both forward and backward directions. If your data structure warrants flexible traversing, you may define iterator classes as a subtype of **java.util.ListIterator**.

variations of iterators

The implementation of the iterator is not efficient. Every time you remove an element through the iterator, the whole list is rebuilt (line 261 in Listing 27.5 BST.java). The client should always use the **delete** method in the **BinraryTree** class to remove an element. To prevent the user from using the **remove** method in the iterator, implement the iterator as follows:

```
public void remove() {
  throw new UnsupportedOperationException
    ("Removing an element from the iterator is not supported");
}
```

After making the **remove** method unsupported by the iterator class, you can implement the iterator more efficiently without having to maintain a list for the elements in the tree. You can use a stack to store the nodes, and the node on the top of the stack contains the element that is to be returned from the **next()** method. If the tree is well-balanced, the maximum stack size will be *O*(log*n*).

Check Point

MyProgrammingLab™

27.11 What is an iterator?

27.12 What method is defined in the **java.lang.Iterable<E>** interface?

27.13 Suppose you delete **extends Iterable<E>** from line 1 in Listing 27.3, Tree.java. Will Listing 27.11 still compile?

27.14 What is the benefit of being a subtype of **Iterable<E>**?

27.6 Case Study: Data Compression

Key Point

Huffman coding compresses data by using fewer bits to encode characters that occur more frequently. The codes for the characters are constructed based on the occurrence of the characters in the text using a binary tree, called the Huffman coding tree.

Compressing data is a common task. There are many utilities available for compressing files. This section introduces Huffman coding, invented by David Huffman in 1952.

In ASCII, every character is encoded in 8 bits. If a text consists of 100 characters, it will take 800 bits to represent the text. The idea of Huffman coding is to use a fewer bits to encode frequently used characters in the text and more bits to encode less frequently used characters to reduce the overall size of the file. In Huffman coding, the characters' codes are constructed based on the characters' occurrence in the text using a binary tree, called the *Huffman coding tree*. Suppose the text is **Mississippi**. Its Huffman tree can be shown as in Figure 27.20a. The left and right edges of a node are assigned a value **0** and **1**, respectively. Each character is a leaf in the tree. The code for the character consists of the edge values in the path from the root to the leaf, as shown in Figure 27.20b. Since **i** and **s** appear more than **M** and **p** in the text, they are assigned shorter codes.

Huffman coding

(a) Huffman coding tree

Character	Code	Frequency
M	000	1
p	001	2
s	01	4
i	1	4

(b) Character code table

FIGURE 27.20 The codes for characters are constructed based on the occurrence of characters in the text using a coding tree.

The coding tree is also used for decoding a sequence of bits into characters. To do so, start with the first bit in the sequence and determine whether to go to the left or right branch of the tree's root based on the bit value. Consider the next bit and continue to go down to the left or right branch based on the bit value. When you reach a leaf, you have found a character. The next bit in the stream is the first bit of the next character. For example, the stream `011001` is decoded to `sip`, with `01` matching `s`, `1` matching `i`, and `001` matching `p`.

decoding

To construct a *Huffman coding tree*, use an algorithm as follows:

construct coding tree

1. Begin with a forest of trees. Each tree contains a node for a character. The weight of the node is the frequency of the character in the text.
2. Repeat the following action to combine trees until there is only one tree: Choose two trees with the smallest weight and create a new node as their parent. The weight of the new tree is the sum of the weight of the subtrees.
3. For each interior node, assign its left edge a value `0` and right edge a value `1`. All leaf nodes represent characters in the text.

Here is an example of building a coding tree for the text `Mississippi`. The frequency table for the characters is shown in Figure 27.20b. Initially the forest contains single-node trees, as shown in Figure 27.21a. The trees are repeatedly combined to form large trees until only one tree is left, as shown in Figures 27.21b–d.

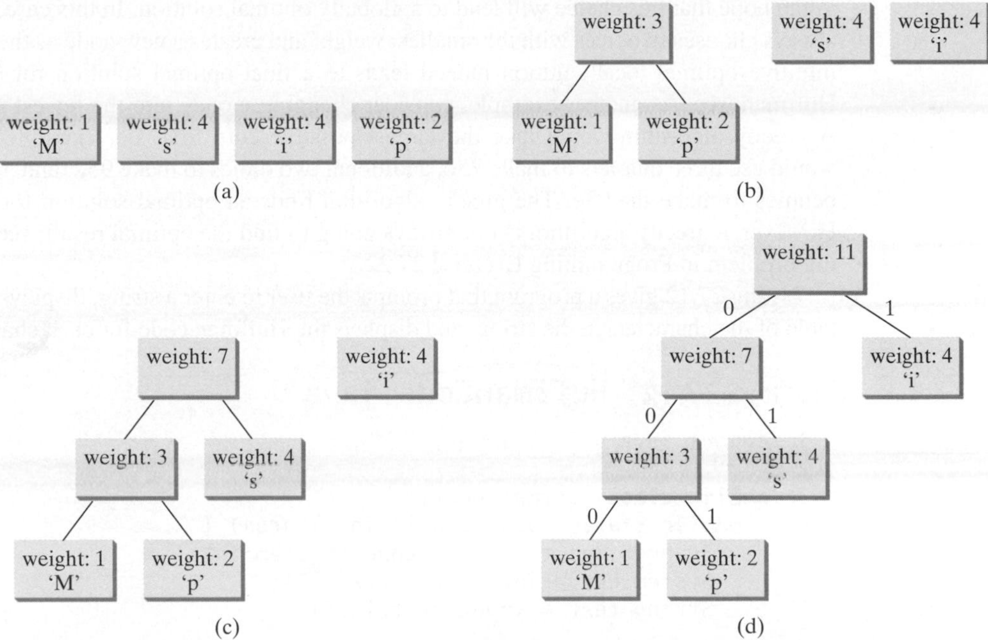

FIGURE 27.21 The coding tree is built by repeatedly combining the two smallest-weighted trees.

It is worth noting that no code is a prefix of another code. This property ensures that the streams can be decoded unambiguously.

prefix property

Pedagogical Note

For an interactive GUI demo to see how Huffman coding works, go to www.cs.armstrong.edu/liang/animation/HuffmanCodingAnimation.html, as shown in Figure 27.22.

Huffman coding animation on Companion Website

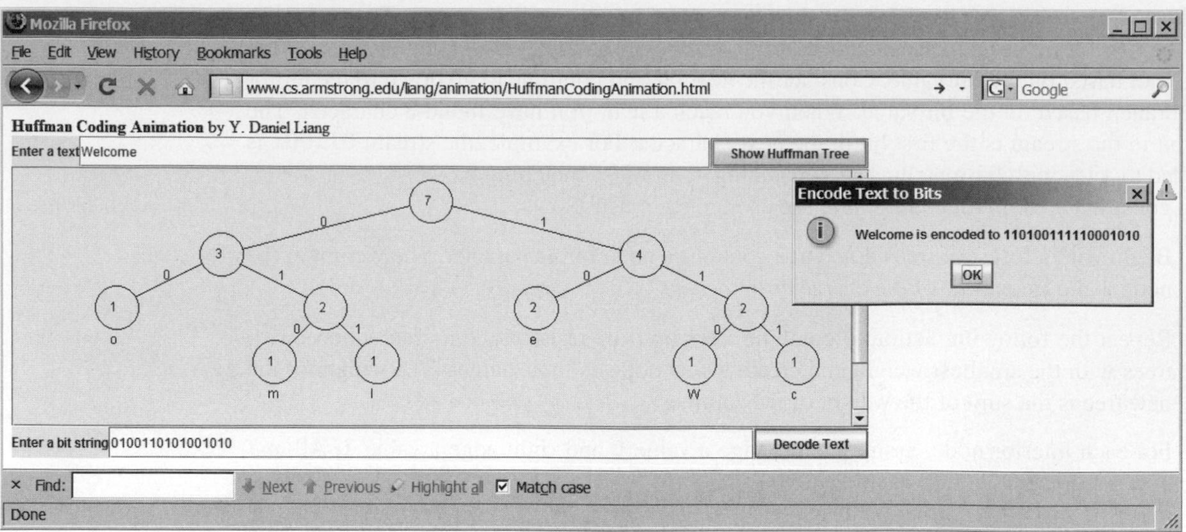

FIGURE 27.22 The animation tool enables you to create and view a Huffman tree, and it performs encoding and decoding using the tree.

greedy algorithm

The algorithm used here is an example of a *greedy algorithm*. A greedy algorithm is often used in solving optimization problems. The algorithm makes the choice that is optimal locally in the hope that this choice will lead to a globally optimal solution. In this case, the algorithm always chooses two trees with the smallest weight and creates a new node as their parent. This intuitive optimal local solution indeed leads to a final optimal solution for constructing a Huffman tree. As another example, consider changing money into the fewest possible coins. A greedy algorithm would take the largest possible coin first. For example, for 98¢, you would use three quarters to make 75¢, additional two dimes to make 95¢, and additional three pennies to make the 98¢. The greedy algorithm finds an optimal solution for this problem. However, a greedy algorithm is not always going to find the optimal result; see the bin packing problem in Programming Exercise 27.22.

Listing 27.12 gives a program that prompts the user to enter a string, displays the frequency table of the characters in the string, and displays the Huffman code for each character.

LISTING 27.12 HuffmanCode.java

count frequency

get Huffman tree

code for each character

```
import java.util.Scanner;

public class HuffmanCode {
  public static void main(String[] args) {
    Scanner input = new Scanner(System.in);
    System.out.print("Enter text: ");
    String text = input.nextLine();

    int[] counts = getCharacterFrequency(text); // Count frequency

    System.out.printf("%-15s%-15s%-15s%-15s\n",
      "ASCII Code", "Character", "Frequency", "Code");

    Tree tree = getHuffmanTree(counts); // Create a Huffman tree
    String[] codes = getCode(tree.root); // Get codes

    for (int i = 0; i < codes.length; i++)
      if (counts[i] != 0) // (char)i is not in text if counts[i] is 0
        System.out.printf("%-15d%-15s%-15d%-15s\n",
```

```
        i, (char)i + "", counts[i], codes[i]);
  }

  /** Get Huffman codes for the characters
   * This method is called once after a Huffman tree is built
   */
  public static String[] getCode(Tree.Node root) {
    if (root == null) return null;
    String[] codes = new String[2 * 128];
    assignCode(root, codes);
    return codes;
  }

  /* Recursively get codes to the leaf node */
  private static void assignCode(Tree.Node root, String[] codes) {
    if (root.left != null) {
      root.left.code = root.code + "0";
      assignCode(root.left, codes);

      root.right.code = root.code + "1";
      assignCode(root.right, codes);
    }
    else {
      codes[(int)root.element] = root.code;
    }
  }

  /** Get a Huffman tree from the codes */
  public static Tree getHuffmanTree(int[] counts) {
    // Create a heap to hold trees
    Heap<Tree> heap = new Heap<Tree>(); // Defined in Listing 25.10
    for (int i = 0; i < counts.length; i++) {
      if (counts[i] > 0)
        heap.add(new Tree(counts[i], (char)i)); // A leaf node tree
    }

    while (heap.getSize() > 1) {
      Tree t1 = heap.remove(); // Remove the smallest-weight tree
      Tree t2 = heap.remove(); // Remove the next smallest
      heap.add(new Tree(t1, t2)); // Combine two trees
    }

    return heap.remove(); // The final tree
  }

  /** Get the frequency of the characters */
  public static int[] getCharacterFrequency(String text) {
    int[] counts = new int[256]; // 256 ASCII characters

    for (int i = 0; i < text.length(); i++)
      counts[(int)text.charAt(i)]++; // Count the characters in text

    return counts;
  }

  /** Define a Huffman coding tree */
  public static class Tree implements Comparable<Tree> {
    Node root; // The root of the tree

    /** Create a tree with two subtrees */
```

getCode

assignCode

getHuffmanTree

getCharacterFrequency

Huffman tree

tree node

```
80      public Tree(Tree t1, Tree t2) {
81        root = new Node();
82        root.left = t1.root;
83        root.right = t2.root;
84        root.weight = t1.root.weight + t2.root.weight;
85      }
86
87      /** Create a tree containing a leaf node */
88      public Tree(int weight, char element) {
89        root = new Node(weight, element);
90      }
91
92      @Override /** Compare trees based on their weights */
93      public int compareTo(Tree t) {
94        if (root.weight < t.root.weight) // Purposely reverse the order
95          return 1;
96        else if (root.weight == t.root.weight)
97          return 0;
98        else
99          return -1;
100     }
101
102     public class Node {
103       char element; // Stores the character for a leaf node
104       int weight; // weight of the subtree rooted at this node
105       Node left; // Reference to the left subtree
106       Node right; // Reference to the right subtree
107       String code = ""; // The code of this node from the root
108
109       /** Create an empty node */
110       public Node() {
111       }
112
113       /** Create a node with the specified weight and character */
114       public Node(int weight, char element) {
115         this.weight = weight;
116         this.element = element;
117       }
118     }
119   }
120 }
```

```
Enter text: Welcome ↵Enter
ASCII Code     Character     Frequency     Code
87             W             1             110
99             c             1             111
101            e             2             10
108            l             1             011
109            m             1             010
111            o             1             00
```

getCharacterFrequency

The program prompts the user to enter a text string (lines 5–7) and counts the frequency of the characters in the text (line 9). The **getCharacterFrequency** method (lines 66–73) creates an array **counts** to count the occurrences of each of the 256 ASCII characters in the text. If a character appears in the text, its corresponding count is increased by **1** (line 70).

The program obtains a Huffman coding tree based on `counts` (line 14). The tree consists of linked nodes. The `Node` class is defined in lines 102–118. Each node consists of properties `element` (storing character), `weight` (storing weight of the subtree under this node), `left` (linking to the left subtree), `right` (linking to the right subtree), and `code` (storing the Huffman code for the character). The `Tree` class (lines 76–119) contains the root property. From the root, you can access all the nodes in the tree. The `Tree` class implements `Comparable`. The trees are comparable based on their weights. The compare order is purposely reversed (lines 93–100) so that the smallest-weight tree is removed first from the heap of trees.

Node class

Tree class

The `getHuffmanTree` method returns a Huffman coding tree. Initially, the single-node trees are created and added to the heap (lines 50–54). In each iteration of the `while` loop (lines 56–60), two smallest-weight trees are removed from the heap and are combined to form a big tree, and then the new tree is added to the heap. This process continues until the heap contains just one tree, which is our final Huffman tree for the text.

getHuffmanTree

The `assignCode` method assigns the code for each node in the tree (lines 34–45). The `getCode` method gets the code for each character in the leaf node (lines 26–31). The element `codes[i]` contains the code for character `(char)i`, where `i` is from `0` to `255`. Note that `codes[i]` is `null` if `(char)i` is not in the text.

assignCode

getCode

27.15 Every internal node in a Huffman tree has two children. Is it true?

27.16 What is a greedy algorithm? Give an example.

Check Point

MyProgrammingLab™

Key Terms

binary search tree 962	Huffman coding 986
binary tree 962	inorder traversal 965
breadth-first traversal 966	postorder traversal 965
depth-first traversal 965	preorder traversal 965
greedy algorithm 988	tree traversal 965

Chapter Summary

1. A *binary search tree* (BST) is a hierarchical data structure. You learned how to define and implement a BST class, how to insert and delete elements into/from a BST, and how to traverse a BST using *inorder*, *postorder*, *preorder*, depth-first, and breadth-first searches.

2. An iterator is an object that provides a uniform way of traversing the elements in a container, such as a set, a list, or a *binary tree*. You learned how to define and implement iterator classes for traversing the elements in a binary tree.

3. *Huffman coding* is a scheme for compressing data by using fewer bits to encode characters that occur more frequently. The codes for characters are constructed based on the occurrence of characters in the text using a binary tree, called the *Huffman coding tree*.

Test Questions

Do the test questions for this chapter online at www.cs.armstrong.edu/liang/intro9e/test.html.

MyProgrammingLab™

Programming Exercises

Sections 27.2–27.6

*27.1 (*Add new methods in BST*) Add the following new methods in **BST**.

```
/** Displays the nodes in a breadth-first traversal */
public void breadthFirstTraversal()

/** Returns the height of this binary tree, i.e., the
 * number of the nodes in the longest path of the root to a leaf */
public int height()
```

*27.2 (*Test full binary tree*) A full binary tree is a binary tree with the leaves on the same level. Add a method in the **BST** class to return true if the tree is a full binary tree. (*Hint*: The number of nodes in a full binary tree is $2^{depth} - 1$.)

```
/** Returns true if the tree is a full binary tree */
boolean isFullBST()
```

27.3 (*Implement inorder traversal without using recursion*) Implement the **inorder method in **BST** using a stack instead of recursion.

27.4 (*Implement preorder traversal without using recursion*) Implement the **preorder method in **BST** using a stack instead of recursion.

27.5 (*Implement postorder traversal without using recursion*) Implement the **postorder method in **BST** using a stack instead of recursion.

27.6 (*Find the leaves*) Add a method in the **BST class to return the number of the leaves as follows:

```
/** Returns the number of leaf nodes */
public int getNumberOfLeaves()
```

27.7 (*Find the nonleaves*) Add a method in the **BST class to return the number of the nonleaves as follows:

```
/** Returns the number of nonleaf nodes */
public int getNumberofNonLeaves()
```

***27.8 (*Implement bidirectional iterator*) The **java.util.Iterator** interface defines a forward iterator. The Java API also provides the **java.util.ListIterator** interface that defines a bidirectional iterator. Study **ListIterator** and define a bidirectional iterator for the **BST** class.

27.9 (*Tree **clone and **equals***) Implement the **clone** and **equals** methods in the **BST** class.

Comprehensive

**27.10 (*BST search visualization*) Write a Java applet that displays a search path, as shown in Figure 27.23a. The applet allows the user to enter a key. If the key is not in the tree, a message dialog box is displayed. Otherwise, the nodes in the path from the root leading to the key are colored.

**27.11 (*BST animation*) The preceding exercise simply highlights a search path. Write a Java applet that animates how a search is performed. First you see that the root is searched, and then a subtree is searched recursively. When a node is

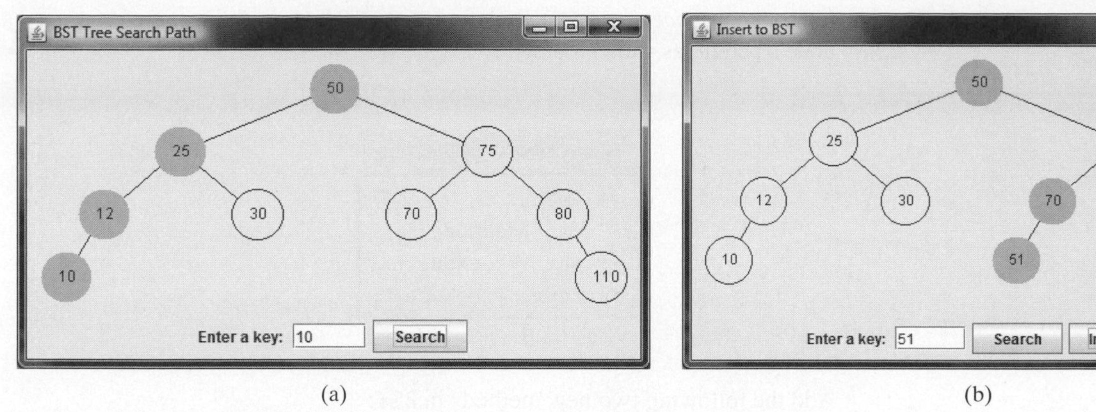

(a) (b)

FIGURE 27.23 (a) The search path is highlighted. (b) The applet animates how an insertion is performed.

searched, the node is highlighted. The search stops when a key is found in the tree, or the applet displays a message that a key is not in the tree.

**27.12 (*BST insert animation*) Add an *Insert* button to the preceding exercise to animate how insertion is performed, as shown in Figure 27.23b. When the *Insert* button is clicked, the applet first animates a search. If the key is already in the tree, display a dialog box. Otherwise, insert the key and repaint the tree.

27.13 (*Add new buttons in* **TreeControl) Modify Listing 27.10, TreeControl.java, to add three new buttons— *Show Inorder, Show Preorder, and Show Postorder*—to display the result in a message dialog box, as shown in Figure 27.24. You need also to modify BST.java to implement the `inorderList()`, `preorderList()`, and `postorderList()` methods so that each of these methods returns a `List` of the node elements in inorder, preorder, and postorder, as follows:

```
public java.util.List<E> inorderList();
public java.util.List<E> preorderList();
public java.util.List<E> postorderList();
```

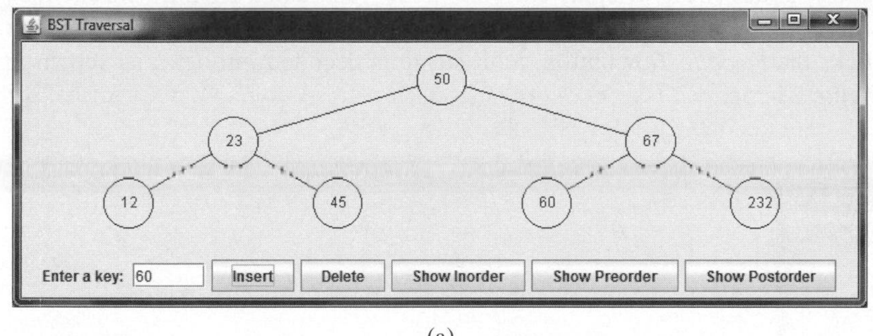

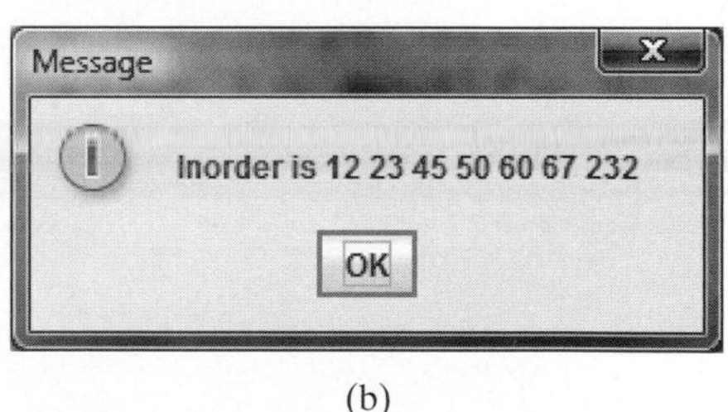

(a) (b)

FIGURE 27.24 When you click the *Show Inorder* button in (a), the tree nodes are displayed in an inorder in a message dialog box in (b).

*27.14 (*Generic* **BST** using **Comparator**) Revise **BST** in Listing 27.5, using a generic parameter and a **Comparator** for comparing objects. Define a new constructor with a **Comparator** as its argument as follows:

```
BST(Comparator<? super E> comparator)
```

***27.15** (*Parent reference for* `BST`) Redefine `TreeNode` by adding a reference to a node's parent, as shown below:

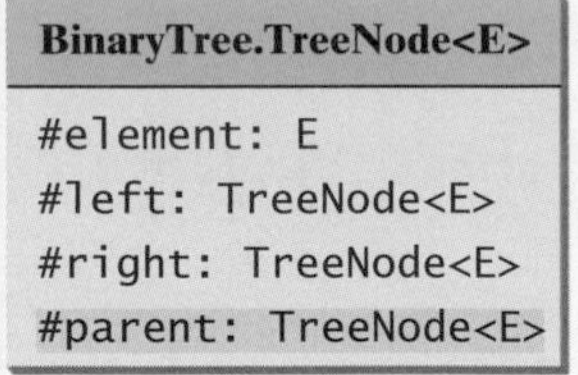

Add the following two new methods in `BST`:

```
/** Returns the parent for the specified node. */
public TreeNode<E> getParent(TreeNode<E> node)

/** Returns the path from the specified node to the root
 * in an array list. */
public ArrayList<TreeNode<E>> getPath(TreeNode<E> node)
```

Write a test program that adds numbers `1`, `2`, . . ., `100` to the tree and displays the paths for all leaf nodes.

****27.16** (*BST animation*) Write a Java applet that animates the binary search tree `insert`, `delete`, and `search` methods, as shown in Figure 27.2.

****27.17** (*Animation: heap*) Write an applet to display a heap visually, as shown in Figure 25.8.

*****27.18** (*Data compression: Huffman coding*) Write a program that prompts the user to enter a file name, then displays the frequency table of the characters in the file and displays the Huffman code for each character.

*****27.19** (*Data compression: Huffman coding animation*) Write an applet that enables the user to enter text and displays the Huffman coding tree based on the text, as shown in Figure 27.25a. Display the weight of the subtree inside the subtree's root circle. Display each leaf node's character. Display the encoded bits for the text in a dialog box, as shown in Figure 27.25b. When the user clicks the *Decode Text* button, a bit string is decoded into text, as shown in Figure 27.25c.

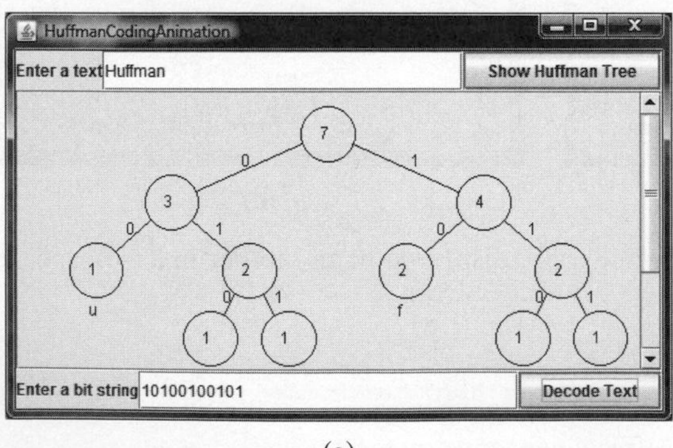

(a)

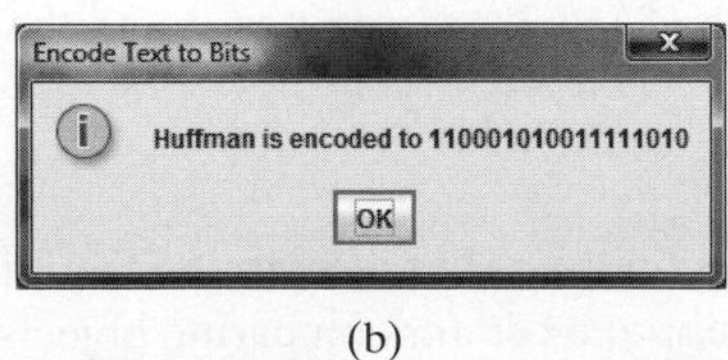

(b)

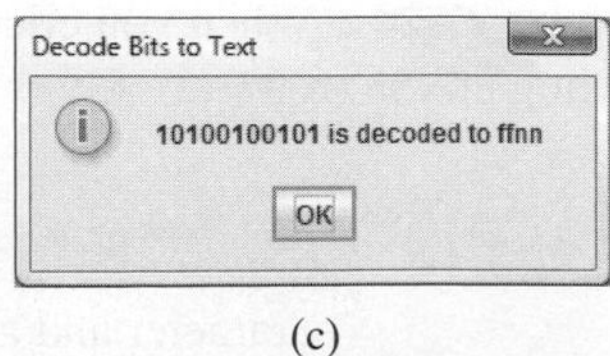

(c)

Figure 27.25 The animation shows the coding tree for a given text string in (a), encoded bits in (b), and the text for the given bit sequence in (c).

*****27.20** (*Compress a file*) Write a program that compresses a source file into a target file using the Huffman coding method. First use `ObjectOutputStream` to output the Huffman codes into the target file, and then use `BitOutputStream` in Programming Exercise 19.17 to output the encoded binary contents to the target file. Pass the files from the command line using the following command:

```
java Exercise27_20 sourcefile targetfile
```

*****27.21** (*Decompress a file*) The preceding exercise compresses a file. The compressed file contains the Huffman codes and the compressed contents. Write a program that decompresses a source file into a target file using the following command:

```
java Exercise27_21 sourcefile targetfile
```

27.22 (*Bin packing using first fit*) Write a program that packs the objects of various weights into containers. Each container can hold a maximum of 10 pounds. The program uses a greedy algorithm that places an object into the first bin in which it would fit. Your program should prompt the user to enter the total number of objects and the weight of each object. The program displays the total number of containers needed to pack the objects and the contents of each container. Here is a sample run of the program:

```
Enter the number of objects: 6
Enter the weights of the objects: 7 5 2 3 5 8
Container 1 contains objects with weight 7 2
Container 2 contains objects with weight 5 3
Container 3 contains objects with weight 5
Container 4 contains objects with weight 8
```

Does this program produce an optimal solution, that is, finding the minimum number of containers to pack the objects?

27.23 (*Bin packing with smallest object first*) Rewrite the preceding program that uses a new greedy algorithm that places an object with the *smallest weight* into the first bin in which it would fit. Your program should prompt the user to enter the total number of objects and the weight of each object. The program displays the total number of containers needed to pack the objects and the contents of each container. Here is a sample run of the program:

```
Enter the number of objects: 6
Enter the weights of the objects: 7 5 2 3 5 8
Container 1 contains objects with weight 2 3 5
Container 2 contains objects with weight 5
Container 3 contains objects with weight 7
Container 4 contains objects with weight 8
```

Does this program produce an optimal solution, that is, finding the minimum number of containers to pack the objects?

27.24 (*Optimal bin packing*) Rewrite the preceding program so that it finds an optimal solution that packs all objects using the smallest number of containers. What is the time complexity of your program?

CHAPTER

28

HASHING

Objectives

- To understand what hashing is and what hashing is used for (§28.2).
- To obtain the hash code for an object and design the hash function to map a key to an index (§28.3).
- To handle collisions using open addressing (§28.4).
- To know the differences among linear probing, quadratic probing, and double hashing (§28.4).
- To handle collisions using separate chaining (§28.5).
- To understand the load factor and the need for rehashing (§28.6).
- To implement `MyHashMap` using hashing (§28.7).
- To implement `MyHashSet` using hashing (§28.8).

28.1 Introduction

Key Point

Hashing is superefficient. It takes O(1) time to search, insert, and delete an element using hashing.

why hashing?

The preceding chapter introduced binary search trees. An element can be found in $O(\log n)$ time in a well-balanced search tree. Is there a more efficient way to search for an element in a container? This chapter introduces a technique called *hashing*. You can use hashing to implement a map or a set to search, insert, and delete an element in $O(1)$ time.

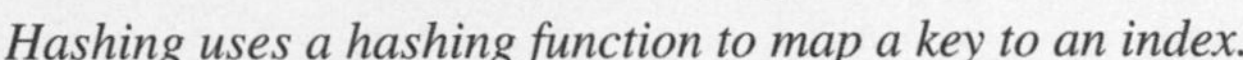

28.2 What Is Hashing?

Key Point

Hashing uses a hashing function to map a key to an index.

map
key
value

Before introducing hashing, let us review map, which is a data structure that is implemented using hashing. Recall that a *map* (introduced in Section 23.5) is a container object that stores entries. Each entry contains two parts: a *key* and a *value*. The key, also called a *search key*, is used to search for the corresponding value. For example, a dictionary can be stored in a map, in which the words are the keys and the definitions of the words are the values.

Note

A map is also called a *dictionary*, a *hash table*, or an *associative array*.

dictionary
hash table
associative array

The Java Collections Framework defines the `java.util.Map` interface for modeling maps. Three concrete implementations are `java.util.HashMap`, `java.util.LinkedHashMap`, and `java.util.TreeMap`. `java.util.HashMap` is implemented using hashing, `java.util.LinkedHashMap` using `LinkedList`, and `java.util.TreeMap` using red-black trees. (The bonus Chapter 48 introduces red-black trees.) You will learn the concept of hashing and use it to implement a map in this chapter.

hash table
hash function
hashing

If you know the index of an element in the array, you can retrieve the element using the index in $O(1)$ time. So does that mean we can store the values in an array and use the key as the index to find the value? The answer is yes—if you can map a key to an index. The array that stores the values is called a *hash table*. The function that maps a key to an index in the hash table is called a *hash function*. As shown in Figure 28.1, a hash function obtains an index from a key and uses the index to retrieve the value for the key. *Hashing* is a technique that retrieves the value using the index obtained from the key without performing a search.

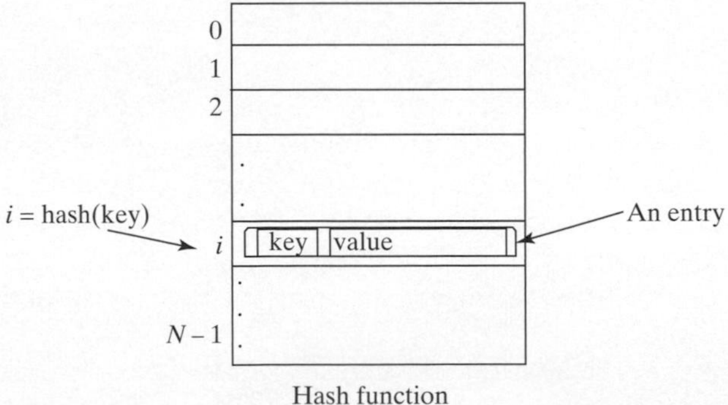

FIGURE 28.1 A hash function maps a key to an index in the hash table.

perfect hash function

How do you design a hash function that produces an index from a key? Ideally, we would like to design a function that maps each search key to a different index in the hash table. Such a function is called a *perfect hash function*. However, it is difficult to find a perfect hash function. When two or more keys are mapped to the same hash value, we say that a *collision* has occurred. Although there are ways to deal with collisions, which are discussed later in this chapter, it is better to avoid collisions in the first place. Thus, you should design a fast and easy-to-compute hash function that minimizes collisions.

collision

28.1 What is a hash function? What is a perfect hash function? What is a collision?

Check Point

MyProgrammingLab™

28.3 Hash Functions and Hash Codes

A typical hash function first converts a search key to an integer value called a hash code, *then compresses the hash code into an index to the hash table.*

Key Point

Java's root class `Object` has the `hashCode` method, which returns an integer hash code. By default, the method returns the memory address for the object. The general contract for the `hashCode` method is as follows:

hash code

hashCode()

1. You should override the `hashCode` method whenever the `equals` method is overridden to ensure that two equal objects return the same hash code.
2. During the execution of a program, invoking the `hashCode` method multiple times returns the same integer, provided that the object's data are not changed.
3. Two unequal objects may have the same hash code, but you should implement the `hashCode` method to avoid too many such cases.

28.3.1 Hash Codes for Primitive Types

For search keys of the type `byte`, `short`, `int`, and `char`, simply cast them to `int`. Therefore, two different search keys of any one of these types will have different hash codes.

byte, short, int, char

For a search key of the type `float`, use `Float.floatToIntBits(key)` as the hash code. Note that `floatToIntBits(float f)` returns an `int` value whose bit representation is the same as the bit representation for the floating number `f`. Thus, two different search keys of the `float` type will have different hash codes.

float

For a search key of the type `long`, simply casting it to `int` would not be a good choice, because all keys that differ in only the first 32 bits will have the same hash code. To take the first 32 bits into consideration, divide the 64 bits into two halves and perform the exclusive-or operation to combine the two halves. This process is called *folding*. The hashing code for a `long` keyword is

long

folding

```
int hashCode = (int)(key ^ (key >> 32));
```

Note that >> is the right-shift operator that shifts the bits 32 positions to the right. For example, `1010110 >> 2` yields `0010101`. The ^ is the bitwise exclusive-or operator. It operates on two corresponding bits of the binary operands. For example, `1010110 ^ 0110111` yields `1100001`. For more on bitwise operations, see Appendix G, Bitwise Operations.

For a search key of the type `double`, first convert it to a `long` value using the `Double.doubleToLongBits` method, and then perform a folding as follows:

double

folding

```
long bits = Double.doubleToLongBits(key);
int hashCode = (int)(bits ^ (bits >> 32));
```

28.3.2 Hash Codes for Strings

Search keys are often strings, so it is important to design a good hash function for strings. An intuitive approach is to sum the Unicode of all characters as the hash code for the string. This approach may work if two search keys in an application don't contain the same letters, but it will produce a lot of collisions if the search keys contain the same letters, such as **tod** and **dot**.

A better approach is to generate a hash code that takes the position of characters into consideration. Specifically, let the hash code be

$$s_0*b^{(N-1)} + s_1*b^{(N-2)} + \ldots + s_{N-1}$$

where s_i is **s.charAt(i)**. This expression is a polynomial for some positive b, so this is called a *polynomial hash code*. Using Horner's rule for polynomial evaluation (see Section 9.4), the hash code can be calculated efficiently as follows:

polynomial hash code

$$(\ldots((s_0*b + s_1)b + s_2)b + \ldots + s_{N-2})b + s_{N-1}$$

This computation can cause an overflow for long strings, but arithmetic overflow is ignored in Java. You should choose an appropriate value b to minimize collisions. Experiments show that good choices for b are 31, 33, 37, 39, and 41. In the **String** class, the **hashCode** is overridden using the polynomial hash code with b being **31**.

28.3.3 Compressing Hash Codes

The hash code for a key can be a large integer that is out of the range for the hash-table index, so you need to scale it down to fit in the index's range. Assume the index for a hash table is between **0** and **N-1**. The most common way to scale an integer to between **0** and **N-1** is to use

```
h(hashCode) = hashCode % N
```

To ensure that the indices are spread evenly, choose **N** to be a prime number greater than **2**.

Ideally, you should choose a prime number for **N**. However, it is time consuming to find a large prime number. In the Java API implementation for **java.util.HashMap**, **N** is set to a value of the power of **2**. There is a good reason for this choice. When **N** is a value of the power of **2**,

```
h(hashCode) = hashCode % N
```

is the same as

```
h(hashCode) = hashCode & (N - 1)
```

The ampersand, **&**, is a bitwise AND operator (see Appendix G, Bitwise Operations). The AND of two corresponding bits yields a **1** if both bits are **1**. For example, assume **N = 4** and **hashCode = 11**, **11 % 4 = 3**, which is the same as **01011 & 00011 = 11**. The **&** operator can be performed much faster than the **%** operator.

To ensure that the hashing is evenly distributed, a supplemental hash function is also used along with the primary hash function in the implementation of **java.util.HashMap**. The supplemental function is defined as:

```
private static int supplementalHash(int h) {
  h ^= (h >>> 20) ^ (h >>> 12);
  return h ^ (h >>> 7) ^ (h >>> 4);
}
```

^ and **>>>** are bitwise exclusive-or and unsigned right-shift operations (also introduced in Appendix G). The bitwise operations are much faster than the multiplication, division, and remainder operations. You should replace these operations with the bitwise operations whenever possible.

The complete hash function is defined as:

```
h(hashCode) = supplementalHash(hashCode) % N
```

This is the same as

```
h(hashCode) = supplementalHash(hashCode) & (N - 1)
```

since `N` is a value of the power of `2`.

MyProgrammingLab™

28.2 What is a hash code? What is the hash code for `Byte`, `Short`, `Integer`, and `Character`?

28.3 How is the hash code for a `Float` object computed?

28.4 How is the hash code for a `Long` object computed?

28.5 How is the hash code for a `Double` object computed?

28.6 How is the hash code for a `String` object computed?

28.7 How is a hash code compressed to an integer representing the index in a hash table?

28.8 If `N` is a value of the power of `2`, is `N / 2` same as `N >> 1`?

28.9 If `N` is a value of the power of `2`, is `m % N` same as `m & (N - 1)` for any integer `m`?

28.4 Handling Collisions Using Open Addressing

Key Point

A collision occurs when two keys are mapped to the same index in a hash table. Generally, there are two ways for handling collisions: open addressing *and* separate chaining.

open addressing

Open addressing is the process of finding an open location in the hash table in the event of a collision. Open addressing has several variations: *linear probing*, *quadratic probing*, and *double hashing*.

28.4.1 Linear Probing

add entry
linear probing

When a collision occurs during the insertion of an entry to a hash table, *linear probing* finds the next available location sequentially. For example, if a collision occurs at `hashTable[k % N]`, check whether `hashTable[(k+1) % N]` is available. If not, check `hashTable[(k+2) % N]` and so on, until an available cell is found, as shown in Figure 28.2.

Note

When probing reaches the end of the table, it goes back to the beginning of the table. Thus, the hash table is treated as if it were circular.

circular hash table

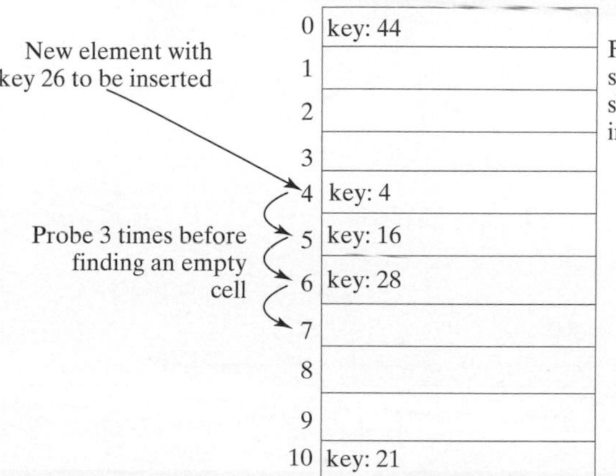

FIGURE 28.2 Linear probing finds the next available location sequentially.

search entry

To search for an entry in the hash table, obtain the index, say `k`, from the hash function for the key. Check whether `hashTable[k % n]` contains the entry. If not, check whether `hashTable[(k+1) % n]` contains the entry, and so on, until it is found, or an empty cell is reached.

remove entry

To remove an entry from the hash table, search the entry that matches the key. If the entry is found, place a special marker to denote that the entry is available. Each cell in the hash table has three possible states: occupied, marked, or empty. Note that a marked cell is also available for insertion.

cluster

Linear probing tends to cause groups of consecutive cells in the hash table to be occupied. Each group is called a *cluster*. Each cluster is actually a probe sequence that you must search when retrieving, adding, or removing an entry. As clusters grow in size, they may merge into even larger clusters, further slowing down the search time. This is a big disadvantage of linear probing.

linear probing animation on Companion Website

Pedagogical Note

For an interactive GUI demo to see how linear probing works, go to www.cs.armstrong.edu/liang/animation/HashingLinearProbingAnimation.html, as shown in Figure 28.3.

28.4.2 Quadratic Probing

quadratic probing

Quadratic probing can avoid the clustering problem that can occur in linear probing. Linear probing looks at the consecutive cells beginning at index *k*. Quadratic probing, on the other

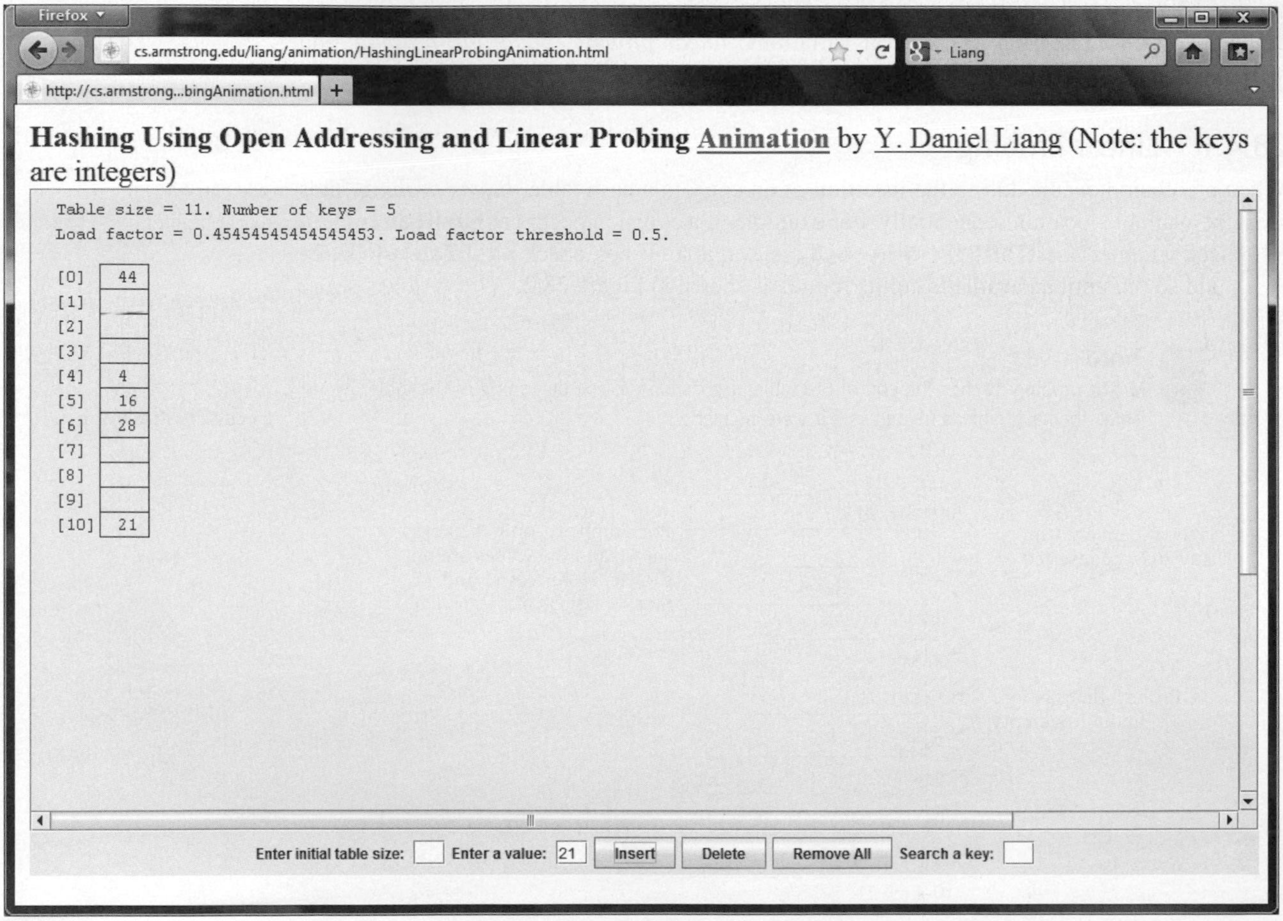

Hashing Using Open Addressing and Linear Probing Animation by Y. Daniel Liang (Note: the keys are integers)

```
Table size = 11. Number of keys = 5
Load factor = 0.45454545454545453. Load factor threshold = 0.5.

[0]  44
[1]
[2]
[3]
[4]  4
[5]  16
[6]  28
[7]
[8]
[9]
[10] 21
```

Enter initial table size: Enter a value: 21 Insert Delete Remove All Search a key:

FIGURE 28.3 The animation tool shows how linear probing works.

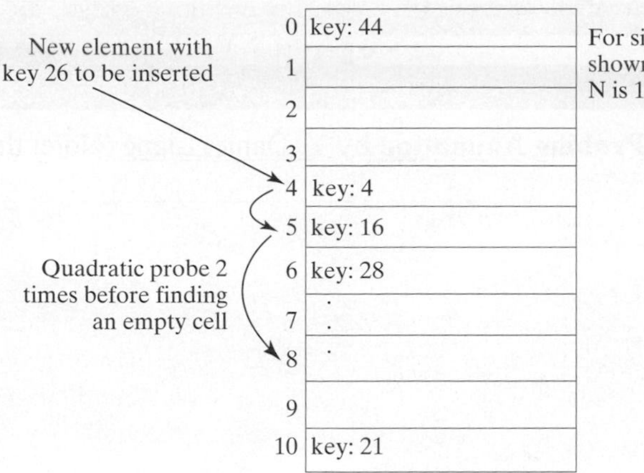

FIGURE 28.4 Quadratic probing increases the next index in the sequence by `j`^{2} for $j = 1, 2, 3, \ldots$.

hand, looks at the cells at indices $(k + j^2)$ % n, for $j \geq 0$, that is, k, $(k + 1)$ % n, $(k + 4)$ % n, $(k + 9)$ % n, . . . , and so on, as shown in Figure 28.4.

Quadratic probing works in the same way as linear probing except for a change in the search sequence. Quadratic probing avoids linear probing's clustering problem, but it has its own clustering problem, called *secondary clustering*; that is, the entries that collide with an occupied entry use the same probe sequence.

secondary clustering

Linear probing guarantees that an available cell can be found for insertion as long as the table is not full. However, there is no such guarantee for quadratic probing.

Pedagogical Note

For an interactive GUI demo to see how quadratic probing works, go to www.cs.armstrong.edu/liang/animation/HashingQuadraticProbingAnimation.html, as shown in Figure 28.5.

quadratic probing animation on Companion Website

28.4.3 Double Hashing

double hashing

Another open addressing scheme that avoids the clustering problem is known as *double hashing*. Starting from the initial index k, both linear probing and quadratic probing add an increment to k to define a search sequence. The increment is `1` for linear probing and `j`^{2} for quadratic probing. These increments are independent of the keys. Double hashing uses a secondary hash function on the keys to determine the increments to avoid the clustering problem.

For example, let the primary hash function `h` and secondary hash function `h'` on a hash table of size `11` be defined as follows:

```
h(k) = k % 11;
h'(k) = 7 - k % 7;
```

For a search key of `12`, we have

```
h(12) = 12 % 11 = 1;
h'(k) = 7 - 12 % 7 = 2;
```

The probe sequence for key `12` starts at index `1` with an increment `2`, as shown in Figure 28.6.

The indices of the probe sequence are as follows: 1, 3, 5, 7, 9, 0, 2, 4, 6, 8, 10. This sequence reaches the entire table. You should design your functions to produce a probe sequence that reaches the entire table. Note that the second function should never have a zero value, since zero is not an increment.

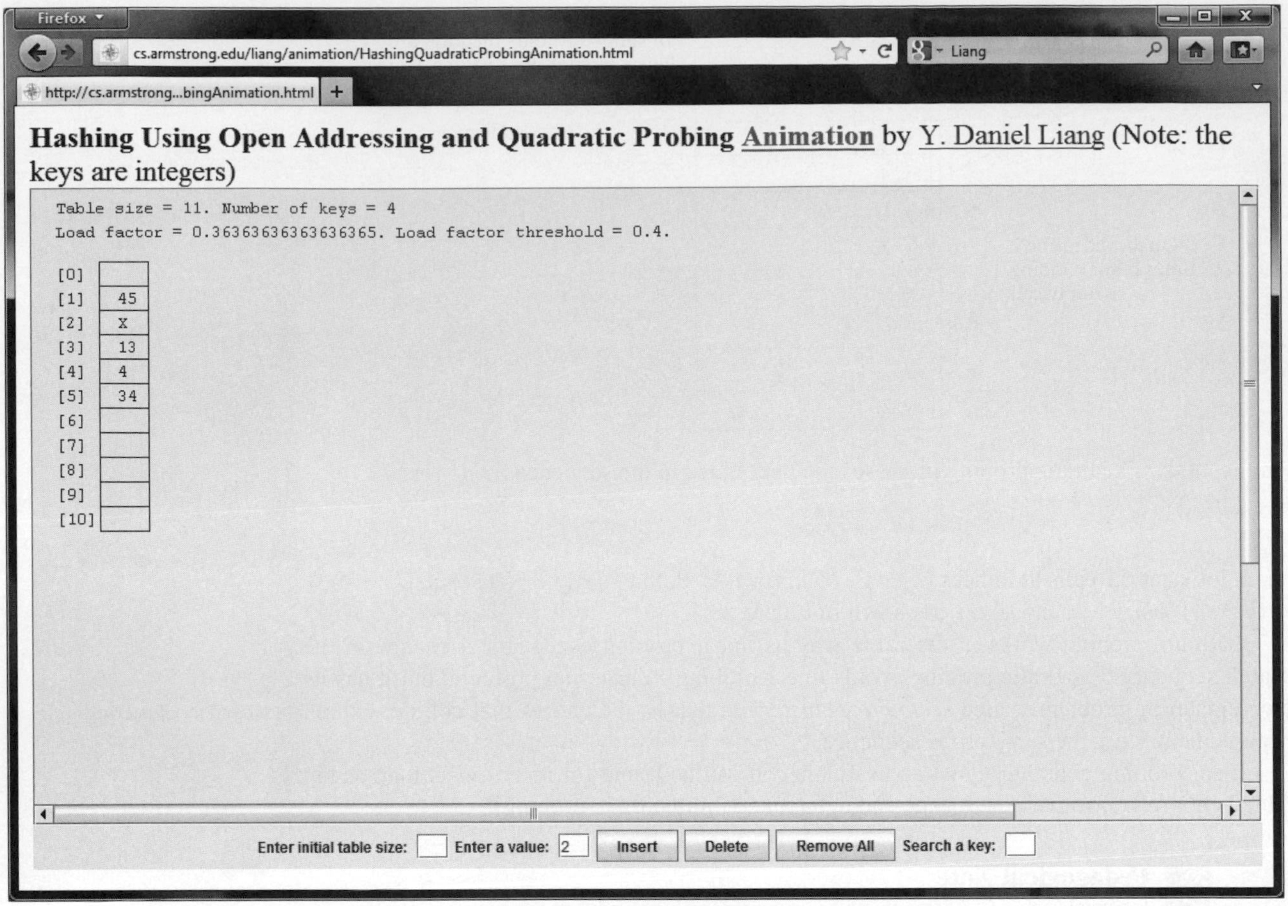

Firefox
cs.armstrong.edu/liang/animation/HashingQuadraticProbingAnimation.html
http://cs.armstrong...bingAnimation.html

Hashing Using Open Addressing and Quadratic Probing Animation by Y. Daniel Liang (Note: the keys are integers)

```
Table size = 11. Number of keys = 4
Load factor = 0.36363636363636365. Load factor threshold = 0.4.

[0]
[1]   45
[2]   X
[3]   13
[4]   4
[5]   34
[6]
[7]
[8]
[9]
[10]
```

Enter initial table size: Enter a value: 2 Insert Delete Remove All Search a key:

FIGURE 28.5 The animation tool shows how quadratic probing works.

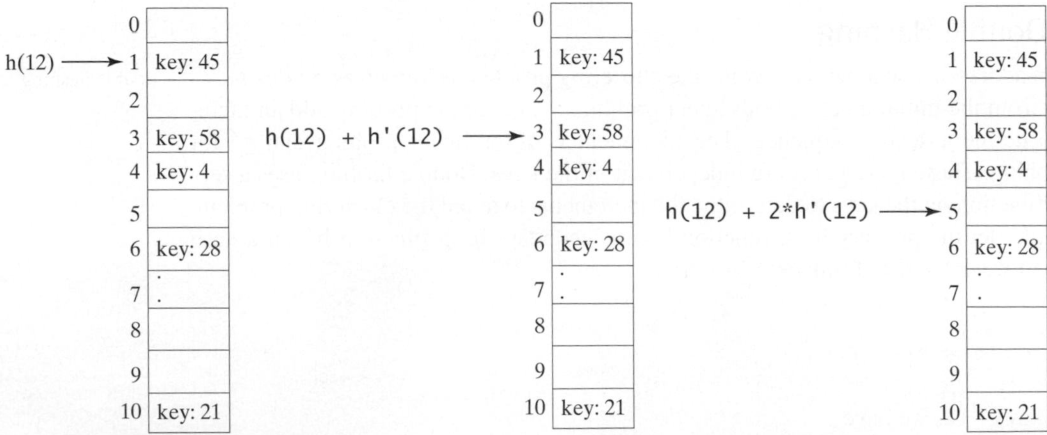

FIGURE 28.6 The secondary hash function in a double hashing determines the increment of the next index in the probe sequence.

MyProgrammingLab™

28.10 What is open addressing? What is linear probing? What is quadratic probing? What is double hashing?

28.11 Describe the clustering problem for linear probing.

28.12 What is secondary clustering?

28.13 Show the hash table of size 11 after inserting entries with keys 34, 29, 53, 44, 120, 39, 45, and 40, using linear probing.

28.14 Show the hash table of size 11 after inserting entries with keys 34, 29, 53, 44, 120, 39, 45, and 40, using quadratic probing.

28.15 Show the hash table of size 11 after inserting entries with keys 34, 29, 53, 44, 120, 39, 45, and 40, using double hashing with the following functions:

```
h(k) = k % 11;
h'(k) = 7 - k % 7;
```

28.5 Handling Collisions Using Separate Chaining

The separate chaining *scheme places all entries with the same hash index in the same location, rather than finding new locations. Each location in the separate chaining scheme uses a* bucket *to hold multiple entries.*

separate chaining

implementing bucket

You can implement a bucket using an array, **ArrayList**, or **LinkedList**. We will use **LinkedList** for demonstration. You can view each cell in the hash table as the reference to the head of a linked list, and elements in the linked list are chained starting from the head, as shown in Figure 28.7.

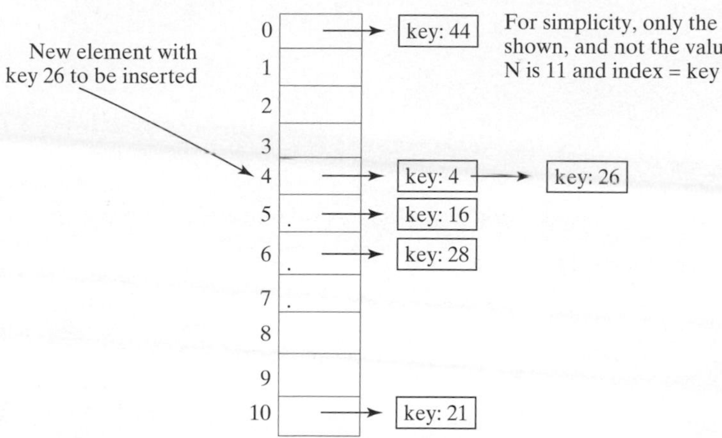

FIGURE 28.7 Separate chaining scheme chains the entries with the same hash index in a bucket.

28.16 Show the hash table of size 11 after inserting entries with the keys 34, 29, 53, 44, 120, 39, 45, and 40, using separate chaining.

Check Point

MyProgrammingLab™

28.6 Load Factor and Rehashing

Key Point

The load factor *measures how full a hash table is. If the load factor is exceeded, increase the hash-table size and reload the entries into the new larger hash table. This is called* rehashing.

rehashing

load factor

Load factor λ *(lambda)* measures how full a hash table is. It is the ratio of the number of elements to the size of the hash table, that is, $\lambda = \frac{n}{N}$, where *n* denotes the number of elements and *N* the number of locations in the hash table.

Note that λ is zero if the map is empty. For the open addressing scheme, λ is between **0** and **1**; λ is **1** if the hash table is full. For the separate chaining scheme, λ can be any value. As λ

increases, the probability of a collision increases. Studies show that you should maintain the load factor under `0.5` for the open addressing scheme and under `0.9` for the separate chaining scheme.

threshold

rehash

Keeping the load factor under a certain threshold is important for the performance of hashing. In the implementation of the `java.util.HashMap` class in the Java API, the threshold `0.75` is used. Whenever the load factor exceeds the threshold, you need to increase the hash-table size and *rehash* all the entries in the map into the new larger hash table. Notice that you need to change the hash functions, since the hash-table size has been changed. To reduce the likelihood of rehashing, since it is costly, you should at least double the hash-table size. Even with periodic rehashing, hashing is an efficient implementation for map.

separate chaining animation on Companion Website

Pedagogical Note

For an interactive GUI demo to see how separate chaining works, go to www.cs.armstrong.edu/liang/animation/HashingUsingSeparateChainingAnimation.html, as shown in Figure 28.8.

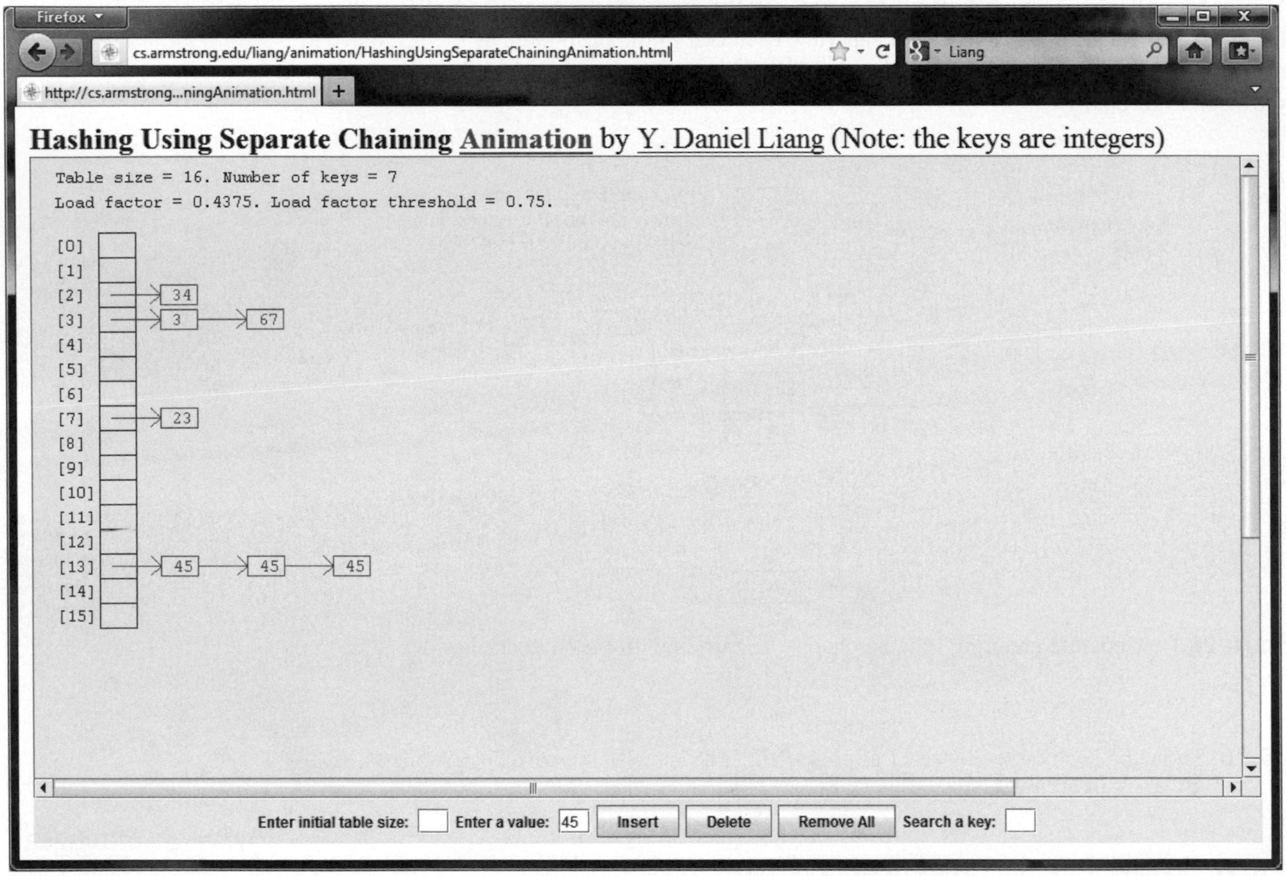

FIGURE 28.8 The animation tool shows how separate chaining works.

28.17 Assume the hash table has the initial size 4 and its load factor is 0.5; show the hash table after inserting entries with the keys 34, 29, 53, 44, 120, 39, 45, and 40, using linear probing.

28.18 Assume the hash table has the initial size 4 and its load factor is 0.5; show the hash table after inserting entries with the keys 34, 29, 53, 44, 120, 39, 45, and 40, using quadratic probing.

28.19 Assume the hash table has the initial size 4 and its load factor is 0.5; show the hash table after inserting entries with the keys 34, 29, 53, 44, 120, 39, 45, and 40, using separate chaining.

28.7 Implementing a Map Using Hashing

A map can be implemented using hashing.

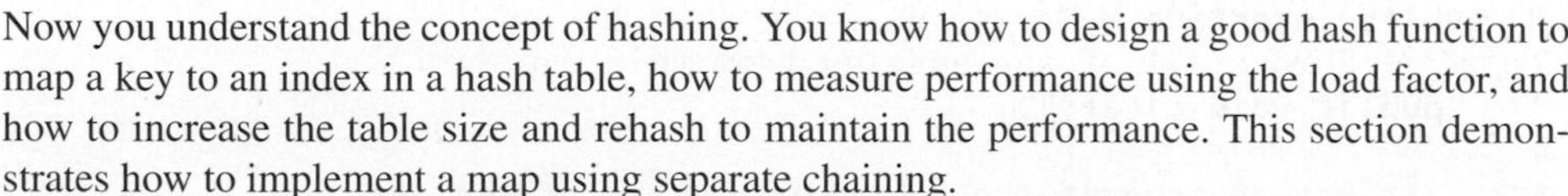

Now you understand the concept of hashing. You know how to design a good hash function to map a key to an index in a hash table, how to measure performance using the load factor, and how to increase the table size and rehash to maintain the performance. This section demonstrates how to implement a map using separate chaining.

We design our custom `Map` interface to mirror `java.util.Map` and name the interface `MyMap` and a concrete class `MyHashMap`, as shown in Figure 28.9.

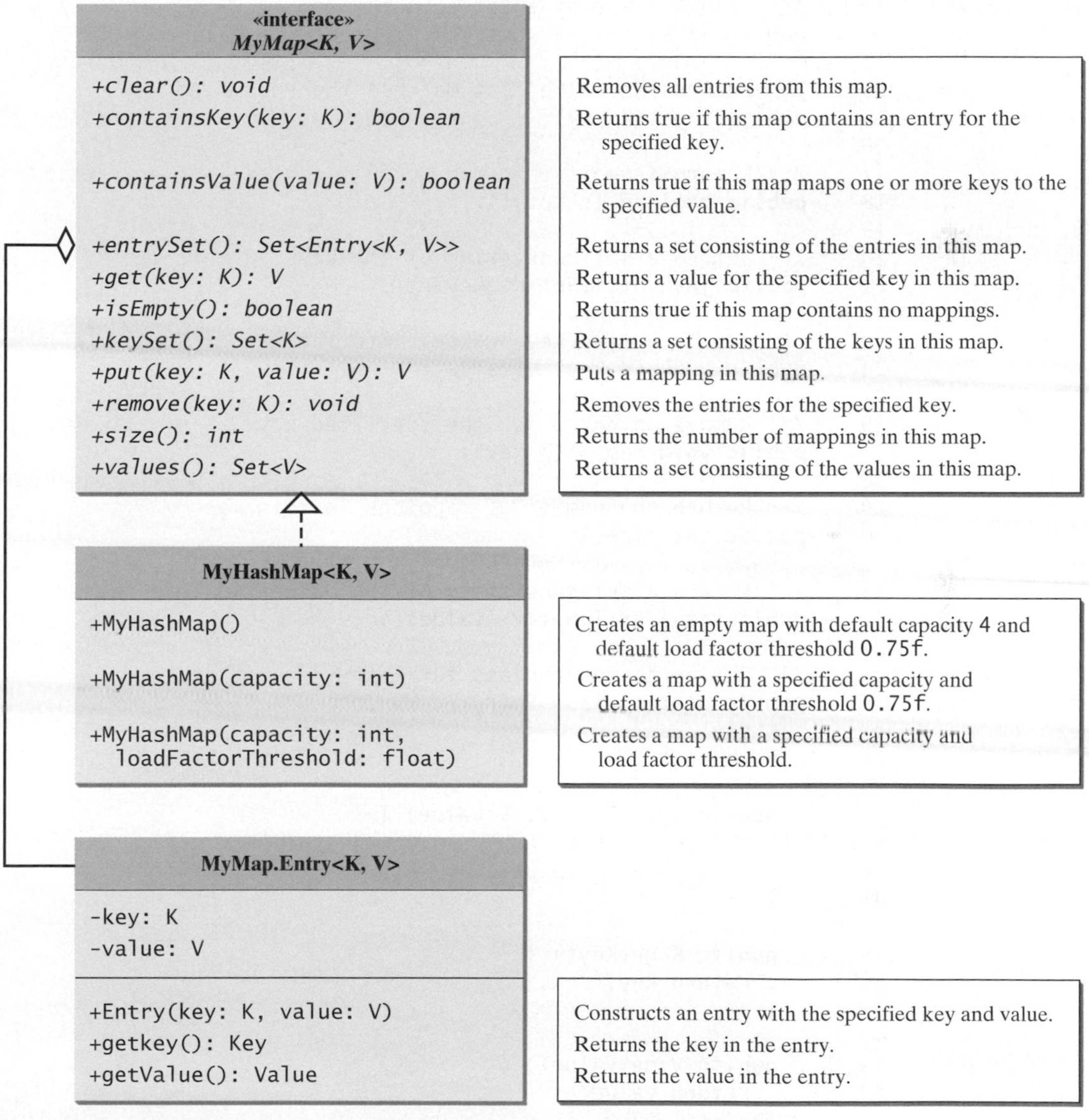

«interface» *MyMap<K, V>*	
`+clear(): void`	Removes all entries from this map.
`+containsKey(key: K): boolean`	Returns true if this map contains an entry for the specified key.
`+containsValue(value: V): boolean`	Returns true if this map maps one or more keys to the specified value.
`+entrySet(): Set<Entry<K, V>>`	Returns a set consisting of the entries in this map.
`+get(key: K): V`	Returns a value for the specified key in this map.
`+isEmpty(): boolean`	Returns true if this map contains no mappings.
`+keySet(): Set<K>`	Returns a set consisting of the keys in this map.
`+put(key: K, value: V): V`	Puts a mapping in this map.
`+remove(key: K): void`	Removes the entries for the specified key.
`+size(): int`	Returns the number of mappings in this map.
`+values(): Set<V>`	Returns a set consisting of the values in this map.

MyHashMap<K, V>	
`+MyHashMap()`	Creates an empty map with default capacity 4 and default load factor threshold `0.75f`.
`+MyHashMap(capacity: int)`	Creates a map with a specified capacity and default load factor threshold `0.75f`.
`+MyHashMap(capacity: int, loadFactorThreshold: float)`	Creates a map with a specified capacity and load factor threshold.

MyMap.Entry<K, V>	
`-key: K`	
`-value: V`	
`+Entry(key: K, value: V)`	Constructs an entry with the specified key and value.
`+getkey(): Key`	Returns the key in the entry.
`+getValue(): Value`	Returns the value in the entry.

FIGURE 28.9 `MyHashMap` implements the `MyMap` interface.

How do you implement **MyHashMap**? If you use an **ArrayList** and store a new entry at the end of the list, the search time will be $O(n)$. If you implement **MyHashMap** using a binary tree, the search time will be $O(\log n)$ if the tree is well balanced. Nevertheless, you can implement **MyHashMap** using hashing to obtain an $O(1)$ time search algorithm. Listing 28.1 shows the **MyMap** interface and Listing 28.2 implements **MyHashMap** using separate chaining.

LISTING 28.1 MyMap.java

```
public interface MyMap<K, V> {
  /** Remove all of the entries from this map */
  public void clear();

  /** Return true if the specified key is in the map */
  public boolean containsKey(K key);

  /** Return true if this map contains the specified value */
  public boolean containsValue(V value);

  /** Return a set of entries in the map */
  public java.util.Set<Entry<K, V>> entrySet();

  /** Return the value that matches the specified key */
  public V get(K key);

  /** Return true if this map doesn't contain any entries */
  public boolean isEmpty();

  /** Return a set consisting of the keys in this map */
  public java.util.Set<K> keySet();

  /** Add an entry (key, value) into the map */
  public V put(K key, V value);

  /** Remove an entry for the specified key */
  public void remove(K key);

  /** Return the number of mappings in this map */
  public int size();

  /** Return a set consisting of the values in this map */
  public java.util.Set<V> values();

  /** Define an inner class for Entry */
  public static class Entry<K, V> {
    K key;
    V value;

    public Entry(K key, V value) {
      this.key = key;
      this.value = value;
    }

    public K getKey() {
      return key;
    }

    public V getValue() {
      return value;
    }
```

interface MyMap
clear
containsKey
containsValue
entrySet
get
isEmpty
keySet
put
remove
size
values
Entry inner class

```

    @Override
    public String toString() {
      return "[" + key + ", " + value + "]";
    }
  }
}
```

Listing 28.2 MyHashMap.java

```
import java.util.LinkedList;

public class MyHashMap<K, V> implements MyMap<K, V> {
  // Define the default hash-table size. Must be a power of 2
  private static int DEFAULT_INITIAL_CAPACITY = 4;

  // Define the maximum hash-table size. 1 << 30 is same as 2^30
  private static int MAXIMUM_CAPACITY = 1 << 30;

  // Current hash-table capacity. Capacity is a power of 2
  private int capacity;

  // Define default load factor
  private static float DEFAULT_MAX_LOAD_FACTOR = 0.75f;

  // Specify a load factor used in the hash table
  private float loadFactorThreshold;

  // The number of entries in the map
  private int size = 0;

  // Hash table is an array with each cell being a linked list
  LinkedList<MyMap.Entry<K,V>>[] table;

  /** Construct a map with the default capacity and load factor */
  public MyHashMap() {
    this(DEFAULT_INITIAL_CAPACITY, DEFAULT_MAX_LOAD_FACTOR);
  }

  /** Construct a map with the specified initial capacity and
   * default load factor */
  public MyHashMap(int initialCapacity) {
    this(initialCapacity, DEFAULT_MAX_LOAD_FACTOR);
  }

  /** Construct a map with the specified initial capacity
   * and load factor */
  public MyHashMap(int initialCapacity, float loadFactorThreshold) {
    if (initialCapacity > MAXIMUM_CAPACITY)
      this.capacity = MAXIMUM_CAPACITY;
    else
      this.capacity = trimToPowerOf2(initialCapacity);

    this.loadFactorThreshold = loadFactorThreshold;
    table = new LinkedList[capacity];
  }

  @Override /** Remove all of the entries from this map */
  public void clear() {
    size = 0;
```

class MyHashMap
default initial capacity
maximum capacity
current capacity
default load factor
load-factor threshold
size
hash table
no-arg constructor
constructor
constructor
clear

```
    removeEntries();
  }

  @Override /** Return true if the specified key is in the map */
```

containsKey

```
  public boolean containsKey(K key) {
    if (get(key) != null)
      return true;
    else
      return false;
  }

  @Override /** Return true if this map contains the value */
```

containsValue

```
  public boolean containsValue(V value) {
    for (int i = 0; i < capacity; i++) {
      if (table[i] != null) {
        LinkedList<Entry<K, V>> bucket = table[i];
        for (Entry<K, V> entry: bucket)
          if (entry.getValue().equals(value))
            return true;
      }
    }

    return false;
  }

  @Override /** Return a set of entries in the map */
```

entrySet

```
  public java.util.Set<MyMap.Entry<K,V>> entrySet() {
    java.util.Set<MyMap.Entry<K, V>> set =
      new java.util.HashSet<MyMap.Entry<K, V>>();

    for (int i = 0; i < capacity; i++) {
      if (table[i] != null) {
        LinkedList<Entry<K, V>> bucket = table[i];
        for (Entry<K, V> entry: bucket)
          set.add(entry);
      }
    }

    return set;
  }

  @Override /** Return the value that matches the specified key */
```

get

```
  public V get(K key) {
    int bucketIndex = hash(key.hashCode());
    if (table[bucketIndex] != null) {
      LinkedList<Entry<K, V>> bucket = table[bucketIndex];
      for (Entry<K, V> entry: bucket)
        if (entry.getKey().equals(key))
          return entry.getValue();
    }

    return null;
  }

  @Override /** Return true if this map contains no entries */
```

isEmpty

```
  public boolean isEmpty() {
    return size == 0;
  }

  @Override /** Return a set consisting of the keys in this map */
```

keySet

```java
  public java.util.Set<K> keySet() {
    java.util.Set<K> set = new java.util.HashSet<K>();

    for (int i = 0; i < capacity; i++) {
      if (table[i] != null) {
        LinkedList<Entry<K, V>> bucket = table[i];
        for (Entry<K, V> entry: bucket)
          set.add(entry.getKey());
      }
    }

    return set;
  }

  @Override /** Add an entry (key, value) into the map */
```

put

```java
  public V put(K key, V value) {
    if (get(key) != null) { // The key is already in the map
      int bucketIndex = hash(key.hashCode());
      LinkedList<Entry<K, V>> bucket = table[bucketIndex];
      for (Entry<K, V> entry: bucket)
        if (entry.getKey().equals(key)) {
          V oldValue = entry.getValue();
          // Replace old value with new value
          entry.value = value;
          // Return the old value for the key
          return oldValue;
        }
    }

    // Check load factor
    if (size >= capacity * loadFactorThreshold) {
      if (capacity == MAXIMUM_CAPACITY)
        throw new RuntimeException("Exceeding maximum capacity");

      rehash();
    }

    int bucketIndex = hash(key.hashCode());

    // Create a linked list for the bucket if not already created
    if (table[bucketIndex] == null) {
      table[bucketIndex] = new LinkedList<Entry<K, V>>();
    }

    // Add a new entry (key, value) to hashTable[index]
    table[bucketIndex].add(new MyMap.Entry<K, V>(key, value));

    size++; // Increase size

    return value;
  }

  @Override /** Remove the entries for the specified key */
```

remove

```java
  public void remove(K key) {
    int bucketIndex = hash(key.hashCode());

    // Remove the first entry that matches the key from a bucket
    if (table[bucketIndex] != null) {
      LinkedList<Entry<K, V>> bucket = table[bucketIndex];
      for (Entry<K, V> entry: bucket)
```

size values hash supplementalHash trimToPowerOf2 removeEntries rehash

```
          if (entry.getKey().equals(key)) {
            bucket.remove(entry);
            size--; // Decrease size
            break; // Remove just one entry that matches the key
          }
      }
  }

  @Override /** Return the number of entries in this map */
  public int size() {
    return size;
  }

  @Override /** Return a set consisting of the values in this map */
  public java.util.Set<V> values() {
    java.util.Set<V> set = new java.util.HashSet<V>();

    for (int i = 0; i < capacity; i++) {
      if (table[i] != null) {
        LinkedList<Entry<K, V>> bucket = table[i];
        for (Entry<K, V> entry: bucket)
          set.add(entry.getValue());
      }
    }

    return set;
  }

  /** Hash function */
  private int hash(int hashCode) {
    return supplementalHash(hashCode) & (capacity - 1);
  }

  /** Ensure the hashing is evenly distributed */
  private static int supplementalHash(int h) {
    h ^= (h >>> 20) ^ (h >>> 12);
    return h ^ (h >>> 7) ^ (h >>> 4);
  }

  /** Return a power of 2 for initialCapacity */
  private int trimToPowerOf2(int initialCapacity) {
    int capacity = 1;
    while (capacity < initialCapacity) {
      capacity <<= 1; // Same as capacity *= 2. <= is more efficient
    }

    return capacity;
  }

  /** Remove all entries from each bucket */
  private void removeEntries() {
    for (int i = 0; i < capacity; i++) {
      if (table[i] != null) {
        table[i].clear();
      }
    }
  }

  /** Rehash the map */
  private void rehash() {
```

```
231       java.util.Set<Entry<K, V>> set = entrySet(); // Get entries
232       capacity <<= 1; // Same as capacity *= 2. <= is more efficient
233       table = new LinkedList[capacity]; // Create a new hash table
234       size = 0; // Reset size to 0
235 
236       for (Entry<K, V> entry: set) {
237         put(entry.getKey(), entry.getValue()); // Store to new table
238       }
239     }
240 
241     @Override /** Return a string representation for this map */
242     public String toString() {
243       StringBuilder builder = new StringBuilder("[");
244 
245       for (int i = 0; i < capacity; i++) {
246         if (table[i] != null && table[i].size() > 0)
247           for (Entry<K, V> entry: table[i])
248             builder.append(entry);
249       }
250 
251       builder.append("]");
252       return builder.toString();
253     }
254   }
```

toString

hash-table parameters

The **MyHashMap** class implements the **MyMap** interface using separate chaining. The parameters that determine the hash-table size and load factors are defined in the class. The default initial capacity is **4** (line 5) and the maximum capacity is 2^{30} (line 8). The current hash-table capacity is designed as a value of the power of **2** (line 11). The default load-factor threshold is **0.75f** (line 14). You can specify a custom load-factor threshold when constructing a map. The custom load-factor threshold is stored in **loadFactorThreshold** (line 17). The data field **size** denotes the number of entries in the map (line 20). The hash table is an array. Each cell in the array is a linked list (line 23).

three constructors

Three constructors are provided to construct a map. You can construct a default map with the default capacity and load-factor threshold using the no-arg constructor (lines 26–28), a map with the specified capacity and a default load-factor threshold (lines 32–34), and a map with the specified capacity and load-factor threshold (lines 38–46).

clear

The **clear** method removes all entries from the map (lines 49–52). It invokes **removeEntries()**, which deletes all entries in the buckets (lines 221–227). The **removeEntries()** method takes *O*(*capacity*) time to clear all entries in the table.

containsKey

The **containsKey(key)** method checks whether the specified key is in the map by invoking the **get** method (lines 55–60). Since the **get** method takes *O*(1) time, the **containsKey(key)** method takes *O*(1) time.

containsValue

The **containsValue(value)** method checks whether the value is in the map (lines 63–74). This method takes *O*(*capacity* + *size*) time. It is actually *O*(*capacity*), since *capacity* > *size*.

entrySet

The **entrySet()** method returns a set that contains all entries in the map (lines 77–90). This method takes *O*(*capacity*) time.

get

The **get(key)** method returns the value of the first entry with the specified key (lines 93–103). This method takes *O*(1) time.

isEmpty

The **isEmpty()** method simply returns true if the map is empty (lines 106–108). This method takes *O*(1) time.

keySet

The **keySet()** method returns all keys in the map as a set. The method finds the keys from each bucket and adds them to a set (lines 111–123). This method takes *O*(*capacity*) time.

put

The **put(key, value)** method adds a new entry into the map. The method first tests if the key is already in the map (line 127), if so, it locates the entry and replaces the old value with the new value in the entry for the key (line 134) and the old value is returned (line 136). If the key is new in the map, the new entry is created in the map (line 156). Before inserting the new entry, the method checks whether the size exceeds the load-factor threshold (line 141). If so, the program invokes `rehash()` (line 145) to increase the capacity and store entries into the new larger hash table.

rehash

The `rehash()` method first copies all entries in a set (line 231), doubles the capacity (line 232), creates a new hash table (line 233), and resets the size to `0` (line 234). The method then copies the entries into the new hash table (lines 236–238). The `rehash` method takes $O(capacity)$ time. If no rehash is performed, the `put` method takes $O(1)$ time to add a new entry.

remove

The `remove(key)` method removes the entry with the specified key in the map (lines 164–177). This method takes $O(1)$ time.

size

The `size()` method simply returns the size of the map (lines 180–182). This method takes $O(1)$ time.

values

The `values()` method returns all values in the map. The method examines each entry from all buckets and adds it to a set (lines 185–197). This method takes $O(capacity)$ time.

hash

The `hash()` method invokes the `supplementalHash` to ensure that the hashing is evenly distributed to produce an index for the hash table (lines 200–208). This method takes $O(1)$ time.

Table 28.1 summarizes the time complexities of the methods in `MyHashMap`.

TABLE 28.1 Time Complexities for Methods in `MyHashMap`

Methods	*Time*
`clear()`	$O(capacity)$
`containsKey(key: Key)`	$O(1)$
`containsValue(value: V)`	$O(capacity)$
`entrySet()`	$O(capacity)$
`get(key: K)`	$O(1)$
`isEmpty()`	$O(1)$
`keySet()`	$O(capacity)$
`put(key: K, value: V)`	$O(1)$
`remove(key: K)`	$O(1)$
`size()`	$O(1)$
`values()`	$O(capacity)$
`rehash()`	$O(capacity)$

Since rehashing does not happen very often, the time complexity for the `put` method is $O(1)$. Note that the complexities of the `clear`, `entrySet`, `keySet`, `values`, and `rehash` methods depend on `capacity`, so to avoid poor performance for these methods you should choose an initial capacity carefully.

Listing 28.3 gives a test program that uses `MyHashMap`.

Listing 28.4 shows the MySet interface and Listing 28.5 implements MyHashSet using separate chaining.

LISTING 28.4 MySet.java

```
public interface MySet<E> extends java.lang.Iterable<E> {
  /** Remove all elements from this set */
  public void clear();

  /** Return true if the element is in the set */
  public boolean contains(E e);

  /** Add an element to the set */
  public boolean add(E e);

  /** Remove the element from the set */
  public boolean remove(E e);

  /** Return true if the set doesn't contain any elements */
  public boolean isEmpty();

  /** Return the number of elements in the set */
  public int size();

  /** Return an iterator for the elements in this set */
  public java.util.Iterator iterator();
}
```

clear
contains
add
remove
isEmpty
size
iterator

LISTING 28.5 MyHashSet.java

```
import java.util.LinkedList;

public class MyHashSet<E> implements MySet<E> {
  // Define the default hash-table size. Must be a power of 2
  private static int DEFAULT_INITIAL_CAPACITY = 4;

  // Define the maximum hash-table size. 1 << 30 is same as 2^30
  private static int MAXIMUM_CAPACITY = 1 << 30;

  // Current hash-table capacity. Capacity is a power of 2
  private int capacity;

  // Define default load factor
  private static float DEFAULT_MAX_LOAD_FACTOR = 0.75f;

  // Specify a load-factor threshold used in the hash table
  private float loadFactorThreshold;

  // The number of elements in the set
  private int size = 0;

  // Hash table is an array with each cell being a linked list
  private LinkedList<E>[] table;

  /** Construct a set with the default capacity and load factor */
  public MyHashSet() {
    this(DEFAULT_INITIAL_CAPACITY, DEFAULT_MAX_LOAD_FACTOR);
  }

```

class MyHashSet
default initial capacity
maximum capacity
current capacity
default max load factor
load-factor threshold
size
hash table
no-arg constructor

```java
  /** Construct a set with the specified initial capacity and
   * default load factor */
```

constructor

```java
  public MyHashSet(int initialCapacity) {
    this(initialCapacity, DEFAULT_MAX_LOAD_FACTOR);
  }

  /** Construct a set with the specified initial capacity
   * and load factor */
```

constructor

```java
  public MyHashSet(int initialCapacity, float loadFactorThreshold) {
    if (initialCapacity > MAXIMUM_CAPACITY)
      this.capacity = MAXIMUM_CAPACITY;
    else
      this.capacity = trimToPowerOf2(initialCapacity);

    this.loadFactorThreshold = loadFactorThreshold;
    table = new LinkedList[capacity];
  }

  @Override /** Remove all elements from this set */
```

clear

```java
  public void clear() {
    size = 0;
    removeElements();
  }

  @Override /** Return true if the element is in the set */
```

contains

```java
  public boolean contains(E e) {
    int bucketIndex = hash(e.hashCode());
    if (table[bucketIndex] != null) {
      LinkedList<E> bucket = table[bucketIndex];
      for (E element: bucket)
        if (element.equals(e))
          return true;
    }

    return false;
  }

  @Override /** Add an element to the set */
```

add

```java
  public boolean add(E e) {
    if (contains(e)) // Duplicate element not stored
      return false;

    if (size > capacity * loadFactorThreshold) {
      if (capacity == MAXIMUM_CAPACITY)
        throw new RuntimeException("Exceeding maximum capacity");

      rehash();
    }

    int bucketIndex = hash(e.hashCode());

    // Create a linked list for the bucket if not already created
    if (table[bucketIndex] == null) {
      table[bucketIndex] = new LinkedList<E>();
    }

    // Add e to hashTable[index]
    table[bucketIndex].add(e);

    size++; // Increase size
```

```

    return true;
  }

  @Override /** Remove the element from the set */
  public boolean remove(E e) {
    if (!contains(e))
      return false;

    int bucketIndex = hash(e.hashCode());

    // Create a linked list for the bucket if not already created
    if (table[bucketIndex] != null) {
      LinkedList<E> bucket = table[bucketIndex];
      for (E element: bucket)
        if (e.equals(element)) {
          bucket.remove(element);
          break;
        }
    }

    size--; // Decrease size

    return true;
  }

  @Override /** Return true if the set contain no elements */
  public boolean isEmpty() {
    return size == 0;
  }

  @Override /** Return the number of elements in the set */
  public int size() {
    return size;
  }

  @Override /** Return an iterator for the elements in this set */
  public java.util.Iterator<E> iterator() {
    return new MyHashSetIterator(this);
  }

  /** Inner class for iterator */
  private class MyHashSetIterator implements java.util.Iterator<E> {
    // Store the elements in a list
    private java.util.ArrayList<E> list;
    private int current = 0; // Point to the current element in list
    private MyHashSet<E> set;

    /** Create a list from the set */
    public MyHashSetIterator(MyHashSet<E> set) {
      this.set = set;
      list = setToList();
    }

    @Override /** Next element for traversing? */
    public boolean hasNext() {
      if (current < list.size())
        return true;

      return false;
```

remove

isEmpty

size

iterator

inner class

```
    }

    @Override /** Get current element and move cursor to the next */
    public E next() {
      return list.get(current++);
    }

    /** Remove the current element and refresh the list */
    public void remove() {
      // Delete the current element from the hash set
      set.remove(list.get(current));
      list.remove(current); // Remove current element from the list
    }
  }

  /** Hash function */
```

hash

```
  private int hash(int hashCode) {
    return supplementalHash(hashCode) & (capacity - 1);
  }

  /** Ensure the hashing is evenly distributed */
```

supplementalHash

```
  private static int supplementalHash(int h) {
    h ^= (h >>> 20) ^ (h >>> 12);
    return h ^ (h >>> 7) ^ (h >>> 4);
  }

  /** Return a power of 2 for initialCapacity */
```

trimToPowerOf2

```
  private int trimToPowerOf2(int initialCapacity) {
    int capacity = 1;
    while (capacity < initialCapacity) {
      capacity <<= 1; // Same as capacity *= 2. <= is more efficient
    }

    return capacity;
  }

  /** Remove all e from each bucket */
  private void removeElements() {
    for (int i = 0; i < capacity; i++) {
      if (table[i] != null) {
        table[i].clear();
      }
    }
  }

  /** Rehash the set */
```

rehash

```
  private void rehash() {
    java.util.ArrayList<E> list = setToList(); // Copy to a list
    capacity <<= 1; // Same as capacity *= 2. <= is more efficient
    table = new LinkedList[capacity]; // Create a new hash table
    size = 0;

    for (E element: list) {
      add(element); // Add from the old table to the new table
    }
  }

  /** Copy elements in the hash set to an array list */
```

setToList

```
  private java.util.ArrayList<E> setToList() {
    java.util.ArrayList<E> list = new java.util.ArrayList<E>();
```

```
210
211     for (int i = 0; i < capacity; i++) {
212       if (table[i] != null) {
213         for (E e: table[i]) {
214           list.add(e);
215         }
216       }
217     }
218
219     return list;
220   }
221
222   @Override /** Return a string representation for this set */
223   public String toString() {
224     java.util.ArrayList<E> list = setToList();
225     StringBuilder builder = new StringBuilder("[");
226
227     // Add the elements except the last one to the string builder
228     for (int i = 0; i < list.size() - 1; i++) {
229       builder.append(list.get(i) + ", ");
230     }
231
232     // Add the last element in the list to the string builder
233     if (list.size() == 0)
234       builder.append("]");
235     else
236       builder.append(list.get(list.size() - 1) + "]");
237
238     return builder.toString();
239   }
240 }
```

toString

MyHashSet vs. MyHashMap

The **MyHashSet** class implements the **MySet** interface using separate chaining. Implementing **MyHashSet** is very similar to implementing **MyHashMap** except for the following differences:

1. The elements are stored in the hash table for **MyHashSet**, but the entries (key/value pairs) are stored in the hash table for **MyHashMap**.
2. **MySet** extends **java.lang.Iterable** and **MyHashSet** implements **MySet** and overrides **iterator()**. So the elements in **MyHashSet** are iterable.

three constructors

Three constructors are provided to construct a set. You can construct a default set with the default capacity and load factor using the no-arg constructor (lines 26–28), a set with the specified capacity and a default load factor (lines 32–34), and a set with the specified capacity and load factor (lines 38–46).

clear

The **clear** method removes all elements from the set (lines 49–52). It invokes **removeElements()**, which clears all table cells (line 190). Each table cell is a linked list that stores the elements with the same hash code. The **removeElements()** method takes $O(capacity)$ time.

contains

The **contains(element)** method checks whether the specified element is in the set by examining whether the designated bucket contains the element (lines 55–65). This method takes $O(1)$ time.

add

The **add(element)** method adds a new element into the set. The method first checks if the element is already in the set (line 69). If so, the method returns false. The method then checks whether the size exceeds the load-factor threshold (line 72). If so, the program invokes **rehash()** (line 76) to increase the capacity and store elements into the new larger hash table.

rehash

The **rehash()** method first copies all elements in a list (line 197), doubles the capacity (line 198), obtains a new threshold (line 198), creates a new hash table (line 199), and resets the size to `0` (line 200). The method then copies the elements into the new larger hash table (lines 202–204). The `rehash` method takes *O*(*capacity*) time. If no rehash is performed, the `add` method takes *O*(1) time to add a new element.

remove

The `remove(element)` method removes the specified element in the set (lines 95–114). This method takes *O*(1) time.

size

The `size()` method simply returns the number of elements in the set (lines 122–124). This method takes *O*(1) time.

iterator

The `iterator()` method returns an instance of `java.util.Iterator`. The `MyHashSetIterator` class implements `java.util.Iterator` to create a forward iterator. When a `MyHashSetIterator` is constructed, it copies all the elements in the set to a list (line 141). The variable `current` points to the element in the list. Initially, `current` is `0` (line 135), which points to the first element in the list. `MyHashSetIterator` implements the methods `hasNext()`, `next()`, and `remove()` in `java.util.Iterator`. Invoking `hasNext()` returns true if `current < list.size()`. Invoking `next()` returns the current element and moves `current` to point to the next element (line 153). Invoking `remove()` removes the current element in the iterator from the set.

hash

The `hash()` method invokes the `supplementalHash` to ensure that the hashing is evenly distributed to produce an index for the hash table (lines 166–174). This method takes *O*(1) time.

Table 28.2 summarizes the time complexity of the methods in `MyHashSet`.

Table 28.2 Time Complexities for Methods in `MyHashSet`

Methods	*Time*
`clear()`	*O*(*capacity*)
`contains(e: E)`	*O*(1)
`add(e: E)`	*O*(1)
`remove(e: E)`	*O*(1)
`isEmpty()`	*O*(1)
`size()`	*O*(1)
`iterator()`	*O*(*capacity*)
`rehash()`	*O*(*capacity*)

Listing 28.6 gives a test program that uses `MyHashSet`.

Listing 28.6 TestMyHashSet.java

create a set
add elements
display elements
set size

```
public class TestMyHashSet {
  public static void main(String[] args) {
    // Create a MyHashSet
    MySet<String> set = new MyHashSet<String>();
    set.add("Smith");
    set.add("Anderson");
    set.add("Lewis");
    set.add("Cook");
    set.add("Smith");

    System.out.println("Elements in set: " + set);
    System.out.println("Number of elements in set: " + set.size());
    System.out.println("Is Smith in set? " + set.contains("Smith"));
```

```
14
15     set.remove("Smith");
16     System.out.print("Names in set in uppercase are ");
17     for (String s: set)
18       System.out.print(s.toUpperCase() + " ");
19
20     set.clear();
21     System.out.println("\nElements in set: " + set);
22   }
23 }
```

remove element

for-each loop

clear set

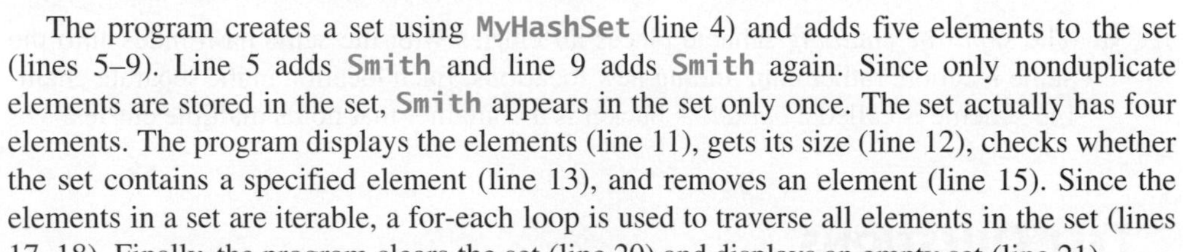

```
Elements in set: [Cook, Anderson, Smith, Lewis]
Number of elements in set: 4
Is Smith in set? true
Names in set in uppercase are COOK ANDERSON LEWIS
Elements in set: []
```

The program creates a set using `MyHashSet` (line 4) and adds five elements to the set (lines 5–9). Line 5 adds `Smith` and line 9 adds `Smith` again. Since only nonduplicate elements are stored in the set, `Smith` appears in the set only once. The set actually has four elements. The program displays the elements (line 11), gets its size (line 12), checks whether the set contains a specified element (line 13), and removes an element (line 15). Since the elements in a set are iterable, a for-each loop is used to traverse all elements in the set (lines 17–18). Finally, the program clears the set (line 20) and displays an empty set (line 21).

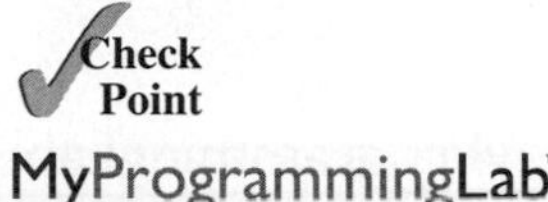

28.25 Why can you use a for-each loop to traverse the elements in a set?

28.26 Describe how the `add(e)` method is implemented in the `MyHashSet` class.

28.27 In Listing 28.5, the `remove` method in the iterator removes the current element from the set. It also removes the current element from the internal list (line 161):

```
list.remove(current); // Remove current element from the list
```

Is this necessary?

Key Terms

associative array 998
cluster 1002
dictionary 998
double hashing 1003
hash code 999
hash function 998
hash map 1016
hash set 1016
hash table 998
linear probing 1001
load factor 1005
open addressing 1001
perfect hash function 998
polynomial hash code 1000
quadratic probing 1002
rehashing 1005
secondary clustering 1003
separate chaining 1005

Chapter Summary

1. A *map* is a data structure that stores entries. Each entry contains two parts: a *key* and a *value*. The key is also called a *search key*, which is used to search for the corresponding value. You can implement a map to obtain $O(1)$ time complexity on searching, retrieval, insertion, and deletion using the hashing technique.

2. A *set* is a data structure that stores elements. You can use the hashing technique to implement a set to achieve $O(1)$ time complexity on searching, insertion, and deletion for a set.

3. *Hashing* is a technique that retrieves the value using the index obtained from a key without performing a search. A typical *hash function* first converts a search key to an integer value called a *hash code*, then compresses the hash code into an index to the *hash table*.

4. A *collision* occurs when two keys are mapped to the same index in a hash table. Generally, there are two ways for handling collisions: *open addressing* and *separate chaining*.

5. Open addressing is the process of finding an open location in the hash table in the event of collision. Open addressing has several variations: *linear probing*, *quadratic probing*, and *double hashing*.

6. The *separate chaining* scheme places all entries with the same hash index into the same location, rather than finding new locations. Each location in the separate chaining scheme is called a *bucket*. A bucket is a container that holds multiple entries.

Test Questions

Do the test questions for this chapter online at www.cs.armstrong.edu/liang/intro9e/test.html.

MyProgrammingLab™

Programming Exercises

****28.1** (*Implement `MyMap` using open addressing with linear probing*) Create a new concrete class that implements `MyMap` using open addressing with linear probing. For simplicity, use `f(key) = key % size` as the hash function, where size is the hash-table size. Initially, the hash-table size is `4`. The table size is doubled whenever the load factor exceeds the threshold (`0.5`).

****28.2** (*Implement `MyMap` using open addressing with quadratic probing*) Create a new concrete class that implements `MyMap` using open addressing with quadratic probing. For simplicity, use `f(key) = key % size` as the hash function, where `size` is the hash-table size. Initially, the hash-table size is `4`. The table size is doubled whenever the load factor exceeds the threshold (`0.5`).

****28.3** (*Implement `MyMap` using open addressing with double hashing*) Create a new concrete class that implements `MyMap` using open addressing with double hashing. For simplicity, use `f(key) = key % size` as the hash function, where `size` is the hash-table size. Initially, the hash-table size is `4`. The table size is doubled whenever the load factor exceeds the threshold (`0.5`).

****28.4** (*Modify `MyHashMap` with duplicate keys*) Modify `MyHashMap` to allow duplicate keys for entries. You need to modify the implementation for the `put(key, value)` method. Also add a new method named `getAll(key)` that returns a set of values that match the key in the map.

****28.5** (*Implement `MyHashSet` using `MyHashMap`*) Implement `MyHashSet` using `MyHashMap`. Note that you can create entries with (`key, key`), rather than (`key, value`).

****28.6** (*Animate linear probing*) Write a Java applet that animates linear probing, as shown in Figure 28.3. You can change the initial size of the hash-table in the applet. Assume the load-factor threshold is `0.75`.

****28.7** (*Animate separate chaining*) Write a Java applet that animates `MyHashMap`, as shown in Figure 28.8. You can change the initial size of the table. Assume the load-factor threshold is `0.75`.

****28.8** (*Animate quadratic probing*) Write a Java applet that animates quadratic probing, as shown in Figure 28.5. You can change the initial size of the hash-table in the applet. Assume the load-factor threshold is `0.75`.

****28.9** (*Compare `MyHashSet` and `MyArrayList`*) `MyArrayList` is defined in Listing 26.3. Write a program that generates `1000000` random integers between `0` and `999999`, shuffles them, and stores them in a `MyArrayList` and in a `MyHashSet`. Generate a list of `1000000` random integers between `0` and `1999999`. For each number in the list, test if it is in the array list and in the hash set. Run your program to display the total test time for the array list and for the hash set.

CHAPTER 29

AVL TREES

Objectives

- To know what an AVL tree is (§29.1).
- To understand how to rebalance a tree using the LL rotation, LR rotation, RR rotation, and RL rotation (§29.2).
- To design the `AVLTree` class by extending the `BST` class (§29.3).
- To insert elements into an AVL tree (§29.4).
- To implement tree rebalancing (§29.5).
- To delete elements from an AVL tree (§29.6).
- To implement the `AVLTree` class (§29.7).
- To test the `AVLTree` class (§29.8).
- To analyze the complexity of search, insertion, and deletion operations in AVL trees (§29.9).

29.1 Introduction

AVL Tree is a balanced binary search tree.

perfectly balanced tree

well-balanced tree

Chapter 27 introduced binary search trees. The search, insertion, and deletion times for a binary tree depend on the height of the tree. In the worst case, the height is $O(n)$. If a tree is *perfectly balanced*–i.e., a complete binary tree—its height is log n. Can we maintain a perfectly balanced tree? Yes, but doing so will be costly. The compromise is to maintain a *well-balanced tree*—that is, the heights of every node's two subtrees are about the same. This chapter introduces AVL trees. Web Chapters 47 and 48 introduce 2-4 trees and red-black trees.

AVL tree

$O(\log n)$

AVL trees are well balanced. AVL trees were invented in 1962 by two Russian computer scientists, G. M. Adelson-Velsky and E. M. Landis (hence the name *AVL*). In an AVL tree, the difference between the heights of every node's two subtrees is 0 or 1. It can be shown that the maximum height of an AVL tree is $O(\log n)$.

balance factor

balanced

left-heavy

right-heavy

The process for inserting or deleting an element in an AVL tree is the same as in a regular binary search tree, except that you may have to rebalance the tree after an insertion or deletion operation. The *balance factor* of a node is the height of its right subtree minus the height of its left subtree. A node is said to be *balanced* if its balance factor is -1, 0, or 1. A node is considered *left-heavy* if its balance factor is -1, and *right-heavy* if its balance factor is +1.

AVL tree animation on Companion Website

Pedagogical Note

For an interactive GUI demo to see how an AVL tree works, go to www.cs.armstrong.edu/liang/animation/AVLTreeAnimation.html, as shown in Figure 29.1.

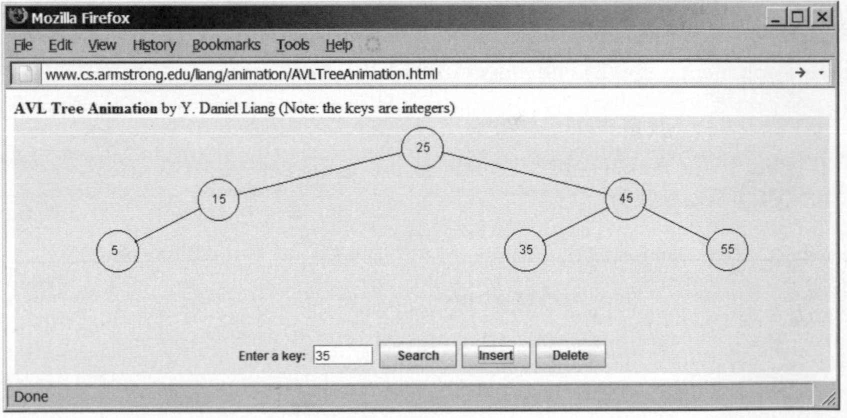

FIGURE 29.1 The animation tool enables you to insert, delete, and search elements.

29.2 Rebalancing Trees

After inserting or deleting an element from an AVL tree, if the tree becomes unbalanced, perform a rotation operation to rebalance the tree.

rotation

If a node is not balanced after an insertion or deletion operation, you need to rebalance it. The process of rebalancing a node is called *rotation*. There are four possible rotations: LL, RR, LR, and RL.

LL rotation

LL imbalance

LL rotation: An *LL imbalance* occurs at a node A, such that A has a balance factor of -2 and a left child B with a balance factor of -1 or 0, as shown in Figure 29.2a. This type of imbalance can be fixed by performing a single right rotation at A, as shown in Figure 29.2b.

RR rotation

RR imbalance

RR rotation: An *RR imbalance* occurs at a node A, such that A has a balance factor of +2 and a right child B with a balance factor of +1 or 0, as shown in Figure 29.3a. This

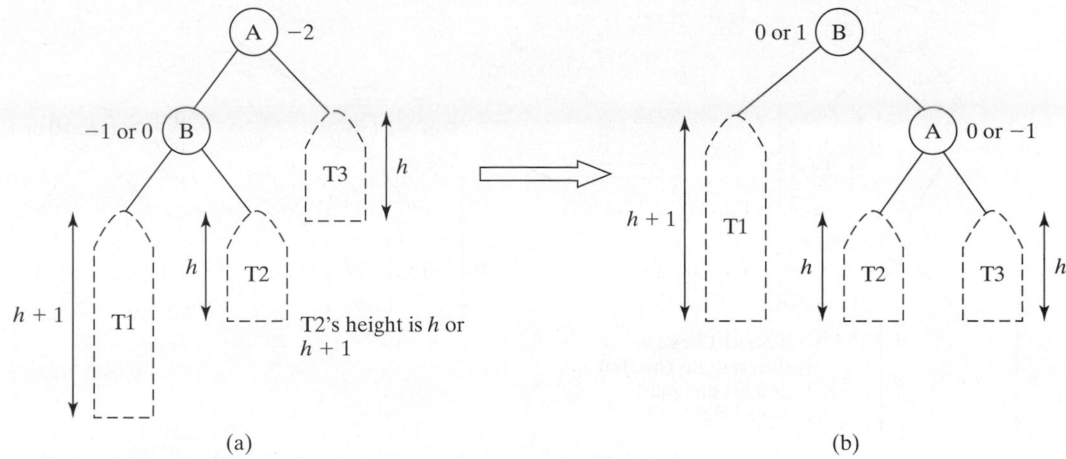

FIGURE 29.2 An LL rotation fixes an LL imbalance.

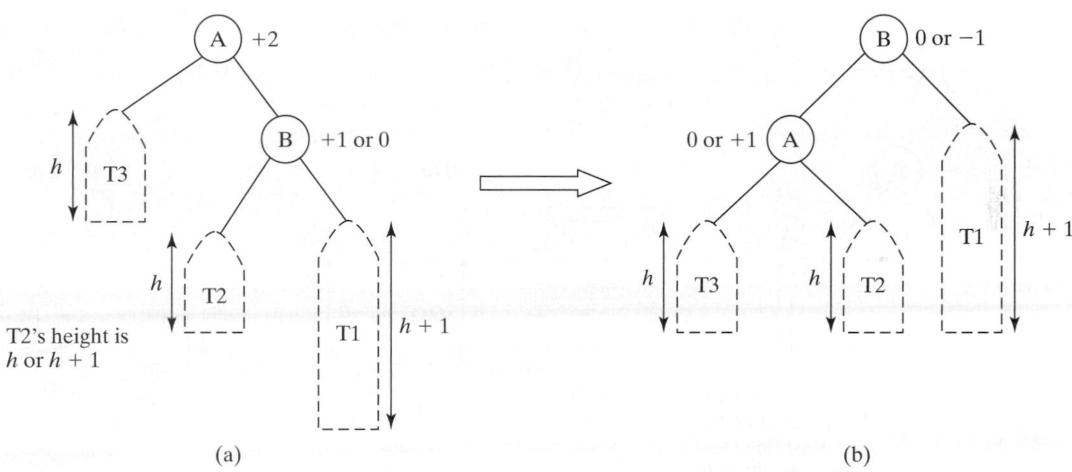

FIGURE 29.3 An RR rotation fixes an RR imbalance.

type of imbalance can be fixed by performing a single left rotation at A, as shown in Figure 29.3b.

LR rotation
LR imbalance

LR rotation: An *LR imbalance* occurs at a node A, such that A has a balance factor of -2 and a left child B with a balance factor of +1, as shown in Figure 29.4a. Assume B's right child is C. This type of imbalance can be fixed by performing a double rotation at A (first a single left rotation at B and then a single right rotation at A), as shown in Figure 29.4b.

RL rotation
RL imbalance

RL rotation: An *RL imbalance* occurs at a node A, such that A has a balance factor of +2 and a right child B with a balance factor of -1, as shown in Figure 29.5a. Assume B's left child is C. This type of imbalance can be fixed by performing a double rotation at A (first a single right rotation at B and then a single left rotation at A), as shown in Figure 29.5b.

29.1 What is an AVL tree? Describe the following terms: balance factor, left-heavy, and right-heavy.

29.2 Show the balance factor of each node in the trees shown in Figure 29.6.

29.3 Describe LL rotation, RR rotation, LR rotation, and RL rotation for an AVL tree.

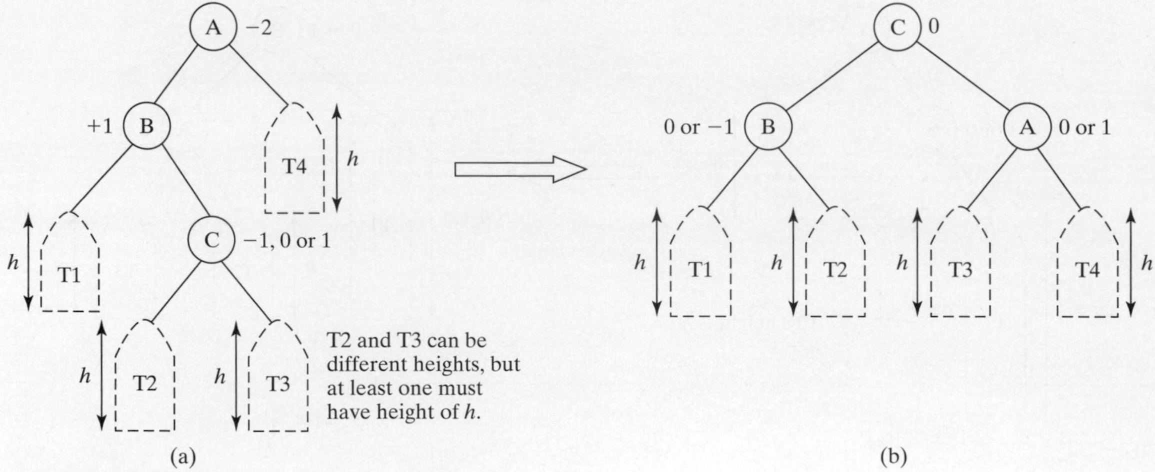

FIGURE 29.4 An LR rotation fixes an LR imbalance.

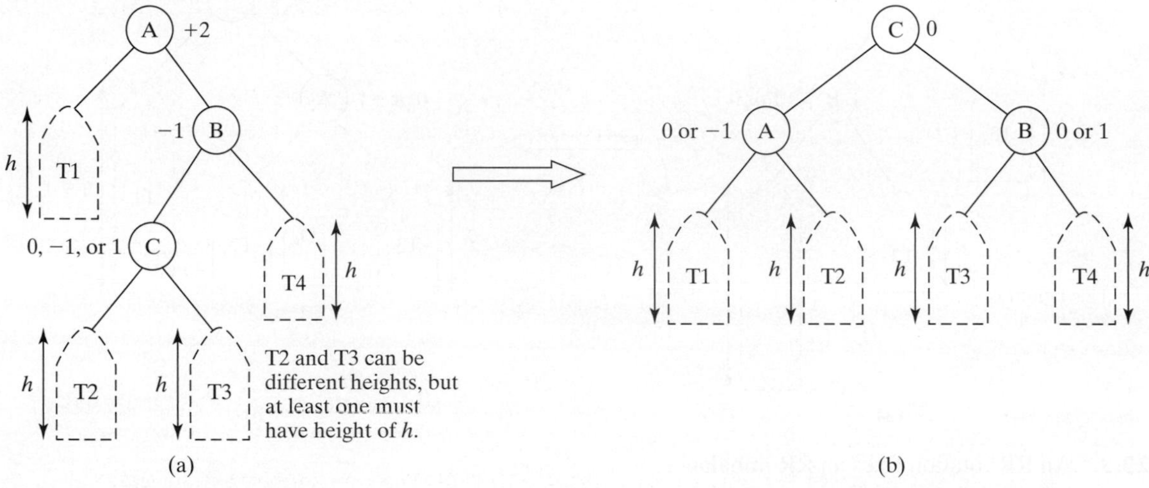

FIGURE 29.5 An RL rotation fixes an RL imbalance.

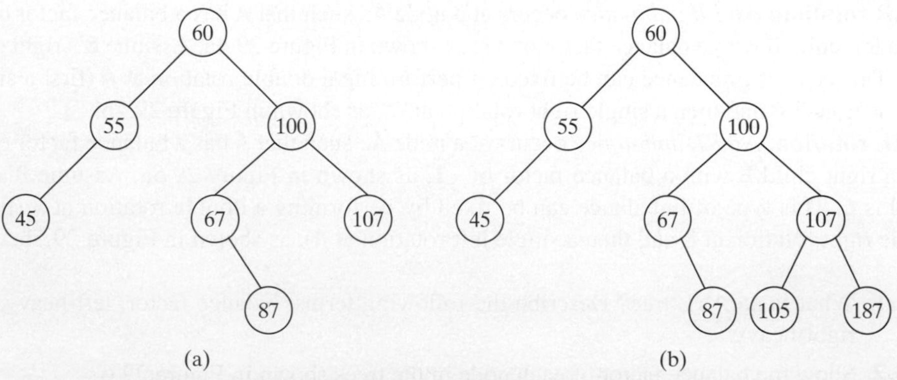

FIGURE 29.6 A balance factor determines whether a node is balanced.

29.3 Designing Classes for AVL Trees

Since an AVL tree is a binary search tree, `AVLTree` *is designed as a subclass of* `BST`.

An AVL tree is a binary tree, so you can define the `AVLTree` class to extend the `BST` class, as shown in Figure 29.7. The `BST` and `TreeNode` classes are defined in Section 27.2.5.

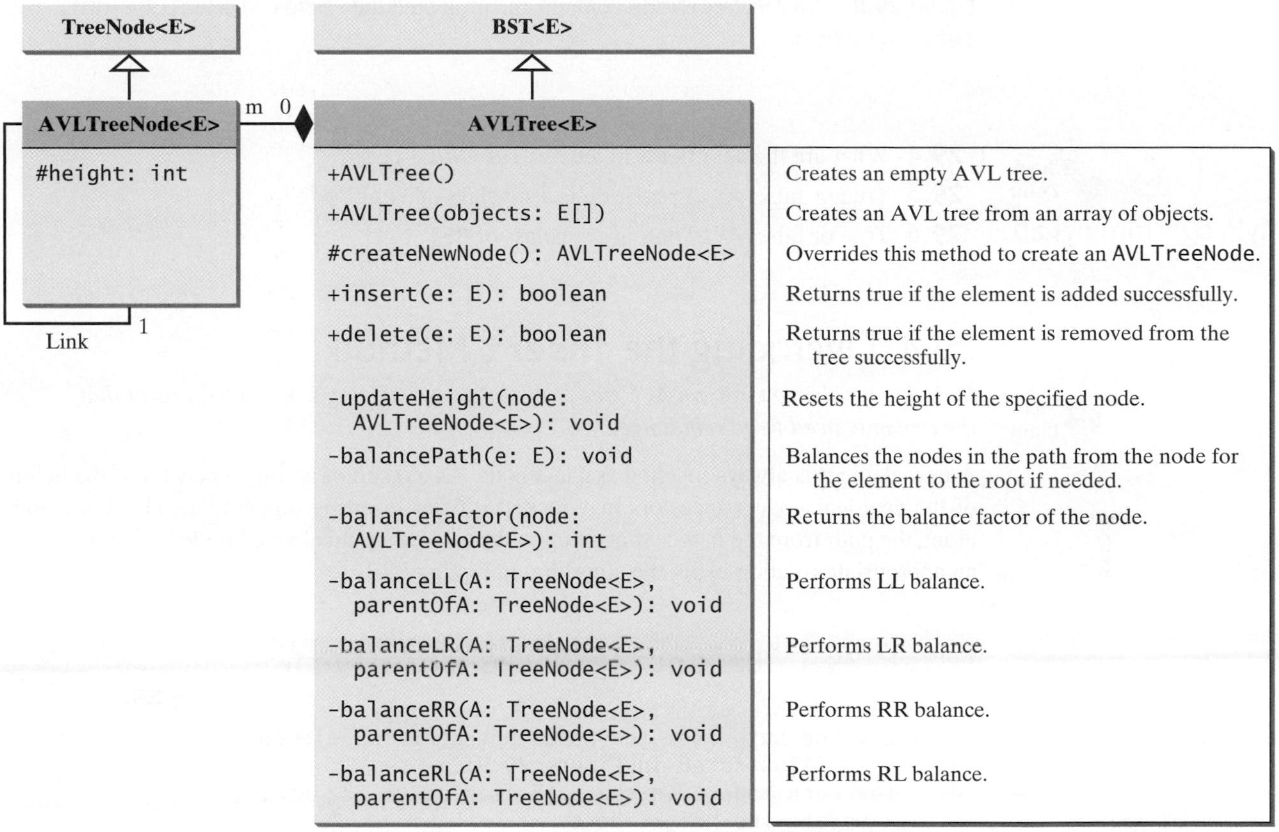

TreeNode<E> ← AVLTreeNode<E> (m — 0, composition with AVLTree<E>; Link 1)

BST<E> ← AVLTree<E>

AVLTreeNode<E>
#height: int

AVLTree<E>	
+AVLTree()	Creates an empty AVL tree.
+AVLTree(objects: E[])	Creates an AVL tree from an array of objects.
#createNewNode(): AVLTreeNode<E>	Overrides this method to create an `AVLTreeNode`.
+insert(e: E): boolean	Returns true if the element is added successfully.
+delete(e: E): boolean	Returns true if the element is removed from the tree successfully.
-updateHeight(node: AVLTreeNode<E>): void	Resets the height of the specified node.
-balancePath(e: E): void	Balances the nodes in the path from the node for the element to the root if needed.
-balanceFactor(node: AVLTreeNode<E>): int	Returns the balance factor of the node.
-balanceLL(A: TreeNode<E>, parentOfA: TreeNode<E>): void	Performs LL balance.
-balanceLR(A: TreeNode<E>, parentOfA: TreeNode<E>): void	Performs LR balance.
-balanceRR(A: TreeNode<E>, parentOfA: TreeNode<E>): void	Performs RR balance.
-balanceRL(A: TreeNode<E>, parentOfA: TreeNode<E>): void	Performs RL balance.

FIGURE 29.7 The `AVLTree` class extends `BST` with new implementations for the `insert` and `delete` methods.

In order to balance the tree, you need to know each node's height. For convenience, store the height of each node in `AVLTreeNode` and define `AVLTreeNode` to be a subclass of `BST.TreeNode`. Note that `TreeNode` is defined as a static inner class in `BST`. `AVLTreeNode` will be defined as a static inner class in `AVLTree`. `TreeNode` contains the data fields `element`, `left`, and `right`, which are inherited by `AVLTreeNode`. Thus, `AVLTreeNode` contains four data fields, as shown in Figure 29.8. AVLTreeNode

In the `BST` class, the `createNewNode()` method creates a `TreeNode` object. This method is overridden in the `AVLTree` class to create an `AVLTreeNode`. Note that the return type of the `createNewNode()` method in the `BST` class is `TreeNode`, but the return type of the `createNewNode()` method in the `AVLTree` class is `AVLTreeNode`. This is fine, since `AVLTreeNode` is a subclass of `TreeNode`. createNewNode()

Searching for an element in an `AVLTree` is the same as searching in a regular binary tree, so the `search` method defined in the `BST` class also works for `AVLTree`.

The `insert` and `delete` methods are overridden to insert and delete an element and perform rebalancing operations if necessary to ensure that the tree is balanced.

node: AVLTreeNode<E>
#element: E #height: int #left: TreeNode<E> #right: TreeNode<E>

FIGURE 29.8 An `AVLTreeNode` contains the protected data fields `element`, `height`, `left`, and `right`.

Check Point
MyProgrammingLab™

29.4 What are the data fields in the `AVLTreeNode` class?

29.5 True or false: `AVLTreeNode` is a subclass of `TreeNode`?

29.6 True or false: `AVLTree` is a subclass of `BST`.

29.4 Overriding the `insert` Method

Key Point

Inserting an element into an AVL tree is the same as inserting it to a BST, except that the tree may need to be rebalanced.

A new element is always inserted as a leaf node. As a result of adding a new node, the heights of the new leaf node's ancestors may increase. After inserting a new node, check the nodes along the path from the new leaf node up to the root. If an unbalanced node is found, perform an appropriate rotation using the algorithm in Listing 29.1.

LISTING 29.1 Balancing Nodes on a Path

```
balancePath(E e) {
  Get the path from the node that contains element e to the root,
    as illustrated in Figure 29.9;
  for each node A in the path leading to the root {
    Update the height of A;
    Let parentOfA denote the parent of A,
      which is the next node in the path, or null if A is the root;

    switch (balanceFactor(A)) {
      case -2: if balanceFactor(A.left) == -1 or 0
                 Perform LL rotation; // See Figure 29.2
               else
                 Perform LR rotation; // See Figure 29.4
               break;
      case +2: if balanceFactor(A.right) == +1 or 0
                 Perform RR rotation; // See Figure 29.3
               else
                 Perform RL rotation; // See Figure 29.5
    } // End of switch
  } // End of for
} // End of method
```

The algorithm considers each node in the path from the new leaf node to the root. Update the height of the node on the path. If a node is balanced, no action is needed. If a node is not balanced, perform an appropriate rotation.

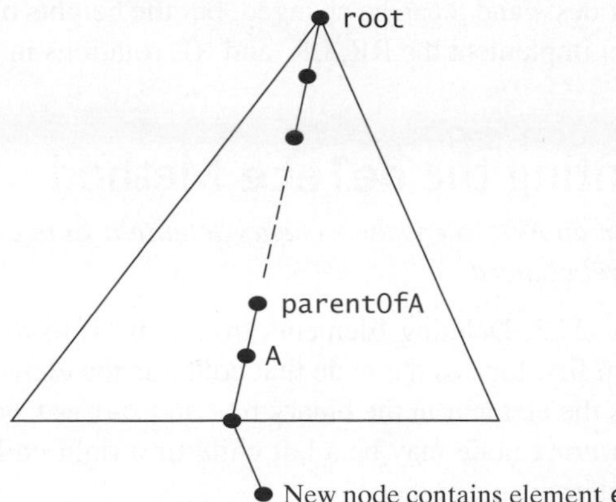

FIGURE 29.9 The nodes along the path from the new leaf node may become unbalanced.

Check Point
MyProgrammingLab™

29.7 For the AVL tree in Figure 29.6a, show the new AVL tree after adding element 40. What rotation do you perform in order to rebalance the tree? Which node was unbalanced?

29.8 For the AVL tree in Figure 29.6a, show the new AVL tree after adding element 50. What rotation do you perform in order to rebalance the tree? Which node was unbalanced?

29.9 For the AVL tree in Figure 29.6a, show the new AVL tree after adding element 80. What rotation do you perform in order to rebalance the tree? Which node was unbalanced?

29.10 For the AVL tree in Figure 29.6a, show the new AVL tree after adding element 89. What rotation do you perform in order to rebalance the tree? Which node was unbalanced?

29.5 Implementing Rotations

Key Point

An unbalanced tree becomes balanced by performing an appropriate rotation operation.

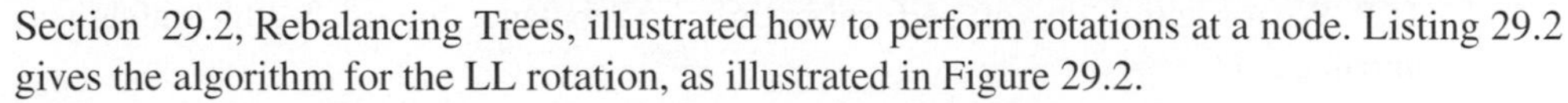

Section 29.2, Rebalancing Trees, illustrated how to perform rotations at a node. Listing 29.2 gives the algorithm for the LL rotation, as illustrated in Figure 29.2.

LISTING 29.2 LL Rotation Algorithm

```
balanceLL(TreeNode A, TreeNode parentOfA) {
  Let B be the left child of A.

  if (A is the root)
    Let B be the new root
  else {
    if (A is a left child of parentOfA)
      Let B be a left child of parentOfA;
    else
      Let B be a right child of parentOfA;
  }

  Make T2 the left subtree of A by assigning B.right to A.left;
  Make A the right child of B by assigning A to B.right;
  Update the height of node A and node B;
} // End of method
```

left child of A

reconnect B's parent

move subtrees

adjust height

Note that the height of nodes A and B can be changed, but the heights of other nodes in the tree are not changed. You can implement the RR, LR, and RL rotations in a similar manner.

29.6 Implementing the delete Method

Deleting an element from an AVL tree is the same as deleing it from a BST, except that the tree may need to be rebalanced.

As discussed in Section 27.3, Deleting Elements from a BST, to delete an element from a binary tree, the algorithm first locates the node that contains the element. Let current point to the node that contains the element in the binary tree and parent point to the parent of the current node. The current node may be a left child or a right child of the parent node. Two cases arise when deleting an element.

Case 1: The current node does not have a left child, as shown in Figure 27.10a. To delete the current node, simply connect the parent node with the right child of the current node, as shown in Figure 27.10b.

The height of the nodes along the path from the parent node up to the root may have decreased. To ensure that the tree is balanced, invoke

```
balancePath(parent.element); // Defined in Listing 29.1
```

Case 2: The current node has a left child. Let rightMost point to the node that contains the largest element in the left subtree of the current node and parentOfRightMost point to the parent node of the rightMost node, as shown in Figure 27.12a. The rightMost node cannot have a right child but it may have a left child. Replace the element value in the current node with the one in the rightMost node, connect the parentOfRightMost node with the left child of the rightMost node, and delete the rightMost node, as shown in Figure 27.12b.

The height of the nodes along the path from parentOfRightMost up to the root may have decreased. To ensure that the tree is balanced, invoke

```
balancePath(parentOfRightMost); // Defined in Listing 29.1
```

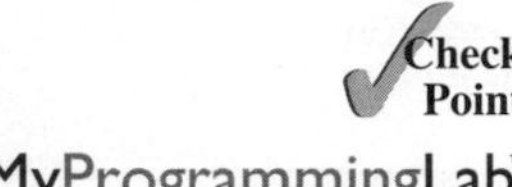

29.11 For the AVL tree in Figure 29.6a, show the new AVL tree after deleting element 107. What rotation do you perform in order to rebalance the tree? Which node was unbalanced?

29.12 For the AVL tree in Figure 29.6a, show the new AVL tree after deleting element 60. What rotation do you perform in order to rebalance the tree? Which node was unbalanced?

29.13 For the AVL tree in Figure 29.6a, show the new AVL tree after deleting element 55. What rotation did you perform in order to rebalance the tree? Which node was unbalanced?

29.14 For the AVL tree in Figure 29.6b, show the new AVL tree after deleting elements 67 and 87. What rotation did you perform in order to rebalance the tree? Which node was unbalanced?

29.7 The AVLTree Class

The AVLTree class extends the BST class to override the insert and delete methods to rebalance the tree if necessary.

Listing 29.3 gives the complete source code for the AVLTree class.

LISTING 29.3 AVLTree.java

```
public class AVLTree<E extends Comparable<E>> extends BST<E> {
  /** Create an empty AVL tree */
  public AVLTree() {
  }

  /** Create an AVL tree from an array of objects */
  public AVLTree(E[] objects) {
    super(objects);
  }

  @Override /** Override createNewNode to create an AVLTreeNode */
  protected AVLTreeNode<E> createNewNode(E e) {
    return new AVLTreeNode<E>(e);
  }

  @Override /** Insert an element and rebalance if necessary */
  public boolean insert(E e) {
    boolean successful = super.insert(e);
    if (!successful)
      return false; // e is already in the tree
    else {
      balancePath(e); // Balance from e to the root if necessary
    }

    return true; // e is inserted
  }

  /** Update the height of a specified node */
  private void updateHeight(AVLTreeNode<E> node) {
    if (node.left == null && node.right == null) // node is a leaf
      node.height = 0;
    else if (node.left == null) // node has no left subtree
      node.height = 1 + ((AVLTreeNode<E>)(node.right)).height;
    else if (node.right == null) // node has no right subtree
      node.height = 1 + ((AVLTreeNode<E>)(node.left)).height;
    else
      node.height = 1 +
        Math.max(((AVLTreeNode<E>)(node.right)).height,
        ((AVLTreeNode<E>)(node.left)).height);
  }

  /** Balance the nodes in the path from the specified
   * node to the root if necessary
   */
  private void balancePath(E e) {
    java.util.ArrayList<TreeNode<E>> path = path(e);
    for (int i = path.size() - 1; i >= 0; i--) {
      AVLTreeNode<E> A = (AVLTreeNode<E>)(path.get(i));
      updateHeight(A);
      AVLTreeNode<E> parentOfA = (A == root) ? null :
        (AVLTreeNode<E>)(path.get(i - 1));

      switch (balanceFactor(A)) {
        case -2:
          if (balanceFactor((AVLTreeNode<E>)A.left) <= 0) {
            balanceLL(A, parentOfA); // Perform LL rotation
          }
          else {
```

no-arg constructor

constructor

create AVL tree node

override insert

balance tree

update node height

balance nodes

get path

consider a node

update height

get height

left-heavy

LL rotation

```
        balanceLR(A, parentOfA); // Perform LR rotation
      }
      break;
    case +2:
      if (balanceFactor((AVLTreeNode<E>)A.right) >= 0) {
        balanceRR(A, parentOfA); // Perform RR rotation
      }
      else {
        balanceRL(A, parentOfA); // Perform RL rotation
      }
    }
  }
}

/** Return the balance factor of the node */
private int balanceFactor(AVLTreeNode<E> node) {
  if (node.right == null) // node has no right subtree
    return -node.height;
  else if (node.left == null) // node has no left subtree
    return +node.height;
  else
    return ((AVLTreeNode<E>)node.right).height -
      ((AVLTreeNode<E>)node.left).height;
}

/** Balance LL (see Figure 29.2) */
private void balanceLL(TreeNode<E> A, TreeNode<E> parentOfA) {
  TreeNode<E> B = A.left; // A is left-heavy and B is left-heavy

  if (A == root) {
    root = B;
  }
  else {
    if (parentOfA.left == A) {
      parentOfA.left = B;
    }
    else {
      parentOfA.right = B;
    }
  }

  A.left = B.right; // Make T2 the left subtree of A
  B.right = A; // Make A the left child of B
  updateHeight((AVLTreeNode<E>)A);
  updateHeight((AVLTreeNode<E>)B);
}

/** Balance LR (see Figure 29.4) */
private void balanceLR(TreeNode<E> A, TreeNode<E> parentOfA) {
  TreeNode<E> B = A.left; // A is left-heavy
  TreeNode<E> C = B.right; // B is right-heavy

  if (A == root) {
    root = C;
  }
  else {
    if (parentOfA.left == A) {
      parentOfA.left = C;
    }
    else {
```

```
          parentOfA.right = C;
        }
      }

      A.left = C.right; // Make T3 the left subtree of A
      B.right = C.left; // Make T2 the right subtree of B
      C.left = B;
      C.right = A;

      // Adjust heights
```

update height

```
      updateHeight((AVLTreeNode<E>)A);
      updateHeight((AVLTreeNode<E>)B);
      updateHeight((AVLTreeNode<E>)C);
    }

    /** Balance RR (see Figure 29.3) */
```

RR rotation

```
    private void balanceRR(TreeNode<E> A, TreeNode<E> parentOfA) {
      TreeNode<E> B = A.right; // A is right-heavy and B is right-heavy

      if (A == root) {
        root = B;
      }
      else {
        if (parentOfA.left == A) {
          parentOfA.left = B;
        }
        else {
          parentOfA.right = B;
        }
      }

      A.right = B.left; // Make T2 the right subtree of A
      B.left = A;
```

update height

```
      updateHeight((AVLTreeNode<E>)A);
      updateHeight((AVLTreeNode<E>)B);
    }

    /** Balance RL (see Figure 29.5) */
```

RL rotation

```
    private void balanceRL(TreeNode<E> A, TreeNode<E> parentOfA) {
      TreeNode<E> B = A.right; // A is right-heavy
      TreeNode<E> C = B.left; // B is left-heavy

      if (A == root) {
        root = C;
      }
      else {
        if (parentOfA.left == A) {
          parentOfA.left = C;
        }
        else {
          parentOfA.right = C;
        }
      }

      A.right = C.left; // Make T2 the right subtree of A
      B.left = C.right; // Make T3 the left subtree of B
      C.left = A;
      C.right = B;

      // Adjust heights
```

update height

```
    updateHeight((AVLTreeNode<E>)A);
    updateHeight((AVLTreeNode<E>)B);
    updateHeight((AVLTreeNode<E>)C);
  }

  @Override /** Delete an element from the AVL tree.
   * Return true if the element is deleted successfully
   * Return false if the element is not in the tree */
```

override delete

```
  public boolean delete(E element) {
    if (root == null)
      return false; // Element is not in the tree

    // Locate the node to be deleted and also locate its parent node
    TreeNode<E> parent = null;
    TreeNode<E> current = root;
    while (current != null) {
      if (element.compareTo(current.element) < 0) {
        parent = current;
        current = current.left;
      }
      else if (element.compareTo(current.element) > 0) {
        parent = current;
        current = current.right;
      }
      else
        break; // Element is in the tree pointed by current
    }

    if (current == null)
      return false; // Element is not in the tree

    // Case 1: current has no left children (See Figure 27.10)
    if (current.left == null) {
      // Connect the parent with the right child of the current node
      if (parent == null) {
        root = current.right;
      }
      else {
        if (element.compareTo(parent.element) < 0)
          parent.left = current.right;
        else
          parent.right = current.right;

        // Balance the tree if necessary
```

balance nodes

```
        balancePath(parent.element);
      }
    }
    else {
      // Case 2: The current node has a left child
      // Locate the rightmost node in the left subtree of
      // the current node and also its parent
      TreeNode<E> parentOfRightMost = current;
      TreeNode<E> rightMost = current.left;

      while (rightMost.right != null) {
        parentOfRightMost = rightMost;
        rightMost = rightMost.right; // Keep going to the right
      }

      // Replace the element in current by the element in rightMost
```

```
239         current.element = rightMost.element;
240
241         // Eliminate rightmost node
242         if (parentOfRightMost.right == rightMost)
243           parentOfRightMost.right = rightMost.left;
244         else
245           // Special case: parentOfRightMost is current
246           parentOfRightMost.left = rightMost.left;
247
248         // Balance the tree if necessary
249         balancePath(parentOfRightMost.element);
250       }
251
252       size--;
253       return true; // Element inserted
254     }
255
256     /** AVLTreeNode is TreeNode plus height */
257     protected static class AVLTreeNode<E extends Comparable<E>>
258         extends BST.TreeNode<E> {
259       protected int height = 0; // New data field
260
261       public AVLTreeNode(E e) {
262         super(e);
263       }
264     }
265   }
```

balance nodes

inner AVLTreeNode class

node height

constructors

The **AVLTree** class extends **BST**. Like the **BST** class, the **AVLTree** class has a no-arg constructor that constructs an empty **AVLTree** (lines 3–4) and a constructor that creates an initial **AVLTree** from an array of elements (lines 7–9).

The **createNewNode()** method defined in the **BST** class creates a **TreeNode**. This method is overridden to return an **AVLTreeNode** (lines 12–14).

insert

The **insert** method in **AVLTree** is overridden in lines 17–26. The method first invokes the **insert** method in **BST**, then invokes **balancePath(e)** (line 22) to ensure that the tree is balanced.

balancePath

The **balancePath** method first gets the nodes on the path from the node that contains element **e** to the root (line 46). For each node in the path, update its height (line 49), check its balance factor (line 53), and perform appropriate rotations if necessary (lines 53–69).

rotations

Four methods for performing rotations are defined in lines 85–182. Each method is invoked with two **TreeNode** arguments—**A** and **parentOfA**—to perform an appropriate rotation at node **A**. How each rotation is performed is illustrated in Figures 29.2–29.5. After the rotation, the heights of nodes **A**, **B**, and **C** are updated for the LL and RR rotations (lines 102, 129, 152, 179).

delete

The **delete** method in **AVLTree** is overridden in lines 187–264. The method is the same as the one implemented in the **BST** class, except that you have to rebalance the nodes after deletion in two cases (lines 33–34).

Check Point

MyProgrammingLab™

29.15 Why is the **createNewNode** method defined protected?

29.16 When is the **updateHeight** method invoked? When is the **balanceFactor** method invoked? When is the **balancePath** method invoked?

29.17 What are data fields in the **AVLTree** class?

29.18 In the **insert** and **delete** methods, once you have performed a rotation to balance a node in the tree, is it possible that there are still unbalanced nodes?

29.8 Testing the AVLTree Class

Key Point

This section gives an example of using the **AVLTree** *class.*

Listing 29.4 gives a test program. The program creates an **AVLTree** initialized with an array of the integers **25**, **20**, and **5** (lines 4–5), inserts elements in lines 9–14, and deletes elements in lines 22–28. Since **AVLTree** is a subclass of **BST** and the elements in a **BST** are iterable, the program uses a for-each loop to traverse all the elements in lines 33–34.

LISTING 29.4 TestAVLTree.java

create an AVLTree
insert 34
insert 50
insert 30
insert 10
delete 34
delete 30
delete 50
delete 5
for-each loop

```
1  public class TestAVLTree {
2    public static void main(String[] args) {
3      // Create an AVL tree
4      AVLTree<Integer> tree = new AVLTree<Integer>(new Integer[]{25,
5        20, 5});
6      System.out.print("After inserting 25, 20, 5:");
7      printTree(tree);
8
9      tree.insert(34);
10     tree.insert(50);
11     System.out.print("\nAfter inserting 34, 50:");
12     printTree(tree);
13
14     tree.insert(30);
15     System.out.print("\nAfter inserting 30");
16     printTree(tree);
17
18     tree.insert(10);
19     System.out.print("\nAfter inserting 10");
20     printTree(tree);
21
22     tree.delete(34);
23     tree.delete(30);
24     tree.delete(50);
25     System.out.print("\nAfter removing 34, 30, 50:");
26     printTree(tree);
27
28     tree.delete(5);
29     System.out.print("\nAfter removing 5:");
30     printTree(tree);
31
32     System.out.print("\nTraverse the elements in the tree: ");
33     for (int e: tree) {
34       System.out.print(e + " ");
35     }
36   }
37
38   public static void printTree(BST tree) {
39     // Traverse tree
40     System.out.print("\nInorder (sorted): ");
41     tree.inorder();
41     System.out.print("\nPostorder: ");
43     tree.postorder();
44     System.out.print("\nPreorder: ");
45     tree.preorder();
46     System.out.print("\nThe number of nodes is " + tree.getSize());
```

```
      System.out.println();
    }
}
```

```
After inserting 25, 20, 5:
Inorder (sorted): 5 20 25
Postorder: 5 25 20
Preorder: 20 5 25
The number of nodes is 3

After inserting 34, 50:
Inorder (sorted): 5 20 25 34 50
Postorder: 5 25 50 34 20
Preorder: 20 5 34 25 50
The number of nodes is 5

After inserting 30
Inorder (sorted): 5 20 25 30 34 50
Postorder: 5 20 30 50 34 25
Preorder: 25 20 5 34 30 50
The number of nodes is 6

After inserting 10
Inorder (sorted): 5 10 20 25 30 34 50
Postorder: 5 20 10 30 50 34 25
Preorder: 25 10 5 20 34 30 50
The number of nodes is 7

After removing 34, 30, 50:
Inorder (sorted): 5 10 20 25
Postorder: 5 20 25 10
Preorder: 10 5 25 20
The number of nodes is 4

After removing 5:
Inorder (sorted): 10 20 25
Postorder: 10 25 20
Preorder: 20 10 25
The number of nodes is 3
Traverse the elements in the tree: 10 20 25
```

Figure 29.10 shows how the tree evolves as elements are added to the tree. After **25** and **20** are added, the tree is as shown in Figure 29.10a. **5** is inserted as a left child of **20**, as shown in Figure 29.10b. The tree is not balanced. It is left-heavy at node **25**. Perform an LL rotation to result in an AVL tree, as shown in Figure 29.10c.

After inserting **34**, the tree is shown in Figure 29.10d. After inserting **50**, the tree is as shown in Figure 29.10e. The tree is not balanced. It is right-heavy at node **25**. Perform an RR rotation to result in an AVL tree, as shown in Figure 29.10f.

After inserting **30**, the tree is as shown in Figure 29.10g. The tree is not balanced. Perform an RL rotation to result in an AVL tree, as shown in Figure 29.10h.

After inserting **10**, the tree is as shown in Figure 29.10i. The tree is not balanced. Perform an LR rotation to result in an AVL tree, as shown in Figure 29.10j.

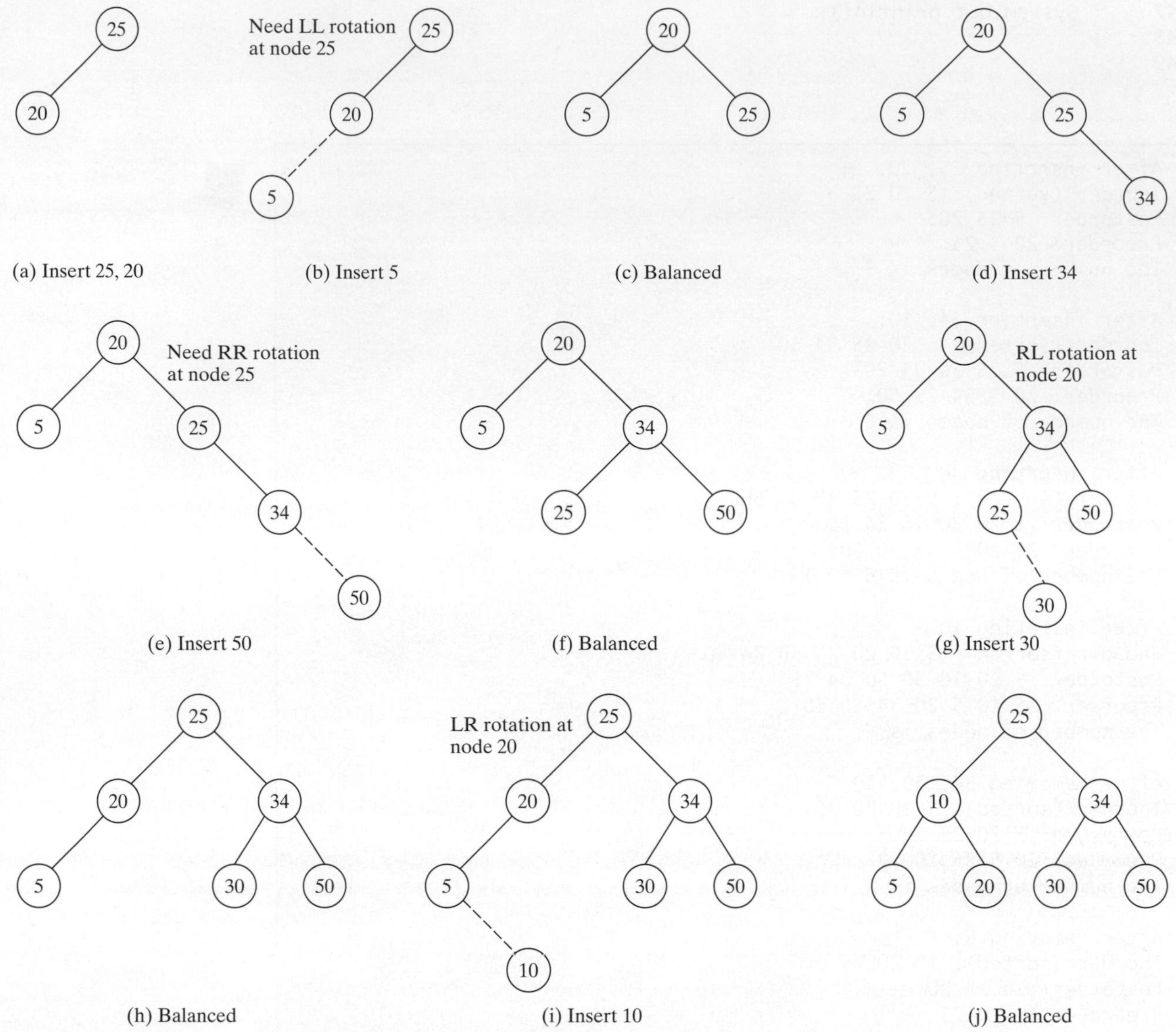

Need LL rotation at node 25

(a) Insert 25, 20 (b) Insert 5 (c) Balanced (d) Insert 34

Need RR rotation at node 25

RL rotation at node 20

(e) Insert 50 (f) Balanced (g) Insert 30

LR rotation at node 20

(h) Balanced (i) Insert 10 (j) Balanced

FIGURE 29.10 The tree evolves as new elements are inserted.

Figure 29.11 shows how the tree evolves as elements are deleted. After deleting 34, 30, and 50, the tree is as shown in Figure 29.11b. The tree is not balanced. Perform an LL rotation to result in an AVL tree, as shown in Figure 29.11c.

After deleting 5, the tree is as shown in Figure 29.11d. The tree is not balanced. Perform an RL rotation to result in an AVL tree, as shown in Figure 29.11e.

MyProgrammingLab™

29.19 Show the change of an AVL tree when inserting 1, 2, 3, 4, 10, 9, 7, 5, 8, 6 into the tree, in this order.

29.20 For the tree built in the preceding question, show its change after 1, 2, 3, 4, 10, 9, 7, 5, 8, 6 are deleted from the tree in this order.

29.21 Can you traverse the elements in an AVL tree using a for-each loop?

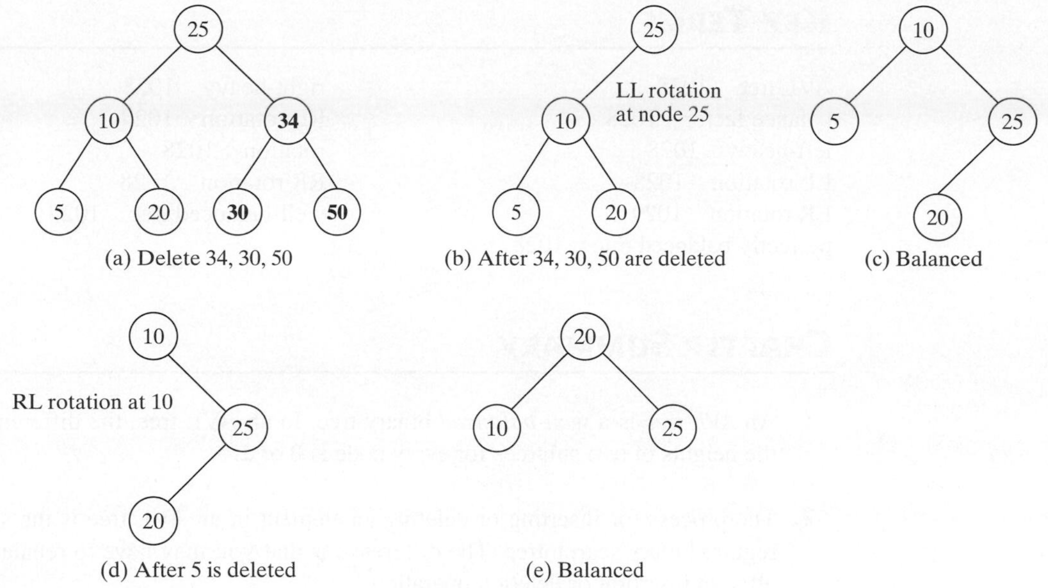

(a) Delete 34, 30, 50 (b) After 34, 30, 50 are deleted (c) Balanced

(d) After 5 is deleted (e) Balanced

FIGURE 29.11 The tree evolves as elements are deleted from the tree.

29.9 AVL Tree Time Complexity Analysis

Since the height of an AVL tree is O(log n), the time complexity of the `search`, `insert`, and `delete` methods in `AVLTree` is O(log n).

The time complexity of the `search`, `insert`, and `delete` methods in `AVLTree` depends on the height of the tree. We can prove that the height of the tree is $O(\log n)$.

tree height

Let $G(h)$ denote the minimum number of the nodes in an AVL tree with height h. Obviously, $G(1)$ is 1 and $G(2)$ is 2. The minimum number of nodes in an AVL tree with height $h \geq 3$ must have two minimum subtrees: one with height $h - 1$ and the other with height $h - 2$. Thus,

$$G(h) = G(h - 1) + G(h - 2) + 1$$

Recall that a Fibonacci number at index i can be described using the recurrence relation $F(i) = F(i - 1) + F(i - 2)$. Therefore, the function $G(h)$ is essentially the same as $F(i)$. It can be proven that

$$h < 1.4405 \log(n + 2) - 1.3277$$

where n is the number of nodes in the tree. Hence, the height of an AVL tree is $O(\log n)$.

The `search`, `insert`, and `delete` methods involve only the nodes along a path in the tree. The `updateHeight` and `balanceFactor` methods are executed in a constant time for each node in the path. The `balancePath` method is executed in a constant time for a node in the path. Thus, the time complexity for the `search`, `insert`, and `delete` methods is $O(\log n)$.

MyProgrammingLab™

29.22 What is the maximum/minimum height for an AVL tree of 3 nodes, 5 nodes, and 7 nodes?

29.23 If an AVL tree has a height of 3, what maximum number of nodes can the tree have? What minimum number of nodes can the tree have?

29.24 If an AVL tree has a height of 4, what maximum number of nodes can the tree have? What minimum number of nodes can the tree have?

Key Terms

AVL tree 1028
balance factor 1028
left-heavy 1028
LL rotation 1028
LR rotation 1029
perfectly balanced tree 1028
right-heavy 1028
RL rotation 1029
rotation 1028
RR rotation 1028
well-balanced tree 1028

Chapter Summary

1. An *AVL tree* is a *well-balanced* binary tree. In an AVL tree, the difference between the heights of two subtrees for every node is `0` or `1`.

2. The process for inserting or deleting an element in an AVL tree is the same as in a regular binary search tree. The difference is that you may have to rebalance the tree after an insertion or deletion operation.

3. Imbalances in the tree caused by insertions and deletions are rebalanced through subtree rotations at the node of the imbalance.

4. The process of rebalancing a node is called a *rotation*. There are four possible rotations: *LL rotation*, *LR rotation*, *RR rotation*, and *RL rotation*.

5. The height of an AVL tree is $O(\log n)$. Therefore, the time complexities for the `search`, `insert`, and `delete` methods are $O(\log n)$.

Test Questions

Do the test questions for this chapter online at www.cs.armstrong.edu/liang/intro9e/test.html.

MyProgrammingLab™

Programming Exercises

***29.1** (*Display AVL tree graphically*) Write an applet that displays an AVL tree along with its balance factor for each node.

29.2 (*Compare performance*) Write a test program that randomly generates 500,000 numbers and inserts them into a `BST`, reshuffles the 500,000 numbers and performs a search, and reshuffles the numbers again before deleting them from the tree. Write another test program that does the same thing for an `AVLTree`. Compare the execution times of these two programs.

*****29.3** (*AVL tree animation*) Write a Java applet that animates the AVL tree `insert`, `delete`, and `search` methods, as shown in Figure 29.1.

****29.4** (*Parent reference for* `BST`) Suppose that the `TreeNode` class defined in `BST` contains a reference to the node's parent, as shown in Programming Exercise 27.15. Implement the `AVLTree` class to support this change. Write a test program that adds numbers `1`, `2`, . . . , `100` to the tree and displays the paths for all leaf nodes.

****29.5** (*The* k*th smallest element*) You can find the *k*th smallest element in a BST in $O(n)$ time from an inorder iterator. For an AVL tree, you can find it in $O(\log n)$

time. To achieve this, add a new data field named `size` in `AVLTreeNode` to store the number of nodes in the subtree rooted at this node. Note that the size of a node v is one more than the sum of the sizes of its two children. Figure 29.12 shows an AVL tree and the `size` value for each node in the tree.

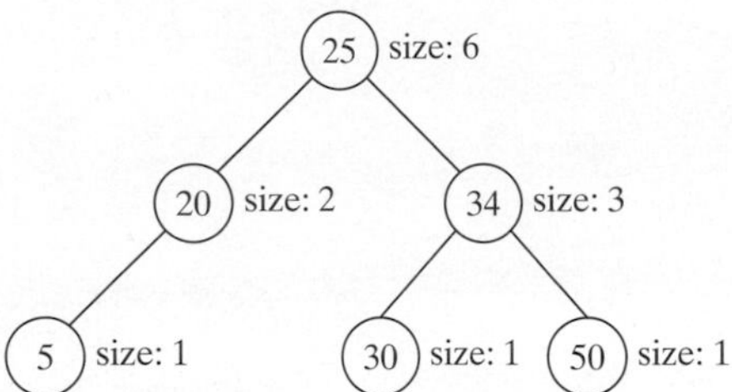

FIGURE 29.12 The `size` data field in `AVLTreeNode` stores the number of nodes in the subtree rooted at the node.

In the `AVLTree` class, add the following method to return the kth smallest element in the tree.

```
public E find(int k)
```

The method returns `null` if `k < 1` or `k > the size of the tree`. This method can be implemented using the recursive method `find(k, root)`, which returns the kth smallest element in the tree with the specified root. Let `A` and `B` be the left and right children of the root, respectively. Assuming that the tree is not empty and $k \leq root.size$, `find(k, root)` can be recursively defined as follows:

$$find(k, root) = \begin{cases} root.element, \text{ if } A \text{ is null and } k \text{ is } 1; \\ B.element, \text{ if } A \text{ is null and } k \text{ is } 2; \\ find(k, A), \text{ if } k <= A.size; \\ root.element, \text{ if } k = A.size + 1; \\ find(k - A.size - 1, B), \text{ if } k > A.size + 1; \end{cases}$$

Modify the `insert` and `delete` methods in `AVLTree` to set the correct value for the `size` property in each node. The `insert` and `delete` methods will still be in $O(\log n)$ time. The `find(k)` method can be implemented in $O(\log n)$ time. Therefore, you can find the kth smallest element in an AVL tree in $O(\log n)$ time.

CHAPTER

30

GRAPHS AND APPLICATIONS

Objectives

- To model real-world problems using graphs and explain the Seven Bridges of Königsberg problem (§30.1).
- To describe the graph terminologies: vertices, edges, simple graphs, weighted/unweighted graphs, and directed/undirected graphs (§30.2).
- To represent vertices and edges using lists, edge arrays, edge objects, adjacency matrices, and adjacency lists (§30.3).
- To model graphs using the `Graph` interface, the `AbstractGraph` class, and the `UnweightedGraph` class (§30.4).
- To display graphs visually (§30.5).
- To represent the traversal of a graph using the `AbstractGraph.Tree` class (§30.6).
- To design and implement depth-first search (§30.7).
- To solve the connected-circle problem using depth-first search (§30.8).
- To design and implement breadth-first search (§30.9).
- To solve the nine-tail problem using breadth-first search (§30.10).

30.1 Introduction

Many real-world problems can be solved using graph algorithms.

problem

Graphs are useful in modeling and solving real-world problems. For example, the problem to find the least number of flights between two cities can be modeled using a graph, where the vertices represent cities and the edges represent the flights between two adjacent cities, as shown in Figure 30.1. The problem of finding the minimal number of connecting flights between two cities is reduced to finding the shortest path between two vertices in a graph.

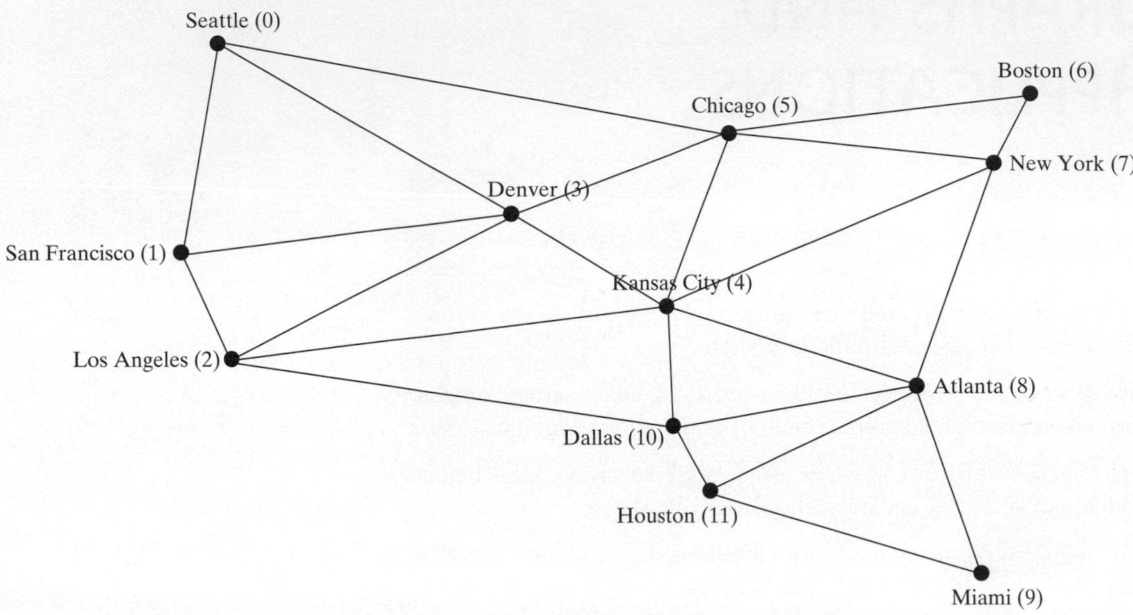

FIGURE 30.1 A graph can be used to model the flights between the cities.

graph theory
Seven Bridges of Königsberg

The study of graph problems is known as *graph theory*. Graph theory was founded by Leonhard Euler in 1736, when he introduced graph terminology to solve the famous *Seven Bridges of Königsberg* problem. The city of Königsberg, Prussia (now Kaliningrad, Russia), was divided by the Pregel River. There were two islands on the river. The city and islands were connected by seven bridges, as shown in Figure 30.2a. The question is, can one take a walk, cross each bridge exactly once, and return to the starting point? Euler proved that it is not possible.

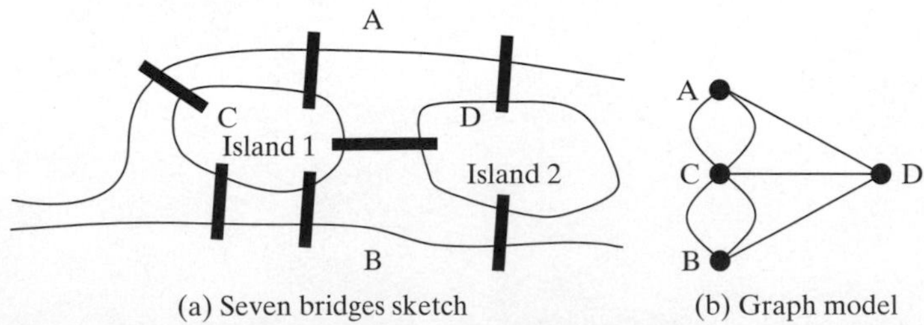

FIGURE 30.2 Seven bridges connected islands and land.

To establish a proof, Euler first abstracted the Königsberg city map by eliminating all streets, producing the sketch shown in Figure 30.2a. Next, he replaced each land mass with a dot, called a *vertex* or a *node*, and each bridge with a line, called an *edge*, as shown in Figure 30.2b. This structure with vertices and edges is called a *graph*.

Looking at the graph, we ask whether there is a path starting from any vertex, traversing all edges exactly once, and returning to the starting vertex. Euler proved that for such a path to exist, each vertex must have an even number of edges. Therefore, the Seven Bridges of Königsberg problem has no solution.

Graph problems are often solved using algorithms. Graph algorithms have many applications in various areas, such as in computer science, mathematics, biology, engineering, economics, genetics, and social sciences. This chapter presents the algorithms for depth-first search and breadth-first search, and their applications. The next chapter presents the algorithms for finding a minimum spanning tree and shortest paths in weighted graphs, and their applications.

30.2 Basic Graph Terminologies

A graph consists of vertices, and edges that connect the vertices.

This chapter does not assume that you have any prior knowledge of graph theory or discrete mathematics. We use plain and simple terms to define graphs.

What is a graph? A *graph* is a mathematical structure that represents relationships among entities in the real world. For example, the graph in Figure 30.1 represents the flights among cities, and the graph in Figure 30.2b represents the bridges among land masses. (what is a graph?)

A graph consists of a nonempty set of vertices (also known as *nodes* or *points*), and a set of edges that connect the vertices. For convenience, we define a graph as G = (V, E), where V represents a set of vertices and E represents a set of edges. For example, V and E for the graph in Figure 30.1 are as follows: (define a graph)

```
V = {"Seattle", "San Francisco", "Los Angeles",
  "Denver", "Kansas City", "Chicago", "Boston", "New York",
  "Atlanta", "Miami", "Dallas", "Houston"};

E = {{"Seattle", "San Francisco"},{"Seattle", "Chicago"},
     {"Seattle", "Denver"}, {"San Francisco", "Denver"},
     ...
    };
```

A graph may be directed or undirected. In a *directed graph*, each edge has a direction, which indicates that you can move from one vertex to the other through the edge. You can model parent/child relationships using a directed graph, where an edge from vertex A to B indicates that A is a parent of B. Figure 30.3a shows a directed graph. (directed vs. undirected graphs)

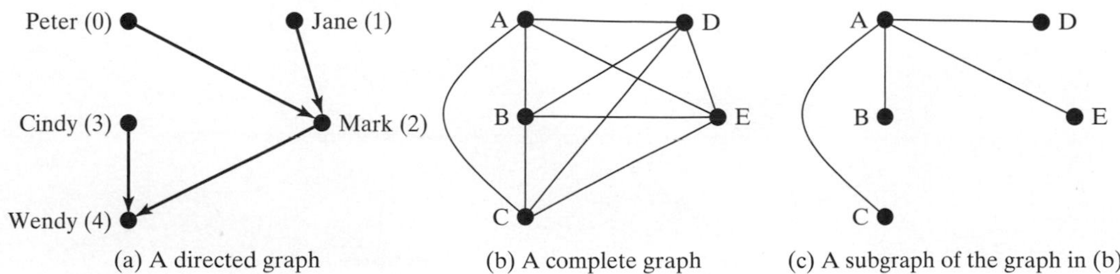

FIGURE 30.3 Graphs may appear in many forms.

In an *undirected graph*, you can move in both directions between vertices. The graph in Figure 30.1 is undirected.

Edges may be weighted or unweighted. For example, you can assign a weight for each edge in the graph in Figure 30.1 to indicate the flight time between the two cities. (weighted vs. unweighted graphs)

adjacent vertices
incident edges
degree
neighbor

Two vertices in a graph are said to be *adjacent* if they are connected by the same edge. Similarly, two edges are said to be *adjacent* if they are connected to the same vertex. An edge in a graph that joins two vertices is said to be *incident* to both vertices. The *degree* of a vertex is the number of edges incident to it.

Two vertices are called *neighbors* if they are adjacent. Similarly, two edges are called *neighbors* if they are adjacent.

loop
parallel edge
simple graph
complete graph
connected graph
subgraph

A *loop* is an edge that links a vertex to itself. If two vertices are connected by two or more edges, these edges are called *parallel edges*. A *simple graph* is one that has doesn't have any loops or parallel edges. In a *complete graph*, every two pairs of vertices are connected, as shown in Figure 30.3b.

A graph is *connected* if there exists a path between any two vertices in the graph. A *subgraph* of a graph *G* is a graph whose vertex set is a subset of that of *G* and whose edge set is a subset of that of *G*. For example, the graph in Figure 30.3c is a subgraph of the graph in Figure 30.3b.

tree
cycle
spanning tree

Assume that the graph is connected and undirected. A connected graph is a *tree* if it does not have cycles. A *cycle* is a closed path that starts from a vertex and ends at the same vertex. A *spanning tree* of a graph *G* is a connected subgraph of *G* and the subgraph is a tree that contains all vertices in G.

graph learning tool on Companion Website

Pedagogical Note

Before we introduce graph algorithms and applications, it is helpful to get acquainted with graphs using the interactive tool at www.cs.armstrong.edu/liang/animation/GraphLearningTool.html, as shown in Figure 30.4. The tool allows you to add/remove/move vertices and draw edges using mouse gestures. You can also find depth-first search (DFS) trees and breadth-first search (BFS) trees, and the shortest path between two vertices.

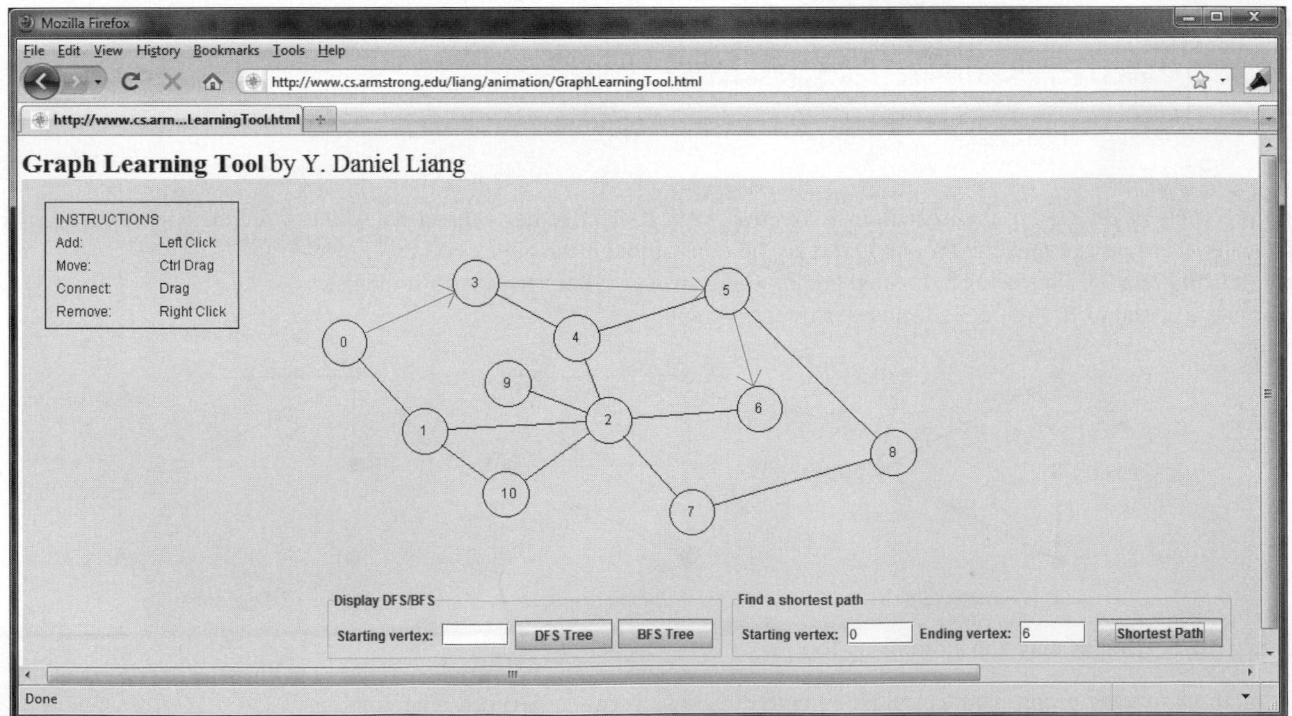

FIGURE 30.4 You can use the tool to create a graph with mouse gestures and show DFS/BFS trees and shortest paths.

30.1 What is the famous *Seven Bridges of Königsberg* problem?

30.2 What is a graph? Explain the following terms: undirected graph, directed graph, weighted graph, degree of a vertex, parallel edge, simple graph, complete graph, connected graph, cycle, subgraph, tree, and spanning tree.

30.3 How many edges are in a complete graph with 5 vertices? How many edges are in a tree of 5 vertices?

30.4 How many edges are in a complete graph with *n* vertices? How many edges are in a tree of *n* vertices?

Check Point

MyProgrammingLab™

30.3 Representing Graphs

Representing a graph is to store its vertices and edges in a program. The data structure for storing a graph is arrays or lists.

Key Point

To write a program that processes and manipulates graphs, you have to store or represent data for the graphs in the computer.

30.3.1 Representing Vertices

The vertices can be stored in an array or a list. For example, you can store all the city names in the graph in Figure 30.1 using the following array:

```
String[] vertices = {"Seattle", "San Francisco", "Los Angeles",
  "Denver", "Kansas City", "Chicago", "Boston", "New York",
  "Atlanta", "Miami", "Dallas", "Houston"};
```

Note

vertex type

The vertices can be objects of any type. For example, you can consider cities as objects that contain the information such as its name, population, and mayor. Thus, you may define vertices as follows:

```
City city0 = new City("Seattle", 608660, "Mike McGinn");
...
City city11 = new City("Houston", 2099451, "Annise Parker");
City[] vertices = {city0, city1, ... , city11};

public class City {
  private String cityName;
  private int population;
  private String mayor;

  public City(String cityName, int population, String mayor) {
    this.cityName = cityName;
    this.population = population;
    this.mayor = mayor;
  }

  public String getCityName() {
    return cityName;
  }

  public int getPopulation() {
    return population;
  }
```

```
    public String getMayor() {
      return mayor;
    }

    public void setMayor(String mayor) {
      this.mayor = mayor;
    }

    public void setPopulation(int population) {
      this.population = population;
    }
  }
```

The vertices can be conveniently labeled using natural numbers 0, 1, 2, . . . , $n - 1$, for a graph for n vertices. Thus, `vertices[0]` represents `"Seattle"`, `vertices[1]` represents `"San Francisco"`, and so on, as shown in Figure 30.5.

`vertices[0]`	Seattle
`vertices[1]`	San Francisco
`vertices[2]`	Los Angeles
`vertices[3]`	Denver
`vertices[4]`	Kansas City
`vertices[5]`	Chicago
`vertices[6]`	Boston
`vertices[7]`	New York
`vertices[8]`	Atlanta
`vertices[9]`	Miami
`vertices[10]`	Dallas
`vertices[11]`	Houston

FIGURE 30.5 An array stores the vertex names.

reference vertex

Note

You can reference a vertex by its name or its index, whichever is more convenient. Obviously, it is easy to access a vertex via its index in a program.

30.3.2 Representing Edges: Edge Array

The edges can be represented using a two-dimensional array. For example, you can store all the edges in the graph in Figure 30.1 using the following array:

```
int[][] edges = {
  {0, 1}, {0, 3}, {0, 5},
  {1, 0}, {1, 2}, {1, 3},
```

```
    {2, 1}, {2, 3}, {2, 4}, {2, 10},
    {3, 0}, {3, 1}, {3, 2}, {3, 4}, {3, 5},
    {4, 2}, {4, 3}, {4, 5}, {4, 7}, {4, 8}, {4, 10},
    {5, 0}, {5, 3}, {5, 4}, {5, 6}, {5, 7},
    {6, 5}, {6, 7},
    {7, 4}, {7, 5}, {7, 6}, {7, 8},
    {8, 4}, {8, 7}, {8, 9}, {8, 10}, {8, 11},
    {9, 8}, {9, 11},
    {10, 2}, {10, 4}, {10, 8}, {10, 11},
    {11, 8}, {11, 9}, {11, 10}
  };
```

This representation is known as the *edge array*. The vertices and edges in Figure 30.3a can be represented as follows:

edge array

```
String[] names = {"Peter", "Jane", "Mark", "Cindy", "Wendy"};

int[][] edges = {{0, 2}, {1, 2}, {2, 4}, {3, 4}};
```

30.3.3 Representing Edges: Edge Objects

Another way to represent the edges is to define edges as objects and store the edges in a **java.util.ArrayList**. The **Edge** class can be defined as follows:

```
public class Edge {
  int u;
  int v;

  public Edge(int u, int v) {
    this.u = u;
    this.v = v;
  }
}
```

For example, you can store all the edges in the graph in Figure 30.1 using the following list:

```
java.util.ArrayList<Edge> list = new java.util.ArrayList<Edge>();
list.add(new Edge(0, 1));
list.add(new Edge(0, 3));
list.add(new Edge(0, 5));
...
```

Storing **Edge** objects in an **ArrayList** is useful if you don't know the edges in advance.

While representing edges using an edge array or **Edge** objects in Section 30.3.2 and earlier in this section may be intuitive for input, it's not efficient for internal processing. The next two sections introduce the representation of graphs using *adjacency matrices* and *adjacency lists*. These two data structures are efficient for processing graphs.

30.3.4 Representing Edges: Adjacency Matrices

Assume that the graph has n vertices. You can use a two-dimensional $n \times n$ matrix, say **adjacencyMatrix**, to represent the edges. Each element in the array is **0** or **1**. **adjacencyMatrix[i][j]** is **1** if there is an edge from vertex i to vertex j; otherwise, **adjacencyMatrix[i][j]** is **0**. If the graph is undirected, the matrix is symmetric, because **adjacencyMatrix[i][j]** is the same as **adjacencyMatrix[j][i]**. For

adjacency matrix

example, the edges in the graph in Figure 30.1 can be represented using an *adjacency matrix* as follows:

```
int[][] adjacencyMatrix = {
  {0, 1, 0, 1, 0, 1, 0, 0, 0, 0, 0, 0}, // Seattle
  {1, 0, 1, 1, 0, 0, 0, 0, 0, 0, 0, 0}, // San Francisco
  {0, 1, 0, 1, 1, 1, 0, 0, 0, 0, 0, 0}, // Los Angeles
  {1, 1, 1, 0, 1, 1, 0, 0, 0, 0, 0, 0}, // Denver
  {0, 0, 1, 1, 0, 1, 0, 1, 1, 0, 1, 0}, // Kansas City
  {1, 0, 0, 1, 1, 0, 1, 1, 0, 0, 0, 0}, // Chicago
  {0, 0, 0, 0, 0, 1, 0, 1, 0, 0, 0, 0}, // Boston
  {0, 0, 0, 0, 1, 1, 1, 0, 1, 0, 0, 0}, // New York
  {0, 0, 0, 1, 1, 0, 0, 1, 0, 1, 1, 1}, // Atlanta
  {0, 0, 0, 0, 0, 0, 0, 0, 1, 0, 0, 1}, // Miami
  {0, 0, 1, 0, 1, 0, 0, 0, 1, 0, 0, 1}, // Dallas
  {0, 0, 0, 0, 0, 0, 0, 0, 1, 1, 1, 0}  // Houston
};
```

ragged array

Note

Since the matrix is symmetric for an undirected graph, to save storage you can use a ragged array.

The adjacency matrix for the directed graph in Figure 30.3a can be represented as follows:

```
int[][] a = {{0, 0, 1, 0, 0}, // Peter
             {0, 0, 1, 0, 0}, // Jane
             {0, 0, 0, 0, 1}, // Mark
             {0, 0, 0, 0, 1}, // Cindy
             {0, 0, 0, 0, 0}  // Wendy
            };
```

30.3.5 Representing Edges: Adjacency Lists

adjacency lists

To represent edges using *adjacency lists*, define an array of lists. The array has *n* entries, and each entry is a linked list. The linked list for vertex *i* contains all the vertices *j* such that there is an edge from vertex *i* to vertex *j*. For example, to represent the edges in the graph in Figure 30.1, you can create an array of linked lists as follows:

```
java.util.LinkedList[] neighbors = new java.util.LinkedList[12];
```

`neighbors[0]` contains all vertices adjacent to vertex `0` (i.e., Seattle), `neighbors[1]` contains all vertices adjacent to vertex `1` (i.e., San Francisco), and so on, as shown in Figure 30.6.

To represent the edges in the graph in Figure 30.3a, you can create an array of linked lists as follows:

```
java.util.LinkedList[] neighbors = new java.util.LinkedList[5];
```

`neighbors[0]` contains all vertices pointed from vertex `0` via directed edges, `neighbors[1]` contains all vertices pointed from vertex `1` via directed edges, and so on, as shown in Figure 30.7. Wendy does not point to any vertex, so `neighbors[4]` is `null`.

adjacency matrices vs. adjacency lists

Note

You can represent a graph using an adjacency matrix or adjacency lists. Which one is better? If the graph is dense (i.e., there are a lot of edges), using an adjacency matrix is preferred. If the graph is very sparse (i.e., very few edges), using adjacency lists is better, because using an adjacency matrix would waste a lot of space.

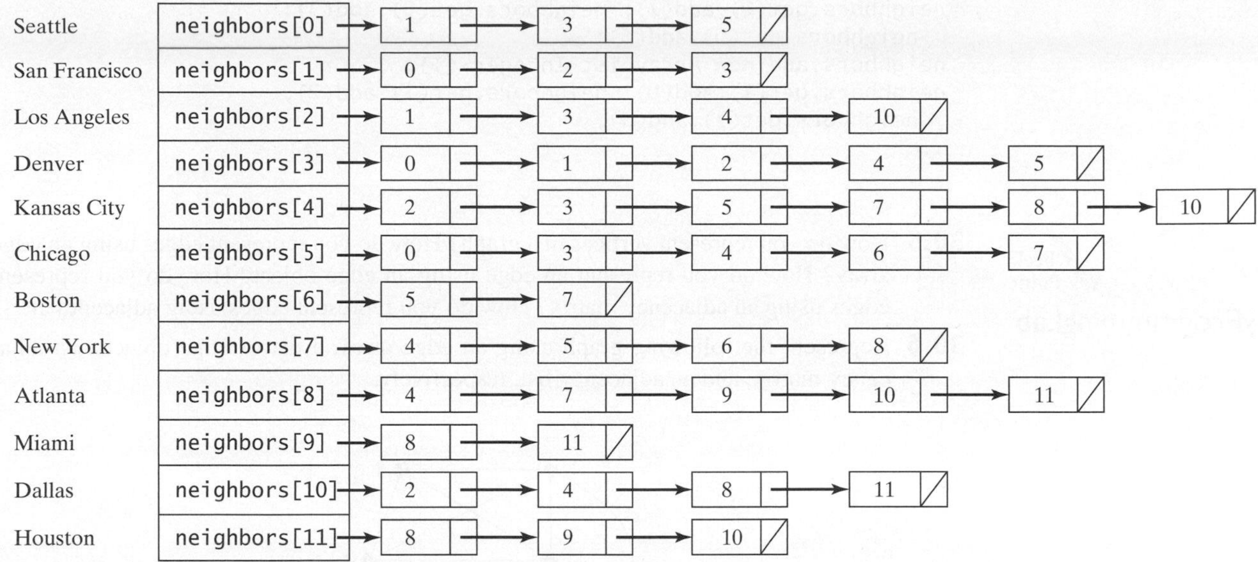

FIGURE 30.6 Edges in the graph in Figure 30.1 are represented using linked lists.

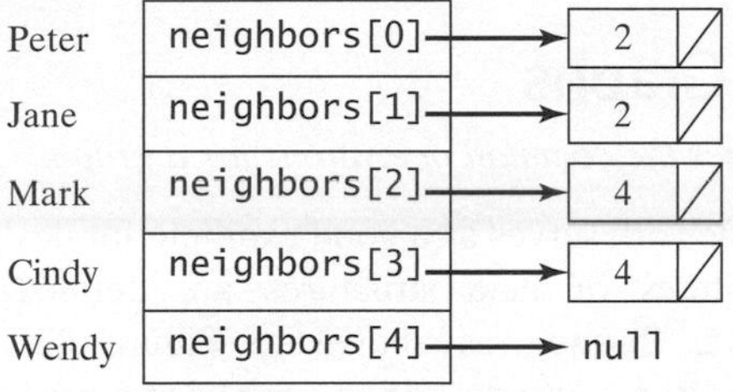

FIGURE 30.7 Edges in the graph in Figure 30.3a are represented using linked lists.

Both adjacency matrices and adjacency lists can be used in a program to make algorithms more efficient. For example, it takes $O(1)$ constant time to check whether two vertices are connected using an adjacency matrix, and it takes linear time $O(m)$ to print all edges in a graph using adjacency lists, where m is the number of edges.

Note

Adjacency matrices and adjacency lists are two common representations for graphs, but they are not the only ways to represent graphs. For example, you can define a vertex as an object with a method **getNeighbors()** that returns all its neighbors. For simplicity, the text will use adjacency lists to represent graphs. Other representations will be explored in the exercises.

other representations

For flexibility and simplicity, we will use array lists to represent arrays. Also, we will use array lists instead of linked lists, because our algorithms only require searching for adjacent vertices in the list. Using array lists is more efficient for our algorithms. Using array lists, the adjacency list in Figure 30.6 can be built as follows:

using `ArrayList`

```
List<ArrayList<Integer>> neighbors
  = new ArrayList<List<Integer>>();
neighbors.add(new ArrayList<Integer>());
```

```
neighbors.get(0).add(1); neighbors.get(0).add(3);
  neighbors.get(0).add(5);
neighbors.add(new ArrayList<Integer>());
neighbors.get(1).add(0); neighbors.get(1).add(2);
  neighbors.get(1).add(3);
...
...
```

30.5 How do you represent vertices in a graph? How do you represent edges using an edge array? How do you represent an edge using an edge object? How do you represent edges using an adjacency matrix? How do you represent edges using adjacency lists?

30.6 Represent the following graph using an edge array, a list of edge objects, an adjacency matrix, and an adjacency list, respectively.

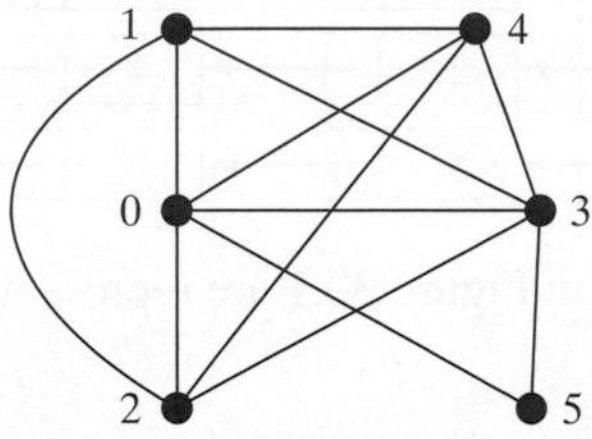

30.4 Modeling Graphs

The* Graph *interface defines the common operations for a graph.

The Java Collections Framework serves as a good example for designing complex data structures. The common features of data structures are defined in the interfaces (e.g., Collection, Set, List, Queue), as shown in Figure 22.1. Abstract classes (e.g., AbstractCollection, AbstractSet, AbstractList) partially implement the interfaces. Concrete classes (e.g., HashSet, LinkedHashSet, TreeSet, ArrayList, LinkedList, PriorityQueue) provide concrete implementations. This design pattern is useful for modeling graphs. We will define an interface named Graph that contains all the common operations of graphs and an abstract class named AbstractGraph that partially implements the Graph interface. Many concrete graphs can be added to the design. For example, we will define such graphs named UnweightedGraph and WeightedGraph. The relationships of these interfaces and classes are illustrated in Figure 30.8.

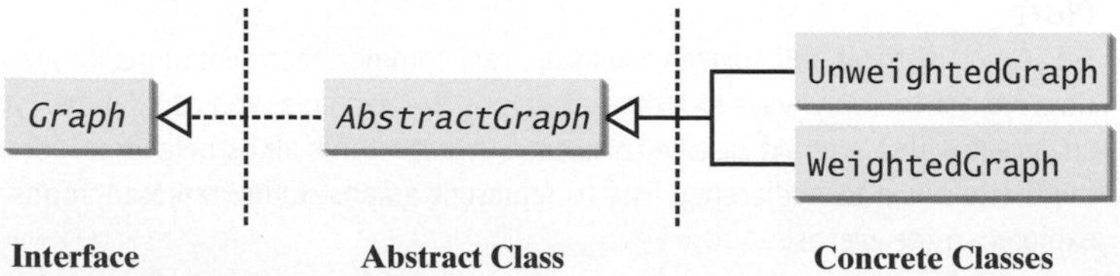

Figure 30.8 Graphs can be modeled using interfaces, abstract classes, and concrete classes.

What are the common operations for a graph? In general, you need to get the number of vertices in a graph, get all vertices in a graph, get the vertex object with a specified index, get the index of the vertex with a specified name, get the neighbors for a vertex, get the degree for a vertex, clear the graph, add a new vertex, add a new edge, perform a depth-first search, and perform a breadth-first search. Depth-first search and breadth-first search will be introduced in the next section. Figure 30.9 illustrates these methods in the UML diagram.

AbstractGraph does not introduce any new methods. A list of vertices and a list of adjacency lists for the vertices are defined in the AbstractGraph class. With these data fields, it is sufficient to implement all the methods defined in the Graph interface.

«interface»
Graph<V>

The generic type V is the type for vertices.

+getSize(): int	Returns the number of vertices in the graph.
+getVertices(): List<V>	Returns the vertices in the graph.
+getVertex(index: int): V	Returns the vertex object for the specified vertex index.
+getIndex(v: V): int	Returns the index for the specified vertex.
+getNeighbors(index: int): List<Integer>	Returns the neighbors of vertex with the specified index.
+getDegree(index: int): int	Returns the degree for a specified vertex index.
+printEdges(): void	Print the edges.
+clear(): void	Clears the graph.
+addVertex(v, V): void	Adds a vertex to the graph.
+addEdge(u: int, v: int): void	Adds an edge to the graph.
+dfs(v: int): AbstractGraph<V>.Tree	Obtains a depth-first search tree starting from v.
+bfs(v: int): AbstractGraph<V>.Tree	Obtains a breadth-first search tree starting from v.

AbstractGraph<V>

#vertices: List<V>	Vertices in the graph.
#neighbors: List<List<Integer>>	Neighbors for each vertex in the graph.
#AbstractGraph()	Constructs an empty graph.
#AbstractGraph(edges: int[][], vertices: V[])	Constructs a graph with the specified edges and vertices stored in arrays.
#AbstractGraph(edges: List<Edge>, vertices: List<V>)	Constructs a graph with the specified edges and vertices stored in lists.
#AbstractGraph(edges: int[][], numberOfVertices: int)	Constructs a graph with the specified edges in an array and the integer vertices 1, 2, ...
#AbstractGraph(edges: List<Edge>, numberOfVertices: int)	Constructs a graph with the specified edges in a list and the integer vertices 1, 2, ...
Inner classes Tree is defined here	

UnweightedGraph<V>

+UnweightedGraph()	Constructs an empty unweighted graph.
+UnweightedGraph(edges: int[][], vertices: V[])	Constructs a graph with the specified edges and vertices in arrays.
+UnweightedGraph(edges: List<Edge>, vertices: List<V>)	Constructs a graph with the specified edges and vertices stored in lists.
+UnweightedGraph(edges: List<Edge>, numberOfVertices: int)	Constructs a graph with the specified edges in an array and the integer vertices 1, 2, ...
+UnweightedGraph(edges: int[][], numberOfVertices: int)	Constructs a graph with the specified edges in a list and the integer vertices 1, 2, ...

FIGURE 30.9 The Graph interface defines the common operations for all types of graphs.

UnweightedGraph simply extends **AbstractGraph** with five constructors for creating the concrete **Graph** instances. **UnweightedGraph** inherits all the methods from **AbstractGraph**, and it does not introduce any new methods.

vertices and their indices

Note

You can create a graph with any type of vertices. Each vertex is associated with an index, which is the same as the index of the vertex in the vertices list. If you create a graph without specifying the vertices, the vertices are the same as their indices.

why AbstractGraph?

Note

The **AbstractGraph** class implements all the methods in the **Graph** interface. So why is it defined as abstract? In the future, you may need to add new methods to the **Graph** interface that cannot be implemented in **AbstractGraph**. To make the classes easy to maintain, it is desirable to define the **AbstractGraph** class as abstract.

Assume all these interfaces and classes are available. Listing 30.1 gives a test program that creates the graph in Figure 30.1 and another graph for the one in Figure 30.3a.

Listing 30.1 TestGraph.java

vertices · edges · create a graph · number of vertices · get vertex · get index · print edges · list of Edge objects

```
public class TestGraph {
  public static void main(String[] args) {
    String[] vertices = {"Seattle", "San Francisco", "Los Angeles",
      "Denver", "Kansas City", "Chicago", "Boston", "New York",
      "Atlanta", "Miami", "Dallas", "Houston"};

    // Edge array for graph in Figure 30.1
    int[][] edges = {
      {0, 1}, {0, 3}, {0, 5},
      {1, 0}, {1, 2}, {1, 3},
      {2, 1}, {2, 3}, {2, 4}, {2, 10},
      {3, 0}, {3, 1}, {3, 2}, {3, 4}, {3, 5},
      {4, 2}, {4, 3}, {4, 5}, {4, 7}, {4, 8}, {4, 10},
      {5, 0}, {5, 3}, {5, 4}, {5, 6}, {5, 7},
      {6, 5}, {6, 7},
      {7, 4}, {7, 5}, {7, 6}, {7, 8},
      {8, 4}, {8, 7}, {8, 9}, {8, 10}, {8, 11},
      {9, 8}, {9, 11},
      {10, 2}, {10, 4}, {10, 8}, {10, 11},
      {11, 8}, {11, 9}, {11, 10}
    };

    Graph<String> graph1 =
      new UnweightedGraph<String>(edges, vertices);
    System.out.println("The number of vertices in graph1: "
      + graph1.getSize());
    System.out.println("The vertex with index 1 is "
      + graph1.getVertex(1));
    System.out.println("The index for Miami is " +
      graph1.getIndex("Miami"));
    System.out.println("The edges for graph1:");
    graph1.printEdges();

    // List of Edge objects for graph in Figure 30.3a
    String[] names = {"Peter", "Jane", "Mark", "Cindy", "Wendy"};
    java.util.ArrayList<AbstractGraph.Edge> edgeList
      = new java.util.ArrayList<AbstractGraph.Edge>();
    edgeList.add(new AbstractGraph.Edge(0, 2));
```

```
39      edgeList.add(new AbstractGraph.Edge(1, 2));
40      edgeList.add(new AbstractGraph.Edge(2, 4));
41      edgeList.add(new AbstractGraph.Edge(3, 4));
42      // Create a graph with 5 vertices
43      Graph<String> graph2 = new UnweightedGraph<String>
44        (edgeList, java.util.Arrays.asList(names));
45      System.out.println("\nThe number of vertices in graph2: "
46        + graph2.getSize());
47      System.out.println("The edges for graph2:");
48      graph2.printEdges();
49    }
50  }
```

create a graph

print edges

```
The number of vertices in graph1: 12
The vertex with index 1 is San Francisco
The index for Miami is 9
The edges for graph1:
Seattle (0): (0, 1) (0, 3) (0, 5)
San Francisco (1): (1, 0) (1, 2) (1, 3)
Los Angeles (2): (2, 1) (2, 3) (2, 4) (2, 10)
Denver (3): (3, 0) (3, 1) (3, 2) (3, 4) (3, 5)
Kansas City (4): (4, 2) (4, 3) (4, 5) (4, 7) (4, 8) (4, 10)
Chicago (5): (5, 0) (5, 3) (5, 4) (5, 6) (5, 7)
Boston (6): (6, 5) (6, 7)
New York (7): (7, 4) (7, 5) (7, 6) (7, 8)
Atlanta (8): (8, 4) (8, 7) (8, 9) (8, 10) (8, 11)
Miami (9): (9, 8) (9, 11)
Dallas (10): (10, 2) (10, 4) (10, 8) (10, 11)
Houston (11): (11, 8) (11, 9) (11, 10)

The number of vertices in graph2: 5
The edges for graph2:
Peter (0): (0, 2)
Jane (1): (1, 2)
Mark (2): (2, 4)
Cindy (3): (3, 4)
Wendy (4):
```

The program creates **graph1** for the graph in Figure 30.1 in lines 3–24. The vertices for **graph1** are defined in lines 3–5. The edges for **graph1** are defined in 8–21. The edges are represented using a two-dimensional array. For each row **i** in the array, **edges[i][0]** and **edges[i][1]** indicate that there is an edge from vertex **edges[i][0]** to vertex **edges[i][1]**. For example, the first row, {**0**, **1**}, represents the edge from vertex **0** (**edges[0][0]**) to vertex **1** (**edges[0][1]**). The row {**0**, **5**} represents the edge from vertex **0** (**edges[2][0]**) to vertex **5** (**edges[2][1]**). The graph is created in line 24. Line 32 invokes the **printEdges()** method on **graph1** to display all edges in **graph1**.

The program creates **graph2** for the graph in Figure 30.3a in lines 35–44. The edges for **graph2** are defined in lines 38–41. **graph2** is created using a list of **Edge** objects in line 44. Line 48 invokes the **printEdges()** method on **graph2** to display all edges in **graph2**.

Note that both **graph1** and **graph2** contain the vertices of strings. The vertices are associated with indices **0**, **1**, . . . , **n-1**. The index is the location of the vertex in **vertices**. For example, the index of vertex **Miami** is **9**.

Now we turn our attention to implementing the interface and classes. Listings 30.2, 30.3, and 30.4 give the **Graph** interface, the **AbstractGraph** class, and the **UnweightedGraph** class, respectively.

LISTING 30.2 Graph.java

getSize
getVertices
getVertex
getIndex
getNeighbors
getDegree
printEdges
clear
addVertex
addEdge
dfs
bfs

```
public interface Graph<V> {
  /** Return the number of vertices in the graph */
  public int getSize();

  /** Return the vertices in the graph */
  public java.util.List<V> getVertices();

  /** Return the object for the specified vertex index */
  public V getVertex(int index);

  /** Return the index for the specified vertex object */
  public int getIndex(V v);

  /** Return the neighbors of vertex with the specified index */
  public java.util.List<Integer> getNeighbors(int index);

  /** Return the degree for a specified vertex */
  public int getDegree(int v);

  /** Print the edges */
  public void printEdges();

  /** Clear graph */
  public void clear();

  /** Add a vertex to the graph */
  public void addVertex(V vertex);

  /** Add an edge to the graph */
  public void addEdge(int u, int v);

  /** Obtain a depth-first search tree starting from v */
  public AbstractGraph<V>.Tree dfs(int v);

  /** Obtain a breadth-first search tree starting from v */
  public AbstractGraph<V>.Tree bfs(int v);
}
```

LISTING 30.3 AbstractGraph.java

no-arg constructor
constructor

```
import java.util.*;

public abstract class AbstractGraph<V> implements Graph<V> {
  protected List<V> vertices = new ArrayList<V>(); // Store vertices
  protected List<List<Integer>> neighbors
    = new ArrayList<List<Integer>>(); // Adjacency lists

  /** Construct an empty graph */
  protected AbstractGraph() {
  }

  /** Construct a graph from edges and vertices stored in arrays */
  protected AbstractGraph(int[][] edges, V[] vertices) {
    for (int i = 0; i < vertices.length; i++)
      this.vertices.add(vertices[i]);

    createAdjacencyLists(edges, vertices.length);
  }
```

```

  /** Construct a graph from edges and vertices stored in List */
  protected AbstractGraph(List<Edge> edges, List<V> vertices) {
    for (int i = 0; i < vertices.size(); i++)
      this.vertices.add(vertices.get(i));

    createAdjacencyLists(edges, vertices.size());
  }

  /** Construct a graph for integer vertices 0, 1, 2 and edge list */
  protected AbstractGraph(List<Edge> edges, int numberOfVertices) {
    for (int i = 0; i < numberOfVertices; i++)
      vertices.add((V)(new Integer(i))); // vertices is {0, 1, ...}

    createAdjacencyLists(edges, numberOfVertices);
  }

  /** Construct a graph from integer vertices 0, 1, and edge array */
  protected AbstractGraph(int[][] edges, int numberOfVertices) {
    for (int i = 0; i < numberOfVertices; i++)
      vertices.add((V)(new Integer(i))); // vertices is {0, 1, ...}

    createAdjacencyLists(edges, numberOfVertices);
  }

  /** Create adjacency lists for each vertex */
  private void createAdjacencyLists(
      int[][] edges, int numberOfVertices) {
    // Create a linked list
    for (int i = 0; i < numberOfVertices; i++) {
      neighbors.add(new ArrayList<Integer>());
    }

    for (int i = 0; i < edges.length; i++) {
      int u = edges[i][0];
      int v = edges[i][1];
      neighbors.get(u).add(v);
    }
  }

  /** Create adjacency lists for each vertex */
  private void createAdjacencyLists(
      List<Edge> edges, int numberOfVertices) {
    // Create a linked list for each vertex
    for (int i = 0; i < numberOfVertices; i++) {
      neighbors.add(new ArrayList<Integer>());
    }

    for (Edge edge: edges) {
      neighbors.get(edge.u).add(edge.v);
    }
  }

  @Override /** Return the number of vertices in the graph */
  public int getSize() {
    return vertices.size();
  }

  @Override /** Return the vertices in the graph */
  public List<V> getVertices() {
```

constructor

constructor

constructor

`getSize`

`getVertices`

```
    return vertices;
  }

  @Override /** Return the object for the specified vertex */
```

getVertex

```
  public V getVertex(int index) {
    return vertices.get(index);
  }

  @Override /** Return the index for the specified vertex object */
```

getIndex

```
  public int getIndex(V v) {
    return vertices.indexOf(v);
  }

  @Override /** Return the neighbors of the specified vertex */
```

getNeighbors

```
  public List<Integer> getNeighbors(int index) {
    return neighbors.get(index);
  }

  @Override /** Return the degree for a specified vertex */
```

getDegree

```
  public int getDegree(int v) {
    return neighbors.get(v).size();
  }

  @Override /** Print the edges */
```

printEdges

```
  public void printEdges() {
    for (int u = 0; u < neighbors.size(); u++) {
      System.out.print(getVertex(u) + " (" + u + "): ");
      for (int j = 0; j < neighbors.get(u).size(); j++) {
        System.out.print("(" + u + ", " +
          neighbors.get(u).get(j) + ") ");
      }
      System.out.println();
    }
  }

  @Override /** Clear graph */
```

clear

```
  public void clear() {
    vertices.clear();
    neighbors.clear();
  }

  @Override /** Add a vertex to the graph */
```

addVertex

```
  public void addVertex(V vertex) {
    vertices.add(vertex);
    neighbors.add(new ArrayList<Integer>());
  }

  @Override /** Add an edge to the graph */
```

addEdge

```
  public void addEdge(int u, int v) {
    neighbors.get(u).add(v);
    neighbors.get(v).add(u);
  }

  /** Edge inner class inside the AbstractGraph class */
```

Edge inner class

```
  public static class Edge {
    public int u; // Starting vertex of the edge
    public int v; // Ending vertex of the edge

    /** Construct an edge for (u, v) */
    public Edge(int u, int v) {
```

```
      this.u = u;
      this.v = v;
    }
  }

  @Override /** Obtain a DFS tree starting from vertex v */
  /** To be discussed in Section 30.7 */
  public Tree dfs(int v) {
    List<Integer> searchOrder = new ArrayList<Integer>();
    int[] parent = new int[vertices.size()];
    for (int i = 0; i < parent.length; i++)
      parent[i] = -1; // Initialize parent[i] to -1

    // Mark visited vertices
    boolean[] isVisited = new boolean[vertices.size()];

    // Recursively search
    dfs(v, parent, searchOrder, isVisited);

    // Return a search tree
    return new Tree(v, parent, searchOrder);
  }

  /** Recursive method for DFS search */
  private void dfs(int v, int[] parent, List<Integer> searchOrder,
      boolean[] isVisited) {
    // Store the visited vertex
    searchOrder.add(v);
    isVisited[v] = true; // Vertex v visited

    for (int i : neighbors.get(v)) {
      if (!isVisited[i]) {
        parent[i] = v; // The parent of vertex i is v
        dfs(i, parent, searchOrder, isVisited); // Recursive search
      }
    }
  }

  @Override /** Starting BFS search from vertex v */
  /** To be discussed in Section 30.9 */
  public Tree bfs(int v) {
    List<Integer> searchOrder = new ArrayList<Integer>();
    int[] parent = new int[vertices.size()];
    for (int i = 0; i < parent.length; i++)
      parent[i] = -1; // Initialize parent[i] to -1

    java.util.LinkedList<Integer> queue =
      new java.util.LinkedList<Integer>(); // list used as a queue
    boolean[] isVisited = new boolean[vertices.size()];
    queue.offer(v); // Enqueue v
    isVisited[v] = true; // Mark it visited

    while (!queue.isEmpty()) {
      int u = queue.poll(); // Dequeue to u
      searchOrder.add(u); // u searched
      for (int w : neighbors.get(u)) {
        if (!isVisited[w]) {
          queue.offer(w); // Enqueue w
          parent[w] = u; // The parent of w is u
          isVisited[w] = true; // Mark it visited
```

dfs method

bfs method

Tree inner class

```
        }
      }
    }

    return new Tree(v, parent, searchOrder);
  }

  /** Tree inner class inside the AbstractGraph class */
  /** To be discussed in Section 30.5 */
  public class Tree {
    private int root; // The root of the tree
    private int[] parent; // Store the parent of each vertex
    private List<Integer> searchOrder; // Store the search order

    /** Construct a tree with root, parent, and searchOrder */
    public Tree(int root, int[] parent, List<Integer> searchOrder) {
      this.root = root;
      this.parent = parent;
      this.searchOrder = searchOrder;
    }

    /** Return the root of the tree */
    public int getRoot() {
      return root;
    }

    /** Return the parent of vertex v */
    public int getParent(int v) {
      return parent[v];
    }

    /** Return an array representing search order */
    public List<Integer> getSearchOrder() {
      return searchOrder;
    }

    /** Return number of vertices found */
    public int getNumberOfVerticesFound() {
      return searchOrder.size();
    }

    /** Return the path of vertices from a vertex to the root */
    public List<V> getPath(int index) {
      ArrayList<V> path = new ArrayList<V>();

      do {
        path.add(vertices.get(index));
        index = parent[index];
      }
      while (index != -1);

      return path;
    }

    /** Print a path from the root to vertex v */
    public void printPath(int index) {
      List<V> path = getPath(index);
      System.out.print("A path from " + vertices.get(root) + " to " +
        vertices.get(index) + ": ");
      for (int i = path.size() - 1; i >= 0; i--)
```

```
259          System.out.print(path.get(i) + " ");
260      }
261
262      /** Print the whole tree */
263      public void printTree() {
264        System.out.println("Root is: " + vertices.get(root));
265        System.out.print("Edges: ");
266        for (int i = 0; i < parent.length; i++) {
267          if (parent[i] != -1) {
268            // Display an edge
269            System.out.print("(" + vertices.get(parent[i]) + ", " +
270              vertices.get(i) + ") ");
271          }
272        }
273        System.out.println();
274      }
275    }
276  }
```

LISTING 30.4 UnweightedGraph.java

```
import java.util.*;

public class UnweightedGraph<V> extends AbstractGraph<V> {
  /** Construct an empty graph */
  public UnweightedGraph() {
  }

  /** Construct a graph from edges and vertices stored in arrays */
  public UnweightedGraph(int[][] edges, V[] vertices) {
    super(edges, vertices);
  }

  /** Construct a graph from edges and vertices stored in List */
  public UnweightedGraph(List<Edge> edges, List<V> vertices) {
    super(edges, vertices);
  }

  /** Construct a graph for integer vertices 0, 1, 2 and edge list */
  public UnweightedGraph(List<Edge> edges, int numberOfVertices) {
    super(edges, numberOfVertices);
  }

  /** Construct a graph from integer vertices 0, 1, and edge array */
  public UnweightedGraph(int[][] edges, int numberOfVertices) {
    super(edges, numberOfVertices);
  }
}
```

no-arg constructor

constructor

constructor

constructor

constructor

The code in the **Graph** interface in Listing 30.2 and the **UnweightedGraph** class in Listing 30.4 are straightforward. Let us digest the code in the **AbstractGraph** class in Listing 30.3.

The **AbstractGraph** class defines the data field **vertices** (line 4) to store vertices and **neighbors** (line 5) to store edges in adjacency lists. **neighbors.get(i)** stores all vertices adjacent to vertex **i**. Four overloaded constructors are defined in lines 9–42 to create a default graph, or a graph from arrays or lists of edges and vertices. The **createAdjacencyLists(int[][] edges, int numberOfVertices)** method creates adjacency lists from edges in an array (lines 45–57). The **createAdjacencyLists(List<Edge> edges, int numberOfVertices)** method creates adjacency lists from edges in a list (lines 60–70).

The `printEdges()` method (lines 103–112) displays all vertices and edges adjacent to each vertex.

The code in lines 146–275 gives the methods for finding a depth-first search tree and a breadth-first search tree, which will be introduced in Sections 30.7 and 30.9, respectively.

MyProgrammingLab™

30.7 Describe the relationships among `Graph`, `AbstractGraph`, and `UnweightedGraph`.

30.8 For the code in Listing 30.1, TestGraph.java, what is `graph1.getIndex("Seattle")`? What is `graph1.getDegree(5)`? What is `graph1.getVertex(4)`?

30.5 Graph Visualization

To display a graph visually, each vertex must be assigned a location.

The preceding section introduced how to model a graph using the `Graph` interface, `AbstractGraph` class, and `UnweightedGraph` class. This section discusses how to display graphs graphically. In order to display a graph, you need to know where each vertex is displayed and the name of each vertex. To ensure a graph can be displayed, we define an interface named `Displayable` that has the methods for obtaining the `x`-and `y`-coordinates and their names, and make vertices instances of `Displayable`, in Listing 30.5.

Listing 30.5 Displayable.java

`Displayable` interface

```
public interface Displayable {
  public int getX(); // Get x-coordinate of the vertex
  public int getY(); // Get y-coordinate of the vertex
  public String getName(); // Get display name of the vertex
}
```

A graph with `Displayable` vertices can now be displayed on a panel named `GraphView`, as shown in Listing 30.6.

Listing 30.6 GraphView.java

extends `JPanel`

```
public class GraphView extends javax.swing.JPanel {
  private Graph<? extends Displayable> graph;

  public GraphView(Graph<? extends Displayable> graph) {
    this.graph = graph;
  }

  @Override
  protected void paintComponent(java.awt.Graphics g) {
    super.paintComponent(g);

    // Draw vertices
    java.util.List<? extends Displayable> vertices
      = graph.getVertices();
    for (int i = 0; i < graph.getSize(); i++) {
      int x = vertices.get(i).getX();
      int y = vertices.get(i).getY();
      String name = vertices.get(i).getName();

      g.fillOval(x - 8, y - 8, 16, 16); // Display a vertex
      g.drawString(name, x - 12, y - 12); // Display the name
    }

    // Draw edges for pair of vertices
    for (int i = 0; i < graph.getSize(); i++) {
```

```
26        java.util.List<Integer> neighbors = graph.getNeighbors(i);
27        int x1 = graph.getVertex(i).getX();
28        int y1 = graph.getVertex(i).getY();
29        for (int v: neighbors) {
30          int x2 = graph.getVertex(v).getX();
31          int y2 = graph.getVertex(v).getY();
32
33          g.drawLine(x1, y1, x2, y2); // Draw an edge for (i, v)
34        }
35      }
36    }
37  }
```

To display a graph on a panel, simply create an instance of **GraphView** by passing the graph as an argument in the constructor (line 4). The class for the graph's vertex must implement the **Displayable** interface in order to display the vertices (lines 13–22). For each vertex index **i**, invoking **graph.getNeighbors(i)** returns its adjacency list (line 26). From this list, you can find all vertices that are adjacent to **i** and draw a line to connect **i** with its adjacent vertex (lines 27–34).

Listing 30.7 gives an example of displaying the graph in Figure 30.1, as shown in Figure 30.10.

LISTING 30.7 DisplayUSMap.java

```
import javax.swing.*;

public class DisplayUSMap extends JApplet {
  private City[] vertices = {new City("Seattle", 75, 50),
    new City("San Francisco", 50, 210),
    new City("Los Angeles", 75, 275), new City("Denver", 275, 175),
    new City("Kansas City", 400, 245),
    new City("Chicago", 450, 100), new City("Boston", 700, 80),
    new City("New York", 675, 120), new City("Atlanta", 575, 295),
    new City("Miami", 600, 400), new City("Dallas", 408, 325),
    new City("Houston", 450, 360) };

  // Edge array for graph in Figure 30.1
  private int[][] edges = {
    {0, 1}, {0, 3}, {0, 5}, {1, 0}, {1, 2}, {1, 3},
    {2, 1}, {2, 3}, {2, 4}, {2, 10},
    {3, 0}, {3, 1}, {3, 2}, {3, 4}, {3, 5},
    {4, 2}, {4, 3}, {4, 5}, {4, 7}, {4, 8}, {4, 10},
    {5, 0}, {5, 3}, {5, 4}, {5, 6}, {5, 7},
    {6, 5}, {6, 7}, {7, 4}, {7, 5}, {7, 6}, {7, 8},
    {8, 4}, {8, 7}, {8, 9}, {8, 10}, {8, 11},
    {9, 8}, {9, 11}, {10, 2}, {10, 4}, {10, 8}, {10, 11},
    {11, 8}, {11, 9}, {11, 10}
  };

  private Graph<City> graph
    = new UnweightedGraph<City>(edges, vertices);

  public DisplayUSMap() {
    add(new GraphView(graph));
  }

  static class City implements Displayable {
    private int x, y;
    private String name;
```

create a graph

create a GraphView

City class

```
36
37     City(String name, int x, int y) {
38       this.name = name;
39       this.x = x;
40       this.y = y;
41     }
42
43     @Override
44     public int getX() {
45       return x;
46     }
47
48     @Override
49     public int getY() {
50       return y;
51     }
52
53     @Override
54     public String getName() {
55       return name;
56     }
57   }
58 }
```

main method omitted

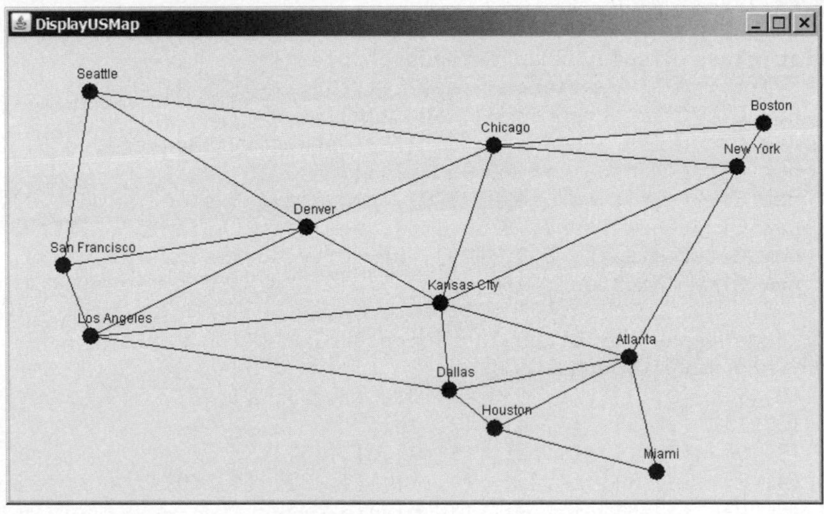

FIGURE 30.10 The graph is displayed in the panel.

The class **City** is defined to model the vertices with their coordinates and names (lines 33–57). The program creates a graph with the vertices of the **City** type (line 27). Since **City** implements **Displayable**, a **GraphView** object created for the graph displays the graph in the panel (line 30).

As an exercise to get acquainted with the graph classes and interfaces, add a city (e.g., Savannah) with appropriate edges into the graph.

MyProgrammingLab™

30.9 For the **graph1** object created in Listing 30.1, TestGraph.java, can you create a **GraphView** object as follows?

```
GraphView view = new GraphView(graph1);
```

30.6 Graph Traversals

Depth-first and breadth-first are two common ways to traverse a graph.

depth-first search
breadth-first search

Graph traversal is the process of visiting each vertex in the graph exactly once. There are two popular ways to traverse a graph: *depth-first traversal* (or *depth-first search*) and *breadth-first traversal* (or *breadth-first search*). Both traversals result in a spanning tree, which can be modeled using a class, as shown in Figure 30.11. Note that `Tree` is an inner class defined in the `AbstractGraph` class. `AbstractGraph<V>.Tree` is different from the `Tree` interface defined in Section 27.2.5. `AbstractGraph.Tree` is a specialized class designed for describing the parent-child relationship of the nodes, whereas the `Tree` interface defines common operations such as searching, inserting, and deleting in a tree. Since there is no need to perform these operations for a spanning tree, `AbstractGraph<V>.Tree` is not defined as a subtype of `Tree`.

AbstractGraph<V>.Tree	
-root: int	The root of the tree.
-parent: int[]	The parents of the vertices.
-searchOrder: List<Integer>	The orders for traversing the vertices.
+Tree(root: int, parent: int[], searchOrder: List<Integer>)	Constructs a tree with the specified root, parent, and searchOrder.
+getRoot(): int	Returns the root of the tree.
+getSearchOrder(): List<Integer>	Returns the order of vertices searched.
+getParent(index: int): int	Returns the parent for the specified vertex index.
+getNumberOfVerticesFound(): int	Returns the number of vertices searched.
+getPath(index: int): List<V>	Returns a list of vertices from the specified vertex index to the root.
+printPath(index: int): void	Displays a path from the root to the specified vertex.
+printTree(): void	Displays tree with the root and all edges.

FIGURE 30.11 The `Tree` class describes the nodes with parent-child relationships.

The `Tree` class is defined as an inner class in the `AbstractGraph` class in lines 208–275 in Listing 30.3. The constructor creates a tree with the root, edges, and a search order.

The `Tree` class defines seven methods. The `getRoot()` method returns the root of the tree. You can get the order of the vertices searched by invoking the `getSearchOrder()` method. You can invoke `getParent(v)` to find the parent of vertex `v` in the search. Invoking `getNumberOfVerticesFound()` returns the number of vertices searched. The method `getPath(index)` returns a list of vertices from the specified vertex index to the root. Invoking `printPath(v)` displays a path from the root to `v`. You can display all edges in the tree using the `printTree()` method.

Sections 30.7 and 30.9 will introduce depth-first search and breadth-first search, respectively. Both searches will result in an instance of the `Tree` class.

30.10 Does `AbstractGraph<V>.Tree` implement the `Tree` interface defined in Listing 27.3 Tree.java?

30.11 What method do you use to find the parent of a vertex in the tree?

30.7 Depth-First Search (DFS)

The depth-first search of a graph starts from a vertex in the graph and visits all vertices in the graph as far as possible before backtracking.

The depth-first search of a graph is like the depth-first search of a tree discussed in Section 27.2.4, Tree Traversal. In the case of a tree, the search starts from the root. In a graph, the search can start from any vertex.

A depth-first search of a tree first visits the root, then recursively visits the subtrees of the root. Similarly, the depth-first search of a graph first visits a vertex, then it recursively visits all the vertices adjacent to that vertex. The difference is that the graph may contain cycles, which could lead to an infinite recursion. To avoid this problem, you need to track the vertices that have already been visited.

The search is called *depth-first* because it searches "deeper" in the graph as much as possible. The search starts from some vertex *v*. After visiting *v*, it next visits an unvisited neighbor of *v*. If *v* has no unvisited neighbor, the search backtracks to the vertex from which it reached *v*. We assume that the graph is connected and the search starting from any vertex can reach all the vertices. If this is not the case, see Programming Exercise 30.4 for finding connected components in a graph.

30.7.1 Depth-First Search Algorithm

The algorithm for the depth-first search is described in Listing 30.8.

LISTING 30.8 Depth-First Search Algorithm

visit v

check a neighbor

recursive search

```
dfs(vertex v) {
  visit v;
  for each neighbor w of v
    if (w has not been visited) {
      dfs(w);
    }
}
```

You can use an array named `isVisited` to denote whether a vertex has been visited. Initially, `isVisited[i]` is `false` for each vertex *i*. Once a vertex, say *v*, is visited, `isVisited[v]` is set to `true`.

Consider the graph in Figure 30.12a. Suppose you start the depth-first search from vertex 0. First visit 0, then any of its neighbors, say 1. Now 1 is visited, as shown in Figure 30.12b. Vertex 1 has three neighbors—0, 2, and 4. Since 0 has already been visited, you will visit either 2 or 4. Let us pick 2. Now 2 is visited, as shown in Figure 30.12c. Vertex 2 has three neighbors: 0, 1, and 3. Since 0 and 1 have already been visited, pick 3. 3 is now visited, as shown in Figure 30.12d. At this point, the vertices have been visited in this order:

```
0, 1, 2, 3
```

Since all the neighbors of 3 have been visited, backtrack to 2. Since all the vertices of 2 have been visited, backtrack to 1. 4 is adjacent to 1, but 4 has not been visited. Therefore, visit 4, as shown in Figure 30.12e. Since all the neighbors of 4 have been visited, backtrack to 1. Since all the neighbors of 1 have been visited, backtrack to 0. Since all the neighbors of 0 have been visited, the search ends.

DFS time complexity

Since each edge and each vertex is visited only once, the time complexity of the `dfs` method is `O(|E| + |V|)`, where `|E|` denotes the number of edges and `|V|` the number of vertices.

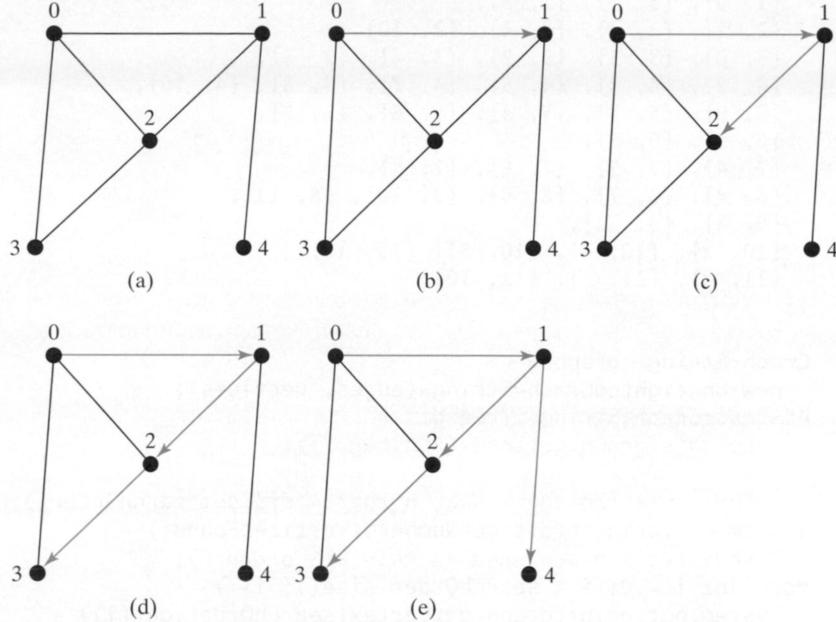

FIGURE 30.12 Depth-first search visits a node and its neighbors recursively.

30.7.2 Implementation of Depth-First Search

The algorithm for DFS in Listing 30.8 uses recursion. It is natural to use recursion to implement it. Alternatively, you can use a stack (see Programming Exercise 30.3).

The `dfs(int v)` method is implemented in lines 146–175 in Listing 30.3. It returns an instance of the `Tree` class with vertex `v` as the root. The method stores the vertices searched in the list `searchOrder` (line 147), the parent of each vertex in the array `parent` (line 148), and uses the `isVisited` array to indicate whether a vertex has been visited (line 153). It invokes the helper method `dfs(v, parent, searchOrder, isVisited)` to perform a depth-first search (line 156).

In the recursive helper method, the search starts from vertex `v`. `v` is added to `searchOrder` in line 166 and is marked as visited (line 167). For each unvisited neighbor of `v`, the method is recursively invoked to perform a depth-first search. When a vertex `i` is visited, the parent of `i` is stored in `parent[i]` (line 171). The method returns when all vertices are visited for a connected graph, or in a connected component.

Listing 30.9 gives a test program that displays a DFS for the graph in Figure 30.1 starting from Chicago. The graphical illustration of the DFS starting from Chicago is shown in Figure 30.13. For an interactive GUI demo of DFS, go to www.cs.armstrong.edu/liang/animation/USMapSearch.html.

U.S. Map Search

LISTING 30.9 TestDFS.java

vertices

edges

```
public class TestDFS {
  public static void main(String[] args) {
    String[] vertices = {"Seattle", "San Francisco", "Los Angeles",
      "Denver", "Kansas City", "Chicago", "Boston", "New York",
      "Atlanta", "Miami", "Dallas", "Houston"};

    int[][] edges = {
      {0, 1}, {0, 3}, {0, 5},
```

create a graph

get DFS

get search order

```
        {1, 0}, {1, 2}, {1, 3},
        {2, 1}, {2, 3}, {2, 4}, {2, 10},
        {3, 0}, {3, 1}, {3, 2}, {3, 4}, {3, 5},
        {4, 2}, {4, 3}, {4, 5}, {4, 7}, {4, 8}, {4, 10},
        {5, 0}, {5, 3}, {5, 4}, {5, 6}, {5, 7},
        {6, 5}, {6, 7},
        {7, 4}, {7, 5}, {7, 6}, {7, 8},
        {8, 4}, {8, 7}, {8, 9}, {8, 10}, {8, 11},
        {9, 8}, {9, 11},
        {10, 2}, {10, 4}, {10, 8}, {10, 11},
        {11, 8}, {11, 9}, {11, 10}
      };

      Graph<String> graph =
        new UnweightedGraph<String>(edges, vertices);
      AbstractGraph<String>.Tree dfs =
        graph.dfs(graph.getIndex("Chicago"));

      java.util.List<Integer> searchOrder = dfs.getSearchOrder();
      System.out.println(dfs.getNumberOfVerticesFound() +
        " vertices are searched in this DFS order:");
      for (int i = 0; i < searchOrder.size(); i++)
        System.out.print(graph.getVertex(searchOrder.get(i)) + " ");
      System.out.println();

      for (int i = 0; i < searchOrder.size(); i++)
        if (dfs.getParent(i) != -1)
          System.out.println("parent of " + graph.getVertex(i) +
            " is " + graph.getVertex(dfs.getParent(i)));
    }
  }
```

```
12 vertices are searched in this DFS order:
  Chicago Seattle San Francisco Los Angeles Denver
  Kansas City New York Boston Atlanta Miami Houston Dallas
parent of Seattle is Chicago
parent of San Francisco is Seattle
parent of Los Angeles is San Francisco
parent of Denver is Los Angeles
parent of Kansas City is Denver
parent of Boston is New York
parent of New York is Kansas City
parent of Atlanta is New York
parent of Miami is Atlanta
parent of Dallas is Houston
parent of Houston is Miami
```

30.7.3 Applications of the DFS

The depth-first search can be used to solve many problems, such as the following:

- Detecting whether a graph is connected. Search the graph starting from any vertex. If the number of vertices searched is the same as the number of vertices in the graph, the graph is connected. Otherwise, the graph is not connected. (See Programming Exercise 30.1.)

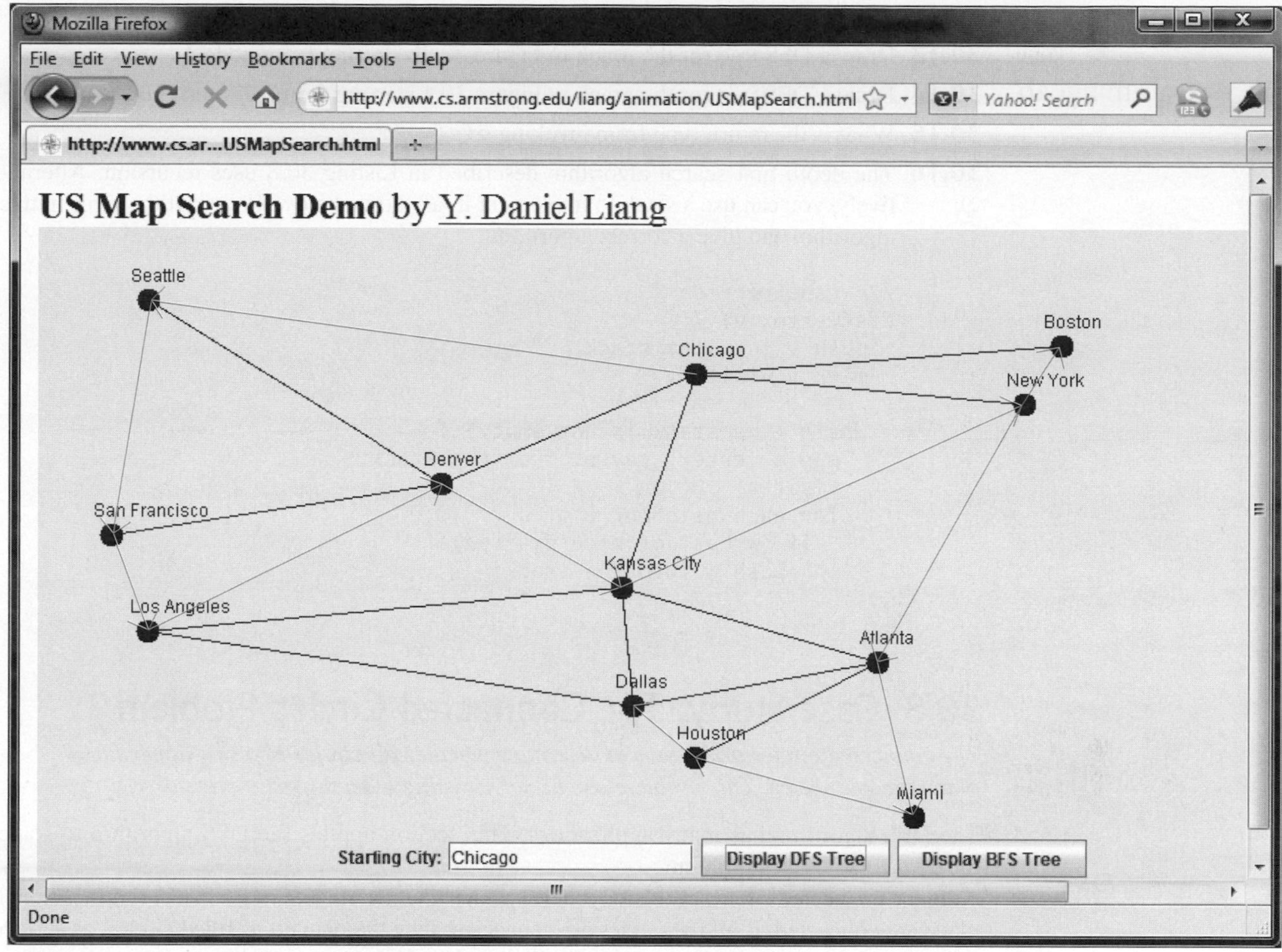

FIGURE 30.13 A DFS search starts from Chicago.

- Detecting whether there is a path between two vertices (see Programming Exercise 30.5).
- Finding a path between two vertices (see Programming Exercise 30.5).
- Finding all connected components. A connected component is a maximal connected subgraph in which every pair of vertices are connected by a path. (See Programming Exercise 30.4.)
- Detecting whether there is a cycle in the graph (see Programming Exercise 30.6).
- Finding a cycle in the graph (see Programming Exercise 30.7).
- Finding a Hamiltonian path/cycle. A *Hamiltonian path* in a graph is a path that visits each vertex in the graph exactly once. A *Hamiltonian cycle* visits each vertex in the graph exactly once and returns to the starting vertex. (See Programming Exercise 30.17.)

The first six problems can be easily solved using the `dfs` method in Listing 30.3. To find a Hamiltonian path/cycle, you have to explore all possible DFSs to find the one that leads to the longest path. The Hamiltonian path/cycle has many applications, including for solving the well-known Knight's Tour problem, which is presented in Supplement VI.C on the Companion Website.

MyProgrammingLab™

30.12 What is depth-first search?

30.13 Draw a DFS tree for the graph in Figure 30.3b starting from node `A`.

30.14 Draw a DFS tree for the graph in Figure 30.1 starting from vertex `Atlanta`.

30.15 What is the return type from invoking `dfs(v)`?

30.16 The depth-first search algorithm described in Listing 30.8 uses recursion. Alternatively, you can use a stack to implement it, as shown below. Point out the error in this algorithm and give a correct algorithm.

```
// Wrong version
dfs(vertex v) {
  push v into the stack;
  mark v visited;

  while (the stack is not empty) {
    pop a vertex, say u, from the stack
    visit u;
    for each neighbor w of u
      if (w has not been visited)
        push w into the stack;
  }
}
```

30.8 Case Study: The Connected Circles Problem

The connected circles problem is to determine whether all circles in a two-dimensional plane are connected. This problem can be solved using a depth-first traversal.

The DFS algorithm has many applications. This section applies the DFS algorithm to solve the connected circles problem.

In the connected circles problem, you determine whether all the circles in a two-dimensional plane are connected. If all the circles are connected, they are painted as filled circles, as shown in Figure 30.14a. Otherwise, they are not filled, as shown in Figure 30.14b.

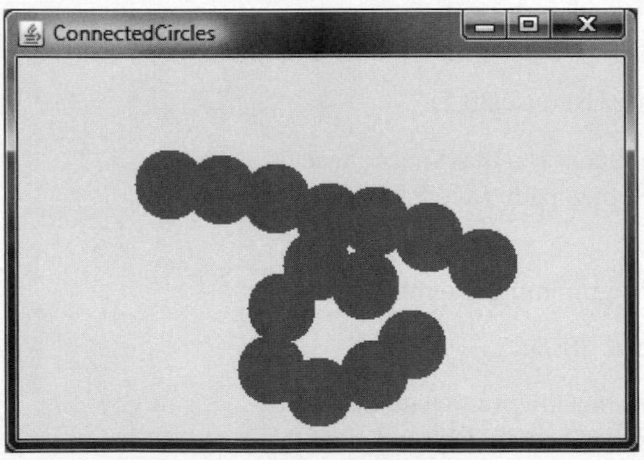

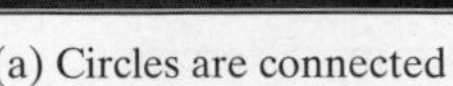
(a) Circles are connected

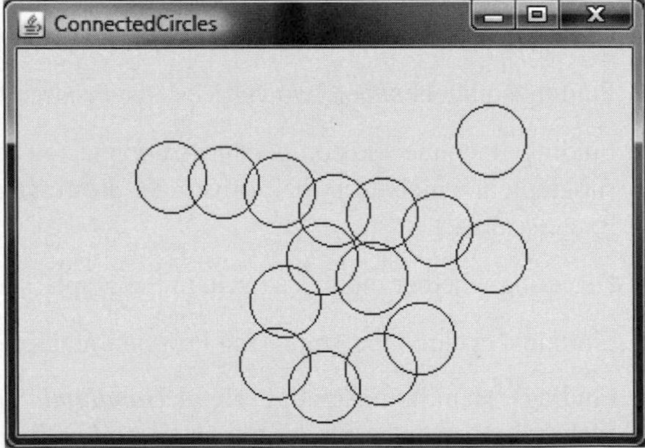

(b) Circles are not connected

FIGURE 30.14 You can apply DFS to determine whether the circles are connected.

We will write a program that lets the user create a circle by clicking a mouse in a blank area that is not currently covered by a circle. As the circles are added, the circles are repainted filled if they are connected or unfilled otherwise.

We will create a graph to model the problem. Each circle is a vertex in the graph. Two circles are connected if they overlap. We apply the DFS in the graph, and if all vertices are found in the depth-first search, the graph is connected.

The program is given in Listing 30.10.

LISTING 30.10 ConnectedCircles.java

```
import java.util.List;
import java.util.ArrayList;
import javax.swing.*;
import java.awt.*;
import java.awt.event.*;

public class ConnectedCircles extends JApplet {
  // Circles are stored in a list
  private List<Circle> circles = new ArrayList<Circle>();

  public ConnectedCircles() {
    add(new CirclePanel()); // Add to circle panel to applet
  }

  /** Panel for displaying circles */
  class CirclePanel extends JPanel {
    public CirclePanel() {
      addMouseListener(new MouseAdapter() {
        @Override
        public void mouseClicked(MouseEvent e) {
          if (!isInsideACircle(e.getPoint())) { // Add a new circle
            circles.add(new Circle(e.getX(), e.getY()));
            repaint();
          }
        }
      });
    }

    /** Returns true if the point is inside an existing circle */
    private boolean isInsideACircle(Point p) {
      for (Circle circle: circles)
        if (circle.contains(p))
          return true;

      return false;
    }

    @Override
    protected void paintComponent(Graphics g) {
      if (circles.size() == 0)
        return; // Nothing to paint

      super.paintComponent(g);

      // Build the edges
      List<AbstractGraph.Edge> edges
        = new ArrayList<AbstractGraph.Edge>();
      for (int i = 0; i < circles.size(); i++)
        for (int j = i + 1; j < circles.size(); j++)
          if (circles.get(i).overlaps(circles.get(j))) {
            edges.add(new AbstractGraph.Edge(i, j));
            edges.add(new AbstractGraph.Edge(j, i));
          }
```

circles in a list

panel for showing circles

mouse clicked

add a new circle

inside circle check

no circles

create edges

create a graph
get a search tree
connected?
connected
not connected
the `Circle` class
contains a point?
two circles overlap
main method omitted

```
54
55       // Create a graph with circles as vertices
56       Graph<Circle> graph
57         = new UnweightedGraph<Circle>(edges, circles);
58       AbstractGraph<Circle>.Tree tree = graph.dfs(0); // a DFS tree
59       boolean isAllCirclesConnected = circles.size() == tree
60           .getNumberOfVerticesFound();
61
62       for (Circle circle : circles) {
63         int radius = circle.radius;
64         if (isAllCirclesConnected) { // All circles are connected
65           g.setColor(Color.RED);
66           g.fillOval(circle.x - radius, circle.y - radius,
67             2 * radius, 2 * radius);
68         } else
69           // circles are not all connected
70           g.drawOval(circle.x - radius, circle.y - radius,
71             2 * radius, 2 * radius);
72       }
73     }
74   }
75
76   private static class Circle {
77     int radius = 20;
78     int x, y;
79
80     Circle(int x, int y) {
81       this.x = x;
82       this.y = y;
83     }
84
85     public boolean contains(Point p) {
86       double d = distance(x, y, p.x, p.y);
87       return d <= radius;
88     }
89
90     public boolean overlaps(Circle circle) {
91       return distance(this.x, this.y, circle.x, circle.y) <= radius
92         + circle.radius;
93     }
94
95     private static double distance(int x1, int y1, int x2, int y2) {
96       return Math.sqrt((x1 - x2) * (x1 - x2) + (y1 - y2) * (y1 - y2));
97     }
98   }
99 }
```

The `Circle` class is defined in lines 76–98. It contains the data fields `x`, `y`, and `radius`, which specify the circle's center location and radius. It also defines the `contains` and `overlaps` methods (lines 85–93) for checking whether a point is inside the circle and whether two circles overlap.

When the user clicks the mouse outside of any existing circle, a new circle is created centered at the mouse point and the circle is added to the list `circles` (line 22).

To detect whether the circles are connected, the program constructs a graph (lines 56–57). The circles are the vertices of the graph. The edges are constructed in lines 46–53. Two circle vertices are connected if they overlap (line 50). The DFS of the graph results in a tree (line 58). The tree's `getNumberOfVerticesFound()` returns the number of vertices searched. If it is equal to the number of circles, all circles are connected (lines 59–60).

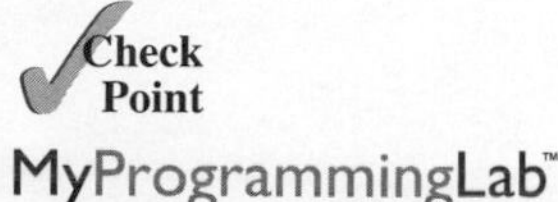

30.17 How is a graph created for the connected circles problem?

30.18 When you click the mouse inside a circle, does the program create a new circle?

30.19 How does the program know if all circles are connected?

30.9 Breadth-First Search (BFS)

The breadth-first search of a graph visits the vertices level by level. The first level consists of the starting vertex. Each next level consists of the vertices adjacent to the vertices in the preceding level.

The breadth-first traversal of a graph is like the breadth-first traversal of a tree discussed in Section 27.2.4, Tree Traversal. With breadth-first traversal of a tree, the nodes are visited level by level. First the root is visited, then all the children of the root, then the grandchildren of the root, and so on. Similarly, the breadth-first search of a graph first visits a vertex, then all its adjacent vertices, then all the vertices adjacent to those vertices, and so on. To ensure that each vertex is visited only once, it skips a vertex if it has already been visited.

30.9.1 Breadth-First Search Algorithm

The algorithm for the breadth-first search starting from vertex *v* in a graph is described in Listing 30.11.

LISTING 30.11 Breadth-First Search Algorithm

```
bfs(vertex v) {
  create an empty queue for storing vertices to be visited;
  add v into the queue;
  mark v visited;

  while (the queue is not empty) {
    dequeue a vertex, say u, from the queue;
    add u into a list of traversed vertices;
    for each neighbor w of u
      if w has not been visited {
        add w into the queue;
        mark w visited;
      }
  }
}
```

create a queue
enqueue v
dequeue into u
u traversed
check a neighbor w
is w visited?
enqueue w

Consider the graph in Figure 30.15a. Suppose you start the breadth-first search from vertex 0. First visit 0, then visit all its neighbors, 1, 2, and 3, as shown in Figure 30.15b. Vertex 1 has three neighbors: 0, 2, and 4. Since 0 and 2 have already been visited, you will now visit just 4, as shown in Figure 30.15c. Vertex 2 has three neighbors, 0, 1, and 3, which have all been visited. Vertex 3 has three neighbors, 0, 2, and 4, which have all been visited. Vertex 4 has two neighbors, 1 and 3, which have all been visited. Hence, the search ends.

Since each edge and each vertex is visited only once, the time complexity of the **bfs** method is **O(|E| + |V|)**, where **|E|** denotes the number of edges and **|V|** the number of vertices.

BFS time complexity

30.9.2 Implementation of Breadth-First Search

The **bfs(int v)** method is defined in the **Graph** interface and implemented in the **AbstractGraph** class in Listing 30.3 (lines 179–204). It returns an instance of the **Tree** class with vertex **v** as the root. The method stores the vertices searched in the list **searchOrder** (line 180), the parent of each vertex in the array **parent** (line 181), uses a linked list for a

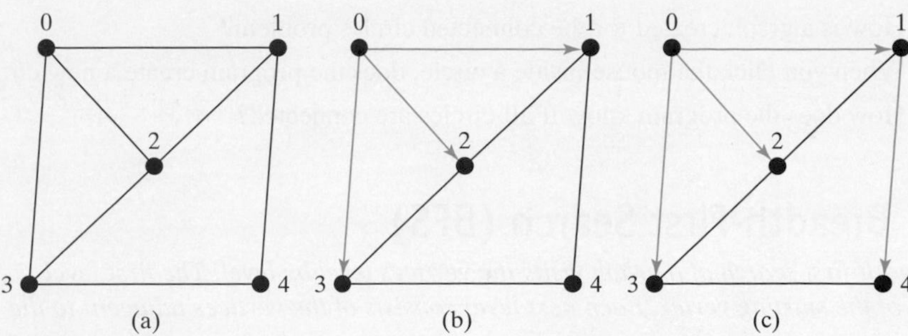

FIGURE 30.15 Breadth-first search visits a node, then its neighbors, then its neighbors's neighbors, and so on.

queue (lines 185–186), and uses the `isVisited` array to indicate whether a vertex has been visited (line 187). The search starts from vertex `v`. `v` is added to the queue in line 188 and is marked as visited (line 189). The method now examines each vertex `u` in the queue (line 192) and adds it to `searchOrder` (line 193). The method adds each unvisited neighbor `w` of `u` to the queue (line 196), sets its parent to `u` (line 197), and marks it as visited (line 198).

Listing 30.12 gives a test program that displays a BFS for the graph in Figure 30.1 starting from Chicago. The graphical illustration of the BFS starting from Chicago is shown in Figure 30.16. For an interactive GUI demo of BFS, go to www.cs.armstrong.edu/liang/animation/USMapSearch.html.

LISTING 30.12 TestBFS.java

vertices
edges
create a graph
create a BFS tree
get search order

```java
public class TestBFS {
  public static void main(String[] args) {
    String[] vertices = {"Seattle", "San Francisco", "Los Angeles",
      "Denver", "Kansas City", "Chicago", "Boston", "New York",
      "Atlanta", "Miami", "Dallas", "Houston"};

    int[][] edges = {
      {0, 1}, {0, 3}, {0, 5},
      {1, 0}, {1, 2}, {1, 3},
      {2, 1}, {2, 3}, {2, 4}, {2, 10},
      {3, 0}, {3, 1}, {3, 2}, {3, 4}, {3, 5},
      {4, 2}, {4, 3}, {4, 5}, {4, 7}, {4, 8}, {4, 10},
      {5, 0}, {5, 3}, {5, 4}, {5, 6}, {5, 7},
      {6, 5}, {6, 7},
      {7, 4}, {7, 5}, {7, 6}, {7, 8},
      {8, 4}, {8, 7}, {8, 9}, {8, 10}, {8, 11},
      {9, 8}, {9, 11},
      {10, 2}, {10, 4}, {10, 8}, {10, 11},
      {11, 8}, {11, 9}, {11, 10}
    };

    Graph<String> graph =
      new UnweightedGraph<String>(edges, vertices);
    AbstractGraph<String>.Tree bfs =
      graph.bfs(graph.getIndex("Chicago"));

    java.util.List<Integer> searchOrder = bfs.getSearchOrder();
    System.out.println(bfs.getNumberOfVerticesFound() +
      " vertices are searched in this order:");
    for (int i = 0; i < searchOrder.size(); i++)
      System.out.println(graph.getVertex(searchOrder.get(i)));
```

```

      for (int i = 0; i < searchOrder.size(); i++)
        if (bfs.getParent(i) != -1)
          System.out.println("parent of " + graph.getVertex(i) +
            " is " + graph.getVertex(bfs.getParent(i)));
    }
  }
```

```
12 vertices are searched in this order:
  Chicago Seattle Denver Kansas City Boston New York
  San Francisco Los Angeles Atlanta Dallas Miami Houston
parent of Seattle is Chicago
parent of San Francisco is Seattle
parent of Los Angeles is Denver
parent of Denver is Chicago
parent of Kansas City is Chicago
parent of Boston is Chicago
parent of New York is Chicago
parent of Atlanta is Kansas City
parent of Miami is Atlanta
parent of Dallas is Kansas City
parent of Houston is Atlanta
```

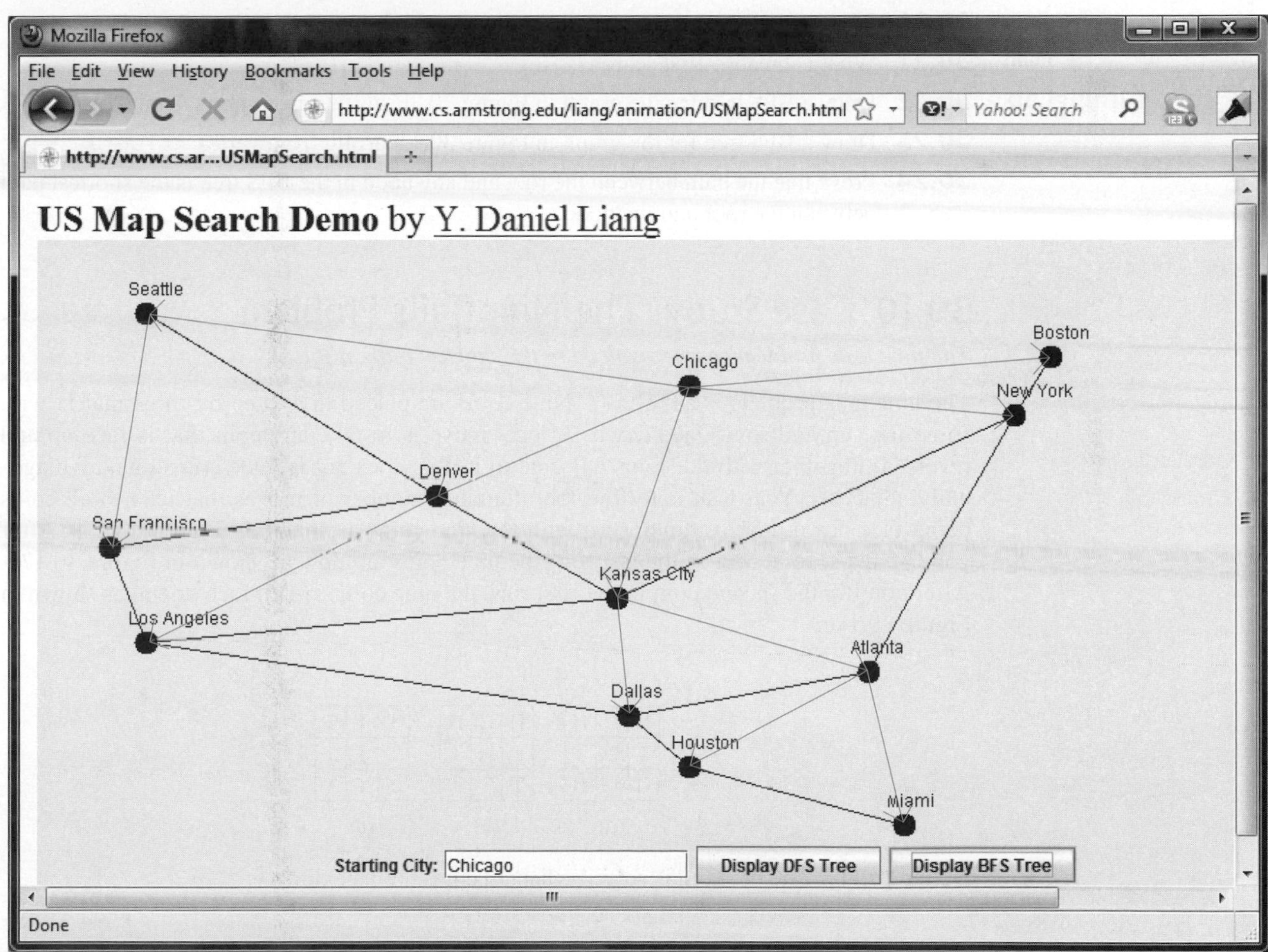

FIGURE 30.16 BFS search starts from Chicago.

30.9.3 Applications of the BFS

Many of the problems solved by the DFS can also be solved using the BFS. Specifically, the BFS can be used to solve the following problems:

- Detecting whether a graph is connected. A graph is connected if there is a path between any two vertices in the graph.
- Detecting whether there is a path between two vertices.
- Finding the shortest path between two vertices. You can prove that the path between the root and any node in the BFS tree is the shortest path between the root and the node. (See Check Point Question 30.24.)
- Finding all connected components. A connected component is a maximal connected subgraph in which every pair of vertices are connected by a path.
- Detecting whether there is a cycle in the graph (see Programming Exercise 30.6).
- Finding a cycle in the graph (see Programming Exercise 30.7).
- Testing whether a graph is bipartite. (A graph is bipartite if the vertices of the graph can be divided into two disjoint sets such that no edges exist between vertices in the same set.) (See Programming Exercise 30.8.)

MyProgrammingLab™

30.20 What is the return type from invoking `bfs(v)`?

30.21 What is breadth-first search?

30.22 Draw a BFS tree for the graph in Figure 30.3b starting from node `A`.

30.23 Draw a BFS tree for the graph in Figure 30.1 starting from vertex `Atlanta`.

30.24 Prove that the path between the root and any node in the BFS tree is the shortest path between the root and the node.

30.10 Case Study: The Nine Tails Problem

The nine tails problem can be reduced to the shortest path problem.

The nine tails problem is as follows. Nine coins are placed in a three-by-three matrix with some face up and some face down. A legal move is to take any coin that is face up and reverse it, together with the coins adjacent to it (this does not include coins that are diagonally adjacent). Your task is to find the minimum number of moves that lead to all coins being face down. For example, start with the nine coins as shown in Figure 30.17a. After you flip the second coin in the last row, the nine coins are now as shown in Figure 30.17b. After you flip the second coin in the first row, the nine coins are all face down, as shown in Figure 30.17c.

H	H	H
T	T	T
H	H	H

(a)

H	H	H
T	H	T
T	T	T

(b)

T	T	T
T	T	T
T	T	T

(c)

FIGURE 30.17 The problem is solved when all coins are face down.

We will write a program that prompts the user to enter an initial state of the nine coins and displays the solution, as shown in the following sample run.

```
Enter the initial nine coins Hs and Ts: HHHTTTHHH ↵Enter

The steps to flip the coins are
HHH
TTT
HHH

HHH
THT
TTT

TTT
TTT
TTT
```

Each state of the nine coins represents a node in the graph. For example, the three states in Figure 30.17 correspond to three nodes in the graph. For convenience, we use a 3 × 3 matrix to represent all nodes and use **0** for heads and **1** for tails. Since there are nine cells and each cell is either **0** or **1**, there are a total of 2^9 (512) nodes, labeled **0**, **1**, . . . , and **511**, as shown in Figure 30.18.

0	0	0
0	0	0
0	0	0

0

0	0	0
0	0	0
0	0	1

1

0	0	0
0	0	0
0	1	0

2

0	0	0
0	0	0
0	1	1

3

.....

1	1	1
1	1	1
1	1	1

511

FIGURE 30.18 There are total of 512 nodes labeled in this order: **0**, **1**, **2**, . . . , **511**.

We assign an edge from node **v** to **u** if there is a legal move from **u** to **v**. Figure 30.19 shows a partial graph. Note there is an edge from **511** to **47**, since you can flip a cell in node **47** to become node **511**.

The last node in Figure 30.18 represents the state of nine face-down coins. For convenience, we call this last node the *target node*. Thus, the target node is labeled **511**. Suppose the initial state of the nine tails problem corresponds to the node **s**. The problem is reduced to finding the shortest path from node **s** to the target node, which is equivalent to finding the path from node **s** to the target node in a BFS tree rooted at the target node.

Now the task is to build a graph that consists of 512 nodes labeled **0**, **1**, **2**, . . . , **511**, and edges among the nodes. Once the graph is created, obtain a BFS tree rooted at node **511**. From the BFS tree, you can find the shortest path from the root to any vertex. We will create a class named **NineTailModel**, which contains the method to get the shortest path from the target node to any other node. The class UML diagram is shown in Figure 30.20.

Visually, a node is represented in a 3 × 3 matrix with the letters **H** and **T**. In our program, we use a single-dimensional array of nine characters to represent a node. For example, the node for vertex **1** in Figure 30.18 is represented as {**'H'**, **'H'**, **'H'**, **'H'**, **'H'**, **'H'**, **'H'**, **'H'**, **'T'**} in the array.

The **getEdges()** method returns a list of **Edge** objects.

The **getNode(index)** method returns the node for the specified index. For example, **getNode(0)** returns the node that contains nine **H**s. **getNode(511)** returns the node that contains nine **T**s. The **getIndex(node)** method returns the index of the node.

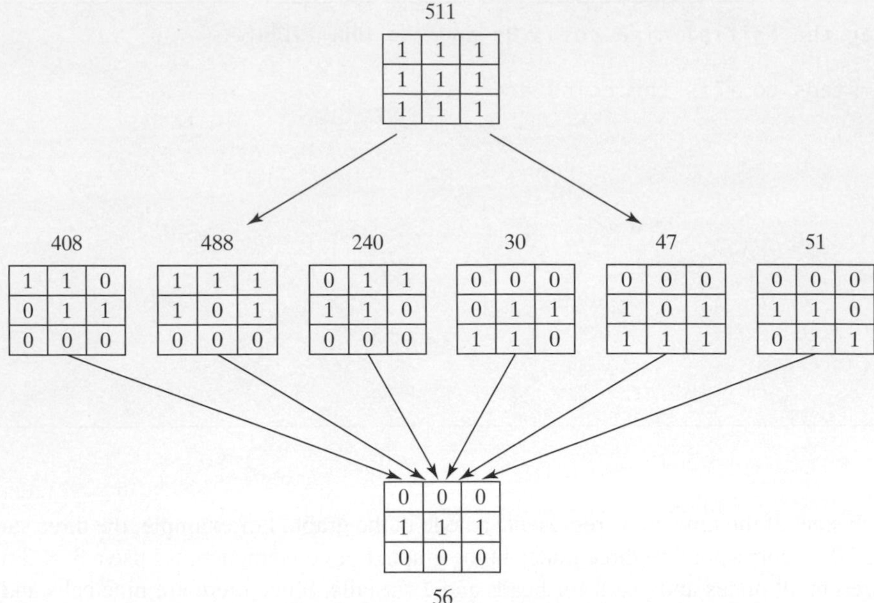

FIGURE 30.19 If node `u` becomes node `v` after cells are flipped, assign an edge from `v` to `u`.

NineTailModel	
`#tree: AbstractGraph<Integer>.Tree`	A tree rooted at node 511.
`+NineTailModel()`	Constructs a model for the nine tails problem and obtains the tree.
`+getShortestPath(nodeIndex: int): List<Integer>`	Returns a path from the specified node to the root. The path returned consists of the node labels in a list.
`-getEdges(): List<AbstractGraph.Edge>`	Returns a list of `Edge` objects for the graph.
`+getNode(index: int): char[]`	Returns a node consisting of nine characters of Hs and Ts.
`+getIndex(node: char[]): int`	Returns the index of the specified node.
`+getFlippedNode(node: char[], position: int): int`	Flips the node at the specified position and returns the index of the flipped node.
`+flipACell(node: char[], row: int, column: int): void`	Flips the node at the specified row and column.
`+printNode(node: char[]): void`	Displays the node on the console.

FIGURE 30.20 The `NineTailModel` class models the nine tails problem using a graph.

Note that the data field **`tree`** is defined as protected so that it can be accessed from the `WeightedNineTail` subclass in the next chapter.

The **`getFlippedNode(char[] node, int position)`** method flips the node at the specified position and its adjacent positions. This method returns the index of the new node. For example, for node `56` in Figure 30.19, flip it at position `0`, and you will get node `51`. If you flip node `56` at position `1`, you will get node `47`.

The **`flipACell(char[] node, int row, int column)`** method flips a node at the specified row and column. For example, if you flip node `56` at row `0` and column `0`, the new node is `408`. If you flip node `56` at row `2` and column `0`, the new node is `30`.

Listing 30.13 shows the source code for NineTailModel.java.

LISTING 30.13 NineTailModel.java

```
import java.util.*;

public class NineTailModel {
  public final static int NUMBER_OF_NODES = 512;
  protected AbstractGraph<Integer>.Tree tree; // Define a tree

  /** Construct a model */
  public NineTailModel() {
    // Create edges
    List<AbstractGraph.Edge> edges = getEdges();

    // Create a graph
    UnweightedGraph<Integer> graph = new UnweightedGraph<Integer>(
      edges, NUMBER_OF_NODES);

    // Obtain a BSF tree rooted at the target node
    tree = graph.bfs(511);
  }

  /** Create all edges for the graph */
  private List<AbstractGraph.Edge> getEdges() {
    List<AbstractGraph.Edge> edges =
      new ArrayList<AbstractGraph.Edge>(); // Store edges

    for (int u = 0; u < NUMBER_OF_NODES; u++) {
      for (int k = 0; k < 9; k++) {
        char[] node = getNode(u); // Get the node for vertex u
        if (node[k] == 'H') {
          int v = getFlippedNode(node, k);
          // Add edge (v, u) for a legal move from node u to node v
          edges.add(new AbstractGraph.Edge(v, u));
        }
      }
    }

    return edges;
  }

  public static int getFlippedNode(char[] node, int position) {
    int row = position / 3;
    int column = position % 3;

    flipACell(node, row, column);
    flipACell(node, row - 1, column);
    flipACell(node, row + 1, column);
    flipACell(node, row, column - 1);
    flipACell(node, row, column + 1);

    return getIndex(node);
  }

  public static void flipACell(char[] node, int row, int column) {
    if (row >= 0 && row <= 2 && column >= 0 && column <= 2) {
      // Within the boundary
      if (node[row * 3 + column] == 'H')
        node[row * 3 + column] = 'T'; // Flip from H to T
      else
        node[row * 3 + column] = 'H'; // Flip from T to H
```

declare a tree

create edges

create graph

create tree

get edges

add an edge

flip cells

flip a cell

```
 59      }
 60    }
 61
 62    public static int getIndex(char[] node) {
 63      int result = 0;
 64
 65      for (int i = 0; i < 9; i++)
 66        if (node[i] == 'T')
 67          result = result * 2 + 1;
 68        else
 69          result = result * 2 + 0;
 70
 71      return result;
 72    }
 73
 74    public static char[] getNode(int index) {
 75      char[] result = new char[9];
 76
 77      for (int i = 0; i < 9; i++) {
 78        int digit = index % 2;
 79        if (digit == 0)
 80          result[8 - i] = 'H';
 81        else
 82          result[8 - i] = 'T';
 83        index = index / 2;
 84      }
 85
 86      return result;
 87    }
 88
 89    public List<Integer> getShortestPath(int nodeIndex) {
 90      return tree.getPath(nodeIndex);
 91    }
 92
 93    public static void printNode(char[] node) {
 94      for (int i = 0; i < 9; i++)
 95        if (i % 3 != 2)
 96          System.out.print(node[i]);
 97        else
 98          System.out.println(node[i]);
 99
100      System.out.println();
101    }
102  }
```

get index for a node (line 62)

For example:
index: 3
node: HHHHHHHTT

H	H	H
H	H	H
H	T	T

get node for an index (line 74)

For example:
node: THHHHHHTT
index: 259

T	H	H
H	H	H
H	T	T

shortest path (line 89)

display a node (line 93)

The constructor (lines 8–18) creates a graph with 512 nodes, and each edge corresponds to the move from one node to the other (line 10). From the graph, a BFS tree rooted at the target node `511` is obtained (line 17).

To create edges, the `getEdges` method (lines 21–37) checks each node `u` to see if it can be flipped to another node `v`. If so, add `(v, u)` to the `Edge` list (line 31). The `getFlippedNode(node, position)` method finds a flipped node by flipping an `H` cell and its neighbors in a node (lines 43–47). The `flipACell(node, row, column)` method actually flips an `H` cell and its neighbors in a node (lines 52–60).

The `getIndex(node)` method is implemented in the same way as converting a binary number to a decimal number (lines 62–72). The `getNode(index)` method returns a node consisting of the letters `H` and `T` (lines 74–87).

The `getShortestpath(nodeIndex)` method invokes the `getPath(nodeIndex)` method to get the vertices in the shortest path from the specified node to the target node (lines 89–91).

The `printNode(node)` method displays a node on the console (lines 93–101).

Listing 30.14 gives a program that prompts the user to enter an initial node and displays the steps to reach the target node.

LISTING 30.14 NineTail.java

```
1  import java.util.Scanner;
2
3  public class NineTail {
4    public static void main(String[] args) {
5      // Prompt the user to enter nine coins' Hs and Ts
6      System.out.print("Enter the initial nine coins Hs and Ts: ");
7      Scanner input = new Scanner(System.in);
8      String s = input.nextLine();
9      char[] initialNode = s.toCharArray();
10
11     NineTailModel model = new NineTailModel();
12     java.util.List<Integer> path =
13       model.getShortestPath(NineTailModel.getIndex(initialNode));
14
15     System.out.println("The steps to flip the coins are ");
16     for (int i = 0; i < path.size(); i++)
17       NineTailModel.printNode(
18         NineTailModel.getNode(path.get(i).intValue()));
19   }
20 }
```

initial node

create model

get shortest path

The program prompts the user to enter an initial node with nine letters with a combination of Hs and Ts as a string in line 8, obtains an array of characters from the string (line 9), creates a graph model to get a BFS tree (line 11), obtains the shortest path from the initial node to the target node (lines 12–13), and displays the nodes in the path (lines 16–18).

30.25 How are the nodes created for the graph in `NineTailModel`?

30.26 How are the edges created for the graph in `NineTailModel`?

30.27 What is returned after invoking `getIndex("HTHTTTHHH".toCharArray())` in Listing 30.13? What is returned after invoking `getNode(46)` in Listing 30.13?

30.28 If lines 26 and 27 are swapped in Listing 30.13, NineTailModel.java, will the program work? Why not?

KEY TERMS

adjacency list 1054
adjacency matrix 1054
adjacent vertices 1050
breadth-first search 1069
complete graph 1050
cycle 1050
degree 1050
depth-first search 1069
directed graph 1049
graph 1049
incident edges 1050
parallel edge 1050
Seven Bridges of Königsberg 1048
simple graph 1050
spanning tree 1050
tree 1050
undirected graph 1049
unweighted graph 1049
weighted graph 1049

Chapter Summary

1. A *graph* is a useful mathematical structure that represents relationships among entities in the real world. You learned how to model graphs using classes and interfaces, how to represent vertices and edges using arrays and linked lists, and how to implement operations for graphs.

2. Graph traversal is the process of visiting each vertex in the graph exactly once. You learned two popular ways for traversing a graph: the *depth-first search* (DFS) and *breadth-first search* (BFS).

3. DFS and BFS can be used to solve many problems such as detecting whether a graph is connected, detecting whether there is a cycle in the graph, and finding the shortest path between two vertices.

Test Questions

Do the test questions for this chapter online at www.cs.armstrong.edu/liang/intro9e/test.html.

MyProgrammingLab™

Programming Exercises

Sections 30.6–30.10

***30.1** (*Test whether a graph is connected*) Write a program that reads a graph from a file and determines whether the graph is connected. The first line in the file contains a number that indicates the number of vertices (`n`). The vertices are labeled as `0`, `1`, . . . , `n-1`. Each subsequent line, with the format `u v1 v2 ...`, describes edges (`u`, `v1`), (`u`, `v2`), and so on. Figure 30.21 gives the examples of two files for their corresponding graphs.

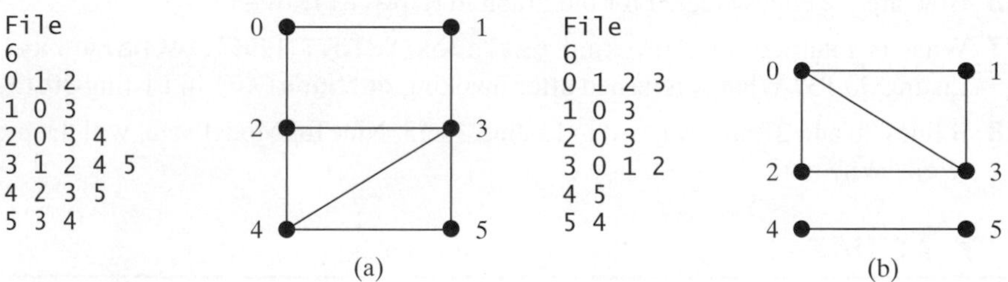

Figure 30.21 The vertices and edges of a graph can be stored in a file.

Your program should prompt the user to enter the name of the file, then it should read data from the file, create an instance `g` of `UnweightedGraph`, invoke `g.printEdges()` to display all edges, and invoke `dfs()` to obtain an instance `tree` of `AbstractGraph.Tree`. If `tree.getNumberOfVerticesFound()` is the same as the number of vertices in the graph, the graph is connected. Here is a sample run of the program:

```
Enter a file name: c:\exercise\GraphSample1.txt ↵Enter
The number of vertices is 6
Vertex 0: (0, 1) (0, 2)
Vertex 1: (1, 0) (1, 3)
Vertex 2: (2, 0) (2, 3) (2, 4)
Vertex 3: (3, 1) (3, 2) (3, 4) (3, 5)
Vertex 4: (4, 2) (4, 3) (4, 5)
Vertex 5: (5, 3) (5, 4)
The graph is connected
```

(*Hint*: Use **new UnweightedGraph(list, numberOfVertices)** to create a graph, where **list** contains a list of **AbstractGraph.Edge** objects. Use **new AbstractGraph.Edge(u, v)** to create an edge. Read the first line to get the number of vertices. Read each subsequent line into a string **s** and use **s.split("[\\s+]")** to extract the vertices from the string and create edges from the vertices.)

***30.2** (*Create a file for a graph*) Modify Listing 30.1, TestGraph.java, to create a file representing **graph1**. The file format is described in Programming Exercise 30.1. Create the file from the array defined in lines 8–21 in Listing 30.1. The number of vertices for the graph is **12**, which will be stored in the first line of the file. The contents of the file should be as follows:

12
0 1 3 5
1 0 2 3
2 1 3 4 10
3 0 1 2 4 5
4 2 3 5 7 8 10
5 0 3 4 6 7
6 5 7
7 4 5 6 8
8 4 7 9 10 11
9 8 11
10 2 4 8 11
11 8 9 10

***30.3** (*Implement DFS using a stack*) The depth-first search algorithm described in Listing 30.8 uses recursion. Implement it without using recursion.

***30.4** (*Find connected components*) Create a new class named **MyGraph** as a subclass of **UnweightedGraph** that contains a method for finding all connected components in a graph with the following header:

```
public List<List<Integer>> getConnectedComponents();
```

The method returns a **List<List<Integer>>**. Each element in the list is another list that contains all the vertices in a connected component. For example, for the graph in Figure 30.21b, **getConnectedComponents()** returns **[[0, 1, 2, 3], [4, 5]]**.

***30.5** (*Find paths*) Add a new method in **AbstractGraph** to find a path between two vertices with the following header:

```
public List<Integer> getPath(int u, int v);
```

The method returns a **List<Integer>** that contains all the vertices in a path from **u** to **v** in this order. Using the BFS approach, you can obtain the shortest path from **u** to **v**. If there isn't a path from **u** to **v**, the method returns **null**.

***30.6** (*Detect cycles*) Add a new method in **AbstractGraph** to determine whether there is a cycle in the graph with the following header:

```
public boolean isCyclic();
```

***30.7** (*Find a cycle*) Add a new method in **AbstractGraph** to find a cycle in the graph with the following header:

```
public List<Integer> getACycle(int u);
```

The method returns a **List** that contains all the vertices in a cycle starting from **u**. If the graph doesn't have any cycles, the method returns **null**.

****30.8** (*Test bipartite*) Recall that a graph is bipartite if its vertices can be divided into two disjoint sets such that no edges exist between vertices in the same set. Add a new method in **AbstractGraph** with the following header to detect whether the graph is bipartite:

```
public boolean isBipartite();
```

****30.9** (*Get bipartite sets*) Add a new method in **AbstractGraph** with the following header to return two bipartite sets if the graph is bipartite:

```
public List<List<Integer>> getBipartite();
```

The method returns a **List** that contains two sublists, each of which contains a set of vertices. If the graph is not bipartite, the method returns **null**.

***30.10** (*Find the shortest path*) Write a program that reads a connected graph from a file. The graph is stored in a file using the same format specified in Exercise 30.1. Your program should prompt the user to enter the name of the file, then two vertices, and should display the shortest path between the two vertices. For example, for the graph in Figure 30.21a, the shortest path between **0** and **5** may be displayed as **0 1 3 5**.

Here is a sample run of the program:

```
Enter a file name: c:\exercise\GraphSample1.txt [Enter]
Enter two vertices (integer indexes): 0 5 [Enter]
The number of vertices is 6
Vertex 0: (0, 1) (0, 2)
Vertex 1: (1, 0) (1, 3)
Vertex 2: (2, 0) (2, 3) (2, 4)
Vertex 3: (3, 1) (3, 2) (3, 4) (3, 5)
Vertex 4: (4, 2) (4, 3) (4, 5)
Vertex 5: (5, 3) (5, 4)
The path is 0 1 3 5
```

****30.11** (*Revise Listing 30.14, NineTail.java*) The program in Listing 30.14 lets the user enter an input for the nine tails problem from the console and displays the result on the console. Write an applet that lets the user set an initial state of the nine coins (see Figure 30.22a) and click the *Solve* button to display the solution, as shown in Figure 30.22b. Initially, the user can click the mouse button to flip a coin. Set a red color on the flipped cells.

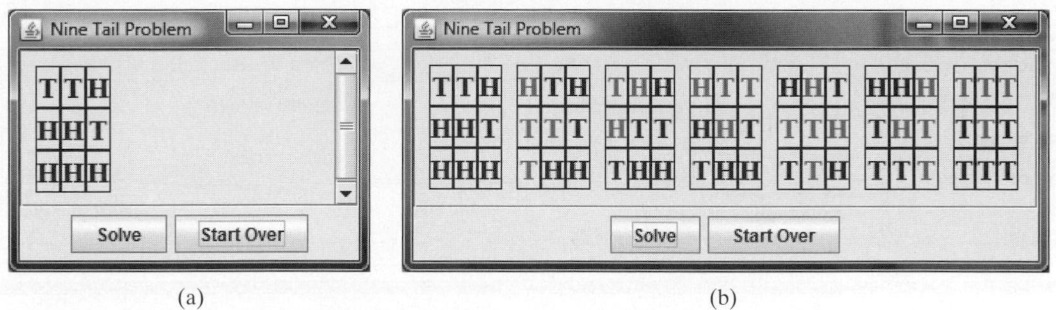

FIGURE 30.22 The applet solves the nine tails problem.

****30.12** (*Variation of the nine tails problem*) In the nine tails problem, when you flip a coin, the horizontal and vertical neighboring cells are also flipped. Rewrite the program, assuming that all neighboring cells including the diagonal neighbors are also flipped.

****30.13** (*4 × 4 16 tails model*) The nine tails problem in the text uses a 3 × 3 matrix. Assume that you have 16 coins placed in a 4 × 4 matrix. Create a new model class named `TailModel16`. Create an instance of the model and save the object into a file named **TailModel16.dat**.

****30.14** (*4 × 4 16 tails view*) Listing 30.14, NineTail.java, presents a solution for the nine tails problem. Revise this program for the 4 × 4 16 tails problem. Your program should read the model object created from the preceding exercise.

****30.15** (*Dynamic graphs*) Write a program that lets the user create a graph dynamically. The user can create a vertex by entering its name and location, as shown in Figure 30.23. The user can also create an edge to connect two vertices. To simplify the program, assume that the vertex names are the same as the vertex indices. You have to add the vertex indices `0`, `1`, . . . , `n`, in this order. The user can specify two vertices and let the program display their shortest path in red.

****30.16** (*Induced subgraph*) Given an undirected graph G = (V, E) and an integer *k*, find an induced subgraph H of G of maximum size such that all vertices of H have a degree >= *k*, or conclude that no such induced subgraph exists. Implement the method with the following header:

```
public static Graph maxInducedSubgraph(Graph edge, int k)
```

The method returns `null` if such a subgraph does not exist.

(*Hint*: An intuitive approach is to remove vertices whose degree is less than *k*. As vertices are removed with their adjacent edges, the degrees of other vertices may be reduced. Continue the process until no vertices can be removed, or all the vertices are removed.)

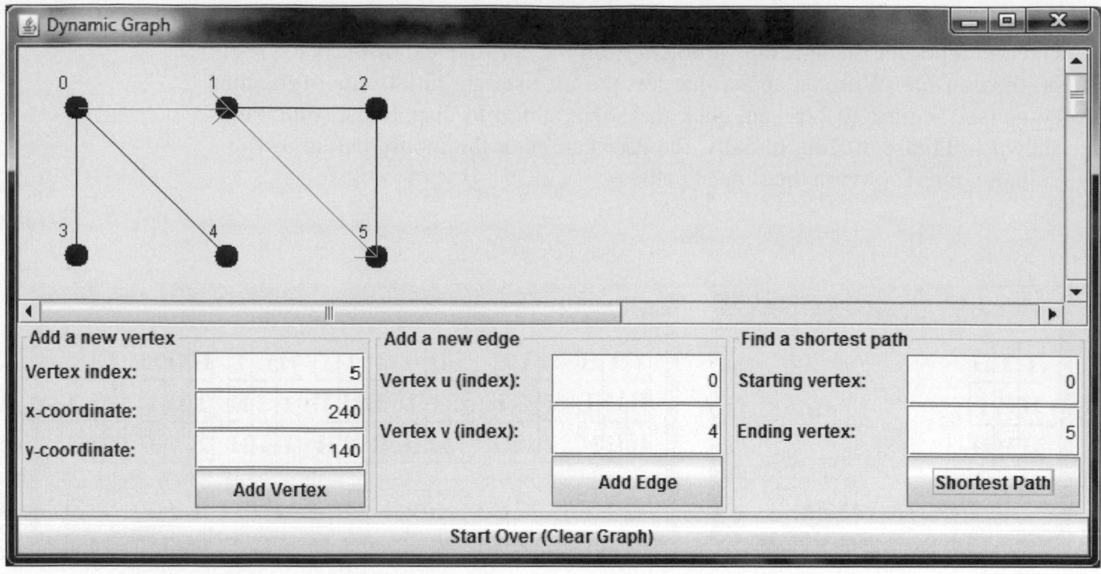

FIGURE 30.23 The program can add vertices and edges and display the shortest path between two specified vertices.

*****30.17** (*Hamiltonian cycle*) The Hamiltonian path algorithm is implemented in Supplement VI.C. Add the following `getHamiltonianCycle` method in the `Graph` interface and implement it in the `AbstractGraph` class:

```
/** Return a Hamiltonian cycle
  * Return null if the graph doesn't contain a Hamiltonian cycle */
public List<Integer> getHamiltonianCycle()
```

*****30.18** (*Knight's Tour cycle*) Rewrite KnightTourApp.java in the case study in Supplement VI.C to find a knight's tour that visits each square in a chessboard and returns to the starting square. Reduce the Knight's Tour cycle problem to the problem of finding a Hamiltonian cycle.

****30.19** (*Display a DFS/BFS tree in a graph*) Modify `GraphView` in Listing 30.6 to add a new data field `tree` with a set method. The edges in the tree are displayed in red. Write a program that displays the graph in Figure 30.1 and the DFS/BFS tree starting from a specified city, as shown in Figures 30.13 and 30.16. If a city not in the map is entered, the program displays a dialog box to alert the user.

***30.20** (*Display a graph*) Write a program that reads a graph from a file and displays it. The first line in the file contains a number that indicates the number of vertices (`n`). The vertices are labeled `0`, `1`, . . . , `n-1`. Each subsequent line, with the format `u x y v1 v2 ...`, describes the position of `u` at (`x`, `y`) and edges (`u`, `v1`), (`u`, `v2`), and so on. Figure 30.24a gives an example of the file for their corresponding graph. Your program prompts the user to enter the name of the file, reads data from the file, and displays the graph on a panel using `GraphView`, as shown in Figure 30.24b.

****30.21** (*Display sets of connected circles*) Modify Listing 30.10, ConnectedCircles.java, to display sets of connected circles in different colors. That is, if two circles are connected, they are displayed using the same color; otherwise, they are not in same color, as shown in Figure 30.25. (*Hint*: See Programming Exercise 30.4.)

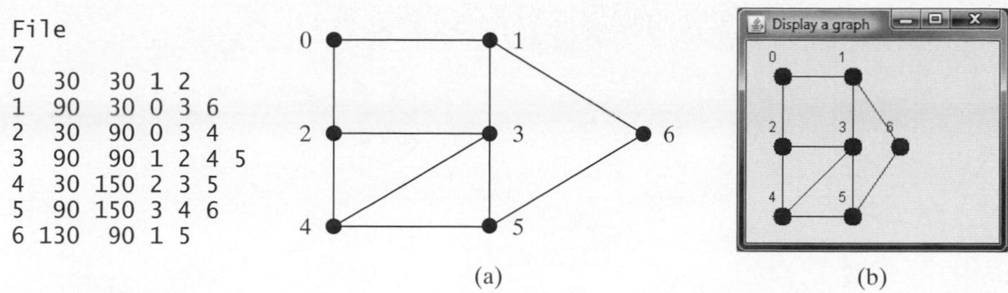

FIGURE 30.24 The program reads the information about the graph and displays it visually.

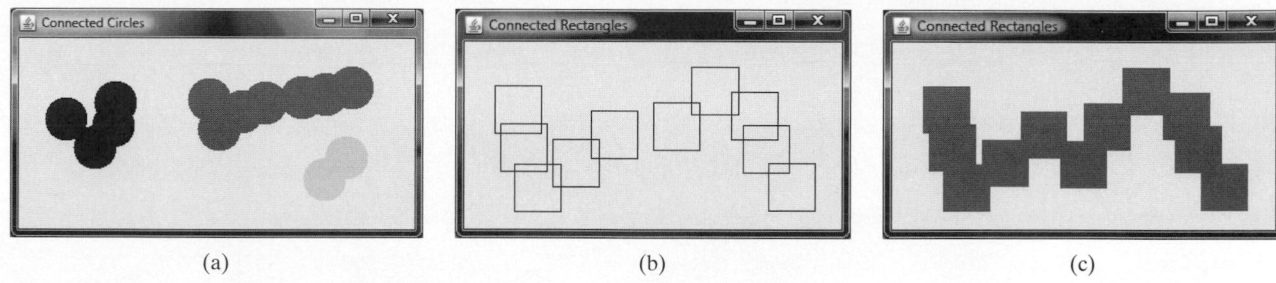

FIGURE 30.25 (a) Connected circles are displayed in the same color. (b) Rectangles are not filled with a color if they are not connected. (c) Rectangles are filled with a color if they are connected.

***30.22** (*Move a circle*) Modify Listing 30.10, ConnectedCircles.java, to enable the user to drag and move a circle.

****30.23** (*Connected rectangles*) Listing 30.10, ConnectedCircles.java, allows the user to create circles and determine whether they are connected. Rewrite the program for rectangles. The program lets the user create a rectangle by clicking a mouse in a blank area that is not currently covered by a rectangle. As the rectangles are added, the rectangles are repainted as filled if they are connected or are unfilled otherwise, as shown in Figure 30.25b–c.

***30.24** (*Remove a circle*) Modify Listing 30.10, ConnectedCircles.java, to enable the user to remove a circle when the mouse is clicked inside the circle.

*****30.25** (*Graph visualization tool*) Develop an applet as shown in Figure 30.4, with the following requirements: (1) The radius of each vertex is 20 pixels. (2) The user clicks the left-mouse button to place a vertex centered at the mouse point, provided that the mouse point is not inside or too close to an existing vertex. (3) The user clicks the right-mouse button inside an existing vertex to remove the vertex. (4) The user presses a mouse button inside a vertex, drags to another vertex, and then releases the button to create an edge. (5) The user drags a vertex while pressing the *CTRL* key to move a vertex. (6) The vertices are numbers starting from `0`. When a vertex is removed, the vertices are renumbered. (7) You can click the *DFS* or *BFS* button to display a DFS or BFS tree from a starting vertex. (8) You can click the *Shortest Path* button to display the shortest path between the two specified vertices.

CHAPTER

31

Weighted Graphs and Applications

Objectives

- To represent weighted edges using adjacency matrices and priority queues (§31.2).
- To model weighted graphs using the `WeightedGraph` class that extends the `AbstractGraph` class (§31.3).
- To design and implement the algorithm for finding a minimum spanning tree (§31.4).
- To define the `MST` class that extends the `Tree` class (§31.4).
- To design and implement the algorithm for finding single-source shortest paths (§31.5).
- To define the `ShortestPathTree` class that extends the `Tree` class (§31.5).
- To solve the weighted nine tails problem using the shortest-path algorithm (§31.6).

31.1 Introduction

A graph is a weighted graph *if each edge is assigned a weight. Weighted graphs have many practical applications.*

problem

Figure 30.1 assumes that the graph represents the number of flights among cities. You can apply the BFS to find the fewest number of flights between two cities. Assume that the edges represent the driving distances among the cities as shown in Figure 31.1. How do you find the minimal total distances for connecting all cities? How do you find the shortest path between two cities? This chapter will address these questions. The former is known as the *minimum spanning tree (MST) problem* and the latter as the *shortest path problem*.

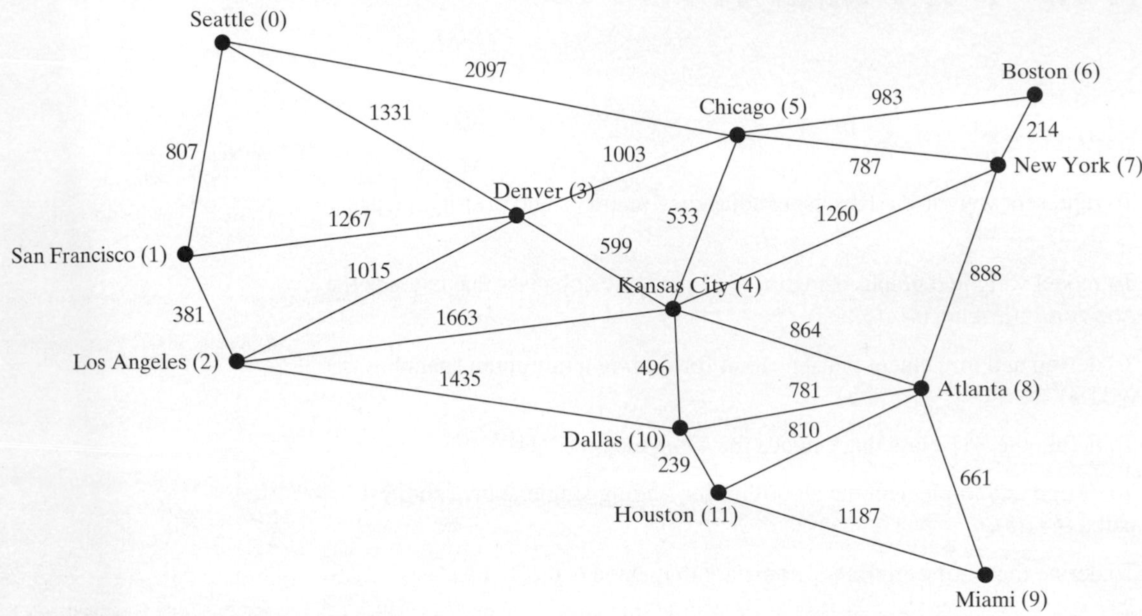

FIGURE 31.1 The graph models the distances among the cities.

The preceding chapter introduced the concept of graphs. You learned how to represent edges using edge arrays, edge lists, adjacency matrices, and adjacency lists, and how to model a graph using the `Graph` interface, the `AbstractGraph` class, and the `UnweightedGraph` class. The preceding chapter also introduced two important techniques for traversing graphs: depth-first search and breadth-first search, and applied traversal to solve practical problems. This chapter will introduce weighted graphs. You will learn the algorithm for finding a minimum spanning tree in Section 31.4 and the algorithm for finding shortest paths in Section 31.5.

weighted graph learning tool on Companion Website

Pedagogical Note

Before we introduce the algorithms and applications for weighted graphs, it is helpful to get acquainted with weighted graphs using the GUI interactive tool at www.cs.armstrong.edu/liang/animation/WeightedGraphLearningTool.html, as shown in Figure 31.2. The tool allows you to enter vertices, specify edges and their weights, view the graph, and find an MST and all shortest paths from a single source, as shown in Figure 31.2.

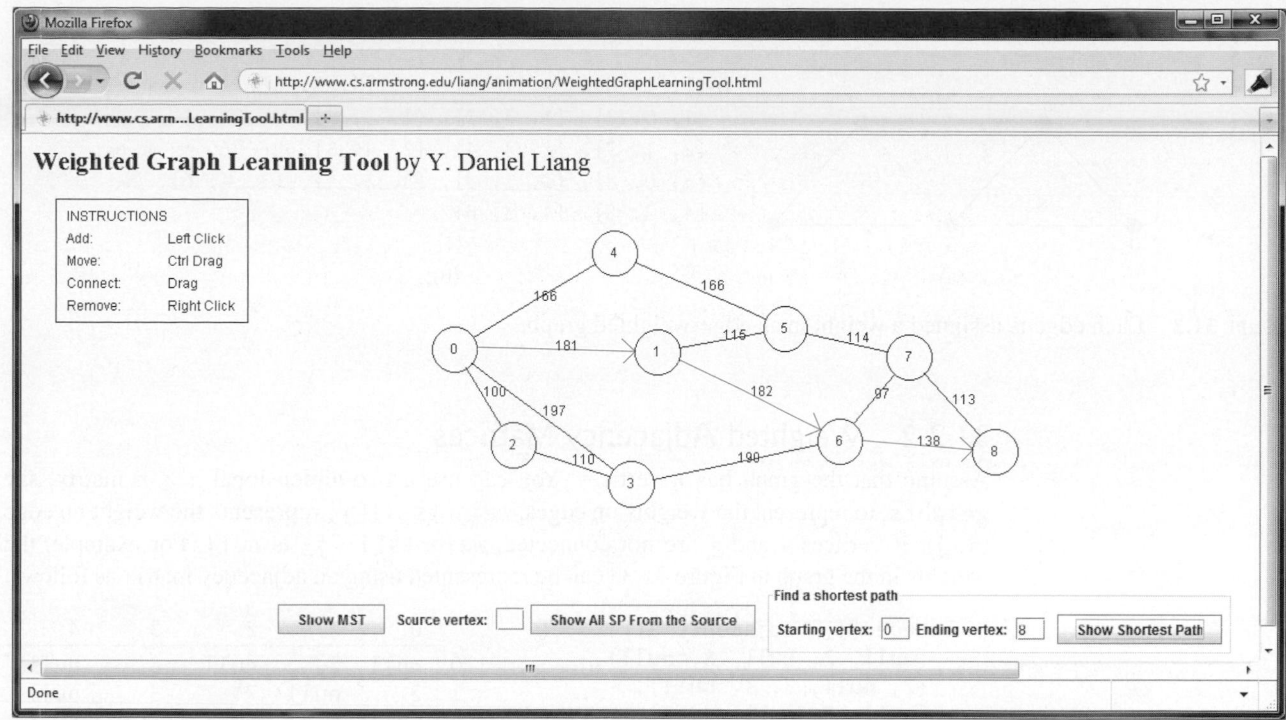

FIGURE 31.2 You can use the tool to create a weighted graph with mouse gestures and show the MST and shortest paths.

31.2 Representing Weighted Graphs

Often it is desirable to use a priority queue to store weighted edges.

Key Point

vertex-weighted graph
edge-weighted graph

There are two types of weighted graphs: vertex weighted and edge weighted. In a *vertex-weighted graph*, each vertex is assigned a weight. In an *edge-weighted graph*, each edge is assigned a weight. Of the two types, edge-weighted graphs have more applications. This chapter considers edge-weighted graphs.

Weighted graphs can be represented in the same way as unweighted graphs, except that you have to represent the weights on the edges. As with unweighted graphs, the vertices in weighted graphs can be stored in an array. This section introduces three representations for the edges in weighted graphs.

31.2.1 Representing Weighted Edges: Edge Array

Weighted edges can be represented using a two-dimensional array. For example, you can store all the edges in the graph in Figure 31.3a using the array in Figure 31.3b.

Note

Weights can be of any type: **Integer**, **Double**, **BigDecimal**, and so on. You can use a two-dimensional array of the **Object** type to represent weighted edges as follows:

```
Object[][] edges = {
  {new Integer(0), new Integer(1), new SomeTypeForWeight(2)},
  {new Integer(0), new Integer(3), new SomeTypeForWeight(8)},
  ...
};
```

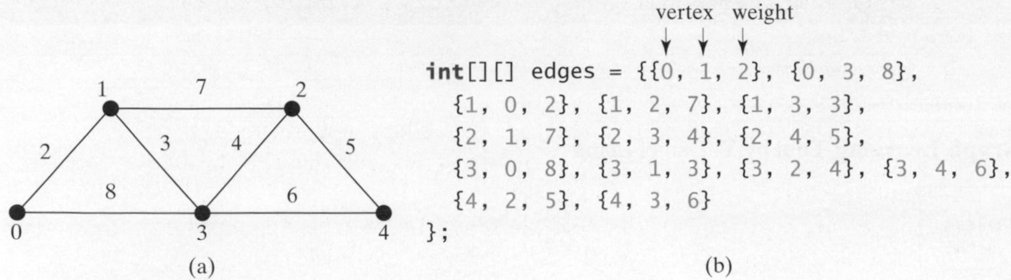

FIGURE 31.3 Each edge is assigned a weight in an edge-weighted graph.

31.2.2 Weighted Adjacency Matrices

Assume that the graph has n vertices. You can use a two-dimensional $n \times n$ matrix, say `weights`, to represent the weights on edges. `weights[i][j]` represents the weight on edge (`i`, `j`). If vertices `i` and `j` are not connected, `weights[i][j]` is `null`. For example, the weights in the graph in Figure 31.3a can be represented using an adjacency matrix as follows:

```
Integer[][] adjacencyMatrix = {
  {null, 2, null, 8, null},
  {2, null, 7, 3, null},
  {null, 7, null, 4, 5},
  {8, 3, 4, null, 6},
  {null, null, 5, 6, null}
};
```

	0	1	2	3	4
0	null	2	null	8	null
1	2	null	7	3	null
2	null	7	null	4	5
3	8	3	4	null	6
4	null	null	5	6	null

31.2.3 Priority Adjacency Lists

Another way to represent the edges is to define edges as objects. The `AbstractGraph.Edge` class was defined to represent an unweighted edge in Listing 30.3. For weighted edges, we define the `WeightedEdge` class as shown in Listing 31.1.

LISTING 31.1 `WeightedEdge.java`

edge weight
constructor
compare edges

```
public class WeightedEdge extends AbstractGraph.Edge
    implements Comparable<WeightedEdge> {
  public double weight;  // The weight on edge (u, v)

  /** Create a weighted edge on (u, v) */
  public WeightedEdge(int u, int v, double weight) {
    super(u, v);
    this.weight = weight;
  }

  @Override  /** Compare two edges on weights */
  public int compareTo(WeightedEdge edge) {
    if (weight > edge.weight)
      return 1;
    else if (weight == edge.weight)
      return 0;
    else
      return -1;
  }
}
```

`AbstractGraph.Edge` is an inner class defined in the `AbstractGraph` class. It represents an edge from vertex `u` to `v`. `WeightedEdge` extends `AbstractGraph.Edge` with a new property `weight`.

To create a `WeightedEdge` object, use `new WeightedEdge(i, j, w)`, where `w` is the weight on edge (`i`, `j`). It is often useful to store a vertex's adjacent edges in a priority queue so that you can remove the edges in increasing order of their weights. For this reason, the `WeightedEdge` class implements the `Comparable` interface.

For unweighted graphs, we use adjacency lists to represent edges. For weighted graphs, we still use adjacency lists, but the lists are priority queues. For example, the adjacency lists for the vertices in the graph in Figure 31.3a can be represented as follows:

```
java.util.PriorityQueue<WeightedEdge>[] queues =
  new java.util.PriorityQueue<WeightedEdge>[5];
```

queues[0]	WeightedEdge(0, 1, 2)	WeightedEdge(0, 3, 8)		
queues[1]	WeightedEdge(1, 0, 2)	WeightedEdge(1, 3, 3)	WeightedEdge(1, 2, 7)	
queues[2]	WeightedEdge(2, 3, 4)	WeightedEdge(2, 4, 5)	WeightedEdge(2, 1, 7)	
queues[3]	WeightedEdge(3, 1, 3)	WeightedEdge(3, 2, 4)	WeightedEdge(3, 4, 6)	WeightedEdge(3, 0, 8)
queues[4]	WeightedEdge(4, 2, 5)	WeightedEdge(4, 3, 6)		

`queues[i]` stores all edges adjacent to vertex `i`.

For flexibility, we will use an array list rather than a fixed-sized array to represent `queues`.

Check Point
MyProgrammingLab™

31.1 For the code `WeightedEdge edge = new WeightedEdge(1, 2, 3.5)`, what is `edge.u`, `edge.v`, and `edge.weight`?

31.2 What is the printout of the following code?

```
List<WeightedEdge> list = new ArrayList<WeightedEdge>();
list.add(new WeightedEdge(1, 2, 3.5));
list.add(new WeightedEdge(2, 3, 4.5));
WeightedEdge e = java.util.Collections.max(list);
System.out.println(e.u);
System.out.println(e.v);
System.out.println(e.weight);
```

31.3 The **WeightedGraph** Class

The `WeightedGraph` class extends `AbstractGraph`.

Key Point

The preceding chapter designed the `Graph` interface, the `AbstractGraph` class, and the `UnweightedGraph` class for modeling graphs. Following this pattern, we design `WeightedGraph` as a subclass of `AbstractGraph`, as shown in Figure 31.4.

`WeightedGraph` simply extends `AbstractGraph` with five constructors for creating concrete `WeightedGraph` instances. `WeightedGraph` inherits all methods from `AbstractGraph`, overrides the `clear` and `addVertex` methods, implements a new `addEdge` method for adding a weighted edge, and also introduces new methods for obtaining minimum spanning trees and for finding all single-source shortest paths. Minimum spanning trees and shortest paths will be introduced in Sections 31.4 and 31.5, respectively.

Listing 31.2 implements `WeightedGraph`. Priority adjacency lists (line 5) are used internally to store adjacent edges for a vertex. When a `WeightedGraph` is constructed, its priority adjacency lists are created (lines 15, 21, 27, and 34). The methods `getMinimumSpanningTree()` (lines 102–159) and `getShortestPath()` (lines 193–246) will be introduced in upcoming sections.

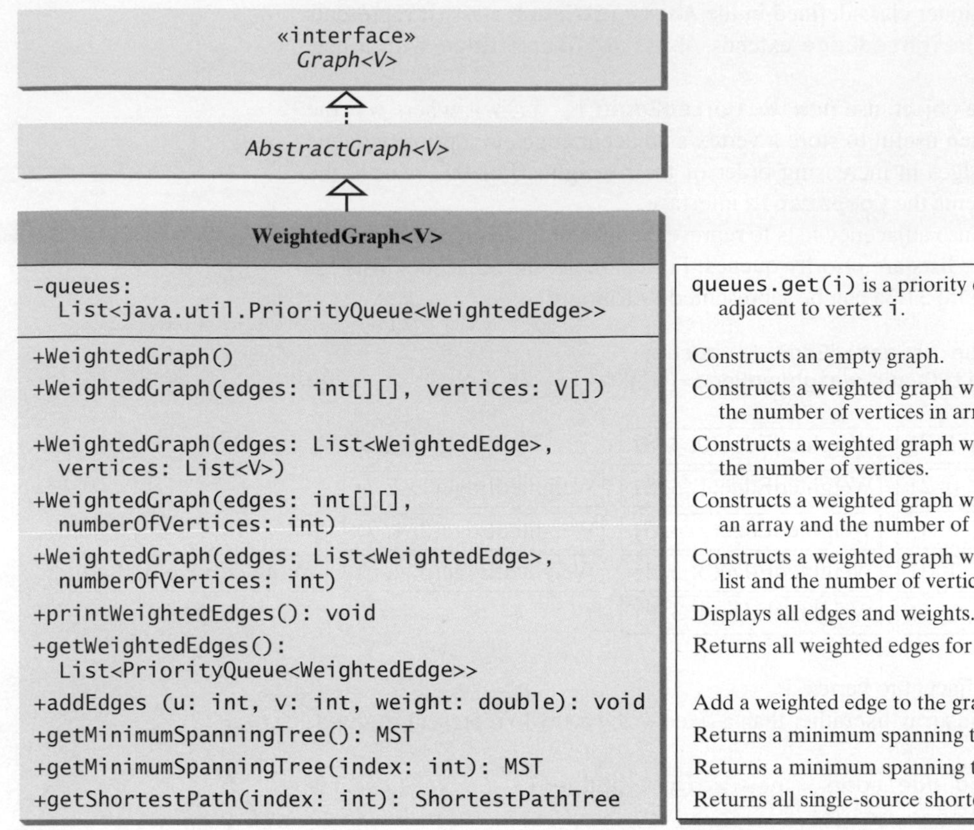

FIGURE 31.4 `WeightedGraph` extends `AbstractGraph`.

LISTING 31.2 WeightedGraph.java

```
import java.util.*;

public class WeightedGraph<V> extends AbstractGraph<V> {
  // Priority adjacency lists
  private List<PriorityQueue<WeightedEdge>> queues
    = new ArrayList<PriorityQueue<WeightedEdge>>();

  /** Construct a WeightedGraph from edges and vertices in arrays */
  public WeightedGraph() {
  }

  /** Construct a WeightedGraph from edges and vertices in arrays */
  public WeightedGraph(int[][] edges, V[] vertices) {
    super(edges, vertices);
    createQueues(edges, vertices.length);
  }

  /** Construct a WeightedGraph from edges and vertices in List */
  public WeightedGraph(int[][] edges, int numberOfVertices) {
    super(edges, numberOfVertices);
    createQueues(edges, numberOfVertices);
  }

  /** Construct a WeightedGraph for vertices 0, 1, 2 and edge list */
  public WeightedGraph(List<WeightedEdge> edges, List<V> vertices) {
    super((List)edges, vertices);
```

priority queue; no-arg constructor; constructor; superclass constructor; create priority queues; constructor; constructor

```
    createQueues(edges, vertices.size());
  }

  /** Construct a WeightedGraph from vertices 0, 1, and edge array */
```

constructor

```
  public WeightedGraph(List<WeightedEdge> edges,
      int numberOfVertices) {
    super((List)edges, numberOfVertices);
    createQueues(edges, numberOfVertices);
  }

  /** Create priority adjacency lists from edge arrays */
```

create priority queues

```
  private void createQueues(int[][] edges, int numberOfVertices) {
    for (int i = 0; i < numberOfVertices; i++) {
      queues.add(new PriorityQueue<WeightedEdge>()); // Create a queue
    }

    for (int i = 0; i < edges.length; i++) {
      int u = edges[i][0];
      int v = edges[i][1];
      int weight = edges[i][2];
      // Insert an edge into the queue
      queues.get(u).offer(new WeightedEdge(u, v, weight));
    }
  }

  /** Create priority adjacency lists from edge lists */
```

create queues

```
  private void createQueues(List<WeightedEdge> edges,
      int numberOfVertices) {
    for (int i = 0; i < numberOfVertices; i++) {
      queues.add(new PriorityQueue<WeightedEdge>()); // Create a queue
    }

    for (WeightedEdge edge: edges) {
      queues.get(edge.u).offer(edge); // Insert an edge into the queue
    }
  }

  /** Display edges with weights */
```

print edges

```
  public void printWeightedEdges() {
    for (int i = 0; i < queues.size(); i++) {
      System.out.print(getVertex(i) + " (" + i + "): ");
      for (WeightedEdge edge : queues.get(i)) {
        System.out.print("(" + edge.u +
          ", " + edge.v + ", " + edge.weight + ") ");
      }
      System.out.println();
    }
  }

  /** Get the edges from the weighted graph */
```

get edges

```
  public List<PriorityQueue<WeightedEdge>> getWeightedEdges() {
    return queues;
  }

  @Override  /** Clear the weighted graph */
```

clear graph

```
  public void clear() {
    vertices.clear();
    neighbors.clear();
    queues.clear();
  }
```

```
  @Override /** Add vertices to the weighted graph */
  public void addVertex(V vertex) {
    super.addVertex(vertex);
    queues.add(new PriorityQueue<WeightedEdge>());
  }

  /** Add edges to the weighted graph */
  public void addEdge(int u, int v, double weight) {
    super.addEdge(u, v);
    queues.get(u).add(new WeightedEdge(u, v, weight));
    queues.get(v).add(new WeightedEdge(v, u, weight));
  }

  /** Get a minimum spanning tree rooted at vertex 0 */
  public MST getMinimumSpanningTree() {
    return getMinimumSpanningTree(0);
  }

  /** Get a minimum spanning tree rooted at a specified vertex */
  public MST getMinimumSpanningTree(int startingVertex) {
    List<Integer> T = new ArrayList<Integer>();
    // T initially contains the startingVertex;
    T.add(startingVertex);

    int numberOfVertices = vertices.size();  // Number of vertices
    int[] parent = new int[numberOfVertices]; // Parent of a vertex
    // Initially set the parent of all vertices to -1
    for (int i = 0; i < parent.length; i++)
      parent[i] = -1;
    double totalWeight = 0;  // Total weight of the tree thus far

    // Clone the priority queue, so to keep the original queue intact
    List<PriorityQueue<WeightedEdge>> queues = deepClone(this.queues);

    // All vertices are found?
    while (T.size() < numberOfVertices) {
      // Search for the vertex with the smallest edge adjacent to
      // a vertex in T
      int v = -1;
      double smallestWeight = Double.MAX_VALUE;
      for (int u : T) {
        while (!queues.get(u).isEmpty() &&
            T.contains(queues.get(u).peek().v)) {
          // Remove the edge from queues[u] if the adjacent
          // vertex of u is already in T
          queues.get(u).remove();
        }

        if (queues.get(u).isEmpty()) {
          continue; // Consider the next vertex in T
        }

        // Current smallest weight on an edge adjacent to u
        WeightedEdge edge = queues.get(u).peek();
        if (edge.weight < smallestWeight) {
          v = edge.v;
          smallestWeight = edge.weight;
          // If v is added to the tree, u will be its parent
          parent[v] = u;
```

Margin notes: add vertex; add edge; minimum spanning tree; start from vertex 0; minimum spanning tree; vertices in tree; add to tree; number of vertices; parent array; initialize parent; total weight; a copy of queues; more vertices?; every u in tree; remove visited vertex; `queues.get(u)` is empty; smallest edge to u; update `smallestWeight`

```
      }
    }  // End of for loop

    if (v != -1)
      T.add(v);  // Add a new vertex to the tree
    else
      break;  // The tree is not connected, a partial MST is found

    totalWeight += smallestWeight;
  } // End of while loop

  return new MST(startingVertex, parent, T, totalWeight);
}

/** Clone an array of queues */
private List<PriorityQueue<WeightedEdge>> deepClone(
  List<PriorityQueue<WeightedEdge>> queues) {
  List<PriorityQueue<WeightedEdge>> copiedQueues =
    new ArrayList<PriorityQueue<WeightedEdge>>();

  for (int i = 0; i < queues.size(); i++) {
    copiedQueues.add(new PriorityQueue<WeightedEdge>());
    for (WeightedEdge e : queues.get(i)) {
      copiedQueues.get(i).add(e);
    }
  }

  return copiedQueues;
}

/** MST is an inner class in WeightedGraph */
public class MST extends Tree {
  private double totalWeight;  // Total weight of the tree's edges

  public MST(int root, int[] parent, List<Integer> searchOrder,
      double totalWeight) {
    super(root, parent, searchOrder);
    this.totalWeight = totalWeight;
  }

  public double getTotalWeight() {
    return totalWeight;
  }
}

/** Find single-source shortest paths */
public ShortestPathTree getShortestPath(int sourceVertex) {
  // T stores the vertices of paths found so far
  List<Integer> T = new ArrayList<Integer>();
  // T initially contains the sourceVertex;
  T.add(sourceVertex);

  // vertices is defined in AbstractGraph
  int numberOfVertices = vertices.size();

  // parent[v] stores the previous vertex of v in the path
  int[] parent = new int[numberOfVertices];
  parent[sourceVertex] = -1;  // The parent of source is set to -1

  // cost[v] stores the cost of the path from v to the source
```

add to tree

update `totalWeight`

clone queue

clone every element

MST inner class

total weight in tree

`getShortestPath`

vertices found

add source

number of vertices

parent array

parent of root

cost array
source cost
a copy of queues
more vertices left?
determine one
remove visited vertex
queues.get(u) is empty
smallest edge to u
update smallestCost
v now found
add to T
create a path
cost
constructor
get cost
print all paths

```
    double[] cost = new double[numberOfVertices];
    for (int i = 0; i < cost.length; i++) {
      cost[i] = Double.MAX_VALUE; // Initial cost set to infinity
    }
    cost[sourceVertex] = 0; // Cost of source is 0

    // Get a copy of queues
    List<PriorityQueue<WeightedEdge>> queues = deepClone(this.queues);

    // Expand T
    while (T.size() < numberOfVertices) {
      int v = -1; // Vertex to be determined
      double smallestCost = Double.MAX_VALUE; // Set to infinity
      for (int u : T) {
        while (!queues.get(u).isEmpty() &&
            T.contains(queues.get(u).peek().v)) {
          queues.get(u).remove(); // Remove the vertex in queue for u
        }

        if (queues.get(u).isEmpty()) {
          // All vertices adjacent to u are in T
          continue;
        }

        WeightedEdge e = queues.get(u).peek();
        if (cost[u] + e.weight < smallestCost) {
          v = e.v;
          smallestCost = cost[u] + e.weight;
          // If v is added to the tree, u will be its parent
          parent[v] = u;
        }
      } // End of for loop

      T.add(v); // Add a new vertex to T
      cost[v] = smallestCost;
    } // End of while loop

    // Create a ShortestPathTree
    return new ShortestPathTree(sourceVertex, parent, T, cost);
  }

  /** ShortestPathTree is an inner class in WeightedGraph */
  public class ShortestPathTree extends Tree {
    private double[] cost; // cost[v] is the cost from v to source

    /** Construct a path */
    public ShortestPathTree(int source, int[] parent,
        List<Integer> searchOrder, double[] cost) {
      super(source, parent, searchOrder);
      this.cost = cost;
    }

    /** Return the cost for a path from the root to vertex v */
    public double getCost(int v) {
      return cost[v];
    }

    /** Print paths from all vertices to the source */
    public void printAllPaths() {
      System.out.println("All shortest paths from " +
```

```
267            vertices.get(getRoot()) + " are:");
268          for (int i = 0; i < cost.length; i++) {
269            printPath(i); // Print a path from i to the source
270            System.out.println("(cost: " + cost[i] + ")"); // Path cost
271          }
272        }
273      }
274    }
```

When you construct a **WeightedGraph** using the no-arg constructor, the superclass's no-arg constructor is invoked. When you construct a **WeightedGraph** using the other four constructors, the superclass's constructor is invoked (lines 14, 20, 26, 33) to initialize the properties **vertices** and **neighbors** in **AbstractGraph**. Additionally, priority queues are created for instances of **WeightedGraph**. The **clear** and **addVertex** methods in **AbstractGraph** are overridden in lines 82–92 to handle the weighted edges. The **addEdge(u, v, weight)** method adds a new edge (**u**, **v**) with the specified weight to the graph (lines 95–99).

Listing 31.3 gives a test program that creates a graph for the one in Figure 31.1 and another graph for the one in Figure 31.3a.

LISTING 31.3 TestWeightedGraph.java

```
public class TestWeightedGraph {
  public static void main(String[] args) {
    String[] vertices = {"Seattle", "San Francisco", "Los Angeles",
      "Denver", "Kansas City", "Chicago", "Boston", "New York",
      "Atlanta", "Miami", "Dallas", "Houston"};

    int[][] edges = {
      {0, 1, 807}, {0, 3, 1331}, {0, 5, 2097},
      {1, 0, 807}, {1, 2, 381}, {1, 3, 1267},
      {2, 1, 381}, {2, 3, 1015}, {2, 4, 1663}, {2, 10, 1435},
      {3, 0, 1331}, {3, 1, 1267}, {3, 2, 1015}, {3, 4, 599},
        {3, 5, 1003},
      {4, 2, 1663}, {4, 3, 599}, {4, 5, 533}, {4, 7, 1260},
        {4, 8, 864}, {4, 10, 496},
      {5, 0, 2097}, {5, 3, 1003}, {5, 4, 533},
        {5, 6, 983}, {5, 7, 787},
      {6, 5, 983}, {6, 7, 214},
      {7, 4, 1260}, {7, 5, 787}, {7, 6, 214}, {7, 8, 888},
      {8, 4, 864}, {8, 7, 888}, {8, 9, 661},
        {8, 10, 781}, {8, 11, 810},
      {9, 8, 661}, {9, 11, 1187},
      {10, 2, 1435}, {10, 4, 496}, {10, 8, 781}, {10, 11, 239},
      {11, 8, 810}, {11, 9, 1187}, {11, 10, 239}
    };

    WeightedGraph<String> graph1 =
      new WeightedGraph<String>(edges, vertices);
    System.out.println("The number of vertices in graph1: "
      + graph1.getSize());
    System.out.println("The vertex with index 1 is "
      + graph1.getVertex(1));
    System.out.println("The index for Miami is " +
      graph1.getIndex("Miami"));
    System.out.println("The edges for graph1:");
    graph1.printWeightedEdges();

    edges = new int[][]{
      {0, 1, 2}, {0, 3, 8},
```

vertices
edges
create graph
print edges
edges

```
39          {1, 0, 2}, {1, 2, 7}, {1, 3, 3},
40          {2, 1, 7}, {2, 3, 4}, {2, 4, 5},
41          {3, 0, 8}, {3, 1, 3}, {3, 2, 4}, {3, 4, 6},
42          {4, 2, 5}, {4, 3, 6}
43        };
44        WeightedGraph<Integer> graph2 =
45          new WeightedGraph<Integer>(edges, 5);     // create graph
46        System.out.println("\nThe edges for graph2:");
47        graph2.printWeightedEdges();                // print edges
48      }
49    }
```

```
The number of vertices in graph1: 12
The vertex with index 1 is San Francisco
The index for Miami is 9
The edges for graph1:
Vertex 0: (0, 1, 807) (0, 3, 1331) (0, 5, 2097)
Vertex 1: (1, 2, 381) (1, 0, 807) (1, 3, 1267)
Vertex 2: (2, 1, 381) (2, 3, 1015) (2, 4, 1663) (2, 10, 1435)
Vertex 3: (3, 4, 599) (3, 5, 1003) (3, 1, 1267)
  (3, 0, 1331) (3, 2, 1015)
Vertex 4: (4, 10, 496) (4, 8, 864) (4, 5, 533) (4, 2, 1663)
  (4, 7, 1260) (4, 3, 599)
Vertex 5: (5, 4, 533) (5, 7, 787) (5, 3, 1003)
  (5, 0, 2097) (5, 6, 983)
Vertex 6: (6, 7, 214) (6, 5, 983)
Vertex 7: (7, 6, 214) (7, 8, 888) (7, 5, 787) (7, 4, 1260)
Vertex 8: (8, 9, 661) (8, 10, 781) (8, 4, 864)
  (8, 7, 888) (8, 11, 810)
Vertex 9: (9, 8, 661) (9, 11, 1187)
Vertex 10: (10, 11, 239) (10, 4, 496) (10, 8, 781) (10, 2, 1435)
Vertex 11: (11, 10, 239) (11, 9, 1187) (11, 8, 810)

The edges for graph2:
Vertex 0: (0, 1, 2) (0, 3, 8)
Vertex 1: (1, 0, 2) (1, 2, 7) (1, 3, 3)
Vertex 2: (2, 3, 4) (2, 1, 7) (2, 4, 5)
Vertex 3: (3, 1, 3) (3, 4, 6) (3, 2, 4) (3, 0, 8)
Vertex 4: (4, 2, 5) (4, 3, 6)
```

The program creates **graph1** for the graph in Figure 31.1 in lines 3–27. The vertices for **graph1** are defined in lines 3–5. The edges for **graph1** are defined in lines 7–24. The edges are represented using a two-dimensional array. For each row **i** in the array, **edges[i][0]** and **edges[i][1]** indicate that there is an edge from vertex **edges[i][0]** to vertex **edges[i][1]** and the weight for the edge is **edges[i][2]**. For example, {**0**, **1**, **807**} (line 8) represents the edge from vertex **0** (**edges[0][0]**) to vertex **1** (**edges[0][1]**) with weight **807** (**edges[0][2]**). {**0**, **5**, **2097**} (line 8) represents the edge from vertex **0** (**edges[2][0]**) to vertex **5** (**edges[2][1]**) with weight **2097** (**edges[2][2]**). Line 35 invokes the **printWeightedEdges()** method on **graph1** to display all edges in **graph1**.

The program creates the edges for **graph2** for the graph in Figure 31.3a in lines 37–45. Line 47 invokes the **printWeightedEdges()** method on **graph2** to display all edges in **graph2**.

traversing priority queue

Note

The adjacent edges for each vertex are stored in a priority queue. When you remove an edge from the queue, the one with the smallest weight is always removed. However, if you traverse the edges in the queue, the edges are not necessarily in increasing order of weights.

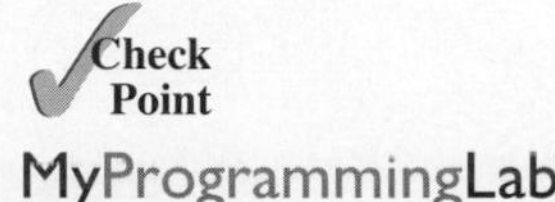

31.3 What is the printout of the following code?

```
PriorityQueue<WeightedEdge> q =
  new PriorityQueue<WeightedEdge>();
q.offer(new WeightedEdge(1, 2, 3.5));
q.offer(new WeightedEdge(1, 6, 6.5));
q.offer(new WeightedEdge(1, 7, 1.5));
System.out.println(q.poll().weight);
System.out.println(q.poll().weight);
System.out.println(q.poll().weight);
```

31.4 What is wrong in the following code? Fix it and show the printout.

```
List<PriorityQueue<WeightedEdge>> queues =
  new ArrayList<PriorityQueue<WeightedEdge>>();
queues.get(0).offer(new WeightedEdge(0, 2, 3.5));
queues.get(0).offer(new WeightedEdge(0, 6, 6.5));
queues.get(0).offer(new WeightedEdge(0, 7, 1.5));
queues.get(1).offer(new WeightedEdge(1, 0, 3.5));
queues.get(1).offer(new WeightedEdge(1, 5, 8.5));
queues.get(1).offer(new WeightedEdge(1, 8, 19.5));
System.out.println(queues.get(0).peek()
  .compareTo(queues.get(1).peek()));
```

31.4 Minimum Spanning Trees

A minimum spanning tree of a graph is a spanning tree with the minimum total weights.

minimum spanning tree

A graph may have many spanning trees. Suppose that the edges are weighted. A *minimum spanning tree* has the minimum total weights. For example, the trees in Figures 31.5b, 31.5c, 31.5d are spanning trees for the graph in Figure 31.5a. The trees in Figures 31.3c and 31.3d are minimum spanning trees.

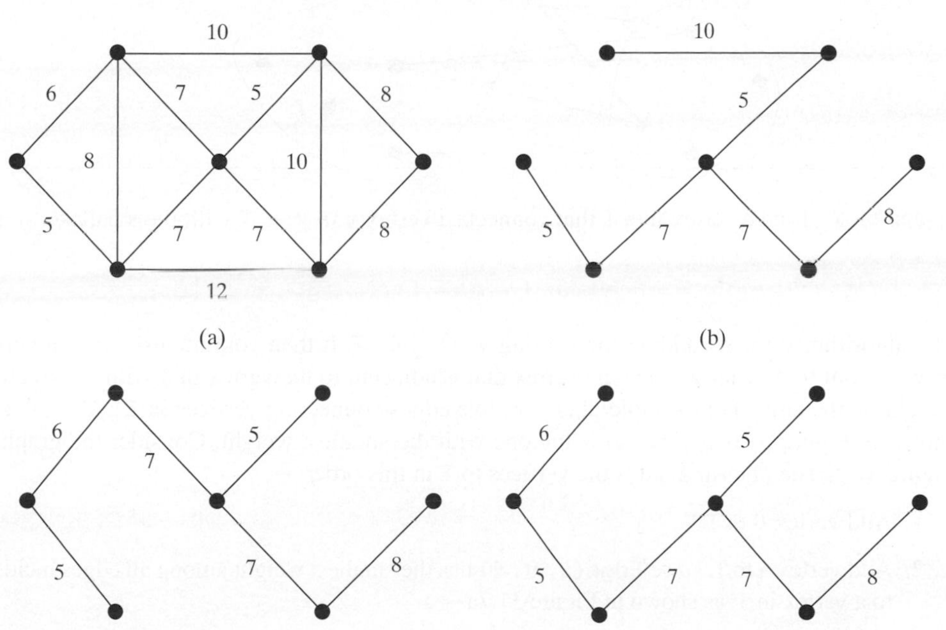

FIGURE 31.5 The trees in (c) and (d) are minimum spanning trees of the graph in (a).

The problem of finding a minimum spanning tree has many applications. Consider a company with branches in many cities. The company wants to lease telephone lines to connect all the branches together. The phone company charges different amounts of money to connect different pairs of cities. There are many ways to connect all branches together. The cheapest way is to find a spanning tree with the minimum total rates.

31.4.1 Minimum Spanning Tree Algorithms

Prim's algorithm

How do you find a minimum spanning tree? There are several well-known algorithms for doing so. This section introduces *Prim's algorithm.* Prim's algorithm starts with a spanning tree T that contains an arbitrary vertex. The algorithm expands the tree by repeatedly adding a vertex with the *lowest-cost* edge incident to a vertex already in the tree. Prim's algorithm is a greedy algorithm, and it is described in Listing 31.4.

LISTING 31.4 Prim's Minimum Spanning Tree Algorithm

add initial vertex
more vertices?
find a vertex
add to tree

```
minimumSpanningTree() {
  Let V denote the set of vertices in the graph;
  Let T be a set for the vertices in the spanning tree;
  Initially, add the starting vertex to T;

  while (size of T < n) {
    find u in T and v in V - T with the smallest weight
      on the edge (u, v), as shown in Figure 31.6;
    add v to T;
  }
}
```

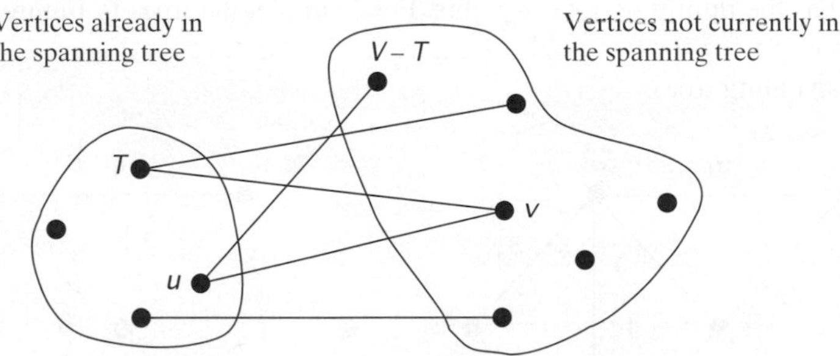

FIGURE 31.6 Find a vertex u in T that connects a vertex v in V – T with the smallest weight.

example

The algorithm starts by adding the starting vertex into T. It then continuously adds a vertex (say v) from V – T into T. v is the vertex that is adjacent to the vertex in T with the smallest weight on the edge. For example, there are five edges connecting vertices in T and V – T as shown in Figure 31.6, and (u, v) is the one with the smallest weight. Consider the graph in Figure 31.7. The algorithm adds the vertices to T in this order:

1. Add vertex 0 to T.
2. Add vertex 5 to T, since Edge(5, 0, 5) has the smallest weight among all edges incident to a vertex in T, as shown in Figure 31.7a.
3. Add vertex 1 to T, since Edge(1, 0, 6) has the smallest weight among all edges incident to a vertex in T, as shown in Figure 31.7b.

4. Add vertex 6 to T, since Edge(6, 1, 7) has the smallest weight among all edges incident to a vertex in T, as shown in Figure 31.7c.
5. Add vertex 2 to T, since Edge(2, 6, 5) has the smallest weight among all edges incident to a vertex in T, as shown in Figure 31.7d.
6. Add vertex 4 to T, since Edge(4, 6, 7) has the smallest weight among all edges incident to a vertex in T, as shown in Figure 31.7e.
7. Add vertex 3 to T, since Edge(3, 2, 8) has the smallest weight among all edges incident to a vertex in T, as shown in Figure 31.7f.

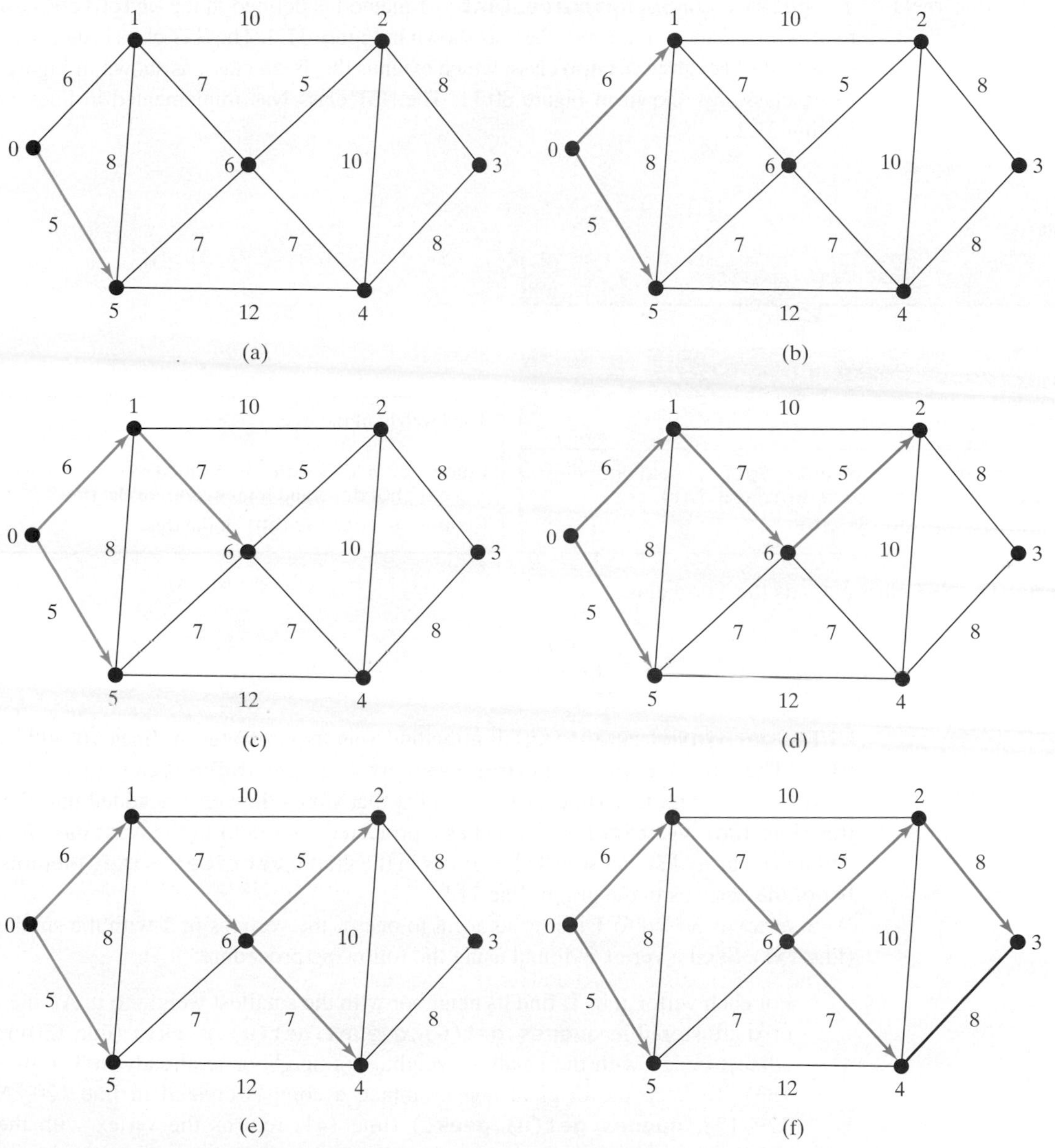

FIGURE 31.7 The adjacent vertices with the smallest weight are added successively to T.

unique tree?

Note

A minimum spanning tree is not unique. For example, both (c) and (d) in Figure 31.5 are minimum spanning trees for the graph in Figure 31.5a. However, if the weights are distinct, the graph has a unique minimum spanning tree.

connected and undirected

Note

Assume that the graph is connected and undirected. If a graph is not connected or directed, the algorithm will not work. You can modify the algorithm to find a spanning forest for any undirected graph. A spanning forest is a graph in which each connected component is a tree.

31.4.2 Implementation of the MST Algorithm

getMinimumSpanningTree()

The **getMinimumSpanningTree(int v)** method is defined in the **WeightedGraph** class. It returns an instance of the **MST** class, as shown in Figure 31.4. The **MST** class is defined as an inner class in the **WeightedGraph** class, which extends the **Tree** class, as shown in Figure 31.8. The **Tree** class was shown in Figure 30.11. The **MST** class was implemented in lines 178–190 in Listing 31.2.

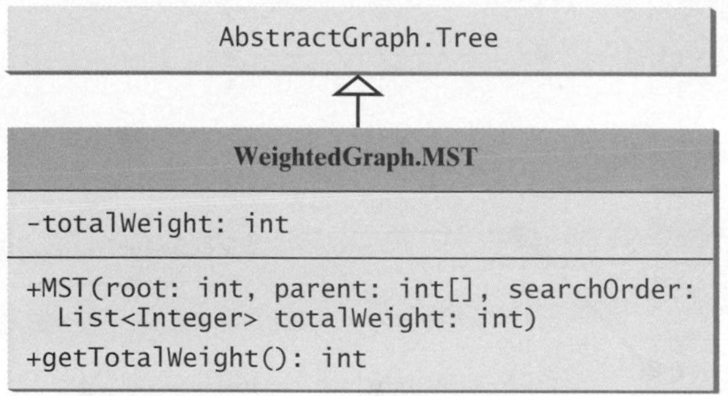

FIGURE 31.8 The **MST** class extends the **Tree** class.

The **getMinimumSpanningTree** method was implemented in lines 107–159 in Listing 31.2. The **getMinimumSpanningTree(int startingVertex)** method first adds **startingVertex** to **T** (line 110). **T** is a list that stores the vertices added into the spanning tree (line 108). **vertices** is defined as a protected data field in the **AbstractGraph** class, and it is an array list that stores all vertices in the graph. **vertices.size()** returns the number of the vertices in the graph (line 112).

A vertex is added to **T** if it is adjacent to one of the vertices in **T** with the smallest weight (line 151). Such a vertex is found using the following procedure:

1. For each vertex **u** in **T**, find its neighbor with the smallest weight to **u**. All the neighbors of **u** are stored in **queues.get(u)**. **queues.get(u).peek()** (line 130) returns the adjacent edge with the smallest weight. If a neighbor is already in **T**, remove it (line 133). To keep the original queues intact, a copy is created in line 120. After lines 129–138, **queues.get(u).peek()** (line 141) returns the vertex with the smallest weight to **u**.
2. Compare all these neighbors and find the one with the smallest weight (lines 141–147).

After a new vertex is added to `T` (line 151), `totalWeight` is updated (line 155). Once all vertices are added to `T`, an instance of `MST` is created (line 158). Note that the method will not work if the graph is not connected. However, you can modify it to obtain a partial MST.

The `MST` class extends the `Tree` class (line 178). To create an instance of `MST`, pass `root`, `parent`, `T`, and `totalWeight` (lines 181). The data fields `root`, `parent`, and `searchOrder` are defined in the `Tree` class, which is an inner class defined in `AbstractGraph`.

For each vertex, the program constructs a priority queue for its adjacent edges. It takes $O(\log|V|)$ time to insert an edge into a priority queue and the same time to remove an edge from the priority queue. Thus, the overall time complexity for the program is $O(|E| \log |V|)$, where $|E|$ denotes the number of edges and $|V|$ the number of vertices.

time complexity

Listing 31.5 gives a test program that displays minimum spanning trees for the graph in Figure 31.1 and the graph in Figure 31.3a, respectively.

LISTING 31.5 TestMinimumSpanningTree.java

```
public class TestMinimumSpanningTree {
  public static void main(String[] args) {
    String[] vertices = {"Seattle", "San Francisco", "Los Angeles",
      "Denver", "Kansas City", "Chicago", "Boston", "New York",
      "Atlanta", "Miami", "Dallas", "Houston"};

    int[][] edges = {
      {0, 1, 807}, {0, 3, 1331}, {0, 5, 2097},
      {1, 0, 807}, {1, 2, 381}, {1, 3, 1267},
      {2, 1, 381}, {2, 3, 1015}, {2, 4, 1663}, {2, 10, 1435},
      {3, 0, 1331}, {3, 1, 1267}, {3, 2, 1015}, {3, 4, 599},
        {3, 5, 1003},
      {4, 2, 1663}, {4, 3, 599}, {4, 5, 533}, {4, 7, 1260},
        {4, 8, 864}, {4, 10, 496},
      {5, 0, 2097}, {5, 3, 1003}, {5, 4, 533},
        {5, 6, 983}, {5, 7, 787},
      {6, 5, 983}, {6, 7, 214},
      {7, 4, 1260}, {7, 5, 787}, {7, 6, 214}, {7, 8, 888},
      {8, 4, 864}, {8, 7, 888}, {8, 9, 661},
        {8, 10, 781}, {8, 11, 810},
      {9, 8, 661}, {9, 11, 1187},
      {10, 2, 1435}, {10, 4, 496}, {10, 8, 781}, {10, 11, 239},
      {11, 8, 810}, {11, 9, 1187}, {11, 10, 239}
    };

    WeightedGraph<String> graph1 =
      new WeightedGraph<String>(edges, vertices);
    WeightedGraph<String>.MST tree1 = graph1.getMinimumSpanningTree();
    System.out.println("Total weight is " + tree1.getTotalWeight());
    tree1.printTree();

    edges = new int[][]{
      {0, 1, 2}, {0, 3, 8},
      {1, 0, 2}, {1, 2, 7}, {1, 3, 3},
      {2, 1, 7}, {2, 3, 4}, {2, 4, 5},
      {3, 0, 8}, {3, 1, 3}, {3, 2, 4}, {3, 4, 6},
      {4, 2, 5}, {4, 3, 6}
    };

    WeightedGraph<Integer> graph2 =
      new WeightedGraph<Integer>(edges, 5);
    WeightedGraph<Integer>.MST tree2 =
```

create vertices

create edges

create `graph1`

MST for `graph1`

total weight

print tree

create edges

create `graph2`

MST for graph2
total weight
print tree

```
43             graph2.getMinimumSpanningTree(1);
44         System.out.println("Total weight is " + tree2.getTotalWeight());
45         tree2.printTree();
46     }
47 }
```

```
Total weight is 6513.0
Root is: Seattle
Edges: (Seattle, San Francisco) (San Francisco, Los Angeles)
  (Los Angeles, Denver) (Denver, Kansas City) (Kansas City, Chicago)
  (New York, Boston) (Chicago, New York) (Dallas, Atlanta)
  (Atlanta, Miami) (Kansas City, Dallas) (Dallas, Houston)

Total weight is 14.0
Root is: 1
Edges: (1, 0) (3, 2) (1, 3) (2, 4)
```

The program creates a weighted graph for Figure 31.1 in line 27. It then invokes **getMinimumSpanningTree()** (line 28) to return an **MST** that represents a minimum spanning tree for the graph. Invoking **printTree()** (line 30) on the **MST** object displays the edges in the tree. Note that **MST** is a subclass of **Tree**. The **printTree()** method is defined in the **Tree** class.

graphical illustration

The graphical illustration of the minimum spanning tree is shown in Figure 31.9. The vertices are added to the tree in this order: Seattle, San Francisco, Los Angeles, Denver, Kansas City, Dallas, Houston, Chicago, New York, Boston, Atlanta, and Miami.

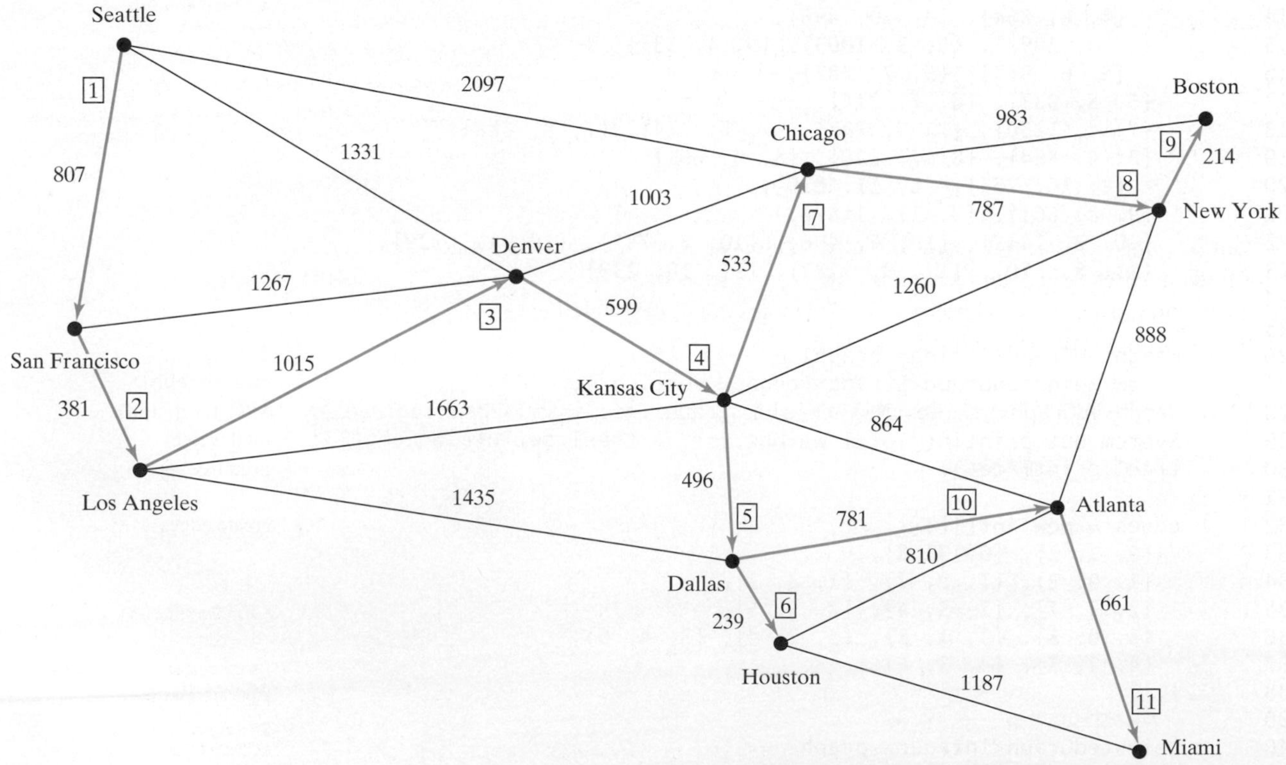

FIGURE 31.9 The edges in the minimum spanning tree for the cities are highlighted.

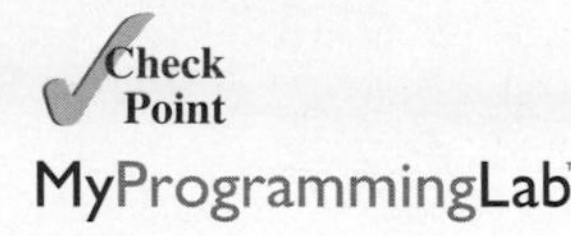

31.5 Find a minimum spanning tree for the following graph.

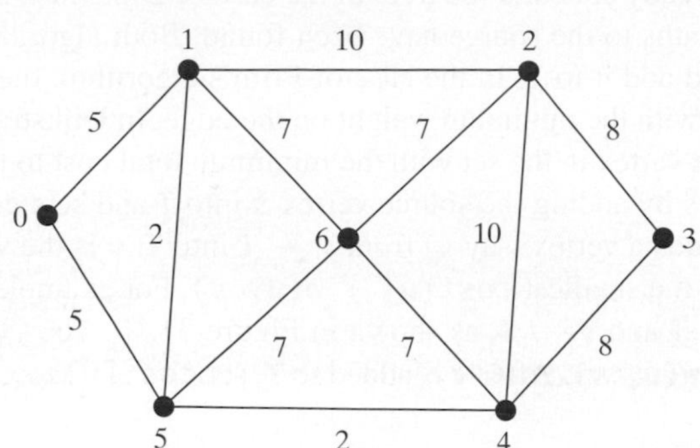

31.6 Is the minimum spanning tree unique if all edges have different weights?

31.7 If you use an adjacency matrix to represent weighted edges, what will be the time complexity for Prim's algorithm?

31.8 What happens to the `getMinimumSpanningTree()` method in `WeightedGraph` if the graph is not connected? Verify your answer by writing a test program that creates an unconnected graph and invokes the `getMinimumSpanningTree()` method. How do you fix the problem by obtaining a partial MST?

31.5 Finding Shortest Paths

The shortest path between two vertices is the path with the minimum total weights.

shortest path
Dijkstra's algorithm
single-source shortest path

Given a graph with nonnegative weights on the edges, a well-known algorithm for finding a *shortest path* between two vertices was discovered by Edsger Dijkstra, a Dutch computer scientist. In order to find a shortest path from vertex `u` to vertex `v`, *Dijkstra's algorithm* finds the shortest path from `u` to all vertices. So *Dijkstra's algorithm* is known as a *single-source* shortest path algorithm. The algorithm uses `cost[v]` to store the cost of the *shortest path* from vertex `v` to the source vertex `s`. `cost[s]` is `0`. Initially assign infinity to `cost[v]` to indicate that no path is found from `v` to `s`. Let `V` denote all vertices in the graph and `T` denote the set of the vertices whose costs are known. Initially, the source vertex `s` is in `T`. The algorithm repeatedly finds a vertex `u` in `T` and a vertex `v` in `V - T` such that `cost[u] + w(u, v)` is the smallest, and moves `v` to `T`. Here, `w(u, v)` denotes the weight on edge (`u`, `v`).

The algorithm is described in Listing 31.6.

Listing 31.6 Dijkstra's Single-Source Shortest-Path Algorithm

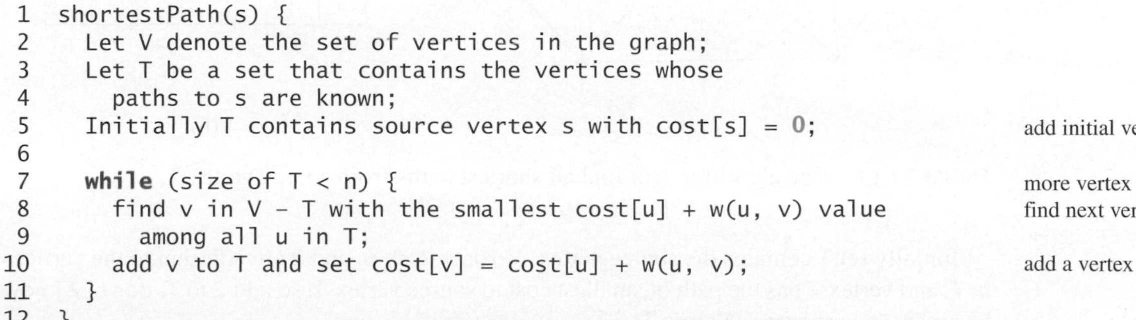

```
shortestPath(s) {
  Let V denote the set of vertices in the graph;
  Let T be a set that contains the vertices whose
    paths to s are known;
  Initially T contains source vertex s with cost[s] = 0;

  while (size of T < n) {
    find v in V - T with the smallest cost[u] + w(u, v) value
      among all u in T;
    add v to T and set cost[v] = cost[u] + w(u, v);
  }
}
```

add initial vertex
more vertex
find next vertex
add a vertex

This algorithm is very similar to Prim's for finding a minimum spanning tree. Both algorithms divide the vertices into two sets: T and V - T. In the case of Prim's algorithm, set T contains the vertices that are already added to the tree. In the case of Dijkstra's, set T contains the vertices whose shortest paths to the source have been found. Both algorithms repeatedly find a vertex from V – T and add it to T. In the case of Prim's algorithm, the vertex is adjacent to some vertex in the set with the minimum weight on the edge. In Dijkstra's algorithm, the vertex is adjacent to some vertex in the set with the minimum total cost to the source.

The algorithm starts by adding the source vertex s into T and sets cost[s] to 0 (line 5). It then continuously adds a vertex (say v) from V - T into T. v is the vertex that is adjacent to a vertex u in T with the smallest cost[u] + w(u, v). For example, there are five edges connecting vertices in T and V - T, as shown in Figure 31.10; (u, v) is the one with the smallest cost[u] + w(u, v). After v is added to T, set cost[v] to cost[u] + w(u, v) (line 10).

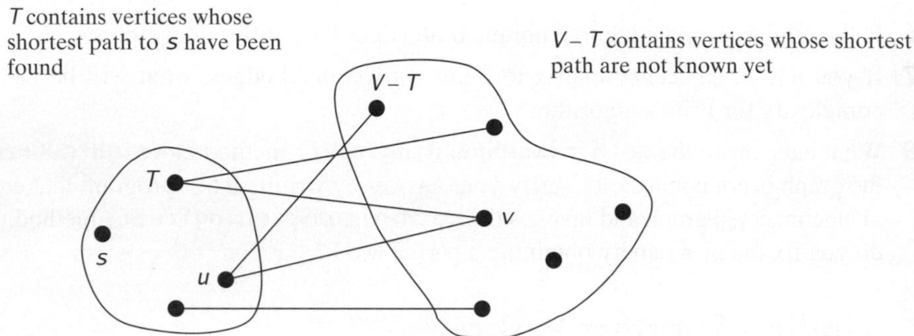

FIGURE 31.10 Find a vertex u in T that connects a vertex v in V - T with the smallest cost[u] + w(u, v).

Let us illustrate Dijkstra's algorithm using the graph in Figure 31.11a. Suppose the source vertex is 1. Therefore, cost[1] is 0 and the costs for all other vertices are initially ∞, as shown in Figure 31.11b. We use the parent[i] to denote the parent of i in the path. For convenience, set the parent of the source node to -1.

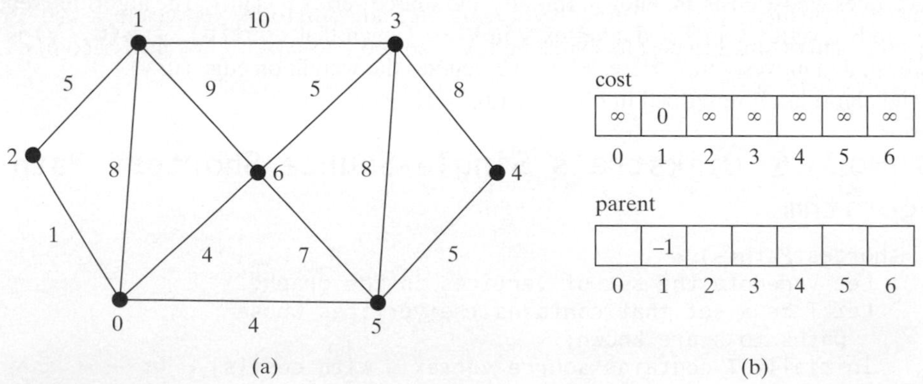

FIGURE 31.11 The algorithm will find all shortest paths from source vertex 1.

Initially set T contains the source vertex. Vertices 2, 0, 6, and 3 are adjacent to the vertices in T, and vertex 2 has the path of smallest cost to source vertex 1, so add 2 to T. cost[2] now becomes 5, as shown in Figure 31.12.

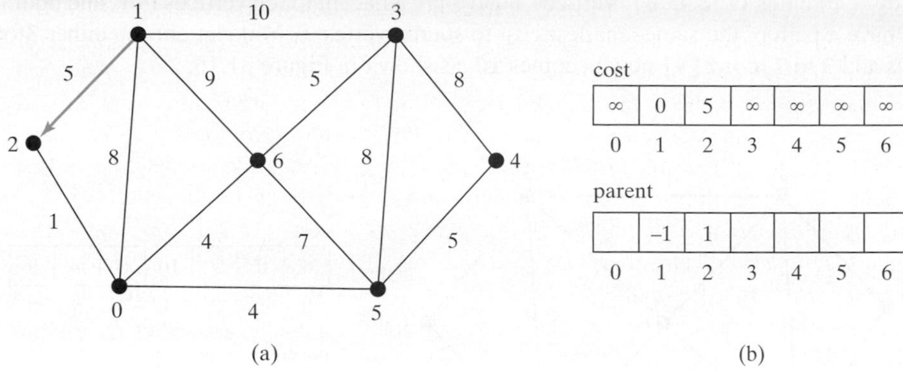

FIGURE 31.12 Now vertices 1 and 2 are in set T.

Now T contains {1, 2}. Vertices 0, 6, and 3 are adjacent to the vertices in T, and vertex 0 has a path of smallest cost to source vertex 1, so add 0 to T. `cost[0]` now becomes 6, as shown in Figure 31.13.

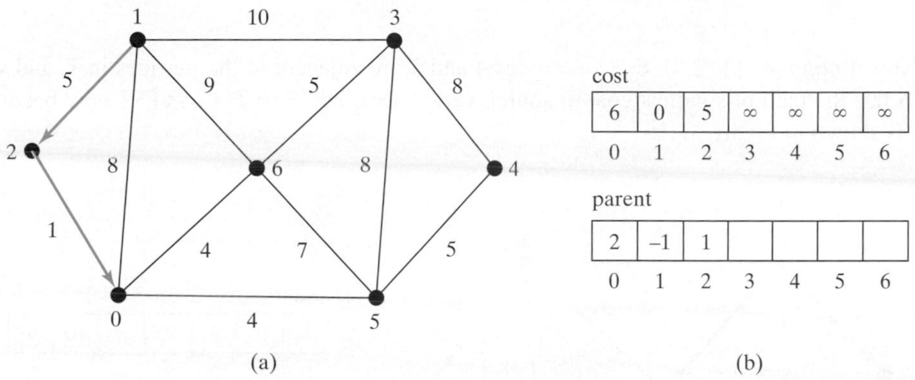

FIGURE 31.13 Now vertices {1, 2, 0} are in set T.

Now T contains {1, 2, 0}. Vertices 3, 6, and 5 are adjacent to the vertices in T, and vertex 6 has the path of smallest cost to source vertex 1, so add 6 to T. `cost[6]` now becomes 9, as shown in Figure 31.14.

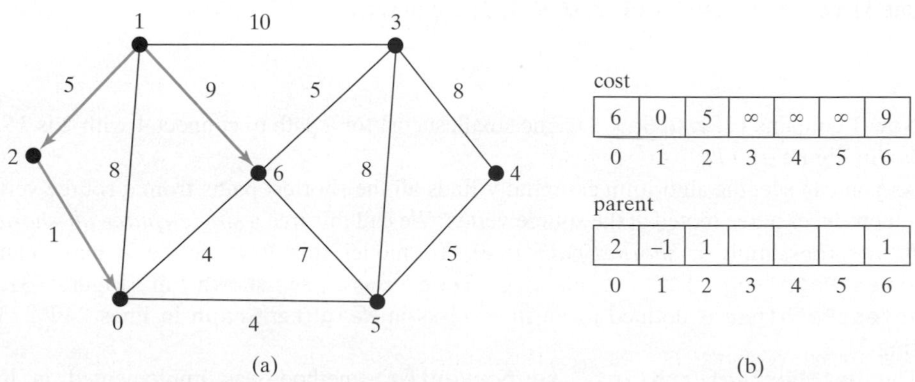

FIGURE 31.14 Now vertices {1, 2, 0, 6} are in set T.

Now T contains {1, 2, 0, 6}. Vertices 3 and 5 are adjacent to the vertices in T, and both vertices have a path of the same smallest cost to source vertex 1. You can choose either 3 or 5. Let us add 3 to T. **cost[3]** now becomes 10, as shown in Figure 31.15.

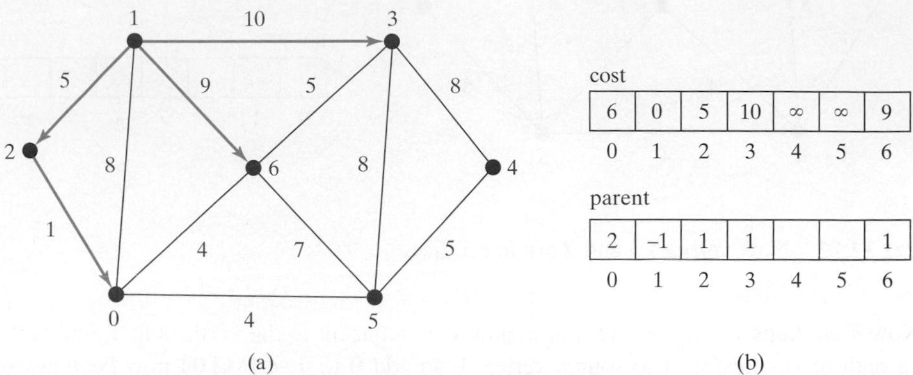

FIGURE 31.15 Now vertices {1, 2, 0, 6, 3} are in set T.

Now T contains {1, 2, 0, 6, 3}. Vertices 4 and 5 are adjacent to the vertices in T, and vertex 5 has the path of smallest cost to source vertex 1, so add 5 to T. **cost[5]** now becomes 10, as shown in Figure 31.16.

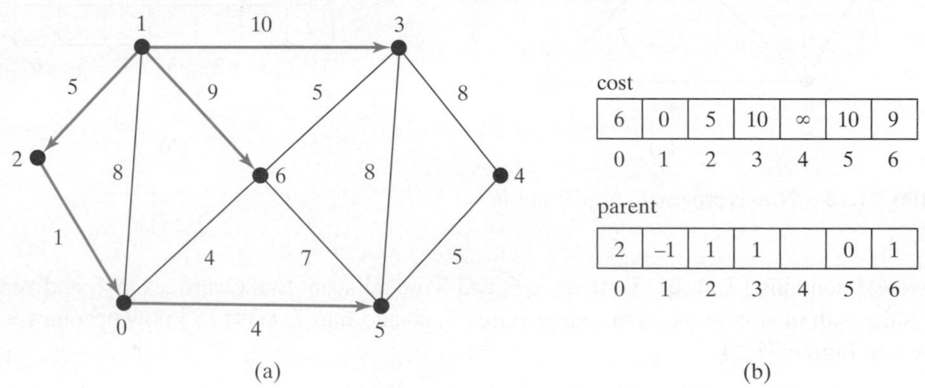

FIGURE 31.16 Now vertices {1, 2, 0, 6, 3, 5} are in set T.

Now T contains {1, 2, 0, 6, 3, 5}. The smallest cost for a path to connect 4 with 1 is 15, as shown in Figure 31.17.

shortest-path tree

As you can see, the algorithm essentially finds all the shortest paths from a source vertex, which produces a tree rooted at the source vertex. We call this tree a *single-source all-shortest-path tree* (or simply a *shortest-path tree*). To model this tree, define a class named **ShortestPathTree** that extends the **Tree** class, as shown in Figure 31.18. **ShortestPathTree** is defined as an inner class in **WeightedGraph** in lines 249–273 in Listing 31.2.

The **getShortestPath(int sourceVertex)** method was implemented in lines 193–246 in Listing 31.2. The method first adds **sourceVertex** to T (line 197). T is a list that

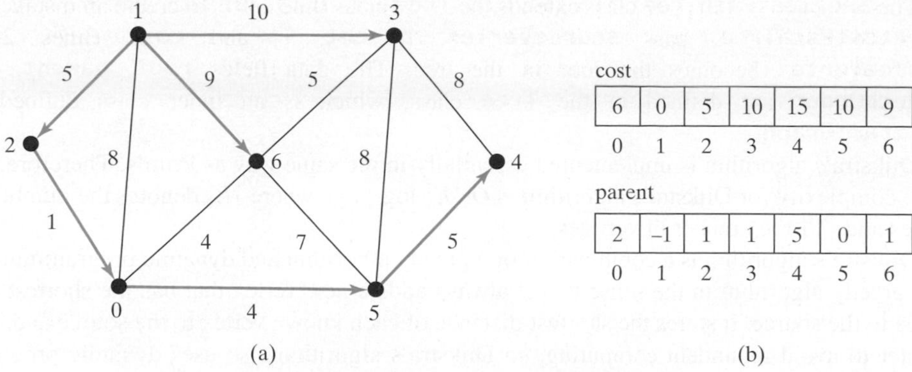

FIGURE 31.17 Now vertices {1, 2, 6, 0, 3, 5, 4} are in set T.

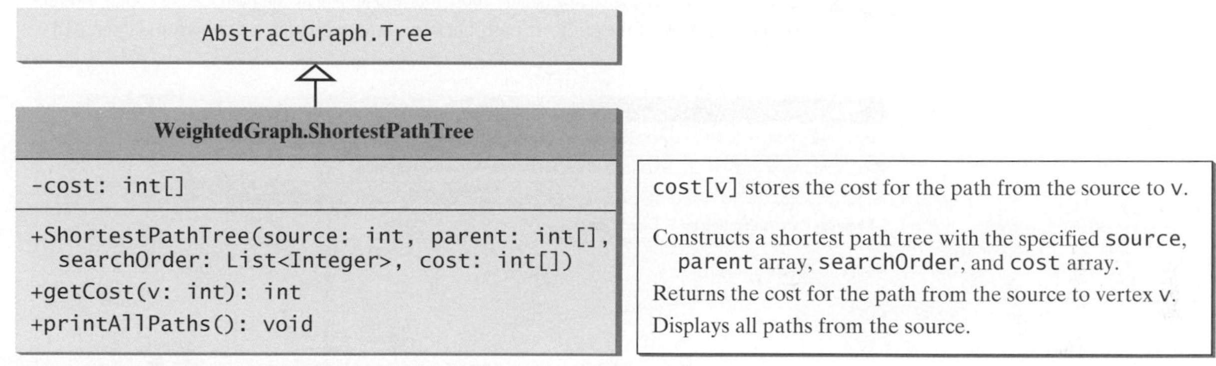

FIGURE 31.18 **WeightedGraph.ShortestPathTree** extends **AbstractGraph.Tree**.

stores the vertices whose paths have been found (line 195). **vertices** is defined as a protected data field in the **AbstractGraph** class, and it is an array that stores all vertices in the graph. **vertices.size()** returns the number of the vertices in the graph (line 200).

Each vertex is assigned a cost. The cost of the source vertex is **0** (line 211). The cost of all other vertices is initially assigned as infinity (line 209).

The method needs to remove the elements from the queues in order to find the one with the smallest total cost. To keep the original queues intact, queues are cloned in line 214.

A vertex is added to **T** if it is adjacent to one of the vertices in **T** with the smallest cost (line 240). Such a vertex is found using the following procedure.

1. For each vertex **u** in **T**, find its incident edge **e** with the smallest weight to **u**. All the incident edges to **u** are stored in **queues.get(u)**. **queues.get(u).peek()** (line 231) returns the incident edge with the smallest weight. If **e.v** is already in **T**, remove **e** from **queues.get(u)** (line 223). After lines 221–229, **queues.get(u).peek()** returns the edge **e**, such that **e** has the smallest weight to **u** and **e.v** is not in **T** (line 231).

2. Compare all these edges and find the one with the smallest value on **cost[u]** + **e.getWeight()** (line 232).

After a new vertex is added to **T** (line 240), the cost of this vertex is updated (line 241). Once all vertices are added to **T**, an instance of **ShortestPathTree** is created (line 245). Note that the method will not work if the graph is not connected. However, you can modify it to obtain the shortest paths to all connected vertices to the source vertex.

ShortestPathTree class

The `ShortestPathTree` class extends the `Tree` class (line 249). To create an instance of `ShortestPathTree`, pass `sourceVertex`, `parent`, `T`, and `cost` (lines 253). `sourceVertex` becomes the root in the tree. The data fields `root`, `parent`, and `searchOrder` are defined in the `Tree` class, which is an inner class defined in `AbstractGraph`.

Dijkstra's algorithm time complexity

Dijkstra's algorithm is implemented essentially in the same way as Prim's. Therefore, the time complexity for Dijkstra's algorithm is $O(|E| \log |V|)$, where $|E|$ denotes the number of edges and $|V|$ the number of vertices.

greedy and dynamic programming

Dijkstra's algorithm is a combination of a greedy algorithm and dynamic programming. It is a greedy algorithm in the sense that it always adds a new vertex that has the shortest distance to the source. It stores the shortest distance of each known vertex to the source and uses it later to avoid redundant computing, so Dijkstra's algorithm also uses dynamic programming.

shortest path animation on Companion Website

Pedagogical Note

Go to www.cs.armstrong.edu/liang/animation/ShortestPathAnimation.html to use a GUI interactive program to find the shortest path between any two cities, as shown in Figure 31.19.

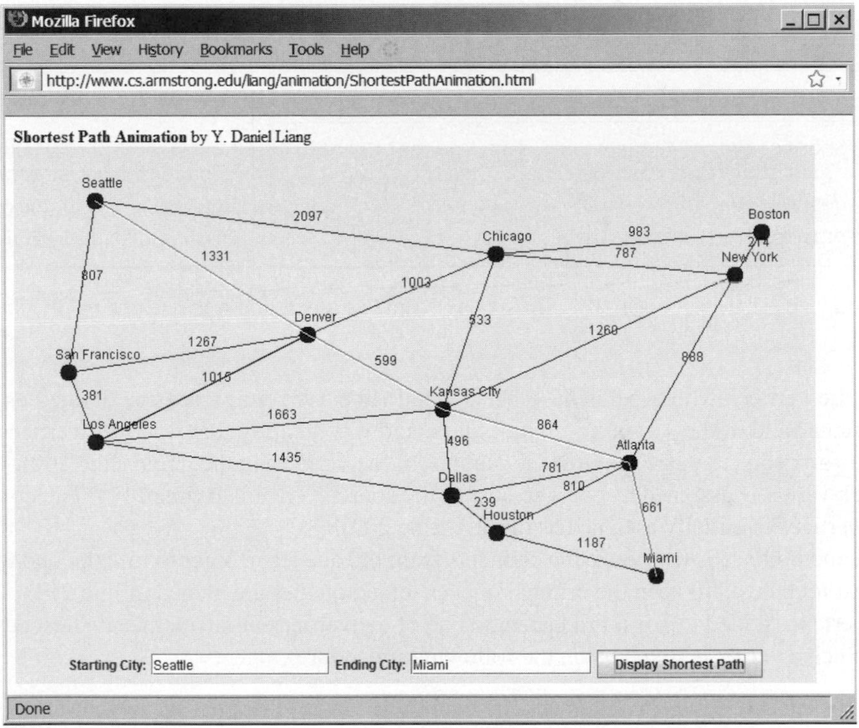

FIGURE 31.19 The animation tool displays a shortest path between two cities.

Listing 31.7 gives a test program that displays the shortest paths from Chicago to all other cities in Figure 31.1 and the shortest paths from vertex `3` to all vertices for the graph in Figure 31.3a, respectively.

LISTING 31.7 TestShortestPath.java

vertices

```
public class TestShortestPath {
  public static void main(String[] args) {
    String[] vertices = {"Seattle", "San Francisco", "Los Angeles",
```

```
      "Denver", "Kansas City", "Chicago", "Boston", "New York",
      "Atlanta", "Miami", "Dallas", "Houston"};

    int[][] edges = {
      {0, 1, 807}, {0, 3, 1331}, {0, 5, 2097},
      {1, 0, 807}, {1, 2, 381}, {1, 3, 1267},
      {2, 1, 381}, {2, 3, 1015}, {2, 4, 1663}, {2, 10, 1435},
      {3, 0, 1331}, {3, 1, 1267}, {3, 2, 1015}, {3, 4, 599},
        {3, 5, 1003},
      {4, 2, 1663}, {4, 3, 599}, {4, 5, 533}, {4, 7, 1260},
        {4, 8, 864}, {4, 10, 496},
      {5, 0, 2097}, {5, 3, 1003}, {5, 4, 533},
        {5, 6, 983}, {5, 7, 787},
      {6, 5, 983}, {6, 7, 214},
      {7, 4, 1260}, {7, 5, 787}, {7, 6, 214}, {7, 8, 888},
      {8, 4, 864}, {8, 7, 888}, {8, 9, 661},
        {8, 10, 781}, {8, 11, 810},
      {9, 8, 661}, {9, 11, 1187},
      {10, 2, 1435}, {10, 4, 496}, {10, 8, 781}, {10, 11, 239},
      {11, 8, 810}, {11, 9, 1187}, {11, 10, 239}
    };

    WeightedGraph<String> graph1 =
      new WeightedGraph<String>(edges, vertices);
    WeightedGraph<String>.ShortestPathTree tree1 =
      graph1.getShortestPath(graph1.getIndex("Chicago"));
    tree1.printAllPaths();

    // Display shortest paths from Houston to Chicago
    System.out.print("Shortest path from Houston to Chicago: ");
    java.util.List<String> path = tree1.getPath(11);
    for (String s: path) {
      System.out.print(s + " ");
    }

    edges = new int[][]{
      {0, 1, 2}, {0, 3, 8},
      {1, 0, 2}, {1, 2, 7}, {1, 3, 3},
      {2, 1, 7}, {2, 3, 4}, {2, 4, 5},
      {3, 0, 8}, {3, 1, 3}, {3, 2, 4}, {3, 4, 6},
      {4, 2, 5}, {4, 3, 6}
    };
    WeightedGraph<Integer> graph2 =
      new WeightedGraph<Integer>(edges, 5);
    WeightedGraph<Integer>.ShortestPathTree tree2 =
      graph2.getShortestPath(3);
    tree2.printAllPaths();
  }
}
```

edges

create graph1

shortest path

create edges

create graph2

print paths

```
All shortest paths from Chicago are:
A path from Chicago to Seattle: Chicago Seattle (cost: 2097)
A path from Chicago to San Francisco:
  Chicago Denver San Francisco (cost: 2270)
A path from Chicago to Los Angeles:
  Chicago Denver Los Angeles (cost: 2018)
A path from Chicago to Denver: Chicago Denver (cost: 1003)
A path from Chicago to Kansas City: Chicago Kansas City (cost: 533)
```

```
A path from Chicago to Chicago: Chicago (cost: 0)
A path from Chicago to Boston: Chicago Boston (cost: 983)
A path from Chicago to New York: Chicago New York (cost: 787)
A path from Chicago to Atlanta:
  Chicago Kansas City Atlanta (cost: 1397)
A path from Chicago to Miami:
  Chicago Kansas City Atlanta Miami (cost: 2058)
A path from Chicago to Dallas:
  Chicago Kansas City Dallas (cost: 1029)
A path from Chicago to Houston:
  Chicago Kansas City Dallas Houston (cost: 1268)

Shortest path from Chicago to Houston:
  Chicago Kansas City Dallas Houston

All shortest paths from 3 are:
A path from 3 to 0: 3 1 0 (cost: 5)
A path from 3 to 1: 3 1 (cost: 3)
A path from 3 to 2: 3 2 (cost: 4)
A path from 3 to 3: 3 (cost: 0)
A path from 3 to 4: 3 4 (cost: 6)
```

The program creates a weighted graph for Figure 31.1 in line 27. It then invokes the **getShortestPath(graph1.getIndex("Chicago"))** method to return a **Path** object that contains all shortest paths from Chicago. Invoking **printAllPaths()** on the **ShortestPathTree** object displays all the paths (line 30).

The graphical illustration of all shortest paths from Chicago is shown in Figure 31.20. The shortest paths from Chicago to the cities are found in this order: Kansas City, New York,

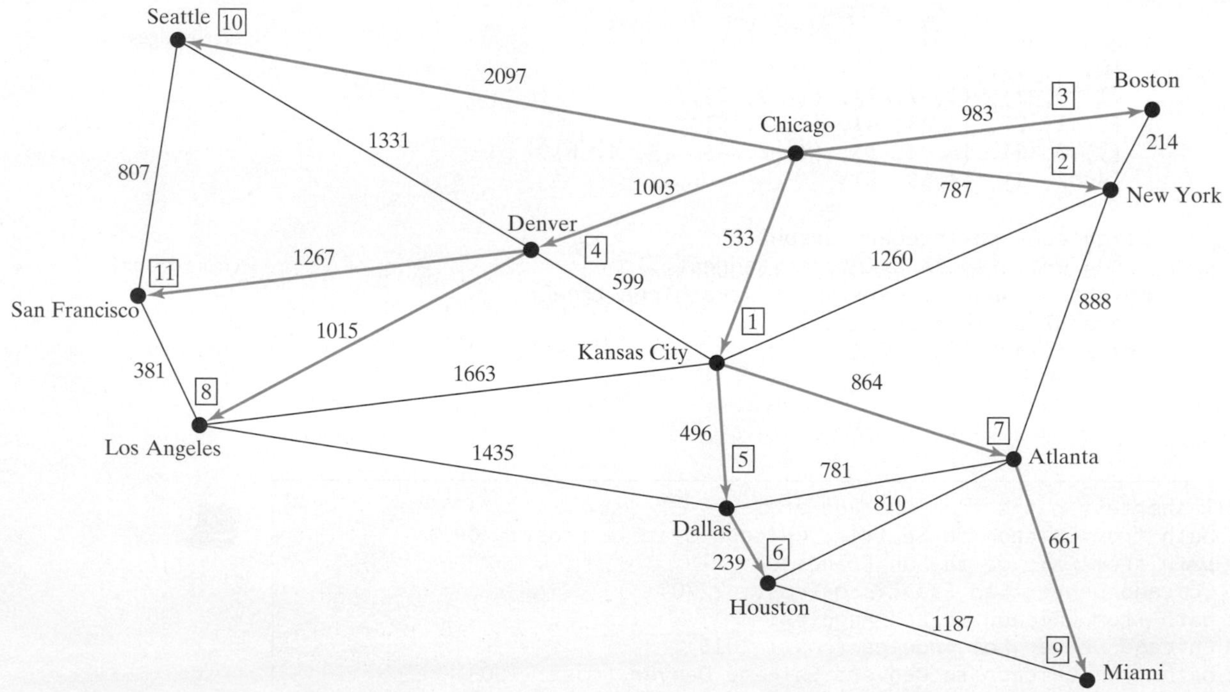

FIGURE 31.20 The shortest paths from Chicago to all other cities are highlighted.

Boston, Denver, Dallas, Houston, Atlanta, Los Angeles, Miami, Seattle, and San Francisco.

Check Point
MyProgrammingLab™

31.9 Trace Dijkstra's algorithm for finding shortest paths from Boston to all other cities in Figure 31.1.

31.10 Is the shortest path between two vertices unique if all edges have different weights?

31.11 If you use an adjacency matrix to represent weighted edges, what would be the time complexity for Dijkstra's algorithm?

31.12 What happens to the `getShortestPath()` method in `WeightedGraph` if the graph is not connected? Verify your answer by writing a test program that creates an unconnected graph and invoke the `getShortestPath()` method.

31.6 Case Study: The Weighted Nine Tails Problem

Key Point

The weighted nine tails problem can be reduced to the weighted shortest path problem.

Section 30.10 presented the nine tails problem and solved it using the BFS algorithm. This section presents a variation of the problem and solves it using the shortest-path algorithm.

The nine tails problem is to find the minimum number of the moves that lead to all coins facing down. Each move flips a head coin and its neighbors. The weighted nine tails problem assigns the number of flips as a weight on each move. For example, you can move from the coins in Figure 31.21a to those in Figure 31.21b by flipping the first coin in the first row and its two neighbors. Thus, the weight for this move is `3`.

H	H	H
T	T	T
H	H	H

(a)

T	T	H
H	T	T
H	H	H

(b)

FIGURE 31.21 The weight for each move is the number of flips for the move.

The weighted nine tails problem can be reduced to finding the shortest path from a starting node to the target node in an edge-weighted graph. The graph has 512 nodes. Create an edge from node `v` to `u` if there is a move from node `u` to node `v`. Assign the number of flips to be the weight of the edge.

Recall that in Section 30.10 we defined a class `NineTailModel` for modeling the nine tails problem. We now define a new class named `WeightedNineTailModel` that extends `NineTailModel`, as shown in Figure 31.22.

The `NineTailModel` class creates a `Graph` and obtains a `Tree` rooted at the target node `511`. `WeightedNineTailModel` is the same as `NineTailModel` except that it creates a `WeightedGraph` and obtains a `ShortestPathTree` rooted at the target node `511`. `WeightedNineTailModel` extends `NineTailModel`. The method `getEdges()` finds all edges in the graph. The `getNumberOfFlips(int u, int v)` method returns the number of flips from node `u` to node `v`. The `getNumberOfFlips(int u)` method returns the number of flips from node `u` to the target node.

Listing 31.8 implements `WeightedNineTailModel`.

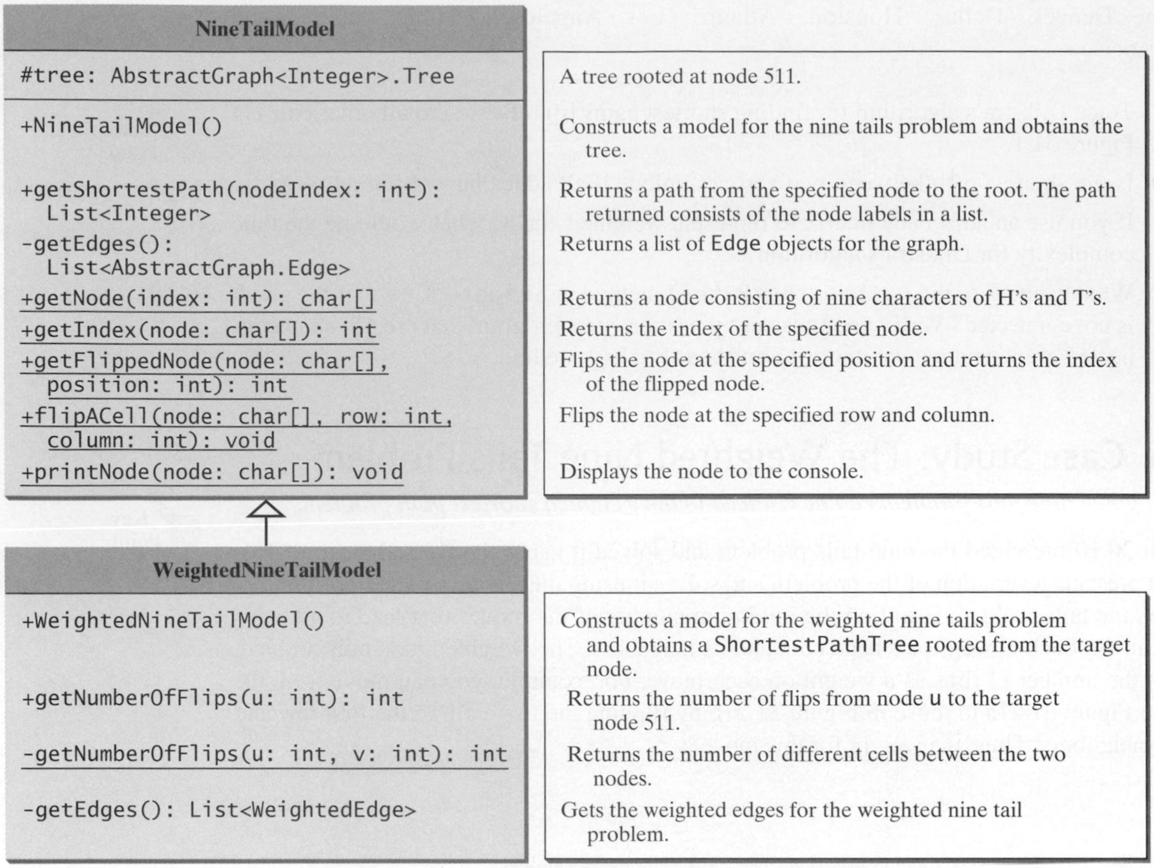

NineTailModel	
#tree: AbstractGraph<Integer>.Tree	A tree rooted at node 511.
+NineTailModel()	Constructs a model for the nine tails problem and obtains the tree.
+getShortestPath(nodeIndex: int): List<Integer>	Returns a path from the specified node to the root. The path returned consists of the node labels in a list.
-getEdges(): List<AbstractGraph.Edge>	Returns a list of Edge objects for the graph.
+getNode(index: int): char[]	Returns a node consisting of nine characters of H's and T's.
+getIndex(node: char[]): int	Returns the index of the specified node.
+getFlippedNode(node: char[], position: int): int	Flips the node at the specified position and returns the index of the flipped node.
+flipACell(node: char[], row: int, column: int): void	Flips the node at the specified row and column.
+printNode(node: char[]): void	Displays the node to the console.

WeightedNineTailModel	
+WeightedNineTailModel()	Constructs a model for the weighted nine tails problem and obtains a ShortestPathTree rooted from the target node.
+getNumberOfFlips(u: int): int	Returns the number of flips from node u to the target node 511.
-getNumberOfFlips(u: int, v: int): int	Returns the number of different cells between the two nodes.
-getEdges(): List<WeightedEdge>	Gets the weighted edges for the weighted nine tail problem.

FIGURE 31.22 The `WeightedNineTailModel` class extends `NineTailModel`.

LISTING 31.8 `WeightedNineTailModel.java`

```
import java.util.*;

public class WeightedNineTailModel extends NineTailModel {
  /** Construct a model */
  public WeightedNineTailModel() {
    // Create edges
    List<WeightedEdge> edges = getEdges();

    // Create a graph
    WeightedGraph<Integer> graph = new WeightedGraph<Integer>(
      edges, NUMBER_OF_NODES);

    // Obtain a shortest path tree rooted at the target node
    tree = graph.getShortestPath(511);
  }

  /** Create all edges for the graph */
  private List<WeightedEdge> getEdges() {
    // Store edges
    List<WeightedEdge> edges = new ArrayList<WeightedEdge>();

    for (int u = 0; u < NUMBER_OF_NODES; u++) {
```

```
23       for (int k = 0; k < 9; k++) {
24         char[] node = getNode(u); // Get the node for vertex u
25         if (node[k] == 'H') {
26           int v = getFlippedNode(node, k);
27           int numberOfFlips = getNumberOfFlips(u, v);
28
29           // Add edge (v, u) for a legal move from node u to node v
30           edges.add(new WeightedEdge(v, u, numberOfFlips));
31         }
32       }
33     }
34
35     return edges;
36   }
37
38   private static int getNumberOfFlips(int u, int v) {
39     char[] node1 = getNode(u);
40     char[] node2 = getNode(v);
41
42     int count = 0; // Count the number of different cells
43     for (int i = 0; i < node1.length; i++)
44       if (node1[i] != node2[i]) count++;
45
46     return count;
47   }
48
49   public int getNumberOfFlips(int u) {
50     return (int)((WeightedGraph<Integer>.ShortestPathTree)tree)
51       .getCost(u);
52   }
53 }
```

get adjacent node

weight

add an edge

number of flips

total number of flips

`WeightedNineTailModel` extends `NineTailModel` to build a `WeightedGraph` to model the weighted nine tails problem (lines 10–11). For each node `u`, the `getEdges()` method finds a flipped node `v` and assigns the number of flips as the weight for edge (`v`, `u`) (line 30). The `getNumberOfFlips(int u, int v)` method returns the number of flips from node `u` to node `v` (lines 38–47). The number of flips is the number of the different cells between the two nodes (line 44).

The `WeightedNineTailModel` obtains a `ShortestPathTree` rooted at the target node `511` (line 14). Note that `tree` is a protected data field defined in `NineTailModel` and `ShortestPathTree` is a subclass of `Tree`. The methods defined in `NineTailModel` use the `tree` property.

The `getNumberOfFlips(int u)` method (lines 49–52) returns the number of flips from node `u` to the target node, which is the cost of the path from node `u` to the target node. This cost can be obtained by invoking the `getCost(u)` method defined in the `ShortestPathTree` class (line 51).

Listing 31.9 gives a program that prompts the user to enter an initial node and displays the minimum number of flips to reach the target node.

LISTING 31.9 WeightedNineTail.java

```
import java.util.Scanner;

public class WeightedNineTail {
  public static void main(String[] args) {
    // Prompt the user to enter the nine coins' Hs and Ts
```

initial node · create model · get shortest path · print node · number of flips

```
6      System.out.print("Enter an initial nine coins' Hs and Ts: ");
7      Scanner input = new Scanner(System.in);
8      String s = input.nextLine();
9      char[] initialNode = s.toCharArray();
10
11     WeightedNineTailModel model = new WeightedNineTailModel();
12     java.util.List<Integer> path =
13       model.getShortestPath(NineTailModel.getIndex(initialNode));
14
15     System.out.println("The steps to flip the coins are ");
16     for (int i = 0; i < path.size(); i++)
17       NineTailModel.printNode(
18         NineTailModel.getNode(path.get(i).intValue()));
19
20     System.out.println("The number of flips is " +
21       model.getNumberOfFlips(NineTailModel.getIndex(initialNode)));
22   }
23 }
```

```
Enter an initial nine coins Hs and Ts: HHHTTTHHH ↵Enter

The steps to flip the coins are
HHH
TTT
HHH

HHH
THT
TTT

TTT
TTT
TTT

The number of flips is 8
```

The program prompts the user to enter an initial node with nine letters with a combination of Hs and Ts as a string in line 8, obtains an array of characters from the string (line 9), creates a model (line 11), obtains the shortest path from the initial node to the target node (lines 12–13), displays the nodes in the path (lines 16–18), and invokes `getNumberOfFlips` to get the number of flips needed to reach the target node (line 21).

MyProgrammingLab™

31.13 Why is the `tree` data field in `NineTailModel` in Section 30.13 defined protected?

31.14 How are the nodes created for the graph in `WeightedNineTailModel`?

31.15 How are the edges created for the graph in `WeightedNineTailModel`?

Key Terms

Dijkstra's algorithm 1111
edge-weighted graph 1095
minimum spanning tree 1105
Prim's algorithm 1106
shortest path 1111
single-source shortest path 1111
vertex-weighted graph 1095

Chapter Summary

1. You can use adjacency matrices or priority queues to represent weighted edges in graphs.

2. A spanning tree of a graph is a subgraph that is a tree and connects all vertices in the graph. You learned how to implement *Prim's algorithm* for finding a *minimum spanning tree*.

3. You learned how to implement *Dijkstra's algorithm* for finding *shortest paths*.

Test Questions

Do the test questions for this chapter online at www.cs.armstrong.edu/liang/intro9e/test.html.

Programming Exercises

MyProgrammingLab™

***31.1** (*Kruskal's algorithm*) The text introduced Prim's algorithm for finding a minimum spanning tree. Kruskal's algorithm is another well-known algorithm for finding a minimum spanning tree. The algorithm repeatedly finds a minimum-weight edge and adds it to the tree if it does not cause a cycle. The process ends when all vertices are in the tree. Design and implement an algorithm for finding an MST using Kruskal's algorithm.

***31.2** (*Implement Prim's algorithm using an adjacency matrix*) The text implements Prim's algorithm using priority queues on adjacent edges. Implement the algorithm using an adjacency matrix for weighted graphs.

***31.3** (*Implement Dijkstra's algorithm using an adjacency matrix*) The text implements Dijkstra's algorithm using priority queues on adjacent edges. Implement the algorithm using an adjacency matrix for weighted graphs.

***31.4** (*Modify weight in the nine tails problem*) In the text, we assign the number of the flips as the weight for each move. Assuming that the weight is three times of the number of flips, revise the program.

***31.5** (*Prove or disprove*) The conjecture is that both `NineTailModel` and `WeightedNineTailModel` result in the same shortest path. Write a program to prove or disprove it. (*Hint*: Let `tree1` and `tree2` denote the trees rooted at node `511` obtained from `NineTailModel` and `WeightedNineTailModel`, respectively. If the depth of a node `u` is the same in `tree1` and in `tree2`, the length of the path from `u` to the target is the same.)

****31.6** (*Weighted 4 × 4 16 tails model*) The weighted nine tails problem in the text uses a 3 × 3 matrix. Assume that you have 16 coins placed in a 4 × 4 matrix. Create a new model class named `WeightedTailModel16`. Create an instance of the model and save the object into a file named **WeightedTailModel16.dat**.

****31.7** (*Weighted 4 × 4 16 tails view*) Listing 31.9, WeightedNineTail.java, presents a view for the nine tails problem. Revise this program for the weighted 4 × 4 16 tails problem. Your program should read the model object created from the preceding exercise.

****31.8** (*Traveling salesperson problem*) The traveling salesperson problem (TSP) is to find the shortest round-trip route that visits each city exactly once and then returns to the starting city. The problem is equivalent to finding the shortest Hamiltonian cycle in Programming Exercise 30.17. Add the following method in the `WeightedGraph` class:

```
// Return the shortest cycle
// Return null if no such cycle exists
public List<Integer> getShortestHamiltonianCycle()
```

***31.9** (*Find a minimum spanning tree*) Write a program that reads a connected graph from a file and displays its minimum spanning tree. The first line in the file contains a number that indicates the number of vertices (`n`). The vertices are labeled as `0`, `1`, ..., `n-1`. Each subsequent line describes the edges in the form of `u1, v1, w1 | u2, v2, w2 | ...`. Each triplet in this form describes an edge and its weight. Figure 31.23 shows an example of the file for the corresponding graph. Note that we assume the graph is undirected. If the graph has an edge (`u`, `v`), it also has an edge (`v`, `u`). Only one edge is represented in the file. When you construct a graph, both edges need to be considered.

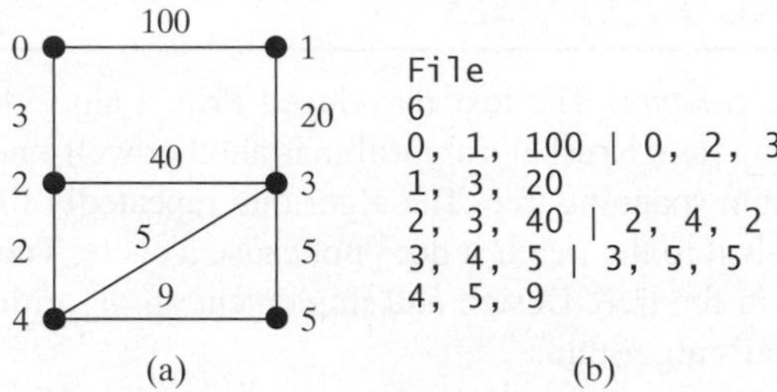

FIGURE 31.23 The vertices and edges of a weighted graph can be stored in a file.

Your program should prompt the user to enter the name of the file, read data from the file, create an instance `g` of `WeightedGraph`, invoke `g.printWeightedEdges()` to display all edges, invoke `getMinimumSpanningTree()` to obtain an instance `tree` of `WeightedGraph.MST`, invoke `tree.getTotalWeight()` to display the weight of the minimum spanning tree, and invoke `tree.printTree()` to display the tree. Here is a sample run of the program:

```
Enter a file name: c:\exercise\WeightedGraphSample.txt [Enter]
The number of vertices is 6
Vertex 0: (0, 2, 3) (0, 1, 100)
Vertex 1: (1, 3, 20) (1, 0, 100)
Vertex 2: (2, 4, 2) (2, 3, 40) (2, 0, 3)
Vertex 3: (3, 4, 5) (3, 5, 5) (3, 1, 20) (3, 2, 40)
Vertex 4: (4, 2, 2) (4, 3, 5) (4, 5, 9)
Vertex 5: (5, 3, 5) (5, 4, 9)
Total weight is 35
Root is: 0
Edges: (3, 1) (0, 2) (4, 3) (2, 4) (3, 5)
```

(*Hint*: Use `new WeightedGraph(list, numberOfVertices)` to create a graph, where `list` contains a list of `WeightedEdge` objects. Use `new WeightedEdge(u, v, w)` to create an edge. Read the first line to get the number of vertices. Read each subsequent line into a string `s` and use `s.split("[\\|]")` to extract the triplets. For each triplet, use `triplet.split("[,]")` to extract vertices and weight.)

***31.10** (*Create a file for a graph*) Modify Listing 31.3, TestWeightedGraph.java, to create a file for representing `graph1`. The file format is described in Programming Exercise 31.9. Create the file from the array defined in lines 7–24 in Listing 31.3. The number of vertices for the graph is `12`, which will be stored in the first line of the file. An edge (`u`, `v`) is stored if `u < v`. The contents of the file should be as follows:

```
12
0, 1, 807 | 0, 3, 1331 | 0, 5, 2097
1, 2, 381 | 1, 3, 1267
2, 3, 1015 | 2, 4, 1663 | 2, 10, 1435
3, 4, 599 | 3, 5, 1003
4, 5, 533 | 4, 7, 1260 | 4, 8, 864 | 4, 10, 496
5, 6, 983 | 5, 7, 787
6, 7, 214
7, 8, 888
8, 9, 661 | 8, 10, 781 | 8, 11, 810
9, 11, 1187
10, 11, 239
```

***31.11** (*Find shortest paths*) Write a program that reads a connected graph from a file. The graph is stored in a file using the same format specified in Programming Exercise 31.9. Your program should prompt the user to enter the name of the file then two vertices, and should display the shortest path between the two vertices. For example, for the graph in Figure 31.23, the shortest path between `0` and `1` can be displayed as `0 2 4 3 1`.

Here is a sample run of the program:

```
Enter a file name: WeightedGraphSample2.txt ↵Enter
Enter two vertices (integer indexes): 0 1 ↵Enter
The number of vertices is 6
Vertex 0: (0, 2, 3) (0, 1, 100)
Vertex 1: (1, 3, 20) (1, 0, 100)
Vertex 2: (2, 4, 2) (2, 3, 40) (2, 0, 3)
Vertex 3: (3, 4, 5) (3, 5, 5) (3, 1, 20) (3, 2, 40)
Vertex 4: (4, 2, 2) (4, 3, 5) (4, 5, 9)
Vertex 5: (5, 3, 5) (5, 4, 9)
A path from 0 to 1: 0 2 4 3 1
```

***31.12** (*Display weighted graphs*) Revise `GraphView` in Listing 30.6 to display a weighted graph. Write a program that displays the graph in Figure 31.1 as shown in Figure 31.24a.

***31.13** (*Display shortest paths*) Revise `GraphView` in Listing 30.6 to display a weighted graph and the shortest path between the two specified cities, as shown in Figure 31.19. You need to add a data field `path` in `GraphView`. If a `path` is not null, the edges in the path are displayed in red. If a city not in the map is entered, the program displays a dialog box to alert the user.

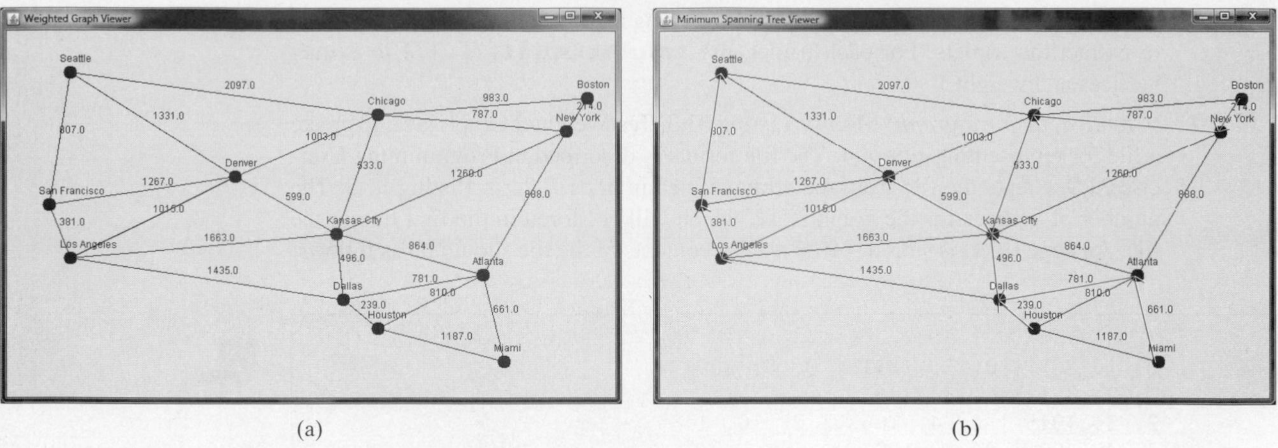

FIGURE 31.24 (a) Exercise 31.12 displays a weighted graph. (b) Exercise 31.14 displays an MST.

***31.14** (*Display a minimum spanning tree*) Revise `GraphView` in Listing 30.6 to display a weighted graph and a minimum spanning tree for the graph in Figure 31.1, as shown in Figure 31.24b. The edges in the MST are shown in red.

*****31.15** (*Dynamic graphs*) Write a program that lets the users create a weighted graph dynamically. The user can create a vertex by entering its name and location, as shown in Figure 31.25. The user can also create an edge to connect two vertices. To simplify the program, assume that vertex names are the same as vertex indices. You have to add the vertex indices `0`, `1`, . . . , and `n`, in this order. The user can specify two vertices and let the program display their shortest path in red.

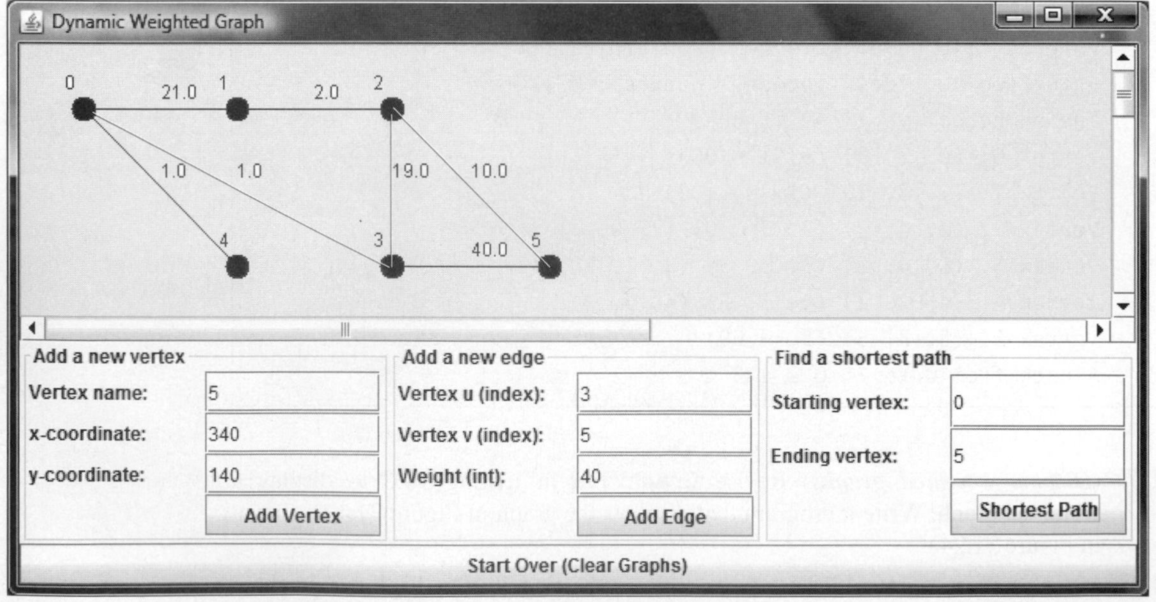

FIGURE 31.25 The program can add vertices and edges and display the shortest path between two specified vertices.

*****31.16** (*Display a dynamic MST*) Write a program that lets the user create a weighted graph dynamically. The user can create a vertex by entering its name and location, as shown in Figure 31.26. The user can also create an edge to connect two vertices. To simplify the program, assume that vertex names are the same as those of vertex indices. You have to add the vertex indices 0, 1, . . ., and n, in this order. The edges in the MST are displayed in red. As new edges are added, the MST is redisplayed.

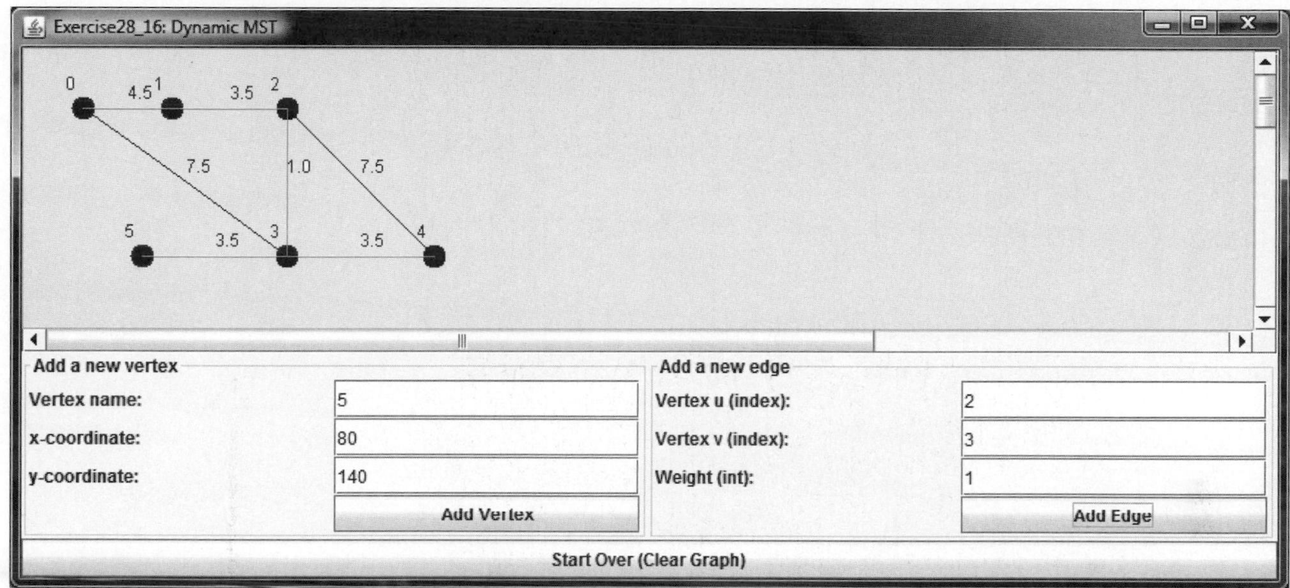

FIGURE 31.26 The program can add vertices and edges and display MST dynamically.

*****31.17** (*Weighted graph visualization tool*) Develop an applet as shown in Figure 31.2, with the following requirements: (1) The radius of each vertex is 20 pixels. (2) The user clicks the left mouse button to place a vertex centered at the mouse point, provided that the mouse point is not inside or too close to an existing vertex. (3) The user clicks the right mouse button inside an existing vertex to remove the vertex. (4) The user presses a mouse button inside a vertex and drags to another vertex and then releases the button to create an edge, and the distance between the two vertices is also displayed. (5) The user drags a vertex while pressing the *CTRL* key to move a vertex. (6) The vertices are numbers starting from 0. When a vertex is removed, the vertices are renumbered. (7) You can click the *Show MST* or *Show All SP From the Source* button to display an MST or SP tree from a starting vertex. (8) You can click the *Show Shortest Path* button to display the shortest path between the two specified vertices.

CHAPTER

32

MULTITHREADING AND PARALLEL PROGRAMMING

Objectives

- To get an overview of multithreading (§32.2).
- To develop task classes by implementing the `Runnable` interface (§32.3).
- To create threads to run tasks using the `Thread` class (§32.3).
- To control threads using the methods in the `Thread` class (§32.4).
- To control animations using threads (§32.5, §32.7).
- To run code in the event dispatch thread (§32.6).
- To execute tasks in a thread pool (§32.8).
- To use synchronized methods or blocks to synchronize threads to avoid race conditions (§32.9).
- To synchronize threads using locks (§32.10).
- To facilitate thread communications using conditions on locks (§§32.11–32.12).
- To use blocking queues to synchronize access to an array queue, linked queue, and priority queue (§32.13).
- To restrict the number of accesses to a shared resource using semaphores (§32.14).
- To use the resource-ordering technique to avoid deadlocks (§32.15).
- To describe the life cycle of a thread (§32.16).
- To create synchronized collections using the static methods in the `Collections` class (§32.17).
- To develop parallel programs using the Fork/Join Framework (§32.18).

32.1 Introduction

Multithreading enables multiple tasks in a program to be executed concurrently.

multithreading

One of the powerful features of Java is its built-in support for *multithreading*—the concurrent running of multiple tasks within a program. In many programming languages, you have to invoke system-dependent procedures and functions to implement multithreading. This chapter introduces the concepts of threads and how to develop multithreading programs in Java.

32.2 Thread Concepts

A program may consist of many tasks that can run concurrently. A thread *is the flow of execution, from beginning to end, of a task.*

thread
task

A *thread* provides the mechanism for running a task. With Java, you can launch multiple threads from a program concurrently. These threads can be executed simultaneously in multiprocessor systems, as shown in Figure 32.1a.

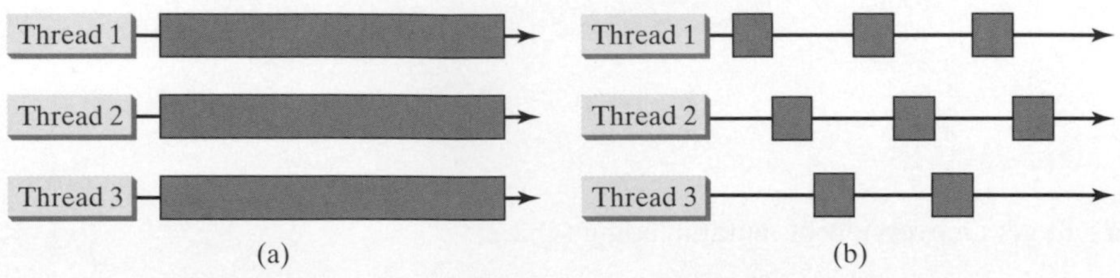

FIGURE 32.1 (a) Here multiple threads are running on multiple CPUs. (b) Here multiple threads share a single CPU.

time sharing

In single-processor systems, as shown in Figure 32.1b, the multiple threads share CPU time, known as *time sharing*, and the operating system is responsible for scheduling and allocating resources to them. This arrangement is practical, because most of the time the CPU is idle. It does nothing, for example, while waiting for the user to enter data.

Multithreading can make your program more responsive and interactive, as well as enhance performance. For example, a good word processor lets you print or save a file while you are typing. In some cases, multithreaded programs run faster than single-threaded programs even on single-processor systems. Java provides exceptionally good support for creating and running threads and for locking resources to prevent conflicts.

task
runnable object
thread

When your program executes as an application, the Java interpreter starts a thread for the `main` method. When your program executes as an applet, the Web browser starts a thread to run the applet. You can create additional threads to run concurrent tasks in the program. In Java, each task is an instance of the `Runnable` interface, also called a *runnable object*. A *thread* is essentially an object that facilitates the execution of a task.

MyProgrammingLab™

32.1 Why is multithreading needed? How can multiple threads run simultaneously in a single-processor system?

32.2 What is a runnable object? What is a thread?

32.3 Creating Tasks and Threads

A task class must implement the `Runnable` *interface. A task must be run from a thread.*

`Runnable` interface

Tasks are objects. To create tasks, you have to first define a class for tasks, which implements the `Runnable` interface. The `Runnable` interface is rather simple. All it contains is the **run** method. You need to implement this method to tell the system how your thread is going to run. A template for developing a task class is shown in Figure 32.2a.

run() method

```
java.lang.Runnable <-------- TaskClass

// Custom task class
public class TaskClass implements Runnable {
  ...
  public TaskClass(...) {
    ...
  }

  // Implement the run method in Runnable
  public void run() {
    // Tell system how to run custom thread
    ...
  }
  ...
}
```

(a)

```
// Client class
public class Client {
  ...
  public void someMethod() {
    ...
    // Create an instance of TaskClass
    TaskClass task = new TaskClass(...);

    // Create a thread
    Thread thread = new Thread(task);

    // Start a thread
    thread.start();
    ...
  }
  ...
}
```

(b)

FIGURE 32.2 Define a task class by implementing the **Runnable** interface.

Once you have defined a **TaskClass**, you can create a task using its constructor. For example,

```
TaskClass task = new TaskClass(...);
```

A task must be executed in a thread. The **Thread** class contains the constructors for creating threads and many useful methods for controlling threads. To create a thread for a task, use

Thread class
creating a task

```
Thread thread = new Thread(task);
```

You can then invoke the **start()** method to tell the JVM that the thread is ready to run, as follows:

creating a thread

```
thread.start();
```

The JVM will execute the task by invoking the task's **run()** method. Figure 32.2b outlines the major steps for creating a task, a thread, and starting the thread.

starting a thread

Listing 32.1 gives a program that creates three tasks and three threads to run them.

- The first task prints the letter *a* 100 times.
- The second task prints the letter *b* 100 times.
- The third task prints the integers 1 through 100.

When you run this program, the three threads will share the CPU and take turns printing letters and numbers on the console. Figure 32.3 shows a sample run of the program.

LISTING 32.1 TaskThreadDemo.java

```
public class TaskThreadDemo {
  public static void main(String[] args) {
    // Create tasks
    Runnable printA = new PrintChar('a', 100);
    Runnable printB = new PrintChar('b', 100);
    Runnable print100 = new PrintNum(100);
```

create tasks

```
C:\book>java TaskThreadDemo
aaaaaaaaaaaaaaaab 1b 2b 3b 4b 5b 6b 7b 8 9 10 11 12 13 14 15 16 17 18 19 20 21 2
2 23 24 25 26bababababababababa 27 28 29 30 31 32 33 34 35 36 37 38 39 40 41 42
43 44 45 46 47 48 49 50 51 52 53 54 55 56 57 58 59 60 61abababababababababbbbbbb
bbbbbbbbbbbbba 62a 63a 64a 65a 66a 67a 68a 69a 70 71 72 73 74 75 76 77 78 79 80 8
1 82 83 84 85 86 87 88abababababababababbbbbbbbbbbbbbbbbbba 89a 90a 91a 92a 93a
94a 95a 96a 97 98 99 100aaaaaaaaaaaaaaaaaabbbbbbbbbbbbbbbbbbbbbbbbbbbbbbbbaaaaaaaaa
aaaaaaaaaaa
C:\book>
```

FIGURE 32.3 Tasks `printA`, `printB`, and `print100` are executed simultaneously to display the letter `a` 100 times, the letter `b` 100 times, and the numbers from 1 to 100.

create threads

```

    // Create threads
    Thread thread1 = new Thread(printA);
    Thread thread2 = new Thread(printB);
    Thread thread3 = new Thread(print100);
```

start threads

```

    // Start threads
    thread1.start();
    thread2.start();
    thread3.start();
  }
}

// The task for printing a character a specified number of times
```

task class

```
class PrintChar implements Runnable {
  private char charToPrint; // The character to print
  private int times; // The number of times to repeat

  /** Construct a task with specified character and number of
   *  times to print the character
   */
  public PrintChar(char c, int t) {
    charToPrint = c;
    times = t;
  }

  @Override /** Override the run() method to tell the system
   *  what task to perform
   */
```

run

```
  public void run() {
    for (int i = 0; i < times; i++) {
      System.out.print(charToPrint);
    }
  }
}

// The task class for printing numbers from 1 to n for a given n
```

task class

```
class PrintNum implements Runnable {
  private int lastNum;

  /** Construct a task for printing 1, 2, ..., n */
  public PrintNum(int n) {
    lastNum = n;
  }

  @Override /** Tell the thread how to run */
```

run

```
  public void run() {
    for (int i = 1; i <= lastNum; i++) {
```

```
55         System.out.print(" " + i);
56       }
57     }
58   }
```

The program creates three tasks (lines 4–6). To run them concurrently, three threads are created (lines 9–11). The `start()` method (lines 14–16) is invoked to start a thread that causes the `run()` method in the task to be executed. When the `run()` method completes, the thread terminates.

Because the first two tasks, `printA` and `printB`, have similar functionality, they can be defined in one task class `PrintChar` (lines 21–41). The `PrintChar` class implements `Runnable` and overrides the `run()` method (lines 36–40) with the print-character action. This class provides a framework for printing any single character a given number of times. The runnable objects `printA` and `printB` are instances of the `PrintChar` class.

The `PrintNum` class (lines 44–58) implements `Runnable` and overrides the `run()` method (lines 53–57) with the print-number action. This class provides a framework for printing numbers from *1* to *n*, for any integer *n*. The runnable object `print100` is an instance of the class `printNum` class.

Note

effect of concurrency

If you don't see the effect of these three threads running concurrently, increase the number of characters to be printed. For example, change line 4 to

```
Runnable printA = new PrintChar('a', 10000);
```

Important Note

run() method

The `run()` method in a task specifies how to perform the task. This method is automatically invoked by the JVM. You should not invoke it. Invoking `run()` directly merely executes this method in the same thread; no new thread is started.

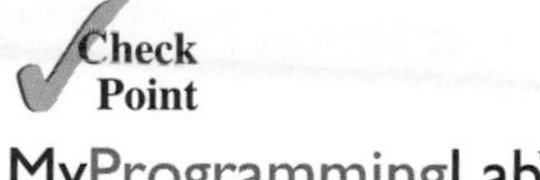

32.3 How do you define a task class? How do you create a thread for a task?

32.4 What would happen if you replaced the `start()` method with the `run()` method in lines 14–16 in Listing 32.1?

```
print100.start();                    print100.run();
printA.start();    Replaced by -->   printA.run();
printB.start();                      printB.run();
```

32.5 What is wrong in the following two programs? Correct the errors.

```
public class Test implements Runnable {
  public static void main(String[] args) {
    new Test();
  }

  public Test() {
    Test task = new Test();
    new Thread(task).start();
  }

  public void run() {
    System.out.println("test");
  }
}
```

(a)

```
public class Test implements Runnable {
  public static void main(String[] args) {
    new Test();
  }

  public Test() {
    Thread t = new Thread(this);
    t.start();
    t.start();
  }

  public void run() {
    System.out.println("test");
  }
}
```

(b)

32.4 The **Thread** Class

The **Thread** *class contains the constructors for creating threads for tasks and the methods for controlling threads.*

Figure 32.4 shows the class diagram for the **Thread** class.

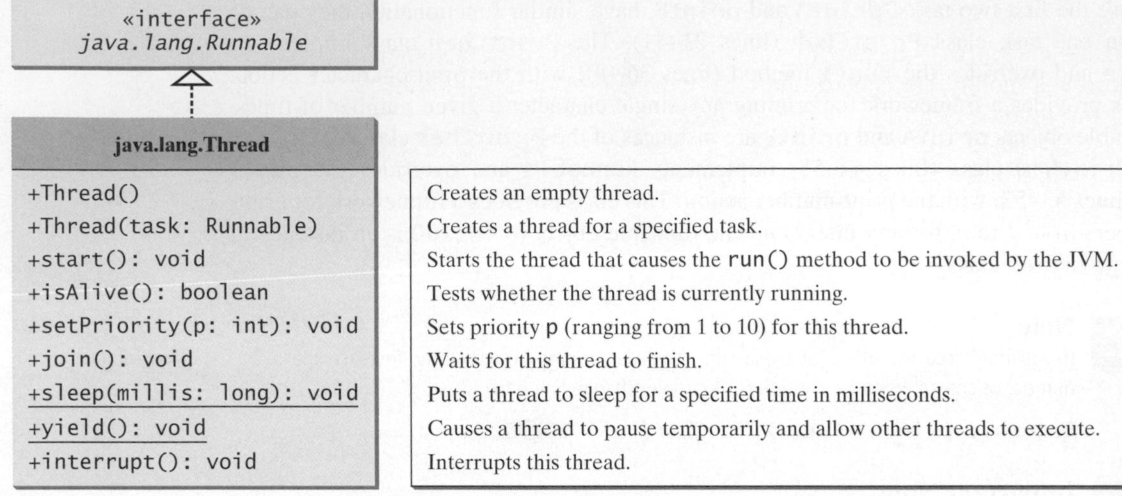

FIGURE 32.4 The **Thread** class contains the methods for controlling threads.

Note

separating task from thread

Since the **Thread** class implements **Runnable**, you could define a class that extends **Thread** and implements the **run** method, as shown in Figure 32.5a, and then create an object from the class and invoke its **start** method in a client program to start the thread, as shown in Figure 32.5b.

java.lang.Thread ◁── CustomThread

```
// Custom thread class
public class CustomThread extends Thread {
  ...
  public CustomThread(...) {
    ...
  }

  // Override the run method in Runnable
  public void run() {
    // Tell system how to perform this task
    ...
  }
  ...
}
```

(a)

```
// Client class
public class Client {
  ...
  public void someMethod() {
    ...
    // Create a thread
    CustomThread thread1 = new CustomThread(...);

    // Start a thread
    thread1.start();
    ...

    // Create another thread
    CustomThread thread2 = new CustomThread(...);

    // Start a thread
    thread2.start();
  }
  ...
}
```

(b)

FIGURE 32.5 Define a thread class by extending the **Thread** class.

This approach is, however, not recommended, because it mixes the task and the mechanism of running the task. Separating the task from the thread is a preferred design.

Note

The **Thread** class also contains the **stop()**, **suspend()**, and **resume()** methods. As of Java 2, these methods were *deprecated* (or *outdated*) because they are known to be inherently unsafe. Instead of using the **stop()** method, you should assign **null** to a **Thread** variable to indicate that it is stopped.

deprecated method

You can use the **yield()** method to temporarily release time for other threads. For example, suppose you modify the code in the **run()** method in lines 53–57 for **PrintNum** in Listing 32.1 as follows:

yield()

```
public void run() {
  for (int i = 1; i <= lastNum; i++) {
    System.out.print(" " + i);
    Thread.yield();
  }
}
```

Every time a number is printed, the thread of the **print100** task is yielded to other threads.

The **sleep(long millis)** method puts the thread to sleep for the specified time in milliseconds to allow other threads to execute. For example, suppose you modify the code in lines 53–57 in Listing 32.1 as follows:

sleep(long)

```
public void run() {
  try {
    for (int i = 1; i <= lastNum; i++) {
      System.out.print(" " + i);
      if (i >= 50) Thread.sleep(1);
    }
  }
  catch (InterruptedException ex) {
  }
}
```

Every time a number (**>= 50**) is printed, the thread of the **print100** task is put to sleep for 1 millisecond.

The **sleep** method may throw an **InterruptedException**, which is a checked exception. Such an exception may occur when a sleeping thread's **interrupt()** method is called. The **interrupt()** method is very rarely invoked on a thread, so an **InterruptedException** is unlikely to occur. But since Java forces you to catch checked exceptions, you have to put it in a **try-catch** block. If a **sleep** method is invoked in a loop, you should wrap the loop in a **try-catch** block, as shown in (a) below. If the loop is outside the **try-catch** block, as shown in (b), the thread may continue to execute even though it is being interrupted.

InterruptedException

```
public void run() {
  try {
    while (...) {
      ...
      Thread.sleep(1000);
    }
  }
  catch (InterruptedException ex) {
    ex.printStackTrace();
  }
}
```

(a) Correct

```
public void run() {
  while (...) {
    try {
      ...
      Thread.sleep(sleepTime);
    }
    catch (InterruptedException ex) {
      ex.printStackTrace();
    }
  }
}
```

(b) Incorrect

join()

You can use the `join()` method to force one thread to wait for another thread to finish. For example, suppose you modify the code in lines 53–57 in Listing 32.1 as follows:

```
public void run() {
  Thread thread4 = new Thread(
    new PrintChar('c', 40));
  thread4.start();
  try {
    for (int i = 1; i <= lastNum; i++) {
      System.out.print (" " + i);
      if (i == 50) thread4.join();
    }
  }
  catch (InterruptedException ex) {
  }
}
```


A new `thread4` is created, and it prints character *c* 40 times. The numbers from `50` to `100` are printed after thread `thread4` is finished.

Java assigns every thread a priority. By default, a thread inherits the priority of the thread that spawned it. You can increase or decrease the priority of any thread by using the `setPriority` method, and you can get the thread's priority by using the `getPriority` method. Priorities are numbers ranging from `1` to `10`. The `Thread` class has the `int` constants `MIN_PRIORITY`, `NORM_PRIORITY`, and `MAX_PRIORITY`, representing `1`, `5`, and `10`, respectively. The priority of the main thread is `Thread.NORM_PRIORITY`.

setPriority(int)

The JVM always picks the currently runnable thread with the highest priority. A lower-priority thread can run only when no higher-priority threads are running. If all runnable threads have equal priorities, each is assigned an equal portion of the CPU time in a circular queue. This is called *round-robin scheduling*. For example, suppose you insert the following code in line 16 in Listing 32.1:

round-robin scheduling

```
thread3.setPriority(Thread.MAX_PRIORITY);
```

The thread for the `print100` task will be finished first.

Tip

The priority numbers may be changed in a future version of Java. To minimize the impact of any changes, use the constants in the `Thread` class to specify thread priorities.

Tip

contention or starvation

A thread may never get a chance to run if there is always a higher-priority thread running or a same-priority thread that never yields. This situation is known as *contention* or *starvation*. To avoid contention, the thread with higher priority must periodically invoke the `sleep` or `yield` method to give a thread with a lower or the same priority a chance to run.

Check Point

MyProgrammingLab™

32.6 Which of the following methods are instance methods in `java.lang.Thread`? Which method may throw an `InterruptedException`? Which of them are deprecated in Java?

`run, start, stop, suspend, resume, sleep, interrupt, yield, join`

32.7 If a loop contains a method that throws an `InterruptedException`, why should the loop be placed inside a `try-catch` block?

32.8 How do you set a priority for a thread? What is the default priority?

32.5 Case Study: Flashing Text

Key Point

You can use a thread to control an animation.

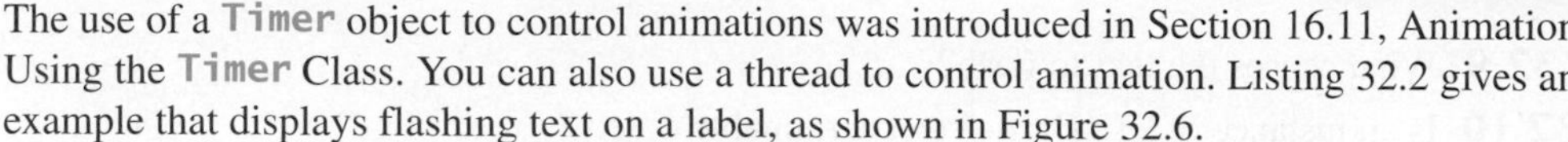

The use of a **Timer** object to control animations was introduced in Section 16.11, Animation Using the **Timer** Class. You can also use a thread to control animation. Listing 32.2 gives an example that displays flashing text on a label, as shown in Figure 32.6.

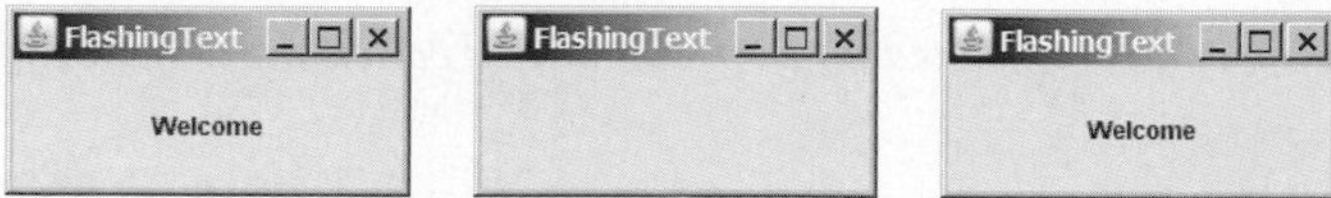

FIGURE 32.6 The text "Welcome" blinks.

LISTING 32.2 FlashingText.java

```
1  import javax.swing.*;
2
3  public class FlashingText extends JApplet implements Runnable {
4    private JLabel jlblText = new JLabel("Welcome", JLabel.CENTER);
5
6    public FlashingText() {
7      add(jlblText);
8      new Thread(this).start();
9    }
10
11   @Override /** Set the text on/off every 200 milliseconds */
12   public void run() {
13     try {
14       while (true) {
15         if (jlblText.getText() == null)
16           jlblText.setText("Welcome");
17         else
18           jlblText.setText(null);
19
20         Thread.sleep(200);
21       }
22     }
23     catch (InterruptedException ex) {
24     }
25   }
26 }
```

implements Runnable (line 3); create a label (line 4); add a label (line 7); start a thread (line 8); how to run (line 12); sleep (line 20); main method omitted

FlashingText implements **Runnable** (line 3), so it is a task class. Line 8 wraps the task in a thread and starts the thread. The **run** method dictates how to run the thread. It sets a text in the label if the label does not have one (line 15), and sets its text as **null** (line 18) if the label has a text. The text is set and unset to simulate a flashing effect.

thread vs. timer

You can use a timer or a thread to control animation. Which one is better? A timer is a source component that fires an **ActionEvent** at a "fixed rate." When an action event occurs, the timer invokes the listener's **actionPerformed** method to handle the event. The timer and event handling run on the same thread. If it takes a long time to handle the event, the actual delay time between the two events will be longer than the requested delay time. In this case, you should run event handling on a separate thread. (The next section gives an example to illustrate the problem and how to fix it by running the event handling on a separate thread.) In general, threads are more reliable and responsive than timers. If you need a precise delay time or a quick response, it is better to use a thread. Otherwise, using a timer is simpler and more efficient. Timers consume less system resources because they run on the GUI event dispatch thread, so you don't need to spawn new threads for timers.

Check Point

MyProgrammingLab™

32.9 What causes the text to flash?

32.10 Is an instance of `FlashingText` a runnable object?

32.6 GUI Event Dispatch Thread

Key Point

GUI event handling code is executed on a special thread called the event dispatch thread.

event dispatch thread

This special thread is also used to run most of Swing methods. Running GUI event handling code and most of Swing methods in the same thread is necessary because most Swing methods are not thread-safe. Invoking them from multiple threads may cause conflicts.

invokeLater
invokeAndWait

In certain situations, you need to run the code in the event dispatch thread to avoid possible conflicts. You can use the static methods `invokeLater` and `invokeAndWait` in the `javax.swing.SwingUtilities` class to run the code in the event dispatch thread. You must put this code in the `run` method of a `Runnable` object and specify the `Runnable` object as the argument to `invokeLater` and `invokeAndWait`. The `invokeLater` method returns immediately, without waiting for the event dispatch thread to execute the code. The `invokeAndWait` method is just like `invokeLater`, except that `invokeAndWait` doesn't return until the event dispatching thread has executed the specified code.

So far, you have launched your GUI application from the `main` method by creating a frame and making it visible. This works fine for most applications, but if it takes a long time to launch a GUI application, problems may occur. To avoid possible problems in this situation, you should launch the GUI creation from the event dispatch thread, as follows:

```
public static void main(String[] args) {
  SwingUtilities.invokeLater(new Runnable() {
    public void run() {
      // The code for creating a frame and setting its properties
    }
  });
}
```

For example, Listing 32.3 gives a simple program that launches the frame from the event dispatch thread.

LISTING 32.3 EventDispatcherThreadDemo.java

create frame

```
import javax.swing.*;

public class EventDispatcherThreadDemo extends JApplet {
  public EventDispatcherThreadDemo() {
    add(new JLabel("Hi, it runs from an event dispatch thread"));
  }

  /** Main method */
  public static void main(String[] args) {
    SwingUtilities.invokeLater(new Runnable() {
      public void run() {
        JFrame frame = new JFrame("EventDispatcherThreadDemo");
        frame.add(new EventDispatcherThreadDemo());
        frame.setSize(200, 200);
        frame.setDefaultCloseOperation(JFrame.EXIT_ON_CLOSE);
        frame.setLocationRelativeTo(null); // Center the frame
```

```
                frame.setVisible(true);
            }
        });
    }
}
```

32.11 What is the event dispatch thread?

32.12 How do you let a task run from the event dispatch thread?

Check Point
MyProgrammingLab™

32.7 Case Study: Clock with Audio

This case study shows the necessity of using threads for certain GUI animations.

This case study creates an applet that displays a running clock that announces the time at one-minute intervals. For example, if the current time is 6:30:00, the applet announces, "six o'clock thirty minutes A.M." If the current time is 20:20:00, the applet announces, "eight o'clock twenty minutes P.M." The program also has a label that displays the digital time, as shown in Figure 32.7.

FIGURE 32.7 The applet displays a clock and announces the time every minute.

To announce the time, the applet plays three audio clips. The first clip announces the hour, the second announces the minute, and the third announces A.M. or P.M. All of the audio files are stored in the directory `audio`, a subdirectory of the applet's class directory. The 12 audio files used to announce the hours are stored in the files **hour0.au**, **hour1.au**, and so on, to **hour11.au**. The 60 audio files used to announce the minutes are stored in the files **minute0.au**, **minute1.au**, and so on, to **minute59.au**. The two audio files used to announce A.M. or P.M. are stored in the file **am.au** and **pm.au**.

audio clips
audio files

You need to play three audio clips on a separate thread to avoid animation delays. To illustrate the problem, let us first write a program without playing the audio on a separate thread.

In Section 13.9, the `StillClock` class was developed to draw a still clock to show the current time. Create an applet named `ClockWithAudio` (Listing 32.4) that contains an instance of `StillClock` to display an analog clock, and an instance of `JLabel` to display the digital time. Override the `init` method to load the audio files. Use a `Timer` object to set and display the current time continuously at every second. When the second is zero, announce the current time.

LISTING 32.4 `ClockWithAudio.java`

```
import java.applet.*;
import javax.swing.*;
import java.awt.event.*;
import java.awt.*;

public class ClockWithAudio extends JApplet {
  protected AudioClip[] hourAudio = new AudioClip[12];
```

audio clips

am clip
pm clip
still clock
timer
label
create audio clips
start timer
stop timer
timer listener
set new time
announce time
announce hour

```
  protected AudioClip[] minuteAudio = new AudioClip[60];

  // Create audio clips for pronouncing am and pm
  protected AudioClip amAudio =
    Applet.newAudioClip(this.getClass().getResource("audio/am.au"));
  protected AudioClip pmAudio =
    Applet.newAudioClip(this.getClass().getResource("audio/pm.au"));

  // Create a clock
  private StillClock clock = new StillClock();

  // Create a timer
  private Timer timer = new Timer(1000, new TimerListener());

  // Create a label to display time
  private JLabel jlblDigitTime = new JLabel("", JLabel.CENTER);

  @Override /** Initialize the applet */
  public void init() {
    // Create audio clips for pronouncing hours
    for (int i = 0; i < 12; i++)
      hourAudio[i] = Applet.newAudioClip(
        this.getClass().getResource("audio/hour" + i + ".au"));

    // Create audio clips for pronouncing minutes
    for (int i = 0; i < 60; i++)
      minuteAudio[i] = Applet.newAudioClip(
        this.getClass().getResource("audio/minute" + i + ".au"));

    // Add clock and time label to the content pane of the applet
    add(clock, BorderLayout.CENTER);
    add(jlblDigitTime, BorderLayout.SOUTH);
  }

  @Override /** Override the applet's start method */
  public void start() {
    timer.start(); // Resume clock
  }

  @Override /** Override the applet's stop method */
  public void stop() {
    timer.stop(); // Suspend clock
  }

  private class TimerListener implements ActionListener {
    @Override
    public void actionPerformed(ActionEvent e) {
      clock.setCurrentTime();
      clock.repaint();
      jlblDigitTime.setText(clock.getHour() + ":" + clock.getMinute()
        + ":" + clock.getSecond());
      if (clock.getSecond() == 0)
        announceTime(clock.getHour(), clock.getMinute());
    }
  }

  /** Announce the current time at every minute */
  public void announceTime(int hour, int minute) {
    // Announce hour
    hourAudio[hour % 12].play();
```

```
68
69       try {
70         // Time delay to allow hourAudio play to finish
71         Thread.sleep(1500);
72
73         // Announce minute
74         minuteAudio[minute].play();
75
76         // Time delay to allow minuteAudio play to finish
77         Thread.sleep(1500);
78       }
79       catch(InterruptedException ex) {
80       }
81
82       // Announce am or pm
83       if (hour < 12)
84         amAudio.play();
85       else
86         pmAudio.play();
87     }
88   }
```

announce minute

announce am

announce pm

main method omitted

The **hourAudio** is an array of twelve audio clips that are used to announce the 12 hours of the day (line 7); the **minuteAudio** is an audio clip that is used to announce the minutes in an hour (line 8). The **amAudio** announces "A.M." (line 11); the **pmAudio** announces "P.M." (line 13).

The **init()** method creates hour audio clips (lines 29–30) and minute audio clips (lines 34–35), and places a clock and a label in the applet (lines 38–39).

An **ActionEvent** is fired by the timer every second. In the listener's **actionPerformed** method (lines 54–61), the clock is repainted with the new current time, and the digital time is displayed in the label.

In the **announceTime** method (lines 65–87), the **sleep()** method (lines 71, 77) is purposely invoked to ensure that one clip finishes before the next clip starts, so that the clips do not interfere with each other.

The applet's **start()** and **stop()** methods (lines 43–50) are overridden to ensure that the timer starts or stops when the applet is restarted or stopped.

When you run the preceding program, you will notice that the second hand does not display at the first, second, and third seconds of the minute. This is because **sleep(1500)** is invoked twice in the **announceTime()** method, which takes three seconds to announce the time at the beginning of each minute. Thus, the next action event is delayed for three seconds during the first three seconds of each minute. As a result of this delay, the time is not updated and the clock is not repainted for these three seconds. To fix this problem, you should announce the time on a separate thread. This can be accomplished by modifying the **announceTime** method. Listing 32.5 gives the new program.

abnormal problem

LISTING 32.5 ClockWithAudioOnSeparateThread.java

```
// Same import statements as in Listing 32.4, so omitted

public class ClockWithAudioOnSeparateThread extends JApplet {
  // Same as in lines 7-62 in Listing 32.4, so omitted

  /** Announce the current time at every minute */
  public void announceTime(int h, int m) {
    new Thread(new AnnounceTimeOnSeparateThread(h, m)).start();
  }
```

omitted

omitted

create a thread

task class

run thread

main method omitted

```
10
11     /** Inner class for announcing time */
12     class AnnounceTimeOnSeparateThread implements Runnable {
13       private int hour, minute;
14
15       /** Get audio clips */
16       public AnnounceTimeOnSeparateThread(int hour, int minute) {
17         this.hour = hour;
18         this.minute = minute;
19       }
20
21       @Override
21       public void run() {
22         // Announce hour
23         hourAudio[hour % 12].play();
24
25         try {
26           // Time delay to allow hourAudio play to finish
27           Thread.sleep(1500);
28
29           // Announce minute
30           minuteAudio[minute].play();
31
32           // Time delay to allow minuteAudio play to finish
33           Thread.sleep(1500);
34         }
35         catch (InterruptedException ex) {
36         }
37
38         // Announce am or pm
39         if (hour < 12)
40           amAudio.play();
41         else
42           pmAudio.play();
43       }
44     }
45   }
```

The new class **ClockWithAudioOnSeparateThread** is the same as **ClockWithAudio** except that the **announceTime** method is new. The new **announceTime** method creates a thread (line 8) for the task of announcing the time. The task class is defined as an inner class (lines 12–44). The **run** method (line 21) announces the time on a separate thread.

When running this program, you will discover that the audio does not interfere with the clock animation because an instance of **AnnounceTimeOnSeparateThread** starts on a separate thread to announce the current time. This thread is independent of the thread on which the **actionPerformed** method runs.

MyProgrammingLab™

32.13 When should you use a timer or a thread to control animation? What are the advantages and disadvantages of using a thread and a timer?

32.8 Thread Pools

A thread pool can be used to execute tasks efficiently.

In Section 32.3, Creating Tasks and Threads, you learned how to define a task class by implementing **java.lang.Runnable**, and how to create a thread to run a task like this:

```
Runnable task = new TaskClass(task);
new Thread(task).start();
```

This approach is convenient for a single task execution, but it is not efficient for a large number of tasks, because you have to create a thread for each task. Starting a new thread for each task could limit throughput and cause poor performance. Using a *thread pool* is an ideal way to manage the number of tasks executing concurrently. Java provides the **Executor** interface for executing tasks in a thread pool and the **ExecutorService** interface for managing and controlling tasks. **ExecutorService** is a subinterface of **Executor**, as shown in Figure 32.8.

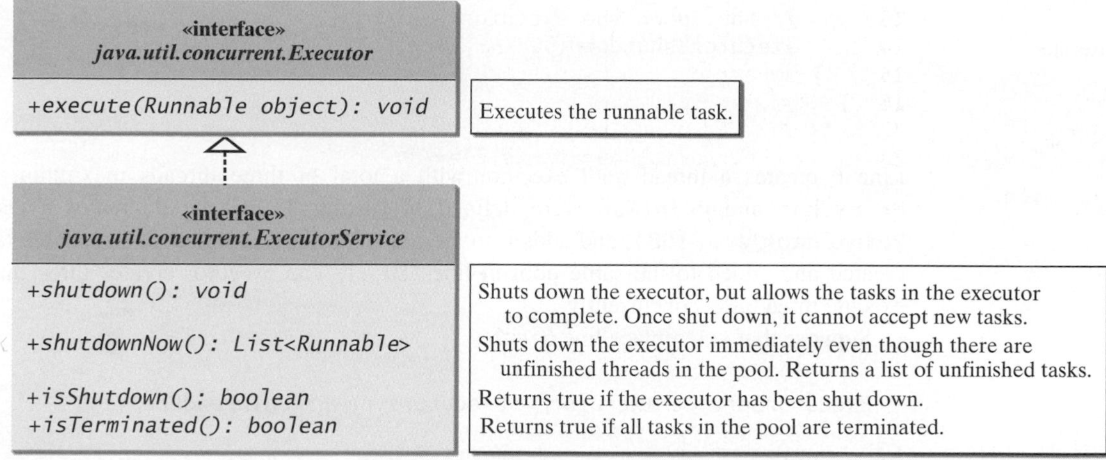

FIGURE 32.8 The **Executor** interface executes threads, and the **ExecutorService** subinterface manages threads.

To create an **Executor** object, use the static methods in the **Executors** class, as shown in Figure 32.9. The **newFixedThreadPool(int)** method creates a fixed number of threads in a pool. If a thread completes executing a task, it can be reused to execute another task. If a thread terminates due to a failure prior to shutdown, a new thread will be created to replace it if all the threads in the pool are not idle and there are tasks waiting for execution. The **newCachedThreadPool()** method creates a new thread if all the threads in the pool are not idle and there are tasks waiting for execution. A thread in a cached pool will be terminated if it has not been used for 60 seconds. A cached pool is efficient for many short tasks.

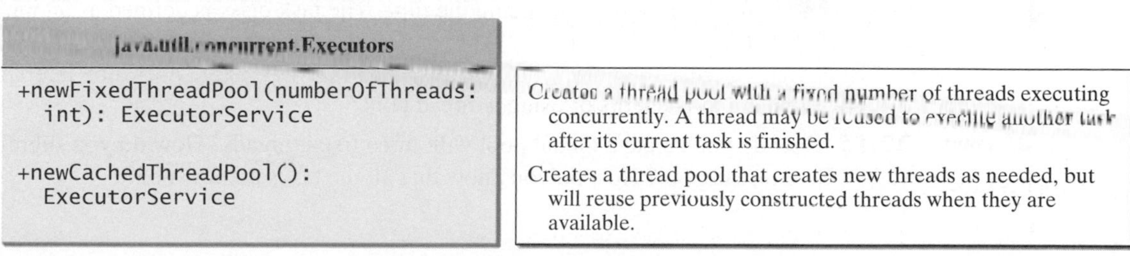

FIGURE 32.9 The **Executors** class provides static methods for creating **Executor** objects.

Listing 32.6 shows how to rewrite Listing 32.1 using a thread pool.

LISTING 32.6 ExecutorDemo.java

```
import java.util.concurrent.*;

public class ExecutorDemo {
```

```
 4   public static void main(String[] args) {
 5     // Create a fixed thread pool with maximum three threads
 6     ExecutorService executor = Executors.newFixedThreadPool(3);
 7
 8     // Submit runnable tasks to the executor
 9     executor.execute(new PrintChar('a', 100));
10     executor.execute(new PrintChar('b', 100));
11     executor.execute(new PrintNum(100));
12
13     // Shut down the executor
14     executor.shutdown();
15   }
16 }
```

create executor

submit task

shut down executor

Line 6 creates a thread pool executor with a total of three threads maximum. Classes `PrintChar` and `PrintNum` were defined in Listing 32.1. Line 9 creates a task, `new PrintChar('a', 100)`, and adds it to the pool. Similarly, another two runnable tasks are created and added to the same pool in lines 10–11. The executor creates three threads to execute three tasks concurrently.

Suppose that you replace line 6 with

```
ExecutorService executor = Executors.newFixedThreadPool(1);
```

What will happen? The three runnable tasks will be executed sequentially, because there is only one thread in the pool.

Suppose you replace line 6 with

```
ExecutorService executor = Executors.newCachedThreadPool();
```

What will happen? New threads will be created for each waiting task, so all the tasks will be executed concurrently.

The `shutdown()` method in line 14 tells the executor to shut down. No new tasks can be accepted, but any existing tasks will continue to finish.

Tip

If you need to create a thread for just one task, use the `Thread` class. If you need to create threads for multiple tasks, it is better to use a thread pool.

MyProgrammingLab™

32.14 What are the benefits of using a thread pool?

32.15 How do you create a thread pool with three fixed threads? How do you submit a task to a thread pool? How do you know that all the tasks are finished?

32.9 Thread Synchronization

Thread synchronization is to coordinate the execution of the dependent threads.

A shared resource may become corrupted if it is accessed simultaneously by multiple threads. The following example demonstrates the problem.

Suppose that you create and launch 100 threads, each of which adds a penny to an account. Define a class named `Account` to model the account, a class named `AddAPennyTask` to add a penny to the account, and a main class that creates and launches threads. The relationships of these classes are shown in Figure 32.10. The program is given in Listing 32.7.

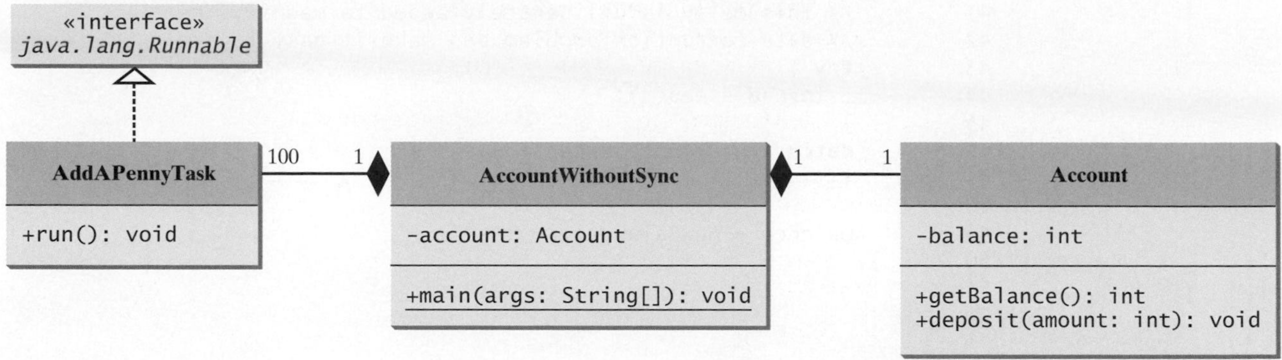

FIGURE 32.10 AccountWithoutSync contains an instance of Account and 100 threads of AddAPennyTask.

LISTING 32.7 AccountWithoutSync.java

```
import java.util.concurrent.*;

public class AccountWithoutSync {
  private static Account account = new Account();

  public static void main(String[] args) {
    ExecutorService executor = Executors.newCachedThreadPool();

    // Create and launch 100 threads
    for (int i = 0; i < 100; i++) {
      executor.execute(new AddAPennyTask());
    }

    executor.shutdown();

    // Wait until all tasks are finished
    while (!executor.isTerminated()) {
    }

    System.out.println("What is balance? " + account.getBalance());
  }

  // A thread for adding a penny to the account
  private static class AddAPennyTask implements Runnable {
    public void run() {
      account.deposit(1);
    }
  }

  // An inner class for account
  private static class Account {
    private int balance = 0;

    public int getBalance() {
      return balance;
    }

    public void deposit(int amount) {
      int newBalance = balance + amount;

```

create executor

submit task

shut down executor

wait for all tasks to terminate

```
41         // This delay is deliberately added to magnify the
42         // data-corruption problem and make it easy to see.
43         try {
44           Thread.sleep(5);
45         }
46         catch (InterruptedException ex) {
47         }
48
49         balance = newBalance;
50       }
51     }
52   }
```

The classes `AddAPennyTask` and `Account` in lines 24–51 are inner classes. Line 4 creates an `Account` with initial balance `0`. Line 11 creates a task to add a penny to the account and submit the task to the executor. Line 11 is repeated 100 times in lines 10–12. The program repeatedly checks whether all tasks are completed in lines 17–18. The account balance is displayed in line 20 after all tasks are completed.

The program creates 100 threads executed in a thread pool `executor` (lines 10–12). The `isTerminated()` method (line 17) is used to test whether the thread is terminated.

The balance of the account is initially `0` (line 32). When all the threads are finished, the balance should be `100`, but the output is unpredictable. As can be seen in Figure 32.11, the answers are wrong in the sample run. This demonstrates the data-corruption problem that occurs when all the threads have access to the same data source simultaneously.

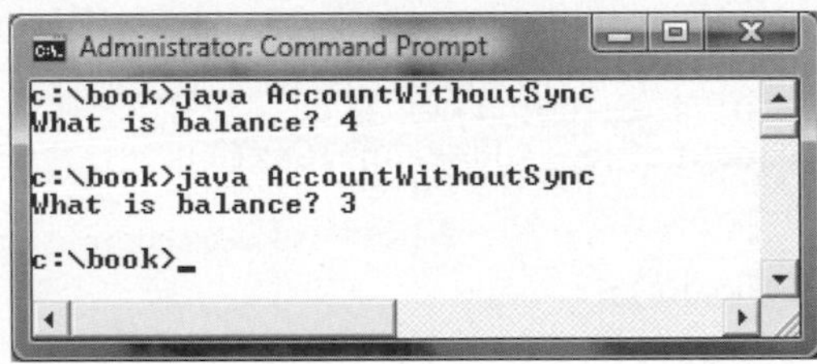

FIGURE 32.11 The `AccountWithoutSync` program causes data inconsistency.

Lines 39–49 could be replaced by one statement:

```
balance = balance + amount;
```

It is highly unlikely, although plausible, that the problem can be replicated using this single statement. The statements in lines 39–49 are deliberately designed to magnify the data-corruption problem and make it easy to see. If you run the program several times but still do not see the problem, increase the sleep time in line 44. This will increase the chances for showing the problem of data inconsistency.

What, then, caused the error in this program? A possible scenario is shown in Figure 32.12.

Step	Balance	Task 1	Task 2
1	0	`newBalance = balance + 1;`	
2	0		`newBalance = balance + 1;`
3	1	`balance = newBalance;`	
4	1		`balance = newBalance;`

FIGURE 32.12 Task 1 and Task 2 both add 1 to the same balance.

In Step 1, Task 1 gets the balance from the account. In Step 2, Task 2 gets the same balance from the account. In Step 3, Task 1 writes a new balance to the account. In Step 4, Task 2 writes a new balance to the account.

The effect of this scenario is that Task 1 does nothing, because in Step 4 Task 2 overrides Task 1's result. Obviously, the problem is that Task 1 and Task 2 are accessing a common resource in a way that causes a conflict. This is a common problem, known as a *race condition*, in multithreaded programs. A class is said to be *thread-safe* if an object of the class does not cause a race condition in the presence of multiple threads. As demonstrated in the preceding example, the `Account` class is not thread-safe.

race condition

thread-safe

32.9.1 The `synchronized` Keyword

To avoid race conditions, it is necessary to prevent more than one thread from simultaneously entering a certain part of the program, known as the *critical region*. The critical region in Listing 32.7 is the entire `deposit` method. You can use the keyword `synchronized` to synchronize the method so that only one thread can access the method at a time. There are several ways to correct the problem in Listing 32.7. One approach is to make `Account` thread-safe by adding the keyword `synchronized` in the `deposit` method in line 38, as follows:

critical region

```
public synchronized void deposit(double amount)
```

A synchronized method acquires a lock before it executes. A lock is a mechanism for exclusive use of a resource. In the case of an instance method, the lock is on the object for which the method was invoked. In the case of a static method, the lock is on the class. If one thread invokes a synchronized instance method (respectively, static method) on an object, the lock of that object (respectively, class) is acquired first, then the method is executed, and finally the lock is released. Another thread invoking the same method of that object (respectively, class) is blocked until the lock is released.

With the `deposit` method synchronized, the preceding scenario cannot happen. If Task 1 enters the method, Task 2 is blocked until Task 1 finishes the method, as shown in Figure 32.13.

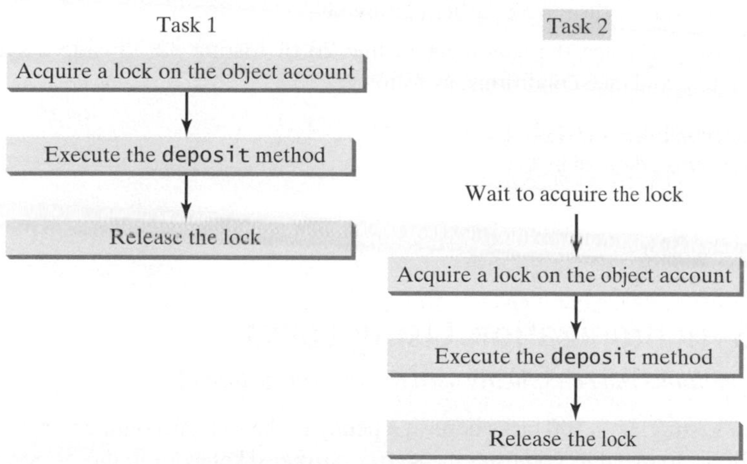

FIGURE 32.13 Task 1 and Task 2 are synchronized.

32.9.2 Synchronizing Statements

Invoking a synchronized instance method of an object acquires a lock on the object, and invoking a synchronized static method of a class acquires a lock on the class. A synchronized statement can be used to acquire a lock on any object, not just *this* object, when executing a

synchronized block

block of the code in a method. This block is referred to as a *synchronized block*. The general form of a synchronized statement is as follows:

```
synchronized (expr) {
  statements;
}
```

The expression **expr** must evaluate to an object reference. If the object is already locked by another thread, the thread is blocked until the lock is released. When a lock is obtained on the object, the statements in the synchronized block are executed, and then the lock is released.

Synchronized statements enable you to synchronize part of the code in a method instead of the entire method. This increases concurrency. You can make Listing 32.7 thread-safe by placing the statement in line 26 inside a synchronized block:

```
synchronized (account) {
  account.deposit(1);
}
```

Note

Any synchronized instance method can be converted into a synchronized statement. For example, the following synchronized instance method in (a) is equivalent to (b):

```
public synchronized void xMethod() {
  // method body
}
```

(a)

```
public void xMethod() {
  synchronized (this) {
    // method body
  }
}
```

(b)

MyProgrammingLab™

32.16 Give some examples of possible resource corruption when running multiple threads. How do you synchronize conflicting threads?

32.17 Suppose you place the statement in line 26 of Listing 32.7 inside a synchronized block to avoid race conditions, as follows:

```
synchronized (this) {
  account.deposit(1);
}
```

Will it work?

32.10 Synchronization Using Locks

Locks and conditions can be explicitly used to synchronize threads.

Recall that in Listing 32.7, 100 tasks deposit a penny to the same account concurrently, which causes conflicts. To avoid it, you used the **synchronized** keyword in the **deposit** method, as follows:

```
public synchronized void deposit(double amount)
```

A synchronized instance method implicitly acquires a lock on the instance before it executes the method.

Java enables you to acquire locks explicitly, which give you more control for coordinating threads. A *lock* is an instance of the **Lock** interface, which defines the methods for

lock

acquiring and releasing locks, as shown in Figure 32.14. A lock may also use the `newCondition()` method to create any number of `Condition` objects, which can be used for thread communications.

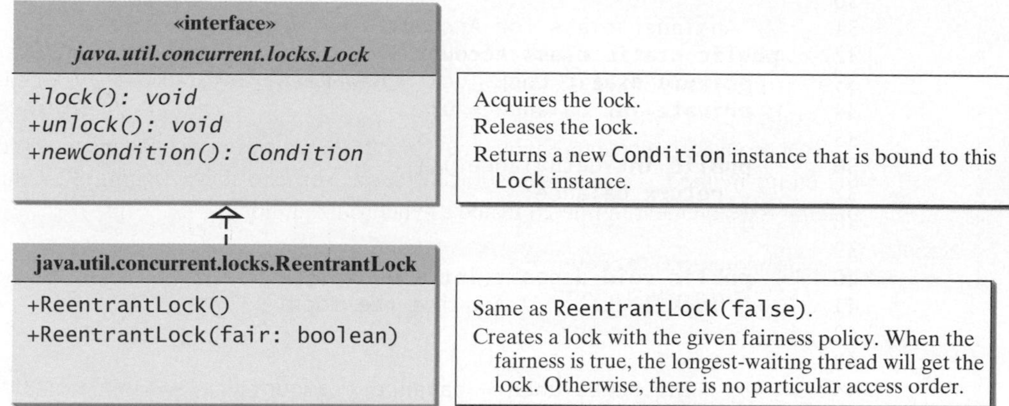

FIGURE 32.14 The `ReentrantLock` class implements the `Lock` interface to represent a lock.

`ReentrantLock` is a concrete implementation of `Lock` for creating mutually exclusive locks. You can create a lock with the specified *fairness policy*. True fairness policies guarantee that the longest-waiting thread will obtain the lock first. False fairness policies grant a lock to a waiting thread arbitrarily. Programs using fair locks accessed by many threads may have poorer overall performance than those using the default setting, but they have smaller variances in times to obtain locks and prevent starvation.

fairness policy

Listing 32.8 revises the program in Listing 32.7 to synchronize the account modification using explicit locks.

LISTING 32.8 AccountWithSyncUsingLock.java

package for locks

```
import java.util.concurrent.*;
import java.util.concurrent.locks.*;

public class AccountWithSyncUsingLock {
  private static Account account = new Account();

  public static void main(String[] args) {
    ExecutorService executor = Executors.newCachedThreadPool();

    // Create and launch 100 threads
    for (int i = 0; i < 100; i++) {
      executor.execute(new AddAPennyTask());
    }

    executor.shutdown();

    // Wait until all tasks are finished
    while (!executor.isTerminated()) {
    }

    System.out.println("What is balance? " + account.getBalance());
  }

  // A thread for adding a penny to the account
```

create a lock

acquire the lock

release the lock

```
25    public static class AddAPennyTask implements Runnable {
26      public void run() {
27        account.deposit(1);
28      }
29    }
30
31    // An inner class for Account
32    public static class Account {
33      private static Lock lock = new ReentrantLock(); // Create a lock
34      private int balance = 0;
35
36      public int getBalance() {
37        return balance;
38      }
39
40      public void deposit(int amount) {
41        lock.lock(); // Acquire the lock
42
43        try {
44          int newBalance = balance + amount;
45
46          // This delay is deliberately added to magnify the
47          // data-corruption problem and make it easy to see.
48          Thread.sleep(5);
49
50          balance = newBalance;
51        }
52        catch (InterruptedException ex) {
53        }
54        finally {
55          lock.unlock(); // Release the lock
56        }
57      }
58    }
59  }
```

Line 33 creates a lock, line 41 acquires the lock, and line 55 releases the lock.

Tip

It is a good practice to always immediately follow a call to **lock()** with a **try-catch** block and release the lock in the **finally** clause, as shown in lines 41–56, to ensure that the lock is always released.

Listing 32.8 can be implemented using a synchronize method for **deposit** rather than using a lock. In general, using **synchronized** methods or statements is simpler than using explicit locks for mutual exclusion. However, using explicit locks is more intuitive and flexible to synchronize threads with conditions, as you will see in the next section.

32.18 How do you create a lock object? How do you acquire a lock and release a lock?

MyProgrammingLab™

32.11 Cooperation among Threads

Key Point

Conditions on locks can be used to coordinate thread interactions.

condition

Thread synchronization suffices to avoid race conditions by ensuring the mutual exclusion of multiple threads in the critical region, but sometimes you also need a way for threads to cooperate. *Conditions* can be used to facilitate communications among threads. A thread can specify what to do under a certain condition. Conditions are objects created by invoking the `newCondition()` method on a `Lock` object. Once a condition is created, you can use its `await()`, `signal()`, and `signalAll()` methods for thread communications, as shown in Figure 32.15. The `await()` method causes the current thread to wait until the condition is signaled. The `signal()` method wakes up one waiting thread, and the `signalAll()` method wakes all waiting threads.

«interface» *java.util.concurrent.Condition*	
+await(): void	Causes the current thread to wait until the condition is signaled.
+signal(): void	Wakes up one waiting thread.
+signalAll(): Condition	Wakes up all waiting threads.

FIGURE 32.15 The `Condition` interface defines the methods for performing synchronization.

thread cooperation example

Let us use an example to demonstrate thread communications. Suppose that you create and launch two tasks: one that deposits into an account, and one that withdraws from the same account. The withdraw task has to wait if the amount to be withdrawn is more than the current balance. Whenever new funds are deposited into the account, the deposit task notifies the withdraw thread to resume. If the amount is still not enough for a withdrawal, the withdraw thread has to continue to wait for a new deposit.

To synchronize the operations, use a lock with a condition: `newDeposit` (i.e., new deposit added to the account). If the balance is less than the amount to be withdrawn, the withdraw task will wait for the `newDeposit` condition. When the deposit task adds money to the account, the task signals the waiting withdraw task to try again. The interaction between the two tasks is shown in Figure 32.16.

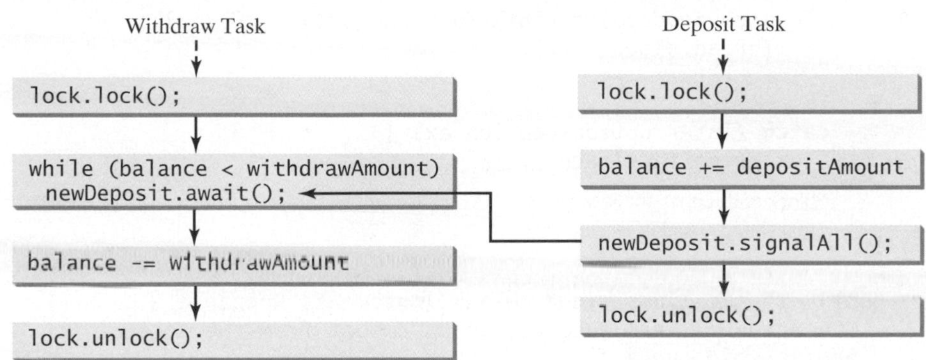

FIGURE 32.16 The condition `newDeposit` is used for communications between the two threads.

You create a condition from a `Lock` object. To use a condition, you have to first obtain a lock. The `await()` method causes the thread to wait and automatically releases the lock on the condition. Once the condition is right, the thread reacquires the lock and continues executing.

Assume that the initial balance is `0` and the amounts to deposit and withdraw are randomly generated. Listing 32.9 gives the program. A sample run of the program is shown in Figure 32.17.

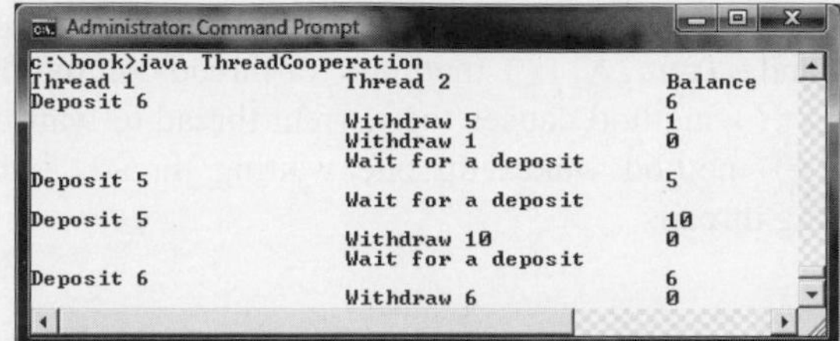

FIGURE 32.17 The withdraw task waits if there are not sufficient funds to withdraw.

LISTING 32.9 ThreadCooperation.java

create two threads

create a lock

create a condition

```
import java.util.concurrent.*;
import java.util.concurrent.locks.*;

public class ThreadCooperation {
  private static Account account = new Account();

  public static void main(String[] args) {
    // Create a thread pool with two threads
    ExecutorService executor = Executors.newFixedThreadPool(2);
    executor.execute(new DepositTask());
    executor.execute(new WithdrawTask());
    executor.shutdown();

    System.out.println("Thread 1\t\tThread 2\t\tBalance");
  }

  public static class DepositTask implements Runnable {
    @Override // Keep adding an amount to the account
    public void run() {
      try { // Purposely delay it to let the withdraw method proceed
        while (true) {
          account.deposit((int)(Math.random() * 10) + 1);
          Thread.sleep(1000);
        }
      }
      catch (InterruptedException ex) {
        ex.printStackTrace();
      }
    }
  }

  public static class WithdrawTask implements Runnable {
    @Override // Keep subtracting an amount from the account
    public void run() {
      while (true) {
        account.withdraw((int)(Math.random() * 10) + 1);
      }
    }
  }

  // An inner class for account
  private static class Account {
    // Create a new lock
    private static Lock lock = new ReentrantLock();

    // Create a condition
    private static Condition newDeposit = lock.newCondition();
```

```
48
49       private int balance = 0;
50
51       public int getBalance() {
52         return balance;
53       }
54
55       public void withdraw(int amount) {
56         lock.lock(); // Acquire the lock
57         try {
58           while (balance < amount) {
59             System.out.println("\t\t\tWait for a deposit");
60             newDeposit.await();
61           }
62
63           balance -= amount;
64           System.out.println("\t\t\tWithdraw " + amount +
65             "\t\t" + getBalance());
66         }
67         catch (InterruptedException ex) {
68           ex.printStackTrace();
69         }
70         finally {
71           lock.unlock(); // Release the lock
72         }
73       }
74
75       public void deposit(int amount) {
76         lock.lock(); // Acquire the lock
77         try {
78           balance += amount;
79           System.out.println("Deposit " + amount +
80             "\t\t\t\t\t" + getBalance());
81
82           // Signal thread waiting on the condition
83           newDeposit.signalAll();
84         }
85         finally {
86           lock.unlock(); // Release the lock
87         }
88       }
89     }
90   }
```

acquire the lock

wait on the condition

release the lock

acquire the lock

signal threads

release the lock

The example creates a new inner class named **Account** to model the account with two methods, **deposit(int)** and **withdraw(int)**, a class named **DepositTask** to add an amount to the balance, a class named **WithdrawTask** to withdraw an amount from the balance, and a main class that creates and launches two threads.

The program creates and submits the deposit task (line 10) and the withdraw task (line 11). The deposit task is purposely put to sleep (line 23) to let the withdraw task run. When there are not enough funds to withdraw, the withdraw task waits (line 59) for notification of the balance change from the deposit task (line 83).

A lock is created in line 44. A condition named **newDeposit** on the lock is created in line 47. A condition is bound to a lock. Before waiting or signaling the condition, a thread must first acquire the lock for the condition. The withdraw task acquires the lock in line 56, waits for the **newDeposit** condition (line 60) when there is not a sufficient amount to withdraw, and releases the lock in line 71. The deposit task acquires the lock in line 76, and signals all waiting threads (line 83) for the **newDeposit** condition after a new deposit is made.

What will happen if you replace the `while` loop in lines 58–61 with the following `if` statement?

```
if (balance < amount) {
  System.out.println("\t\t\tWait for a deposit");
  newDeposit.await();
}
```

The deposit task will notify the withdraw task whenever the balance changes. `(balance < amount)` may still be true when the withdraw task is awakened. Using the `if` statement, the withdraw task may wait forever. Using the loop statement, the withdraw task will have a chance to recheck the condition. Thus you should always test the condition in a loop.

Caution

ever-waiting threads

Once a thread invokes `await()` on a condition, the thread waits for a signal to resume. If you forget to call `signal()` or `signalAll()` on the condition, the thread will wait forever.

Caution

`IllegalMonitorState-Exception`

A condition is created from a `Lock` object. To invoke its method (e.g., `await()`, `signal()`, and `signalAll()`), you must first own the lock. If you invoke these methods without acquiring the lock, an `IllegalMonitorStateException` will be thrown.

Locks and conditions were introduced in Java 5. Prior to Java 5, thread communications were programmed using the object's built-in monitors. Locks and conditions are more powerful and flexible than the built-in monitor, so you can ignore this section. *However*, if you are working with legacy Java code, you may encounter Java's built-in monitor.

Java's built-in monitor

monitor

A *monitor* is an object with mutual exclusion and synchronization capabilities. Only one thread at a time can execute a method in the monitor. A thread enters the monitor by acquiring a lock on it and exits by releasing the lock. *Any object can be a monitor*. An object becomes a monitor once a thread locks it. Locking is implemented using the `synchronized` keyword on a method or a block. A thread must acquire a lock before executing a synchronized method or block. A thread can wait in a monitor if the condition is not right for it to continue executing in the monitor. You can invoke the `wait()` method on the monitor object to release the lock so that some other thread can get in the monitor and perhaps change the monitor's state. When the condition is right, the other thread can invoke the `notify()` or `notifyAll()` method to signal one or all waiting threads to regain the lock and resume execution. The template for invoking these methods is shown in Figure 32.18.

Task 1

```
synchronized (anObject) {
  try {
    // Wait for the condition to become true
    while (!condition)
      anObject.wait();

    // Do something when condition is true
  }
  catch (InterruptedException ex) {
    ex.printStackTrace();
  }
}
```

resume

Task 2

```
synchronized (anObject) {
  // When condition becomes true
  anObject.notify(); or anObject.notifyAll();
  ...
}
```

FIGURE 32.18 The `wait()`, `notify()`, and `notifyAll()` methods coordinate thread communication.

The `wait()`, `notify()`, and `notifyAll()` methods must be called in a synchronized method or a synchronized block on the receiving object of these methods. Otherwise, an `IllegalMonitorStateException` will occur.

When `wait()` is invoked, it pauses the thread and simultaneously releases the lock on the object. When the thread is restarted after being notified, the lock is automatically reacquired.

The `wait()`, `notify()`, and `notifyAll()` methods on an object are analogous to the `await()`, `signal()`, and `signalAll()` methods on a condition.

32.19 How do you create a condition on a lock? What are the `await()`, `signal()`, and `signalAll()` methods for?

32.20 What would happen if the `while` loop in line 58 of Listing 32.9 were changed to an `if` statement?

```
while (balance < amount)   --Replaced by-->   if (balance < amount)
```

32.21 Why does the following class have a syntax error?

```
import javax.swing.*;

public class Test extends JApplet implements Runnable {
  public void init() throws InterruptedException {
    Thread thread = new Thread(this);
    thread.sleep(1000);
  }

  public synchronized void run() {
  }
}
```

32.22 What is a possible cause for `IllegalMonitorStateException`?

32.23 Can the `wait()`, `notify()`, and `notifyAll()` be invoked from any object? What is the purpose of these methods?

32.24 What is wrong in the following code?

```
synchronized (object1) {
  try {
    while (!condition) object2.wait();
  }
  catch (InterruptedException ex) {
  }
}
```

32.12 Case Study: Producer/Consumer

This section gives the classic Consumer/Producer example for demonstrating thread coordination.

Suppose you use a buffer to store integers, and that the buffer size is limited. The buffer provides the method `write(int)` to add an `int` value to the buffer and the method `read()` to read and delete an `int` value from the buffer. To synchronize the operations, use a lock with two conditions: `notEmpty` (i.e., the buffer is not empty) and `notFull` (i.e., the buffer is not full). When a task adds an `int` to the buffer, if the buffer is full, the task will wait for the `notFull` condition. When a task deletes an `int` from the buffer, if the buffer is empty, the task will wait for the **notEmpty** condition. The interaction between the two tasks is shown in Figure 32.19.

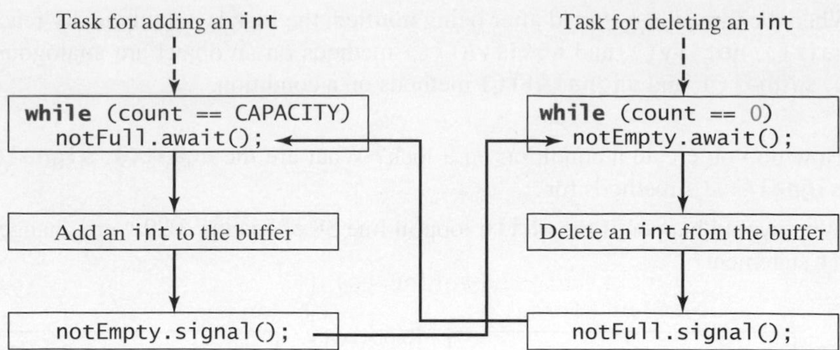

FIGURE 32.19 The conditions **notFull** and **notEmpty** are used to coordinate task interactions.

Listing 32.10 presents the complete program. The program contains the **Buffer** class (lines 48–95) and two tasks for repeatedly adding and consuming numbers to and from the buffer (lines 16–45). The **write(int)** method (line 60) adds an integer to the buffer. The **read()** method (line 77) deletes and returns an integer from the buffer.

The buffer is actually a first-in, first-out queue (lines 50–51). The conditions **notEmpty** and **notFull** on the lock are created in lines 57–58. The conditions are bound to a lock. A lock must be acquired before a condition can be applied. If you use the **wait()** and **notify()** methods to rewrite this example, you have to designate two objects as monitors.

LISTING 32.10 ConsumerProducer.java

create a buffer (line 5)
create two threads (line 9)
producer task (line 16)

```
1  import java.util.concurrent.*;
2  import java.util.concurrent.locks.*;
3
4  public class ConsumerProducer {
5    private static Buffer buffer = new Buffer();
6
7    public static void main(String[] args) {
8      // Create a thread pool with two threads
9      ExecutorService executor = Executors.newFixedThreadPool(2);
10     executor.execute(new ProducerTask());
11     executor.execute(new ConsumerTask());
12     executor.shutdown();
13   }
14
15   // A task for adding an int to the buffer
16   private static class ProducerTask implements Runnable {
17     public void run() {
18       try {
19         int i = 1;
20         while (true) {
21           System.out.println("Producer writes " + i);
22           buffer.write(i++); // Add a value to the buffer
23           // Put the thread to sleep
24           Thread.sleep((int)(Math.random() * 10000));
25         }
26       } catch (InterruptedException ex) {
```

```
        ex.printStackTrace();
      }
    }
  }

  // A task for reading and deleting an int from the buffer
  private static class ConsumerTask implements Runnable {
    public void run() {
      try {
        while (true) {
          System.out.println("\t\t\tConsumer reads " + buffer.read());
          // Put the thread to sleep
          Thread.sleep((int)(Math.random() * 10000));
        }
      } catch (InterruptedException ex) {
        ex.printStackTrace();
      }
    }
  }

  // An inner class for buffer
  private static class Buffer {
    private static final int CAPACITY = 1; // buffer size
    private java.util.LinkedList<Integer> queue =
      new java.util.LinkedList<Integer>();

    // Create a new lock
    private static Lock lock = new ReentrantLock();

    // Create two conditions
    private static Condition notEmpty = lock.newCondition();
    private static Condition notFull = lock.newCondition();

    public void write(int value) {
      lock.lock(); // Acquire the lock
      try {
        while (queue.size() == CAPACITY) {
          System.out.println("Wait for notFull condition");
          notFull.await();
        }

        queue.offer(value);
        notEmpty.signal(); // Signal notEmpty condition
      } catch (InterruptedException ex) {
        ex.printStackTrace();
      } finally {
        lock.unlock(); // Release the lock
      }
    }

    public int read() {
      int value = 0;
      lock.lock(); // Acquire the lock
      try {
        while (queue.isEmpty()) {
          System.out.println("\t\t\tWait for notEmpty condition");
          notEmpty.await();
        }

        value = queue.remove();
```

consumer task

create a lock

create a condition

create a condition

acquire the lock

wait for notFull

signal notEmpty

release the lock

acquire the lock

wait for notEmpty

signal notFull

release the lock

```
          notFull.signal(); // Signal notFull condition
        } catch (InterruptedException ex) {
          ex.printStackTrace();
        } finally {
          lock.unlock(); // Release the lock
          return value;
        }
      }
    }
  }
```

A sample run of the program is shown in Figure 32.20.

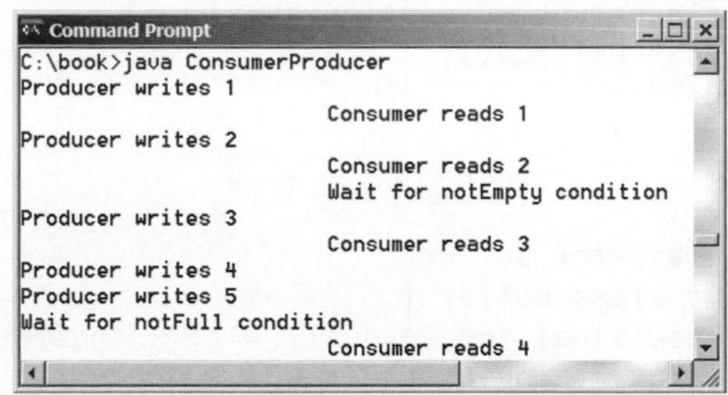

FIGURE 32.20 Locks and conditions are used for communications between the Producer and Consumer threads.

MyProgrammingLab™

32.25 Can the `read` and `write` methods in the `Buffer` class be executed concurrently?

32.26 When invoking the `read` method, what happens if the queue is empty?

32.27 When invoking the `write` method, what happens if the queue is full?

32.13 Blocking Queues

Java Collections Framework provides `ArrayBlockingQueue`, `LinkedBlockingQueue`, *and* `PriorityBlockingQueue` *for supporting blocking queues.*

blocking queue

Queues and priority queues were introduced in Section 22.9. A *blocking queue* causes a thread to block when you try to add an element to a full queue or to remove an element from an empty queue. The `BlockingQueue` interface extends `java.util.Queue` and provides the synchronized `put` and `take` methods for adding an element to the tail of the queue and for removing an element from the head of the queue, as shown in Figure 32.21.

Three concrete blocking queues—`ArrayBlockingQueue`, `LinkedBlockingQueue`, and `PriorityBlockingQueue`—are provided in Java, as shown in Figure 32.22. All are in the `java.util.concurrent` package. `ArrayBlockingQueue` implements a blocking queue using an array. You have to specify a capacity or an optional fairness to construct an `ArrayBlockingQueue`. `LinkedBlockingQueue` implements a blocking queue using a linked list. You can create an unbounded or bounded `LinkedBlockingQueue`. `PriorityBlockingQueue` is a priority queue. You can create an unbounded or bounded priority queue.

unbounded queue

Note

The `put` method will never block an unbounded `LinkedBlockingQueue` or `PriorityBlockingQueue`.

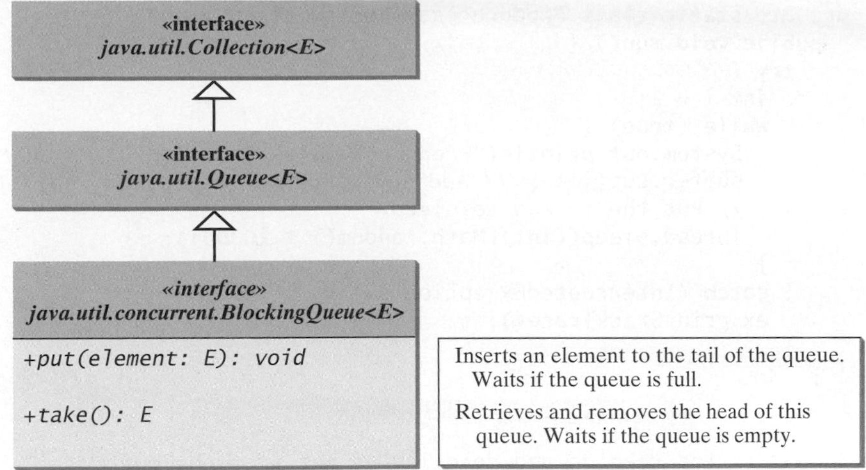

FIGURE 32.21 `BlockingQueue` is a subinterface of `Queue`.

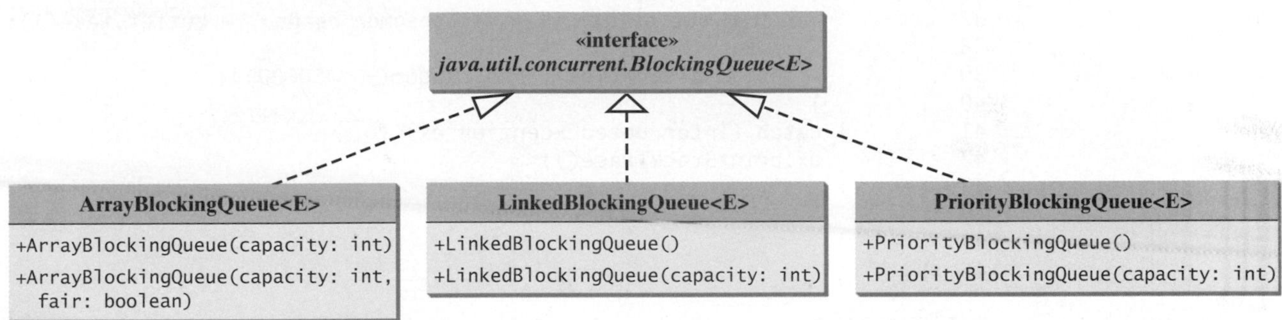

FIGURE 32.22 `ArrayBlockingQueue`, `LinkedBlockingQueue`, and `PriorityBlockingQueue` are concrete blocking queues.

Listing 32.11 gives an example of using an `ArrayBlockingQueue` to simplify the Consumer/Producer example in Listing 32.10. Line 5 creates an `ArrayBlockingQueue` to store integers. The Producer thread puts an integer into the queue (line 22), and the Consumer thread takes an integer from the queue (line 37).

LISTING 32.11 ConsumerProducerUsingBlockingQueue.java

```
 1 import java.util.concurrent.*;
 2 
 3 public class ConsumerProducerUsingBlockingQueue {
 4   private static ArrayBlockingQueue<Integer> buffer =
 5     new ArrayBlockingQueue<Integer>(2);
 6 
 7   public static void main(String[] args) {
 8     // Create a thread pool with two threads
 9     ExecutorService executor = Executors.newFixedThreadPool(2);
10     executor.execute(new ProducerTask());
11     executor.execute(new ConsumerTask());
12     executor.shutdown();
13   }
14 
15   // A task for adding an int to the buffer
```

create a buffer

create two threads

producer task

put

consumer task

take

```
    private static class ProducerTask implements Runnable {
      public void run() {
        try {
          int i = 1;
          while (true) {
            System.out.println("Producer writes " + i);
            buffer.put(i++); // Add any value to the buffer, say, 1
            // Put the thread to sleep
            Thread.sleep((int)(Math.random() * 10000));
          }
        } catch (InterruptedException ex) {
          ex.printStackTrace();
        }
      }
    }

    // A task for reading and deleting an int from the buffer
    private static class ConsumerTask implements Runnable {
      public void run() {
        try {
          while (true) {
           System.out.println("\t\t\tConsumer reads " + buffer.take());
            // Put the thread to sleep
            Thread.sleep((int)(Math.random() * 10000));
          }
        } catch (InterruptedException ex) {
          ex.printStackTrace();
        }
      }
    }
  }
```

In Listing 32.10, you used locks and conditions to synchronize the Producer and Consumer threads. In this program, hand coding is not necessary, because synchronization is already implemented in `ArrayBlockingQueue`.

MyProgrammingLab™

32.28 What is a blocking queue? What blocking queues are supported in Java?

32.29 What method do you use to add an element to an `ArrayBlockingQueue`? What happens if the queue is full?

32.30 What method do you use to retrieve an element from an `ArrayBlockingQueue`? What happens if the queue is empty?

32.14 Semaphores

Semaphores *can be used to restrict the number of threads that access a shared resource.*

semaphore

In computer science, a *semaphore* is an object that controls the access to a common resource. Before accessing the resource, a thread must acquire a permit from the semaphore. After finishing with the resource, the thread must return the permit back to the semaphore, as shown in Figure 32.23.

To create a semaphore, you have to specify the number of permits with an optional fairness policy, as shown in Figure 32.24. A task acquires a permit by invoking the semaphore's `acquire()` method and releases the permit by invoking the semaphore's `release()` method. Once a permit is acquired, the total number of available permits in a semaphore is reduced by `1`. Once a permit is released, the total number of available permits in a semaphore is increased by `1`.

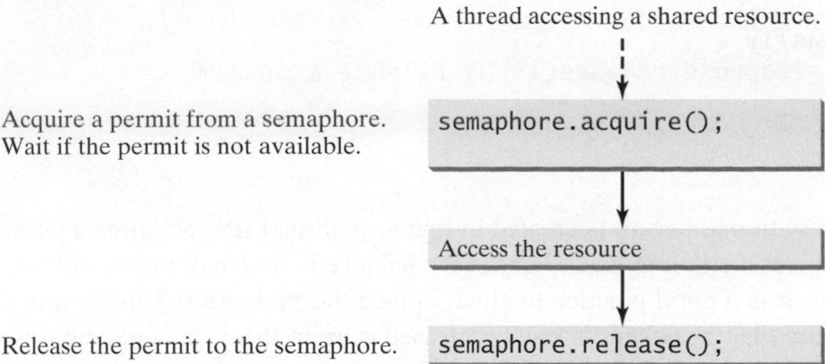

FIGURE 32.23 A limited number of threads can access a shared resource controlled by a semaphore.

java.util.concurrent.Semaphore	
`+Semaphore(numberOfPermits: int)`	Creates a semaphore with the specified number of permits. The fairness policy is false.
`+Semaphore(numberOfPermits: int, fair: boolean)`	Creates a semaphore with the specified number of permits and the fairness policy.
`+acquire(): void`	Acquires a permit from this semaphore. If no permit is available, the thread is blocked until one is available.
`+release(): void`	Releases a permit back to the semaphore.

FIGURE 32.24 The **Semaphore** class contains the methods for accessing a semaphore.

A semaphore with just one permit can be used to simulate a mutually exclusive lock. Listing 32.12 revises the **Account** inner class in Listing 32.9 using a semaphore to ensure that only one thread at a time can access the **deposit** method.

LISTING 32.12 New Account Inner Class

```
// An inner class for Account
private static class Account {
  // Create a semaphore
  private static Semaphore semaphore = new Semaphore(1);
  private int balance = 0;

  public int getBalance() {
    return balance;
  }

  public void deposit(int amount) {
    try {
      semaphore.acquire(); // Acquire a permit
      int newBalance = balance + amount;

      // This delay is deliberately added to magnify the
      // data-corruption problem and make it easy to see
      Thread.sleep(5);

      balance = newBalance;
    }
    catch (InterruptedException ex) {
```

create a semaphore

acquire a permit

release a permit

```
23       }
24       finally {
25         semaphore.release(); // Release a permit
26       }
27     }
28   }
```

A semaphore with one permit is created in line 4. A thread first acquires a permit when executing the deposit method in line 13. After the balance is updated, the thread releases the permit in line 25. It is a good practice to always place the `release()` method in the `finally` clause to ensure that the permit is finally released even in the case of exceptions.

MyProgrammingLab™

32.31 What are the similarities and differences between a lock and a semaphore?

32.32 How do you create a semaphore that allows three concurrent threads? How do you acquire a semaphore? How do you release a semaphore?

32.15 Avoiding Deadlocks

Key Point

Deadlocks can be avoided by using a proper resource ordering.

deadlock

Sometimes two or more threads need to acquire the locks on several shared objects. This could cause a *deadlock*, in which each thread has the lock on one of the objects and is waiting for the lock on the other object. Consider the scenario with two threads and two objects, as shown in Figure 32.25. Thread 1 has acquired a lock on `object1`, and Thread 2 has acquired a lock on `object2`. Now Thread 1 is waiting for the lock on `object2`, and Thread 2 for the lock on `object1`. Each thread waits for the other to release the lock it needs, and until that happens, neither can continue to run.

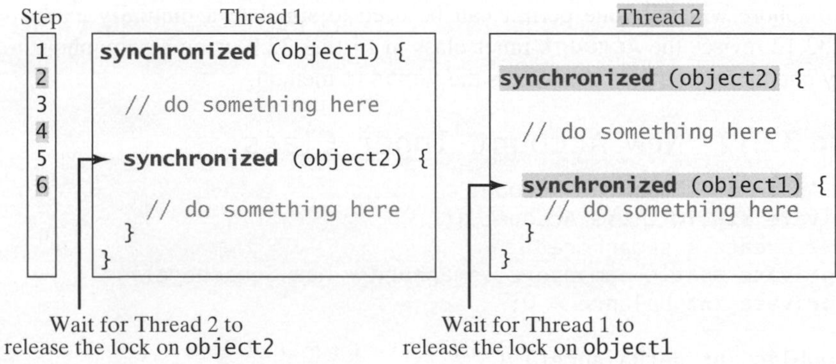

FIGURE 32.25 Thread 1 and Thread 2 are deadlocked.

resource ordering

Deadlock is easily avoided by using a simple technique known as *resource ordering*. With this technique, you assign an order to all the objects whose locks must be acquired and ensure that each thread acquires the locks in that order. For the example in Figure 32.25, suppose that the objects are ordered as `object1` and `object2`. Using the resource ordering technique, Thread 2 must acquire a lock on `object1` first, then on `object2`. Once Thread 1 acquires a lock on `object1`, Thread 2 has to wait for a lock on `object1`. Thus, Thread 1 will be able to acquire a lock on `object2` and no deadlock will occur.

MyProgrammingLab™

32.33 What is a deadlock? How can you avoid deadlock?

32.16 Thread States

A thread state indicates the status of thread.

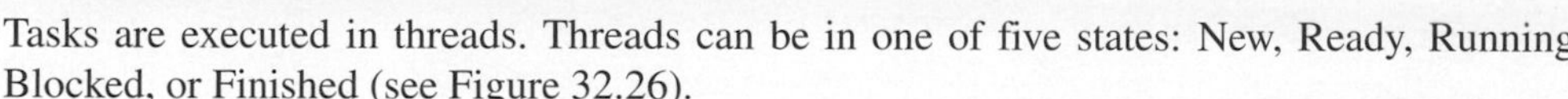

Tasks are executed in threads. Threads can be in one of five states: New, Ready, Running, Blocked, or Finished (see Figure 32.26).

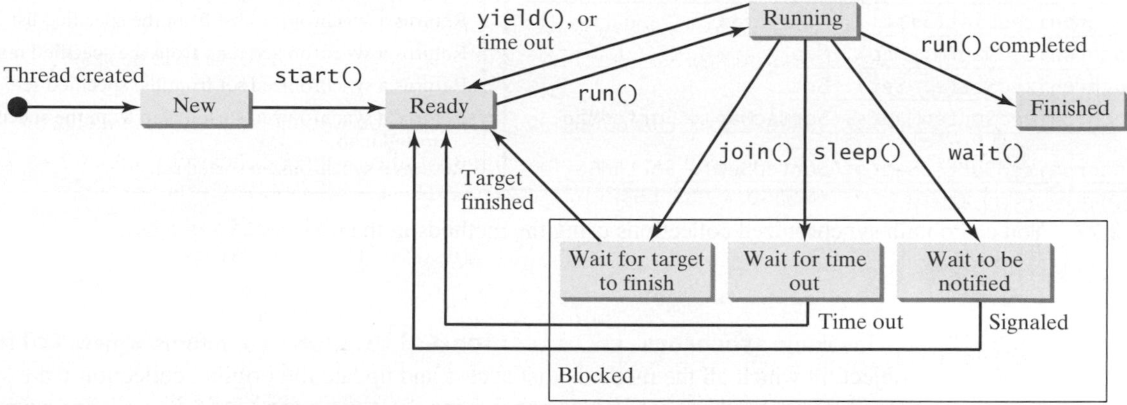

Figure 32.26 A thread can be in one of five states: New, Ready, Running, Blocked, or Finished.

When a thread is newly created, it enters the ***New** state*. After a thread is started by calling its `start()` method, it enters the ***Ready** state*. A ready thread is runnable but may not be running yet. The operating system has to allocate CPU time to it.

When a ready thread begins executing, it enters the ***Running** state*. A running thread can enter the ***Ready*** state if its given CPU time expires or its `yield()` method is called.

A thread can enter the ***Blocked** state* (i.e., become inactive) for several reasons. It may have invoked the `join()`, `sleep()`, or `wait()` method. It may be waiting for an I/O operation to finish. A blocked thread may be reactivated when the action inactivating it is reversed. For example, if a thread has been put to sleep and the sleep time has expired, the thread is reactivated and enters the **Ready** state.

Finally, a thread is ***Finished*** if it completes the execution of its `run()` method.

The `isAlive()` method is used to find out the state of a thread. It returns `true` if a thread is in the **Ready**, **Blocked**, or **Running** state; it returns `false` if a thread is new and has not started or if it is finished.

The `interrupt()` method interrupts a thread in the following way: If a thread is currently in the **Ready** or **Running** state, its interrupted flag is set; if a thread is currently blocked, it is awakened and enters the **Ready** state, and a `java.lang.InterruptedException` is thrown.

32.34 What is a thread state? Describe the states for a thread.

32.17 Synchronized Collections

Java Collections Framework provides synchronized collections for lists, sets, and maps.

The classes in the Java Collections Framework are not thread-safe; that is, their contents may become corrupted if they are accessed and updated concurrently by multiple threads. You can protect the data in a collection by locking the collection or by using synchronized collections. synchronized collection

The **Collections** class provides six static methods for wrapping a collection into a synchronized version, as shown in Figure 32.27. The collections created using these methods are called *synchronization wrappers*.

synchronization wrapper

java.util.Collections	
+synchronizedCollection(c: Collection): Collection	Returns a synchronized collection.
+synchronizedList(list: List): List	Returns a synchronized list from the specified list.
+synchronizedMap(m: Map): Map	Returns a synchronized map from the specified map.
+synchronizedSet(s: Set): Set	Returns a synchronized set from the specified set.
+synchronizedSortedMap(s: SortedMap): SortedMap	Returns a synchronized sorted map from the specified sorted map.
+synchronizedSortedSet(s: SortedSet): SortedSet	Returns a synchronized sorted set.

FIGURE 32.27 You can obtain synchronized collections using the methods in the **Collections** class.

Invoking **synchronizedCollection(Collection c)** returns a new **Collection** object, in which all the methods that access and update the original collection **c** are synchronized. These methods are implemented using the **synchronized** keyword. For example, the **add** method is implemented like this:

```
public boolean add(E o) {
  synchronized (this) {
    return c.add(o);
  }
}
```

Synchronized collections can be safely accessed and modified by multiple threads concurrently.

Note

The methods in **java.util.Vector**, **java.util.Stack**, and **java.util.Hashtable** are already synchronized. These are old classes introduced in JDK 1.0. Starting with JDK 1.5, you should use **java.util.ArrayList** to replace **Vector**, **java.util.LinkedList** to replace **Stack**, and **java.util.Map** to replace **Hashtable**. If synchronization is needed, use a synchronization wrapper.

fail-fast

The synchronization wrapper classes are thread-safe, but the iterator is *fail-fast*. This means that if you are using an iterator to traverse a collection while the underlying collection is being modified by another thread, then the iterator will immediately fail by throwing **java.util.ConcurrentModificationException**, which is a subclass of **RuntimeException**. To avoid this error, you need to create a synchronized collection object and acquire a lock on the object when traversing it. For example, to traverse a set, you have to write the code like this:

```
Set hashSet = Collections.synchronizedSet(new HashSet());

synchronized (hashSet) { // Must synchronize it
  Iterator iterator = hashSet.iterator();

  while (iterator.hasNext()) {
    System.out.println(iterator.next());
  }
}
```

Failure to do so may result in nondeterministic behavior, such as a `ConcurrentModificationException`.

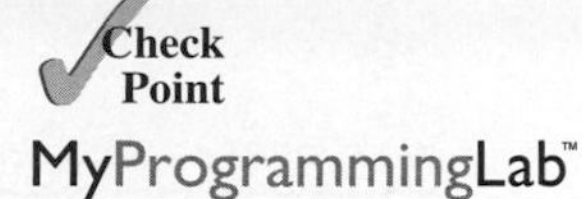

32.35 What is a synchronized collection? Is `ArrayList` synchronized? How do you make it synchronized?

32.36 Explain why an iterator is fail-fast.

32.18 Parallel Programming

The Fork/Join Framework is used for parallel programming in Java.

The widespread use of multicore systems has created a revolution in software. In order to benefit from multiple processors, software needs to run in parallel. JDK 7 introduces the new Fork/Join Framework for parallel programming, which utilizes the multicore processors. JDK 7 feature

The *Fork/Join Framework* is illustrated in Figure 32.28 (the diagram resembles a fork, hence its name). A problem is divided into nonoverlapping subproblems, which can be solved independently in parallel. The solutions to all subproblems are then joined to obtain the overall solution for the problem. This is the parallel implementation of the divide-and-conquer approach. In JDK 7's Fork/Join Framework, a *fork* can be viewed as an independent task that runs on a thread. Fork/Join Framework

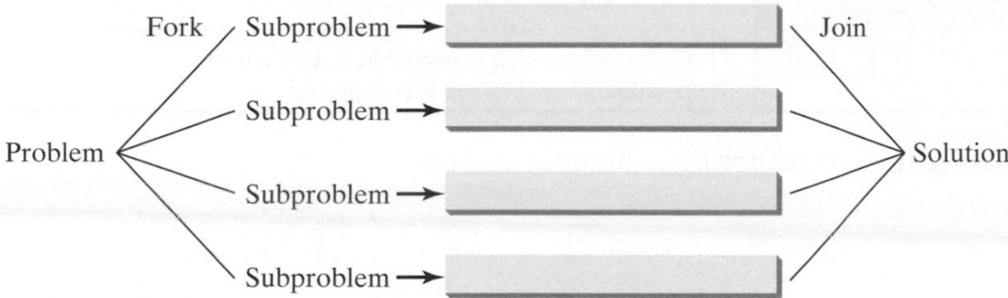

FIGURE 32.28 The nonoverlapping subproblems are solved in parallel.

The framework defines a task using the `ForkJoinTask` class, as shown in Figure 32.29, and executes a task in an instance of `ForkJoinPool`, as shown in Figure 32.30. `ForkJoinTask` `ForkJoinPool`

`ForkJoinTask` is the abstract base class for tasks. A `ForkJoinTask` is a thread-like entity, but it is much lighter than a normal thread, because huge numbers of tasks and subtasks can be executed by a small number of actual threads in a `ForkJoinPool`. The tasks are primarily coordinated using `fork()` and `join()`. Invoking `fork()` on a task arranges asynchronous execution, and invoking `join()` waits until the task is completed. The `invoke()` and `invokeAll(tasks)` methods implicitly invoke `fork()` to execute the task and `join()` to wait for the tasks to complete, and return the result, if any. Note that the static method `invokeAll` takes a variable number of `ForkJoinTask` arguments using the `...` syntax, which was introduced in Section 6.9.

The Fork/Join Framework is designed to parallelize divide-and-conquer solutions, which are naturally recursive. `RecursiveAction` and `RecursiveTask` are two subclasses of `ForkJoinTask`. To define a concrete task class, your class should extend `RecursiveAction` or `RecursiveTask`. `RecursiveAction` is for a task that doesn't return a value, and `RecursiveTask` is for a task that does return a value. Your task class should override the `compute()` method to specify how a task is performed. `RecursiveAction` `RecursiveTask`

We now use a merge sort to demonstrate how to develop parallel programs using the Fork/Join Framework. The merge sort algorithm (introduced in Section 25.3) divides the

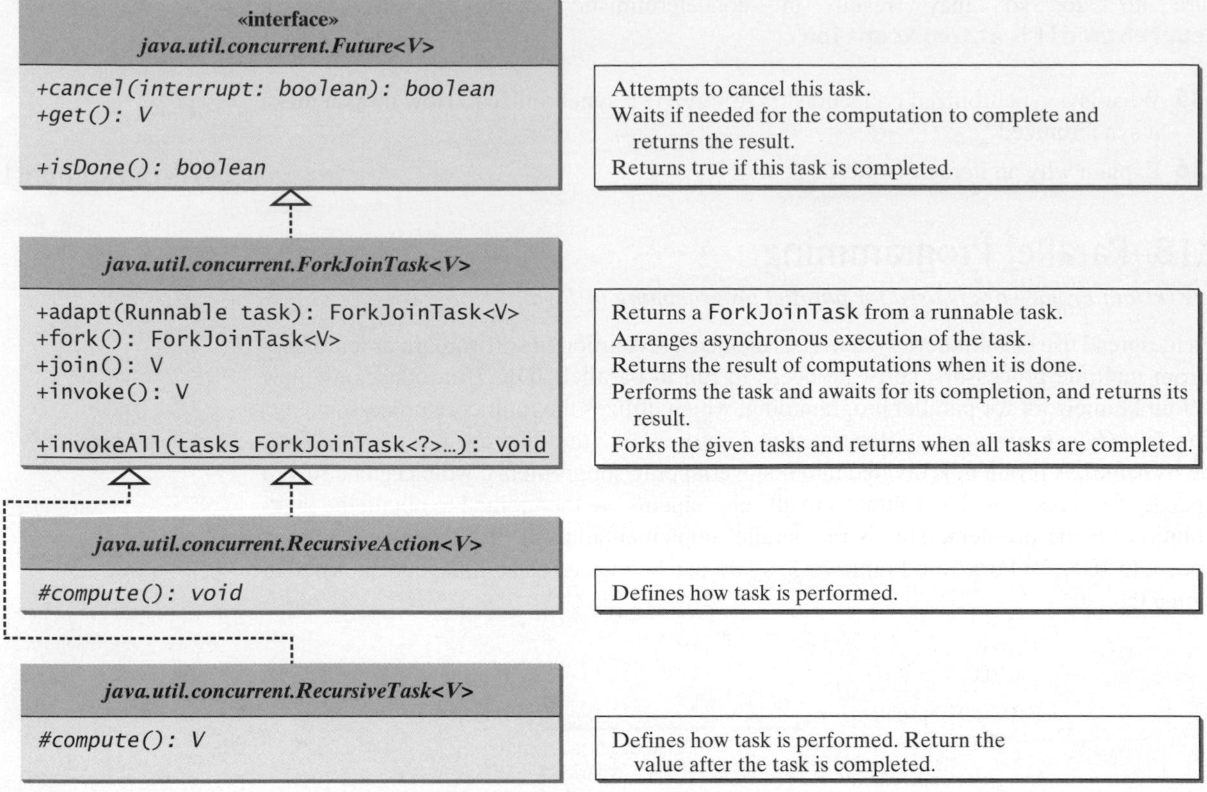

FIGURE 32.29 The ForkJoinTask class defines a task for asynchronous execution.

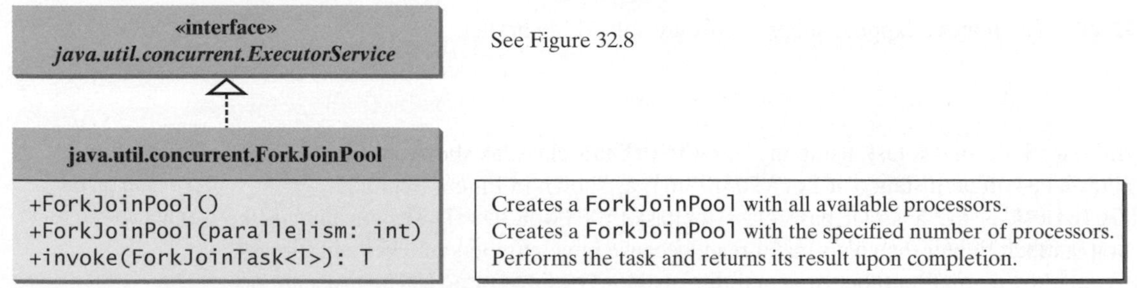

FIGURE 32.30 The ForkJoinPool executes Fork/Join tasks.

array into two halves and applies a merge sort on each half recursively. After the two halves are sorted, the algorithm merges them. Listing 32.13 gives a parallel implementation of the merge sort algorithm and compares its execution time with a sequential sort.

LISTING 32.13 ParallelMergeSort.java

```
import java.util.concurrent.RecursiveAction;
import java.util.concurrent.ForkJoinPool;

public class ParallelMergeSort {
  public static void main(String[] args) {
```

```
    final int SIZE = 7000000;
    int[] list1 = new int[SIZE];
    int[] list2 = new int[SIZE];

    for (int i = 0; i < list1.length; i++)
      list1[i] = list2[i] = (int)(Math.random() * 10000000);

    long startTime = System.currentTimeMillis();
    parallelMergeSort(list1); // Invoke parallel merge sort
    long endTime = System.currentTimeMillis();
    System.out.println("\nParallel time with "
      + Runtime.getRuntime().availableProcessors() +
      " processors is " + (endTime - startTime) + " milliseconds");

    startTime = System.currentTimeMillis();
    MergeSort.mergeSort(list2); // MergeSort is in Listing 25.5
    endTime = System.currentTimeMillis();
    System.out.println("\nSequential time is " +
      (endTime - startTime) + " milliseconds");
  }

  public static void parallelMergeSort(int[] list) {
    RecursiveAction mainTask = new SortTask(list);
    ForkJoinPool pool = new ForkJoinPool();
    pool.invoke(mainTask);
  }

  private static class SortTask extends RecursiveAction {
    private final int THRESHOLD = 500;
    private int[] list;

    SortTask(int[] list) {
      this.list = list;
    }

    @Override
    protected void compute() {
      if (list.length < THRESHOLD)
        java.util.Arrays.sort(list);
      else {
        // Obtain the first half
        int[] firstHalf = new int[list.length / 2];
        System.arraycopy(list, 0, firstHalf, 0, list.length / 2);

        // Obtain the second half
        int secondHalfLength = list.length - list.length / 2;
        int[] secondHalf = new int[secondHalfLength];
        System.arraycopy(list, list.length / 2,
          secondHalf, 0, secondHalfLength);

        // Recursively sort the two halves
        invokeAll(new SortTask(firstHalf),
          new SortTask(secondHalf));

        // Merge firstHalf with secondHalf into list
        MergeSort.merge(firstHalf, secondHalf, list);
      }
    }
  }
}
```

invoke parallel sort

invoke sequential sort

create a `ForkJoinTask`

create a `ForkJoinPool`

execute a task

define concrete `ForkJoinTask`

perform the task

sort a small list

split into two parts

solve each part

merge two parts

```
Parallel time with 2 processors is 2829 milliseconds
Sequential time is 4751 milliseconds
```

Since the sort algorithm does not return a value, we define a concrete `ForkJoinTask` class by extending `RecursiveAction` (lines 33–64). The `compute` method is overridden to implement a recursive merge sort (lines 42–63). If the list is small, it is more efficient to be solved sequentially (line 44). For a large list, it is split into two halves (lines 47–54). The two halves are sorted concurrently (lines 57–58) and then merged (line 61).

The program creates a main `ForkJoinTask` (line 28), a `ForkJoinPool` (line 29), and places the main task for execution in a `ForkJoinPool` (line 30). The `invoke` method will return after the main task is completed.

When executing the main task, the task is split into subtasks and the subtasks are invoked using the `invokeAll` method (lines 57–58). The `invokeAll` method will return after all the subtasks are completed. Note that each subtask is further split into smaller tasks recursively. Huge numbers of subtasks may be created and executed in the pool. The Fork/Join Framework automatically executes and coordinates all the tasks efficiently.

The `MergeSort` class is defined in Listing 25.5. The program invokes `MergeSort.merge` to merge two sorted sublists (line 61). The program also invokes `MergeSort.mergeSort` (line 21) to sort a list using merge sort sequentially. You can see that the parallel sort is much faster than the sequential sort.

Note that the loop for initializing the list can also be parallelized. However, you should avoid using `Math.random()` in the code, because it is synchronized and cannot be executed in parallel (see Programming Exercise 32.12). The `parallelMergeSort` method only sorts an array of `int` values, but you can modify it to become a generic method (see Programming Exercise 32.13).

In general, a problem can be solved in parallel using the following pattern:

```
if (the program is small)
  solve it sequentially;
else {
  divide the problem into nonoverlapping subproblems;
  solve the subproblems concurrently;
  combine the results from subproblems to solve the whole problem;
}
```

Listing 32.14 develops a parallel method that finds the maximal number in a list.

LISTING 32.14 ParallelMax.java

invoke max

```
import java.util.concurrent.*;

public class ParallelMax {
  public static void main(String[] args) {
    // Create a list
    final int N = 9000000;
    int[] list = new int[N];
    for (int i = 0; i < list.length; i++)
      list[i] = i;

    long startTime = System.currentTimeMillis();
    System.out.println("\nThe maximal number is " + max(list));
    long endTime = System.currentTimeMillis();
    System.out.println("The number of processors is " +
      Runtime.getRuntime().availableProcessors());
    System.out.println("Time is " + (endTime - startTime)
```

```
17            + " milliseconds");
18      }
19
20      public static int max(int[] list) {
21        RecursiveTask<Integer> task = new MaxTask(list, 0, list.length);
22        ForkJoinPool pool = new ForkJoinPool();
23        return pool.invoke(task);
24      }
25
26      private static class MaxTask extends RecursiveTask<Integer> {
27        private final static int THRESHOLD = 1000;
28        private int[] list;
29        private int low;
30        private int high;
31
32        public MaxTask(int[] list, int low, int high) {
33          this.list = list;
34          this.low = low;
35          this.high = high;
36        }
37
38        @Override
39        public Integer compute() {
40          if (high - low < THRESHOLD) {
41            int max = list[0];
42            for (int i = low; i < high; i++)
43              if (list[i] > max)
44                max = list[i];
45            return new Integer(max);
46          }
47          else {
48            int mid = (low + high) / 2;
49            RecursiveTask<Integer> left = new MaxTask(list, low, mid);
50            RecursiveTask<Integer> right = new MaxTask(list, mid, high);
51
52            right.fork();
53            left.fork();
54            return new Integer(Math.max(left.join().intValue(),
55              right.join().intValue()));
56          }
57        }
58      }
59    }
```

create a `ForkJoinTask`
create a `ForkJoinPool`
execute a task
define concrete `ForkJoinTask`
perform the task
solve a small problem
split into two parts
fork right
fork left
join tasks

```
The maximal number is 8999999
The number of processors is 2
Time is 44 milliseconds
```

Since the algorithm returns an integer, we define a task class for fork join by extending **RecursiveTask<Integer>** (lines 26–58). The **compute** method is overridden to return the max element in a **list[low..high]** (lines 39–57). If the list is small, it is more efficient to be solved sequentially (lines 40–46). For a large list, it is split into two halves (lines 48–50). The tasks **left** and **right** find the maximal element in the left half and right half, respectively. Invoking **fork()** on the task causes the task to be executed (lines 52–53). The **join()** method awaits for the task to complete and then returns the result (lines 54–55).

MyProgrammingLab™

32.37 How do you define a ForkJoinTask? What are the differences between RecursiveAction and RecursiveTask?

32.38 How do you tell the system to execute a task?

32.39 What method can you use to test if a task has been completed?

32.40 How do you create a ForkJoinPool? How do you place a task into a ForkJoinPool?

Key Terms

condition 1150
deadlock 1162
event dispatch thread 1138
fail-fast 1164
fairness policy 1149
Fork/Join Framework 1165
lock 1148
monitor 1154
multithreading 1130
race condition 1147
semaphore 1160
synchronization wrapper 1164
synchronized block 1148
thread 1130
thread-safe 1147

Chapter Summary

1. Each task is an instance of the Runnable interface. A *thread* is an object that facilitates the execution of a task. You can define a task class by implementing the Runnable interface and create a thread by wrapping a task using a Thread constructor.

2. After a thread object is created, use the start() method to start a thread, and the sleep(long) method to put a thread to sleep so that other threads get a chance to run.

3. A thread object never directly invokes the run method. The JVM invokes the run method when it is time to execute the thread. Your class must override the run method to tell the system what the thread will do when it runs.

4. To prevent threads from corrupting a shared resource, use *synchronized* methods or blocks. A *synchronized method* acquires a *lock* before it executes. In the case of an instance method, the lock is on the object for which the method was invoked. In the case of a static (class) method, the lock is on the class.

5. A synchronized statement can be used to acquire a lock on any object, not just *this* object, when executing a block of the code in a method. This block is referred to as a *synchronized block*.

6. You can use explicit locks and *conditions* to facilitate communications among threads, as well as using the built-in monitor for objects.

7. *Deadlock* occurs when two or more threads acquire locks on multiple objects and each has a lock on one object and is waiting for the lock on the other object. The *resource ordering technique* can be used to avoid deadlock.

8. The JDK 7's Fork/Join Framework is designed for developing parallel programs. You can define a task class that extends RecursiveAction or RecursiveTask and execute the tasks concurrently in ForkJoinPool, and obtains the overall solution after all tasks are completed.

TEST QUESTIONS

Do the test questions for this chapter online at www.cs.armstrong.edu/liang/intro9e/test.html.

PROGRAMMING EXERCISES

MyProgrammingLab™

Sections 32.1–32.5

***32.1** (*Revise Listing 32.1*) Rewrite Listing 32.1 to display the output in a text area, as shown in Figure 32.31.

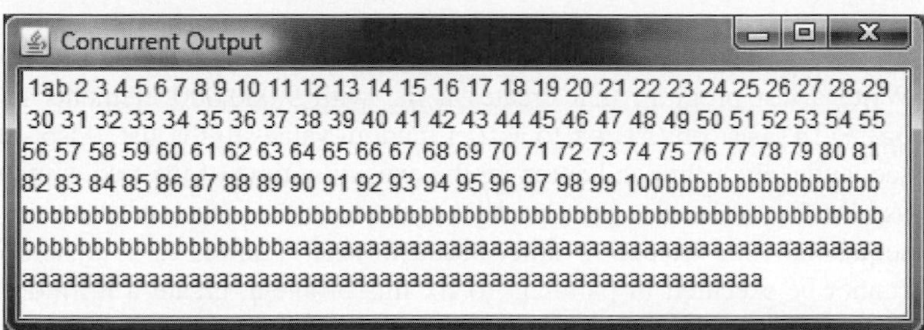

FIGURE 32.31 The output from three threads is displayed in a text area.

32.2 (*Racing cars*) Rewrite Programming Exercise 18.17 using a thread to control car racing. Compare the program with Programming Exercise 18.17 by setting the delay time to 10 in both programs. Which one runs the animation faster?

32.3 (*Raise flags*) Rewrite Programming Exercise 18.23 using a thread to animate a flag being raised. Compare the program with Programming Exercise 18.23 by setting the delay time to 10 in both programs. Which one runs the animation faster?

Sections 32.8–32.12

32.4 (*Synchronize threads*) Write a program that launches 1,000 threads. Each thread adds `1` to a variable `sum` that initially is `0`. You need to pass `sum` by reference to each thread. In order to pass it by reference, define an `Integer` wrapper object to hold `sum`. Run the program with and without synchronization to see its effect.

32.5 (*Run fans*) Rewrite Programming Exercise 18.11 using a thread to control the fan animation.

32.6 (*Bouncing balls*) Rewrite Programming Exercise 18.19 using a thread to animate bouncing ball movements.

32.7 (*Control a group of clocks*) Rewrite Programming Exercise 18.14 using a thread to control the clock animation.

32.8 (*Account synchronization*) Rewrite Listing 32.9, ThreadCooperation.java, using the object's `wait()` and `notifyAll()` methods.

32.9 (*Demonstrate* `ConcurrentModificationException`) The iterator is *fail-fast*. Write a program to demonstrate it by creating two threads that concurrently access and modify a set. The first thread creates a hash set filled with numbers, and adds a new number to the set every second. The second thread obtains an iterator for the set and traverses the set back and forth through the iterator every second. You will receive a `ConcurrentModificationException` because the underlying set is being modified in the first thread while the set in the second thread is being traversed.

***32.10** (*Use synchronized sets*) Using synchronization, correct the problem in the preceding exercise so that the second thread does not throw a `ConcurrentModificationException`.

Section 32.15

***32.11** (*Demonstrate deadlock*) Write a program that demonstrates deadlock.

Section 32.18

***32.12** (*Parallel array initializer*) Implement the following method using the Fork/Join Framework to assign random values to the list.

```
public static void parallelAssignValues(double[] list)
```

Write a test program that creates a list with 9,000,000 elements and invokes `parallelAssignValues` to assign random values to the list. Also implement a sequential algorithm and compare the execution time of the two. Note that if you use `Math.random()`, your parallel code execution time will be worse than the sequential code execution time, because `Math.random()` is synchronized and cannot be executed in parallel. To fix this problem, create a `Random` object for assigning random values to a small list.

32.13 (*Generic parallel merge sort*) Revise Listing 32.13, ParallelMergeSort.java, to define a generic `parallelMergeSort` method as follows:

```
public static void <E extends Comparable<E>>
  parallelMergeSort(E[] list)
```

***32.14** (*Parallel quick sort*) Implement the following method in parallel to sort a list using quick sort (see Listing 25.7).

```
public static void parallelQuickSort(int[] list)
```

Write a test program that times the execution time for a list of size 9,000,000 using this parallel method and a sequential method.

***32.15** (*Parallel sum*) Implement the following method using Fork/Join to find the sum of a list.

```
public static double parallelSum(double[] list)
```

Write a test program that finds the sum in a list of 9,000,000 double values.

***32.16** (*Parallel matrix addition*) Programming Exercise 7.5 describes how to perform matrix addition. Suppose you have multiple processors, so you can speed up the matrix addition. Implement the following method in parallel.

```
public static double[][] parallelAddMatrix(
  double[][] a, double[][] b)
```

Write a test program that times the execution time for adding two $2{,}000 \times 2{,}000$ matrices.

***32.17** (*Parallel matrix multiplication*) Programming Exercise 7.6 describes how to perform matrix multiplication. Suppose you have multiple processors, so you can speed up the matrix multiplication. Implement the following method in parallel.

```
public static double[][] parallelMultiplyMatrix(
  double[][] a, double[][] b)
```

Write a test program that times the execution time for multiplying two 2,000 × 2,000 matrices.

***32.18** (*Parallel Eight Queens*) Revise Listing 24.10, EightQueens.java, to develop a parallel algorithm that finds all solutions for the Eight Queens problem. (*Hint*: Launch eight subtasks, each of which places the queen in a different column in the first row.)

Comprehensive

*****32.19** (*Sorting animation*) Write an animation applet for selection sort, insertion sort, and bubble sort, as shown in Figure 32.32. Create an array of integers 1, 2, . . . , 50. Shuffle it randomly. Create a panel to display the array in a histogram. You should invoke each sort method in a separate thread. Each algorithm uses two nested loops. When the algorithm completes an iteration in the outer loop, put the thread to sleep for 0.5 seconds, and redisplay the array in the histogram. Color the last bar in the sorted subarray.

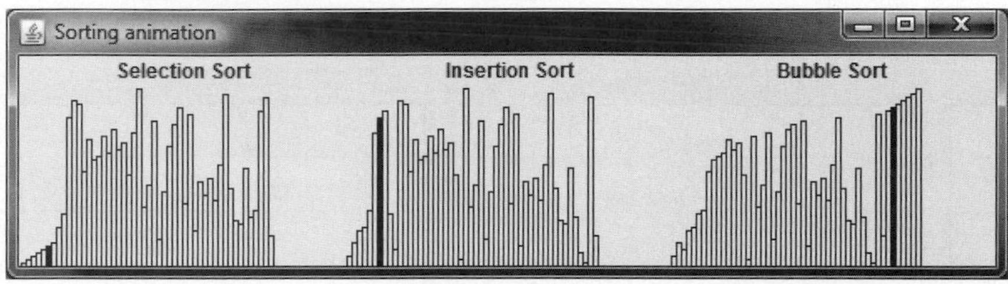

(a) Sorting in progress

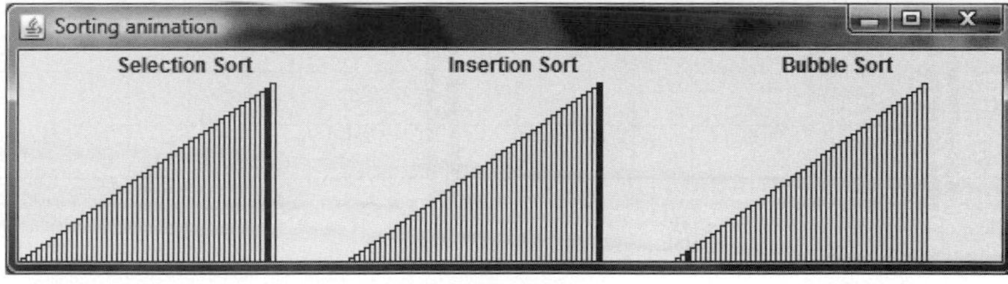

(b) Sorted

FIGURE 32.32 Three sorting algorithms are illustrated in the animation.

*****32.20** (*Sudoku search animation*) Modify Programming Exercise 24.21 to display the intermediate results of the search. As shown in Figure 32.33a, the number 2 is placed in the first row and last column, because 2 already appears in the same row. This number is invalid, so the next value, 3, is placed in Figure 32.33b. This number is also invalid, because 3 already appears in the same row; so the next value, 4, is placed in Figure 32.33c. The animation displays all the search steps.

*****32.21** (*Eight Queens animation*) Modify Listing 24.10, EightQueens.java, to display the intermediate results of the search. As shown in Figure 32.34a, the current row being searched is highlighted. When the user clicks the mouse button, a position for the row is found and a queen is placed in the row, as shown in Figure 32.34b.

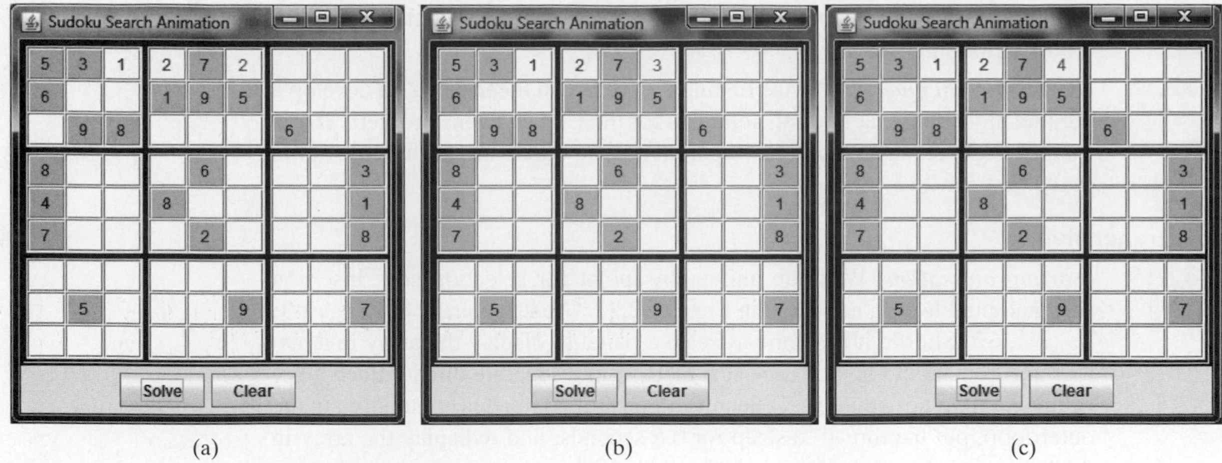

(a) (b) (c)

Figure 32.33 The intermediate search steps are displayed in the animation for the Sudoku problem.

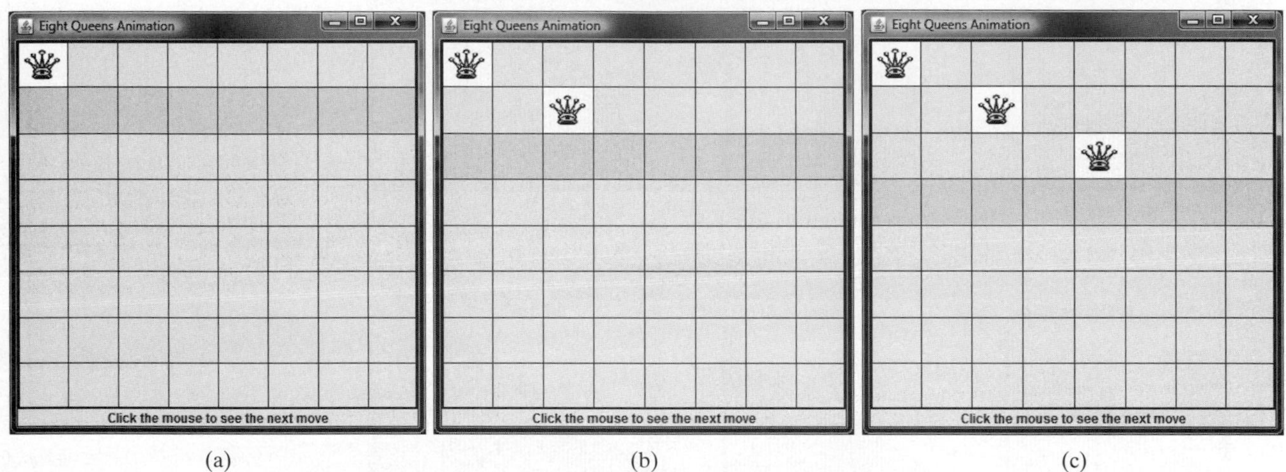

(a) (b) (c)

Figure 32.34 The intermediate search steps are displayed in the animation for the Eight Queens problem.

CHAPTER

33

NETWORKING

Objectives

- To explain terms: TCP, IP, domain name, domain name server, stream-based communications, and packet-based communications (§33.2).
- To create servers using server sockets (§33.2.1) and clients using client sockets (§33.2.2).
- To implement Java networking programs using stream sockets (§33.2.3).
- To develop an example of a client/server application (§33.2.4).
- To obtain Internet addresses using the `InetAddress` class (§33.3).
- To develop servers for multiple clients (§33.4).
- To develop applets that communicate with the server (§33.5).
- To send and receive objects on a network (§33.6).
- To develop an interactive tic-tac-toe game played on the Internet (§33.7).

33.1 Introduction

Computer networking is to send and receive messages among computers on the Internet.

To browse the Web or send email, your computer must be connected to the Internet. The *Internet* is the global network of millions of computers. Your computer can connect to the Internet through an Internet Service Provider (ISP) using a dialup, DSL, or cable modem, or through a local area network (LAN).

IP address

When a computer needs to communicate with another computer, it needs to know the other computer's address. An *Internet Protocol* (IP) address uniquely identifies the computer on the Internet. An IP address consists of four dotted decimal numbers between `0` and `255`, such as `130.254.204.33`. Since it is not easy to remember so many numbers, they are often mapped to meaningful names called *domain names*, such as liang.armstrong.edu. Special servers called *Domain Name Servers* (DNS) on the Internet translate host names into IP addresses. When a computer contacts liang.armstrong.edu, it first asks the DNS to translate this domain name into a numeric IP address and then sends the request using the IP address.

domain name
domain name server

TCP

The Internet Protocol is a low-level protocol for delivering data from one computer to another across the Internet in packets. Two higher-level protocols used in conjunction with the IP are the *Transmission Control Protocol* (TCP) and the *User Datagram Protocol* (UDP). TCP enables two hosts to establish a connection and exchange streams of data. TCP guarantees delivery of data and also guarantees that packets will be delivered in the same order in which they were sent. UDP is a standard, low-overhead, connectionless, host-to-host protocol that is used over the IP. UDP allows an application program on one computer to send a datagram to an application program on another computer.

stream-based
packet-based

Java supports both stream-based and packet-based communications. *Stream-based communications* use TCP for data transmission, whereas *packet-based communications* use UDP. Since TCP can detect lost transmissions and resubmit them, transmissions are lossless and reliable. UDP, in contrast, cannot guarantee lossless transmission. Stream-based communications are used in most areas of Java programming and are the focus of this chapter. Packet-based communications are introduced in Supplement III.U, Networking Using Datagram Protocol.

33.2 Client/Server Computing

Java provides the `ServerSocket` *class for creating a server socket and the* `Socket` *class for creating a client socket. Two programs on the Internet communicate through a server socket and a client socket using I/O streams.*

socket

Networking is tightly integrated in Java. The Java API provides the classes for creating sockets to facilitate program communications over the Internet. *Sockets* are the endpoints of logical connections between two hosts and can be used to send and receive data. Java treats socket communications much as it treats I/O operations; thus, programs can read from or write to sockets as easily as they can read from or write to files.

Network programming usually involves a server and one or more clients. The client sends requests to the server, and the server responds. The client begins by attempting to establish a connection to the server. The server can accept or deny the connection. Once a connection is established, the client and the server communicate through sockets.

The server must be running when a client attempts to connect to the server. The server waits for a connection request from a client. The statements needed to create sockets on a server and a client are shown in Figure 33.1.

33.2.1 Server Sockets

server socket

To establish a server, you need to create a *server socket* and attach it to a *port*, which is where the server listens for connections. The port identifies the TCP service on the socket. Port numbers range from 0 to 65536, but port numbers 0 to 1024 are reserved for privileged services.

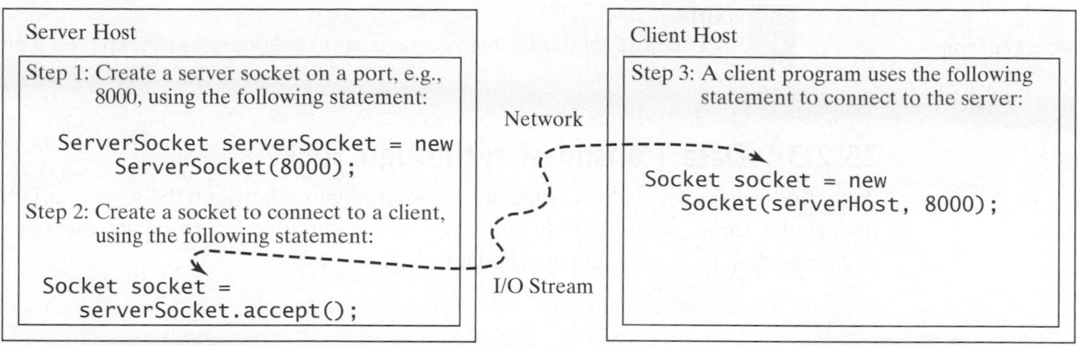

FIGURE 33.1 The server creates a server socket and, once a connection to a client is established, connects to the client with a client socket.

For instance, the email server runs on port 25, and the Web server usually runs on port 80. You can choose any port number that is not currently used by other programs. The following statement creates a server socket `serverSocket`:

```
ServerSocket serverSocket = new ServerSocket(port);
```

Note

Attempting to create a server socket on a port already in use would cause the `java.net.BindException`. BindException

33.2.2 Client Sockets

After a server socket is created, the server can use the following statement to listen for connections:

```
Socket socket = serverSocket.accept();
```

This statement waits until a client connects to the server socket. The client issues the following statement to request a connection to a server: connect to client

```
Socket socket = new Socket(serverName, port);
```

This statement opens a socket so that the client program can communicate with the server. `serverName` is the server's Internet host name or IP address. The following statement creates a socket on the client machine to connect to the host 130.254.204.33 at port 8000: client socket use IP address

```
Socket socket = new Socket("130.254.204.33", 8000)
```

Alternatively, you can use the domain name to create a socket, as follows: use domain name

```
Socket socket = new Socket("liang.armstrong.edu", 8000);
```

When you create a socket with a host name, the JVM asks the DNS to translate the host name into the IP address.

Note

A program can use the host name `localhost` or the IP address `127.0.0.1` to refer to the machine on which a client is running. localhost

Note

UnknownHostException

The Socket constructor throws a java.net.UnknownHostException if the host cannot be found.

33.2.3 Data Transmission through Sockets

After the server accepts the connection, communication between the server and client is conducted the same as for I/O streams. The statements needed to create the streams and to exchange data between them are shown in Figure 33.2.

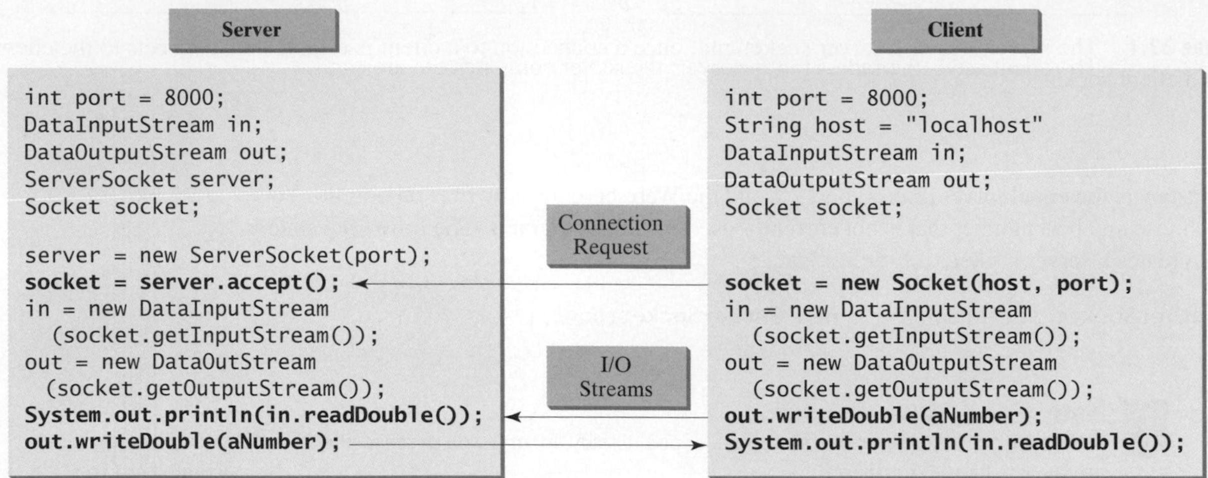

FIGURE 33.2 The server and client exchange data through I/O streams on top of the socket.

To get an input stream and an output stream, use the getInputStream() and getOutputStream() methods on a socket object. For example, the following statements create an InputStream stream called input and an OutputStream stream called output from a socket:

```
InputStream input = socket.getInputStream();
OutputStream output = socket.getOutputStream();
```

The InputStream and OutputStream streams are used to read or write bytes. You can use DataInputStream, DataOutputStream, BufferedReader, and PrintWriter to wrap on the InputStream and OutputStream to read or write data, such as int, double, or String. The following statements, for instance, create the DataInputStream stream input and the DataOutput stream output to read and write primitive data values:

```
DataInputStream input = new DataInputStream
  (socket.getInputStream());
DataOutputStream output = new DataOutputStream
  (socket.getOutputStream());
```

The server can use input.readDouble() to receive a double value from the client, and output.writeDouble(d) to send the double value d to the client.

Tip

Recall that binary I/O is more efficient than text I/O because text I/O requires encoding and decoding. Therefore, it is better to use binary I/O for transmitting data between a server and a client to improve performance.

33.2.4 A Client/Server Example

This example presents a client program and a server program. The client sends data to a server. The server receives the data, uses it to produce a result, and then sends the result back to the client. The client displays the result on the console. In this example, the data sent from the client comprise the radius of a circle, and the result produced by the server is the area of the circle (see Figure 33.3).

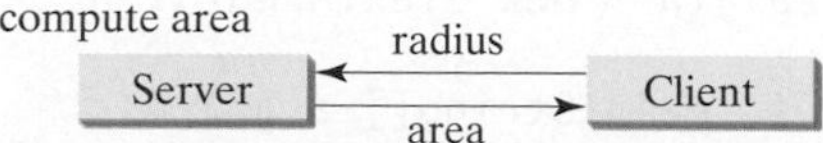

FIGURE 33.3 The client sends the radius to the server; the server computes the area and sends it to the client.

The client sends the radius through a `DataOutputStream` on the output stream socket, and the server receives the radius through the `DataInputStream` on the input stream socket, as shown in Figure 33.4a. The server computes the area and sends it to the client through a `DataOutputStream` on the output stream socket, and the client receives the area through a `DataInputStream` on the input stream socket, as shown in Figure 33.4b. The server and client programs are given in Listings 33.1 and 33.2. Figure 33.5 contains a sample run of the server and the client.

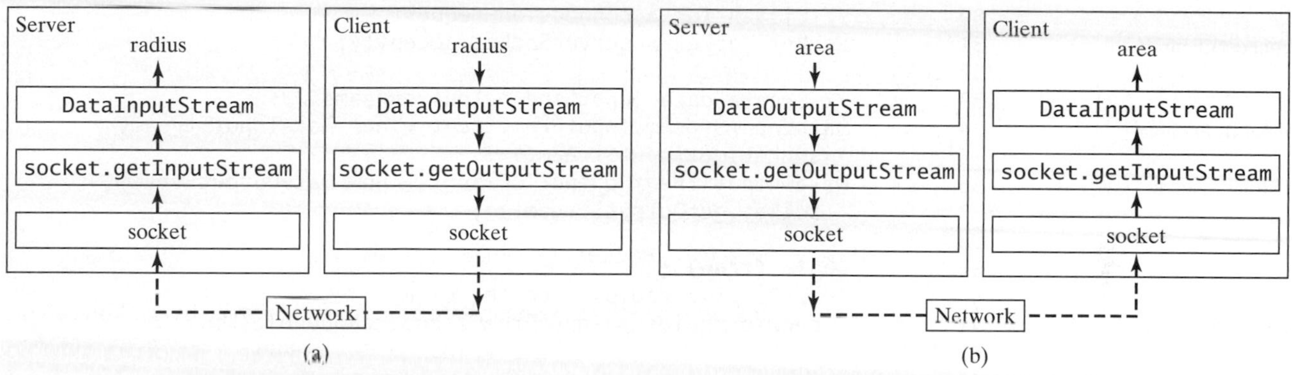

FIGURE 33.4 (a) The client sends the radius to the server. (b) The server sends the area to the client.

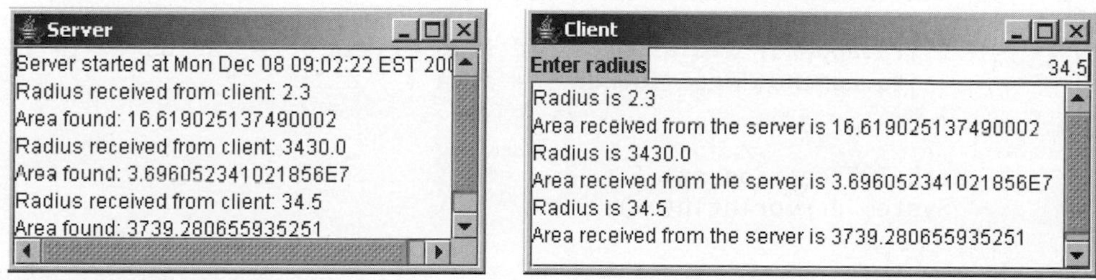

FIGURE 33.5 The client sends the radius to the server. The server receives it, computes the area, and sends the area to the client.

LISTING 33.1 Server.java

```
import java.io.*;
import java.net.*;
import java.util.*;
import java.awt.*;
import javax.swing.*;

public class Server extends JFrame {
  // Text area for displaying contents
  private JTextArea jta = new JTextArea();

  public static void main(String[] args) {
    new Server();
  }

  public Server() {
    // Place text area on the frame
    setLayout(new BorderLayout());
    add(new JScrollPane(jta), BorderLayout.CENTER);

    setTitle("Server");
    setSize(500, 300);
    setDefaultCloseOperation(JFrame.EXIT_ON_CLOSE);
    setVisible(true); // It is necessary to show the frame here!

    try {
      // Create a server socket
      ServerSocket serverSocket = new ServerSocket(8000);
      jta.append("Server started at " + new Date() + '\n');

      // Listen for a connection request
      Socket socket = serverSocket.accept();

      // Create data input and output streams
      DataInputStream inputFromClient = new DataInputStream(
        socket.getInputStream());
      DataOutputStream outputToClient = new DataOutputStream(
        socket.getOutputStream());

      while (true) {
        // Receive radius from the client
        double radius = inputFromClient.readDouble();

        // Compute area
        double area = radius * radius * Math.PI;

        // Send area back to the client
        outputToClient.writeDouble(area);

        jta.append("Radius received from client: " + radius + '\n');
        jta.append("Area found: " + area + '\n');
      }
    }
    catch(IOException ex) {
      System.err.println(ex);
    }
  }
}
```

launch server

server socket

connect client

input from client

output to client

read radius

write area

LISTING 33.2 Client.java

```
import java.io.*;
import java.net.*;
import java.awt.*;
import java.awt.event.*;
import javax.swing.*;

public class Client extends JFrame {
  // Text field for receiving radius
  private JTextField jtf = new JTextField();

  // Text area to display contents
  private JTextArea jta = new JTextArea();

  // IO streams
  private DataOutputStream toServer;
  private DataInputStream fromServer;

  public static void main(String[] args) {
    new Client();
  }

  public Client() {
    // Panel p to hold the label and text field
    JPanel p = new JPanel();
    p.setLayout(new BorderLayout());
    p.add(new JLabel("Enter radius"), BorderLayout.WEST);
    p.add(jtf, BorderLayout.CENTER);
    jtf.setHorizontalAlignment(JTextField.RIGHT);

    setLayout(new BorderLayout());
    add(p, BorderLayout.NORTH);
    add(new JScrollPane(jta), BorderLayout.CENTER);

    jtf.addActionListener(new TextFieldListener());

    setTitle("Client");
    setSize(500, 300);
    setDefaultCloseOperation(JFrame.EXIT_ON_CLOSE);
    setVisible(true); // It is necessary to show the frame here!

    try {
      // Create a socket to connect to the server
      Socket socket = new Socket("localhost", 8000);
      // Socket socket = new Socket("130.254.204.33", 8000);
      // Socket socket = new Socket("liang.armstrong.edu", 8000);

      // Create an input stream to receive data from the server
      fromServer = new DataInputStream(
        socket.getInputStream());

      // Create an output stream to send data to the server
      toServer =
        new DataOutputStream(socket.getOutputStream());
    }
    catch (IOException ex) {
      jta.append(ex.toString() + '\n');
    }
```

launch client

register listener

request connection

input from server

output to server

write radius

read radius

```
58    }
59
60    private class TextFieldListener implements ActionListener {
61      @Override
62      public void actionPerformed(ActionEvent e) {
63        try {
64          // Get the radius from the text field
65          double radius = Double.parseDouble(jtf.getText().trim());
66
67          // Send the radius to the server
68          toServer.writeDouble(radius);
69          toServer.flush();
70
71          // Get area from the server
72          double area = fromServer.readDouble();
73
74          // Display to the text area
75          jta.append("Radius is " + radius + "\n");
76          jta.append("Area received from the server is "
77            + area + '\n');
78        }
79        catch (IOException ex) {
80          System.err.println(ex);
81        }
82      }
83    }
84  }
```

You start the server program first, then start the client program. In the client program, enter a radius in the text field and press *Enter* to send the radius to the server. The server computes the area and sends it back to the client. This process is repeated until one of the two programs terminates.

The networking classes are in the package `java.net`. You should import this package when writing Java network programs.

The `Server` class creates a `ServerSocket serverSocket` and attaches it to port 8000, using this statement (line 27 in Server.java):

```
ServerSocket serverSocket = new ServerSocket(8000);
```

The server then starts to listen for connection requests, using the following statement (line 31 in Server.java):

```
Socket socket = serverSocket.accept();
```

The server waits until a client requests a connection. After it is connected, the server reads the radius from the client through an input stream, computes the area, and sends the result to the client through an output stream.

The `Client` class uses the following statement to create a socket that will request a connection to the server on the same machine (localhost) at port 8000 (line 43 in Client.java).

```
Socket socket = new Socket("localhost", 8000);
```

If you run the server and the client on different machines, replace `localhost` with the server machine's host name or IP address. In this example, the server and the client are running on the same machine.

If the server is not running, the client program terminates with a `java.net.ConnectException`. After it is connected, the client gets input and output streams—wrapped by data input and output streams—in order to receive and send data to the server.

If you receive a `java.net.BindException` when you start the server, the server port is currently in use. You need to terminate the process that is using the server port and then restart the server.

What happens if the `setVisible(true)` statement in line 23 in Server.java is moved after the `try-catch` block in line 56 in Server.java? The frame will not be displayed, because the `while` loop in the `try-catch` block will not finish until the program terminates.

Note

When you create a server socket, you have to specify a port (e.g., 8000) for the socket. When a client connects to the server (line 43 in Client.java), a socket is created on the client. This socket has its own local port. This port number (e.g., 2047) is automatically chosen by the JVM, as shown in Figure 33.6. client socket port

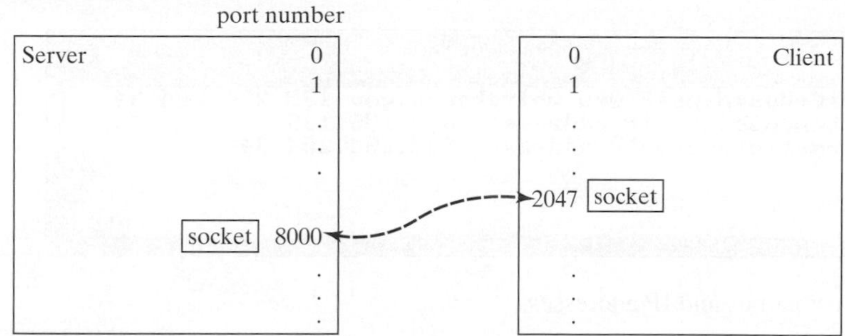

FIGURE 33.6 The JVM automatically chooses an available port to create a socket for the client.

To see the local port on the client, insert the following statement in line 46 in Client.java.

```
System.out.println("local port: " + socket.getLocalPort());
```

Check Point
MyProgrammingLab™

33.1 How do you create a server socket? What port numbers can be used? What happens if a requested port number is already in use? Can a port connect to multiple clients?

33.2 What are the differences between a server socket and a client socket?

33.3 How does a client program initiate a connection?

33.4 How does a server accept a connection?

33.5 How are data transferred between a client and a server?

33.3 The **InetAddress** Class

Key Point

The server program can use the `InetAddress` *class to obtain the information about the IP address and host name for the client.*

Occasionally, you would like to know who is connecting to the server. You can use the `InetAddress` class to find the client's host name and IP address. The `InetAddress` class models an IP address. You can use the following statement in the server program to get an instance of `InetAddress` on a socket that connects to the client.

```
InetAddress inetAddress = socket.getInetAddress();
```

Next, you can display the client's host name and IP address, as follows:

```
System.out.println("Client's host name is " +
  inetAddress.getHostName());
```

```
System.out.println("Client's IP Address is " +
  inetAddress.getHostAddress());
```

You can also create an instance of `InetAddress` from a host name or IP address using the static `getByName` method. For example, the following statement creates an `InetAddress` for the host `liang.armstrong.edu`.

```
InetAddress address = InetAddress.getByName("liang.armstrong.edu");
```

Listing 33.3 gives a program that identifies the host name and IP address of the arguments you pass in from the command line. Line 7 creates an `InetAddress` using the `getByName` method. Lines 8–9 use the `getHostName` and `getHostAddress` methods to get the host's name and IP address. Figure 33.7 shows a sample run of the program.

FIGURE 33.7 The program identifies host names and IP addresses.

LISTING 33.3 `IdentifyHostNameIP.java`

get an `InetAddress` (line 7)
get host name (line 8)
get host IP (line 9)

```
1  import java.net.*;
2
3  public class IdentifyHostNameIP {
4    public static void main(String[] args) {
5      for (int i = 0; i < args.length; i++) {
6        try {
7          InetAddress address = InetAddress.getByName(args[i]);
8          System.out.print("Host name: " + address.getHostName() + " ");
9          System.out.println("IP address: " + address.getHostAddress());
10       }
11       catch (UnknownHostException ex) {
12         System.err.println("Unknown host or IP address " + args[i]);
13       }
14     }
15   }
16 }
```

Check Point

MyProgrammingLab™

33.6 How do you obtain an instance of `InetAddress`?

33.7 What methods can you use to get the IP address and hostname from an `InetAddress`?

33.4 Serving Multiple Clients

Key Point

A server can serve multiple clients. The connection to each client is handled by one thread.

Multiple clients are quite often connected to a single server at the same time. Typically, a server runs continuously on a server computer, and clients from all over the Internet can connect to it. You can use threads to handle the server's multiple clients simultaneously—simply create a thread for each connection. Here is how the server handles the establishment of a connection:

```
while (true) {
  Socket socket = serverSocket.accept(); // Connect to a client
  Thread thread = new ThreadClass(socket);
  thread.start();
}
```

The server socket can have many connections. Each iteration of the `while` loop creates a new connection. Whenever a connection is established, a new thread is created to handle communication between the server and the new client, and this allows multiple connections to run at the same time.

Listing 33.4 creates a server class that serves multiple clients simultaneously. For each connection, the server starts a new thread. This thread continuously receives input (the radius of a circle) from clients and sends the results (the area of the circle) back to them (see Figure 33.8). The client program is the same as in Listing 33.2. A sample run of the server with two clients is shown in Figure 33.9.

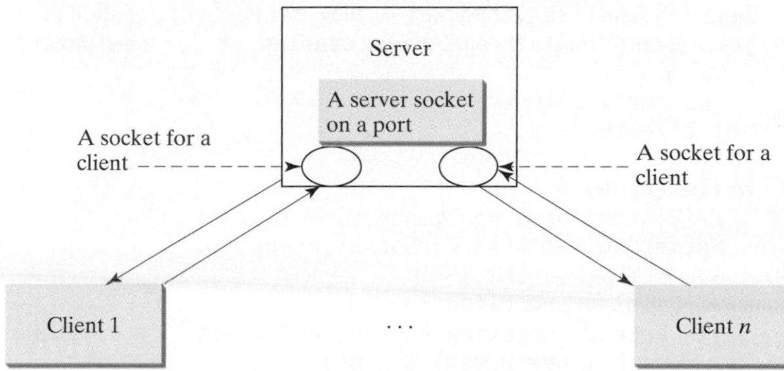

FIGURE 33.8 Multithreading enables a server to handle multiple independent clients.

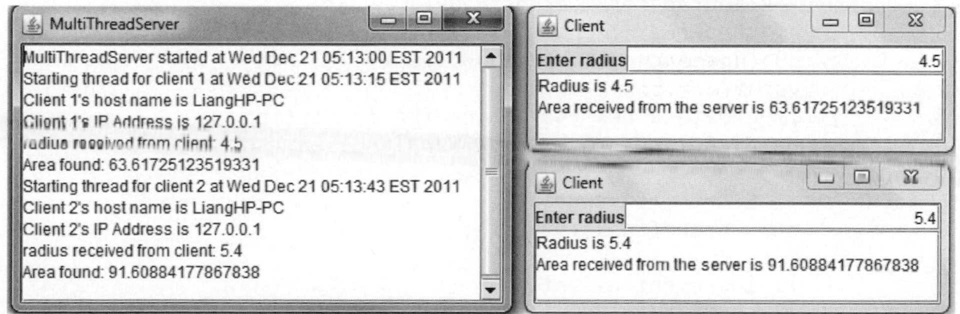

FIGURE 33.9 The server spawns a thread in order to serve a client.

LISTING 33.4 MultiThreadServer.java

```
import java.io.*;
import java.net.*;
import java.util.*;
import java.awt.*;
import javax.swing.*;
```

server socket
connect client
network information
create task
start thread
task class

```java

public class MultiThreadServer extends JFrame {
  // Text area for displaying contents
  private JTextArea jta = new JTextArea();

  public static void main(String[] args) {
    new MultiThreadServer();
  }

  public MultiThreadServer() {
    // Place text area on the frame
    setLayout(new BorderLayout());
    add(new JScrollPane(jta), BorderLayout.CENTER);

    setTitle("MultiThreadServer");
    setSize(500, 300);
    setDefaultCloseOperation(JFrame.EXIT_ON_CLOSE);
    setVisible(true); // It is necessary to show the frame here!

    try {
      // Create a server socket
      ServerSocket serverSocket = new ServerSocket(8000);
      jta.append("MultiThreadServer started at " + new Date() + '\n');

      // Number a client
      int clientNo = 1;

      while (true) {
        // Listen for a new connection request
        Socket socket = serverSocket.accept();

        // Display the client number
        jta.append("Starting thread for client " + clientNo +
          " at " + new Date() + '\n');

        // Find the client's host name and IP address
        InetAddress inetAddress = socket.getInetAddress();
        jta.append("Client " + clientNo + "'s host name is "
          + inetAddress.getHostName() + "\n");
        jta.append("Client " + clientNo + "'s IP Address is "
          + inetAddress.getHostAddress() + "\n");

        // Create a new thread for the connection
        HandleAClient task = new HandleAClient(socket);

        // Start the new thread
        new Thread(task).start();

        // Increment clientNo
        clientNo++;
      }
    }
    catch(IOException ex) {
      System.err.println(ex);
    }
  }

  // Inner class
  // Define the thread class for handling new connection
  class HandleAClient implements Runnable {
```

I/O

```
 66     private Socket socket; // A connected socket
 67 
 68     /** Construct a thread */
 69     public HandleAClient(Socket socket) {
 70       this.socket = socket;
 71     }
 72 
 73     @Override /** Run a thread */
 74     public void run() {
 75       try {
 76         // Create data input and output streams
 77         DataInputStream inputFromClient = new DataInputStream(
 78           socket.getInputStream());
 79         DataOutputStream outputToClient = new DataOutputStream(
 80           socket.getOutputStream());
 81 
 82         // Continuously serve the client
 83         while (true) {
 84           // Receive radius from the client
 85           double radius = inputFromClient.readDouble();
 86 
 87           // Compute area
 88           double area = radius * radius * Math.PI;
 89 
 90           // Send area back to the client
 91           outputToClient.writeDouble(area);
 92 
 93           jta.append("radius received from client: " +
 94             radius + '\n');
 95           jta.append("Area found: " + area + '\n');
 96         }
 97       }
 98       catch(IOException e) {
 99         System.err.println(e);
100       }
101     }
102   }
103 }
```

The server creates a server socket at port 8000 (line 27) and waits for a connection (line 35). When a connection with a client is established, the server creates a new thread to handle the communication (line 49). It then waits for another connection in an infinite `while` loop (lines 33–56).

The threads, which run independently of one another, communicate with designated clients. Each thread creates data input and output streams that receive and send data to a client.

33.8 How do you make a server serve multiple clients?

33.5 Applet Clients

The client can be an applet that connects to the server running on the host from which the applet is loaded.

Because of security constraints, applets can connect only to the host from which they were loaded. Therefore, the HTML file must be located on the machine on which the server is running. You can obtain the server's host name by invoking `getCodeBase().getHost()` on an applet, so you can write the applet without the host name fixed. The following is an example of how to use an applet to connect to a server.

The applet shows the number of visits made to a Web page. The count should be stored in a file on the server side. Every time the page is visited or reloaded, the applet sends a request to the server, and the server increases the count and sends it to the applet. The applet then displays the new count in a message, such as **You are visitor number 11**, as shown in Figure 33.10. The server and client programs are given in Listings 33.5 and 33.6.

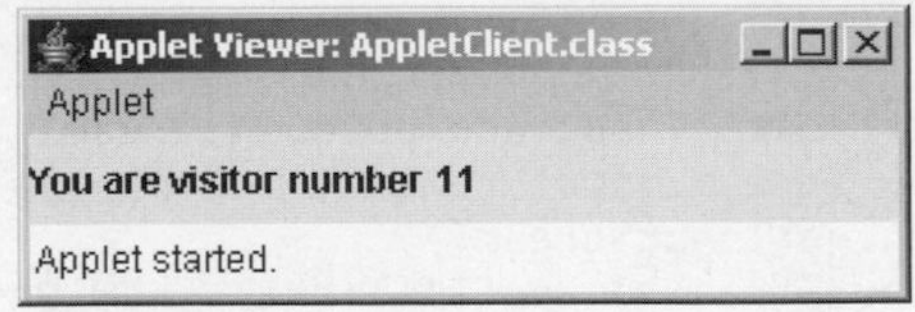

FIGURE 33.10 The applet displays the access count on a Web page.

LISTING 33.5 CountServer.java

```
import java.io.*;
import java.net.*;

public class CountServer {
  private RandomAccessFile raf;
  private int count; // Count the access to the server

  public static void main(String[] args) {
    new CountServer();
  }

  public CountServer() {
    try {
      // Create a server socket
      ServerSocket serverSocket = new ServerSocket(8000);
      System.out.println("Server started ");

      // Create or open the count file
      raf = new RandomAccessFile("count.dat", "rw");

      // Get the count
      if (raf.length() == 0)
        count = 0;
      else
        count = raf.readInt();

      while (true) {
        // Listen for a new connection request
        Socket socket = serverSocket.accept();

        // Create a DataOutputStream for the socket
        DataOutputStream outputToClient =
          new DataOutputStream(socket.getOutputStream());

        // Increase count and send the count to the client
        count++;
        outputToClient.writeInt(count);

        // Write new count back to the file
        raf.seek(0);
```

launch server
server socket
random access file
new file
get count
connect client
send to client
update count

```
41             raf.writeInt(count);
42           }
43         }
44         catch(IOException ex) {
45           ex.printStackTrace();
46         }
47       }
48     }
```

The server creates a **ServerSocket** in line 15 and creates or opens a file using **RandomAccessFile** in line 19. It reads the count from the file in lines 22–33. The server then waits for a connection request from a client (line 29). After a connection with a client is established, the server creates an output stream to the client (lines 32–33), increases the count (line 36), sends the count to the client (line 37), and writes the new count back to the file. This process continues in an infinite `while` loop to handle all clients.

LISTING 33.6 AppletClient.java

```
import java.io.*;
import java.net.*;
import javax.swing.*;

public class AppletClient extends JApplet {
  // Label for displaying the visit count
  private JLabel jlblCount = new JLabel();

  // Indicate if it runs as application
  private boolean isStandAlone = false;

  // Host name or IP address
  private String host = "localhost";

  /** Initialize the applet */
  public void init() {
    add(jlblCount);

    try {
      // Create a socket to connect to the server
      Socket socket;
      if (isStandAlone)
        socket = new Socket(host, 8000);
      else
        socket = new Socket(getCodeBase().getHost(), 8000);

      // Create an input stream to receive data from the server
      DataInputStream inputFromServer =
        new DataInputStream(socket.getInputStream());

      // Receive the count from the server and display it on label
      int count = inputFromServer.readInt();
      jlblCount.setText("You are visitor number " + count);

      // Close the stream
      inputFromServer.close();
    }
    catch (IOException ex) {
      ex.printStackTrace();
    }
  }
```

for standalone

for applet

receive count

```
43    /** Run the applet as an application */
44    public static void main(String[] args) {
45      // Create a frame
46      JFrame frame = new JFrame("Applet Client");
47
48      // Create an instance of the applet
49      AppletClient applet = new AppletClient();
50      applet.isStandAlone = true;
51
52      // Get host
53      if (args.length == 1) applet.host = args[0];
54
55      // Add the applet instance to the frame
56      frame.add(applet, java.awt.BorderLayout.CENTER);
57
58      // Invoke init() and start()
59      applet.init();
60      applet.start();
61
62      // Display the frame
63      frame.pack();
64      frame.setVisible(true);
65    }
66  }
```

The client is an applet. When it runs as an applet, it uses `getCodeBase().getHost()` (line 25) to return the IP address for the server. When it runs as an application, it passes the URL from the command line (line 53). If the URL is not passed from the command line, by default `localhost` is used for the URL (line 13).

The client creates a socket to connect to the server (lines 21–25), creates an input stream from the socket (lines 28–29), receives the count from the server (line 32), and displays it in the text field (line 33).

33.6 Sending and Receiving Objects

Key Point

A program can send and receive objects from another program.

In the preceding examples, you learned how to send and receive data of primitive types. You can also send and receive objects using `ObjectOutputStream` and `ObjectInputStream` on socket streams. To enable passing, the objects must be serializable. The following example demonstrates how to send and receive objects.

The example consists of three classes: StudentAddress.java (Listing 33.7), StudentClient.java (Listing 33.8), and StudentServer.java (Listing 33.9). The client program collects student information from a client and sends it to a server, as shown in Figure 33.11.

FIGURE 33.11 The client sends the student information in an object to the server.

The `StudentAddress` class contains the student information: name, street, city, state, and zip. The `StudentAddress` class implements the `Serializable` interface. Therefore, a `StudentAddress` object can be sent and received using the object output and input streams.

LISTING 33.7 StudentAddress.java

```
public class StudentAddress implements java.io.Serializable {
  private String name;
  private String street;
  private String city;
  private String state;
  private String zip;

  public StudentAddress(String name, String street, String city,
    String state, String zip) {
    this.name = name;
    this.street = street;
    this.city = city;
    this.state = state;
    this.zip = zip;
  }

  public String getName() {
    return name;
  }

  public String getStreet() {
    return street;
  }

  public String getCity() {
    return city;
  }

  public String getState() {
    return state;
  }

  public String getZip() {
    return zip;
  }
}
```

serialized

The client sends a **StudentAddress** object through an **ObjectOutputStream** on the output stream socket, and the server receives the **Student** object through the **ObjectInputStream** on the input stream socket, as shown in Figure 33.12. The client uses

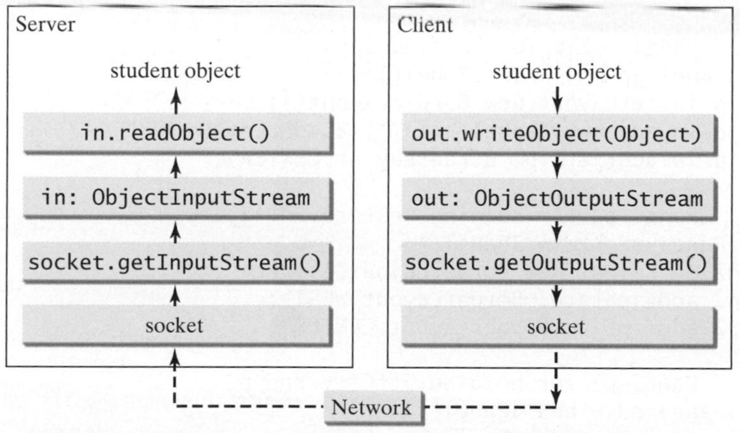

FIGURE 33.12 The client sends a **StudentAddress** object to the server.

the `writeObject` method in the `ObjectOutputStream` class to send data about a student to the server, and the server receives the student's information using the `readObject` method in the `ObjectInputStream` class. The server and client programs are given in Listings 33.8 and 33.9.

LISTING 33.8 StudentClient.java

create UI

```
import java.io.*;
import java.net.*;
import java.awt.*;
import java.awt.event.*;
import javax.swing.*;
import javax.swing.border.*;

public class StudentClient extends JApplet {
  private JTextField jtfName = new JTextField(32);
  private JTextField jtfStreet = new JTextField(32);
  private JTextField jtfCity = new JTextField(20);
  private JTextField jtfState = new JTextField(2);
  private JTextField jtfZip = new JTextField(5);

  // Button for sending a student's address to the server
  private JButton jbtRegister = new JButton("Register to the Server");

  // Indicate if it runs as application
  private boolean isStandAlone = false;

  // Host name or IP address
  String host = "localhost";

  public void init() {
    // Panel p1 for holding labels Name, Street, and City
    JPanel p1 = new JPanel();
    p1.setLayout(new GridLayout(3, 1));
    p1.add(new JLabel("Name"));
    p1.add(new JLabel("Street"));
    p1.add(new JLabel("City"));

    // Panel jpState for holding state
    JPanel jpState = new JPanel();
    jpState.setLayout(new BorderLayout());
    jpState.add(new JLabel("State"), BorderLayout.WEST);
    jpState.add(jtfState, BorderLayout.CENTER);

    // Panel jpZip for holding zip
    JPanel jpZip = new JPanel();
    jpZip.setLayout(new BorderLayout());
    jpZip.add(new JLabel("Zip"), BorderLayout.WEST);
    jpZip.add(jtfZip, BorderLayout.CENTER);

    // Panel p2 for holding jpState and jpZip
    JPanel p2 = new JPanel();
    p2.setLayout(new BorderLayout());
    p2.add(jpState, BorderLayout.WEST);
    p2.add(jpZip, BorderLayout.CENTER);

    // Panel p3 for holding jtfCity and p2
    JPanel p3 = new JPanel();
    p3.setLayout(new BorderLayout());
    p3.add(jtfCity, BorderLayout.CENTER);
```

```
    p3.add(p2, BorderLayout.EAST);

    // Panel p4 for holding jtfName, jtfStreet, and p3
    JPanel p4 = new JPanel();
    p4.setLayout(new GridLayout(3, 1));
    p4.add(jtfName);
    p4.add(jtfStreet);
    p4.add(p3);

    // Place p1 and p4 into StudentPanel
    JPanel studentPanel = new JPanel(new BorderLayout());
    studentPanel.setBorder(new BevelBorder(BevelBorder.RAISED));
    studentPanel.add(p1, BorderLayout.WEST);
    studentPanel.add(p4, BorderLayout.CENTER);

    // Add the student panel and button to the applet
    add(studentPanel, BorderLayout.CENTER);
    add(jbtRegister, BorderLayout.SOUTH);

    // Register listener
    jbtRegister.addActionListener(new ButtonListener());

    // Find the IP address of the Web server
    if (!isStandAlone)
      host = getCodeBase().getHost();
  }

  /** Handle button action */
  private class ButtonListener implements ActionListener {
    @Override
    public void actionPerformed(ActionEvent e) {
      try {
        // Establish connection with the server
        Socket socket = new Socket(host, 8000);

        // Create an output stream to the server
        ObjectOutputStream toServer =
          new ObjectOutputStream(socket.getOutputStream());

        // Get text field
        String name = jtfName.getText().trim();
        String street = jtfStreet.getText().trim();
        String city = jtfCity.getText().trim();
        String state = jtfState.getText().trim();
        String zip = jtfZip.getText().trim();

        // Create a StudentAddress object and send to the server
        StudentAddress s =
          new StudentAddress(name, street, city, state, zip);
        toServer.writeObject(s);
      }
      catch (IOException ex) {
        System.err.println(ex);
      }
    }
  }

  /** Run the applet as an application */
  public static void main(String[] args) {
    // Create a frame
```

register listener

get server name

server socket

output stream

send to server

```
        JFrame frame = new JFrame("Register Student Client");

        // Create an instance of the applet
        StudentClient applet = new StudentClient();
        applet.isStandAlone = true;

        // Get host
        if (args.length == 1) applet.host = args[0];

        // Add the applet instance to the frame
        frame.add(applet, BorderLayout.CENTER);

        // Invoke init() and start()
        applet.init();
        applet.start();

        // Display the frame
        frame.pack();
        frame.setVisible(true);
    }
}
```

LISTING 33.9 StudentServer.java

```
import java.io.*;
import java.net.*;

public class StudentServer {
  private ObjectOutputStream outputToFile;
  private ObjectInputStream inputFromClient;

  public static void main(String[] args) {
    new StudentServer();
  }

  public StudentServer() {
    try {
      // Create a server socket
      ServerSocket serverSocket = new ServerSocket(8000);
      System.out.println("Server started ");

      // Create an object output stream
      outputToFile = new ObjectOutputStream(
        new FileOutputStream("student.dat", true));

      while (true) {
        // Listen for a new connection request
        Socket socket = serverSocket.accept();

        // Create an input stream from the socket
        inputFromClient =
          new ObjectInputStream(socket.getInputStream());

        // Read from input
        Object object = inputFromClient.readObject();

        // Write to the file
        outputToFile.writeObject(object);
        System.out.println("A new student object is stored");
      }
```

server socket

output to file

connect to client

input stream

get from client

write to file

```
37      }
38      catch(ClassNotFoundException ex) {
39        ex.printStackTrace();
40      }
41      catch(IOException ex) {
42        ex.printStackTrace();
43      }
44      finally {
45        try {
46          inputFromClient.close();
47          outputToFile.close();
48        }
49        catch (Exception ex) {
50          ex.printStackTrace();
51        }
52      }
53    }
54  }
```

On the client side, when the user clicks the *Register to the Server* button, the client creates a socket to connect to the host (line 87), creates an `ObjectOutputStream` on the output stream of the socket (lines 90–91), and invokes the `writeObject` method to send the `StudentAddress` object to the server through the object output stream (line 103).

On the server side, when a client connects to the server, the server creates an `ObjectInputStream` on the input stream of the socket (lines 27–28), invokes the `readObject` method to receive the `StudentAddress` object through the object input stream (line 31), and writes the object to a file (line 34).

This program can run either as an applet or as an application. To run it as an application, the host name is passed as a command-line argument.

33.9 Can an applet connect to a server that is different from the machine where the applet is located?

33.10 How do you find the host name of an applet?

33.11 How do you send and receive an object?

33.7 Case Study: Distributed Tic-Tac-Toe Games

This section develops an applet that enables two players to play the tic-tac-toe game on the Internet.

In Section 18.9, Case Study: Developing a Tic-Tac-Toe Game, you developed an applet for a tic-tac-toe game that enables two players to play the game on the same machine. In this section, you will learn how to develop a distributed tic-tac-toe game using multithreads and networking with socket streams. A distributed tic-tac-toe game enables users to play on different machines from anywhere on the Internet.

You need to develop a server for multiple clients. The server creates a server socket and accepts connections from every two players to form a session. Each session is a thread that communicates with the two players and determines the status of the game. The server can establish any number of sessions, as shown in Figure 33.13.

For each session, the first client connecting to the server is identified as player 1 with token `X`, and the second client connecting is identified as player 2 with token `O`. The server notifies the players of their respective tokens. Once two clients are connected to it, the server starts a thread to facilitate the game between the two players by performing the steps repeatedly, as shown in Figure 33.14.

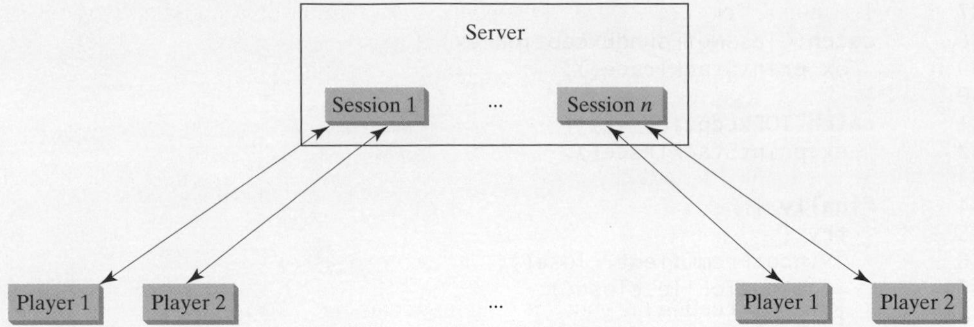

Figure 33.13 The server can create many sessions, each of which facilitates a tic-tac-toe game for two players.

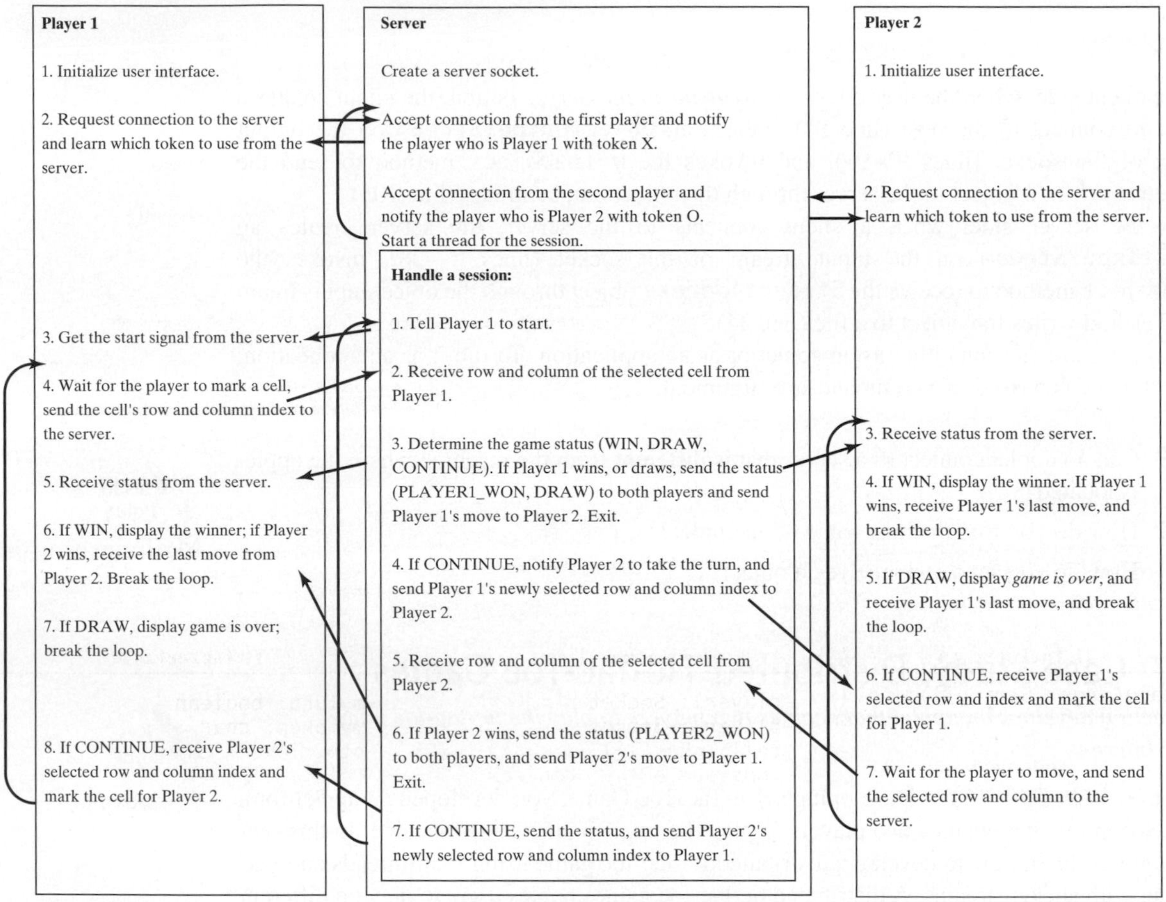

Player 1

1. Initialize user interface.

2. Request connection to the server and learn which token to use from the server.

3. Get the start signal from the server.

4. Wait for the player to mark a cell, send the cell's row and column index to the server.

5. Receive status from the server.

6. If WIN, display the winner; if Player 2 wins, receive the last move from Player 2. Break the loop.

7. If DRAW, display game is over; break the loop.

8. If CONTINUE, receive Player 2's selected row and column index and mark the cell for Player 2.

Server

Create a server socket.

Accept connection from the first player and notify the player who is Player 1 with token X.

Accept connection from the second player and notify the player who is Player 2 with token O. Start a thread for the session.

Handle a session:

1. Tell Player 1 to start.

2. Receive row and column of the selected cell from Player 1.

3. Determine the game status (WIN, DRAW, CONTINUE). If Player 1 wins, or draws, send the status (PLAYER1_WON, DRAW) to both players and send Player 1's move to Player 2. Exit.

4. If CONTINUE, notify Player 2 to take the turn, and send Player 1's newly selected row and column index to Player 2.

5. Receive row and column of the selected cell from Player 2.

6. If Player 2 wins, send the status (PLAYER2_WON) to both players, and send Player 2's move to Player 1. Exit.

7. If CONTINUE, send the status, and send Player 2's newly selected row and column index to Player 1.

Player 2

1. Initialize user interface.

2. Request connection to the server and learn which token to use from the server.

3. Receive status from the server.

4. If WIN, display the winner. If Player 1 wins, receive Player 1's last move, and break the loop.

5. If DRAW, display *game is over*, and receive Player 1's last move, and break the loop.

6. If CONTINUE, receive Player 1's selected row and index and mark the cell for Player 1.

7. Wait for the player to move, and send the selected row and column to the server.

Figure 33.14 The server starts a thread to facilitate communications between the two players.

The server does not have to be a graphical component, but creating it as a frame in which game information can be viewed is user-friendly. You can create a scroll pane to hold a text area in the frame and display game information in the text area. The server creates a thread to handle a game session when two players are connected to the server.

The client is responsible for interacting with the players. It creates a user interface with nine cells, and displays the game title and status to the players in the labels. The client class is very similar to the `TicTacToe` class presented in the case study in Section 18.9. However, the client in this example does not determine the game status (win or draw); it simply passes the moves to the server and receives the game status from the server.

Based on the foregoing analysis, you can create the following classes:

- `TicTacToeServer` serves all the clients in Listing 33.11.
- `HandleASession` facilitates the game for two players. This class is defined in TicTacToeServer.java.
- `TicTacToeClient` models a player in Listing 33.12.
- `Cell` models a cell in the game. It is an inner class in `TicTacToeClient`.
- `TicTacToeConstants` is an interface that defines the constants shared by all the classes in the example in Listing 33.10.

The relationships of these classes are shown in Figure 33.15.

LISTING 33.10 TicTacToeConstants.java

```
public interface TicTacToeConstants {
  public static int PLAYER1 = 1; // Indicate player 1
  public static int PLAYER2 = 2; // Indicate player 2
```

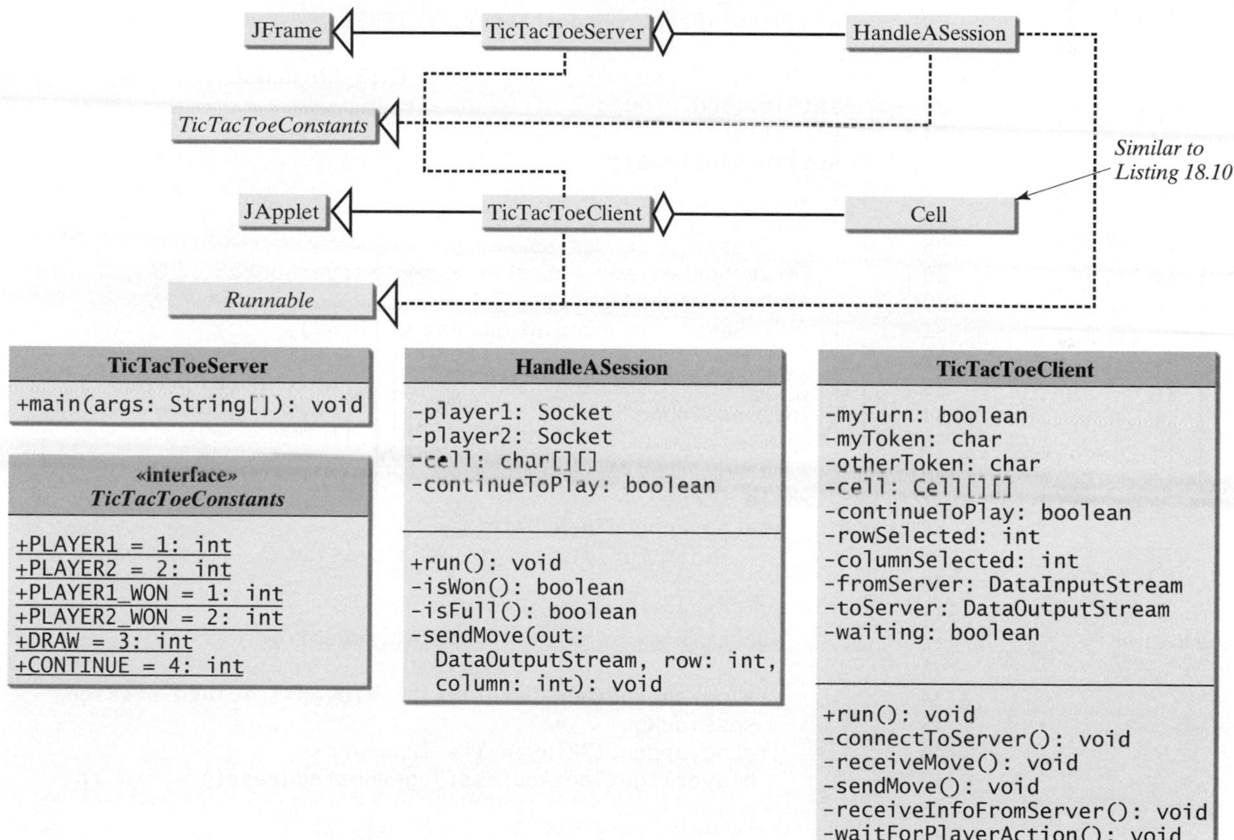

FIGURE 33.15 `TicTacToeServer` creates an instance of `HandleASession` for each session of two players. `TicTacToeClient` creates nine cells in the UI.

```
  public static int PLAYER1_WON = 1; // Indicate player 1 won
  public static int PLAYER2_WON = 2; // Indicate player 2 won
  public static int DRAW = 3; // Indicate a draw
  public static int CONTINUE = 4; // Indicate to continue
}
```

LISTING 33.11 TicTacToeServer.java

```
import java.io.*;
import java.net.*;
import javax.swing.*;
import java.awt.*;
import java.util.Date;

public class TicTacToeServer extends JFrame
    implements TicTacToeConstants {
  public static void main(String[] args) {
    TicTacToeServer frame = new TicTacToeServer();   // run server
  }

  public TicTacToeServer() {
    JTextArea jtaLog = new JTextArea();   // create UI

    // Create a scroll pane to hold text area
    JScrollPane scrollPane = new JScrollPane(jtaLog);

    // Add the scroll pane to the frame
    add(scrollPane, BorderLayout.CENTER);

    setDefaultCloseOperation(JFrame.EXIT_ON_CLOSE);
    setSize(300, 300);
    setTitle("TicTacToeServer");
    setVisible(true);

    try {
      // Create a server socket
      ServerSocket serverSocket = new ServerSocket(8000);   // server socket
      jtaLog.append(new Date() +
        ": Server started at socket 8000\n");

      // Number a session
      int sessionNo = 1;

      // Ready to create a session for every two players
      while (true) {
        jtaLog.append(new Date() +
          ": Wait for players to join session " + sessionNo + '\n');

        // Connect to player 1
        Socket player1 = serverSocket.accept();   // connect to client

        jtaLog.append(new Date() + ": Player 1 joined session " +
          sessionNo + '\n');
        jtaLog.append("Player 1's IP address" +
          player1.getInetAddress().getHostAddress() + '\n');

        // Notify that the player is Player 1
        new DataOutputStream(   // to player1
          player1.getOutputStream()).writeInt(PLAYER1);

```

```
        // Connect to player 2
        Socket player2 = serverSocket.accept();

        jtaLog.append(new Date() +
          ": Player 2 joined session " + sessionNo + '\n');
        jtaLog.append("Player 2's IP address" +
          player2.getInetAddress().getHostAddress() + '\n');

        // Notify that the player is Player 2
        new DataOutputStream(
          player2.getOutputStream()).writeInt(PLAYER2);

        // Display this session and increment session number
        jtaLog.append(new Date() + ": Start a thread for session " +
          sessionNo++ + '\n');

        // Create a new thread for this session of two players
        HandleASession task = new HandleASession(player1, player2);

        // Start the new thread
        new Thread(task).start();
      }
    }
    catch(IOException ex) {
      System.err.println(ex);
    }
  }
}

// Define the thread class for handling a new session for two players
class HandleASession implements Runnable, TicTacToeConstants {
  private Socket player1;
  private Socket player2;

  // Create and initialize cells
  private char[][] cell =  new char[3][3];

  private DataInputStream fromPlayer1;
  private DataOutputStream toPlayer1;
  private DataInputStream fromPlayer2;
  private DataOutputStream toPlayer2;

  // Continue to play
  private boolean continueToPlay = true;

  /** Construct a thread */
  public HandleASession(Socket player1, Socket player2) {
    this.player1 = player1;
    this.player2 = player2;

    // Initialize cells
    for (int i = 0; i < 3; i++)
      for (int j = 0; j < 3; j++)
        cell[i][j] = ' ';
  }

  @Override /** Implement the run() method for the thread */
  public void run() {
    try {
      // Create data input and output streams
```

to player2

a session for two players

```
      DataInputStream fromPlayer1 = new DataInputStream(
        player1.getInputStream());
      DataOutputStream toPlayer1 = new DataOutputStream(
        player1.getOutputStream());
      DataInputStream fromPlayer2 = new DataInputStream(
        player2.getInputStream());
      DataOutputStream toPlayer2 = new DataOutputStream(
        player2.getOutputStream());

      // Write anything to notify player 1 to start
      // This is just to let player 1 know to start
      toPlayer1.writeInt(1);

      // Continuously serve the players and determine and report
      // the game status to the players
      while (true) {
        // Receive a move from player 1
        int row = fromPlayer1.readInt();
        int column = fromPlayer1.readInt();
        cell[row][column] = 'X';

        // Check if Player 1 wins
        if (isWon('X')) {
          toPlayer1.writeInt(PLAYER1_WON);
          toPlayer2.writeInt(PLAYER1_WON);
          sendMove(toPlayer2, row, column);
          break; // Break the loop
        }
        else if (isFull()) { // Check if all cells are filled
          toPlayer1.writeInt(DRAW);
          toPlayer2.writeInt(DRAW);
          sendMove(toPlayer2, row, column);
          break;
        }
        else {
          // Notify player 2 to take the turn
          toPlayer2.writeInt(CONTINUE);

          // Send player 1's selected row and column to player 2
          sendMove(toPlayer2, row, column);
       }

        // Receive a move from Player 2
        row = fromPlayer2.readInt();
        column = fromPlayer2.readInt();
        cell[row][column] = 'O';

        // Check if Player 2 wins
        if (isWon('O')) {
          toPlayer1.writeInt(PLAYER2_WON);
          toPlayer2.writeInt(PLAYER2_WON);
          sendMove(toPlayer1, row, column);
          break;
        }
        else {
          // Notify player 1 to take the turn
          toPlayer1.writeInt(CONTINUE);

          // Send player 2's selected row and column to player 1
```

```
            sendMove(toPlayer1, row, column);
          }
        }
      }
      catch(IOException ex) {
        System.err.println(ex);
      }
    }

    /** Send the move to other player */
    private void sendMove(DataOutputStream out, int row, int column)
        throws IOException {
      out.writeInt(row); // Send row index
      out.writeInt(column); // Send column index
    }

    /** Determine if the cells are all occupied */
    private boolean isFull() {
      for (int i = 0; i < 3; i++)
        for (int j = 0; j < 3; j++)
          if (cell[i][j] == ' ')
            return false; // At least one cell is not filled

      // All cells are filled
      return true;
    }

    /** Determine if the player with the specified token wins */
    private boolean isWon(char token) {
      // Check all rows
      for (int i = 0; i < 3; i++)
        if ((cell[i][0] == token)
            && (cell[i][1] == token)
            && (cell[i][2] == token)) {
          return true;
        }

      /** Check all columns */
      for (int j = 0; j < 3; j++)
        if ((cell[0][j] == token)
            && (cell[1][j] == token)
            && (cell[2][j] == token)) {
          return true;
        }

      /** Check major diagonal */
      if ((cell[0][0] == token)
          && (cell[1][1] == token)
          && (cell[2][2] == token)) {
        return true;
      }

      /** Check subdiagonal */
      if ((cell[0][2] == token)
          && (cell[1][1] == token)
          && (cell[2][0] == token)) {
        return true;
      }

```

```
    /** All checked, but no winner */
    return false;
  }
}
```

LISTING 33.12 TicTacToeClient.java

create UI

```
import java.awt.*;
import java.awt.event.*;
import javax.swing.*;
import javax.swing.border.LineBorder;
import java.io.*;
import java.net.*;

public class TicTacToeClient extends JApplet
    implements Runnable, TicTacToeConstants {
  // Indicate whether the player has the turn
  private boolean myTurn = false;

  // Indicate the token for the player
  private char myToken = ' ';

  // Indicate the token for the other player
  private char otherToken = ' ';

  // Create and initialize cells
  private Cell[][] cell =  new Cell[3][3];

  // Create and initialize a title label
  private JLabel jlblTitle = new JLabel();

  // Create and initialize a status label
  private JLabel jlblStatus = new JLabel();

  // Indicate selected row and column by the current move
  private int rowSelected;
  private int columnSelected;

  // Input and output streams from/to server
  private DataInputStream fromServer;
  private DataOutputStream toServer;

  // Continue to play?
  private boolean continueToPlay = true;

  // Wait for the player to mark a cell
  private boolean waiting = true;

  // Indicate if it runs as application
  private boolean isStandAlone = false;

  // Host name or IP address
  private String host = "localhost";

  @Override /** Initialize UI */
  public void init() {
    // Panel p to hold cells
    JPanel p = new JPanel();
    p.setLayout(new GridLayout(3, 3, 0, 0));
```

```
    for (int i = 0; i < 3; i++)
      for (int j = 0; j < 3; j++)
        p.add(cell[i][j] = new Cell(i, j));

    // Set properties for labels and borders for labels and panel
    p.setBorder(new LineBorder(Color.black, 1));
    jlblTitle.setHorizontalAlignment(JLabel.CENTER);
    jlblTitle.setFont(new Font("SansSerif", Font.BOLD, 16));
    jlblTitle.setBorder(new LineBorder(Color.black, 1));
    jlblStatus.setBorder(new LineBorder(Color.black, 1));

    // Place the panel and the labels for the applet
    add(jlblTitle, BorderLayout.NORTH);
    add(p, BorderLayout.CENTER);
    add(jlblStatus, BorderLayout.SOUTH);

    // Connect to the server
    connectToServer();
  }

  private void connectToServer() {
    try {
      // Create a socket to connect to the server
      Socket socket;
      if (isStandAlone)
        socket = new Socket(host, 8000);
      else
        socket = new Socket(getCodeBase().getHost(), 8000);

      // Create an input stream to receive data from the server
      fromServer = new DataInputStream(socket.getInputStream());

      // Create an output stream to send data to the server
      toServer = new DataOutputStream(socket.getOutputStream());
    }
    catch (Exception ex) {
      System.err.println(ex);
    }

    // Control the game on a separate thread
    Thread thread = new Thread(this);
    thread.start();
  }

  @Override
  public void run() {
    try {
      // Get notification from the server
      int player = fromServer.readInt();

      // Am I player 1 or 2?
      if (player == PLAYER1) {
        myToken = 'X';
        otherToken = 'O';
        jlblTitle.setText("Player 1 with token 'X'");
        jlblStatus.setText("Waiting for player 2 to join");

        // Receive startup notification from the server
        fromServer.readInt(); // Whatever read is ignored

```

connect to server

standalone

applet

input from server

output to server

```
        // The other player has joined
        jlblStatus.setText("Player 2 has joined. I start first");

        // It is my turn
        myTurn = true;
      }
      else if (player == PLAYER2) {
        myToken = 'O';
        otherToken = 'X';
        jlblTitle.setText("Player 2 with token 'O'");
        jlblStatus.setText("Waiting for player 1 to move");
      }

      // Continue to play
      while (continueToPlay) {
        if (player == PLAYER1) {
          waitForPlayerAction(); // Wait for player 1 to move
          sendMove(); // Send the move to the server
          receiveInfoFromServer(); // Receive info from the server
        }
        else if (player == PLAYER2) {
          receiveInfoFromServer(); // Receive info from the server
          waitForPlayerAction(); // Wait for player 2 to move
          sendMove() ; // Send player 2's move to the server
        }
      }
    }
    catch (Exception ex) {
    }
  }

  /** Wait for the player to mark a cell */
  private void waitForPlayerAction() throws InterruptedException {
    while (waiting) {
      Thread.sleep(100);
    }

    waiting = true;
  }

  /** Send this player's move to the server */
  private void sendMove() throws IOException {
    toServer.writeInt(rowSelected); // Send the selected row
    toServer.writeInt(columnSelected); // Send the selected column
  }

  /** Receive info from the server */
  private void receiveInfoFromServer() throws IOException {
    // Receive game status
    int status = fromServer.readInt();

    if (status == PLAYER1_WON) {
      // Player 1 won, stop playing
      continueToPlay = false;
      if (myToken == 'X') {
        jlblStatus.setText("I won! (X)");
      }
      else if (myToken == 'O') {
```

```
          jlblStatus.setText("Player 1 (X) has won!");
          receiveMove();
        }
      }
      else if (status == PLAYER2_WON) {
        // Player 2 won, stop playing
        continueToPlay = false;
        if (myToken == 'O') {
          jlblStatus.setText("I won! (O)");
        }
        else if (myToken == 'X') {
          jlblStatus.setText("Player 2 (O) has won!");
          receiveMove();
        }
      }
      else if (status == DRAW) {
        // No winner, game is over
        continueToPlay = false;
        jlblStatus.setText("Game is over, no winner!");

        if (myToken == 'O') {
          receiveMove();
        }
      }
      else {
        receiveMove();
        jlblStatus.setText("My turn");
        myTurn = true; // It is my turn
      }
    }

    private void receiveMove() throws IOException {
      // Get the other player's move
      int row = fromServer.readInt();
      int column = fromServer.readInt();
      cell[row][column].setToken(otherToken);
    }

    // An inner class for a cell
    public class Cell extends JPanel {
      // Indicate the row and column of this cell in the board
      private int row;
      private int column;

      // Token used for this cell
      private char token = ' ';

      public Cell(int row, int column) {
        this.row = row;
        this.column = column;
        setBorder(new LineBorder(Color.black, 1)); // Set cell's border
        addMouseListener(new ClickListener()); // Register listener
      }

      /** Return token */
      public char getToken() {
        return token;
      }
```

model a cell

register listener

draw X

draw O

mouse listener

main method omitted

```

    /** Set a new token */
    public void setToken(char c) {
      token = c;
      repaint();
    }

    @Override /** Paint the cell */
    protected void paintComponent(Graphics g) {
      super.paintComponent(g);

      if (token == 'X') {
        g.drawLine(10, 10, getWidth() - 10, getHeight() - 10);
        g.drawLine(getWidth() - 10, 10, 10, getHeight() - 10);
      }
      else if (token == 'O') {
        g.drawOval(10, 10, getWidth() - 20, getHeight() - 20);
      }
    }

    /** Handle mouse click on a cell */
    private class ClickListener extends MouseAdapter {
      @Override
      public void mouseClicked(MouseEvent e) {
        // If cell is not occupied and the player has the turn
        if (token == ' ' && myTurn) {
          setToken(myToken);  // Set the player's token in the cell
          myTurn = false;
          rowSelected = row;
          columnSelected = column;
          jlblStatus.setText("Waiting for the other player to move");
          waiting = false; // Just completed a successful move
        }
      }
    }
  }
}
```

The server can serve any number of sessions simultaneously. Each session takes care of two players. The client can be a Java applet or a Java application. To run a client as a Java applet from a Web browser, the server must run from a Web server. Figures 33.16 and 33.17 show sample runs of the server and the clients.

FIGURE 33.16 `TicTacToeServer` accepts connection requests and creates sessions to serve pairs of players.

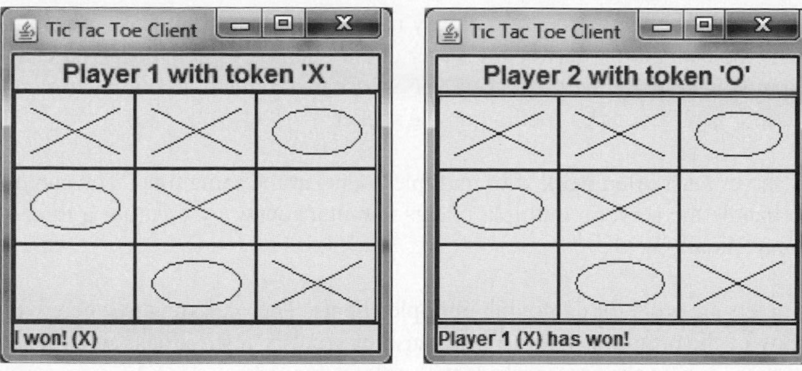

FIGURE 33.17 `TicTacToeClient` can run as an applet or an application.

The `TicTacToeConstants` interface defines the constants shared by all the classes in the project. Each class that uses the constants needs to implement the interface. Centrally defining constants in an interface is a common practice in Java. For example, all the constants shared by Swing classes are defined in `java.swing.SwingConstants`.

Once a session is established, the server receives moves from the players in alternation. Upon receiving a move from a player, the server determines the status of the game. If the game is not finished, the server sends the status (`CONTINUE`) and the player's move to the other player. If the game is won or a draw, the server sends the status (`PLAYER1_WON`, `PLAYER2_WON`, or `DRAW`) to both players.

The implementation of Java network programs at the socket level is tightly synchronized. An operation to send data from one machine requires an operation to receive data from the other machine. As shown in this example, the server and the client are tightly synchronized to send or receive data.

Check Point
MyProgrammingLab™

33.12 Will the program work if lines 48-49 in Listing 33.12 TicTacToeClient.java

```
@Override /** Initialize UI */
public void init() {
```

is changed to

```
public TicTacToeClient() {
```

33.13 If a player does not have the turn, but clicks on an empty cell, will the code in line 254 in Listing 33.12 be executed and will the code in line 255 be executed?

Chapter Summary

1. Java supports stream sockets and datagram sockets. *Stream sockets* use TCP (Transmission Control Protocol) for data transmission, whereas *datagram sockets* use UDP (User Datagram Protocol). Since TCP can detect lost transmissions and resubmit them, transmissions are lossless and reliable. UDP, in contrast, cannot guarantee lossless transmission.

2. To create a server, you must first obtain a server socket, using `new ServerSocket(port)`. After a server socket is created, the server can start to listen for connections, using the `accept()` method on the server socket. The client requests a connection to a server by using `new Socket(serverName, port)` to create a client socket.

3. Stream socket communication is very much like input/output stream communication after the connection between a server and a client is established. You can obtain an input stream using the `getInputStream()` method and an output stream using the `getOutputStream()` method on the socket.

4. A server must often work with multiple clients at the same time. You can use threads to handle the server's multiple clients simultaneously by creating a thread for each connection.

5. Applets are good for deploying multiple clients. They can run anywhere with a single copy of the program. However, because of security restrictions, an applet client can connect only to the server where the applet is loaded.

Test Questions

Do the test questions for this chapter online at www.cs.armstrong.edu/liang/intro9e/test.html.

MyProgrammingLab™

Programming Exercises

Section 33.2

*33.1 (*Loan server*) Write a server for a client. The client sends loan information (annual interest rate, number of years, and loan amount) to the server (see Figure 33.18a). The server computes monthly payment and total payment and sends them back to the client (see Figure 33.18b). Name the client Exercise33_1Client and the server Exercise33_1Server.

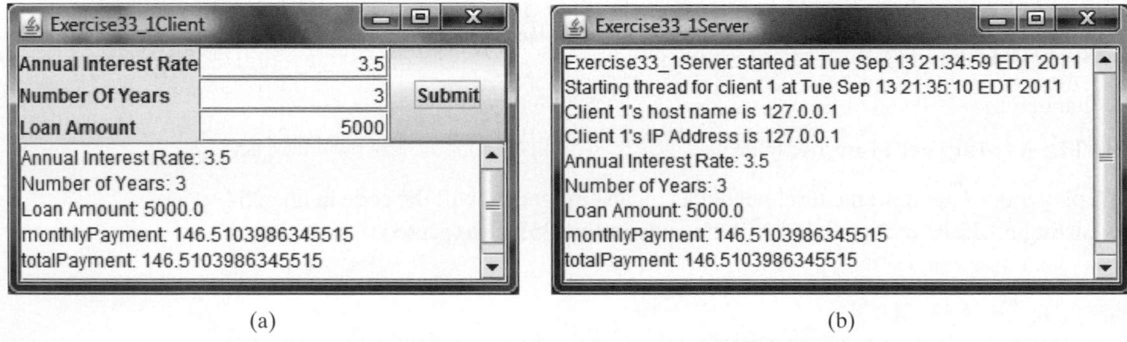

Figure 33.18 The client in (a) sends the annual interest rate, number of years, and loan amount to the server and receives the monthly payment and total payment from the server in (b).

33.2 (*Network I/O using* `Scanner` *and* `PrintWriter`) Rewrite the server and client programs in Listings 33.1 and 33.2 using a `Scanner` for input and a `PrintWriter` for output. Name the server Exercise33_2Server and the client Exercise33_2Client.

Sections 33.3–33.4

*33.3 (*Loan server for multiple clients*) Revise Exercise 33.1 to write a server for multiple clients.

Section 33.5

33.4 (*Web visit count*) Section 33.5, Applet Clients, created an applet that shows the number of visits made to a Web page. The count is stored in a file on the server side. Every time the page is visited or reloaded, the applet sends a request to the server, and the server increases the count and sends it to the applet. The count is stored using a random-access file. When the applet is loaded, the server reads the count from the file, increases it, and saves it back to the file. Rewrite the program to improve its performance. Read the count from the file when the server starts, and save the count to the file when the server stops, using the *Stop* button, as shown in Figure 33.19. When the server is alive, use a variable to store the count. Name the client Exercise33_4Client and the server Exercise33_4Server. The client program should be the same as in Listing 33.6. Rewrite the server as a GUI application with a *Stop* button that exits the server.

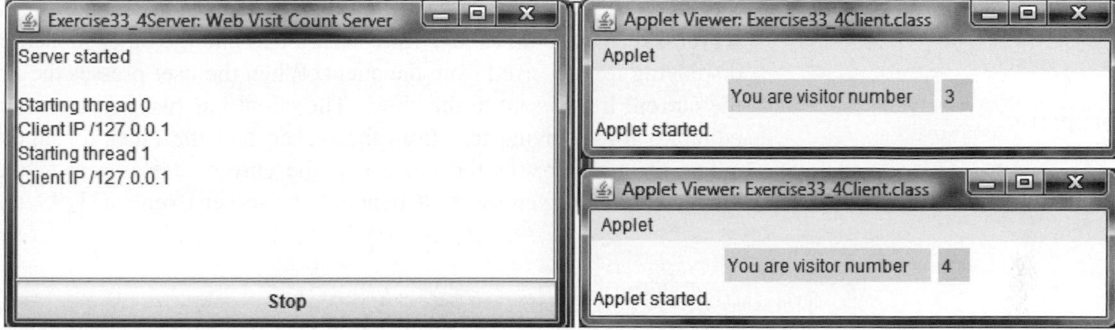

FIGURE 33.19 The applet displays how many times this Web page has been accessed. The server stores the count.

33.5 (*Create a stock ticker in an applet*) Write an applet like the one in Programming Exercise 18.16. Assume that the applet gets the stock index from a file named **Ticker.txt** stored on the Web server. Enable the applet to run as a standalone.

Section 33.6

33.6 (*Display and add addresses*) Develop a client/server application to view and add addresses, as shown in Figure 33.20.

- Define an `Address` class to hold the name, street, city, state, and zip in an object.
- The user can use the buttons *First*, *Next*, *Previous*, and *Last* to view an address, and the *Add* button to add a new address.
- Limit the concurrent connections to two clients.

Name the client Exercise33_6Client and the server Exercise33_6Server.

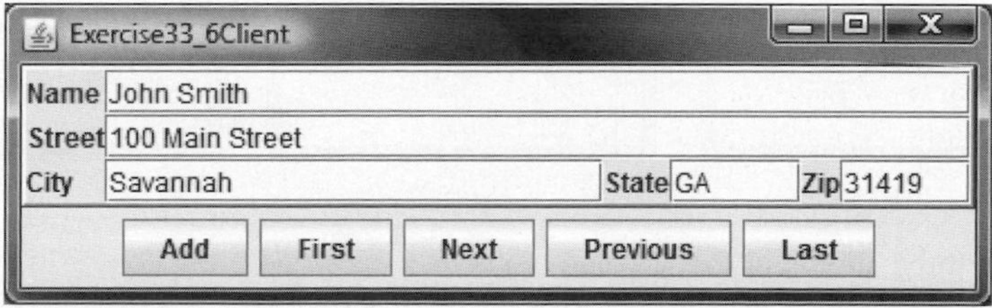

FIGURE 33.20 You can view and add an address in this applet.

***33.7** (*Transfer last 100 numbers in an array*) Programming Exercise 24.12 retrieves the last 100 prime numbers from a file **PrimeNumbers.dat**. Write a client program that requests the server to send the last 100 prime numbers in an array. Name the server program Exercise33_7Server and the client program Exercise33_7Client. Assume that the numbers of the `long` type are stored in **PrimeNumbers.dat** in binary format.

***33.8** (*Transfer last 100 numbers in an `ArrayList`*) Programming Exercise 24.12 retrieves the last 100 prime numbers from a file **PrimeNumbers.dat**. Write a client program that requests the server to send the last 100 prime numbers in an `ArrayList`. Name the server program Exercise33_8Server and the client program Exercise33_8Client. Assume that the numbers of the `long` type are stored in **PrimeNumbers.dat** in binary format.

Section 33.7

****33.9** (*Chat*) Write a program that enables two users to chat. Implement one user as the server (Figure 33.21a) and the other as the client (Figure 33.21b). The server has two text areas: one for entering text and the other (noneditable) for displaying text received from the client. When the user presses the *Enter* key, the current line is sent to the client. The client has two text areas: one (non-editable) for receiving text from the server, and the other for entering text. When the user presses the *Enter* key, the current line is sent to the server. Name the client Exercise33_9Client and the server Exercise33_9Server.

FIGURE 33.21 The server and client send text to and receive text from each other.

*****33.10** (*Multiple client chat*) Write a program that enables any number of clients to chat. Implement one server that serves all the clients, as shown in Figure 33.22. Name the client Exercise33_10Client and the server Exercise33_10Server.

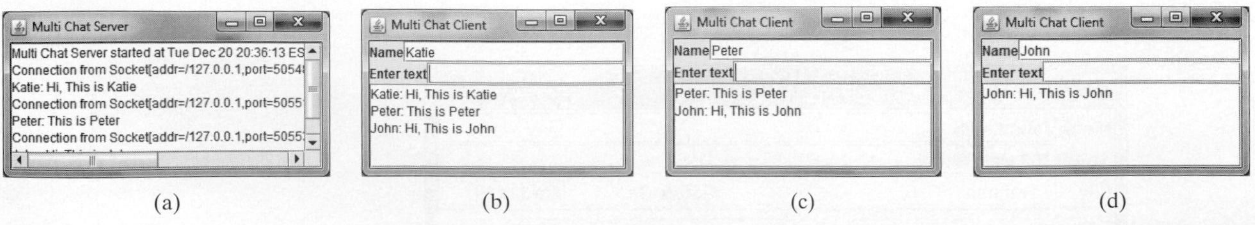

FIGURE 33.22 The server starts in (a) with three clients in (b), (c), and (d).

CHAPTER

34

Java Database Programming

Objectives

- To understand the concepts of databases and database management systems (§34.2).
- To understand the relational data model: relational data structures, constraints, and languages (§34.2).
- To use SQL to create and drop tables and to retrieve and modify data (§34.3).
- To learn how to load a driver, connect to a database, execute statements, and process result sets using JDBC (§34.4).
- To use prepared statements to execute precompiled SQL statements (§34.5).
- To use callable statements to execute stored SQL procedures and functions (§34.6).
- To explore database metadata using the `DatabaseMetaData` and `ResultSetMetaData` interfaces (§34.7).

34.1 Introduction

Java provides the API for developing database applications that works with any relational database systems.

You may have heard a lot about database systems. Database systems are everywhere. Your social security information is stored in a database by the government. If you shop online, your purchase information is stored in a database by the company. If you attend a university, your academic information is stored in a database by the university. Database systems not only store data, they also provide means of accessing, updating, manipulating, and analyzing data. Your social security information is updated periodically, and you can register for courses online. Database systems play an important role in society and in commerce.

This chapter introduces database systems, the SQL language, and how to develop database applications using Java. If you already know SQL, you can skip Sections 34.2 and 34.3.

34.2 Relational Database Systems

SQL is the standard database language for defining and accessing databases.

database system

A *database system* consists of a database, the software that stores and manages data in the database, and the application programs that present data and enable the user to interact with the database system, as shown in Figure 34.1.

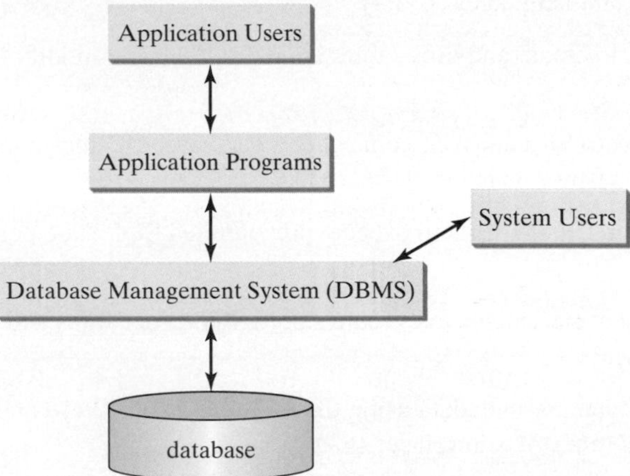

FIGURE 34.1 A database system consists of data, database management software, and application programs.

A *database* is a repository of data that form information. When you purchase a database system—such as MySQL, Oracle, IBM's DB2 and Informix, Microsoft SQL Server, or Sybase—from a software vendor, you actually purchase the software comprising a *database management system* (DBMS). Database management systems are designed for use by professional programmers and are not suitable for ordinary customers. Application programs are built on top of the DBMS for customers to access and update the database. Thus, application programs can be viewed as the *interfaces* between the database system and its users. Application programs may be standalone GUI applications or Web applications, and may access several different database systems in the network, as shown in Figure 34.2.

DBMS

Most of today's database systems are *relational database systems*. They are based on the relational data model, which has three key components: structure, integrity, and language.

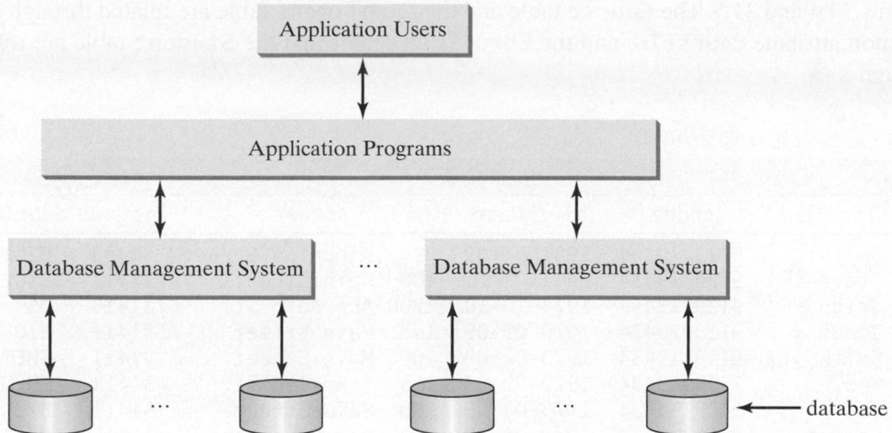

FIGURE 34.2 An application program can access multiple database systems.

Structure defines the representation of the data. *Integrity* imposes constraints on the data. *Language* provides the means for accessing and manipulating data.

34.2.1 Relational Structures

relational model

The relational model is built around a simple and natural structure. A *relation* is actually a table that consists of nonduplicate rows. Tables are easy to understand and easy to use. The relational model provides a simple yet powerful way to represent data.

tuple

attribute

A row of a table represents a *record*, and a column of a table represents the *value of a single attribute* of the record. In relational database theory, a row is called a *tuple* and a column is called an *attribute*. Figure 34.3 shows a sample table that stores information about the courses offered by a university. The table has eight tuples, and each tuple has five attributes.

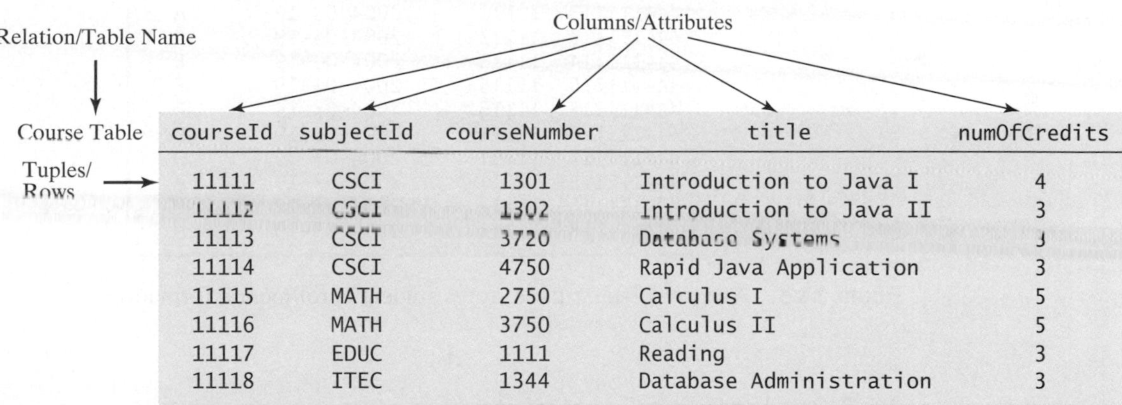

courseId	subjectId	courseNumber	title	numOfCredits
11111	CSCI	1301	Introduction to Java I	4
11112	CSCI	1302	Introduction to Java II	3
11113	CSCI	3720	Database Systems	3
11114	CSCI	4750	Rapid Java Application	3
11115	MATH	2750	Calculus I	5
11116	MATH	3750	Calculus II	5
11117	EDUC	1111	Reading	3
11118	ITEC	1344	Database Administration	3

FIGURE 34.3 A table has a table name, column names, and rows.

Tables describe the relationship among data. Each row in a table represents a record of related data. For example, "11111", "CSCI", "1301", "Introduction to Java I", and "4" are related to form a record (the first row in Figure 34.3) in the `Course` table. Just as data in the same row are related, so too data in different tables may be related through common attributes. Suppose the database has two other tables, `Student` and `Enrollment`, as shown in

Figures 34.4 and 34.5. The Course table and the Enrollment table are related through their common attribute courseId, and the Enrollment table and the Student table are related through ssn.

Student Table

ssn	firstName	mi	lastName	phone	birthDate	street	zipCode	deptID
444111110	Jacob	R	Smith	9129219434	1985-04-09	99 Kingston Street	31435	BIOL
444111111	John	K	Stevenson	9129219434	null	100 Main Street	31411	BIOL
444111112	George	K	Smith	9129213454	1974-10-10	1200 Abercorn St.	31419	CS
444111113	Frank	E	Jones	9125919434	1970-09-09	100 Main Street	31411	BIOL
444111114	Jean	K	Smith	9129219434	1970-02-09	100 Main Street	31411	CHEM
444111115	Josh	R	Woo	7075989434	1970-02-09	555 Franklin St.	31411	CHEM
444111116	Josh	R	Smith	9129219434	1973-02-09	100 Main Street	31411	BIOL
444111117	Joy	P	Kennedy	9129229434	1974-03-19	103 Bay Street	31412	CS
444111118	Toni	R	Peterson	9129229434	1964-04-29	103 Bay Street	31412	MATH
444111119	Patrick	R	Stoneman	9129229434	1969-04-29	101 Washington St.	31435	MATH
444111120	Rick	R	Carter	9125919434	1986-04-09	19 West Ford St.	31411	BIOL

Figure 34.4 A Student table stores student information.

Enrollment Table

ssn	courseId	dateRegistered	grade
444111110	11111	2004-03-19	A
444111110	11112	2004-03-19	B
444111110	11113	2004-03-19	C
444111111	11111	2004-03-19	D
444111111	11112	2004-03-19	F
444111111	11113	2004-03-19	A
444111112	11114	2004-03-19	B
444111112	11115	2004-03-19	C
444111112	11116	2004-03-19	D
444111113	11111	2004-03-19	A
444111113	11113	2004-03-19	A
444111114	11115	2004-03-19	B
444111115	11115	2004-03-19	F
444111115	11116	2004-03-19	F
444111116	11111	2004-03-19	D
444111117	11111	2004-03-19	D
444111118	11111	2004-03-19	A
444111118	11112	2004-03-19	D
444111118	11113	2004-03-19	B

Figure 34.5 An Enrollment table stores student enrollment information.

34.2.2 Integrity Constraints

integrity constraint

An *integrity constraint* imposes a condition that all the legal values in a table must satisfy. Figure 34.6 shows an example of some integrity constraints in the Subject and Course tables.

In general, there are three types of constraints: domain constraints, primary key constraints, and foreign key constraints. *Domain constraints* and *primary key constraints* are known as *intrarelational constraints*, meaning that a constraint involves only one relation. The *foreign key constraint* is *interrelational*, meaning that a constraint involves more than one relation.

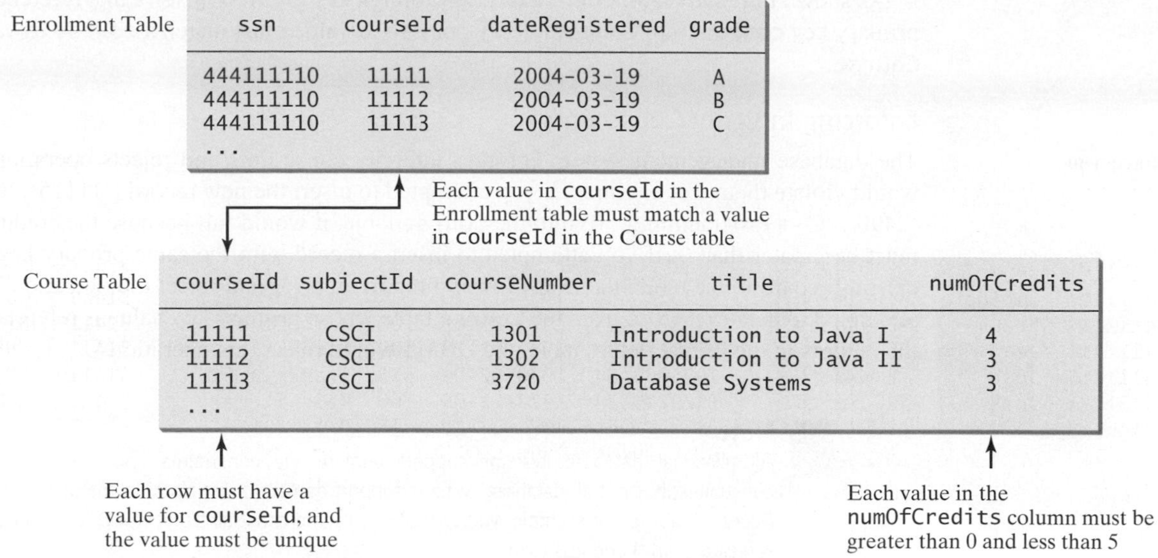

FIGURE 34.6 The **Enrollment** table and the **Course** table have integrity constraints.

Domain Constraints

Domain constraints specify the permissible values for an attribute. Domains can be specified using standard data types, such as integers, floating-point numbers, fixed-length strings, and variant-length strings. The standard data type specifies a broad range of values. Additional constraints can be specified to narrow the ranges. For example, you can specify that the **numOfCredits** attribute (in the **Course** table) must be greater than 0 and less than 5. You can also specify whether an attribute can be **null**, which is a special value in a database meaning unknown or not applicable. As shown in the **Student** table, **birthDate** may be **null**.

domain constraint

Primary Key Constraints

To understand *primary keys*, it is helpful to know superkeys, keys, and candidate keys. A *superkey* is an attribute or a set of attributes that uniquely identifies the relation. That is, no two tuples have the same values on a superkey. By definition, a relation consists of a set of distinct tuples. The set of all attributes in the relation forms a superkey.

primary key constraint

superkey

A *key* **K** is a minimal superkey, meaning that any proper subset of **K** is not a superkey. A relation can have several keys. In this case, each of the keys is called a *candidate key*. The *primary key* is one of the candidate keys designated by the database designer. The primary key is often used to identify tuples in a relation. As shown in Figure 34.6, **courseId** is the primary key in the **Course** table.

Foreign Key Constraints

In a *relational database*, data are related. Tuples in a relation are related, and tuples in different relations are related through their common attributes. Informally speaking, the common attributes are foreign keys. The *foreign key constraints* define the relationships among relations.

relational database

foreign key constraint

Formally, a set of attributes *FK* is a *foreign key* in a relation *R* that references relation *T* if it satisfies the following two rules:

- The attributes in *FK* have the same domain as the primary key in *T*.
- A nonnull value on *FK* in *R* must match a primary key value in *T*.

As shown in Figure 34.6, **courseId** is the foreign key in **Enrollment** that references the primary key **courseId** in **Course**. Every **courseId** value must match a **courseId** value in **Course**.

Enforcing Integrity Constraints

auto enforcement

The database management system enforces integrity constraints and rejects operations that would violate them. For example, if you attempted to insert the new record ('11115', 'CSCI', '2490', 'C++ Programming', 0) into the **Course** table, it would fail because the credit hours must be greater than **0**; if you attempted to insert a record with the same primary key as an existing record in the table, the DBMS would report an error and reject the operation; if you attempted to delete a record from the **Course** table whose primary key value is referenced by the records in the **Enrollment** table, the DBMS would reject this operation.

Note

All relational database systems support primary key constraints and foreign key constraints, but not all database systems support domain constraints. In the Microsoft Access database, for example, you cannot specify the constraint that **numOfCredits** is greater than **0** and less than **5**.

MyProgrammingLab™

34.1 What are superkeys, candidate keys, and primary keys?

34.2 What is a foreign key?

34.3 Can a relation have more than one primary key or foreign key?

34.4 Does a foreign key need to be a primary key in the same relation?

34.5 Does a foreign key need to have the same name as its referenced primary key?

34.6 Can a foreign key value be null?

34.3 SQL

Structured Query Language (SQL) *is the* language *for defining tables and integrity constraints and for accessing and manipulating data.*

SQL

database language

SQL (pronounced "S-Q-L" or "sequel") is the universal language for accessing relational database systems. Application programs may allow users to access a database without directly using SQL, but these applications themselves must use SQL to access the database. This section introduces some basic SQL commands.

standard SQL

Note

There are many relational database management systems. They share the common SQL language but do not all support every feature of SQL. Some systems have their own extensions to SQL. This section introduces standard SQL supported by all systems.

SQL can be used on MySQL, Oracle, Sybase, IBM DB2, IBM Informix, Borland InterBase, MS Access, or any other relational database system. This chapter uses MySQL to demonstrate SQL and uses MySQL, Access, and Oracle to demonstrate Java database programming. The Companion Web site contains the following supplements on how to install and use three popular databases: MySQL, Oracle, and Access:

MySQL Tutorial

Oracle Tutorial

Access Tutorial

- Supplement IV.B: Tutorial for MySQL
- Supplement IV.C: Tutorial for Oracle
- Supplement IV.D: Tutorial for Microsoft Access

34.3.1 Creating a User Account on MySQL

Assume that you have installed MySQL 5 with the default configuration. To match all the examples in this book, you should create a user named *scott* with the password *tiger*. You can perform the administrative tasks using the MySQL Workbench or using the command line. MySQL Workbench is a GUI tool for managing MySQL databases. Here are the steps to create a user from the command line:

1. From the DOS command prompt, type

   ```
   mysql -uroot -p
   ```

   You will be prompted to enter the root password, as shown in Figure 34.7.

2. At the mysql prompt, enter

   ```
   use mysql;
   ```

3. To create user **scott** with password **tiger**, enter

   ```
   create user 'scott'@'localhost' identified by 'tiger';
   ```

4. To grant privileges to **scott**, enter

   ```
   grant select, insert, update, delete, create, create view, drop,
     execute, references on *.* to 'scott'@'localhost';
   ```

   - If you want to enable remote access of the account from any IP address, enter

     ```
     grant all privileges on *.* to 'scott'@'%'
       identified by 'tiger';
     ```

   - If you want to restrict the account's remote access to just one particular IP address, enter

     ```
     grant all privileges on *.* to 'scott'@'ipAddress'
       identified by 'tiger';
     ```

5. Enter

   ```
   exit;
   ```

   to exit the MySQL console.

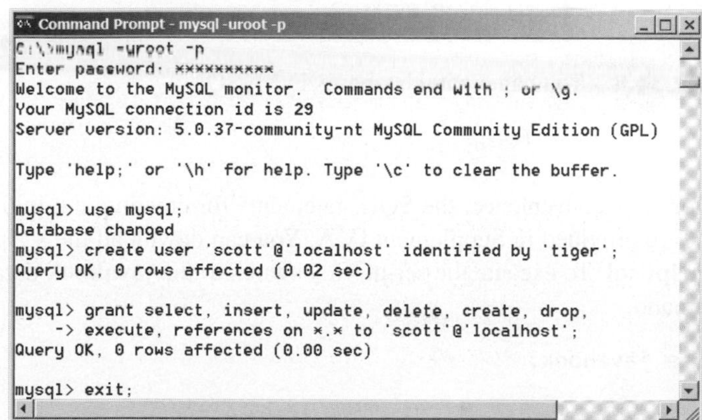

FIGURE 34.7 You can access a MySQL database server from the command window.

Note

stop mysql
start mysql

On Windows, your MySQL database server starts every time your computer starts. You can stop it by typing the command `net stop mysql` and restart it by typing the command `net start mysql`.

By default, the server contains two databases named **mysql** and **test**. The **mysql** database contains the tables that store information about the server and its users. This database is intended for the server administrator to use. For example, the administrator can use it to create users and grant or revoke user privileges. Since you are the owner of the server installed on your system, you have full access to the mysql database. However, you should not create user tables in the mysql database. You can use the **test** database to store data or create new databases. You can also create a new database using the command `create database` ***`databasename`*** or delete an existing database using the command `drop database` ***`databasename`***.

34.3.2 Creating a Database

To match the examples in the book, you should create a database named **javabook**. Here are the steps to create it:

1. From the DOS command prompt, type

   ```
   mysql -uscott -ptiger
   ```

   to login to mysql, as shown in Figure 34.8.
2. At the mysql prompt, enter

   ```
   create database javabook;
   ```

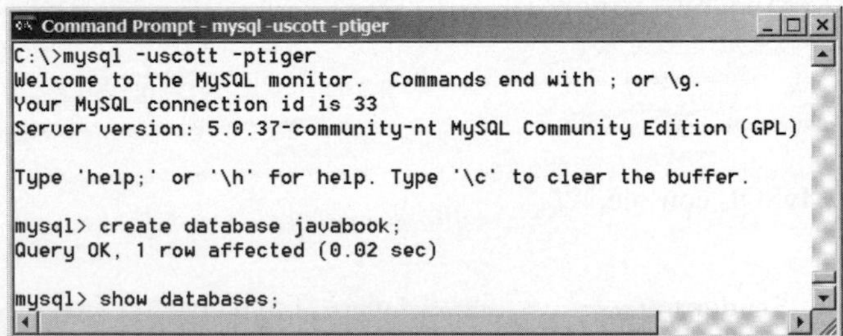

FIGURE 34.8 You can create databases in MySQL.

For your convenience, the SQL statements for creating and initializing tables used in the book are provided in Supplement IV.A. You can download the script for MySQL and save it to **script.sql**. To execute the script, first switch to the **javabook** database using the following command:

```
use javabook;
```

and then type

run script file

```
source script.sql;
```

as shown in Figure 34.9.

```
Welcome to the MySQL monitor.  Commands end with ; or \g.
Your MySQL connection id is 2
Server version: 5.1.35-community MySQL Community Server (GPL)

Type 'help;' or '\h' for help. Type '\c' to clear the current input statement.

mysql> create database javabook;
Query OK, 1 row affected (0.03 sec)

mysql> use javabook;
Database changed
mysql> source script.sql;
```

FIGURE 34.9 You can run SQL commands in a script file.

Note

You can populate the javabook database using the script from Supplement IV.A.

populating database

34.3.3 Creating and Dropping Tables

Tables are the essential objects in a database. To create a table, use the `create table` statement to specify a table name, attributes, and types, as in the following example:

create table

```
create table Course (
  courseId char(5),
  subjectId char(4) not null,
  courseNumber integer,
  title varchar(50) not null,
  numOfCredits integer,
  primary key (courseId)
);
```

This statement creates the `Course` table with attributes `courseId`, `subjectId`, `courseNumber`, `title`, and `numOfCredits`. Each attribute has a data type that specifies the type of data stored in the attribute. `char(5)` specifies that `courseId` consists of five characters. `varchar(50)` specifies that `title` is a variant-length string with a maximum of 50 characters. `integer` specifies that `courseNumber` is an integer. The primary key is `courseId`.

The tables `Student` and `Enrollment` can be created as follows:

```
create table Student (
  ssn char(9),
  firstName varchar(25),
  mi char(1),
  lastName varchar(25),
  birthDate date,
  street varchar(25),
  phone char(11),
  zipCode char(5),
  deptId char(4),
  primary key (ssn)
);
```

```
create table Enrollment (
  ssn char(9),
  courseId char(5),
  dateRegistered date,
  grade char(1),
  primary key (ssn, courseId),
  foreign key (ssn) references
    Student(ssn),
  foreign key (courseId) references
    Course(courseId)
);
```

Note

SQL keywords are not case sensitive. This book adopts the following naming conventions: Tables are named in the same way as Java classes, and attributes are named in the same way as Java variables. SQL keywords are named in the same way as Java keywords.

naming convention

If a table is no longer needed, it can be dropped permanently using the **drop table** command. For example, the following statement drops the **Course** table:

drop table

```
drop table Course;
```

If a table to be dropped is referenced by other tables, you have to drop the other tables first. For example, if you have created the tables **Course**, **Student**, and **Enrollment** and want to drop **Course**, you have to first drop **Enrollment**, because **Course** is referenced by **Enrollment**.

Figure 34.10 shows how to enter the **create table** statement from the MySQL console.

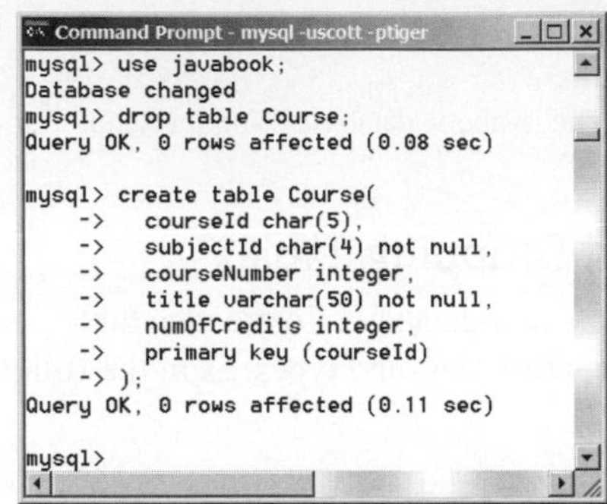

FIGURE 34.10 A table is created using the **create table** statement.

If you make typing errors, you have to retype the whole command. To avoid retyping, you can save the command in a file, and then run the command from the file. To do so, create a text file to contain commands, named, for example, **test.sql**. You can create the text file using any text editor, such as Notepad, as shown in Figure 34.11a. To comment a line, precede it with two dashes. You can now run the script file by typing **source test.sql** from the SQL command prompt, as shown in Figure 34.11b.

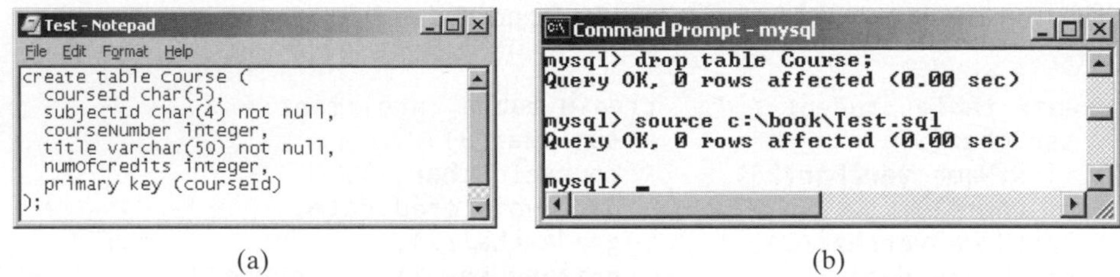

FIGURE 34.11 (a) You can use Notepad to create a text file for SQL commands. (b) You can run the SQL commands in a script file from MySQL.

34.3.4 Simple Insert, Update, and Delete

Once a table is created, you can insert data into it. You can also update and delete records. This section introduces simple insert, update, and delete statements.

The syntax to insert a record into a table is:

```
insert into tableName [(column1, column2, ..., column)]
values (value1, value2, ..., valuen);
```

For example, the following statement inserts a record into the **Course** table. The new record has the **courseId** '11113', **subjectId** 'CSCI', **courseNumber** '3720', **title** 'Database Systems', and **creditHours** 3.

```
insert into Course (courseId, subjectId, courseNumber, title, numOfCredits)
values ('11113', 'CSCI', '3720', 'Database Systems', 3);
```

The column names are optional. If they are omitted, all the column values for the record must be entered, even though the columns have default values. String values are case sensitive and enclosed inside single quotation marks in SQL.

The syntax to update a table is:

```
update tableName
set column1 = newValue1 [, column2 = newValue2, ...]
[where condition];
```

For example, the following statement changes the **numOfCredits** for the course whose **title** is Database Systems to 4.

```
update Course
set numOfCredits = 4
where title = 'Database Systems';
```

The syntax to delete records from a table is:

```
delete [from] tableName
[where condition];
```

For example, the following statement deletes the Database Systems course from the **Course** table:

```
delete Course
where title = 'Database Systems';
```

The following statement deletes all the records from the **Course** table:

```
delete Course;
```

34.3.5 Simple Queries

To retrieve information from tables, use a **select** statement with the following syntax:

```
select column-list
from table-list
[where condition];
```

The **select** clause lists the columns to be selected. The **from** clause refers to the tables involved in the query. The optional **where** clause specifies the conditions for the selected rows.

Query 1: Select all the students in the CS department, as shown in Figure 34.12.

```
select firstName, mi, lastName
from Student
where deptId = 'CS';
```

```
mysql> select firstName, mi, lastName
    -> from Student
    -> where deptId = 'CS';
+-----------+------+----------+
| firstName | mi   | lastName |
+-----------+------+----------+
| George    | R    | Heintz   |
| Joy       | P    | Kennedy  |
+-----------+------+----------+
2 rows in set (0.16 sec)

mysql>
```

FIGURE 34.12 The result of the **select** statement is displayed in the MySQL console.

34.3.6 Comparison and Boolean Operators

SQL has six comparison operators, as shown in Table 34.1, and three Boolean operators, as shown in Table 34.2.

TABLE 34.1 Comparison Operators

Operator	*Description*
=	Equal to
<> or !=	Not equal to
<	Less than
<=	Less than or equal to
>	Greater than
>=	Greater than or equal to

TABLE 34.2 Boolean Operators

Operator	*Description*
not	Logical negation
and	Logical conjunction
or	Logical disjunction

Note

The comparison and Boolean operators in SQL have the same meanings as in Java. In SQL the **equal to** operator is =, but in Java it is ==. In SQL the **not equal to** operator is <> or !=, but in Java it is !=. The **not**, **and**, and **or** operators are **!**, **&&** (**&**), and **||** (**|**) in Java.

Query 2: Get the names of the students who are in the CS dept and live in the ZIP code 31411.

```
select firstName, mi, lastName
from Student
where deptId = 'CS' and zipCode = '31411';
```

Note

To select all the attributes from a table, you don't have to list all the attribute names in the select clause. Instead, you can just use an *asterisk* (*), which stands for all the attributes. For example, the following query displays all the attributes of the students who are in the CS dept and live in ZIP code 31411:

```
select *
from Student
where deptId = 'CS' and zipCode = '31411';
```

34.3.7 The `like`, `between-and`, and `is null` Operators

SQL has a `like` operator that can be used for pattern matching. The syntax to check whether a string `s` has a pattern `p` is

`s like p` or `s not like p`

You can use the wildcard characters `%` (percent symbol) and _ (underline symbol) in the pattern `p`. `%` matches zero or more characters, and _ matches any single character in `s`. For example, `lastName like '_mi%'` matches any string whose second and third letters are `m` and `i`. `lastName not like '_mi%'` excludes any string whose second and third letters are `m` and `i`.

Note

In earlier versions of MS Access, the wildcard character is *, and the character ? matches any single character.

The `between-and` operator checks whether a value `v` is between two other values, `v1` and `v2`, using the following syntax:

`v between v1 and v2` or `v not between v1 and v2`

`v between v1 and v2` is equivalent to `v >= v1 and v <= v2`, and `v not between v1 and v2` is equivalent to `v < v1 or v > v2`.

The `is null` operator checks whether a value `v` is `null` using the following syntax:

`v is null` or `v is not null`

Query 3: Get the Social Security numbers of the students whose grades are between 'C' and 'A'.

```
select ssn
from Enrollment
where grade between 'C' and 'A';
```

34.3.8 Column Alias

When a query result is displayed, SQL uses the column names as column headings. Usually the user gives abbreviated names for the columns, and the columns cannot have spaces when the table is created. Sometimes it is desirable to give more descriptive names in the result heading. You can use the column aliases with the following syntax:

```
select columnName [as] alias
```

Query 4: Get the last name and ZIP code of the students in the CS department. Display the column headings as "Last Name" for lastName and "Zip Code" for zipCode. The query result is shown in Figure 34.13.

```
Command Prompt - mysql
mysql> select lastName as "Last Name", zipCode as "Zip Code"
    -> from Student
    -> where deptId = 'CS';
+-----------+----------+
| Last Name | Zip Code |
+-----------+----------+
| Heintz    | 31419    |
| Kennedy   | 31412    |
+-----------+----------+
2 rows in set (0.00 sec)

mysql>
```

FIGURE 34.13 You can use a column alias in the display.

```
select lastName as "Last Name", zipCode as "Zip Code"
from Student
where deptId = 'CS';
```

Note

The **as** keyword is optional in MySQL and Oracle, but it is required in MS Access.

34.3.9 The Arithmetic Operators

You can use the arithmetic operators * (multiplication), / (division), + (addition), and - (subtraction) in SQL.

Query 5: Assume that a credit hour is 50 minutes of lectures, and get the total minutes for each course with the subject CSCI. The query result is shown in Figure 34.14.

```
select title, 50 * numOfCredits as "Lecture Minutes Per Week"
from Course
where subjectId = 'CSCI';
```

```
Command Prompt - mysql
mysql> select title, 50 * numOfCredits as "Lecture Minutes Per Week"
    -> from Course
    -> where subjectId = 'CSCI';
+-------------------------+--------------------------+
| title                   | Lecture Minutes Per Week |
+-------------------------+--------------------------+
| Intro to Java I         |                      200 |
| Intro to Java II        |                      150 |
| Database Systems        |                      150 |
| Rapid Java Application  |                      150 |
+-------------------------+--------------------------+
4 rows in set (0.00 sec)

mysql>
```

FIGURE 34.14 You can use arithmetic operators in SQL.

34.3.10 Displaying Distinct Tuples

SQL provides the **distinct** keyword, which can be used to eliminate duplicate tuples in the result. Figure 34.15a displays all the subject IDs used by the courses and Figure 34.15b displays all the distinct subject IDs used by the courses using the following statement.

```
select distinct subjectId as "Subject ID"
from Course;
```

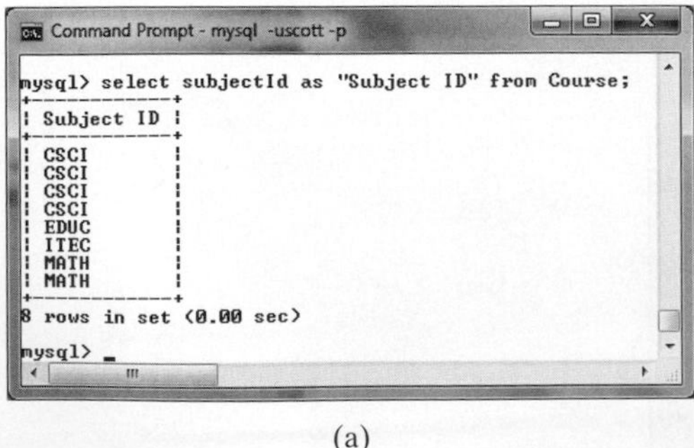

(a)

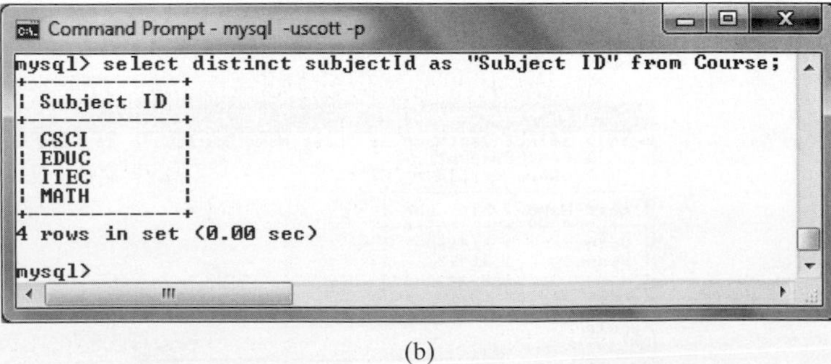

(b)

FIGURE 34.15 (a) The duplicate tuples are displayed. (b) The distinct tuples are displayed.

When there is more than one column in the `select` clause, the `distinct` keyword applies to the whole tuple in the result. For example, the following statement displays all tuples with distinct `subjectId` and `title`, as shown in Figure 34.16. Note that some tuples may have the same `subjectId`, but different `title`. These tuples are distinct.

```
select distinct subjectId, title
from Course;
```

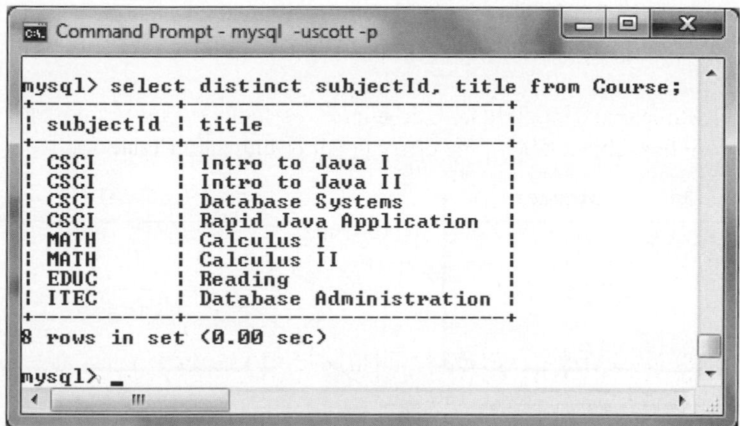

FIGURE 34.16 The keyword `distinct` applies to the entire tuple.

34.3.11 Displaying Sorted Tuples

SQL provides the `order by` clause to sort the output using the following syntax:

```
select column-list
from table-list
[where condition]
[order by columns-to-be-sorted];
```

In the syntax, `columns-to-be-sorted` specifies a column or a list of columns to be sorted. By default, the order is ascending. To sort in descending order, append the `desc` keyword. You could also append the `asc` keyword after `columns-to-be-sorted`, but it is not necessary. When multiple columns are specified, the rows are sorted based on the first column, then the rows with the same values on the first column are sorted based on the second column, and so on.

Query 6: List the full names of the students in the CS department, ordered primarily on their last names in descending order and secondarily on their first names in ascending order. The query result is shown in Figure 34.17.

```
Command Prompt - mysql
mysql> select lastName, firstName, deptId
    -> from Student
    -> where deptId = 'CS'
    -> order by lastName desc, firstName asc;
+----------+-----------+--------+
| lastName | firstName | deptId |
+----------+-----------+--------+
| Kennedy  | Joy       | CS     |
| Heintz   | George    | CS     |
+----------+-----------+--------+
2 rows in set (0.02 sec)

mysql> _
```

FIGURE 34.17 You can sort results using the `order by` clause.

```
select lastName, firstName, deptId
from Student
where deptId = 'CS'
order by lastName desc, firstName asc;
```

34.3.12 Joining Tables

Often you need to get information from multiple tables, as demonstrated in the next query.

Query 7: List the courses taken by student Jacob Smith. To solve this query, you need to join tables `Student` and `Enrollment`, as shown in Figure 34.18.

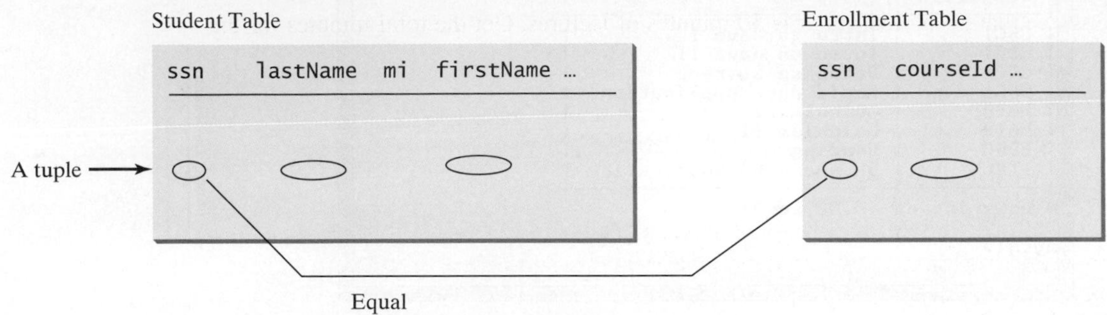

FIGURE 34.18 `Student` and `Enrollment` are joined on `ssn`.

You can write the query in SQL:

```
select distinct lastName, firstName, courseId
from Student, Enrollment
where Student.ssn = Enrollment.ssn and
  lastName = 'Smith' and firstName = 'Jacob';
```

The tables `Student` and `Enrollment` are listed in the `from` clause. The query examines every pair of rows, each made of one item from `Student` and another from `Enrollment`, and selects the pairs that satisfy the condition in the `where` clause. The rows in `Student` have the last name, Smith, and the first name, Jacob, and both rows from `Student` and `Enrollment` have the same `ssn` values. For each pair selected, `lastName` and `firstName` from `Student` and `courseId` from `Enrollment` are used to produce the result, as shown in Figure 34.19. `Student` and `Enrollment` have the same attribute `ssn`. To distinguish them in a query, use `Student.ssn` and `Enrollment.ssn`.

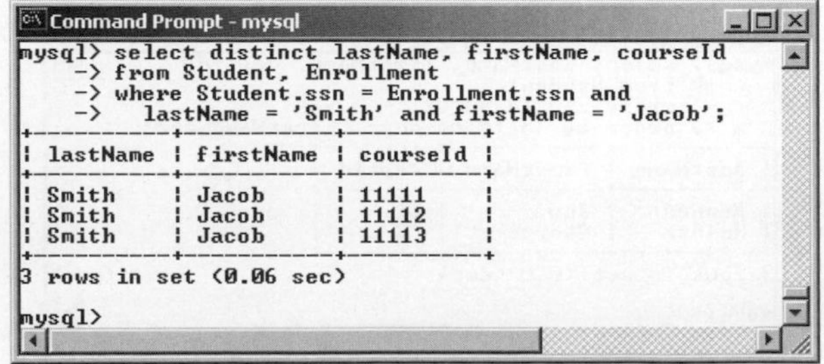

FIGURE 34.19 Query 7 demonstrates queries involving multiple tables.

For more features of SQL, see Supplement IV.H and Supplement IV.I.

Check Point
MyProgrammingLab™

34.7 Create the tables `Course`, `Student`, and `Enrollment` using the `create table` statements in Section 34.3.3, Creating and Dropping Tables. Insert rows into the `Course`, `Student`, and `Enrollment` tables using the data in Figures 34.3, 34.4, and 34.5.

34.8 List all CSCI courses with at least four credit hours.

34.9 List all students whose last names contain the letter *e* two times.

34.10 List all students whose birthdays are null.

34.11 List all students who take Math courses.

34.12 List the number of courses in each subject.

34.13 Assume that each credit hour is 50 minutes of lectures. Get the total minutes for the courses that each student takes.

34.4 JDBC

JDBC is the Java API for accessing relational database.

The Java API for developing Java database applications is called *JDBC*. JDBC is the trademarked name of a Java API that supports Java programs that access relational databases. JDBC is not an acronym, but it is often thought to stand for Java Database Connectivity.

JDBC provides Java programmers with a uniform interface for accessing and manipulating a wide range of relational databases. Using the JDBC API, applications written in the Java programming language can execute SQL statements, retrieve results, present data in a user-friendly interface, and propagate changes back to the database. The JDBC API can also be used to interact with multiple data sources in a distributed, heterogeneous environment.

The relationships between Java programs, JDBC API, JDBC drivers, and relational databases are shown in Figure 34.20. The JDBC API is a set of Java interfaces and classes used to write Java programs for accessing and manipulating relational databases. Since a JDBC driver serves as the interface to facilitate communications between JDBC and a proprietary database, JDBC drivers are database specific and are normally provided by the database vendors. You need MySQL JDBC drivers to access the MySQL database, and Oracle JDBC drivers to

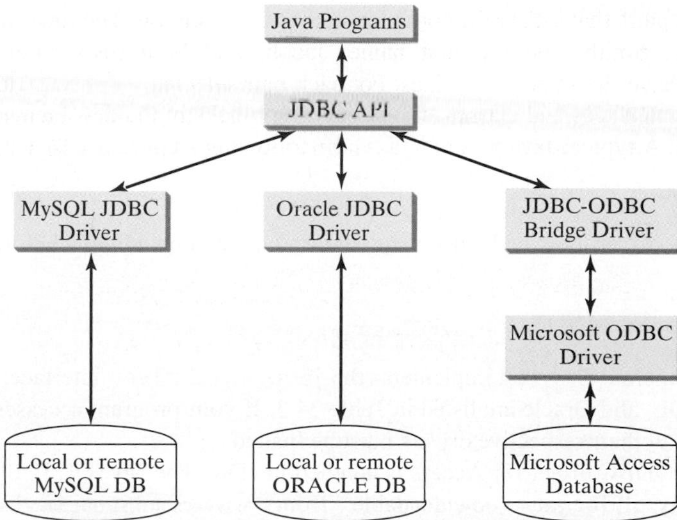

FIGURE 34.20 Java programs access and manipulate databases through JDBC drivers.

access the Oracle database. For the Access database, use the JDBC-ODBC bridge driver included in the JDK. ODBC is a technology developed by Microsoft for accessing databases on the Windows platform. An ODBC driver is preinstalled on Windows. The JDBC-ODBC bridge driver allows a Java program to access any ODBC data source.

34.4.1 Developing Database Applications Using JDBC

The JDBC API is a Java application program interface to generic SQL databases that enables Java developers to develop DBMS-independent Java applications using a uniform interface.

The JDBC API consists of classes and interfaces for establishing connections with databases, sending SQL statements to databases, processing the results of SQL statements, and obtaining database metadata. Four key interfaces are needed to develop any database application using Java: `Driver`, `Connection`, `Statement`, and `ResultSet`. These interfaces define a framework for generic SQL database access. The JDBC API defines these interfaces, and the JDBC driver vendors provide the implementation for the interfaces. Programmers use these interfaces.

The relationship of these interfaces is shown in Figure 34.21. A JDBC application loads an appropriate driver using the `Driver` interface, connects to the database using the `Connection` interface, creates and executes SQL statements using the `Statement` interface, and processes the result using the `ResultSet` interface if the statements return results. Note that some statements, such as SQL data definition statements and SQL data modification statements, do not return results.

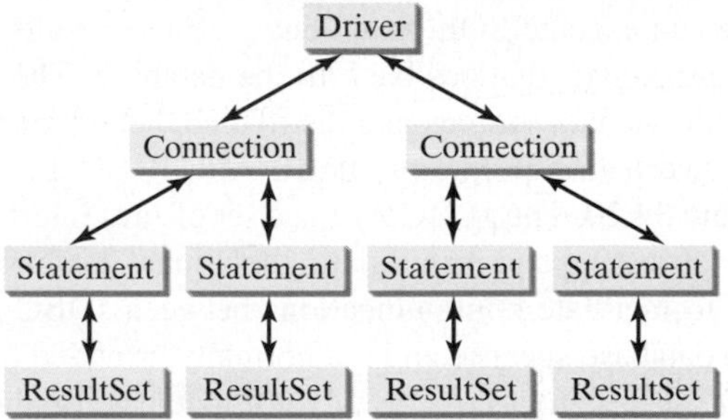

FIGURE 34.21 JDBC classes enable Java programs to connect to the database, send SQL statements, and process results.

The JDBC interfaces and classes are the building blocks in the development of Java database programs. A typical Java program takes the following steps to access a database.

1. Loading drivers.

An appropriate driver must be loaded using the statement shown below before connecting to a database.

```
Class.forName("JDBCDriverClass");
```

A driver is a concrete class that implements the `java.sql.Driver` interface. The drivers for Access, MySQL, and Oracle are listed in Table 34.3. If your program accesses several different databases, all their respective drivers must be loaded.

mysqljdbc.jar

The JDBC-ODBC driver for Access is bundled in JDK. The MySQL JDBC driver is contained in **mysqljdbc.jar** (downloadable from www.cs.armstrong.edu/liang/intro9e/book/lib/mysqljdbc.jar). The Oracle JDBC driver is contained in ojdbc6.jar (downloadable from www.cs.armstrong.edu/liang/intro9e/book/lib/ojdbc6.jar). To use the MySQL and Oracle drivers,

TABLE 34.3 JDBC Drivers

Database	*Driver Class*	*Source*
Access	`sun.jdbc.odbc.JdbcOdbcDriver`	Already in JDK
MySQL	`com.mysql.jdbc.Driver`	Companion Web site
Oracle	`oracle.jdbc.driver.OracleDriver`	Companion Web site

you have to add **mysqljdbc.jar** and **ojdbc6.jar** in the classpath using the following DOS command on Windows: ojdbc6.jar

```
set classpath=%classpath%;c:\book\mysqljdbc.jar;c:\book\ojdbc6.jar
```

If you use an IDE such as Eclipse or NetBeans, you need to add these jar files into the library in the IDE.

Note

`com.mysql.jdbc.Driver` is a class in **mysqljdbc.jar**, and `oracle.jdbc.driver.OracleDriver` is a class in **ojdbc6.jar. mysqljdbc.jar** and **ojdbc6.jar** contain many classes to support the driver. These classes are used by JDBC, but not directly by JDBC programmers. When you use a class explicitly in the program, it is automatically loaded by the JVM. The driver classes, however, are not used explicitly in the program, so you have to write the code to tell the JVM to load them. why load a driver?

Note

Java 6 supports automatic driver discovery, so you don't have to load the driver explicitly. At the time of this writing, however, this feature is not supported for all database drivers. To be safe, load the driver explicitly. automatic driver discovery

2. Establishing connections.

To connect to a database, use the static method `getConnection(databaseURL)` in the `DriverManager` class, as follows:

```
Connection connection = DriverManager.getConnection(databaseURL);
```

where `databaseURL` is the unique identifier of the database on the Internet. Table 34.4 lists the URL patterns for the Access, MySQL, and Oracle databases.

TABLE 34.4 JDBC URLs

Database	*URL Pattern*
Access	`jdbc:odbc:dataSource`
MySQL	`jdbc:mysql://hostname/dbname`
Oracle	`jdbc:oracle:thin:@hostname:port#:oracleDBSID`

For an ODBC data source, the `databaseURL` is `jdbc:odbc:dataSource`. An ODBC data source can be created using the ODBC Data Source Administrator on Windows. See Supplement IV.D, Tutorial for Microsoft Access, on how to create an ODBC data source for an Access database. connect Access DB

Suppose a data source named ExampleMDBDataSource has been created for an Access database. The following statement creates a Connection object:

```
Connection connection = DriverManager.getConnection
  ("jdbc:odbc:ExampleMDBDataSource");
```

The databaseURL for a MySQL database specifies the host name and database name to locate a database. For example, the following statement creates a Connection object for the local MySQL database javabook with username *scott* and password *tiger*:

connect MySQL DB

```
Connection connection = DriverManager.getConnection
  ("jdbc:mysql://localhost/javabook", "scott", "tiger");
```

Recall that by default MySQL contains two databases named *mysql* and *test*. Section 34.3.2, Creating a Database, created a custom database named javabook. We will use javabook in the examples.

The databaseURL for an Oracle database specifies the *hostname*, the *port#* where the database listens for incoming connection requests, and the *oracleDBSID* database name to locate a database. For example, the following statement creates a Connection object for the Oracle database on liang.armstrong.edu with the username *scott* and password *tiger*:

connect Oracle DB

```
Connection connection = DriverManager.getConnection
  ("jdbc:oracle:thin:@liang.armstrong.edu:1521:orcl",
   "scott", "tiger");
```

3. Creating statements.

If a Connection object can be envisioned as a cable linking your program to a database, an object of Statement can be viewed as a cart that delivers SQL statements for execution by the database and brings the result back to the program. Once a Connection object is created, you can create statements for executing SQL statements as follows:

```
Statement statement = connection.createStatement();
```

4. Executing statements.

SQL data definition language (DDL) and update statements can be executed using executeUpdate(String sql), and an SQL query statement can be executed using executeQuery(String sql). The result of the query is returned in ResultSet. For example, the following code executes the SQL statement create table Temp (col1 char(5), col2 char(5)):

```
statement.executeUpdate
  ("create table Temp (col1 char(5), col2 char(5))");
```

This next code executes the SQL query select firstName, mi, lastName from Student where lastName = 'Smith':

```
// Select the columns from the Student table
ResultSet resultSet = statement.executeQuery
  ("select firstName, mi, lastName from Student where lastName "
    + " = 'Smith'");
```

5. Processing ResultSet.

The ResultSet maintains a table whose current row can be retrieved. The initial row position is null. You can use the next method to move to the next row and the various get methods to retrieve values from a current row. For example, the following code displays all the results from the preceding SQL query.

```
// Iterate through the result and print the student names
while (resultSet.next())
  System.out.println(resultSet.getString(1) + " " +
    resultSet.getString(2) + " " + resultSet.getString(3));
```

The `getString(1)`, `getString(2)`, and `getString(3)` methods retrieve the column values for `firstName`, `mi`, and `lastName`, respectively. Alternatively, you can use `getString("firstName")`, `getString("mi")`, and `getString("lastName")` to retrieve the same three column values. The first execution of the `next()` method sets the current row to the first row in the result set, and subsequent invocations of the `next()` method set the current row to the second row, third row, and so on, to the last row.

Listing 34.1 is a complete example that demonstrates connecting to a database, executing a simple query, and processing the query result with JDBC. The program connects to a local MySQL database and displays the students whose last name is `Smith`.

LISTING 34.1 SimpleJDBC.java

```
 1 import java.sql.*;
 2
 3 public class SimpleJdbc {
 4   public static void main(String[] args)
 5       throws SQLException, ClassNotFoundException {
 6     // Load the JDBC driver
 7     Class.forName("com.mysql.jdbc.Driver");
 8     System.out.println("Driver loaded");
 9
10     // Connect to a database
11     Connection connection = DriverManager.getConnection
12       ("jdbc:mysql://localhost/javabook" , "scott", "tiger");
13     System.out.println("Database connected");
14
15     // Create a statement
16     Statement statement = connection.createStatement();
17
18     // Execute a statement
19     ResultSet resultSet = statement.executeQuery
20       ("select firstName, mi, lastName from Student where lastName "
21       + " = 'Smith'");
22
23     // Iterate through the result and print the student names
24     while (resultSet.next())
25       System.out.println(resultSet.getString(1) + "\t" +
26         resultSet.getString(2) + "\t" + resultSet.getString(3));
27
28     // Close the connection
29     connection.close();
30   }
31 }
```

load driver

connect database

create statement

execute statement

get result

close connection

The statement in line 7 loads a JDBC driver for MySQL, and the statement in lines 11–13 connects to a local MySQL database. You can change them to connect to an Access or Oracle database. The program creates a `Statement` object (line 16), executes an SQL statement and returns a `ResultSet` object (lines 19–21), and retrieves the query result from the `ResultSet` object (lines 24–26). The last statement (line 29) closes the connection and releases resources related to the connection.

Note

If you run this program from the DOS prompt, specify the appropriate driver in the classpath, as shown in Figure 34.22.

run from DOS prompt

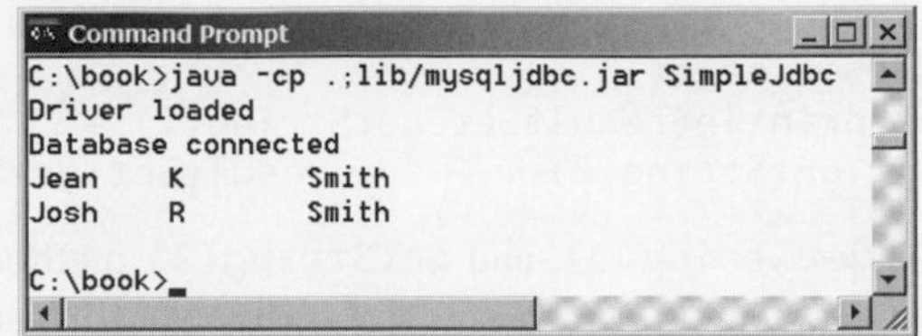

FIGURE 34.22 You must include the driver file to run Java database programs.

The classpath directory and jar files are separated by commas. The period (`.`) represents the current directory. For convenience, the driver files are placed under the **lib** directory.

the semicolon issue

Caution

Do not use a semicolon (`;`) to end the Oracle SQL command in a Java program. The semicolon may not work with the Oracle JDBC drivers. It does work, however, with the other drivers used in the book.

auto commit

Note

The `Connection` interface handles transactions and specifies how they are processed. By default, a new connection is in autocommit mode, and all its SQL statements are executed and committed as individual transactions. The commit occurs when the statement completes or the next execute occurs, whichever comes first. In the case of statements returning a result set, the statement completes when the last row of the result set has been retrieved or the result set has been closed. If a single statement returns multiple results, the commit occurs when all the results have been retrieved. You can use the `setAutoCommit(false)` method to disable autocommit, so that all SQL statements are grouped into one transaction that is terminated by a call to either the `commit()` or the `rollback()` method. The `rollback()` method undoes all the changes made by the transaction.

34.4.2 Accessing a Database from a Java Applet

If you are using the JDBC-ODBC bridge driver, your program cannot run as an applet from a Web browser because the ODBC driver contains non-Java native code. The JDBC drivers for MySQL and Oracle are written in Java and can run from the JVM in a Web browser. This section gives an example that demonstrates connecting to a database from a Java applet. The applet lets the user enter the SSN and the course ID to find a student's grade, as shown in Figure 34.23. The code in Listing 34.2 uses the MySQL database on the localhost.

FIGURE 34.23 A Java applet can access the database on the server.

LISTING 34.2 FindGrade.java

```
import javax.swing.*;
import java.sql.*;
import java.awt.*;
import java.awt.event.*;

public class FindGrade extends JApplet {
  private JTextField jtfSSN = new JTextField(9);
  private JTextField jtfCourseId = new JTextField(5);
  private JButton jbtShowGrade = new JButton("Show Grade");

  // Statement for executing queries
  private Statement stmt;

  /** Initialize the applet */
  public void init() {
    // Initialize database connection and create a Statement object
    initializeDB();

    jbtShowGrade.addActionListener(new ActionListener() {
      @Override
      public void actionPerformed(ActionEvent e) {
        jbtShowGrade_actionPerformed(e);
      }
    });

    JPanel jPanel1 = new JPanel();
    jPanel1.add(new JLabel("SSN"));
    jPanel1.add(jtfSSN);
    jPanel1.add(new JLabel("Course ID"));
    jPanel1.add(jtfCourseId);
    jPanel1.add(jbtShowGrade);

    add(jPanel1, BorderLayout.NORTH);
  }

  private void initializeDB() {
    try {
      // Load the JDBC driver
      Class.forName("com.mysql.jdbc.Driver");
//        Class.forName("oracle.jdbc.driver.OracleDriver");
      System.out.println("Driver loaded");

      // Establish a connection
      Connection connection = DriverManager.getConnection
        ("jdbc:mysql://localhost/javabook", "scott", "tiger");
//      ("jdbc:oracle:thin:@liang.armstrong.edu:1521:orcl",
//       "scott", "tiger");
      System.out.println("Database connected");

      // Create a statement
      stmt = connection.createStatement();
    }
    catch (Exception ex) {
      ex.printStackTrace();
    }
  }

  private void jbtShowGrade_actionPerformed(ActionEvent e) {
```

button listener

load driver

Oracle driver commented

connect to MySQL database

connect to Oracle commented

create statement

```
59        String ssn = jtfSSN.getText();
60        String courseId = jtfCourseId.getText();
61        try {
62          String queryString = "select firstName, mi, " +
63            "lastName, title, grade from Student, Enrollment, Course " +
64            "where Student.ssn = '" + ssn + "' and Enrollment.courseId "
65            + "= '" + courseId +
66            "' and Enrollment.courseId = Course.courseId " +
67            " and Enrollment.ssn = Student.ssn";
68
69          ResultSet rset = stmt.executeQuery(queryString);
70
71          if (rset.next()) {
72            String firstName = rset.getString(1);
73            String mi = rset.getString(2);
74            String lastName = rset.getString(3);
75            String title = rset.getString(4);
76            String grade = rset.getString(5);
77
78            // Display result in a dialog box
79            JOptionPane.showMessageDialog(null, firstName + " " + mi +
80              " " + lastName + "'s grade on course " + title + " is " +
81              grade);
82          } else {
83            // Display result in a dialog box
84            JOptionPane.showMessageDialog(null, "Not found");
85          }
86        }
87        catch (SQLException ex) {
88          ex.printStackTrace();
89        }
90      }
91    }
```

execute statement

show result

main method omitted

The `initializeDB()` method (lines 36–56) loads the MySQL driver (line 39), connects to the MySQL database on host `liang.armstrong.edu` (lines 44–45) and creates a statement (line 51).

You can run the applet as a standalone from the `main` method (note that the listing for the `main` method is omitted for all the applets in the book for brevity) or test the applet using the appletviewer utility, as shown in Figure 34.23. If this applet is deployed on the server where the database is located, any client on the Internet can run it from a Web browser. Since the client may not have a MySQL driver, you should specify the driver in the archive attribute in the applet tag, as follows:

```
<applet
  code = "FindGrade"
  archive = "FindGrade.jar, lib/mysqljdbc.jar"
  width = 380
  height = 80
>
</applet>
```

Note

create archive file

For information on how to *create an archive file*, see Supplement III.Q, Packaging and Deploying Java Projects. The FindGrade.jar file can be created using the following command:

```
c:\book>jar -cf FindGrade.jar FindGrade.class
  FindGrade$1.class
```

Note

To access the database from an applet, *security restrictions* make it necessary for the applet to be downloaded from the server where the database is located. Therefore, you have to deploy the applet on the server.

applet security restriction

Note

There is a *security hole* in this program. If you enter `1' or true or '1` in the `SSN` field, you will get the first student's score, because the query string now becomes

security hole

```
select firstName, mi, lastName, title, grade
from Student, Enrollment, Course
where Student.ssn = '1' or true or '1' and
      Enrollment.courseId = ' ' and
      Enrollment.courseId = Course.courseId and
      Enrollment.ssn = Student.ssn;
```

You can avoid this problem by using the `PreparedStatement` interface, which is discussed in the next section.

Check Point

MyProgrammingLab™

34.14 What are the advantages of developing database applications using Java?

34.15 Describe the following JDBC interfaces: `Driver`, `Connection`, `Statement`, and `ResultSet`.

34.16 How do you load a JDBC driver? What are the driver classes for MySQL, Access, and Oracle?

34.17 How do you create a database connection? What are the URLs for MySQL, Access, and Oracle?

34.18 How do you create a `Statement` and execute an SQL statement?

34.19 How do you retrieve values in a `ResultSet`?

34.20 Does JDBC automatically commit a transaction? How do you set autocommit to false?

34.5 PreparedStatement

Key Point

`PreparedStatement` enables you to create parameterized SQL statements.

Once a connection to a particular database is established, it can be used to send SQL statements from your program to the database. The `Statement` interface is used to execute static SQL statements that don't contain any parameters. The `PreparedStatement` interface, extending `Statement`, is used to execute a precompiled SQL statement with or without parameters. Since the SQL statements are precompiled, they are efficient for repeated executions.

A `PreparedStatement` object is created using the `preparedStatement` method in the `Connection` interface. For example, the following code creates a `PreparedStatement` for an SQL `insert` statement:

```
Statement preparedStatement = connection.prepareStatement
  ("insert into Student (firstName, mi, lastName) " +
   "values (?, ?, ?)");
```

This `insert` statement has three question marks as placeholders for parameters representing values for `firstName`, `mi`, and `lastName` in a record of the `Student` table.

As a subinterface of `Statement`, the `PreparedStatement` interface inherits all the methods defined in `Statement`. It also provides the methods for setting parameters in the object of `PreparedStatement`. These methods are used to set the values for the parameters before executing statements or procedures. In general, the set methods have the following name and signature:

```
setX(int parameterIndex, X value);
```

where *X* is the type of the parameter, and `parameterIndex` is the index of the parameter in the statement. The index starts from 1. For example, the method `setString(int parameterIndex, String value)` sets a `String` value to the specified parameter.

The following statements pass the parameters `"Jack"`, `"A"`, and `"Ryan"` to the placeholders for `firstName`, `mi`, and `lastName` in `preparedStatement`:

```
preparedStatement.setString(1, "Jack");
preparedStatement.setString(2, "A");
preparedStatement.setString(3, "Ryan");
```

After setting the parameters, you can execute the prepared statement by invoking `executeQuery()` for a SELECT statement and `executeUpdate()` for a DDL or update statement.

The `executeQuery()` and `executeUpdate()` methods are similar to the ones defined in the `Statement` interface except that they don't have any parameters, because the SQL statements are already specified in the `preparedStatement` method when the object of `PreparedStatement` is created.

Using a prepared SQL statement, Listing 34.2 can be improved as in Listing 34.3.

LISTING 34.3 FindGradeUsingPreparedStatement.java

```
import javax.swing.*;
import java.sql.*;
import java.awt.*;
import java.awt.event.*;

public class FindGradeUsingPreparedStatement extends JApplet {
  private JTextField jtfSSN = new JTextField(9);
  private JTextField jtfCourseId = new JTextField(5);
  private JButton jbtShowGrade = new JButton("Show Grade");

  // PreparedStatement for executing queries
  private PreparedStatement preparedStatement;

  /** Initialize the applet */
  public void init() {
    // Initialize database connection and create a Statement object
    initializeDB();

    jbtShowGrade.addActionListener(new ActionListener() {
      @Override
      public void actionPerformed(ActionEvent e) {
        jbtShowGrade_actionPerformed(e);
      }
    });

    JPanel jPanel1 = new JPanel();
    jPanel1.add(new JLabel("SSN"));
    jPanel1.add(jtfSSN);
    jPanel1.add(new JLabel("Course ID"));
    jPanel1.add(jtfCourseId);
    jPanel1.add(jbtShowGrade);

```

```
    add(jPanel1, BorderLayout.NORTH);
  }

  private void initializeDB() {
    try {
      // Load the JDBC driver
      Class.forName("com.mysql.jdbc.Driver");
//      Class.forName("oracle.jdbc.driver.OracleDriver");
      System.out.println("Driver loaded");

      // Establish a connection
      Connection connection = DriverManager.getConnection
        ("jdbc:mysql://localhost/javabook", "scott", "tiger");
//      ("jdbc:oracle:thin:@liang.armstrong.edu:1521:orcl",
//       "scott", "tiger");
      System.out.println("Database connected");

      String queryString = "select firstName, mi, " +
        "lastName, title, grade from Student, Enrollment, Course " +
        "where Student.ssn = ? and Enrollment.courseId = ? " +
        "and Enrollment.courseId = Course.courseId";

      // Create a statement
      preparedStatement = connection.prepareStatement(queryString);
    }
    catch (Exception ex) {
      ex.printStackTrace();
    }
  }

  private void jbtShowGrade_actionPerformed(ActionEvent e) {
    String ssn = jtfSSN.getText();
    String courseId = jtfCourseId.getText();
    try {
      preparedStatement.setString(1, ssn);
      preparedStatement.setString(2, courseId);
      ResultSet rset = preparedStatement.executeQuery();

      if (rset.next()) {
        String lastName = rset.getString(1);
        String mi = rset.getString(2);
        String firstName = rset.getString(3);
        String title = rset.getString(4);
        String grade = rset.getString(5);

        // Display result in a dialog box
        JOptionPane.showMessageDialog(null, firstName + " " + mi +
          " " + lastName + "'s grade on course " + title + " is " +
          grade);
      }
      else {
        // Display result in a dialog box
        JOptionPane.showMessageDialog(null, "Not found");
      }
    }
    catch (SQLException ex) {
      ex.printStackTrace();
    }
  }
}
```

load driver

connect database

placeholder

prepare statement

execute statement

show result

main method omitted

This example does exactly the same thing as Listing 34.2 except that it uses the prepared statement to dynamically set the parameters. The code in this example is almost the same as in the preceding example. The new code is highlighted.

A prepared query string is defined in lines 50–53 with `ssn` and `courseId` as parameters. An SQL prepared statement is obtained in line 56. Before executing the query, the actual values of `ssn` and `courseId` are set to the parameters in lines 67–68. Line 69 executes the prepared statement.

34.21 Describe prepared statements. How do you create instances of `PreparedStatement`? How do you execute a `PreparedStatement`? How do you set parameter values in a `PreparedStatement`?

34.22 What are the benefits of using prepared statements?

34.6 CallableStatement

`CallableStatement` enables you to execute SQL stored procedures.

IN parameter
OUT parameter
IN OUT parameter

The `CallableStatement` interface is designed to execute SQL-stored procedures. The procedures may have `IN`, `OUT` or `IN OUT` parameters. An `IN` parameter receives a value passed to the procedure when it is called. An `OUT` parameter returns a value after the procedure is completed, but it doesn't contain any value when the procedure is called. An `IN OUT` parameter contains a value passed to the procedure when it is called, and returns a value after it is completed. For example, the following procedure in Oracle PL/SQL has `IN` parameter `p1`, `OUT` parameter `p2`, and `IN OUT` parameter `p3`.

```
create or replace procedure sampleProcedure
  (p1 in varchar, p2 out number, p3 in out integer) is
begin
  /* do something */
end sampleProcedure;
/
```

Note

The syntax of stored procedures is vendor specific. We use both Oracle and MySQL for demonstrations of stored procedures in this book.

A `CallableStatement` object can be created using the `prepareCall(String call)` method in the `Connection` interface. For example, the following code creates a `CallableStatement cstmt` on `Connection connection` for the procedure `sampleProcedure`.

```
CallableStatement callableStatement = connection.prepareCall(
  "{call sampleProcedure(?, ?, ?)}");
```

`{call sampleProcedure(?, ?, ...)}` is referred to as the *SQL escape syntax*, which signals the driver that the code within it should be handled differently. The driver parses the escape syntax and translates it into code that the database understands. In this example, `sampleProcedure` is an Oracle procedure. The call is translated to the string `begin sampleProcedure(?, ?, ?); end` and passed to an Oracle database for execution.

You can call procedures as well as functions. The syntax to create an SQL callable statement for a function is:

```
{? = call functionName(?, ?, ...)}
```

CallableStatement inherits PreparedStatement. Additionally, the CallableStatement interface provides methods for registering the OUT parameters and for getting values from the OUT parameters.

Before calling an SQL procedure, you need to use appropriate set methods to pass values to IN and IN OUT parameters, and use registerOutParameter to register OUT and IN OUT parameters. For example, before calling procedure sampleProcedure, the following statements pass values to parameters p1 (IN) and p3 (IN OUT) and register parameters p2 (OUT) and p3 (IN OUT):

```
callableStatement.setString(1, "Dallas"); // Set Dallas to p1
callableStatement.setLong(3, 1); // Set 1 to p3
// Register OUT parameters
callableStatement.registerOutParameter(2, java.sql.Types.DOUBLE);
callableStatement.registerOutParameter(3, java.sql.Types.INTEGER);
```

You can use execute() or executeUpdate() to execute the procedure depending on the type of SQL statement, then use get methods to retrieve values from the OUT parameters. For example, the next statements retrieve the values from parameters p2 and p3.

```
double d = callableStatement.getDouble(2);
int i = callableStatement.getInt(3);
```

Let us define a MySQL function that returns the number of the records in the table that match the specified firstName and lastName in the Student table.

```
/* For the callable statement example. Use MySQL version 5 */
drop function if exists studentFound;

delimiter //

create function studentFound(first varchar(20), last varchar(20))
  returns int
begin
  declare result int;

  select count(*) into result
  from Student
  where Student.firstName = first and
    Student.lastName = last;

  return result;
end;
//

delimiter ;
/* Please note that there is a space between delimiter and ; */
```

If you use an Oracle database, the function can be defined as follows:

```
create or replace function studentFound
  (first varchar2, last varchar2)
  /* Do not name firstName and lastName. */
  return number is
  numberOfSelectedRows number := 0;
begin
  select count(*) into numberOfSelectedRows
  from Student
```

```
  where Student.firstName = first and
    Student.lastName = last;

  return numberOfSelectedRows;
end studentFound;
/
```

Suppose the function **studentFound** is already created in the database. Listing 34.4 gives an example that tests this function using callable statements.

LISTING 34.4 TestCallableStatement.java

```
import java.sql.*;

public class TestCallableStatement {
  /** Creates new form TestTableEditor */
  public static void main(String[] args) throws Exception {
    Class.forName("com.mysql.jdbc.Driver");
    Connection connection = DriverManager.getConnection(
      "jdbc:mysql://localhost/javabook",
      "scott", "tiger");
//    Connection connection = DriverManager.getConnection(
//      ("jdbc:oracle:thin:@liang.armstrong.edu:1521:orcl",
//      "scott", "tiger");

    // Create a callable statement
    CallableStatement callableStatement = connection.prepareCall(
      "{? = call studentFound(?, ?)}");

    java.util.Scanner input = new java.util.Scanner(System.in);
    System.out.print("Enter student's first name: ");
    String firstName = input.nextLine();
    System.out.print("Enter student's last name: ");
    String lastName = input.nextLine();

    callableStatement.setString(2, firstName);
    callableStatement.setString(3, lastName);
    callableStatement.registerOutParameter(1, Types.INTEGER);
    callableStatement.execute();

    if (callableStatement.getInt(1) >= 1)
      System.out.println(firstName + " " + lastName +
        " is in the database");
    else
      System.out.println(firstName + " " + lastName +
        " is not in the database");
  }
}
```

load driver
connect database
create callable statement
enter fistName
enter lastName
set IN parameter
set IN parameter
register OUT parameter
execute statement
get OUT parameter

```
Enter student's first name: Jacob ↵Enter
Enter student's last name: Smith ↵Enter
Jacob Smith is in the database
```

```
Enter student's first name: John ↵Enter
Enter student's last name: Smith ↵Enter
John Smith is not in the database
```

The program loads a MySQL driver (line 6), connects to a MySQL database (lines 7–9), and creates a callable statement for executing the function `studentFound` (lines 15–16).

The function's first parameter is the return value; its second and third parameters correspond to the first and last names. Before executing the callable statement, the program sets the first name and last name (lines 24–25) and registers the `OUT` parameter (line 26). The statement is executed in line 27.

The function's return value is obtained in line 29. If the value is greater than or equal to `1`, the student with the specified first and last name is found in the table.

34.23 Describe callable statements. How do you create instances of `CallableStatement`? How do you execute a `CallableStatement`? How do you register `OUT` parameters in a `CallableStatement`?

34.7 Retrieving Metadata

The database metadata such as database URL, username, JDBC driver name can be obtained using the `DatabaseMetaData` *interface and result set metadata such as table column count and column names can be obtained using the* `ResultSetMetaData` *interface.*

database metadata

JDBC provides the `DatabaseMetaData` interface for obtaining database-wide information, and the `ResultSetMetaData` interface for obtaining information on the specific `ResultSet`.

34.7.1 Database Metadata

The `Connection` interface establishes a connection to a database. It is within the context of a connection that SQL statements are executed and results are returned. A connection also provides access to database metadata information that describes the capabilities of the database, supported SQL grammar, stored procedures, and so on. To obtain an instance of `DatabaseMetaData` for a database, use the `getMetaData` method on a `Connection` object like this:

```
DatabaseMetaData dbMetaData = connection.getMetaData();
```

If your program connects to a local MySQL database, the program in Listing 34.5 displays the database information statements shown in Figure 34.24.

LISTING 34.5 TestDatabaseMetaData.java

```
import java.sql.*;

public class TestDatabaseMetaData {
  public static void main(String[] args)
      throws SQLException, ClassNotFoundException {
    // Load the JDBC driver
    Class.forName("com.mysql.jdbc.Driver");
    System.out.println("Driver loaded");

    // Connect to a database
    Connection connection = DriverManager.getConnection
      ("jdbc:mysql://localhost/javabook", "scott", "tiger");
    System.out.println("Database connected");

    DatabaseMetaData dbMetaData = connection.getMetaData();
    System.out.println("database URL: " + dbMetaData.getURL());
    System.out.println("database username: " +
```

load driver

connect database

database metadata

get metadata

```
          dbMetaData.getUserName());
        System.out.println("database product name: " +
          dbMetaData.getDatabaseProductName());
        System.out.println("database product version: " +
          dbMetaData.getDatabaseProductVersion());
        System.out.println("JDBC driver name: " +
          dbMetaData.getDriverName());
        System.out.println("JDBC driver version: " +
          dbMetaData.getDriverVersion());
        System.out.println("JDBC driver major version: " +
          dbMetaData.getDriverMajorVersion());
        System.out.println("JDBC driver minor version: " +
          dbMetaData.getDriverMinorVersion());
        System.out.println("Max number of connections: " +
          dbMetaData.getMaxConnections());
        System.out.println("MaxTableNameLength: " +
          dbMetaData.getMaxTableNameLength());
        System.out.println("MaxColumnsInTable: " +
          dbMetaData.getMaxColumnsInTable());

        // Close the connection
        connection.close();
      }
    }
```

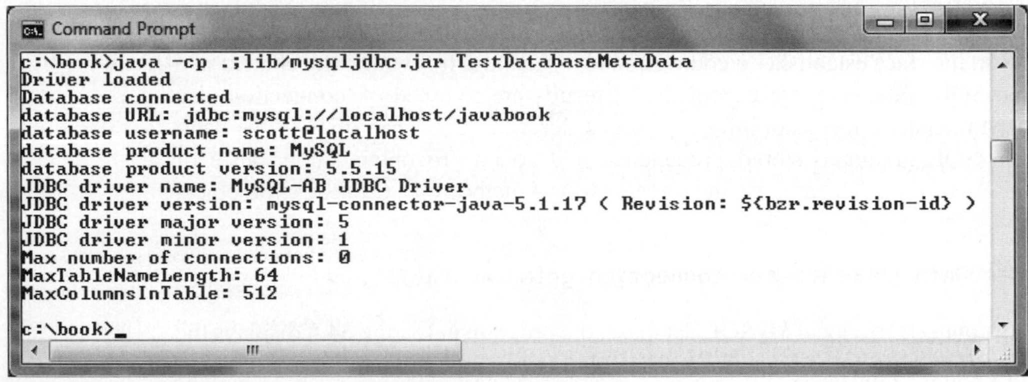

FIGURE 34.24 The DatabaseMetaData interface enables you to obtain database information.

34.7.2 Obtaining Database Tables

You can identify the tables in the database through database metadata using the getTables method. Listing 34.6 displays all the user tables in the test database on a local MySQL database. Figure 34.25 shows a sample output of the program.

LISTING 34.6 FindUserTables.java

```
import java.sql.*;

public class FindUserTables {
  public static void main(String[] args)
      throws SQLException, ClassNotFoundException {
    // Load the JDBC driver
    Class.forName("com.mysql.jdbc.Driver");
```

load driver

```
8       System.out.println("Driver loaded");
9
10      // Connect to a database
11      Connection connection = DriverManager.getConnection
12        ("jdbc:mysql://localhost/javabook", "scott", "tiger");
13      System.out.println("Database connected");
14
15      DatabaseMetaData dbMetaData = connection.getMetaData();
16
17      ResultSet rsTables = dbMetaData.getTables(null, null, null,
18        new String[] {"TABLE"});
19      System.out.print("User tables: ");
20      while (rsTables.next())
21        System.out.print(rsTables.getString("TABLE_NAME") + " ");
22
23      // Close the connection
24      connection.close();
25    }
26  }
```

connect database

database metadata

obtain tables

get table names

```
C:\book>java -cp .;lib/mysqljdbc.jar FindUserTables
Driver loaded
Database connected
User tables: account address college course csci1301 csci1302 csci4990 departmen
t enrollment faculty quiz staff student subject taughtby
C:\book>
```

FIGURE 34.25 You can find all the tables in the database.

Line 17 obtains table information in a result set using the **getTables** method. One of the columns in the result set is TABLE_NAME. Line 21 retrieves the table name from this result set column.

34.7.3 Result Set Metadata

The **ResultSetMetaData** interface describes information pertaining to the result set. A **ResultSetMetaData** object can be used to find the types and properties of the columns in a **ResultSet**. To obtain an instance of **ResultSetMetaData**, use the **getMetaData** method on a result set like this:

```
ResultSetMetaData rsMetaData = resultSet.getMetaData();
```

You can use the **getColumnCount()** method to find the number of columns in the result and the **getColumnName(int)** method to get the column names. For example, Listing 34.7 displays all the column names and contents resulting from the SQL SELECT statement ***select * from Enrollment***. The output is shown in Figure 34.26.

LISTING 34.7 TestResultSetMetaData.java

```
import java.sql.*;

public class TestResultSetMetaData {
  public static void main(String[] args)
      throws SQLException, ClassNotFoundException {
    // Load the JDBC driver
    Class.forName("com.mysql.jdbc.Driver");
    System.out.println("Driver loaded");
```

load driver

connect database · create statement · create result set · result set metadata · column count · column name

```
    // Connect to a database
    Connection connection = DriverManager.getConnection
      ("jdbc:mysql://localhost/javabook", "scott", "tiger");
    System.out.println("Database connected");

    // Create a statement
    Statement statement = connection.createStatement();

    // Execute a statement
    ResultSet resultSet = statement.executeQuery
      ("select * from Enrollment");

    ResultSetMetaData rsMetaData = resultSet.getMetaData();
    for (int i = 1; i <= rsMetaData.getColumnCount(); i++)
      System.out.printf("%-12s\t", rsMetaData.getColumnName(i));
    System.out.println();

    // Iterate through the result and print the students' names
    while (resultSet.next()) {
      for (int i = 1; i <= rsMetaData.getColumnCount(); i++)
        System.out.printf("%-12s\t", resultSet.getObject(i));
      System.out.println();
    }

    // Close the connection
    connection.close();
  }
}
```

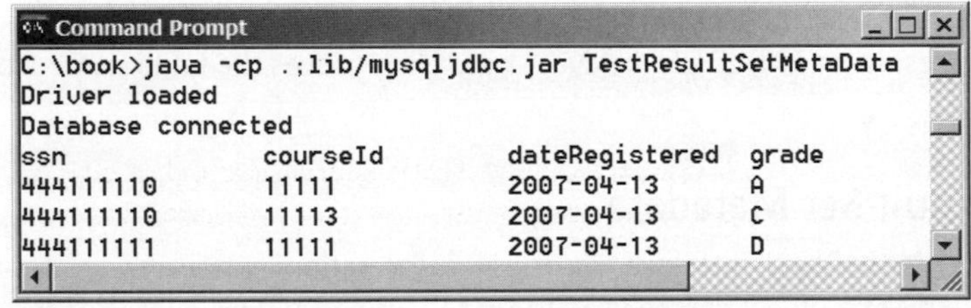

```
C:\book>java -cp .;lib/mysqljdbc.jar TestResultSetMetaData
Driver loaded
Database connected
ssn          courseId     dateRegistered grade
444111110    11111        2007-04-13     A
444111110    11113        2007-04-13     C
444111111    11111        2007-04-13     D
```

Figure 34.26 The `ResultSetMetaData` interface enables you to obtain result set information.

MyProgrammingLab™

34.24 What is `DatabaseMetaData` for? Describe the methods in `DatabaseMetaData`. How do you get an instance of `DatabaseMetaData`?

34.25 What is `ResultSetMetaData` for? Describe the methods in `ResultSetMetaData`. How do you get an instance of `ResultSetMetaData`?

34.26 How do you find the number of columns in a result set? How do you find the column names in a result set?

Key Terms

database system 1212
domain constraint 1215
foreign key constraint 1215
integrity constraint 1214
primary key constraint 1215
relational database 1215
Structured Query Language (SQL) 1216

CHAPTER SUMMARY

1. This chapter introduced the concepts of *database systems*, *relational databases*, *relational data models*, *data integrity*, and *SQL*. You learned how to develop database applications using Java.

2. The Java API for developing Java database applications is called *JDBC*. JDBC provides Java programmers with a uniform interface for accessing and manipulating a wide range of relational databases.

3. The JDBC API consists of classes and interfaces for establishing connections with databases, sending SQL statements to databases, processing the results of SQL statements, and obtaining database metadata.

4. Since a JDBC driver serves as the interface to facilitate communications between JDBC and a proprietary database, JDBC drivers are database specific. A JDBC-ODBC bridge driver is included in JDK to support Java programs that access databases through ODBC drivers. If you use a driver other than the JDBC-ODBC bridge driver, make sure it is in the classpath before running the program.

5. Four key interfaces are needed to develop any database application using Java: `Driver`, `Connection`, `Statement`, and `ResultSet`. These interfaces define a framework for generic SQL database access. The JDBC driver vendors provide implementation for them.

6. A JDBC application loads an appropriate driver using the `Driver` interface, connects to the database using the `Connection` interface, creates and executes SQL statements using the `Statement` interface, and processes the result using the `ResultSet` interface if the statements return results.

7. The `PreparedStatement` interface is designed to execute dynamic SQL statements with parameters. These SQL statements are precompiled for efficient use when repeatedly executed.

8. Database *metadata* is information that describes the database itself. JDBC provides the `DatabaseMetaData` interface for obtaining database-wide information and the `ResultSetMetaData` interface for obtaining information on the specific `ResultSet`.

TEST QUESTIONS

Do the test questions for this chapter online at www.cs.armstrong.edu/liang/intro9e/test.html.

PROGRAMMING EXERCISES

MyProgrammingLab™

*34.1 (*Access and update a `Staff` table*) Write a Java applet that views, inserts, and updates staff information stored in a database, as shown in Figure 34.27a. The *View* button displays a record with a specified ID. The `Staff` table is created as follows:

```
create table Staff (
  id char(9) not null,
```

```
    lastName varchar(15),
    firstName varchar(15),
    mi char(1),
    address varchar(20),
    city varchar(20),
    state char(2),
    telephone char(10),
    email varchar(40),
    primary key (id)
);
```

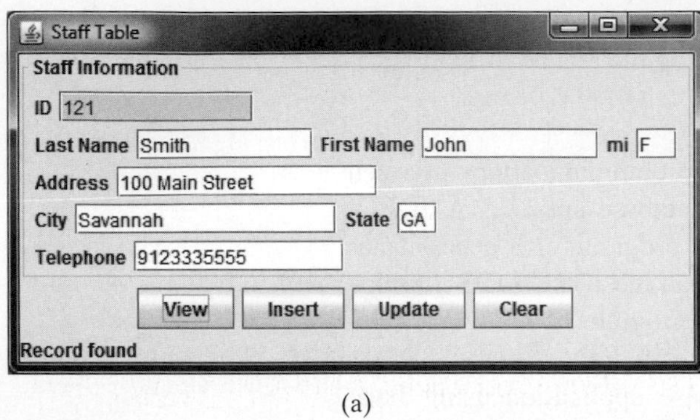

(a)

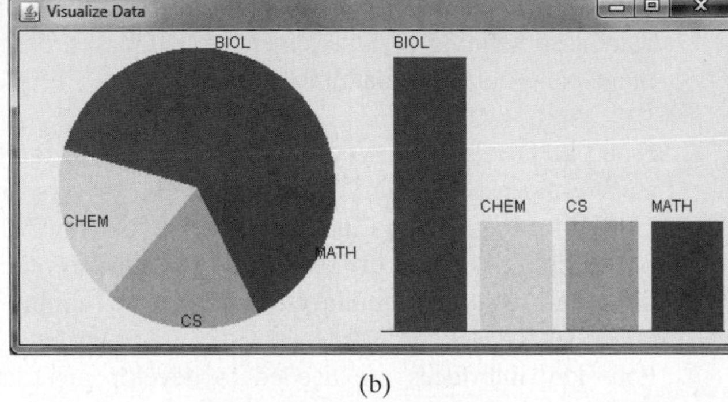

(b)

FIGURE 34.27 (a) The applet lets you view, insert, and update staff information. (b) The `PieChart` and `BarChart` components display the query data obtained from the data module.

****34.2** (*Visualize data*) Write a program that displays the number of students in each department in a pie chart and a bar chart, as shown in Figure 34.27b. The number of students for each department can be obtained from the `Student` table (see Figure 34.4) using the following SQL statement:

```
select deptId, count(*)
from Student
where deptId is not null
group by deptId;
```

***34.3** (*Connection dialog*) Develop a class named `DBConnectionPanel` that enables the user to select or enter a JDBC driver and a URL and to enter a username and password, as shown in Figure 34.28. When the *OK* button is clicked, a `Connection` object for the database is stored in the `connection` property. You can then use the `getConnection()` method to return the connection.

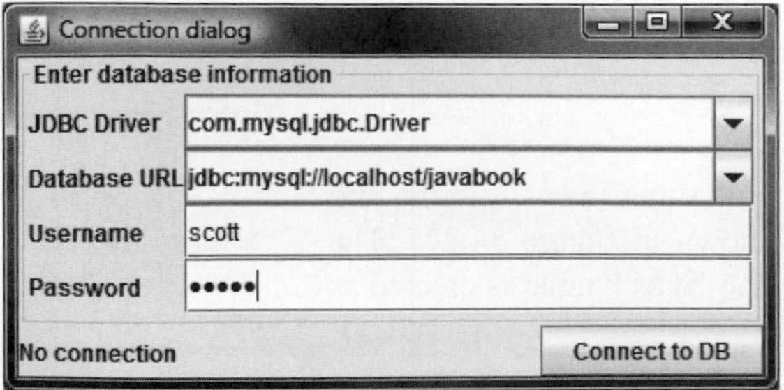

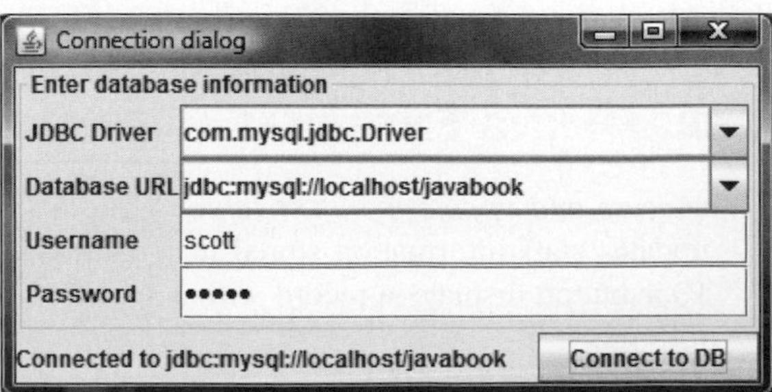

FIGURE 34.28 The `DBConnectionPanel` component enables the user to enter database information.

***34.4** (*Find grades*) Listing 34.2, FindGrade.java, presented an applet that finds a student's grade for a specified course. Rewrite the program to find all the grades for a specified student, as shown in Figure 34.29.

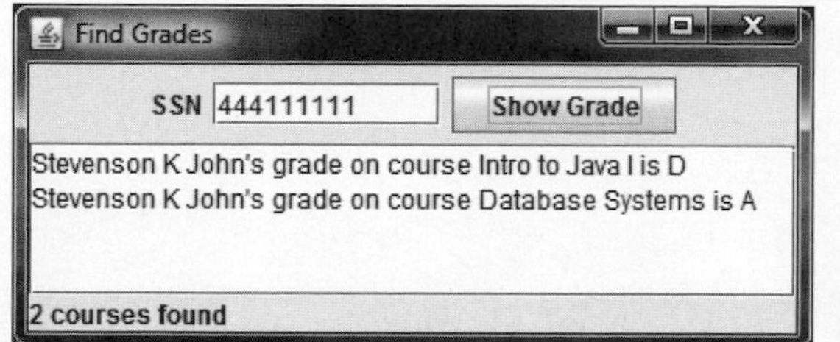

FIGURE 34.29 The program displays the grades for the courses for a specified student.

***34.5** (*Display table contents*) Write a program that displays the content for a given table. As shown in Figure 34.30a, you enter a table and click the *Show Contents* button to display the table contents in the text area.

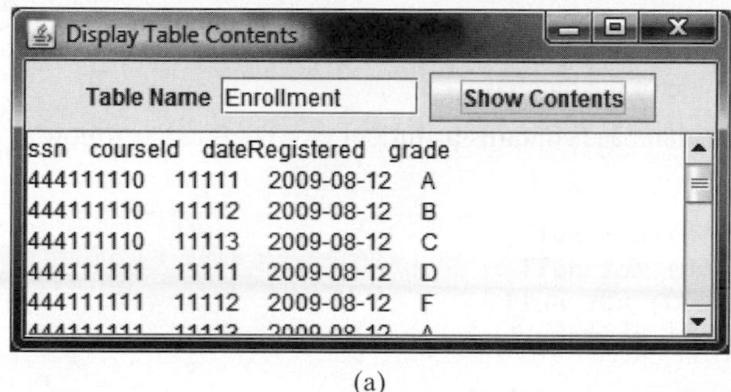

(a)

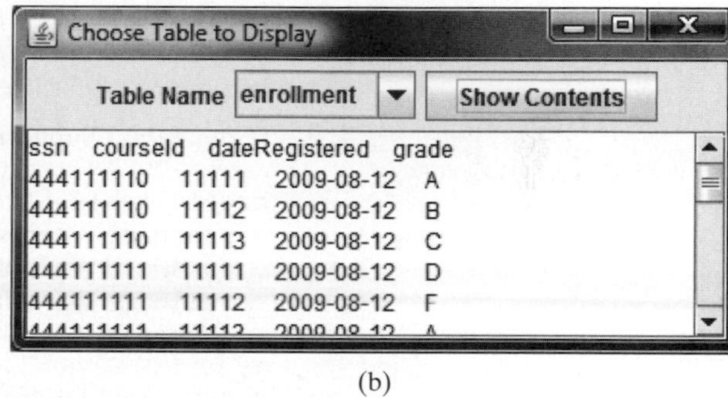

(b)

FIGURE 34.30 (a) Enter a table name to display the table contents. (b) Select a table name from the combo box to display its contents.

***34.6** (*Find tables and showing their contents*) Write a program that fills in table names in a combo box, as shown in Figure 34.30b. You can select a table from the combo box to display its contents in the text area.

****34.7** (*Populate Quiz table*) Create a table named `Quiz` as follows:

```
create table Quiz(
  questionId int,
  question varchar(4000),
  choicea varchar(1000),
  choiceb varchar(1000),
  choicec varchar(1000),
  choiced varchar(1000),
  answer varchar(5));
```

The `Quiz` table stores multiple-choice questions. Suppose the multiple-choice questions are stored in a text file accessible from www.cs.armstrong.edu/liang/data/Quiz.txt in the following format:

```
1. question1
a. choice a
b. choice b
```

```
c. choice c
d. choice d
Answer:cd

2. question2
a. choice a
b. choice b
c. choice c
d. choice d
Answer:a

...
```

Write a program that reads the data from the file and populate it into the `Quiz` table.

*34.8 (*Populate Salary table*) Create a table named `Salary` as follows:

```
create table Salary(
  firstName varchar(100),
  lastName varchar(100),
  rank varchar(15),
  salary float);
```

Obtain the data for salary from http://cs.armstrong.edu/liang/data/Salary.txt and populate it into the `Salary` table in the database.

*34.9 (*Copy table*) Suppose the database contains a student table defined as follows:

```
create table Student1 (
  username varchar(50) not null,
  password varchar(50) not null,
  fullname varchar(200) not null,
  constraint pkStudent primary key (username)
);
```

Create a new table named `Student2` as follows:

```
create table Student2 (
  username varchar(50) not null,
  password varchar(50) not null,
  firstname varchar(100),
  lastname varchar(100),
  constraint pkStudent primary key (username)
);
```

A full name is in the form of `firstname mi lastname` or `firstname lastname`. For example, `John K Smith` is a full name. Write a program that copies table `Student1` into `Student2`. Your task is to split a full name into `firstname`, `mi`, and `lastname` for each record in `Student1` and store a new record into `Student2`.

*34.10 (*Record unsubmitted exercises*) The following three tables store information on students, assigned exercises, and exercise submission in LiveLab. LiveLab is an automatic grading system for grading programming exercises.

```
create table AGSStudent (
  username varchar(50) not null,
  password varchar(50) not null,
  fullname varchar(200) not null,
  instructorEmail varchar(100) not null,
```

```
  constraint pkAGSStudent primary key (username)
);

create table ExerciseAssigned (
  instructorEmail varchar(100),
  exerciseName varchar(100),
  maxscore double default 10,
  constraint pkCustomExercise primary key
    (instructorEmail, exerciseName)
);

create table AGSLog (
  username varchar(50), /* This is the student's user name */
  exerciseName varchar(100), /* This is the exercise assigned */
  score double default null,
  submitted bit default 0,
  constraint pkLog primary key (username, exerciseName)
);
```

The `AGSStudent` table stores the student information. The `ExerciseAssigned` table assigns the exercises by an instructor. The `AGSLog` table stores the grading results. When a student submits an exercise, a record is stored in the `AGSLog` table. However, there is no record in `AGSLog` if a student did not submit the exercise.

Write a program that adds a new record for each student and an assigned exercise to the student in the `AGSLog` table if a student has not submitted the exercise. The record should have the default values on `score` and `submitted`. For example, if the tables contain the following data in `AGSLog` before you run this program, the `AGSLog` table now contains the new records after the program runs.

AGSStudent

username	password	fullname	instructorEmail
abc	p1	John Roo	t@gmail.com
cde	p2	Yao Mi	c@gmail.com
wbc	p3	F3	t@gmail.com

ExerciseAssigned

instructorEmail	exerciseName	maxScore
t@gmail.com	e1	10
t@gmail.com	e2	10
c@gmail.com	e1	4
c@gmail.com	e4	20

AGSLog

username	exerciseName	score	submitted
abc	e1	9	1
wbc	e2	7	1

AGSLog after the program runs

username	exerciseName	score	submitted
abc	e1	9	1
wbc	e2	7	1
abc	e2		0
wbc	e1		0
cde	e1		0
cde	e4		0

APPENDIXES

APPENDIX A

Java Keywords

The following fifty keywords are reserved for use by the Java language:

abstract	**double**	**int**	**super**
assert	**else**	**interface**	**switch**
boolean	**enum**	**long**	**synchronized**
break	**extends**	**native**	**this**
byte	**final**	**new**	**throw**
case	**finally**	**package**	**throws**
catch	**float**	**private**	**transient**
char	**for**	**protected**	**try**
class	**goto**	**public**	**void**
const	**if**	**return**	**volatile**
continue	**implements**	**short**	**while**
default	**import**	**static**	
do	**instanceof**	**strictfp***	

The keywords **goto** and **const** are C++ keywords reserved, but not currently used, in Java. This enables Java compilers to identify them and to produce better error messages if they appear in Java programs.

The literal values **true**, **false**, and **null** are not keywords, just like literal value 100. However, you cannot use them as identifiers, just as you cannot use 100 as an identifier. In the code listing, we use the keyword color for **true**, **false**, and **null** to be consistent with their coloring in Java IDEs.

assert is a keyword added in JDK 1.4 and **enum** is a keyword added in JDK 1.5.

---

*The **strictfp** keyword is a modifier for a method or class that enables it to use strict floating-point calculations. Floating-point arithmetic can be executed in one of two modes: *strict* or *nonstrict*. The strict mode guarantees that the evaluation result is the same on all Java Virtual Machine implementations. The nonstrict mode allows intermediate results from calculations to be stored in an extended format different from the standard IEEE floating-point number format. The extended format is machine-dependent and enables code to be executed faster. However, when you execute the code using the nonstrict mode on different JVMs, you may not always get precisely the same results. By default, the nonstrict mode is used for floating-point calculations. To use the strict mode in a method or a class, add the **strictfp** keyword in the method or the class declaration. Strict floating-point may give you slightly better precision than nonstrict floating-point, but the distinction will only affect some applications. Strictness is not inherited; that is, the presence of **strictfp** on a class or interface declaration does not cause extended classes or interfaces to be strict.

APPENDIX B

The ASCII Character Set

Tables B.1 and B.2 show ASCII characters and their respective decimal and hexadecimal codes. The decimal or hexadecimal code of a character is a combination of its row index and column index. For example, in Table B.1, the letter **A** is at row 6 and column 5, so its decimal equivalent is 65; in Table B.2, letter **A** is at row 4 and column 1, so its hexadecimal equivalent is 41.

TABLE B.1 ASCII Character Set in the Decimal Index

	0	*1*	*2*	*3*	*4*	*5*	*6*	*7*	*8*	*9*
0	nul	soh	stx	etx	eot	enq	ack	bel	bs	ht
1	nl	vt	ff	cr	so	si	dle	dcl	dc2	dc3
2	dc4	nak	syn	etb	can	em	sub	esc	fs	gs
3	rs	us	sp	!	”	#	$	%	&	’
4	(	)	*	+	,	–	.	/	0	1
5	2	3	4	5	6	7	8	9	:	;
6	<	=	>	?	@	A	B	C	D	E
7	F	G	H	I	J	K	L	M	N	O
8	P	Q	R	S	T	U	V	W	X	Y
9	Z	[	\	]	∧	—	‘	a	b	c
10	d	e	f	g	h	i	j	k	l	m
11	n	o	p	q	r	s	t	u	v	w
12	x	y	z	{	|	}	~	del		

TABLE B.2 ASCII Character Set in the Hexadecimal Index

	0	*1*	*2*	*3*	*4*	*5*	*6*	*7*	*8*	*9*	*A*	*B*	*C*	*D*	*E*	*F*
0	nul	soh	stx	etx	eot	enq	ack	bel	bs	ht	nl	vt	ff	cr	so	si
1	dle	dcl	dc2	dc3	dc4	nak	syn	etb	can	em	sub	esc	fs	gs	rs	us
2	sp	!	”	#	$	%	&	’	(	)	*	+	,	–	.	/
3	0	1	2	3	4	5	6	7	8	9	:	;	<	=	>	?
4	@	A	B	C	D	E	F	G	H	I	J	K	L	M	N	O
5	P	Q	R	S	T	U	V	W	X	Y	Z	[	\	]	∧	—
6	‘	a	b	c	d	e	f	g	h	i	j	k	l	m	n	o
7	p	q	r	s	t	u	v	w	x	y	z	{	|	}	~	del

Appendix C

Operator Precedence Chart

The operators are shown in decreasing order of precedence from top to bottom. Operators in the same group have the same precedence, and their associativity is shown in the table.

Operator	*Name*	*Associativity*
()	Parentheses	Left to right
()	Function call	Left to right
[]	Array subscript	Left to right
.	Object member access	Left to right
++	Postincrement	Right to left
--	Postdecrement	Right to left
++	Preincrement	Right to left
--	Predecrement	Right to left
+	Unary plus	Right to left
-	Unary minus	Right to left
!	Unary logical negation	Right to left
(type)	Unary casting	Right to left
new	Creating object	Right to left
*	Multiplication	Left to right
/	Division	Left to right
%	Remainder	Left to right
+	Addition	Left to right
-	Subtraction	Left to right
<<	Left shift	Left to right
>>	Right shift with sign extension	Left to right
>>>	Right shift with zero extension	Left to right
<	Less than	Left to right
<=	Less than or equal to	Left to right
>	Greater than	Left to right
>=	Greater than or equal to	Left to right
instanceof	Checking object type	Left to right

Operator	*Name*	*Associativity*
`==`	Equal comparison	Left to right
`!=`	Not equal	Left to right
`&`	(Unconditional AND)	Left to right
`^`	(Exclusive OR)	Left to right
`|`	(Unconditional OR)	Left to right
`&&`	Conditional AND	Left to right
`||`	Conditional OR	Left to right
`?:`	Ternary condition	Right to left
`=`	Assignment	Right to left
`+=`	Addition assignment	Right to left
`-=`	Subtraction assignment	Right to left
`*=`	Multiplication assignment	Right to left
`/=`	Division assignment	Right to left
`%=`	Remainder assignment	Right to left

Appendix D

Java Modifiers

Modifiers are used on classes and class members (constructors, methods, data, and class-level blocks), but the **final** modifier can also be used on local variables in a method. A modifier that can be applied to a class is called a *class modifier*. A modifier that can be applied to a method is called a *method modifier*. A modifier that can be applied to a data field is called a *data modifier*. A modifier that can be applied to a class-level block is called a *block modifier*. The following table gives a summary of the Java modifiers.

Modifier	*Class*	*Constructor*	*Method*	*Data*	*Block*	*Explanation*
(default)*	√	√	√	√	√	A class, constructor, method, or data field is visible in this package.
public	√	√	√	√		A class, constructor, method, or data field is visible to all the programs in any package.
private		√	√	√		A constructor, method, or data field is only visible in this class.
protected		√	√	√		A constructor, method, or data field is visible in this package and in subclasses of this class in any package.
static			√	√	√	Define a class method, a class data field, or a static initialization block.
final	√		√	√		A final class cannot be extended. A final method cannot be modified in a subclass. A final data field is a constant.
abstract	√		√			An abstract class must be extended. An abstract method must be implemented in a concrete subclass.
native			√			A native method indicates that the method is implemented using a language other than Java.

*Default access doesn't have a modifier associated with it. For example: **class Test {}**

Modifier	*Class*	*Constructor*	*Method*	*Data*	*Block*	*Explanation*
`synchronized`			√		√	Only one thread at a time can execute this method.
`strictfp`	√		√			Use strict floating-point calculations to guarantee that the evaluation result is the same on all JVMs.
`transient`				√		Mark a nonserializable instance data field.

The modifiers default (no modifier), `public`, `private`, and `protected` are known as *visibility* or *accessibility modifiers* because they specify how classes and class members are accessed.

The modifiers `public`, `private`, `protected`, `static`, `final`, and `abstract` can also be applied to inner classes.

APPENDIX E

Special Floating-Point Values

Dividing an integer by zero is invalid and throws ArithmeticException, but dividing a floating-point value by zero does not cause an exception. Floating-point arithmetic can overflow to infinity if the result of the operation is too large for a double or a float, or underflow to zero if the result is too small for a double or a float. Java provides the special floating-point values POSITIVE_INFINITY, NEGATIVE_INFINITY, and NaN (Not a Number) to denote these results. These values are defined as special constants in the Float class and the Double class.

If a positive floating-point number is divided by zero, the result is POSITIVE_INFINITY. If a negative floating-point number is divided by zero, the result is NEGATIVE_INFINITY. If a floating-point zero is divided by zero, the result is NaN, which means that the result is undefined mathematically. The string representations of these three values are Infinity, -Infinity, and NaN. For example,

```
System.out.print(1.0 / 0); // Print Infinity
System.out.print(-1.0 / 0); // Print -Infinity
System.out.print(0.0 / 0); // Print NaN
```

These special values can also be used as operands in computations. For example, a number divided by POSITIVE_INFINITY yields a positive zero. Table E.1 summarizes various combinations of the /, *, %, +, and - operators.

TABLE E.1 Special Floating-Point Values

x	*y*	*x/y*	*x*y*	*x%y*	*x + y*	*x − y*
Finite	± 0.0	± infinity	± 0.0	NaN	Finite	Finite
Finite	± infinity	± 0.0	± 0.0	x	± infinity	infinity
± 0.0	± 0.0	NaN	± 0.0	NaN	± 0.0	± 0.0
± infinity	Finite	± infinity	± 0.0	NaN	± infinity	± infinity
± infinity	± infinity	NaN	± 0.0	NaN	± infinity	infinity
± 0.0	± infinity	± 0.0	NaN	± 0.0	± infinity	± 0.0
NaN	Any	NaN	NaN	NaN	NaN	NaN
Any	NaN	NaN	NaN	NaN	NaN	NaN

Note
If one of the operands is NaN, the result is NaN.

APPENDIX F

Number Systems

F.1 Introduction

Computers use binary numbers internally, because computers are made naturally to store and process 0s and 1s. The binary number system has two digits, 0 and 1. A number or character is stored as a sequence of 0s and 1s. Each 0 or 1 is called a *bit* (binary digit). binary numbers

In our daily life we use decimal numbers. When we write a number such as 20 in a program, it is assumed to be a decimal number. Internally, computer software is used to convert decimal numbers into binary numbers, and vice versa. decimal numbers

We write computer programs using decimal numbers. However, to deal with an operating system, we need to reach down to the "machine level" by using binary numbers. Binary numbers tend to be very long and cumbersome. Often hexadecimal numbers are used to abbreviate them, with each hexadecimal digit representing four binary digits. The hexadecimal number system has 16 digits: 0–9 and A–F. The letters A, B, C, D, E, and F correspond to the decimal numbers 10, 11, 12, 13, 14, and 15. hexadecimal number

The digits in the decimal number system are 0, 1, 2, 3, 4, 5, 6, 7, 8, and 9. A decimal number is represented by a sequence of one or more of these digits. The value that each digit represents depends on its position, which denotes an integral power of 10. For example, the digits 7, 4, 2, and 3 in decimal number 7423 represent 7000, 400, 20, and 3, respectively, as shown below:

$$\boxed{7\,|\,4\,|\,2\,|\,3} = 7 \times 10^3 + 4 \times 10^2 + 2 \times 10^1 + 3 \times 10^0$$

$$10^3 \ 10^2 \ 10^1 \ 10^0 = 7000 + 400 + 20 + 3 = 7423$$

The decimal number system has ten digits, and the position values are integral powers of 10. We say that 10 is the *base* or *radix* of the decimal number system. Similarly, since the binary number system has two digits, its base is 2, and since the hex number system has 16 digits, its base is 16. base radix

If 1101 is a binary number, the digits 1, 1, 0, and 1 represent 1×2^3, 1×2^2, 0×2^1, and 1×2^0, respectively:

$$\boxed{1\,|\,1\,|\,0\,|\,1} = 1 \times 2^3 + 1 \times 2^2 + 0 \times 2^1 + 1 \times 2^0$$

$$2^3 \ 2^2 \ 2^1 \ 2^0 = 8 + 4 + 0 + 1 = 13$$

If 7423 is a hex number, the digits 7, 4, 2, and 3 represent 7×16^3, 4×16^2, 2×16^1, and 3×16^0, respectively:

$$\boxed{7\,|\,4\,|\,2\,|\,3} = 7 \times 16^3 + 4 \times 16^2 + 2 \times 16^1 + 3 \times 16^0$$

$$16^3 \ 16^2 \ 16^1 \ 16^0 = 28672 + 1024 + 32 + 3 = 29731$$

F.2 Conversions Between Binary and Decimal Numbers

binary to decimal

Given a binary number $b_n b_{n-1} b_{n-2} \ldots b_2 b_1 b_0$, the equivalent decimal value is

$$b_n \times 2^n + b_{n-1} \times 2^{n-1} + b_{n-2} \times 2^{n-2} + \ \ldots \ + b_2 \times 2^2 + b_1 \times 2^1 + b_0 \times 2^0$$

Here are some examples of converting binary numbers to decimals:

Binary	**Conversion Formula**	**Decimal**
10	$1 \times 2^1 + 0 \times 2^0$	2
1000	$1 \times 2^3 + 0 \times 2^2 + 0 \times 2^1 + 0 \times 2^0$	8
10101011	$1 \times 2^7 + 0 \times 2^6 + 1 \times 2^5 + 0 \times 2^4 + 1 \times 2^3 + 0 \times 2^2 + 1 \times 2^1 + 1 \times 2^0$	171

decimal to binary

To convert a decimal number d to a binary number is to find the bits b_n, b_{n-1}, b_{n-2}, . . . , b_2, b_1, and b_0 such that

$$d = b_n \times 2^n + b_{n-1} \times 2^{n-1} + b_{n-2} \times 2^{n-2} + \ldots + b_2 \times 2^2 + b_1 \times 2^1 + b_0 \times 2^0$$

These bits can be found by successively dividing d by 2 until the quotient is 0. The remainders are b_0, b_1, b_2, . . . , b_{n-2}, b_{n-1}, and b_n.

For example, the decimal number 123 is 1111011 in binary. The conversion is done as follows:

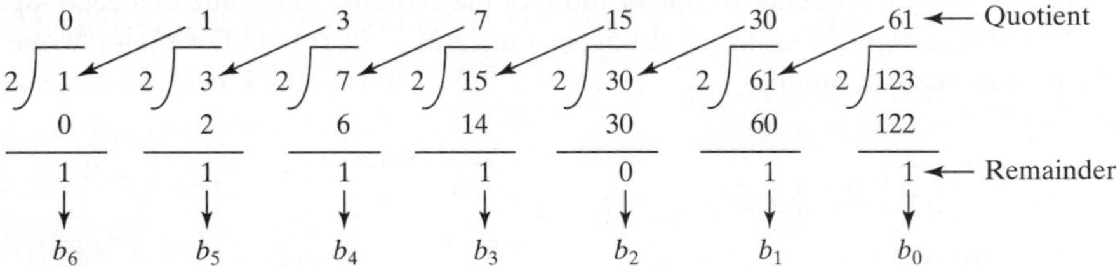

Tip

The Windows Calculator, as shown in Figure F.1, is a useful tool for performing number conversions. To run it, search for *Calculator* from the *Start* button and launch Calculator, then under *View* select *Scientific*.

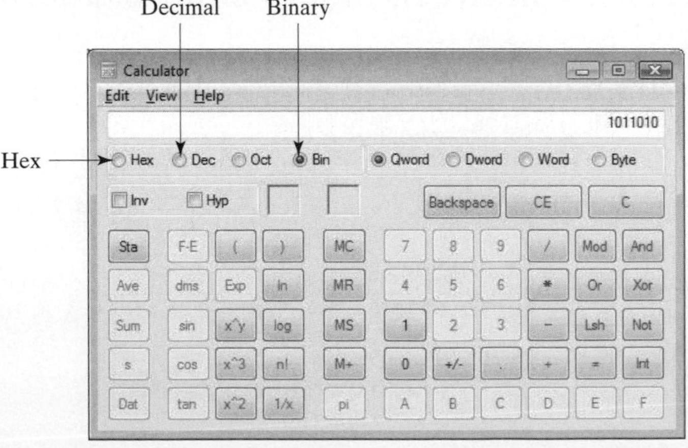

FIGURE F.1 You can perform number conversions using the Windows Calculator.

F.3 Conversions Between Hexadecimal and Decimal Numbers

Given a hexadecimal number $h_n h_{n-1} h_{n-2} \ldots h_2 h_1 h_0$, the equivalent decimal value is

hex to decimal

$$h_n \times 16^n + h_{n-1} \times 16^{n-1} + h_{n-2} \times 16^{n-2} + \ldots + h_2 \times 16^2 + h_1 \times 16^1 + h_0 \times 16^0$$

Here are some examples of converting hexadecimal numbers to decimals:

Hexadecimal	**Conversion Formula**	**Decimal**
7F	$7 \times 16^1 + 15 \times 16^0$	127
FFFF	$15 \times 16^3 + 15 \times 16^2 + 15 \times 16^1 + 15 \times 16^0$	65535
431	$4 \times 16^2 + 3 \times 16^1 + 1 \times 16^0$	1073

To convert a decimal number d to a hexadecimal number is to find the hexadecimal digits $h_n, h_{n-1}, h_{n-2}, \ldots, h_2, h_1$, and h_0 such that

decimal to hex

$$d = h_n \times 16^n + h_{n-1} \times 16^{n-1} + h_{n-2} \times 16^{n-2} + \ldots + h_2 \times 16^2 + h_1 \times 16^1 + h_0 \times 16^0$$

These numbers can be found by successively dividing d by 16 until the quotient is 0. The remainders are $h_0, h_1, h_2, \ldots, h_{n-2}, h_{n-1}$, and h_n.

For example, the decimal number 123 is 7B in hexadecimal. The conversion is done as follows:

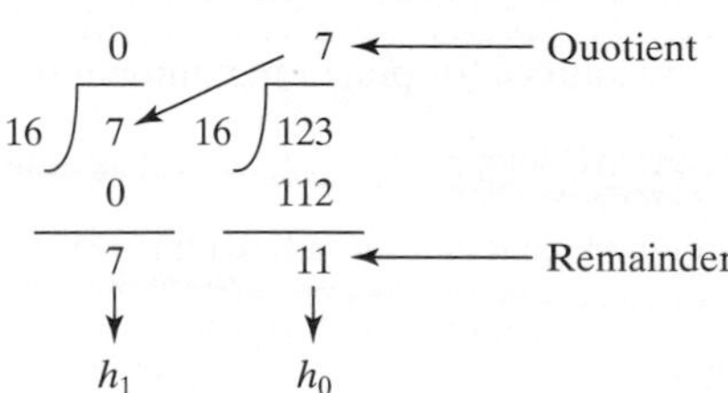

F.4 Conversions Between Binary and Hexadecimal Numbers

To convert a hexadecimal to a binary number, simply convert each digit in the hexadecimal number into a four-digit binary number, using Table F.1.

hex to binary

For example, the hexadecimal number 7B is 1111011, where 7 is 111 in binary, and B is 1011 in binary.

To convert a binary number to a hexadecimal, convert every four binary digits from right to left in the binary number into a hexadecimal number.

binary to hex

For example, the binary number 1110001101 is 38D, since 1101 is D, 1000 is 8, and 11 is 3, as shown below.

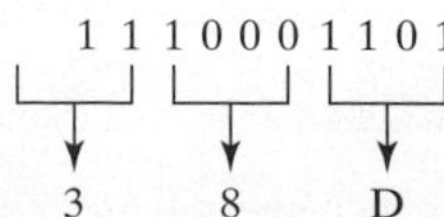

TABLE F.1 Converting Hexadecimal to Binary

Hexadecimal	*Binary*	*Decimal*
0	0000	0
1	0001	1
2	0010	2
3	0011	3
4	0100	4
5	0101	5
6	0110	6
7	0111	7
8	1000	8
9	1001	9
A	1010	10
B	1011	11
C	1100	12
D	1101	13
E	1110	14
F	1111	15

Note

Octal numbers are also useful. The octal number system has eight digits, 0 to 7. A decimal number 8 is represented in the octal system as 10.

Here are some good online resources for practicing number conversions:

- http://forums.cisco.com/CertCom/game/binary_game_page.htm
- http://people.sinclair.edu/nickreeder/Flash/binDec.htm
- http://people.sinclair.edu/nickreeder/Flash/binHex.htm

F.1 Convert the following decimal numbers into hexadecimal and binary numbers:

`100; 4340; 2000`

F.2 Convert the following binary numbers into hexadecimal and decimal numbers:

`1000011001; 100000000; 100111`

F.3 Convert the following hexadecimal numbers into binary and decimal numbers:

`FEFA9; 93; 2000`

APPENDIX G

Bitwise Operations

To write programs at the machine-level, often you need to deal with binary numbers directly and perform operations at the bit-level. Java provides the bitwise operators and shift operators defined in Table G.1.

The bit operators apply only to integer types (`byte`, `short`, `int`, and `long`). A character involved in a bit operation is converted to an integer. All bitwise operators can form bitwise assignment operators, such as =, |=, <<=, >>=, and >>>=.

TABLE G.1

Operator	*Name*	*Example (using bytes in the example)*	*Description*
&	Bitwise AND	10101110 & 10010010 yields 10000010	The AND of two corresponding bits yields a 1 if both bits are 1.
|	Bitwise inclusive OR	10101110 | 10010010 yields 10111110	The OR of two corresponding bits yields a 1 if either bit is 1.
^	Bitwise exclusive OR	10101110 ^ 10010010 yields 00111100	The XOR of two corresponding bits yields a 1 only if two bits are different.
~	One's complement	~10101110 yields 01010001	The operator toggles each bit from 0 to 1 and from 1 to 0.
<<	Left shift	10101110 << 2 yields 10111000	The operator shifts bits in the first operand left by the number of bits specified in the second operand, filling with 0s on the right.
>>	Right shift with sign extension	10101110 >> 2 yields 11101011 00101110 >> 2 yields 00001011	The operator shifts bit in the first operand right by the number of bits specified in the second operand, filling with the highest (sign) bit on the left.
>>>	Unsigned right shift with zero extension	10101110 >>> 2 yields 00101011 00101110 >>> 2 yields 00001011	The operator shifts bit in the first operand right by the number of bits specified in the second operand, filling with 0s on the left.

INDEX

C

F

H

I

J

M

X

Java Quick Reference

Console Input

```
Scanner input = new Scanner(System.in);
int intValue = input.nextInt();
long longValue = input.nextLong();
double doubleValue = input.nextDouble();
float floatValue = input.nextFloat();
String string = input.next();
```

Console Output

```
System.out.println(anyValue);
```

GUI Input Dialog

```
String string = JOptionPane.showInputDialog(
  "Enter input");
int intValue = Integer.parseInt(string);
double doubleValue =
  Double.parseDouble(string);
```

Message Dialog

```
JOptionPane.showMessageDialog(null,
  "Enter input");
```

Primitive Data Types

byte	8 bits
short	16 bits
int	32 bits
long	64 bits
float	32 bits
double	64 bits
char	16 bits
boolean	true/false

Arithmetic Operators

+	addition
-	subtraction
*	multiplication
/	division
%	remainder
++var	preincrement
--var	predecrement
var++	postincrement
var--	postdecrement

Assignment Operators

=	assignment
+=	addition assignment
-=	subtraction assignment
*=	multiplication assignment
/=	division assignment
%=	remainder assignment

Relational Operators

<	less than
<=	less than or equal to
>	greater than
>=	greater than or equal to
==	equal to
!=	not equal

Logical Operators

&&	short circuit AND
||	short circuit OR
!	NOT
^	exclusive OR

if Statements

```
if (condition) {
  statements;
}

if (condition) {
  statements;
}
else {
  statements;
}

if (condition1) {
  statements;
}
else if (condition2) {
  statements;
}
else {
  statements;
}
```

switch Statements

```
switch (intExpression) {
  case value1:
    statements;
    break;
  ...
  case valuen:
    statements;
    break;
  default:
    statements;
}
```

loop Statements

```
while (condition) {
  statements;
}

do {
  statements;
} while (condition);

for (init; condition;
  adjustment) {
  statements;
}
```

Companion Web site: www.pearsonhighered.com/liang